Houghton Mifflin Harcourt

GRADE 6

Common Core Assessment Readiness

D1063114

ISBN   978-0-547-87633-7
11 12 13   0982   22 21 20 19 18 17
4500650974   B C D E F G

Contents

Ratios and Proportional Relationships

Understand ratio concepts and use ratio reasoning to solve problems.

6.RP.1 Understand the concept of a ratio and use ratio language to describe a ratio relationship between two quantities. **1**

6.RP.2 Understand the concept of a unit rate a/b associated with a ratio $a:b$ with $b \neq 0$, and use rate language in the context of a ratio relationship. **3**

6.RP.3 Use ratio and rate reasoning to solve real-world and mathematical problems, e.g., by reasoning about tables of equivalent ratios, tape diagrams, double number line diagrams, or equations.

    a. Make tables of equivalent ratios relating quantities with whole-number measurements, find missing values in the tables, and plot the pairs of values on the coordinate plane. Use tables to compare ratios. **5**

    b. Solve unit rate problems including those involving unit pricing and constant speed. **7**

    c. Find a percent of a quantity as a rate per 100 (e.g., 30% of a quantity means 30/100 times the quantity); solve problems involving finding the whole, given a part and the percent. **9**

    d. Use ratio reasoning to convert measurement units; manipulate and transform units appropriately when multiplying or dividing quantities. **11**

The Number System

Apply and extend previous understandings of multiplication and division to divide fractions by fractions.

6.NS.1 Interpret and compute quotients of fractions, and solve word problems involving division of fractions by fractions, e.g., by using visual fraction models and equations to represent the problem. **13**

Compute fluently with multi-digit numbers and find common factors and multiples.

6.NS.2 Fluently divide multi-digit numbers using the standard algorithm. **15**

6.NS.3 Fluently add, subtract, multiply, and divide multi-digit decimals using the standard algorithm for each operation. **17**

6.NS.4 Find the greatest common factor of two whole numbers less than or equal to 100 and the least common multiple of two whole numbers less than or equal to 12. Use the distributive property to express a sum of two whole numbers 1–100 with a common factor as a multiple of a sum of two whole numbers with no common factor. **19**

Apply and extend previous understandings of numbers to the system of rational numbers.

6.NS.5 Understand that positive and negative numbers are used together to describe quantities having opposite directions or values (e.g., temperature above/below zero, elevation above/below sea level, credits/debits, positive/negative electric charge); use positive and negative numbers to represent quantities in real-world contexts, explaining the meaning of 0 in each situation. **21**

6.NS.6 Understand a rational number as a point on the number line. Extend number line diagrams and coordinate axes familiar from previous grades to represent points on the line and in the plane with negative number coordinates.

    a. Recognize opposite signs of numbers as indicating locations on opposite sides of 0 on the number line; recognize that the opposite of the opposite of a number is the number itself, e.g., $-(-3) = 3$, and that 0 is its own opposite. **23**

    b. Understand signs of numbers in ordered pairs as indicating locations in quadrants of the coordinate plane; recognize that when two ordered pairs differ only by signs, the locations of the points are related by reflections across one or both axes.

    c. Find and position integers and other rational numbers on a horizontal or vertical number line diagram; find and position pairs of integers and other rational numbers on a coordinate plane. **25**

6.NS.7 Understand ordering and absolute value of rational numbers.

    a. Interpret statements of inequality as statements about the relative position of two numbers on a number line diagram. **27**

    b. Write, interpret, and explain statements of order for rational numbers in real-world contexts. **29**

    c. Understand the absolute value of a rational number as its distance from 0 on the number line; interpret absolute value as magnitude for a positive or negative quantity in a real-world situation. **31**

    d. Distinguish comparisons of absolute value from statements about order.

6.NS.8 Solve real-world and mathematical problems by graphing points in all four quadrants of the coordinate plane. Include use of coordinates and absolute value to find distances between points with the same first coordinate or the same second coordinate. **33**

Expressions and Equations

Apply and extend previous understandings of arithmetic to algebraic expressions.

6.EE.1 Write and evaluate numerical expressions involving whole-number exponents. **35**

6.EE.2   Write, read, and evaluate expressions in which letters stand for numbers.

     a. Write expressions that record operations with numbers and with letters standing for numbers.   **37**

     b. Identify parts of an expression using mathematical terms (sum, term, product, factor, quotient, coefficient); view one or more parts of an expression as a single entity.   **39**

     c. Evaluate expressions at specific values of their variables. Include expressions that arise from formulas used in real-world problems. Perform arithmetic operations, including those involving whole-number exponents, in the conventional order when there are no parentheses to specify a particular order (Order of Operations).   **41**

6.EE.3   Apply the properties of operations to generate equivalent expressions.   **43**

6.EE.4   Identify when two expressions are equivalent (i.e., when the two expressions name the same number regardless of which value is substituted into them).   **45**

Reason about and solve one-variable equations and inequalities.

6.EE.5   Understand solving an equation or inequality as a process of answering a question: which values from a specified set, if any, make the equation or inequality true? Use substitution to determine whether a given number in a specified set makes an equation or inequality true.   **47**

6.EE.6   Use variables to represent numbers and write expressions when solving a real-world or mathematical problem; understand that a variable can represent an unknown number, or, depending on the purpose at hand, any number in a specified set.   **49**

6.EE.7   Solve real-world and mathematical problems by writing and solving equations of the form $x + p = q$ and $px = q$ for cases in which p, q and x are all nonnegative rational numbers.   **51**

6.EE.8   Write an inequality of the form $x > c$ or $x < c$ to represent a constraint or condition in a real-world or mathematical problem. Recognize that inequalities of the form $x > c$ or $x < c$ have infinitely many solutions; represent solutions of such inequalities on number line diagrams.   **53**

Represent and analyze quantitative relationships between dependent and independent variables.

6.EE.9   Use variables to represent two quantities in a real-world problem that change in relationship to one another; write an equation to express one quantity, thought of as the dependent variable, in terms of the other quantity, thought of as the independent variable. Analyze the relationship between the dependent and independent variables using graphs and tables, and relate these to the equation.   **55**

Geometry

Solve real-world and mathematical problems involving area, surface area, and volume.

6.G.1   Find the area of right triangles, other triangles, special quadrilaterals, and polygons by composing into rectangles or decomposing into triangles and other shapes; apply these techniques in the context of solving real-world and mathematical problems.   **57**

6.G.2   Find the volume of a right rectangular prism with fractional edge lengths by packing it with unit cubes of the appropriate unit fraction edge lengths, and show that the volume is the same as would be found by multiplying the edge lengths of the prism. Apply the formulas $V = lwh$ and $V = bh$ to find volumes of right rectangular prisms with fractional edge lengths in the context of solving real-world and mathematical problems.   **59**

6.G.3   Draw polygons in the coordinate plane given coordinates for the vertices; use coordinates to find the length of a side joining points with the same first coordinate or the same second coordinate. Apply these techniques in the context of solving real-world and mathematical problems.   **61**

6.G.4   Represent three-dimensional figures using nets made up of rectangles and triangles, and use the nets to find the surface area of these figures. Apply these techniques in the context of solving real-world and mathematical problems.   **63**

Statistics and Probability

Develop understanding of statistical variability.

6.SP.1   Recognize a statistical question as one that anticipates variability in the data related to the question and accounts for it in the answers.   **65**

6.SP.2   Understand that a set of data collected to answer a statistical question has a distribution which can be described by its center, spread, and overall shape.   **67**

6.SP.3   Recognize that a measure of center for a numerical data set summarizes all of its values with a single number, while a measure of variation describes how its values vary with a single number.   **69**

Summarize and describe distributions.

6.SP.4   Display numerical data in plots on a number line, including dot plots, histograms, and box plots.   **71**

6.SP.5   Summarize numerical data sets in relation to their context, such as by:

    a. Reporting the number of observations.   **73**

    b. Describing the nature of the attribute under investigation, including how it was measured and its units of measurement.

    c. Giving quantitative measures of center (median and/or mean) and variability (interquartile range and/or mean absolute deviation), as well as describing any overall pattern and any striking deviations from the overall pattern with reference to the context in which the data were gathered.   **75**

    d. Relating the choice of measures of center and variability to the shape of the data distribution and the context in which the data were gathered.   **77**

Some of the assessment items for the Standards for Mathematical Content cited in the preceding Contents also involve one or more of the following Standards for Mathematical Practice.

Standards for Mathematical Practice

MP.1 Make sense of problems and persevere in solving them.

MP.2 Reason abstractly and quantitatively.

MP.3 Construct viable arguments and critique the reasoning of others.

MP.4 Model with mathematics.

MP.5 Use appropriate tools strategically.

MP.6 Attend to precision.

MP.7 Look for and make use of structure.

MP.8 Look for and express regularity in repeated reasoning.

6.RP.1

SELECTED RESPONSE
Select the correct answer.

1. A snow blower requires a fuel mixture ratio of 40:1 (gas to oil). Which expression represents this ratio?

   (A) $\dfrac{40}{1}$

   (B) 1×40

   (C) 40×1

   (D) $\dfrac{1}{40}$

2. A rectangular yard is 10 feet long by 7 feet wide. What is the ratio of the width of the yard to the perimeter of the yard?

   (A) 7 to 17

   (B) 7 to 34

   (C) 17 to 34

   (D) 34 to 7

3. Steve earns $8 per hour. His older brother earns $2 more per hour than Steve. What is the ratio of the money Steve earns in an hour to the money his brother earns in an hour?

   (A) $8 to $2

   (B) $2 to $8

   (C) $10 to $8

   (D) $8 to $10

4. A man mixed 2 teaspoons of sugar into his large coffee but then added one more teaspoon of sugar because it was not sweet enough. What is the ratio of teaspoons of sugar to one large coffee?

   (A) 3:1

   (B) 2:1

   (C) 1:3

   (D) 1:2

Select all correct answers.

5. A punch bowl contained 2 liters of ginger ale, 1 liter of orange juice, and 1 liter of raspberry juice. Select all the true statements.

   (A) The ratio of the ginger ale to the entire punch bowl is 1 to 4.

   (B) The ratio of orange juice to ginger ale is 2 to 1.

   (C) The ratio of the juices to the ginger ale is 2 to 2.

   (D) The ratio of the entire punch bowl to the juices is 2 to 4.

   (E) The ratio of the orange juice to the raspberry juice is 1 to 1.

6. A restaurant worker was told to make every ham sandwich with 2 tomato slices and 3 pickle slices. Select all true statements.

   (A) A worker makes three ham sandwiches. Taken together, the sandwiches will have a ratio of total number of tomato slices to total number of pickle slices of 6:9.

   (B) For every ham sandwich, the ratio of tomato slices to pickle slices is 3:2.

   (C) A worker makes five sandwiches. The ratio of total number of tomato slices to total number of pickle slices is 7:8.

   (D) On every ham sandwich, the ratio of tomato slices to pickle slices is 2:3.

   (E) Once a ham sandwich is made, there will be a ratio of 2 tomato slices to 1 ham sandwich.

CONSTRUCTED RESPONSE

7. In Ken's meatball recipe, for every 5 cups of bread crumbs, 9 pounds of ground beef are used. Write this ratio using a fraction. Label the numbers in the fraction.

8. For every pizza Eric's family ate, Eric ate 2 of the 8 pieces. If Eric's family bought 2 pizzas, write the ratio of the total number of pieces Eric ate to the total number of pieces the family ate.

_____

_____

9. A middle school has the fifth and sixth grades. There are 100 fifth grade boys and 110 fifth grade girls. There are 7 fewer sixth grade boys than fifth grade boys, and there are 10 more sixth grade girls than sixth grade boys What is the ratio of girls to boys in the middle school? Show your work.

_____

_____

_____

_____

_____

10. A particular school has a teacher to student ratio of 1 teacher to 11 students.

a. Express the teacher to student ratio using the symbol ":".

_____

b. Express the teacher to student ratio as a fraction.

_____

c. Are there more teachers or students? Explain how you know.

_____

_____

_____

_____

11. On a package of rice, the directions say that the ratio of cups of water to cups of uncooked rice should be $1:\frac{1}{2}$.

a. What is the total number of cups of ingredients needed if you want to cook $\frac{1}{2}$ cup of uncooked rice?

_____

b. Susan says that the ratio of cups of water to total cups of ingredients is 1:2 because there is twice as much water as there is rice. Is this the correct ratio? Explain why or why not, and if not, give the correct ratio.

_____

_____

_____

_____

_____

_____

12. At the end of the season, Erica's basketball team has a win-to-loss ratio of 3:2.

a. What is the ratio of wins to games played?

_____

b. Can you use the ratio you found in part a to conclude that the total number of games Erica's team played in one season is 5? Explain why or why not.

_____

_____

_____

_____

6.RP.2

SELECTED RESPONSE
Select the correct answer.

1. A 5-pound bag of cat food costs $11.25. What is the unit price of the cat food in dollars per pound?

   Ⓐ $0.44 per pound

   Ⓑ $2.25 per pound

   Ⓒ $6.25 per pound

   Ⓓ $56.25 per pound

2. Three pounds of fish costs $14.97 at the market. What is the unit price of the fish in dollars per pound?

   Ⓐ $4.99

   Ⓑ $11.97

   Ⓒ $14.97

   Ⓓ $44.91

3. Bill drove 315 miles in 7 hours, Alisha drove 235 miles in 5 hours, and Joanne drove 414 miles in 9 hours. Which person drove at an average speed of 47 miles per hour?

   Ⓐ Alisha

   Ⓑ Joanne

   Ⓒ Bill

   Ⓓ Both Joanne and Bill

Select all correct answers.

4. For each store, calculate the unit price per ounce of potato chips. Which stores sell potato chips at a unit rate of $0.17 per ounce?

Potato Chip Prices		
Store	**Cost**	**Ounces**
A	$1.69	8
B	$2.99	16
C	$3.74	20
D	$4.08	24
E	$5.44	32

   Ⓐ Store A

   Ⓑ Store B

   Ⓒ Store C

   Ⓓ Store D

   Ⓔ Store E

5. Which of the rates shown here correspond to a unit rate of $6 per sandwich?

   Ⓐ Spending $42 to buy 7 sandwiches

   Ⓑ Spending $108 to buy 18 sandwiches

   Ⓒ Spending $40 to buy 5 sandwiches

   Ⓓ Spending $100 to buy 16 sandwiches

   Ⓔ Spending $42 to buy 6 sandwiches

Match each quantity with the correct unit rate.

_____ 6. A 30-ounce bottle of fruit juice costs $4.80.

_____ 7. 16 ounces of ground turkey costs $2.40.

_____ 8. A 32-ounce bottle of laundry detergent costs $6.72.

_____ 9. A 20-ounce bag of potato chips costs $3.80.

_____ 10. A 32-ounce bottle of shampoo costs $5.76.

A $0.15 per ounce

B $0.16 per ounce

C $0.17 per ounce

D $0.18 per ounce

E $0.19 per ounce

F $0.20 per ounce

G $0.21 per ounce

H $0.22 per ounce

CONSTRUCTED RESPONSE

11. A group of 180 students is divided into 20 teams for a competition.

    a. Write a unit rate that represents the number of students on one team.

    _____

    b. Part way through the competition, the students are gathered together and divided into 15 teams. If there are still 180 students in the competition, how many students are on each team now?

    _____

12. A deli sells ham for $2.98 per half pound. Kyle incorrectly says that the unit rate is $1.49 per pound. His calculations are shown below. Explain Kyle's mistake and determine the correct price per pound. Show your work.

$$\frac{\$2.98 \div 2}{\frac{1}{2} \text{ pound} \div 2} = \frac{\$1.49}{1 \text{ pound}}$$

    _____

    _____

    _____

    _____

13. A grocery store sells Swiss cheese for $5.90 a pound. To the nearest cent, what is the cost per ounce of Swiss cheese? Round your answer to the nearest cent and show your work.

    _____

    _____

    _____

    _____

14. Three wholesalers are having special deals on chicken this week. Wholesaler A is selling 10 pounds of chicken for $40.00, wholesaler B is selling 15 pounds of chicken for $45.00, and wholesaler C is selling 20 pounds of chicken for $50. Which wholesaler has the best price on chicken? Show your work.

    _____

    _____

    _____

15. John and Maria are spending the afternoon hiking in the desert. They purchased six bottles of water for $9.00, two protein bars for lunch for $5.00, and some peanuts for $3.00 as a snack. Suppose they start hiking at 11:30 A.M. and finish the hike at 3:45 P.M. What is the unit rate of money spent to hours hiked? Show your work.

    _____

    _____

    _____

    _____

    _____

    _____

    _____

    _____

    _____

    _____

    _____

6.RP.3b

SELECTED RESPONSE

Select the correct answer.

1. If 4 gallons of milk cost $16.76, how much would 7 gallons of milk cost?

   Ⓐ $4.19

   Ⓑ $29.33

   Ⓒ $67.04

   Ⓓ $117.32

2. John drives to the beach, which is 270 miles away. In 2 hours, he drives 120 miles. If he continues at that speed, how long will it take him to get to the beach?

   Ⓐ 2 hours

   Ⓑ 2.5 hours

   Ⓒ 4 hours

   Ⓓ 4.5 hours

3. The yard care staff can mow 45 lawns in a 10-hour work day. Each of the 9 workers can mow the same number of lawns per hour. How many lawns can one worker mow per hour?

   Ⓐ 0.5 lawn per hour

   Ⓑ 0.9 lawn per hour

   Ⓒ 4.5 lawns per hour

   Ⓓ 5 lawns per hour

4. A car travels 304 miles on 16 gallons of gas. How far can the car go on 5 gallons?

   Ⓐ 3.2 miles

   Ⓑ 60.8 miles

   Ⓒ 80 miles

   Ⓓ 95 miles

5. The last time Robert filled up his car with gas, he paid $24.50 for 7 gallons. This time, he needs 15 gallons. If the price is the same, how much will he pay?

   Ⓐ $52.50

   Ⓑ $32.50

   Ⓒ $11.43

   Ⓓ $3.50

CONSTRUCTED RESPONSE

6. A moving company has one large truck for furniture and one small truck for boxes. During one move, it took the large truck 4 hours to travel 180 miles. It took the small truck 3 hours to make the same trip.

   a. Assume both trucks traveled at constant speeds. How fast did each truck travel?

   _____

   _____

   b. The following week, the company was hired for a 225-mile move. If each truck traveled at the same speed it had the previous week, how long did the trip take for each truck?

   _____

   _____

   _____

   _____

7. Two shoppers bought meat at a supermarket deli. The first bought 3 pounds of meat for $9.87. The second bought 4 pounds of meat for $16.76. Neither of the shoppers had a coupon or a discount card. Can you tell if both shoppers bought the same kind of meat? Explain why or why not.

   _____

   _____

   _____

   _____

   _____

8. Lupita bought 7 pounds of pretzels at a local wholesaler for $16.80. Her friend Charles bought 5 pounds of pretzels at the supermarket for $12.75. Charles thinks he got the better deal because $12.75 is less than $16.80.

   a. Is Charles's reasoning correct? Explain why or why not.

   _____

   _____

   _____

   _____

   _____

   _____

   _____

   _____

   _____

   b. How much would Charles have spent if he had purchased the same amount of pretzels as Lupita?

   _____

   _____

   _____

   _____

   _____

9. Sam is renting one of two cars to go on a 300-mile trip. The first car can travel 75 miles on 5 gallons of gas. The second car can travel 240 miles on 20 gallons of gas. Each car costs the same to rent, and Sam wants to rent the car with the better gas mileage. Sam estimates that he will pay $49.42 for every 14 gallons of gas he has to buy. Which car should Sam rent, and how much money should Sam bring for gas? Explain your reasoning.

   _____

   _____

   _____

   _____

10. A band Martha likes just released a new album. A digital music service is selling the 12-song album for $9.96. The service also allows purchase of individual songs off the album, with 3 songs selling for $1.29 and 9 selling for $0.99. Martha likes all of the $1.29 songs and 6 of the $0.99 songs. She is considering buying just those songs or buying the whole album. What is the better deal in terms of price per song? Show your work.

   _____

   _____

   _____

   _____

   _____

6.RP.3c

SELECTED RESPONSE
Select the correct answer.

1. What is 5% of 200?

   Ⓐ $\dfrac{1}{40}$

   Ⓑ 10

   Ⓒ 40

   Ⓓ 1,000

2. What is 120% of 50?

   Ⓐ 2.4

   Ⓑ 6

   Ⓒ 60

   Ⓓ 6,000

3. A 15% tip on a diner bill is $2.55. How much is the bill?

   Ⓐ $0.17

   Ⓑ $0.38

   Ⓒ $17.00

   Ⓓ $38.25

4. 56.25% of what number is 168.75?

   Ⓐ 3

   Ⓑ 94.9219

   Ⓒ 300

   Ⓓ 9,492.19

Select all correct answers.

5. Choose all statements that are true.

   Ⓐ 15% of 15 is 1.

   Ⓑ 5% of 50 is 10.

   Ⓒ 10% of 100 is 10.

   Ⓓ 2% of 100 is 5.

   Ⓔ 3% of 200 is 6.

Match each library with its total number of books.

_____ 6. 30 books represent 2% of the total books at library 1.

_____ 7. 45 books represent 5% of the total books at library 2.

_____ 8. 60 books represent 1% of the total books at library 3.

_____ 9. 75 books represent 10% of the total books at library 4.

_____ 10. 90 books represent 3% of the total books at library 5.

A 750 books
B 900 books
C 1,500 books
D 2,000 books
E ~~3,000 books~~
F 6,000 books

CONSTRUCTED RESPONSE

11. The state sales tax rate for North Carolina is 4.75%. The state sales tax rate for South Carolina is 6%. Shandra would like to buy a cookbook with a list price of $20.

    a. If Shandra buys this book in North Carolina, how much would she pay for sales tax?

    _____

    b. If she buys the same book on a trip to South Carolina, how much more sales tax would she pay compared to North Carolina?

    _____

12. a. 1.5% of what number is 60? 15% of what number is 60? 150% of what number is 60?

_____

_____

_____

_____

b. What pattern do you notice in part a?

_____

_____

_____

_____

_____

c. 2.5% of 2,000 is 50. Explain how to use the pattern you described in part b to find 25% of what number is 50.

_____

_____

_____

_____

_____

_____

13. Jane will receive 18% less of her regular pay when she retires. Her regular pay is $500 per week.

a. How much would she receive per week if she retires today?

_____

_____

_____

b. Explain how you can calculate this using 100% − 18% = 82%.

_____

_____

_____

_____

c. Show why these calculations are equivalent in general. (*Hint*: Write an expression for finding an amount *A* minus *n*% of *A*. Write another expression for finding (100 − *n*)% of *A*, and then use algebra to show that these two expressions are the same.)

_____

_____

_____

_____

_____

_____

6.RP.3d

SELECTED RESPONSE

Select the correct answer.

1. Heather's desk is 3 feet long. About how long is it in meters? Use 1 foot ≈ 0.305 meter.

   Ⓐ 0.00915 meter

   Ⓑ 0.9015 meter

   Ⓒ 0.915 meters

   Ⓓ 9.15 meters

2. A large container at a party holds 9 liters of lemonade. About how many gallons of lemonade does the container hold? Use 1 gallon ≈ 3.79 liters.

   Ⓐ 0.4 gallon

   Ⓑ 2.4 gallons

   Ⓒ 12.8 gallons

   Ⓓ 34.1 gallons

3. Joan mails a package that weighs 140 grams. About how many ounces is the package? Use 1 ounce ≈ 28.4 grams.

   Ⓐ 0.2 ounce

   Ⓑ 4.9 ounces

   Ⓒ 168.4 ounces

   Ⓓ 403.3 ounces

4. A printing company makes plastic banners 15 feet long by 6 feet wide. An overseas customer wants to know about how many square meters the banner is. Use 1 foot ≈ 0.305 meter.

   Ⓐ 8.37 square meters

   Ⓑ 27.5 square meters

   Ⓒ 90.0 square meters

   Ⓓ 900 square meters

Select all correct answers.

5. Choose all measurements that are equivalent to 45 meters.

   Ⓐ 450 centimeters

   Ⓑ 4,500 centimeters

   Ⓒ 0.045 kilometer

   Ⓓ 0.45 kilometer

   Ⓔ 4,500 millimeters

Select the correct answer for each lettered part.

6. John knows he can safely lift 30 pounds without help. He needs to move the following packages. Can he lift each safely without help? Use the following:
   1 pound ≈ 0.454 kilogram
   1 ounce ≈ 28.4 grams
   1 kilogram = 1,000 grams

   a. 9.08 kilograms ○ Yes ○ No

   b. 9,080 grams ○ Yes ○ No

   c. 460 ounces ○ Yes ○ No

   d. 46 kilograms ○ Yes ○ No

CONSTRUCTED RESPONSE

7. A chemist has a beaker with 4 fluid ounces of a solution. The chemist needs 500 milliliters for an experiment. About how many more milliliters does the chemist need? Use 1 fluid ounce ≈ 29.6 milliliters and show your work.

   _____

   _____

   _____

   _____

   _____

8. How many square centimeters of paper do you need to wrap the box shown below? Use 1 inch = 2.54 centimeters. Round your final answer to the nearest whole square centimeter. Show your work.

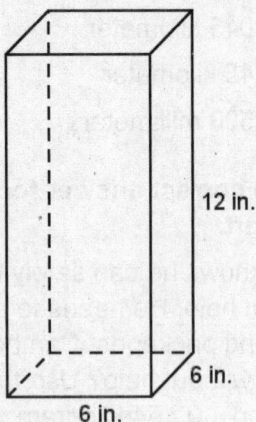

12 in.

6 in.

6 in.

_____

_____

_____

_____

9. Jorge wants to buy new vinyl flooring for his kitchen. The kitchen floor is 12 feet by 15 feet. How many square yards is the floor? Show your work.

_____

_____

_____

_____

_____

_____

10. Tisha orders a carpet for a room that measures 270 square feet. The salesman says the carpet costs $12.00 per square yard. He explains that since there are 3 square feet for every square yard, Tisha needs 90 square yards of carpeting, which costs $1,080. What error did the salesman make? What should be the actual cost of the carpet?

_____

_____

_____

_____

_____

11. A recipe includes the following juices. The measurements are given in milliliters.

a. Find the amount of each in cups to complete the table. Use 1 fluid ounce ≈ 29.6 milliliters and 1 cup = 8 fluid ounces. Round to the nearest cup as necessary.

Juice	Milliliters	Cups
Cranberry	3,500	
Orange	950	
Lemon	240	

b. One quart of cranberry juice equals 4 cups. How many quarts of cranberry juice are needed for the recipe? If you can only buy whole quarts of juice, will there be cranberry juice left over? Explain.

_____

_____

_____

_____

6.NS.1

SELECTED RESPONSE
Select the correct answer.

1. You have $\frac{7}{8}$ cup of sour cream to make tacos. If each taco requires $\frac{1}{16}$ cup of sour cream, how many tacos can you make?

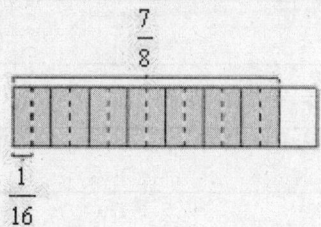

$$\frac{7}{8}$$

$$\frac{1}{16}$$

   (A) $\frac{7}{128}$ taco   (C) 14 tacos

   (B) $\frac{1}{14}$ taco   (D) 15 tacos

2. How many $\frac{1}{2}$-cup servings are there in $\frac{7}{8}$ cup of peanut butter?

   (A) $\frac{1}{16}$ (C) $\frac{4}{7}$

   (B) $\frac{7}{16}$ (D) $1\frac{3}{4}$

3. Carl wants to plant a garden that is $1\frac{1}{2}$ yards long and has an area of $3\frac{1}{2}$ square yards. How wide should the garden be?

   (A) $\frac{3}{7}$ yard   (C) $2\frac{1}{3}$ yards

   (B) 2 yards   (D) $5\frac{1}{4}$ yards

4. Divide. $\frac{3}{7} \div \frac{17}{19}$

   (A) $\frac{3}{133}$ (C) $\frac{51}{133}$

   (B) $\frac{57}{119}$ (D) $\frac{119}{57}$

5. Nima uses $\frac{2}{3}$ cup peanuts, $\frac{1}{2}$ cup cashews, $\frac{3}{4}$ cup pecans, and some raisins in a recipe that makes $2\frac{1}{4}$ cups of trail mix. How many cups of peanuts are there per cup of trail mix?

   (A) $\frac{2}{9}$ (C) $\frac{8}{27}$

   (B) $\frac{3}{9}$ (D) $\frac{27}{8}$

6. Jerry is tiling the wall behind his sink. The tiles he's using are square with sides that measure $1\frac{3}{4}$ inches. If the area of wall he's tiling is 42 inches long and $29\frac{3}{4}$ inches high, how many tiles will he need?

   (A) 17

   (B) 24

   (C) 408

   (D) $1249\frac{1}{2}$

CONSTRUCTED RESPONSE

7. The following division is being performed using multiplication by the reciprocal. Find the missing numbers.

$$\frac{5}{12} \div \frac{?}{3} = \frac{5}{12} \cdot \frac{?}{10} = \frac{1}{?}$$

_____

_____

8. Ida is cutting a $\frac{11}{12}$-foot wooden board into $\frac{3}{16}$-foot sections to do some detail work on a model she is building. How many whole $\frac{3}{16}$-foot sections are there in the $\frac{11}{12}$-foot wooden board? Explain your answer and show your work.

_____

_____

_____

_____

_____

9. Baruka has $\frac{1}{2}$ gallon of milk left in the fridge.

a. How many $\frac{5}{64}$-gallon (10-ounce) servings of milk does she have left? Show your work.

_____

_____

_____

b. If she drinks 10 ounces of milk a day, how many days of milk does she have left? Explain.

_____

_____

_____

_____

10. Juan was presented with the following problem on a math test: "Divide $\frac{3}{4}$ by $\frac{5}{7}$. Show your work." His work is shown below. What was Juan's error? Correct his work and state the correct quotient.

$$\frac{5}{7} \div \frac{3}{4} = \frac{5}{7} \cdot \frac{4}{3} = \frac{20}{21}$$

_____

_____

_____

_____

_____

_____

11. Consider the division statement $\frac{1}{4} \div \frac{7}{16}$.

a. Describe a real world situation that might involve this expression.

_____

_____

_____

_____

_____

b. Find the quotient.

_____

_____

c. Interpret the quotient in terms of the situation you described in part a.

_____

_____

_____

6.NS.2

SELECTED RESPONSE

Select the correct answer.

1. Divide. $196 \div 28$

   Ⓐ 6

   Ⓑ 6 R27

   Ⓒ 7 R1

   Ⓓ 7

2. Divide. $98\overline{)308}$

   Ⓐ 3

   Ⓑ 3 R14

   Ⓒ 4

   Ⓓ 14 R3

3. An art teacher has 192 containers of paint for 17 students. If the teacher wants to provide each student with an equal number of containers, how many containers will be left over?

   Ⓐ 0

   Ⓑ 5

   Ⓒ 7

   Ⓓ 18

4. A local theater can seat 2,254 people. The seats are arranged into 98 rows. Each row has the same number of seats. How many seats are there in each row?

   Ⓐ 15 　　 Ⓒ 23

   Ⓑ 20 　　 Ⓓ 32

Select all correct answers.

5. The event staff for a local concert hall has 73 tickets to sell. If they sell all of the tickets at the same price, they will have $438. Which of the following people have enough money to buy a ticket?

   Ⓐ Celia has $4.50.

   Ⓑ Louis has $7.00.

   Ⓒ Jan has $6.50.

   Ⓓ Nicola has $6.00.

   Ⓔ Chuck has $5.00.

CONSTRUCTED RESPONSE

6. A skyscraper with 102 floors is 1,326 feet tall. Each floor is the same height. How tall is each floor? Show your work.

   _____

   _____

   _____

   _____

   _____

7. An apple orchard harvested 3,584 apples and separated them evenly into 112 bags.

   a. How many apples are in each bag?

   _____

   _____

   _____

   b. If 56 apples were placed in each bag instead, how many bags would be left over?

   _____

   _____

   _____

8. A movie streaming service charges its customers $15 a month. Martina has $98 saved up. Will she have any money left over if she pays for the maximum amount of months she can afford? Explain.

   _____

   _____

   _____

   _____

   _____

9. Maurice says that 1079 ÷ 62 is 16 with a remainder of 87.

   a. Without seeing his work, how can you tell Maurice divided incorrectly?

   _____

   _____

   _____

   _____

   b. Maurice is correct about this fact: $16 \times 62 + 87 = 1079$. Explain how you can use that fact to find the correct quotient and remainder for 1079 ÷ 62 without actually dividing. Then find the quotient.

   _____

   _____

   _____

   _____

   _____

   _____

10. The administrator of the school is dividing 342 students into 38 equal groups to do a team-building exercise. One of the guidance counselors says that the exercise will be most effective if there are 7 or fewer students in a group.

    a. Explain why the administrator's plan is not as effective as it can be.

    _____

    _____

    _____

    _____

    _____

b. How many groups should there be? Will all the groups have the same number of students? Explain.

   _____

   _____

   _____

   _____

11. a. Find 117 ÷ 13, 118 ÷ 13, and 119 ÷ 13.

    _____

    _____

    _____

    b. Without dividing, what is the quotient of 120 ÷ 13? Use the pattern you found in the first three problems to explain your answer.

    _____

    _____

    _____

    _____

    _____

    _____

    _____

    c. According to the pattern, 130 ÷ 13 should be 9 with a remainder of 13. Explain why that is incorrect and find the correct quotient.

    _____

    _____

    _____

    _____

    _____

6.NS.3

SELECTED RESPONSE

Select the correct answer.

1. Add. 13.389 + 1.24
   - (A) 13.513
   - (B) 14.529
   - (C) 14.62
   - (D) 14.629 ●

2. Subtract. 102.596 − 10.478
   - (A) 92.118 ●
   - (B) 92.128
   - (C) 112.122
   - (D) 192.118

3. Multiply. 1.8762 × 4.2
   - (A) 7.88004 ●
   - (B) 78.8004
   - (C) 788.004
   - (D) 7,880.04

4. Divide. 0.09975 ÷ 0.007
   - (A) 1.425
   - (B) 14.25
   - (C) 142.5
   - (D) 1,425

Match each multiplication expression with its product.

A 5. 2.986 × 1.26   A 376,236

G 6. 0.2986 × 0.126   B 37,623.6

D 7. 29.86 × 12.6   C 3,762.36

B 8. 298.6 × 126   D 376.236

E 9. 2.986 × 12.6   E 37.6236

F 10. 2,986 × 126   F 3.76236

C 11. 298.6 × 12.6   G 0.376236

H 12. 2.986 × 0.126   H 0.0376236

CONSTRUCTED RESPONSE

13. Elsa has $45.78 in her savings account and $21.38 in her wallet.

    a. How much money does Elsa have?

    _____

    _____

    b. If Elsa puts half of the money in her wallet in the bank, how much money will she have in her savings account?

    _____

    _____

    _____

    _____

14. Mariposa needs a number of 0.3125-inch strips of wood for a model she is building. How many of these strips can she get from a 5.625-inch wooden board? Show your work.

_____

_____

_____

_____

_____

15. Jean-Paul incorrectly states that $4.2874 + 1.286 = 4.416$. His work is shown below. Explain Jean-Paul's mistake and correct his work.

```
     1   1   1
  4. 2   8   7   4
+    1.  2   8   6
  ─────────────────
  4. 4   1   6   0
```

Jean-Paul mistake is that he needed to a line the decimal and thats how he gets it wrong

16. At a local gas station, regular gasoline sells for $3.499 per gallon, while premium gasoline sells for $3.879 per gallon.

a. Find the difference in price between the two types of gasoline.

The different is .620 gallons

b. How much does a person save on 15.25 gallons of gas by buying regular instead of premium? Show your work, and round your answer to the nearest whole cent.

_____

_____

17. Shen earns $9.60 per hour at his part-time job. Last month, he worked 7.25 hours the first week, 8.75 hours the second week, 5.5 hours the third week, and 6.75 hours the fourth week. Shen puts half of his paycheck in the bank every other week starting with the first.

a. How much money did Shen earn each week?

_____

_____

_____

_____

b. How much money did he put in the bank last month? Show your work.

_____

_____

_____

_____

c. How much money did Shen have to spend from his 4 paychecks? Show your work.

_____

_____

_____

18. Pablo wants to buy a steak at the grocery store. He has two options. The first is 1.37 pounds and costs $9.59. The second is 1.75 pounds and costs $10.85. Which is the better buy? Explain.

_____

_____

_____

_____

_____

_____

6.NS.4

SELECTED RESPONSE

Select the correct answer.

1. Find the greatest common factor of 12 and 18.

   Ⓐ 1

   Ⓑ 2

   Ⓒ 3

   Ⓓ 6

2. Find the least common multiple of 8 and 10.

   Ⓐ 32

   Ⓑ 40

   Ⓒ 50

   Ⓓ 80

3. Find the greatest common factor of 7 and 11.

   Ⓐ 1

   Ⓑ 7

   Ⓒ 11

   Ⓓ 77

4. Find the least common multiple of 6 and 12.

   Ⓐ 6

   Ⓑ 12

   Ⓒ 24

   Ⓓ 72

5. Factor out the greatest common factor of the expression below using the distributive property.

$$90 + 60$$

   Ⓐ 30(3 + 2)

   Ⓑ 10(9 + 6)

   Ⓒ 15(6 + 4)

   Ⓓ 6(15 + 10)

CONSTRUCTED RESPONSE

6. Is it possible to use the distributive property to rewrite 85 + 99 as a product of a whole number greater than 1 and a sum of two whole numbers? Explain your answer.

   _____

   _____

   _____

   _____

   _____

7. Charlie and Dasha are roommates, and they have a dog. If neither of them is home, they hire someone to watch the dog. Charlie must go on business trips every 6 months, while Dasha must go on business trips every 9 months. If they both just got back from business trips, how many months will it be before they need to hire someone to look after the dog again? Explain your answer.

   _____

   _____

   _____

   _____

8. Salvatore is making some party favors for his birthday party. He has 96 pencils and 80 boxes of raisins. He wants each party favor to be the same, and he wants to use all of the pencils and raisins. Find the GCF of 96 and 80 to figure out how many party favors he can make. How many pencils and boxes of raisins will be in each one?

   _____

   _____

Name _____ Date _____ Class_____

9. a. What is the LCM of two numbers when one number is a multiple of the other? Give an example.

_____

_____

_____

_____

_____

b. What is the LCM of two numbers that have no common factors greater than 1? Give an example.

_____

_____

_____

_____

_____

_____

10. a. Find the greatest common factor of 3 and 5.

_____

b. Find the greatest common factor of 11 and 13.

_____

_____

c. Use your results from parts a and b to make a conjecture about the GCF of any pair of prime numbers.

_____

_____

_____

_____

11. Consider the sum 36 + 45.

a. Use the distributive property to rewrite the sum as the product of a whole number other than 1 and a sum of two whole numbers.

_____

b. Write the sum as the product of a whole number different from the one you chose in part a and a sum of two whole numbers.

_____

c. Can this be done in more than two ways? Explain.

_____

_____

_____

_____

12. A baker has 72 vanilla cupcakes and 80 chocolate cupcakes. She wants to make platters that have both kinds of cupcakes, and she wants to have the same number of each kind on each platter.

a. Can the baker make 10 platters of cupcakes with no cupcakes left over? Explain why or why not.

_____

_____

_____

_____

_____

b. What is the greatest number of platters she can make with no cupcakes left over? How many of each kind of cupcake will be on each platter?

_____

_____

_____

_____

6.NS.5

SELECTED RESPONSE

Select the correct answer.

1. Carlos deposited $28.50 into his bank account after making a $20.00 withdrawal to pay for some school supplies. Represent these situations as signed numbers.

   Ⓐ 28.50, 20.00

   Ⓑ –28.50, –20.00

   Ⓒ 28.50, –20.00

   Ⓓ –28.50, 20.00

2. In Barrow, Alaska, the northernmost town in the United States, the record high temperature is 79 °F, recorded on July 13, 1993. The record low is 56 °F below zero, recorded on February 3, 1924. Represent these situations as signed numbers.

   Ⓐ 79, 56

   Ⓑ –79, –56

   Ⓒ 79, –56

   Ⓓ –79, 56

3. While on vacation in Australia, Brent and Giselle decide to explore the Great Barrier Reef. Brent decides to go snorkeling near the surface at a depth of 5 feet below sea level. Giselle is an experienced scuba diver and decides to explore a little deeper at 80 feet below sea level. Represent these situations as signed numbers.

   Ⓐ 5, 80

   Ⓑ –5, –80

   Ⓒ 5, –80

   Ⓓ –5, 80

Select all correct answers.

4. Choose all the situations that can be described with a negative number.

   Ⓐ The Titanic rests at a depth of about 12,000 feet.

   Ⓑ The temperature of the photosphere of the Sun is approximately 5,505 °C.

   Ⓒ The height of the Taipei 101 skyscraper in Taiwan is 1,671 feet.

   Ⓓ The average high temperature in Antarctica in January is 15 °F below zero.

   Ⓔ The world record for deepest scuba dive is 1,083 feet.

   Ⓕ The world record for highest base jump from a building is 2,205 feet above sea level.

CONSTRUCTED RESPONSE

5. An object's elevation is its height above some fixed point. The most commonly used point is sea level. The word "altitude" is used to describe an object's position above sea level, whereas the word "depth" is used to describe an object's position below sea level. Express each of the following situations as a signed number or zero.

   a. An airplane at an altitude of 30,000 feet

   _____

   b. A submarine at a depth of 1,200 feet

   _____

   c. A boat on the surface of the ocean

   _____

6. In golf, par is the number of strokes an average player should need to complete a particular hole. If a golfer scores under par, the score is reported as a negative number representing the number of strokes less than par. If a golfer scores over par, the score is reported as a positive number. Scoring par exactly is represented by 0. Express each of the following scores as a signed number or zero.

a. Margaret completed 18 holes with an overall score of 9 under par.

_____

b. Anika completed the last hole with a score of 1 over par.

_____

c. Johan completed 9 holes on par.

_____

d. Seamus completed the first hole of the tournament with a score of 2 under par.

_____

7. In a standard savings account, the term "credit" is used to describe a deposit of money into the account. The term "debit" is used to describe a withdrawal of money from the account. Describe what a positive number, a negative number, and zero mean in this context.

_____

_____

_____

_____

_____

8. Use a signed number to represent each of the following situations. Then describe what 0 represents in the same situation.

a. Salazar dives to a depth of 73 feet.

_____

_____

_____

b. Nu deposits $16.78 into her bank account.

_____

_____

_____

c. Overnight, the temperature drops by 15 °F.

_____

_____

_____

9. Write two situations that could be described by each of the following numbers.

a. 50

_____

_____

_____

b. −50

_____

_____

_____

6.NS.6a, 6.NS.6b

SELECTED RESPONSE

Select the correct answer.

1. Describe the locations of 3 and −3 with respect to 0 on a number line.

   Ⓐ 3 is to the right of 0, and −3 is to the right of 0.

   Ⓑ 3 is to the left of 0, and −3 is to the left of 0.

   Ⓒ 3 is to the left of 0, and −3 is to the right of 0.

   Ⓓ 3 is to the right of 0, and −3 is to the left of 0.

2. What is the opposite of 12?

   Ⓐ −12

   Ⓑ $-\dfrac{1}{12}$

   Ⓒ $\dfrac{1}{12}$

   Ⓓ 12

3. In which quadrant is $\left(3, -\dfrac{4}{5}\right)$?

   Ⓐ Quadrant I

   Ⓑ Quadrant II

   Ⓒ Quadrant III

   Ⓓ Quadrant IV

4. If the point (−1.9, −2) is reflected across the *x*-axis, which quadrant will it be in?

   Ⓐ Quadrant I

   Ⓑ Quadrant II

   Ⓒ Quadrant III

   Ⓓ Quadrant IV

5. Choose the correct sign description of a point in Quadrant I.

   Ⓐ (+, +)

   Ⓑ (−, −)

   Ⓒ (+, −)

   Ⓓ (−, +)

Select all correct answers.

6. Which pairs of numbers lie on opposite sides of 0 on a number line?

   Ⓐ 8, 7

   Ⓑ −10, 10

   Ⓒ −4, 9

   Ⓓ −8, −15

   Ⓔ −21, 21

   Ⓕ 2, 200

CONSTRUCTED RESPONSE

7. Graph −5, 0, 2, and 4 on the number line. Then, graph their opposites on the same number line.

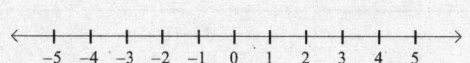

8. Elevation is measured as a distance above or below sea level. Sea level has an elevation of 0 feet. Johanna is standing on a hillside 35 feet above sea level, and Marcus is exploring a cave at an elevation that is the opposite of Johanna's elevation. What is Marcus's elevation?

_____

9. The point (1.235, −987) is in Quadrant IV. What kind of reflection would move this point from Quadrant IV to Quadrant III? Which coordinate(s) would change signs?

_____

_____

_____

_____

_____

_____

_____

10. To celebrate the 100th anniversary of the opening of their school, the teachers organize a treasure hunt for the students. One of the clues states, "Think of the main office as 0 on a number line. You will find the next clue in the room that is the opposite of the teachers' lounge." Use the diagram below to determine where the students should go to find the next clue. Explain.

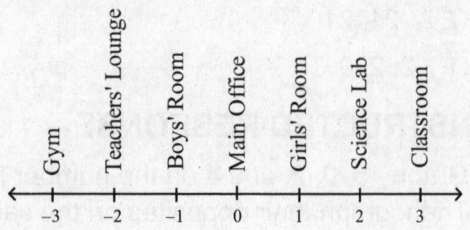

_____

_____

_____

11. a. Find the opposites of −8, 1, and 7.

_____

   b. Find the opposites of the opposites from part a.

_____

   c. What do you notice about a number and the opposite of its opposite?

_____

_____

12. Consider the ordered pair $\left(\frac{2}{3}, y\right)$. Find a value of y that places the ordered pair in each quadrant. If it is not possible for the ordered pair to be in a certain quadrant, explain why.

_____

_____

13. The following graph shows the point (−4, 3). It also shows the points that result when (−4, 3) is reflected across the x-axis and the y-axis.

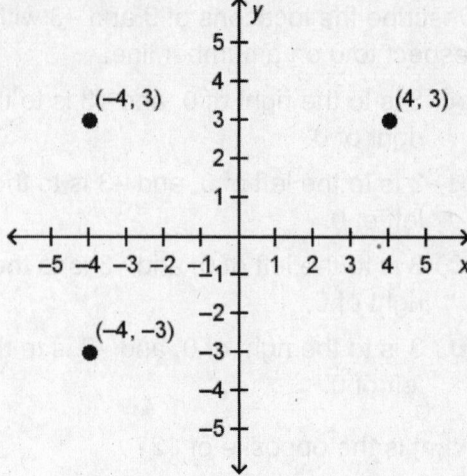

   a. The point (−4, 3) reflected across the x-axis is (−4, −3). What do you notice about the signs of the coordinates?

_____

_____

   b. The point (−4, 3) reflected across the y-axis is (4, 3). What do you notice about the signs of the coordinates?

_____

_____

   c. What do you think would happen to the signs of the coordinates of (−4, 3) if it were reflected across the x-axis and then the result was reflected across the y-axis? Explain your answer and provide the resulting point.

_____

_____

_____

6.NS.6c

SELECTED RESPONSE

Select the correct answer.

1. Where is $\frac{2}{3}$ on a number line?

   (A) Between –3 and –2

   (B) Between –1 and 0

   (C) Between 0 and 1

   (D) Between 2 and 3

2. Identify the point on the number line.

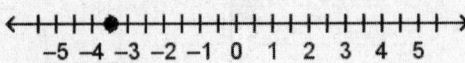

   (A) –4

   (B) –3.5

   (C) 3.5

   (D) 4

3. Identify the coordinates of the point.

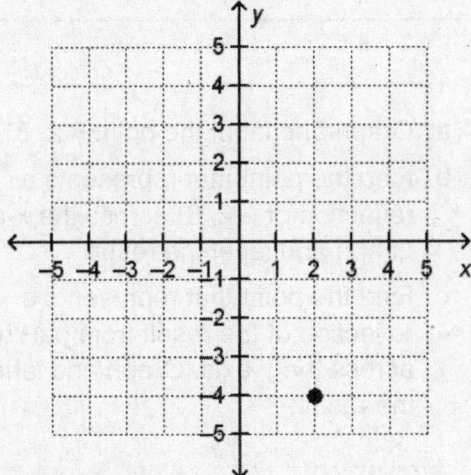

   (A) (–2, –4)

   (B) (–4, –2)

   (C) (–4, 2)

   (D) (2, –4)

4. Describe the process of graphing $\left(\frac{4}{5}, \frac{1}{3}\right)$ on a coordinate plane.

   (A) Starting at the origin, move $\frac{4}{5}$ unit in the positive x-direction. Then, move $\frac{1}{3}$ unit in the positive y-direction.

   (B) Starting at the origin, move $\frac{4}{5}$ unit in the negative x-direction. Then, move $\frac{1}{3}$ unit in the negative y-direction.

   (C) Starting at the origin, move $\frac{4}{5}$ unit in the positive x-direction. Then, move $\frac{1}{3}$ unit in the negative y-direction.

   (D) Starting at the origin, move $\frac{4}{5}$ unit in the negative x-direction. Then, move $\frac{1}{3}$ unit in the positive y-direction.

Select all correct answers.

5. What numbers are graphed on the vertical number line?

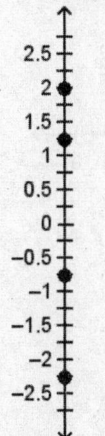

   (A) –2.5   (E) 1

   (B) –2.25   (F) 1.25

   (C) –1.75   (G) 2

   (D) –0.75   (H) 2.5

CONSTRUCTED RESPONSE

6. Graph and label (0.75, –1.25), (1.5, 2), (–0.25, –1.75), and (–1, 0.75).

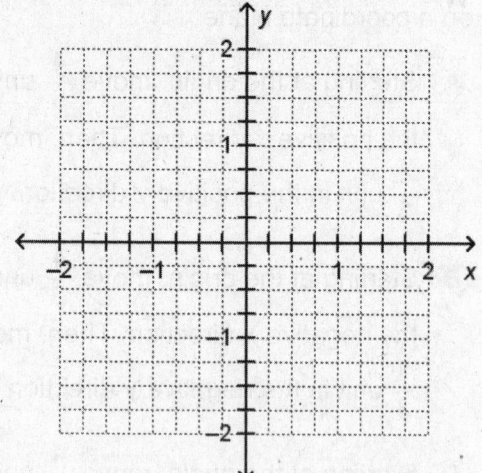

7. A group of students is participating in a tug-of-war contest. The rope is laid out in a straight line with a knot in the middle. The students are positioned according to the following diagram. The object of the game for both teams is to pull the knot 2 units in their direction. The first team to do so wins the contest. Assume that each team pulls in a straight line. If Holden's side wins, find the final positions of Holden and Marishka. Explain your answers using a number line.

Juan Phoebe Holden | Knot | Marishka Ming Thomas

–6 –5 –4 –3 –2 –1 0 1 2 3 4 5 6

_____
_____
_____
_____

8. Below is a map showing various places in relation to Carlos's house at the origin. Find the coordinates of the library, the school, the bike shop, and the baseball field.

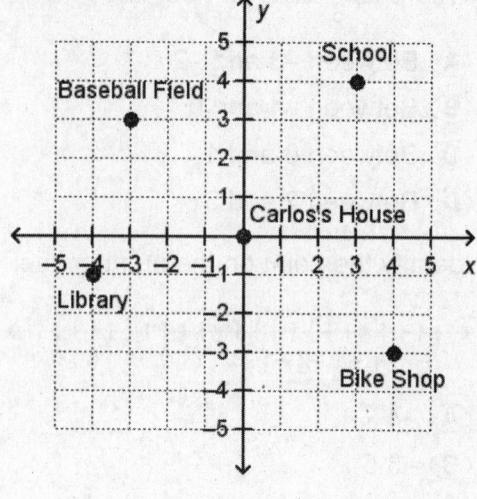

_____
_____
_____
_____

9. a. Graph and label the point (–2, 8).

b. Find the point that represents a reflection of (–2, 8) across the x-axis. Graph and label the result.

c. Find the point that represents a reflection of the result from part b across the y-axis. Graph and label the result.

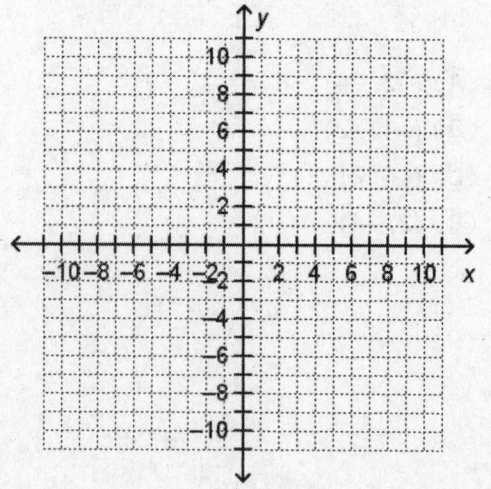

6.NS.7a

SELECTED RESPONSE
Select the correct answer.

1. If $-3 > -7$ and $1 > -7$, where are -3 and 1 relative to -7 on a number line?

   Ⓐ -3 and 1 are both to the right of -7.

   Ⓑ -3 and 1 are both to the left of -7.

   Ⓒ -3 is to the right of -7 and 1 is to the left of -7.

   Ⓓ -3 is to the left of -7 and 1 is to the right of -7.

2. If $\frac{4}{3} > \frac{3}{5}$ and $\frac{1}{2} < \frac{3}{5}$, where are $\frac{4}{3}$ and $\frac{1}{2}$ relative to $\frac{3}{5}$ on a number line?

   Ⓐ $\frac{4}{3}$ and $\frac{1}{2}$ are both to the right of $\frac{3}{5}$.

   Ⓑ $\frac{4}{3}$ and $\frac{1}{2}$ are both to the left of $\frac{3}{5}$.

   Ⓒ $\frac{4}{3}$ is to the right of $\frac{3}{5}$, and $\frac{1}{2}$ is to the left of $\frac{3}{5}$.

   Ⓓ $\frac{4}{3}$ is to the left of $\frac{3}{5}$, and $\frac{1}{2}$ is to the right of $\frac{3}{5}$.

3. A number x is to the left of 10.2 on a number line. Which inequality describes this situation?

   Ⓐ $x > 10.2$

   Ⓑ $x < 10.2$

   Ⓒ $-10.2 < x$

   Ⓓ $x < -10.2$

4. On a number line, a number p is to the right of 18. Which of the following choices describes this situation?

   Ⓐ $18 > p$ Ⓒ $p < -18$

   Ⓑ $-18 > p$ Ⓓ $p > 18$

Select all correct answers.

5. Which statements are equivalent to the inequality $-2.5 < \frac{8}{13}$?

   Ⓐ -2.5 is to the left of $\frac{8}{13}$ on a number line.

   Ⓑ $\frac{8}{13}$ is to the right of -2.5 on a number line.

   Ⓒ $\frac{8}{13}$ is to the left of -2.5 on a number line.

   Ⓓ -2.5 is less than $\frac{8}{13}$.

   Ⓔ -2.5 is to the right of $\frac{8}{13}$ on a number line.

   Ⓕ $\frac{8}{13} < -2.5$

   Ⓖ $\frac{8}{13} > -2.5$

   Ⓗ $\frac{8}{13}$ is less than -2.5.

CONSTRUCTED RESPONSE

6. Describe the positions of 10 and 17 relative to each other on a number line in two different ways, given that $17 > 10$.

   _____

   _____

   _____

7. $0.001 < x$ and $x < 10,000$. Is x between 0.001 and 10,000, to the left of 0.001, or to the right of 10,000? Explain your reasoning.

   _____

   _____

8. Look at the following inequalities.

$$1,000,000 > \frac{7}{23}, \ 0 < \frac{7}{23}, \ 22 > \frac{7}{23},$$

$$-1,000 < \frac{7}{23}, \ -\frac{18}{19} < \frac{7}{23}, \ \frac{7}{23} > 0.2,$$

$$\frac{7}{23} < \frac{1}{2}, \ \frac{7}{23} < 4\frac{1}{6}$$

a. Which of the numbers above are to the right of $\frac{7}{23}$ on a number line?

_____

_____

b. Which of the numbers above are to the left of $\frac{7}{23}$ on a number line?

_____

_____

9. Consider the three points on the number line.

a. Pick any two of the points and write an inequality statement. Explain your answer using the positions of the two numbers relative to each other on the number line.

_____

_____

_____

_____

_____

b. Could the relationship between the two numbers you chose be represented in a different way? If so, write the inequality.

_____

10. Matthias says that the inequality $1 > -2.2$ is true because 1 is to the right of -2.2 on a number line. Helga says that the inequality is true because -2.2 is to the left of 1 on a number line. Who is correct? Explain your answer by graphing 1 and -2.2 on a number line and interpreting the result.

_____

_____

_____

_____

11. Consider the inequality $-5.5 < -4$.

a. Graph the two numbers on a number line.

b. Describe the positions of -5.5 and -4 relative to each other on a number line in two different ways.

_____

_____

_____

_____

c. Write an inequality using -5.5 and a number to the left of -5.5 on the number line.

_____

d. Write an inequality using -4 and a number to the right of -4 on the number line.

_____

6.NS.7b

SELECTED RESPONSE
Select the correct answer.

1. The thermometer at Bruce's house shows a temperature of –2 °F. The thermometer at Zan's house reads –5 °F. Which inequality represents this situation? Whose thermometer shows a warmer temperature?

   Ⓐ –2 °F < –5 °F; Bruce's thermometer shows a warmer temperature.

   Ⓑ –2 °F < –5 °F; Zan's thermometer shows a warmer temperature.

   Ⓒ –2 °F > –5 °F; Bruce's thermometer shows a warmer temperature.

   Ⓓ –2 °F > –5 °F; Zan's thermometer shows a warmer temperature.

2. Marco and Randy decide to have a foot race on a local field. Marco can maintain a speed of 8 miles per hour, while Randy runs at 6 miles per hour. Which inequality represents this situation? Who is faster?

   Ⓐ 8 mph > 6 mph; Marco is faster.

   Ⓑ 8 mph > 6 mph; Randy is faster.

   Ⓒ 8 mph < 6 mph; Marco is faster.

   Ⓓ 8 mph < 6 mph; Randy is faster.

3. In a cooking class, each student needs $\frac{2}{3}$ cup of sugar for a recipe. Zach has $\frac{3}{4}$ cup of sugar at his cooking station, while Suzanne has $\frac{1}{2}$ cup at her cooking station. Who has enough sugar to make the recipe?

   Ⓐ Zach has enough sugar.

   Ⓑ Suzanne has enough sugar.

   Ⓒ Zach and Suzanne both have enough sugar.

   Ⓓ Neither Zach nor Suzanne has enough sugar.

4. Anthony has $53.43 in his savings account, Maxine has $54.78, Rodolfo has $54.98, and Nicola has $53.29. Who has saved the most money? Who has saved the least?

   Ⓐ Maxine has saved the most money, and Anthony has saved the least.

   Ⓑ Maxine has saved the most money, and Nicola has saved the least.

   Ⓒ Rodolfo has saved the most money, and Nicola has saved the least.

   Ⓓ Rodolfo has saved the most money, and Anthony has saved the least.

Select all correct answers.

5. Jack needs a piece of wood at least $\frac{13}{16}$ inch long for some detail work on a project he is working on. Which of the following lengths of wood would meet his requirements?

   Ⓐ $\frac{1}{2}$ inch

   Ⓑ $\frac{7}{8}$ inch

   Ⓒ $\frac{3}{4}$ inch

   Ⓓ $\frac{27}{32}$ inch

   Ⓔ $\frac{5}{8}$ inch

CONSTRUCTED RESPONSE

6. A recipe calls for $\frac{2}{3}$ cup strawberries, $\frac{1}{4}$ cup sugar, $\frac{1}{2}$ cup walnuts, and $\frac{3}{4}$ cup flour. Order the amounts from least to greatest. Which ingredient does the recipe require the least amount of?

   _____

7. While climbing a mountain, Chuck and Marissa decided to take separate trails and meet at the peak. Chuck took the easier trail and was at an elevation of about 425 feet after an hour. Marissa took the more advanced trail and made it to 550 feet in an hour. Marissa started to get tired and was only able to climb 150 more feet in the next hour. Since Chuck took the easier trail, he was able to climb an additional 350 feet in the second hour. Write inequalities that express their locations on the mountain after 1 hour and after 2 hours. Who was at a higher elevation after 2 hours?

_____

_____

_____

8. Sally plants four flowers in her garden and measures their heights (Height 1). One month later, she measures their heights again (Height 2). Which flower grew the most? Show your work.

Flower	Height 1	Height 2
1	$6\frac{1}{2}$ in.	$8\frac{5}{16}$ in.
2	$7\frac{3}{4}$ in.	$8\frac{1}{4}$ in.
3	$5\frac{7}{8}$ in.	$9\frac{3}{16}$ in.
4	$6\frac{5}{16}$ in.	$7\frac{1}{2}$ in.

_____

_____

_____

_____

_____

9. The record low temperatures for three towns in Alaska are given in the table below. Write three inequalities using three different pairs of temperatures. Which of the three towns has the highest record low?

Town	Record Low
Anchorage	$-34\ °F$
Barrow	$-56\ °F$
Juneau	$-22\ °F$

_____

_____

_____

10. Sam and Nima have part-time jobs for the summer. Over the last three weeks, Sam has made deposits of $40.25, $58.50, and $28.40 into his savings account. During the same time, his sister Nima has deposited $60.85, $20.00, and $62.13 into her savings account.

a. Write an inequality that compares Sam's total deposits with Nima's total deposits. Who deposited more money?

_____

_____

b. Sam and Nima both make withdrawals from their accounts. Nima withdraws $37.28. After the withdrawals, Sam has more money in his account than Nima does. What is the largest amount Sam could have withdrawn for this to be true? Explain your reasoning.

_____

_____

_____

_____

6.NS.7c, 6.NS.7d

SELECTED RESPONSE
Select the correct answer.

1. Marlene is about to write a check for $103.48 to pay for groceries. When she subtracts the amount of the check from her account balance, she sees that the new balance would be –$28.80. Rather than overdraw her checking account, Marlene asks the cashier to remove some items. For Marlene to be able to pay by check without overdrawing her account, what is the minimum value of the items the cashier must remove?

    (A) –$103.48

    (B) –$28.80

    (C) $28.80

    (D) $103.48

2. Which of the following pairs of numbers have the same absolute value?

    (A) –1, 0.1

    (B) $-\frac{1}{2}, \frac{1}{2}$

    (C) 0, 1

    (D) –4, –40

3. How do the numbers –3 and 2 compare? How do their absolute values compare?

    (A) –3 is greater than 2, but 2 has the greater absolute value.

    (B) 2 is greater than –3, but –3 has the greater absolute value.

    (C) –3 is greater than 2, and –3 has the greater absolute value.

    (D) 2 is greater than –3, and 2 has the greater absolute value.

4. Which is greater, $\frac{9}{13}$ or $1\frac{2}{3}$? Which number has the greater absolute value?

    (A) $-\frac{9}{13}$ is greater than $1\frac{2}{3}$, but $1\frac{2}{3}$ has the greater absolute value.

    (B) $1\frac{2}{3}$ is greater than $-\frac{9}{13}$, but $-\frac{9}{13}$ has the greater absolute value.

    (C) $-\frac{9}{13}$ is greater than $1\frac{2}{3}$, and $-\frac{9}{13}$ has the greater absolute value.

    (D) $1\frac{2}{3}$ is greater than $-\frac{9}{13}$, and $1\frac{2}{3}$ has the greater absolute value.

Select all correct answers.

5. Which numbers have an absolute value of 2?

    (A) –3

    (B) –2

    (C) –1

    (D) 0

    (E) 1

    (F) 2

    (G) 3

CONSTRUCTED RESPONSE

6. Identify the pairs of numbers on the number line that have the same absolute value.

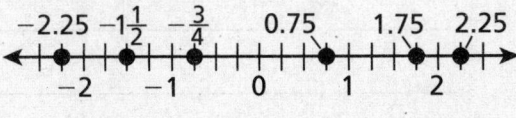

_____

_____

_____

7. Both Vince and Betty use their debit cards to make purchases. After their purchases, Vince's checking account balance shows a transaction of –$25.00, while Betty's shows –$18.25. Who spent more money? Justify your answer by writing an inequality.

_____

_____

_____

8. Find two numbers a and b with the following properties.

a. $a > b$, $|a| > |b|$

_____

b. $a > b$, $|a| < |b|$

_____

c. $a > b$, $|a| = |b|$

_____

9. Monica is hiking in California's Death Valley. Along her route, she sees a sign that says "282 feet below sea level." Elevation is the height above or below a fixed point. Positive elevations indicate heights above the point, and negative elevations indicate heights below the point.

a. What is the elevation of the sign relative to sea level? Explain.

_____

_____

b. How far up or down must Monica hike from the sign to reach sea level? Explain.

_____

_____

10. In a town, Talbot Street is the main commercial center. The number line shown represents Talbot Street, where each unit represents 100 feet.

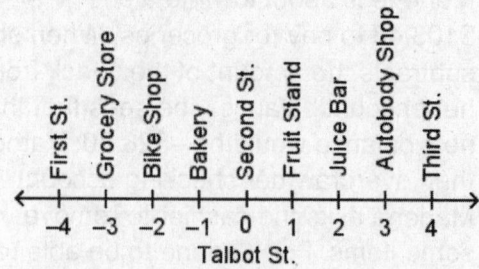

a. Yvette and Naomi are at the intersection of Second Street and Talbot Street. If Yvette goes to the grocery store and Naomi goes to the fruit stand, who travels farther from Second Street? Justify your answer.

_____

_____

_____

b. Anzelm is at the intersection of First Street and Talbot Street. How many feet is Anzelm from Second Street? Justify your answer.

_____

_____

_____

11. Suppose a and b are two negative numbers. If $a > b$, is it possible that $|a| > |b|$? Explain your answer, using a number line and examples as needed.

_____

_____

_____

_____

_____

_____

6.NS.8

SELECTED RESPONSE

Select the correct answer.

1. On a coordinate plane, point *A* is located at (−5, 3). To get to point *B*, move 8 units to the right, 6 units down, and 1 unit to the left. What are the coordinates of point *B*?

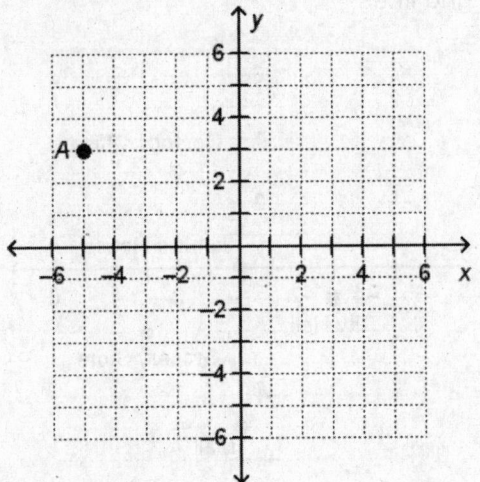

Ⓐ (−12, 9)

Ⓑ (−12, −3)

Ⓒ (2, −3)

Ⓓ (2, 9)

2. What is the distance between point *A* at (−7, 5) and point *B* at (2, 5)?

Ⓐ −9

Ⓑ 5

Ⓒ 9

Ⓓ 10

3. North is the positive *y*-direction on a coordinate plane, and 1 unit on the plane represents 1 foot. A soccer ball is kicked directly east from point (−3, 4). The ball travels a horizontal distance of 23 feet through the air and rolls an extra 14 feet. Where does the ball stop?

Ⓐ (34, 4)

Ⓑ (−40, 4)

Ⓒ (20, 4)

Ⓓ (11, 4)

CONSTRUCTED RESPONSE

4. Jerry and Meena are riding their bicycles through the city to meet at the park, as shown on the coordinate plane. On the coordinate plane, north is in the positive *y*-direction, and 1 unit represents 1 city block. Jerry starts at the point (2, −5) and rides north toward the park at the point (2, 1). Meena starts at east of the park at the point (5, 1) and rides west toward the park. How far does each person travel to reach the park?

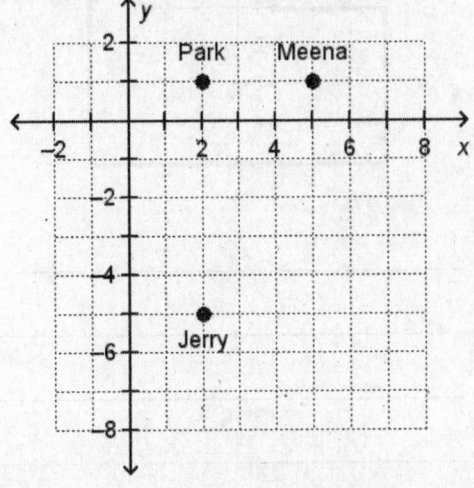

_____

_____

_____

5. Point *A* is located at (−3, 1), point *B* is located at (−3, −4), and point *C* is located at (3, 1) on a coordinate plane.

a. What is the distance between points *A* and *B*?

_____

_____

b. What is the distance between points *A* and *C*?

_____

_____

6. Ravel wants to build a fence around his garden. The shape of his garden is shown on the coordinate plane, where each unit represents 1 foot. Use absolute values to find the length of each section of fence. How many feet of fence does Ravel need? Show your work.

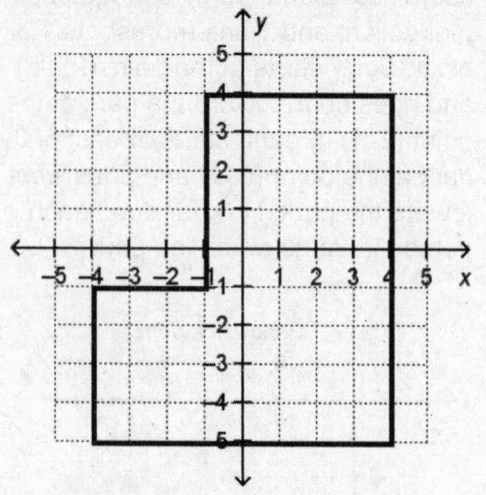

_____

_____

_____

_____

_____

_____

_____

_____

_____

_____

_____

_____

_____

_____

_____

7. Jamie's house is in the center of town, at point (0, 0). He is doing some errands in town and stops at the other four labeled points on the coordinate plane. One unit on the coordinate plane represents 1 block. He travels 4 blocks to his first stop. His second stop is 7 blocks from his first stop. He can only travel on the sidewalks, which are represented by the grid lines.

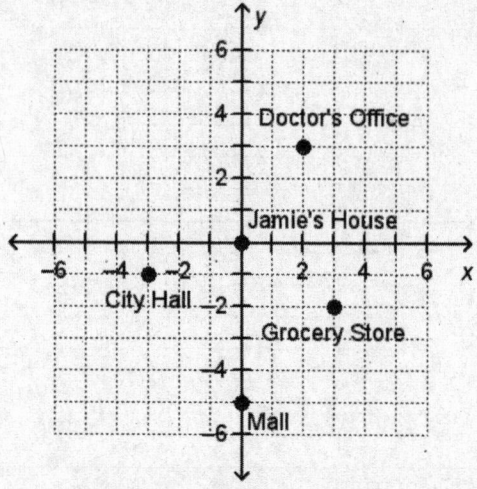

a. Where did Jamie go first? List all possible answers. Justify your answers.

_____

_____

_____

_____

_____

b. Where did Jamie go second? List all possible answers. Justify your answers.

_____

_____

_____

_____

_____

6.EE.1

SELECTED RESPONSE

Select the correct answer.

1. Which exponential expression equals
   $5 \times 5 \times 5 \times 5 \times 5 \times 5$?

   (A) 5^5

   (B) 5^6

   (C) 6^5

   (D) 5^7

2. Which is the expanded form of 7^5?

   (A) $7 \times 7 \times 7 \times 7 \times 7 \times 7$

   (B) $5 \times 5 \times 5 \times 5 \times 5 \times 5 \times 5$

   (C) $7 \times 7 \times 7 \times 7$

   (D) $7 \times 7 \times 7 \times 7 \times 7$

3. Which is the expanded form of $3^2 \times 3^5$?

   (A) $3 \times 3 \times 3 \times 3 \times 3 \times 3 \times 3$

   (B) $9 \times 9 \times 9 \times 9 \times 9 \times 9 \times 9 \times 9 \times 9 \times 9$

   (C) $3 \times 3 \times 3 \times 3 \times 3 \times 3 \times 3 \times 3 \times 3 \times 3$

   (D) $9 \times 9 \times 9 \times 9 \times 9 \times 9 \times 9$

4. Which is the value of 6^4?

   (A) 216

   (B) 1,296

   (C) 4,096

   (D) 7,776

Select all correct answers.

5. Which of the following expressions is
   equal to 64?

   (A) 2^4

   (B) 8^2

   (C) 6^3

   (D) 2^6

   (E) 4^3

Match each exponential expression with its expanded form.

_____ 6. $2^3 \times 5^4$

_____ 7. $9^3 \times 11^5$

_____ 8. 12^5

_____ 9. $2^4 \times 5^4$

_____ 10. $9^4 \times 11^5$

A $2 \times 2 \times 2 \times 2 \times 5 \times 5 \times 5 \times 5$

B $12 \times 12 \times 12 \times 12 \times 12 \times 12 \times 12$

C $9 \times 9 \times 9 \times 9 \times 11 \times 11 \times 11 \times 11 \times 11$

D $5 \times 5 \times 5 \times 5 \times 5 \times 3 \times 3 \times 3$

E $5 \times 5 \times 5 \times 2 \times 2$

F $9 \times 9 \times 9 \times 11 \times 11 \times 11 \times 11 \times 11$

G $2 \times 2 \times 2 \times 5 \times 5 \times 5 \times 5$

H $12 \times 12 \times 12 \times 12 \times 12$

CONSTRUCTED RESPONSE

11. Louis evaluated the expression $3^5 + 6^3$, but he made a mistake. His work is shown.
    Identify Louis's mistake and show how to find the correct answer.

    $3^5 + 6^3 = 5 \times 5 \times 5 + 3 \times 3 \times 3 \times 3 \times 3 \times 3$

    $\qquad = 854$

    _____

    _____

12. Evaluate $11^2 \times 2^3 + 3^5 + 9^3$. Show your work.

_____

_____

_____

_____

_____

_____

_____

_____

13. A square has a side length of 8 centimeters.

a. The area of a square is the square of the side length. Write and evaluate an exponential expression for the area of the given square.

_____

_____

b. If the given square is one side of a cube, the surface area of the cube will be 6 times the area of the square. Write and evaluate an exponential expression for the surface area of the cube.

_____

_____

c. If the given square is one side of a cube, the volume of the cube will be the cube of the side length of the square. Write and evaluate an exponential expression for the volume of the cube.

_____

_____

14. Kerry puts pennies into a jar every day. On the first day, she puts 2 pennies into the jar. On the second day, she adds double the number of pennies she put into the jar on the first day. On the third day, she adds double the number of pennies she put into the jar on the second day. This pattern follows for a week.

a. Write exponential expressions for the number of pennies put into the jar on the second, third, and fourth days.

_____

_____

_____

_____

b. What pattern do you notice in the expressions you wrote for part a?

_____

_____

_____

_____

c. Write an expression in exponential form for the number of pennies she puts into the jar on the seventh day. Expand and evaluate the expression.

_____

_____

_____

_____

d. How much money will be in the jar at the end of the week?

_____

_____

_____

SELECTED RESPONSE

Select the correct answer.

1. Which expression below represents "*k* more than 8"?

   Ⓐ $8k$

   Ⓑ $8 + k$

   Ⓒ $8 - k$

   Ⓓ $\dfrac{8}{k}$

2. Which statement below could be represented by the expression $7 - t$?

   Ⓐ *t* less than 7

   Ⓑ 7 times *t*

   Ⓒ *t* more than 7

   Ⓓ 7 less than *t*

3. Which statement below CANNOT be represented by the expression $t - 16$?

   Ⓐ 16 less than *t*

   Ⓑ *t* decreased by 16

   Ⓒ *t* less than 16

   Ⓓ 16 subtracted from *t*

4. Marcus and Judy are picking apples. At the end of the day, Marcus has *a* apples. Judy has 5 times as many apples as Marcus. How many apples does Judy have in terms of *a*?

   Ⓐ $a - 5$

   Ⓑ $5 + a$

   Ⓒ $\dfrac{5}{a}$

   Ⓓ $5a$

Select all correct answers.

5. Which of the following statements could be represented by the expression $d - 10$?

   Ⓐ 10 less than *d*

   Ⓑ 10 more than *d*

   Ⓒ *d* decreased by 10

   Ⓓ *d* less than 10

   Ⓔ *d* minus 10

   Ⓕ *d* increased by 10

6. Which of the following indicates that the operation is addition?

   Ⓐ 8 plus *j*

   Ⓑ *k* fewer than 10

   Ⓒ *r* increased by 7

   Ⓓ 14 divided by *n*

   Ⓔ 11 decreased by *h*

   Ⓕ 6 more than *s*

Select the correct answer for each lettered part.

7. Choose the operation that is indicated by each statement.

   a. 5 more than *n*   ○ +   ○ −   ○ ×   ○ ÷

   b. 11 fewer than *w*   ○ +   ○ −   ○ ×   ○ ÷

   c. *k* divided by 4   ○ +   ○ −   ○ ×   ○ ÷

   d. *y* less than 8   ○ +   ○ −   ○ ×   ○ ÷

   e. 2 times *r*   ○ +   ○ −   ○ ×   ○ ÷

   f. 9 increased by *g*   ○ +   ○ −   ○ ×   ○ ÷

CONSTRUCTED RESPONSE

8. Rebecca and Clark are playing baseball. During the first hour, Rebecca has *r* hits and Clark has 3 more hits than Rebecca. During the second hour, Clark has *c* hits and Rebecca hits 5 fewer than twice the number of Clark's hits.

   a. Write an expression for the number of hits Clark made in the first hour.

   _____

   b. Write an expression for the number of hits Rebecca made in the second hour.

   _____

9. The zoo has lions, tigers, and bears. There are *t* tigers in the zoo.

   a. How many lions are in the zoo if there are 3 more lions that tigers?

   _____

   b. How many bears are in the zoo if the number of bears is two times the number of lions?

   _____

10. a. Write an expression represented by the statement "3 more than *n*."

   _____

   b. Write an expression represented by the statement "*n* increased by 3."

   _____

   c. Write an expression represented by the statement "*n* plus 3."

   _____

   d. What can you say about the statements in parts a through c in terms of the expressions they represent?

   _____

   _____

11. A construction crew is installing lights in a room. The room has an area of *s* square feet. The number of lights required in the room is *s* divided by 5.

   a. How many lights are required in the room?

   _____

   b. The construction crew has 10 more lights than the number of lights required. Use your answer from part a to write an expression for the number of lights the construction crew has.

   _____

   c. Some of the lights are broken, so it turns out that the construction crew has 15 fewer lights than the number of lights required. Use your answer from part a to write an expression for the number of lights the construction crew has.

   _____

   d. After receiving a new shipment, the construction crew has twice the number of required lights. Use your answer from part a to write an expression for the number of lights the construction crew has.

   _____

12. Trudy is ordering pies from Sal. Trudy orders 3 more apple pies than *c* cherry pies. Sal gives Trudy *c* cherry pies and *c* − 3 apple pies. Explain Sal's mistake and correct it.

   _____

   _____

   _____

   _____

6.EE.2b

SELECTED RESPONSE

Select the correct answer.

1. Which expression is the product of two factors?

    Ⓐ $8(5 + n)$

    Ⓑ $2 + h$

    Ⓒ $\dfrac{x}{3}$

    Ⓓ $t - 9$

2. In the expression $n + 23$, what is 23?

    Ⓐ A coefficient

    Ⓑ A factor

    Ⓒ A term

    Ⓓ A sum

3. Which expression is a quotient?

    Ⓐ $9r$

    Ⓑ $\dfrac{b}{12}$

    Ⓒ $15 + d$

    Ⓓ $m - 4$

4. Which is the coefficient in the expression $23y + 5$?

    Ⓐ y

    Ⓑ 5

    Ⓒ $23y$

    Ⓓ 23

Select the correct answer for each lettered part.

5. Identify each expression as a sum, a difference, a product, or a quotient.

a. $4t$	○ Sum	○ Difference	○ Product	○ Quotient
b. $6 - u$	○ Sum	○ Difference	○ Product	○ Quotient
c. $f + 10$	○ Sum	○ Difference	○ Product	○ Quotient
d. $27(v + 3)$	○ Sum	○ Difference	○ Product	○ Quotient
e. $42 + k$	○ Sum	○ Difference	○ Product	○ Quotient
f. $\dfrac{t}{13}$	○ Sum	○ Difference	○ Product	○ Quotient

CONSTRUCTED RESPONSE

6. Write the expression represented by the statement "7 times the sum of 2 and x." Identify the factors in the expression.

   _____

   _____

   _____

7. Identify two sums in the expression $14 + b + 27d$. Identify the terms of each.

   _____

   _____

   _____

   _____

8. Identify each product in the expression $14n + 2 + 6k$ and then identify the coefficients in each product.

_____

_____

_____

9. a. Identify the terms of the expression $7x^2 + 2y - 8$. Identify which terms in the expression are products and find the coefficients in those products.

_____

_____

b. List the order of operations used to evaluate the expression. What is the value of the expression at $x = 2$ and $y = -1$?

_____

_____

_____

_____

_____

10. Lara says the factors of the expression $(5 + s)(k + 7)$ are 5, s, k, and 7. Is this correct? If not, explain what Lara found and write the correct factors.

_____

_____

_____

_____

_____

11. Use the expression $56xy + 5 - 6x + \dfrac{y}{20}$, for the following questions.

a. Identify two sums.

_____

_____

b. Identify the terms of the expression.

_____

_____

c. Identify a product of two factors. Find the coefficient in the product.

_____

_____

d. Identify the quotient.

_____

12. Identify all sums, products, and factors in the expression.

$$(x + 5)(y + 9) + (2 + x)(y + 23)$$

_____

_____

_____

_____

_____

_____

_____

_____

_____

_____

_____

_____

6.EE.2c

SELECTED RESPONSE
Select the correct answer.

1. Helen bought notebooks and pencils for school. The number of pencils she bought is given by $6(n-3)$, where n is the number of notebooks she bought. How many pencils did Helen buy if she bought 5 notebooks?

   (A) 2 pencils

   (B) 12 pencils

   (C) 27 pencils

   (D) 48 pencils

2. In what order should the operations be performed to evaluate $6x^2 - 2$ at $x = 3$?

   (A) First, multiply 6 by 3. Then, square the result. Finally, subtract 2 from the result.

   (B) First, find 3^2. Then, subtract 2 from the result. Finally, multiply the result by 6.

   (C) First, find 3^2. Then, multiply the result by 6. Finally, subtract 2 from the result.

   (D) First, multiply 6 by 3. Then, subtract 2 from the result. Finally, square the result.

3. What is the value of the expression $\frac{8}{n} - \frac{1}{2}n^2$ at $n = 4$?

   (A) −6

   (B) −2

   (C) 2

   (D) 24

4. The area of a triangle is given by the formula $A = \frac{1}{2}bh$. What is the area of the triangle if $b = 5$ and $h = 4$?

   (A) 2   (C) 4.5

   (B) 2.5   (D) 10

Select all correct answers.

5. Which expressions are equal to 41 when evaluated at $d = 4$?

   (A) $9d + 5$

   (B) $7 + 3d^2$

   (C) $10d - 1$

   (D) $11d - \dfrac{12}{d}$

   (E) $d^3 - 23$

CONSTRUCTED RESPONSE

6. A rectangular box with dimensions ℓ by w by h has a surface area A given by $A = 2\ell w + 2\ell h + 2wh$. Its volume V is given by $V = \ell wh$. If the dimensions of the box are given as 5 feet by 3 feet by 2.5 feet, what is the surface area and volume of the box? Show your work.

   _____

   _____

   _____

   _____

   _____

   _____

   _____

   _____

7. Evaluate the expression $\frac{1}{4}y + 10 + y^2$ for $y = 8$.

   _____

   _____

   _____

8. Mandy has q quarters. The number of nickels she has is 4 times the number of quarters. She has 10 more dimes than quarters.

   a. Write expressions for the number of nickels and dimes Mandy has.

   _____

   _____

   b. How many nickels and dimes does she have if she has $5 in quarters?

   _____

   _____

   _____

9. Evaluate the expression $11k + 9 - k^2 - \dfrac{15}{k}$ at $k = 5$. Show your work.

   _____

   _____

   _____

   _____

   _____

10. Mark incorrectly evaluated the expression $4x + 12 - x^2$ at $x = 2$. His work is shown. Identify and correct Mark's mistake. Show your work.

$$4(2) + 12 - 2^2 = 4(2) + 10^2$$
$$= 4(2) + 100$$
$$= 8 + 100$$
$$= 108$$

   _____

   _____

   _____

   _____

   _____

11. Rosa is putting cube-shaped tissue boxes into a shipping crate. Each tissue box has a side length of 4 inches.

   a. The volume V of a cube is given by $V = s^3$, where s is the side length of the cube. What is the volume of one tissue box?

   _____

   b. If 32 tissue boxes fit into the crate without any gaps or space left over, what is the volume of the crate? Explain how you find your answer.

   _____

   _____

   _____

   _____

   c. Can you tell what the dimensions of the crate are if you only know its volume? Explain why and give the dimensions, or explain why not.

   _____

   _____

12. Tyler is planting a garden. The garden will contain mums that cost $7 each and daisies that cost $10 for 3.

   a. Write an expression for the cost of m mums and d daisies.

   _____

   _____

   b. How much will it cost for 7 mums and 6 daisies? Show your work.

   _____

   _____

   c. How much will it cost for 3 mums and 9 daisies? Show your work.

   _____

   _____

6.EE.3

SELECTED RESPONSE
Select the correct answer.

1. Which expression is equivalent to $12x - 3x$?

   Ⓐ $x(12 - 3)$

   Ⓑ $8x$

   Ⓒ $3(3x - x)$

   Ⓓ 9

2. What property is used to say that the expression $5x + 7 - 2x$ is equivalent to the expression $5x - 2x + 7$?

   Ⓐ Commutative property of addition

   Ⓑ Commutative property of multiplication

   Ⓒ Associative property of addition

   Ⓓ Distributive property

3. What expression is equivalent to the expression $(1 + 4x) + 2x$?

   Ⓐ $7x$

   Ⓑ $5x + 2x$

   Ⓒ $1 + 6x$

   Ⓓ $x(4 + 2)$

4. The expression $11x^3 - 6y + 2x^3$ is simplified as follows. Which property is NOT used to simplify the expression?

   $$11x^3 - 6y + 2x^3 = 11x^3 + 2x^3 - 6y$$
   $$= x^3(11 + 2) - 6y$$
   $$= x^3(13) - 6y$$
   $$= 13x^3 - 6y$$

   Ⓐ Commutative property of addition

   Ⓑ Commutative property of multiplication

   Ⓒ Associative property of multiplication

   Ⓓ Distributive property

Select all correct answers.

5. The expression $(y + 14x) - 5x - x^2$ is simplified as follows. Which properties of operations are used to simplify the expression?

   $$(y + 14x) - 5x - x^2 = y + (14x - 5x) - x^2$$
   $$= y + x(14 - 5) - x^2$$
   $$= y + x(9) - x^2$$
   $$= y + 9x - x^2$$

   Ⓐ Commutative property of addition

   Ⓑ Commutative property of multiplication

   Ⓒ Associative property of addition

   Ⓓ Associative property of multiplication

   Ⓔ Distributive property

CONSTRUCTED RESPONSE

6. a. Use the distributive property to write $23y - (7x - 2y) + x$ without parentheses.

   _____

   _____

   _____

   b. Use the commutative property of addition to collect like terms.

   _____

   _____

   c. Simplify the result from part b.

   _____

   _____

7. Simplify the expression $(2x + 3y) + y$ using the properties of operations. Show your work.

   _____

   _____

8. Amy is buying fruit for a party she is having. She buys the fruit over a 3-day period. The first day, she buys a apples and n nectarines. The second day, she buys twice as many apples as she bought the first day. On the third day, she buys 10 bananas.

   a. Write an expression for the total number of pieces of fruit Amy buys. Do not simplify.

   _____

   b. Explain how to use the order of operations to simplify the expression. Show your work.

   _____

   _____

   _____

   _____

   _____

   _____

   _____

   _____

9. A rectangular prism has length a, width b, and height c.

   a. Using the formula $A = \ell w$, find the area of each face of the prism and write an expression for the sum of the areas. Collect like terms, and then use the distributive property to simplify the expression so that there are three terms inside the parentheses. Show your work.

   _____

   _____

   _____

   _____

   b. Use the result from part a to write an expression for the total surface area of a cube with side length a. Use the properties of operations to simplify the expression to one term. Show your work.

   _____

   _____

   _____

   _____

   _____

   _____

10. Laura mistakenly found that the expression $4x - 6y$ is equivalent to the expression $12x - 18y - 4(2x + 3y)$. Her work is shown. Find and correct Laura's mistake. Use the properties of operations to correctly simplify $12x - 18y - 4(2x + 3y)$ to two terms. Show your work.

$$12x - 18y - 4(2x + 3y) = 12x - 18y - 8x + 12y \quad \text{Distributive property}$$
$$= 12x - 8x - 18y + 12y \quad \text{Commutative property of addition}$$
$$= 4x - 6y \quad \text{Combine like terms.}$$

_____

_____

_____

_____

6.EE.4

SELECTED RESPONSE

Select the correct answer.

1. Which expression is NOT equivalent to the expression $11 - (3x + 2)$?

   Ⓐ $11 - 3x - 2$

   Ⓑ $9 - 3x$

   Ⓒ $11 - 3x + 2$

   Ⓓ $11 + (-3x - 2)$

2. Which expression is equivalent to $12x - 3(x + 2)$?

   Ⓐ $12x + 6$

   Ⓑ $12x - 6$

   Ⓒ $9x + 6$

   Ⓓ $9x - 6$

3. Which pair of expressions are equivalent?

   Ⓐ $4x - 2 + 5x$ and $7x$

   Ⓑ $(11 + 3x) - x$ and $11 + 2x$

   Ⓒ $12(x - 2)$ and $12x - 2$

   Ⓓ $9x(4)$ and $13x$

Select all correct answers.

4. Which expressions are equivalent to the expression $2x - (-3x + 8y) + 8$?

   Ⓐ $2x + (3x + 8y) + 8$

   Ⓑ $2x + (3x - 8y) + 8$

   Ⓒ $(2x + 3x) - 8y + 8$

   Ⓓ $3x + 8$

   Ⓔ $5x - 8y + 8$

Match each expression with an equivalent expression.

____ 5. $3x - 2 + 8x$

____ 6. $4x - (2x + 1)$

____ 7. $11(x - 1) + 2$

____ 8. $4(3x)$

____ 9. $-13x + 5x$

A $12x$

B $2x - 1$

C $7x$

D $11x - 9$

E $11x - 2$

F $2x + 1$

G $-8x$

CONSTRUCTED RESPONSE

10. Blaine and Tanya are selling pumpkins and tomatoes at a farm stand. Blaine sells p pumpkins and t tomatoes on the first day. The second day he sells double what he sells the first day. Over both days, Tanya sells triple what Blaine sells on the first day.

    a. Write an expression for the total number of pumpkins and tomatoes Blaine sold both days.

    _____

    b. Write an expression for the total number of pumpkins and tomatoes Tanya sold both days.

    _____

    c. Did Blaine and Tanya sell the same amount? Explain.

    _____

11. Peter is making cookies. He needs to add a total of $2\frac{1}{4}$ cups of flour and $2\frac{2}{3}$ cups of sugar per batch. At the beginning of the recipe, he only adds $1\frac{3}{4}$ cups of flour and $\frac{2}{3}$ cup of sugar per batch. He adds $\frac{1}{2}$ cup of flour and $1\frac{1}{3}$ cups of sugar per batch later in the recipe.

   a. Write an expression for the number of cups of flour Peter added to make b batches of cookies.

   _____

   b. Write an expression for the number of cups of sugar Peter added to make b batches of cookies.

   _____

   c. Simplify the expressions from parts a and b. Did Peter add enough flour and sugar to his cookies?

   _____

   _____

   _____

12. Show that the expression $(8x - 12y) + y + 2(3 + 3x)$ is equivalent to the expression $-11y + 6 + 14x$.
   Use the properties of operations to justify your steps.

   _____

   _____

   _____

   _____

   _____

13. Nick is finding the perimeter of a garden. The measurements of the garden are given below. Nick's expression for the perimeter is $2n + 1 + 2n + 4n + 5$.

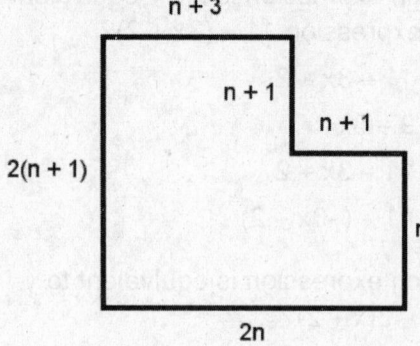

   a. Write an expression for the perimeter of the garden.

   _____

   b. Simplify the expression from part a to two terms. Show your work.

   _____

   _____

   _____

   c. Is Nick's expression for the perimeter correct? Show your work.

   _____

   _____

   _____

   _____

   _____

   _____

   _____

   _____

   _____

6.EE.5

SELECTED RESPONSE

Select the correct answer.

1. For what value of x is the equation $4 = 12x - 2$ true?

   Ⓐ $\dfrac{1}{6}$

   Ⓑ $\dfrac{1}{2}$

   Ⓒ 2

   Ⓓ 6

2. Which values from the set $\{1, 2, 3, 4, 5, 6\}$ are solutions of $9 < 2x + 3$?

   Ⓐ $x = \{1, 2\}$

   Ⓑ $x = \{3, 4, 5, 6\}$

   Ⓒ $x = \{4, 5, 6\}$

   Ⓓ $x = \{1, 2, 3, 4, 5, 6\}$

3. What is a common solution of $x - 8 \le 2$ and $7 \le 2x - 13$?

   Ⓐ 9

   Ⓑ 10

   Ⓒ 11

   Ⓓ The inequalities do not have a common solution.

4. Rachel is typing a 1,500-word report. Her progress is represented by the equation $1,500 = 500 + 50t$, where t is the number of minutes spent typing. If she does not take a break, how many minutes does Rachel need to type to finish her report?

   Ⓐ 10 minutes

   Ⓑ 20 minutes

   Ⓒ 30 minutes

   Ⓓ 40 minutes

Select all correct answers.

5. Which statements below are true when $x = 5$?

   Ⓐ $3 = 2x - 7$

   Ⓑ $3 < 2x - 9$

   Ⓒ $2 \le x + 6$

   Ⓓ $18 = 6x - 12$

   Ⓔ $3 = 2 + x$

CONSTRUCTED RESPONSE

6. Is 4 a solution of $7 \le 5x - 16$? Show your work.

   _____

   _____

   _____

   _____

7. Do all of the values from the set $\{5, 6, 7\}$ make the inequality $9x - 3 < 60$ true? Explain.

   _____

   _____

   _____

   _____

8. What value(s) from the set $\{0, 1, 2\}$ make the equation $4x + 9 = 13$ true? Show your work.

   _____

   _____

   _____

   _____

   _____

9. What values from the set of natural numbers make the inequality $6 + 2x > 8$ true? Explain.

_____

_____

_____

_____

_____

_____

_____

10. Kyle is saving his money to buy a computer for $300. He has already saved $75, and plans to save an additional $22.50 each day.

   a. Write an equation for the number of days Kyle will need to save in order to buy the computer.

_____

   b. If Kyle saves for 10 days, will he have enough money to buy the computer? Explain.

_____

_____

_____

_____

_____

_____

11. a. Which values from the set $\{1, 2, 3, 4\}$ are solutions of $11 \geq 2x + 5$? Show your work.

_____

_____

_____

_____

   b. Which values from the set $\{1, 2, 3, 4\}$ are solutions of $11 > 2x + 5$? Show your work.

_____

_____

_____

_____

_____

   c. How are your answers from parts a and b different?

_____

_____

_____

_____

12. Jasmine says that 2 and 3 are solutions of the inequality $16 \geq 11x - 6$. Is Jasmine correct? Explain. Show your work.

_____

_____

_____

_____

6.EE.6

SELECTED RESPONSE

Select the correct answer.

1. There are red and blue marbles in a bowl. There are twice as many blue marbles as red marbles. What expression represents the number of blue marbles?

   (A) $2b$, where b is the number of blue marbles

   (B) $2r$, where r is the number of red marbles

   (C) $r + 2$, where r is the number of red marbles

   (D) $\dfrac{b}{2}$, where b is the number of blue marbles

2. x is 4 less than a number y. What expression represents the value of x?

   (A) $x - 4$

   (B) $y - 4$

   (C) $x + 4$

   (D) $y + 4$

3. Kyle starts with $15.00 and saves $3.50 each day. What expression represents the total amount Kyle saves?

   (A) $3.50

   (B) $15.00

   (C) $3.5t + 15$, where t is the number of days

   (D) $15t + 3.5$, where t is the number of days

4. The product of two different numbers is 132. If one of the numbers is x, what expression represents the value of the other number?

   (A) $\dfrac{132}{x}$

   (B) $132x$

   (C) $132 - x$

   (D) $x + 132$

Select all correct answers.

5. Joan has 3 fewer dogs than rabbits. If r is the number of rabbits Joan has, which expressions represent the total number of animals Joan has?

   (A) r

   (B) $r + (r - 3)$

   (C) $r - 3$

   (D) $2r - 3$

   (E) $r + (r + 3)$

CONSTRUCTED RESPONSE

6. Paulo and Marie are collecting quarters. The number of quarters Paulo has is 3 times the quantity of 5 fewer than the number of quarters Marie has. Write an expression for the number of quarters Paulo in terms of the number of quarters Marie has. Define any variables used.

   _____

   _____

   _____

   _____

7. The value of x is 3 more than half the value of y.

   a. Write an expression for the value of x in terms of y.

   _____

   b. What is the value of x if $y = 7$? Show your work.

   _____

   _____

   _____

   _____

8. Daisies and tulips are planted in a garden. There are 11 fewer tulips planted than daisies.

   a. Write an expression that represents the number of tulips in terms of the number of daisies. Define any variables used.

_____

_____

   b. If 18 daisies are planted, how many tulips are planted?

_____

_____

9. Elena is selling tickets for an amusement park. She sells triple the number of student tickets as adult tickets and she sells 8 fewer senior tickets than adult tickets.

   a. Write expressions for the number of adult tickets, student tickets, and senior tickets, using *a* as the number of adult tickets.

_____

_____

_____

   b. Using your answers from part b, write a simplified expression for the total number of tickets Elena sells.

_____

_____

   c. If Elena sells 15 adult tickets, does she sell at least 100 total tickets? Show your work.

_____

_____

10. A group of students collect a number of shells on the beach. They sort the shells into three piles based on the size of each shell. The first pile has half as many shells as the number they collected. The second pile has 10 fewer shells than the first pile. The third pile has the remaining shells.

   a. Write simplified expressions for the number of shells in each pile in terms of the total number of shells. Define any variables used.

_____

_____

_____

_____

_____

_____

_____

_____

   b. If there are 22 shells in the first pile, how many total shells did the students collect? Explain two ways you could find the total number of shells.

_____

_____

_____

_____

_____

_____

_____

6.EE.7

SELECTED RESPONSE

Select the correct answer.

1. Which of these equations has the same solution as the equation $x + 5 = 12$?

   Ⓐ $x + 5 = 7$

   Ⓑ $x + 8 = 15$

   Ⓒ $x + 7 = 12$

   Ⓓ $x + 12 = 20$

2. Thomas put $\frac{1}{4}$ of the c coins he had in his pocket into the jar under his bed. He put 16 coins into the jar. The equation that models this situation is $\frac{1}{4}c = 16$. How many coins did Thomas have in his pocket?

   Ⓐ 4 coins

   Ⓑ 12 coins

   Ⓒ 20 coins

   Ⓓ 64 coins

3. What is the procedure for solving the equation $\frac{1}{2}x = 16$?

   Ⓐ Add $\frac{1}{2}$ to both sides of the equation.

   Ⓑ Subtract $\frac{1}{2}$ from both sides of the equation.

   Ⓒ Multiply both sides of the equation by 2.

   Ⓓ Multiply both sides of the equation by $\frac{1}{2}$.

4. There are 6 blue shirts and g green shirts in a drawer. There are 11 shirts total in the drawer. What equation models this situation?

   Ⓐ $6 + g = 11$

   Ⓑ $6g = 11$

   Ⓒ $6 - g = 11$

   Ⓓ $\frac{1}{6}g = 11$

CONSTRUCTED RESPONSE

5. What is the solution of the equation $3 + x = 9$? Show your work.

   _____

   _____

   _____

6. Sally measured the height of a flower growing in her garden. The flower was $3\frac{1}{4}$ inches tall. Over the next week, the flower grew h inches and measured $4\frac{1}{8}$ inches tall. Write an equation that models the situation. Then solve the equation and state how much the flower grew during the week.

   _____

   _____

   _____

7. The sum of 6 and another number is 23. Write and solve an equation to find the other number. Show your work.

   _____

   _____

   _____

8. Cho is driving a car. He gets to his destination, which is 72 miles away, in 1 hour and 30 minutes.

   a. The equation $d = rt$ can be used to model Cho's drive, where d is the distance traveled, r is the speed of the car, and t is the amount of time spent traveling. Substitute Cho's time and distance into the equation.

   _____

   b. Solve the equation in part a to find Cho's speed. Show your work.

   _____

   _____

   _____

9. Kirk owns a bakery and is making muffins. Each batch of muffins uses $\frac{2}{3}$ cup of milk. He has 1 gallon of milk to use.

   a. If Kirk uses $\frac{1}{4}$ gallon of milk in total, how many batches of muffins did he make? Write and solve an equation to find the answer. Show your work. (Hint: There are 16 cups in 1 gallon.)

   _____

   _____

   _____

   b. Kirk earned $108 from selling the muffins. How much money did he earn per batch? Write and solve an equation to find how much money Kirk earned per batch.

   _____

   _____

   _____

   _____

10. Lauren incorrectly solves the equation $\frac{4}{5} + x = \frac{13}{5}$. Her work is shown below. Explain Lauren's mistake and find the correct solution. Show your work.

$$\frac{4}{5} + x = \frac{13}{5}$$
$$\frac{4}{5} + \frac{4}{5} + x = \frac{13}{5} + \frac{4}{5}$$
$$x = \frac{17}{5}$$

   _____

   _____

   _____

   _____

11. Adam is saving money to buy a computer. He saves s dollars each week. After 7 weeks, he has $315 saved.

   a. Write an equation that models the situation.

   _____

   b. How much does Adam save each week? Show your work.

   _____

   _____

   _____

   c. The computer Adam wants to buy is $450. How many more weeks does he have to save to buy the computer? Write an equation to model this situation and solve. Show your work.

   _____

   _____

   _____

6.EE.8

SELECTED RESPONSE

Select the correct answer.

1. What inequality has the solutions graphed on the number line?

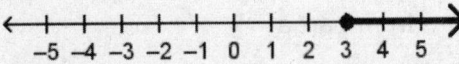

   A) $x < 3$

   B) $x \leq 3$

   C) $x > 3$

   D) $x \geq 3$

2. All of the students in a class are older than 10 years. What inequality represents the ages a of the students?

   A) $a < 10$

   B) $a \leq 10$

   C) $a > 10$

   D) $a \geq 10$

3. Dianne is 5 feet and 6 inches tall. Manuel is taller than Dianne. What inequality represents Manuel's height h in feet? Recall that there are 12 inches in a foot.

   A) $h < 5.6$

   B) $h > 5.6$

   C) $h < 5.5$

   D) $h > 5.5$

4. Jay jogs daily for exercise. He jogs faster than 3.5 miles per hour every day. Which inequality represents Jay's jogging speeds s?

   A) $s < 3.5$

   B) $s \leq 3.5$

   C) $s > 3.5$

   D) $s \geq 3.5$

Select all correct answers.

5. Which inequalities share some solutions with $x \geq 3$?

   A) $x > 3$

   B) $x < 0$

   C) $x \leq 3$

   D) $x \geq 5$

   E) $x < 3$

CONSTRUCTED RESPONSE

6. Jenna eats dinner at a restaurant. Her bill is $14.50. Jenna pays her bill and leaves a tip. Write an inequality to represent the total cost of Jenna's dinner.

   _____

7. Describe the values graphed on the number line in words. The number line represents the solutions of what inequality? How many solutions does this inequality have?

   _____

   _____

   _____

8. Graph the solutions of $x < 2$ and $x \leq 2$ on the number lines. How are the solutions of the inequalities similar? How are they different?

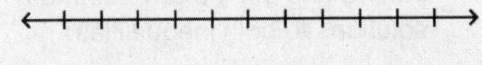

   _____

   _____

   _____

   _____

9. Keith wrote the inequality $x < 4$ to represent the statement "a number x is less than 4." He graphed the solutions of the inequality on the number line shown. Did Keith write the inequality and graph the solutions correctly? Explain.

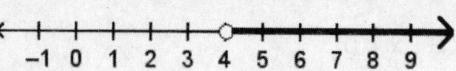

_____

_____

_____

_____

_____

_____

10. a. The value of n is less than 20. Write the inequality that represents the value of n and graph the solutions on the number line.

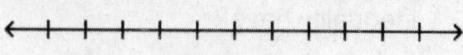

_____

b. The value of m is greater than 5. Write the inequality that represents the value of m and graph the solutions on the number line.

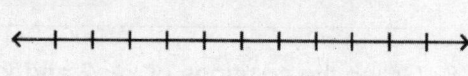

_____

c. Describe the solutions graphed in parts a and b. Find any common solutions to both inequalities.

_____

_____

_____

_____

11. Savannah's daily commute from home to work is more than 35 miles each way.

a. Write an inequality that represents this situation.

_____

b. Graph the solutions of the inequality from part a.

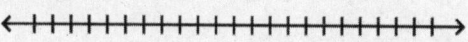

c. If Savannah travels 35 miles from home, is it possible she is at work? Explain.

_____

_____

_____

12. The graph on the number line shows the different amounts of money in dollars that Liam saves weekly.

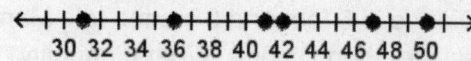

a. Liam wants to save as much as or more than he did the week during which he saved the least. Write an inequality that represents this situation.

_____

b. Describe the solutions of the inequality from part a in terms of the situation.

_____

_____

_____

c. Does every solution of the inequality represent a realistic amount? Explain.

_____

_____

_____

6.EE.9

SELECTED RESPONSE
Select the correct answer.

1. The graph below shows the relationship between the number of miles a person walks and the number of hours spent walking. What equation best describes the relationship between the two variables?.

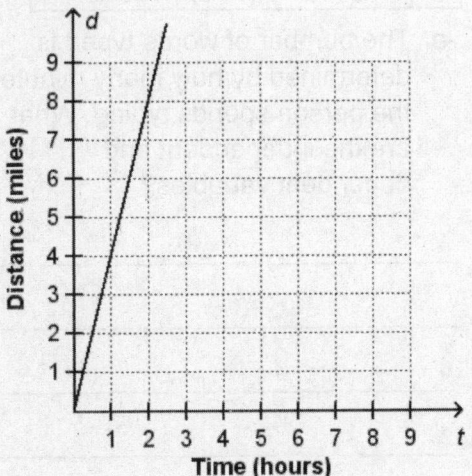

Ⓐ $t = 4d$

Ⓑ $d = 4t$

Ⓒ $t = d$

Ⓓ $d = \dfrac{1}{4}t$

2. A gardener is growing tomato plants. One plant starts out 5 cm tall. It grows a constant 2 cm every week. What equation represents the height h of the plant after t weeks?

Ⓐ $t = 5h + 2$

Ⓑ $t = 2h + 5$

Ⓒ $h = 5t + 2$

Ⓓ $h = 2t + 5$

3. The table below shows the balance of a savings account after t weeks, where money is being withdrawn at a constant rate. Peter can find the balance of the account based on how many weeks have passed. What are the independent and dependent variables, and how do they change?

Time (weeks), t	Balance (dollars), b
0	850
1	800
2	750
3	700

Ⓐ As the independent variable t increases by 1, the dependent variable b increases by 50.

Ⓑ As the independent variable t increases by 1, the dependent variable b decreases by 50.

Ⓒ As the independent variable b increases by 1, the dependent variable t increases by 50.

Ⓓ As the independent variable b increases by 1, the dependent variable t decreases by 50.

Select all correct answers.

4. Gloria is an artist. She sets a goal to paint 2 pieces every month. She has already painted 5 pieces. The number of pieces Gloria paints depends on the number of months she spends painting. Which statements describe the number of pieces p Gloria paints over t months if she meets her goal?

Ⓐ p is the independent variable and t is the dependent variable.

Ⓑ t is the independent variable and p is the dependent variable.

Ⓒ p increases by 2 as t increases by 1.

Ⓓ t increases by 2 as p increases by 1.

Ⓔ The equation representing the situation is $p = 2t + 5$.

CONSTRUCTED RESPONSE

5. An online bookstore is having a sale. All paperback books are $6.00, with a flat shipping fee of $2.50. Write an equation that represents the total cost c based on buying b books. Identify the independent and dependent variables and how the dependent variable changes in relation to the independent variable.

_____

_____

_____

_____

6. The graph below shows the relationship between the number of pencils bought and the cost. Describe the relationship between the two variables. Use this relationship to write an equation relating the two variables.

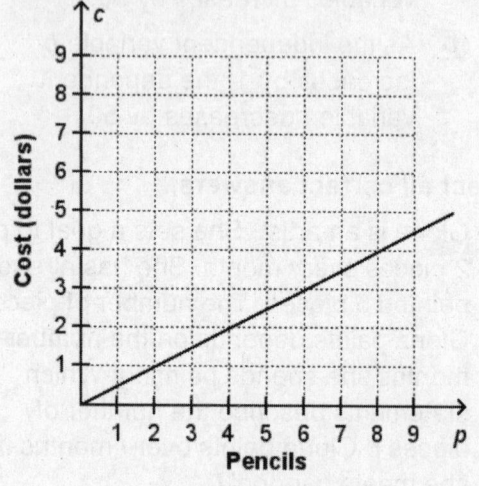

_____

_____

_____

_____

7. The table below shows the number of words w a person types after t minutes. The number of words typed per minute is a constant 52.

Time (minutes), t	Number of words, w
0	0
1	52
2	104
3	156

a. The number of words typed is determined by how many minutes the person spends typing. What are the independent and dependent variables?

_____

_____

_____

_____

_____

_____

_____

_____

_____

b. Graph the values from the table.

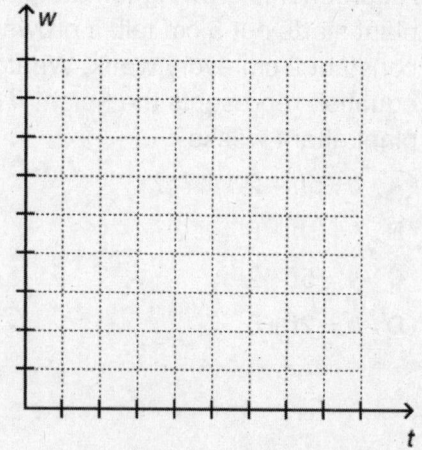

c. Write an equation that represents the situation.

_____

6.G.1

SELECTED RESPONSE
Select the correct answer.

1. What is the area of the triangle below?

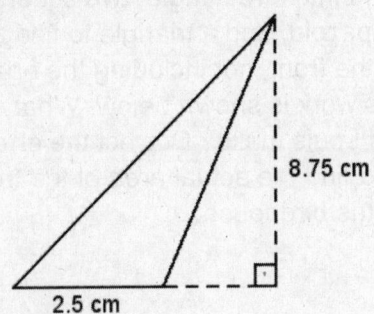

8.75 cm

2.5 cm

Ⓐ 5.625 cm²

Ⓑ 10.9375 cm²

Ⓒ 11.25 cm²

Ⓓ 21.875 cm²

2. What is the area of the triangle in the figure below?

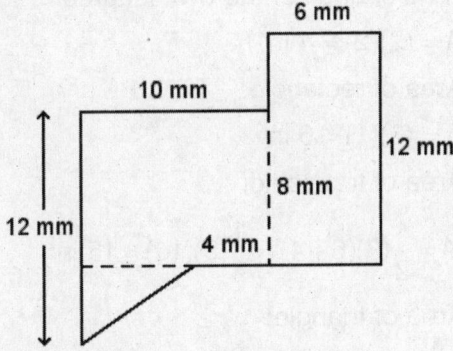

6 mm

10 mm

12 mm

8 mm

12 mm

4 mm

Ⓐ 12 mm²

Ⓑ 20 mm²

Ⓒ 36 mm²

Ⓓ 60 mm²

3. What is the area of this shape?

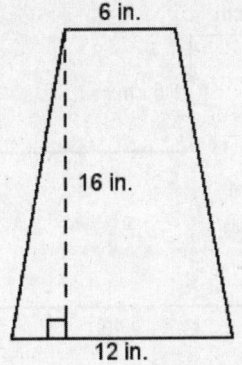

6 in.

16 in.

12 in.

Ⓐ 48 in²   Ⓒ 144 in²

Ⓑ 96 in²   Ⓓ 288 in²

4. What is the area of the following rhombus?

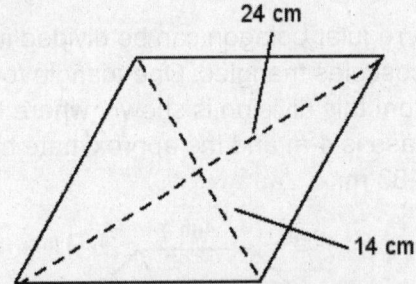

24 cm

14 cm

Ⓐ 76 cm²   Ⓒ 336 cm²

Ⓑ 168 cm²   Ⓓ 672 cm²

CONSTRUCTED RESPONSE

5. Draw a rectangle using this triangle and an exact copy of it. What is the area of the resulting rectangle?

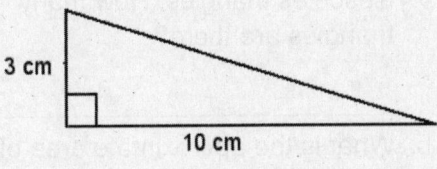

3 cm

10 cm

_____

_____

6. Find the area of the polygon below by dividing it into two rectangles using one vertical line. Show your work.

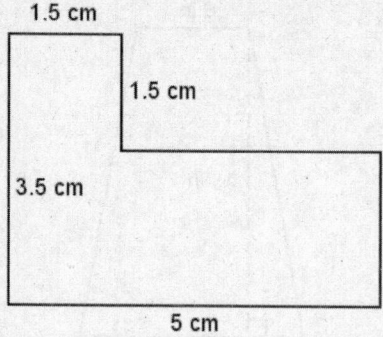

1.5 cm

1.5 cm

3.5 cm

5 cm

_____

_____

_____

7. A regular octagon can be divided into isosceles triangles. One triangle formed from this division is shown, where the base is 4 m and the approximate height is 4.83 m.

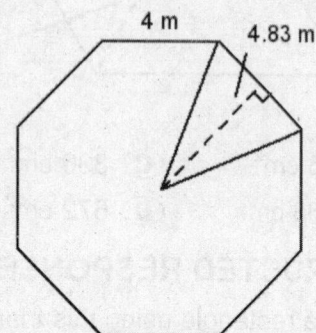

4 m

4.83 m

a. Using the figure above as a start, finish dividing the octagon into isosceles triangles. How many triangles are there?

_____

b. What is the approximate area of the octagon? Show your work.

_____

_____

_____

8. Louis is building a birdhouse. He sketches the front of the birdhouse, which is shown below. The shaded region is a rectangular opening with a base of 4 in. and a height of 2 in. Louis divided the front into a rectangle, two squares, a trapezoid, and a triangle to find the area of the front, not including the opening. His work is shown below. What error did Louis make? Correct the error and find the actual area of the front of the birdhouse.

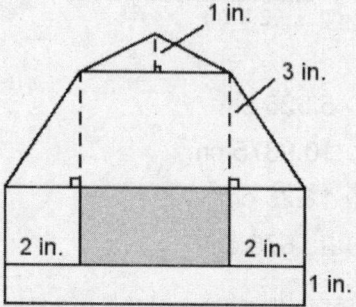

1 in.

3 in.

2 in.   2 in.

1 in.

Area of each of the two squares:

$A = (2)(2) = 4$ in^2

Area of rectangle:

$A = (6)(1) = 6$ in^2

Area of trapezoid:

$A = \frac{1}{2}(3)(6+4) = \frac{1}{2}(3)(10) = 15$ in^2

Area of triangle:

$A = \frac{1}{2}(4)(1) = 2$ in^2

The area of the front of the birdhouse is
4 in^2 + 4 in^2 + 6 in^2 + 15 in^2 + 2 in^2 = 31 in^2.

_____

_____

_____

_____

_____

_____

Grade 6   58   Common Core Assessment Readiness

6.G.2

SELECTED RESPONSE
Select the correct answer.

1. What is the volume of the rectangular prism?

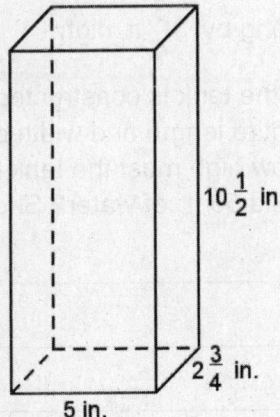

10 $\frac{1}{2}$ in.

2 $\frac{3}{4}$ in.

5 in.

(A) $18\frac{1}{4}$ in^3

(B) $28\frac{7}{8}$ in^3

(C) $52\frac{1}{2}$ in^3

(D) $144\frac{3}{8}$ in^3

2. A brick has a length of $2\frac{2}{5}$ cm, a width of $\frac{4}{5}$ cm, and a height of 1 cm. How many $\frac{1}{5}$-cm cubes can fit along the length of the brick?

(A) 4

(B) 5

(C) 12

(D) 240

3. If 300 cubes can fit in the rectangular prism below, what is the edge length of each cube?

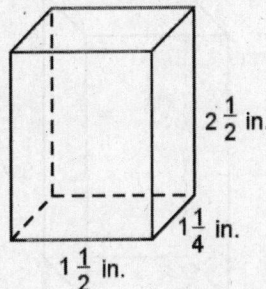

2 $\frac{1}{2}$ in.

1 $\frac{1}{4}$ in.

1 $\frac{1}{2}$ in.

(A) $\frac{1}{64}$ in.

(B) $\frac{7}{400}$ in.

(C) $\frac{1}{4}$ in.

(D) $4\frac{11}{16}$ in.

Select all correct answers.

4. Which dimensions describe a rectangular prism with a volume of $\frac{3}{50}$ cubic units?

(A) $\frac{2}{5}$ unit $\times \frac{1}{4}$ unit $\times \frac{3}{5}$ unit

(B) $1\frac{2}{3}$ unit $\times \frac{1}{4}$ unit $\times \frac{5}{9}$ unit

(C) $\frac{6}{7}$ unit $\times \frac{7}{10}$ unit $\times \frac{1}{5}$ unit

(D) $\frac{3}{5}$ unit $\times \frac{3}{10}$ unit $\times \frac{1}{3}$ unit

(E) $\frac{4}{7}$ unit $\times 2\frac{5}{8}$ units $\times \frac{1}{25}$ unit

CONSTRUCTED RESPONSE

5. Use the formula for volume $V = \ell wh$ to find the volume of the rectangular prism shown. Show your work.

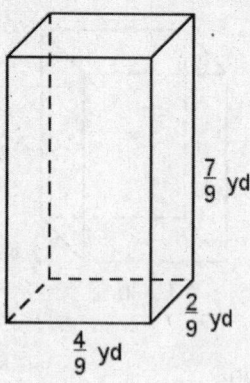

$\frac{7}{9}$ yd

$\frac{2}{9}$ yd

$\frac{4}{9}$ yd

_____

_____

_____

_____

_____

6. How many cubes with side length $\frac{1}{2}$ m would fit inside the rectangular prism shown below? Show your work.

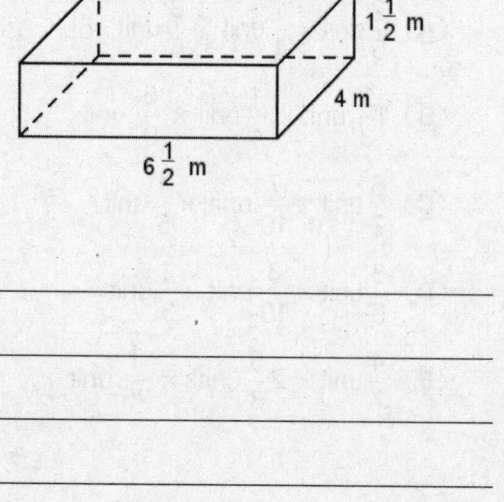

$1\frac{1}{2}$ m

4 m

$6\frac{1}{2}$ m

_____

_____

_____

_____

_____

7. A homeowner wants to construct a tank in the shape of a rectangular prism to collect rainwater runoff from her roof. The homeowner would like to hide the tank in a space under the deck between the supports. The space is $2\frac{1}{2}$ ft wide by 12 ft long by $3\frac{3}{4}$ ft high.

a. If the tank is constructed using the entire length and width of the space, how high must the tank be in order to hold 50 ft³ of water? Show your work.

_____

_____

_____

_____

_____

_____

_____

_____

_____

b. If the tank is constructed using the entire length and height of the space, how wide must the tank be in order to hold 50 ft³ of water? Show your work.

_____

_____

_____

_____

_____

_____

_____

_____

6.G.3

SELECTED RESPONSE
Select the correct answer.

1. What is the length of $\overline{CD}$ in the figure?

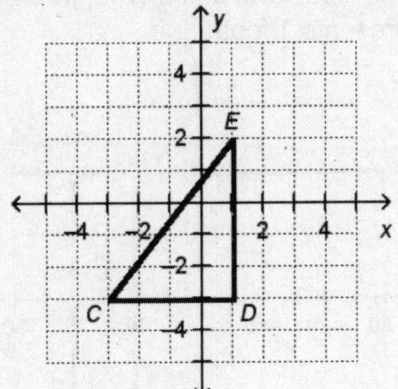

Ⓐ 2 units

Ⓑ 3 units

Ⓒ 4 units

Ⓓ 5 units

2. Which name best describes the polygon with vertices (0, 0), (4, 8), (12, 8), and (16, 0)?

Ⓐ Triangle

Ⓑ Square

Ⓒ Trapezoid

Ⓓ Pentagon

3. A rectangular plot of land is represented on a map by the vertices (10, 10), (10, 90), (70.5, 90), and (70.5, 10), where the x- and y-coordinates are measured in yards. What is the area of the plot of land?

Ⓐ 1,560 yd^2

Ⓑ 4,840 yd^2

Ⓒ 5,445 yd^2

Ⓓ 6,345 yd^2

Select all correct answers.

4. A rectangle has one vertex at (0, 4). The rectangle has at least one side with a length of 6 units. Which vertices could represent the other three vertices of the rectangle?

Ⓐ (0, –2), (–2, –2), and (–2, 4)

Ⓑ (3, 4), (3, 1), and (0, 1)

Ⓒ (6, 4), (0, 2), and (6, 2)

Ⓓ (–6, 4), (0, 5), and (–6, 5)

Ⓔ (0, 6), (2, 6), and (2, 4)

Select the correct answer for all lettered parts.

5. A line segment has endpoints (–1, –1) and (–1, 2). Could the given vertex form a triangle if connected to the endpoints of the line segment?

a. (6, 2)	○ Yes	○ No
b. (–1, 6)	○ Yes	○ No
c. (–1, 0)	○ Yes	○ No
d. (–4, 8)	○ Yes	○ No

CONSTRUCTED RESPONSE

6. The figure below is a regular hexagon. One unit on the graph represents 1 centimeter. What is the perimeter of the hexagon? Explain how you found your answer.

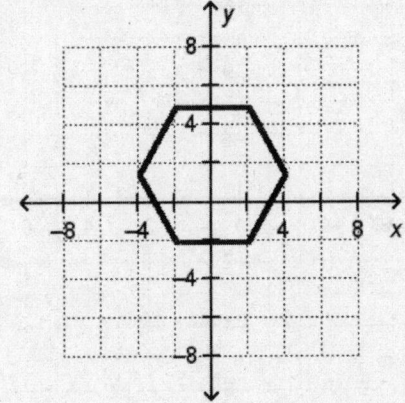

_____

_____

_____

7. A town requires that angled parking spaces have a "curb length" of 9 feet. The curb length is the distance from one angled line to the next as measured along the curb. One plan for angled spaces is shown below. Do these angled parking spaces meet the town's requirement? Explain why or why not. Each unit on the graph represents 1 foot.

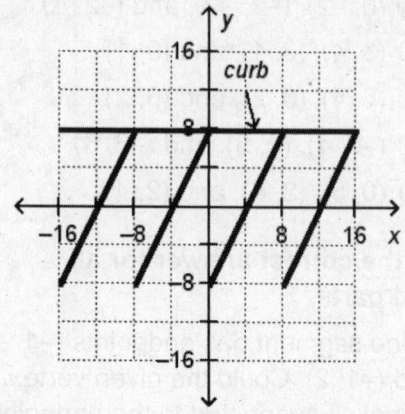

_____

_____

_____

_____

8. Graph the shape that has vertices A(−3, −2), B(−1, 2), C(4, 2), and D(2, −2). What kind of shape is it?

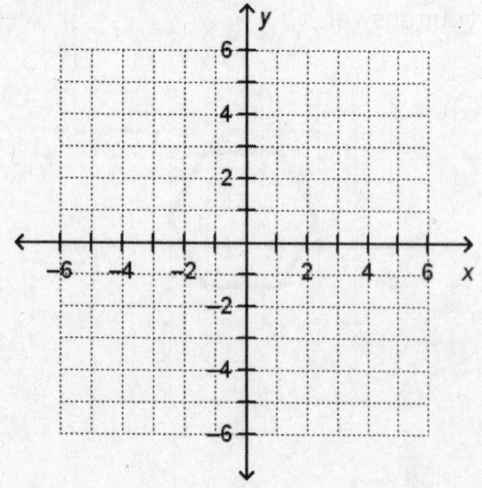

_____

9. Sarah wants to plant a flower bed next to her driveway. The position of the driveway and the road are shown on the map below. She has chosen the point (10, 10) to be one of the vertices of the flower bed. One unit on the graph represents 1 foot.

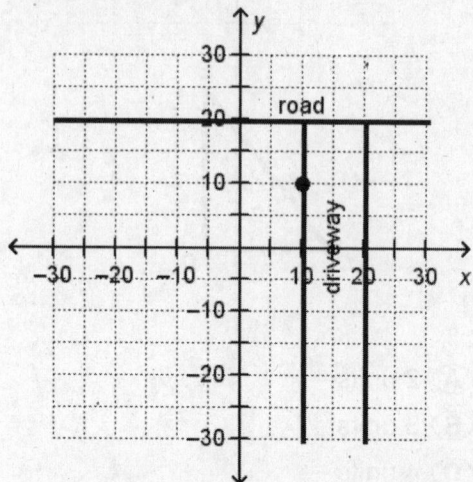

a. Sarah's first plan is to make the flower bed a square with a side length of 5 feet. Graph two possible locations for the flower bed.

b. Sarah changes her mind and decides to make the flower bed a rectangle that measures 30 feet by 5 feet. She wants the side that measures 30 feet to lie along the edge of the driveway. She still wants (10, 10) to be a vertex. Are there still two possible locations for Sarah's flower bed? Explain why or why not, and graph all possible locations.

_____

_____

_____

_____

_____

_____

_____

_____

_____

6.G.4

SELECTED RESPONSE

Select the correct answer.

1. What three-dimensional figure can be formed by folding the net shown?

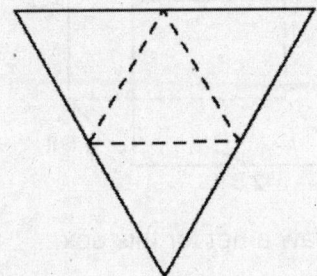

- (A) Rectangular prism
- (B) Square pyramid
- (C) Triangular pyramid
- (D) Triangular prism

2. The net of a square pyramid is shown. Find the surface area of the pyramid.

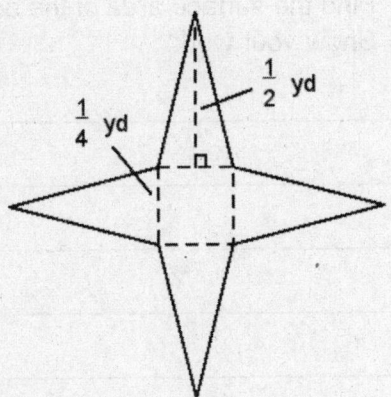

- (A) $\frac{1}{8}$ yd^2
- (B) $\frac{1}{4}$ yd^2
- (C) $\frac{5}{16}$ yd^2
- (D) $\frac{9}{16}$ yd^2

3. An aquarium has the dimensions shown in the net below. What is the surface area of the aquarium?

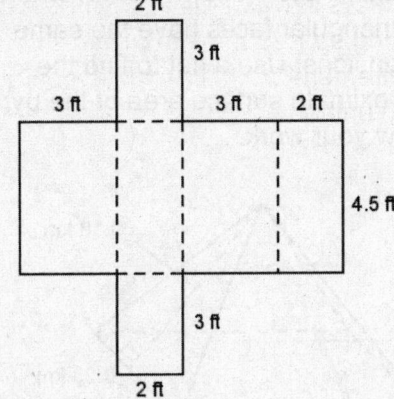

- (A) 27 ft^2
- (B) 28.5 ft^2
- (C) 45 ft^2
- (D) 57 ft^2

Select all correct answers.

4. Which of the following areas correspond to the area of a face of the rectangular prism that can be formed by the net shown?

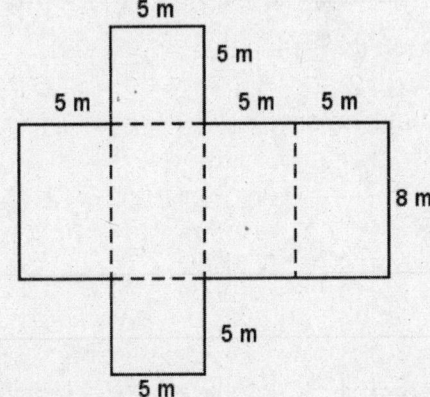

- (A) 25 m^2
- (B) 40 m^2
- (C) 65 m^2
- (D) 80 m^2
- (E) 90 m^2

CONSTRUCTED RESPONSE

5. Hector is visiting the pyramids in Egypt. He wants to know the surface area of the Pyramid of Giza. The approximate dimensions are shown below, where all of the triangular faces have the same dimensions. Use a net to find the approximate surface area of the pyramid. Show your work.

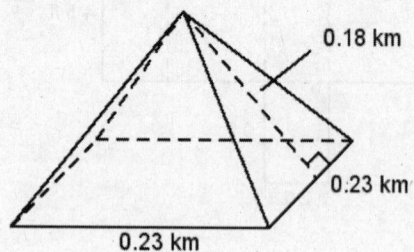

0.18 km

0.23 km

0.23 km

_____

_____

_____

_____

_____

_____

6. An employee of a store's gift wrapping center is wrapping 8 gifts, each in the same size box. The dimensions of the box are shown below.

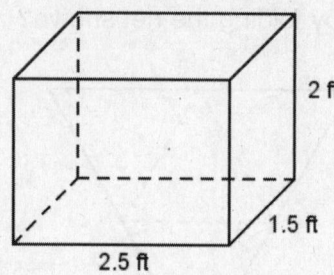

2 ft

1.5 ft

2.5 ft

a. Draw a net for this box.

b. Find the surface area of the box. Show your work.

_____

_____

_____

_____

c. If there is only 160 square feet of wrapping paper left, will the employee be able to wrap all of the gifts? Explain.

_____

_____

_____

_____

6.SP.1

SELECTED RESPONSE

Select the correct answer.

1. Which of the following questions is statistical?

    (A) How many hours did you sleep last night?

    (B) How many hours did the students in your class sleep last night?

    (C) How many hours did your friend spend reading last night?

    (D) How many hours did your teacher spend reading on Saturday?

2. What statement best describes the question "How many computer games does Christopher have right now?"

    (A) The question is statistical because it does not involve a data set with items that vary.

    (B) This question is statistical because there is variation in the resulting data set.

    (C) This is not a statistical question because it does not involve a data set with items that vary.

    (D) This is not a statistical question because there is variation in the resulting data set.

3. Nancy wants to know more about the music her friends listen to. Which of her questions below is NOT a statistical question?

    (A) If I make a list of musical styles, how many of my friends like each style?

    (B) How many songs does each of my friends have?

    (C) What is my best friend's favorite song?

    (D) How many songs does each of my friends buy in one month?

4. Mia plants 20 flowers of different types in her garden. Which of the following questions is NOT a statistical question about the flowers?

    (A) What was the total cost of the flowers?

    (B) How tall is the shortest flower?

    (C) How many of each type of flower is there?

    (D) How many flowers have 5 petals?

Select all correct answers.

5. Glenn wants to learn more about his classmates. Which of the following are statistical questions that Glenn can ask?

    (A) Is Jennifer wearing glasses today?

    (B) How tall is Jeremy?

    (C) How tall are all of the students?

    (D) How many students brought lunch today?

    (E) How old are the students?

    (F) How many students brought lunch each day over the past month?

CONSTRUCTED RESPONSE

6. A zookeeper asks, "How many animals were in the zoo each month of last year?" Is this question statistical or not? Explain your reasoning.

    _____

    _____

    _____

    _____

    _____

    _____

    _____

    _____

    _____

7. The following questions were asked about Brian's weekly exercise routine.

   1. How long did Brian spend exercising last week?

   2. How long does Brian spend on each type of exercise each week?

  a. What is the difference between the results of each question?

_____

_____

_____

  b. Which question is statistical? Explain.

_____

_____

_____

_____

_____

  c. Rewrite the question that is not statistical into one that is. The subject should still be about Brian's exercise routine.

_____

_____

_____

_____

8. Claire is comparing refrigerators at an appliance store. She asks the following questions.

   1. What are the prices of the refrigerators?

   2. How much does it cost to deliver the refrigerator?

   3. What are the volumes of the refrigerators in cubic feet?

  a. State whether each question is statistical or not. Explain.

_____

_____

_____

  b. Write one statistical question, different from the ones above, about the refrigerators.

_____

_____

_____

_____

  c. One store has 10 refrigerators that are the exact same model in stock. If Claire asks how many cubic feet each of the 10 refrigerators has, is this a statistical question? Explain why or why not.

_____

_____

_____

_____

_____

6.SP.2

SELECTED RESPONSE

Select the correct answer.

1. The test scores for a class are shown. What is the average test score?

   79, 80, 92, 92, 81, 100, 88, 98, 71, 100, 91, 90

   (A) 71   (C) 90.5
   (B) 88.5   (D) 92

2. Find the interquartile range of the data displayed in the box plot shown.

   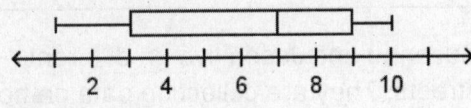

   (A) 9   (C) 6
   (B) 7   (D) 3

3. What is the median of the data set shown?

   34, 86, 12, 56, 21, 98, 72, 34, 21, 34, 45, 23, 97, 44

   (A) 34   (C) 44
   (B) 39   (D) 53

4. The number of people per household for a street with 15 houses is shown. What statement best describes the shape of the distribution of the data set?

   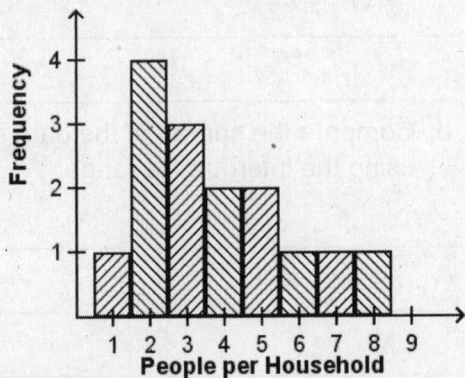

   (A) Skewed right
   (B) Skewed left
   (C) Symmetric
   (D) Has two peaks

Select all correct answers.

5. Which of the following statements accurately describe the data displayed in the dot plot shown?

   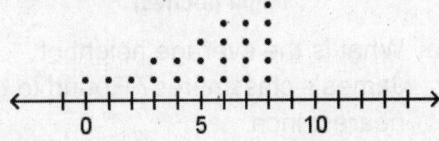

   (A) The distribution is right skewed.
   (B) The distribution is left skewed.
   (C) The distribution is symmetric.
   (D) The mean is approximately 5.4.
   (E) The median is 6.
   (F) The mode is 0.

CONSTRUCTED RESPONSE

6. Gianna is keeping track of how much money she spends each week. Her data is shown.

   $75, $123, $36, $86, $57, $89, $41, $70, $148, $80

   a. Find the median of the data set. Show your work.

   _____

   _____

   _____

   _____

   b. Find the interquartile range of the data set. Show your work.

   _____

   _____

   _____

   _____

7. James asked each of his classmates how tall they are. The data that he collected is shown in the plot below.

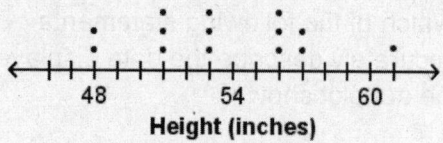

Height (inches)

a. What is the average height of James's classmates? Round to the nearest inch.

_____

b. Are more of James's classmates taller or shorter than this average? Explain your answer.

_____

_____

8. The number of runs Jackie's baseball team scored per game throughout a part of one season is shown below.

3, 7, 8, 9, 2, 4, 5, 1, 0, 7, 2, 4

a. Construct a box plot from the given data set. Show your work.

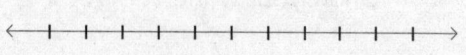

_____

_____

b. Describe the shape of the distribution of the data set.

_____

c. The median number of runs Jackie's rival team scored during the same time was 5. How does Jackie's baseball team's median number of runs compare to the rival team's median number of runs?

_____

_____

9. The number of hours Linda sleeps each night for two weeks is shown. Find the mean absolute deviation, rounding to the nearest whole number. Explain how this value describes the distribution of the data.

8, 7, 6.5, 8, 9, 10, 7.5, 9.5, 8, 9.5, 10, 7, 8, 7

_____

_____

_____

_____

10. Suzanne and Jason live on different streets. They are collecting data on how many gallons of water per day the residents of their streets use. This data is shown below.

Suzanne's street: 100, 92, 83, 75, 95, 112, 80, 73

Jason's street: 81, 62, 98, 74, 82, 100, 121, 93, 76, 72

a. On average, do the residents of Suzanne's street or Jason's street use more gallons of water per day?

_____

_____

_____

b. Compare the spread of the data sets using the interquartile range.

_____

_____

_____

_____

_____

_____

6.SP.3

SELECTED RESPONSE
Select the correct answer.

1. The number of touchdowns scored by one football team in each game during a season is shown. What was the mean of the touchdowns the team scored during that season?

   2, 4, 1, 0, 4, 3, 2, 4, 5, 1, 0, 3, 6, 4, 2, 3

   (A) 2.75 touchdowns
   (B) 3 touchdowns
   (C) 3.14 touchdowns
   (D) 4 touchdowns

2. Jesse asked how many magazine subscriptions each house on his street had. These numbers are shown. What is the interquartile range of the data set?

   1, 0, 2, 3, 4, 1, 0, 0, 4, 1, 2, 2, 1

   (A) 0.5 subscription
   (B) 1 subscription
   (C) 2 subscriptions
   (D) 2.5 subscriptions

3. The number of showtimes for one movie over several days is shown. What is the mean absolute deviation?

   9, 6, 8, 9, 7, 4, 3, 5, 2, 4

   (A) 2.1 showtimes
   (B) 5.5 showtimes
   (C) 5.7 showtimes
   (D) 11.4 showtimes

Select all correct answers.

4. Which measures describe the variation in a data set?

   (A) Mean
   (B) Median
   (C) Mode
   (D) Mean absolute deviation
   (E) Interquartile range
   (F) Range

For the data set shown, match each measure of center or measure of variability with its value(s).

2, 6, 8, 3, 4, 6, 2, 6, 8, 5, 6, 2, 7, 8, 4, 3, 2, 7, 3, 4

_____ 5. Mean

_____ 6. Median

_____ 7. Mode(s)

_____ 8. Mean absolute deviation

_____ 9. Interquartile range

_____ 10. Range

A 4.8
B 3.5
C 1.9
D 2 and 6
E 4.5
F 6

CONSTRUCTED RESPONSE

11. The daily maximum temperatures, in degrees Fahrenheit, for one town during one week in summer are shown below.

    93, 99, 89, 76, 68, 97, 71

    a. Find the mean and the mean absolute deviation. Show your work. Round your answers to the nearest tenth of a degree.

    _____

    b. Explain the difference between the interpretations of the mean and the mean absolute deviation. Which is a measure of center? Which is a measure of spread?

    _____

12. The data set shows the number of hours Marissa jogs daily. What is the average number of hours that Marissa's jogging times vary from her mean jogging time? Show your work and round your final answer to the nearest hour.

    4, 4, 1, 6, 5, 4, 6, 3, 3

    _____

    _____

13. Alex asks several households how many cars they have. The number of cars in the households is shown.

1, 0, 3, 2, 1, 1, 0, 2, 2, 2

  a. Find the median of the data set.

_____

  b. Is the median a measure of center or a measure of spread?

_____

14. Sara's basketball team has 10 players. The number of points each player scored during a recent game is shown.

6, 10, 12, 8, 9, 13, 15, 7, 8, 10

  a. Find the median.

_____

_____

_____

  b. Find the interquartile range.

_____

_____

_____

  c. If the interquartile range for another basketball team is 3 points, do the scores tend to vary more or less than the scores of Sara's team? Explain how you know.

_____

_____

_____

_____

_____

15. Naomi works at an ice cream shop. She is keeping track of how many customers come into the store every hour for one day. Each dot on the dot plot represents an hour period that Naomi's shop is open.

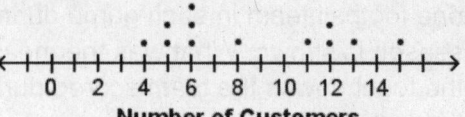

Number of Customers

  a. What is the mean of the data set rounded to the nearest whole number?

_____

  b. What is the median of the data set rounded to the nearest whole number?

_____

  c. How can you find the mode(s) of the data set using the dot plot? Find the mode.

_____

_____

16. Landon asks everyone in his class to pick a number between 1 and 10. These numbers are shown.

9, 7, 8, 3, 6, 9, 10, 5, 3, 2, 6, 9, 6, 7

Landon claims the mode is 6 and the range is $10 - 1 = 9$. Is he correct? If he is not correct, find the correct value(s) and show your work.

_____

_____

_____

_____

_____

_____

_____

_____

SELECTED RESPONSE
Select all correct answers.

1. Which values are needed to display a set of data using a box plot?

   (A) Mean

   (B) Median

   (C) Mode

   (D) Mean absolute deviation

   (E) Lower quartile

   (F) Upper quartile

   (G) Greatest value

   (H) Least value

Select the correct answer for each lettered part.

2. If the data shown is displayed using a dot plot, how many dots will go over each value?

   2, 3, 7, 4, 10, 1, 3, 7, 12, 1, 10, 2, 1, 1, 3, 6, 6, 8, 9, 11, 2

a. 2	○ 1 dot	○ 3 dots
b. 5	○ 0 dots	○ 1 dot
c. 6	○ 2 dots	○ 3 dots
d. 9	○ 1 dot	○ 4 dots

Select the correct answer.

3. The amount of rainfall, in inches, for one town is shown. If this data is displayed using a histogram and equally sized intervals, which intervals can be used?

   1.3, 2.5, 0.6, 1.2, 1, 1.3, 0.1, 0.5, 1, 2.6, 1.8, 1.4, 2

   (A) 0 to 0.9 inches and 1 to 1.9 inches

   (B) 0 to 0.5 inches, 0.6 to 1.5 inches, and 1.6 to 3 inches

   (C) 0 to 1 inches, 0.5 to 2 inches, and 1.5 to 3 inches

   (D) 0 to 0.9 inches, 1 to 1.9 inches, and 2 to 2.9 inches

4. Which box plot correctly displays the data set shown?

   2, 5, 7, 2, 11, 13, 5, 7, 1, 10, 10, 2, 3, 5, 1, 11

   (A)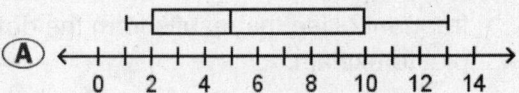

   (B)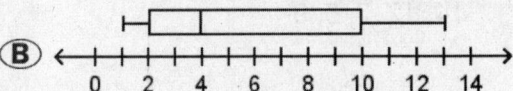

   (C)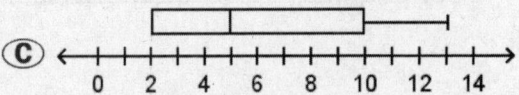

   (D)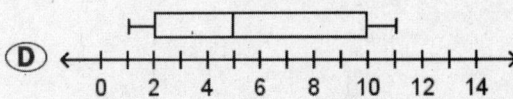

5. What is the median of the data shown in the histogram?

   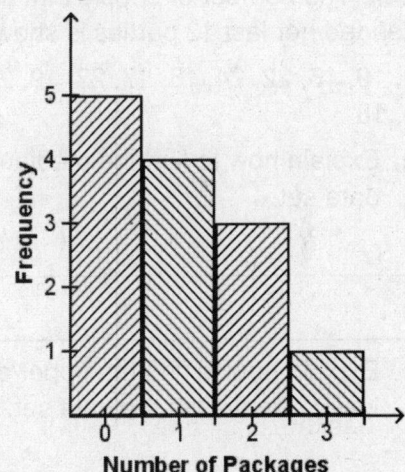

   (A) 0   (C) 1.5

   (B) 1   (D) 2

CONSTRUCTED RESPONSE

6. Oliver owns a bicycle store. The number of bikes that he sells each month for 18 months is shown. Use a dot plot to display this data. What number of bicycles sold per month was the most frequent? Use the results from the dot plot to explain.

   5, 11, 12, 4, 9, 5, 11, 4, 10, 11, 4, 5, 10, 14, 12, 3, 5, 9

   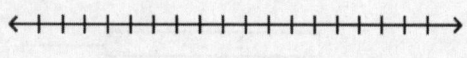

   _____

   _____

   _____

7. Jennifer is having her annual party next week. The number of people that have attended her last 12 parties is shown.

   20, 19, 16, 22, 24, 18, 17, 22, 19, 22, 18, 18

   a. Explain how to find the median of the data set.

   _____

   _____

   b. Explain how to find the upper and lower quartiles of the data set.

   _____

   _____

   c. Use parts a and b to display the data using a box plot.

   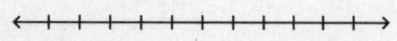

   d. What is the interquartile range of the data?

   _____

   _____

8. Jamie asks his classmates how many hours of television they watch daily. This data is shown.

   2, 6, 4, 1, 0, 3, 6, 2, 3, 5, 3, 1, 6, 0, 4, 6, 2, 7, 2, 2, 5

   a. Use a dot plot to display the data.

   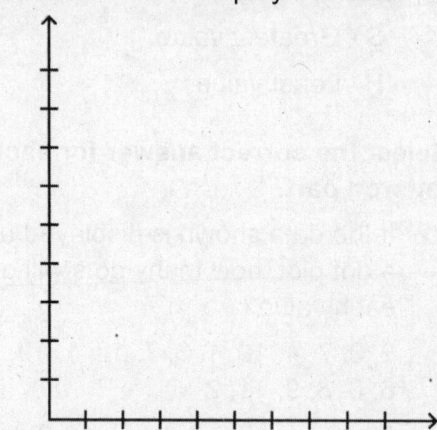

   b. Use a histogram with four equally sized intervals to display the data.

   c. Compare the shape of your graph from part a with the shape of your graph from part b. Explain why the shapes are different.

   _____

   _____

   _____

   _____

   _____

   _____

   _____

   _____

   _____

   _____

6.SP.5a, 6.SP.5b

SELECTED RESPONSE
Select the correct answer.

1. Colleen is training over the summer for a triathlon. The amount of time that she spends training daily is displayed on the dot plot shown. How many days did Colleen spend training?

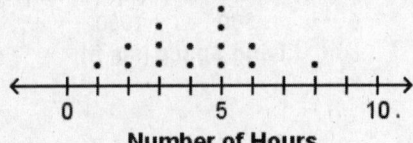

Number of Hours

- Ⓐ 7
- Ⓑ 8
- Ⓒ 15
- Ⓓ The number of days cannot be determined.

2. A traffic engineer is collecting counts of how many cars are on one street during a specific time each day. The results are shown in the histogram. How many days did the traffic engineer collect data?

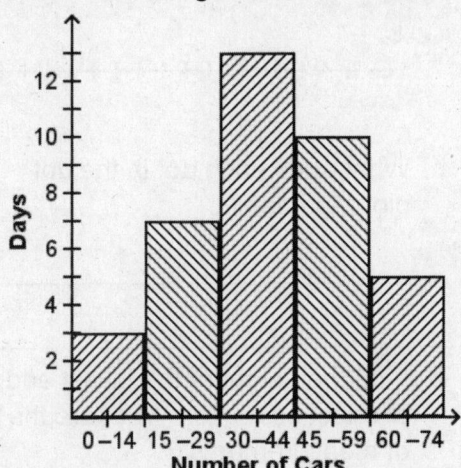

- Ⓐ 13
- Ⓑ 38
- Ⓒ 74
- Ⓓ The number of days cannot be determined.

3. The dean of a university is looking at the number of students who were enrolled in school during previous years. This data is shown in the table. What do the data values represent?

Year	Students Enrolled
2000	700
2001	841
2002	978
2003	1,200
2004	1,345
2005	1,498
2006	1,612
2007	1,766
2008	2,000

- Ⓐ The average number of students enrolled in school each year
- Ⓑ The most number of students enrolled in school between the years 2000 and 2008
- Ⓒ The number of students enrolled in school each month
- Ⓓ The number of students enrolled in school each year

Select all correct answers.

4. Roberto asks "How old are you?" to each of his classmates, and then records the data he receives. Which units can Roberto use to record his data?

- Ⓐ Days
- Ⓑ Inches
- Ⓒ Grams
- Ⓓ Months
- Ⓔ Years

CONSTRUCTED RESPONSE

5. Three different data sets are displayed on the following graphs. Can the number of observations in each data set be determined from its graph? If so, give the number of observations. If not, explain.

a.

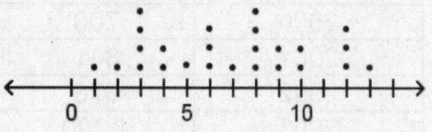

_____

_____

_____

b.

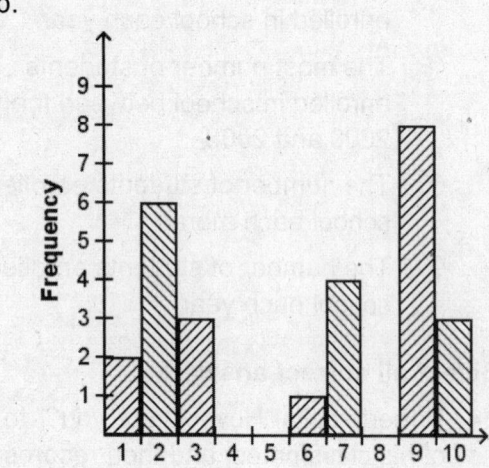

_____

_____

_____

c.

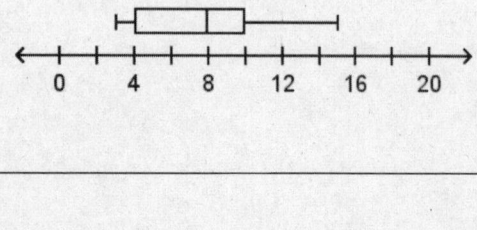

_____

_____

_____

6. Frank is moving to a different city and needs to rent an apartment. He asks several realtors in the city about available apartments. The dot plot shows the data he gathered for these apartments. What does each dot represent? In what units are the data values measured?

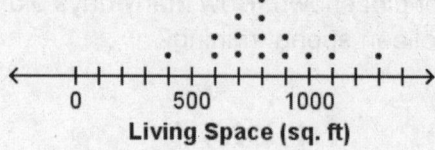

_____

_____

_____

7. Gabrielle collected the heights, in inches, of her coworkers. This data is shown.

65, 70, 60, 58, 60, 63, 65, 66, 72, 72, 63, 62, 63, 66, 63, 68, 68, 66

a. Construct a dot plot of the data Gabrielle collected.

b. What does each dot in the dot plot represent?

_____

_____

c. Find the height of the tallest and shortest coworker. What are the units of measurements?

_____

_____

d. Can Gabrielle use a different unit of measurement when collecting her data? Explain.

_____

_____

_____

6.SP.5c

SELECTED RESPONSE
Select all correct answers.

1. The dot plot shown displays the amount of money, in millions of dollars, that different companies spend on television advertising in one year. Which of the following statements describe the data set?

**Amount Spent on Advertising
(in millions of dollars)**

Ⓐ The overall pattern of the distribution is skewed left.

Ⓑ The overall pattern of the distribution is skewed right.

Ⓒ The overall pattern of the distribution is symmetric.

Ⓓ The average amount spent on television advertising is $10.10.

Ⓔ The average amount spent on television advertising is $10.1 million.

Ⓕ The median amount spent on television advertising is $10.50.

Ⓖ The median amount spent on television advertising is $10.5 million.

Select the correct answer.

2. Lianna planted several plants in her garden. The heights, in centimeters, of these plants after one month are shown. What is the mean height of Lianna's plants? Round your answer to the nearest tenth of a centimeter.

6, 9, 5.1, 12.8, 7.3, 16, 14.8, 9, 11.7, 12.4

Ⓐ 6.0 centimeters

Ⓑ 9.5 centimeters

Ⓒ 10.4 centimeters

Ⓓ 16.0 centimeters

3. Ina wants to buy a new computer, so she compares the prices of different computers. Her results are shown in the box plot, in hundreds of dollars. What is the interquartile range of the prices for computers?

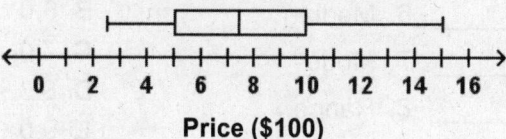

Price ($100)

Ⓐ $5.00

Ⓑ $12.50

Ⓒ $500.00

Ⓓ $1,250.00

4. Fred asked each of his classmates how many times they went to the beach over summer break. He displayed the data using the histogram shown. Which statement best describes the pattern of the distribution?

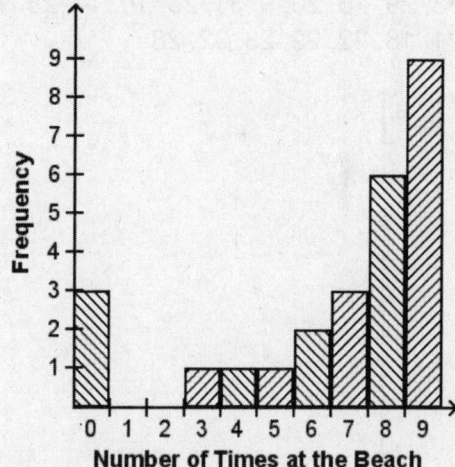

Number of Times at the Beach

Ⓐ Skewed left with one deviation from the overall pattern at the value 0

Ⓑ Skewed left with no deviations from the overall pattern

Ⓒ Skewed right with one deviation from the overall pattern at the value 0

Ⓓ Skewed right with no deviations from the overall pattern

Using the data set shown, match the measures of center and spread with their corresponding values. Round answers to the nearest tenth as needed.

3, 7, 9, 2, 11, 6, 13, 12, 15, 9, 3, 6, 13, 9, 10, 5

_____ 5. Mean   **A** 3.3

_____ 6. Median   **B** 6.0

_____ 7. Mode   **C** 7.0

_____ 8. Range   **D** 8.3

_____ 9. Mean absolute   **E** 9.0
        deviation   **F** 12.0

_____ 10. Interquartile range   **G** 13.0

CONSTRUCTED RESPONSE

11. Shawn is researching the daily fiber intake, in grams, of a group of people. His findings are listed below. Construct a histogram to display the data, using four equally sized intervals. Describe the overall pattern of the distribution.

33, 29, 16, 20, 9, 31, 23, 10, 14, 28, 17, 21, 16, 22, 29, 23, 32, 28

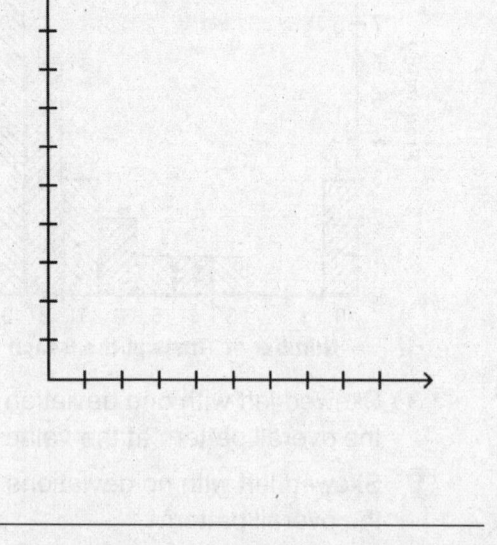

_____

_____

_____

12. Elijah works for a local car dealership. To make sure their customers are satisfied with the service, Elijah surveys a group of customers after their visit. The survey asks the customers to rate their service on a scale from 0 to 10, with 0 being the worst and 10 being the best. The survey results are shown.

3, 6, 9, 0, 4, 10, 9, 8, 4, 6, 6, 7, 9, 10, 5

a. Find the mode or modes of the dealership's ratings.

_____

b. Find the dealership's average rating. Is this value above or below the median rating?

_____

_____

13. A company is hiring for positions that require experience in biology. The years of experience in biology for several applicants are given.

2, 1, 3, 6, 2, 11, 0, 1, 5, 7, 3, 0, 4, 0, 2, 11, 1, 0

a. What is the range of years of experience the applicants have?

_____

b. Construct a dot plot using the given data.

$\longleftarrow\!\!+\!+\!+\!+\!+\!+\!+\!+\!+\!+\!+\!+\!+\!+\!+\!+\!\longrightarrow$

c. Describe the overall pattern of the distribution, including any deviations from the overall pattern.

_____

_____

_____

SELECTED RESPONSE
Select the correct answer.

1. Does the mean or median best describe a typical value in the data set shown?

   19, 18, 19, 18, 19, 19, 1, 19, 18, 19, 18

   Ⓐ Mean

   Ⓑ Median

   Ⓒ Neither describe a value in the data well.

   Ⓓ Both describe a value in the data well.

2. The dot plot shown displays the heights, in inches, of the students in one class. Which measure of variability best describes how spread out the heights of the students are?

   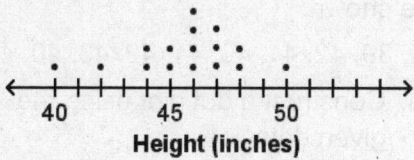

   Height (inches)

   Ⓐ Mean

   Ⓑ Median

   Ⓒ Mean absolute deviation

   Ⓓ Interquartile range

3. The exam scores from the most recent math test are shown. What is the value of the measure that best describes a typical exam score?

   93, 88, 76, 91, 92, 96, 100, 96, 74, 89, 94, 91

   Ⓐ 90

   Ⓑ 91.5

   Ⓒ 96

   Ⓓ 100

4. What measure best describes the variability of the data set displayed using the box plot shown?

   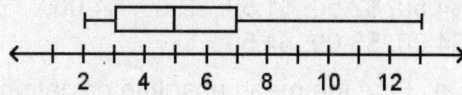

   Ⓐ Mean

   Ⓑ Median

   Ⓒ Mean absolute deviation

   Ⓓ Interquartile range

5. The number of miles Cynthia travels each day is shown. What are the values of the measures of center and variability that best describe the data set?

   57, 40, 35, 60, 56, 57, 59

   Ⓐ The mean 52 miles and the mean absolute deviation about 8 miles

   Ⓑ The median 57 miles and the interquartile range 19 miles

   Ⓒ The mean 57 miles and the mean absolute deviation 19 miles

   Ⓓ The median 52 miles and the interquartile range about 8 miles

Select all correct answers.

6. Which measures of center and variability best describe the data set shown?

   17, 19, 15, 12, 10, 21, 2, 16, 18, 19, 20, 16, 11, 12, 17

   Ⓐ Mean

   Ⓑ Median

   Ⓒ Mode

   Ⓓ Mean absolute deviation

   Ⓔ Interquartile range

   Ⓕ Range

CONSTRUCTED RESPONSE

7. Hector is selling some of his books. The prices for each book are shown.

$1.50, $5.50, $4.00, $3.00, $2.50,
$1.50, $2.50, $1.50, $2.00, $4.00,
$1.00, $3.00, $4.50

a. Find the mean absolute deviation of the book prices.

_____

b. Find the interquartile range of the book prices.

_____

c. Which measure best describes the variability of the prices of Hector's books? Explain.

_____

_____

_____

8. Jocelyn is studying the traffic flow at a certain intersection in the city. The approximate number of cars, in thousands, that pass through the intersection daily are shown.

9, 10, 11, 12, 11, 13, 12, 13, 8, 14, 11, 9, 10, 11

a. Find the mean of the data set. Round to the nearest thousand as needed.

_____

b. Find the median of the data set. Round to the nearest thousand as needed.

_____

c. Which measure best describes the typical number of cars passing through the intersection? Explain.

_____

_____

_____

9. What measures of center and variability best describe the data set displayed in the histogram? Explain.

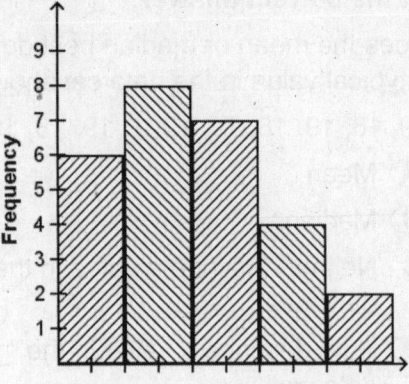

_____

_____

10. The salaries, in thousands of dollars, of different workers at a company are shown.

41, 39, 42, 41, 40, 41, 42, 43, 40, 41

a. Construct a dot plot using the given data.

⟵+++++++++++++++++++++⟶

b. Describe the overall shape of the distribution of the data. What does this tell you about the measure of center that best describes the data set?

_____

_____

c. Calculate and interpret all appropriate measures of center and variability to describe the data set. Round your answers to the nearest dollar as needed.

_____

_____

_____

ECONOMICS TODAY

THE MACRO VIEW

ECONOMICS TODAY

Fourth Canadian Edition

THE MACRO VIEW

Roger LeRoy Miller
Institute for University Studies
Arlington, Texas

Brenda Abbott
Northern Alberta Institute of Technology

Sam Fefferman
Northern Alberta Institute of Technology

Ronald K. Kessler
British Columbia Institute of Technology

Terrence Sulyma
Northern Alberta Institute of Technology

PEARSON

Addison
Wesley

Toronto

Library and Archives Canada Cataloguing in Publication

Economics today : the macro view / Roger LeRoy Miller . . . [et al.].—4th Canadian ed.

First Canadian ed. written by: Roger LeRoy Miller, Nancy W. Clegg.
Includes index.
ISBN 978-0-321-53767-6

1. Macroeconomics.   I. Miller, Roger LeRoy

HB172.5.M54 2008   339   C2008-900986-X

ISBN-13: 978-0-321-53767-6
ISBN-10: 0-321-53767-X

Vice President, Editorial Director: Gary Bennett
Acquisitions Editor: Don Thompson
Marketing Manager: Leigh-Anne Graham
Developmental Editors: Kimberley Hermans and Megan Dunkley
Production Editors: Laura Neves and Cheryl Jackson
Copy Editor: Nicole Mellow
Proofreader: Marg Bukta
Production Coordinator: Andrea Falkenberg
Compositor: Integra
Photo and Permissions Researcher: Sandy Cooke
Art Director: Miguel Angel Acevedo
Cover and Interior Designer: Sonya V. Thursby, Opus House Incorporated
Cover Image: Getty Images

1 2 3 4 5   12 11 10 09 08
Printed and bound in the United States of America.

My married name is Abbott, my maiden name is Novakowski. Two families united from different backgrounds, one from PEI, the other from Alberta, one English, one Ukrainian/Polish, a true multicultural family.

—B.A./B.N.

I would like to thank my loving family—Brenda, Tara, Amy, and Shane—for all their patience and support.

—S.F.

For my children, Elizabeth and Anne, never far from my heart as they move into the world.

—R.K.

To John and Mary Sulyma for instilling in me a thirst for knowledge and love of learning. To Andrea, Drew, and Vanya for their love and support.

—T.S.

BRIEF CONTENTS

PREFACE   xv
ACKNOWLEDGMENTS   xviii

Part 1   Introduction   1

Chapter 1   The Nature of Economics   1
            APPENDIX A   Reading and Working with Graphs   21
Chapter 2   Production Possibilities and Economic Systems   29
            APPENDIX B   The Production Possibilities Curve and
            Comparative Advantage   57
Chapter 3   Demand and Supply   63

Part 2   Dimensions of Macroeconomics   95

Chapter 4   Introduction to Macroeconomics   95
Chapter 5   Measuring the Economy's Performance   125

**Part 3   National Income Determination and the
            Government Sector**   155

Chapter 6   Modelling Real GDP and the Price Level in the
            Long Run   155
Chapter 7   Economic Growth and Development   180
Chapter 8   Modelling Real GDP and the Price Level in the
            Short Run   207
            APPENDIX C   Classical and Keynesian Macro Analyses   230
Chapter 9   Consumption, Investment, and the Multiplier   237
            APPENDIX D   The Keynesian Cross and the Multiplier   265
            APPENDIX E   The Algebra of the Keynesian Expenditure
            Model   266
Chapter 10 The Public Sector   269
Chapter 11 Fiscal Policy and the Public Debt   291
            APPENDIX F   Fiscal Policy: A Keynesian Perspective   316

Part 4   Money, Monetary Policy, and Stabilization   319

Chapter 12 Money and the Banking System   319
Chapter 13 Money Creation and Deposit Insurance   338
Chapter 14 The Bank of Canada and Monetary Policy   355
            APPENDIX G   Monetary Policy: A Keynesian Perspective   384
Chapter 15 Issues in Stabilization Policy   386

Part 5   Global Economics   418

Chapter 16 Comparative Advantage and the Open Economy   418
Chapter 17 Exchange Rates and the Balance of Payments   445

ANSWERS TO ODD-NUMBERED PROBLEMS   472
ANSWERS TO "FOR CRITICAL ANALYSIS" QUESTIONS   487
GLOSSARY   503
INDEX   512

CONTENTS

PREFACE   xv

ACKNOWLEDGMENTS   xviii

Part 1 Introduction   1

Chapter 1 The Nature of Economics   1

1.1 Scarcity   2
1.2 Defining Economics   3
     EXAMPLE 1-1 **The Economics of Web Page Design**   4
1.3 Rational Decision Making   5
     EXAMPLE 1-2 **The Opportunity Cost of Finding a Mate—Lower on the Internet?**   7
     EXAMPLE 1-3 **What Does a Year at College Really Cost?**   8
     POLICY EXAMPLE 1-1 **Chinese Smuggling**   9
     EXAMPLE 1-4 **Giving Charity to Oneself?**   10
1.4 The Scientific Method   10
     EXAMPLE 1-5 **The Science Behind Cold-fX®**   12
     EXAMPLE 1-6 **An Economic Model of Crime**   13
1.5 Positive versus Normative Economics   14
1.6 Economic Policy and Socioeconomic Goals   14
     ISSUES AND APPLICATIONS: **Bottled Water: The Hummer of Beverages?**   16

     APPENDIX A **Reading and Working with Graphs**   21
     Direct and Inverse Relationships   21
     Constructing a Graph   21
     The Slope of a Line (A Linear Curve)   25

Chapter 2 Production Possibilities and Economic Systems   29

2.1 The Production Possibilities Curve   30
2.2 Applications of the Production Possibilities Curve   31
     EXAMPLE 2-1 **Skipping Class without Skipping Lectures**   32
     EXAMPLE 2-2 **One Laptop per Child**   33
     POLICY EXAMPLE 2-1 **The Multibillion Dollar Park**   36
2.3 Consumption Goods versus Capital Goods   37
     EXAMPLE 2-3 **Canadian Post-Secondary Education Pays Off Big Time!**   39
2.4 Specialization and Greater Productivity   41
     EXAMPLE 2-4 **Why Men Marry: Is It for Love or the Marriage Premium?**   42
2.5 Economic Systems   44
2.6 Capitalism in More Depth   45
     POLICY EXAMPLE 2-2 **Canadian Politics: Rights, Left, and Centre**   48
     ISSUES AND APPLICATIONS: **Private or Public Auto Insurance: What Is Best for Canada?**   49

     APPENDIX B **The Production Possibilities Curve and Comparative Advantage**   57
     Before Specialization and Trade   57

After Specialization and Before Trade   58
After Specialization and After Trade   58

Chapter 3   Demand and Supply   63

3.1   The Law of Demand   64
    EXAMPLE 3-1   Why RFID Tags Are Catching On Fast   68
3.2   Shifts in Demand   68
    EXAMPLE 3-2   Chocaholics Beware   69
    EXAMPLE 3-3   Brunettes Now Have More Fun   70
    EXAMPLE 3-4   Garth Brooks, Used CDs, and the Law of Demand   72
3.3   The Law of Supply   73
3.4   Shifts in Supply   76
    EXAMPLE 3-5   Surge in Electronics Sales Follows Dramatic Drop in LCD Prices   78
3.5   Putting Demand and Supply Together   79
3.6   Changes in Equilibrium   82
    POLICY EXAMPLE 3-1   Having a Cow Over Milk Prices   84
    EXAMPLE 3-6   Air Canada Stock Price Spins Out of Free Fall   86
    ISSUES AND APPLICATIONS: Is Canada the Prescription for Lower Drug Prices in the U.S.?   88

Part 2   Dimensions of Macroeconomics   95

Chapter 4   Introduction to Macroeconomics   95

4.1   The Importance of Macroeconomics   96
4.2   Economic Activity and Business Fluctuations   97
    EXAMPLE 4-1   Technology and Long Cycles   99
4.3   Unemployment   101
    POLICY EXAMPLE 4-1   Challenges of Measuring the Unemployment Rate in China   105
    EXAMPLE 4-2   Translating Employment into Hours on the Job   106
    POLICY EXAMPLE 4-2   Policymakers Promote Measured Full Employment in India   108
4.4   Inflation and Deflation   108
    EXAMPLE 4-3   Do Rising Nominal Wages Mean Rising Real Wages, Too?   112
    EXAMPLE 4-4   British Columbia Coal Mines   113
    EXAMPLE 4-5   Hyperinflation   116
4.5   International Trade   117
4.6   Government Policies   117
    ISSUES AND APPLICATIONS: Hyperinflation and the Collapse of the Zimbabwean Economy   119

Chapter 5   Measuring the Economy's Performance   125

5.1   Economic Activity and the Circular Flow   126
5.2   Measuring Gross Domestic Product   129
    POLICY EXAMPLE 5-1   The Economic Cost of Pollution   132
    EXAMPLE 5-1   The Underground Economy   133
5.3   Two Main Methods of Measuring GDP   134
    EXAMPLE 5-2   Variability of GDP Expenditure Components   137

EXAMPLE 5-3 **World GDP May Be Understated**   140

5.4   Other Components of GDP and National Income
           Accounting   140
           EXAMPLE 5-4 **Correcting GDP for Price Level Changes,
           1997–2006**   142

5.5   Limitations of GDP   144
           EXAMPLE 5-5 **Comparing Standards of Living**   146

           EXAMPLE 5-6 **Purchasing Power Parity Comparisons
           of World Incomes**   147

           ISSUES AND APPLICATIONS: **Setting Goals for a Nation:
           What Do We Aim For?**   148

Part 3   National Income Determination and the
           Government Sector   155

Chapter 6 Modelling Real GDP and the Price Level in the
           Long Run   155

6.1   The Long-Run Aggregate Supply Curve   156
6.2   Shifts in Long-Run Aggregate Supply   159
           POLICY EXAMPLE 6-1 **Regulation and Economic Growth**   160

           EXAMPLE 6-1 **Terrorism and Economic Growth**   161

6.3   Aggregate Demand   162
           EXAMPLE 6-2 **Interest Rate Hikes and a Hot Loonie
           Are Hurting Ontario**   167

6.4   Long-Run Equilibrium, the Price Level,
           and Economic Growth   168
           EXAMPLE 6-3 **Information Technologies and Long-Run
           Aggregate Supply**   170

6.5   Causes of Inflation   170
           EXAMPLE 6-4 **The Economic Challenge of Age**   172

           EXAMPLE 6-5 **When Aggregate Demand Gets Out of
           Control, Watch Out!**   173

           ISSUES AND APPLICATIONS: **Why the 2004 Tsunami
           Did Not Swamp Asian Economies**   174

Chapter 7 Economic Growth and Development   180

7.1   Defining Economic Growth   181
           EXAMPLE 7-1 **Growth Rates around the World**   181

           EXAMPLE 7-2 **What If Canada Had Grown a Little Bit
           Less or More Each Year?**   183

7.2   Modelling Economic Growth   184
           EXAMPLE 7-3 **Productivity Gains**   187

           EXAMPLE 7-4 **How Does Canadian Productivity Compare
           with the Rest of the World?**   187

7.3   Fundamental Determinants of Economic Growth   188
           POLICY EXAMPLE 7-1 **The Mystery of Capitalism**   189

7.4   New Growth Theory and What Determines Growth   191
           POLICY EXAMPLE 7-2 **Competing on Creativity**   193

7.5   The Costs and Benefits of Economic Growth   195
           POLICY EXAMPLE 7-3 **Ottawa and the Kyoto Accord**   196

7.6   International Economic Development   197
           POLICY EXAMPLE 7-4 **The End of Poverty**   201

ISSUES AND APPLICATIONS: Winners and Losers in the
Brain-Drain Game   202

Chapter 8   Modelling Real GDP and the Price Level in the
             Short Run   207

8.1   The Short-Run Aggregate Supply Curve   208
       EXAMPLE 8-1 Changing the Slope of the Short-Run
       Aggregate Supply Schedule?   212
8.2   Shifts in the Aggregate Supply Curves   213
8.3   Equilibrium   215
       POLICY EXAMPLE 8-1 The Bank of Canada and Output Gaps   216
       EXAMPLE 8-2 A Tale of Two Economies   218
8.4   The Long-Run Adjustment Process   219
       EXAMPLE 8-3 Rising Labour Costs Reduce
       Productivity Gains   220
8.5   Aggregate Demand and Supply in an Open Economy   220
       EXAMPLE 8-4 Rising Canadian Loonie   222
8.6   Inflation and in the Short Run   222
       EXAMPLE 8-5 The Effect of World War I   223
       EXAMPLE 8-6 Why Have Unemployment Rates Fallen in
       North America with only Low Rates of Inflation?   224
       ISSUES AND APPLICATIONS: Oil Price Changes Shock
       the North American Economy   225
       APPENDIX C: Classical and Keynesian Macro Analyses   230
       Keynesian Economics and the Keynesian
       Short-Run Aggregate Supply Curve   234

Chapter 9   Consumption, Investment, and the Multiplier   237

9.1   Saving and Consumption   238
       POLICY EXAMPLE 9-1 Spending on Human Capital:
       Investment or Consumption?   239
9.2   Determinants of Planned Consumption and
       Planned Saving   240
       EXAMPLE 9-1 U.S. Consumers Are Bloodied But Unbowed   243
9.3   Determinants of Investment   244
       EXAMPLE 9-2 Changes in Investment and the Great Depression 246
9.4   Equilibrium in the Keynesian Model   247
       EXAMPLE 9-3 Oil Sands Investment Continues to Grow   252
9.5   The Multiplier   252
       POLICY EXAMPLE 9-2 The Multiplier Effect of Forced Housing
       Investment in China   255
9.6   The Relationship between Total Planned
       Expenditures and the Aggregate Demand Curve   256
       ISSUES AND APPLICATIONS: Can Stock Market Crashes
       Affect the Economy?   256
       APPENDIX D: The Keynesian Cross and the Multiplier   265
       APPENDIX E: The Algebra of the Keynesian Expenditure Model 266

Chapter 10   The Public Sector   269

10.1   Economic Functions of Government   270
       POLICY EXAMPLE 10-1 Who Should Pay the High Cost
       of a Legal System?   270
       EXAMPLE 10-1 Are Lighthouses a Public Good?   272

10.2	The Political Functions of Government	273
	POLICY EXAMPLE 10-2 **Do Government-Funded Sports Stadiums Have a Net Positive Effect on Local Economies?**	274
	EXAMPLE 10-2 **Child Care Spaces**	274
10.3	Tax Rates and the Canadian Tax System	279
	POLICY EXAMPLE 10-3 **Tax Freedom Day Around the World**	280
	EXAMPLE 10-3 **Employment Insurance**	282
	ISSUES AND APPLICATIONS: **Should We Switch to a Flat Tax?**	286

Chapter 11 Fiscal Policy and the Public Debt   291

11.1	Fiscal Policy	292
	POLICY EXAMPLE 11-1 **Did Roosevelt's New Deal Really Provide a Stimulus?**	294
11.2	Government Budgets and Finances	295
	POLICY EXAMPLE 11-2 **The Baby Boom Generation Moves into Retirement Years**	299
11.3	Federal Budget Deficits in an Open Economy	301
11.4	Possible Offsets to Fiscal Policy	302
	POLICY EXAMPLE 11-3 **Boosting Tax Revenues via International Tax Competition**	305
11.5	Discretionary Fiscal Policy in Practice	306
11.6	Automatic Stabilizers	307
	POLICY EXAMPLE 11-4 **Keynesian Fiscal Policy Loses Its Lustre**	310
	ISSUES AND APPLICATIONS: **How Much Government Is Enough?**	311
	APPENDIX F: **Fiscal Policy: A Keynesian Perspective**	316
	Changes in Government Spending	316
	Changes in Taxes	317
	The Balanced-Budget Multiplier	317
	The Fixed-Price Level Assumption	318

Part 4 Money, Monetary Policy, and Stabilization   319

Chapter 12 Money and the Banking System   319

12.1	The Functions of Money	320
	EXAMPLE 12-1 **Will Barter Make a Comeback on the Web?**	321
	EXAMPLE 12-2 **Converting Dollars into African Vouchers on the Web**	322
12.2	Monetary Standards, or What Backs Money	323
	EXAMPLE 12-3 **E-Gold-Backed E-Money**	323
	EXAMPLE 12-4 **Is Gold Worth Its Weight?**	324
12.3	Defining the Canadian Money Supply	325
	EXAMPLE 12-5 **Eliminating the $1 and $2 Bills**	326
	EXAMPLE 12-6 **Why McDonald's Wants Your Card, Not Your Cash**	327
	EXAMPLE 12-7 **Credit Cards and Canadians**	327
	EXAMPLE 12-8 **What Will Digital Cash Replace?**	328
12.4	The Canadian Financial System	330
	EXAMPLE 12-9 **Why Banks Want Their Customers to Go Online**	332

ISSUES AND APPLICATIONS: **The Dollarization Movement: Is the U.S. Fed Destined to be a Multinational Central Bank?** 335

Chapter 13 Money Creation and Deposit Insurance 338

13.1 Links between Changes in the Money Supply and Other Economic Variables 339
13.2 The Origins of Fractional Reserve Banking 339
13.3 Reserves 340

POLICY EXAMPLE 13-1 **Are Reserve Requirements on the Way Out or In?** 341

13.4 The Relationship between Reserves and Total Deposits 342
13.5 The Money Multiplier 346
13.6 Deposit Insurance and Flawed Bank Regulation 347

POLICY EXAMPLE 13-2 **Bailouts That Cost Taxpayers Millions** 349

ISSUES AND APPLICATIONS: **Deregulating the Financial Services Industry** 350

Chapter 14 The Bank of Canada and Monetary Policy 355

14.1 Central Banks and the Bank of Canada 356
EXAMPLE 14-1 **Is Canadian Tire Money Real Money?** 358

14.2 The Money Supply and Tools of Monetary Policy 359
EXAMPLE 14-2 **Determining the Price of Bonds** 362

POLICY EXAMPLE 14-1 **The Determination of the Target for the Overnight Rate** 363

14.3 The Demand for Money 364
EXAMPLE 14-3 **The Choice between Cash and Savings Accounts in Colombia** 366

14.4 Monetary Policy in Action: The Transmission Mechanism 367

EXAMPLE 14-4 **Unfortunately for Germany, the Crude Quantity Theory Worked Very Well** 370

EXAMPLE 14-5 **Inflation and Money Growth Throughout the World** 370

POLICY EXAMPLE 14-2 **Monetary Policy: Where Are We Now?** 372

14.5 Effectiveness of Monetary Policy 374

POLICY EXAMPLE 14-3 **Political Uncertainty and Monetary Targeting** 377

ISSUES AND APPLICATIONS: **Is the Bank of Canada Independent and, If Not, Does It Matter?** 378

APPENDIX G: **Monetary Policy: A Keynesian Perspective** 384

Increasing the Money Supply 384
Decreasing the Money Supply 385
Arguments against Monetary Policy 385

Chapter 15 Issues in Stabilization Policy 386

Active versus Passive Policy Making 387
15.1 The Natural Rate of Unemployment 387
EXAMPLE 15-1 **Canada's Natural Rate of Unemployment** 388

EXAMPLE 15-2 **Monetary Policy and Aggregate Demand: The Bank of Japan Tries to Have It Both Ways** 390

15.2   The Phillips Curve   391

     EXAMPLE 15-3 **Distinguishing between the Natural Rate of**
     Unemployment and the NAIRU   392

15.3   The Importance of Expectations   393

     EXAMPLE 15-4 **The Effects of Higher Inflation on**
     Inflation Expectations   394

15.4   Rational Expectations and the New Classical Model   396

     EXAMPLE 15-5 **Higher Interest Rates and "Tight" Monetary**
     Policy   399

15.5   Real Business Cycle Theory   401
15.6   Suppy-Side Economics   402

     EXAMPLE 15-6 **Islam and Supply-Side Economics**   404

15.7   Alternative Models for Active Policy Making   405

     EXAMPLE 15-7 **Job Cuts or Pay Reductions: Which Are**
     Less Harmful to Workers' Morale?   406

     EXAMPLE 15-8 **Henry Ford and the Efficiency Wage Model**   406

     EXAMPLE 15-9 **The French Government's Direct Approach**
     to Reducing Unemployment   407

     ISSUES AND APPLICATIONS: **The Bank of Canada's High**
     Interest Rate Policy   411

Part 5   Global Economics   418

    Chapter 16   Comparative Advantage and the Open Economy   418

16.1   The Worldwide Importance, Trends, and
     Patterns of International Trade   419

     EXAMPLE 16-1 **The Importance of International Trade in**
     Various Countries   420

     EXAMPLE 16-2 **U.S. Consumers Go Online to Import**
     Canadian Pharmaceuticals   421

16.2   Why We Trade: Comparative Advantage and
     Exhausting Mutual Gains from Exchange   422

     EXAMPLE 16-3 **International Trade and the Alphabet**   426

     EXAMPLE 16-4 **The Importation of Priests into Spain**   427

16.3   International Competitiveness   427

     EXAMPLE 16-5 **Do Legal Restrictions Reduce the**
     International Competitiveness of Middle Eastern Nations?   428

16.4   Arguments against Free Trade   429

     EXAMPLE 16-6 **Dumping Chinese Garlic**   430

     POLICY EXAMPLE 16-1 **Who Is Dumping on Whom?**   430

     EXAMPLE 16-7 **Unfair Competition from Low-Wage**
     Countries   432

16.5   Ways to Restrict Foreign Trade   432
16.6   International Trade Agreements   434

     POLICY EXAMPLE 16-2 **Should Canadian Farmers**
     Be Subsidized?   436

     ISSUES AND APPLICATIONS: **Do Regional Trade Agreements**
     Help or Hinder International Trade?   437

    Chapter 17   Exchange Rates and the Balance of Payments   445

17.1   The Balance of Payments and International Capital
     Movements   446
17.2   Accounting Identities   446

EXAMPLE 17-1 Perhaps the Trade Situation Isn't So Bad After All   448

EXAMPLE 17-2 Does Canada's Frequent Current Account Deficit Mean It Has a Weak Economy?   449

17.3   Determining Foreign Exchange Rates   452

EXAMPLE 17-3 Central European Currency Values Are Up, So Exports Are Down   453

17.4   Factors That Can Induce Changes in Equilibrium Exchange Rates   457

17.5   The Gold Standard and the International Monetary Fund   459

POLICY EXAMPLE 17-1 Should We Go Back to the Gold Standard?   460

17.6   Fixed versus Floating Exchange Rates   461

POLICY EXAMPLE 17-2 Can Foreign Exchange Rates Be Fixed Forever?   462

ISSUES AND APPLICATIONS: A Major Foreign Exchange Flop   465

ANSWERS TO ODD-NUMBERED PROBLEMS   472

ANSWERS TO "FOR CRITICAL ANALYSIS" QUESTIONS   487

GLOSSARY   503

INDEX   512

PREFACE

From the Authors

In creating *Economics Today: The Macro View*, Fourth Canadian Edition, substantial revisions to the previous edition were made, based on the helpful suggestions and comments provided by adopters and reviewers. We were careful to ensure that any changes we made to the third edition would maintain the straightforward and approachable style that has made this book so popular in post-secondary institutions across Canada.

As instructors with extensive teaching experience in both college and university settings, we want to continue to present a text that students can relate to based on their personal, social, and career interests. We also hope that this book will encourage students to broaden their interests to include local, national, and global economic issues. Many of our students will not take subsequent economics courses; in that case, we want them to be ready for the world, and not just for intermediate economics courses.

The approach used in *Economics Today: The Macro View*, Fourth Canadian Edition, is based on the belief that students learn more when they are involved and engaged in the material they are studying. The presentation of issues and applications in a Canadian setting is a major strength of this text. Each chapter begins with an issue that introduces certain economic principles; those principles are presented throughout the chapter, and at the end of the chapter an Issues and Applications section explains how those principles can be applied to that issue. This section ends with For Critical Analysis questions, which help reinforce the theory at hand and encourage the students to reflect on economics in the "real" world—their world.

In addition, each chapter contains numerous short Examples and Policy Examples that further illustrate the points being made in the text. Each of these examples is accompanied by For Critical Analysis questions, which encourage students to actively apply the economic principles presented in the chapter. Mindful of the importance of global events to Canada's economic well-being, we have used many examples and issues that connect Canada with the rest of the world. Suggested solutions to all of the For Critical Analysis questions are provided at the end of the text.

For this fourth Canadian edition we have reorganized and consolidated material within chapters; updated numerous Issues and Applications and Example boxes; included additional Canadian and international comparisons and examples; and added new end-of-chapter questions and exercises.

Below is a sample of some of the new issues discussed in the Fourth Canadian Edition:

- Bottled Water: The Hummer of Beverages? (Chapter 1 Issues and Applications)
- One Laptop per Child (Example 2-2)
- Why RFID Tags Are Catching On Fast (Example 3-1)
- Interest Rate Hikes and a Hot Loonie are Hurting Ontario (Example 6-2)
- Competing on Creativity (Policy Example 7-2)
- The Bank of Canada and Output Gaps (Policy Example 8-1)
- E-Gold-Backed E-Money (Example 12-3)
- The Effects of Higher Inflation on Inflation Expectations (Example 15-4)
- U.S. Consumers Go Online to Import Canadian Pharmaceuticals (Example 16-2)
- Should Canadian Farmers Be Subsidized? (Policy Example 16-2)

In addition, we have made several important changes to chapter content. For example,

- The chapter on long-run aggregate supply (Chapter 6) has been placed before the chapter on economic growth (Chapter 7).
- In Chapter 6, Modelling Real GDP and the Price Level in the Long Run, we have integrated our discussion of the multiplier into the section on aggregate demand.
- In Chapter 7, Economic Growth and Development, we have added a new section on modelling economic growth.
- In Chapter 12, Money and the Banking System, we have extended our discussion of asymmetrical information, adverse selection, and moral hazard in banking. We have also added new material on financial intermediation across national boundaries.
- In Chapter 15, Issues in Stabilization Policy, we have significantly revised our discussions of new Keynesian inflation dynamics and active versus passive policy-making.

In the end, we believe that *Economics Today: The Macro View* and the MyEconLab will provide students with a relevant and interesting resource—one that will present students with a "window of the world" that will help them in their personal lives as citizens and professionals. We hope that you will enjoy this book and begin to appreciate the many ways in which economics can be a part of your day-to-day activities.

Economic Principles in Practice

CHAPTER OPENING ISSUES. Each opening issue motivates student interest in the key chapter concepts. The issue presented is revisited in the Issues and Applications section at the culmination of the chapter.

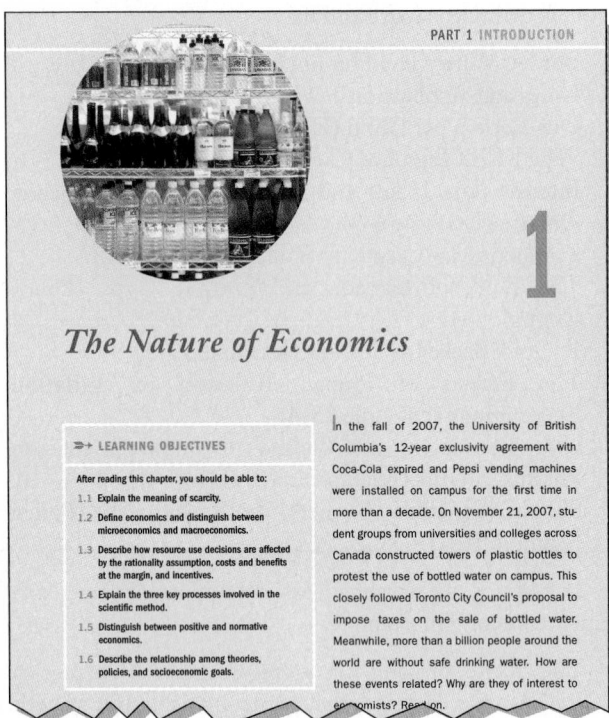

POLICY EXAMPLES. Many of the economic debates reported in the media involve important policy issues. Here, students are presented with various key policy questions on both the domestic and international fronts. Each Policy Example is followed by a For Critical Analysis question that encourages students to consider exactly what is involved in the discussion and what the further ramifications might be. Suggested solutions to these questions are provided at the back of the text and in the Instructor's Manual.

POLICY EXAMPLE 1-1   Chinese Smuggling

In the recent past, the Chinese government recruited an antismuggling police force to try to stop the annual flow of tens of billions of dollars in illegal contraband. One example of "illegal contraband" was cigarettes. Domestic taxes on cigarettes were so high that many Chinese cigarette manufacturers exported half their output, which they then smuggled back into China. Another example was diesel fuel. The Chinese government fixed the price of diesel fuel at levels above prices elsewhere in the world. This gave consumers of diesel fuel an incentive to smuggle cheaper foreign-produced diesel fuel into the country.

Why did China need an antismuggling police force when it already employed an army of border guards and customs inspectors? The answer is that the returns on smuggling were so high that many existing border guards and customs inspectors became smugglers themselves. Thus, the government felt that new police officers were needed, in part, to watch over the existing cadre of "law enforcers."

On July 18, 2006, the London School of Hygiene and Tropical Medicine, at the University of London, reported that new research based on the internal documents of one of the world's biggest tobacco companies, British American Tobacco (BAT), suggests that BAT had restructured its operations to control and expand the contraband trade in China.

As smoking is declining in the world's richer nations, tobacco companies are seeking to increase sales in other countries. China is regarded as the ultimate prize among tobacco's emerging markets—one in three of all cigarettes smoked are smoked there and the nation has the largest number of smokers in the world (350 million). BAT's internal documents state that their exports from Hong Kong, intended for the contraband Chinese market, are the "key to the future" for BAT.

SOURCE: "RESEARCH REVEALS TOBACCO COMPANY'S ROLE IN CHINA'S CIGARETTE SMUGGLING CRISIS." TUESDAY JULY 18, 2006. LONDON SCHOOL OF HYGIENE AND TROPICAL MEDICINE PRESS.

For critical analysis: What actions could the government take to remove the incentives to smuggle cigarettes and diesel fuel?

ISSUES AND APPLICATIONS. The Issues and Applications feature is designed to encourage students not just to apply economic concepts, but also to think critically about them. Each begins with the concepts being applied in this instance, and is followed by For Critical Analysis questions that could be used to prompt in-class discussions. Suggested answers to these questions are given at the back of the text, as well as in the Instructor's Manual at the end of the appropriate chapter.

EXAMPLES. Many thought-provoking and relevant examples highlight Canadian, as well as international, events and demonstrate economic principles. The For Critical Analysis questions that follow encourage students to apply the knowledge and information gained from the example. Possible answers to the questions are provided at the back of the text and in the Instructor's Manual.

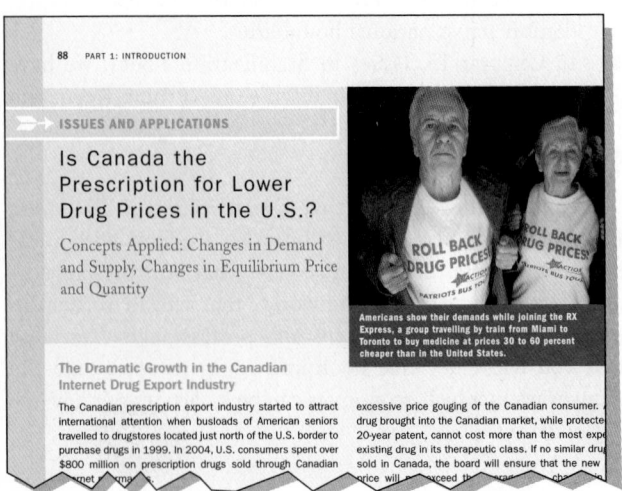

EXAMPLE 2-1   Skipping Class without Skipping Lectures

At Harvard University, there is a department called the Instructional Computing Group. Employees videotape about 30 courses per semester and place them on the university's internal website for students to review if they missed class.

Every student, naturally, has his or her own subjective estimate of the expected value of the next-best alternative to attending class. For each student, the value of an hour spent in class depends in part on what time of the day the class meets. Harvard's online lecture-review system permits students to reallocate the uses of their time. If a student would rather be in a rowboat on the Charles River at 1:00 on a spring afternoon instead of attending her Harvard economics class, she can miss the class. Then she can view the class lecture, say, at 5:00, when she rates the value of that study activity to be higher than her next-highest-valued activity for that hour of the day.

Of course, there is still an opportunity cost associated with skipping the actual class meeting. The student misses out on the opportunity to ask questions of her professor during the lecture and to interact with other class members. Nevertheless, there is evidence that many Harvard students prefer to reallocate their daily schedule in favour of virtual class attendance—professors in some of the courses with videotaped lectures have been increasingly concerned about noticeable drops in physical attendance in class meetings.

For critical analysis:

1. What opportunity costs (sacrifices) might you incur when you skip your classes?

2. In classes where group discussion or group work is an essential feature of the learning...

Pedagogy With a Purpose

This fourth Canadian edition of *Economics Today: The Macro View* is loaded with the same highly regarded pedagogy of the previous edition. It helps students apply what they learn.

FOR CRITICAL ANALYSIS. At the end of each Example and Policy Example, students are asked to reflect on real-world problems by answering For Critical Analysis questions. The answers to the questions are found at the end of the student text and in the Instructor's Manual.

DID YOU KNOW THAT . . . ? Each chapter starts with a provocative question to engage students' interest and lead them into the content of the chapter.

LEARNING OBJECTIVES. On the first page of each chapter, several learning objectives are presented, giving purpose and focus to the chapter. These are then fully reviewed at the end of the chapter.

GRAPHS. Articulate and precise, the four-colour graphs illustrate key concepts.

KEY TERMS. Key terms are printed in bold type, and are defined in the margin of the text the first time they appear. These terms are also reproduced alphabetically in the Glossary at the end of the text.

CONCEPTS IN BRIEF. At the end of each major section in each chapter, Concepts in Brief summarizes the main points, thus reinforcing students' knowledge as well as testing their learning. The Concepts in Brief are organized around the chapter's learning objectives.

MYECONLAB SUMMARY CHART. Each chapter ends with a chart linking the learning objectives with the MyEconLab study plan. It identifies what students should know after reading each chapter and where to go when they need to practise.

PROBLEMS. A variety of problems support each chapter, with each problem linked to the appropriate learning objective in the chapter. Answers for all odd-numbered problems are provided at the back of the textbook. The complete set of problem answers (both even- and odd-numbered) appears in the Instructor's Manual.

Teaching/Learning Package

Instructor's Resource CD-ROM

This resource provides all of the following supplements in one convenient package.

- **Instructor's Manual.** The Instructor's Manual has been adapted for this fourth Canadian edition of *Economics Today*. This extensive manual includes chapter overviews, objectives, and outlines; points to emphasize, including more theoretical issues for those who wish to stress theory; suggested questions for further class discussion; answers to the For Critical Analysis questions and end-of-chapter problems from the text; and selected references.
- **Pearson Education Canada TestGen.** This software enables instructors to view and edit the existing testbank questions, add new questions, and generate custom tests. It includes a minimum of 100 multiple-choice questions, 10 short-answer questions, and 5 essay questions per chapter.
- **PowerPoint Presentations.** PowerPoint Presentations are available for each chapter of the text to highlight and illustrate important ideas.

MyEconLab

This text is fully integrated with MyEconLab, a robust online learning system featuring lots of practice exercises and study tools as well as a personalized study plan generated to suit your individual study needs. The site is available 24 hours a day so you can study where you want, how you want, and when you want.

MyEconLab is found at **www.myeconlab.com.** Follow the simple registration instructions on the Access Code card bound into every new copy of this text.

ACKNOWLEDGMENTS

We could not have completed the fourth Canadian edition without the help of a terrific team of professionals at Pearson Education Canada. Thanks to Don Thompson, our Acquisitions Editor, for giving us this opportunity! Our Developmental Editor, Kimberley Hermans, was a constant source of timely advice and encouragement. Laura Neves, Production Editor, guided the book through the final stages with a calm and sure hand. Our Copy Editor, Nicole Mellow, juggled four authors and four different writing styles with great dexterity.

We would also like to thank the following professors who helped with the development of this text by offering us their insightful comments and constructive criticisms:

Aurelia Best, Centennial College
Ron Bianchi, Vanier College
Jim Butko, Niagara College
Philippe Ghayad, Dawson College and Concordia University
Susan Kamp, University of Alberta
Carl Weston, Mohawk College

In completing this work, we sincerely appreciate the support and patience we have received from each of our families.

Finally, we would like to thank our colleagues and students at Northern Alberta Institute of Technology and British Columbia Institute of Technology for their valuable advice and support during the writing of this book.

Brenda Abbott

Sam Fefferman

Ronald K. Kessler

Terrence Sulyma

1

The Nature of Economics

➡ **LEARNING OBJECTIVES**

After reading this chapter, you should be able to:

1.1 **Explain the meaning of scarcity.**

1.2 **Define economics and distinguish between microeconomics and macroeconomics.**

1.3 **Describe how resource use decisions are affected by the rationality assumption, costs and benefits at the margin, and incentives.**

1.4 **Explain the three key processes involved in the scientific method.**

1.5 **Distinguish between positive and normative economics.**

1.6 **Describe the relationship among theories, policies, and socioeconomic goals.**

In the fall of 2007, the University of British Columbia's 12-year exclusivity agreement with Coca-Cola expired and Pepsi vending machines were installed on campus for the first time in more than a decade. On November 21, 2007, student groups from universities and colleges across Canada constructed towers of plastic bottles to protest the use of bottled water on campus. This closely followed Toronto City Council's proposal to impose taxes on the sale of bottled water. Meanwhile, more than a billion people around the world are without safe drinking water. How are these events related? Why are they of interest to economists? Read on.

MyEconLab helps you master each objective and study more efficiently. See end of chapter for details.

DID YOU KNOW THAT... ?

In 2006, 82 percent of all Canadian households owned a computer, with more than 50 percent owning more than one. Seventy-five percent of Canadians had Internet access from home and three-quarters of these individuals had high speed access. The most popular online activities include conducting bank transactions (62%), researching trips (60%) and comparison shopping (52%).

While the average family spends more than 32 hours online per week, 50 percent of Canadians with Internet access have yet to make an online purchase.

The world around us continues to change rapidly, and much of that change stems from the significant decline in cost and increase in convenience associated with information technology. Since 1961, the average cost of computer processing equipment has fallen at a rate of 19 percent per year. Your own decisions about what type of computer to buy, how to access the Internet, and how much time you spend online each week involve an untold number of variables. But, as you will see, there are economic underpinnings for nearly all the decisions you make.

SOURCE: "The 2006 Canadian Inter@ctive Reid Report." Ipos Reid, http://www.ipsos_ca/pdf/CIFG.pdf.

1.1 Scarcity

You can't have it all! You were probably first exposed to this very important economics lesson when, as a toddler, your parents denied your request to buy you a new toy at the supermarket. You undoubtedly experienced this same lesson many times over by the time you enrolled in this course. After you graduate, you may face such choices as buying a brand new car, putting a down payment on a condo, travelling to faraway places, or getting married and starting a family. As a senior member of your community, you may have to choose between spending tax dollars on building a new hospital and improving the education system for the next generation.

Whenever individuals or communities cannot obtain everything they desire, choices occur. Choices occur because of the fundamental economic problem of *scarcity*. Scarcity is the most basic concept in all of economics.

Scarcity The condition that arises because wants always exceed what can be produced with limited resources.

> **Scarcity** refers to the condition that arises because wants always exceed what can be produced with limited resources.

As a result of scarcity, we do not and cannot have enough income and wealth to satisfy our every desire.

Scarcity is not the same thing as poverty. Scarcity occurs among the rich as well as the poor. Even the richest person faces scarcity because available time is limited. Low income levels do not create more scarcity. High income levels do not create less scarcity.

Scarcity and Wants

Wants refer to the goods and services that we wish to consume as well as the goals that we seek to achieve. **Goods** are physical items that we as consumers are willing to pay for, such as meat, jeans, DVDs, and cars. **Services** are the tasks performed by others that we as consumers are willing to pay for, such as haircuts, education, and medical, dental, and legal services. The goals that we seek to achieve can be individual or social in nature. The important thing to note is that we are referring to goods, services, and goals that require the use of our limited resources.

Goods The physical items that consumers are willing to pay for.

Services The tasks performed by others that consumers are willing to pay for.

Scarcity and Resources

The scarcity concept arises from the fact that resources are insufficient to satisfy our every desire. Resources are the inputs used in the production of the things that we want. **Production** can be defined as virtually any activity that results in the conversion of resources into goods and services. Production includes delivering things from one part of the country to another. It includes taking ice from an ice tray to put in your soft-drink glass.

Production Any activity that results in the conversion of resources into goods and services.

The resources used in production are called *factors of production,* and some economists use the terms *resources* and *factors of production* interchangeably. The total quantity of all resources that an economy has at any one time determines what that economy can produce.

Factors of production can be classified in many ways. Here is one such classification:

Land Nonhuman gifts of nature.

Labour Productive contributions made by individuals who work.

Physical capital Factories and equipment used in production.

Human capital The education and training of workers.

Entrepreneurship Human resources that perform the functions of risk taking, organizing, managing, and assembling other factors of production to make business ventures.

1. **Land** encompasses all the nonhuman gifts of nature, including timber, water, fish, minerals, and the original fertility of the land. It is often called the *natural resource.*
2. **Labour** is the human resource, which includes all productive contributions made by individuals who work, such as steelworkers, ballet dancers, and professional baseball players.
3. **Physical capital** consists of the factories and equipment used in production. It also includes improvements to natural resources, such as irrigation ditches.
4. **Human capital** is the economic characterization of the education and training of workers. How much the nation produces depends not only on how many hours people work but also on how productive they are, and that, in turn, depends in part on education and training. To become more educated, individuals have to devote time and resources, just as a business has to devote resources if it wants to increase its physical capital. Whenever a worker's skills increase, human capital has been improved.
5. **Entrepreneurship** is actually a subdivision of labour and involves human resources that perform the functions of risk taking, organizing, managing, and assembling the other factors of production to make business ventures. Entrepreneurship also encompasses taking risks that involve the possibility of losing large sums of wealth on new ventures. It includes new methods of doing common things, and generally experimenting with any type of new thinking that could lead to making more money income. Without entrepreneurship, virtually no business organization could operate.

Rent Income earned by land.

Wages Income earned by labour.

Interest Income earned by capital.

Profit Income earned by the entrepreneur.

When resources are used to produce goods and services, they earn income. The incomes earned by land, labour, capital, and entrepreneurship are referred to as **rent, wages, interest,** and **profit,** respectively.

1.2 Defining Economics

What is economics exactly? *Economics* is one of the social sciences and, as such, seeks explanations of real events. All social sciences analyze human behaviour. The physical sciences, on the other hand, generally analyze the behaviour of electrons, atoms, and other nonhuman phenomena.

Economics A social science that studies how people allocate their limited resources to satisfy their wants.

> **Economics** is a social science that studies how people allocate their limited resources to satisfy their wants. That is, economics is concerned with how individuals, groups, and societies respond to the economic problem of scarcity.

Resources are limited relative to wants. Consumers, managers, business owners, citizens, and politicians must continually make choices among alternative courses of action. For example, as a consumer, you choose how to spend your limited income on a vast array of goods and services. If you own a business or manage a government department, you will have to decide what resources to hire in order to best promote the goals of your organization, while working within a limited budget. As a citizen and potential politician, you make decisions that affect how limited tax dollars are used for the betterment of society. Economics helps us study how such choices can be made.

As Example 1–1 suggests, even a web page designer, who prefers to engage in artistic endeavours, must practise economics on a regular basis.

| EXAMPLE 1-1 | The Economics of Web Page Design |

Over 22 million Canadians use the Internet every month. In 2006, 84 percent of Canadians had access to the Internet from any location, with British Columbia having the highest access (92 percent). Almost 90 percent of Canadians aged 18 to 54 had Internet access. Seventy-five percent of Canadians had Internet access from home and three-quarters of these individuals had high-speed access. Canadians between the ages of 15 to 54 years spent an average of 13.3 hours per week, or approximately two hours per day, on the Internet. During the month of September 2006 alone, Canadians spent 45.78 billion minutes on the Internet, a 20 percent increase over September 2005.

Companies that want to sell their products realize that these Internet use statistics suggest that advertisements posted on the Net can potentially reach very large audiences, not only in Canada but worldwide as well. These companies also know that when individuals access the Internet, the home pages of the individuals are typically those of their Internet service provider, a popular search engine, such as Yahoo!, or their favourite media website. Consequently, many companies advertise on these web pages. In 2006, Canadian online advertising ballooned to a record $1.01 billion for the year. This represents an increase of 80 percent over the 2005 level of online advertising.

The owner of any web page that carries advertising faces the economic problem of scarcity. For example, advertisers widely consider the home page of Yahoo! search engine as "prime real estate" because so many people see it each day. But there is relatively little space on the computer screen to view Yahoo!'s opening page, without having to scroll farther down the screen. Thus, when Yahoo! allocates space to promote its own services and products, it gives up space that it could sell to advertisers. On the other hand, if Yahoo! fills up too much of its prime screen space with ads, some users will switch to a less cluttered search engine. Web designers try to minimize the placement of ads on valuable prime screen space by using animations that can feature a number of different ads on the same space on a web page. However, Net surfers are only willing to spend a limited amount of time to view such animations. All these considerations make web design a crucial economic concern.

For critical analysis: What are the "unlimited wants" and "limited resources" that face a person in charge of designing a frequently visited web page?

SOURCES: "ONLINE ADVERTISING RESEARCH STUDY." IAB CANADA. http://www.iabcanada.com/iab_resources/quick_facts.shtml; "THE CANADIAN INTERNET FACT PAGE." IPSOS REID. http://www.ipsos-reid.com/ca/data/dsp_little_cdn_fact_book.cfm; "CANADIANS SPEND OVER 45 BILLION MINUTES ONLINE." IAB CANADA NEWSLETTER, DECEMBER 7, 2006. http://www.iabcanada.com/newsletters/061207.shtml; THE 2006 CANADIAN INTER@CTIVE REID REPORT: FACT GUIDE. THE DEFINITIVE RESOURCE ON CANADIANS AND THE INTERNET. IPSOS REID. http://www.ipsos.ca/pdf/CIFG.pdf; "2006 CANADIAN ONLINE ADVERTISING TOPS $1 BILLION DOLLARS." IAB CANADA NEWSLETTER, APRIL 30, 2007. http://www.iabcanada.com/newsletters/070430.shtm.

Microeconomics versus Macroeconomics

Economics is typically divided into two fields of study: *microeconomics* and *macroeconomics*.

Microeconomics studies decision making undertaken by individuals and by firms in specific parts of the economy. It is like looking through a microscope to focus on individual households, firms, industries, and occupations.

Macroeconomics studies the behaviour of the economy as a whole. It deals with economywide phenomena, such as changes in unemployment, the general price level, and national income.

Microeconomic analysis, for example, is concerned with the effects of changes in the price of gasoline relative to that of other energy sources. It examines the effects of new taxes on a specific product or industry. If price controls were to be reinstituted in Canada, how individual firms and consumers would react to them would be in the realm of microeconomics. The raising of wages by an effective union strike would also be analyzed using the tools of microeconomics.

Microeconomics The study of decision making undertaken by individuals and by firms in specific parts of the economy.

Macroeconomics The study of the behaviour of the economy as a whole.

Aggregates Economywide measures.

By contrast, such issues as the rate of inflation, the amount of economywide unemployment, and the yearly growth in the output of goods and services in the nation all fall into the domain of macroeconomic analysis. In other words, macroeconomics deals with **aggregates**, or economywide measures, such as total output in an economy.

The Power of Economic Analysis

Knowing that an economic problem of scarcity exists every time you make a decision is not enough. As you study economics, you will be encouraged to develop a framework of analysis that will allow you to effectively analyze possible solutions to each economic problem—whether you are a student trying to decide how much studying time you should devote to a course, a consumer making the choice between renting and owning your next home, a business owner interested in setting the most profitable price for your product, or a government leader searching for the policy that would most effectively create jobs in your province. The remainder of this chapter is concerned with introducing you to a powerful framework of analysis that includes the *economic way of thinking*, the *scientific approach*, and *policy analysis* based on valued economic goals.

Indeed, just as taking an art or literature appreciation class increases the pleasure you receive when you view paintings or read novels, taking an economics course will increase your understanding when viewing news clips on the Internet, watching the news on TV, listening to newscasts on the radio, or reading newspapers.

➤➔ **CONCEPTS IN BRIEF**

Learning Objective 1.1: Explain the meaning of scarcity.
- Scarcity refers to the condition that arises because wants always exceed what can be produced with the available limited resources. Scarcity is ever present in both rich and poor nations.
- Limited resources include such items as land, labour, physical capital, human capital, and entrepreneurship. Wants refer to the goods and services that we wish to consume as well as the goals that we seek to achieve.

Learning Objective 1.2: Define economics and distinguish between microeconomics and macroeconomics.
- Economics is a social science that studies how people allocate limited resources to satisfy unlimited wants.
- The field of economics can be further subdivided into microeconomics and macroeconomics.
- Microeconomics focuses on the specific parts of the economy, such as the individual household, firm, industry, or occupation.
- Macroeconomics focuses on the behaviour of the economy as a whole and seeks to explain economywide phenomena, such as changes in unemployment, the general price level, and national income.
- Economics offers a useful framework of analysis that includes the economic way of thinking, the scientific approach, and policy analysis.

1.3 Rational Decision Making

Economic way of thinking Assumes that the typical response to an economic problem of scarcity is rational behaviour.

The **economic way of thinking** assumes that the typical response to an economic problem of scarcity is rational behaviour. That is, individuals behave as if they compare the costs and benefits of different possible choices when they make resource use decisions. They behave in this manner in order to further their own self-interest.

Economists presume that individuals act *as if* motivated by self-interest and respond predictably to opportunities for gain. This central insight of economics was first clearly articulated by Adam Smith in 1776. Smith wrote in his most famous book, *An Inquiry into the Nature and Causes of the Wealth of Nations*, that "it is not from the benevolence of the butcher, the brewer, or the baker that we expect our dinner, but from their regard to their own interest." Otherwise stated, the *typical* person about whom economists make behavioural predictions is assumed to look out for his or her own self-interest in a rational manner. The word *typical* is very important. Economists know that not all people respond in the same way when faced with the same circumstances. If offered a free trip to Hawaii for participating in a marketing experiment, for example, most people will take part. There inevitably will be some who do not want to go to Hawaii, perhaps because they do not like travelling, so they will not participate in the study. But, *on average*, the promised trip to Hawaii will be sufficient to attract participants because people behave in a predictably self-interested way.

The Rationality Assumption

Rationality assumption An individual makes decisions based on maximizing his or her own self-interest.

The **rationality assumption** of economics, simply stated, is as follows:

> An individual makes decisions based on maximizing his or her own self-interest.

The distinction here is between what people may think—the realm of psychology and psychiatry and perhaps sociology—and what they do. Economics does *not* involve itself in analyzing individual or group thought processes. Economics looks at what people actually do in life with their limited resources. It does little good to criticize the rationality assumption by stating, "Nobody thinks that way" or "I never think that way" or "How unrealistic! That's as irrational as anyone can get!"

Take the example of driving. When you consider passing another car on a two-lane highway with oncoming traffic, you have to make very quick decisions: You must estimate the speed of the car you are going to pass, the speed of the oncoming cars, the distance between your car and the oncoming cars, and your car's potential rate of acceleration. If we were to apply a model to your behaviour, we would use the laws of calculus. In actual fact, you and most other drivers in such a situation do not actually think of using the laws of calculus, but we could predict your behaviour *as if* you understood the laws of calculus.

In practical terms, the rationality assumption implies that an individual will adopt a course of action if the action's relevant benefits exceed its relevant costs. Let us proceed to examine what we mean by *relevant* costs and benefits.

Opportunity Cost

The natural fact of scarcity implies that we must make choices. One of the most important results of this fact is that every choice made (or not made, for that matter) means that some opportunity had to be sacrificed. Every choice involves giving up another opportunity to do or use something else.

Consider a practical example. Every choice you make to study one more hour of economics requires that you give up the opportunity to do any of the following activities: study more of another subject, listen to music, sleep, browse at a local store, read a novel, or work out at the gym. Many more opportunities are forgone if you choose to study economics for an additional hour.

Because there were so many alternatives from which to choose, how could you determine the value of what you gave up to engage in that extra hour of studying economics? First of all, no one else can tell you the answer because only you can *subjectively* put a value on each alternative. Only you know the value of another hour of sleep or of an hour looking for the latest CDs. That means that only you can determine the highest-valued alternative that you had to sacrifice in order to study economics one more hour. It is you who must come up with the *subjective* estimate of the expected value of the best alternative.

The value of the best alternative that must be sacrificed to satisfy a want is called *opportunity cost*. The **opportunity cost** of any action is the value of what is given up—the highest-ranked alternative—because a choice was made. When you study one more hour, there may be many alternatives available for the use of that hour, but assume that you can do only one thing in that hour—your highest-ranked alternative. What is important is the choice that you would have made if you had not studied one more hour. Your opportunity cost is the *highest-ranked* alternative, not *all* alternatives.

Opportunity cost The value of the best alternative that must be given up because a choice was made.

> In economics, cost is a forgone opportunity.

In this chapter's Issues and Applications we use the concept of *opportunity cost* to assess the value of allocating tens of billions of dollars a year of limited resources to the manufacture of bottled water products such as Aquafina and Dasani, which contribute to pollution and solid waste, despite the fact that we already have a much cheaper source of safe water flowing from our municipal water systems. The opportunity costs are that we forgo the option to have a healthier environment and we forgo allocating the invested resources to important causes such as providing drinking water to the billion people around the world who don't have access to safe water.

In Example 1–2 we will examine how the relatively high opportunity cost of searching for a compatible romantic partner has helped create an industry based in cyberspace.

EXAMPLE 1-2   ## The Opportunity Cost of Finding a Mate—Lower on the Internet?

For many single people looking for a companion, the biggest difficulty is not necessarily a lack of potential mates. The problem is that the time spent dating in search of "Ms. Right" or "Mr. Right" could otherwise be devoted to alternative activities, the highest-valued of which is the opportunity cost of time spent on each date.

This provides a fundamental rationale for the existence of such Internet-based companies as Match.com. For about $35 per month, a person looking for "that special someone" with desired characteristics, similar interests, and so on can enter personal information into a database and be matched, by computer, with someone else. According to the company's "director of flirting and dating," its business is all "about numbers, and it's also about time." In short, it is about the high opportunity cost of finding a compatible partner. For the really picky who face especially high opportunity costs of screening candidate mates for very specific characteristics, there are special Internet services available, albeit at higher prices. Goodgenes.com is open to graduates of Ivy League universities and a select group of other top-notch colleges and universities. For Jewish men and women, there is JDate.com, and Matrimony.org helps link Islamic singles. There is even Singleswithscruples.com, which provides assistance to those who face the high opportunity cost of finding currently unattached individuals who are not morally or ethically challenged.

For critical analysis: Why do the prices charged by websites specializing in people who share very specific characteristics tend to be higher than the prices charged by general dating services, such as Match.com?

Making Decisions at the Margin

As you progress through this text, you will be reminded frequently that in order to rationally evaluate a possible course of action, you must compare the action's *marginal benefit* with its *marginal cost*. **Marginal benefit** refers to all the *extra* benefits that one receives in pursuing a course of action, while **marginal cost** refers to all the *extra* costs or sacrifices incurred. In order to ensure that you properly identify the marginal cost relevant to your decision at hand, you must be careful not to include *sunk costs*. **Sunk costs** refer to irreversible costs incurred prior to your decision.

As an example, suppose you are in the process of estimating the extra (marginal) transportation costs associated with a Nova Scotia vacation that you are planning to take. You own your car and you have paid the annual insurance and car licence fee long before contemplating this vacation. If you decide to use your own car for this trip, the annual licence fee and insurance are sunk costs that are not relevant to the decision of travelling to Nova Scotia. As such, you should not include these two costs in your estimate of the extra (marginal) transportation costs. To better understand the notion of marginal and sunk costs, we refer you to Example 1–3: "What Does a Year at College Really Cost?"

Marginal benefit All the *extra* benefits that one receives in pursuing a course of action.

Marginal cost All the *extra* costs or sacrifices incurred.

Sunk costs Irreversible costs incurred prior to your decision.

Making decisions at the margin will often reveal that there can be too much of a good thing! As an example, suppose that at a time when marijuana use is at an all-time low, one of the contenders for prime minister, in a federal election campaign, proposes a policy for eliminating all marijuana use in Canada. While this type of zero tolerance policy proposal can win votes, if implemented, it can result in the transfer of a massive amount of policing resources away from the prevention of serious violent crimes in order to achieve a very small reduction in marijuana use. In other words, the marginal cost of the zero tolerance policy far exceeds the marginal benefit!

EXAMPLE 1–3   **What Does a Year at College Really Cost?**

Jane Sanders is currently earning $2000 per month working full time in Hamilton, Ontario. She lives in a one-bedroom apartment and pays $700 per month in rent. Her monthly food, personal care, and entertainment expenses are $500 per month. Since she does not own a vehicle, she pays $65 per month for a bus pass.

Jane is in the process of estimating the extra cost related to the decision to enroll full time in the first year of a business program at a college in the Hamilton area. If she enrolls, she will give up her full-time job for the eight-month period of the first-year program. If Jane goes to college, she plans to continue to live in her one-bedroom apartment, take the bus to the college campus, and maintain her current lifestyle. Jane estimates that her decision to enroll in college for the first year (eight-month period) will cost $13 720, estimated as follows:

TABLE 1-1

Rent	$700 × 8 =	$ 5 600
Food, Personal Care, Entertainment	$500 × 8 =	$ 4 000
Public Transportation	$ 65 × 8 =	$ 520
Tuition, Books, College Fees		$ 3 600
Total Cost		**$13 720**

For critical analysis: Did Jane correctly determine the extra cost related to the decision to enroll in college full time for eight months? What else must Jane try to estimate in order to make a rational decision? Explain.

Responding to Incentives

If it is reasonable to assume that individuals make decisions by comparing marginal costs and benefits, then we are in a position to better understand and predict how people respond to incentives. We define an **incentive** as an inducement to take a particular action. The inducement can be a reward, or a "carrot," which would take the form of an increase in benefit or a decrease in cost. Alternatively, the inducement can be a punishment, or a "stick," in the form of an increase in cost or a decrease in benefit. To the extent that a change in incentives implies a change in the relation between the marginal costs and benefits associated with various choices, individual decisions will change.

> **Incentive** Inducement to take a particular action.

Indeed, much of human behaviour can be explained in terms of how individuals respond to changing incentives over time. School students are motivated to do better by a variety of incentive systems, ranging from gold stars and certificates of achievement when they are young to better grades with accompanying promises of a "better life" as they get older. The rapid growth in Internet use noted in Example 1–1 can be explained in terms of increased incentives due to the decline in cost and increase in convenience associated with information technology.

In Policy Example 1–1: Chinese Smuggling you are asked to help the Chinese government reduce the incentives to smuggle cigarettes and diesel fuel by identifying actions that either increase the marginal cost or decrease the marginal benefit of this type of illegal activity.

POLICY EXAMPLE 1-1   **Chinese Smuggling**

In the recent past, the Chinese government recruited an antismuggling police force to try to stop the annual flow of tens of billions of dollars in illegal contraband. One example of "illegal contraband" was cigarettes. Domestic taxes on cigarettes were so high that many Chinese cigarette manufacturers exported half their output, which they then smuggled back into China. Another example was diesel fuel. The Chinese government fixed the price of diesel fuel at levels above prices elsewhere in the world. This gave consumers of diesel fuel an incentive to smuggle cheaper foreign-produced diesel fuel into the country.

Why did China need an antismuggling police force when it already employed an army of border guards and customs inspectors? The answer is that the returns on smuggling were so high that many existing border guards and customs inspectors became smugglers themselves. Thus, the government felt that new police officers were needed, in part, to watch over the existing cadre of "law enforcers."

On July 18, 2006, the London School of Hygiene and Tropical Medicine, at the University of London, reported that new research based on the internal documents of one of the world's biggest tobacco companies, British American Tobacco (BAT), suggests that BAT had restructured its operations to control and expand the contraband trade in China.

As smoking is declining in the world's richer nations, tobacco companies are seeking to increase sales in other countries. China is regarded as the ultimate prize among tobacco's emerging markets—one in three of all cigarettes smoked are smoked there and the nation has the largest number of smokers in the world (350 million). BAT's internal documents state that their exports from Hong Kong, intended for the contraband Chinese market, are the "key to the future" for BAT.

SOURCE: "RESEARCH REVEALS TOBACCO COMPANY'S ROLE IN CHINA'S CIGARETTE SMUGGLING CRISIS." TUESDAY JULY 18, 2006. LONDON SCHOOL OF HYGIENE AND TROPICAL MEDICINE PRESS.

For critical analysis: What actions could the government take to remove the incentives to smuggle cigarettes and diesel fuel?

Defining Self-Interest

Self-interest does not always mean increasing one's wealth as measured in dollars and cents. We assume that individuals seek many goals, not just increased monetary wealth. Thus, the self-interest part of our economic-person assumption includes goals relating to prestige, friendship, love, power, helping others, creating works of art, and many other matters. The giving of gifts can be considered a form of charity that is, nonetheless, in the self-interest of the giver. As Example 1–4 explains, donors may even expect to get some of their giving back.

➥ **CONCEPTS IN BRIEF**

Learning Objective 1.3: Describe how resource use decisions are affected by the rationality assumption, costs and benefits at the margin, and incentives.
- The economic way of thinking assumes that the typical response to an economic problem is rational behaviour.
- The rationality assumption suggests that an individual makes decisions based on maximizing his or her own self-interest.
- In order to maximize self-interest, an individual will use his or her resources in satisfying those wants where the marginal (extra) benefit exceeds the marginal (extra) cost. Marginal cost is measured in terms of opportunity cost, which is the highest-valued alternative that must be sacrificed to satisfy a want.
- A change in marginal cost or marginal benefit will change the incentives that an individual faces and will lead to a change in resource use decisions.

| EXAMPLE 1-4 | **Giving Charity to Oneself?** |

Economists have long recognized that charitable giving is in the self-interest of the donors. It makes them feel that they are contributing to society, helping the less fortunate and, more pragmatically, saving on the income tax they pay. But perhaps there are other reasons as well. Let us look at some of the evidence from the year 2004, the most recent year for which these data are available.

FIGURE 1-1 *Percentage of Household Income Spent on Donations by Level of Household Income, Donors Aged 15 and Older, Canada, 2004*

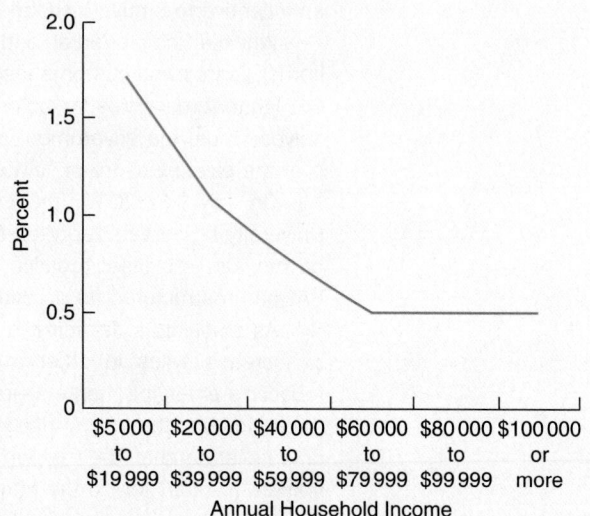

SOURCE: ADAPTED FROM THE STATISTICS CANADA PUBLICATION "CARING CANADIANS, INVOLVED CANADIANS: HIGHLIGHTS FROM THE 2004 CANADA SURVEY OF GIVING, VOLUNTEERING AND PARTICIPATING," 2004, CATALOGUE 71-542-XIE, SEPTEMBER 7, 2007, PAGE 20.

Although donors with higher household incomes make larger dollar donations, they tend to give a smaller *percentage* of their overall pretax income to charity. As the accompanying figure shows, those household incomes of less than $20 000 donated 1.7 percent of their pre-tax income to charitable and nonprofit organizations, while those with incomes of $100 000 or more contributed about 0.5 percent of their pretax income.

One explanation that would make this giving pattern *rational* is that the poorer households are those most likely to have used charity in the past or to need it in the future. Perhaps these households, unable to build large savings accounts to help them through periods of economic misfortune, look to public charity as a kind of insurance and to their donations as the premiums they pay for it.

For critical analysis: Can you devise an explanation for this pattern of giving charity among the lower-income households, using the notions of costs and benefits?

SOURCE: *2004 CANADA SURVEY OF GIVING, VOLUNTEERING AND PARTICIPATING.* IMAGINE CANADA. http://www.givingandvolunteering.ca/aboutus.asp.

1.4 The Scientific Method

Models or theories Simplified representations of the real world used to understand and predict economic phenomena.

Economics is a social science that makes use of the same kinds of methods used in other sciences, such as biology, physics, and chemistry. Similar to these other sciences, economics engages in key processes that include making assumptions, forming models or theories, and testing these models with real-world facts. Economic **models** or **theories** are simplified representations of the real world that we use to help us understand and predict economic phenomena in the real world. There are, of course, differences among the sciences. The social sciences, especially economics, make little use of laboratory methods in which changes in variables can be explained under controlled conditions. Rather, social scientists, and especially economists, usually have to examine what has already happened in the real world to test their models.

Models and Realism

At the outset, it must be emphasized that no model in *any* science, and therefore no economic model, is complete in the sense that it captures *every* detail or interrelationship that exists. Indeed, a model, by definition, is an abstraction from reality. It is conceptually impossible to construct a perfectly complete realistic model. For example, in physics, we cannot account for every molecule and its position, nor every atom and subparticle. Not only would such a model be prohibitively expensive to build but also working with it would be impossibly complex.

The nature of scientific model building is such that the model should capture only the essential relationships that are sufficient to analyze the particular problem or answer the particular question with which we are concerned. *An economic model cannot be faulted as unrealistic simply because it does not represent every detail of the real world.* A map of a city that shows only major streets is not necessarily unrealistic if, in fact, all you need to know is how to navigate through the city using major streets. As long as a model is realistic in terms of shedding light on the *central* issue at hand or forces at work, it may be useful.

A map is a basic model. It is always a simplified representation, always unrealistic. But it is also useful in making (refutable) predictions about the world. If the model—the map—predicts that when you take Campus Avenue to the north, you always reach the campus, that is a (refutable) prediction. If our goal is to explain observed behaviour, the simplicity or complexity of the model we use is irrelevant. If a simple model can explain observed behaviour in repeated settings just as well as a complex one, the simple model has some value and is probably easier to use.

Assumptions

Every model, or theory, is based on a set of assumptions. Assumptions define the conditions under which a model is meant to apply. By eliminating detail that is not considered to be essential to the economic phenomena under investigation, assumptions help simplify a model.

In the theory of the firm, we assume that, typically, firms attempt to maximize profits when deciding how much of a product to produce in an industry. This assumption leads to an economic model of the firm that provides numerous predictions about how the firm will react to various events and incentives. As an example, one prediction would be that if a firm can sell its product at a higher price, it will tend to produce more of this product. Another prediction would be that if a major cost of producing this product increases, such as energy costs, the firm will likely reduce the level of production of this product. Finally, this model would predict that if the government lowered the taxes imposed on the firms in this industry, this would entice firms to increase their supply of this product.

While the owners of the firms in the industry under investigation may well have a variety of other motives for producing the product, the profit-maximizing assumption model is valid to the extent that it consistently provides accurate predictions of real-world behaviour.

THE *CETERIS PARIBUS* ASSUMPTION: ALL OTHER THINGS BEING EQUAL. Constructing a model typically involves making generalizations of how variables in our environment relate to each other. It would be impossible to isolate the effects of changes in one variable on another variable if we always had to worry about the many additional variables that might also enter the analysis. As in other sciences, economics uses the **ceteris paribus** **assumption**, which is the assumption that nothing changes except the factor or factors being studied. *Ceteris paribus* means "other things being constant" or "other things being equal."

Ceteris paribus [KAY-ter-us PEAR-uh-bus] assumption The assumption that nothing changes except the factor or factors being studied; "other things being constant," or "other things equal."

Consider an example taken from economics. One of the most important determinants of how much of a particular product a family buys is the price of that product relative to other products. We know that in addition to relative prices, other factors influence decisions about making purchases. Some of them have to do with income, others with tastes, and yet others with custom and religious beliefs. Whatever these other factors are, we hold them constant when we look at the relationship between changes in prices and changes in how much of a given product people will purchase. As Example 1–5 illustrates, Canadian researchers applied the *ceteris paribus* assumption in designing a scientific study to test the effectiveness of a popular anti-cold formulation created in Canada.

EXAMPLE 1-5   **The Science Behind COLD-fX®**

On October 5, 2005, the *Canadian Medical Association Journal* published the results of a scientific study that showed COLD-fX® , an anti-cold formulation, reduced the incidence and frequency of recurrent colds by more than half. COLD-fX® also cut the duration of colds and significantly reduced their severity. Shortly after the research results were published, the stock price of CV Technologies, the company manufacturing COLD-fX® , reached an all-time high of $4.74 per share, an increase of 166 percent over the previous year's stock price!

Research subjects for the COLD-fX® study were required to be in good general health, to be between 18 and 65 years of age, and to have contracted at least two colds in the past year. Subjects were excluded if they had been vaccinated against influenza in the previous six months.

Volunteers who qualified for the study were randomly assigned to receive either the ginseng extract that makes up COLD-fX® or a placebo, which was made to look exactly like the COLD-fX® capsule except that the placebo did not contain any type of medication. All subjects were instructed to take two capsules per day for a period of six months following the onset of influenza season. They were instructed not to take any other cold medication while involved in the study. All observations and analyses were performed by a statistician under double-blind conditions. That is, the statistician did not know which subjects were actually taking COLD-fX® or the placebo. Similarly, each subject did not know whether he or she was taking COLD-fX® or the placebo.

For critical analysis: The COLD-fX® study is interested in examining the relationship between which two variables? Explain how the study attempts to apply the *ceteris paribus* assumption.

SOURCES: "INTERACTIVE CHARTS. CV TECHNOLOGIES." CTVGLOBEMEDIA. http://www.globeinvestor.com. (ACCESSED MAY 12, 2007.); GERALD N. PREDY, VINTI GOEL, RAY LOVLIN, ALLAN DONNER, LARRY STITT, AND TAPAN K. BASU. "EFFICACY OF AN EXTRACT OF NORTH AMERICAN GINSENG CONTAINING POLY-FURANOSYL-PYRANOSYL-SACCHARIDES FOR PREVENTING UPPER RESPIRATORY TRACT INFECTIONS: A RANDOMIZED CONTROLLED TRIAL." *CMAJ*, OCTOBER 25, 2005: 173 (9). DOI:10.1503/CMAJ.1041470.

Testing Models

We generally do not attempt to determine the usefulness, or "goodness," of a model merely by evaluating how realistic its assumptions are. Rather, we consider a model good if it yields usable predictions and implications for the real world. In other words, can we use the model to predict what will happen in the world around us?

Once we have determined that the model does predict real-world phenomena, the scientific approach to the analysis of the world around us requires that we consider evidence. Evidence is used to test the usefulness of a model. This is why we call economics an *empirical* science, **empirical** meaning using real-world data to test the usefulness of a model. Economists are often engaged in empirically testing their models.

Empirical Using real-world data to test the usefulness of a model.

Consider two competing models for the way students act when doing complicated probability problems to choose the best gambles. One model predicts that, on the basis of the assumption of rational self-interest, students who are paid more for better performance will, in fact, perform better on average during the experiment. A competing model might be that students whose last names start with the letters A through L will do better than students with last names starting with M through Z, irrespective of how much they are paid. The model that consistently predicts more accurately is the model that we would normally choose. In this example, the "alphabet" model did not work well: The first letter of the last name of the students who actually did the experiment was irrelevant in predicting how well they would perform the mathematical calculations necessary to choose the correct gambles. The model based on rational self-interest predicted well, in contrast.

Models of Behaviour, Not Thought Processes

Take special note of the fact that economists' models do not relate to the way people *think*; they relate to the way people *act*, to what they do in life with their limited resources. Models tend to generalize human behaviour. Normally, the economist does not attempt to predict how people will think about a particular topic, such as a higher price of oil products, accelerated inflation, or higher taxes. Rather, the task at hand is to predict how people will act, which may be quite different from what they say they will do (much to the consternation of poll takers and market researchers). The people involved in examining thought processes are psychologists and psychiatrists, who are not usually economists.

Example 1–6 provides you with an economic model that is used to explain and predict criminal behaviour.

EXAMPLE 1-6   **An Economic Model of Crime**

As you may suspect, numerous sociological, cultural, psychological, and physiological theories are used to explain criminal behaviour. Traits such as deviance, abnormality, depravity, insanity, and genetics are used to characterize those who break the law. In this Example, we will present an economic model of crime, based on the rationality assumption. That is, in an economic model of criminal behaviour, individuals compare the marginal costs and marginal benefits of engaging in an illegal act (as opposed to a legal act). If the marginal benefits of engaging in a crime exceed its marginal costs, the individual will commit the crime.

What might be included in the marginal benefits of engaging in a crime? For many crimes, such as property theft, identity theft, financial fraud, drug trafficking, and tax evasion, part of the marginal benefit would be the extra monies received. Other marginal benefits might prove to be psychological in nature, such as the thrill of danger, peer approval, retribution, the need to feed an addiction, or even a sense of accomplishment.

What about the marginal costs of committing an illegal act? The costs would include material costs (equipment, guns, vehicles), psychological costs (guilt, anxiety, fear, aversion to risk), expected punishment costs, and opportunity costs.

The expected punishment costs are a combination of the probability of being "caught" (arrested and convicted) and the severity of the penalty when convicted. If there is a high probability of being caught and/or there is a large penalty when convicted, this results in a relatively large marginal cost of committing a crime.

The opportunity cost of committing a crime consists of the net benefit of the legal activity that is forgone while planning, performing, and concealing the criminal act. The lower an individual's income from legal activity, the lower the opportunity cost of committing a crime.

As with any scientific model, the validity of the economic model of crime depends on testing the model's predictions with real world evidence. Numerous studies have found a clear negative association between high costs of punishment and crime rates. These studies suggest that the probability of getting caught is a stronger deterrent to criminal action than the severity of the penalty when convicted. Studies also indicate that individuals are more apt to engage in crimes when they earn low incomes in an environment of significant income inequality. In other words, one is more apt to commit a crime when there is a lot to gain and little to lose.

For critical analysis: Based on the economic model of crime, predict how each of the following would affect the crime rate: an increase in the unemployment rate; a decrease in conviction rates.

SOURCE: EIDE, E., (1999). "ECONOMICS OF CRIMINAL BEHAVIOUR." HANDBOOK OF LAW AND ECONOMICS, 8100, 345–389. (ADOBE ACROBAT DOCUMENT - 145KB) http://www.staff.lboro.ac.uk/~ecrs3/Econ%20of%20Criminology/media/Eide%20(1999).pdf.

The economic model of crime presented in Example 1–6 above can prove useful in identifying incentives that help to reduce specific crimes. As an example, the cigarette smuggling problem in China, noted in Policy Example 1–1, could be reduced by decreasing the benefits derived from smuggling cigarettes into the country. If the Chinese government reduced the taxes imposed on cigarettes legally sold in the country, this would reduce the price and profit that criminals would get from smuggling cigarettes from outside the country.

1.5 Positive versus Normative Economics

Economic theory uses *positive analysis,* a value-free approach to inquiry. No subjective or moral judgments enter into the analysis. Positive analysis relates to such statements as "If *A,* then *B.*" For example, "If the price of gasoline goes up relative to all other prices, then the amount of it that people will buy will fall." That is a positive economic statement. It is a statement of *what is,* and its validity can be tested by observing the facts. It is not a statement of anyone's value judgment or subjective feelings. For many problems analyzed in the hard sciences, such as physics and chemistry, the analyses are considered to be virtually value-free. After all, how can someone's values enter into a theory of molecular behaviour? But economists face a different problem. They deal with the behaviour of individuals, not molecules. That makes it more difficult to stick to what we consider to be value-free or *positive economics* without reference to our feelings. **Positive economics** refers to analysis that can be tested by observing the facts.

> **Positive economics** refers to analysis that can be tested by observing the facts.

> **Normative economics** refers to analysis based on value judgments made about what ought to be.

When our values are interjected into the analysis, we enter the realm of *normative economics,* involving *normative analysis.* **Normative economics** refers to analysis based on value judgments made about what ought to be. A positive economic statement is: "If the price of gas rises, people will buy less." If we add to that analysis the statement "so we should not allow the price to go up," we have entered the realm of normative economics—we have expressed a value judgment. In fact, any time you see the word *should,* you will know that values are entering into the discussion. Just remember that positive statements are concerned with *what is,* whereas normative statements are concerned with *what ought to be.*

In the last section of this chapter, we will introduce the important social and economic goals that governments try to achieve when they design economic policy. Normative analysis is often encountered when you examine the various goals that form the basis of policy. As an example, in this chapter's Issues and Applications, you will see that the proposal to tax bottled water is, in part, based on certain goals, such as "a pollution-free environment," which are normative in nature.

A Warning: Recognize Normative Analysis

It is easy to define positive economics. It is quite another matter to catch all unlabelled normative statements in a textbook such as this one (or any other), even though the authors go over the manuscript many times before it is printed. Therefore, do not get the impression that a textbook's authors will be able to keep all personal values out of the book. They will slip through. In fact, the very choice of which topics to include in an introductory textbook involves normative economics. There is no value-free, or objective, way to decide which topics to include in a textbook. The authors' values ultimately make a difference when choices have to be made. But from your own stand-point, you might want to be able to recognize when you are engaging in normative, as opposed to positive, economic analysis. Reading this text will help equip you for that task.

1.6 Economic Policy and Socioeconomic Goals

As we noted above, economic models will enhance your ability to understand and predict behaviour. In the chapters to come, we will illustrate how these models prove useful in for-mulating, assessing, and reacting to government policies that affect you as a consumer, an employee, an investor, a business owner, and a concerned citizen.

Policies Action plans designed to achieve goals.

Most government economic **policies** are action plans designed to achieve commonly accepted socioeconomic goals. The goals that are most frequently considered, when forming and evaluating economic policies, are described below.

1. Full Employment: an economy in which people looking for work find jobs reasonably quickly.
2. Efficiency: an economy in which resources are allocated to the production of goods and services in a way that achieves maximum benefit for society.
3. Economic Growth: an economy with the ability to increase its rate of production over time to enhance society's well being.
4. Price Stability: an economy in which prices remain relatively stable over time.
5. Equity: an economy that moves closer toward some social consensus of fairness. An example often used as a basis of economic policy is the goal of a *more equitable distribution of income*, which aims to reduce the level of poverty in the economy.

Theory and Policy

Economic theory plays a useful role in helping us understand how existing and proposed policies relate to major socioeconomic goals. As you progress through this text, you will be surprised at the frequency with which a proposed policy is shown to conflict with the very goals it is meant to promote, once you employ the relevant economic model.

For example, a local politician may propose a rent control policy aimed at reducing apartment rents in order to make housing more affordable to the poor. That is, the rent control policy is aimed at promoting a more equitable distribution of income. However, once you become familiar with the demand-and-supply model presented in Chapter 4, you will see that this policy will more likely conflict with the goal of an equitable distribution of income because of the resulting shortages in livable accommodation. Moreover, this same policy will also conflict with the goal of full employment to the extent that construction workers are laid off as fewer new apartments are being built.

We hope that you will enjoy the challenge of using economic models to formulate superior alternative policies. A superior policy refers to a plan of action that promotes as many socioeconomic goals as possible with minimal goal conflict. In the rent control example, you may find that relevant economic theory suggests that a policy of increasing competition in the apartment construction and rental industries may prove to be the superior policy. By increasing the supply of affordable, quality housing units, the goals of full employment and equitable distribution can both be promoted!

➤ **CONCEPTS IN BRIEF**

Learning Objective 1.4: Explain the three key processes involved in the scientific method.
- In using the scientific method one makes assumptions, constructs models or theories, and tests these models with the facts.
- Assumptions define the conditions under which a model is meant to apply. A model is a simplification of reality. We consider a model useful if it does a good job of predicting real-world phenomena.

Learning Objective 1.5: Distinguish between positive and normative economics.
- Positive economics is value-free and relates to statements that can be tested by such facts as "If *A*, then *B*." Normative economics involves value judgments, and normative statements typically contain such words as "should" or "ought to." Positive statements are prevalent in economic theories, whereas normative statements are often encountered in the goals used to evaluate policy.

Learning Objective 1.6: Describe the relationship among theories, policies, and socioeconomic goals.
- Policies refer to action plans aimed at promoting various important socioeconomic goals.
- Models or theories are used to identify how specific policies affect goals.
- Key socioeconomic goals include full employment, efficiency, economic growth, price stability, and equity.

Bottled Water: The Hummer of Beverages?

Concepts Applied: Economics, Microeconomics versus Macroeconomics, Opportunity Cost, Economic Way of Thinking, Incentives, Policy Analysis

In Canada, consumption of bottled water exceeds that of coffee, tea, apple juice, milk, and beer.

The Rapid Growth of the Bottled Water Industry

Everyone knows that water is an essential resource. Yet, more than a billion people around the world don't have access to safe, clean water. The worldwide demand for water is doubling every 20 years, to the point that two-thirds of the people on this planet may be facing severe water shortages by the year 2025.

Despite the fact that clean and safe tap water is available in developed nations such as Canada and the U.S., the bottled water market has been exploding in North America. Today, close to one-fifth of the population relies exclusively on bottled water for their daily hydration. In Canada, bottled water consumption exceeds coffee, tea, apple juice, milk, and beer consumption.

The global bottled water industry is dominated by four companies: Coca-Cola (Dasani), Pepsi (Aquafina), Nestlé (Perrier), and Danone (Evian). In response to growing interest in healthier lifestyles and declining demand for soft drinks, these companies have been promoting bottled water as a more desirable option than tap water. North Americans spend more than US$11 billion per year drinking over 8 billion gallons of bottled water. Currently, bottled water is the fastest growing and most profitable segment of the beverage industry in North America. Within the next ten years, industry analysts project that bottled water could overtake soft drinks as the leading beverage.

Critics of the bottled water industry argue that its rapid growth is not due to informed individual consumer choices but rather is in response to the deceptive and non-competitive practices of the large beverage companies. Moreover, these critics point to the significant resource costs and environmental degradation related to the bottled water industry. The specific arguments are explained below.

Concerns Related to the Bottled Water Industry

Consumers can be easily misled by the "pure," "crisp," "fresh," and "sparkling" glossy advertising of the leading brands of bottled water. The product has often been depicted as coming from pristine natural spring and glacier-like environments, when in fact the water comes from municipal water sources (the same as tap water) or from borehole ground water wells located near the bottling plants. In response to consumer demands, industry leader Aquafina (Pepsi) has agreed to print "Public Water Source" on Aquafina labels. To date, Coke (Dasani) has not followed suit, even though its water source is the same as tap water.

One might have legitimate health-related concerns over the fact that while cities such as Toronto test their water quality every few hours, bottled water plants are publicly inspected only once every three to six years. To date, companies such as Coke have refused to publicly report on the health and quality of their bottled water in ways required of public water systems.

Through the widespread use of exclusivity contracts with schools, colleges, and universities, Coca-Cola and Pepsi have conducted successful marketing campaigns aimed at weaning the younger generation off of tap water in favour of bottled water. The University of British Columbia (UBC) was the first university in Canada to sign an exclusivity contract with Coca-Cola in 1995. Under this contract, UBC was to receive $8.5 million dollars in return for giving Coke the exclusive right to sell its products on campus. This contract excluded all Coke competitors from selling their products at UBC. During the contract period it was reported that over 40% of water fountains were removed or disabled on the UBC campus. Needless to say, these exclusivity contracts set the stage for Coke to charge high prices for its bottled water products.

We must question whether the bottled water industry is squandering our limited resources in producing a product that is arguably no better than tap water, which is available at a much lower cost. A 1.5 litre bottle of Aquafina costs around $2.70, but the same amount of water taken from the Montreal municipal system costs 1/500th of a cent. The extra costs for the higher priced bottled water include what some might consider unnecessary "purifying" of already good quality water, creating plastic bottles, packaging, advertising, marketing, transportation, and a healthy profit. Globally, an estimated US$100 billion is spent every year on the purchase of bottled water. It is estimated that it would only take US$30 billion to halve the number of people who do not have ready access to clean, safe, drinking water, and achieve one of the Millennium Development Goals established by the UN in 2000.

Yet another concern has to do with bottled water's impact on the environment. The plastic bottles create carbon dioxide (CO_2) when they are made, trucked to the store, and later disposed of in a landfill or recycled. It is estimated that the energy required to manufacture a single plastic one-litre bottle, fill it with water, truck it to a typical retail location, and then bury it in a landfill creates about .23 pounds of CO_2. That's equivalent to what an average car would emit in driving about half a kilometer.

Policies Aimed at Slowing Growth in the Bottled Water Industry

What types of policies might the government employ in order to reduce the degree to which our limited resources are used to produce bottled water? If we apply the economic way of thinking to those who manufacture and sell bottled water, any policy which reduces the marginal benefit or increases the marginal cost of supplying this product will reduce its production.

Starting January 1, 2008, Chicago began levying a tax of 5 cents per litre of bottled water sold in its city, thereby increasing the marginal cost of selling this product. In the latter part of 2007, Toronto City Council was reviewing a proposal to impose a tax of 5 cents per litre on water bottled in Ontario and 10 cents per litre for water bottled outside of the province.

The Industry Response to the Proposed Toronto Tax

The Canadian Bottled Water Association (CBWA), representing the major bottled water manufacturers, mounted a strong campaign opposing Toronto's proposed tax on the sale of bottled water. The CBWA argued that it is unfair and unwise to impose a discriminatory tax on a single grocery item, especially a healthy beverage alternative. The CBWA also noted that imposing a tax within Toronto would drive consumers to buy their food and beverage items outside the city limits, which could harm local businesses and create unemployment.

For critical analysis:

1. Explain how this issue relates to the concepts of scarcity, opportunity cost, and the meaning of economics.
2. This issue focuses on production and consumption related to one industry in Canada. Is this a microeconomic or macroeconomic focus? Explain.
3. How might the government affect the marginal benefit derived from supplying bottled water so as to reduce the amount of resources used in the production of bottled water?
4. How does this issue apply to policy analysis?

SOURCES: "NOVEMBER 21ST CAMPUS DAY OF ACTION: UPDATE AND RESULTS." *INSIDE THE BOTTLE.* DECEMBER 2, 2007. http://www.insidethebottle.org/november-21st-campus-day-action-update-and-results; GRANT, KELLY. "TORONTO MULLS BOTTLED-WATER TAX; SEVERAL U.S. CITIES HAVE ADOPTED SIMILAR MEASURE." *NATIONAL POST.* NOVEMBER 21, 2007. PG A1; POLARIS INSTITUTE. "WATER ROYALTIES COMING SOON: QUEBEC EYES B.C. AND ONTARIO MODELS." NOVEMBER 27, 2007. http://www.polarisinstitute.org/water_royalties_coming_soon_quebec_eyes_b_c_and_ontario_models.

⇒→ SUMMARY

Here is what you should know after reading this chapter. MyEconLab will help you identify what you know, and where to go when you need to practise. We suggest that as soon as you review one of the Learning Objective sections below, you then proceed to go through the related section in MyEconLab.

⟨Ⅹ⟩ **myecon**lab

⇒→ LEARNING OBJECTIVES	KEY TERMS	MYECONLAB PRACTICE
1.1 Scarcity. Scarcity refers to the condition that arises because human wants in terms of goods, services, and goals always exceed what can be produced with the available limited resources—land, labour, entrepreneurship, and physical and human capital. Economics is a social science that studies how people allocate limited resources to satisfy unlimited wants.	scarcity, 2 goods, 2 services, 2 production, 2 land, 3 labour, 3 physical capital, 3 human capital, 3 entrepreneurship, 3 rent, 3 wages, 3 interest, 3 profit, 3	• **MyEconLab** Study Plan 1.1
1.2 Defining Economics. Economics is usually divided into microeconomics, which is the study of individual decision making by households and firms, and macroeconomics, which is the study of economy-wide phenomena such as inflation, unemployment, and national income.	economics, 3 microeconomics, 4 macroeconomics, 4 aggregates, 5	• **MyEconLab** Study Plan 1.2
1.3 Rational Decision Making. Benefits at the Margin, Incentives, and Resource Use. Under the rationality assumption, the individual will employ resources in uses where the marginal benefit exceeds the marginal cost so as to maximize his or her own self-interest. Marginal cost is measured in terms of opportunity cost, which is the highest-valued alternative that must be sacrificed to satisfy a want. A change in marginal cost or marginal benefit will change the incentives that an individual faces and will lead to a change in resource use decisions.	economic way of thinking, 5 rationality assumption, 6 opportunity cost, 6 marginal benefit, 7 marginal cost, 7 sunk costs, 7 incentive, 8	• **MyEconLab** Study Plan 1.3
1.4 The Scientific Method. In using the scientific method, one makes assumptions, constructs models or theories, and tests these models with the facts. Models are simplified representations of the real world that make predictions that can be tested by the facts.	models or theories, 10 *ceteris paribus* assumption, 11 empirical, 12	• **MyEconLab** Study Plan 1.4

➡ LEARNING OBJECTIVES	KEY TERMS	MYECONLAB PRACTICE
1.5 Positive versus Normative Economics. Positive economics deals with *what is*, whereas normative economics deals with what *ought to be*. Positive statements are of the "if . . . then" nature and are testable by facts. By contrast, normative statements are based on subjective value judgments.	positive economics, 14 normative economics, 14	• **MyEconLab** Study Plan 1.5
1.6 Economic Policy and Socioeconomic Goals. Theories can help us identify how various policies affect socioeconomic goals, such as full employment, efficiency, economic growth, price stability, and equity.	policies, 15	• **MyEconLab** Study Plan 1.6

➡ PROBLEMS

(Answers to the odd-numbered problems appear at the back of the book.)

LO 1.1 Explain the meaning of scarcity.

1. Identify the factor of production that best relates to each of the following:
   a. a degree in engineering
   b. underground oil reserves
   c. the factor that earns profit
   d. a newly constructed pulp and paper mill
   e. the factor that earns wages

LO 1.2 Define economics and distinguish between microeconomics and macroeconomics.

2. According to Example 1–1, "The Economics of Web Page Design," what aspects of web design make it an "economic concern"?

3. Categorize the following issues as either a microeconomic issue or a macroeconomic issue.
   a. The national unemployment rate increases.
   b. The wage increases of nurses do not keep up with the wage increases of doctors.
   c. The price of cigarettes increases due to a tax imposed on cigarette manufacturers.
   d. The Canadian annual inflation rate exceeds the average annual increase in Canadian wages.
   e. The nation's total annual rate of production declines.

   f. In response to strong competition, a Canadian retail corporation files for bankruptcy.

LO 1.3 Describe how resource use decisions are affected by the rationality assumption, costs and benefits at the margin, and incentives.

4. In order to spend a winter in Victoria, B.C., Paul Dafoe rents out his Montreal condo, as well as his car, to a married couple attending university. Paul estimates that the total cost associated with his decision to winter in Victoria for the eight-month period is $15 000. He calculates this total cost by adding the following costs: round trip airfare; eight months' rental fees for a Victoria condo; estimated total grocery, personal care, and entertainment expenses while staying in Victoria; and total rental car expenses incurred in Victoria. Is $15 000 the correct marginal cost associated with Paul's decision to winter in Victoria? Explain.

5. Jon Krechen is currently earning $3000 per month working full time as a computer technical support person for a college situated in Toronto. Jon lives in a one-bedroom apartment and pays $1000 per month in rent. Jon's monthly living expenses, including food, personal care, taxes, insurance, and entertainment amount to $1600 per month. Since Jon does not own a vehicle he pays $75 per month for a bus pass.

Jon is in the process of estimating the marginal (extra) cost related to his decision to enroll full-time in an intensive two-month computer networking course in the Toronto area. While taking the computer course, Jon will be on a two-month leave without pay from the college where he works. Jon will continue to live in the same apartment and will travel by bus to the training centre offering the computer course. Jon estimates that his living expenses will be the same as if he were working. The tuition, books, and fees related to taking the computer course are $4500. Compute Jon's marginal cost of taking the two-month computer course.

6. Recent Canadian studies indicate that Canadians in the lower income brackets tend to donate more time, per year, to volunteer activities, compared to individuals who earn higher levels of income. Is this observation consistent with rational behaviour? Explain.

7. Your bank advertises that cash withdrawals from your bank machine are "free" if you always keep a minimum monthly balance of $5000 in your chequing account. In this case, are your cash withdrawals truly "free"? Explain.

8. According to Example 1–2, "The Opportunity Cost of Finding a Mate—Lower on the Internet?", what economic concept helps explain the popularity of online dating websites? Explain.

9. The mayor of a Canadian city justifies the construction of a beautiful new city hall on the basis of there being sufficient tax dollars available to pay for this project. Is the mayor's decision to construct the city hall a rational one? Explain.

10. Since health care is an essential service, all health-care services should be provided free of charge. Moreover, the government should continue to increase the resources to health care until all hospital waitlists across the nation disappear. Is this view consistent with making decisions at the margin? Explain.

LO 1.4 Explain the three key processes involved in the scientific method.

11. Give a refutable implication (one that can be tested by evidence from the real world) for each of the following models:
    a. The accident rate of drivers is inversely related to their age.
    b. The rate of inflation is directly related to the rate of change in the nation's money supply.

    c. The wages of professional basketball players are directly related to their high-school grade-point averages.
    d. The rate at which bank employees are promoted is inversely related to their frequency of absenteeism.

12. Consider the following statements on the basis of positive economic analysis that assumes *ceteris paribus*. List one other thing that might change and thus alter the outcome stated.
    a. Increased demand for laptop computers will drive up their price.
    b. Falling gasoline prices will result in additional vacation travel.
    c. A reduction in corporate income tax rates will result in more people working.

LO 1.5 Distinguish between positive and normative economics.

13. Identify which of the following statements use positive economic analysis and which use normative analysis.
    a. Increasing the minimum wage will reduce employment opportunities for young people.
    b. A teacher should earn a higher salary than a hockey player, since the teacher's job is far more valuable to society.
    c. Everyone should enjoy free access to dental care.
    d. If the price of admission to each NHL hockey game is reduced, there will be an increase in ticket sales for each NHL game.

LO 1.6 Describe the relationship among theories, policies, and socioeconomic goals.

14. Identify which socioeconomic goal(s) may be promoted and which goal(s) may be conflicted with, for each policy listed below.
    a. Policy: In order to provide free public-health services, the government severely taxes Canadian corporation profits.
    b. Policy: The government raises the rate of income tax on all employees. The extra tax dollars raised are used to compensate upper-income investors who were swindled by fraud schemes.
    c. Policy: The government increases the monthly benefits (payments) to those collecting welfare. These people immediately spend the extra income on new goods and services.
    d. Policy: The government levies a special tax on all luxury goods. The taxes collected are used to keep college and university tuition fees relatively low.

APPENDIX A

READING AND WORKING WITH GRAPHS

A graph is a visual representation of the relationship between variables. In this appendix, we will stick to just two variables: an **independent variable**, which can change freely in value, and a **dependent variable**, which changes only as a result of changes in the value of the independent variable. For example, if nothing else is changing in your life, your weight depends on the amount of food you eat. Food is the independent variable and weight the dependent variable.

Independent variable A variable whose value is determined independently of, or outside, the equation under study.

Dependent variable A variable whose value changes according to changes in the value of one or more independent variables.

A table is a list of numerical values showing the relationship between two (or more) variables. Any table can be converted into a graph, which is a visual representation of that list. Once you understand how a table can be converted to a graph, you will understand what graphs are and how to construct and use them.

Consider a practical example. A conservationist may try to convince you that driving at lower highway speeds will help you conserve gas. Table A–1 shows the relationship between speed—the independent variable—and the distance you can go on a litre of gas at that speed—the dependent variable. This table does show a pattern of sorts. As the data in the first column get larger in value, the data in the second column get smaller.

TABLE A–1

Gas Consumption as a Function of Driving Speed

Kilometres per Hour	Kilometres per Litre
70	11
80	10
90	9
100	8
110	7
120	6
130	5

Now, let us take a look at the different ways in which variables can be related.

Direct and Inverse Relationships

Two variables can be related in different ways, some simple, others more complex. For example, a person's weight and height are often related. If we measured the height and weight of thousands of people, we would surely find that taller people tend to weigh more than shorter people. That is, we would discover that there is a **direct relationship** between height and weight. By this, we simply mean that an increase in one variable is usually associated with an increase in the related variable. This can easily be seen in part (a) of Figure A–1.

Direct relationship A relationship between two variables that is positive, meaning that an increase in one variable is associated with an increase in the other, and a decrease in one variable is associated with a decrease in the other.

Inverse relationship A relationship between two variables that is negative, meaning that an increase in one variable is associated with a decrease in the other, and a decrease in one variable is associated with an increase in the other.

Let us look at another simple way in which two variables can be related. Much evidence indicates that as the price of a specific commodity rises, the amount purchased decreases—there is an **inverse relationship** between the variable's price per unit and quantity purchased. A table listing the data for this relationship would indicate that for higher and higher prices, smaller and smaller quantities would be purchased. We see this relationship in part (b) of Figure A–1.

Constructing a Graph

Let us now examine how to construct a graph to illustrate a relationship between two variables.

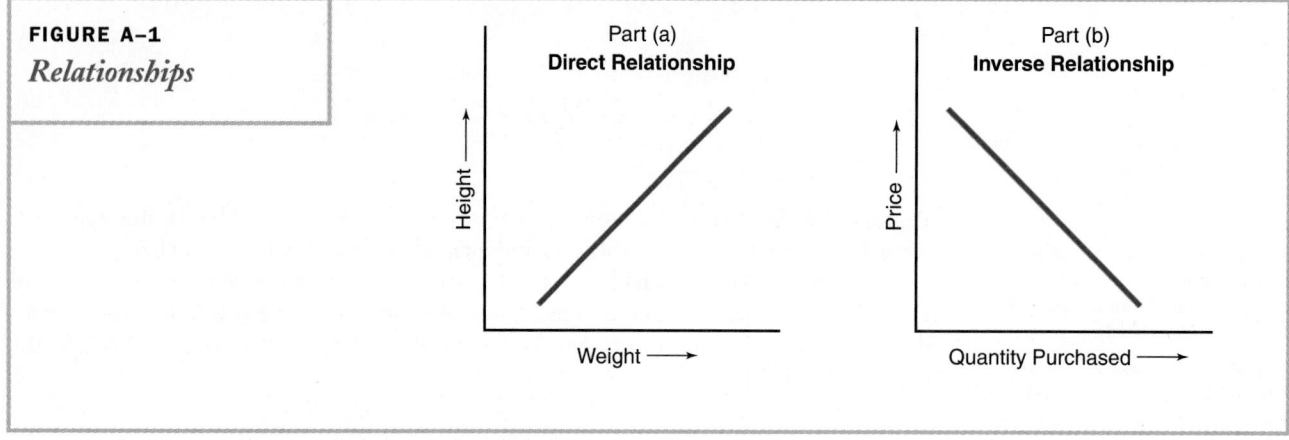

FIGURE A–1
Relationships

Part (a)
Direct Relationship

Height ——→

Weight ——→

Part (b)
Inverse Relationship

Price ——→

Quantity Purchased ——→

A Number Line

Number line A line that can be divided into segments of equal length, each associated with a number.

The first step is to become familiar with what is called a **number line.** One is shown in Figure A–2. There are two things that you should know about it.

1. The points on the line divide the line into equal segments.
2. The numbers associated with the points on the line increase in value from left to right; saying it the other way around, the numbers decrease in value from right to left. However you say it, what we are describing is formally called an *ordered set of points.*

On the number line, we have shown the line segments—that is, the distance from 0 to 10 or the distance between 30 and 40. They all appear to be equal and, indeed, are equal to 13 mm. When we use a distance to represent a quantity, such as barrels of oil, graphically, we are scaling the number line. In the example shown, the distance between 0 and 10 might represent 10 barrels of oil, or the distance from 0 to 40 might represent 40 barrels. Of course, the scale may differ on different number lines. For example, a distance of 1 cm could represent 10 units on one number line but 5000 units on another. Note that on our number line, points to the left of 0 correspond to negative numbers and points to the right of 0 correspond to positive numbers.

Of course, we can also construct a vertical number line. Consider the one in Figure A–3. As we move up this vertical number line, the numbers increase in value; conversely, as we descend, they decrease in value. Below 0 the numbers are negative, and above 0 the numbers are positive. And as on the horizontal number line, all the line segments are equal. This line is divided into segments such that the distance between −2 and −1 is the same as the distance between 0 and 1.

Combining Vertical and Horizontal Number Lines

By drawing the horizontal and vertical lines on the same sheet of paper, we are able to express the relationships between variables graphically. We do this in Figure A–4.

We draw them (1) so that they intersect at each other's 0 point, and (2) so that they are perpendicular to each other. The result is a set of coordinate axes, where each line is called an axis. When we have two axes, they span a plane.

FIGURE A–2
Horizontal Number Line

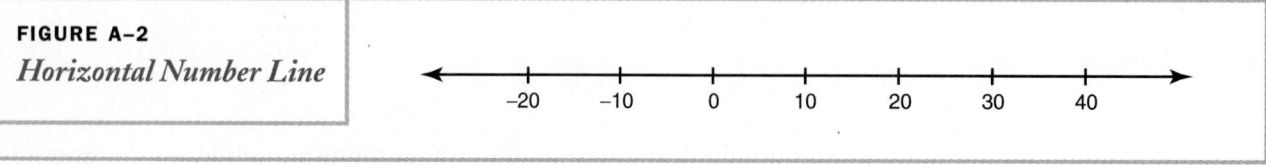

−20   −10   0   10   20   30   40

FIGURE A–3
Vertical Number Line

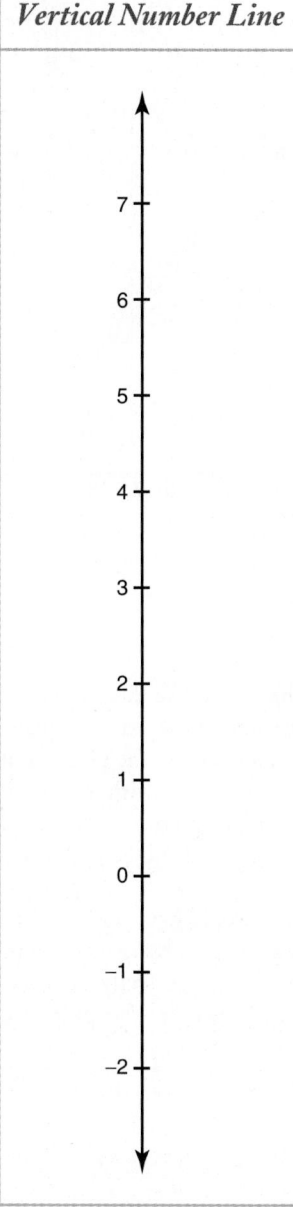

FIGURE A–4
A Set of Coordinate Axes

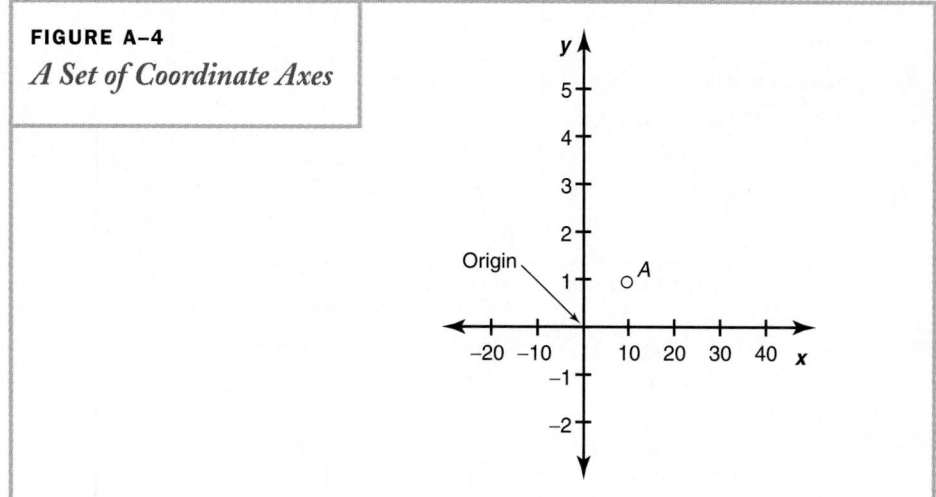

y-axis The vertical axis in a graph.

x-axis The horizontal axis in a graph.

Origin The intersection of the *y*-axis and the *x*-axis in a graph.

For one number line, you need only one number to specify any point on the line; equivalently, when you see a point on the line, you know that it represents one number or one value. With a coordinate value system, you need two numbers to specify a single point in the plane; when you see a single point on a graph, you know that it represents two numbers or two values.

The basic things that you should know about a coordinate number system are that the vertical number line is referred to as the **y-axis**, the horizontal number line is referred to as the **x-axis**, and the point of intersection of the two lines is referred to as the **origin.**

Any point such as A in Figure A–4 represents two numbers—a value of x and a value of y. But we know more than that; we also know that point A represents a positive value of y because it is above the x-axis, and we know that it represents a positive value of x because it is to the right of the y-axis.

Point A represents a "paired observation" of the variables x and y; in particular, in Figure A–4, A represents an observation of the pair of values $x = 10$ and $y = 1$. Every point in the coordinate system corresponds to a paired observation of x and y, which can be simply written (x, y)—the x-value is always specified first, then the y-value. When we give the values associated with the position of point A in the coordinate number system, we are, in effect, giving the coordinates of that point. A's coordinates are $x = 10$, $y = 1$, or $(10, 1)$.

Graphing Numbers in a Table

Consider Table A–2. Column 1 shows different prices for T-shirts, and column 2 gives the number of T-shirts purchased per week at these prices. Note the pattern of these numbers. As the price of a T-shirt falls, the number of T-shirts purchased per week increases. Therefore, an inverse relationship exists between these two variables, and as soon as we represent it on a graph, you will be able to see the relationship. We can graph this relationship using a coordinate number system—a vertical and a horizontal number line for each of these two variables. Such a graph is shown in part (b) of Figure A–5.

TABLE A–2
T-Shirts Purchased

(1) Price of a T-Shirt	(2) Number of T-Shirts Purchased per Week
$10	20
9	30
8	40
7	50
6	60
5	70

FIGURE A–5

Graphing the Relationship between T-Shirts Purchased and Price

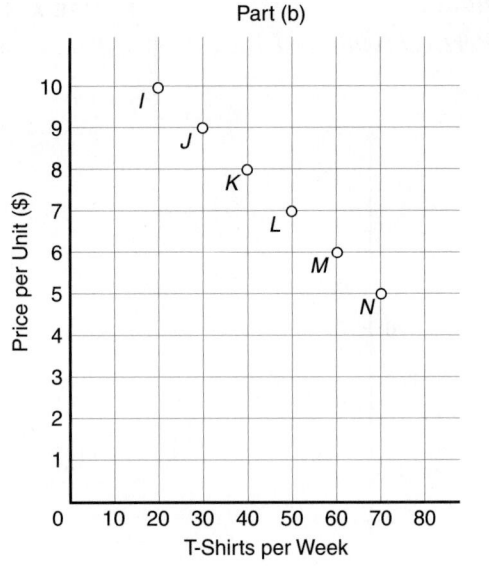

Part (a)

T-Shirts Purchased per Week	Price per T-Shirt	Point on Graph
20	$10	I (20, 10)
30	9	J (30, 9)
40	8	K (40, 8)
50	7	L (50, 7)
60	6	M (60, 6)
70	5	N (70, 5)

In economics, it is conventional to put dollar values on the *y*-axis. We therefore construct a vertical number line for price and a horizontal number line, the *x*-axis, for quantity of T-shirts purchased per week. The resulting coordinate system allows the plotting of each of the paired observation points; in part (a), we repeat Table A–2, with a column added expressing these points in paired-data (*x, y*) form. For example, point *J* is the paired observation (30, 9). It indicates that when the price of a T-shirt is $9, 30 will be purchased per week.

If it were possible to sell parts of a T-shirt ($\frac{1}{2}$ or $\frac{1}{20}$ shirt), we would have observations at every possible price. That is, we would be able to connect our paired observations, represented as lettered points. Let us assume that we can make T-shirts perfectly divisible. We would then have a line that connects these points, as shown in the graph in Figure A–6.

FIGURE A–6

Connecting the Observation Points

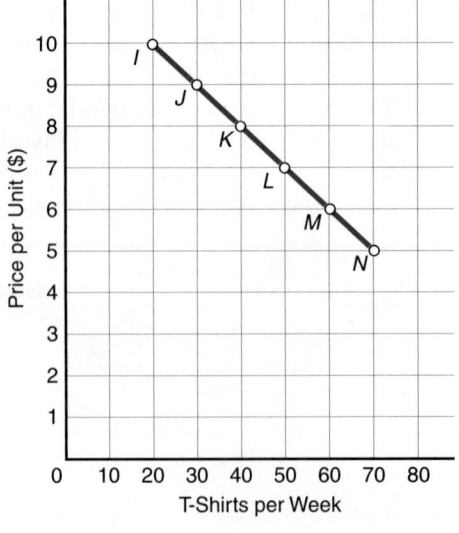

In short, we have now represented the data from the table in the form of a graph. Note that an inverse relationship between two variables shows up on a graph as a line or curve that slopes downward from left to right. (You might as well get used to the idea that economists call a straight line a "curve," even though it may not curve at all. Much of economists' data turn out to be curves, so they refer to everything represented graphically, even straight lines, as curves.)

The Slope of a Line (A Linear Curve)

An important property of a curve represented on a graph is its *slope*. Consider Figure A–7, which represents the quantities of shoes per week that a seller is willing to offer at different prices. Note that in part (a) of Figure A–7, as in Figure A–5, we have expressed the coordinates of the points in parentheses in paired-data form.

The *slope* of a line is defined as the change in the *y*-values divided by the corresponding change in the *x*-values as we move along the line. Let us move from point *E* to point *D* in part (b) of Figure A–7. As we move, we note that the change in the *y*-values, which is the change in price, is +$20 because we have moved from a price of $20 to a price of $40 per pair. As we move from *E* to *D*, the change in the *x*-values is +80; the number of pairs of shoes willingly offered per week rises from 80 to 160 pairs. The slope calculated as a change in the *y*-values divided by the change in the *x*-values is, therefore,

$$\frac{20}{80} = \frac{1}{4}$$

It may be helpful for you to think of slope as a "rise" (movement in the vertical direction) over a "run" (movement in the horizontal direction). We show this abstractly in Figure A–8. The slope is measured by the amount of rise divided by the amount of run. In the example in Figure A–8, and of course in Figure A–7, the amount of rise is positive and so is the amount of run. That is because it is a direct relationship. We show an inverse relationship in Figure A–9. The slope is still equal to the rise divided by the run, but in this case, the rise and the run have opposite signs because the curve slopes downward. That means that the slope will have to be negative and that we are dealing with an inverse relationship.

FIGURE A–7
A Positively Sloped Curve

Part (a)

Pairs of Shoes Offered per Week	Price per Pair	Point on Graph
400	$100	A (400, 100)
320	80	B (320, 80)
240	60	C (240, 60)
160	40	D (160, 40)
80	20	E (80, 20)

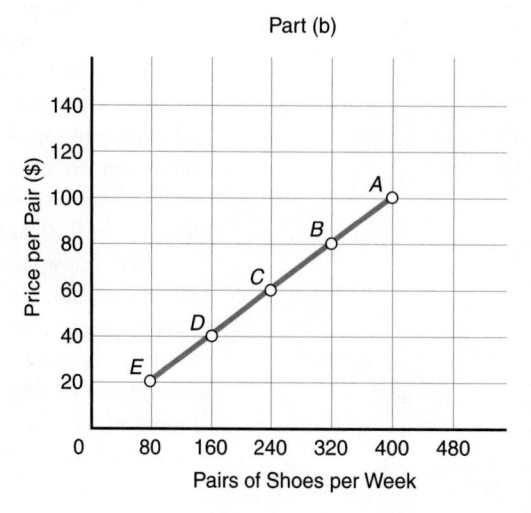
Part (b)

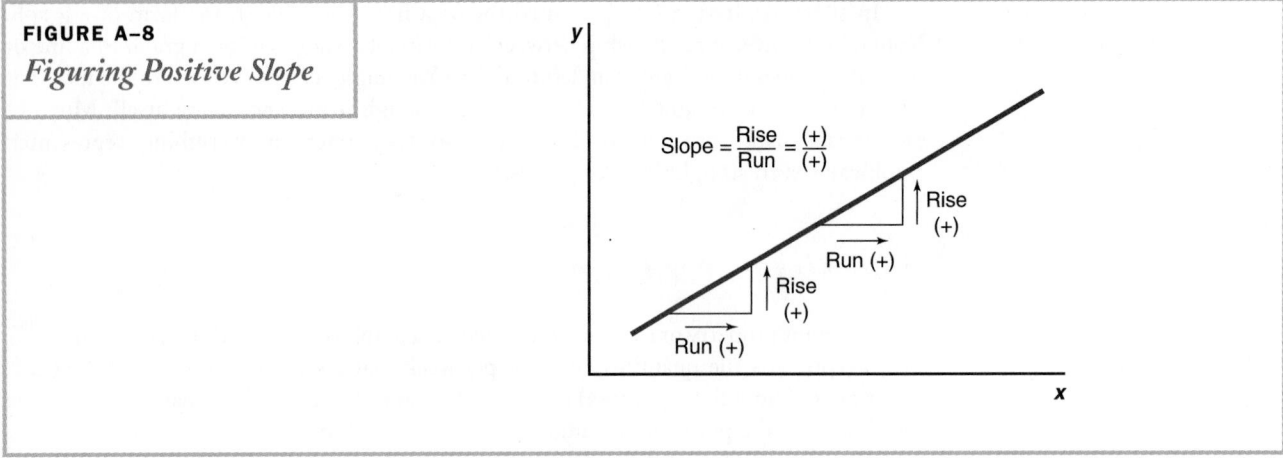

FIGURE A–8

Figuring Positive Slope

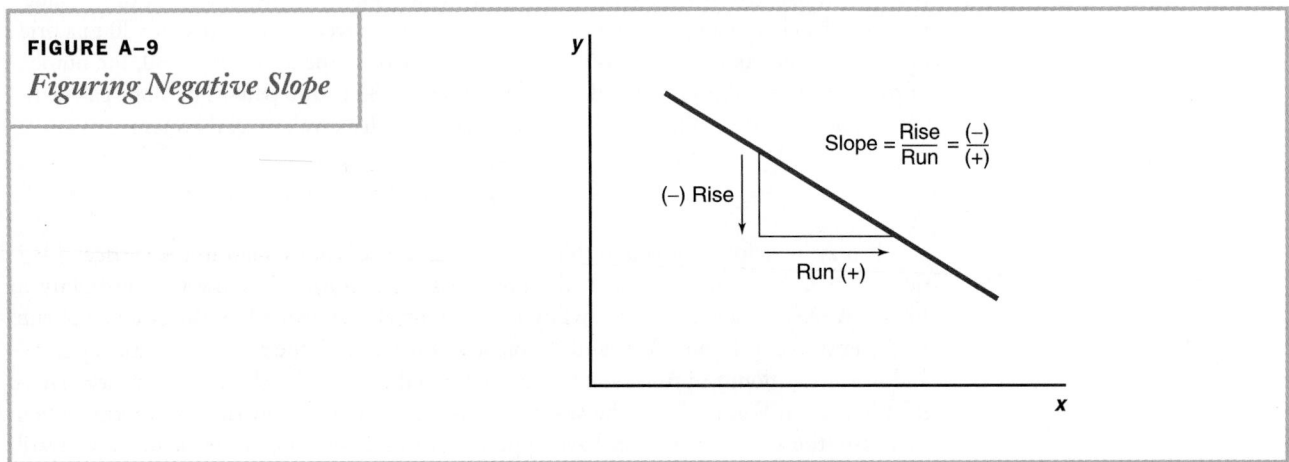

FIGURE A–9

Figuring Negative Slope

Now, let us calculate the slope for a different part of the curve in part (b) of Figure A–7. We will find the slope as we move from point B to point A. Again, we note that the slope, or rise over run, from B to A equals

$$\frac{20}{80} = \frac{1}{4}$$

A specific property of a straight line is that its slope is the same between any two points; in other words, the slope is constant at all points on a straight line in a graph.

We conclude that for our example in Figure A–7, the relationship between the price of a pair of shoes and the number of pairs of shoes willingly offered per week is linear, which simply means "in a straight line," and our calculations indicate a constant slope. Moreover, we calculate a direct relationship between these two variables, which turns out to be an upward-sloping (from left to right) curve. Upward-sloping curves have positive slopes—in this case, it is +1/4.

We know that an inverse relationship between two variables shows up as a downward-sloping curve—rise over run will be a negative slope because the rise and run have opposite signs as shown in Figure A–9. When we see a negative slope, we know that increases in one variable are associated with decreases in the other. Therefore, we say that downward-sloping curves have negative slopes. Can you verify that the slope of the graph representing the relationship between T-shirt prices and the quantity of T-shirts purchased per week in Figure A–6 is –1/10?

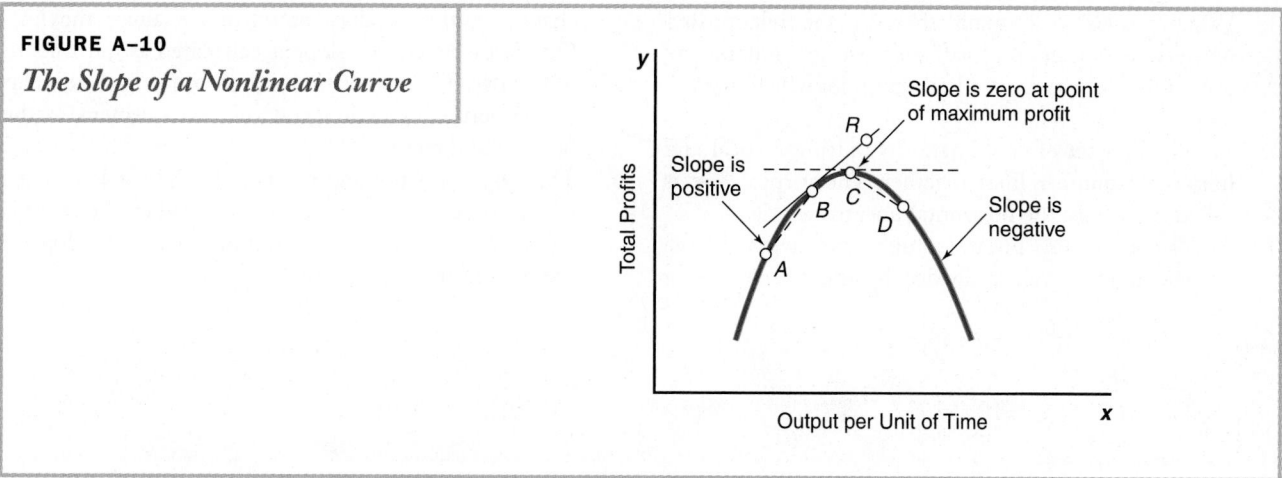

Slopes of Nonlinear Curves

The graph presented in Figure A–10 indicates a *nonlinear* relationship between two variables—total profits and output per unit of time. Inspection of this graph indicates that at first, increases in output lead to increases in total profits; that is, total profits rise as output increases. But beyond some output level, further increases in output cause decreases in total profits.

Can you see how this curve rises at first, reaches a peak at point *C*, and then falls? This curve relating total profits to output levels appears mountain-shaped.

Considering that this curve is nonlinear (it is obviously not a straight line), should we expect a constant slope when we compute changes in *y* divided by corresponding changes in *x* in moving from one point to another? A quick inspection, even without specific numbers, should lead us to conclude that the slopes of lines joining different points in this curve, such as between *A* and *B*, *B* and *C*, or *C* and *D*, will *not* be the same. The curve slopes upward (in a positive direction) for some values and downward (in a negative direction) for other values. In fact, the slope of the line between any two points on this curve will be different from the slope of the line between any two other points. Each slope will be different as we move along the curve.

Instead of using a line between two points to discuss slope, mathematicians and economists prefer to discuss the slope *at a particular point*. The slope at a point on the curve, such as point *B* in the graph in Figure A–10, is the slope of a line *tangent* to that point. A tangent line is a straight line that touches a curve at only one point. For example, it might be helpful to think of the tangent at *B* as the straight line that just "kisses" the curve at point *B*.

To calculate the slope of a tangent line, you need to have some additional information besides the two values of the point of tangency. For example, in Figure A–10, if we knew that the point *R* also lay on the tangent line and we knew the two values of that point, we could calculate the slope of the tangent line. We could calculate rise over run between points *B* and *R*, and the result would be the slope of the line tangent to the one point *B* on the curve.

APPENDIX SUMMARY

1. Direct relationships involve a dependent variable changing in the same direction as the change in the independent variable.

2. Inverse relationships involve the dependent variable changing in the opposite direction of the change in the independent variable.

3. When we draw a graph showing the relationship between two economic variables, we are holding all other things constant (the Latin term for which is *ceteris paribus*).
4. We obtain a set of coordinates by putting vertical and horizontal number lines together. The vertical line is called the *y*-axis; the horizontal line, the *x*-axis.
5. The slope of any linear (straight-line) curve is the change in the *y*-values divided by the corresponding

change in the *x*-values as we move along the line. Otherwise stated, the slope is calculated as the amount of rise over the amount of run, where rise is movement in the vertical direction and run is movement in the horizontal direction.
6. The slope of a nonlinear curve changes; it is positive when the curve is rising and negative when the curve is falling. At a maximum or minimum point, the slope of the nonlinear curve is zero.

➡ APPENDIX PROBLEMS

(Answers to the odd-numbered problems appear at the back of the book.)

A-1. Explain which is the independent variable and which is the dependent variable in the following examples.

   a. Once you determine the price of a notebook at your college bookstore, you will decide how many notebooks to buy.

   b. You will decide how many credit hours to register for this semester once the university tells you how many work-study hours you will be assigned.

   c. You are anxious to receive your Economics exam grade because you studied many hours in the weeks preceding the exam.

A-2. For the following items, state whether a direct or an indirect relationship exists.

   a. The number of hours you study for an exam and your exam mark.

   b. The price of pizza and the quantity purchased.

   c. The number of games your college basketball team won last year and the number of season tickets sold this year.

A-3. Complete the schedule and plot the following function:

$y = 3x$

x	y
4	
3	
2	
1	
0	
−1	
−2	
−3	
−4	

A-4. Review Figure A–4, and then state whether the following paired observations are on, above, or below the *x*-axis and on, to the left of, or to the right of the *y*-axis.

   a. (−10, 4)

   b. (20, −2)

   c. (10, 0)

A-5. Calculate the slope for the function you graphed in Problem A-3.

A-6. Complete the schedule and plot the following function:

$y = x^2$

x	y
4	
3	
2	
1	
0	
−1	
−2	
−3	
−4	

A-7. Indicate at each ordered pair whether the slope of the curve you plotted in Problem A-6 is positive, negative, or zero.

A-8. State whether the following functions imply a positive or negative relationship between *x* and *y*.

   a. $y = 5x$

   b. $y = 3 + x$

   c. $y = -3x$

Production Possibilities and Economic Systems

➤ **LEARNING OBJECTIVES**

After reading this chapter, you should be able to:

2.1 Define the production possibilities curve and identify its assumptions.

2.2 Use the production possibilities curve to illustrate the concepts of scarcity, trade-offs, unemployment, productive efficiency, allocative efficiency, increasing opportunity cost, and economic growth.

2.3 Use the production possibilities curve to explain the trade-off between consumption goods and capital goods.

2.4 Distinguish between absolute advantage and comparative advantage and use these concepts to explain how specialization and trade can increase production and consumption.

2.5 Explain the differences between the pure capitalist, pure command, and mixed economic systems.

2.6 Describe the features of pure capitalism and explain how capitalism answers the three basic economic questions.

myeconlab

MyEconLab helps you master each objective and study more efficiently. See end of chapter for details.

High and soaring Canadian car insurance rates created havoc for politicians and consumers alike in 2003. The issue of skyrocketing auto insurance almost toppled the once very popular New Brunswick Conservative government during the summer 2003 provincial election. In October 2003, in his first speech as Ontario's new premier, Dalton McGuinty announced a freeze on Ontario auto insurance rates. Within days, the free-enterprise Alberta Conservative government followed suit with its own 18-month rate freeze.

In October 2005, the Consumer Association of Canada completed a study involving 714 Canadian communities and close to 4 000 000 insurance quotes. Consistent with previous findings, car insurance rates tend to be significantly lower in those Canadian provinces where this service is provided by government, and not the private sector. The concepts presented in this chapter will help you understand both the public benefits and costs related to delivering services, such as auto insurance, under different economic systems.

DID YOU KNOW THAT...

Identity theft is the fastest growing fraud in both Canada and the United States. The phone rings up to 1200 times a day at the Canadian PhoneBusters antifraud call centre, but the dozen or so call-takers are so swamped that most victims hang up while they are waiting in the queue. In 2006, according to PhoneBusters, about 7800 victims reported losses of $16.3 million, which falls dramatically short of the number of cases of identity theft that are suspected to occur in Canada. This amounts to an annual increase of 90 percent over the losses of $8.6 million reported in 2005 in Canada.

One hard drive stolen from a computer at a Regina data management company contained names, addresses, dates of birth, social insurance numbers, pension statements, personal records for workers' compensation, and personal applications for provincial government rebates for over 300 000 Canadians. In January 2007, it was reported that as many as 2 million credit cards were affected when computer hackers stole customer information from the U.S. parent company of Canadian retailers Winners and HomeSense. Thieves use this stolen information to gain unlawful access to personal bank accounts and credit cards and to fraudulently apply for loans. In economics, identity theft can be viewed as a form of capital investment undertaken by dishonest individuals, as explained in this chapter.

SOURCE: "PUBLIC ADVISORY: SPECIAL REPORT FOR CONSUMERS ON IDENTITY THEFT." MAY 21, 2003. THE DEPARTMENT OF THE SOLICITOR GENERAL OF CANADA. http://www.sgc.gc.ca/publications/policing/Identity_Theft_Consumers_e.asp. (ACCESSED NOVEMBER 29, 2003); "STATISTICS ON IDENTITY THEFT." SEPTEMBER 2003. PHONEBUSTERS. http://www.phonebusters.com/Eng/Statistics/idtheft_canada_stats_2003.html (ACCESSED NOVEMBER 29, 2003); "IDENTITY THEFT IN CANADA." EXPOSITOR STAFF. BRANTFORD, ONTARIO. CANADIAN CREDIT CENTRE. FEBRUARY 1, 2003. ACCESSED NOVEMBER 29, 2003. ARTICLE CREDIT: COPYRIGHT 2003. THE LEADER-POST (REGINA) COPYRIGHT 2003, CANWEST GLOBAL COMMUNICATIONS CORP; PHONEBUSTERS. "STATISTICS ON IDENTITY THEFT." JANUARY 2007. http://www.phonebusters.com/english/statistics_E05.html. (ACCESSED JULY 11, 2007.)

2.1 The Production Possibilities Curve

We begin this chapter by introducing an economic model called the production possibilities curve. We will use this model to sharpen your understanding of concepts discussed in Chapter 1, such as scarcity, choice, opportunity cost, efficiency, full employment, and economic growth. As well, we will illustrate how production possibilities can be expanded through specialization and trade. Finally, we will complete this chapter by examining the different economic systems that nations and industries can use to determine production possibilities.

Production possibilities curve (PPC) A curve that represents all possible production combinations of two goods that can be produced.

The **production possibilities curve (PPC)** is a curve representing all possible production combinations of two goods that can be produced under the following assumptions:

1. The nation's resources—land, labour, capital, and entrepreneurship—are fully and efficiently employed producing just these two goods (or services).
2. The production is measured over a specific period of time—for example, one year.
3. The quantity and quality of resources used to produce these two goods are fixed over this period of time.
4. The technology is fixed over this period of time.

Technology Society's pool of applied knowledge concerning how goods and services can be produced.

Technology is defined as society's pool of applied knowledge concerning how goods and services can be produced by managers, workers, engineers, scientists, and craftspeople, using land and capital. You can think of technology as the formula (or recipe) used to combine factors of production. When better formulas are developed, more production can be obtained from the same amount of resources. The level of technology sets the limit on the amount and types of goods and services that we can derive from any given amount of resources. The production possibilities curve is drawn under the assumption that we use the best technology that we currently have available and that this technology does not change over the time period under study.

Production Possibilities Curve: An Example

Figure 2–1 describes a production possibilities curve for Canada for the two goods automobiles and newsprint for 2007 (the data in Figure 2–1 are hypothetical). We assume for the moment that automobiles and newsprint are the only two goods that can be produced in Canada.

Part (a) of Figure 2–1 gives the various production combinations of automobiles and newsprint, assuming full and efficient employment of resources and a fixed level of resources and technology. If all resources are devoted to automobile production (point A), 3 million autos can be produced per year. Instead, if Canada decides to devote all her resources to newsprint production (point G), 6 million tonnes of newsprint per year can be produced. In between are other alternative possible production combinations. All of these production combinations are plotted as points A, B, C, D, E, F, and G in part (b) of Figure 2–1. Once these points are connected with a smooth curve, Canada's production possibilities curve is constructed.

Note that this production possibilities curve indicates the *maximum* quantity of one good that can be produced in 2007, given some quantity of the other good that is to be produced. Therefore, if we are given that 2 million autos are to be produced in 2007, then the maximum amount of newsprint that can be produced in 2007 is 4 million tonnes at point E on the curve.

2.2 *Applications of the Production Possibilities Curve*

We now turn to examine how we can apply the production possibilities curve model to better understand concepts introduced in Chapter 1.

FIGURE 2–1

A Society's Trade-Off between Automobiles and Newsprint

The production of automobiles is measured in millions of units per year, while the production of newsprint is measured in millions of tonnes per year. The various combinations are given in part (a) and plotted in part (b). Connecting the points A–G with a relatively smooth line gives the production possibilities curve for automobiles and newsprint. Point R lies outside the production possibilities curve and is therefore unattainable at the point in time for which the graph is drawn. Point S lies inside the production possibilities curve and therefore represents an inefficient use of available resources or unemployment.

Part (a)

Combination	Newsprint (millions of tonnes per year)	Automobiles (millions of units per year)
A	0	3.0
B	1	2.9
C	2	2.7
D	3	2.4
E	4	2.0
F	5	1.4
G	6	0

Part (b)

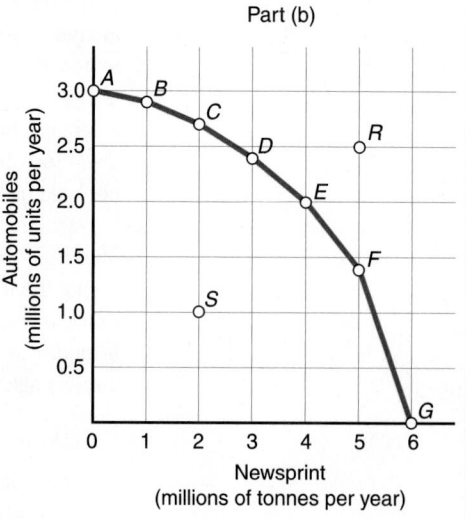

The Production Possibilities Curve, Scarcity, and Trade-Offs

Recall from the previous chapter that *scarcity* refers to the condition that arises because wants always exceed what can be produced with limited resources. The production possibilities curve in Figure 2–1 can be viewed as a boundary that separates the attainable production combinations, on or inside the curve, from the unattainable points outside of the curve (such as point *R* in Figure 2–1). That is, even though we are assuming that the resources are being fully and efficiently employed using the most up-to-date technology, Canada faces a *limit*, in terms of what it can produce, as portrayed by the production possibilities curve. The existence of this boundary, in the face of unlimited wants, gives us a vision of the economic problem of scarcity.

The fact that the production possibilities curve slopes downward to the right suggests that due to scarcity, society is forced to make choices that involve trade-offs. In Figure 2–1 you can clearly see that if Canada is currently at point *E* in the current year, and chooses to move to point *F*, next year, when it can produce additional tonnes of newsprint, Canada has to trade off some automobile production. Note that trade-offs will occur anywhere *on* the production possibilities curve.

As a student, you face the scarcity problem of using a limited amount of time to achieve both your academic and personal goals. Every time you attend a class or a study group session you trade off the opportunity to spend that time learning in a different manner or engaging in a work- or leisure-related activity. As Example 2–1 illustrates, new technologies are changing the nature of the trade-offs students face when they consider whether they will attend their next class or choose the best alternative use of their time.

EXAMPLE 2–1   **Skipping Class without Skipping Lectures**

At Harvard University, there is a department called the Instructional Computing Group. Employees videotape about 30 courses per semester and place them on the university's internal website for students to review if they missed class.

Every student, naturally, has his or her own subjective estimate of the expected value of the next-best alternative to attending class. For each student, the value of an hour spent in class depends in part on what time of the day the class meets. Harvard's online lecture-review system permits students to reallocate the uses of their time. If a student would rather be in a rowboat on the Charles River at 1:00 on a spring afternoon instead of attending her Harvard economics class, she can miss the class. Then she can view the class lecture, say, at 5:00, when she rates the value of that study activity to be higher than her next-highest-valued activity for that hour of the day.

Of course, there is still an opportunity cost associated with skipping the actual class meeting. The student misses out on the opportunity to ask questions of her professor during the lecture and to interact with other class members. Nevertheless, there is evidence that many Harvard students prefer to reallocate their daily schedule in favour of virtual class attendance—professors in some of the courses with videotaped lectures have been increasingly concerned about noticeable drops in physical attendance in class meetings.

For critical analysis:

1. What opportunity costs (sacrifices) might you incur when you skip your classes?
2. In classes where group discussion or group work is an essential feature of the learning process, who bears some of the additional costs of higher absenteeism rates resulting from posting lectures on the Web?

The Production Possibilities Curve and Unemployment

Recall that full employment is one of the important socioeconomic goals identified in Chapter 1. Our simple production possibilities model helps us better understand the importance of this goal. Suppose in Figure 2–1 Canada failed to achieve the goal of full employment. Where, roughly speaking, would Canada's production combination be located—inside, on, or outside of the production possibilities curve? The answer would be somewhere *inside* the production possibilities curve, such as point S in Figure 2–1. When Canada is inside her production possibilities curve, this clearly shows that a major cost of unemployment is that society forgoes some production of goods and services. That is, unemployment leads to a lower standard of living for society as a whole. If Canada were to eliminate this unemployment and move from point S to point E, would this involve a trade-off? The answer is no, as the extra production would be derived from putting unemployed workers back to work, allowing more of both goods to be produced.

The Production Possibilities Curve and Efficiency

The production possibilities curve can be used to define the notion of efficiency. Whenever the economy is operating on the PPC at such points as A, B, C, or D, we say that its production is efficient. Such points as S in Figure 2–1, which lie below the production possibilities curve, are said to represent production situations that are not efficient.

PRODUCTIVE EFFICIENCY. Efficiency can mean many things to many people. Even within economics, there are different types of efficiency. Here, we are discussing efficiency in production, or **productive efficiency**, which occurs when a given output level is produced at minimal cost. Alternatively stated, productive efficiency occurs when a given level of inputs is used in a manner that produces the maximum output possible, given the level of technology.

A simple commonsense definition of productive efficiency is getting the most out of what we have as an economy. Clearly, we are not getting the most out of what we have if we are at point S in part (b) of Figure 2–1. We can move from point S to, say, point C, thereby increasing the total quantity of automobiles produced without any decrease in the total quantity of newsprint produced. We can move from point S to point E, for example, and have both more automobiles and more newsprint. Point S is called a **productively inefficient point**, which is defined as any point below the production possibilities curve, assuming resources are fully employed.

Example 2–2 below describes a global initiative designed to educate children in the poorest regions of the world in a productively efficient (minimal cost) manner.

Productive efficiency Occurs when a given output level is produced at minimal cost.

Productively inefficient point Any point below the production possibilities curve, assuming resources are fully employed.

EXAMPLE 2-2	**One Laptop per Child**

Most of the nearly 2 billion children in the developing world are inadequately educated or uneducated. One in three does not complete the fifth grade. Children are resigned to poverty and isolation, never knowing what the light of learning could mean to their lives. At the same time, their governments struggle to compete in a very dynamic, social, and global information economy.

Attempting to enhance the education of children living in the developing (poorer) nations using traditional "bricks and mortar" educational resources—building schools, hiring teachers, buying textbooks—seems to be too expensive a task, and hence unrealistic. As an example, in Canada, it costs on average over $10 000 per year for every student in the traditional education system. Given the resources that poor countries can reasonably allocate to education—sometimes less than $20 per year per pupil—a worldwide nonprofit association called "One Laptop per Child (OLPC)" is seeking to bring education to children (and their parents) in poorer nations through the creation of a laptop costing less than $100 per child. OLPC has currently developed the XO laptop, a machine designed for "learning learning."

The XO Laptop has been designed to provide the most engaging wireless network available at a cost of $100 per unit. The laptops are connected to each other and to the

continued

Internet. The children in the neighbourhood are thus permanently connected to chat, share information on the web, gather by videoconference, make music together, edit texts, read e-books, and enjoy the use of collaborative games online. As the children grow and pursue new ideas, the software, content, resources, and tools should be able to grow with them. The battery of the laptop can work for many hours and it can be charged in special gang chargers in the school or by mechanical or solar power—so there is no need to have electricity. The unique XO display allows the use of the laptop under a bright sun, enabling the user to work outside in the wild, if need be.

For critical analysis: Explain how the One Laptop per Child concept promotes productive efficiency.

SOURCES: "MISSION." ONE LAPTOP PER CHILD. http://www.laptop.org/en/vision/mission/index.shtml; "LAPTOP." ONE LAPTOP PER CHILD. http://www.laptop.org/en/laptop/; "EDUCATIONAL EXPENDITURES. THE PEOPLE." CANADA E-BOOK. STATISTICS CANADA. http://www43.statcan.ca/02/02c/02c_001_e.htm.

Allocative efficiency Producing the mix of goods and services most valued by consumers.

ALLOCATIVE EFFICIENCY. The concept of **allocative efficiency** is concerned with producing the mix of goods and services most valued by consumers. While all the points along the production possibilities curve in Figure 2–1 are productively efficient, only one production combination on this curve will be allocatively efficient. Suppose that point E in part (b) of Figure 2–1 is the most highly valued combination. If Canada ends up producing this combination, it is being allocatively efficient.

Stated in terms of the concepts learned in Chapter 1, if society were to move away from point E, in either direction, the marginal benefit derived from this move would be less than the marginal cost associated with this move. In other words, the extra value derived from producing a different combination of cars and newsprint would be less than the value given up by departing from point E. If the firms that produce these goods make decisions on the basis of society's marginal benefits and marginal costs, rational behaviour has the potential to lead us to this allocatively efficient production combination.

In this chapter's Issues and Applications, the merits of providing auto insurance via privately owned companies is compared with the merits of having the government administer auto insurance in Canada. One of the advantages of private auto insurance is that each injured individual can take the necessary legal action to ensure that the dollar value of the compensation resulting from an accident claim (marginal benefit) is sufficient to cover the full marginal cost related to the individual's injuries and losses sustained from the accident. In this way, private auto insurance promotes allocative efficiency. In contrast, under public auto insurance, the government dictates the maximum insurance payouts to injured parties for claims, such as those relating to the pain and suffering incurred in an accident. Since these maximum payouts are often set in a manner that attempts to reduce the total cost of these claims, the public insurance system may tend to underallocate resources in the payment of claims to injured individuals.

The Production Possibilities Curve and Opportunity Cost

We have re-created the curve in Figure 2–1 as Figure 2–2. Each combination, A through G, of automobiles and newsprint is represented on the production possibilities curve. Starting with the production of zero newsprint, Canada could produce 3 million automobiles with its available resources and technology. When we increase production of newsprint from zero to 1 million tonnes per year, we have to give up the automobile production represented by that first vertical arrow, Aa. From part (a) of Figure 2–1 you can see that this is 0.1 million autos a year (3.0 million – 2.9 million). Again, if we increase production of newsprint by 1 million tonnes per year, we go from B to C. In order to do

FIGURE 2-2

The Law of Increasing Relative Cost

Consider equal increments of newsprint production, as measured on the horizontal axis. All the horizontal arrows—*aB*, *bC*, and so on-are of equal length (1 million tonnes). The opportunity cost of going from 5 million tonnes of newsprint per year to 6 million (*Ff*) is much greater than going from zero tonnes to 1 million tonnes (*Aa*). The opportunity cost of each additional equal increase in newsprint production rises.

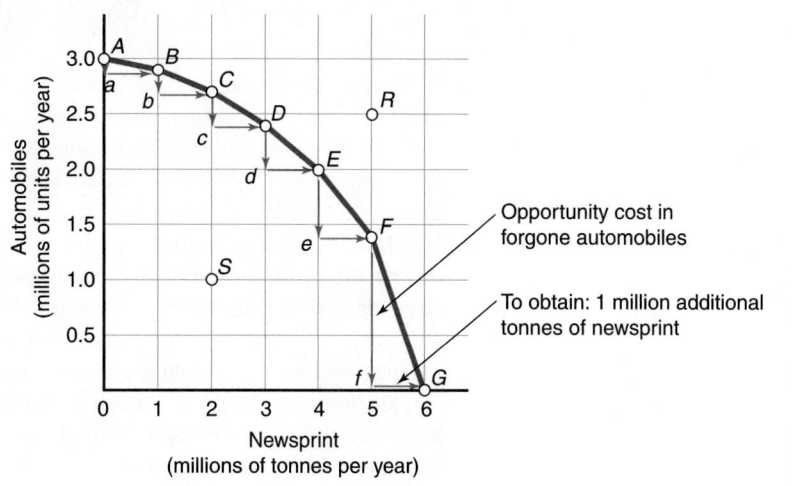

so, we have to give up the vertical distance *Bb*, or 0.2 million automobiles a year. By the time we go from 5 million to 6 million tonnes of newsprint, to obtain that 1 million tonne increase we have to forgo the vertical distance *Ff*, or 1.4 million automobiles. In other words, the opportunity cost of the last 1 million tonnes of newsprint is 1.4 million autos, compared with 0.1 million autos, the opportunity cost for the first million tonnes of newsprint (starting at zero production).

Consider equal increments of newsprint production, as measured on the horizontal axis. All the horizontal arrows—*aB*, *bC*, and so on—are of equal length (1 million tonnes). The opportunity cost of going from 5 million tonnes of newsprint per year to 6 million (*Ff*) is much greater than going from zero tonnes to 1 million tonnes (*Aa*). The opportunity cost of each additional equal increase in newsprint production rises.

Law of increasing relative cost
When society takes more resources and applies them to the production of any specific good, the opportunity cost increases for each additional unit produced.

LAW OF INCREASING RELATIVE COST. What we are observing is called the **law of increasing relative cost**: When society takes more resources and applies them to the production of any specific good, the opportunity cost increases for each additional unit produced. The reason that, as a country, we face the law of increasing relative cost (which causes the production possibilities curve to bow outward) is that certain resources are better suited for producing some goods than they are for others. Resources are generally not *perfectly* adaptable for alternative uses. When increasing the output of a particular good, producers must use less adaptable resources than those already used in order to produce the additional output. Hence the cost of producing the additional units increases. In our hypothetical example here, at first, the mechanical technicians in the automobile industry would shift over to producing newsprint. After a while, though, upholstery specialists and windshield installers would also be asked to help. Clearly, they would be less effective in making newsprint.

As a rule of thumb, the more *specialized the resources, the more bowed the production possibilities curve*. At the other extreme, if all resources are equally suitable for newsprint production or automobile production, the curves in Figures 2–1 and 2–2 would approach a straight line representing a constant opportunity cost situation.

Policy Example 2–1 describes recent policy decisions made by the government of British Columbia that affect the production combination of two highly valued types of goods—natural-wilderness-area-related goods and energy-related goods (oil and gas). This example encourages you to apply the concepts of opportunity cost and allocative efficiency to evaluate policies that affect the way in which our resources are used.

POLICY EXAMPLE 2-1 **The Multibillion Dollar Park**

In October 1997, the British Columbia NDP government established the Muskwa-Kechika land-use area, a wilderness area larger than Switzerland, located in the northeast part of the province. In 2000, more land was added, bringing the total Muskwa-Kechika Management Area (M-KMA) to 6.3 million hectares, which made it the largest land-use decision of its kind in North America.

The management intent for the M-KMA is to maintain in perpetuity the wilderness quality, the diversity and abundance of wildlife, and the ecosystems on which the wildlife depends. One of the primary challenges is to be able to prevent corporate interests from exploiting the region's natural resources by engaging in logging, oil and gas drilling, and mining practices that would jeopardize the area's natural beauty and wildlife.

On June 25, 2003, the British Columbia Liberal government announced that it would allow exploration of extensive natural gas deposits, with a potential development value of $16 billion, in parts of the M-KMA.

According to the "2005–06 Muskwa-Kechika Management Area Annual Report to the Premier and Public," resource extraction for energy products such as oil and natural gas is permitted in 75 percent of the area, while 25 percent is designated under the provincial park system. In this report it was noted that the intent is to use "best practices" to ensure that resource extraction occurs with minimal reduction in the quality of the natural wilderness area. For example, in extracting oil and gas for energy production, methods used to reduce negative impacts include building winter ice and snow roads that will be deactivated once the activity at well sites has been completed, conducting heliportable exploration drilling, timing activities so they are coordinated with other resource users such as guide outfitters, and coordinating resource road development with other industry companies.

For critical analysis: Sketch the appropriate two-good production possibilities curve, assuming the law of increasing relative cost and illustrating the trade-off indicated in this example. On this production possibilities curve sketch the allocatively efficient point *E*, which we assume is halfway down the curve you sketched. Sketch another point *F*, which is on the curve but in the direction of more energy products (oil and gas) when compared to point *E*. What is the opportunity cost of moving from point *E* to *F*? If British Columbia's economy moved from point *E* to point *F*, how would the marginal benefit of such a move compare with the marginal cost of such a move? Explain.

SOURCE: "MUSKWA-KECHIKA, BC'S WORKING WILDERNESS, 2005–06, REPORT TO THE PREMIER AND THE PUBLIC." MUSKWA-KECHIKA MANAGEMENT AREA. MUSKWA-KECHIKA ADVISORY BOARD. http://www.muskwa-kechika.com/pdf/2005–2006annual_report.pdf.

The Production Possibilities Curve and Economic Growth

During any particular time period, a society cannot be outside the production possibilities curve. Over time, however, it is possible to have more of everything. This occurs through economic growth. Figure 2–3 shows the production possibilities curve for automobiles and newsprint shifting outward. The two additional curves represent new choices open to an economy that has experienced economic growth. Such economic growth occurs because of many things, including increases in the quantity of resources available, increases in the productivity of existing resources, and changes in technology.

Scarcity still exists, however, no matter how much economic growth there is. At any point in time, we will always be on some production possibilities curve; thus, we will always face trade-offs. The more we want of one thing, the less we can have of others.

If a country experiences economic growth, the production possibilities curve between automobiles and newsprint will move outward, as is shown in Figure 2–3. This takes time and does not occur automatically. One reason it will occur involves the choice about how much to consume today.

FIGURE 2–3

Economic Growth Allows for More of Everything

If the country experiences economic growth, the production possibilities curve between automobiles and newsprint will shift out, as shown. This takes time, however, and it does not occur automatically. This means, therefore, that we can have more automobiles and more newsprint only after a period of time during which we have experienced economic growth.

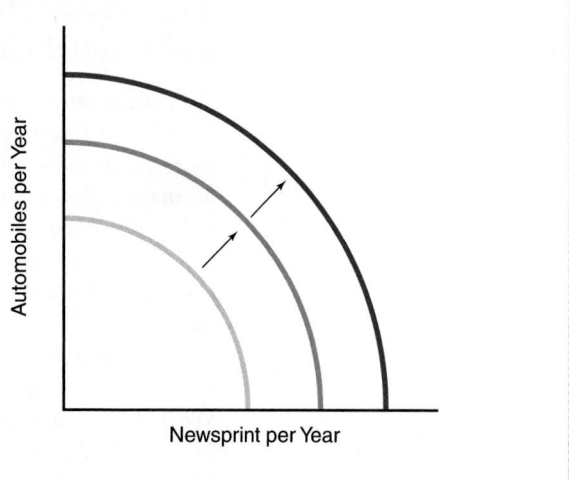

2.3 Consumption Goods versus Capital Goods

Consumption The use of goods and services for direct personal satisfaction.

The production possibilities curve and economic growth can be used to examine the trade-off between present consumption and future consumption. **Consumption** is the use of goods and services for direct personal satisfaction. These goods and services are what we call consumption or consumer goods—food, clothes, and entertainment, for example. And we have already defined physical capital as the manufactured goods, such as machines and factories, used to make other goods and services.

Why We Make Capital Goods

Why would we be willing to use productive resources to make things—capital goods—that we cannot consume directly? For one thing, capital goods enable us to produce larger quantities of consumer goods or to produce them less expensively than we otherwise could. Before fish are "produced" for the market, such equipment as fishing boats, nets, and poles are produced first. Imagine how expensive it would be to obtain fish for the market without using these capital goods. Catching fish with one's hands is not an easy task. The price per fish would be very high if capital goods were not used.

Forgoing Current Consumption

Whenever we use productive resources to make capital goods, we are implicitly forgoing current consumption. We are waiting until some time in the future to consume the fruits that will be reaped from the use of capital goods. In effect, when we forgo current consumption to invest in capital goods, we are engaging in an economic activity that is forward looking—we do not get instant utility or satisfaction from our activity.

At the start of this chapter, in the *Did You Know That* section, we noted the rapid growth of identity theft in Canada. Even an individual contemplating a theft faces a choice between increased current consumption versus increased capital accumulation. That is, instead of breaking into a home to steal a consumer item, such as a TV or stereo, the identity thief uses sophisticated electronic devices to steal the identity of others. While securing the identity of others does not, in itself, provide immediate self-gratification in terms of current consumption, it does allow the sophisticated thief the ability to enhance his or her future consumption through the fraudulent use of credit cards and debit cards. Just as a new machine can reduce the costs of a legitimate business, identity theft lowers the cost of engaging in illegal activity by reducing the probability of being "caught in the act." That is, identity thieves often acquire the personal data of others, without ever having any direct contact with the victims. Indeed, identity theft can be viewed as a form of capital investment undertaken by dishonest individuals.

The Trade-Off between Consumption Goods and Capital Goods

To have more consumer goods in the future, we must accept fewer consumer goods today. In other words, an opportunity cost is involved here. Every time we make a choice for more goods today, we incur an opportunity cost of fewer goods tomorrow, and every time we make a choice of more goods in the future, we incur an opportunity cost of fewer goods today. With the resources that we do not use to produce consumer goods for today, we invest in capital goods that will produce more consumer goods for us later. The trade-off is shown in Figure 2–4. On the left in part (a), you can see this trade-off depicted as a production possibilities curve between capital goods and consumption goods.

Assume that we are willing to give up $1 billion worth of consumption today. We will be at point *A* in the left-hand diagram of part (a). This will allow the economy to grow. We will have more future consumption because we invested in more capital goods today. In the right-hand diagram of part (a), we see two goods represented, food and recreation. The production possibilities curve will move outward if we collectively decide to restrict consumption each year and invest in capital goods.

In part (b), we show the results of our willingness to forgo more current consumption. We move to point *C*, where we have much fewer consumer goods today, but produce a lot more capital goods. This leads to more future growth in this simplified model, and thus, the production possibilities curve in the right-hand side of part (b) shifts outward more than it did in the right-hand side of part (a).

In other words, the more we give up today, the more we can have tomorrow, provided, of course, that the capital goods are productive in future periods and that society desires the consumer goods produced by this additional capital.

FIGURE 2–4

Capital Goods and Growth

In part (a), the nation chooses not to consume $1 billion, so it invests that amount in capital goods. In part (b), it chooses even more capital goods. The PPC moves even farther to the right on the right-hand diagram in part (b) as a result.

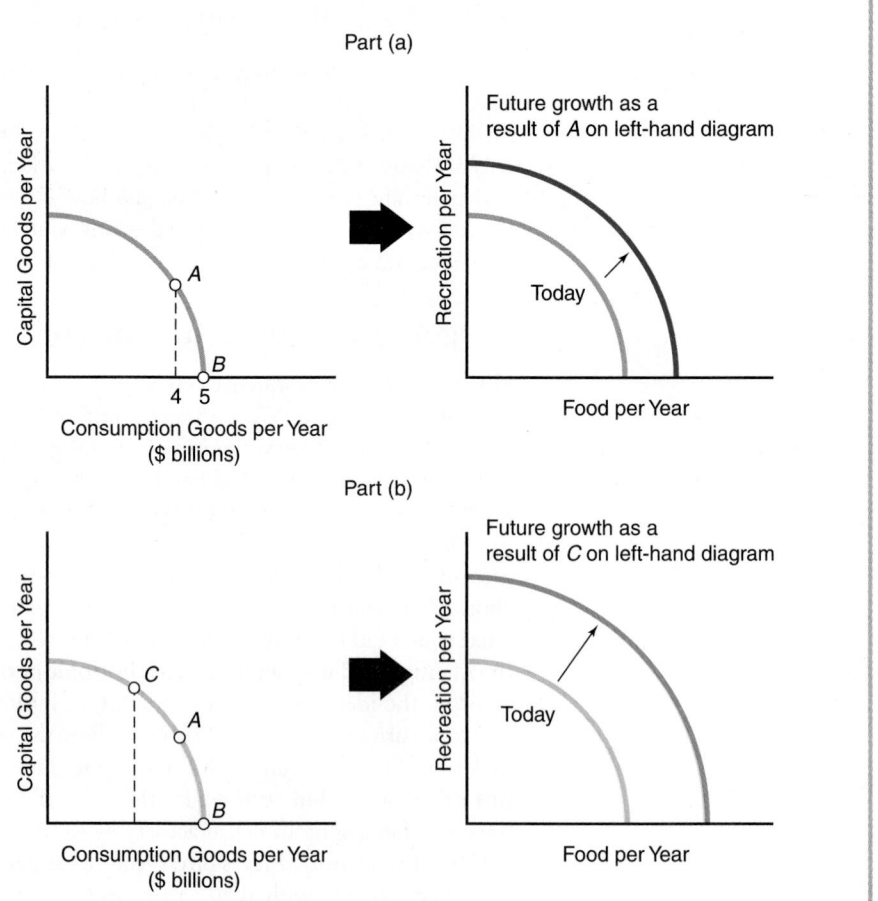

At the individual consumer's level, one's decision to enroll in a post-secondary educational institution, on a full-time basis, entails a trade-off between additional capital goods and additional consumer goods. As we noted in Chapter 1, the decision to enroll in a college or university on a full-time basis entails the extra costs of lost employment income for eight months per year, as well as additional out-of-pocket costs, such as tuition, fees, and textbooks. These additional educational costs mean that the individual full-time student sacrifices some current consumption goods when enrolled in a post-secondary institution.

So, what does an individual gain when he or she purchases additional years of post-secondary education? Since post-secondary education is a form of human capital, the student should be more productive upon graduation and therefore should earn a higher level of income in future years. This means that the college or university graduate will be able to consume a greater quantity of consumer goods in the future. Example 2–3 examines whether the facts support the view that Canadian post-secondary education is a productive form of human capital.

EXAMPLE 2-3   **Canadian Post-Secondary Education Pays Off Big Time!**

Canadian college and university students can indeed look forward to a higher level of consumption upon graduation, and their future prospects continually improve as they accumulate even greater levels of post-secondary education, according to the information presented in this example.

In Table 2–1 below, the Canadian inflation rate has been applied to data from a 2002 study undertaken by the Ministry of Learning for the Government of Alberta. The table shows estimates of the 2007 average annual salaries earned by individuals in Canada who have attained different levels of education. An individual with a college diploma earned an annual average income of $37 106, which was $6633 in excess of the $30 473 annual average income earned by a high-school graduate. An individual with a university bachelor's degree earned an annual average income of $46 481, which was $9376 in excess of the $37 106 annual average income earned by a graduate with a college diploma. Finally, an individual with a university masters or doctorate degree earned an annual average income of $56 719, which was $10 238 in excess of the $46 481 annual average income earned by a graduate with a bachelor's degree.

Table 2–1 also presents annualized percentage rates of returns for each of the three post-secondary education achievement levels for Canada for 2007. These rates of return are computed by utilizing a sophisticated compound interest formula to compare the extra annual income gained (marginal benefit) with the extra annual costs (marginal cost), including the extra forgone income, tuition, fees, and textbook costs associated with each of the three levels of post-secondary education. The rates of return calculations in the table assume that a typical student enrolls full time in a post-secondary education institute at 19 years of age and, upon graduation, works until he or she is 60 years of age.

As you can see from the accompanying table, the annual percentage rates of return are 12 percent, 15 percent, and 13 percent for a diploma, a bachelor's degree, and a masters/ doctorate degree, respectively. The fact that each rate of return is positive implies that, for each level of post-secondary education, the marginal benefit exceeds the marginal cost, making the investment a productive one. What is perhaps even more impressive is that each rate of return compares very favourably with other alternate investments available. In June 2007, a two-year term deposit of between $5000 and $100 000 at a typical Canadian chartered bank earned a mere 3 percent a year, while a ten-year term deposit for the same dollar investment earned just 3.55 percent per year. Clearly, an investment in post-secondary education in Canada pays off big time!

continued

TABLE 2–1	Highest Level of Education Achieved	2007 Canadian Annual Average Salary	Annual Rate of Return in Percent
	High-School Graduate	$30 473	
	College Diploma Graduate	$37 106	12%
	Bachelor Degree Graduate	$46 481	15%
	Masters/Doctorate Degree Graduate	$56 719	13%

For critical analysis: Sketch two identical production possibilities curves for 2007 for the two goods—post-secondary education and current consumption goods. On the first production possibilities curve show point A that describes the production combination chosen by a 2007 high-school graduate who decides not to enroll in post-secondary education. On the second production possibilities curve, show point B that describes the production combination chosen by a 2007 high-school graduate who decides to seek and obtain a bachelor's degree. For each of the two production possibilities curves, roughly sketch the appropriate 2020 production possibilities curve.

SOURCE: "POST-SECONDARY EDUCATION PAYS OFF BIG—ESPECIALLY FOR ALBERTANS." MINISTRY OF LEARNING. GOVERNMENT OF ALBERTA. SEPTEMBER 8, 2003. http://www.learning.gov.ab.ca/news/2003/ September/ nr-PostSecPays.asp. (ACCESSED NOVEMBER 8, 2003.); STATISTICS CANADA. CONSUMER PRICE INDEX (CPI), 2001. BASKET CONTENT: ALL ITEMS: CANADA. CANSIM II SERIES V735319. TABLE NUMBER: 326000.

➡→ **CONCEPTS IN BRIEF**

Learning Objective 2.1: Define the production possibilities curve and identify its assumptions.

- The production possibilities curve describes all possible combinations of two goods that can be produced, assuming (1) full and efficient employment of resources, (2) a fixed time period, (3) fixed quantity and quality of resources, and (4) fixed technology.

Learning Objective 2.2: Use the production possibilities curve to illustrate the concepts of scarcity, trade-offs, unemployment, productive efficiency, allocative efficiency, increasing opportunity cost, and economic growth.

- The production possibilities curve emphasizes that there is a limit to what can be produced, despite the fact that human wants are unlimited. This illustrates the scarcity problem.
- The downward-sloping nature of the production possibilities curve implies that more of one good results in less of the other desirable good, which illustrates a trade-off situation.
- An increasing opportunity cost situation is depicted by a "bowed-out" production possibilities curve. This occurs when resources are not equally productive when used to produce different goods.
- Unemployment is reflected in a production combination inside the production possibilities curve. This illustrates that unemployment results in lost production.
- Each production combination on the production possibilities curve is productively efficient in that each combination represents the maximum level of output that can be produced with a fixed amount of resources. Allocative efficiency is achieved when the nation produces the production combination, on the production possibilities curve, that society values the most.
- Economic growth is illustrated by an outward shift, over time, in the production possibilities curve.

Learning Objective 2.3: Use the production possibilities curve to explain the trade-off between consumption goods and capital goods.

➣ A production possibilities curve that involves capital goods and consumption goods illustrates that when we use more of our resources to produce capital goods and promote economic growth, we must forgo present consumption goods.

2.4 Specialization and Greater Productivity

Individuals and societies have sought to increase their production possibilities through specialization. **Specialization** involves working at a relatively well-defined, limited endeavour, such as accounting or teaching. Individuals, regions, and nations produce a narrow range of products. Most people, in fact, do specialize. For example, you could probably change the oil in your car if you wanted to. Typically, though, you would take your car to a garage and let the mechanic do it. You benefit by letting the garage mechanic specialize in changing the oil and in completing other repairs on your car. The specialist has all the proper equipment to do the work and will likely get the job finished sooner than you could. Specialization usually leads to greater productivity, not only for each individual but also for the country.

> **Specialization** Involves working at a relatively well-defined, limited endeavour; individuals, regions, and nations produce a narrow range of products.

Absolute Advantage

Specialization occurs because different individuals and different nations have different skills. Sometimes, it seems that some individuals are better at doing everything than anyone else and are said to have an **absolute advantage**, the ability to perform a task using the fewest number of labour hours. A president of a large company might be able to type better than any of the typists, file better than any of the file clerks, and wash windows better than any of the window washers. The president has an absolute advantage in all these endeavours—by using fewer labour hours for each task than anyone else in the company. The president does not, however, spend time doing those other activities. Why not? Because a president is paid the most for undertaking managerial duties and specializes in that one particular task despite having an absolute advantage in all tasks. Indeed, absolute advantage is irrelevant in predicting how the president's time is spent; only *comparative advantage* matters.

> **Absolute advantage** The ability to perform a task using the fewest number of labour hours.

Comparative Advantage

Comparative advantage is the ability to perform an activity at the lowest opportunity cost. You have a comparative advantage in one activity whenever you have the lowest opportunity cost of performing that activity. Take the example of a lawyer and her secretary who can both review law cases and type legal opinions. Suppose the lawyer can review two law cases or type one legal opinion in one hour. At the same time, her secretary can review one law case or type one legal opinion in one hour. Here, the lawyer has an absolute advantage in reviewing law cases and seemingly is just as good as her secretary at typing legal opinions. Is there any reason for the lawyer and her secretary to "trade"? The answer is yes, because such trading will lead to higher output.

> **Comparative advantage** The ability to perform an activity at the lowest opportunity cost.

Consider the scenario of no trading. Assume that during each eight-hour day, the lawyer and her secretary devote half of their day to reviewing law cases and half to typing legal opinions. The lawyer would review eight law cases (4 hours × 2 per hour) and type four legal opinions (4 × 1). During that same period, the secretary would review four law cases (4 × 1) and type four legal opinions (4 × 1). Each day the combined output for the lawyer and her secretary would be 12 reviewed law cases and eight typed legal opinions.

If the lawyer specialized only in reviewing law cases and her secretary specialized only in typing legal opinions, their combined output would rise to 16 reviewed law cases

(8 × 2) and eight typed legal opinions (8 × 1). Overall, production would increase by four law cases per day.

The lawyer has a comparative advantage in reviewing cases. In the time it takes her to review one case (one-half hour) she could have typed one-half of a legal opinion. Her opportunity cost of reviewing the law case is therefore one-half of a legal opinion. The secretary, however, gives up typing an entire legal opinion each time she reviews a case. Since the lawyer's opportunity cost of reviewing law cases is less than her secretary's, she has the comparative advantage in reviewing law cases. See if you can work out why the secretary has a comparative advantage in typing legal opinions.

You may be convinced that everybody can do everything better than you. In this extreme situation, do you still have a comparative advantage? The answer is yes. To discover your comparative advantage, you need to find a job in which your *disadvantage* relative to others is the smallest. You do not have to be a mathematical genius to figure this out. The market tells you very clearly by offering you the highest income for the job for which you have the smallest disadvantage compared with others. Stated differently, to find your comparative advantage, no matter how much better everybody else can do the jobs that you want to do, you simply find which job maximizes your income.

The coaches of sports teams are constantly faced with determining each player's comparative advantage. Former Blue Jay Dave Winfield was originally one of the best pitchers in college baseball, winning the most valuable player award for pitching for the University of Minnesota Golden Bears in the 1973 College World Series. After he was drafted by the San Diego Padres, the coach decided to make him an outfielder, even though he was one of the best pitchers on the roster. The coach wanted Winfield to concentrate on his hitting. Good pitchers do not bring in as many fans as home-run kings. Dave Winfield's comparative advantage was clearly in hitting homers, rather than practising and developing his pitching game.

Scarcity, Self-Interest, and Specialization

In Chapter 1, you learned about the assumption of rational self-interest. It says that for the purposes of our analyses, we assume that individuals are rational in that they will do what is in their own self-interest. They will not consciously carry out actions that will make them worse off. In this chapter, you learned that scarcity requires people to make choices. We assume that they make choices based on their self-interest and attempt to maximize benefits net of opportunity cost. In so doing, individuals recognize their comparative advantage and end up specializing. Ultimately, when people specialize, they increase the money they make and become richer, as illustrated by Example 2–4.

EXAMPLE 2–4   **Why Men Marry: Is It for Love or the Marriage Premium?**

Earnings of married men are typically 10 to 20 percent higher than those of unmarried men. This wage differential between married and unmarried men is known as the "marriage premium."

It is likely that the efforts of these men's wives account for the marriage premium. If a wife devotes most of her time to managing the household, the husband has more time to devote to his job, which helps boost his earnings. The estimates displayed provide support for this idea. The figure shows that the marriage premium for husbands with stay-at-home wives is about 10 times as large as for husbands with wives who have jobs outside the home. If the trend toward more women with jobs outside the home continues, more men will have to devote their time to household activities, and the average marriage premium for men is likely to decline.

continued

FIGURE 2–5 *Estimates of the Marriage Premium*

Married men with stay-at-home wives earn about 31 percent more than men who have never been married. Married men with wives who work outside the home full time earn only about 3 percent more.

SOURCE: HYUNBAE CHUN AND INJAE LEE, "WHY DO MARRIED MEN EARN MORE: PRODUCTIVITY OR MARRIAGE SELECTION?" *ECONOMIC INQUIRY* 39 (APRIL 2001), PP. 307–319.

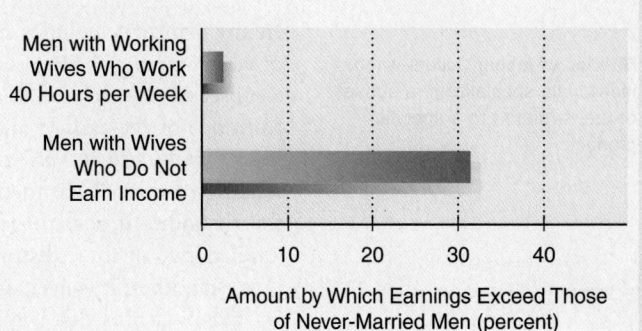

Amount by Which Earnings Exceed Those of Never-Married Men (percent)

For critical analysis: How might you use the concept of specialization to explain the marriage premium? Explain.

Comparative Advantage and Trade Among Nations

Though most of our analysis of absolute advantage, comparative advantage, and specialization has dealt with individuals or firms, it is equally applicable to countries. First, consider Canada. The Prairie provinces have a comparative advantage in the production of grains and other agricultural goods. Ontario and Quebec in Central Canada tend to specialize in industrialized production, such as automobiles and newsprint. Not surprisingly, grains are shipped from the Prairies to Central Canada, and automobiles are shipped in the reverse direction. Such specialization and trade allow for higher incomes and standards of living. If both the Prairies and Central Canada were politically defined as separate countries, the same analysis would still hold, but we would call it international trade. Indeed, Europe is smaller than Canada in area, but instead of one nation, Europe has 15. What we call *interprovincial trade* in Canada is called *international trade* in Europe. There is no difference, however, in the economic results—both yield greater economic efficiency and higher average incomes.

Political problems that do not normally arise within a particular nation often do between nations. For example, if Nova Scotia crab fishers develop a cheaper method of harvesting crabs than fishers in British Columbia, British Columbia fishers will lose out. They cannot do much about the situation, except try to lower their own costs of production. If crab fishers in Alaska, however, develop a cheaper method, both Nova Scotia and British Columbia fishers can (and likely will) try to raise political barriers to prevent Alaskan fishers from freely selling their product in Canada. Canadian crab fishers will use such arguments as "unfair" competition and loss of Canadian jobs. In so doing, they are only partly right: Crab-fishing jobs may decline in Canada, but jobs will not necessarily decline overall. If the argument of Canadian crab fishers had any validity, every time a region in Canada developed a better way to produce a product manufactured somewhere else in the country, employment in Canada would decline. That has never happened and never will.

When countries specialize where they have a comparative advantage and then trade with the rest of the world, the average standard of living in the world rises. In effect, international trade allows the world to move from inside the global production possibilities curve toward the curve itself, thereby improving worldwide economic efficiency.

The Division of Labour

Division of labour Occurs when individuals specialize in a subset of tasks related to a specific product.

In any firm that includes specialized human and nonhuman resources, there is a division of labour among those resources. **Division of labour** occurs when individuals specialize in a subset of tasks related to a specific product. The best-known example of all time comes from one of the earliest and perhaps most famous economists, Adam Smith, who, in his book *The Wealth of Nations* (1776), illustrated the benefits of a division of labour in the making of pins: "One man draws out the wire, another straightens it, a third cuts it, a fourth points it, a fifth grinds it at the top for receiving the head; to make the head requires two or three distinct operations; to put it on is a peculiar business, to whiten the pins is another; it is even a trade by itself to put them into the paper."

Making pins this way allowed 10 workers without very much skill to make almost 48 000 pins "of a middling size" in a day. One worker, toiling alone, could have made perhaps 20 pins a day; therefore, 10 workers could have produced 200. Division of labour allowed for an increase in the daily output of the pin factory from 200 to 48 000! (Smith did not attribute all of the gain to the division of labour according to talent but credited also the use of machinery and the fact that less time was spent shifting from task to task.)

What we are discussing here involves a division of the resource called labour into different kinds of labour. The different kinds of labour are organized in such a way as to increase the amount of output possible from the fixed resources available. We can, therefore, talk about an organized division of labour within a firm leading to increased output.

➤ CONCEPTS IN BRIEF

Learning Objective 2.4: Distinguish between absolute advantage and comparative advantage and use these concepts to explain how specialization and trade can increase production and consumption.

- Absolute advantage refers to the ability to produce one unit of a product at a lower labour cost than another producer. Comparative advantage refers to the ability to produce a unit of a product at a lower opportunity cost than another producer.
- With a given set of resources, specialization results in a higher output and, therefore, greater material well-being.
- Individuals must specialize in their areas of comparative advantage in order to reap the gains from specialization and trade.
- When individuals specialize in a subset of tasks related to a specific product, according to their comparative advantage, production is further enhanced. Such specialization is called division of labour.

2.5 Economic Systems

In the remainder of this chapter, we will study some of the established social arrangements that different nations use in choosing their production possibilities that, realistically, can include millions of goods and services being produced to satisfy the wants of millions of consumers.

Economic system The social arrangements or institutional means through which resources are used to satisfy human wants.

At any point in time, every nation has its own **economic system**, which can be defined as the social arrangements or institutional means through which resources are used to satisfy human wants. No matter what institutional means—marketplace or government—a nation chooses to use, the following three basic economic questions must always be answered because of the economic problem of scarcity.

1. *What and how much will be produced?* Literally billions of different things could be produced with society's scarce resources but not all at the same time. Some mechanism must exist that causes some things to be produced and others to remain as either inventors' pipe dreams or individuals' unfulfilled desires.
2. *How will it be produced?* There are many ways to produce a desired item. It is possible to use more labour and less capital or *vice versa*. It is possible to use more unskilled labour and fewer units of skilled labour. Somehow, in some way, a decision must be made as to the particular mix of inputs, the way they should be organized, and how they are brought together at a particular place.

3. *For whom will it be produced?* Once a commodity is produced, who should get it? In a modern economy, individuals and businesses purchase commodities with money income. The question then is what mechanism is there to distribute income, which then determines how commodities are distributed throughout the economy.

Not long ago, in response to the problem of scarcity, textbooks presented two extreme economic systems as possible polar alternatives for the industrialized nations to consider— the *pure command economy* versus the *pure capitalist economy*— in order to answer the three basic economic questions. Despite the fact that many countries have recently moved away from a command economy, it is appropriate to review both types of economic systems. This is because many informed citizens within Canada and other capitalist economies feel that elements of the command economy should prevail in the provision of important services, such as health care, education, and national security.

Pure Command Economy

Pure command economy An economic system characterized by public ownership of all property resources.

Public (government) ownership of all property resources characterizes a pure command economy. A **pure command economy** is an economic system characterized by public ownership of all property resources. The three basic economic questions—What, How, For Whom—are answered in a very centralized manner by government or the "state." Detailed five-year plans are formulated by the central authorities in order to respond to the three basic economic questions.

Until recently, such nations as Russia and China used the pure command economy to make their resource-allocation decisions. In the past, this type of system has typically been associated with nations practising communism or socialism.

Pure Capitalist Economy

Pure capitalist economy An economic system characterized by private ownership of all property resources.

In contrast to the pure command economy, a **pure capitalist economy** is an economic system characterized by private ownership of all property resources. Households and firms interacting through a system of markets answer the three basic economic questions— What, How, For Whom—in a decentralized manner. The pure capitalist economy goes by other names, such as *capitalism, market economy*, or *price system*.

Mixed Economic Systems

Mixed economy An economic system in which decisions about how resources are used are made partly by the private sector and partly by the public sector.

The pure command and the pure capitalist systems are extreme economic systems. Real world economies, which typically fall somewhere between these two extreme systems, are called mixed economies. In **mixed economies**, decisions about how resources are used are made partly by the private sector and partly by the public sector. As an example, Canada is referred to as a mixed capitalist system. This is because, while the majority of products are produced in the private sector, there are other goods and services provided by the government.

2.6 Capitalism in More Depth

Since there has been a global trend away from pure command economies toward capitalist economies, we will describe pure capitalism in more depth below.

Features of Capitalism

In elaborating on the pure capitalist economy, we will periodically refer to the Circular Flow Model presented in Figure 2–6.

Key features of pure capitalism include:

1. *Private ownership of resources:* Individual households and individual firms own the productive resources in pure capitalism. As described in Figure 2–6, households have two essential roles in capitalism—they supply resources to firms, and they demand

FIGURE 2-6

Circular Flow Model

This model describes how households and firms interact through
both product and factor markets
in a pure capitalist economy. In
the product markets, the households demand goods and services, while the firms supply the
goods and services. In the factor
markets, these roles are reversed.
That is, households supply the
resources, and the firms demand
the resources.

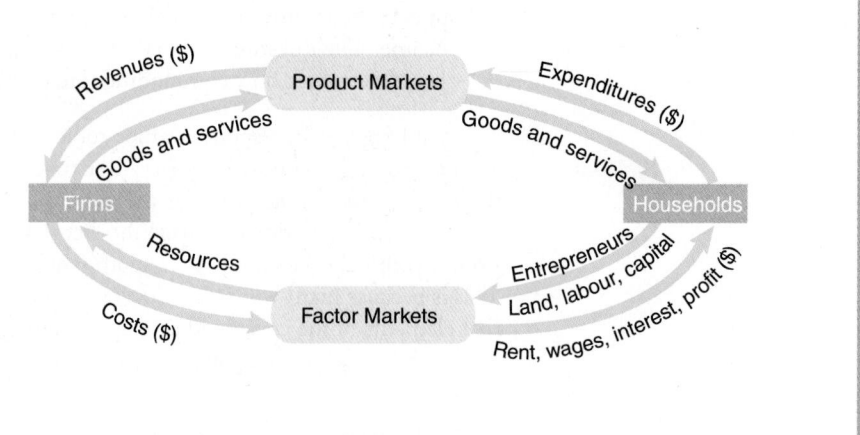

goods and services with the income received from supplying resources. Firms, in turn, demand or hire resources in order to supply goods and services to households.

2. *Self-interest:* The primary motive underlying decisions made by households and firms in pure capitalism is the pursuit of self-interest. More specifically, firms attempt to maximize their own profit, when deciding what resources to demand or hire and what products to supply. Similarly, households are assumed to attempt to maximize individual wealth and other personal goals when deciding on where to supply their resources. When demanding goods and services, households attempt to maximize self-satisfaction or utility.

3. *Consumer sovereignty:* The pure capitalist system is to serve the household in its con-
sumer role. Operationally, this means that capitalism is to produce the mix of goods and services that consumers desire, at the lowest possible prices.

4. *Markets and prices:* The Circular Flow Diagram in Figure 2–6 indicates the two broad types of markets that exist in pure capitalism—product markets and factor (resource) markets. When consumer demand changes or resource availability changes, this sets off changes in relative prices in affected product and factor markets. These price changes ultimately reallocate resources in line with the change in consumer demand or resource availability. While we will examine how prices are determined in individual markets in the chapters that follow, we will provide a simple example below.

Suppose that consumer demand for red wine increases and consumer demand for cigarettes decreases. Referring to the product markets in Figure 2–6, the price of red wine will increase, while the price of cigarettes will decrease. The higher price for red wine serves as a signal to firms that red wine is now relatively more profitable to produce than cigarettes.

Driven by the profit motive, the red wine firms will increase their demand to hire resources, while the cigarette firms will decrease their demand for resources, to reduce their losses. Prices will now change in the factor markets in Figure 2–6. Prices (i.e., wages) of resources (i.e., employees) that engage in the production of red wine will increase relative to the prices offered to resources in the cigarette industry. Resources, guided by self-interest, will move out of cigarette production and into the production of red wine. Eventually, red wine production will increase. Note how this system of markets and prices operates to reallocate resources in line with changes in consumer demand, thus promoting consumer sovereignty.

5. *Competition:* In order to ensure that the self-interests of firms and resources work to the best interests of consumers, it is necessary that many independent sellers and buyers compete in each market. This will be more fully explained in the subsequent chapters of this text.

6. *Limited government:* To the extent that competition exists in each market, the "invisible hand" of self-interest will serve to promote consumer sovereignty. Hence, allocating resources to meet changes in consumer demand does not require the "heavy hand" of

Laissez-faire French term for "leave it alone"; the government should leave it (the economy) alone or "let it be."

Three Ps Private property, Profits, and Prices inherent in capitalism.

government. The French have termed this feature of capitalism "**laissez-faire,**" which means that the government should leave it (the economy) alone or "let it be."

One way to remember some of the important attributes of the market economy is by thinking of capitalism's **Three Ps**: Private property, Profits, and Prices.

Capitalism and the Three Economic Questions

Now that we have reviewed the essential features of pure capitalism, we can proceed to examine how this economic system operates to answer the three basic economic questions—What, How, For Whom.

WHAT AND HOW MUCH WILL BE PRODUCED? Since firms can enhance profits by producing what consumers are willing to buy, we can see that consumer demand plays an important role in deciding what goods and services are produced. In more formal terms, the profit motive and competition lead firms to promote allocative efficiency—that is, firms will produce the mix of goods and services most wanted by society. However, we must keep in mind that if the highest price that consumers are willing to pay for a good is less than the lowest resource cost at which the good can be produced, no profit will result, and none of this good will be produced. In other words, resource availability also plays a role in determining what goods and services are produced.

HOW WILL IT BE PRODUCED? The question of how output will be produced in a pure capitalist system relates to the efficient use of scarce inputs. Consider the possibility of using only two types of resources, capital and labour. A firm may have the options given in Table 2–2. It can use various combinations of labour and capital to produce the same amount of output.

TABLE 2-2

Production Costs for 100 Units of Product X

Technique A or B can be used to produce the same output. Obviously, B will be used because its total cost is less than A's. Using production technique B will generate a $2 savings for every 100 units produced.

Inputs	Input Unit Price	A Production Technique A (input units)	Cost	B Production Technique B (input units)	Cost
Labour	$10	5	$50	4	$40
Capital	8	4	32	5	40
Total cost of 100 units			82		80

Two hypothetical combinations are given in Table 2–2. How then is it decided which combination will be used? Under pure capitalism, the least cost combination (technique B, in our example) will be chosen by firms because it will maximize profits. In other words, in pure capitalism, competition and the profit motive encourage firms to achieve productive efficiency.

FOR WHOM WILL IT BE PRODUCED? This last question involves how households share in the consumption of the goods and services produced. This, in turn, is based on the distribution of money incomes and wealth among households. Households with higher levels of income and wealth will get to purchase and consume a greater portion of the goods produced in the economy.

What determines the distribution of wealth and money income among different households? This distribution is based on the quantities, qualities, and types of the various human and nonhuman resources that different households own and supply to the marketplace. Households that own large quantities of resources that are highly in demand in the marketplace will earn high levels of income.

It should be noted that many current debates regarding economic systems apply to individual industries within a national economy. The central question posed in this chapter's Issues and Applications is: "What economic system should be used to best provide auto insurance in Canada?" As this Issues and Applications section points out, different economic systems are currently being used to provide auto insurance in Canada, depending on the province in which one resides.

As Policy Example 2–2 outlines, political factors also play a role in issues surrounding the use of alternate economic systems to allocate and distribute our limited economic resources, goods, and services.

POLICY EXAMPLE 2-2   **Canadian Politics: Right, Left, and Centre**

In Chapter 1, it was noted that Canadian government policies are, in part, based on economic theories applied to government efforts that attempt to achieve key socioeconomic goals. To more fully understand how policies are determined, it is important to recognize that political factors often play an important role. That is, policies are frequently guided by the principles of the political party of the government in power. In Canada the three major political parties at both the federal and provincial levels are the Conservatives, the New Democrats, and the Liberals. The Conservative Party, often referred to as the right-wing party, seeks to move the economy more toward the pure capitalist model, with private ownership and competition, decentralized individual decision making through free markets, and a laissez-faire approach to the economy. The New Democrats, who sit on the left side of the political landscape, place a high priority on: serving the interests of labour and working families; promoting social justice; reducing poverty and inequality; protecting the rights of minorities; and ensuring public funding and provision of social programs and services. Often the principles of the New Democrats tend to move various industries and services in the direction of a command system, with more government involvement. The Liberal Party, known as the centralists, supports a variety of policies from both the right and the left ends of the political spectrum, seemingly guided by public opinion as identified through political polls. The current federal Liberal Party emphasizes the importance of balancing the government budget with providing affordable social programs. Liberals typically favour mixed economic systems. Voters who wish to avoid extreme shifts in policies often vote for the Liberals.

For critical analysis: State whether each of the following policies is more consistent with the principles of the Conservatives or New Democrats. Policy A: Waiting time for surgeries is reduced through the expansion of government-funded surgical units located in government-run hospitals. Policy B: Waiting time for surgeries is reduced through the provision of new surgical services through privately owned health-care clinics.

SOURCE: "FOUNDING PRINCIPLES. GETTING THINGS DONE FOR ALL OF US." THE CONSERVATIVE PARTY OF CANADA. http://www.conservative.ca. (ACCESSED JUNE 1, 2007.); "ISSUES. NDP." THE NDP PARTY OF CANADA. http://www.ndp.ca/ (ACCESSED JUNE 1, 2007.); "VISION. LIBERAL—STRONGER TOGETHER." LIBERAL PARTY OF CANADA. http://www.liberal.ca/default_e.aspx. (ACCESSED JUNE 1, 2007.)

➥→ CONCEPTS IN BRIEF

Learning Objective 2.5: Explain the differences between the pure capitalist, pure command, and mixed economic systems.

- In a pure command system, the government owns the resources, and the three basic questions—What, How, For Whom—are answered in a centralized manner by government. In pure capitalism, resources are privately owned, and the basic questions are answered in a decentralized manner by individual firms and households interacting in markets.

- In a mixed economic system, there is some private as well as some public ownership of resources. In some sectors of the economy, the government answers the three basic questions, while in other sectors, individual households and firms answer these questions.

Learning Objective 2.6: Describe the features of pure capitalism and explain how capitalism answers the three basic economic questions.

- The key features of pure capitalism include private ownership of resources, self-interest motives, consumer sovereignty, markets and prices, competition and limited government. In short, think of the three *P*s—Private property, Profits, and Prices.

✦ In capitalism, consumer demand and resource availability determine what goods and services will be produced. Due to the profit motive, the least-cost method of production will be chosen when deciding how the goods will be produced. Who gets what is based on each consumer's level of wealth and income. This, in turn, depends on the degree to which individual households own marketable resources, and the price of these resources.

ISSUES AND APPLICATIONS

Private or Public Auto Insurance: What Is Best for Canada?

Concepts Applied: Capitalist, Command, and Mixed Systems; Productive Efficiency; Allocative Efficiency; and Equity

Ontario NDP Leader Howard Hampton points to a map of Canada to show that the gap between Ontario drivers and drivers in public auto insurance provinces is growing wider during a campaign stop in Peterborough, Ontario, in September 2003.

In response to public outrage over skyrocketing car insurance premiums, the Consumers' Association of Canada completed a comprehensive report on auto insurance rates in Canada in September 2003. In presenting the report, the association noted that government-owned, or public, auto insurance systems offer the lowest premiums for Canadian drivers.

Provincial Automobile Insurance Rates

Figure 2–7, taken from the report, compares the average annual auto insurance premiums among provinces, assuming the same insurance coverage, vehicle, driving record, and claims history. The average premiums are based on over 7000 rate quotes across Canada. All quotes assume an insurance coverage of $2 million liability, $500 collision deductible, and $300 comprehensive deductible. As you can see from this figure, the annual car insurance premiums are significantly lower in the provinces of British Columbia, Saskatchewan, Manitoba, and Quebec, where the mandatory insurance is provided by a government monopoly.

FIGURE 2–7

Comparison of Average Auto Insurance Rates by Province, 2003

SOURCE: REVIEW OF AUTOMOBILE INSURANCE RATES. CONSUMERS' ASSOCIATION OF CANADA. SEPTEMBER 2003, P. 11. ACCESSED NOVEMBER 11, 2003. http://www.cacbc.com/reports/ CAC%20National%20Auto%20Rates% 20Study%202003%20.pdf. COPYRIGHT CONSUMERS' ASSOCIATION OF CANADA.

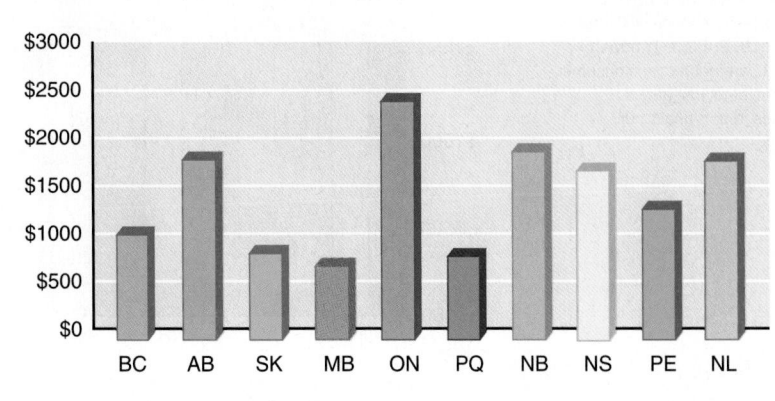

The Consumers' Association of Canada's report also noted the differences in the annual rate of increase in premiums between the private and public insurance systems in 2003. While premiums were escalating by up to 70 percent per year in the six provinces where privately owned insurance companies operate, Manitoba's publicly run auto insurance system was increasing annual premiums by only 7.2 percent.

To add fuel to the fire, in provinces offering private insurance, individuals can pay significantly higher premiums based on such criteria as age, gender, and marital status, regardless of the driving record or type of vehicle being insured. In New Brunswick, in 2003, older drivers who drove newer, much more expensive cars, and who had driving convictions, paid up to $2000 less for auto insurance, compared with young drivers with clean driving records. A 2002 Ford Taurus SE was more than $7000 cheaper for an 18-year-old male with a clean driving record to insure in Saskatoon's public insurance system than in Toronto or St John's, where private insurance companies operate. In provinces with public auto insurance, where rates were not based on age or gender, a young driver with a clean record paid a lower premium than an older driver with driving convictions.

Follow-Up Study

On October 15, 2005, the Consumer Association of Canada published a follow-up study comparing the automobile insurance rates in different provinces, keeping factors constant such as the driver's vehicle, driving record, claims history, deductibles and liability, and other types of coverage.

Similar to the 2003 study, the insurance rates continue to be significantly lower in British Columbia, Manitoba, and Saskatchewan where the mandatory insurance is provided by a government monopoly.

Providing Auto Insurance: Two Extreme Models

To better understand the significant differences in automobile premiums being charged across provinces and across customers within the same province, we will first contrast the two extreme economic systems that are possible in the provision of car insurance.

Under the pure capitalist or pure market model, privately owned, for-profit insurance companies sell the mandatory auto insurance policies, and the claims are paid out according to a decentralized tort-based or fault-based system.

In a fault-based system, the injured party must first prove that the other party is at fault, and then the injured party can bring legal action for recovery of damages against the person who caused the accident. The claim for recovery of damages will typically include monies to replace lost wages, out-of-pocket expenses, medical expenses, damages to the vehicle, and an amount to compensate for the pain and suffering related to injuries sustained as a result of the accident. If the injured party and the party at fault cannot agree on the amount of the total claim, the matter will eventually go to court. The fault-based system awards damages in a very decentralized manner, as the amount of each accident claim is assessed on the merits of each individual situation.

FIGURE 2-8

Comparison of Average Auto Insurance Rates by Province: October 2005

SOURCE: "NATIONAL STUDY OF AUTOMOBILE INSURANCE RATES: THIRD RELEASE." CONSUMER'S ASSOCIATION OF CANADA. OCTOBER 19, 2005. P. 7. https://secure2.baremetal.com/consumer/pdfs/cac_auto_ins_atlantic_provinces_report-final1.pdf.

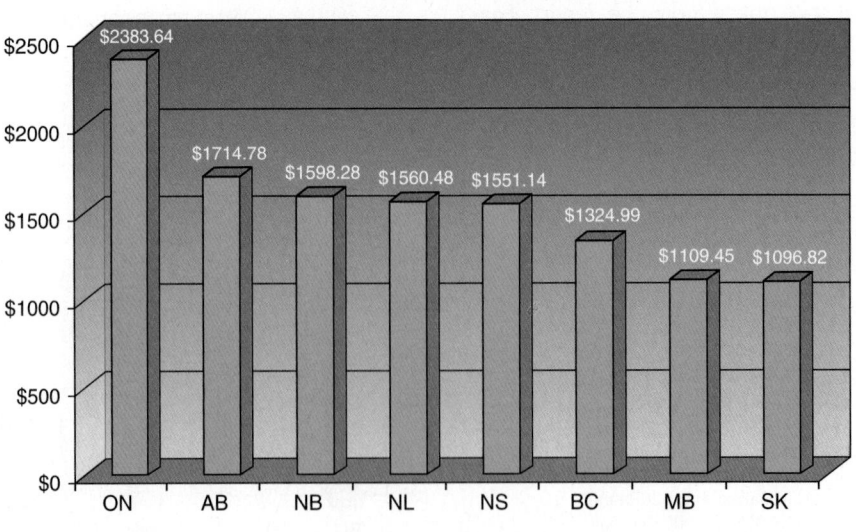

Average Auto Insurance Rates by Province
714 Communities, 3 985 162 Quotations

Province	Rate
ON	$2383.64
AB	$1714.78
NB	$1598.28
NL	$1560.48
NS	$1551.14
BC	$1324.99
MB	$1109.45
SK	$1096.82

At the other extreme, auto insurance can be delivered in a manner resembling a pure command economic system. In this model, the one government-owned Crown Corporation (public monopoly) provides all mandatory auto insurance for the entire province, and the claims are paid out on a pure no-fault basis.

In a pure no-fault system, one's own insurance company (or the government monopoly) pays for the damages that one incurs, regardless of fault. A comprehensive predetermined compensation schedule would dictate the maximum payment for specific types of losses, expenses, and injuries. In a pure no-fault system, one's individual right to sue for damages is eliminated.

The Advantages of Using the Command Model

It is interesting to note that Manitoba, the province that charges the lowest average annual auto insurance premiums, according to the Consumers' Association of Canada's study, operates an insurance system that most closely resembles the pure command model. That is, Manitoba Public Insurance (MPI), a government-owned monopoly, provides the mandatory car insurance, and the claims are paid out on a no-fault basis.

So, how can a pure command system result in lower auto insurance premiums when compared with the pure capitalist model? First, there are factors inherent in the public system that make it more productively efficient. Due to its no-fault feature, the system does not have to employ the expensive legal and court-related resources to establish fault and to establish the extent of the legal damages experienced by each injured party in each accident. As well, the amount of benefits paid out per claim to compensate an injured party for pain and suffering is significantly lower in the public system.

Since the government is the sole organization providing mandatory car insurance in the province, it does not have to employ resources to market its services to the customer. Moreover, as the sole provider, the public insurance organization is able to avoid the duplication in administrative resources that typically occurs when numerous private car insurance companies compete with each other in the same province. Because the public system can offer the same insurance coverage with minimal use of resources, it is able to keep its costs down and, in turn, charge low premiums.

A public insurance organization, such as Manitoba Public, does not have to raise premiums to a point where profits have to be earned on its operations, as is the case with privately run companies. Unlike the provincially owned public insurance providers, multinational private insurance corporations face the added pressure of raising premiums in order to recoup losses incurred in past global disasters, such as the September 11 terrorist attacks in the United States.

The Advantages of Using the Capitalist Model

In a series of recent studies, the Fraser Institute, a Canadian organization that promotes market-based policies,

defends the use of the capitalist model in providing mandatory auto insurance. The Institute argues that a public auto insurance system results in more accidents and imposes greater burdens on the health-care system when compared with private insurance. After examining two private insurance provinces and three public insurance provinces, they note that the number of collisions and the number of collision related deaths, injuries, and hospital admissions is significantly higher, per 100 000 population or per vehicle kilometres travelled, in those provinces with public insurance. This difference is most pronounced for males between the ages of 16 and 25 years. The Institute suggests that since the public insurance system fails to charge higher premiums for certain high-risk classes, such as the younger male class, it encourages too many risky drivers to take to the road, and it shifts collision costs to other drivers—primarily female, safer, and older drivers. As well, the expensive lawsuits that accompany the fault system can provide incentives for safer driving.

Another benefit of the pure capitalist approach to auto insurance relates to the goal of allocative efficiency. A fault-based insurance system provides the opportunity for each injured individual to take the necessary legal action to ensure that the dollar value of the compensation resulting from an accident claim (marginal benefit) is sufficient to cover the full marginal cost related to the individual's injuries and losses sustained from the accident.

As an example, two individuals may suffer the same physical injury in an accident, but the pain and suffering experienced by one of the individuals would be significantly greater if that individual could no longer engage in his or her favourite hobby—playing the piano. The fault-based insurance system could enable the piano lover to receive a higher level of compensation based on the higher level of pain and suffering (i.e., the higher level of marginal cost). In contrast, the pure command model's no-fault system would likely pay out the same level of benefits to both injured individuals.

Using a Mixed System

Despite the potential benefits of using a pure capitalist approach in the provision of auto insurance, Canadians residing in the private insurance jurisdictions are putting political pressure on their provincial governments to play an active role in the auto insurance industry. Many of the private insurance provinces are moving toward a mixed economic system of providing auto insurance. While privately owned corporations continue to provide the car insurance in these provinces, the provincial governments are proposing to fix the premium rates and set maximum dollar limits for the payout of certain types of claims, such as pain and suffering. These governments have a difficult task ahead of them as they attempt to strike an acceptable balance between affordable premiums, public safety, equity, and their own political party's commitment to promote a capitalist provincial economy.

For critical analysis:

1. Explain how the pure command model of providing auto insurance can promote productive efficiency.
2. Explain how the pure capitalist model of providing auto insurance can promote the goals of public safety and allocative efficiency.
3. Explain what equity (fairness) trade-offs are involved when choosing the pure command model of providing auto insurance.
4. A provincial government freezes the premiums charged by private insurance companies but lets the fault system determine the payment of claims. What problems will likely occur with this mixed system policy?

SOURCES: REVIEW OF AUTOMOBILE INSURANCE RATES. CONSUMERS' ASSOCIATION OF CANADA. SEPTEMBER 2003, P. 5. http://www.cacbc.com/reports/CAC%20National%20Auto%20Rates%20Study%202003%20.pdf. (ACCESSED NOVEMBER 11, 2003.); AUTO INSURANCE RATE COMPARISON STUDY—JULY 28, 2003. CONSUMERS' ASSOCIATION OF CANADA. JULY 2003, P. 3. http://www.cacbc.com/reports/July%2028,2003%20Report%20Auto%20NB.pdf. (Accessed November 11, 2003.); SGI 2003 RATE COMPARISON PROFILES. http://www.sgi.sk.ca/sgi_internet/rates/2003_rate_profiles.html#. (ACCESSED NOVEMBER 11, 2003.); MULLINS, MARK. "PUBLIC AUTO INSURANCE: A MORTALITY WARNING FOR MOTORISTS." FRASER INSTITUTE SEPTEMBER 2003, PP. 1–4. http://www.fraserinstitute.ca/admin/books/files/auto-insur.pdf. (ACCESSED NOVEMBER 14, 2003.)

SUMMARY

Here is what you should know after reading this chapter. MyEconLab will help you identify what you know, and where to go when you need to practise. We suggest that as soon as you review one of the Learning Objective sections below, you then proceed to go through the related section in MyEconLab.

LEARNING OBJECTIVES	KEY TERMS	MYECONLAB PRACTICE
2.1 The Production Possibilities Curve. The production possibilities curve describes all possible combinations of two goods that can be produced, assuming full and efficient employment of resources, a fixed time period, fixed quantity and quality of resources, and fixed technology.	production possibilities curve, 30 technology, 30	• **MyEconLab** Study Plan 2.1
2.2 Applications of the Production Possibilities Curve. The production possibilities curve illustrates the scarcity problem by acting as a production boundary in the face of unlimited wants. Its downward slope implies a trade-off—more of one good means less of another. An increasing opportunity cost situation is shown by a "bowed out" production possibilities curve. Unemployment is reflected by a point inside the curve, signifying lost production. Any production combination on the curve is productively efficient and the one combination that society values the most is allocatively efficient. Economic growth shifts the production possibilities curve outward over time.	productive efficiency, 33 productively inefficient point, 33 allocative efficiency, 34 law of increasing relative cost, 35	• **MyEconLab** Study Plan 2.2

➡ LEARNING OBJECTIVES	KEY TERMS	MYECONLAB PRACTICE
2.3 Consumption Goods versus Capital Goods. A production possibilities curve that involves capital goods and consumption goods illustrates that when we use more of our resources to produce capital goods that enhance future consumption, we must forgo present consumption goods.	consumption, 37	• **MyEconLab** Study Plan 2.3
2.4 Specialization and Greater Productivity. Absolute advantage refers to the ability to produce one unit of a product at a lower labour cost than another producer. Comparative advantage refers to producing a unit of a product at a lower opportunity cost than another producer. According to the comparative advantage principle, the combined production of two producers can be increased if each producer specializes according to comparative advantage. The terms of trade principle states that each producer will gain from specialization and trade, if the terms of trade are between each producer's opportunity cost of production.	specialization, 41 absolute advantage, 41 comparative advantage, 41 division of labour, 44	• **MyEconLab** Study Plan 2.4
2.5 Economic Systems. In a pure command system, the government owns the resources and the three basic questions—what, how, for whom—are answered in a centralized manner by government. In pure capitalism, resources are privately owned and the basic questions are answered in a decentralized manner by individual firms and households interacting in markets. In a mixed economic system, where there is both private and public ownership of resources, the basic questions are partly answered by government and partly by individual firms and households in markets.	economic system, 44 pure command economy, 45 pure capitalist economy, 45 mixed economy, 45	• **MyEconLab** Study Plan 2.5
2.6 Capitalism in More Depth. The key features of pure capitalism include private ownership of resources, self-interest motives, consumer sovereignty, markets and prices, competition, and limited government. Consumer demand and resource availability determine *what* goods and services will be produced; the least costly method will be chosen in deciding *how* the goods will be produced; the degree to which households own marketable resources will determine *for whom* goods are produced.	laissez-faire, 47 three *P*s, 47	• **MyEconLab** Study Plan 2.6

PROBLEMS

(Answers to the odd-numbered problems appear at the back of the book.)

LO 2.1, LO 2.2 Define the production possibilities curve and identify its assumptions; use the production possibilities curve to illustrate the concepts of scarcity, trade-offs, unemployment, productive efficiency, allocative efficiency, increasing opportunity cost, and economic growth.

1. The production possibilities curve for the nation of Epica for the two goods, factories and yachts, for 2008 is described in the accompanying graph.

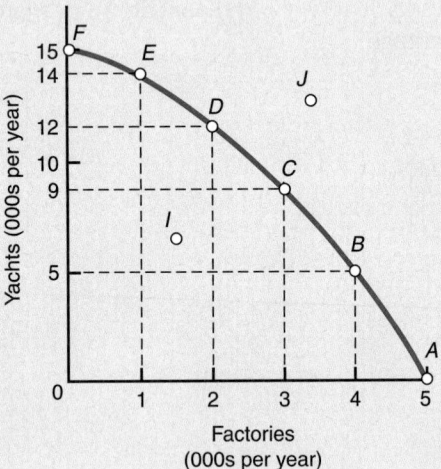

a. If Epica produces 12 000 yachts in 2008, what is the maximum amount of factories that can be produced in 2008?
b. If Epica devotes all its resources to the production of factories, what is the maximum amount of factories that can be produced in 2008?
c. What factors prevent Epica from producing the combination at point *J* in 2008?
d. If Epica is at point *I* in 2008, this situation could conflict with what two socioeconomic goals?
e. What is the opportunity cost of producing an additional factory when moving: (i) from point *E* to *D*? (ii) from point *C* to *B*?
f. What is the opportunity cost of producing an additional yacht when moving: (i) from point *A* to *B*? (ii) from point *E* to *F*?
g. What economic law is illustrated by your answers to parts (e) and (f) above?
h. If society values production combination *D* the most, but Epica is producing combination *C*, this situation conflicts with what socioeconomic goal?
i. How will economic growth affect Epica's production possibilities curve over time?

2. The production possibilities curve for the nation of Fantasia for the two goods, TVs and business machines, for 2007 is described in the accompanying graph.

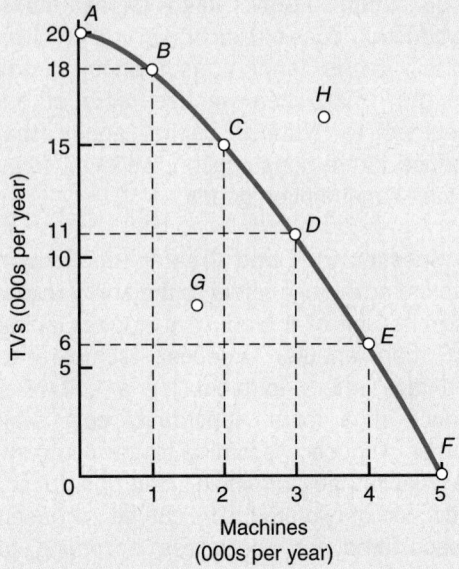

a. If Fantasia produces 2000 machines in 2007, what is the maximum number of TVs that can be produced in 2007?
b. What factors prevent Fantasia from producing the combination at point *H* in 2007?
c. If Fantasia completely specializes in the production of TVs in 2007, what maximum number of TVs could it produce per year?
d. If Fantasia is at point *G* in 2007, this situation could conflict with what two socioeconomic goals?
e. What is the opportunity cost of producing an additional machine when moving from: (i) point *A* to point *B*? (ii) point *D* to point *E*?
f. What economic law is illustrated by your answers to part (e) above?
g. Which of the points *A, B, C, D, E, F, G,* and *H* are productively efficient?
h. If society values the production combination at point *D* the most, but Fantasia is currently producing at point *C*, this situation conflicts with what socioeconomic goal?
i. Which one of the two points—*B* or *E*—would lead to a greater rate of economic growth? Why? What important trade-off is illustrated here?
j. How will economic growth affect Fantasia's production possibilities curve over time?

3. The following table illustrates the marks a student can earn on examinations in economics and biology if the student uses all available hours for study.

Economics	Biology
100	40
90	50
80	60
70	70
60	80
50	90
40	100

Plot this student's production possibilities curve. Does this PPC illustrate increasing or constant opportunity costs?

4. The following sets of numbers represent hypothetical production possibilities for a country in 2008. Plot these points on graph paper.

Cheese	Apples
4	0
3	1.6
2	2.4
1	2.8
0	3.0

Does the law of increasing relative cost seem to hold? Why? On the same graph, plot and draw the production possibilities curve that will represent 10 percent economic growth.

5. Construct a production possibilities curve for a country facing increasing opportunity costs for producing food and video games. Show how the PPC changes given the following events:
   a. A new and better fertilizer is developed.
   b. There is a surge in labour that can be employed in both the agriculture sector and the video game sector.
   c. A new programming language is invented that is less costly to code and is more memory-efficient, enabling the use of smaller games cartridges.
   d. A heat wave and drought result in a decrease of 10 percent in usable farmland.

LO 2.3 Use the production possibilities curve to explain the trade-off between consumption goods and capital goods.

6. Two countries, Workland and Playland, have similar populations and identical production possibilities curves but different preferences. The production possibilities combinations are as follows:

Point	Capital Goods	Consumption Goods
A	0	20
B	1	19
C	2	17
D	3	14
E	4	10
F	5	5

Playland is located at point *B* on the PPC, and Workland is located at point *E*. Assume that this situation continues into the future and that all other things remain the same.
   a. What is Workland's opportunity cost of capital goods in terms of consumption goods?
   b. What is Playland's opportunity cost of capital goods in terms of consumption goods?
   c. How would the PPCs of Workland and Playland be expected to compare with each other 50 years in the future?

7. If, by going to college, you give up the chance to work in your mother's business for 35 hours per week at $7 per hour, what would be your opportunity cost of earning a two-year college diploma? What incentives exist to make you incur that opportunity cost? What are you giving up today in order to have more in the future? Assume that you will need to spend 60 weeks in college to earn a diploma.

LO 2.4 Distinguish between absolute advantage and comparative advantage and use these concepts to explain how specialization and trade can increase production and consumption.

8. What two economic concepts presented in this chapter help explain the marriage premium described in Example 2–4, "Why Men Marry: Is It for Love or the Marriage Premium?"?

9. You can wash, fold, and iron a basket of laundry in two hours and prepare a meal in one hour. Your roommate can wash, fold, and iron a basket of laundry in three hours and prepare a meal in one hour. Should you and your roommate specialize in particular tasks? Why? And if so, who should specialize in which task? Calculate how much labour time you save if you choose to "trade" an appropriate task with your roommate, as opposed to doing it yourself.

LO 2.5, 2.6 Explain the differences between the pure capitalist, pure command, and mixed economic systems; describe the features of pure capitalism and explain how capitalism answers the three basic economic questions.

10. Noah and Nora are partners in a fast food submarine sandwich shop. In one hour, Noah can prepare ten sandwiches and 30 pasta salads. In the same hour, Nora can prepare ten sandwiches and 20 pasta salads.
   a. Who has the absolute advantage in preparing pasta salads?
   b. Who has the comparative advantage in preparing sandwiches?
   c. For each hour spent on specializing in preparing the items in which each partner has a comparative advantage, what will be the net gain in production?

11. Toby and Tony are partners in their popular downtown Italian eatery. In one hour, Toby can produce ten gourmet pizzas and five lasagne supremes. In the same

hour, Tony can prepare five gourmet pizzas and five lasagne supremes.

a. Who has the absolute advantage in producing pizzas?

b. Who has the comparative advantage in producing the lasagne?

c. For each hour spent on specializing in preparing the items in which each partner has a comparative advantage, what will be the net gain in production?

12. State whether each of the following policies is more consistent with the principles of the Conservative party or the New Democratic party.

Policy A: The Canadian government provides tax cuts to parents of young children that amount to $100 per child.

Policy B: The Canadian government expands day-care spaces through the expansion of government-owned and -operated day-care services.

13. What features of capitalism help explain how consumer sovereignty can be achieved with limited government involvement?

14. Briefly explain how capitalism answers the three basic economic questions.

15. The table gives the production techniques and input prices for 100 units of product X.

Production Technique			
Input	Input Unit Price	A (units)	B (units)	C (units)
Labour	$10	6	5	4
Capital	8	5	6	7

a. In a market system, which techniques will be used to produce 100 units of product X?

b. If the market price of a unit of X is $1, which technique will lead to the greatest profit?

c. The output of X is still 100 units, but the price of labour and capital changes so that labour is $8 and capital is $10. Which production technique will be used?

d. Using the information in part (c), what is the potential profit of producing 100 units of X?

APPENDIX B

THE PRODUCTION POSSIBILITIES CURVE AND COMPARATIVE ADVANTAGE

The gains from specialization and trade can be effectively illustrated by the production possibilities curve model. Let us assume that two Canadian family farms, the Pulets and the Dowbys, can produce chicken and perogies on each of their farm operations. The Pulets can produce one kilogram of chicken per hour or one kilogram of perogies per hour. The Dowbys can produce two kilograms of chicken per hour or eight kilograms of perogies per hour. Armed with this productivity information, we can proceed to construct production possibilities for each family farm.

Before Specialization and Trade

We will construct a daily production possibilities curve for the two products, chicken and perogies, for each family farm, by assuming that each family works an eight-hour day.

The Pulets' production possibilities curve in Figure B–1 part (a) shows that in a typical day, if they devote all eight hours to producing perogies, they can produce eight kilograms of perogies per day, which is at point *A*. Alternatively, if the Pulets devote all of the eight hours to producing chicken, they can produce eight kilograms of chicken per day, which is at point *B* in Figure B–1 part (a). Currently, the Pulets are not specializing and trading, and so they are producing and consuming six kilograms of perogies and two kilograms of chicken on a daily basis, which is at point *C* in Figure B–1 part (a).

The Dowbys' production possibilities curve in Figure B–1 part (b) shows that in a typical day, if they devote all eight hours to producing perogies, they can produce 64 kilograms of perogies per day, which is at point *A*. Alternatively, if the Dowbys devote all of the eight hours to producing chicken, they can produce 16 kilograms of chicken per day, which is at point *B* in Figure B–1 part (b). Currently, the Dowbys are not specializing and trading, and so they are producing and consuming 48 kilograms of perogies and four kilograms of chicken on a daily basis, which is at point *C* in Figure B–1 part (b).

FIGURE B–1

The Before-Specialization, Before-Trade Production Possibilities

In part (a), the Pulets have chosen to produce and consume two kilograms of chicken and six kilograms of perogies. In part (b), the Dowbys have chosen to produce and consume four kilograms of chicken and 48 kilograms of perogies.

Part (a)
Pulets' Production Possibilities Curve

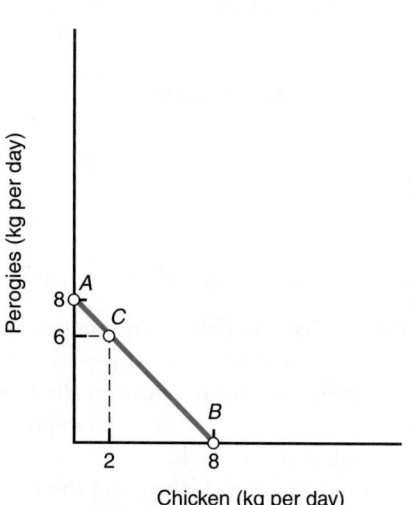

Part (b)
Dowbys' Production Possibilities Curve

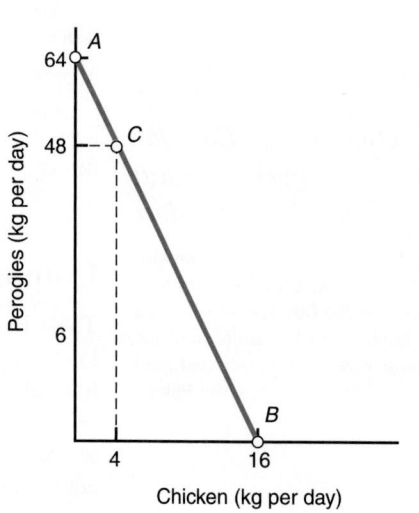

You will notice that both production possibilities curves are assumed to be straight lines. This implies that the opportunity cost of production will stay constant as each farm specializes in the production of one of its products. This assumption will simplify our production possibilities illustration of the gains from trade and specialization.

Figure B–1 illustrates that the Dowbys can produce more of both products, when compared with the Pulets, despite the fact that both family farms are employing the same level of total labour input on a daily basis. This implies that the Dowbys can produce a kilogram of each product at a lower labour cost than the Pulets. In other words, the Dowbys have the absolute advantage in the production of chicken and in the production of perogies.

Since the Dowbys have the absolute advantage in the production of each product, it may appear that there would be no incentive for the Dowbys to specialize and trade with the Pulets. However, as we will explain below, the Pulets do have the comparative advantage in the production of chicken, and therefore, the Dowbys can increase their consumption possibilities by specializing and trading with the Pulets.

After Specialization and Before Trade

As noted in Chapter 2, we can identify the family farm that has the comparative advantage in each product by computing opportunity costs.

Opportunity Costs Incurred by the Pulets

According to Figure B–1 part (a), if the Pulets switch production possibilities from point *A* to point *B*, eight additional kilograms of chicken can be produced by giving up eight kilograms of perogies. Therefore, one additional kilogram of chicken has an opportunity cost or sacrifice of one kilogram of perogies on the Pulets' farm. If the Pulets switch production possibilities from point *B* to point *A* in Figure B–1 part (a), you can see that one additional kilogram of perogies has an opportunity cost of one kilogram of chicken. These opportunity costs are summarized in Table B–1.

Opportunity Costs Incurred by the Dowbys

According to Figure B–1 part (b), if the Dowbys switched production possibilities from point *A* to point *B*, 16 additional kilograms of chicken can be produced by giving up 64 kilograms of perogies. Therefore, one additional kilogram of chicken has an opportunity cost of four kilograms of perogies. If the Dowbys were to switch production possibilities from point *B* to point *A* in Figure B–1 part (b), you can see that one additional kilogram of perogies has an opportunity cost of one-quarter of a kilogram of chicken. These opportunity costs are summarized in Table B–1.

TABLE B–1

Opportunity Costs for Each Farm for Each Product

The Pulets can produce a kilogram of chicken at a lower opportunity cost than the Dowbys. The Dowbys can produce a kilogram of perogies at a lower opportunity cost than the Pulets.

	Opportunity cost of 1 kg of chicken:	Opportunity cost of 1 kg of perogies:
Pulets	1 kg of perogies	1 kg of chicken
Dowbys	4 kg of perogies	1/4 = 0.25 kg of chicken

Comparative Advantage Principle

Table B–1 indicates that the Pulets can produce an additional kilogram of chicken at a lower opportunity cost, one kilogram of perogies, than the Dowbys' opportunity cost of four kilograms of perogies. This implies that the Dowbys can produce an additional kilogram of the other product, perogies, at a lower opportunity cost than the Pulets (0.25 kilograms versus one kilogram of chicken). In other words, the Pulets have the comparative advantage in the production of chicken, and the Dowbys have the comparative advantage in the production of perogies.

Comparative Advantage Principle states that the combined production of two producers can be enhanced if each producer specializes in the product in which it has the comparative advantage.

The **Comparative Advantage Principle** states that the combined production of two producers can be enhanced if each producer specializes in the product in which it has the comparative advantage. According to this principle, the combined daily production of both family farms can be increased by having the Pulets specialize in the production of chicken and the Dowbys specialize in the production of perogies.

Figure B–1 part (a) reminds us that before specialization, the Pulets were producing two kilograms of chicken and six kilograms of perogies. Figure B–1 part (b) indicates that before specialization, the Dowbys were producing four kilograms of chicken and 48 kilograms of perogies. Therefore, the combined family farm production before specialization was 2 + 4 = 6 kilograms of chicken and was 6 + 48 = 54 kilograms of perogies.

According to Figure B–1 part (a), if the Pulets specialized in the production of chicken, they would switch production possibilities to point *B* and produce eight kilograms of chicken and zero kilograms of perogies per day. Figure B–1 part (b) indicates that if the Dowbys specialized in perogies, they would switch production possibilities to point *A* and produce 64 kilograms of perogies and zero kilograms of chicken per day. Note that by specializing according to comparative advantage, the combined family farm production of chicken has increased from six kilograms to eight kilograms per day. Similarly, the combined family farm production of perogies has increased from 54 kilograms to 64 kilograms per day.

After Specialization and After Trade

With each family farm specializing according to comparative advantage, the need will arise to trade the surplus production between family farms. Under specialization, the only way the Pulets can obtain perogies is by trading off some chicken. Similarly, the Dowbys will have to trade some of their perogies in order to consume some chicken. In trading with each other, the question now becomes, how much of one product should each farm trade away in order to get an additional kilogram of the other product?

The Terms of Trade Principle

Terms of trade The amount of one product that must be traded in order to obtain an additional unit of another product.

Terms of Trade Principle Each producer will gain from specialization and trade if the terms of trade are between the producers' opportunity costs of production.

The **terms of trade** for chicken is the amount of the other product, perogies, that must be traded in order to obtain one additional kilogram of chicken. The **Terms of Trade Principle** states that each producer will gain from specialization and trade if the terms of trade is between the producers' opportunity costs of production.

As an example, a mutually beneficial terms of trade for one kilogram of chicken would be anywhere between one kilogram of perogies (opportunity cost at the Pulets farm) and four kilograms of perogies (opportunity cost at the Dowbys farm). Thus, one acceptable terms of trade for one kilogram of chicken would be two kilograms of perogies. Assuming this terms of trade and assuming that the Pulets end up trading five kilograms of their chicken in exchange for 10 kilograms of perogies with the Dowbys, Table B–2 illustrates how both family farms can increase their consumption possibilities.

THE PULETS' GAIN FROM TRADE. According to Table B–2, if the Pulets specialize and produce eight kilograms of chicken and then trade away five kilograms of chicken for 10 kilograms of perogies, they end up consuming 8 − 5 = 3 kilograms of chicken and 0 + 10 = 10 kilograms of perogies, after specialization and after trade. On the basis of point *C* of Figure B–1, the Pulets produced and consumed only two kilograms of chicken and six kilograms of perogies, before specialization and trade. In other words, specialization and trade increased the Pulets' consumption of chicken and perogies by one kilogram and four kilograms per day, respectively.

Figure B–2 part (a) describes the Pulets' gain as a rightward shift from point *C* on the Pulets' production possibilities curve to point *C1* on the Pulets' new consumption possibilities curve. Note that the slope of the Pulets' new consumption possibilities curve is 2, which is based on the terms of trade for one kilogram of chicken.

THE DOWBYS' GAIN FROM TRADE. Table B–2 also describes how the Dowbys can enhance their consumption possibilities with the terms of trade of two kilograms of perogies for one kilogram of chicken. Before trade and specialization, the Dowbys produced and consumed four kilograms of chicken and 48 kilograms of perogies (point *C* in Figure B–1 part (b)). After trade and specialization, the Dowbys can consume five kilograms of chicken and 54 kilograms of perogies. Specialization and trade increased the Dowbys' consumption of chicken and perogies by one kilogram and six kilograms per day, respectively.

Figure B–2 part (b) describes the Dowbys' gain as a rightward shift from point *C* on the Dowbys' production possibilities curve to point *C1* on the Dowbys' new consumption possibilities curve. Again, note that the slope of the Dowbys' new consumption possibilities curve is 2, which is based on the terms of trade for one kilogram of chicken.

In summary, we have just shown how the Dowbys can benefit by specializing and trading with the Pulets, despite the fact that the Dowbys have the absolute advantage in both products. This is because the opportunity costs of production differ between both family farms. In other words, *the gains from specialization and trade are based on comparative advantage and not absolute advantage.*

TABLE B–2

Gains from Specialization and Trade

After specialization and trade, the Pulets gain one kilogram of chicken and four kilograms of perogies. The Dowbys gain one kilogram of chicken and six kilograms of perogies.

Farm	(1) Production Before Specialization	(2) Production After Specialization	(3) Trade: Sells (–) Buys (+)	(4) = (2) + (3) Consumption After Specialization and Trade	(5) = (4) – (1) Gains from Specialization and Trade
Pulets					
Chicken	2 kg	8 kg	–5 kg	8 – 5 = 3 kg	3 – 2 = +1 kg
Perogies	6 kg	0 kg	+10 kg	0 + 10 = 10 kg	10 – 6 = +4 kg
Dowbys					
Chicken	4 kg	0 kg	+5 kg	0 + 5 = 5 kg	5 – 4 = +1 kg
Perogies	48 kg	64 kg	–10 kg	64 – 10 = 54 kg	54 – 48 = +6 kg

FIGURE B–2

After-Specialization, After-Trade Consumption Possibilities

In part (a) and part (b), specialization and trade allow both the Pulets and the Dowbys to increase their consumption possibilities beyond their production possibilities.

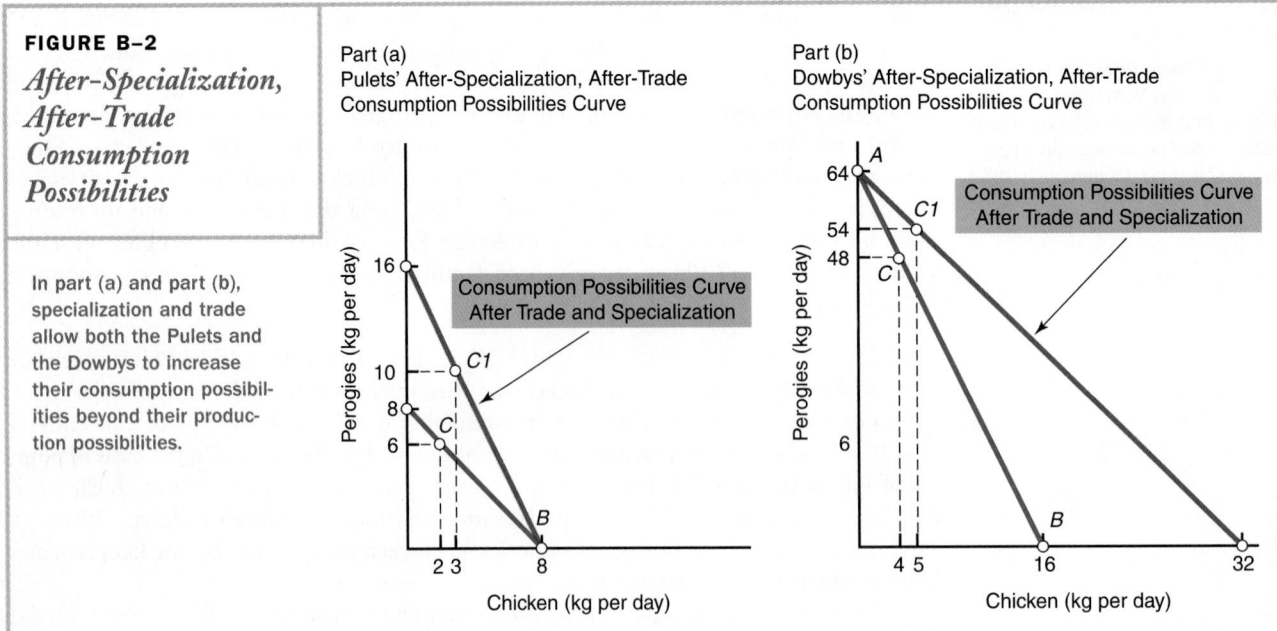

Part (a)
Pulets' After-Specialization, After-Trade Consumption Possibilities Curve

Part (b)
Dowbys' After-Specialization, After-Trade Consumption Possibilities Curve

APPENDIX SUMMARY

1. Absolute advantage refers to the ability to produce one unit of a product at a lower labour cost than another producer. Comparative advantage refers to the ability to produce a unit of a product at a lower opportunity cost than another producer.

2. According to the Comparative Advantage Principle, the combined production of two producers can be increased if each producer specializes according to comparative advantage. This principle applies even in those cases where one producer has the absolute advantage in both product areas.

3. The terms of trade for one product, *A*, is the amount of the other product, *B*, that must be traded in order to obtain one additional unit of *A*.

4. The Terms of Trade Principle states that each producer will gain from specialization and trade if the terms of trade is between the producers' opportunity costs of production. In this case, consumption possibilities can exceed production possibilities.

APPENDIX PROBLEMS

(Answers to the odd-numbered problems appear at the back of the book.)

B–1. Answer each of the following on the basis of the before-specialization and trade production possibilities for the Martin and the Richard families described in the accompanying two graphs. Before specialization and trade, each family is producing and consuming production combination *C*.

a. Which family has the absolute advantage in the production of each product?

b. Compute the opportunity cost of producing one litre of beer for each family.

c. Which family has the comparative advantage in the production of each product?

d. Before specialization, each family is producing combination *C* on its respective production possibilities curve. Assuming that each family decides to specialize in its area of comparative advantage, compute the gains in total combined production for each product.

e. In order for both families to share the gains from specialization, the terms of trade for one litre of beer should be somewhere between ___ and ___ litres of wine.

Martins' Production Possibilities

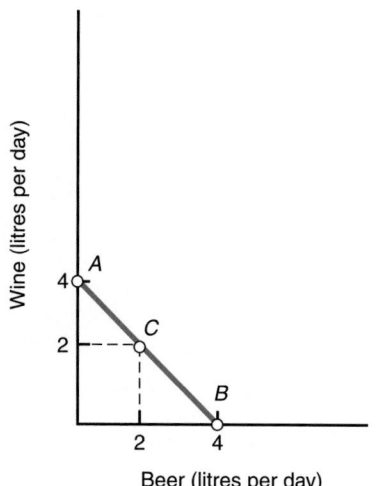

Richards' Production Possibilities

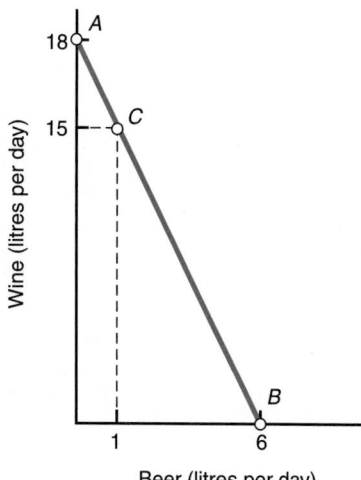

B-2. Answer each of the following on the basis of the before-specialization and trade production possibilities for the nations of Mazland and Attica for the two products, cell phones and digital cameras, as shown in the accompanying graphs. Before specialization and trade, each nation is producing and consuming production combination *C*.

a. Which nation has the absolute advantage in the production of each product?

b. Compute the opportunity cost of producing one camera for each nation.

c. Which nation has the comparative advantage in the production of each product?

d. Before specialization, both nations are producing combination *C* on their respective production possibilities curve. Assuming that each nation decides to specialize in its area of comparative advantage, compute the gains in total combined production for each product.

e. In order for both nations to share the gains from specialization, the terms of trade for one camera should be somewhere between ___ and ___ phones.

Mazland's Production Possibilities

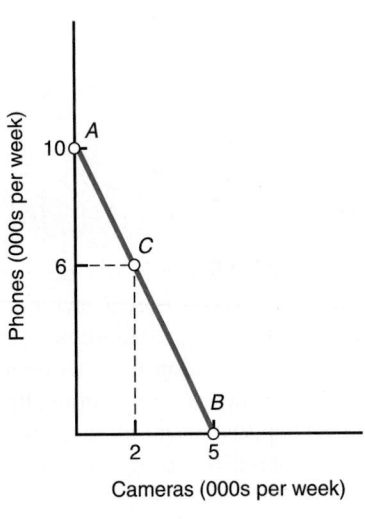

Attica's Production Possibilities

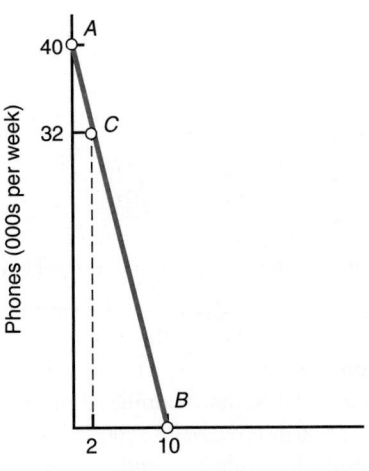

3

Demand and Supply

➡️ **LEARNING OBJECTIVES**

After reading this chapter, you should be able to:

3.1 Explain the law of demand.

3.2 Distinguish between a change in quantity demanded and a change in demand.

3.3 Explain the law of supply.

3.4 Distinguish between a change in quantity supplied and a change in supply.

3.5 Explain how the forces of demand and supply interact to determine equilibrium price and quantity.

3.6 Describe how changes in demand and supply can change equilibrium price and quantity.

MyEconLab helps you master each objective and study more efficiently. See end of chapter for details.

It started in 1999, with busloads of American seniors travelling to Canada to purchase low-priced prescription drugs. It is estimated that in 2004 U.S. consumers spent over $800 million on pharmaceuticals sold by Canadian Internet drugstores. For this Canadian export industry to flourish, Canadian health professionals have to co-sign prescriptions for U.S. patients they have not seen. In 2007, as the U.S. congress pushes to expand this drug trade with Canada, Canadian politicians and consumer groups are lobbying to restrict pharmaceutical exports to the United States.

The theory presented in this chapter will help you understand why selling drugs online is such a contentious issue in both Canada and the United States.

More than 200 million North American residences owned wireless cellular phones in 2006. This is a huge jump from the mere 200 000 who owned them in 1985. Since 1992, two out of every three new telephone numbers in North America have been assigned to cellular phones. In Canada, the use of cellphones is about to surpass the use of traditional wire-line phones. In 2006, there were 18 million wireless subscribers and roughly the same number of wire-line phone subscribers in Canada. These numbers do not include the 740 000 subscribers using cable telephony services.

There are several reasons for the spectacular growth in cellular phone use, not the least being the dramatic reduction in both price and size due to improved and cheaper computer chips that go into making them. There is something else at work, though. It has to do with crime. In a recent survey, 46 percent of new cellular phone users said that personal safety was the main reason they bought a portable phone. The tools of demand and supply, presented in this chapter, will help you to better understand how prices can be declining in an industry that is experiencing explosive growth.

SOURCES: STEVE ROSENBUSH, ROGER CROCKETT, CHRISTOPHER PALMERI, AND PETER BURROWS. "A WIRELESS WORLD: IN A FEW YEARS MOBILE PHONES WILL DOMINATE U.S. COMMUNICATIONS." *BUSINESS WEEK,* ISSUE 3855, OCTOBER 27, 2003, P. 110., "CELLPHONE USE SET TO SURPASS LAND LINES; WIRELESS HIGH-GROWTH," *EDMONTON JOURNAL*, MAY 15, 2007, FINAL EDITION, P. E3; KRISTEN BECKMAN, "FROM THE FIRST CELL-PHONE CALL TO 200 MILLION WIRELESS SUBSCRIBERS... CELEBRATING 25 YEARS OF COVERING THE WIRELESS INDUSTRY," MAY 22, 2006, RCR WIRELESS NEWS, 12 VOLUME 25, NUMBER 21. COPYRIGHT © 2006 CRAIN COMMUNICATIONS, INC. ALL RIGHTS RESERVED.

3.1 The Law of Demand

Demand Refers to the quantities of a specific good or service that individuals are willing to purchase at various possible prices, other things being constant.

Law of demand The observation that there is an inverse relationship between the price of any good and its quantity demanded, holding other factors equal.

Demand has a special meaning in economics. It refers to the quantities of specific goods or services that individuals, either singly or as a group, will purchase at various possible prices, other things being constant. We can, therefore, talk about the demand for microprocessor chips, French fries, compact disc players, and health care.

Associated with the concept of demand is the **law of demand**, which can be stated as follows:

> When the price of a good goes up, people buy less of it, other things being equal. When the price of a good goes down, people buy more of it, other things being equal.

The law of demand tells us that the quantity demanded of any commodity is inversely related to its price, other things being equal. In an inverse relationship, one variable moves up in value when the other moves down. The law of demand states that a change in price causes the quantity demanded to change in the *opposite* direction.

Note that we tacked onto the end of the law of demand the statement "other things being equal." We referred to this in Chapter 1 as the *ceteris paribus* assumption. It means, for example, that when we predict that people will buy fewer CD players if their price goes up, we are holding constant the price of all other goods in the economy as well as people's incomes. Implicitly, therefore, if we are assuming that no other prices change when we examine the price behaviour of CD players, we are looking at the *relative* price of CD players.

The law of demand is supported by millions of observations of how people behave in the marketplace. Theoretically, it can be derived from an economic model based on rational behaviour, as was discussed in Chapter 1. Basically, if nothing else changes and the price of a good falls, the lower price induces us to buy more over a certain period of time. This is because we can enjoy additional net gains that were unavailable at the higher price. For the most part, if you examine your own purchasing behaviour, you will see that it generally follows the law of demand.

Relative Prices versus Money Prices

Relative price Any commodity's price in terms of another commodity.

Money price The actual price that you pay in dollars and cents for any good or service at any point in time.

The **relative price** of any commodity is its price in terms of another commodity. The actual price that you pay in dollars and cents for any good or service at any point in time is called its **money price**. Consider an example that you might hear quite often around older friends or relatives. "When I bought my first new car, it cost only $1500." The implication, of course, is that the price of cars today is outrageously high because the average new car might cost $20 000. But that is not an accurate comparison. What was the price of the average house during that same year? Perhaps it was only $12 000. By comparison, then, given that houses today average about $200 000, the current price of a new car does not sound so far out of line, does it?

The point is that comparing money prices during different time periods does not tell you much. You have to find out relative prices. Consider a simplified example of the price comparison of prerecorded DVDs versus prerecorded videocassettes between last year and this year. In Table 3–1, we show the money prices of DVDs and videocassettes for two years during which time both have gone up. That means that we have to pay out more for DVDs and more for videocassettes in today's dollars. If we look, though, at the relative prices of DVDs and videocassettes, we find that last year, DVDs were twice as expensive as videocassettes, whereas this year they are only 1.5 times as expensive. Conversely, if we compare videocassettes to DVDs, last year they cost only half as much as DVDs, but today they cost about 67 percent as much. In the one-year period, though both prices have gone up in money terms, the relative price of DVDs has fallen (and equivalently, the relative price of videocassettes has risen).

TABLE 3-1

Money Price versus Relative Price

The money prices of both DVDs and videocassettes have risen. But the relative price of DVDs has fallen (or conversely, the relative price of videocassettes has risen).

	Money Price		Relative Price	
	Last Year	This Year	Last Year	This Year
DVDs	$20	$24	$20 / $10 = 2.0	$24 / $16 = 1.5
Videocassettes	$10	$16	$10 / $20 = 0.5	$16 / $24 = 0.67

When evaluating the effects of price changes, we must always compare prices per *constant-quality unit*. Sometimes, relative price changes occur because the quality of a product improves, thereby bringing about a decrease in the item's effective price per constant-quality unit.

The Demand Schedule

Let us take a hypothetical demand situation to see how the inverse relationship between the price and the quantity demanded looks (holding other things equal). We will consider the quantity of rewriteable DVDs demanded *per year* by one person. Without stating the *time dimension*, we could not make sense out of this demand relationship because the numbers would be different if we were talking about the quantity demanded per month or the quantity demanded per decade.

In addition to implicitly or explicitly stating a time dimension for a demand relationship, we are also implicitly referring to constant-quality units of the good or service in question. Prices are always expressed in constant-quality units in order to avoid the problem of comparing commodities that are, in fact, not truly comparable.

In part (a) of Figure 3–1, we see that if the price were $1 per DVD, 50 of them would be bought each year by our representative individual, but if the price were $5 per DVD, only 10 would be bought each year. This reflects the law of demand. Part (a) is also simply called *demand*, or a *demand schedule*, because it gives a schedule of alternative quantities demanded per year at different possible prices.

The Demand Curve

Tables expressing relationships between two variables can be represented in graphical terms. To do this, we need only construct a graph that has the price per constant-quality DVD on the vertical axis, and the quantity measured in constant-quality DVDs per year on the horizontal axis. All we have to do is take combinations *A* through *E* from part (a) of Figure 3–1 and plot those points in part (b). Now we connect the points with a smooth line, and *voilà*, we have a *demand curve*.[1] It is downward-sloping

---

[1]Even though we call them "curves," for the purposes of exposition, we often draw straight lines. In many real-world situations, demand and supply curves will, in fact, be lines that do curve. To connect the points in part (b) with a line, we assume that for all prices in between the ones shown, the quantities demanded will be found along that line.

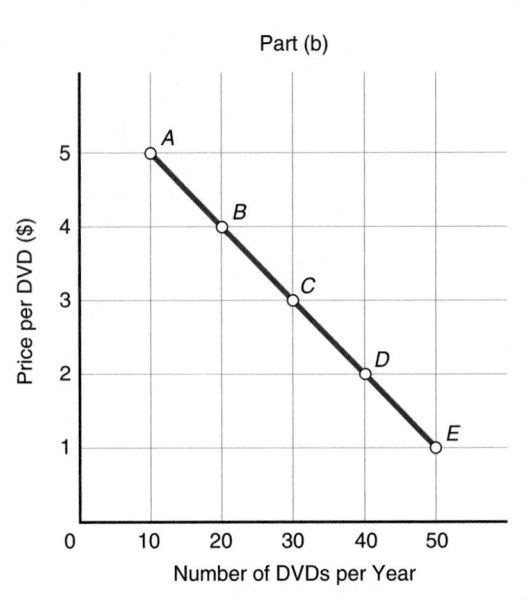

FIGURE 3–1

The Individual Demand Schedule and the Individual Demand Curve

In part (a), we show combinations A through E of the quantities of DVDs demanded, measured in constant-quality units at prices ranging from $5 down to $1 per DVD. In part (b), we plot combinations A through E on a grid. The result is the individual demand curve for DVDs.

Part (a)

Combination	Price per Constant-Quality DVD	Quantity of Constant-Quality DVDs per Year
A	$5	10
B	4	20
C	3	30
D	2	40
E	1	50

Demand curve A graphical representation of the law of demand.

(from left to right) to indicate the inverse relationship between the price of DVDs and the quantity demanded per year. Our presentation of demand schedules and curves applies equally well to all commodities, including toothpicks, hamburgers, textbooks, credit, and labour services. Remember, the **demand curve** is simply a graphical representation of the law of demand.

Individual versus Market Demand Curves

Market All of the arrangements that individuals have for exchanging with one another.

Market demand Determined by adding the individual demand at each price for all the consumers in the market.

The demand schedule shown in part (a) of Figure 3–1 and the resulting demand curve shown in part (b) are both given for one individual. As we shall see, determining price in the **market** (all of the arrangements that individuals have for exchanging with one another) depends on, among other things, the *market demand* for a particular commodity. The way in which we measure a **market demand** schedule and derive a market demand curve for DVDs or any other commodity is by adding the individual demand at each price for all consumers in the market. Suppose that the market for DVDs consists of only two buyers: buyer 1, for whom we have already shown the demand schedule in Figure 3–1, and buyer 2, whose demand schedule is displayed in Figure 3–2, part (a), column 3. Column 1 of Figure 3–2, part (a) shows the price, and column 2 gives the quantity demanded by buyer 1 (data taken` directly from Figure 3–1). Column 4 states the total quantity demanded at each price, obtained by adding columns 2 and 3. Graphically, in part (d) of Figure 3–2, we add the demand curves of buyer 1 [part (b)] and buyer 2 [part (c)] to derive the market demand curve.

There are, of course, literally millions of potential consumers for DVDs. We will assume that the summation of all of the consumers in the market results in a demand schedule, given in part (a) of Figure 3–3, and a demand curve, given in part (b). The quantity demanded is now measured in millions of units per year. Remember, part (b) in Figure 3–3 shows the market demand curve for the millions of users of DVDs. The "market" demand curve that we derived in Figure 3–2 assumed that there were only two buyers in the entire market. This is why that demand curve is not a smooth line—whereas the true market demand curve in part (b) of Figure 3–3 is—and has no kinks.

You have likely heard about the increased interest in using technology such as radio frequency identification tags (RFID tags) to track items such as manufacturing, wholesale, and retail merchandise; precious jewellery and art; and library books at all times in their life cycle. As Example 3–1 implies, the increased use of RFID tags can be illustrated graphically as a downward movement along the demand curve for RFID tags.

FIGURE 3-2

The Horizontal Summation of Two Demand Schedules

Part (a) shows how to sum the demand schedule for one buyer with that of another buyer. Column 2 shows the quantity demanded by buyer 1, taken from part (a) of Figure 3-1. Column 4 is the sum of columns 2 and 3. We plot the demand curve for buyer 1 in part (b) and the demand curve for buyer 2 in part (c). When we add those two demand curves horizontally, we get the market demand curve for two buyers, shown in part (d).

Part (a)

(1) Price per DVD	(2) Buyer 1 Quantity Demanded	(3) Buyer 2 Quantity Demanded	(4) = (2) + (3) Combined Quantity Demanded per Year
$5	10	10	20
4	20	20	40
3	30	40	70
2	40	50	90
1	50	60	110

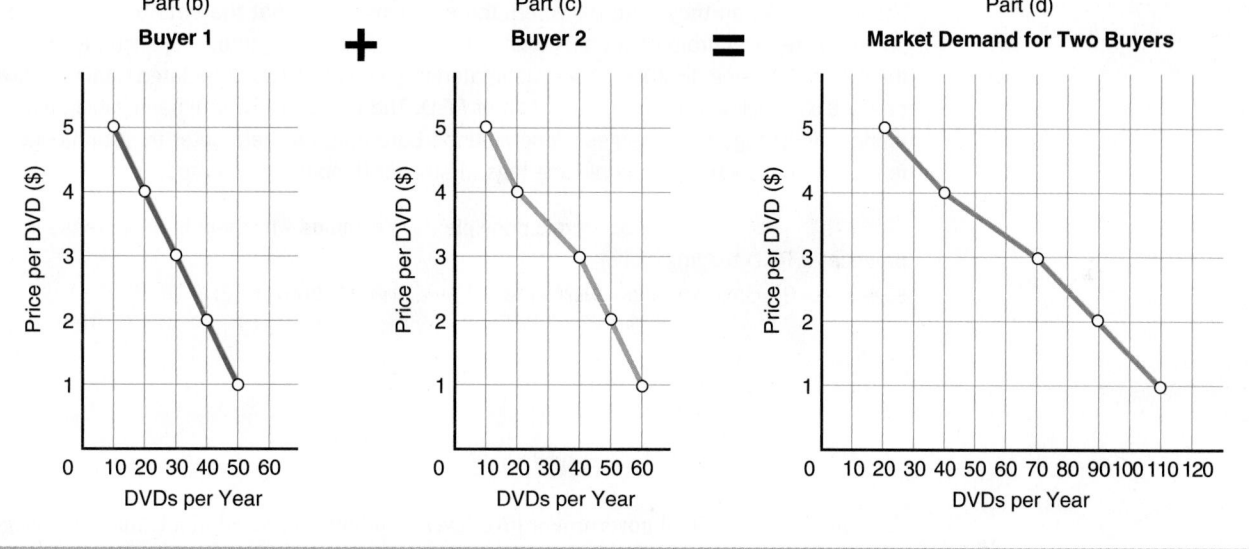

FIGURE 3-3

The Market Demand Schedule for DVDs

In part (a), we add up the millions of existing demand schedules for DVDs. In part (b), we plot the quantities from part (a) on a grid; connecting them produces the market demand curve for DVDs.

Part (a)

Price per Constant-Quality DVD	Total Quantity Demanded of Constant-Quality DVDs per Year (millions)
$5	20
4	40
3	60
2	80
1	100

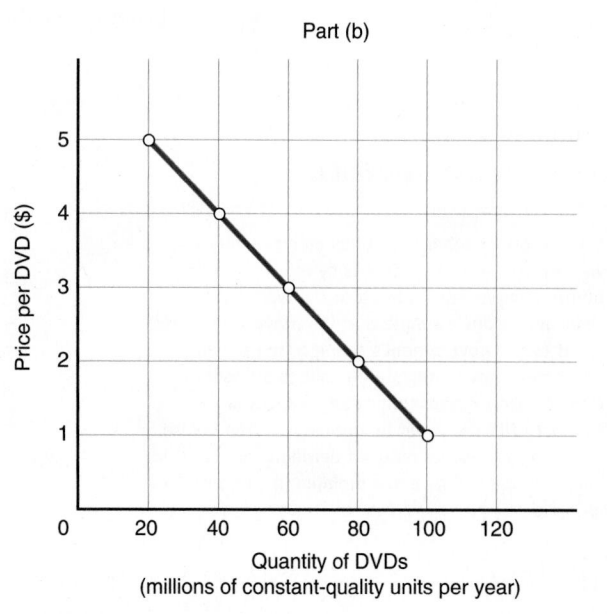

Why RFID Tags Are Catching On Fast

An RFID tag contains a tiny microchip and a radio antenna, and it emits a unique signal that a computer-operated reader can use to track any item to which the tag is attached. In principle, any tagged item can be tracked as it travels in planes, trucks, and ships, through ports and warehouses, onto retailers' shelves, through checkout lines, and into homes and offices.

Just a couple of years ago, the price of an RFID tag was about 30 cents. It has now dropped to 15 cents, and in just a few more years the price is likely to decline to not much more than a nickel. Given the trend in RFID prices, an increasing number of tags have been put to use by retailers, hospitals, trucking firms, airlines, railroads, and shipping lines.

In June 2006, Staples Business Depot piloted RFID tagging with four suppliers and one retail location in Toronto. Suppliers placed RFID tags on pallets and cases bound for Staples, and when they were delivered, the company found that the time to process each pallet was reduced from nearly 18 minutes to less than three minutes, significantly reducing the cost of handling. In 2006, it was estimated that Wal-Mart and other large retailers saved nearly $100 million due to the adoption of RFID. The European central bank, which already embeds RFID tags in the largest denomination Euro notes to help deter theft and counterfeiting, is now contemplating placing tags in smaller denomination notes.

For critical analysis: What economic principle (law) explains why there is an increase in the practice of RFID tagging?

Source: Ken Hunt, "Are you reading me?" *Globe and Mail*, April 12, 2007, p. 28.

3.2 Shifts in Demand

Assume that the federal government gives every student registered in a Canadian college, university, or technical school a personal computer that uses DVDs. The demand curve shown in part (b) of Figure 3–3 is no longer an accurate representation of the total market demand for DVDs. There will now be an increase in the number of DVDs demanded *at each and every possible price*. What we have to do is shift the curve outward, or to the right, to represent the rise in demand. The demand curve in Figure 3–4 will shift from D_1 to D_2. Take any price, say, $3 per DVD. Originally, before the federal government giveaway of personal computers, the amount demanded at $3 was 60 million DVDs per year. After

FIGURE 3–4

A Shift in the Demand Curve

If some factor other than price changes, the only way we can show its effect is by moving the entire demand curve, say, from D_1 to D_2. We have assumed in our example that the move was precipitated by the government's giving a free personal computer to every registered college student in Canada. That meant that at all prices, a larger number of DVDs would be demanded than before. Curve D_3 represents reduced demand compared to curve D_1, caused by a law prohibiting computers on campus.

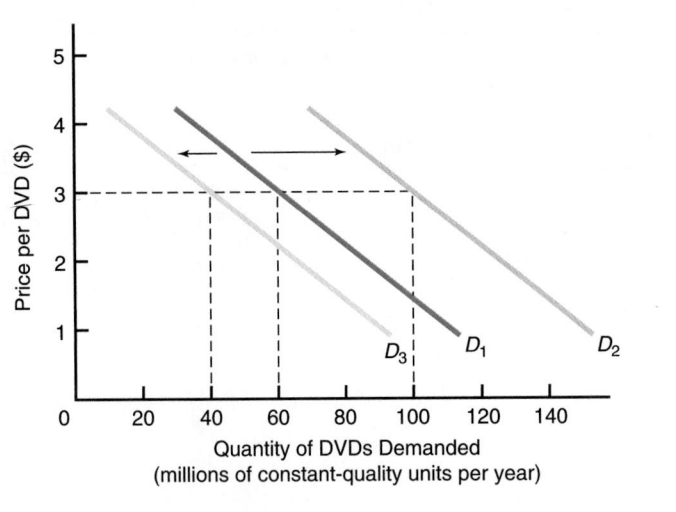

the government giveaway, however, the quantity demanded at $3 is 100 million DVDs per year. What we have seen is a shift in the demand for DVDs.

The shift can also go in the opposite direction. What if colleges uniformly outlawed the use of personal computers by students? Such a regulation would cause a shift inward—to the left—of the demand curve for DVDs. In Figure 3–4, the demand curve would shift to D_3; the amount demanded would now be less at each and every possible price.

The Other Determinants of Demand

The demand curve in part (b) of Figure 3–3 is drawn with other things held constant, specifically all of the other factors that determine how much will be bought. There are many such determinants. The major ones are income; tastes and preferences; the prices of related goods; expectations regarding future prices, future incomes, and future product availability; and population (market size). Let us examine each determinant more closely.

INCOME. For most goods, an increase in income will lead to an increase in demand. The phrase *increase in demand* always refers to a comparison between two different demand curves. Thus, for most goods, an increase in income will lead to a rightward shift in the position of the demand curve from, say, D_1 to D_2 in Figure 3–4. You can avoid confusion about shifts in curves by always relating a rise in demand to a rightward shift in the demand curve and a fall in demand to a leftward shift in the demand curve.

Goods for which the demand rises when income rises are called **normal goods**. Most goods, such as shoes, computers, and CDs, are "normal goods." For some goods, however, demand *falls* as income rises. These are called **inferior goods**. Beans might be an example. As households get richer, they tend to spend less and less on beans and more and more on meat. (The terms *normal* and *inferior* are merely part of the economist's terminology; no value judgments are implied by or associated with them.)

Remember, a shift to the left in the demand curve represents a fall in demand, and a shift to the right represents a rise, or increase, in demand.

Example 3–2 describes the long-term trends affecting the global demand for chocolate bars. After reading this example, we will ask you to explain how the market demand curve for chocolate bars is shifting.

Normal goods Goods for which demand rises as income rises.

Inferior goods Goods for which demand falls as income rises.

EXAMPLE 3–2   **Chocoholics Beware**

In April 2007, Hershey Co. and Mars Inc., two of the world's largest chocolate bar makers, announced that they will be hiking the prices they charge retailers in the United States for their chocolate bars by as much as 5 percent. Industry observers predict that consumers can expect the price of the average chocolate bar to increase by about five cents (U.S.). Canadian consumers can expect a similar hike in the near future. In Canada, in 2007, the most popular chocolate bars sell for $1.19 (Canadian) in corner stores and $1.25 in vending machines.

Higher incomes in developing countries like China, as well as the perceived cancer-fighting antioxidant health benefits of eating dark chocolate, are enhancing the long-term demand for chocolate bars.

The chocolate manufacturers are also being affected by the same input cost pressures as other food suppliers. Escalating world oil prices and the desire of countries such as the United States and China to be more energy self-sufficient have caused an increasing amount of sugar and corn, key ingredients for candy bars, to be used for the production of environment-friendly fuels, such as ethanol, instead of serving as inputs to food and candy products. As a result, the costs of making chocolate bars have significantly increased.

For critical analysis: According to this example, are chocolate bars normal or inferior goods in China? Explain. Using a diagram, explain what is happening to the global market demand curve for chocolate bars.

SOURCE: DANA FLAVELLE, "COCOA FINDS ITS SWEET SPOT; AS PRICES FOR THE FLAVOURFUL BEANS SOAR ON GLOBAL MARKETS, IT MAY BE TIME TO STOCK UP ON CHOCOLATE," TORONTO STAR, APRIL 6, 2007, ONTARIO EDITION, P. F1.

TASTES AND PREFERENCES. A change in consumer tastes in favour of a good can shift its demand curve outward to the right. When Frisbees® became the rage, the demand curve for them shifted outward to the right; when the rage died out, the demand curve shifted inward to the left. Fashions depend to a large extent on people's tastes and preferences. Economists have little to say about the determination of tastes; they have no "good" theories of taste determination or why people buy one brand of a product rather than others. Advertisers, however, do have various theories that they use in trying to make consumers prefer their products to those of competitors.

Example 3–3 illustrates how taste-related factors have recently affected the demand for hair dye.

EXAMPLE 3–3 **Brunettes Now Have More Fun**

In the 1960s, manufacturers of hair dye aired television and radio commercials claiming that "Blondes Have More Fun" and that "Gentlemen Prefer Blondes." For years thereafter, purchases of blonde hair colourings were a significantly higher share of total U.S. expenditures on hair dyes.

Women's tastes in hair colour began to change in the mid-2000s, however. More of the top female stars of stage and screen are brunettes, such as Jennifer Lopez and Catherine Zeta-Jones. In addition, there has been an increase in U.S. populations of Hispanic, Asian, and Arabic women, whose natural hair shades tend to be brunette colours. Finally, graying women from the baby boom generation born between the mid-1940s and the late 1950s have found that darker shades better cover gray and require less maintenance.

For critical analysis: Explain how various taste-related factors have shifted the demand curve for brunette hair dyes.

PRICES OF RELATED GOODS: SUBSTITUTES AND COMPLEMENTS. Demand schedules are always drawn with the prices of all other commodities held constant. In other words, when deriving a given demand curve, we assume that only the price of the good under study changes. For example, when we draw the demand curve for butter, we assume that the price of margarine is held constant. When we draw the demand curve for stereo speakers, we assume that the price of stereo amplifiers is held constant. When we refer to *related goods*, we are talking about goods for which demand is interdependent. If a change in the price of one good shifts the demand for another good, those two goods are related. There are two types of related goods: *substitutes* and *complements*. We can define and distinguish between substitutes and complements in terms of how the change in price of one commodity affects the demand for its related commodity.

Substitutes Two goods are substitutes when either one can be used to satisfy a similar want.

Two goods are **substitutes** when either one can be used to satisfy a similar want. Butter and margarine are substitutes. Let us assume that each originally cost $4 per kilogram. If the price of butter remains the same and the price of margarine falls from $4 to $2 per kilogram, people will buy more margarine and less butter. The demand curve for butter will shift inward to the left. If, conversely, the price of margarine rises from $4 to $6 per kilogram, people will buy more butter and less margarine. The demand curve for butter will shift outward to the right. An increase in the price of margarine will lead to an increase in the demand for butter, and an increase in the price of butter will lead to an increase in the demand for margarine. For substitutes, a price change in the substitute will cause a change in demand *in the same direction*.

Complements Two goods are complements if both are used together for consumption or enjoyment.

Two goods are **complements** if both are used together for consumption or enjoyment. For complements, the situation is reversed. Consider stereo speakers and stereo amplifiers. We draw the demand curve for speakers with the price of amplifiers held

CHAPTER 3: DEMAND AND SUPPLY

constant. If the price per constant-quality unit of stereo amplifiers decreases from, say, $500 to $200, that will encourage more people to purchase component stereo systems. They will now buy more speakers than before at any given price. The demand curve for speakers will shift outward to the right. If, by contrast, the price of amplifiers increases from $200 to $500, fewer people will purchase component stereo systems. The demand curve for speakers will shift inward to the left. To summarize, a decrease in the price of amplifiers leads to an increase in the demand for speakers. An increase in the price of amplifiers leads to a decrease in the demand for speakers. Thus, for complements, a price change in a product will cause a change in demand *in the opposite direction*.

EXPECTATIONS.   Consumers' expectations regarding future prices, future incomes, and future availability may prompt them to buy more or less of a particular good without a change in its current money price. For example, consumers getting wind of a scheduled 100 percent price increase in DVDs next month may buy more of them today at today's prices. Today's demand curve for DVDs will shift from D_1 to D_2 in Figure 3–4 on page 68. The opposite would occur if a decrease in the price of DVDs were scheduled for next month.

Expectations of a rise in income may cause consumers to want to purchase more of everything today at today's prices. Again, such a change in expectations of higher future income will cause a shift in the demand curve from D_1 to D_2 in Figure 3–4. Finally, expectations that goods will not be available at any price will induce consumers to stock up now, increasing current demand.

POPULATION.   An increase in the population in an economy (holding per-capita income constant) often shifts the market demand outward for most products. This is because an increase in population means an increase in the number of buyers in the market. Conversely, a reduction in the population will shift most market demand curves inward because of the reduction in the number of buyers in the market.

The rapid growth of Canadian Internet pharmacies selling prescription drugs to American consumers is highlighted in this chapter's Issues and Applications. Much of this growth can be explained in terms of some of the nonprice determinants mentioned above. That is, the higher prices of substitute products, such as prescription drugs sold by American pharmacies, have resulted in a significant increase in American consumer demand for the cheaper Canadian prescription drugs. As well, Internet and fax technology has made it very easy to promote and sell Canadian prescription drugs to virtually any location in the United States. This, in turn, has increased the population or number of American buyers wishing to purchase prescription drugs from Canadian online pharmacies. As a result of these changes in nonprice determinants, the market demand curve for prescription drugs sold by Canadian Internet pharmacies has been shifting to the right.

Changes in Demand versus Changes in Quantity Demanded

We have made repeated references to demand and to quantity demanded. It is important to realize that there is a difference between a *change in demand* and a *change in quantity demanded*.

Demand refers to a schedule of planned rates of purchase and depends on a great many nonprice determinants. Whenever there is a change in a nonprice determinant, there will be a change in demand—a shift in the entire demand curve to the right or to the left.

Quantity demanded is a specific quantity at a specific price, represented by a single point on a demand curve. When price changes, quantity demanded changes according to the law of demand, and there will be a movement from one point to another along the same demand curve. Look at Figure 3–5. At a price of $3 per DVD, 60 million DVDs per year are demanded. If the price falls to $1, quantity demanded

FIGURE 3–5
Movement along a Given Demand Curve

A change in price changes the quantity of a good demanded. This can be represented as movement along a given demand schedule. If, in our example, the price of DVDs falls from $3 to $1 apiece, the quantity demanded will increase from 60 million to 100 million units per year.

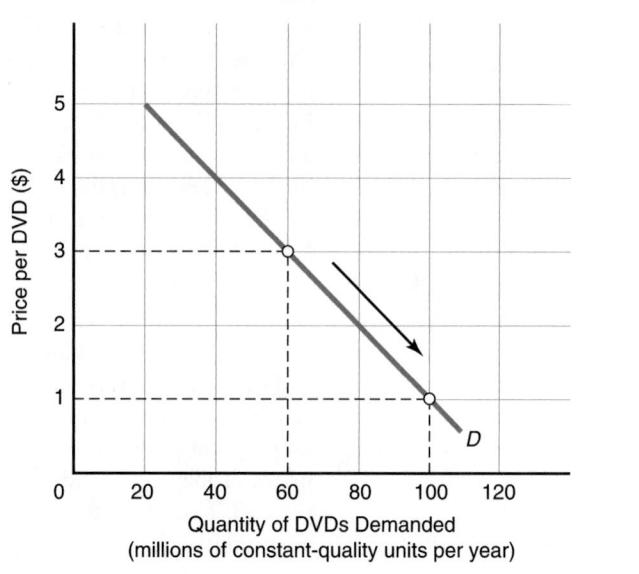

increases to 100 million per year. This movement occurs because the current market price for the product changes. In Figure 3–5, you can see the arrow pointing down the given demand curve *D*.

When you think of demand, think of the entire curve. Quantity demanded, in contrast, is represented by a single point on the demand curve.

> A change or shift in demand causes the *entire* curve to move. The *only* thing that can cause the entire curve to move is a change in a determinant *other than its own price*.

In economic analysis, we cannot emphasize too much the following distinction that must constantly be made:

> A change in a good's own price leads to a change in quantity demanded, for any given demand curve, other things held constant. This is a movement *along* the curve.

A change in any other determinant of demand leads to a change in demand. This causes a shift *of* the curve.

As Example 3–4 explains, knowing the difference between a change in quantity demanded and a change in demand will help you understand the effects that a used or secondary market has on the market for a new good.

EXAMPLE 3–4   **Garth Brooks, Used CDs, and the Law of Demand**

A few years ago, country singer Garth Brooks tried to prevent his latest album from being sold to any retail chain or store that also sold used CDs. His argument was that the used-CD market deprived labels and artists of earnings. His announcement came after a giant American retailer started selling used CDs side by side with new releases, at half the price. Brooks, along with the distribution arms of Sony, Warner Music, Capitol-EMI, and MCA were trying to quash the used-CD market. This shows that none of these parties understood the law of demand.

continued

Let us say the price of a new CD is $15. The existence of a secondary used-CD market means that to people who choose to resell their CDs for $5, the net cost of a new CD is, in fact, only $10. Because we know that quantity demanded is inversely related to price, more copies of a new CD will be sold at a price of $10 than of the same CD at a price of $15. Taking only this force into account, eliminating the used-CD market will reduce the sale of new CDs.

But there is another force at work here, too. Used CDs are substitutes for new CDs. If used CDs are not available, some people who would have purchased them will instead purchase new CDs. If this second effect outweighs the incentive to buy less because of the higher effective price, then Brooks' attempt to suppress the used-CD market is correct.

For critical analysis: Sketch a demand curve for the product "new music CDs." On this same graph, describe the various effects that the used-CD market has on the "quantity demanded" and the "demand" for "new music CDs."

➤➔ **CONCEPTS IN BRIEF**

Learning Objective 3.1: Explain the law of demand.
- The law of demand states that there is an inverse relationship between the quantity demanded of a good and its price.
- The law of demand applies when other nonprice determinants, such as income and the prices of all other goods, are held constant.
- Graphically, the law of demand is illustrated by a downward-sloping demand curve.
- The market demand curve is derived by summing the quantity demanded by all individuals in the market at each price.

Learning Objective 3.2: Distinguish between a change in quantity demanded and a change in demand.
- A change in quantity demanded occurs when there is a change in the good's own price. A change in quantity demanded is described as a movement along the good's demand curve.
- A change in demand occurs when there is a change in a determinant other than the good's own price. A change in demand is described as a shift in the entire demand curve. An increase in demand is shown as a rightward shift and a decrease in demand is shown as a leftward shift.
- Nonprice determinants that shift the demand curve for a good include (1) income, (2) tastes and preferences, (3) prices of related goods, (4) expectations about future prices or future incomes, and (5) population or number of buyers in the market.

3.3 The Law of Supply

Supply Refers to the quantities of a specific good or service that firms are willing to sell at various possible prices, other things being constant.

Law of supply The observation that there is a direct relationship between the price of any good and its quantity supplied, holding other factors constant.

The other side of the market for a product involves the quantities of goods and services that *firms* are prepared to *supply* to the market. The **supply** of any good or service is the amount that firms are willing to sell at various possible prices, other things being constant. The relationship between price and quantity supplied, called the **law of supply**, can be summarized as follows:

At higher prices, a larger quantity will generally be supplied than at lower prices, all other things held constant. At lower prices, a smaller quantity will generally be supplied than at higher prices, all other things held constant.

There is generally a direct relationship between quantity supplied and price. Producers are normally willing to produce and sell more of their product at a higher price than at a lower price, other things being constant. At $5 per DVD, 3M, Sony, Maxell,

Fuji, and other manufacturers would almost certainly be willing to supply a larger quantity than at $1 per unit, assuming, of course, that no other prices in the economy had changed.

As with the law of demand, millions of instances in the real world have given us confidence in the law of supply. On a theoretical level, the law of supply is based on a model in which producers and sellers seek to make the most gain possible from their activities. For example, as a DVD manufacturer attempts to produce more and more DVDs over the same time period, it will eventually have to hire more workers and overutilize its machines. Only if offered a higher price per DVD will the manufacturer be willing to incur these extra costs. That is why the law of supply implies a direct relationship between price and quantity supplied.

The Supply Schedule

Just as we were able to construct a demand schedule, we can construct a *supply schedule*, which is a table relating prices to the quantity supplied at each price. A supply schedule can also be referred to simply as *supply*. It is a set of planned production rates that depends on the price of the product. We show the individual supply schedule for a hypothetical producer in part (a) of Figure 3–6. At $1 per DVD, for example, this producer will supply 200 000 DVDs per year; at $5, it will supply 550 000 DVDs per year.

The Supply Curve

Supply curve An upward-sloping curve that shows the direct relationship between price and quantity supplied.

We can convert the supply schedule in part (a) of Figure 3–6 into a *supply curve*, just as we created a demand curve in Figure 3–1. All we do is take the price–quantity combinations from part (a) of Figure 3–6 and plot them in part (b). We have labelled these combinations *F* through *J*. Connecting these points, we obtain the **supply curve**, an upward-sloping curve that shows the typically direct relationship between price and quantity supplied. Again, we have to remember that we are talking about quantity supplied *per year*, measured in constant-quality units.

FIGURE 3–6

The Individual Producer's Supply Schedule and Supply Curve for DVDs

Part (a) shows that at higher prices, a hypothetical supplier will be willing to provide a greater quantity of DVDs. We plot the various price-quantity combinations in part (a) on the grid in part (b). When we connect these points, we find the individual supply curve for DVDs. It is positively sloped.

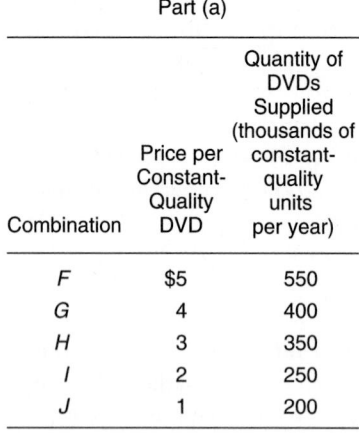

Part (a)

Combination	Price per Constant-Quality DVD	Quantity of DVDs Supplied (thousands of constant-quality units per year)
F	$5	550
G	4	400
H	3	350
I	2	250
J	1	200

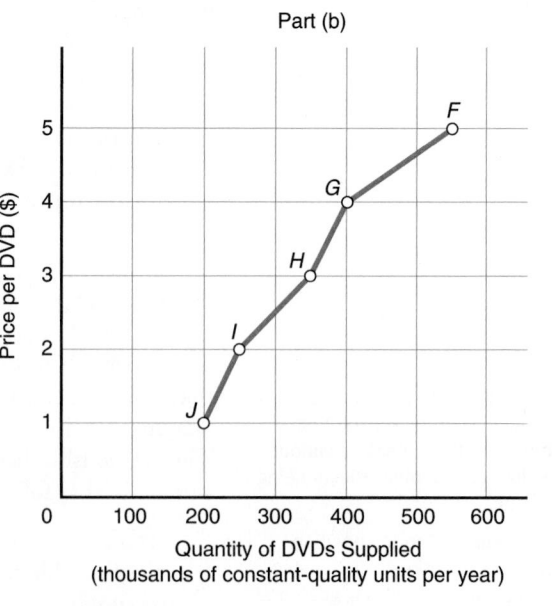

Part (b)

The Market Supply Curve

Just as we had to add the individual demand curves to get the market demand curve, we need to add the individual producers' supply curves to get the market supply curve. Look at Figure 3–7, in which we horizontally sum two typical DVD manufacturers' supply curves. Supplier 1's data are taken from Figure 3–6; supplier 2 is added. The numbers are presented in part (a). The graphical representation of supplier 1 is in part (b), of supplier 2 in part (c), and of the summation in part (d). The result, then, is the supply curve for DVDs for suppliers 1 and 2.

There are many more suppliers of DVDs, however. The total market supply schedule and total market supply curve for DVDs are represented in Figure 3–8, with the curve in part (b) obtained by adding all of the supply curves, such as those shown in parts (b) and (c) of Figure 3–7. Note the difference between the market supply curve with only two suppliers in Figure 3–7 and the one with a large number of suppliers—the entire true market—in part (b) of Figure 3–8. There are no kinks in the true total market supply curve because there are so many suppliers.

Observe what happens at the market level when price changes. If the price is $3, the quantity supplied is 60 million DVDs. If the price goes up to $4, the quantity supplied increases to 80 million per year. If the price falls to $2, the quantity supplied decreases to 40 million DVDs per year. Changes in quantity supplied are represented by movements along the supply curve in part (b) of Figure 3–8.

FIGURE 3–7

Horizontal Summation of Supply Curves

In part (a), we show the data for two individual suppliers of DVDs. Adding how much each is willing to supply at different prices, we arrive at the combined quantities supplied in column 4. When we plot the values in columns 2 and 3 on grids in parts (b) and (c) and add them horizontally, we obtain the combined supply curve for the two suppliers in question, shown in part (d).

Part (a)

(1) Price per DVD	(2) Supplier 1 Quantity Supplied (thousands)	(3) Supplier 2 Quantity Supplied (thousands)	(4) = (2) + (3) Combined Quantity Supplied per Year (thousands)
$5	550	350	900
4	400	300	700
3	350	200	550
2	250	150	400
1	200	100	300

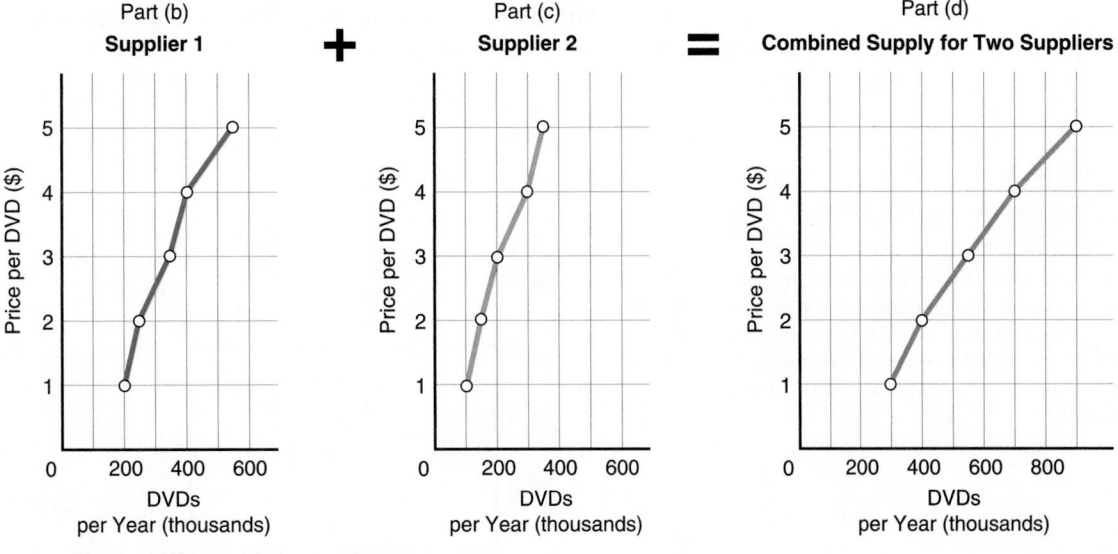

FIGURE 3–8

The Market Supply Schedule and the Market Supply Curve for DVDs

In part (a), we show the summation of all the individual producers' supply schedules; in part (b), we graph the resulting supply curve. It represents the market supply curve for DVDs and is upward sloping.

Part (a)

Price per Constant-Quality DVD	Quantity of DVDs Supplied (millions of constant-quality units per year)
$5	100
4	80
3	60
2	40
1	20

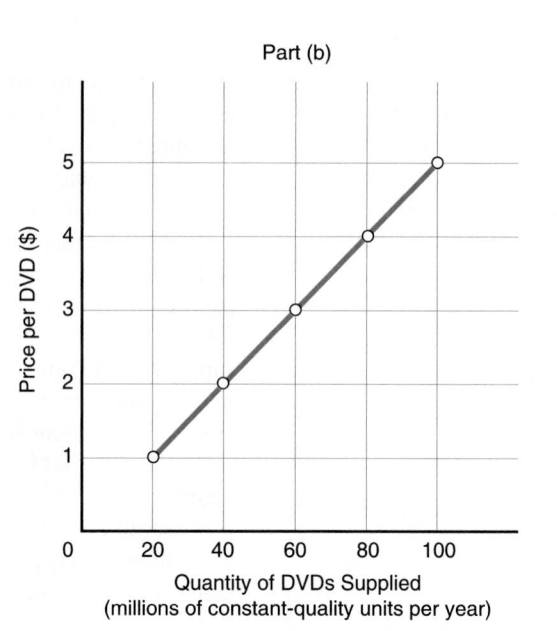

Part (b)

3.4 Shifts in Supply

When we looked at demand, we found out that any change in anything relevant other than the price of the good or service caused the demand curve to shift inward or outward. The same is true for the supply curve. If something relevant changes apart from the price of the product or service being supplied, we will see the entire supply curve shift.

Consider an example. A new method of putting magnetic material on DVDs has been invented. It reduces the cost of producing a DVD by 50 percent. In this situation, DVD producers will supply more of their product at all prices because their cost of so doing has fallen dramatically. Competition among DVD manufacturers to produce more at every price will shift the supply schedule of DVDs outward to the right from S_1 to S_2 in Figure 3–9. At a price of $3, the quantity supplied was originally 60 million DVDs per

FIGURE 3–9

A Shift in the Supply Curve

If the cost of producing DVDs were to fall dramatically, the supply curve would shift rightward from S_1 to S_2 such that at all prices, a larger quantity would be forthcoming from suppliers. Conversely, if the cost of production rose, the supply curve would shift leftward to S_3.

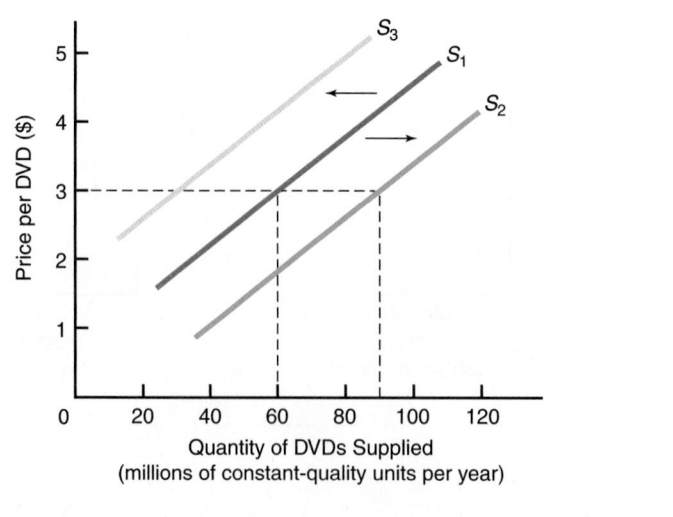

year, but now the quantity supplied (after the reduction in the costs of production) at $3 a DVD will be 90 million DVDs a year. (This is similar to what has happened to the supply curve of personal computers and fax machines in recent years as the price of the computer memory chip has fallen.)

Now, consider the opposite case. If the cost of the magnetic material needed for making DVDs doubles, the supply curve in Figure 3–9 will shift from S_1 to S_3. At each price, the number of DVDs supplied will fall due to the increase in the price of raw materials.

The Other Determinants of Supply

When supply curves are drawn, only the price of the good in question changes, and it is assumed that other things remain constant. The other things assumed constant are the costs of resources (inputs) used to produce the product, technology and productivity, taxes and subsidies, producers' price expectations, and the number of firms in the industry. These are the major nonprice determinants of supply. If any of them changes, there will be a shift in the supply curve.

COST OF INPUTS USED TO PRODUCE THE PRODUCT. If one or more input prices fall, the supply curve will shift outward to the right; that is, more will be supplied at each price. The opposite will be true if one or more inputs become more expensive. For example, when we draw the supply curve of new cars, we are holding the cost of steel (and other inputs) constant. If the price of steel decreases, the supply curve for new cars will shift *outward to the right*. When we draw the supply curve of blue jeans, we are holding the cost of cotton fixed. The supply curve for blue jeans will shift inward to the left if the price of cotton *increases*.

TECHNOLOGY AND PRODUCTIVITY. Supply curves are drawn by assuming a given technology, or "state of the art." When the available production techniques change, the supply curve will shift. For example, when a better, cheaper, production technique for DVDs becomes available, the supply curve will shift to the right. A larger quantity will be forthcoming at every price because the cost of production is lower.

TAXES AND SUBSIDIES. Certain taxes, such as a per-unit tax, are effectively an addition to production costs and therefore reduce the supply. If the supply curve were S_1 in Figure 3–9, a per-unit tax increase would shift it to S_3. A subsidy would do the opposite; it would shift the curve to S_2. Every producer would get from the government a "gift" of a few cents for each unit produced.

PRICE EXPECTATIONS. A change in the expectation of a future relative price of a product can affect a producer's current willingness to supply, just as price expectations affect a consumer's current willingness to purchase. For example, DVD suppliers may withhold part of their current supply from the market if they anticipate higher prices in the future. The current amount supplied at all prices will decrease.

NUMBER OF FIRMS IN THE INDUSTRY. In the short run, when firms can only change the number of employees they use, we hold the number of firms in the industry constant. In the long run, the number of firms (or the size of some existing firms) may change. If the number of firms increases, the supply curve will shift outward to the right. If the number of firms decreases, it will shift inward to the left.

Example 3–5 describes how some of the determinants of supply, noted above, have affected the markets relating to popular electronic products. Indeed, the current trends in supply may help us predict whether Plasma or LCD will dominate the flat screen TV markets in the future.

EXAMPLE 3-5 | **Surge in Electronics Sales Follows Dramatic Drop in LCD Prices**

Beginning in 2004, the prices of liquid crystal displays (LCDs), which are key components in many electronic devices, plummeted. Worldwide, manufacturers of cell phones, computers, electronic hand-held gadgets, and flat screen TVs dramatically increased production—particularly for those brands made up of LCDs. Market research indicates that the average North American price of an LCD TV in the most popular 30- to 34-inch size averaged US$780 in the first quarter ending in March 2007, down 45.7 percent from US$1437 a year earlier.

Industry observers predict that in 2007, LCD TV prices will fall by 30 percent or more, compared with a decline of 15 to 20 percent for plasma TVs, due to ample LCD panel supplies. They forecast that the plasma TV market will start shrinking in 2009 after hitting $24 billion in 2008, while they see LCD TV demand reaching $75 billion in 2008 and $93 billion in 2010. Large corporations such as Sony and Taiwan's Chunghwa Picture Tubes have already made decisions to halt production of plasma TVs in order to increase their focus on LCD flat screens. About 80 percent of global flat screen research and development spending is being allocated to LCD panels, with the remaining 20 percent to plasma and some other technologies.

Largely due to the falling LCD prices, Best Buy Co. noted that same-store sales at 168 Future Shop and Best Buy stores in Canada rose 14 percent in the fourth quarter ended March 2007, compared to a year earlier.

For critical analysis: With the aid of a diagram explain what has been happening to the market supply curve for LCD flat screen TVs and why. In a separate diagram, sketch the predicted effects on the supply curve for plasma TVs in 2009 and after.

SOURCES: KIYOSHI TAKENAKA, "SHIFT TO BIG-SCREEN TVS FAVOURS LCD OVER PLASMA: QUALITY RISING AS PRICE GAP NARROWS," *CALGARY HERALD*, DECEMBER 4, 2006, FINAL EDITION, P. B7; "TV SALES ENHANCE BEST BUY PICTURE; SAME-STORE SALES UP 14% IN CANADA," *CALGARY HERALD*, APRIL 5, 2007, FINAL EDITION, P. D10.

Changes in Supply versus Changes in Quantity Supplied

We cannot overstress the importance of distinguishing between a movement along the supply curve—which occurs only when the product's price changes—and a shift in the supply curve—which occurs only with changes in other nonprice factors. A change in price always brings about a change in quantity supplied along a given supply curve. We move from one point to another along the same supply curve. This is specifically called a *change in quantity supplied*.

When you think of *supply*, think of the entire curve. Quantity supplied is represented by a single point on the curve.

A change in supply causes the entire curve to shift. The *only* thing that can cause the entire curve to shift is a change in a determinant *other than price*.

Consequently,

A change in the price leads to a change in the quantity supplied, other things being constant. This is a *movement along* the curve.

A change in any other determinant of supply leads to a change in supply. This causes a *shift of* the curve.

➤→ CONCEPTS IN BRIEF

Learning Objective 3.3: Explain the law of supply.

- The law of supply states that there is a direct relationship between the quantity of a good supplied and its price.
- The law of supply applies when other things—such as technology and productivity, cost of inputs, government taxes and subsidies, expectations about future prices, and number of firms—are held constant.
- Graphically, the law of supply is illustrated by an upward-sloping supply curve.
- The market supply curve is derived by summing the quantity supplied by all firms in the market at each price.

Learning Objective 3.4: Distinguish between a change in quantity supplied and a change in supply.

- A change in quantity supplied occurs when there is a change in the good's own price. A change in quantity supplied is described as a movement along the good's supply curve.
- A change in supply occurs when there is a change in a determinant other than the good's own price. A change in supply is described as a shift in the entire supply curve. An increase in supply is shown as a rightward shift, and a decrease in supply is shown as a leftward shift.
- Nonprice determinants that shift the supply curve for a good include (1) cost of inputs, (2) technology and productivity, (3) taxes and subsidies, (4) expectations about future prices, and (5) number of firms in the market.

3.5 Putting Demand and Supply Together

In the sections on supply and demand, we tried to confine each discussion to supply or demand only. But you have probably already realized that we cannot view the world just from the supply side or just from the demand side. There is an interaction between the two. In this section, we will discuss how they interact and how that interaction determines the prices that prevail in our economy. Understanding how demand and supply interact is essential to understanding how prices are determined in our economy and other economies in which the forces of supply and demand are allowed to work.

Let us first combine the demand and supply schedules and then combine the curves.

Demand and Supply Schedules Combined

Let us place part (a) from Figure 3–3 (the market demand schedule) and part (a) from Figure 3–8 (the market supply schedule) together in part (a) of Figure 3–10. Column 1 shows the price; column 2, the quantity supplied per year at any given price; and column 3, the quantity demanded. Column 4 is merely the difference between columns 2 and 3, or the difference between the quantity supplied and the quantity demanded. In column 5, we label those differences as either excess quantity supplied (a surplus), or excess quantity demanded (a shortage). For example, at a price of $2, only 40 million DVDs would be supplied, but the quantity demanded would be 80 million. The difference is 40 million, which we label as excess quantity demanded (a shortage). At the other end of the scale, a price of $5 per DVD would elicit 100 million in quantity supplied, but quantity demanded would drop to 20 million. This leaves a difference of 80 million units, which we call excess quantity supplied (a surplus).

What do you notice about the price of $3? At that price, the quantity supplied and the quantity demanded per year are both 60 million. The difference, then, is zero. There is neither excess quantity demanded (shortage) nor excess quantity supplied (surplus). Hence the price of $3 is very special. It is called the **market clearing price** or **equilibrium price**—the price at which market quantity demanded equals market quantity supplied. The market clearing price of $3 clears the market of all excess supply or excess demand. We refer to this price as the equilibrium price, in the sense that this is the price at which

Market clearing price or **equilibrium price** The price at which market quantity demanded equals market quantity supplied.

FIGURE 3–10

Putting Demand and Supply Together

In part (a), we see that at the price of $3, the quantity supplied and the quantity demanded are equal, resulting in neither an excess in the quantity demanded nor an excess in the quantity supplied. We call this price the equilibrium, or market clearing, price. In part (b), the intersection of the supply and demand curves is at *E*, at a price of $3 per constant-quality DVD and a quantity of 60 million per year. At point *E*, there is neither an excess in the quantity demanded nor an excess in the quantity supplied. At a price of $1, the quantity supplied will be only

20 million DVDs per year, but the quantity demanded will be 100 million. The difference is excess quantity demanded at a price of $1. The price will rise, and so we will move from point *A* up the supply curve and point *B* up the demand curve to point *E*. At the other extreme, $5 elicits a quantity supplied of 100 million but a quantity demanded of only 20 million. The difference is excess quantity supplied at a price of $5. The price will fall, and so we will move down the demand curve and the supply curve to the equilibrium price, $3 per DVD.

Part (a)

(1) Price per Constant-Quality DVD	(2) Quantity Supplied (DVDs per year)	(3) Quantity Demanded (DVDs per year)	(4) Difference (2) − (3) (DVDs per year)	(5) Condition
$5	100 million	20 million	80 million	Excess quantity supplied (surplus)
4	80 million	40 million	40 million	Excess quantity supplied (surplus)
3	60 million	60 million	0	Market clearing price—equilibrium (no surplus, no shortage)
2	40 million	80 million	−40 million	Excess quantity demanded (shortage)
1	20 million	100 million	−80 million	Excess quantity demanded (shortage)

Part (b)

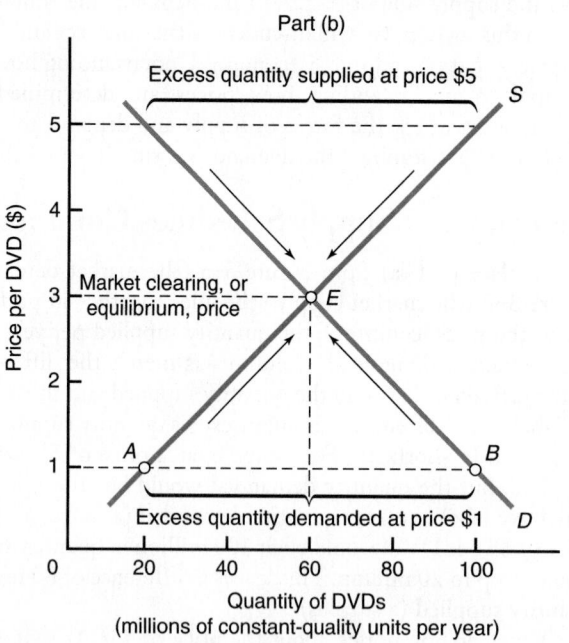

there is no tendency for change. At this price, consumers are able to buy all that they wish to purchase and suppliers are able to sell all that they wish to supply.

We can define **equilibrium** in general as a point from which there tends to be no movement unless demand or supply changes. Any movement away from this point will set in motion certain forces that will cause movement back to it. Therefore, equilibrium is a stable point. Any point that is not at equilibrium is unstable and cannot be maintained.

Equilibrium A point from which there tends to be no movement unless demand or supply changes.

Demand and Supply Curves Combined

The equilibrium point occurs where supply and demand intersect. Part (b) from Figure 3–3 and part (b) from Figure 3–8 are combined as part (b) in Figure 3–10. The only difference now is that the horizontal axis measures both the quantity supplied and the quantity demanded per year. Everything else is the same. The demand curve is labelled *D*, the supply curve *S*. We have labelled the intersection of the two curves as point *E*, for equilibrium. That corresponds to a market clearing price of $3, at which both the quantity supplied and the quantity demanded are 60 million units per year. There is neither a surplus nor a shortage. Point *E*, the equilibrium point, always occurs at the intersection of the supply and demand curves. This is the price toward which the market price will automatically tend to gravitate.

Shortages

The demand and supply curves in Figure 3–10 represent a situation of equilibrium. But a non–market-clearing, or disequilibrium, price will bring into play forces that cause the price to change and move toward the market clearing price. Then, equilibrium is again sustained. Look once more at part (b) in Figure 3–10. Suppose that instead of being at the market clearing price of $3 per DVD, for some reason, the market price is $1 per DVD. At this price, the quantity demanded (100 million), exceeds the quantity supplied (20 million). We have a situation of excess quantity demanded at the price of $1. This is usually called a **shortage**. Consumers of DVDs would find that they could not buy all that they wished at $1 apiece. But forces will cause the price to rise: Competing consumers will bid up the price, and suppliers will raise the price and increase output, whether explicitly or implicitly. (Remember, some buyers would pay $5 or more, rather than do without DVDs. They do not want to be left out.) We would move from points *A* and *B* toward point *E*. The process would stop when the price again reached $3 per DVD.

Shortage A situation in which the quantity demanded exceeds the quantity supplied at a price below the market clearing price.

Surpluses

Now, let us repeat the experiment with the market price at $5 per DVD, rather than at the market clearing price of $3. Clearly, the quantity supplied will exceed the quantity demanded at that price. The result will be an excess quantity supplied at $5 per unit. This is often called a **surplus**, a situation in which quantity supplied is greater than quantity demanded at a price above the market clearing price. Given the curves in part (b) in Figure 3–10, however, there will be forces pushing the price back down toward $3 per DVD: Competing suppliers will attempt to reduce their inventories by cutting prices and reducing output, and consumers will offer to purchase more at lower prices. Suppliers will want to reduce inventories, which will be above their optimal level; that is, there will be an excess over what each seller believes to be the most profitable stock of DVDs. After all, inventories are costly to hold. But consumers may find out about such excess inventories and see the possibility of obtaining increased quantities of DVDs at a decreased price. It benefits consumers to attempt to obtain a good at a lower price, and they will therefore try to do so. If the two forces of supply and demand are unrestricted, they will bring the price back to $3 per DVD.

Surplus A situation in which quantity supplied is greater than quantity demanded at a price above the market clearing price.

3.6 *Changes in Equilibrium*

Shifts in Demand or Supply

When a nonprice determinant of demand or supply changes, this will result in a shift in the demand or the supply curve for the product under study. In turn, this will cause the product's equilibrium price and equilibrium quantity to change. In certain situations, it is possible to predict in which direction the equilibrium price and equilibrium quantity will change. Specifically, whenever one curve is stable while the other curve shifts, we can tell what will happen to price and quantity. Consider the four possibilities in Figure 3–11. Each possibility starts with the equilibrium price of DVDs equal to $3.00 ($P_1$) and the equilibrium quantity equal to 60 million DVDs (Q_1).

FIGURE 3–11

Shifts in Demand or Supply

In part (a), the supply curve is stable at S. The demand curve shifts outward, or increases, from D_1 to D_2. The equilibrium price increases from P_1 to P_2 and the equilibrium quantity increases from Q_1 to Q_2. In part (b), with the supply curve stable, the demand curve shifts to the left or decreases. In this case, the equilibrium price decreases from P_1 to P_3, while the equilibrium quantity decreases from Q_1 to Q_3. In part (c), the demand curve is stable at D. Now the supply curve shifts to the right or increases. This results in a decrease in the equilibrium price from P_1 to P_2 but an increase in equilibrium quantity from Q_1 to Q_2. In part (d), with the demand curve stable at D, there is a leftward shift, or a decrease in the supply. While this causes the equilibrium price to increase from P_1 to P_3, the equilibrium quantity decreases from Q_1 to Q_3.

Part (a) An increase in demand: $P_e \uparrow Q_e \uparrow$

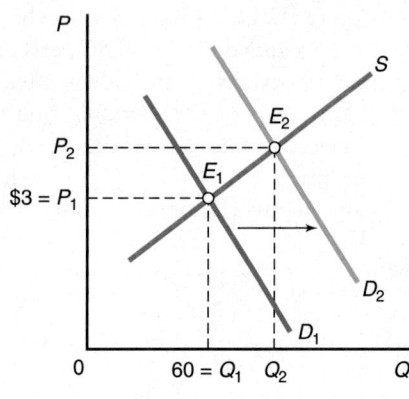

Part (b) A decrease in demand: $P_e \downarrow Q_e \downarrow$

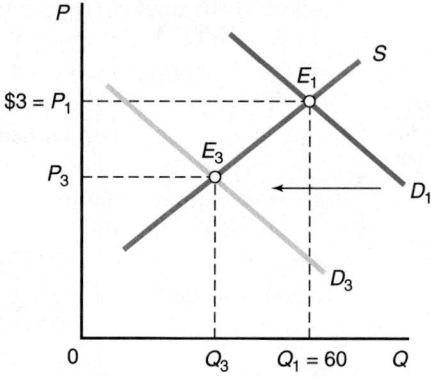

Part (c) An increase in supply: $P_e \downarrow Q_e \uparrow$

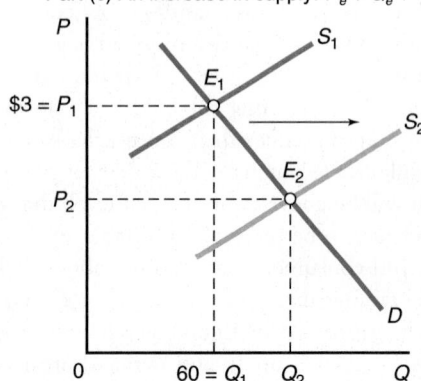

Part (d) A decrease in supply: $P_e \uparrow Q_e \downarrow$

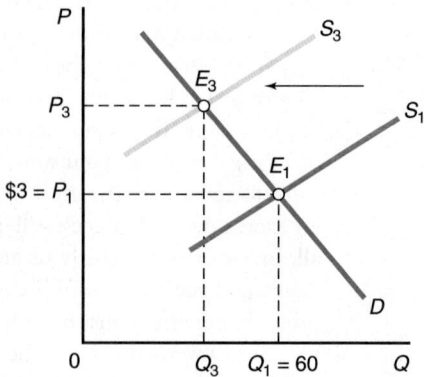

INCREASE IN DEMAND. In Figure 3–11 part (a), the supply curve remains stable but *demand increases* from D_1 to D_2. Note that the result is both *an increase in the equilibrium price* of DVDs from P_1 to P_2 and an *increase in equilibrium quantity* from Q_1 to Q_2 ($P_e\uparrow Q_e\uparrow$).

Nonprice determinants that can cause an increase in demand include an increase in income with DVDs being a normal good; an increase in the price of a substitute good for DVDs; a decrease in the price of a complement good for DVDs; an increase in population or number of buyers; a change in tastes that favours DVDs; and expectations that DVD prices will increase in the future.

In the example "Chocoholics Beware," we noted how increased incomes in large nations such as China and taste factors such as the perceived health benefits of eating dark chocolate have caused an increase in demand for chocolate. According to Figure 3–11(a), this increase in demand helps to explain why chocolate prices increased in 2007.

DECREASE IN DEMAND. In Figure 3–11 part (b), the supply curve remains stable but *demand decreases* from D_1 to D_3. Note that the result is both a *decrease in the equilibrium price* of DVDs from P_1 to P_3 and a *decrease in equilibrium quantity* from Q_1 to Q_3 ($P_e\downarrow Q_e\downarrow$).

INCREASE IN SUPPLY. In Figure 3–11 part (c), the demand curve remains stable but *supply increases* from S_1 to S_2. Note that the result is a *decrease in the equilibrium price* of DVDs from P_1 to P_2 and an *increase in equilibrium quantity* from Q_1 to Q_2 ($P_e\downarrow Q_e\uparrow$).

Nonprice determinants that can cause an increase in supply include a decline in the costs of inputs used to manufacture DVDs; a technological change increasing the productivity of manufacturing DVDs; a reduction in taxes imposed on DVD manufacturers; an increase in the subsidies enjoyed by DVD manufacturers; and an increase in the number of firms manufacturing DVDs.

In the example "Surge in Electronics Sales Follows Dramatic Drop in LCD Prices," we illustrate how the increase in supply of LCD flat screen TVs has been significantly increasing due to the decline in a key cost of input—LCD panels. Figure 3–11 part (c) explains how this increase in supply has led to a decline in the price of LCD flat screen TVs relative to comparable plasma TVs. Even though in 2007 the prices of LCD TVs are still typically higher than for the same size plasma TVs, the price gap has significantly narrowed.

DECREASE IN SUPPLY. In Figure 3–11 part (d), the demand curve remains stable but *supply decreases* from S_1 to S_3. Note that the result is both an *increase in the equilibrium price* of DVDs from P_1 to P_3 and a *decrease in equilibrium quantity* from Q_1 to Q_3 ($P_e\uparrow Q_e\downarrow$).

In addition to the demand factors noted above, supply shifts also help to explain the rising chocolate bar prices described in the example "Chocoholics Beware." You may recall that government policies aimed at increasing the supply of the alternative fuel ethanol are driving up the prices of corn, sugar, cattle feed, and therefore milk. This is causing the costs of key inputs in the production of chocolate to increase. Figure 3–11 part (d) explains how this translates into higher chocolate prices by shifting the supply curve of chocolate to the left.

According to this chapter's Issues and Applications, Canadian Internet pharmacies have been making a lot of money buying prescription drugs from American drug manufacturers and then reselling these same drugs to American consumers at relatively low retail prices. As this practice grows, it threatens to reduce overall drug prices in the United States, which, in turn, can reduce the profits earned by the American drug manufacturers. As a result, the American drug manufacturers are beginning to cut back the quantity of prescription drugs distributed to Canadian Internet pharmacies. To the extent that these cutbacks significantly reduce the supply of drugs available to Canadian pharmacies, this can result in higher equilibrium drug prices paid by Canadian consumers, as explained in Figure 3–11 part (d).

The principles of supply and demand presented above are powerful tools that will allow you to predict the future effects that current events will have on markets that affect you. Presumably, you will be able to react to these predictions in a manner that promotes your self-interest.

As Policy Example 3–1 illustrates, supply and demand can also prove useful when evaluating government policies that interfere with market outcomes.

POLICY EXAMPLE 3–1   **Having a Cow Over Milk Prices**

Globally, milk prices are rising at an all-time record rate. Fluid milk futures, which predict future prices, advanced to a record $19.15 on May 3, 2007, and have risen 63 percent compared to the previous year. Skim-milk powder, the benchmark for world trade, has risen 60 percent in six months to a record $1.58 a pound on May 4, 2007 on the Chicago Mercantile Exchange—seven times higher than the five-year average.

Industry observers predict that milk prices will not likely fall anytime soon due to the trends in demand and supply. The demand for milk has been growing significantly in China, India, and Latin America. While the 2.5 billion people in China and India are drinking more milk than ever, they still have a long way to go before catching up with the North American per-capita average demand of 25 ounces a day—almost four times the amount in India and 19 times more than in China. Chinese consumers, who drink an average of 1.3 ounces of milk a day, are predicted to increase demand for milk by as much as 15 percent annually for the next three years.

Governments such as Canada and the United States have been encouraging the production of environment friendly fuel alternatives such as ethanol, which currently requires that massive amounts of corn be diverted away from feeding animals including dairy cows. As a result, the cost of corn, a primary source of livestock feed, has advanced 55 percent in the past year on the Chicago Board of Trade. In addition, there has been a reduction in government subsidies given to dairy farmers in Europe and the United States, which has slowed global milk production.

For critical analysis: Sketch an initial global demand and supply curve and equilibrium price for milk. Show how events described in this example have shifted the demand curve for milk and how this affects the equilibrium price. In a separate supply and demand diagram, show how the government policies—incentives to produce more ethanol and reduction of dairy farm subsidies—have shifted the supply curve for milk and how this affects the equilibrium price.

SOURCE: "EXPLORING THE LAND OF MILK AND MONEY; PRICES SKYROCKET AS WORLD GETS TASTE FOR DAIRY PRODUCTS AND SUPPLIES DWINDLE," EDMONTON JOURNAL, MAY 15, 2007, FINAL EDITION, P. E5.

When Both Demand and Supply Shift

Each example given in Figure 3–11 shows a predictable outcome for equilibrium price and quantity based on a shift in either the demand curve holding the supply curve constant or the supply curve holding the demand curve constant. Often, we want to predict the changes in equilibrium price and quantity in market situations where *multiple nonprice determinants* are changing at the same time, resulting in shifts in *both* demand and supply. As you will see below, unless you know the full extent of each individual shift in demand and supply, the overall outcome will be *indeterminate* for *either* equilibrium price *or* equilibrium quantity.

INCREASE IN DEMAND AND INCREASE IN SUPPLY. Suppose the price of CDs, a substitute for DVDs, significantly increases, causing an *increase in demand* for DVDs. At the same time, new technology reduces the cost of manufacturing DVDs, resulting in an *increase in supply* of DVDs. To predict the overall effect on the equilibrium price and quantity of DVDs, we suggest that you begin by analyzing the effect of *each individual shift* on equilibrium price and quantity using the appropriate part in Figure 3–11.

According to part (a) in Figure 3–11, an *increase in demand* for DVDs will cause the *equilibrium price to increase* and the *equilibrium quantity to increase* ($P_e\uparrow Q_e\uparrow$). Similarly, part (c) in Figure 3.11 suggests that *an increase in supply* will cause *the equilibrium price to decrease* and the *equilibrium quantity to increase* ($P_e\downarrow Q_e\uparrow$).

If you now combine the effects of both shifts, you can conclude that the *equilibrium quantity will certainly increase*, but the overall effect on equilibrium price is *indeterminate*, meaning that it could go up or down or stay the same, depending on the extent of the shift in both curves. Figure 3–12 describes a situation where the supply shifts by a larger amount than the demand shifts, resulting in an overall decrease in the equilibrium price of DVDs.

In the Did You Know? section at the beginning of this chapter it was noted that cellphone prices have been declining despite the fact that the demand for cellphones has been significantly increasing worldwide. Now that you have been exposed to the tools of demand and supply, you are in a better position to understand these trends in the cellular phone industry.

The smaller computer chips that have been invented have reduced the size and increased the portability of cellular phones, resulting in an increase in demand for cellular phones. As well, the concern for personal safety has increased the demand for cellular phones. At the same time, new technology has significantly reduced the cost of the computer chips used in the manufacture of cellular phones, and this has increased the supply of cellular phones. Since you know that the price of cellular phones has been declining, you can conclude that the increase in supply has exceeded the increase in demand in the cellular phone industry. As Figure 3–12 illustrates, this situation leads to a decline in equilibrium price and a substantial increase in equilibrium quantity, explaining what has often been called the " cellular phone explosion."

DECREASE IN DEMAND AND DECREASE IN SUPPLY. Suppose the average household income declines, causing a *decrease in demand* for DVDs. At the same time, the number of firms manufacturing DVDs declines, resulting in *a decrease in supply* of DVDs. On the basis of parts (b) and (d) of Figure 3–11, you can conclude that the *equilibrium*

FIGURE 3–12

An Increase in Demand and Supply

The original equilibrium price is $3 per DVD, and the original equilibrium quantity is 60 million DVDs, which is determined by the intersection of D_1 and S_1. With an increase in demand and supply, the new demand curve is D_2, and the new supply curve is S_2. The new equilibrium price and quantity, located at the intersection of D_2 and S_2, is $2.50 and 120 million DVDs, respectively. The overall result is that the equilibrium price decreases and the equilibrium quantity increases significantly.

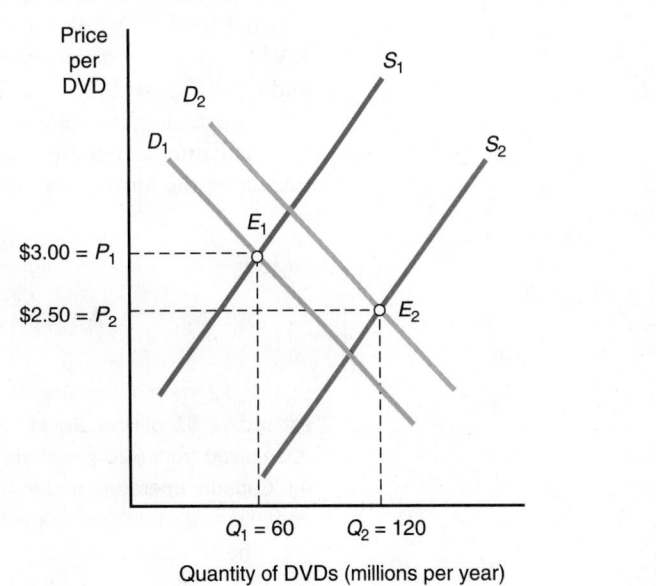

FIGURE 3–13

A Decrease in Demand and Supply

The original equilibrium price is $3 per DVD, and the original equilibrium quantity is 60 million DVDs, which is determined by the intersection of D_1 and S_1. With a decrease in demand and supply, the new demand curve is D_3 and the new supply curve is S_3. The new equilibrium price and quantity, located at the intersection of D_3 and S_3 is $2.75 and 20 million DVDs, respectively. The overall result is that the equilibrium price decreases and the equilibrium quantity decreases significantly.

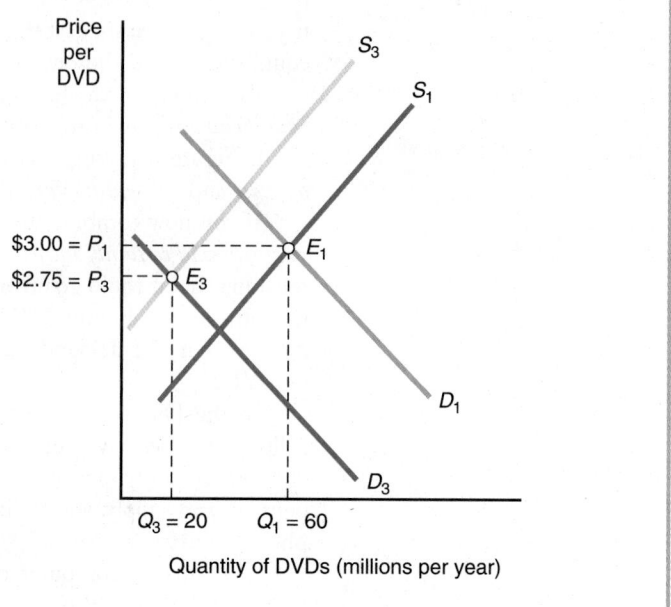

quantity will certainly decrease, but the overall *effect on equilibrium price is indeterminate.* If after further investigation, you determine that the decrease in demand (pulling the price down) far exceeds the decrease in supply (pushing the price up), you can predict that the equilibrium price will decline, as illustrated in Figure 3–13.

INCREASE IN DEMAND AND DECREASE IN SUPPLY. Suppose consumers, expecting the prices of DVDs to skyrocket in the future, increase their demand for DVDs in the current period. At the same time, the government imposes a new tax on DVD manufacturers, causing a *decrease in supply* of DVDs. On the basis of parts (a) and (d) of Figure 3–11, you can conclude that the *equilibrium price will certainly increase,* but the overall *effect on equilibrium quantity is indeterminate.*

DECREASE IN DEMAND AND INCREASE IN SUPPLY. Suppose the price of DVD players, a complement of DVDs, significantly increases, causing a decrease in demand for DVDs. At the same time, the government provides subsidies to Canadian DVD manufacturers, resulting in an increase in supply of DVDs. On the basis of parts (b) and (c) of Figure 3–11, you can conclude that the *equilibrium price will certainly decrease,* but the overall *effect on equilibrium quantity is indeterminate.*

As Example 3–6 explains, industry supply and demand trends can have a significant impact on the fortunes or misfortunes of major Canadian corporations.

EXAMPLE 3–6   **Air Canada Stock Price Spins Out of Free Fall**

In the 12 months ending September 30, 2003, Air Canada mounted an annual loss exceeding $1 billion. Between July 2000 and December 2003, Air Canada's stock price nose-dived from $20 per share to $0.94 per share. Between April 2003 and October 2004, Air Canada operated under bankruptcy-court protection from creditors. A review of the demand and supply trends affecting international air carriers helps to explain, at least in part, the company's dismal financial situation.

continued

The terrorist attacks of September 11, 2001, had significantly reduced air travel globally. Due to these attacks, air carriers have been faced with increased security costs. Rising fuel and labour costs have also cut into airline profits. Many businesses are increasingly using the Internet and video and teleconferencing technologies in order to communicate at a distance.

In October 2004, Air Canada emerged from bankruptcy-court protection with a new parent company, ACE Aviation Holdings, and with a stock price exceeding $20. Since 2004, Air Canada has been consistently increasing its "load" factor (proportion of seats filled) to a post-9/11 record level of 84 percent in May 2007. Factors leading to its growth in seats sold include: passengers being less fearful of terrorist attacks on airlines; Air Canada offering flights that use smaller, more cost-efficient jets on shorter regional routes; the addition of more international flights to growth areas like China; and the demise of Canadian competitors such as Jetsgo, Canada 3000, CanJet, and Harmony.

For critical analysis: With the aid of a graph, explain what happened to the market demand, market supply, and equilibrium quantity for the air travel services provided by international air carriers between 2001 and 2003. Between 2004 and 2007, what has happened to the demand curve for Air Canada airline services and why?

SOURCES: "AIR CANADA." GLOBEINVESTOR.COM. DECEMBER 13, 2003. http://investdb.theglobeandmail. com/invest/investSQL/gx.company_prof?company_id=168356; "AIRLINES INDUSTRY PROFILE." INDUSTRY CENTER. YAHOO!FINANCE. DECEMBER 13, 2003. http://biz.yahoo.com/ic/prof/4.html; "AIRLINES REPORT RECORD LOADS," *CALGARY HERALD*, JUNE 7, 2007, FINAL EDITION, P. D1.FRO.

⇒ CONCEPTS IN BRIEF

Learning Objective 3.5: Explain how the forces of demand and supply interact to determine equilibrium price and quantity.

- ❧ Equilibrium price and quantity occur where market demand equals market supply. Graphically, equilibrium occurs where the market demand curve intersects the market supply curve.
- ❧ The forces of surpluses and shortages ensure that the market will stabilize at equilibrium. Whenever the price is greater than the equilibrium price, there is an excess quantity supplied (surplus). This surplus puts downward pressure on price. Whenever the price is below the equilibrium price, there is an excess quantity demanded (shortage). This shortage puts upward pressure on price.

Learning Objective 3.6: Describe how changes in demand and supply can change equilibrium price and quantity.

- ❧ An increase in demand will cause the equilibrium price and quantity to increase. A decrease in demand will cause the equilibrium price and quantity to decrease.
- ❧ An increase in supply will cause the equilibrium price to decrease and the equilibrium quantity to increase. A decrease in supply will cause the equilibrium price to increase and the equilibrium quantity to decrease.
- ❧ When both demand and supply change in the same direction, the equilibrium quantity will also change in the same direction, but the equilibrium price might increase, decrease, or remain the same.
- ❧ When both demand and supply change in opposite directions, the equilibrium price will change in the same direction as demand, but the equilibrium quantity might increase, decrease, or remain the same.

Is Canada the Prescription for Lower Drug Prices in the U.S.?

Concepts Applied: Changes in Demand and Supply, Changes in Equilibrium Price and Quantity

Americans show their demands while joining the RX Express, a group travelling by train from Miami to Toronto to buy medicine at prices 30 to 60 percent cheaper than in the United States.

The Dramatic Growth in the Canadian Internet Drug Export Industry

The Canadian prescription export industry started to attract international attention when busloads of American seniors travelled to drugstores located just north of the U.S. border to purchase drugs in 1999. In 2004, U.S. consumers spent over $800 million on prescription drugs sold through Canadian Internet pharmacies.

This rapidly growing Canadian export industry is based on the fact that many popular brand name prescription drugs sell for significantly lower prices in Canada than in the U.S. Table 3–2 compares average Canadian and U.S. list prices for a select number of brand name prescription drugs (in U.S. dollars) taken from both U.S. and Canadian online pharmacies on June 24, 2007. As you can see, the average Canadian price for the eight selected drugs is $124.55, which is 40 percent of the average U.S. price ($307.70).

Why are brand name prescription drugs so much cheaper in Canada than in the U.S.? A number of factors help to explain this difference.

In Canada, brand name prescription drugs are regulated by the Patent Medicine Prices Review Board so as to avoid excessive price gouging of the Canadian consumer. A new drug brought into the Canadian market, while protected by a 20-year patent, cannot cost more than the most expensive existing drug in its therapeutic class. If no similar drugs are sold in Canada, the board will ensure that the new drug's price will not exceed the average price charged in other countries where the drug is currently sold. In Canada, throughout the patent period, a drug's price cannot increase faster than the Canadian Consumer Price Index. Since there is no such form of government price control in the U.S., prescription drug companies can charge higher prices to U.S. consumers.

In Canada, provincial governments pay for about 45 percent of outpatient drugs, about double what U.S. governments pay. This gives the provinces significant "buying power" over the drug companies selling the drugs. If the drug companies want to have their drugs covered by a provincial government drug insurance plan, they need to charge prices that are competitive with similar drugs insured by the plan.

TABLE 3–2	Prescription Drug	Description	U.S. Online Price (US$)	Canadian Online Price (US$)
Online Prices of Prescription Drugs in Canada and the United States	Clarinex 5 mg, 30 pills	Oral antihistamine	$ 91.47	$ 43.00
	Coumadin 5 mg, 100 pills	Blood thinner	86.56	47.03
	Lipitor 20 mg, 90 pills	Cholesterol reducer	321.30	116.00
	Mobic 15 mg, 90 pills	Anti-osteoarthritis	438.87	120.90
	Prevacid 15 mg, 100 pills	Antacid	466.62	235.18
	Risperdal 1 mg, 120 pills	Antipsychotic	464.32	159.94
	Celexa 20 mg, 100 pills	Antidepressant	287.97	159.38
	Celebrex 200 mg, 90 pills	Anti-arthritis	304.46	115.00
	Average Price		307.70	124.55

SOURCES: "PRESCRIPTIONS." DRUGSTORE.COM. http://www.drugstore.com/pharmacy/prices/. (ACCESSED JUNE 24, 2007.); "FIND DRUGS" CHEAP RXMEDS.COM. http://www.cheaprxmeds.com/content/find_drugs/. (ACCESSED JUNE 24, 2007.)

The Online Purchase Process: An Illegal Form of Reimportation

So how do U.S. consumers go about purchasing prescription drugs from Canadian Internet pharmacies? Canadian Internet pharmacies advertise the cheaper Canadian drug prices on the web. After surfing the web, U.S. consumers choose the specific Canadian Internet pharmacies to import their drugs from. They then fax their U.S. doctors' drug prescriptions to these Canadian pharmacies. Upon paying Canadian doctors a fee to co-sign the U.S. drug prescriptions, the Canadian Internet pharmacies mail out the drug orders directly to the homes of the U.S. consumers.

Throughout the U.S., American entrepreneurs recognized that there were many millions of people who don't have Internet access and so they began opening up "storefront" operations in the U.S. that performed the Internet purchases and faxes on behalf of the U.S. consumers. These storefront operations significantly expanded the imports of prescription drugs from Canada.

The online purchase process, described above, has frequently been referred to as drug reimportation. That is because many of the drugs sold by the Canadian Internet pharmacies are actually developed, patented, and manufactured in the U.S. by large multinational drug companies. The multinational companies distribute these drugs to large wholesalers who, in turn, sell them to Canadian Internet pharmacies. When American consumers end up buying the drugs from Canadian Internet pharmacies, these goods are, in essence, reimported back into the U.S.

U.S. Opposition to Large-Scale Drug Reimportation

Strictly speaking, the reimportation of pharmaceuticals into the U.S. is illegal. The U.S. Food and Drug Administration (FDA) is responsible for enforcing this law. While the FDA continues to allow individual American consumers to import 90-day supplies of Canadian pharmaceuticals, it has recently been successful in getting the U.S. courts to shut down many of the American storefront operations that were facilitating large-scale purchases from Canadian Internet suppliers. The FDA has justified these shutdowns by mounting publicity campaigns suggesting that Internet pharmacies can lead to the sale of counterfeit prescription drugs, threatening the safety of American consumers.

If drug reimportation were allowed to take place on a large-scale basis, this would serve to lower the price that the multinational drug companies get from selling their brand name prescription drugs on their home turf—in the U.S. Hence, these multinational companies have supported the recent moves to shut down storefront operations facilitating reimportation. Moreover, six large U.S. multinational drug companies have threatened to restrict the sale of brand name drugs to Canadian Internet pharmacies.

U.S. Support for Large-Scale Drug Reimportation

A number of U.S. politicians have been promoting large-scale drug reimportation. Such a move would help to ensure that necessary prescription drugs remain affordable for low-income American families. As well, drug reimportation would significantly improve the efficiency of numerous municipal and state insurance plans by lowering drug costs. The mayor of Springfield, Massachusetts, recently made the decision to purchase all the prescription drugs for his city's health insurance plan from Canadian Internet pharmacies. The states of Iowa, Illinois, Michigan, and Minnesota are all considering similar measures. In January 2007, the U.S. Senate and House of Representatives introduced bills supporting large-scale drug reimportation.

Canadian Concerns with Large-Scale Drug Importation

Even in Canada there have been recent moves to reduce the practice of drug reimportation. Provincial medical associations have been reprimanding some of the Canadian doctors who have facilitated reimportation by co-signing the U.S prescriptions faxed to Canadian Internet pharmacies. The actions of these doctors have been viewed as unethical in that they are authorizing prescriptions for U.S patients who they have not examined.

If drug reimportation is allowed to expand on a large-scale basis, this could have detrimental effects for Canadian drug consumers. The large U.S. multinational drug companies will cut off shipment of popular prescription drugs to the Canadian market, or they will pressure the Canadian government to relax the drug price controls in exchange for resuming shipments of key drugs. Either way Canada loses. Canadians could be deprived of much needed medicines, or wind up paying much higher drug prices.

For critical analysis:

1. Identify the various nonprice determinants that result in an increase in demand for the prescription drugs sold by Canadian Internet pharmacies.
2. Identify the various nonprice determinants that result in a decrease in supply of the prescription drugs sold by Canadian Internet pharmacies.
3. Suppose the U.S. government legalizes the reimportation of prescription drugs from Canadian Internet pharmacies. At the same time, suppose the multinational drug manufacturers significantly cut back the quantity of prescription drugs distributed to Canadian Internet pharmacies. Predict the effect that these two events will have on the equilibrium price and quantity of prescription drugs sold to Canadian consumers.

SOURCES: John Graham, "Prescription Drug Prices in Canada and the US—Part 4, Canadian Prescriptions for American Patients Are Not the Solution," September 2003. Fraser Institute. http://www.fraserinstitute.ca/shared/readmore.asp?sNav=pb&id= 580. (Accessed December 20, 2003.); Barrie McKenna, "Canadian Drugs Not Prescription for U.S. Health Ills," *The Globe and Mail*, November 7, 2003; Standing Committee on Health #020. House of Commons Canada. February 14, 2005. http://cmte.parl.gc.ca/ Content/HOC/Committee/381/HESA/Evidence/EV1630121/HESA EV20-E.PDF; "Top pharmacist pans U.S. drug bill," *Leader Post*, Regina SK, January 25, 2007, final edition, p. C12.

⇒→ SUMMARY

Here is what you should know after reading this chapter. MyEconLab will help you identify what you know, and where to go when you need to practise. We suggest that as soon as you review one of the Learning Objective sections below, you then proceed to go through the related section in MyEconLab.

⇒→ LEARNING OBJECTIVES	KEY TERMS	MYECONLAB PRACTICE
3.1 The Law of Demand. According to the law of demand, other things being equal, households will purchase fewer units of a good at a higher price and more units of a good at a lower price. This law is described by a downward-sloping demand curve.	demand, 64 law of demand, 64 relative price, 64 money price, 64 demand curve, 66 market, 66 market demand, 66	• **MyEconLab** Study Plan 3.1
3.2 Shifts in Demand. A change in the good's own price causes a change in quantity demanded, which is a movement along the same demand curve. A change in demand is described as a shift in the entire demand curve caused by a change in a non-price determinant, such as income, tastes, prices of related goods, expectations, and number of buyers. An increase in demand means that the demand curve shifts rightward, while a decrease in demand implies a leftward shift.	normal goods, 69 inferior goods, 69 substitutes, 70 complements, 70	• **MyEconLab** Study Plan 3.2
3.3 The Law of Supply. According to the law of supply, firms will produce and offer for sale more units of a good at a higher price and fewer units of a good at a lower price. This law is described by an upward-sloping supply curve.	supply, 73 law of supply, 73 supply curve, 74	• **MyEconLab** Study Plan 3.3
3.4 Shifts in Supply. A change in the good's own price causes a change in quantity supplied, which is a movement along the same supply curve. A change in supply is described as a shift in the entire supply curve caused by a change in a non-price determinant such as input prices, technology and productivity, taxes and subsidies, price expectations, and number of sellers. An increase in supply means that the supply curve shifts rightward, while a decrease in supply implies a leftward shift.		• **MyEconLab** Study Plan 3.4
3.5 Putting Demand and Supply Together. The equilibrium price and equilibrium quantity occur where market demand equals	market clearing price or equilibrium price, 79	• **MyEconLab** Study Plan 3.5

➤→ LEARNING OBJECTIVES	KEY TERMS	MYECONLAB PRACTICE
market supply. Graphically, equilibrium occurs where the market demand curve intersects the market supply curve. At this point, the plans of sellers and buyers match, meaning that shortages and surpluses are eliminated.	equilibrium, 81 shortage, 81 surplus, 81	
3.6 Changes in Equilibrium. An increase in demand will cause equilibrium price and quantity to increase, whereas a decrease in demand will cause equilibrium price and quantity to decrease. An increase in supply will cause equilibrium price to decrease and equilibrium quantity to increase, while a decrease in supply will cause equilibrium price to increase and equilibrium quantity to decrease. When both demand and supply change in the same direction, the equilibrium quantity will also change in the same direction, but the equilibrium price might increase, decrease, or remain the same. When both demand and supply change in opposite directions, the equilibrium price will change in the same direction as demand, but the equilibrium quantity might increase, decrease, or remain the same.		• **MyEconLab** Study Plan 3.6

➤→ PROBLEMS

(Answers to the odd-numbered problems appear at the back of the book.)

LO 3.1, 3.2 Explain the law of demand; distinguish between a change in quantity demanded and a change in demand.

1. Examine the following table, and then answer the questions.

	Price per Unit Last Year	Price per Unit Today
Heating oil	$1.00	$2.00
Natural gas	$0.80	$3.20

What has happened to the absolute price of heating oil? Of natural gas? What has happened to the price of heating oil relative to the price of natural gas? What has

happened to the relative price of natural gas? Will consumers, through time, change their relative purchases? If so, how?

2. Give an example of a complement and a substitute in consumption for each of the following items:
    a. Bacon
    b. Coffee
    c. Automobiles

3. Consider the market for Canadian beef. Explain whether each of the following events would cause an increase in demand, a decrease in demand, an increase in quantity demanded, or a decrease in quantity demanded. Also describe how each event will affect the demand curve for Canadian beef.

a. The price of chicken decreases.

b. Household income increases, and beef is a normal good.

c. The price of Canadian beef decreases.

d. A Canadian cow is found to have mad cow disease.

e. The Canadian government raises the price of Canadian beef.

LO 3.3, 3.4 Explain the law of supply; distinguish between a change in quantity supplied and a change in supply.

4. Consider the market for newly constructed bungalow homes in Canada. Explain whether each of the following events would cause an increase in supply, a decrease in supply, an increase in quantity supplied, or a decrease in quantity supplied. Also describe how each event will affect the supply curve for new Canadian bungalow homes.

a. The price of lumber skyrockets in Canada.

b. The Canadian government lowers the price of new bungalow homes in Canada.

c. New technology is developed that significantly reduces the cost of building new bungalows.

d. The Canadian government provides subsidies to builders of new Canadian bungalows.

e. The price of Canadian bungalows increases.

LO 3.5, 3.6 Explain how the forces of demand and supply interact to determine equilibrium price and quantity; describe how changes in demand and supply can change equilibrium price and quantity.

5. Suppose that, in a recent market period, an industry-wide survey determined the following relationship between the price of rock music CDs and the quantity supplied and demanded.

Price	Quantity Demanded	Quantity Supplied
$ 9	100 million	40 million
$10	90 million	60 million
$11	80 million	80 million
$12	70 million	100 million
$13	60 million	120 million

a. What is the equilibrium price and equilibrium quantity?

b. If the industry price is $13, is there a shortage or a surplus of CDs? How much is the shortage or surplus? Will the price stay at $13? Explain.

c. If the industry price is $10, is there a shortage or a surplus of CDs? How much is the shortage or surplus? Will the price stay at $10? Explain.

6. Refer to Example 3–2, "Chocoholics Beware," and use a demand and supply diagram (for chocolate bars) to describe the changes in supply that have occurred in the chocolate bar market in 2007. Show graphically how these changes in supply will affect the equilibrium price of chocolate bars.

7. Suppose that a survey for a later market period indicates that the quantities supplied in the table in Problem 5 are unchanged. The quantity demanded, however, has increased by 30 million at each price. Construct the resulting demand curve in the illustration you made for Problem 5. Is this an increase or a decrease in demand? What is the new equilibrium quantity and the new market price? Give two examples that might cause such a change.

8. In Policy Example 3–1, "Having a Cow Over Milk Prices," it was noted that milk prices were increasing at record rates globally in 2007. With the aid of a supply and demand diagram focusing on the product pizza, explain how the increase in the price of milk will affect the equilibrium price and quantity for pizza. Keep in mind that the amount paid for cheese accounts for approximately 30 percent of the cost of each pizza.

9. In the market for rock music CDs, explain whether the following events would cause an increase or decrease in demand or an increase or decrease in the quantity demanded. Also explain what happens to the equilibrium quantity and the equilibrium price.

a. The price of CD packaging material declines.

b. The price of CD players declines.

c. The price of cassette tapes increases dramatically.

d. A booming economy increases the income of the typical CD buyer.

e. Many rock fans suddenly develop a fondness for country music.

10. Consider the market for laptop computers. Explain whether the following events would cause an increase or decrease in supply or an increase or decrease in the quantity supplied. Illustrate each, and show what would happen to the equilibrium market price, given a typical downward-sloping demand curve.

a. The price of memory chips used in laptop computers declines.

b. The price of memory chips used in desktop personal computers declines.

c. The number of manufacturers of laptop computers increases.

d. The prices of computer peripherals, printers, fax–modems, and scanners decrease.

11. The following diagram describes the hypothetical monthly demand and supply conditions for eggs in a small provincial market.

a. If the price in the egg market above was initially at $1.40 per dozen, there would be a (surplus or shortage) equal to ___ thousands of dozens of eggs per week. Will the price stay at $1.40?

b. If the price in the egg market above was initially at $0.80 per dozen, there would be a (surplus or

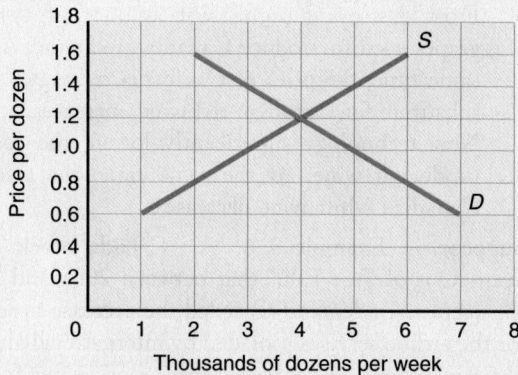

Thousands of dozens per week

shortess) equal to ___ thousands of dozens of eggs per week. Will the price stay at $0.80?

c. Determine the equilibrium price and equilibrium quantity in the egg market described above.

d. In the egg market described above, explain whether each of the following events would cause an increase or decrease in demand or supply. Also explain what happens to the equilibrium price and quantity.

   i. Studies show that daily use of eggs reduces the risk of getting serious diseases.

   ii. The cost of feeding chickens significantly increases.

   iii. Average consumer income increases, and eggs are an inferior good.

   iv. The government provides a subsidy to egg producers. A subsidy is a situation where the government pays the egg producers a set amount per dozen produced.

12. Airline routes are typically controlled by imposing a quota on the number of airline companies that may use the route and the number of flights on the route. Consequently, the government restricts the number of round-trip seats available on these flight routes. Suppose that the following table describes the daily demand and supply schedules for seats on round-trip flights between Toronto and Vancouver.

Price per seat ($)	Quantity Demanded (no. of seats)	Quantity Supplied (no. of seats)
200	2000	1200
300	1800	1400
400	1600	1600
500	1400	1800
600	1200	2000

a. What is the equilibrium price and quantity for the Toronto-to-Vancouver airline seats? How much, in total dollars, do passengers spend on this route each day?

b. Suppose the government limits the daily number of round-trip seats to ensure that only 1200 seats

can be made available on the Toronto-to-Vancouver route. What will be the new price per round-trip seat on this route? With the quota policy, do passengers end up spending more or less each day on this same route in total dollars? Can you think of how this quota policy might actually benefit the passengers (consumers) in the longer run?

13. The following diagram describes the hypothetical monthly demand and supply for one-bedroom apartments in a small college town.

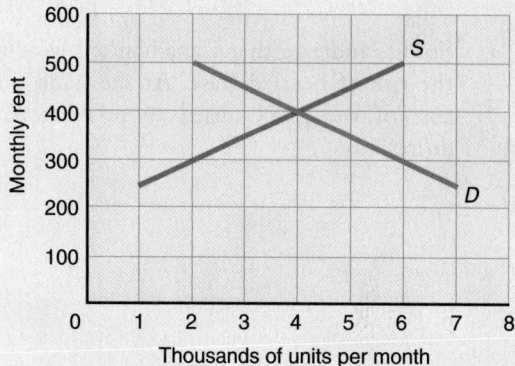

Thousands of units per month

a. What is the equilibrium monthly rent (price) and equilibrium monthly quantity?

b. Suppose that the mayor of this town decides to make housing more affordable for the local college students by imposing a rent control that holds the price of a one-bedroom apartment to $300 per month.

This rent control policy will result in a (shortage or surplus) of _____ units per month.

c. What will this rent control policy do to the market for two-bedroom apartments that are not regulated by the government? What will happen to the equilibrium price and quantity for the unregulated two-bedroom apartments?

14. In May 2000, the Canadian government imposed a tax on bicycles imported from Taiwan and China. Show how this tax affects the market for Taiwanese and Chinese bicycles, shifting the appropriate curve and indicating a new market equilibrium quantity and price. In a separate graph, show the effect of the tax on Canadian-made bicycles, shifting the appropriate curve and indicating the new market equilibrium and price.

15. The following diagram describes the market for Canadian red wine. Explain how each of the following sets of events will affect the equilibrium price and equilibrium quantity of Canadian red wine. Note that in some cases, your answer will be "indeterminate," meaning that with the given information, you cannot predict the direction of change.

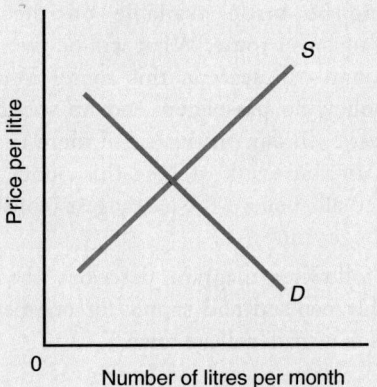

a. Studies indicate that Canadian red wine reduces the risk of heart disease. At the same time, the cost of the grapes used to produce red wine decreases.

b. Frost destroys a significant amount of the red grapes used to produce Canadian red wine. At the same time, the price of California red wine, a key substitute for Canadian red wine, increases.

c. New technology significantly lowers the cost of producing wine. At the same time, the price of Canadian white wine decreases.

16. Suppose, in Example 3–6, "Air Canada Stock Price Spins Out of Free Fall," that between 2001 and 2003 the decrease in demand exceeded the decrease in supply for the airline services provided by international airlines like Air Canada. What would these market trends have done to the fares that Air Canada charged its customers? In turn, what would this have done to the magnitude of Air Canada's losses? Hint: Sketch the appropriate demand and supply curves to determine how the equilibrium price would have changed.

4

Introduction to Macroeconomics

➤ LEARNING OBJECTIVES

After reading this chapter, you should be able to:

4.1 Explain why the study of macroeconomics is important.

4.2 Describe economic activity and business fluctuations and explain their effects.

4.3 Calculate the rate of unemployment and discuss the three kinds of unemployment.

4.4 Explain how inflation is measured and describe the effects of inflation and deflation.

4.5 Explain why trade is an important issue for Canadians.

4.6 Name the basic economic policies available to government.

In 2007, the inflation rate in Zimbabwe was running at over 10 000 percent. In July of that year, in an attempt to lower inflation, the government ordered that prices of basic goods be dropped by 50 percent. As a result, shoppers rioted in the capital city due to the overwhelming demand for the items that were on sale. At the same time, unemployment was over 80 percent and the output of the economy had declined by an estimated 50 percent. The economy of Zimbabwe has fallen apart, and people have great difficulty obtaining the basic necessities of life.

How does an economy work, and how does it affect you? How does the government measure inflation, unemployment, and economic output? These are the basic questions of this chapter.

MyEconLab helps you master each objective and study more efficiently. See end of chapter for details.

A widely respected magazine, *The Economist*, tries to provide notice of the beginning of a business downturn by tracking what it calls the "*R*-word Index." This is the number of times that the word *recession*—the technical term economists use to describe a downturn—appears in a computer database of stories appearing in print media outlets, such as the *New York Times* and the *Washington Post*. In contrast, months *after* business slowdowns began in 1981, 1990, and (in the United States) 2001, economists determined the exact month that each economic downturn officially began. When *The Economist* looked back at these official starting dates, it found in each case that the *R*-word Index jumped noticeably at almost the same time. Apparently, it does not take long for the media to catch on when an economic downturn begins.

A central objective of macroeconomics—the study of the structure and performance of the national economy—is to understand the sources of change in overall economic activity. Such changes also have important implications for inflation and unemployment.

4.1 The Importance of Macroeconomics

The study of the "big picture" economic issues is the basis for macroeconomics. Economists study these issues by looking backward at what happened in the past and by predicting what will happen in the future. Looking to the past requires a solid grounding in the *measurement* of the relevant economic variables. These variables measure the broad picture of the economy. Looking to the future requires that we have *models* to understand the relationship between the variables. (Refer back to Chapter 1 to review how models are built.)

These macroeconomic variables measure the economic outcomes of the economy, such as the amount it produces, the number of people employed, and what the price of that output is. These variables can be somewhat difficult to measure because they are broad aggregates of what is happening in many individual markets. Nevertheless, these outcomes affect us all in our daily lives.

What can we do as a society to improve the situation here and elsewhere? What role does government play in helping improve the performance of our economy? By studying macroeconomics, economists hope to understand and improve these outcomes to make us all better off. In macroeconomics, corrective actions are usually undertaken by government and can include a host of different policies that are under its control. Governments around the world try to influence the economic performance of their economies. They know about the problems we have outlined and try to improve their economies for the benefit of their citizens. They want their economies to grow, to have low rates of unemployment and inflation, and to see stable trading and financial investment with other nations. There are a number of major policies that governments have used in a variety of ways to try to improve their economies, and we will look at these later in this book.

However, having a better idea about the future can also affect your personal decision making. Such questions as "Should I buy a house?" or "Is this a good time to expand my business?" require decisions strongly affected by the macroeconomic environment. Modelling allows us to get a glimpse of how those actions may affect us in the future and take corrective action today.

So, what are you hoping to get out of the study of macroeconomics? You want to get through your studies, of course, but more importantly, you are learning several things. You are learning an important way of thinking. You are also learning about some of the economic choices that have to be made, and just as importantly, the trade-offs that are made. You are learning about the institutions that operate and affect the world around you. Finally, as a citizen, you are becoming better informed about the policies that your leaders are making and will be able to make better decisions to help choose the leaders that you want.

As we mentioned at the beginning of this section, economists need to have a clear understanding of what they are actually measuring before they can make their assessment. Economists measure many variables, and it is important to understand that there are two kinds: stocks and flows.

FIGURE 4–1

Visualizing Stocks and Flows

Unemployment at any point in time is some number that represents a stock, such as the amount of water in a bathtub. People who lose their job constitute a new flow into the bathtub. Those who find a job can be thought of as the water that flows out the drain.

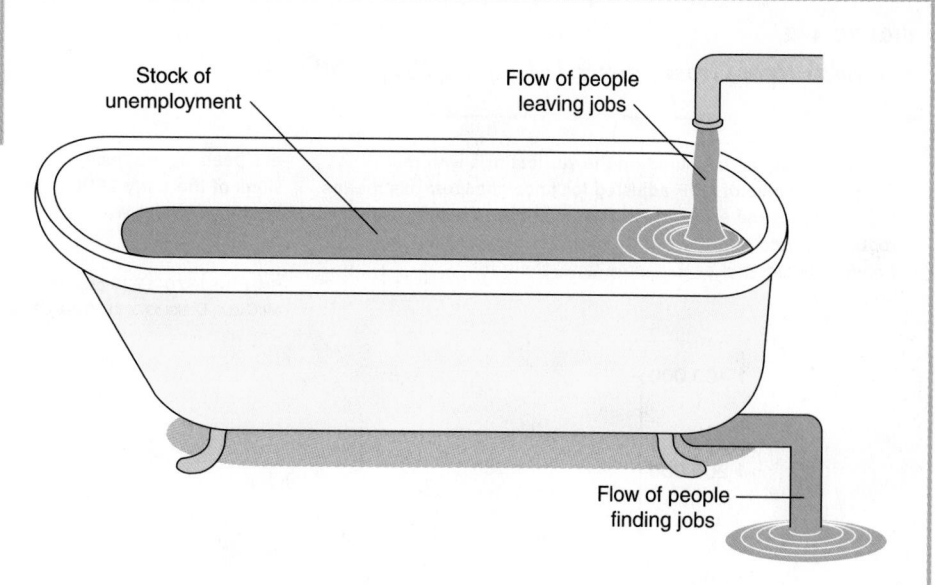

Stock of unemployment

Flow of people leaving jobs

Flow of people finding jobs

Stock A quantity of something at a given point in time.

Flow A quantity measured per unit of time that shows how fast something is changing.

In general, a **stock** is the quantity of something at a given point in time—for example, an inventory of goods or a bank account. Stocks are defined independently of time, although they are assessed at a particular point in time.

A **flow** is a quantity measured per unit of time that shows how fast something is changing—for example, something that occurs over time, such as the income you make per week or per year, or the number of individuals who leave their job in a month. Picturing a bathtub, as illustrated in Figure 4-1, is a good way of remembering how stocks and flows work.

In this chapter, we will introduce the three most important variables that economists use to assess and understand an economy. These variables are gross domestic product (GDP), unemployment, and inflation. In later chapters, we will spend more time modelling how these variables get determined. The first variable, GDP, measures economic activity.

4.2 Economic Activity and Business Fluctuations

Gross domestic product (GDP) The value of all goods and services produced in a country in a year.

Economic growth The increase in economic output that nations have experienced over time.

Measuring the economic output of a country and looking at how that output changes over time is a fundamental cornerstone of macroeconomics. Economic output in macroeconomics is defined as the value of all goods and services produced in a country in a year, and is called **gross domestic product (GDP)**. (We will look at how GDP is measured in the next chapter.) When we look back into history, we see that most nations have experienced substantial increases in economic output (measured by the increase in GDP) over time. This increase is called **economic growth**.

High economic growth for a country, sustained over a long period of time, usually means that the people living there experience higher standards of living. With higher standards of living, people have more of the goods and services that they like having, such as food items, cars, and houses. It also shows up in the ability to buy more education, health care, and sanitation, and so a country with a large GDP (relative to the size of its population) is also usually a country with a long life expectancy and high levels of education. If we were to look at poorer nations, with their problems of inadequate food and shelter and short life expectancy, the major economic difference would be that the high-income countries (like Canada) have experienced long periods of high economic growth, while the poorer nations have not.

Figure 4–2 shows how Canada's economic output has changed since 1870. Note that we produce about 150 times as much as we did in 1870! In Chapter 7, we will look at a simple model of production and examine the sources of this tremendous increase in output.[1]

---

[1]Note that the vertical axis measures real GDP, which means that GDP has been adjusted for changing prices. We will look at this in more detail in Chapter 5.

Canada's output is measured on the vertical axis with real GDP, which is the value of GDP adjusted for price changes; this means that it removes the effect of inflation in comparing the value of production. Note that the long-term trend for production is strongly upward, and at the same time, there h

ave been severe fluctuations in that trend, such as the recessions of the early 1890s, the Great Depression of 1930–38, the booms of World War I and II, and the recessions of the 1980s and 1990s.

SOURCES: 1870–1926 DATA: *PERSPECTIVES ON CANADIAN ECONOMIC HISTORY* MCCALLA, DOUGLAS, AND MICHAEL HUBERMAN, PP. 160–161, 1994 (DATA HAVE

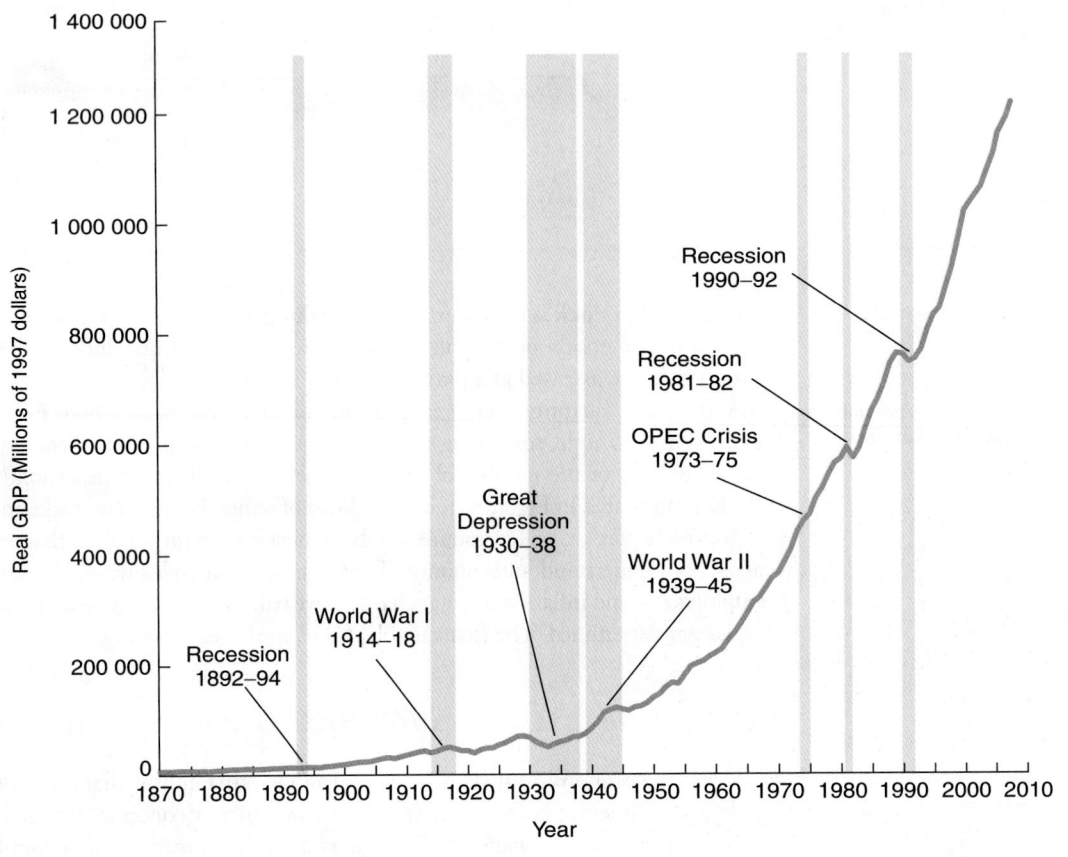

If you look at Figure 4–2, you will see that the record of economic activity has been on a long-term growth trend upward but is not entirely smooth. There are "hills and valleys" in economic activity, and some of the major ones are noted on the figure. The ups and downs in overall economic activity are sometimes called **business fluctuations**. When business fluctuations are positive, they are called **expansions**—accelerations in the pace of national economic activity. The opposite of an expansion is a **contraction**, which is a decline in economic output. The top of an expansion is usually called a *peak,* and the bottom of a contraction is usually called a *trough.* If the contractionary phase of business fluctuations goes on for two consecutive quarters or more, we call it a **recession**. An extremely deep recession is called a **depression**.

Business fluctuations are sometimes called *business cycles*, but that term is less appropriate because the word *cycle* implies a predetermined or automatic recurrence, and that does not seem to be what happens. What Canada and other countries have experienced are contractions and expansions that vary greatly in length and severity.

Business fluctuations The ups and downs in overall economic activity.

Expansion An acceleration in the pace of national economic activity.

Contraction A decline in economic output.

Recession A contractionary business fluctuation where economic output declines for two consecutive quarters or more.

Depression An extremely deep recession.

Why Do We Care about Business Fluctuations?

Why should we concern ourselves with business fluctuations? The first reason is that a contraction in the economy means that we are losing billions of dollars in GDP because we are producing fewer goods and services than we otherwise could. A 3 percent decline in GDP (a moderate recession) is about $40 billion in goods and services, or about $1200 in income per person in Canada. That could be a new TV, a DVD player, and a gaming box for everyone! To put this in perspective, during the Great Depression, GDP fell by about 30 percent.

The second concern is that the contraction phase is usually accompanied by unemployment. The loss of income we experience is not equal for everyone because some people lose their jobs—and, thus, their income—while others continue to work. This means that the loss of GDP is unevenly distributed across the population and can be quite devastating for some. As a society, we generally want to minimize this impact upon people's lives.

Thirdly, the expansion phase has its own problems. Expansion phases can (but do not necessarily) result in a rapid rise in average prices for goods and services across the economy, which we call **inflation**.

Inflation A rise in average prices for goods and services across the economy.

When prices rise in an unanticipated or rapid manner, it can cause income and wealth to be redistributed in ways that are detrimental to society. People who are not able to adjust to rising prices, such as people on fixed incomes, lose purchasing power and can be impoverished by the inflation.

What causes these fluctuations? One theory is that they are caused by the adoption of new technology, as Example 4–1 explains.

EXAMPLE 4–1   **Technology and Long Cycles**

During the 1920s, a Russian economist named Nikolai Kondratieff studied business fluctuations. He thought that capitalist economies regularly went through cycles of 50 years or so, from bust to boom and back to bust, driven by technological changes. It all starts when scientists make a technological breakthrough. Businesses then expand to produce and incorporate the new technology into industry, creating an upswing in the economy. However, markets eventually become saturated with the new products, and output starts to decline. The economy then enters the contractionary phase of the cycle. What puts an end to the contraction? Yet another new scientific discovery.

More recent economists have built on Kondratieff's work, and offer the following as evidence to support his theory. In 1709, Englishman Abraham Darby discovered a way to make good-quality iron in a coke-fired furnace. This discovery led to all kinds of new industrial uses for iron, including steam engines. Steam power then helped drive the Industrial Revolution in England, which began in the mid-1700s and peaked around 1815. The English economy fell into a depression shortly thereafter.

The next discovery was an economical way to make steel, thus advancing railway technology. The world's first railway opened in England in 1825 and its subsequent proliferation led to a 30-year boom that began in the 1840s. The inevitable recession followed, when scientists began work on chemicals, electricity, and automobiles. These new discoveries fuelled economic expansion from the late 1890s until the Great Depression.

During the Great Depression, new discoveries were made in airplane technology and in consumer goods, such as refrigerators and televisions. Manufacture of these products drove the expansion of the 1950s and 1960s. The economic decline of the 1970s saw scientists working on microprocessors and biotechnology, which drive the present-day expansion. If Kondratieff's theory holds, the good times we are now experiencing should last until the 2020s.

For critical analysis: What recent technological changes have occurred that might explain the slowdown in economic activity that occurred in 2001?

FIGURE 4–3
Idealized Business Cycle

This diagram shows what an idealized busi-ness cycle would go through: from peak to trough and back again in a regular cycle around a long-term growth trend.

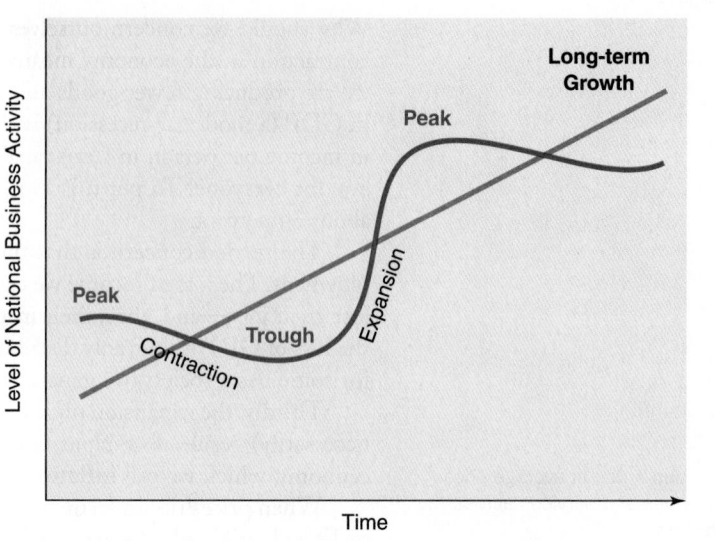

Figure 4–3 shows a stylized version of how typical business fluctuations occur around a long-term growth trend. Starting at a peak, the economy goes into a contraction (reces-sion). Then, an expansion starts and moves up to its peak, higher than the last one, and then the sequence starts over again.

Figure 4–4 shows the *percentage change* in real GDP and the unemployment rate from 1926 to 2007. Note that there are big swings in activity in the early years and that when the GDP is decreasing, unemployment is usually increasing. While it is difficult to pin-point the exact time a contraction or expansion begins or ends, the economy experienced approximately seven cycles of expansion and contraction over the period illustrated in Figure 4–4.

CONCEPTS IN BRIEF

Learning Objective 4.1: Explain why the study of macroeconomics is important.

- Studying macroeconomics allows us to understand the "big issues" in our economy, such as economic growth, inflation, and unemployment.
- Governments try to use this understanding of the economy to create economic growth and to keep inflation low and their citizens working. Understanding economics helps us as individuals make economic decisions and understand our political choices.
- Model building is an important part of macroeconomics because it allows us to anticipate problems and take corrective action.

Learning Objective 4.2: Describe economic activity and business fluctuations and explain their effects.

- Economic growth is important because it helps determine our standard of living. With economic growth, people can have more of the things that they desire, such as cars, houses, and vacations.
- Economic growth is measured as the increase in real GDP. Canadian real GDP has grown about 150 times in value since Confederation.
- Deviations from the long-term economic growth trend are called business fluctua-tions (or the business cycle), which consist of expansions and contractions in overall economic activity.
- The lowest point of a contraction is called the trough and is usually associated with high unemployment and contracting GDP; the highest point of an expansion is called the peak and is sometimes accompanied by inflation.
- A recession is a downturn in business activity for two consecutive quarters.

FIGURE 4-4
Business Fluctuations Peak-to-Peak, 1926–2007

The solid line shows changes in real national output from year to year, while the shaded area shows the unemployment rate in each year. Note that on average, when output is falling during a contraction, unemployment is rising, and when output is rising during an expansion, unemployment is falling.

SOURCES: ADAPTED FROM THE STATISTIC CANADA CANSIM TABLES 380–0040, 380–0003, 384–0035, 282–0086, JULY 2007, AND FROM THE STATISTICS CANADA PUBLICATION *HISTORICAL STATISTICS OF CANADA*, SECOND EDITION, CATALOGUE 11-516, 1983, SERIES D233.

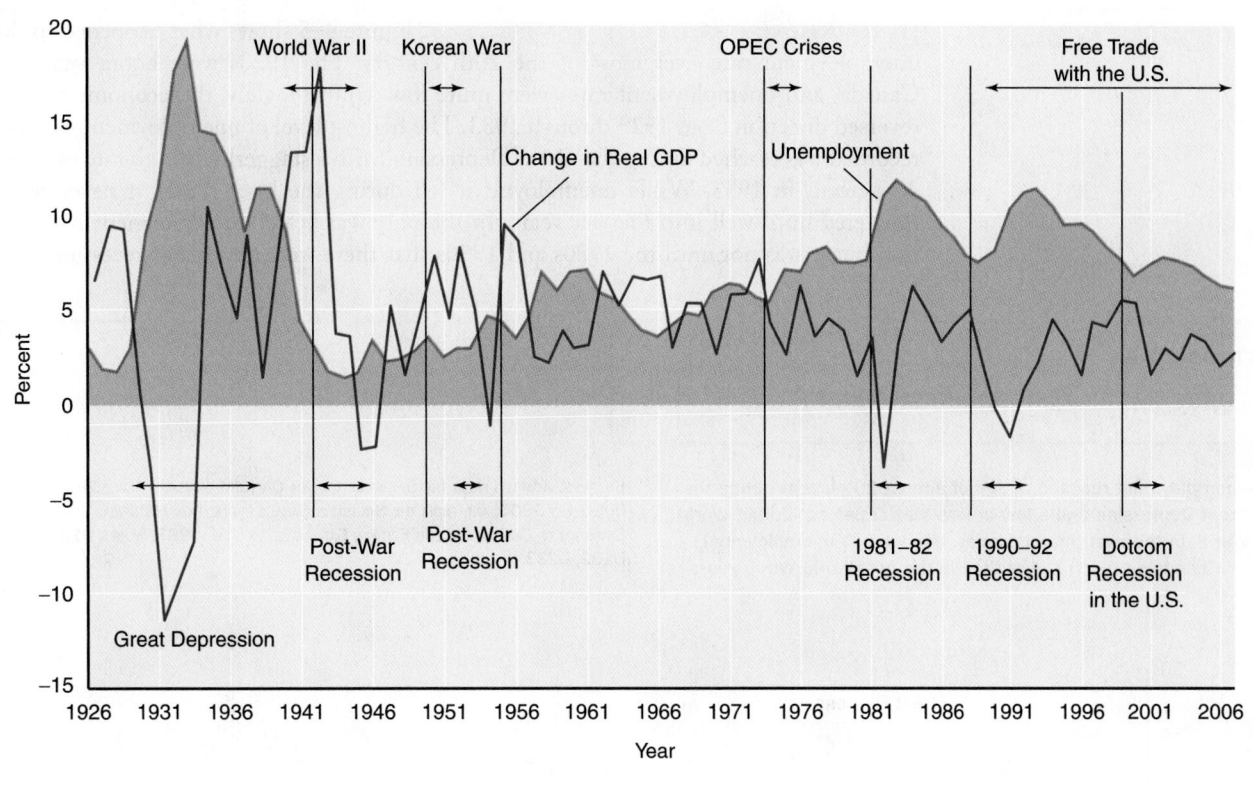

4.3 Unemployment

As we have already mentioned, unemployment is one important aspect of recessions. Unemployment is not just confined to recessions, however, but is a normal part of a functioning economy at all times. Labour is one of the primary resources used in producing Canada's GDP and accounts for about 70 percent of the income created from producing that GDP. Not using labour, then, represents a major loss to the economy.

Why Do We Care about Unemployment?

Firstly, most people depend on labour income. We know unemployment creates personal hardship and results in lost GDP. Secondly, the loss of GDP when workers are unemployed can be very large and ultimately affects us all, even if we are not personally unemployed.

One researcher has estimated that at the beginning of the 1990s, when the unemployment rate was about 10.5 percent and factories were running at 72 percent of their capacity, the amount of output that the economy lost due to idle resources was almost 6 percent of the total production throughout Canada, or about $80 billion in today's money. That represents about $80 billion worth of schools, houses, restaurant meals, cars, and movies that *could have been produced* but were not. (In other words, Canada was somewhere inside the production possibilities curve that we talked about in Chapter 2). It also represents a huge loss to the government in terms of taxes as well as a big increase in support payments for the unemployed, all of which affects even those of us who are not unemployed. It is no wonder that policy makers closely watch the unemployment figures published by Statistics Canada.

On a more personal level, being unemployed often results in hardship and failed opportunities as well as a loss of self-respect. Psychology researchers believe that being fired creates as much stress as the death of a close friend. Because of the difficulties to individuals and to society that accompany unemployment, it is very important both politically and economically to try to minimize unemployment. As many politicians have found to their regret, having a declining economy at the time of an election can result in a change in government! The numbers that we present about unemployment can never fully convey its true cost.

HISTORICAL UNEMPLOYMENT RATES. Figure 4–5 shows what happened to the unemployment rate over most of the 20th century. The 1920s were boom years for Canada, and unemployment rates were quite low. Unfortunately, the economy rapidly reversed direction from 1929 through 1933. The highest level of unemployment we have recorded was reached during the Great Depression, with a staggeringly high rate of about 20 percent in 1933. While unemployment fell during the later 1930s, it never really recovered until well into the war years. In the post-war years, unemployment rates did rise, but it was not until the 1980s and 1990s that there were two major recessions and

FIGURE 4–5
Eighty-Seven Years of Unemployment

Unemployment reached a high of almost 20 percent during the Great Depression and a low of less than 2 percent during World War II. In the past three decades, the average unemployment rate has been much higher than in the post-World War II years.

SOURCES: ADAPTED FROM THE STATISTICS CANADA CANSIM DATABASE, TABLE 282-0086 JULY 2007, AND FROM THE STATISTICS CANADA PUBLICATION *HISTORICAL STATISTICS OF CANADA*, SECOND EDITION, CATALOGUE 11-516, 1983, SERIES D129, D132, D233.

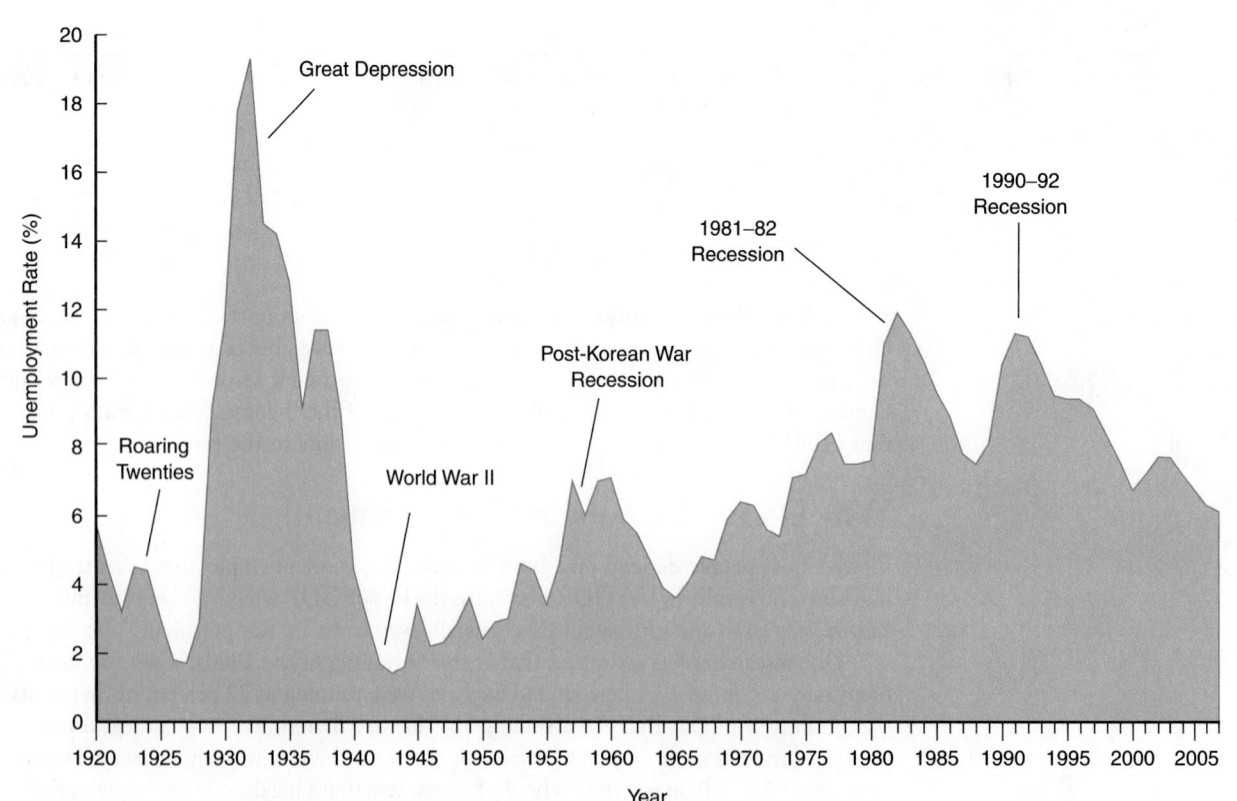

unemployment rates once again reached the "double digits." Unemployment today is lower than it has been for most of the last 25 years.

Measuring Employment, Unemployment, and the Labour Force

In order to measure unemployment, Statistics Canada breaks down Canada's population of about 32.5 million people into various subgroupings. First, Statistics Canada identifies that many millions of people are too young to participate in the production of GDP, and so it defines the number of people of working age as being those 15 years of age and older, which (in May 2007) represents about 26.5 million people (this group is called the "**working age population**"). This group is further subdivided as shown in Figure 4–6.

Figure 4–6 presents the working age population of individuals 15 years of age or older broken into three subgroups: (1) employed, (2) unemployed, and (3) not in the labour force. Those who have work of any sort (as little as one hour per week) are considered **employed**. **Unemployed** are those who are willing and able to work, and who are actively looking for work. The **labour force** is the total of these two groups—the number of employed plus the number of unemployed. Anyone 15 years of age or older who is neither unemployed or employed is referred to as "not in the labour force." This group includes people like homemakers, full-time students, and retired persons.

In May 2007, the labour force amounted to 18.06 million people: 16.964 million were employed and 1.097 million were unemployed. To calculate the unemployment rate, we simply divide the number of unemployed by the number of people in the labour force and multiply by 100:

$$\text{Unemployment rate} = \frac{\text{Number of unemployed}}{\text{Labour force}} \times 100$$

In May 2007, the unemployment rate was $(1.097 \div 18.06) \times 100 = 6.1$ percent.

THE ARITHMETIC DETERMINATION OF UNEMPLOYMENT. Knowing the rate of unemployment at a given moment does not really tell us *why* people are unemployed. During any single year more than 1.3 million of the 18 million people in the labour force will have either changed jobs or taken new jobs. In every single *month*, about 785 000 workers will have quit, been laid off (told that they will be rehired later), or been permanently fired; another 940 000 will have gone to new jobs or returned to old ones. In the process, more than 3 million persons will have reported themselves unemployed at one time or another during any single year. Because there are continually people in transition among employment, unemployment, and not being in the labour force at any point in time, the relationship between the unemployment rate and employment is not simple. People leaving their job are shown in Figure 4–7 as two arrows pointing away from the employed group, toward the pool of unemployed, or out of the labour force entirely. In the same way, people "not in the labour force" or unemployed have two choices about where to go.

Working age population The number of people 15 years of age and older.

Employed The number of adults aged 15 years or older who have work.

Unemployed The total number of adults aged 15 years or older who are willing and able to work, and who are actively looking for work but have not found a job.

Labour force The total number of adults aged 15 years or older who either have a job or are looking and available for a job; the number of employed plus the number of unemployed.

FIGURE 4–6

Understanding the Working Age Population and Unemployment

The working age population of 26.505 million can be broken down into three groups: people who are employed, those who are unemployed, and those not in the labour force. The blue and orange areas represent the labour force—those employed and unemployed. The numbers are for May 2007.

SOURCE: ADAPTED FROM THE STATISTICS CANADA CANSIM DATABASE, TABLE 282-0001.

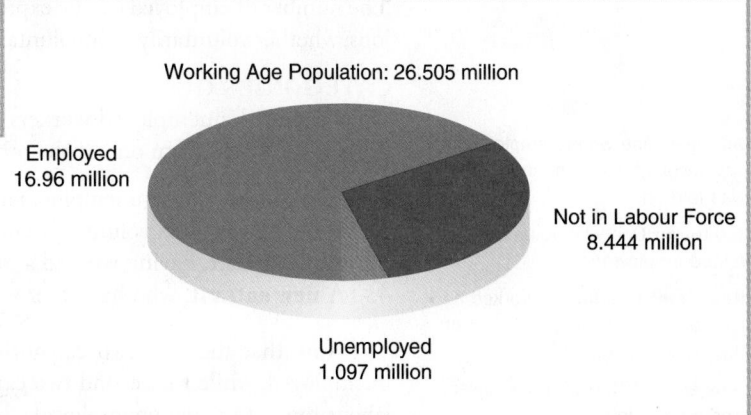

Working Age Population: 26.505 million

Employed 16.96 million

Not in Labour Force 8.444 million

Unemployed 1.097 million

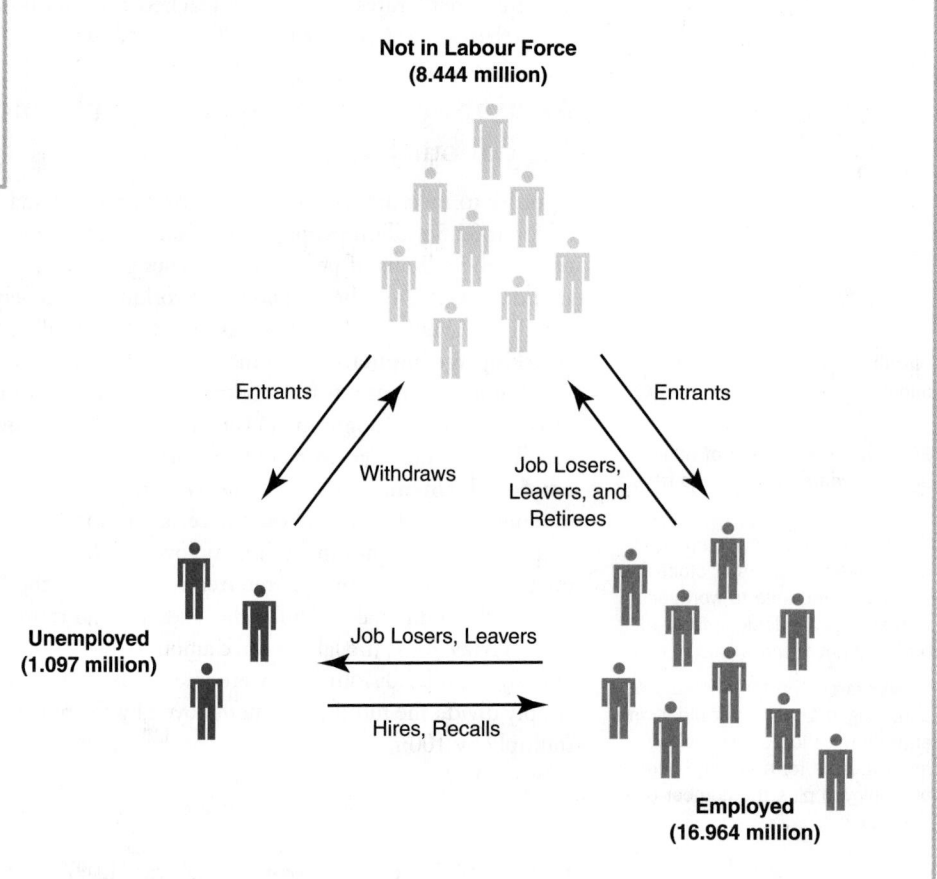

FIGURE 4–7

Understanding the Working Age Population and Unemployment

The working age population is in constant flux among the three subgroups. People are moving among the various groups as they move through their working life and as they enter and leave the workplace for a variety of reasons.

Source: Adapted from the Statistics Canada CANSIM database, Table 282-0001.

It is possible that people may choose to leave the labour force when they leave their jobs, such as when people quit their jobs to go back to school. In this case, it would appear that the unemployment rate has risen slightly, even though the number of people unemployed has remained the same. In the same way, it is possible for employment to rise and for the unemployment rate to rise. This has happened in the past at the ends of recessions. People who have not been looking for work during the recession notice that employment prospects are rising, and so they begin to search for work. Those that find work may go directly from being "not in the labour force" to being employed, while those that do not immediately find work now count as unemployed. The latter two groups are entrants to the labour force.

The number of unemployed can be expressed as some number at any given point in time. It is a stock of individuals who do not have a job but are actively looking for one. The number of employed can be expressed the same way. The number of people departing jobs, whether voluntarily or involuntarily, is a flow, as is the number of people finding jobs.

CATEGORIES OF INDIVIDUALS WHO ARE WITHOUT WORK. Once defined as unemployed, unemployed workers may fall into any one of four categories on the basis of their transition from one of the other two categories:

1. A **job loser**, whose unemployment was involuntarily terminated or who was laid off.
2. A **job leaver**, who voluntarily ended employment.
3. A **re-entrant**, having worked a job before but having been out of the labour force.
4. A **new entrant**, who has never worked at a job.

Note that the first two categories represent a movement from being employed to unemployed, while the second two categories represent movement from being "not in the labour force" to being unemployed.

Job loser One whose employment was involuntarily terminated or who was laid off.

Job leaver One who voluntarily ended employment.

Re-entrant One having worked a job before but having been out of the labour force.

New entrant One who has never worked at a job.

DURATION OF UNEMPLOYMENT. If you are out of a job for a week, your situation is typically much less serious than if you are out of a job for 14 weeks. An increase in the duration of unemployment can increase the unemployment rate because workers stay unemployed longer, thereby creating a greater number of them at any given time. The most recent information on duration of unemployment paints the following picture: 39.4 percent of those who become unemployed find a new job by the end of one month, 27.5 percent find a job within three months, and 14.5 percent are still unemployed after six months. When overall business activity goes into a downturn, the duration of unemployment tends to rise, thereby causing much of the increase in the estimated unemployment rate. In a sense, then, it is the increase in the duration of unemployment during a downturn in national economic activity that generates the bad news that concerns policy makers in Ottawa. Furthermore, the 14.5 percent who stay unemployed longer than six months are the ones who create the pressure on the federal government to "do something." What the government has typically done in the past is extend and supplement unemployment benefits. However, with the Employment Insurance plan implemented in mid-1996, employment insurance benefits are more difficult to get. The Canadian government hopes this will act as an incentive to the unemployed to look harder for work.

THE DISCOURAGED WORKER PHENOMENON. Critics of the published unemployment rate calculated by the federal government believe that there exist numerous *discouraged workers* and "hidden unemployed." Though there is no exact definition or way to measure *discouraged workers*, Statistics Canada defines **discouraged workers** as people who have dropped out of the labour force and are no longer looking for a job because they believe that the job market has little to offer them. To what extent do we want to include in the measured labour force those individuals who voluntarily choose not to look for work or those who take only two minutes a day to scan the "want ads" and then decide that there are no jobs?

Discouraged workers People who have dropped out of the labour force and are no longer looking for a job because they believe that the job market has little to offer them.

Some economists argue that people who work part-time but are willing to work full-time should be classified as "semi-hidden" unemployed. Estimates of this category of unemployment range as high as 2.5 million workers at any one time. Offsetting this factor, though, is *overemployment*. An individual working 50 or 60 hours a week—or a full-time *and* part-time job—is still counted as only one full-time worker. Similarly, as shown in Policy Example 4–1, we see how China's employement policies can affect measured unemployment rates in ways that make it seem lower than it actually is, a form of "hidden" employment.

POLICY EXAMPLE 4–1 Challenges of Measuring the Unemployment Rate in China

In recent years, the Chinese government's official estimate of the unemployment rate has hovered between 4 and 5 percent. This figure takes into account only members of the nation's labour force who permanently reside in urban areas. Measurement of China's labour force and unemployment rate fails to encompass all of the roughly 115 million people who migrate each year from rural areas in search of jobs in cities. Most of these migrant workers do find jobs in urban areas, but millions do not. In addition, China's government has not yet developed a way to determine how many of the millions of people laid off from state-owned firms have obtained positions with private firms.

Studies of unemployment in China suggest that the average annual unemployment rate for the nation as a whole during the mid-2000s has actually been somewhere between 7 and 13 percent. In a nation with a labour force exceeding 760 million people, this means that it is likely that between 15 million and 60 million more residents of China are unemployed than government figures indicate.

For Critical Analysis: Why might total unemployment of migrant workers in China be likely to reflect all four major types of unemployment?

Labour force participation rate
The proportion of working age individuals who are employed or seeking employment.

LABOUR FORCE PARTICIPATION. The way in which we define unemployment and membership in the labour force will affect what is known as the **labour force participation rate**. It is defined as the proportion of working age individuals who are employed or seeking employment. (If there are discouraged, or hidden, unemployed within any particular group, the labour force participation rate for that particular group will drop as these people are counted as "not in the labour force.")

Figure 4–8 illustrates the labour force participation rates since 1945. The major change has been the increase in female labour force participation. From a low of 23.2 percent in 1950, the female labour force participation rate climbed steadily to a high of 62 percent in 2007. At the same time, however, the number of hours worked is also changing. Because of differences between countries and over time, the same participation rate may mean quite different things, as we can see in Example 4–2.

FIGURE 4–8

Labour Force Participation Rate by Gender

Participation rates for men have generally been falling since World War II, while female participation rates have been rising much more rapidly. Overall, participation rates have risen about 10 percent.

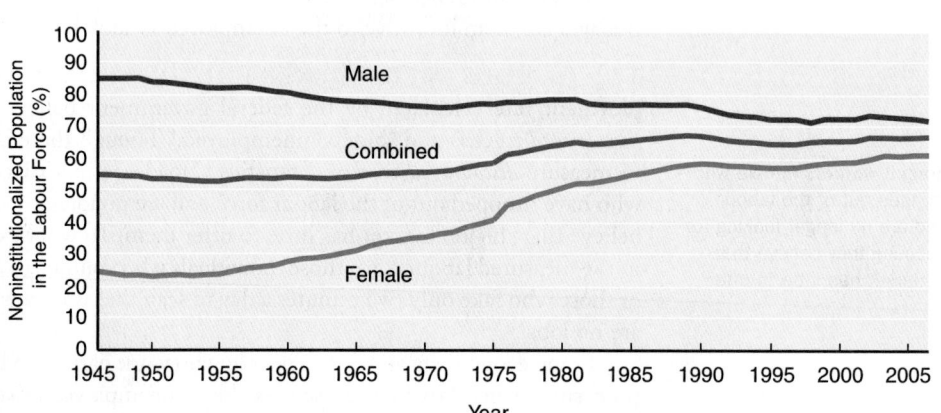

SOURCES: ADAPTED FROM THE STATISTICS CANADA CANSIM DATABASE, TABLE 282-0086, JULY 2007 AND FROM THE STATISTICS CANADA PUBLICATION *HISTORICAL STATISTICS OF CANADA*, SECOND EDITION, CATALOGUE 11-516, 1983, SERIES D146-149.

| EXAMPLE 4–2 | **Translating Employment into Hours on the Job** |

The average number of hours that an individual works in a given year can vary considerably from nation to nation. In Canada, workers averaged 1706 hours per year, while in the United States, for instance, a typical employed worker is on the job 1978 hours per year; the comparable figure in Norway is 1376 hours per year. This means that relative to a worker in Norway, the typical American worker devotes the equivalent of more than 15 additional 40-hour weeks to work each year.

The average American worker spends more time on the job than a typical worker in most other developed nations. Only in the Czech Republic and South Korea do people spend even more time at work. A typical South Korean resident works almost 800 hours more than an average Canadian worker, and nearly 1400 hours more than a resident of Norway. This means that for every hour that an individual in Norway spends on the job, someone in South Korea is at work 50 minutes longer.

For critical analysis: Does the fact that a typical individual in South Korea works more hours per year than an average resident of Norway necessarily imply that the South Korean worker produces more output of a comparable good or service in that time?

Different Kinds of Unemployment

Economists generally divide the group of unemployed into three broad categories that reflect different reasons for unemployment. These categories are called *frictional*, *structural*, and *cyclical* unemployment.

Frictional unemployment is the unemployment that arises from the continuous flow of individuals from job to job and in and out of employment, which includes those seeking a job for the first time. There will always be some frictional unemployment because new jobs cannot be found instantly. In the labour market, the cost of time involved in looking for a job, being interviewed, negotiating the pay, and so on is a *transaction cost*, and it is never zero. To eliminate frictional unemployment, we would have to prevent workers from leaving their present jobs until they had already lined up other jobs at which they would start working immediately, and we would have to guarantee first-time job seekers a job *before* they started looking. It is unrealistic, then, to think we could ever have a *zero* unemployment rate.

A second kind of unemployment is *structural unemployment*. Structural changes in our economy cause some workers to become unemployed permanently or for very long periods of time because they cannot find jobs that use their particular skills. **Structural unemployment** occurs when there is a mismatch of available jobs and available skills. For example, a shipbuilding company in Nova Scotia may have job openings for qualified shipwrights, but all the qualified shipwrights live in British Columbia. Or a printing firm may update its technology, making the skills of its existing workforce obsolete. The firm hires new workers and lays off the old, who are now structurally unemployed. **Seasonal unemployment** (unemployment that varies with the seasons of the year) is a form of structural unemployment because skills are not needed for part of the year. This occurs in the tourism and construction industries, for example.

Cyclical unemployment is related to business fluctuations and is defined as unemployment associated with changes in business conditions—primarily recessions and depressions. The way to lessen cyclical unemployment would be to reduce the intensity, duration, and frequency of ups and downs of business activity. Economic policy makers attempt, through their policies, to reduce cyclical unemployment by keeping business activity on an even keel.

Full Employment

Does full employment mean that everybody has a job? No, because not everyone is looking for a job—full-time students and full-time homemakers, for example, are not. Is it possible for everyone who is looking for a job to always find one? No, because transaction costs in the labour market are not zero.

We will always have some frictional unemployment as individuals move in and out of the labour force, seek higher-paying jobs, and move to different parts of the country. Full employment is, therefore, a vague concept implying some sort of balance or equilibrium in an ever-shifting labour market. In general, **full employment** occurs if only workers who are between jobs and those whose skills are not needed in the economy are unemployed, or, in other words, the demand for jobs is equal to the supply of (useable) workers. In order to carry out appropriate policies to reduce unemployment, it is important to know when the economy has reached full employment. Economists estimate this through the **natural rate of unemployment**, which is the rate of unemployment that prevails when only frictional unemployment and structural unemployment exist, thereby excluding cyclical unemployment. As an indication of how difficult it is to identify which type of unemployment is which, however, the Government of Canada and the Bank of Canada estimate that the natural rate of unemployment is somewhere between 7.4 and 9.5 percent. Given that the current rate of unemployment is near or even below the bottom of this range, it is not surprising to see reports of labour shortages in newspapers. In Policy Example 4-2, we have a look at how the government of India has artificially tried to reach full employment.

Frictional unemployment The unemployment that arises from the continuous flow of individuals from job to job and in and out of employment, which includes those seeking a job for the first time.

Structural unemployment Unemployment that occurs when there is a mismatch of available jobs and available skills.

Seasonal unemployment Unemployment that varies with the seasons of the year.

Cyclical unemployment Unemployment associated with changes in business conditions—primarily recessions and depressions.

Full employment Occurs if only workers who are between jobs and those whose skills are not needed in the economy are unemployed.

Natural rate of unemployment The rate of unemployment that prevails when only frictional unemployment and structural unemployment exist.

POLICY EXAMPLE 4-2   **Policymakers Promote Measured Full Employment in India**

Since 2005, the Indian government has extended a standing guarantee of employment, at a government-established wage, to one person per household for at least 100 days per year. Those employed under this policy engage in such activities as building rural roads and planting mango and orange groves. During the time that the government honours its commitment, those people put to work on such tasks are no longer unemployed. Consequently, the measured unemployment rate in India has been reduced.

For Critical Analysis Who provides the funds required to honour the government's guarantee and reduce India's unemployment rate?

➡️ CONCEPTS IN BRIEF

Learning Objective 4.3: Calculate the rate of unemployment and discuss the three kinds of unemployment.

- Unemployment is a concern because of the loss of GDP and personal hardships that result.
- The working age population is the group of people 15 years of age and older. This population is divided into three subgroups: the employed, the unemployed, and those not in the labour force. The labour force is the sum of the employed and the unemployed.
- The flow of people moving among the three groups of the working-age population determines the stock of the employed, the unemployed, and those not in the labour force. The unemployed are job losers, re-entrants, job leavers, and new entrants to the labour force.
- The duration of unemployment also affects the unemployment rate. The number of unemployed workers can remain the same, but if the duration of unemployment increases, the measured unemployment rate will go up.
- Frictional unemployment occurs because of transaction costs in the labour market. Structural unemployment occurs when there is a poor match of workers' skills and abilities with available jobs. Cyclical unemployment exists when the economy is in recession and firms have laid off employees.
- The natural rate of unemployment is the rate of unemployment that occurs when only frictional unemployment and structural unemployment exist.

4.4 Inflation and Deflation

During World War II, you could buy bread for 10 to 15 cents a loaf and have milk delivered fresh to your door costing about 25 cents per half-gallon (2.25 litres). The average price of a new car was less than $1000, and the average house cost less than $5000. Today, bread, milk, cars, and houses all cost more—a lot more. Prices are now 13 times what they were in 1940. Clearly, this country has experienced quite a bit of *inflation* since then. We define **inflation** as an upward movement in the average level of prices. The opposite of inflation is **deflation**, defined as a downward movement in the average level of prices.

Note that these definitions depend on the *average* level of prices. This means that even during a period of inflation, some prices can be falling if other prices are rising at a faster rate. The prices of computers and computer-related equipment have dropped dramatically since the 1960s, even though there has been general inflation. Inflation is measured in Canada using the **Consumer Price Index (CPI)**, which is a weighted average of the prices of a specified set of goods and services purchased by wage earners in urban areas.

Inflation An upward movement in the average level of prices.

Deflation A downward movement in the average level of prices.

Consumer Price Index (CPI) A weighted average of the prices of a specified set of goods and services purchased by wage earners in urban areas.

Historical Changes in the CPI

The CPI has shown a fairly dramatic trend upward since about World War II. Figure 4–9 shows the annual rate of change in the CPI since 1870. Prior to World War II, there were numerous periods of deflation along with periods of inflation. Persistent year-in and year-out inflation seems to be a post–World War II phenomenon, at least in Canada. As far back as the time before Confederation, prices used to rise during war periods and then fall back to more normal levels afterward. This occurred during the War of 1812 and World War I. Consequently, the overall price level in 1940 was not much different from 150 years earlier. Other countries have not been so fortunate, however, as you will discover in the Issues and Applications section.

Measuring the Rate of Inflation

How do we come up with a measure of the rate of inflation? This is, indeed, a thorny problem for government statisticians. It is easy to determine how much the price of an individual commodity has risen: if last year a light bulb cost 50 cents and this year it costs 75 cents, there has been a 50 percent rise in the price of that light bulb over a one-year

---

FIGURE 4–9

Inflation in Canada

Inflation has often been associated with wars (see World War I, World War II, and the Korean War), and deflation is usually associated with a depression. However, during the 1970s, inflation was rising and sustained for many years, only falling back to about 2 percent in the mid-1990s, where it currently sits.

SOURCE: ADAPTED FROM THE STATISTICS CANADA CANSIM DATABASE, TABLE 326-0020; A. GREEN AND A. URQUHART, "NEW ESTIMATES OF OUTPUT GROWTH IN CANADA," *PERSPECTIVES ON CANADIAN ECONOMIC HISTORY*, 1994.

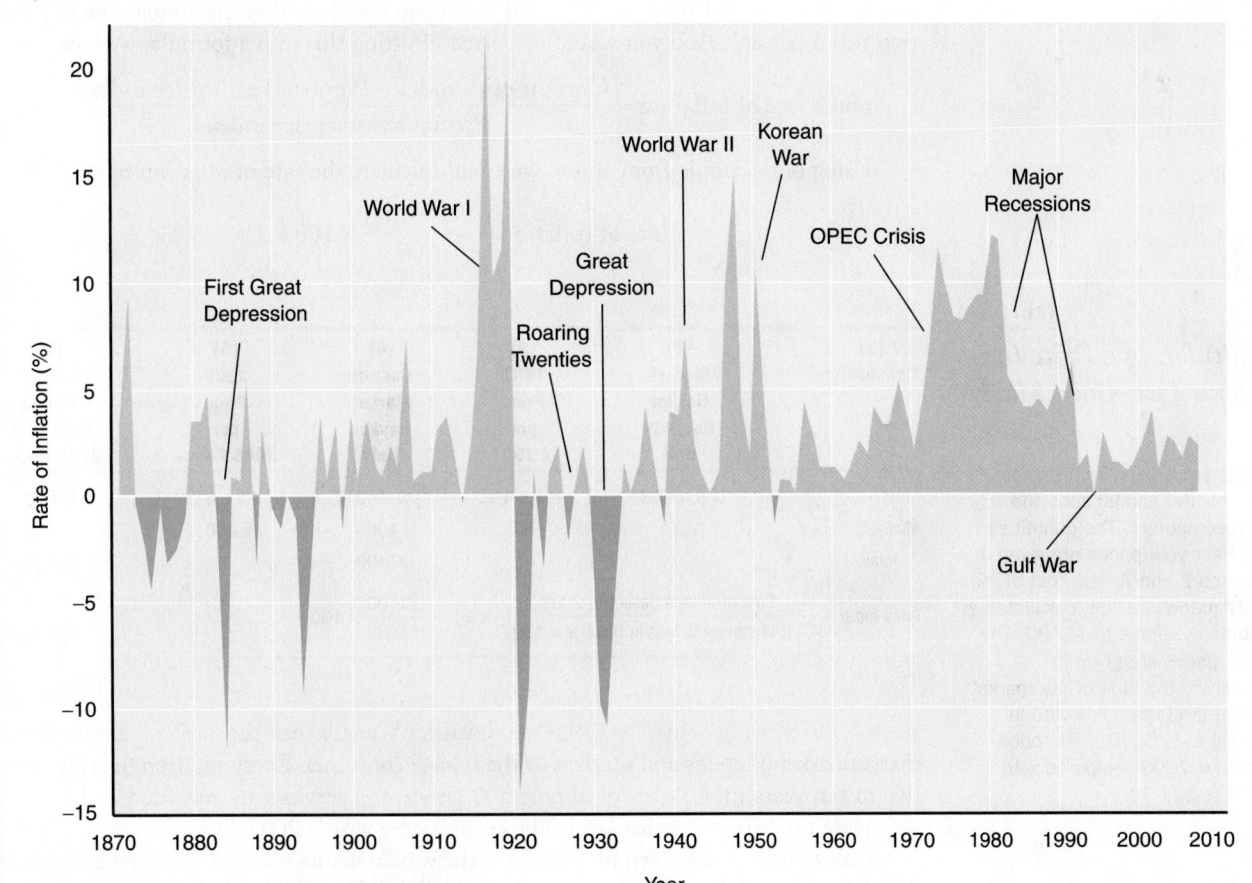

period. We can express the change in the price of the individual light bulb in one of several ways: The price has gone up 25 cents; the price is one and a half (1.5) times as high; the price has risen by 50 percent. An *index number* of this price rise is simply the second way (1.5) multiplied by 100, meaning that the index number would be 150. We multiply by 100 to eliminate decimals because it is easier to think in terms of percentage changes using integers (whole numbers). This is the standard convention adopted for convenience in dealing with index numbers or price levels.

COMPUTING A PRICE INDEX. The measurement problem becomes more complicated when it involves a large number of goods, some whose prices have risen faster than others and some with prices that have fallen. What we have to do is pick a representative bundle, a so-called "market basket," of goods and services and compare the cost of that market basket of goods over time. When we do this, we obtain a **price index**, which is defined as the cost of a market basket of goods in a given year, expressed as a percentage of the cost of that identical market basket of goods in some starting year, known as the **base year**—the year that is chosen as the point of reference for comparison of prices in other years.

Price index The cost of a market basket of goods and services in a given year expressed as a percentage of the cost of the same market basket during a base year.

Base year The year that is chosen as the point of reference for comparison of prices in other years.

$$\text{Price index} = \frac{\text{Cost of market basket in a given year}}{\text{Cost of market basket in base year}} \times 100$$

In the base year the price index will always be 100 because the year is the same in the numerator and in the denominator; therefore, the fraction equals 1, and when we multiply it by 100, we get 100.

A simple numerical example is given in Table 4–1. In the table, there are only two goods in the market basket—corn and microcomputers. The *quantities* in the basket remain the same between the base year, 1997, and the current year, 2008; only the *prices* change. Such a *fixed-quantity* price index is the easiest to compute because the statisticians need only look at prices of goods and services sold every year, rather than actually observing how much of these goods and services consumers actually purchase each year.

You can use a price index to calculate the annual rate of inflation. If the price index rose from 100 to 103 between 2007 and 2008, you could say that the annual rate of inflation was 3 percent. And you would be correct. Putting this into a formula, we have

$$\text{Annual rate of inflation} = \frac{\text{Current price index} - \text{Previous year's price index}}{\text{Previous year's price index}} \times 100$$

Using our example from above, we could calculate the rate of inflation to be

$$\text{Rate of inflation} = \frac{103 - 100}{100} \times 100 = 3\%$$

TABLE 4–1

Calculating a Price Index for a Two-Good Market Basket

In this simplified example, there are only two goods: corn and microcomputers. The quantities and base-year prices are given in columns 2 and 3. The cost of the 1997 market basket, calculated in column 4, comes to $1400. The 2008 prices are given in column 5. The cost of the market basket in 2008, calculated in column 6, is $1700. The price index for 2008 compared with 1997 is 121.43.

(1) Commodity	(2) Market Basket Quantity Unit	(3) 1997 Price per in 1997	(4) Cost of Market Basket Unit	(5) 2008 Price per 2008 Prices	(6) Cost of Market Basket at 2008 Prices
Corn	100 bushels	$ 4	$ 400	$ 8	$ 800
Microcomputers	2	500	1000	450	900
Totals			$1400		$1700

$$\text{Price index} = \frac{\text{Cost of market basket in 2008}}{\text{Cost of market basket in base year 1997}} \times 100 = \frac{\$1700}{\$1400} \times 100 = 121.43$$

THE CONSUMER PRICE INDEX. Statistics Canada has the task of identifying a market basket of goods and services of the typical consumer. Every so often (usually every five to ten years), the prices of almost 500 goods and services are recorded and used to formulate the base year price level. The current base year is 2002.

Economists have known for years that the way Statistics Canada measures changes in the CPI is flawed. Specifically, Statistics Canada has been unable to account for the way consumers substitute less expensive items for higher-priced items. The reason is that the CPI is a fixed-quantity price index (like the index in Table 4–1), meaning that each month Statistics Canada samples only prices, rather than relative quantities purchased by consumers. In addition, Statistics Canada has been unable to take account of quality changes as they occur. Even if it captures the dramatically falling prices of personal computers, it has been unable to reflect the dramatic improvement in quality. Finally, the CPI ignores the introduction of new products.

Inflation and the Purchasing Power of Money

Purchasing power The amount of goods and services a given amount of money can buy.

The value of a dollar does not stay constant when there is inflation. The value of money is usually talked about in terms of the *purchasing power* of money. A dollar's **purchasing power** is the amount of goods and services that it can buy. Consequently, another way of defining inflation is as a decline in the purchasing power of money. The higher the rate of inflation, the greater is the drop in the purchasing power of money.

Nominal value The value of something in today's dollars.

Real values Values that have been corrected for the changes in prices.

One of the most important uses for inflation measures is to be able to distinguish between nominal and real values. A **nominal value** refers to the value of something in today's dollars or its "money face value." **Real values** are those that have been corrected for the changes in prices. Real values involve our command over goods and services—purchasing power—and therefore depend on a set of prices. In many instances where we want to make meaningful comparisons, we must first adjust the nominal values to their real value equivalents. Consider this example: Nominal income per person in 1960 was only about $2250 per year. In 2003, nominal income was $37 400. Were people really that badly off in 1961? No, for nominal income in 1961 is expressed in 1961 dollars, not in the prices of today and so cannot be directly compared. In today's dollars, the per-person income of 1961 would be closer to $14 950, or about 40 percent of today's income per person. (The uncorrected 1961 data show per-person income to be only about 6 percent of today's income.)

How Are People Hurt by Inflation?

Real income Measures how much you can purchase with a given amount of income.

You can tell if you have been hurt by inflation by calculating the change in your *real income*. Your **real income** measures how much you can purchase with a given amount of income. If you could purchase two loaves of bread with the money earned during one hour of work last year, and you can still purchase that bread with the earnings from the same number of hours of work this year, then your purchasing power, or your real income, has not changed. If you cannot purchase two loaves of bread with the earnings from one hour of work but can only afford one and a half loaves, then your real income has declined. Conversely, if you can purchase more than two loaves of bread, your real income has increased. To determine the effect of inflation on your real income, calculate the percentage increase (or decrease) in your income in dollars and subtract the annual rate of inflation. Let us assume, for example, that your income increases 4 percent and inflation is 3 percent. What has happened to your real income?

$$\% \text{ change in real income} = 4\% - 3\% = 1\%$$

In other words, inflation has not hurt you because your income has risen faster than the rate of inflation. Inflation may also affect the value of some assets, and in particular, those with a fixed face value, such as cash, in a similar way. Example 4–3 shows how real income changed for industrial wage earners for the years 1994–2003.

Costs of Inflation

THE RESOURCE COST. Some economists believe that the main cost of unanticipated inflation is the opportunity cost of resources used to protect against inflation and the distortions introduced as firms attempt to plan for the long run. Individuals have to spend time and resources to figure out ways to cover themselves in case inflation is different from what it has been in the past. That may mean spending a longer time working out more complicated contracts for employment, for purchases of goods in the future, and for purchases of raw materials.

Repricing, or menu, cost of inflation A direct cost incurred by inflation in that it requires that price lists be changed.

Inflation incurs a direct cost in that it requires that price lists be changed. This is called the **repricing, or menu, cost of inflation**. The higher the rate of inflation, the higher the repricing cost of inflation because of the time spent simply repricing items. Imagine the repricing cost of Zimbabwe's rapid inflation in 2007 (as in Example 4-5 on page 116) compared with that in Canada, where the average inflation rate rarely reaches double digits.

TAXES AND INFLATION. Inflation creates major problems with the tax structure of the country and, in particular, with interest earned. The tax system works by taxing *nominal* income so that when inflation and interest rates rise together, the effective tax on earned interest is even greater.

For example, suppose that the real interest rate is 5 percent per year and the marginal tax rate is 40 percent. With no inflation, the real interest rate is 5 percent, and 40 percent is taxable. The real *after-tax* interest earned is 3 percent. Now, suppose that inflation rises to 5 percent and the interest rate rises to 10 percent. Thus, the lender must now pay 4 percent to government, leaving a nominal 6 percent *after-tax*. However, because inflation is 5 percent, the real *after-tax* interest rate has now dropped to 1 percent. Effectively, the tax rate has become 67 percent. The higher the inflation rate, the higher is the effect and the smaller is the incentive to save money.

EXAMPLE 4-3 **Do Rising Nominal Wages Mean Rising Real Wages, Too?**

The decade from 1994 to 2007 was good for Canada. Unemployment was generally low, and wages were rising. Or were they?

Figure 4–10 shows the course of average nominal and real industrial wages over the decade. Average nominal weekly wages rose from $592.67 to $765.35 in the year 2007, an increase of about 29 percent. But over the same period, the Consumer Price Index (2002 = 100) had risen from 85.2 to about 112.1, an increase of about 32 percent. On average, then, workers experienced a *decrease* in their real wages of about 2.5 percent, the opposite of what the increase in nominal wages would suggest.

FIGURE 4–10

Average Nominal and Real Earnings

Average nominal industrial wages were on the rise from 1994–2007, but the rise in the price level actually reduced real wages.

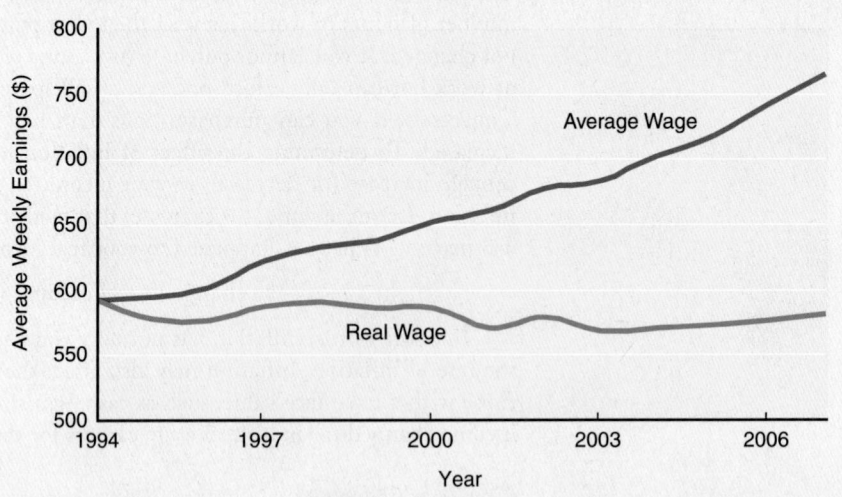

For critical analysis: Who benefits from lower wages?

SOURCE: ADAPTED FROM THE STATISTICS CANADA CANSIM DATABASE, TABLE 281-0028 AND TABLE 176-003 JULY 2007.

UNCERTAINTY. Another major problem with inflation is that usually it does not proceed perfectly evenly. Consequently, the rate of inflation is not exactly what people anticipate. When this is so, the purchasing power of money changes in unanticipated ways. Because money is what we use as the measuring rod of the value of transactions we undertake, we have a more difficult time figuring out what we have really paid for things. As a result, resources tend to be used trying to reduce this uncertainty, rather than seeking more profitable ways to produce things.

Anticipated versus Unanticipated Inflation

Any contract that specifies prices into the future must take future inflation into account. We will see that the effects on individuals and the economy are vastly different, depending on how well people anticipate inflation.

Anticipated inflation is the rate of inflation that individuals believe will occur in the future. If the rate of inflation this year turns out to be 10 percent, and that is about what most people thought it was going to be, we are in a situation of fully anticipated inflation. **Unanticipated inflation** occurs when the rate of inflation is different from what people believed it would be. For example, if the inflation rate in a particular year turns out to be 10 percent when, on average, people thought it was going to be 4 percent, there will have been 6 percent unanticipated inflation.

When people anticipate inflation and the decline in purchasing power that results, they will try to protect themselves. In wage contracts, for example, workers and their employers will negotiate a wage increase to cover the inflation rate. If the rate of inflation is correctly anticipated, then the contract will keep the purchasing power of the wages at what people thought they would be and not experience the decline in real incomes we saw in Example 4–3. Some wage contracts have **cost-of-living adjustments (COLAs)**, which are automatic increases in wage rates to take account of the increases in the price level and, thus, avoid having to anticipate inflation.

Situations of unanticipated rising inflation and unanticipated falling inflation have both occurred in the past 30 years. Both situations can create severe problems for people who have entered into long-term contracts. In Example 4–4, we see how unanticipated falling inflation forced some coal mines out of business and cost the government billions of dollars.

Anticipated inflation The rate of inflation that individuals believe will occur in the future.

Unanticipated inflation The rate of inflation that is different from what people believed it would be.

Cost-of-living adjustments (COLAs) Automatic increases in wage rates to take account of the increases in the price level.

EXAMPLE 4–4	**British Columbia Coal Mines**

During the 1970s, there were a couple of oil crises, and the price of oil jumped from a few dollars a barrel to about $40. The projections of price increases for energy were all pointing upward, perhaps to $80 a barrel. The price of coal rose with the price of oil. Japanese steel companies needed to find a steady and reliable source of coal that they could count on for their needs. So, in Canada, the federal and provincial governments worked together with two coal mine companies (which included some partnered Japanese steel companies that were to buy the coal) to build and open two coal mines in the northeast of British Columbia. A new town called Tumbler Ridge would be built for the workers, and the mines were to be called Quintette and Bullmoose.

Because these mines were far away from the ocean, there would need to be a new electric rail line (about 300 km long through the mountains) and a coal loading facility built in Prince Rupert. The terminal was built to store 12 million tonnes of coal a year, and load 8000 tonnes of coal onto a ship in one hour. The governments wanted economic activity to increase in this part of the province, and so agreed to spend billions of dollars creating these facilities. The coal companies spent more billions getting the coal mines running. By 1983, the mines were built and coal was being shipped to Japan.

Yet, by 2003, both coal mines were shut down, and the houses in Tumbler Ridge sold for next to nothing. The economic activity in that area was brought to a halt, and billions of dollars were lost. Why?

The answer is that the price expectations of the firms and the governments were completely wrong. The recession of the early 1980s meant a large decline in the demand for oil, and the higher price of oil meant that new oil sources were found, such as in Mexico.

continued

Instead of continuing to rise, the price of oil declined, and the coal price fell instead of rising. The Japanese steel companies, which had originally agreed to buy the coal at high prices, were able to use a clause in their contract to get out of the agreement, and a new lower price for coal was set. Eventually, the coal price fell so much that it was not worthwhile to dig the coal out of the ground. The mines were shut down and the workers laid off.

For critical analysis: Natural gas companies offer two types of contracts to their customers. One rate fluctuates with the short-term rates, and the other is a fixed rate for several years. How must the customers structure their purchases of natural gas so they do not get caught in a price squeeze the way Tumbler Ridge was caught?

Real Interest Rates and Inflation

Whenever money is borrowed or lent, a rate of interest is specified in the contract. But what happens if inflation is not anticipated correctly? With unanticipated positive inflation, for example, creditors lose and debtors gain. In most situations, unanticipated inflation benefits borrowers because they are not charged a nominal interest rate that fully covers the rate of inflation that actually occurred. Why? Because the lender did not anticipate inflation correctly. Lenders (such as banks) attempt to protect themselves against inflation by charging nominal interest rates to reflect anticipated inflation. A special type of mortgage called an adjustable-rate mortgage does just that: The interest rate varies according to what happens to overall interest rates in the economy. Creditors will gain and debtors lose in a situation of *falling* inflation and interest rates.

Nominal rate of interest The market rate of interest expressed in today's dollars.

Let us look at an example of a hypothetical world in which there is no inflation and anticipated inflation is zero. In that world, you may be able to borrow money—to buy a car or computer, for example—at a **nominal rate of interest** (the market rate of interest expressed in today's dollars) of, say, 10 percent. If you borrow the money to purchase a computer or a car and your anticipated rate of inflation turns out to be accurate, neither you nor the lender will have been fooled. The dollars you pay back in the years to come will be just as valuable in terms of purchasing power as the dollars you borrowed.

Real rate of interest The nominal rate of interest minus the anticipated rate of inflation.

What you want to know when you borrow money is the *real* rate of interest that you will have to pay. The **real rate of interest** is defined as the nominal rate of interest minus the anticipated rate of inflation. If you were able to borrow money at 10 percent and you anticipated a 10 percent rate of inflation, your real rate of interest would be zero—lucky you. (Of course, the lender will not be happy with this situation and will want a higher rate of interest to lend in the future.) In effect, we say that the nominal rate of interest is the real rate of interest plus an *inflationary premium* that takes into account the effect of anticipated inflation. Over the time period shown in Figure 4–11, the real rate of interest averaged about 5.1 percent.

REAL-WORLD PRICE INDEXES. Government statisticians calculate a number of price indexes. The most often quoted are the *Consumer Price Index,* the *Producer Price Index,* and the *GDP deflator.* The Consumer Price Index (CPI) measures changes only in the level of prices of goods and services purchased by wage earners in urban areas. The **Producer Price Index (PPI)** measures what has happened to the price level for commodities that firms purchase from other firms. The **GDP deflator** measures changes in the level of prices of all new goods and services produced in the economy. The most general indicator of inflation is the GDP deflator because it measures the changes in the prices of everything produced in the economy.

Producer Price Index (PPI) A price index that measures what has happened to the price level for commodities that firms purchase from other firms.

GDP deflator A price index that measures changes in the level of prices of all new goods and services produced in the economy.

THE GDP DEFLATOR. The broadest price index reported in Canada is the GDP deflator, where GDP stands for gross domestic product, or annual total income. Unlike the CPI and the PPIs, the GDP deflator is not based on a fixed market basket of goods and services. The basket is allowed to change with people's consumption and investment patterns. In this sense, the changes in the GDP deflator reflect both price changes and the public's market responses to those price changes. Why? Because new expenditure patterns are allowed to show up in the GDP deflator as people respond to changing prices.

FIGURE 4–11

Interest Rates and Inflation Rates Tend to Move Together

This figure shows how Canadian five-year interest rates and the inflation rate move together. As you can see, the interest rate increases at about the same time as inflation rates go up. When inflation rose rapidly in 1979 and 1980, interest rates soon followed. When inflation declined in the 1990s to about 2 percent, nominal interest rates had again fallen to between 5 and 8 percent.

Source: Derived from Statistics Canada CANSIM Database series: v122497, v737344.

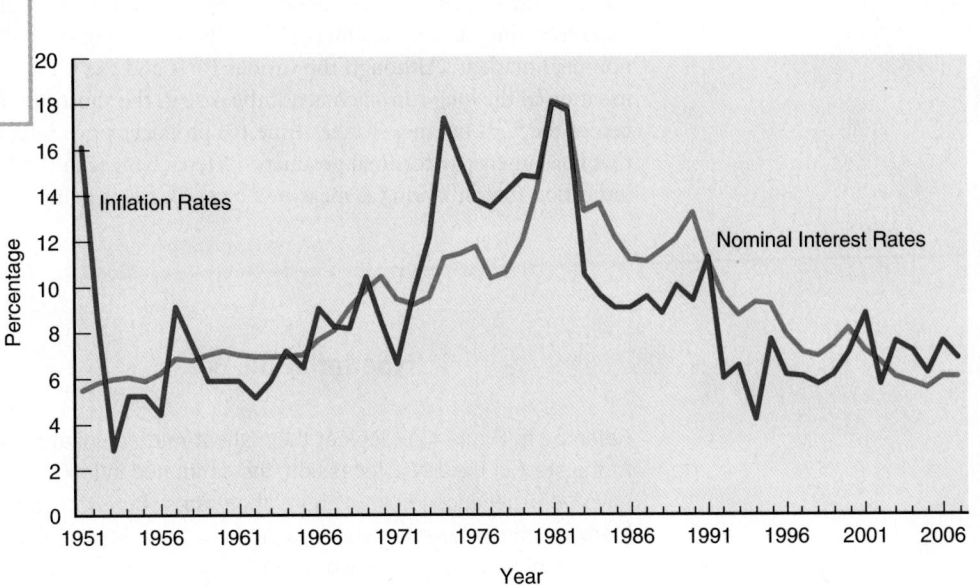

CALCULATING THE GDP DEFLATOR. The GDP deflator is calculated somewhat differently from the CPI.[2] In this measure of the price level, we first gather separate data on the quantity of output and prices. We then determine the market value of that output *as if the base year prices had prevailed.* These values are then added up to determine that year's real GDP.

Once this value is known, we then determine the *implicit* value of the price level by dividing nominal GDP by the calculated real GDP, or in formula terms:

$$\text{GDP deflator} = \frac{\text{Nominal GDP}}{\text{Real GDP}} \times 100$$

If we use the previous example numbers to start and add the quantities for the 2005 year, then we can calculate "real GDP" and the GDP deflator, using 1997 as the base year, as shown in Table 4–2.

TABLE 4–2

Calculating "Real GDP" and the GDP Deflator

(1) Commodity	(2) 1997 Market Basket Price	(3) 2005 Market Basket Quantity	(4) Cost 2005 Basket in 1997 dollars (real GDP)	(5) 2005 Market Basket Price	(6) Cost 2005 Basket in 2005 dollars (nominal GDP)	(7) GDP Deflator (implicit price index)
Corn	$ 4	120	$ 480	8	$ 960	
Microcomputers	500	5	2500	450	2250	
Totals			$2980		$3210	$\frac{\$3210}{\$2980} \times 100 = 107.72$

Note that we get a somewhat different value for inflation than from using the CPI method.

---

[2]Statistics Canada also uses a different method to calculate real GDP and the GDP deflator, called *chain weighting.* This method takes into account the relative changes in the different components of GDP, rather than using a fixed-weight method.

PRODUCER PRICE INDICES (PPI). There are a number of PPIs, including one for food materials, another for intermediate goods (goods used in the production of other goods), and one for finished goods. Most of the producer prices included are in mining, manufacturing, and agriculture. The PPIs can be considered general-purpose indexes for nonretail markets. Although the various PPIs and the CPI generally show the same rate of inflation in the long run, such is not the case in the short run. Most often, the PPIs increase before the CPI because it takes time for producer price increases to show up in the prices that consumers pay for final products. Often, changes in the PPIs are watched closely as an indication that inflation (as measured by the CPI) is going to increase or decrease.

EXAMPLE 4–5   **Hyperinflation**

Referring to Figure 4–9, look at the highest rates of inflation that Canada has experienced. At the start of the 1981 recession, the estimated inflation rate was over 10 percent. Rarely have we experienced such high inflation rates. Consider, in contrast, the rest of the world. Many countries have experienced and continue to experience hyperinflation, an extreme form of inflation, during which average prices rise very rapidly. In 1989, Argentina had an inflation rate of 4923 percent; the following year, in Peru, the rate was 7481 percent; and as we note in the Issues and Applications at the end of this chapter, Zimbabwe experienced inflation of 5000 percent in June of 2007. Russia's 1995 inflation rate of 340 percent seems almost modest in comparison. One of the most extreme hyperinflations ever to occur was in Germany in 1923, when prices increased by 700 billion percent.

For critical analysis: As a consumer, how would your behaviour change during a period of hyperinflation?

➤➤ CONCEPTS IN BRIEF

Learning Objective 4.4: Explain how inflation is measured and describe the effects of inflation and deflation.

- Inflation is a rise in the average price level of goods and services in an economy. It is measured using a standardized basket of goods. Once we pick a market basket of goods, we can construct a price index that compares the cost of that market basket today with the cost of the same market basket in a base year.
- The Consumer Price Index is the most widely used price index in Canada. It reflects a market basket of goods typically purchased in urban areas.
- Nominal values are those that reflect current prices. Real values are those that are corrected for changes in prices. Without correcting for price changes, some comparisons of economic prices may not be accurate.
- People are hurt by inflation because it reduces their real income.
- Inflation creates direct costs for society because of the cost of repricing items, tax bracket movement not related to real income changes, and the uncertainty it creates.
- Whenever inflation is greater than anticipated, it redistributes income in society. For example, creditors lose and debtors gain. The redistribution works in reverse when inflation is lower than anticipated.
- People use a variety of means to correct for inflation, such as COLA clauses in labour contracts and variable interest rates. Interest rates typically move in the same direction as inflation in order to maintain real returns to lenders.
- Other price indexes include the Producer Price Index and the GDP deflator, which measures the average price level of *all* new, domestically produced final goods and services in our economy.

4.5 International Trade

Open economy An economy that engages extensively in trading and investment with other countries.

Closed economy An economy that isolates itself from other countries.

Most of the world's industrialized nations engage in extensive trading and investment relationships with other countries, making them **open economies.** (A **closed economy** is one that isolates itself from other countries.)

The size of the trade and financial flows between countries have been growing faster than the rate of growth of GDP, and so countries are now more interrelated than they ever have been before. Canada trades about 40 percent of its production, primarily with the United States.

Why do we want to study international trade and financial markets? Because many jobs and much of what Canada produces and consumes comes through international trade. Indeed, the very reason that Europeans originally came to Canada was to harvest and export its raw materials—fish, fur, and lumber. An old saying goes, "When the United States sneezes, Canada catches a cold." This saying reflects the fact that most of Canada's trade is with the United States, and so when there is an economic downturn in the United States, Canada's economy usually follows the same trend. Economists want to understand how the business cycle can be transmitted from country to country.

Trade balances are another consideration. Exports and imports are not usually equal in any given year. During and following World War II, Canada's exports were greater than its imports because Canada was sending large quantities of supplies to countries damaged by the war. When exports exceed imports, then there is a **trade surplus.**

Trade surplus When exports exceed imports.

In Canada, trade surpluses again emerged during the 1990s. The corresponding trade deficits that are occurring elsewhere are often a reflection of some underlying financial or political problem, and economists seek to understand why they happen. On balance, Canada has generally exported more than it imports and therefore has a trade surplus.

Exchange rate The amount of money that can be purchased with one unit of foreign currency.

One important influence on trade is the **exchange rate**, which is the amount of Canadian money that can be purchased with one unit of foreign currency.

For Canada, the Canada–United States exchange rate is the most important, as 80 percent of Canada's trade and much of its international financial dealings are with the United States. As the value of Canada's currency goes up or down, the prices of purchasing imports and exports are directly affected. For example, a higher valued Canadian dollar means that Canadians can purchase imports more cheaply but have a harder time selling exports.

4.6 Government Policies

As we mentioned at the beginning of this chapter, governments have an understanding of how macroeconomics works and try to use their policies and spending powers to influence the stability and growth of the economy. Just as importantly, some policies may have unintended economic consequences. All of these government policies may have some substantial effect on the economy.

Government Program Spending

Governments around the world try to influence the economic performance of their economies. They know about the problems we have outlined and try to improve their economies for the benefit of their citizens. They want their economies to grow, to have low rates of unemployment and inflation, and to see stable trading and financial investment with other nations. There are a number of major policies that governments have used in a variety of ways to try to improve the economy.

Mixed economies Economies in which there is a mix of direct intervention by the government and the marketplace.

While Canada and other Western nations depend on the marketplace for determining much of what is produced, you also can see that the governments do not allow all decisions to be made by the marketplace. Governments engage in many types of program spending, distributing many of these goods for free or at subsidized prices. For example, most Western countries have public health-care and education systems, which are usually free or heavily subsidized. Because of this mix of direct intervention by the government and the marketplace, these economies are referred to as **mixed economies.**

Stabilization Policies

Fiscal policy The policies of government spending and taxation, in short, the government budget.

Monetary policy The policies that governments have over short-term interest rates and the rate of growth of the nation's money supply.

A second form of intervention by governments is in the form of fiscal and monetary policies. **Fiscal policy** refers to the policies of government spending and taxation, in short, the government budget. This includes the system of payments made to various groups, such as employment insurance and old age security. (We will examine these policies in greater detail in Chapter 11.) **Monetary policy** refers to the policies that governments have over short-term interest rates and the rate of growth of the nation's money supply. Monetary policies are controlled by a central bank, which in Canada is called the Bank of Canada. (We will look at monetary policy in Chapter 14.) Governments use these stabilization policies primarily to reduce the size of the business fluctuations that occur during a business cycle. During a recession, they are used to spur the economy (thus reducing unemployment), and during an expansion, to restrict it (thus keeping down inflation).

Trade Policies

International trade is actually quite highly regulated and is the subject of very important international and bilateral agreements that Canada has entered into over the years. (We will examine the role of these agreements in Chapters 16 and 17 in greater detail.) These policies are primarily aimed at promoting long-term growth.

Tariffs Government taxes applied to imported goods.

Trade has been regulated by agreements since before Canada was a nation. Early in Canada's history, **tariffs** (government taxes applied to imported goods) were the primary means of encouraging economic growth in a country, and most countries had them. Companies could avoid the tariff if they established a local production facility that would then create jobs within the country.

Tariff policies are now supplemented by a variety of policies that restrict the quantity of imports, such as *import* quotas and *voluntary export* agreements. Because of the increasing variety of policies and the complexity of products sold internationally, new international agreements have been negotiated. These new trade agreements have evolved through a number of stages. Now the World Trade Organization (WTO) regulates trade internationally. Within that framework, Canada has signed special deals with the United States and Mexico, and this arrangement is called the North American Free Trade Agreement (NAFTA). The deals spell out how tariffs and other policies can or cannot be applied and how disputes between nations are to be resolved.

Floating exchange rate Occurs when countries let supply and demand determine the value of their currency.

Closely related to trade policies are exchange rate policies. Countries are not always content to let supply and demand determine the value of their currency (called a **floating exchange rate)** but want to intervene to influence currency values. This is usually done in an attempt to encourage trade between countries, as an exchange rate that is steadier reduces the risk of making cross-border deals.

➡→ CONCEPTS IN BRIEF

Learning Objective 4.5: Explain why trade is an important issue for Canadians.
- ✦ Canada trades extensively with the United States and other countries. We also have an open investment policy that allows cross-country investment to occur.
- ✦ The value of the Canadian dollar has a large impact on the amount of trade that occurs.

Learning Objective 4.6: Name the basic economic policies available to government.
- ✦ Governments use these stabilization policies primarily to reduce the size of the business fluctuations that occur during a business cycle. The primary stabilization policies are fiscal and monetary policies.
- ✦ Trade policies regulate the flow of trade among countries. Tariffs were the first method by which governments attempted to encourage local investment. Trade is now governed by international agreements.
- ✦ Exchange rate policies have been used to try to encourage a stable economy. Today, the government of Canada allows the exchange rate to fluctuate according to supply and demand.

Hyperinflation and the Collapse of the Zimbabwean Economy

Concepts Applied: Hyperinflation, Unemployment, Gross Domestic Product

Rampant inflation caused rioting in Zimbabwe in 2007.

Hyperinflation

In May 2006, a single piece of toilet paper in Harare, the capital of Zimbabwe, cost $417 Zimbabwe dollars. A roll of toilet paper cost $147 750. A year later, that same piece of paper costs approximately 38 times as much or about $16 000 Zimbabwe dollars. Inflation in June of 2007 was approximately 5000 percent annually, which means that prices were more than doubling every month, and by December had risen to at least 10 000 percent. As a result of the rapid inflation, most of the economy was working on a barter system. Figure 4–12 shows the official rate of inflation as measured by the Zimbabwe central bank. This rapid rate of price increases is called hyperinflation.

Economic Output

Real GDP in Zimbabwe has declined every year since 1998 and is approximately half of what it was 20 years ago. At the same time, the population increased by approximately 25 percent. Unemployment is running over 80 percent and has been for

several years. Over 80 percent of the population lives below the poverty line. Figure 4–13 shows how poorly Zimbabwe performed in the last decade.

Government Economic Policies

The Zimbabwe government argued that inflation was the result of collusion between businesses and the West in order to destabilize the country. In June of 2007, the government ordered that prices of basic goods be slashed by 50 percent in an attempt to reduce inflation. Store owners that refused to open were arrested. The owners said that there was no point opening their stores as they would lose money selling at those prices. Where stores did open, there were scenes of near looting, and soldiers had to be deployed to restore order. Most stores did not restock their shelves.

FIGURE 4–12

Zimbabwe Inflation 1999–2007

SOURCE: RESERVE BANK OF ZIMBABWE.

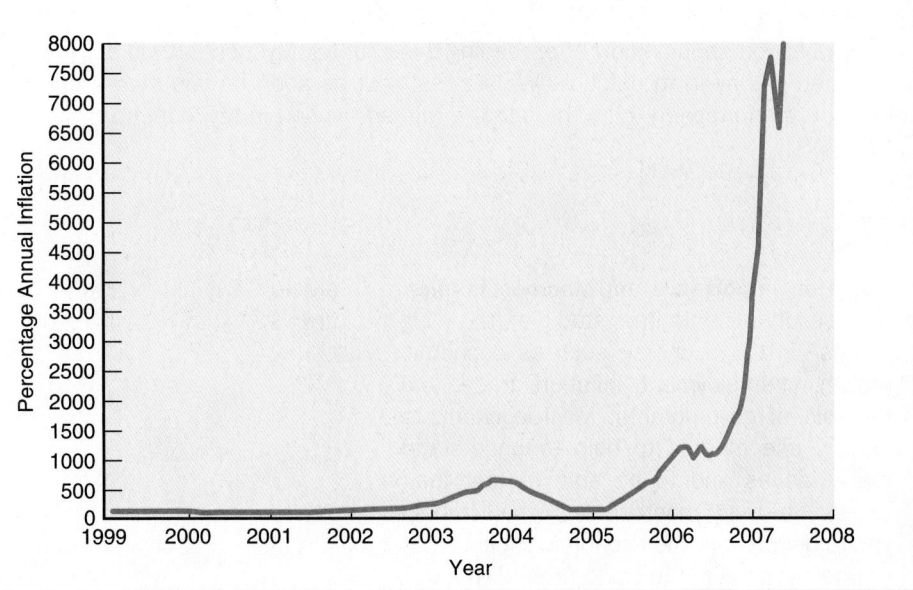

FIGURE 4–13

Zimbabwe GDP Growth

Source: International Monetary Fund, World Economic Outlook Database, April 2007. Estimates from 2005–2008.

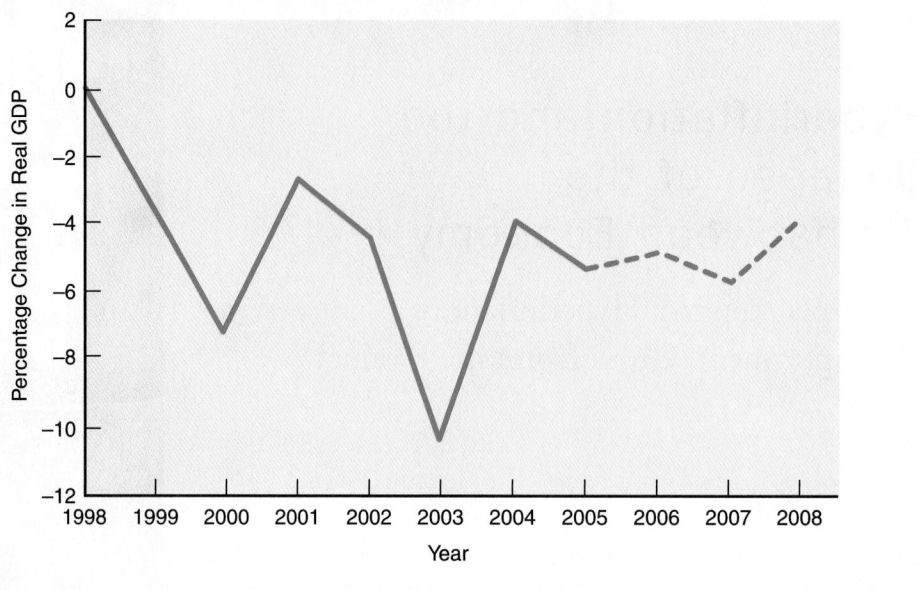

Zimbabwe's problems are clearly not the result of any conspiracy but rather some basic economic policies that have run awry. Economic observers agree that four things caused the collapse of Zimbabwe's economy.

First, Zimbabwe confiscated many of the farms previously owned by farmers who remained in Zimbabwe after the colonial era and gave them to people incapable of working them appropriately. These farms were responsible for a large portion of the economic output of the country, and the lack of protection for property has resulted in a large capital flight out of the country. Second, the government printed trillions of dollars that it used to purchase foreign exchange (needed for oil, for example) and to pay the army and civil servants. Third, up to a quarter of the population has gone into exile for a variety of reasons, primarily political and economic. Fourth, hyperinflation has caused the emergence of a barter economy as the dominant means of exchange.

For critical analysis:

1. Why is a barter economy likely to be less efficient than one based on monetary exchange?
2. Why does printing money and spending it not necessarily create more output?

Sources: New York Times: nytimes.com/2006/05/02/world/Africa/02zimbabwe.html; The Globe and Mail: Friday, July 13, 2007; CIA Factbook 2007: www.cia.gov; http://allafrica.com/stories/200706141025.html

 SUMMARY

Here is what you should know after reading this chapter. MyEconLab will help you identify what you know, and where to go when you need to practice. We suggest that as soon as you review one of the Learning Objective sections below, you then proceed to go through the related section in MyEconLab.

myeconlab

LEARNING OBJECTIVES	KEY TERMS	MYECONLAB PRACTICE
4.1 The Importance of Macroeconomics. Macroeconomics is the study of the "big issues" in the economy, such as economic growth, unemployment, inflation, trade, and the role of governments. Macroeconomists usually use models to help to understand these issues and to be able to test their ideas. Studying macroeconomics will help you to understand the economic choices that are being made in the world around you.	stock, 97 flow, 97	• **MyEconLab** Study Plan 4.1

➡ LEARNING OBJECTIVES	**KEY TERMS**	**MYECONLAB PRACTICE**
4.2 Economic Activity and Business Fluctuations. Economic growth is defined as an increase in Gross Domestic Product (GDP). It is one of the best indicators of the standard of living of a nation. Economic growth allows a nation to buy more goods and services and to invest more in the education and health care of the people. Growth is also closely linked to an increasing life span. Business fluctuations (or business cycles as they are sometimes called) occur when the economy deviates from its long-term growth trend. A positive increase in GDP is called an expansion and a decline is called a contraction. A long contraction is referred to as recession and is usually accompanied by high unemployment. If an expansion phase is too rapid, it can result in inflation.	gross domestic product (GDP), 97 economic growth, 97 business fluctuations, 98 expansion, 98 contraction, 98 recession, 98 depression, 98 inflation, 99	• **MyEconLab** Study Plan 4.2
4.3 Unemployment. Unemployment causes a loss of possible GDP production and so the country loses out on goods and services that might have been produced. It also has a big impact on the personal lives of individuals who become unemployed. The labour force consists of all persons who are employed plus those who are unemployed. Those persons over age 15 who are classified as "not in the labour force" are full-time students, homemakers, and retired persons. The rate of unemployment is obtained by dividing the number of unemployed by the size of the labour force. Labour force participation rates have increased dramatically for women since World War II. Unemployment is usually categorized into three types: frictional, structural, and cyclical. Workers who are temporarily unemployed because they are searching for a job are frictionally unemployed. The structurally unemployed lack the skills currently required by prospective employers. People who are unemployed due to business contractions are cyclically unemployed. The natural rate of unemployment includes the frictionally unemployed and structurally unemployed. When the economy has only frictional and structural unemployment, it is considered to be at full employment.	working age population, 103 employed, 103 unemployed, 103 labour force, 103 job loser, 104 job leaver, 104 re-entrant, 104 new entrant, 104 discouraged workers, 105 labour force participation rate, 106 frictional unemployment, 107 structural unemployment, 107 seasonal unemployment, 107 cyclical unemployment, 107 full employment, 107 natural rate of unemployment, 107	• **MyEconLab** Study Plan 4.3

➡ LEARNING OBJECTIVES	KEY TERMS	MYECONLAB PRACTICE

4.4 Inflation and Deflation. Inflation is a general increase in average prices. Inflation reduces the purchasing power of money. The most commonly used measure of changes in general prices is the Consumer Price Index (CPI), which is a weighted average of the prices of consumer goods and services commonly purchased.
 	
    Inflation, if not anticipated, can result in a redistribution of wealth and income among different groups in society. Since borrowing is a contract with a future repayment, interest rates must be set with an anticipated rate of inflation. If inflation is higher than anticipated, then the borrower gains at the expense of the lender. In order to avoid the effects of inflation, contracts that specify future prices often include clauses that adjust for inflation, such as cost-of-living allowance clauses in wage contracts. Nominal values are those that are stated in current dollars, while real values are those that are corrected for price changes. Interest rates include a component to account for inflation; when inflation rises, nominal rates of interest will also rise. Other price indexes include the Producer Price Index (PPI) and the GDP deflator.
	inflation, 108
	deflation, 108
	Consumer Price Index
	   (CPI), 108
	price index, 110
	base year, 110
	purchasing power, 111
	nominal value, 111
	real values, 111
	real income, 111
	repricing, or menu,
	   cost of inflation,
	   112
	anticipated inflation,
	   113
	unanticipated
	   inflation, 113
	cost-of-living
	   adjustments
	   (COLAs), 113
	nominal rate of
	   interest, 114
	real rate of
	   interest, 114
	Producer Price Index
	   (PPI), 114
	GDP deflator, 114
		• **MyEconLab** Study Plan 4.4

4.5 International Trade. Trade accounts for about 40 percent of Canadian GDP. Most of that trade is with the United States. Canada typically has a trade surplus with much of the rest of the world. The exchange rate is the amount of Canadian currency that it costs to buy one unit of foreign currency. Most of our international financial dealings are also with the United States.	open economy, 117 closed economy, 117 trade surplus, 117 exchange rate, 117	• **MyEconLab** Study Plan 4.5

4.6 Government Policies. The Canadian government uses a variety of policies to try to steer and grow the economy. Stabilization policies that seek to stabilize the business cycle include fiscal policy and monetary policy. Trade policies attempt to regulate international trade. These policies include tariffs, quotas, and exchange rate policies, as well as being a signatory to international agreements.	mixed economies,
	   117
	fiscal policy, 118
	monetary policy, 118
	tariffs, 118
	floating exchange
	   rate, 118
		• **MyEconLab** Study Plan 4.6

PROBLEMS

LO 4.1 Explain why the study of macroeconomics is important.

1. Economists spend much of their time looking at models of economic behaviour. What is the advantage of using models over trying to use the "real thing"? Why might it be impossible to use the "real thing" in economics?

2. When you have finished your studies, what do you expect the economy to be like? Will the general state of the economy have an effect on your future plans? How?

LO 4.2 Describe economic activity and business fluctuations and explain their effects.

3. Compare your lifestyle today with that of the original European settlers in Canada. How has economic growth affected lifestyle?

4. In January 2003, a country's economic activity reached a peak, and a trough occured in July 2003. The next peak occured in August 2004, and another trough occured in November 2005. Finally, there was another peak in October 2006. How many months long was each contraction and each expansion?

5. What are the major symptoms of a recession?

6. What sometimes occurs when we have too rapid an economic expansion?

7. What part of the "business cycle" are we currently in? How would we find out?

LO 4.3 Calculate the rate of unemployment and discuss the three kinds of unemployment.

8. An economic slump occurs and two things happen:
   - Many people stop looking for work because they know that the probability of finding a job is low.
   - Many people who become laid off start doing work at home, such as growing food, painting, and repairing their houses and cars.

   Which of these events implies that the official unemployment rate overstates unemployment, and which implies the opposite?

9. Assume that the labour force consists of 100 people and that every month, five individuals become unemployed, while five others who were unemployed find jobs.
   a. What is the frictional unemployment rate?
   b. What is the average duration of unemployment?
   c. Now, assume that the only type of unemployment in this economy is frictional. What is the unemployment rate?
   d. Suppose that a system of unemployment compensation is instituted and the average duration of unemployment rises to two months. What will the unemployment rate for this economy be now?

e. Does a higher unemployment rate necessarily mean that the economy is weaker or that labourers are worse off?

10. Look back to Example 4–2, "Translating Employment into Hours on the Job." Even accounting for the differences in hours worked, American workers produce more per hour than Canadian workers. What might account for this difference?

11. The Government of Canada has established an electronic job bank on the Internet at jb-ge.hrdc-drhc.gc.ca. How could such a job bank reduce frictional unemployment? Why would it not likely have much effect on cyclical unemployment?

12. Why is the natural rate of unemployment never zero?

13. Categorize each of the following unemployed persons as cyclically, frictionally, or structurally unemployed.
    a. A pulp mill worker is laid off because of excess inventory in British Columbia.
    b. A fish plant worker is laid off because of lack of fish in the cod fishery in Newfoundland.
    c. A typist is laid off because employees have been given their own computers.
    d. A plumber quits his job in Quebec and moves to Toronto to find work.

14. Suppose you are given the following information:

Total Population	30 million
Working-Age Population	20 million
Unemployed	0.75 million

a. If the labour force participation rate is 70 percent, what is the size of the labour force?
b. How many workers are employed?
c. What is the unemployment rate?

LO 4.4 Explain how inflation is measured and describe the effects of inflation and deflation.

15. The data in the table below give unit prices and quantities sold for three consumption goods in an economy.

	Prices per Unit		Quantities Sold	
	2006	**2008**	**2006**	**2008**
Pop	$1	$1	10	15
Chocolate Bars	$2	$4	30	35
Indigestion Pills	$5	$6	20	20

a. Calculate the consumer price index (CPI) for 2008, assuming that the base year is 2006.
b. What is the inflation rate between 2006 and 2008?

c. Now, assume that these three goods make up the economy's entire production. Using 2006 as a base year, what is the GDP deflator in 2008?

16. Explain the following:

    a. Suppose that the nominal interest rate is currently 12 percent. If the anticipated inflation rate is zero, what is the real interest rate?

    b. The anticipated inflation rate rises to 13 percent, while the nominal interest rate remains at 12 percent. Does it make sense to lend money under these circumstances?

17. Columns 1 and 3 in the table below show employment and the price level in the economy. Assume that the labour force in the economy is 10 million. Compute and enter in column 2 the unemployment rate at each level of employment. For each row (except the first), compute and enter in column 4 the annual rate of inflation.

(1) Employment (millions of workers)	(2) Unemployment Rate (%)	(3) Price Level	(4) Rate of Inflation (%)
9.0		1.00	
9.1		1.08	
9.2		1.17	
9.3		1.28	
9.4		1.42	
9.5		1.59	
9.6		1.81	
9.7		2.10	

18. Suppose that in 2010 there is a sudden, unanticipated burst of inflation. Consider the situations faced by the following individuals. Who gains, and who loses?

    a. A homeowner whose wages will keep pace with inflation in 2010 but whose monthly mortgage interest payments to a credit union will remain fixed.

    b. An apartment landlord who has guaranteed his tenants that their monthly rent payments during 2010 will be the same as they were during 2009.

    c. A banker who made an auto loan that the auto buyer will repay at a fixed rate of interest during 2010.

    d. A retired individual who earns a pension with fixed monthly payments from her past employer during 2010.

19. Look back to Example 4–4, "British Columbia Coal Mines." Banks in the 1960s offered mortgages for up to 25 years and yet today are only offering 10-year mortgages. Why would they no longer be interested in long-term mortgages? How is this similar to the problem Tumbler Ridge faced?

20. Holders of cash lose during inflationary times. Who gains from their loss?

LO 4.5 Explain why trade is an important issue for Canadians.

21. What products do you own that were made in other countries?

22. What firms in your area export their products to other countries?

LO 4.6 Name the basic economic policies available to government.

23. Explain the basic purpose of stabilization policies. Why might one be preferred over the other in trying to control the economy?

24. Why would a trade agreement with the United States encourage international trade? How might it benefit producers to have access to a large market instead of just a small one?

25. Name the two basic stabilization policies the government uses.

26. Describe how the government has used tariffs to try and spur economic growth.

5

Measuring the Economy's Performance

➤ **LEARNING OBJECTIVES**

After reading this chapter, you should be able to:

5.1 Describe economic activity and the circular flow of income and output.

5.2 Explain the measurement of gross domestic product (GDP).

5.3 Explain the two main methods of computing GDP: the expenditure and income approaches.

5.4 Explain how various subcomponents of GDP are calculated.

5.5 Understand the limitations of GDP.

MyEconLab helps you master each objective and study more efficiently. See end of chapter for details.

Statistics Canada, Canada's official statistical gathering agency, regularly issues reports on the state of the economy. Each day, Statistics Canada issues new information in a news release called *The Daily*. These reports focus on economic activity, inflation, and unemployment. The economic activity information—probably the most important—tells us that we have some of the highest standards of living in the world; however, measuring the value of economic output is not the same as measuring the well-being of our society. How do we know if we are doing "better?"

In this chapter, you will learn how the economy's economic activity is actually measured and, just as importantly, what it does not measure. At the end of the chapter, we will examine an alternative measure of how well off we are.

DID YOU KNOW THAT...

Canada's economy produces about *150 times* as much in value as it did in 1870! This record is not unique, however, as most industrial nations have had the same record of growth. In some cases, other nations have had even higher rates of growth over this time period. This massive increase in production is central to many of the issues we face in the modern world, such as pollution, environmental degradation, and social and cultural changes.

Even though we produce far more than we once did, the *physical weight* of what we produce has hardly changed. We produce about six times as much as we did 50 years ago, but only a small portion of the growth of our economy comes from physical materials. The remaining part comes from the ability to produce products with less material or using materials that are lighter than old ones. Soup cans weigh about half of what they used to, for example.

The types of products manufactured have also changed dramatically. A tonne of steel has an inflation-adjusted price of about $500. At this price, the production of rolled steel contributes only about $0.50 per kilogram to Canada's output. A microprocessor, by way of contrast, has a price of about $500 and weighs about 0.01 kg, which implies a $50 000-per-kilogram contribution to output. Many products, such as computer programs, have no weight at all, and so they push the average weight of our output down even more.

5.1 Economic Activity and the Circular Flow

In Chapter 4 we learned that the main measure of economic activity is gross domestic product (GDP), which we formally define as the total market value of all final goods and services produced in the economy during a year. GDP is a *flow of production*, measuring how much is produced in a period of time. A country is able to produce goods and services at a certain rate, just as you receive income at a certain rate. Statistics Canada and similar organizations in other countries measure economic activity and its various components using a system called **national income accounting**.

National income accounting
A measurement system used to measure national economic activity and its various components.

Consider this: Your income flow might be at a rate of $5000 per year or $50 000 per year. Suppose you are told that someone earns $500. Would you consider this a good salary? There is no way to answer that question unless you know whether the person is earning $500 per month, or $500 per week, or $500 per hour. You have to specify a time period for all flows. Your income received is a flow, which can be contrasted with your total accumulated savings, which is a stock measured at a point in time. From your employer's point of view, this represents a flow of expenses that pays for your labour. Therefore, for most measures in this chapter, there is an implicit or explicit period of time.

The measurement of all this activity as a series of flows goes back to a doctor named François Quesnay, who drew an analogy between the flow of blood in the body and the economic activity in 1750. The primary economic activity of the country is the flow of goods and services from businesses to consumers and payments from consumers to businesses. These basic flows are represented in a diagram, shown in Figure 5-1, called the circular flow, which is a simple model of the economy.

The concept of a circular flow of economic activity involves two principles:

1. In every economic exchange, the seller receives exactly the same amount that the buyer spends.
2. Goods and services flow in one direction, and money payments flow in the other.

In the simple economy shown in Figure 5–1, there are only businesses and households. It is assumed that businesses sell their *entire* output *immediately* to households and that households spend their *entire* income *immediately* on consumer products. Households receive their income by selling the use of whatever factors of production they own, such as labour services.

Profits Explained

We have indicated in Figure 5–1 that profit is a cost of production. You might be under the impression that profits are not part of the cost of producing goods and services; but profits

FIGURE 5–1

The Circular Flow of Income and Output

Businesses provide final goods and services to households (upper clockwise arrow), who in turn pay for them with money (upper counterclockwise arrow). Money flows in a counterclockwise direction and can be thought of as a circular flow. The dollar value of output is identical to total income because profits are defined as being equal to total business receipts minus business outlays for wages, rents, and interest.

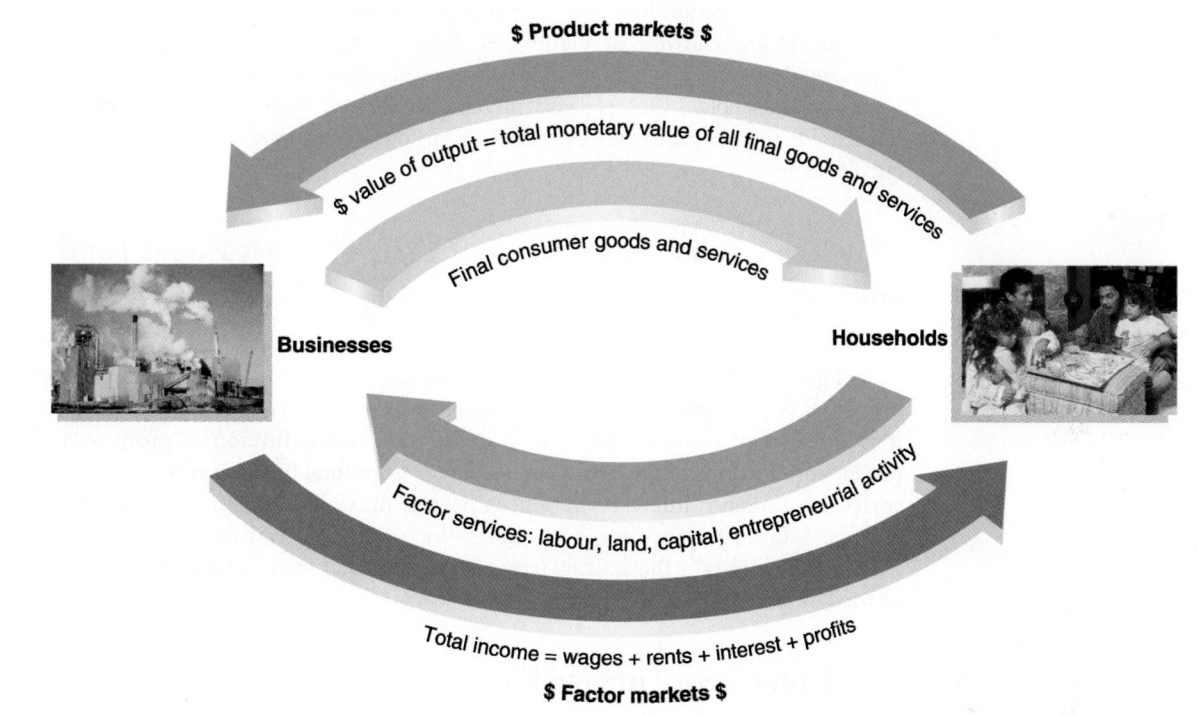

$ Product markets $

$ value of output = total monetary value of all final goods and services

Final consumer goods and services

Businesses

Households

Factor services: labour, land, capital, entrepreneurial activity

Total income = wages + rents + interest + profits

$ Factor markets $

are, indeed, a part of this cost because businesspeople and entrepreneurs must be rewarded for providing their services or they will not provide them. Their reward, if any, is profit. The reward—the profit—is included in the cost of the factors of production. If there were no expectations of profit, entrepreneurs would not incur the risk associated with the organization of productive activities. That is why we consider profits as a cost of doing business.

Total Income or Total Output

Total income The total of all individuals' incomes; the annual cost of producing the entire output of final goods and services.

At the bottom of Figure 5–1 is an arrow that goes from businesses to households, labelled "Total income." What would be a good definition of **total income**? If you answered "the total of all individuals' incomes," you would be right. But all income is actually a payment for something, whether it be wages paid for labour services, rent paid for the use of land, interest paid for the use of capital, or profits paid to entrepreneurs. It is the amount paid to the resource suppliers. Therefore, total income can also be defined as the annual *cost* of producing the entire output of **final goods and services**—goods and services that are at their final stage of production and will not be transformed into yet other goods or services.

Final goods and services Goods and services that are at their final stage of production and will not be transformed into yet other goods or services.

The arrow at the top of Figure 5–1, going from households to businesses, represents the dollar value of output in the economy. It represents the total monetary value of all final goods and services consumed by households. Business receipts are the opposite side of household expenditures. When households purchase goods and services with money, that money becomes a *business receipt*. Every transaction, therefore, simultaneously involves an expenditure as well as a receipt.

PRODUCT MARKETS. Transactions in which households buy goods and services take place in the product markets—that is where households are the buyers and businesses are the sellers of consumer goods. *Product market* transactions are represented in the upper arrows in Figure 5–1. Note that consumer goods and services flow to household demanders, while money flows in the opposite direction to business suppliers.

FACTOR MARKETS. *Factor market* transactions are represented by the lower arrows in Figure 5–1. In the factor market, households are the sellers; they sell such resources as labour, land, capital, and entrepreneurial ability. Businesses are the buyers in factor markets; business expenditures represent receipts or, more simply, income for households. Also, in the lower arrows of Figure 5–1, factor services flow from households to businesses, while the money paid for these services flows in the opposite direction from businesses to households. Observe also the circular flow of money (counterclockwise) from households to businesses and back again from businesses to households; it is an endless circular flow.

Why the Dollar Value of Total Output Must Equal Total Income

Total income represents the income received by households in payment for the production of goods and services. Why must total income be identical to the dollar value of total output? First, as Figure 5–1 shows, spending by one group is income to another. Second, it is a matter of simple accounting and the economic definition of profit as a cost of production. Profit is defined as what is *left over* from total business receipts after all other costs—wages, rents, interest—have been paid. If the dollar value of total output is $1000 and the total of wages, rent, and interest for producing that output is $900, profit is $100. Profit is always the *residual* item that makes total income equal to the dollar value of total output.

The Enhanced Circular Flow

Figure 5–2 shows a more complicated version of the circular flow diagram that includes two other sectors (governments and foreigners) and an important additional market, the financial market. The simplified version we just discussed still represents the majority of the total flow in the economy and is shown on this diagram with the large arrows. The flow of goods and services is omitted for clarity.

Financial markets show the possibility of saving and borrowing. Households take a part of their income and save it in a variety of financial instruments, ranging from ordinary savings accounts to shares and bonds. This money re-enters the circular flow through the borrowing of businesses, which use it to finance their purchase of capital goods (such as property, plant, and equipment). Money may also be borrowed and lent internationally as well as to governments (which is not shown).

Foreigners are shown in this diagram because we trade and invest with the rest of the world. Many products we purchase are made in other countries, and we sell much of what we produce to people in other countries. Because we have open financial markets, we may also wish to purchase assets or lend money in other countries, and foreigners own many assets in Canada.

Governments collect taxes from both individuals and businesses and use that money to purchase goods and services for their operation. Additionally, a large part of government revenue is returned to households as transfer payments (such as employment insurance and old age security), which add to household income.

Note now that the total monetary value of the goods and services is the sum of spending by all sectors, not just households. Total expenditure (also called *aggregate expenditure*) is equal to consumer, government, foreign, and business expenditures, all of which flow through the product markets. This expenditure is equal to the monetary value of output.

FIGURE 5–2
Enhanced Circular Flow

With this enhanced circular flow, the role of governments and foreigners is shown. Governments collect taxes, which they use to pay for their two primary forms of spending: transfer payments and ordinary goods and services. Foreigners also purchase goods and services (adding business output), and we purchase goods and services abroad.

Because all groups in the economy are able to borrow and lend, financial markets form a crucial role in "recycling" savings. These savings form the basis for many purchases, in particular, the purchases of capital goods by businesses.

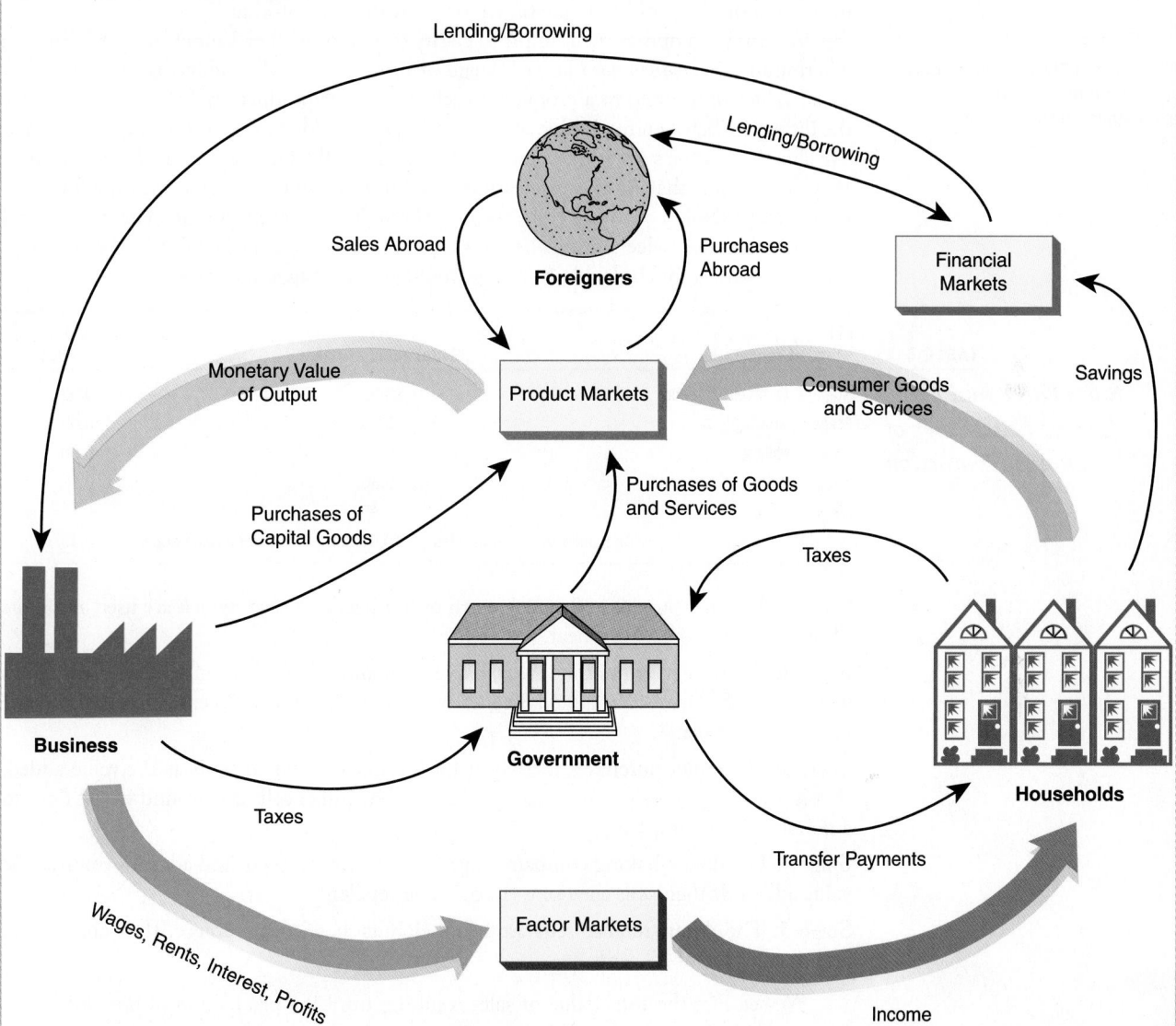

5.2 Measuring Gross Domestic Product

We have already mentioned that policy makers need information about the state of the national economy. Historical statistical records on the performance of the national economy aid economists in testing their theories about how the economy really works. We keep tabs on the health of the economy through national income accounting. Policy gurus use national income accounting for formulating policies that will enhance the nation's economy. National income accounting uses the concepts you encountered in the circular flow diagram to measure national production and its various components.

While we have already defined GDP as the total market value of all final goods and services produced in the economy during a year, it is just as important to understand what is *not* being measured by GDP. Economists have carefully defined what is to be included, and what is not. Below are some explanations on what is excluded from GDP measurements.

Avoid Double Counting

Intermediate goods Goods used up entirely in the production of final goods.

GDP does not count **intermediate goods** (goods used up entirely in the production of final goods) because to do so would be to count them twice. For example, even though grain that a farmer produces may be that farmer's final product, it is not the final product for the nation. It is sold to make bread. Bread is the final product.

Value added The amount of dollar value contributed to a product at each stage of its production.

We can use a numerical example to clarify this point further. Our example will involve determining the *value added* at each stage of production. **Value added** is the amount of dollar value contributed to a product at each stage of its production. In Table 5–1, we see the difference between total value of all sales and value added in the production of a donut. We also see that the sum of the values added is equal to the sale price to the final consumer. It is the 45 cents that is used to measure GDP, not the 96 cents. If we used the 96 cents, we would be double counting from stages 2 through 5, for each intermediate good would be counted at least twice—once when it was produced and again when selling the good that was made with it. Such double counting would grossly exaggerate the GDP.

TABLE 5–1

Sales Value and Value Added at Each Stage of Donut Production

(1) Stage of Production	(2) Dollar Value of Sales		(3) Value Added
Stage 1: Fertilizer and seed	$0.03		$0.03
Stage 2: Growing	0.06		0.03
Stage 3: Milling	0.12		0.06
Stage 4: Baking	0.30		0.18
Stage 5: Retailing	0.45		0.15
	Total dollar value of all sales	$0.96	Total value added	$0.45

Stage 1: A farmer purchases 3 cents' worth of fertilizer and seed, which are used as factors of production in growing wheat.

Stage 2: The farmer grows the wheat, harvests it, and sells it to a miller for 6 cents. Thus we see that the farmer has added 3 cents' worth of value. Those 3 cents represent income paid to the farmer.

Stage 3: The miller purchases the wheat for 6 cents and adds 6 cents as the value added; that is, there is 6 cents for the miller as income. The miller sells the ground wheat flour to a donut-baking company.

Stage 4: The donut-baking company buys the flour for 12 cents and adds 18 cents as the value added. It then sells the donut to the final retailer.

Stage 5: The donut retailer sells fresh hot donuts at 45 cents apiece, thus creating an additional value of 15 cents.

We see that the total value of sales resulting from the production of one donut was 96 cents, but the total value added was 45 cents, which is exactly equal to the retail price. The total value added is equal to the sum of all income payments or to the final retail sale price of the good.

Exclusion of Financial Transactions, Transfer Payments, and Second-Hand Goods

Remember that GDP is the measure of the value of all final goods and services *produced* in one year. Many transactions occur that have nothing to do with final goods and services produced. There are financial transactions, transfers of the ownership of pre-existing goods, and other transactions that should not and do not get included in our measure of GDP.

FINANCIAL TRANSACTIONS. There are three general categories of purely financial transactions: (1) the buying and selling of securities, (2) government transfer payments, and (3) private transfer payments.

1. *Securities.* When you purchase existing shares in the Bank of Nova Scotia, someone else has sold them to you. In essence, there was merely a *transfer* of ownership rights. You paid $100 to obtain the share certificate. Someone else received the $100 and gave up the share certificate. No productive activity took place at that time. Hence, the $100 transaction is not included when we measure gross domestic product.

2. *Government transfer payments.* Transfer payments are payments for which no productive services are provided in exchange at the same time. The most obvious government transfer payments are old age security benefits, veterans' payments, welfare payments, and unemployment compensation. The recipients make no contribution to current production in return for such transfer payments (although they may have made contributions in the past to receive them). Government transfer payments are not included in GDP.

3. *Private transfer payments.* Are you receiving money from your parents in order to attend school? Has a wealthy relative ever given you a gift of money? If so, you have been the recipient of a private transfer payment. This is simply a transfer of funds from one individual to another. As such, it does not constitute productive activity and is not included in gross domestic product.

TRANSFER OF SECOND-HAND GOODS. If I sell you my two-year-old minivan, no current production is involved. I transfer to you the ownership of a vehicle that was produced two years ago; in exchange, you transfer to me $20 000. The original purchase price of the minivan was included in GDP in the year it was produced. To include it again when I sell it to you would be counting the value of the van a second time.

NONMARKET AND HOUSEHOLD TRANSACTIONS. GDP measures only market transactions when money exchanges hands for goods or services. People are not paid in the marketplace for household production tasks such as home improvements, cleaning, and child care; therefore, this type of production is not included in GDP. The production transactions of volunteers, since they are unpaid, are not counted as part of GDP as well. As a result, GDP understates productive activity in the economy.

QUALITY IMPROVEMENTS. Improvements in quality, not just increases in quantity, contribute to economic well being. A computer that you could buy today for $3000 is clearly superior to one you could have purchased three years ago for much more. Cars today last longer and are safer, more comfortable, and more fuel efficient. Failure to account for quality improvements means that GDP understates increases in our real economic well being. GDP is only a quantitative measure.

Furthermore, when we calculate GDP, we use price indexes that take into account only price changes and not changes in quality. Therefore, these indexes create a downward bias to the real GDP calculations.

LEISURE. Leisure time contributes to our economic welfare. If our income stays the same, but we have more leisure time, then we feel better off. In the twentieth century, average income increased and average hours of work decreased from over 50 hours per week to less than 40 hours per week, and most people receive more paid vacations and holidays. These benefits are not reflected in GDP, and the improvement in economic welfare is understated.

COMPOSITION AND DISTRIBUTION OF OUTPUT. GDP does not distinguish between those things that are a benefit to society and those that are not. For example, a switchblade used for crime and a music CD that have the same price are weighed equally in the composition of GDP.

Further, GDP measures do not tell us anything about the distribution of income among individuals in society. It does not distinguish between most of the output going to a small elite versus the same output more evenly distributed.

THE ENVIRONMENT. GDP growth comes at the expense of the environment, but GDP does not account for these costs. Environmental problems such as pollution, congestion, waste, and noise accompany GDP growth but the effects are not deducted from GDP calculations. In fact, when an oil spill, a flood, or an ice storm occurs, the clean-up effort adds to GDP but there is no deduction for the effect on the environment. GDP will, therefore, overstate the value of economic growth in these cases. Policy Example 5-1 shows how this omission can be very significant when measuring GDP.

POLICY EXAMPLE 5–1 | **The Economic Cost of Pollution**

China has begun to look at the economic cost of pollution. In March 2004, China launched the Green GDP Accounting Research Project and conducted an accounting analysis on the physical quantification of environmental pollution, imputed treatment costs, and environmental degradation costs for 42 industries and three regions of east, central, and west China. In a report issued in September 2006, China estimated the cost of pollution at $67.7 billion (U.S.) or about 3 percent of its GDP. About 55 percent of the cost was in water pollution, 43 percent for air pollution, and the remainder of about 1 percent in solid wastes. The report did not take into account soil and ground pollution.

For some areas, inclusion of the significant local pollution problems as a reduction in output would have reduced measured GDP growth quite significantly. Many areas were still placing GDP above all else, and local officials were resisting the report. In July 2007, a second report—on the number of people likely to die prematurely because of air pollution—was cancelled because of the embarrassment these reports were causing the government. That report was expected to show that air pollution kills 750 000 people annually in China.

For critical analysis: What industries are likely to have caused significant air and water pollution?

SOURCE: VANCOUVER SUN, TUESDAY JULY 24TH, 2007 PAGE D9 http://english.gov.cn/2006-09/11/content_384596.htm

---

The Underground Economy

The underground economy (see Example 5–1) is the part of the economy which is deliberately hidden from the government. This activity is unreported in GDP accounts and means that GDP is understated.

If the underground economy is stable as a proportion of the economy over time, its omission will not pose a problem for policy makers. However, shifts from the underground to the rest of the economy, or shifts in the opposite direction, can cause distortions in assessing overall economic activity that could mislead policy makers. For example, the introduction of the goods and services tax during the early 1990s probably resulted in a shift toward the underground economy. As a result of that shift, measured GDP indicated that growth was slower than what was really happening in the economy.

OTHER EXCLUDED TRANSACTIONS. Many other transactions are not included in GDP for practical reasons:

- Household production—home cleaning, child care, and other tasks performed by people within their own households and for which they are not paid through the marketplace. The size of these activities is very large. The value of household production alone is estimated to be between 34 and 54 percent of GDP!
- Otherwise legal underground transactions—those that are legal but not reported and hence not taxed, such as paying housekeepers in cash that is not declared as income.
- Illegal underground (or "shadow") activities—these include prostitution, illegal gambling, and the sale of illicit drugs.

EXAMPLE 5–1   **The Underground Economy**

Economists typically estimate the size of a country's underground economy as a percentage of GDP tabulated by its national governments. Of course, trying to estimate this number is difficult because individuals engaged in these activities are attempting to hide their income from the government!

Current estimates indicate that the size of the underground economy as a percentage of official GDP ranges from a low 7.5 percent in Switzerland to a high of 28.5 percent in Greece.

Explaining the Underground Economy

Although there are many reasons that people may engage in transactions that go unrecorded in official statistics, many underground endeavours are aimed at avoiding taxes. In Canada, individuals sometimes offer not to charge GST if they are "paid in cash." The benefit for the seller, of course, is to avoid paying income tax on that income.

So, one possible hypothesis is that the relative size of a nation's underground economy is likely to rise when there is an increase in those portions of reported income for which people have to pay taxes. Figure 5–3 matches the proportionate size of the underground economies of selected nations with each nation's average taxes as a percentage of labour income. As you can see, overall, there does appear to be a positive relationship—illustrated by the line that best fits the relationship—between the relative size of a nation's underground economy and the overall tax burden imposed by the government. This implies that a government that seeks to fund increased spending on social and public-works programs with higher taxes may find its efforts frustrated by a shift of taxable activities to the underground economy.

FIGURE 5–3

Relative Size of the Underground Economy and Total Tax and Social Underground Burden in Selected Nations

The relative size of a nation's underground economy tends to increase with the tax and social security burden.

SOURCE: FRIEDRICH SCHNEIDER, "THE INCREASE OF THE SIZE OF THE SHADOW ECONOMY OF EIGHTEEN OECD COUNTRIES: SOME PRELIMINARY EXPLANATIONS." CENTER FOR ECONOMIC STUDIES IFO INSTITUTE FOR ECONOMIC RESEARCH WORKING PAPER NO. 306, JUNE 2000.

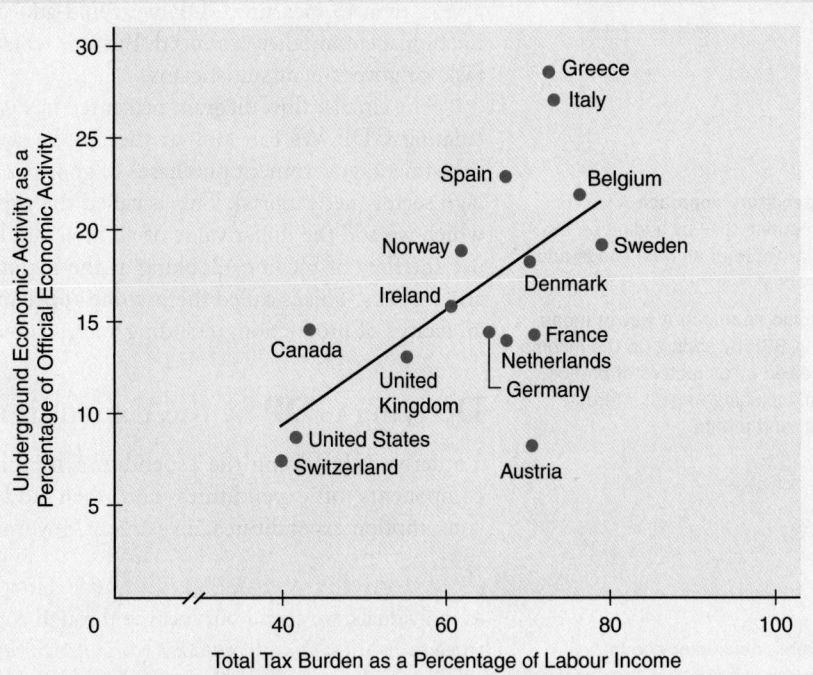

For critical analysis: Does the existence of underground economies cast doubts on the value of comparing nations' economic performance using official data?

➤→ CONCEPTS IN BRIEF

Learning Objective 5.1: Describe economic activity and the circular flow of income and output.

- In the circular flow of income and output, households sell factor services to businesses that pay for those factor services. The receipt of payments is total income. Businesses sell goods and services to households that pay for them.
- The dollar value of total output is equal to the total monetary value of all final goods and services produced.
- The dollar value of final output must always equal total income.
- GDP is the total market value of final goods and services produced in the economy during a one-year period by factors of production within the country's borders. It represents the flow of production over that one-year period.

Learning Objective 5.2: Explain the measurement of gross domestic product (GDP).

- To avoid double counting when measuring GDP, we look only at the value of final goods and services produced or, alternatively, at total value added created.
- When measuring GDP, we must exclude purely financial transactions, such as the buying and selling of securities; government transfer payments; private transfer payments; and the transfer of second-hand goods.
- Many other transactions are excluded from GDP: household services rendered by homemakers, underground economy transactions, and illegal economic activities. Leisure activities and the costs to the environment from production are also not measured.

5.3 Two Main Methods of Measuring GDP

If the definition of GDP is the total value of all final goods and services produced during a year, then to measure GDP, we could add up the prices times the quantities of every individual commodity produced. But this would involve a monumental, if not impossible, task for government statisticians.

The circular flow diagram presented in Figure 5–2 gives us a shortcut method for calculating GDP. We can look at the *flow of expenditures*, which consists of consumption, investment, government purchases of goods and services, and net expenditures in the foreign sector (net exports). This is called the **expenditure approach** to measuring GDP, in which we add the dollar value of all final goods and services. Alternatively, we could also use the flow of income—looking at the income received by everybody producing goods and services. This is called the **income approach**, in which we add the income received by all factors of production, including wages, interest, rent, and profits.

Deriving GDP by the Expenditure Approach

To derive GDP using the expenditure approach, we must look at each of the separate components of expenditures and then add them together. These components are consumption expenditures, investment, government expenditures, and net exports.

CONSUMPTION EXPENDITURES. How do we spend our income? As households or as individuals, we spend our income through consumption expenditure (C), which falls into three categories: *durable consumer goods*, *nondurable consumer goods*, and *services*. **Durable consumer goods** are *arbitrarily* defined as items that last more than three years; they include automobiles, furniture, and household appliances. **Nondurable consumer goods** are all the rest—consumer goods that are used up within three years, such as food and gasoline. **Services** are intangible commodities purchased by consumers: medical care, education, and so on.

Housing expenditures constitute a major proportion of anybody's annual expenditure. Rental payments are automatically included in consumption expenditure estimates. People who own their homes, however, do not make rental payments. Consequently, government statisticians estimate what is called the *implicit rental value* of owner-occupied homes. It

---

Expenditure approach A way of computing GDP by adding up the dollar value of all final goods and services.

Income approach A way of measuring GDP by adding up the income received by all factors of production, including wages, interest, rent, and profits.

Durable consumer goods Consumer items that last more than three years.

Nondurable consumer goods Consumer goods that are used up within three years.

Services Intangible commodities purchased by consumers.

is equal to the amount of rent you would have to pay if you did not own the house but were renting it from someone else.

GROSS PRIVATE DOMESTIC INVESTMENT. We now turn our attention to **gross private domestic investment** (*I*)—the creation of capital goods that can yield production and hence consumption in the future—undertaken by businesses. When economists refer to investment, they are referring to additions to productive capacity. **Investment** may be thought of as an activity that uses resources today in such a way that they allow for greater production in the future and hence greater consumption in the future. When a business buys new equipment or puts up a new factory, it is investing; it is increasing its capacity to produce in the future.

The layperson's notion of investment often relates to the purchase of shares and bonds. For our purposes, such transactions simply represent the *transfer of ownership* of assets called shares and bonds and is referred to by economists as saving. Thus, you must keep in mind the fact that in economics, investment refers *only* to additions to productive capacity, not to transfers of assets.

Investments expenditures are broken into three components. We have already mentioned the first one, which involves a firm buying equipment or putting up a new factory. A **producer durable**, or a **capital good**, is simply a good that is purchased not to be consumed in its current form but to be used to make other goods and services and has an expected service life of more than three years. The purchase of such equipment and factories—capital goods—is called **fixed investment**.

The second type of investment has to do with the change in inventories of raw materials and finished goods. Firms do not immediately sell off all their products to consumers. Some of this final product is usually held in inventory waiting to be sold. Firms hold inventories to meet future expected orders for their products. When a firm increases its inventories of finished products, it is engaging in **inventory investment**. Inventories consist of all finished goods on hand, goods in process, and raw materials.

The reason that we can think of a change in inventories as being a type of investment is that an increase in such inventories provides for future increased consumption possibilities. When inventory investment is zero, the firm is neither adding to nor subtracting from the total stock of goods or raw materials on hand. Thus, if the firm keeps the same amount of inventories throughout the year, inventory *investment* has been zero. Whenever inventories are decreasing, inventory investment is negative; whenever they are increasing, inventory investment is positive.

In estimating gross private domestic investment, government statisticians also add consumer expenditures on *new* residential structures as a third component of investments. New housing represents an addition to our future productive capacity in the sense that a new house can generate housing services in the future.

GOVERNMENT EXPENDITURES. In addition to personal consumption expenditures, there are government purchases of goods and services (*G*). The government buys goods and services from private firms and pays wages and salaries to government employees. Generally, we value goods and services at the prices at which they are sold. But many government goods and services are not sold in the market. Therefore, we cannot use their market value when computing GDP. The value of these goods, therefore, is considered equal to their cost. For example, the value of a newly built road is considered equal to its construction cost and is included in the GDP for the year it was built.

NET EXPORTS (FOREIGN EXPENDITURES). To get an accurate representation of gross domestic product, we must include the foreign sector. As Canadians, we purchase foreign goods, or *imports*. The goods that foreigners purchase from us are our *exports*. To get an idea of the *net* expenditures from the foreign sector, we subtract the value of imports from the value of exports to get net exports (*X* − *M*) for a year:

Net exports (*X* − *M*) = Total exports − Total imports

Gross private domestic investment The creation of capital goods that can yield production and hence consumption in the future.

Investment An activity that uses resources today in such a way that they allow for greater production in the future and hence greater consumption in the future.

Producer durable, or capital good A good that is purchased not to be consumed in its current form but to be used to make other goods and services and has an expected service life of more than three years.

Fixed investment The purchase of capital goods.

Inventory investment Investment made when a firm increases its inventories of finished products.

To understand why we subtract imports, rather than ignoring them altogether, consider that we are using the expenditures approach. If we want to estimate *domestic* output, we have to subtract Canada's expenditures on the goods of other nations.

Mathematical Representation Using the Expenditure Approach

We have just defined the components of GDP using the expenditure approach. When we add them all together, we get a definition for GDP, which is as follows:

$$\text{GDP} = C + I + G + (X - M)$$

Where

$$C = \text{Consumption expenditures}$$
$$I = \text{Investment expenditures}$$
$$G = \text{Government expenditures}$$
$$X - M = \text{Net exports}$$

THE HISTORICAL PICTURE. To get an idea of the relationship among C, I, G, and $X - M$, look at Figure 5–4, which shows GDP, personal consumption expenditures, government purchases, and gross private domestic investment plus net exports from 1926 to 2006. When we add up the expenditures of the household, business, government, and foreign sectors, we get GDP. (Note the scale on the vertical axis.)

Example 5–2 reveals some important information about the sources of GDP variation. You might think that the consumption (C) component is the most important in determining how GDP changes because it is the largest. In fact, most of the variability in GDP can be traced to the changes in investment and net exports.

FIGURE 5–4

Eighty Years of GDP and Its Components

Here we see a display of gross domestic product, personal consumption expenditures, government purchases, gross private domestic investment, and net exports for the years 1926–2006. You can clearly see a dramatic decline during the Great Depression of the 1930s in investment and net exports, and the effect of increased government spending during World War II.

Source: Adapted from Statistics Canada, Historical Statistics of Canada Series F14-32, CANSIM table 380-0017.

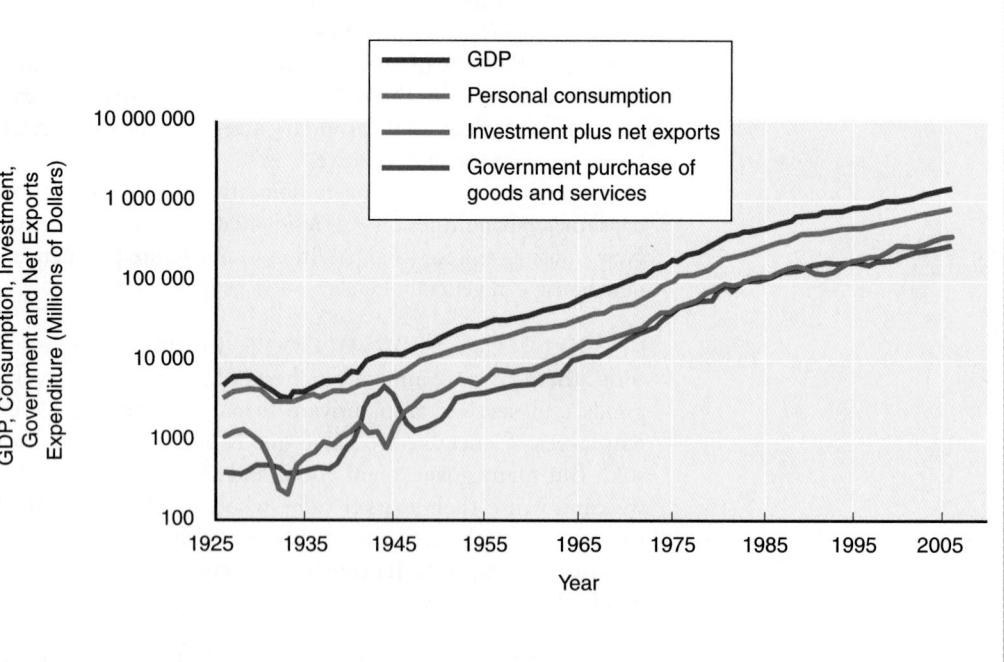

| EXAMPLE 5–2 | **Variability of Nominal GDP Expenditure Components** |

The variation in three components of nominal GDP is shown on the graph in Figure 5–5. Each line shows how much the component varies from the previous year. During the past 30 years, investment (red) has had the largest changes year to year, varying from a high of over +30 percent to a low of almost −15 percent. Consumption (blue) has the lowest variation. Note that the investment component was strongly negative during the last two recessions of 1981–82 and 1990–92. The green shows the variation in net exports. (Government spending variation is not shown for the sake of clarity.)

FIGURE 5–5

Variability of Nominal GDP Components

SOURCE: ADAPTED FROM THE STATISTICS CANADA CANSIM DATABASE, TABLE 380-0017.

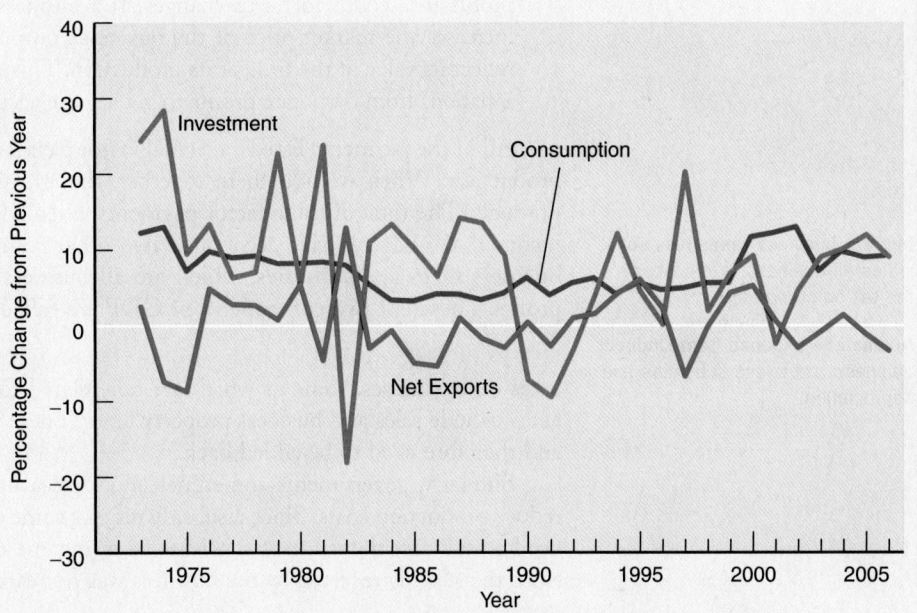

For critical analysis:

1. Why might investment fall dramatically when there is a recession?

2. What technological changes occurring in the 1980s and 1990s kept businesses investing?

3. Why might net exports turn strongly positive during a recession (as it did in 1982)? (Hint: Remember that net exports is made of two parts, imports and exports).

Deriving GDP by the Income Approach

If you go back to the circular flow diagram in Figure 5–1, you see that the product markets are at the top of the diagram and the factor markets are at the bottom. We can calculate the value of the circular flow of income and product by looking at expenditures—which we just did—or by looking at total factor payments. Factor payments are called income. Using the income approach, we calculate gross domestic product as the sum of all earnings from the factors of production plus taxes less subsidies, in order to generate a comparable number to the expenditure approach.

1. *Wages.* The most important category is, of course, wages, including salaries and other forms of labour income, such as income in kind and incentive payments. We also count payroll deductions for employment insurance and pension plans (both the employees' and the employers' contributions) and other fringe benefits.

2. *Corporate profits before taxes.* Businesses either pay out their profits before taxes to their shareholders—the households—or reinvest them in the business. Regardless of the distribution, these corporate profits are counted as income.

3. *Interest and investment income.* Here, interest payments do not equal the sum of all payments for the use of funds in a year. Instead, interest is expressed in net, rather than in gross, terms. Net interest received by households is the difference between the interest they receive (from savings accounts, certificates of deposit, and the like) and the interest they pay (to banks for mortgages, credit cards, and other loans).

4. *Farm and nonincorporated nonfarm business income.* This category includes income earned by owners of businesses who supply their own labour and capital to their businesses. It could also be referred to as "proprietors' income." Rent and imputed rents are also included here.

5. *Inventory valuation adjustment.* Our final category allows for an adjustment to corporate profits to account for price changes. If a business is holding inventory and inflation increases the market price of the business's output, the value of that output will not reflect its value at the time of its production. This category is subtracted (in the case of inflation) from corporate profits to get a more accurate measure of new production.

All of the payments listed are actual factor payments made to owners of the factors of production. When we add them together, though, we do not yet have gross domestic product. (The total of these factor payments when added together is called net domestic income.) We have to take account of two other components: depreciation and **indirect business taxes less subsidies**, which are all business taxes except the tax on corporate profits. These last two components of GDP are called **nonincome expense items**.

Indirect business taxes less subsidies All business taxes except the tax on corporate profits.

Nonincome expense items Indirect business taxes less subsidies and depreciation.

INDIRECT BUSINESS TAXES LESS SUBSIDIES. Governments impose a variety of taxes on businesses, some of which are not related to sales or income. Indirect business taxes include sales and business property taxes. These taxes are part of the income earned and therefore need to be added back.

Similarly, governments sometimes subsidize a business by giving it money to help reduce production costs. Since a subsidy returns some of the taxes paid to the business, we need to subtract the value of subsidies from income earned by the factor of production, since the subsidy received by the business was not earned through production.

DEPRECIATION. We must also *add* depreciation to go from net domestic income to gross domestic product. Why? Depreciation can be thought of as the portion of the current year's GDP that is used to replace physical capital consumed in the process of production. Depreciation happens because of the reduction in the value of capital goods over a one-year period due to physical wear and tear and also to obsolescence. In the course of a year, machines and structures wear out or are used up in the production of domestic product. For example, houses deteriorate as they are occupied, and machines need repairs or they will fall apart and stop working. Most capital, or durable, goods depreciate. Because somebody has paid for the replacement, depreciation must be added as a component of gross domestic product.

Figure 5–6 shows GDP for 2006 calculated using the expenditure approach and the income approach, an amount of approximately \$1.4 trillion. (This amount represents about 3 percent of world GDP, as we see in Example 5–3.) Regardless of the method you use, you will come out with the same number. There are usually statistical discrepancies, but they are normally relatively small.

➤◆ CONCEPTS IN BRIEF

Learning Objective 5.3: Explain the two main methods of computing GDP: the expenditure and income approaches.

◆ The expenditure approach to measuring GDP requires that we add up consumption expenditures, gross private investment, government purchases, and net exports. Consumption expenditures include consumer durables, consumer nondurables, and services.

FIGURE 5–6

Measuring GDP by the Income and Expenditure Approaches 2006 (in millions of 2006 dollars)

By using the two different methods of computing the output of the economy, we come up with the same value for GDP. One approach focuses on expenditures, or the flow of spending by final consumers. The other approach concentrates on the income generated, or the flow of costs in making GDP.

SOURCE: ADAPTED FROM THE STATISTICS CANADA CANSIM DATABASE, TABLES 380-0017 AND 380-0016.

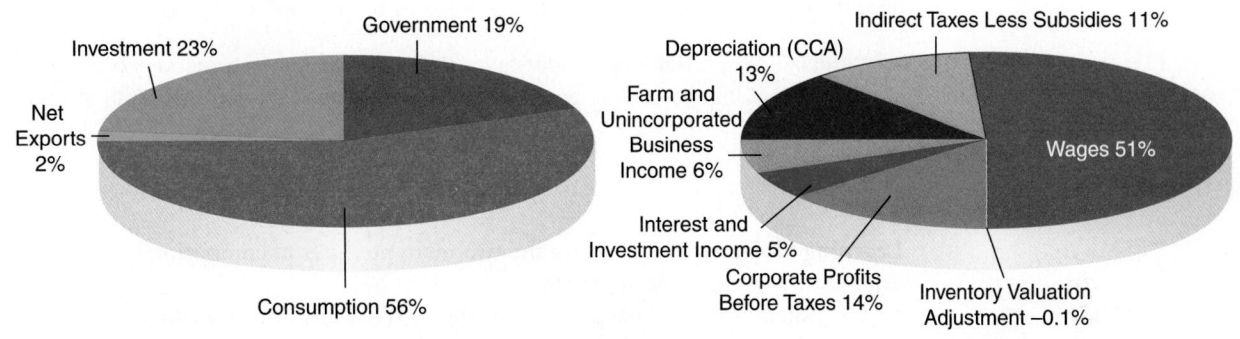

Expenditure Point of View—Product Flow		Income Point of View—Cost Flow	
Expenditures by Different Sectors:		**Domestic Income (at Factor Cost):**	
Household Sector		*Wages*	
Personal expenditure on consumer goods and services	803 502	Wages, salaries, and supplementary labour income	737 382
Government Sector		*Profits*	
Government current expenditure on goods and services	279 806	Corporation profits before taxes	198 859
Business Sector		Government business enterprise profits before taxes	13 823
Gross investment	326 004	*Farm and nonincorporated nonfarm income*	
Foreign Sector		Net income of nonfarm unincorporated business, including rent	85 980
Exports of goods and services	524 706	Accrued net income of farm operators from farm production	344
Deduct: Imports of goods and services	−487 660	*Interest and investment income*	
		Interest and miscellaneous investment income	65 310
Statistical discrepancy	−51	*Nonincome expense items*	
Gross domestic product at market prices	**1 446 307**	Inventory valuation adjustment	−1 775
		Taxes less subsidies, on factors of production	64 421
		Taxes less subsidies, on products	97 161
		Depreciation (capital consumption allowances)	184 750
		Statistical discrepancy	52
		Gross domestic product at market prices	**1 446 307**

> **EXAMPLE 5-3** **World GDP May Be Understated**
>
> To measure global GDP, economists commonly begin by converting the value of each nation's GDP into U.S. dollars. They do this by multiplying the nation's GDP by the exchange rate of the dollar for that nation's currency unit. Then the economists add up the dollar values of the GDPs of all nations to obtain a dollar value of global GDP. Using this method, current world GDP is less than $40 trillion per year, or just below 3.5 times U.S. GDP.
>
> A problem with using exchange rates to convert other nations' GDPs into dollar values is that prices tend to be lower in less-developed nations than in developed countries. Thus, a U.S. dollar can often purchase more goods and services in those nations than it can in developed nations. When the calculation of global GDP is adjusted to take this fact into account, the U.S. dollar value of world GDP jumps to well over $50 trillion.
>
> **For Critical Analysis:** How might understating GDP this year relative to last year bias estimates of the growth of the total output produced by an average resident of planet Earth this year?

➤ CONCEPTS IN BRIEF

Learning Objective 5.3: Explain the two main methods of computing GDP: the expenditure and income approaches.

- The expenditure approach to measuring GDP requires that we add up consumption expenditures, gross private investment, government purchases, and net exports. Consumption expenditures include consumer durables, consumer nondurables, and services.
- Gross private domestic investment *excludes* transfers of asset ownership. It includes only additions to the productive capacity of a nation, repairs on existing capital goods, and changes in business inventories.
- We value government expenditures at their cost because we do not usually have market prices at which to value government goods and services.
- To derive GDP using the income approach, we first add up all factor payments, including wages, corporate profits, interest and investment income, farm and non-incorporated nonfarm business income, and inventory valuation adjustment.
- To get an accurate estimate of GDP with this method, we must also add indirect business taxes less subsidies as well as depreciation to those total factor payments.

5.4 Other Components of GDP and National Income Accounting

There is a whole variety of different measures of economic activity other than GDP and its subcomponents. For example, gross domestic product does not really tell how much income people have access to for spending purposes. To get to those kinds of data, we must make some adjustments to our measurements.

Depreciation and Net Domestic Product

Depreciation Reduction in the value of capital goods over a one-year period due to physical wear and tear and also to obsolescence; also called *capital consumption allowance*.

Net domestic product (NDP) The sum of all incomes arising from production, or ownership of assets used in production, within the economic territory of a country or region.

We have used the terms *gross domestic product* and *gross private domestic investment* without really indicating what *gross* means. The dictionary defines it as "without deduction," as opposed to *net*. Deductions for what, you might ask. The deductions are for something we call **depreciation**, a reduction in the value of capital goods over a one-year period due to physical wear and tear and also obsolescence. An estimate of depreciation is subtracted from gross domestic product to arrive at a figure called **net domestic product (NDP)**, which we define as the sum of all incomes arising from production, or ownership of assets used in production, within the economic territory of a country or region. Taxes and subsidies on factors of production are also included since the size of these components is directly linked to the production decisions of producers. NDP differs from GDP in that NDP excludes capital consumption allowances. NDP can be calculated as follows:

$$\text{NDP} = \text{GDP} - \text{Depreciation}$$

Capital consumption allowance Another name for *depreciation*, the amount of the capital stock that has been consumed over a one-year period.

Depreciation is also called **capital consumption allowance** because it is the amount of the capital stock that has been consumed over a one-year period. In essence, it equals the amount a business would have to put aside to repair and replace deteriorating machines. Because we know that

$$\text{GDP} = C + I + G + (X - M)$$

we know that the formula for NDP is

$$\text{NDP} = C + I + G + (X - M) - \text{Depreciation}$$

What is the significance of this number? Net domestic product (NDP) represents the total market value of goods and services available for both consumption—used in a broader sense here to mean "resource exhaustion"—and net additions to the economy's stock of capital.

Net investment Measurement of *changes* in capital stock over time.

A closely related measure is **net investment**, which measures *changes* in capital stock over time. Net investment is calculated as

$$\text{Net investment} = I - \text{Depreciation}$$

Net investment has been positive nearly every year in which we have measured it. This is consistent with an expanding economy and means that the economy is making net additions to its capital stock. Because depreciation does not vary greatly from year to year as a percentage of GDP, we get a similar picture of what is happening to our national economy by looking at either NDP or GDP data.

Net National Income at Basic Prices

Net national income (NNI) The income available to Canadians for ownership of resources.

We know that net domestic product (NDP) represents the total market value of goods and services available for both consumption and net additions to the economy's stock of capital. NDP does not, however, represent the income available to individuals within that economy because it includes indirect business taxes, such as sales taxes as well as income paid out to and received from outside the country. (Note that we have some foreign ownership in Canada, and some ownership by Canadians abroad, so the income from these investments is also included or excluded accordingly.) We therefore need to adjust NDP to arrive at the figure for all factor income of resource owners. The result is called **net national income (NNI)** at basic prices which represents the income available to the factors of production that are owned by Canadians—in simpler words, it is the income earned by the factors of production for producing GDP.

Personal Income (PI)

Personal income (PI) Income received by the factors of production prior to the payment of personal income taxes.

Net national income does not actually represent what is available to individuals to spend—because some people obtain income for which they have provided no concurrent good or service, and others earn income but do not receive it. In the former category are mainly recipients of transfer payments from government, such as old age security, welfare, and employment insurance benefits. These payments represent shifts of funds within the economy by way of government, where no good or service is concurrently rendered in exchange. The other category, income earned but not received, consists primarily of corporate retained earnings. When transfer payments are added and when income earned but not received is subtracted, we end up with **personal income (PI)**—income received by the factors of production prior to the payment of personal income taxes.

Disposable Personal Income (DPI)

Disposable personal income (DPI) Personal income after all personal income taxes have been subtracted.

Everybody knows that you do not get to take home all of your salary. To get **disposable personal income (DPI)**, we subtract all personal income taxes from personal income. This is the income that individuals have left for consumption and saving.

TABLE 5-2

Going from GDP to Disposable Income, 2006

GDP	**1 446 307**
Deprecation (CCA)	-184 750
Discrepancy	-52
Net domestic product (NDP) at market prices	**1 261 505**
Taxes less subsidies on products	-97 161
Net investment income	-10 754
Net national income at basic prices	**1 153 590**
Undistributed corporate profits	-110 661
Corporate taxes and other earnings not paid to persons	-102 826
Government and other transfer payments	147 720
Personal income	**1 087 823**
Personal income tax and nontax payments	-251 895
Disposable income (DPI)	**835 928**
Personal consumption expenses	-801 810
Personal savings and transfers	**34 118**

SOURCE: ADAPTED FROM STATISTICS CANADA CANSIM DATABASE, TABLES 380-0029, 380-0030, AND 380-0012.

Personal Savings (S)

Personal savings (S) is the amount that is left over from disposable personal income after consumption.

Deriving the Components of GDP

Table 5–2 takes you through the steps necessary to derive the various components of GDP. It shows how you go from gross domestic product to net domestic product, to net national income, to personal income, to disposable personal income, and then to personal savings.

We have completed our rundown of the different ways the GDP can be computed and of the different variants of national income and product. What we have not yet touched on is the difference between national income measured in this year's dollars and national income representing real goods and services.

Real and Nominal GDP

If a compact disc (CD) costs $15 this year, 10 CDs have a market value of $150. If a CD costs $20 next year, the same 10 CDs will have a market value of $200. In this case, there is no increase in the total quantity of CDs, but the market value will have increased by one-third. Apply this to every single good and service produced and sold in Canada and you realize that changes in GDP, measured in nominal dollars, may not be a very useful indication of economic activity. (Statistics Canada uses the term **current dollars** to indicate nominal dollars.) If we are really interested in variations in the real output of the economy, we must correct GDP (and just about everything else we look at) for changes in the average of overall prices from year to year. Basically, we first need to generate an index that approximates the changes in average prices. We then must divide that estimate into the value of output in current dollars to adjust the value of output to what is called **real dollars,** or dollars corrected for general price level changes. (Statistics Canada uses the term *constant dollars* to indicate real dollars.) This price-corrected GDP is called **real GDP.** Refer to Example 5–4 that follows.

EXAMPLE 5-4	**Correcting GDP for Price Level Changes, 1997–2006**

Let us take a numerical example to see how we can adjust GDP for changes in prices. We must pick an appropriate price index in order to adjust for these price level changes. We mentioned the Consumer Price Index, the Producer Price Index, and the GDP deflator in

Chapter 4. Let us use the GDP deflator to adjust our figures. Table 5–3 gives 10 years of GDP figures. Nominal GDP figures are shown in the second column. The price level index (GDP deflator) is in the third column, with base year of 2002 when the GDP deflator equals 100. The fourth column shows real (inflation-adjusted) GDP in 2002 dollars.

The formula for real GDP is

$$\text{Real GDP} = \frac{\text{Nominal GDP}}{\text{Price level}} \times 100$$

TABLE 5-3

Correcting GDP for Price Changes

Year	Nominal GDP (Millions of current dollars per year)	Price Level Index (2002 = 100)	Real GDP (Millions of dollars in 2002 dollars)	Real GDP percentage change
1997	882 733	92.54	953 944	4.4%
1998	914 973	92.13	993 136	4.1%
1999	982 441	93.80	1 047 431	5.5%
2000	1 076 577	97.64	1 102 562	5.3%
2001	1 108 048	98.97	1 119 626	1.5%
2002	1 152 905	100.00	1 152 905	3.0%
2003	1 213 175	103.19	1 175 635	2.0%
2004	1 290 828	106.64	1 210 412	3.0%
2005	1 375 080	110.31	1 246 582	3.0%
2006	1 446 307	113.06	1 279 239	2.6%

SOURCE: ADAPTED FROM STATISTICS CANADA TABLE 380-0002
NOTE: FIGURES FOR THE PRICE LEVEL INDEX ARE ROUNDED.

To calculate real GDP using nominal GDP and the GDP deflator, do the following steps. The base year is 2002, so the price index must equal 100. In 2002, nominal GDP was $1 152.9 billion, and so too was real GDP expressed in 2002 dollars. In 2005, the price index was 110.31. Thus, to correct 2005's nominal GDP for inflation, we divide the price index, 110.31, into the nominal GDP figure of $1 375.1 billion and then multiply it by 100. The result is $1 246.6 billion, which is 2005's GDP expressed in terms of the purchasing power of dollars in 2002. What about a situation when the price level is lower than in 2002? Look at 1997. Here the price index shown in the third column is 92.54. That means that in 1997, the average of all prices was about 92.5 percent of prices in 2002. To obtain 1997 GDP expressed in terms of 2002 purchasing power, we divide nominal GDP, $827.3 billion, by 92.54 and then multiply by 100. The result is a larger number—$953.9 billion. The fourth column in Table 5–3 is a better measure of how the economy has performed than the second column, which shows only nominal GDP changes.

For critical analysis: A few years ago, the base year for the GDP deflator was 1997. What does a change in the base year for the price level index affect?

Plotting Nominal and Real GDP

Nominal GDP and real GDP from 1970 to 2006 are plotted in Figure 5–7. Notice that there is quite a big gap between the two GDP figures, reflecting the amount of inflation that has occurred. Note further that the choice of a base year is arbitrary. We have chosen 2002 as the base year in our example. This happens to be the base year recently used by the government.

➤ CONCEPTS IN BRIEF

Learning Objective 5.4: Explain how various subcomponents of GDP are calculated.
  ✦ To obtain net domestic product (NDP), we subtract from GDP the year's deprecia-tion of the existing capital stock. Net domestic product represents the total market

value of goods and services available for both consumption and net additions to the economy's stock of capital.

↘ To obtain net national income, we subtract indirect business taxes less subsidies and net investment income from net domestic product. Net national income gives us a measure of all factor payments to resource owners.

↘ To obtain personal income, we must add government transfer payments, such as old age security benefits and employment insurance. We must subtract income earned but not received by resource owners, such as corporate retained earnings, corporate income taxes, and business social security taxes.

↘ To obtain disposable personal income, we subtract all personal income taxes from personal income. Disposable personal income is income that individuals actually have for consumption or saving.

5.5 Limitations of GDP

GDP measures aggregate domestic economic activity reasonably accurately. It does *not* measure social and economic well being.

Recognizing the Limitations of GDP

Like any statistical measure, GDP is a concept that can be both well used and misused. Economists find it especially valuable as an overall indicator of a nation's economic performance. But it is important to realize that GDP has significant weaknesses. Because it includes only the value of goods and services traded in markets, it excludes nonmarket production, such as the household services of homemakers discussed earlier. This can cause some problems in comparing the GDP of an industrialized country with the GDP of a predominantly agrarian nation in which nonmarket production is relatively more important. It also causes problems if nations have different definitions of legal versus

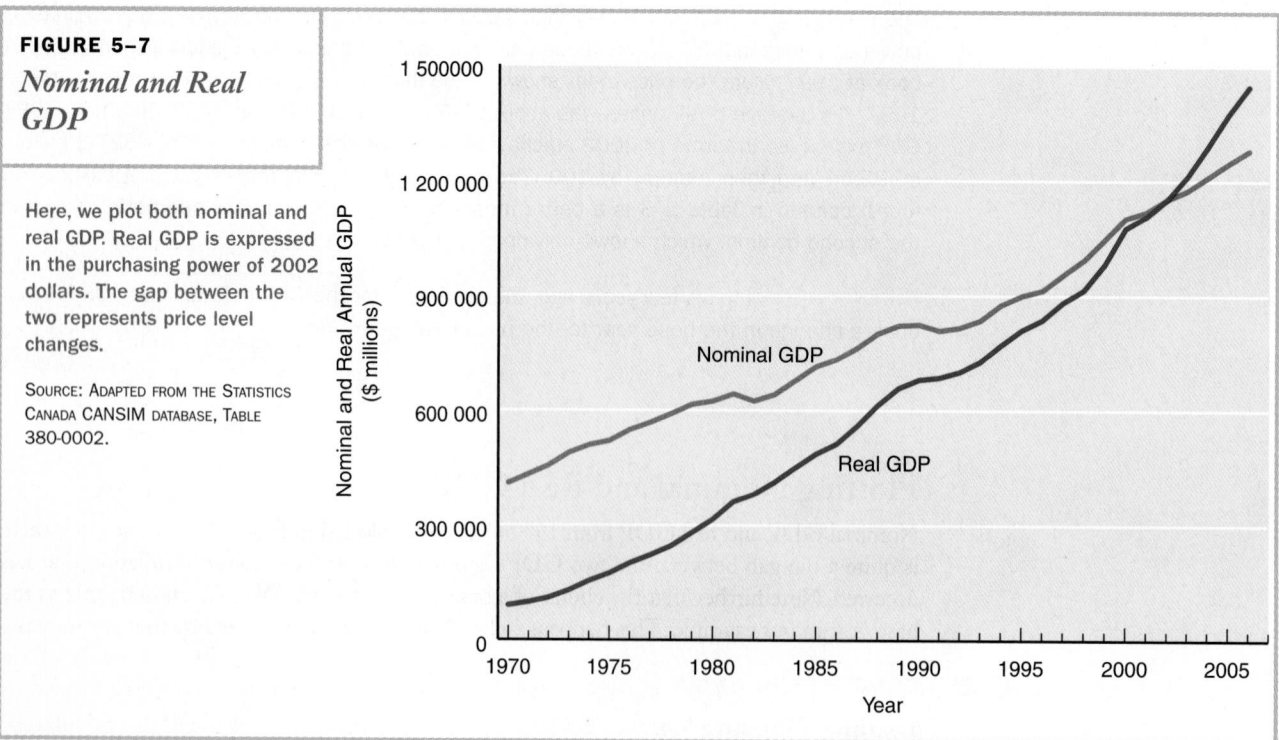

FIGURE 5–7

Nominal and Real GDP

Here, we plot both nominal and real GDP. Real GDP is expressed in the purchasing power of 2002 dollars. The gap between the two represents price level changes.

Source: Adapted from the Statistics Canada CANSIM database, Table 380-0002.

illegal activities. For instance, a nation with legalized gambling will count the value of gambling services, which has a reported market value as a legal activity. But in a country in which gambling is illegal, individuals who provide such services will not report the market value of gambling activities, and so they will not be counted in that country's GDP. This can complicate comparing the GDP of a nation where gambling is legal with the GDP of a country that prohibits gambling.

Furthermore, although GDP is often used as a benchmark measure for standard-of-living calculations, it is not necessarily a good measure of the well-being of a nation. No measured figure of total national annual income can account for the changes in the degree of labour market discrimination, declines or improvements in personal safety, or the quantity or quality of leisure time. Measured GDP also says little about our environmental quality of life. As the now-defunct Soviet Union illustrated to the world, the large-scale production of such goods as minerals, electricity, and irrigation for farming can have negative effects on the environment: deforestation caused by strip mining, pollution of air and soil by particulate emissions or nuclear accidents at power plants, and erosion of the natural balance between water and salt in bodies of water, such as the Aral Sea. Hence, it is important to recognize the following point:

> GDP is a measure of the value of production in terms of market prices and an indicator of economic activity. It is not a measure of a nation's overall welfare.

Nonetheless, GDP is a relatively accurate and useful measure to map changes in a country's domestic economic performance. Understanding GDP is, thus, important for recognizing changes in economic performance over time.

Comparing Living Standards throughout the World

It is relatively easy to compare the standard of living of a family in Montreal with that of one living in Saskatoon. Both families get paid in dollars and can buy the same goods and services at Canadian Tire, McDonald's, and Sobeys. It is not so easy, however, to make a similar comparison between a family living in Canada and one in, say, India. The first problem concerns money. Indians get paid in rupees, their national currency, and buy goods and services with that currency. That means that just as we can compare families in Montreal and Saskatoon, we can compare the living standards of a family in New Delhi with one in Mumbai. But how do we compare the average standard of living in India with that in Canada?

Per-capita real GDP The amount of real GDP per person.

One way we can make a better comparison is through the measure of per-capita real GDP. Looking at changes in GDP alone can be deceiving, particularly if the population size is significantly different. If real GDP over a 10-year period went up 100 percent, you might jump to the conclusion that the material well being of the economy had increased by the same amount. But what if the population increased by 200 percent during the same period? What would you say then? Certainly, the amount of real GDP per person, or **per-capita real GDP**, would have fallen even though total GDP had risen. What we must do to account for price changes and population changes is first deflate GDP and then divide by the total population. We do this calculation for each year. If we were to look at certain less-developed countries, we would find that in many cases, even though real GDP has risen over the past several decades, per-capita real GDP has remained constant or fallen because the population has grown just as rapidly or more quickly.

However, even adjusting for per-capita income does not tell the whole story of the relative well being of countries. We need to look beyond income to other factors, such as life expectancy and literacy levels, to get a truer picture of living standards. In Example 5-5, you will see that the United Nations has attempted to do just that.

EXAMPLE 5-5   Comparing Standards of Living

In 1990, the United Nations Development Programme (UNDP) declared that comparing per-capita incomes across nations did not provide a balanced picture of relative standards of living. Therefore, the UNDP created a Human Development Index (HDI), which takes into account the real GDP of each country, the life expectancy at birth, as well as the educational attainments of its citizens. By combining these factors, the UNDP hoped to illustrate that the size of an economy measured by its GDP does not necessarily indicate the state of human well-being.

The 1995 HDI declared Canada, among 174 countries studied, as the best place in the world to live in, although our per-capita income ranked third behind the United States and Hong Kong. The second overall was the United States, and the third was Japan. The Netherlands and Norway were placed fourth and fifth. The top five developing nations on the HDI were Cyprus, Barbados, Bahamas, Korea, and Argentina.

To illustrate the difficulty of using real GDP as a measure of human well-being, the UNDP points out that while New Zealand and Switzerland ranked 14th and 15th on the HDI, New Zealand's real per-capita income was US$12 600 compared with Switzerland's US$35 760. Both Ecuador and Morocco had per-capita incomes of about US$1000, but Ecuador was placed 64th, while Morocco was placed 123rd.

After the release of the 1995 HDI, Informetrica (a Canadian think tank) applied the same criteria to evaluate Canadian provinces. The result? Saskatchewan is the best province in the best country to live in.

For critical analysis: Which country's citizens enjoy a greater economic well-being: New Zealand's or Switzerland's? What must make up the difference in economic well-being in closing the HDI ranking?

Foreign Exchange Rates

Foreign exchange rate The price of one currency in terms of another.

In the last chapter, you heard about exchange rates and their influence on trade. Now, we will use them to convert foreign measurements to Canadian equivalents. The price we pay for foreign currency is calculated by looking up the **foreign exchange rate** (the price of one currency in terms of another). Those rates are published daily in major newspapers throughout the world and can be found on the Internet for any given moment. If you know that you can exchange $1 for 6 Swiss francs, the exchange rate is 6 to 1 (in other words, a Swiss franc is worth about 17 cents). So, if Swiss incomes per capita are, say 100 000 Swiss francs, that translates to $17 000 at an exchange rate of 6 Swiss francs to $1. For years statisticians calculated relative GDP by simply adding up each country's GDP in its local currency and dividing by each respective dollar exchange rate.

True Purchasing Power

Purchasing power parity Calculating an exchange rate whereby money would have the same value in all countries.

The problem with simply using foreign exchange rates to convert other countries' GDP and per-capita GDP into dollars is that not all goods and services are bought and sold in a world market. Restaurant food, housecleaning services, and home repairs do not get exchanged across countries. In countries that have very low wages, those kinds of services are much cheaper than foreign exchange rate computations would imply. Government statistics claiming that per-capita income in some poor country is only $300 a year seem shocking. But such statistics do not tell you the true standard of living of the people in that country. Only by looking at what is called *purchasing power parity* can you determine other countries' true standards of living compared with ours. **Purchasing power parity** means that we calculate an exchange rate whereby money would have the same value in all countries. Example 5-6 shows how this measure has been applied by the International Monetary Fund to make more appropriate comparisons of relative GDP.

EXAMPLE 5-6   **Purchasing Power Parity Comparisons of World Incomes**

A few years ago, the International Monetary Fund accepted the purchasing power parity approach as the correct one. It started presenting international statistics on each country's GDP relative to every other's based on purchasing power parity. The results were surprising. As you can see from Table 5–4, China's per-capita GDP is higher based on purchasing power parity than when measured at market foreign exchange rates.

For Critical Analysis: What is the percentage increase in China's per-capita GDP when one switches from foreign exchange rates to purchasing power parity?

TABLE 5-4

Comparing GDP Internationally

Country	Annual GDP Based on Purchasing Power Parity (Billions of U.S. dollars)	Per-Capita GDP Based on Purchasing Power Parity (U.S. dollars)	Per-Capita GDP Based on Foreign Exchange Rates (U.S. dollars)
United States	11 693	39 820	41 440
Japan	3 809	29 810	37 050
China	7 634	5 890	1 500
Germany	2 324	28 170	30 690
France	1 779	29 460	30 370
Russia	1 392	9 680	3 400
Indonesia	757	3 480	1 140
Italy	1 613	28 020	26 280
United Kingdom	1 882	31 430	33 630
Brazil	1 460	7 940	3 220
Canada	1 178	35 600	32 590

SOURCE: WORLD BANK.

➤ **CONCEPTS IN BRIEF**

Learning Objective 5.5: Understand the limitations of GDP.

- To correct nominal GDP for price changes, we use the GDP deflator. To get real GDP, divide nominal GDP by the deflator and multiply by 100. Real GDP can then be compared to see if the economy is actually producing more.
- We can divide the population into real GDP to obtain per-capita real GDP, a better measure of the standard of living of the population.
- Statisticians often calculate relative GDP by adding up each country's GDP in its local currency and dividing by the dollar exchange rate.
- Because not all goods and services are bought and sold in the world market, we must correct exchange rate conversions of other countries' GDP figures in order to take into account differences in the true cost of living across countries.

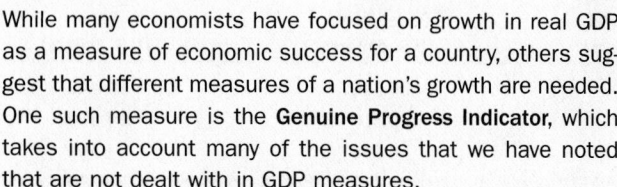

Progress or villainy?

Setting Goals for a Nation: What Do We Aim For?

Concepts Applied: Economic Growth, GDP, National Income Accounting

While many economists have focused on growth in real GDP as a measure of economic success for a country, others suggest that different measures of a nation's growth are needed. One such measure is the **Genuine Progress Indicator,** which takes into account many of the issues that we have noted that are not dealt with in GDP measures.

Some 32 years ago the U.S. economic research think tank, Redefining Progress, devised an alternative measurement for growth called the Genuine Progress Indicator—the GPI—to begin addressing the problems caused by using only GDP as the yardstick for progress. The researchers at this think tank want to reverse much of the unhealthy focus on GDP as the only measure of progress, noting that the architects of the GDP—John Maynard Keynes (U.K.) and Simon Kuznets (U.S.)—did caution against using GDP as a measure of the welfare of a nation. In 1962 Kuznets lamented that "the welfare of a nation can scarcely be inferred from a measurement of national income as defined by the GDP ... goals for 'more' growth should specify of what and for what."

The researchers note that the ideal economic or GDP hero is a chain-smoking terminal cancer patient going through an expensive divorce whose car is totalled in a 20-car pileup, while he is munching on take-out fast food and chatting on a cellphone. All add to GDP growth. The GDP villain is non-smoking, eats home-cooked wholesome meals, and cycles to work. The litany of crimes against genuine progress that GDP accounting sustains includes:

- GDP adds up all money transactions without accounting for costs.
- GDP takes no account of the inequality of income, wealth, and spending power.
- GDP treats crime, imprisonment, divorce, and other forms of family and social breakdown as economic gain, yet the value of housework, parenting, and volunteering count for nothing.
- GDP increases with each environmental calamity, each polluting activity, and then again in repairing the damage.
- GDP does not account for the depletion or degradation of natural resources and the environment.
- GDP treats war expenditures as economic gain both during the destruction and the rebuilding phases.

- GDP ignores the liabilities of living on debt and foreign borrowing.

In contrast to the GDP, the GPI attempts to measure the costs and benefits of human, social, natural, and human-made capital, by adjusting national income figures for these various factors. While U.S. GDP per capita has shown relentless real (adjusted for inflation) positive growth since 1950, the U.S. GPI per capita has been sinking ever since the mid-1970s. In fact, the 1990s saw the largest erosion of the real GPI, which declined at an average annual rate of 2.7 percent, compared with per capita GDP growth of 1.4 percent. The main factors driving the decline in the U.S. GPI include:

- income inequality (the gap between the rich and everyone else) has risen 18 percent, reaching its highest level in 50 years: by 1997 the top 20 percent of households were getting almost 48 percent of the national income while the lowest 20 percent of households got only 4 percent;
- negative costs from the depletion of nonrenewable resources (oil, gas, coal);
- negative costs of lost leisure time and family breakdown; and
- increasing foreign indebtedness.

While similar GPI accounting work in Canada has only just begun, the results are similar. Professor Ron Colman, director of the GPI Atlantic Project, has estimated the value of unpaid housework/parenting, volunteerism, and the cost of crime. Colman has estimated that modern two-parent working Canadian families, despite numerous household innovations, are actually spending more time working for pay and at unpaid housework and childcare than 100 years ago. He suggests that Canadian and U.S. households appear to be caught in a cycle of earning less, spending more, going deeper into debt, and working harder to pay for their increased expenses.

For these researchers, the GPI gives concrete expression to something many Canadians and Americans sense about the economy; that we are living off natural, human, and social capital. They argue that we are cannibalizing both the social structure and the natural habitat to keep the GDP growing at the rate the experts and money markets deem necessary. Yet the nation's economic reportage and debate proceed as though this erosion of real wealth does not exist.

The indicators that should alert us to such tendencies serve to hide them instead.

New national and provincial accounting systems like the GPI might not necessarily lead to smarter economic policies. However, retiring the laments of Kuznets and economic ghosts of Keynes will go a long way toward ensuring governments begin to account for genuine well being and the true state of our natural, social, and human capital. This journey must be taken with hopeful expectations to reclaim, as per T.S. Eliot, "the wisdom we have lost in knowledge and the knowledge we have lost in information."

CONDENSED FROM *THE GENUINE PROGRESS INDICATOR—A PRINCIPLED APPROACH TO ECONOMICS* BY MARK ANIELSKI.

SOURCE: *ENCOMPASS MAGAZINE*, OCT–NOV 1999, VOL. 4 NO. 1.

For critical analysis:

1. Much of the growth in Newfoundland's economy in the last few years can be attributed to the development of offshore oil projects. Why would the GPI give a smaller measure of progress to this development when compared to GDP measures?
2. Which of the "crimes against genuine progress that GDP accounting sustains" do you agree should be deducted from GDP measures? Why?
3. Many activities that are now bought and sold were, in previous generations, done at home, with the biggest changes occurring for women. Does this change in lifestyle mean we have "progressed?" Why or why not?

➡ SUMMARY

Here is what you should know after reading this chapter. MyEconLab will help you identify what you know, and where to go when you need to practise. We suggest that as soon as you review one of the Learning Objective sections below, you then proceed to go through the related section in MyEconLab.

Ⓧ myeconlab

➡ LEARNING OBJECTIVES	KEY TERMS	MYECONLAB PRACTICE
5.1 Economic Activity and the Circular Flow. GDP is a flow concept; it is measured in a period of time. The circular flow of income is a model of how income and output flows between households and businesses. The money received by households in exchange for their factor services is returned through the goods and services market to businesses. This circular flow model provides two approaches to measuring GDP.	national income accounting, 126 total income, 127 final goods and services, 127	• **MyEconLab** Study Plan 5.1
5.2 Measuring Gross Domestic Product (GDP). Gross domestic product is defined as the market value of all final goods and services produced during one year by domestic factors of production. Economists try to estimate GDP in order to evaluate the productive performance of an economy during a year. GDP must use only final goods and services, or else GDP would be exaggerated. We must avoid double counting because intermediate goods are included in the value of final goods sold in the market. GDP does not include many transactions in the economy that are not related to production, such as financial transactions or the sale of second-hand goods, and also does not include transactions which are not a market transaction or are not declared to the government.	intermediate goods, 130 value added, 130	• **MyEconLab** Study Plan 5.2

➤→ LEARNING OBJECTIVES	KEY TERMS	MYECONLAB PRACTICE
5.3 Two Main Methods of Measuring GDP. The expenditure approach to GDP counts expenditures on *all* final goods and services. The four types of expenditure are consumption on goods and services, investment expenditure on all investment goods, government spending on goods and services, and net export expenditure, which is the sum of exports less the value of imports. The income approach to GDP estimation sums the wages, profits, interest, and other receipts of income earners. Because depreciation is not a direct form of payment for a factor, we must add depreciation to national income at factor cost to calculate GDP via the income approach. Similarly, indirect business taxes (such as excise, sales, and property taxes) less subsidies are automatically reflected in the expenditure approach but not included in factor payments, and so they must be added to national income at factor cost.	expenditure approach, 134 income approach, 134 durable consumer goods, 134 nondurable consumer goods, 134 services, 134 gross private domestic investment, 135 investment, 135 producer durable, or capital good, 135 fixed investment, 135 inventory investment, 135 indirect business taxes less subsidies, 138 nonincome expense items, 138	• **MyEconLab** Study Plan 5.3
5.4 Other Components of GDP and National Income Accounting. GDP can be broken down to reflect the personal income that individuals receive and how that income is spent. Usually economists are interested in three specific numbers: personal income, disposable personal income, and personal savings. When the price level is rising (during periods of inflation) nominal GDP estimates would overstate true productive activity. Thus, we need to take into account price level changes by deflating nominal GDP to get real GDP, which can be compared between different time periods.	depreciation, 140 net domestic product (NDP), 140 capital consumption allowance, 141 net investment, 141 net national income (NNI), 141 personal income (PI), 141 disposable personal income (DPI), 141 personal savings (S), 142 current dollars, 142 real dollars, 142 real GDP, 142	• **MyEconLab** Study Plan 5.4
5.5 Limitations of GDP. When we look at how living standards are changing, it is important to look at real GDP per capita (real GDP divided by the population of the country). This figure gives a rough estimate of how standards of living can be compared between years and between countries. When comparing real GDP per capita across countries, exchange rates are altered	per-capita GDP, 145 foreign exchange rate, 146 purchasing power parity, 146	• **MyEconLab** Study Plan 5.5

➤➤ **LEARNING OBJECTIVES**   **KEY TERMS**   **MYECONLAB PRACTICE**

to reflect the purchasing power of the various currencies used, rather than the actual exchange rate. This calculation gives a better measure of living standards across different countries. Even with this correction, however, economists agree that other measures of human welfare, such as life expectancy and education levels, are needed to compare how well we are doing.

➤➤ PROBLEMS

LO 5.1 Describe the circular flow of income and output.

1. Are the arrows on the circular flow diagram a stock concept or a flow concept?

2. State where the following transactions would be initially recorded in the enhanced circular flow diagram.
   a. A consumer buys bread at the local store.
   b. A grocery store pays its employees.
   c. People in France go to see a Quebec-made movie.
   d. A firm constructs a house.
   e. A couple from Detroit stay overnight in Windsor.
   f. Bell Canada buys a satellite from an American producer.

LO 5.2 Explain the measurement of gross domestic product (GDP).

3. Suppose fires destroy many houses in Ontario. What would be the effect on GDP? Why would the country not necessarily be any better off after the houses are rebuilt?

4. Why are transfer payments, such as EI and welfare, excluded from the calculation of GDP?

5. Look back at Example 5–1, "The Underground Economy." Create a hypothesis about the size of the underground economy, higher unemployment, and welfare benefits.

6. At the top of a sheet of paper, write the headings "Production Activity" and "Nonproduction Activity." List each of the following under one of these headings by determining which would go into our measure of GDP.
   a. Mr. X sells his used car to Mr. Y.
   b. Joe's used car lot sells a car to Mr. Z and makes a $50 profit doing so.
   c. Merrill Lynch receives a brokerage commission for selling shares.
   d. Ms. Arianas buys 100 Dofasco shares.
   e. Mrs. LeMaistre cooks and keeps house for her family.
   f. Mr. Singh mows his own lawn.
   g. Mr. Singh mows lawns for a living.
   h. Mr. Smith receives a welfare payment.
   i. Mrs. Johnson sends her daughter $500 for a semester of studies at College University.

7. What happens to the official measure of GDP in each of the following situations?
   a. A man marries his housekeeper, who then quits working for wages.
   b. A drug addict marries her supplier.
   c. Homemakers perform the same jobs but switch houses and charge each other for their services.

8. Which of the following are production activities that are included in GDP? Which are not?
   a. Mr. King paints his own house.
   b. Mr. King paints houses for a living.
   c. Mrs. King earns income by taking baby photos in her home photography studio.
   d. Mrs. King takes photos of planets and stars as part of her astronomy hobby.
   e. E*Trade charges fees to process Internet orders for share trades.
   f. Mr. Ho purchases 300 shares via an Internet trade order.
   g. Mrs. Ho receives a social security payment.
   h. Ms. Chavez makes a $300 payment for an Internet-based course on share trading.
   i. Mr. Langham sells a used laptop computer to his neighbour.

9. Explain what happens to the official measure of GDP in each of the following situations:

   a. A woman who makes a living charging for investment advice on her Internet website marries one of her clients, to whom she now provides advice at no charge.

   b. A tennis player who won two top professional tournaments earlier this year as an amateur turns professional and continues his streak by winning two more before the year is out.

   c. A company that had been selling used firearms illegally finally gets around to obtaining an operating licence and performing background checks, as specified by law, prior to each gun sale.

10. Each year, Johan typically does all his own landscaping and yard work. He spends $200 per year on mulch for his flower beds, $225 per year on flowers and plants, $50 on fertilizer for his lawn, and $245 on gasoline and lawn mower maintenance. The lawn and garden store where he obtains his mulch and fertilizer charges other customers $500 for the service of spreading that much mulch in flower beds and $50 for the service of distributing fertilizer over a yard the size of Johan's. Paying a professional yard care service to mow his lawn would require an expenditure of $1200 per year, but in that case Johan would not have to buy gasoline or maintain his own lawn mower.

    a. In a normal year, how much does Johan's landscaping and yard work contribute to GDP?

    b. Suppose that Johan has developed allergy problems this year and will have to reduce the amount of his yard work. He can wear a mask while running his lawn mower, so he will keep mowing his yard, but he will pay the lawn and garden centre to spread mulch and distribute fertilizer. How much will all the work on Johan's yard contribute to GDP this year?

    c. As a follow-up to part (b), at the end of the year, Johan realizes that his allergies are growing worse and that he will have to arrange for all his landscaping and yard work to be done by someone else next year. How much will he contribute to GDP next year?

LO 5.3 Explain the two main methods of computing GDP: the expenditure and income approaches.

11. Explain which expenditure component of GDP would be affected by these transactions, if any.

    a. The federal government legalizes marijuana.
    b. An individual sells his own house.
    c. An individual sells his house through a real estate broker.

    d. You buy a pizza.
    e. Your parents buy a bottle of Chilean wine.
    f. Newfoundland repaves the Trans-Canada Highway.

12. Why would a new house be included in the investment component of GDP but not a car purchased by a household? Why would a car purchased by a business be included as part of the investment component?

13. Why would "Farm and Nonincorporated Nonfarm Business Income" be separately calculated from wages or corporate profits?

14. Define what depreciation is and why it is important to include it as part of the addition to get gross domestic product using the income approach.

15. Study the following table; then answer the questions.

Stage of Production	Sales Receipts	Intermediate Costs	Value Added
Coal	$2	$0	$2
Steel	5	2	3
Manufactured autos	8	5	3
Sold autos	9	8	1

    a. What is the intermediate good for steel production? How much did it cost?

    b. What is the value added resulting from auto manufacturing?

    c. If automobiles are the only final goods produced in this economy, what would be the GDP via the expenditures approach?

    d. If automobiles are the only final goods produced in this economy, what would be the GDP obtained using the income approach?

LO 5.4 Explain how various subcomponents of GDP are calculated.

16. Given the following information, calculate:

    a. Gross Domestic Product
    b. Net Domestic Product
    c. Net National Income

Government purchases	$ 500
Wages, salaries, and supplementary labour income	$2000
Depreciation (capital consumption allowances)	$ 400
Gross investment	$ 800
Consumption	$2000
Exports	$1600
Imports	$1650
Indirect business taxes less subsidies	$ 150

17. Consider the following hypothetical data for a hypothetical economy in 2008 (in trillions of dollars), and assume that there are no statistical discrepancies or other adjustments.

Profit	2.8
Indirect business taxes	0.8
Rent	0.7
Interest	0.8
Wages	8.2
Depreciation	1.3
Consumption	11.0
Exports	1.5
Government and business transfer payments	2.0
Personal income taxes and nontax payments	1.7
Imports	1.7
Corporate taxes and retained earnings	0.5
Employment insurance taxes	2.0
Government spending	1.8

a. What is the net domestic product? GDP?
b. What is the gross private domestic investment?
c. What is the personal income? Personal disposable income?

18. The following are a year's data for a hypothetical economy:

	Billions of Dollars
Consumption	400
Government spending	350
Gross private domestic investment	150
Exports	150
Imports	100
Depreciation	50
Indirect business taxes less subsidies	25

a. On the basis of the data, what is the value of GDP? NDP? NNI?
b. Suppose that in the next year, exports increase to $175 billion, imports increase to $200 billion, and consumption falls to $350 billion. What will GDP be in that year?
c. If the value of depreciation (capital consumption allowance) should ever exceed that of gross private domestic investment, how would this affect the future productivity of the nation?

19. Fill in the blanks in the following table:

Year	Nominal GDP	Real GDP	GDP Deflator (1997 = 100)
1997	125	___	___
2004	250	200	___
2007	275	___	122.22

20. Look back at Table 5–3, which explains how to correct GDP for price level changes. The fourth column of that table gives real GDP in terms of 2002 constant dollars. Change the base year to 2006. Recalculate the price level index, and then recalculate real GDP—that is, express the fourth column in terms of 2006 dollars instead of 2002 dollars.

21. Consider the following table for the economy of a nation whose residents produce five goods:

	2006		2011	
Good	Price	Quantity	Price	Quantity
Shampoo	$ 2	15	$ 4	20
DVD drives	200	10	250	10
Books	40	5	50	4
Milk	3	10	4	3
Candy	1	40	2	20

Assuming a 2006 base year:
a. What is the nominal GDP for 2006 and 2011?
b. What is the real GDP for 2006 and 2011?

22. In the table for Problem 21, if 2006 is the base year, what is the price index for 2006? For 2011? (Round decimal fractions to the nearest tenth.)

23. Consider the following table for the economy of a nation whose residents produce four goods:

	2007		2008	
Good	Price	Quantity	Price	Quantity
Computers	$1 000	10	$800	15
Bananas	6	3 000	11	1 000
Televisions	100	500	150	300
Cookies	1	10 000	2	10 000

Assuming 2008 as the base year:
a. What is the nominal GDP for 2007 and 2008?
b. What is the real GDP for 2007 and 2008?

24. In the table for Problem 23, if 2008 is the base year, what is the price index for 2007? (Round decimal fractions to the nearest tenth.)

25. Consider the following diagram, and answer the questions below.

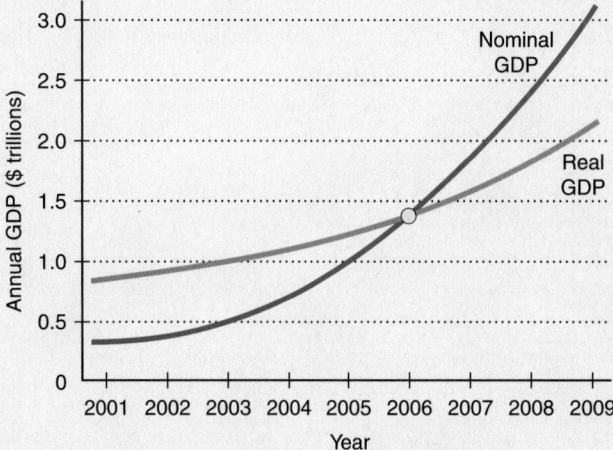

a. What is the base year? Explain.
b. Has this country experienced inflation or deflation since the base year? How can you tell?

LO 5.5 Understand the limitations of GDP.

26. Look back to Example 5–5, "Comparing Standards of Living." Why is GDP not a good measure of national welfare by itself? Why would life expectancy be a better measure? (Hint: What happens if most of the GDP of a country is earned by a small proportion of the population?)

27. Refer back to Example 5–4, "Comparing Standards of Living." It is also known that Canadians enjoy more leisure time than do Americans. Why would leisure time be important for national welfare but not show up in GDP?

28. Explain what happens to the official measure of GDP in each of the following situations:

    a. Air quality improves significantly throughout the United States, but there are no effects on aggregate production or on market prices of final goods and services.

    b. The American government spends considerably less on antipollution efforts this year than it did in recent years.

    c. The quality of cancer treatment increases, so patients undergo fewer treatments, which hospitals continue to provide at the same price as before.

29. Suppose that early in a year, a hurricane hits a town in Nova Scotia and destroys a substantial number of homes. A portion of this stock of housing, which had a market value of $100 million (not including the market value of the land), was uninsured. The owners of the residences spent a total of $5 million during the rest of the year to pay salvage companies to help them save their remaining belongings. A small percentage of uninsured owners had sufficient resources to spend a total of $15 million during the year to pay the construction companies to rebuild their homes. Some were able to devote their own time, the opportunity cost of which was valued at $3 million, to work on rebuilding their homes. The remaining, however, chose to sell their land at its market value and abandon the remains of their houses. What was the combined effect of these transactions on GDP for this year? (Hint: Which transactions took place in the markets for final goods and services?) In what ways, if any, does the effect on GDP reflect a loss in welfare for these individuals?

30. Suppose that in 2011, geologists discover large reserves of oil under the tundra in the Yukon. These reserves have a market value estimated at $50 billion at current oil prices. Oil companies spend $1 billion to hire workers and move and position equipment to begin exploratory pumping during that same year. In the process of loading some of the oil onto the tankers at a port, one company accidentally creates a spill into a bay and ultimately pays more than $1 billion to other companies to clean it up. The oil spill kills thousands of birds, seals, and other wildlife. What was the combined effect of these events on GDP for this year? (Hint: Which transactions took place in the markets for final goods and services?) In what ways, if any, does the effect on GDP reflect a loss in national welfare?

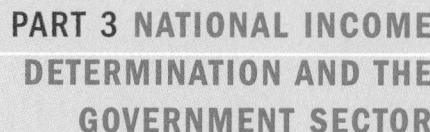

6

Modelling Real GDP and the Price Level in the Long Run

➤ LEARNING OBJECTIVES

After reading this chapter, you should be able to:

6.1 Understand and model the concept of long-run aggregate supply.

6.2 Describe the effect of economic growth on the long-run aggregate supply curve.

6.3 Explain why the aggregate demand curve slopes downward and list key factors that cause this curve to shift.

6.4 Discuss the effect of economic growth on the long-run equilibrium of the economy.

6.5 Evaluate likely reasons for persistent inflation in recent decades.

In Chapters 4 and 5 you learned the basics of the economic issues that face all economies—economic activity, inflation, and unemployment—and about the measurement of these important variables. Now, we want to look beyond simply measuring what has happened in the past; we want to understand what affects our economic performance. We will look at vital issues such as: What causes our GDP to grow? What causes inflation? What creates business fluctuations?

In this chapter and Chapter 7, you will learn how to study the economy with the aggregate demand–aggregate supply model. This model will give you a framework for understanding the economic performance of an economy.

MyEconLab helps you master each objective and study more efficiently. See end of chapter for details.

DID YOU KNOW THAT...

When economic analysts forecast how quickly the Canadian economy will grow in future years, they have to estimate how much consumers will spend, how much businesses will produce in response, *and* how these two events will interact to change the price level across the economy. No wonder it is so difficult to come up with reliable estimates! To make matters worse, unforeseen events—called "shocks" to the economy—occur and often make existing forecasts look way off the mark. In 2003, for example, the economy faced shocks from mad cow disease, forest fires, SARS, grasshoppers, a hurricane, and a widespread electricity blackout! Even with all these shocks, however, the long-term growth of the economy has been upward. In this chapter, you will learn about one model economists use to explain changes in output and the price level in our economy.

6.1 The Long-Run Aggregate Supply Curve

In Chapter 2, we showed the derivation of the production possibilities curve (PPC). At any point in time, the economy can be inside or on the PPC but never outside it. However, regardless of whether resources are fully employed or not, the sum total of all goods and services produced is the nation's real output, or real GDP. Economists refer to the total of all planned production for the entire economy as the **aggregate supply** of real output.

Aggregate supply The total of all planned production for the entire economy.

The Long-Run Aggregate Supply Curve

In this chapter we examine a basic model for studying the economy's long-term performance. We are then able to examine what causes the upward trend in GDP that we learned about in Chapter 4. In the next chapter, we will look at how growth happens in the economy. Finally, in Chapter 8, we will look at how economists model economic fluctuations (where GDP deviates from the long-run trend), and how is it related to the other two variables we examined: unemployment and inflation. Begin by looking at Figure 6–1.

Long-run aggregate supply curve A vertical line representing the long-run aggregate supply of goods and services in the economy.

Modelling Production and Real GDP

Aggregate production function Models the relationship between the inputs to production available in the economy and the total output of an economy (usually measured as real GDP).

THE AGGREGATE PRODUCTION FUNCTION. The **aggregate production function** models the relationship between the inputs to production available in the economy (such as labour, capital, natural resources, and technology) and the total output of an economy (usually measured as real GDP).

FIGURE 6–1
The Aggregate Production Function

In this graph we can see a range of employment between 16 and 18 million workers. When 16 million workers are employed, the economy is able to produce $1.3 trillion of real GDP (point A). At a level of employment of 17 million workers, the economy is able to produce $1.4 trillion of real GDP (point B), and at 18 million workers, the economy is able to produce $1.46 trillion of real GDP (point C).

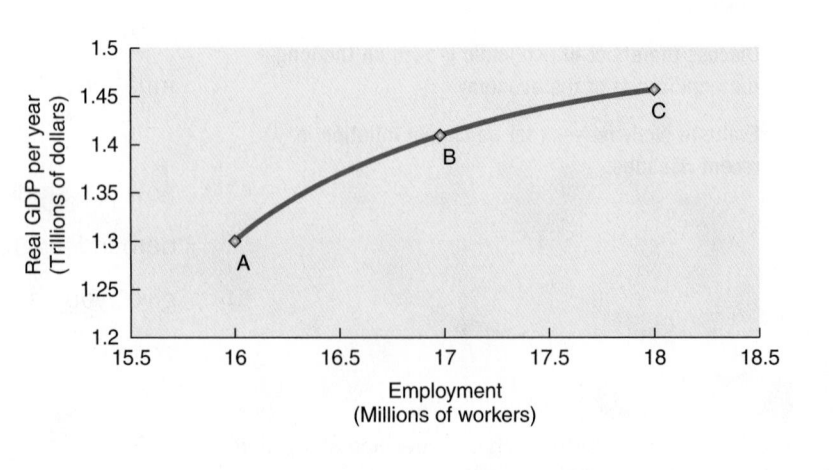

Labour is by far the most important resource in an economy, so the production function is usually drawn showing the relationship between total output and total employment with all other determinants of production unchanged. Labour usage typically varies more quickly than other factors of production. An example is shown in Figure 6–1.

The shape of the aggregate production function in Figure 6–1 is not a straight line, but rather the slope of the curve diminishes as we increase the employment level. Why is that? The reason is that the economy experiences **diminishing marginal returns** as employment increases. Diminishing marginal returns means that even though we increase employment, the additional output those additional workers can make is not as great as that of previous workers. In our example, the 1 million workers we employed when moving from A to B added $100 billion of real GDP, but the next 1 million workers (from B to C) added only $60 billion of real GDP.

Diminishing marginal returns
Even though we increase employment, the additional output those additional workers can make is not as great as that of previous workers.

Why do diminishing returns happen? Think of a single production plant and remember our assumption that all other inputs to production, other than labour, are fixed. The firm is able to increase production by adding workers. However, with a fixed amount of equipment, the ability of workers to add productive output is limited by the amount of equipment available to use. While more workers may use the equipment on more shifts, for example, eventually the opportunities for increasing the output this way are limited, thus additional output is not as great. The economy experiences this limitation in the same way.

The Labour Market

Figure 6-2, part (a) models the labour market for the economy. The demand for labour is derived from the desire by firms to produce real GDP, and the supply represents the willingness of the workers in the economy to provide labour. The labour market is in equilibrium at the natural rate of employment, L_1, and a real wage of w_1. With employment L_1, **the economy can produce a real GDP of Y_p**, the level of potential output for the economy, as shown in part (b).

FIGURE 6–2

Employment, the Production Function, and the Economy's Long-Run Aggregate Supply Curve

At a point in time, a nation's endowment of resources and technology define the position of the supply and demand for labour, as shown in part (a). The equilibrium in this market determines the amount of labour actually used to produce the nation's output, which combined with the available capital and technology results in the production of real GDP, as shown in part (b). In the long run, this level of production is independent of the price of the final goods and services produced, because people have full information and will fully adjust, and therefore the *LRAS* is vertical as shown in part (c).

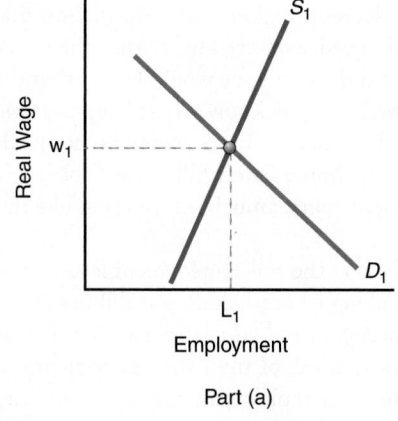

Part (a)

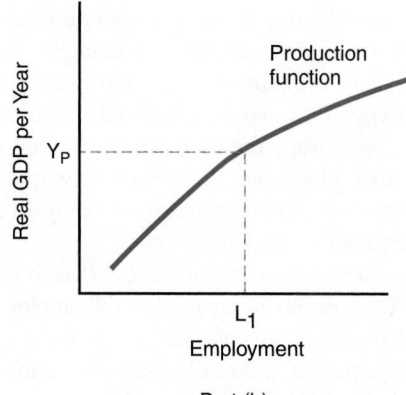

Part (b)

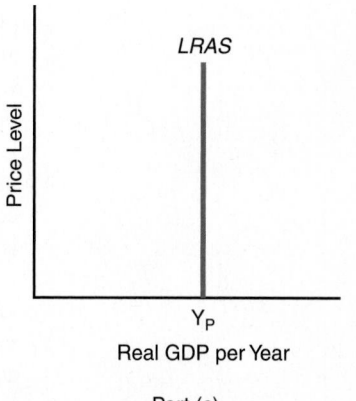

Part (c)

Potential output The amount the economy can produce when all resources are fully employed.

Long-run aggregate supply The output of the economy under conditions of full employment of the available resources. It can alternatively be viewed as the potential level of real GDP after full adjustment has occurred.

Constant dollars The value of a sum measured in base year prices. If the values were measured at the prices that prevailed at the time measured it would be referred to as current dollars.

Long-run aggregate supply curve A vertical line representing the long-run aggregate supply of goods and services in the economy.

Endowments The various resources in an economy, including both physical resources and human resources, such as ingenuity and management skills.

Full-information The assumption that all economic players are able to find and incorporate into their decision making any information that affects them.

Full-adjustment The assumption that all markets will adjust to their long-run equilibrium values without impediment.

This level of output corresponds to one point on the long-run trend for economic activity that we looked at in Chapter 4. It is often called **potential output** because it represents the amount we can produce when we fully employ our available resources. In terms of unemployment, we would have only frictional and structural unemployment in the economy.

Figure 6-2 models the relationship between labour supply, employment, and aggregate production in an economy. Producers in the economy wish to employ L_1 workers and will use those workers to make Y_p output when the labour market is at equilibrium. This is now shown in Figure 6-2 (c) as a vertical line which demonstrates that the economy produces at potential output, labelled *LRAS* for **long-run aggregate supply**. This level of production is some amount of real GDP, say, $1.5 trillion of real GDP, as measured in **constant dollars**—the value of a sum measured in base year prices. If the values were measured at the prices that prevailed at the time measured, it would be referred to as current dollars. Note that the **long-run aggregate supply curve** is drawn vertically, indicating that it does not depend on the price of those goods (although its position is still determined by technology and **endowments**—the various resources that exist in an economy, including both physical resources and human resources such as ingenuity and management skills). Why is it vertical?

The answer is that this model of production assumes that the labour market (and other resource markets) will have adjusted to its market equilibrium. Given the supply and demand for workers, and a fixed technology and capital, there is only one level of production possible. We are assuming that markets can freely move to their equilibrium values, and thus achieve an equilibrium level of employment (full employment), wage rates, and output. A change in the level of prices of goods and services has no effect on real output (real GDP) in the long run because higher output prices will be accompanied by comparable changes in input prices. Producers will, therefore, have no incentive to increase or decrease output, and suppliers of resources (e.g., workers) will also have no incentive to change their supply either as they receive the same real prices. We summarize this way of looking at this level of production by saying that the potential level of output, Y_p, is the **full-information** and **full-adjustment** level of output.

The assumptions of full information and full adjustment can be difficult to understand, so let us take a simple example. Imagine that you work in a unionized environment, where the employment contracts are regularly signed for three years. The contract fixes the price of labour when signed so that both sides know what the wages will be. On the other hand, there is no similar restriction on the price being charged by the business for the output that is being produced. Suppose that shortly after a contract is signed, inflation in the economy rises unexpectedly from 2 percent to 5 percent. In the *short run* (when adjustments to input prices cannot be made), the business is free to raise its prices in line with the inflation rate, but for the remainder of the union contract, wages are fixed for the employees. At the end of the three years, the employees are able to renegotiate their contract to bring their wages back in line with the higher inflation rate and to compensate for the lost purchasing power they encountered from the unexpected inflation. This ability to adjust input prices is assumed to happen for *all markets* (not just the labour market) in the *long run*.

Full information is a similar sort of assumption. We assume that all of the economic players are able to find and incorporate into their decision making any information that affects them. From our previous example, the unionized workers know what their true value is to the company they are negotiating with, and the company would know what the productivity of the workers is. Similarly, unemployed workers know where they can find jobs and what wage they can expect to receive for their labour. There would be no involuntary unemployment, then, because workers would immediately fill vacant jobs, and adjust their wage expectations accordingly. In reality, of course, much information like this is not available to everyone.

Another way of viewing the *LRAS* is to think of it as the full-employment level of real GDP. When the economy reaches full employment along its production possibilities curve, no further adjustments will occur unless a change occurs in the other variables that we are assuming constant and stable. Some economists like to think of the *LRAS* as occurring at the level of real GDP consistent with the natural rate of unemployment, the unemployment rate that occurs in an economy with full adjustment in the long run. As we discussed in

FIGURE 6-3

The Production Possibilities and the Economy's Long-Run Aggregate Supply Curve

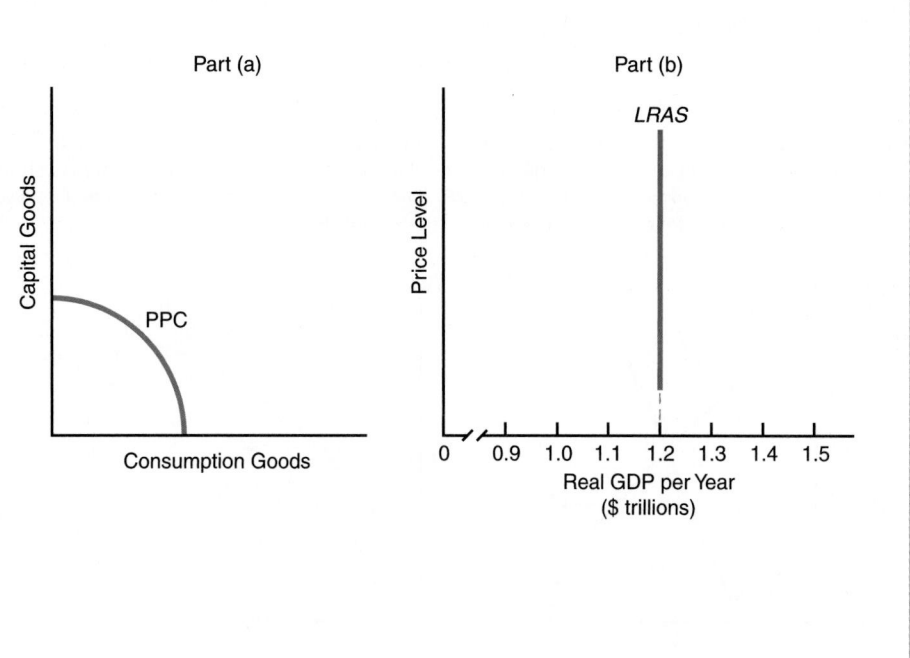

At a point in time, a nation's base of resources and its technological capabilities define the position of its production possibilities curve, as shown in part (a). This defines the real GDP that the nation can produce when resources are fully employed, which determines the position of the long-run aggregate supply curve (*LRAS*) displayed in part (b). Because people have complete information and input prices adjust fully to changes in output prices in the long run, the *LRAS* is vertical.

Chapter 4, many economists like to think of the natural rate of unemployment as consisting of frictional and structural unemployment.

Note that the PPC model also can be related to the *LRAS* . In Figure 6-3, the *LRAS* represents the level of production when the economy is fully employed, which is represented on the PPC model as production anywhere on the PPC curve itself.

6.2 Shifts in Long-Run Aggregate Supply

In the previous chapter, we learned that new technologies, more human and physical capital, or more resources, such as labour, can increase output in an economy. This increase in output will be shown as an increase in the *LRAS* curve. In Figure 6-4, part (c) we see that the *LRAS* curve has shifted to the right as we improve available technology in the economy.

A similar increase in the *LRAS* would occur if we increase the productivity of labour with more human capital or if we invest in new capital. Because we have had population increases, capital stock accumulation, and new technology available in Canada, we have had economic growth for most of Canada's history; aggregate real GDP and long-run aggregate supply have increased. Besides these basic sources of growth, there are other factors necessary for growth to occur. In Policy Example 6-1, one economist suggests that the regulation of industries has been significant in reducing our potential output. As well, we will examine some of the necessary preconditions for growth in greater detail in Chapter 7, and see how it applies to a variety of countries around the world.

We may conclude that in a growing economy, the *LRAS* shifts ever farther to the right over time. If it were the case that the pace at which the *LRAS* shifts rightward were constant, real GDP would increase at a steady annual rate. As shown in Figure 6–5, this means that real GDP would increase along a long-run, or *trend,* path that is an upward-sloping line. Thus, if the *LRAS* shifts rightward from $1.5 trillion to $1.6 trillion between 2007 and 2009 and then increases at a steady pace of $50 billion per year every year thereafter, in 2011 long-run real GDP will equal $1.7 trillion, in 2013 it will equal $1.9 trillion, and so on.

FIGURE 6–4 *Increased Productivity and LRAS*

In this figure, new technology shifts *LRAS* to the right. In part (b), the new technology increases productivity and thereby shifts up the production function from PF_1 to PF_2. This creates greater demand for labour as the productivity of that labour is increased so demand shifts from D_1 to D_2 in part (a). A new (higher) wage rate is established, and a new high potential production level is possible, shown as a shift in the *LRAS* from $LRAS_1$ to $LRAS_2$.

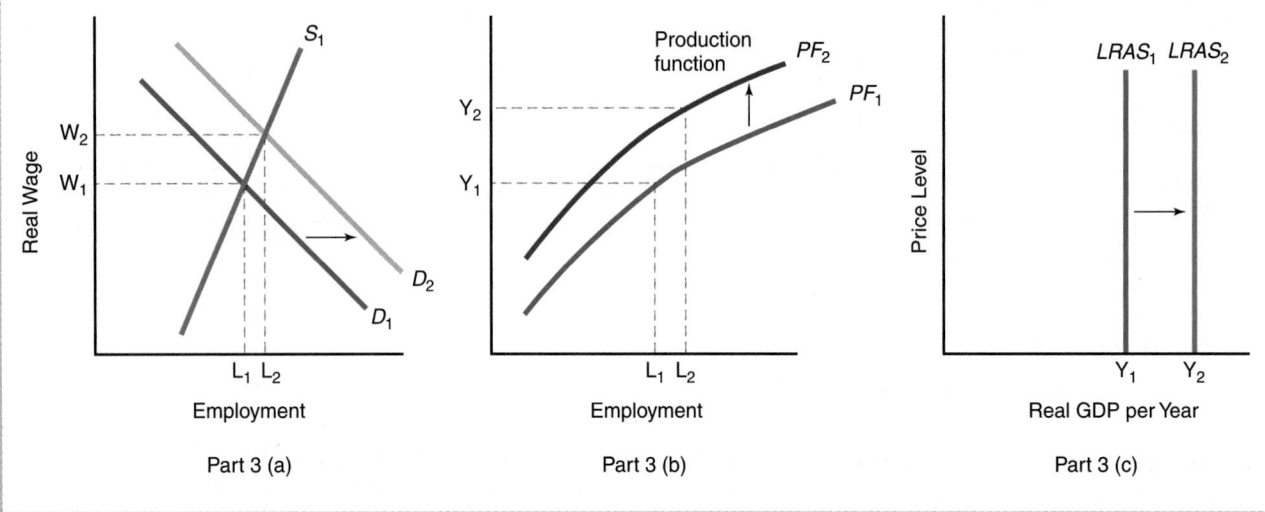

Part 3 (a)

Part 3 (b)

Part 3 (c)

Is it possible for *LRAS* to shift left? Yes, there have been periods of time when growth has been zero or negative. Before the Industrial Revolution, growth was very slow. Without technological advances, productivity was much slower to advance. In general, whenever resources are diverted away from productive activities, rightward shifts in *LRAS* will tend to be slower, as explained in Policy Example 6–1 and Example 6–1.

POLICY EXAMPLE 6-1 **Regulation and Economic Growth**

If government regulation of activities in product and labour markets can be measured by the sheer volume of published regulations, then the scope of regulation has increased tremendously since 1950. To satisfy health and safety, environmental, labour, and various other regulations, companies must shift resources away from producing goods and services. Consequently, the regulation of economic activities creates an opportunity cost for society: forgone production of real GDP.

John Dawson of Appalachian State University and John Seater of North Carolina State University have estimated the degree to which federal regulations have reduced U.S. real GDP growth. They calculated that the trend rate of annual growth of real GDP is almost one percentage point lower due to regulatory growth. Thus, if there had been no increase in federal regulations since the early 1950s, the economy's long-run aggregate supply curve would have shifted much farther to the right over the past five decades. Dawson and Seater estimate that in the absence of increased government regulation, U.S. real GDP would be at least 40 percent higher today.

For critical analysis: How do the various activities involved in satisfying government regulations get counted in real GDP? (Hint: Income payments must be made to owners of resources directed toward meeting regulatory requirements.)

FIGURE 6–5

A Sample Long-Run Growth Path for Real GDP

Year-to-year shifts in the long-run aggregate supply curve yield a long-run trend path for real GDP growth. In this example, real GDP grows by a steady amount of $500 billion each year.

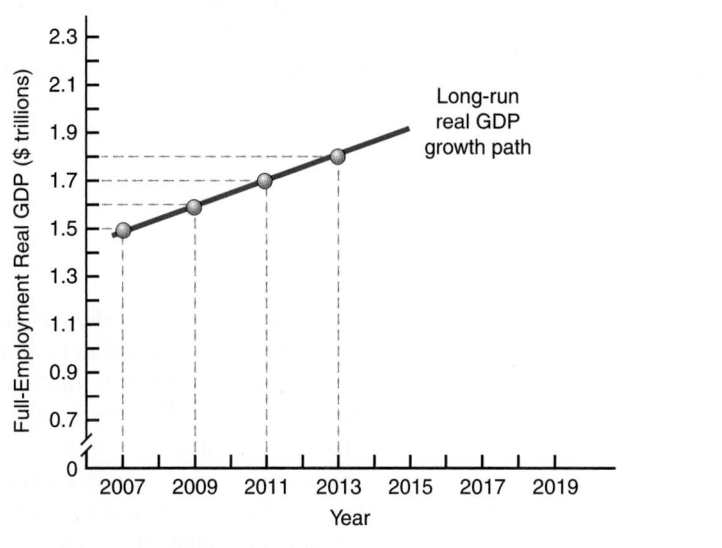

EXAMPLE 6-1   **Terrorism and Economic Growth**

During the days after terrorists slammed wide-bodied jets into the World Trade Center and the Pentagon in the United States on September 11, 2001, trucking firms paid drivers to work overtime reparking trucks in plain view and under security lights. During the months that followed, numerous trucking companies began installing electric fences around their parking lots and hiring more security guards. In busy harbours, ships waited for hours to have their loads searched by customs agents before they could dock and begin unloading boxes and crates. Airlines began imposing "security surcharges" on airfreight shipments to help cover the expense of scanning all items.

The total economywide cost of extra security measures implemented in the United States after September 2001 has been estimated to be as high as $20 billion per year. This is about 2 percent of the nation's annual freight transportation expenses.

Resources diverted to making people, other resources, and produced goods and services more secure cannot be used to produce additional goods and services. Thus, the production possibilities curve for the United States cannot shift as far rightward each year as it did before terrorism became a national worry. Nevertheless, the nation's productive capabilities will continue to increase over time, although the long-run supply curve must shift rightward at a slower pace than it would have if so many resources had not been re-allocated to providing greater security.

For critical analysis: Could the terrorist attacks on September 11, 2001, have had a direct effect on the long-run aggregate supply curve? (Hint: How did the attacks affect the total amount of resources available to produce goods and services?)

➡️ **CONCEPTS IN BRIEF**

Learning Objective 6.1: Understand and model the concept of long-run aggregate supply.

- Aggregate production shows the relationship between available resources and the output of the economy. Long-run aggregate supply is the level of production with all such resources being fully employed.
- The long-run aggregate supply curve, *LRAS*, is a vertical line determined by amounts of available resources, such as labour and capital, and by technology and resource productivity, not by the price level prevailing in the economy. The position of the *LRAS* gives the full-information and full-adjustment levels of real output of goods and services.

Learning Objective 6.2: Describe the effect of economic growth on the long-run aggregate supply curve.

↖ If labour or capital increases from year to year or if the productivity of either of these resources rises from one year to the next, the *LRAS* shifts rightward. In a growing economy, therefore, real GDP gradually rises over time.

6.3 *Aggregate Demand*

In equilibrium, individuals, businesses, and governments purchase all the goods and services produced, valued in billions of real dollars. As explained in Chapters 4 and 5, GDP is the dollar value of total expenditures on domestically produced final goods and services. Because all expenditures are made by individuals, firms, or governments, the total value of these expenditures must be what each of these sectors decides it shall be. The decisions of individuals, managers of firms, and government officials determine the annual dollar value of total expenditures. You can certainly see this in your role as a private individual. You decide what the total dollar amount of your expenditures will be in a year. You decide how much you want to spend and how much you want to save. Thus, if we want to know what determines the total value of GDP, the answer would be clear: the spending decisions of individuals like you; firms; and municipal, provincial, and federal governments. In an open economy, we must also include foreign individuals, firms, and governments (foreigners, for short) that decide to spend their money income in Canada.

In the same way, simply measuring the amount that is spent by firms for resources (as we did in Chapter 5) does not tell us about how firms meet demand. They often have to find new workers and machines, borrow money and other resources, and pay for them. What if those resources are in limited supply? What difference does it make if firms have to pay more for those resources? How do these decisions affect the long-run growth of the economy?

Simply stating that the dollar value of total expenditures in this country depends on what individuals, firms, governments, and foreigners decide to do really does not tell us much, though. Two important issues remain:

1. What determines the total amount that individuals, firms, governments, and foreigners want to spend?
2. What determines the equilibrium price level and the rate of inflation (or deflation)?

The *LRAS* tells us only about the economy's long-run, or trend, real GDP. To answer these additional questions, we must consider another important concept. This is **aggregate demand**, which is the total of all planned real expenditures for the entire economy.

> **Aggregate demand** The total of all planned real expenditures for the entire economy.

Aggregate Demand

The **aggregate demand curve**, *AD*, gives the various quantities of all final commodities demanded at various price levels, all other things held constant. Recall the components of GDP that you studied in Chapter 5: consumption spending, investment expenditures, government purchases, and net exports. They are all components of aggregate demand. Since the price level has a very important influence on aggregate demand, it is plotted against the price level. Throughout this chapter and the next, whenever you see the aggregate demand curve, realize that it is a shorthand way of talking about the components of GDP that are modelled by economists. We are looking at what influences and affects spending and production, not just how much took place. In Chapter 9, you will look more closely at the relationship between these components and, in particular, how consumption spending depends on income.

> **Aggregate demand curve** A curve that gives the various quantities of all final commodities demanded at various price levels, all other things held constant.

The Aggregate Demand Curve

The aggregate demand curve gives the total amount of *real* domestic output that will be purchased at each price level. This consists of the output of final goods and services in the economy—everything produced for final use by households, businesses, governments, and foreign residents. It includes socks, shoes, medical and legal services, computers, and millions of other goods and services that people buy each year. A graphic representation of the aggregate demand curve is seen in Figure 6–6. On the horizontal axis is measured real gross domestic output, or real GDP. For our measure of the price level, we use the GDP price deflator on the vertical axis. The aggregate demand curve is labelled *AD*. If the GDP deflator is 110, aggregate quantity demanded is $1.2 trillion per year (point *A*). At the price level 130, it is $1.1 trillion per year (point *B*). At the price level 150, it is $1.0 trillion per year (point *C*). The higher the price level, the lower is the total real output demanded by the economy, everything else remaining constant, as shown by the arrow along *AD* in Figure 6–6. Conversely, the lower the price level, the higher is the total real output demanded by the economy, everything else staying constant. We will see in a moment why aggregate demand is shown with a negative slope in Figure 6–6.

Let us take the year 2006. Looking at the Statistics Canada preliminary statistics reveals the following information:

- Nominal GDP was $1446.3 billion.
- The price level as measured by the GDP deflator was 113.06 (base year is 2002, for which the index equals 100).
- Real GDP (output) was $1279.2 billion in 2002 dollars.

What can we say about 2006? Given the dollar cost of buying goods and services and all of the other factors that go into spending decisions by individuals, firms, governments, and foreigners, the total amount of real domestic output demanded by firms, individuals, governments, and foreign residents was $1279.2 billion in 2006 (in terms of 2002 dollars).

What Happens When the Price Level Rises?

What if the price level in the economy rose to 120 tomorrow? What would happen to the amount of real goods and services that individuals, firms, governments, and foreigners wish to purchase in Canada? When we asked that question about individual commodities in Chapter 3 the answer was obvious: The quantity demanded would fall if the price went up. Now we are talking about the price level—the average price of all goods and services in the economy. The answer is still that the total quantities of real

FIGURE 6–6

The Aggregate Demand Curve

The aggregate demand curve, *AD*, slopes downward. If the price level is 110, we will be at point *A* with $1.2 trillion of real GDP demanded per year. As the price level increases to 130 and to 150, we will move up to the aggregate demand curve to points *B* and *C*. Real GDP demanded declines.

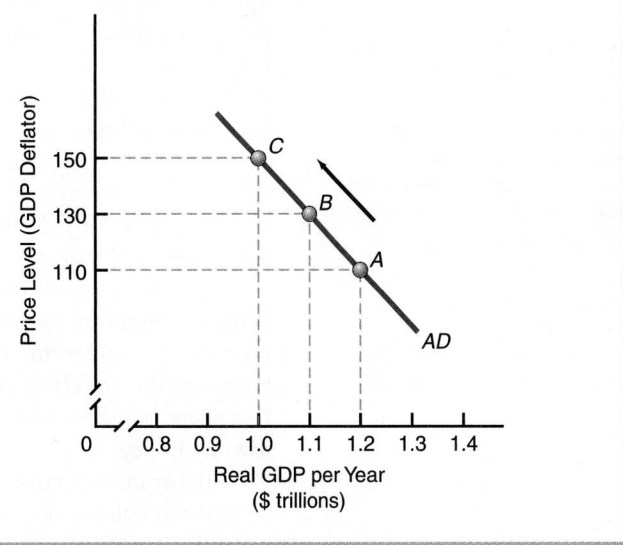

goods and services demanded would fall, but the reasons are different. Remember that in Chapter 3 when the price of one good or service went up, the consumer would substitute other goods and services. For the entire economy, when the price level goes up, the consumer does not simply substitute one good for another, for now we are dealing with the demand for all goods and services in the entire country. There are economy-wide reasons that cause the aggregate demand curve to slope downward. They involve at least three distinct forces: the real-balance effect, the interest rate effect, and the open economy effect.

THE REAL-BALANCE EFFECT. A rise in the price level will have a direct effect on spending. Individuals, firms, governments, and foreigners carry out transactions using money. Money, in this context, only consists of currency and coins that you have in your pocket (or stashed away) right now. Because people use money to purchase goods and services, the amount of money that people have influences the amount of goods and services they want to buy. For example, if you found a $10 bill on the sidewalk, the amount of money you had would rise. Given your greater level of money balances—currency, in this case—you would almost surely increase your spending on goods and services. Similarly, if while on a trip downtown you had your pocket picked, there would be an effect on your desired spending—probably to reduce it.

While increases in the price level do not take money out of your wallet, they do reduce your *purchasing power*. A 5 percent increase in prices means that all of the money you have in your wallet will buy 5 percent less goods and services. Suppose on your shopping trip downtown, instead of having your pocket picked, it turned out that the sale that you thought was on today actually ended yesterday. You have the same amount of money, but it will buy less than you expected. As a result of the price increase, you would ultimately buy fewer goods and services.

> **Real-balance effect** Price level increases reduce the real value of cash balances which, in turn, reduces desired expenditures on the quantity of aggregate goods and services, all other things held constant. (The opposite occurs if the price level declines.)

Because it relates to the real value of your cash balances (which is part of your wealth), this response is called the **real-balance effect** (or sometimes the *wealth effect*). While your nominal cash balances may remain the same, an increase in the price level will reduce the real value of those cash balances which, in turn, reduces desired expenditures on the quantity of aggregate goods and services, all other things held constant. (The opposite occurs if the price level declines.)

When you think of the real-balance effect, just think of what happens to your real wealth if you have, say, a $100 bill hidden under your mattress. If the price level increases by 10 percent, the purchasing power of that $100 bill drops by 10 percent, and so not only may you feel less wealthy, you actually are. This will reduce your spending on all goods and services by some small amount.

THE INTEREST RATE EFFECT. There is the second—more subtle but equally important—*indirect* effect on your desire to spend. As the price level rises, interest rates will rise (assuming the amount of money in circulation remains constant). This raises borrowing costs for consumers and businesses. They will borrow less and consequently spend less. The fact that a higher price level pushes up interest rates and thereby reduces borrowing and spending is known as the **interest rate effect**.

> **Interest rate effect** A higher price level pushes up interest rates and thereby reduces borrowing and spending. (The opposite occurs if the price level declines.)

Because most people and businesses use cash in their everyday transactions, a certain amount of cash is needed for the smooth running of business. Suppose, for example, that the place where you buy lunch raises its prices from $5 to $7 for the daily special. While you would normally carry $5 in your wallet for purchasing the special, now you will need $7. You are therefore carrying less of your money in the bank and more in your wallet. In the same way, the restaurant where you buy your lunches will be carrying more cash in its till every day. When this happens across the economy, the net effect of everyone trying to get more money out of the bank means that there is less money for banks to lend out, and so interest rates (the price of borrowing money) rise.

Higher interest rates make it less attractive for people to buy houses and cars. Higher interest rates also make it less profitable for firms to install new equipment and to erect new office buildings. Whether we are talking about individuals or firms, the indirect effect of a rise in the price level will cause a higher level of interest rates, which, in turn, reduces the amount of goods and services that people are willing to purchase when the price level rises. Therefore, an increase in the price level will tend to reduce the quantity of aggregate goods and services demanded. (The opposite occurs if the price level declines.)

THE OPEN ECONOMY EFFECT. Remember from Chapter 5 that GDP includes net exports—the difference between exports and imports. In an open economy, we buy imports from other countries and ultimately pay for them through the foreign exchange market. The same is true for foreigners who purchase our goods (exports). Given any set of exchange rates between the Canadian dollar and other currencies, an increase in the price level in Canada makes Canadian goods more expensive relative to foreign goods. Foreigners have downward-sloping demand curves for Canadian goods. When the relative prices of Canadian goods go up, foreigners buy fewer Canadian goods and more of their own. In Canada, the relatively cheaper foreign goods now result in Canadians wanting to buy more foreign goods rather than Canadian goods. The result is a fall in exports and a rise in imports when the domestic price level rises. That means that a price level increase tends to reduce net exports, thereby reducing the amount of real goods and services purchased in Canada. (The opposite occurs if the price level declines.) This is known as the **open economy effect** or sometimes called the substitution effect.

Open economy effect A price level increase tends to reduce net exports, thereby reducing the amount of real goods and services purchased in Canada. (The opposite occurs if the price level declines.)

What Happens When the Price Level Falls?

What about the reverse? Suppose now that the GDP deflator falls to 100 from an initial level of 120. You should be able to trace the three effects on desired purchases of goods and services. Specifically, how do the real-balance, interest rate, and open economy effects cause people to want to buy more? You should come to the conclusion that the lower the price level, the greater is the quantity of output of goods and services demanded.

The aggregate demand curve, *AD*, shows the quantity of aggregate output that will be demanded at alternative price levels. It is downward sloping, as is the demand curve for individual goods. The higher the price level, the lower is the quantity of aggregate output demanded, and vice versa.

Aggregate Demand versus Individual Demand

Even though the aggregate demand curve, *AD*, in Figure 6–6 looks quite similar to the individual demand curve, *D*, to which you were introduced in Chapter 3, it is not the same. When we derive the aggregate demand curve, we are looking at the entire economic system. The aggregate demand curve, *AD*, differs from an individual demand curve, *D*, because we are looking at the entire circular flow of income and product when we construct *AD*.

Shifts in the Aggregate Demand Curve

In Chapter 3, you learned that any time a nonprice determinant of demand changed, the demand curve shifted inward to the left or outward to the right. The same analysis holds for the aggregate demand curve, except that we are now talking about the non–price-level determinants of aggregate demand. So, when we ask the question, "What determines the position of the aggregate demand curve?" the fundamental proposition is as follows:

> Any non–price-level change that increases aggregate spending (on domestic goods) shifts *AD* to the right. Any non–price-level change that decreases aggregate spending (on domestic goods) shifts *AD* to the left.

The list of potential determinants of the position of the aggregate demand curve is virtually without limit. Some of the most important "curve shifters" with respect to aggregate demand are presented in Table 6–1. An example of how a change in one of these determinants alters the aggregate demand is drawn in Figure 6–7.

TABLE 6-1 *Determinants of Aggregate Demand*	Changes That Cause an Increase in Aggregate Demand	Changes That Cause a Decrease in Aggregate Demand
Aggregate demand consists of the demand for consumption goods, investment goods, government purchases, and net exports. Consequently, any change in the demand for any one of these components of real GDP will cause a change in aggregate demand. Here are some possibilities.	A drop in the foreign exchange value of the dollar	A rise in the foreign exchange value of the dollar
	Increased security about jobs and future income	Decreased security about jobs and future income
	Improvements in economic conditions in other countries	Declines in economic conditions in other countries
	A reduction in real interest rates (nominal interest rates corrected for inflation) not due to price level changes	A rise in real interest rates (nominal interest rates corrected for inflation) not due to price level changes
	Tax decreases	Tax increases
	An increase in the amount of money in circulation	A decrease in the amount of money in circulation

Aggregate Demand and the Multiplier

Economists have come to understand that new spending in an economy can have a larger impact on the economy than the amount of the original transaction. Formally, we would say that **the multiplier** is the number by which an expenditure is multiplied to get the final change in aggregate demand.

The multiplier The multiplier is the number by which an expenditure is multiplied to get the final change in aggregate demand.

So where does the multiplier effect come from? The multiplier effect happens because income received by one group is being spent on goods and services produced by another group, reflecting the circular flow of the economy that we studied in Chapter 5. So when a new expenditure is made, there is new income created, which creates secondary spending. However, it is clear from the enhanced version of the circular flow, not every dollar earned is spent domestically. Some portion of the spending "leaks out" to savings, another portion to foreigners through the purchase of imports, and a final portion is paid to the government in taxes.

Let us look at a simple numerical example. Suppose that planned investment increases by $10 billion. This could occur, for example, if interest rates were lowered. This increase in investment also means an increase in aggregate demand of $10 billion, shifting the *AD* curve to the right by $10 billion. For those who create the investment goods (such as the construction workers and building suppliers), they experience an increase in income of $10 billion. They will now take the income, pay their taxes, put some aside as savings, and spend the rest (some of it on imports).

That's not the end of the story, though. This additional spending will provide additional income for other individuals (the pub owners on Friday afternoon, for example). Thus we may see a secondary round of spending, perhaps of $6 billion (the other $4 billion having leaked away). Now out of this $6 billion increased real income, what will be the resulting increase in expenditures? Some of the $6 billion will "leak out," and some of it will create income for a third group of people, and so on.

FIGURE 6-7
Aggregate Demand Curve Shift

Any non–price-level determinant that causes a decrease in total planned expenditure will shift the aggregate demand curve left from AD_1 to AD_2. For example, a rise in interest rates will reduce investment expenditure and, thus, reduce planned expenditure.

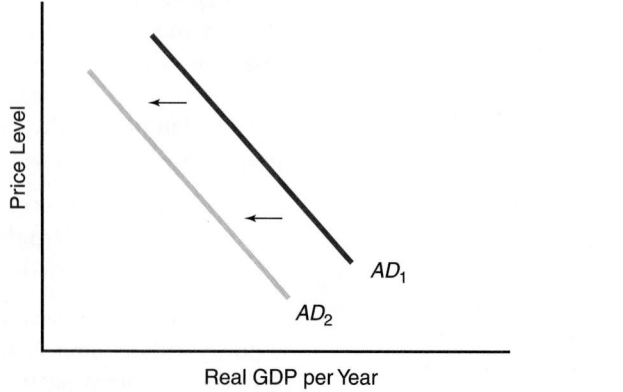

FIGURE 6–8

The Multiplier Effect on AD

An initial expenditure on new goods and services will result in an amplified effect on aggregate demand. The initial impact is shown as the shift from AD_0 to AD_1, while the multiplier effect continues the movement to the right to AD_2.

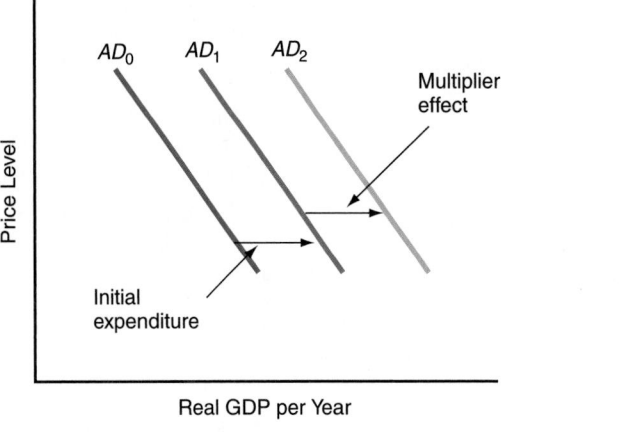

This spending/leakage pattern continues until it goes to zero. The total spending will be a combination of the original $10 billion, the $6 billion of the secondary income earners, and the spending of all the tertiary people.

Thus, the aggregate demand curve will experience a larger shift than you might expect from a single transaction. It does not change the general direction of the aggregate demand curve shift, but rather amplifies it. The shift we see in Figure 6-8 consists of two parts, one based on the original transaction, and the other based on the multiplier effect.

EXAMPLE 6–2   **Interest Rate Hikes and a Hot Loonie Are Hurting Ontario**

Interest rate increases and the rising Canadian dollar have been hurting Ontario's manufacturing industries. The Canadian dollar has risen by 50 percent since 2002 in value against the U.S. dollar, our major trading partner, and interest rates are higher.

A higher Canadian dollar means lower revenue from international sales. Higher interest rates reduce the profitability of companies. The high value of the loonie has been cited as the major cause of the loss 50 000 manufacturing jobs, and the rate of job creation in Ontario has been far below the national average.

The Canadian federal government gave a tax break to businesses by introducing a two-year capital cost allowance for new investments and equipment. The government hoped to encourage higher productivity amongst manufacturers in order to offset the increases in costs and loss in revenue.

For critical analysis: Graph the appropriate shift in the aggregate demand curve to reflect these two events. Why is the effect of these two events likely to affect industries that are not involved in exports?

SOURCE: GLOBE AND MAIL, PAGE B4, JULY 11, 2007. "RATE HIKE, HOT LOONIE HURTING ONTARIO: SORBARA"

➤ **CONCEPTS IN BRIEF**

Learning Objective 6.3: Explain why the aggregate demand curve slopes downward and list key factors that cause this curve to shift.

- Aggregate demand is the total of all planned expenditures in the economy, and aggregate supply is the total of all planned production in the economy. The aggregate demand curve shows the various quantities of all commodities demanded at various price levels; it is downward sloping.

- There are three reasons the aggregate demand curve is downward sloping: the direct effect, the indirect effect, and the open economy effect.

- The real-balance effect occurs because price level changes alter the real value of cash balances, thereby causing people to desire to spend more or less, depending on whether the price level decreases or increases.
- The interest rate effect is caused via interest rate changes that mimic price level changes. At higher interest rates, people desire to buy fewer houses and cars, and vice versa.
- The open economy effect occurs because of the substitution of foreign goods for domestic goods when the domestic price level increases and a shift away from foreign goods when the domestic price level decreases.
- The multiplier effect will shift the aggregate demand curve farther than the amount of the original transaction because of the circular flow nature of the economy.

6.4 Long-Run Equilibrium, the Price Level, and Economic Growth

As noted in Chapter 3, equilibrium occurs where the demand and supply curves intersect. The same is true for the economy as a whole, as shown in Figure 6–9: The equilibrium price level occurs at the point where the aggregate demand curve *(AD)* crosses the long-run aggregate supply curve *(LRAS)*. At this equilibrium price level of 120, the total of all planned real expenditures for the entire economy is equal to total planned production. Thus, the equilibrium depicted in Figure 6–9 is the economy's *long-run equilibrium*.

Long-run macroeconomic equilibrium occurs because of the adjustment process discussed in section 6.1 that occurs when the economy operates at levels other than potential output. Take a look at Figure 6-9. If the economy were at price level 140, the aggregate demand for production would be less than the firms would be willing to make in the long run. Firms would experience declining sales and reduce their demand for labour and other inputs. This situation puts pressure on wages and prices to decline to their equilibrium values. Similarly, if aggregate demand exceeds *LRAS*, there will be an increase in wages that will result in a higher price level. We will examine this wage adjustment process more fully in Chapter 8.

The Effects of Economic Growth on the Price Level

We now have a basic theory of how real output and the price level are determined in the long run when all of a nation's resources can change over time and all input prices

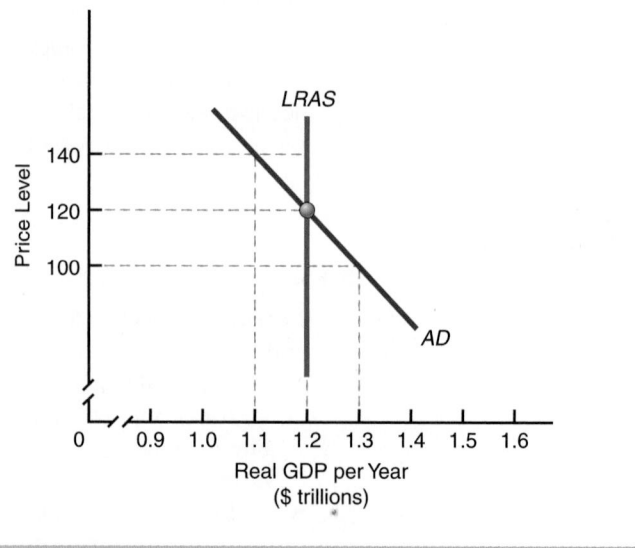

FIGURE 6–9
Long-Run Economywide Equilibrium

For the economy as a whole, long-run equilibrium occurs at the price level where the aggregate demand curve crosses the long-run aggregate supply curve. At this long-run equilibrium price level, which is 120 in the diagram, total planned real expenditures equal total planned production at full employment, which, in our example, is a real GDP of $1.2 trillion.

can adjust fully to changes in the overall level of prices of goods and services that firms produce. Let us begin by evaluating the effects of economic growth on the nation's price level.

GROWTH AND DEFLATION. Take a look at part (a) of Figure 6–10, which shows what happens, other things being equal, when the *LRAS* shifts rightward over time. If the economy were to grow steadily during, say, a 10-year interval, the long-run aggregate supply schedule would shift to the right, from $LRAS_1$ to $LRAS_2$. In the figure, this results in a downward movement along the aggregate demand schedule. The equilibrium price level falls, from 120 to 60. Thus, if all factors that affect total planned real expenditures are unchanged so that the aggregate demand curve does not noticeably move during the 10-year period of real GDP growth, the growing economy in the example would experience deflation. This is known as **secular deflation**, or a persistently declining price level resulting from economic growth in the presence of relatively unchanged aggregate demand.

Between 1872 and 1894 in the U.S. and Canada, the price of bricks fell by 50 percent, the price of sugar by 67 percent, the price of wheat by 69 percent, the price of nails by 70 percent, and the price of copper by nearly 75 percent. Some critics offered a proposal for ending deflation: Americans wanted the government to issue new money backed by silver. As we discussed earlier, an increase in the quantity of money in circulation causes the aggregate demand curve to shift to the right. It is clear from part (b) of Figure 6–10 that the increase in the quantity of money would indeed have pushed the price level back upward.

At that time, steam powered the industrial growth that generated secular deflation. Today, information technologies provide much of the fuel for the engine of economic growth.

A similar situation of deflation is occurring in modern-day Japan because of the deflationary effects of new technology. Since 1998, Japan's real GDP has increased in every year except 2002, when it briefly and very slightly declined. As long-run aggregate supply

Secular deflation A persistently declining price level resulting from economic growth in the presence of relatively unchanged aggregate demand.

FIGURE 6–10
Secular Deflation versus Long-Run Price Stability in a Growing Economy

Part (a) illustrates what happens when economic growth occurs without a corresponding increase in aggregate demand. The result is a decline in the price level over time, known as *secular deflation.* Part (b) shows that in principle, secular deflation can be avoided if the aggregate demand curve shifts rightward at the same pace that the long-run aggregate supply curve shifts to the right.

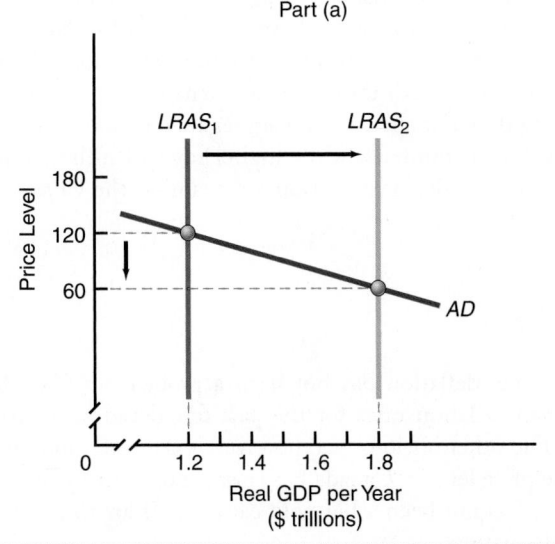

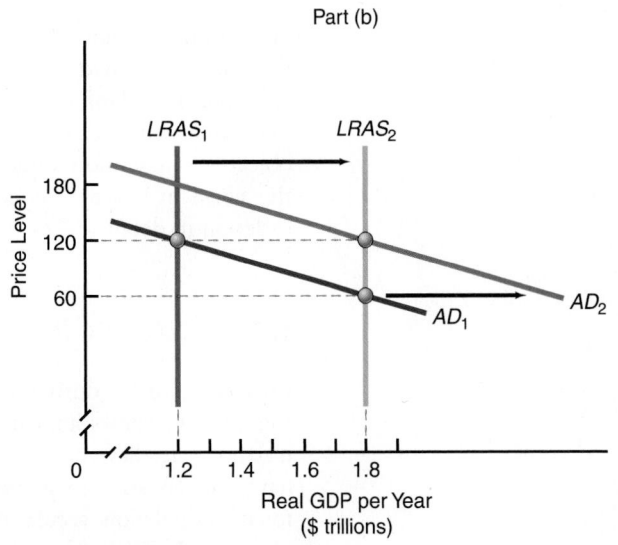

has steadily shifted rightward, the price level has gradually declined. Consequently, Japan has experienced deflation every year since 1998. During this period, Japan's price level has decreased at an annual rate of just over 0.5 percent. Example 6-3 suggests how these new technologies are leading to productivity enhancements that are driving down prices in Japan and elsewhere.

EXAMPLE 6-3 | **Information Technologies and Long-Run Aggregate Supply**

The most promising technologies today are chiefly due to communication among computers. Such communication relates to connections, rather than computations. It enhances and extends the relationships between all businesses and all people. Productivity enhancements that result may be a fundamental way that information technologies are likely to contribute to economic growth.

In addition, the growth of the Internet has allowed for the creation of more entrepreneurial talent by people whose creative lives have become enmeshed in the Web. Remember from Chapter 2 that an important factor of production is entrepreneurship. If the "new" economy does, indeed, create more entrepreneurship, the long-run aggregate supply curve (*LRAS*) may be moving outward to the right faster than it would have otherwise.

For critical analysis: How does entrepreneurship contribute to growth?

Economic Growth Without Changing Prices

Look at Figure 6-10, part (b). We start in equilibrium with AD_1 and $LRAS_1$, at a price level of 120. Real GDP per year is $1.2 trillion. Economic growth occurs due to labour force expansion, capital investments, and other occurrences. The result is a rightward shift in the long-run aggregate supply curve to $LRAS_2$. Therefore, it is possible to achieve real GDP of $1.8 trillion without any increase in the price level. The new output level is reached without a change in the overall price level.

In the world just hypothesized, aggregate demand shifts outward so that at the same price level, 120, it intersects the new long-run aggregate supply curve, $LRAS_2$, at the rate of real GDP that is consistent with full employment and potential output. Firms sell all the output produced at the new level without changing prices.

INFLATION IS THE NORM. Finally, it is possible for aggregate demand to shift outward faster than *LRAS*. Most countries in the world have some level of inflation as the norm. In Canada, we have established a 2 percent inflation rate as the most desirable rate. The Bank of Canada is entrusted with the power to change interest rates to make that happen, by either slowing down or speeding up aggregate demand. Such an objective is common amongst developed countries, while higher rates of inflation are the norm in less-developed countries. In the next section we examine the causes of inflation in detail.

6.5 *Causes of Inflation*

Of course, so far during your lifetime, deflation has not been a problem in Canada. Figure 6–11 shows annual Canadian inflation rates for the past few decades. Clearly, inflation rates have been variable. The other obvious fact, however, is that inflation rates have been consistently *positive*. The price level in Canada has *risen* almost every year. For today's population, secular deflation has not been a big political issue. If anything, it is secular *inflation* that has plagued the nation.

FIGURE 6–11
Inflation Rates in Canada

Canadian inflation rates rose considerably during the 1970s but have declined to much lower levels since the 1990s. Nevertheless, Canada has experienced some inflation every year since 1954.

SOURCE: ADAPTED FROM THE STATISTICS CANADA CANSIM DATABASE, SERIES 737344.

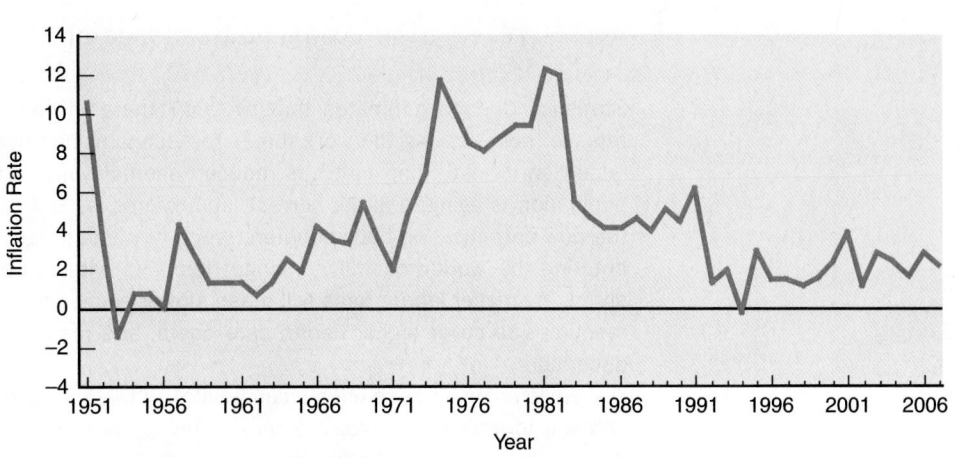

FIGURE 6–12
Explaining Persistent Inflation

As shown in part (a), it is possible for a decline in long-run aggregate supply to cause a rise in the price level. Long-run aggregate supply *increases*, however, in a growing economy, so this cannot explain the observation of persistent Canadian inflation. Part (b) provides the actual explanation of persistent inflation in Canada and most other nations today, which is that increases in aggregate demand push up the long-run equilibrium price level. Thus, it is possible to explain persistent inflation in a growing economy if the aggregate demand curve shifts rightward at a faster pace than the long-run aggregate supply curve, as shown in part (b).

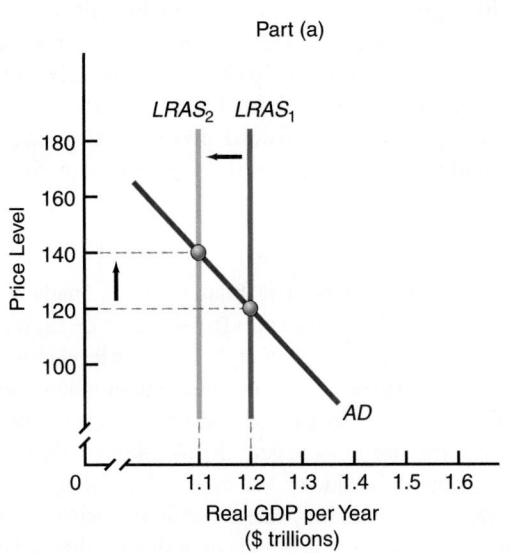

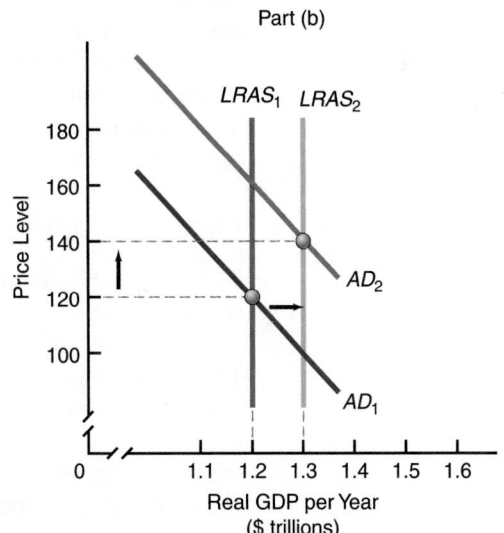

Supply-Side Inflation?

What causes such persistent inflation? The model provides two possible explanations for inflation. One potential rationale is depicted in part (a) of Figure 6–12, which shows a rise in the price level caused by a *decline in long-run aggregate supply*. Hence one possible reason for persistent inflation would be continual reductions in the production of real output. Example 6–4 provides one example of how this might happen in the future.

EXAMPLE 6-4   ## The Economic Challenge of Age

Statistics Canada estimates that by 2017 there will not be enough young people to replace those leaving the work force. The economy has been humming along for years, based on robust hiring that has reduced unemployment to 30-year lows. However, the population is aging, and the current labour force is no longer growing as retirees equal the new entrants. As baby boomers reach retirement age, the number of young people entering the workforce will no longer keep up with retirees, and the work force will shrink. A smaller labour force will mean slower economic growth, a strain on government resources to cover higher health care costs, and pressure on younger workers to produce more.

While some of these effects can be slowed by allowing people to retire later in life, the only way to maintain Canada's output is through productivity gains. However, gains in productivity have not been forthcoming in Canada for the last 10 years. The major policy proposals to increase productivity include more investment in education, lower corporate taxes, and tax incentives to encourage the purchase of machinery and equipment and increase corporate spending on training.

For critical analysis: Using the diagrams in Figure 6-2, show how this decline in the work force will affect the supply of labour, wage rates, and the long-run aggregate supply curve.

SOURCE: GLOBE AND MAIL, JULY 18, 2007, "THE ECONOMIC CHALLENGE OF AGE", PAGE A1, A6

Recall now the factors that would cause the aggregate supply schedule to shift leftward. One might be reductions in labour force participation, higher marginal tax rates on wages, or the provision of government benefits that give households incentives *not* to supply labour services to firms. Although tax rates and government benefits have increased during recent decades, so has the Canadian population. Nevertheless, the significant overall rise in real GDP that has taken place during the past few decades tells us that population growth and productivity gains have dominated other factors. In fact, the aggregate supply schedule has actually shifted *rightward,* not leftward, over time. Consequently, this supply-side explanation for persistent inflation *cannot* be the correct explanation.

Demand-Side Inflation

This leaves only one other explanation for the persistent inflation that Canada has experienced in recent decades. This explanation is depicted in part (b) of Figure 6–12. If aggregate demand increases for a given level of long-run aggregate supply, the price level must increase. The reason is that at an initial price level, such as 120, people desire to purchase more goods and services than firms are willing and able to produce, given the currently available resources and technology. As a result, the rise in aggregate demand leads only to a general rise in the price level, such as the increase to a value of 140 depicted in the figure.

From a long-run perspective, we are left with only one possibility: Persistent inflation in a growing economy is possible only if the aggregate demand curve shifts rightward over time at a faster pace than rightward progression of the long-run aggregate supply curve. Thus, in contrast to the experience of people who lived in the latter portion of the 19th century, in which aggregate demand grew too slowly relative to aggregate supply to maintain price stability, your grandparents, your parents, and you have lived in times during which aggregate demand grew too *speedily.* The result has been a continual upward drift in the price level, or long-term inflation. Hyperinflation can be explained by the very rapid expansion of aggregate demand (usually due to excessive printing of money) and some examples of modern inflation are discussed in Example 6–5.

Figure 6–13 shows that real output has grown in most years since 1970. Nevertheless, this economic growth has been accompanied by higher prices every single year.

FIGURE 6–13

Economic Growth and Inflation in Canada, 1961 to the Present

This figure shows the points where aggregate demand and aggregate supply have intersected for the odd-numbered years (and 2006) from 1961 to the present. Canada has experienced economic growth over this period, but not without inflation.

SOURCES: ADAPTED FROM THE STATISTICS CANADA CANSIM DATABASE, TABLE 380-0003.

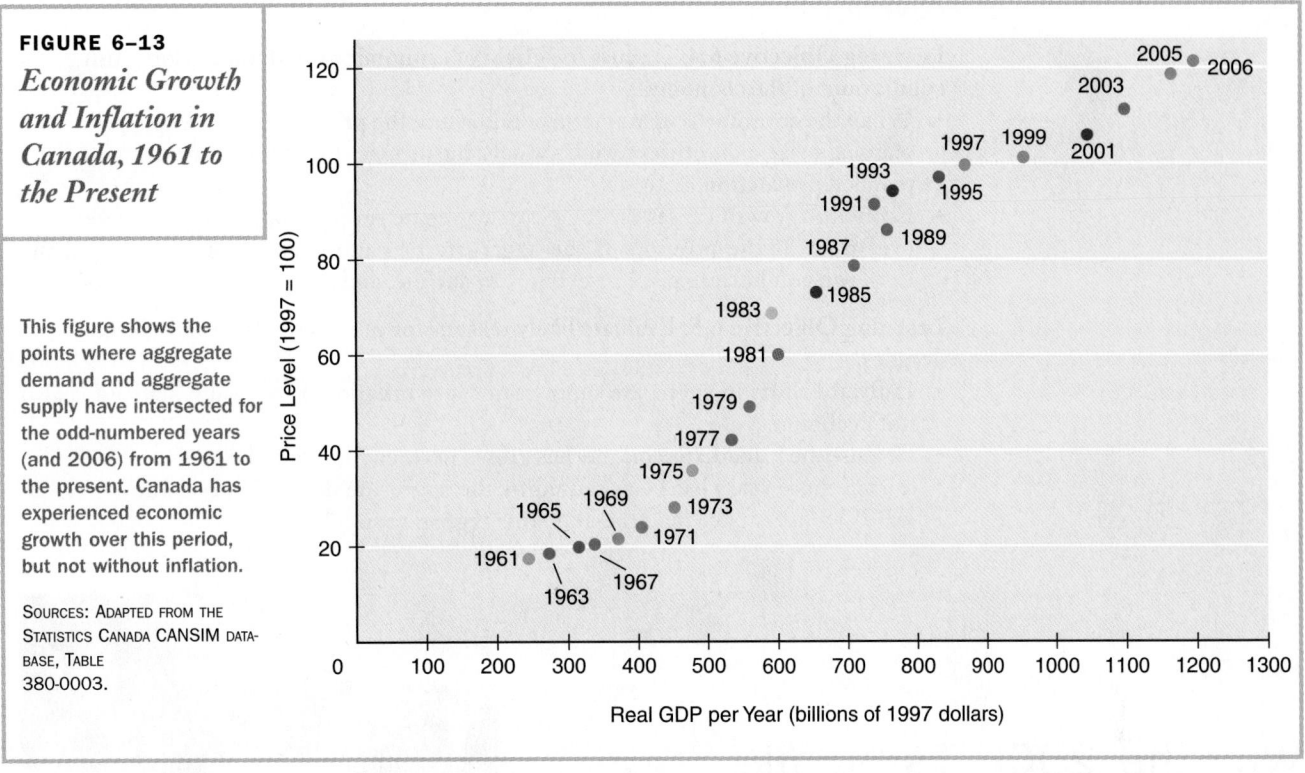

EXAMPLE 6–5

When Aggregate Demand Gets Out of Control, Watch Out!

A country's long-run aggregate supply increases gradually as the nation's capability to produce real GDP increases, typically at a single-digit annual rate of growth. If aggregate demand increases at a much faster rate, the result can be a dramatic increase in the price level.

Table 6–2 shows that some of the highest recorded inflation rates have occurred during the past 80 years. Nevertheless, Hungary's 1946 inflation rate in excess of 2 million percent per month is the highest ever recorded.

For critical analysis: How could the governments of any of these nations have prevented the rapid price growth they experienced?

TABLE 6–2

High-Inflation Episodes

Various nations have experienced extremely high rates of inflation at different times in history.

SOURCE: PIERRE SIKLOS, "INFLATION AND HYPERINFLATION," WORKING PAPER, WILFRID LAURIER UNIVERSITY, AUGUST 2000.

Country	Year Ended	Duration (months)	Average Monthly Inflation Rate (%)
Argentina	1990	11	66
Austria	1922	11	47
Bolivia	1985	18	48
Brazil	1990	4	68
Georgia	1994	13	44
Germany	1923	15	3 990
Greece	1944	13	365
Hungary	1946	12	2 345 000
Peru	1989	8	48
Poland	1990	4	41
Russia	1924	37	57
Ukraine	1993	14	1 024
Yugoslavia	1989	4	51
Zaire (Congo)	1994	36	665
Zimbabwe	Currently ongoing	–	2 000

➔ CONCEPTS IN BRIEF

Learning Objective 6.4: Discuss the effect of economic growth on the long-run equilibrium of the economy.

- When the economy is in long-run equilibrium, the price level adjusts to equate total planned real expenditures by individuals, businesses, and the government with total planned production by firms.
- Economic growth causes the long-run aggregate supply schedule to shift rightward over time. If the position of the aggregate demand curve does not change, the long-run equilibrium price level tends to decline, and there is secular deflation.

Learning Objective 6.5: Evaluate likely reasons for persistent inflation in recent decades.

- Leftward shifts in aggregate supply can cause inflation if aggregate demand is also not declining.
- Because the Canadian economy has grown in recent decades, the persistent inflation during those years has been caused by the aggregate demand curve shifting rightward at a faster pace than the long-run aggregate supply curve.

➔➔ ISSUES AND APPLICATIONS

Why the 2004 Tsunami Did Not Swamp Asian Economies

Concepts Applied: Long-Run Aggregate Supply, Aggregate Demand, Long-Run, Equilibrium

The 2004 tsunami devastated communities throughout southeast Asia but did not stall their economies.

The estimated death toll of 240 000 resulting from the Indian Ocean earthquake and tsunami event of December 26, 2004, exceeded the tallies of all other earthquakes recorded since the year 1556, when a massive Chinese earthquake killed approximately 830 000 people. In spite of this huge human toll and the considerable property damage inflicted by the tsunami, however, most of the economies of the affected southeast-Asian nations were barely bumped from their long-run growth paths.

Dire Predictions for the Future

Why did some media observers suggest that the 2004 tsunami event might deal a lingering blow to the economies of the affected nations? These observers apparently felt that there would be a long-lasting negative effect on the nations' abilities to continue producing goods and services. This caused the observers to be concerned that long-run aggregate supply would decrease.

In a nongrowing economy, reductions in productive capability caused by the tsunami damage could certainly have generated a reduction in aggregate supply. This is why the media observers suggested that the affected nations' price levels would jump, resulting in sudden inflation, and that real GDP would drop, leading to recession.

The Reality of the Long Run

In fact, as part (a) of Table 6–3 shows, inflation rates in the major southeast-Asian nations most affected by the tsunami of late 2004 did increase in 2005. Only in Indonesia did inflation noticeably spike, however. In the other nations, where foreign tourism spending is typically 3 to 5 percent of aggregate planned expenditures, declines in aggregate demand generated by a tourism drop-off helped reduce price increases. In any event, all four nations' inflation rates quickly dropped back to levels consistent with longer-term trends.

Of the nations listed in Table 6–3, not a single country experienced a decline in real GDP during the years following the tsunami event. In fact, in 2005, real GDP grew at an annual rate

TABLE 6-3

Inflation Rates and Real GDP Growth Rates in Selected Southeast-Asian Nations

Although southeast-Asian inflation rates rose in the year following the tsunami disaster that occurred at the end of 2004, rates of inflation quickly returned to levels closer to long-run trends. Real GDP growth rates dropped only very slightly in Malaysia and Thailand, and rates of growth of real GDP actually increased in Indonesia and Sri Lanka.

SOURCE: INTERNATIONAL MONETARY FUND, WORLD ECONOMIC OUTLOOK, VARIOUS ISSUES.

(a) Inflation Rates				
	2004	**2005**	**2006**	**2007**
Indonesia	6.1	10.5	14.2	6.6
Malaysia	1.4	3.0	3.1	2.7
Sri Lanka	7.9	10.6	8.0	7.0
Thailand	2.8	4.5	3.6	2.2

(b) Real GDP Growth Rates				
	2004	**2005**	**2006**	**2007**
Indonesia	5.1	5.6	5.0	6.0
Malaysia	7.1	5.3	5.5	5.8
Sri Lanka	5.4	5.9	5.6	6.2
Thailand	6.2	4.4	5.0	5.4

of at least 5 percent in all four nations. Malaysia and Thailand experienced a slight falloff in real GDP growth during the year following the 2004 disaster. These slightly reduced growth rates perhaps reflected a tsunami effect on productive capabilities that tended to reduce the extent to which the aggregate supply curve shifted rightward. In Indonesia and Sri Lanka, however, real GDP growth actually *increased* in the year following the tsunami calamity. The pace of economic growth might have been even faster in these two nations in the absence of the tsunami event. Nevertheless, the event failed to depress the rate at which long-run aggregate supply increased in the two countries.

For critical analysis

1. What are some possible reasons that the fast-growing nations listed in Table 6–3 may have recently experienced inflation instead of secular deflation?

2. Why do you suppose that the long-run negative macroeconomic effects of the tsunami disaster were greater in the very slow-growing African nation of Somalia than in the nations of southeast Asia?

➡ SUMMARY

Here is what you should know after reading this chapter. MyEconLab will help you identify what you know, and where to go when you need to practise. We suggest that as soon as you review one of the Learning Objective sections below, you then proceed to go through the related section in MyEconLab.

➡ LEARNING OBJECTIVES	KEY TERMS	MYECONLAB PRACTICE
6.1. The Long-Run Aggregate Supply Curve. The long-run aggregate supply curve is vertical at the amount of real GDP that firms plan to produce when they have full information and when complete adjustment of input prices to any changes in output prices has taken place. This is the full-employment level of real output, or the output level at which the natural rate of unemployment— the sum of frictional and structural unemployment as a percentage of the labour force—arises. This is also the economy's potential output.	aggregate supply, 156 long-run aggregate supply curve, 156 aggregate production function, 156 diminishing marginal returns, 157 potential output, 158 long-run aggregate supply, 158 constant dollars, 158 long-run aggregate supply curve, 158 endowments, 158 full-information, 158 full-adjustment, 158	• **MyEconLab** Study Plan 6.1

➡➜ LEARNING OBJECTIVES	KEY TERMS	MYECONLAB PRACTICE
6.2. Economic Growth and Long-Run Aggregate Supply. Economic growth is an expansion of a country's ability to produce. Thus, the *LRAS* curve shifts rightward when the economy grows. In a growing economy, the changes in full-employment output defined by the shifting long-run aggregate supply curve define the nation's long-run, or trend, growth path.		• **MyEconLab** Study Plan 6.2
6.3. Aggregate Demand. A rise in the price level reduces the real value of cash balances in the hands of the public, which induces people to cut back on spending. This is the real-balance effect. In addition, higher interest rates typically accompany increases in the price level, and this interest rate effect induces people to cut back on borrowing and, consequently, spending. Finally, a rise in the price level at home causes domestic goods to be more expensive relative to foreign goods so that there is a fall in exports and a rise in imports, both of which cause domestic planned expenditures to fall. These three factors together account for the downward slope of the aggregate demand curve. A shift in the aggregate demand curve results from a change in total planned real expenditures at any given price level and may be caused by a number of factors, including changes in security about jobs and future income, tax changes, variations in the quantity of money in circulation, changes in real interest rates, movements in exchange rates, and changes in economic conditions in other countries.	aggregate demand, 162 aggregate demand curve, 162 real-balance effect, 164 interest rate effect, 164 open economy effect, 165 the multiplier, 166	• **MyEconLab** Study Plan 6.3
6.4. Long-Run Equilibrium, the Price Level, and Economic Growth. In a long-run economywide equilibrium, the price level adjusts until total planned real expenditures equal total planned production. Thus, the long-run equilibrium price level is determined at the point where the aggregate demand curve intersects the long-run aggregate supply curve. If the aggregate demand curve is stationary during a period of economic growth, the long-run aggregate supply curve shifts rightward along the aggregate demand curve. The long-run equilibrium price level	secular deflation, 169	• **MyEconLab** Study Plan 6.4

→ LEARNING OBJECTIVES	KEY TERMS	MYECONLAB PRACTICE

falls and there is deflation. Economic growth has in this way generated secular deflation in some countries.

- **MyEconLab** Study Plan 6.5

6.5. Causes of Inflation: One event that can induce inflation is a decline in long-run aggregate supply because this causes the long-run aggregate supply curve to shift leftward along the aggregate demand curve. In a growing economy, however, the long-run aggregate supply curve generally shifts rightward. This indicates that a much more likely cause of persistent inflation is a pace of aggregate demand growth that exceeds the pace at which long-run aggregate supply increases.

→ PROBLEMS

(Answers to the odd-numbered problems appear at the back of the book.)

LO 6.1 Understand the concept of long-run aggregate supply.

1. Many economists view the natural rate of unemployment as the level observed when the economy is producing real GDP consistent with the position of its long-run aggregate supply curve. How can there be positive unemployment in this situation?

2. Suppose that the long-run aggregate supply curve is positioned at a real GDP level of $1.2 trillion, and the long-run equilibrium price level (in index number form) is 115. What is the full-employment level of *nominal* GDP?

LO 6.2 Describe the effect of economic growth on the long-run aggregate supply curve.

3. Continuing from Problem 2, suppose that the full-employment level of *nominal* GDP in the following year rises to $1.42 trillion. The long-run equilibrium price level, however, remains unchanged. By how much (in real dollars) has the long-run aggregate supply curve shifted to the right in the following year?

4. A country's long-run equilibrium price level has increased, but the position of its aggregate demand schedule has not changed. What has happened? What specific factors might have accounted for this event?

5. Refer back to Example 6–3, "Information Technologies and Long-Run Aggregate Supply." The prices of computers have been falling for many years. Why might this be happening? What effect will this have on the overall price level?

LO 6.3 Explain why the aggregate demand curve slopes downward and list key factors that cause this curve to shift.

6. Suppose that there is a sudden rise in the price level (and aggregate demand has not shifted). What will happen to economywide spending on purchases of goods and services? Why?

7. In the discussion of why the *AD* curve slopes downward from left to right, note that nothing was said about what happens to the quantity of real output demanded when the price level rises and causes wealth to fall for people in businesses who own mortgages on houses and buildings. Why not? (Hint: What is the *net* effect to the whole economy when the price level rises and causes a wealth loss to lenders who get paid back in fixed nominal dollars?)

8. How is aggregate demand affected when the price level in a foreign economy decreases? What happens to aggregate demand when the price level in the local economy falls?

9. Explain whether each of the following events would cause a movement along or a shift in the position of the

AD curve, other things being equal. In each case, explain the direction of the movement along the curve or shift in its position.

a. Deflation has occurred during the past year.
b. Real GDP levels of all the nation's major trading partners have declined.
c. There has been a decline in the foreign exchange value of the nation's currency.
d. The price level has increased this year.

10. What effect will an economic recession in the European Community have on the economy of Canada? Show how this would be modelled using the aggregate demand and long-run aggregate supply curves.

LO 6.4 Discuss the effect of economic growth on the long-run equilibrium of the economy.

11. Suppose that the position of a nation's long-run aggregate supply curve has not changed but its long-run equilibrium price level has increased. Which of the following factors might account for this event?

a. A rise in the value of the domestic currency relative to other world currencies
b. An increase in the quantity of money in circulation
c. An increase in the labour force participation rate
d. A decrease in taxes
e. A rise in the real incomes of countries that are key trading partners of this nation
f. Increased long-run economic growth

12. Suppose that during a given year, the quantity of Canadian real GDP that can be produced in the long run rises from $1.19 trillion to $1.2 trillion with no change in the various factors that influence aggregate demand. What will happen to the Canadian long-run equilibrium price level during this particular year?

13. Explain whether each of the following events would cause a movement along or a shift in the position of the *LRAS* curve, other things being equal. In each case, explain the direction of the movement along the curve or shift in its position.

a. Last year, businesses invested in new capital equipment, so this year the nation's capital stock is higher than it was last year.
b. There has been an 8 percent increase in the quantity of money in circulation that has shifted the *AD* curve.
c. A hurricane of unprecedented strength has damaged oil rigs, factories, and ports all along the nation's coast.
d. Inflation has occurred during the past year as a result of rightward shifts of the *AD* curve.

14. Consider the accompanying diagram when answering the questions that follow.

a. Suppose that the current price level is P_2. Explain why the price level will decline toward P_1.
b. Suppose that the current price level is P_3. Explain why the price level will rise toward P_1.

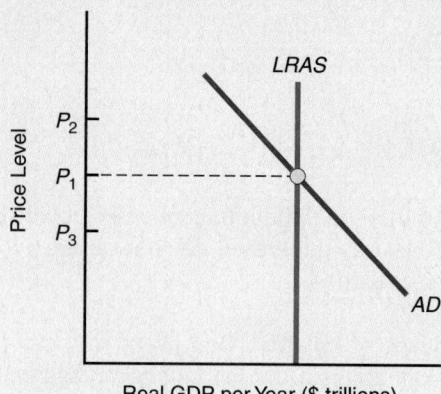

Real GDP per Year ($ trillions)

15. What might happen in the long run if countries were to ban Canadian exports of beef because of "mad cow disease"? Be sure to address what will happen to both aggregate demand and the long-run aggregate supply. How might Canadian producers "fully adjust" to this situation?

16. Assume that the position of a nation's aggregate demand curve has not changed, but the long-run equilibrium price level has declined. Other things being equal, which of the following factors might account for this event?

a. An increase in labour productivity
b. A decrease in the capital stock
c. A decrease in the quantity of money in circulation
d. The discovery of new mineral resources used to produce various goods
e. A technological improvement

17. In this chapter, you learned that if aggregate demand is unchanged, we can predict that deflation accompanies economic growth. On the basis of what you learned in Chapter 4 about the effects of expected and unexpected inflation, is predictable deflation necessarily undesirable? Support your position.

LO 6.5 Evaluate likely reasons for persistent inflation in recent decades.

18. This year, a nation's long-run equilibrium real GDP and price level both increased. Which of the following combinations of factors might simultaneously account for *both* occurrences?

a. An isolated earthquake at the beginning of the year destroyed part of the nation's capital stock, and the nation's government significantly reduced its purchases of goods and services.
b. There was a minor technological improvement at the end of the previous year, and the quantity of money in circulation rose significantly during the year.
c. Labour productivity increased somewhat throughout the year, and consumers significantly increased their total planned purchases of goods and services.

d. The capital stock increased somewhat during the year, and the quantity of money in circulation declined considerably.

19. For each question below, suppose that the economy *begins* at the long-run equilibrium point A. Identify

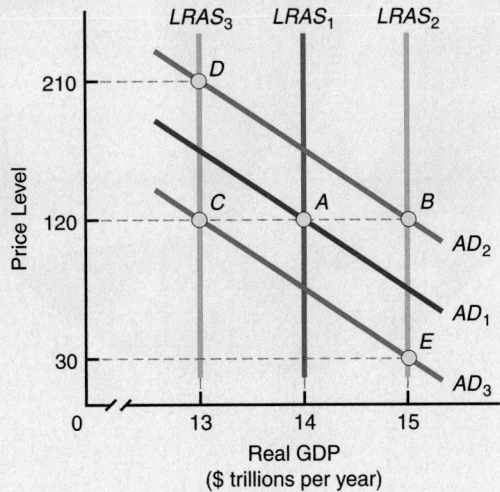

which of the other points on the diagram—points B, C, D, or E—could represent a *new* long-run equilibrium after the described events take place and move the economy away from point A.

a. Significant productivity improvements occur, and the quantity of money in circulation increases.

b. No new capital investment takes place, and a fraction of the existing capital stock depreciates and becomes unusable. At the same time, the government imposes a large tax increase on the nation's households.

c. More efficient techniques for producing goods and services are adopted throughout the economy at the same time that the government reduces its spending on goods and services.

7

Economic Growth and Development

The difference in the standard of living across different countries around the world is more extreme than ever before in our history. Some countries, like Canada, the United States, and much of Europe, have done very well, and few, if any, people in these countries do not have the income to buy food. Other countries have high proportions of people who live in extreme poverty; in sub-Saharan Africa for example, nearly 50 percent live in extreme poverty. Some countries, such as China and India, have been successful in recent years in creating economic growth that has lifted many of their citizens out of extreme poverty.

At the same time, though, many of the best-educated people in these poor countries are immigrating to Canada, creating a so-called "brain drain." What effect does this immigration have on

➤ **LEARNING OBJECTIVES**

After reading this chapter, you should be able to:

7.1 Define economic growth and explain some of the limitations of that definition.

7.2 Explain and model economic growth.

7.3 Describe the fundamental determinants of economic growth.

7.4 Understand the basis of new growth theory.

7.5 Outline some of the costs and benefits of economic growth.

7.6 Discuss the fundamental factors that contribute to international economic development.

MyEconLab helps you master each objective and study more efficiently. See end of chapter for details.

the Canadian economy and on the economies of the poorer countries? The relationships between economic growth and natural resources, human and physical capital, and technology are the focus of this chapter.

DID YOU KNOW THAT...

Only twice in the last 50 years has real GDP fallen from one year to the next: in 1982 and 1991. This nearly unblemished records points to the fact that the Canadian economy has done very well over the long haul. While not the highest per capita GDP in the world, we are still amongst the best. Even more interesting to young people is the fact that at current growth rates, their incomes may well exceed the combined income of both of their parents in their lifetime.

Clearly, the annual rate of income growth for a typical individual makes a big difference to everyone, including you. By choosing to enroll in this course at an institution of higher education, you have already demonstrated that you would prefer a higher income in the future. Obviously, you want to make sure that you experience economic growth as an individual. Now, it is time to consider economic growth for the nation as a whole.

7.1 Defining Economic Growth

Economic growth Increases in per-capita real GDP measured by the rate of change in per-capita real GDP per year.

Most people have a general idea of what economic growth means. When a nation grows economically, its citizens must be better off in at least some ways, usually in terms of their material well being. Typically, though, we do not measure the well being of any nation solely in terms of its total output of real goods and services or in terms of real gross domestic product (GDP) without making some adjustments. After all, India has a GDP about 15 times as large as that of Denmark. The population in India, though, is about 200 times greater than that of Denmark. Consequently, we view India as a relatively poor country and Denmark as a relatively rich country. Thus, when we measure economic growth, we must adjust for population growth. Our formal definition becomes this: **Economic growth** occurs when there are increases in *per-capita* real GDP, measured by the rate of change in per-capita real GDP per year. Figure 7–1 presents the historical record of real GDP per person in Canada. Read Example 7–1 to see how Canada stacks up against the world.

EXAMPLE 7–1   **Growth Rates around the World**

Table 7–1 shows the annual average rate of growth of real income per person in selected countries. Note that during the time period under study, Canada is positioned about midway in the pack. Even though we are one of the world's richest countries, our rate of economic growth in recent decades has not been particularly high. The reason that Canada's per-capita income has remained higher than per-capita incomes in most other nations is that Canada has been able to sustain growth over many decades, as we see in Figure 7.1. This is something that most other countries have so far been unable to accomplish.

For critical analysis: "The largest change is from zero to one." Does this statement have anything to do with relative growth rates in poorer versus richer countries?

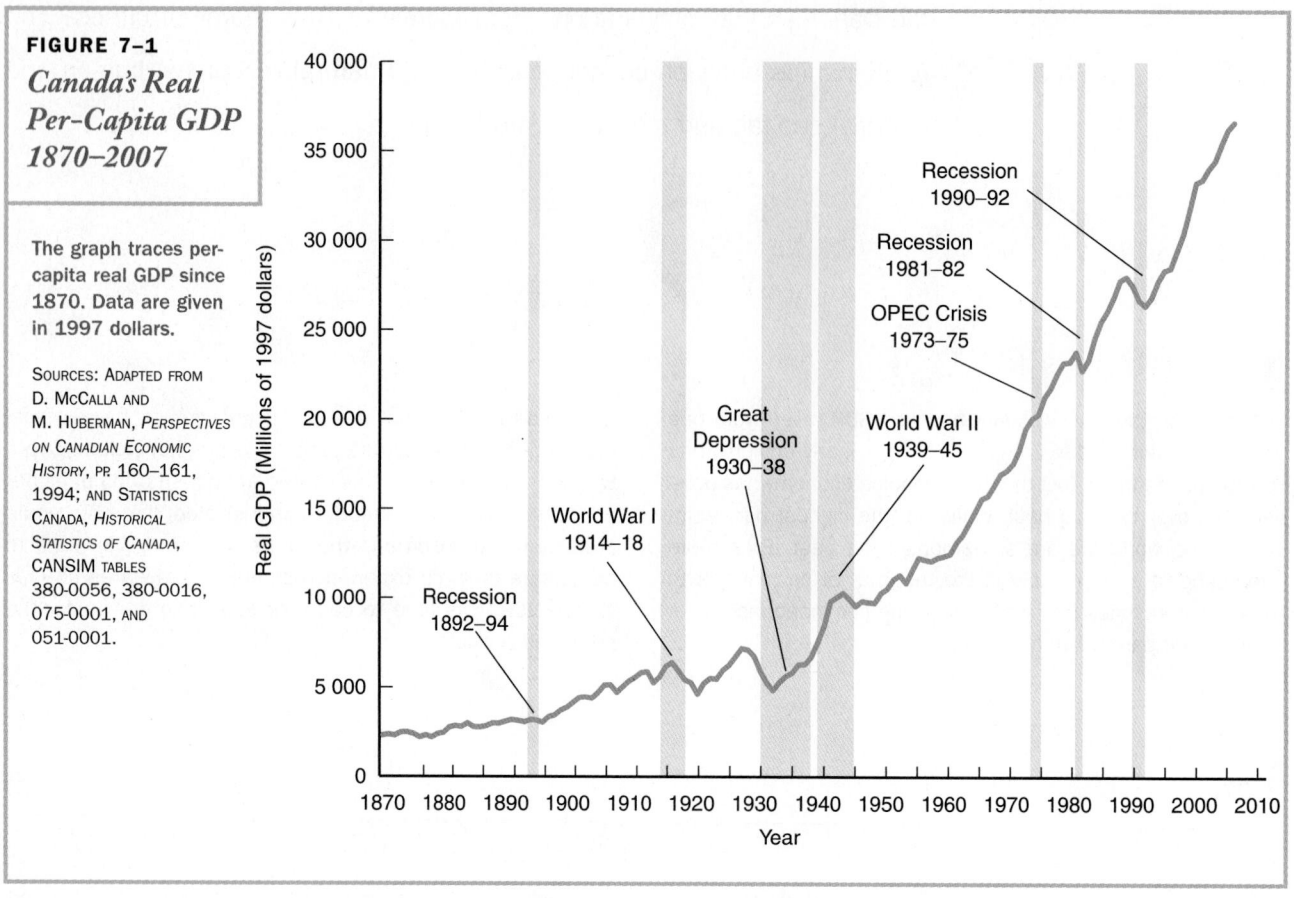

FIGURE 7–1

Canada's Real Per-Capita GDP 1870–2007

The graph traces per-capita real GDP since 1870. Data are given in 1997 dollars.

SOURCES: ADAPTED FROM D. McCALLA AND M. HUBERMAN, PERSPECTIVES ON CANADIAN ECONOMIC HISTORY, PP. 160–161, 1994; AND STATISTICS CANADA, HISTORICAL STATISTICS OF CANADA, CANSIM TABLES 380-0056, 380-0016, 075-0001, AND 051-0001.

One of the fundamental reasons that Canada has stayed near the top of the world in living standards and has improved so much from the time of Confederation is that it has sustained economic growth for many years. While the percentage differences in Table 7–1 are small, the effects of those differences over many years accumulate to very big differences. Canadian per-capita real GDP has grown by a factor of 15 since 1870, even though the average yearly increase has been about 2 percent. Example 7–2 shows how even a small difference in growth rates can make a big difference in standards of living over many years.

TABLE 7–1

Per-Capita Growth Rates in Various Countries

Country	Average Annual Rate of Growth of Real Income Per Capita, 1990–2007 (%)
Brazil	2.4
France	2.5
Japan	3.1
Germany	3.1
Sweden	3.2
Canada	3.4
United States	3.8
Turkey	4.6
Indonesia	4.7
India	5.3
Malaysia	5.4
China	9.4

SOURCES: WORLD BANK, INTERNATIONAL MONETARY FUND AND AUTHORS' ESTIMATES.

EXAMPLE 7–2	What If Canada Had Grown a Little Bit Less or More Each Year?

In 1870, the per-person real GDP expressed in 2004 dollars was $2604. That figure had grown to $39 327 by the middle of 2004. The average economic growth rate was, therefore, about 2 percent per year. What if the Canadian growth rate over the same century and a third had been simply 1 percent less—only 1 percent per year? Per-capita real GDP in 2004 would have been only about 25 percent of what it actually was! Canada would now rank somewhere around 38th on the scale of per-capita income throughout the world. We would be poorer than Greece or Portugal.

Consider a rosier scenario: What if the Canadian economic rate of growth had been 1 point higher, or 3 percent per year? Today's per-capita real GDP would be more than three times its actual value, or about $136 700! This would have about doubled the highest per-capita income in the world today!

For critical analysis: What difference to overall income does a 0.4 percent difference in growth rates make to per-capita income over 17 years? (Note that this is the difference between Canada's and the United States' growth rates in the table.) How does your standard of living differ from your parents' or grandparents'?

Problems in Definition

Our definition of economic growth says nothing about the *distribution* of output and income. A nation might grow very rapidly in terms of increases in per-capita real output, and at the same time its poor people remain poor or become even poorer. Within Canada, economic development has been very uneven, with some regions enjoying much higher standards of living than others. Therefore, in assessing the economic growth record of any nation, we must be careful to pinpoint which income groups have benefited the most from such growth.

The Human Development Index (HDI), developed by the United Nations (UN) to measure how nations are developing, recognizes this problem by measuring income, education, and life expectancy. The index measures these three basic indicators of human development because the UN wants to capture more than just income in its assessment. For the publishers of this index, how a nation's income is spent is just as important as how much it earns. So, even though Canada is not first in any of these three categories, we have come out on top because of how we spend our income.

Real standards of living can go up without any positive economic growth. This second problem with our definition occurs if individuals are, on average, enjoying more leisure by working fewer hours but producing as much as they did before. For example, if per-capita real GDP in Canada remained at $20 000 a year for a decade, we could not automatically jump to the conclusion that Canadians were, on average, no better off. What if, during that same 10-year period, average hours worked fell from 37 per week to 33 per week? That would mean that during the 10 years under study, individuals in the labour force were "earning" four hours more leisure a week. Actually, nothing so extreme has occurred in this country, but something similar has. Average hours worked per week fell steadily until the 1960s, at which time they levelled off. That means that during much of the history of this country, the increase in per-capita real GDP *understated* the actual economic growth that we were experiencing because we were enjoying more and more leisure time as things progressed.

➤→ **CONCEPTS IN BRIEF**

Learning Objective 7.1: Define economic growth and explain some of the limitations of that definition.
- ◆ Economic growth can be defined as the increase in real per-capita output measured by its rate of change per year.

- Economic growth sustained over many years has allowed countries to dramatically increase their GDP.
- The definition of economic growth does not reflect how a nation distributes its goods and services. It does not reflect how this distribution affects its population in terms of literacy or longevity, and it does not capture increases in leisure that can also be "bought" with economic growth.

7.2 Modelling Economic Growth

Let us say that you are required to type 10 term papers and homework assignments a year. You have a laptop to do it, but you are not very good at typing. You end up spending an average of two hours per typing job. The next summer, you buy a typing tutorial for practising on your laptop and spend a few minutes a day improving your typing speed. The following term, you spend only one hour typing per assignment, thereby saving 10 hours a semester. You have become more productive. This concept of productivity relates to your ability (and everyone else's) to produce the same output in fewer labour hours. Thus, **labour productivity** is normally measured by dividing the total real domestic output (real GDP) by the number of workers or the number of labour hours. Labour productivity increases whenever average output produced per worker during a specified time period increases. Clearly, there is a relationship between economic growth and increases in labour productivity.

Labour productivity Measured by dividing the total real domestic output (real GDP) by the number of workers or the number of labour hours.

Statistics Canada defines labour productivity as the cumulative contribution to per-capita GDP of three components: contributions from changes in capital intensity (the amount of capital per hour worked); the contribution from changes in labour composition (involving more highly educated or more experienced workers); and growth in multifactor productivity, which is generally everything that cannot be accounted for by labour and capital. If everything else remains constant, improvements in labour productivity ultimately lead to economic growth and higher living standards.

In the same way, increases in real GDP are closely linked to the productivity of all underlying inputs in production, capital, labour, and technology. An increase in the amount of resources available or productivity of any of these input resources contributes to overall growth. For example, there is a very strong relationship between the average level of education and the standard of living both for individuals and for countries. In the Western economies, new technologies have been a source of much economic growth in the past 100 years.

Let us look again at how our *AD-AS* model relates to these sources of growth.

Adding More Workers

Population increases typically represent an increase in the available labour supply for a country. In Canada, population has increased from 3.6 million in 1870 to 33 million today, partially through natural population increase and also through immigration. With more workers, the potential production in an economy increases. In our aggregate production model, this is shown in Figure 7-2 with an increase in the labour supply from S_1 to S_2.

In part (a) this increase in supply shows that the real wage rate will fall from W_1 to W_2. Simultaneously, the labour employed will increase from L_1 to L_2 because a lower real wage encourages employers to hire more workers.

Part (b) shows the effect of a greater labour force on real GDP. Because more workers are employed, more can be produced, thus increasing potential GDP from Y_1 to Y_2. Part (c) shows a greater output is now possible, shifting $LRAS_1$ to $LRAS_2$.

Unfortunately, the increase in the labour force will be larger than the increase in real GDP because of the economy's diminishing returns. While more workers allow for greater output, the additional output is not enough to maintain the real wage for workers, and so living standards would fall. (In the Issues and Applications section at the end of the chapter, we look at some of the other effects immigration has on Canada and the "sending" nations.)

So how has real GDP *per person* managed to grow over time so dramatically while a country's population is growing? The answer lies in the other factors of production and the technology available.

FIGURE 7-2 *Increasing Population*

As more population enters an economy, the supply of labour increases and drives down wages. If wages are permanently lower, this encourages greater production of real GDP while increasing the quantity of labour demanded.

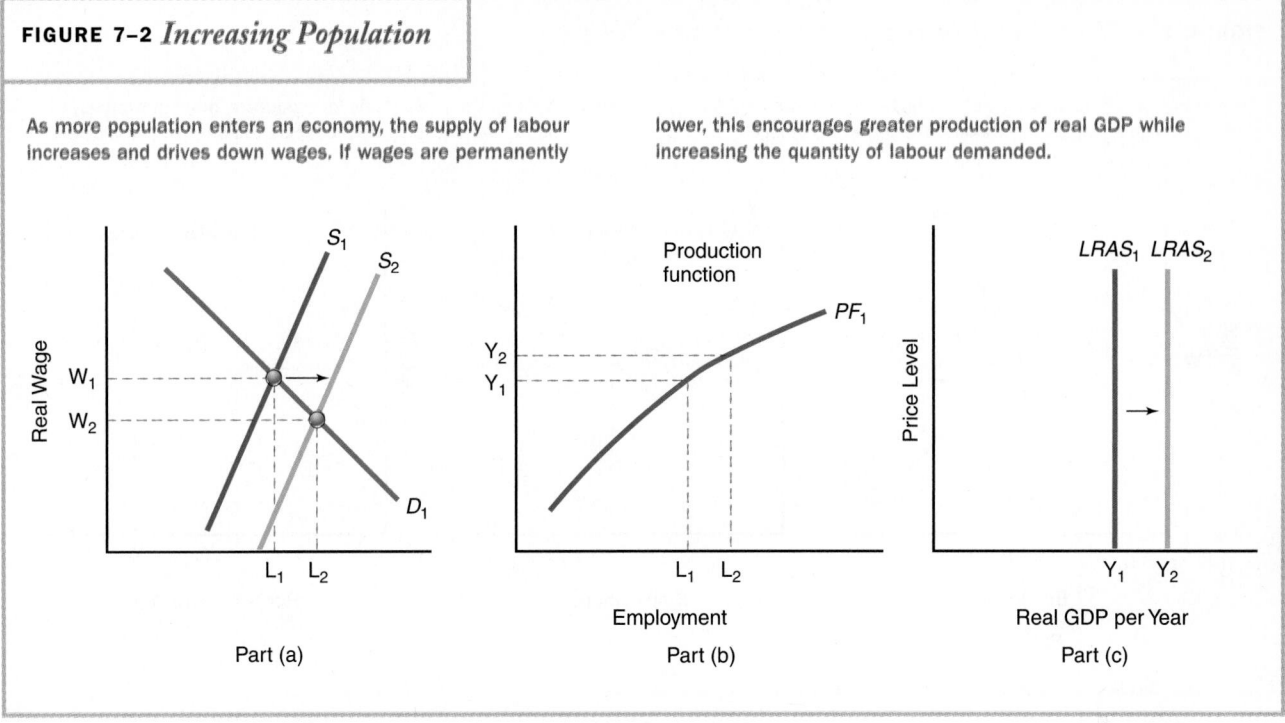

Part (a)   Part (b)   Part (c)

Changes in the Production Function

Suppose now we see an improvement in technology that improves the productivity of labour. This situation is modelled in Figure 7-3 and is shown as an upward shift of the production function. Such shifts could also occur because of an increase in physical capital, human capital, or other available natural resources.

This increase in productivity will mean an increase in the demand for labour, as shown in part (a). Before the change, producers would use L_1 labour at the W_1 real wage rate. However, if workers are now more productive, then employers will find it more profitable to hire more workers at wage W_1, and similarly for every wage rate. This increase in demand moves the demand curve from D_1 to D_2, the real wage rate rises to W_2, the equilibrium level of employment rises to L_2, and the equilibrium potential output increases to Y_2. The increase in real wage rate is a reflection of the increased productivity of labour. Notice that if the labour force of the country is unchanged, this would result in a lower natural rate of unemployment.

There are three general factors that can increase the productivity of labour: an increase in physical capital, an increase in human capital, and an advance in technology. All of these factors have been at work to increase the ability of an individual worker to produce more with an hour of labour. While population has been growing (and thus putting pressure on wages to fall), the increases in physical and human capital and advances in technology have increased the demand for labour faster than the supply has increased. For example, the amount of physical capital in Canada has roughly doubled since 1980, while the population has only increased by about a third.

One common misunderstanding of economic growth is that new technology or increases in the use of machinery leads to unemployment and declining real wages. Such an argument has been put forward by many observers over time, and one modern version was put forward by Jeremy Rifkin in his book, *The End of Work*, published in 1995. Rifkin predicted that there would not be enough work to absorb all the workers that technologies such as the Internet and computers were displacing in modern society. Most observers at the time disagreed, and Rifkin was wrong. Clearly the economies of Canada and the United States have grown larger and adopted new technologies, while unemployment has

FIGURE 7–3 *The Effect of Increasing Labour Productivity*

Greater labour productivity results in a higher overall demand for labour and higher wages for workers. The increased labour productivity reduces labour costs for producers, making workers more valuable and encouraging producers to hire more employees.

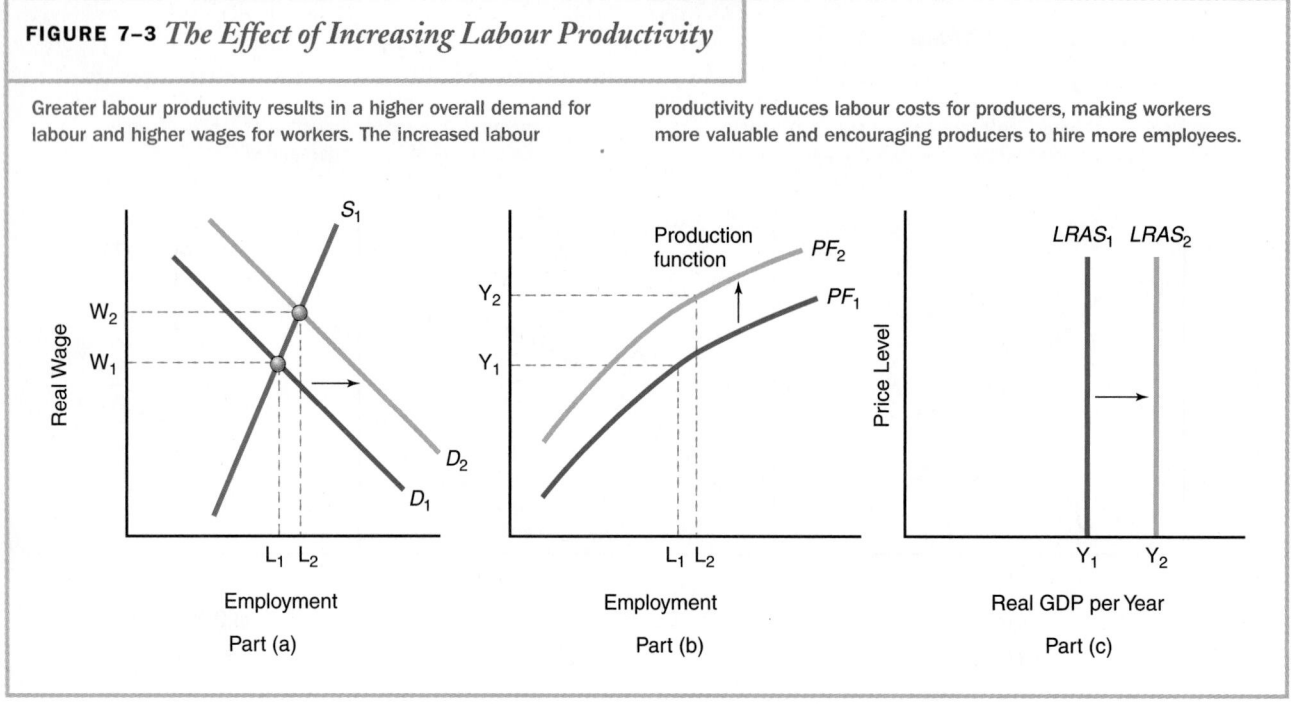

fallen to lower levels than when his book was written. While new machinery may displace workers from their jobs, the overall economy absorbs workers fast enough to keep them employed. Someone has to build the machines and create the new technology!

If we are interested in maintaining economic growth and a rising standard of living, then we will need to examine how we can encourage the creation of new physical capital, form new human capital, and help advance new technologies.

PRODUCTIVITY GROWTH IN CANADA. Although productivity growth seemed to lag in Canada from the mid-1970s through the mid-1980s, there is quite a bit of evidence that it has been on the rise since then. Figure 7–4 traces productivity growth in the manufacturing and service sectors of the economy.

FIGURE 7–4
Nonfarm Canadian Productivity Growth

Whereas productivity growth in the services sector was relatively robust until the early 1980s, productivity in the manufacturing sector has been increasing almost consistently since the 1960s. The recessions of the 1980s and 1990s slowed productivity growth in both sectors.

SOURCE: ADAPTED FROM STATISTICS CANADA CANSIM DATABASE, TABLE 380-0005 AND TABLE 380-012

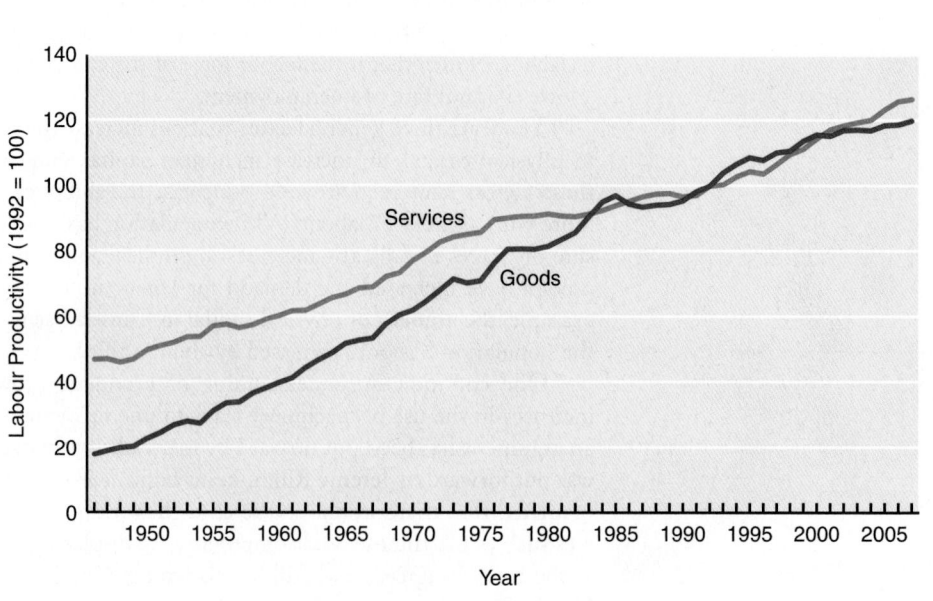

What is the source of the productivity gains in Canada? Statistics Canada suggests that much of the gain in productivity is due to investment in capital, while a smaller amount comes from better technology and better education. You can read more about this issue in Example 7-3. How is Canada doing when compared to the rest of the world? In Example 7-4, The World Economic Forum suggests that we are amongst the best in the world, but we could do better. The Canadian government has recently suggested that investments in equipment and machinery by businesses would be beneficial to our long-term economic growth strategy.

EXAMPLE 7–3 | **Productivity Gains**

A study by Statistics Canada suggests that about 55 percent of the growth in labour productivity in the business sector during the last four decades was due to investment in capital. The study suggests that gains in worker skills accounted for about 20 percent of the increase and technological change accounted for the remaining 25 percent.

Labour productivity grew approximately 2.1 percent annually from 1961 to 2005. During the same period, there was a marked decline in the share of labour compensation paid to people with high school or less education, declining from 89.2 percent to 31.8 percent, while the share of labour compensation of workers with university degrees increased from 7.1 percent to 23.5 percent between 1961 and 2003.

For critical analysis: What effect would taxes on machinery and equipment have on productivity? Show this effect using the model you just learned.

SOURCE: THE DAILY, STATISTICS CANADA, JUNE 25, 2007

EXAMPLE 7–4 | **How Does Canadian Productivity Compare with that of the Rest of the World?**

One way economists use productivity is as a rough measure of competitiveness: The more productive the resources, all else held constant, the lower is the cost of the product. However, in measures of productivity and competitiveness, all else is not held constant. For example, some countries have governments that encourage high productivity by making access to education or new technology easy. Other countries have governments that discourage growth of productivity by enforcing regulations that make labour market changes in response to technology changes difficult.

The World Economic Forum is one body that tries to measure relative productivity among 50 countries. It ranks countries in order of their ability to achieve sustained high rates of growth in GDP per capita using nine different factors it believes explain sustained economic growth. In Table 7–2, you will note that Canada is ranked 16th among the top 25 countries, down from 8th in 1996. We are now below many countries that we might not think of as particularly productive, such as Iceland or Israel.

For critical analysis: Could Canada move up in the list because of events in other countries? Would that mark an improvement in Canada's competitiveness?

continued

TABLE 7-2

Country	2006 Rank	Country	2006 Rank
Switzerland	1	Iceland	14
Finland	2	Israel	15
Sweden	3	Canada	16
Denmark	4	Austria	17
Singapore	5	France	18
United States	6	Australia	19
Japan	7	Belgium	20
Germany	8	Ireland	21
Netherlands	9	Luxembourg	22
United Kingdom	10	New Zealand	23
Hong Kong SAR	11	Korea, Rep	24
Norway	12	Estonia	25
Taiwan, China	13		

7.3 Fundamental Determinants of Economic Growth

Economic growth does not occur in a vacuum. It is not some predetermined fate of a nation. Rather, economic growth depends on certain fundamental factors. One of the most important factors that affect the rate of economic growth—and hence long-term living standards—is the rate of saving.

A basic proposition in economics is that if you want more tomorrow, you have to take less today.

> To have more consumption in the future, you have to consume less today and save the difference between your consumption and your income.

This reduction in consumption frees up resources to be used for economic investment in physical and human capital—fundamental resources needed for growth.

On a national basis, this implies that higher saving rates mean higher living standards in the long run, all other things held constant. Concern has been growing in Canada that we are not saving enough, that is, our rate of saving may be too low. Saving is important because if all income is consumed each year, there is nothing left over to be used by business for investment. If there is no investment in our capital stock, there could be little hope of much economic growth.

The relationship between the rate of saving and per-capita real GDP is shown in Figure 7–5.

Other Determinants of Economic Growth

There are a number of other factors that influence the growth of an economy. A number of political and economic institutions have been identified as important to encouraging growth. Supply-side economists (whose theories we will study later) often focus on these factors, since they are particularly interested in stimulating growth.

PROPERTY RIGHTS AND ENTREPRENEURSHIP. If you were in a country where bank accounts and businesses were periodically expropriated by the government, how willing would you be to leave your financial assets in a savings account or to invest in a business? Certainly, you would be less willing than if such things never occurred. In general, the more certain private property rights are, the more capital accumulation there will be. People will be willing to invest their savings in endeavours that will increase their wealth in future years. This requires that property rights in their wealth be sanctioned and enforced by government. In fact, some economic historians have attempted to show that

FIGURE 7–5

Relationship between Rate of Saving and Per-Capita Real GDP

This diagram shows the combination of per-capita real GDP and the rate of saving expressed as the average percentage of annual real GDP for many nations since 1960. Centrally planned economies and major oil-producing countries are not shown.

SOURCE: ROBERT SUMMERS AND ALAN HESTON, "A NEW SET OF INTERNATIONAL COMPARISONS OF REAL PRODUCT AND PRICE LEVEL," *REVIEW OF INCOME AND WEALTH*, MARCH 1988.

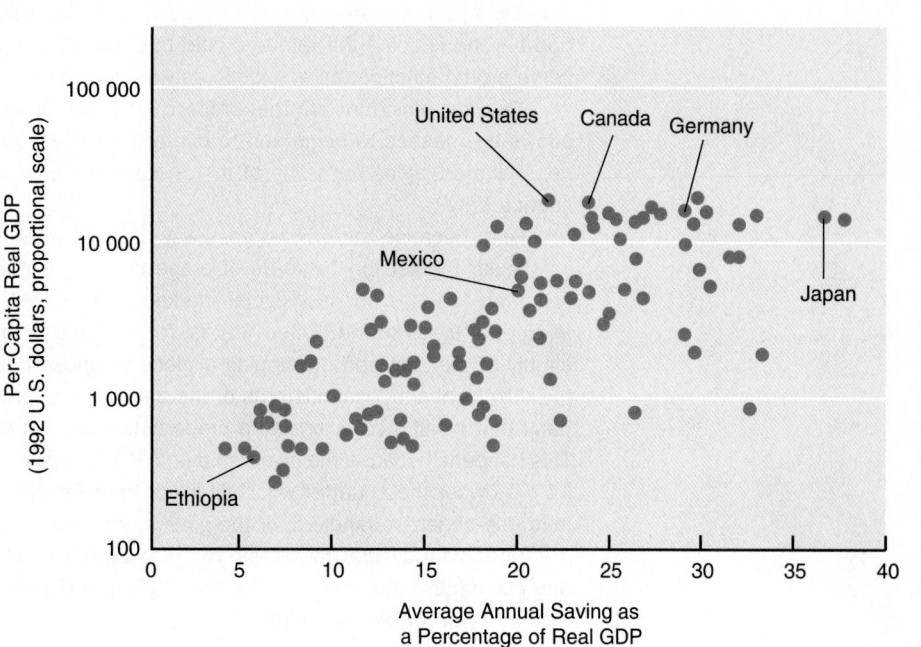

it was the development of well-defined private property rights and legal structure that allowed Western Europe to increase its growth rate after many centuries of stagnation. The ability and certainty with which they can reap the gains from investing also determine the extent to which business owners in other countries will invest capital in the developing countries. The threat of nationalization that hangs over some developing nations probably stands in the way of foreign investments that would allow these nations to develop more rapidly.

The legal structure of a nation is closely tied to the degree with which its citizens use their own entrepreneurial skills. In Chapter 1, we identified entrepreneurship as the fifth factor of production. Entrepreneurs are the risk takers who seek out new ways to do things and create new products. To the extent that entrepreneurs are allowed to capture the rewards from their entrepreneurial activities, they will seek to engage in those activities. In countries in which such rewards cannot be captured because of a lack of property rights, there will be less entrepreneurship. Typically, this results in fewer investments and a lower rate of growth.

In Policy Example 7–1 we see how the lack of property rights has hindered economic development and entrepreneurship in the Third World.

POLICY EXAMPLE 7–1 | **The Mystery of Capitalism**

Hernando de Soto writes in his book *The Mystery of Capitalism*[1] about the fundamental issues of this chapter, development of modern economies in the Third World. He asks a fundamental question: What stops these economies from increasing their productivity and bringing so many people out of poverty? His answer is one that seems simple but is difficult for us in the West to see because our system is something we take for granted.

De Soto shows that the lack of an integrated system of property (as we have in developed countries) greatly hinders the development of an economy. It is because of the lack

continued

---

[1]de Soto, Hernando. *The Mystery of Capitalism*. (c) 2000 Basic Books.

of access to that system that the property that exists in Third World countries cannot function beyond keeping the rain and cold out. The property that people own in the West can serve a dual function, an economic as well as a physical function.

The economic function that property can perform is to serve as a source of value that allows businesses to begin and to operate. In short, people in the West can start a business by mortgaging the value of their house to the bank. In underdeveloped nations, they cannot. Why?

First, because there is no easy way to know what the value of a property is. There is no regular market for the value of property in poor areas, such as slums. Property rights are often "passed on" in irregular markets, without reference to a central land title office. In pioneer times in the United States, for example, property rights were often established simply by clearing and developing a piece of unused land. Their "sweat equity" was captured by local and legal customs of the age. Second, there is no easy way to ensure to the bank that it will receive title to a property (should the entrepreneur fail to repay the loan). This happens because the ownership and title to a property are tied up with multiple claims. (Is the owner the squatter who has lived there for many years and worked to improve the land, the absentee landlord, or the government that has not been paid back taxes?) Third, it is often very difficult for people to go through a legal system of transferring property. In one experiment, de Soto found it took between 6 and 14 years to gain access to desert land in Egypt for development!

Because of the lack of property rights, the savings that people have tied up in their own properties cannot be used to fund a simple business. We know from our earlier discussions that access to savings is a fundamental prerequisite to any economic investment, but in the Third World, the estimated $10 trillion in assets is completely "dead." Creating a legal system that endows the poor with access to their own capital will empower them to develop their own lives and economies, to "pick themselves up by their own bootstraps."

For critical analysis: Many entrepreneurs begin their businesses out of their homes or garages. Why is this not as easy in Third World countries?

SOME OTHER FACTORS. *Market-driven economies* generally seem better at growth than are nonmarket economies. The economies with the highest standard of living all have capitalist markets as a basic institution. Within those systems, almost all have some methods for redistributing income to the poorest in society. Governments usually play an important role in regulation, protecting the market system from monopolies and other side effects of production, such as pollution. Countries that have corrupt government bureaucracies do not do as well either.

Political stability is an important prerequisite for economic growth. We need only to look at how all the gains from many years of economic growth in Yugoslavia were lost when the country fell apart because of civil war in the 1990s. New investment in war-torn countries is often difficult to find, even though that investment can be critical for starting over.

Population growth and immigration can affect economic growth in several ways. Population growth means an increase in the amount of labour, which, as we have previously learned, is one component of economic growth. Immigration also helps economic growth. Most studies indicate that immigrants have a high labour force participation rate and a lower unemployment rate than other Canadians. This should, in the long run, boost potential output. In addition, on average, immigrants have more education than other Canadians and call upon the social programs less frequently. Not all researchers agree about these theories, however, and they are still the focus of much research.

7.4 New Growth Theory and What Determines Growth

What are the forces that make productivity grow in Canada and elsewhere? A simple arithmetic definition of economic growth has already been given. Growth rates of capital and labour plus the growth rate in their productivity are simply defined as the components of economic growth. Economists have had good data on the growth of the labour force as well as the growth of the physical capital stock in Canada. But when you add those two growth rates together, you still do not get the total economic growth rate in Canada. The difference has to be due to improvements in productivity. Economists typically labelled this "improvements in technology," and that was that. More recently, proponents of what is now called the **new growth theory** suggest that new technology can be encouraged by having appropriate incentives in place, such as research and development subsides.

Consider some startling statistics about the growth in technology. Microprocessor speeds may increase from 4000 megahertz to 10 000 megahertz by the year 2015. By that same year, the size of the thinnest circuit line within a transistor may decrease by 90 percent. The typical memory capacity (RAM) of computers will jump from 512 megabytes, or about eight times the equivalent text in the *Encyclopaedia Britannica*, to 128 gigabytes—a 250-fold increase. Predictions are that computers may become as powerful as the human brain by 2020.

Technology: A Separate Factor of Production

We now recognize that technology must be viewed as a separate factor of production that is sensitive to rewards. In other words, one of the major foundations of new growth theory is this:

> The greater the rewards, the more technological advances we will get.

Let us first consider several aspects of technology here, starting with research and development.

Research and Development

A certain amount of technological advancement results from research and development (R & D) activities that have as their goal the development of specific new materials, new products, and new machines. How much spending a nation devotes to R & D can have an impact on that nation's long-term economic growth. Part of how much a nation spends depends on what businesses decide is worth spending. That, in turn, depends on their expected rewards from successful R & D. If your company develops a new way to produce computer memory chips, how much will it be rewarded? The answer depends on whether others can freely copy the new technique.

PATENTS. To protect new techniques developed through R & D, we have a system of **patents**, protections whereby the federal government gives the patent holder the exclusive right to make, use, and sell an invention for a period, typically 20 years in Canada. One can argue that this special position given to owners of patents increases expenditures on R & D and therefore adds to long-term economic growth. Figure 7-6 shows that U.S. patent grants fell during the 1970s, increased steadily after 1982, surged from 1995 until 2001, and are rising again after 2006. This pattern of patent grants roughly mirrors the period of slow economic growth that occurred in North America in the 1970s and 1980s.

POSITIVE EXTERNALITIES AND R & D. Positive externalities are benefits from an activity that are not fully internalized by the instigator of the activity. In the case of R & D spending, a certain amount of the benefits go to other companies that do not have to pay for them. In particular, according to economists David Coe and Elhanan Helpman, about a quarter of the global benefits of R & D investment in the top seven industrialized

New growth theory A theory that technology must be examined from the point of view of what drives it.

Patent A government protection that gives an inventor the exclusive right to make, use, or sell an invention for a limited period of time, typically 20 years in Canada.

FIGURE 7–6
U.S. Patent Grants

The U.S. Patent and Trademark Office gradually began awarding more patent grants between the early 1980s and the mid-1990s. After 1995, the number of patents granted each year increased significantly until 2001.

SOURCE: U.S. PATENT AND TRADEMARK OFFICE.

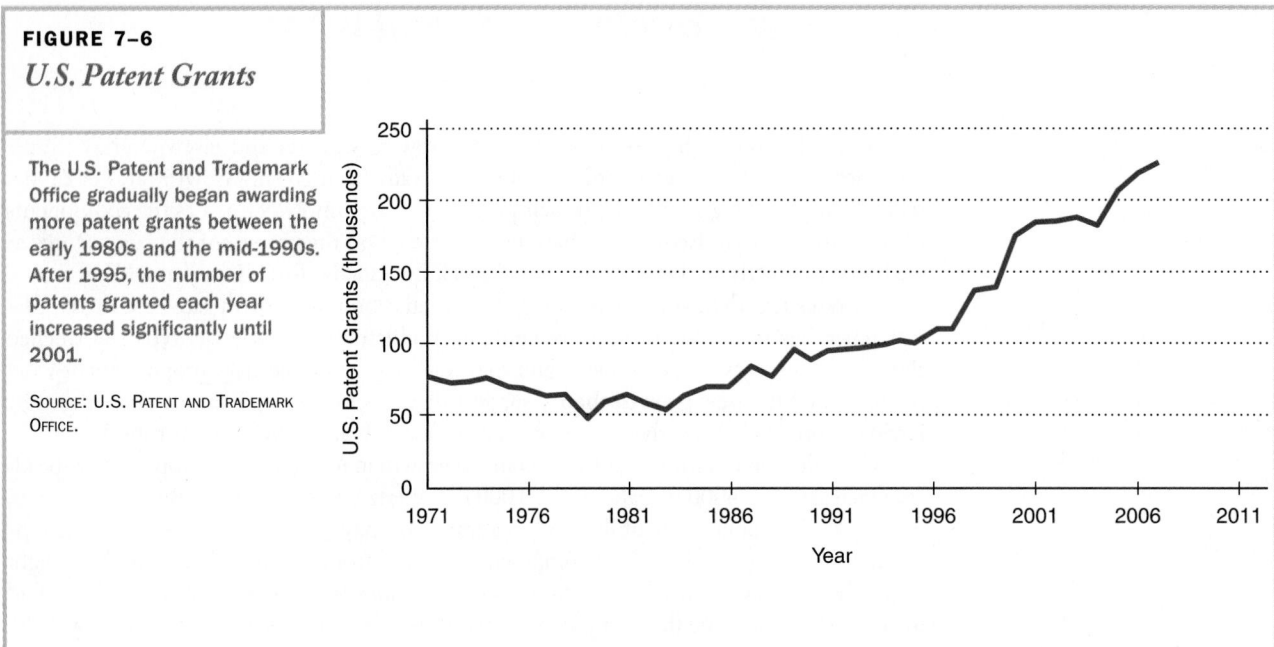

countries go to foreigners. For every 1 percent rise in the stock of research and development in North America alone, for example, productivity in the rest of the world increases by about 0.04 percent. One country's R & D expenditures benefit foreigners because foreigners are able to import goods from technologically advanced countries and then use them as inputs in making their own industries more efficient. In addition, countries that import high-tech goods are able to imitate the technology.

The Open Economy and Economic Growth

People who study economic growth today tend to emphasize the importance of the openness of the economy. Free trade encourages a more rapid spread of technology and industrial ideas. Moreover, open economies may experience higher rates of economic growth because their own industries have access to a bigger market. When trade barriers are erected in the form of tariffs and the like, domestic industries become isolated from global technological progress. This occurred for many years in former communist countries and in many developing countries in Latin America and elsewhere. Figure 7–7 shows the relationship between economic growth and the openness as measured by the level of protectionism of a given economy.

Innovation and Knowledge

Innovation The transformation of something new, such as an invention, into something that benefits the economy either by lowering production costs or providing new goods and services.

We tend to think of technological progress as, say, the invention of the transistor. But invention means nothing by itself; *innovation* is required. **Innovation** involves the transformation of something new, such as an invention, into something that benefits the economy either by lowering production costs or providing new goods and services. Indeed, the new growth theorists believe that real wealth creation comes from innovation and that invention is but one aspect of innovation.

Historically, technologies have moved relatively slowly from invention to innovation to widespread use, and the dispersion of new technology remains, for the most part, slow and uncertain. The inventor of the transistor thought it might be used to make better hearing aids. At the time it was invented, the only reference to it in *The New York Times* was in a small weekly column called "News of Radio." When the laser was invented, no one really knew what it could be used for. It was initially used to help in navigation, measurement, and chemical research. Today, it is used in the reproduction of music, printing, surgery, and telecommunications. Tomorrow, who knows?

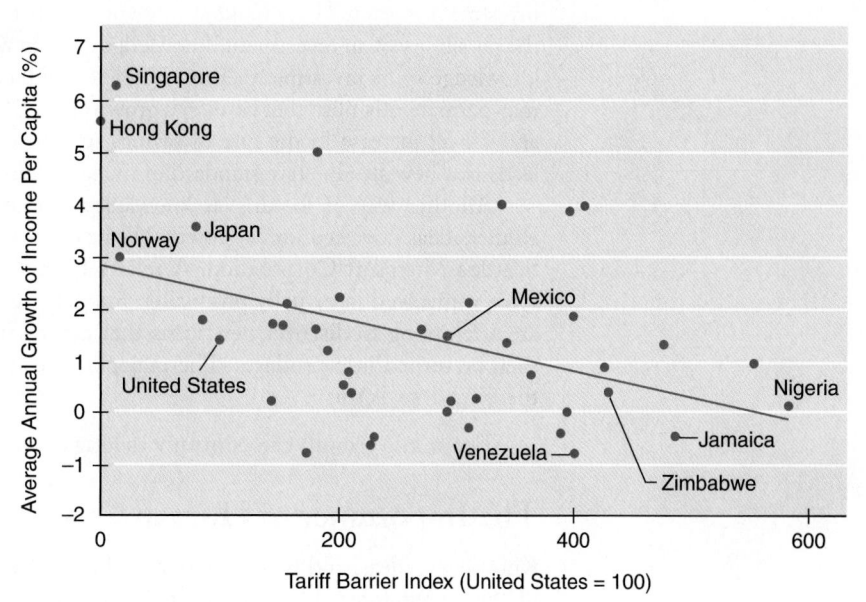

FIGURE 7–7

The Relationship between Economic Growth and Tariff Barriers to International Trade

Nations with low tariff barriers are relatively open to international trade and have tended to have higher average annual rates of per-capita income growth since 1965.

SOURCE: WORLD BANK.

Much innovation involves small improvements in the use of an existing technology. Such improvements develop from experimentation and discovery. Another possible source of innovation and invention may come with new immigrants who bring new ideas to the firms they work for. Policy Example 7–2 shows a strong link between the ability to attract these new immigrants and economic growth.

POLICY EXAMPLE 7–2 | **Competing on Creativity**

Richard Florida, a professor at Carnegie Mellon University, has written about the ability of countries and cities to create new technologies: "The most successful city-regions anywhere are the ones with a social environment that is open to creativity and diversity of all sorts. The ability to attract creative people in arts and culture, and to be open to people of different ethnic, racial, and lifestyle groups, provides distinct advantages to regions in generating innovations, growing and attracting high-technology industries, and spurring economic growth." The benefits of this new knowledge soon spread to the rest of the country.

Using the key factors identified by Professor Florida, the Institute for Competitiveness and Prosperity in Ontario ranked cities in Canada for their ability to compete for these immigrants. The Institute's study used the key factors correlated to the success of high-tech industries, which were the proportion of people who are foreign-born, a high measure of social tolerance, and a high score for cultural diversity. Toronto, Montreal, and Vancouver are all among the top-ranking cities in North America when compared to their American counterparts.

For critical analysis: What government policies encourage this kind of social environment in Canada?

The Importance of Ideas and Knowledge

Economist Paul Romer has added at least one important factor that determines the rate of economic growth. He contends that production and manufacturing knowledge is just as important as the other determinants and perhaps even more so. He considers knowledge a factor of production that, like capital, has to be paid for by forgoing current consumption.

Economies must therefore invest in knowledge just as they invest in machines. Because past investment in capital may make it more profitable to acquire more knowledge, there exists the possibility of an investment–knowledge cycle in which investment spurs knowledge and knowledge spurs investment. A once-and-for-all increase in a country's rate of investment may permanently raise that country's growth rate. (According to traditional theory, a once-and-for-all increase in the rate of saving, and therefore in the rate of investment, simply leads to a new steady-state standard of living but not one that continues to increase.)

Another way of looking at knowledge is that it is a store of ideas. According to Romer, ideas drive economic growth. We have become, in fact, an idea economy. Consider Seattle's Microsoft Corporation. A relatively small percentage of that company's labour force is involved in actually producing products. Rather, a majority of Microsoft workers are attempting to discover new ideas that can be translated to computer codes that can then be turned into products. The major conclusion that Romer and other new growth theorists draw is this:

Economic growth can continue as long as we keep coming up with new ideas.

The Importance of Human Capital

Knowledge, ideas, and productivity are all tied together. One of the threads is the quality of the labour force. Increases in the productivity of the labour force are a function of increases in human capital, the fourth factor of production discussed in Chapter 1. Recall that human capital is the knowledge and skills that people in the workforce acquire through education, on-the-job training, and self-teaching. To increase your own human capital, you have to invest by forgoing income-earning activities while you attend school. Society also has to invest in the form of libraries and teachers. According to the new growth theorists, human capital is at least as important as physical capital, particularly when trying to explain international differences in living standards.

One can argue that policy changes that increase human capital will lead to more technological improvements. One of the reasons concerned citizens, policy makers, and politicians are looking for a change in Canada's school system is that our educational system seems to be falling behind that of other countries. This lag is greatest in science and mathematics—precisely the areas that are required for developing better technologies.

The Role of Government in Encouraging Growth

Governments have an important role to play in economic growth, and governments can help or hinder the process through their policies. Governments play a large role in the factors listed on page 190, by supporting competitive markets and private property, encouraging political stability, and controlling immigration. While many of these actions are political in nature, they have important effects on the economy of a country as well; without them, the opportunity for growth is likely to be very limited.

At the same time, governments have chosen to take direct action in encouraging economic development. Governments encourage investment in human capital by subsidizing both primary and postsecondary education. Many studies have shown investment in education to be worthwhile both for the individuals and for government itself, as it will receive higher taxes in the future from better-paid citizens. Governments also have encouraged growth through investment in infrastructures, such as roads and electricity. These and similar policies have been used in most countries around the world as the basis for economic growth and development for many years.

Another form of government action is through reduction in taxes on activities that encourage growth. The Canadian government encourages savings through Registered Retirement Savings Plans (RRSPs), which defer taxes until people retire. The Canadian government has also encouraged the development of new technology through its Scientific Tax Research Credits, which give tax breaks to companies engaging in scientific research. We will look at this topic in a broader way in Chapter 15.

Finally, the government may choose to give or lend money directly to businesses. These kinds of policies are often controversial, as they conflict with the natural forces of the marketplace. Why should one failing business be subsidized, and not one that is surviving? While many such loans and subsidies do help businesses during an important startup phase, sometimes they are misused to achieve political ends, not economic ones.

➤→ **CONCEPTS IN BRIEF**

Learning Objective 7.2: Explain and model economic growth.
- ⚓ Productivity is the cumulative contribution to per-capita GDP of three components: contributions from changes in capital intensity; contributions from changes in labour composition; and growth in multifactor productivity, which is generally everything that cannot be accounted for by labour and capital.
- ⚓ Each of these sources of new productivity can increase *LRAS*. Increases in the amount of labour can lower wages because of an increase in labour supply, while increases in capital and new technology shift up the aggregate production function and increase the demand for labour, thereby increasing wages.

Learning Objective 7.3: Describe the fundamental determinants of economic growth.
- ⚓ One fundamental determinant of the rate of growth is the rate of saving and investment. To have more consumption in the future, we have to save and invest, rather than consume everything today. In general, countries that have had higher rates of saving have had higher rates of growth in real GDP.

Learning Objective 7.4: Understand the basis of new growth theory.
- ⚓ New growth theory argues that the greater the rewards, the more rapid the pace of technology will be. And greater rewards spur research and development.
- ⚓ The openness of an economy seems to correlate with its economic rate of growth.
- ⚓ Invention and innovation are not the same thing. Inventions are useless until innovation transforms them into things that people find valuable.
- ⚓ According to the new growth economists, economic growth can continue as long as we keep coming up with new ideas.
- ⚓ Increases in human capital can lead to greater rates of economic growth. These come about by increased education, on-the-job training, and self-teaching.
- ⚓ Government actions can make a substantial difference in supporting economic growth through subsidization of some basic investments, such as education and infrastructure, and by giving tax breaks to activities that encourage growth.

7.5 *The Costs and Benefits of Economic Growth*

The growth that Western economies have experienced is controversial. Many people believe that economic growth is generally good. Many others have looked at the cost of that growth and wonder if it is worth the cost. Let us look at how these two groups differ in their ideas about growth.

Limits to Growth

Humanity is very aware of the limited resources that the world holds. Since World War II, the population of the world has increased from 2.5 billion to 6 billion people. At the current rates of population growth, the world population will reach 10 billion within our lifetimes. With the strong economic growth that has occurred, each person in the many nations of the world consumes much more of the world's resources now than a person did 50 years ago. When all these factors are combined, the strain on the earth is tremendous and has clearly had some detrimental effects.

ENVIRONMENTAL DISASTERS. The partial destruction of the ozone layer, global warming due to the emission of greenhouse gases, the collapse of the East Coast fishery, acid rain, and the destruction of rain forests are all signs that the earth is approaching its limit. Without a radical change in the way that the earth's resources and pollution are managed, there is little doubt that there will be disastrous consequences. Already, weather watchers have noted the increase in hurricane activity in the Atlantic Ocean. They suggest that the resulting destruction of property and loss of lives are caused by global warming.

UNEVEN CONSUMPTION AROUND THE WORLD.   Others suggest that the problem of pollution worsens with high levels of consumption that occur in the developed nations. They argue that the excessive use of resources by Western countries is a poor example for the rest of the world. The destruction of the rain forest in Brazil by ranchers, for example, is linked to the consumption of beef. If we consumed less beef, they argue, then there would be less incentive for the clearing of the tropical rain forests for farms. If all countries were to consume oil at the rate that Canada does, there would need to be a tenfold increase in oil production, leading to extra greenhouse gas emissions and increasing global warming.

POVERTY FOR SOME PEOPLE CAUSES MORE ENVIRONMENTAL PRESSURE.   In much of the world, poverty results in environmental stress through over-harvesting of fuel wood, fish, and endangered species; poor waste disposal; and wasteful agricultural practices. In 1972, at the first United Nations Conference on the Environment, which took place in Stockholm, the developing countries took the position that environmental concerns were not their main problem. They would not support any environmental restrictions that would deprive them of the prospect of prosperity enjoyed by the developed countries. On the other hand, most of the population growth in the next 50 years will occur in these nations, and so it becomes more important to find better ways to deal with the environmental costs of population growth.

THE BRUNDTLAND COMMISSION.   In response to these issues, the United Nations created the World Commission on Environment and Development. The Brundtland Commission's report, *Our Common Future*, published in 1987, described environmental degradation, poverty, a rapidly growing human population, the arms race, and wars as interlocking crises demanding action on all fronts. It defined a new term—sustainable development—with the following statement: "Humanity has the ability to make development sustainable—to ensure that it meets the needs of the present without compromising the ability of future generations to meet their own needs." (See Policy Example 7–3.)

POLICY EXAMPLE 7–3   **Ottawa and the Kyoto Accord**

The Conservative government in Canada has announced that it will be impossible to reach the Kyoto Accord targets for carbon emission reductions agreed to in 2002. The government has also stated that it has no intention of attempting to reach those targets; instead, it will set up new targets of its own. Even the previous Liberal government, which signed the Accord, did not take substantial measures to reach those targets. While all political parties now agree that we should reduce CO_2 emissions, little has been done. In fact, CO_2 emissions have been rising in Canada.

For critical analysis: What kinds of taxes and incentives could the government use to reduce CO_2 pollution? What effect would these taxes have on business and economic growth? If a new industry were to be located in your neighbourhood, how much pollution would you be willing to accept?

Benefits of Economic Growth

The main benefit of economic growth is the higher standard of living that usually comes with it. There can be little doubt that people are better off now than they were at the turn of the century. They are healthier, live longer, are better educated, and enjoy many more material goods than they did in the past.

A HIGHER STANDARD OF LIVING. Economic growth can also allow society to buy many goods and services that it could not previously afford. The higher economic growth allows for greater spending on education, health, and income redistribution programs. It also allows for society to clean up the environment without lowering existing living standards.

HIGHER INCOME RESULTING IN LESS POPULATION GROWTH. In the Third World countries and in Canada's own history, higher incomes have generally resulted in a reduction in birth rates. Almost paradoxically, the growth of incomes and, in particular, the education of women, reduce population growth and the resulting stress on the environment. Healthy people with reasonably high incomes tend to have fewer children.

NEW TECHNOLOGIES TO SOLVE THESE PROBLEMS. Growth advocates also point out that new technologies that accompany economic growth have come along, throughout history, to deal with the issues of the day. For example, as oil has begun to be used up, new "enhanced recovery" methods have allowed for greater use of existing oil fields. Recycling technology has made it worthwhile to recycle old paper just as forests began to be in short supply. In the future, as oil disappears, firms will have a greater incentive to develop solar and fusion power as replacements. Both these technologies will also be less polluting and provide more power than does the existing technology.

7.6 *International Economic Development*

How did the developed countries travel paths of growth from extreme poverty to relative riches? That is the essential issue of **development economics**, which is the study of why some countries grow and develop while others do not and of policies that might help the developing economies get richer. It is not enough simply to say that people in different countries are different and that is why some countries are rich and some countries are poor. Economists do not deny that different cultures have different work ethics, but they are unwilling to accept such a pat explanation for the differences in economic development among nations.

Development economics The study of why some countries grow and develop while others do not and of policies that might help the developing economies get richer.

Look at any world map. About four-fifths of the countries you will see on the map are considered relatively poor. The goal of economists who study development is to help the more than 4 billion people with low living standards reach the level of the 2 billion people who have at least moderately high living standards.

Putting World Poverty into Perspective

Most North Americans cannot even begin to understand the reality of poverty in the world today. At least one-half, if not two-thirds, of the world's population lives at subsistence levels, with just enough to eat for survival. Indeed, the World Bank estimates that nearly 30 percent of the world's people live on less than $1 per day. The official poverty line in Canada is set above the average income of at least half the human beings on the planet. This is not to say that we should ignore domestic problems with the poor and homeless simply because they are living better than many people elsewhere in the world. Rather, it is necessary for North Americans to maintain an appropriate perspective on what are considered problems for this country relative to what are considered problems elsewhere.

The Relationship between Population Growth and Economic Development

World population is growing at the rate of just over 2.4 people a second. That amounts to 210 500 a day or 76.9 million a year. Today, there are almost 6.5 billion people on earth. By 2050, according to the United Nations, there will be 9.3 billion. Part (a) of Figure 7–8 shows which countries are growing the most. Part (b) emphasizes an implication of

FIGURE 7–8

Expected Growth in World Population

Part (a) shows that Asia and Africa are expected to gain the most in population by the year 2050. Part (b) indicates that population will increase dramatically in the developing countries through 2050, while industrially advanced nations will grow very little in population in the first half of this century.

SOURCE: UNITED NATIONS.

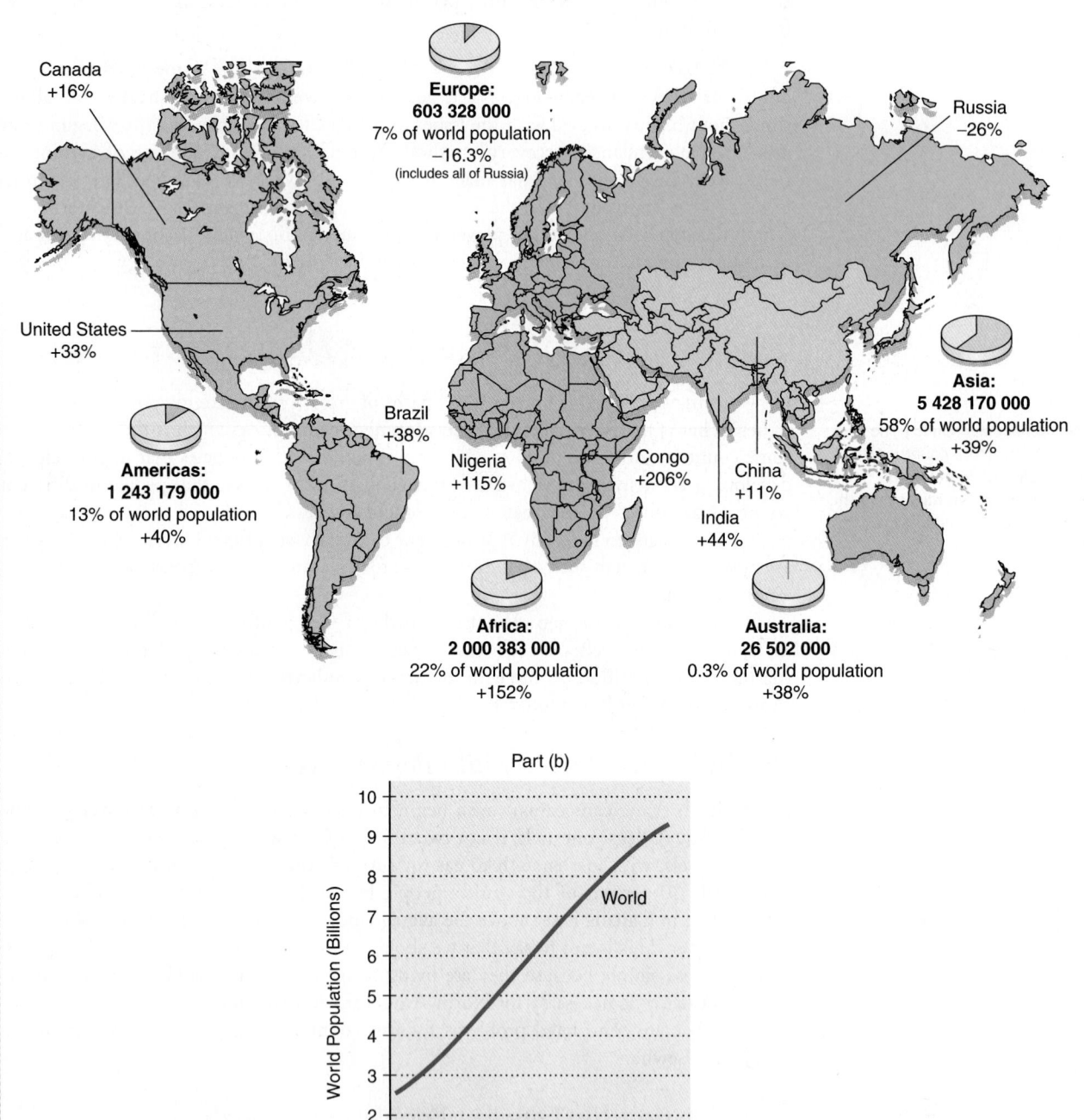

Part (a)

Canada
+16%

Europe:
603 328 000
7% of world population
−16.3%
(includes all of Russia)

Russia
−26%

United States
+33%

Brazil
+38%

Americas:
1 243 179 000
13% of world population
+40%

Nigeria
+115%

Congo
+206%

China
+11%

India
+44%

Asia:
5 428 170 000
58% of world population
+39%

Africa:
2 000 383 000
22% of world population
+152%

Australia:
26 502 000
0.3% of world population
+38%

Part (b)

World

Industrially advanced countries

part (a), which is that virtually all the growth in population is occurring in the developing nations. Many developed countries are expected to experience decreases in population over the next several decades.

Ever since the Reverend Thomas Robert Malthus wrote *An Essay on the Principle of Population* in 1798, excessive population growth has been a concern. Modern-day Malthusians are able to generate great enthusiasm for the concept that population growth is bad. Over and over, media pundits and a number of scientists tell us that rapid population growth threatens economic development and the quality of life.

MALTHUS WAS PROVEN WRONG. Nevertheless, Malthus's prediction that population would outstrip food supplies has never been supported by the facts, according to economist Nicholas Eberstadt of the Harvard Center for Population Studies. As the world's population has grown, so has the world's food supply, measured by calories per person. Furthermore, the price of food, corrected for inflation, has been falling steadily for more than a century. That means that the supply of food has been expanding faster than the rise in demand caused by increased population.

GROWTH LEADS TO SMALLER FAMILIES. Furthermore, economists have found that as nations become richer, average family size declines. Otherwise stated, the more economic development occurs, the slower the population growth rate becomes. This has certainly been true in Western Europe and in the former Soviet Union, where populations in some countries are actually declining. Predictions of birth rates in the developing countries have often turned out to be overstated if those countries experience rapid economic growth. This was the case in Hong Kong, Mexico, Taiwan, and Colombia. Recent research on population and economic development has revealed that social and economic modernization has been accompanied by what might be called a fertility revolution—the spread of deliberate family size limitation within marriage and a decline in childbearing. Modernization reduces infant mortality, which, in turn, reduces the incentive for couples to have many children to make sure that a certain number survive to adulthood. Modernization also lowers the demand for children for a variety of reasons, not the least being that couples in the more developed countries do not need to rely on their children to take care of them in old age.

The Stages of Development: Agriculture to Industry to Services

If we analyze the development of the modern-day rich nations, we find that they went through three stages. First is the agricultural stage, when most of the population is involved in agriculture. Then comes the manufacturing stage, when much of the population becomes involved in the industrial sector of the economy. And finally there is a shift toward services. That is exactly what happened in Canada The so-called tertiary, or service, sector of the economy continues to grow, whereas the manufacturing sector (and its share of employment) is declining in relative importance.

Of particular significance, however, is the requirement for early specialization in a nation's comparative advantage (see Chapter 2). The doctrine of comparative advantage is particularly appropriate for the developing countries of the world. If trading is allowed among nations, a country is normally best off if it produces what it has a comparative advantage in producing and imports the rest (for more details, see Chapter 2). This means that many developing countries should continue to specialize in agricultural production or in labour-intensive manufactured goods.

Keys to Economic Development

One theory of development states that for a country to develop, it must have a large natural resource base. This theory goes on to assert that much of the world is running out of natural resources, thereby limiting economic growth and development. Only the narrowest definition of a natural resource, however, could lead to such an opinion. In broader terms, a natural resource is something occurring in nature that we can use for our own purposes. As emphasized by new growth theory, natural resources, therefore, include knowledge of the use of something. The natural resources that we could define several hundred years ago did not, for example, include hydroelectric power—no one knew that such a natural resource existed or how to bring it into existence.

Natural resources by themselves are not a prerequisite for or a guarantee of economic development, as demonstrated by Japan's extensive development despite a lack of domestic oil resources and by Brazil's slow pace of development in spite of a vast array of natural resources. Resources must be transformed into something usable for either investment or consumption.

Economists have found that four factors seem to be highly related to the pace of economic development:

1. *An educated population.* Both theoretically and empirically, we know that a more educated workforce aids economic development because it allows individuals to build on the ideas of others. According to economists David Gould and Roy Ruffin, increasing the rate of enrollment in secondary schools in the less-developed nations by only 2 percentage points—from 8 percent to 10 percent—raises the average rate of economic growth by half a percent per year. Thus, we must conclude that the developing countries can advance more rapidly if they invest more heavily in secondary education. Or stated in the negative, economic development cannot be sustained if a nation allows a sizable portion of its population to remain uneducated. Education allows young people who grow up poor to acquire skills that enable them to avoid poverty as adults.

2. *Establishing a system of property rights.* As noted earlier, if you were in a country in which bank accounts and businesses were periodically expropriated by the government, you would be reluctant to leave your money in a savings account or to invest in a business. Expropriation of private property rarely takes place in the developed countries. It has occurred in numerous developing countries, however. For example, private property was once nationalized in Chile and still is, for the most part, in Cuba. Economists have found that other things being equal, the more certain private property rights are, the more private capital accumulation and economic growth there will be.

3. *Letting "creative destruction" run its course.* Twentieth-century economist Joseph Schumpeter championed the concept of "creative destruction," through which new businesses ultimately create new jobs and economic growth after first destroying old jobs, old companies, and old industries. Such change is painful and costly, but it is necessary for economic advancement. Nowhere is this more important than in the developing countries, where the principle is often ignored. Many developing nations have had a history of supporting current companies and industries by discouraging new technologies and new companies from entering the marketplace. The process of creative destruction has not been allowed to work its magic in these countries.

4. *Limiting protectionism.* Open economies experience faster economic development than economies closed to international trade. Trade encourages individuals and businesses to discover ways to specialize so that they can become more productive and earn higher incomes. Increased productivity and subsequent increases in economic growth are the results. Thus, the less government protects the domestic economy by imposing trade barriers, the faster that economy will experience economic development. According to a study by economists Nouriel Roubini and Xavier Sala-i-Martin, when a country goes from being relatively open to relatively closed via government-enacted trade barriers, it will have a 2.5-percentage-point decrease in its annual rate of economic growth. While some of these themes are common to most economists, comprehensive ideas about economics are being developed by Jeffrey Sachs, as briefly outlined in Policy Example 7–4.

POLICY EXAMPLE 7-4   **The End of Poverty**

Jeffrey Sachs is the director of the Earth Institute at Columbia University and is a long-time advisor and advocate for international development. In his book, *The End of Poverty*, he advocates for a systematic approach to ending extreme poverty around the world. His book argues that economists need to look more deeply at the causes of poverty in each country rather than prescribing one answer to the world's problems.

He divides his analysis of extreme poverty into broad categories:

1. Poverty Trap – demographic, health, ethnic, and infrastructure issues
2. Economic Policy – analysis of the business environment, trade and investment policies, and investment in human capital
3. Fiscal Framework and Fiscal Trap – issues related to government spending and borrowing
4. Physical Geography – transportation, population density, agronomic conditions, and disease ecology issues
5. Governance – issues related to politics, ethnic conflict, political and civil rights, corruption, and internal violence
6. Cultural Barriers – gender, ethnic, and religious divisions
7. Geopolitics – international security, international sanctions, trade barriers, and cross-border issues

In his analysis, the poorest of the world could be brought out of extreme poverty with the additional expenditure of approximately $140 billion per year for 10 years. This spending could be met within the existing stated goals of development aid amounting to 0.7 percent of GDP from western countries.

Canada has not been particularly good at meeting this stated goal. Canada has been giving about 0.3 percent of its GDP in international aid. Professor Sachs states that it would cost each Canadian approximately $100 per year to provide comprehensive malaria control across Africa and potentially save 1 million lives per year, yet the Canadian government is not prepared to spend this money.

For critical analysis: Imagine if all the roads and train tracks connecting cities in Canada were reduced to simple mud tracks (as in most Third World countries). What would happen to Canada's GDP?

SOURCES: *THE END OF POVERTY* BY JEFFREY SACHS © 2005. PENGUIN BOOKS THE VANCOUVER SUN, JUNE 25, 2007 "STINGY RECORD ON AID TO AFRICA NOT EXACTLY CANADA'S FINEST HOUR" BY JEFFREY SACHS. P. A9.

➤➤ **CONCEPTS IN BRIEF**

Learning Objective 7.5: Outline some of the costs and benefits of economic growth.

- Economic growth results in environmental disasters, such as the destruction of the ozone layer. Sustainable development, a concept first suggested by the Brundtland Commission, is suggested as an alternative economic model for the future.
- Economic growth benefits people through a higher standard of living. People can consume more goods and services, such as education, health, and can afford income redistribution. Income growth in poor nations usually results in a slower population growth. As well, new technologies can be used to clean up environmental problems.

Learning Objective 7.6: Discuss the fundamental factors that contribute to international economic development.

- Although many people believe that population growth hinders economic development, there is little evidence to support that notion. What is clear is that economic development tends to lead to a reduction in the rate of population growth.
- Historically, there are three stages of economic development: the agricultural stage, the manufacturing stage, and the service-sector stage, when a large part of the workforce is employed in providing services.

- Although one theory of economic development holds that a sizable natural resource base is the key to a nation's development, this fails to account for the importance of the human element: The labour force must be capable of using a country's natural resources.
- Fundamental factors contributing to the pace of economic development are training and education, a well-defined system of property rights, allowing new generations of companies and industries to replace older generations, and promoting an open economy by allowing international trade.

 ISSUES AND APPLICATIONS

Winners and Losers in the Brain-Drain Game

Concepts Applied: Economic Growth, Immigration and Growth, Human Capital

Contrary to popular belief, Canada is actually a winner in the brain-drain game.

When a nation loses some of its best-educated workers, it experiences a *brain drain*. Nations that undergo brain drains experience an outflow of human capital and thereby lose a key productive resource. Of course, the movement of well-trained people to other countries generates a "brain gain" for these recipient nations.

The Losers

Figure 7–9 shows the countries of the world that experience the largest brain drains. Depicted in the figure are the percentages of college graduates who leave these nations to live and work in more industrialized nations.

It is not a coincidence that the nations that appear in Figure 7–9 are among those with the lowest per-capita real GDP levels in the world. Because real GDP levels are low in these nations, incomes are low. As a consequence, job opportunities for well-trained people are few. Naturally, this gives highly skilled people incentives to move to other nations where they can find more challenging work and earn higher incomes. Industrialized nations, such as Canada and the United States, are typically the locations where such jobs are more readily available.

As you have learned in this chapter, however, the significant losses of college graduates depicted in Figure 7–9 represent huge outflows of human capital from these nations. These decreases in human capital damage the countries'

prospects for economic growth. Stunted economic growth in turn causes incomes to remain low, thereby perpetuating a brain-drain cycle for these nations.

The Winners

Of course, the countries receiving immigrants from the nations in Figure 7–9 experience a "brain gain." Steady inflows of immigrants from these nations are a source of human capital that promotes economic growth in the recipient countries.

For instance, many highly skilled individuals from Jamaica and Haiti are among the nearly 240 000 people who now migrate to Canada each year. More than half of all new skilled jobs in Canada are filled by immigrants. Indeed, present estimates indicate that by 2011, immigrants are likely to provide *all* of the growth in Canada's *entire* labour force.

Canada is an extreme example of the countries, including the United States, that are winners in the world's brain-drain game. As described earlier, those nations that experience brain drains lose human capital, and this loss contributes to lower economic growth rates in those nations. For the foreseeable future, therefore, it appears likely that the losers will continue to lose, and the winners will continue to win.

FIGURE 7–9

Nations with the Largest Percentage Emigrations of Skilled Workers

Countries with the largest proportionate brain drains to industrialized nations include nations with levels of per-capita real GDP that are among the world's lowest.

SOURCE: ORGANIZATION FOR ECONOMIC COOPERATION AND DEVELOPMENT.

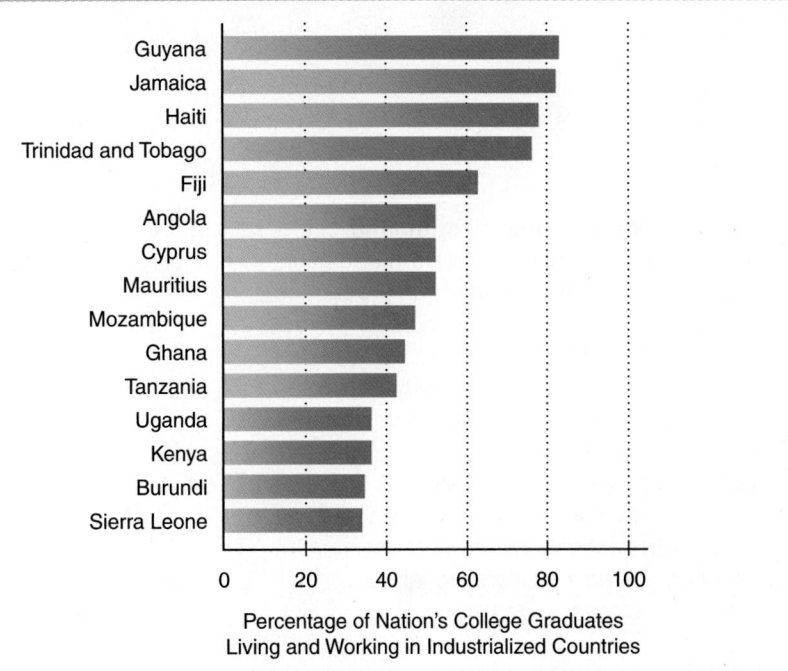

Percentage of Nation's College Graduates
Living and Working in Industrialized Countries

For critical analysis:

1. What might nations with relatively low levels of per-capita real GDP, such as those in Figure 7–9, do to try to slow down the brain drains they are experiencing?
2. Why might some people in the nations currently experiencing "brain drains," such as some condition residents, favour policies aimed at restricting immigration of highly skilled workers from abroad?
(Hint: Immigration of well-trained workers increases the supply of workers in Canadian markets for skilled labour. How does this affect the market wages earned by skilled workers in Canada?)

SUMMARY

Here is what you should know after reading this chapter. MyEconLab will help you identify what you know, and where to go when you need to practise. We suggest that as soon as you review one of the Learning Objective sections below, you then proceed to go through the related section in MyEconLab.

myeconlab

LEARNING OBJECTIVES	KEY TERMS	MYECONLAB PRACTICE
7.1 Defining Economic Growth. The rate of economic growth is the annual rate of change in per-capita real GDP. This measure of the growth of a nation's economy takes into account both its growth in overall production of goods and services and the growth of its population. Canada has been able to achieve a high standard of living because of sustained economic growth over many years. The definition of growth does not take into account changes in the distribution of income or the effect that leisure time has on economic welfare.	economic growth, 181	• **MyEconLab** Study Plan 7.1

LEARNING OBJECTIVES	**KEY TERMS**	**MYECONLAB PRACTICE**
7.2 Modelling Economic Growth. The aggregate production function models the relationship between the inputs to production available in the economy to output. Labour supply increases by themselves will increase output but also reduce productivity and wages because of diminishing returns. However, there are three factors that increase the productivity of labour: an increase in physical capital, an increase in human capital, and an advance in technology. All of these factors have been at work to increase labour productivity and increase wages.	labour productivity, 184	• **MyEconLab** Study Plan 7.2
7.3 Fundamental Determinants of Economic Growth. Savings are a key determinant of capital accumulation. Higher savings rates contribute to greater investment and hence increased capital accumulation and economic growth. Private property and the legal structures of an economy can help or hinder growth. Market-driven economies seem to do better at creating growth than do other economies. Political stability, population growth, and immigration can also help boost economic growth.		• **MyEconLab** Study Plan 7.3
7.4 New Growth Theory and What Determines Growth. This is a relatively recent theory that examines why individuals and businesses conduct research into inventing and developing new technologies and how this process interacts with the rate of economic growth. This theory emphasizes how rewards for technological innovation contribute to higher economic growth rates. A key implication of the theory is that ideas and knowledge are crucial elements of the growth process.	new growth theory, 191 patent, 191 innovation, 192	• **MyEconLab** Study Plan 7.4
7.5 The Costs and Benefits of Economic Growth. Economic growth has many benefits, but some costs as well. We have a higher standard of living when compared with previous generations. We have more material goods, better education, longer life span, and less poverty. At the same time, there is a significant and growing impact upon the environment that detracts from those benefits. The ability of the environment to absorb the ever-increasing pollution created by our		• **MyEconLab** Study Plan 7.5

	LEARNING OBJECTIVES	KEY TERMS	MYECONLAB PRACTICE

economic activity is being questioned by many economists and environmentalists.

7.6 International Economic Development. The key characteristics shared by nations that succeed in attaining higher levels of economic development are significant opportunities for their citizens to obtain training and education, protection of property rights, policies that permit new companies and industries to replace older ones, and the avoidance of protectionist barriers that hinder international trade.

development economics, 197

• **MyEconLab** Study Plan 7.6

PROBLEMS

(Answers to the odd-numbered problems appear at the back of the book.)

LO 7.1 Define economic growth and explain some of the limitations of that definition.

1. Consider the following table, which describes growth-rate data for four countries between 2001 and 2010:

	Annual Growth Rate (%)			
Country	J	K	L	M
Nominal GDP	20	15	10	5
Price level	5	3	6	2
Population	5	8	2	1

   a. Which country has the largest rate of output growth per capita?
   b. Which country has the smallest rate of output growth per capita?

2. In 2008, a nation's population was 10 million. Its nominal GDP was $40 billion, and its price index was 100. In 2009, its population had increased to 12 million, its nominal GDP had risen to $57.6 billion, and its price index had increased to 120. What was this nation's economic growth rate during the year?

3. Between the start of 2008 and the start of 2009, a country's economic growth rate was 4 percent. Its population did not change during the year, nor did its price level. What was the rate of increase of the country's nominal GDP during this one-year interval?

LO 7.2 Explain and model economic growth.

4. This table shows some data for Canada from Statistics Canada.

Year	Real GDP (constant 2002 dollars)	Hours worked (millions)	Capital Cost
2004	1 210 412	23 416.2	394 697.2
2005	1 246 582	23 625.5	413 106.6

   a. Calculate the growth of real GDP from 2004 to 2005.
   b. Calculate labour productivity in 2004 and 2005.
   c. Calculate the rate of labour productivity growth from 2004 to 2005.
   d. Calculate the increased percentage of capital from 2004 to 2005.
   e. Assume one-third of the increase in capital accumulation was the resulting proportionate increase in labour productivity. Calculate the remaining productivity increase due to increased labour skills and technological change. How does this compare to the results found by Statistics Canada in Example 7-3?

5. Population and employment in Canada has been rising. In the aggregate production function model, the increase in population should lower wages, but historically real wages have risen. Explain how this is possible, and show this result using the aggregate production function and the labour market diagram.

6. Many economists have found a strong link between education and per-capita income. Why would it make sense to call education "human capital"?

LO 7.3 Describe the fundamental determinants of economic growth.

7. The graph shows the production possibilities curve for an economy. Which of the labelled points would be associated with the highest feasible growth rate for this economy?

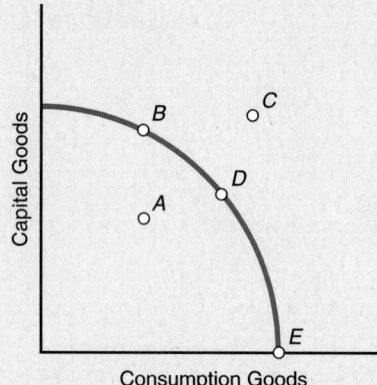

8. Many countries in Africa have extremely large potential stocks of natural resources. Nonetheless, those natural resources often remain unexploited. Give reasons why this situation continues to exist.

LO 7.4 Understand the basis of new growth theory.

9. What existing government policies encourage the development of new technologies?

10. The United States has many more Nobel Prize winners than Japan, but Japan's per-capita income is just as high as that of the United States. Why might it be an advantage to be a "late adopter" of technology?

LO 7.5 Outline some of the costs and benefits of economic growth.

11. Suppose that you are shown the following data for two countries, known only as country X and country Z:

Country	GDP	Population
X	$ 81 billion	9 million
Z	$135 billion	90 million

a. From this information, which country would you expect to be classified as a developing country? Why?

b. Now suppose that you were also given the following data:

Country	Life Expectancy at Birth (years)	Infant Mortality per 1000 Live Births	Literacy (%)
X	70	15	60
Z	58	50	70

Are these figures consistent with your answer to part (a)?

c. Should we expect the developing country identified in part (a) to have a much greater population density than the other country?

12. Refer back to Policy Example 7–3, "Ottawn and the Kyoto Accord." Developing nations such as China often accept very high levels of pollutions in exchange for higher economic growth. Why are enviromentalist concerned about China's high rate of economic growth?

LO 7.6 Discuss the fundamental factors that contribute to international economic development.

13. An increasing number of Chinese and Indian citizens who immigrated to Canada are now returning to their home countries to work. Why are these two countries experiencing a "reverse brain drain"? How do you think this might influence the economic development of these two countries?

14. Why would rising education for women lead to fewer children? What role would the opportunity cost of lost wages play in this decision?

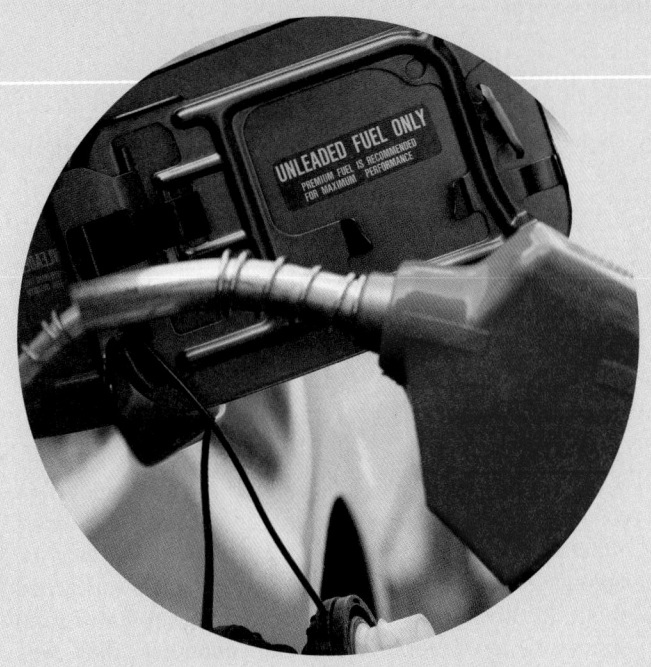

8

Modelling Real GDP and the Price Level in the Short Run

➤ **LEARNING OBJECTIVES**

After reading this chapter, you should be able to:

8.1 Explain the concept of the short-run aggregate supply curve.

8.2 Understand what factors cause shifts in the short-run and long-run aggregate supply curves.

8.3 Evaluate the effects of aggregate demand and supply shocks on equilibrium real output in the short run.

8.4 Explain the long-run adjustment process.

8.5 Explain how an open economy affects aggregate demand and aggregate supply.

8.6 Explain short-run inflation in the economy.

MyEconLab helps you master each objective and study more efficiently. See end of chapter for details.

Between 1999 and 2007, the price of a barrel of crude oil increased from about US$15 to over US$99. Some media outlets compared this increase to the oil price run-up from 1973 to 1981 and there was considerable belief that this might cause another recession in North America. But media observers ignored two important points. First, the oil price increase during the 2000s could not be compared directly with the price jump of the 1970s without adjusting for inflation. Second, they failed to note that U.S. producers rely less on oil to produce goods and services today than did producers in the 1970s. In Canada, the largest exporter of oil to the United States, the recent increase in the price of oil has been accompanied by record low unemployment rates. In this chapter, you will learn why these lapses have caused many in the media to overestimate the negative effects of the oil price increase of the 2000s on the North American economy.

DID YOU KNOW THAT... ❓

The Kobe earthquake in 1995 is instructive when contemplating the economic effects of human and natural disasters, such as Hurricane Katrina that struck the United States in 2005. All told, the total loss to Japan's economy was close to 2 percent of Japan's real GDP at the time, or about $150 billion in 2004 dollars. Nevertheless, in less than two years, the Kobe region's annual contribution to Japan's real GDP had very nearly returned to its prequake level.

Such events can have a significant impact on a nation's real GDP. The long-run effects, though, are often less dramatic. The starting point for understanding how variations in a nation's productive capacity can exert effects on real GDP and the price level is the long-run aggregate supply model of the economy, which we learned about in Chapter 6. As you will see later on, however, an approach to understanding the economy that was developed during the 20th century can do much to help disentangle how natural and human-made disasters affect GDP and the price level in the short run versus the long run.

8.1 *The Short-Run Aggregate Supply Curve*

The fluctuations that we encounter in the economy are modelled somewhat differently from the long-term growth we modelled in the previous chapter. Economists believe that the responsiveness of the economy to changes in prices and profitability is different in a short period of time than over longer periods of time. There are some rigidities in the economy that make the response of firms different in the short run (which creates market imbalances) and the long run (where these imbalances in various markets work themselves out). We model the short-run response of firms using the short-run aggregate supply (*SRAS*), while the aggregate demand curve remains the same as we learned in Chapter 6.

Aggregate Supply versus Individual Supply

Short-run aggregate supply The relationship between aggregate supply and the price level in the short run, all other things held constant.

Short-run aggregate supply (or *SRAS* for short) is defined as the relationship between aggregate supply and the price level in the short run, all other things held constant. The higher the price level, the greater is the aggregate quantity supplied; the lower the price level, the lesser is the aggregate quantity supplied.

Although aggregate supply seems to be the same idea as supply for an individual commodity, the two concepts are not exactly the same. A supply curve for an individual product reflects a change in the price of that individual product relative to the prices of other goods, whereas the aggregate supply curve shows the effects of changes in the price level for the entire economy. Because we are aggregating many products, we cannot ignore the effects that has on related markets, such as the markets for the input resources being used.

Short-Run Aggregate Supply versus Long-Run Aggregate Supply

How does *SRAS* differ from the long-run aggregate supply we studied in Chapter 6? The short-run aggregate supply represents the relationship between the price level and the real output of goods and services in the economy *without* full adjustment and full information. Price changes in the output of firms will have a *temporary* effect on the firm's profitability and hence will move the economy *temporarily along* the production function and *temporarily* increase the quantity of labour demanded. In the long run, that temporary advantage disappears as the prices of inputs readjust. The real level of profitability and the real wages and prices of resources return to what they were, and real GDP returns to its potential output at the *LRAS*. The key difference between these outcomes is that for some period of time, real wages are reduced below their long-run value. Economists believe that wages are relatively *inflexible* or *rigid* and do not change as easily as prices of other goods and services, thus creating a temporary imbalance in the labour market.

Figure 8–1 shows *LRAS* and *SRAS* curves. The *SRAS* is drawn under the assumption that all determinants of aggregate supply other than the price level will be held constant. Most notably, we hold constant the prices of the inputs used in the production of real goods and services, and labour, as shown in part (a), is also held constant. What does this mean? As the price level rises, real wages for labour fall from W_1 to W_2, as shown in part (a). It therefore becomes profitable for all firms to expand production. Otherwise stated, changes in the price level in the short run can affect real output because some production costs are fixed in nominal terms. Therefore, an increase in the price level increases expected profits and the desirability of producing more. Aggregate production, therefore, increases to Y_2. The connection of all such possible points of output and the price level is called the **short-run aggregate supply curve**. Because output expands in the short run with a higher price level, it has a positive slope.

Let us examine a concrete example. Suppose that the bottlers of Screech (a Newfoundland rum) pay their workers $12 per hour, and the selling price of Screech (at the wholesale level) is $4 per bottle. From the workers' point of view, the real wage of the workers is three bottles of Screech. Or, in other words, the bottlers must sell three bottles to pay for one hour of labour.

Suppose that the price of Screech rises to $6. This means that the real wage of the worker has fallen to two bottles of rum. Obviously, the profit of the firm increases because with the same amount of labour, it earns much more from each bottle sold. Firms respond to this change in the real wage rate and the profit in several ways. The primary way in which firms respond in the short run is to increase their production by hiring more

Short-run aggregate supply curve
An upward-sloping line representing the short-run aggregate supply of goods and services in the economy.

FIGURE 8–1 *Deriving the SRAS Curve*

The quantity of real GDP produced will increase in the short run as prices rise because the profitability of firms' production will increase. The economy moves off of the *LRAS* curve to production level Y_2 at price P_2 in part (c). Input costs will be lower as real wages fall relative to the general price level, encouraging

firms to make more (W_2 to W_1 in part (a)). While the firm experiences diminishing returns from this increased production, it also is able to offset these returns with the lower wages paid for labour.

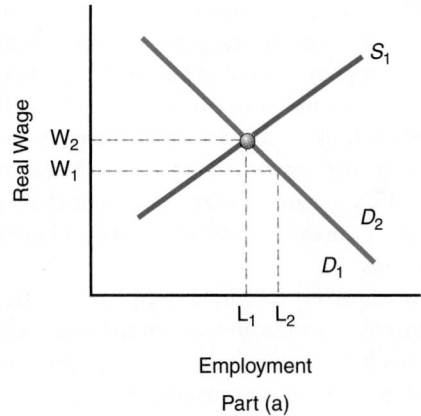

Part (a)

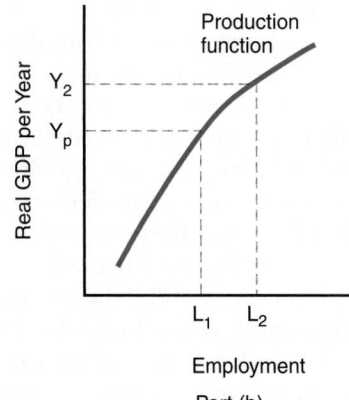

Part (b)

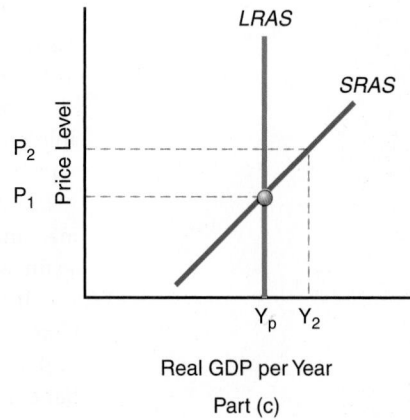

Part (c)

workers and using their machinery more intensively. In the long run, of course, it would be possible to add machinery and capacity as well. If profits are high, there is a strong incentive to increase this capacity.

If the price of Screech were to fall, firms would find their profitability falling as the real wages of the workers are increased. Again, firms respond in the short run by reducing output or even shutting down. If this persists in the long run, and profits are too low, then the firm may exit the industry. This could be voluntarily through selling off its assets or through bankruptcy.

Why Can Output Be Expanded in the Short Run?

In the short run, if the price level rises, output can be expanded (even beyond the economist's notion of the normal capacity of a firm). That is to say, the overall economy can temporarily produce beyond its normal limits or capacity for a variety of reasons:

1. In the short run, most labour contracts implicitly or explicitly call for flexibility in hours of work at the given wage rate. Therefore, firms can use existing workers more intensively in a variety of ways: they can get them to work harder; they can get them to work more hours per day; and they can get them to work more days per week. Workers can also be switched from *uncounted* production, such as maintenance, to *counted* production, which generates counted output. The distinction between counted and uncounted is simply what is measured in the marketplace, particularly by government statisticians and accountants. If a worker cleans a machine, there is no measured output. But if that worker is put on the production line and helps increase the number of units produced each day, measured output will go up. That worker's production has then been counted.

2. Existing capital equipment can be used more intensively. Machines can be worked more hours per day. Some can be made to work at a faster speed. Maintenance can be delayed.

3. Finally, and just as importantly, if nominal wage rates are held constant, a higher price level means that profits go up, which induces firms to hire more workers. The duration of unemployment falls, and thus, the unemployment rate falls. And people who were previously not in the labour force (homemakers and younger or older workers) can be induced to enter.

All of these adjustments allow national output to rise as the price level increases without adding more equipment or machinery.

Capacity utilization A measure of how intensively plant and equipment are being used.

CAPACITY UTILIZATION The ability to adjust output through the intensive use of existing plant and equipment is called **capacity utilization**. Figure 8–2 shows how Canada's capacity utilization has varied over the past 20 years. Capacity utilization signals how the economy is doing and whether there is the ability to increase output in the short run. Why does this matter?

If factories and machinery are operating well below their normal output, firms can easily increase their output to meet rising demand by putting existing plant and equipment to more intensive use. This, in turn, means very little money is spent to buy new machines, build new plants, and hire people to work. On the other hand, if nearly all currently available production capacity is being used, then firms will likely increase their prices in the short run, and in the long run, add capacity to keep with strong demand (and thus shift *LRAS*). If you look back to Figure 5–5 on page 137, you can see that investment in new machinery declined during the recessionary periods of the early 1980s and 1990s and grew again as the economy recovered from those recessions.

It is important to note that the definition of capacity utilization used by Statistics Canada is based on a survey of firms whereby capacity is a measurement of the *theoretical engineering (or potential)* capacity of the capital stock of various industries (i.e., running flat out 24 hours per day). We are more interested in the *economic* capacity, or the capacity at which the firm would want to operate over long periods of time. The difference between these two definitions is that operating at the theoretical potential may be extremely

FIGURE 8–2

Capacity Utilization Changes Over the Last 20 Years

Capacity utilization has varied widely over the past 20 years. Utilization varies in concert with business fluctuations.

SOURCE: STATISTICS CANADA TABLE 028-0002

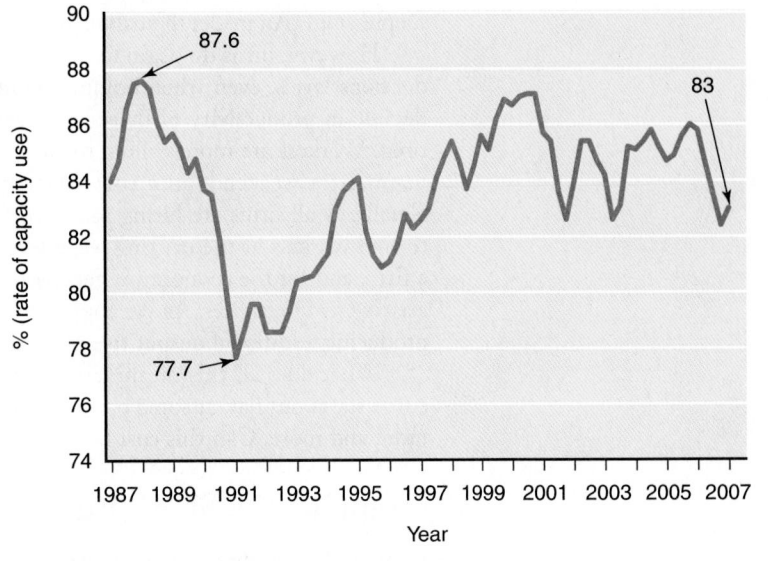

expensive for reasons we note below. Firms will not want to operate at this high level of production unless they can recover the costs through high prices. All this suggests that there is an optimal or normal level of capacity utilization, and indeed many economists assume that market-style economies operate at their normal capacity in good times and only dip below capacity in recessions. An examination of Figure 8-2 shows that most of the time the Canadian economy operates at between 80 percent and 85 percent of capacity, so we can safely assume that normal capacity is in that range.

The Shape of the Short-Run Aggregate Supply Curve

The *SRAS* curve is drawn with a nearly flat segment, then an upward-sloping section, and finally a very steep or vertical portion, as shown in Figure 8–3. Why is it drawn this way?

A flat *SRAS* curve implies that price increases are not necessary to induce firms to produce more. When the economy is operating well below its potential output, the cost of increasing output may not change because there are plenty of workers to hire and lots of unused machinery available. No bottlenecks or shortages are created and diminishing returns are minimal. Such a flat segment is sometimes called the "Keynesian" aggregate supply curve

FIGURE 8–3

The Short-Run Aggregate Supply Curve

The short-run aggregate supply curve, *SRAS*, slopes upward because with fixed input prices, at a higher price level, firms make more profits and desire more output. They use workers and capital more intensively. At price level 100, $1100 billion of real GDP per year is supplied. If the price level rises to 120, $1200 billion of real GDP per year will be supplied.

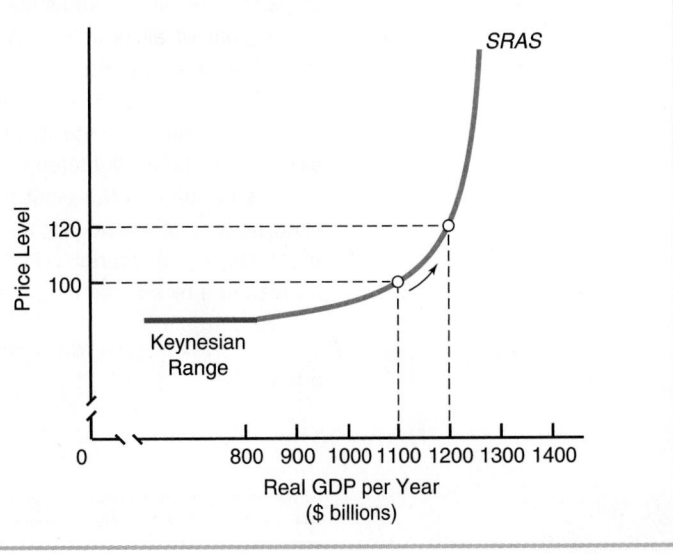

after John Maynard Keynes, an economist who wrote about a similar situation in the Great Depression. (An in-depth analysis of his theories is presented in Appendix C.)

However, firms do begin to experience diminishing returns as they increase their productions levels; even when holding input prices constant, costs are rising because of the decline in productivity of these resources. Why? There are several reasons. Workers get tired. Workers are more willing to work one extra weekend than they are willing to work many extra weekends in a row. Machines cannot go on forever without maintenance. Finally, as all firms are hiring more workers from the same pool, it becomes more costly to find workers at the existing wage level. Once we have reached the normal capacity for a firm, and for the economy, it gets harder and harder to produce more and more *with the existing set of resources.* As we approach the theoretical limit of the economy, the costs of producing additional output rise more sharply.

What does all this mean? Simply put, that although the short-run aggregate supply curve starts out flat, at some point, it must get steeper and steeper as firms try to produce more and more. Can this cost be reduced? Perhaps, as explained in Example 8–1.

Graphing the Short-Run Aggregate Supply Curve

Look back at Figure 8–3. There you see the short-run aggregate supply curve, *SRAS*. As we have drawn it, after a real GDP of $1200 billion, it starts to become steeper and steeper, and by the time it gets close to $1300 billion, it is very steep indeed.[1] If the price index, as represented by the GDP deflator, is 100, the economy will supply $1100 billion per year of real GDP in Figure 8–3. If the GDP deflator increases to 120, the economy will move up the *SRAS* to $1200 billion of real GDP per year.

EXAMPLE 8–1	**Changing the Slope of the Short-Run Aggregate Supply Schedule?**

Evidence has been increasing that the short-run aggregate supply curve (*SRAS*) has become less steeply sloped since the early 1990s. Some economists credit widespread deregulation in the 1970s and 1980s with laying a foundation for a more shallowly sloped *SRAS* curve. The increase in domestic and international rivalry among sellers of goods and services, they argue, has made consumers much more sensitive to price differences across products. In equilibrium, therefore, the general level of prices exhibits change, relative to years past, in response to a given change in output—hence a less steeply sloped *SRAS* curve.

Now, continuing developments in information technologies promise to take this trend a step further. For the first time ever, information technologies are the biggest job creators. Depending on whose statistics you look at, such industries are producing between 25 and 40 percent of all new jobs. An information economy is fundamentally different from an industrial economy. Software and databases, for example, can be scaled up to gigantic capacity at little cost. Indeed, because of the ease of communicating data over the Internet, they have unlimited capacity at the very beginning. In other words, capacity as previously defined may be an outdated concept.

Hence, beyond the point at which the *SRAS* curve crosses the *LRAS* curve, there will likely be less of a tendency for the *SRAS* curve to bend upward as Canada becomes more of an information economy. Perhaps today's and especially tomorrow's *SRAS* will have to be represented by a curve that is more nearly horizontal.

For critical analysis: Why does a constant marginal cost to expanding production imply a flat *SRAS*?

---

[1] If there is a maximum short-run amount of output, at some point, the *SRAS* becomes vertical. However, there is always some way to squeeze a little bit more out of an economic system, and so the *SRAS* does not necessarily have to become vertical, just extremely steep.

8.2 *Shifts in the Aggregate Supply Curves*

Just as there were non–price-level factors that could cause a shift in the aggregate demand curve, there are non–price-level factors that can cause a shift in the aggregate supply curve. The analysis here is not quite so simple as the analysis for the non–price-level determinants for aggregate demand, for here we are dealing with both the short run and the long run—*SRAS* and *LRAS*. Still, anything other than the price level that affects supply will shift at least one of the aggregate supply curves.

Shifts in Short-Run Aggregate Supply

Some events, particularly those that are short-lived, will temporarily shift *SRAS* but not *LRAS*. These events do *not* affect the *LRAS* because they do not affect our *capability* of producing; they only affect the *desirability* of producing. In other words, firms *could* still produce (they have not gotten rid of any machinery, and the workers are still available), but they *choose* not to produce because it is less profitable to do so. One of the most obvious is a temporary shift in input prices, particularly those caused by external events that are not expected to last forever. Wage rate increases, for example, only affect the desirability of producing, not our capability of producing.

Consider the possibility of an announced 90-day embargo of oil from the Middle East to Canada. Oil is an important input in many production activities. The 90-day oil embargo will cause at least a temporary increase in the price of this input. You can see what happens in Figure 8–4. *LRAS* remains fixed, but *SRAS*₁ shifts to *SRAS*₂ reflecting the increase in input prices—the higher price of oil. This is because the rise in costs at each level of real GDP per year requires a higher price level to cover those costs.

Let us consider another example using the 90-day oil embargo as the basis for discussion. WestJet Airlines uses tremendous amounts of fuel in flying its aircraft, about 17 percent of its total costs. With a steep increase in these fuel costs (and perhaps indirectly other costs), it would mean that many flights would no longer be profitable to operate. How would WestJet react?

In the short run, WestJet would cut back on its flights, starting with the ones that are the least profitable (and now losing money). It is unlikely, though, that it would (or even could) immediately sell off its planes. Temporarily, these planes would be grounded. The employees working those flights might be temporarily laid off. Customers attempting to use those flights would either have to use a competitor's flight or switch to a different time. WestJet might also temporarily raise its prices to reflect the extra costs, which would reduce the sales of flights.

If this pattern is repeated across the economy, we would model it as a shift in the *SRAS* to the left. Higher prices are needed to maintain the same level of output.

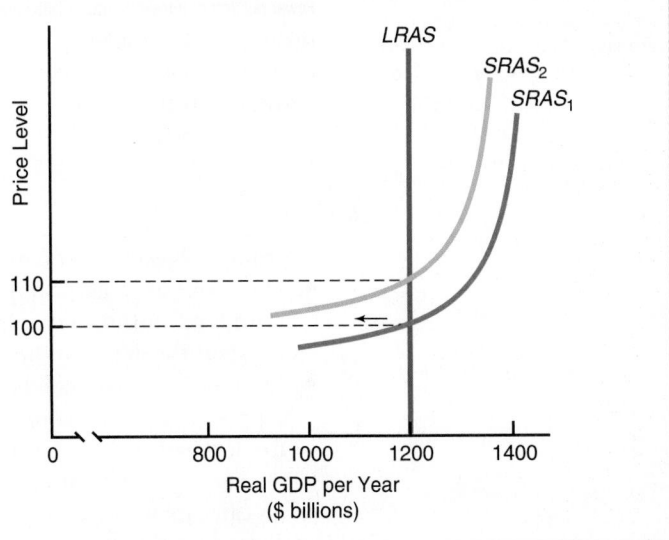

FIGURE 8–4

Shifts in SRAS Only

A temporary increase in an input price will shift the short-run aggregate supply curve from *SRAS*₁ to *SRAS*₂. The desirability of producing is reduced, even though the capability of production is unaffected.

FIGURE 8–5

Shifts in Both Short- and Long-Run Aggregate Supply

Initially, the two supply curves are $SRAS_1$ and $LRAS_1$. Now consider a big oil find in Manitoba in an area where no one thought oil existed. This shifts $LRAS_1$ to $LRAS_2$ at $1250 billion of real GDP. $SRAS_1$ also shifts outward horizontally to $SRAS_2$.

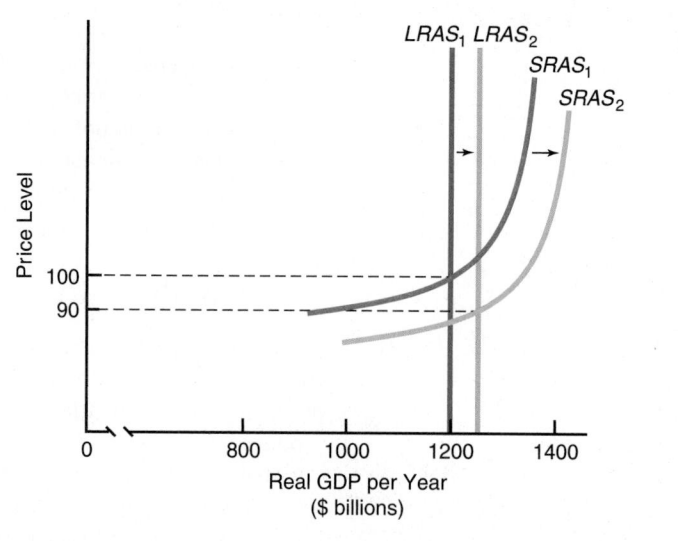

Shifts in Both Short- and Long-Run Aggregate Supply

There is a set of events that cause a shift in both the short-run aggregate supply curve and the long-run aggregate supply curve. In Chapter 6 we learned that the *LRAS* curve will shift rightward with an increase in the amount of labour and natural resources used, the accumulation of capital, and improvements in the productivity of labour and capital, which is usually brought about by increases in available technology and knowledge. Any such change in long-run supply will change short-run supply as well.

Look at Figure 8–5. Initially, the two curves are $SRAS_1$ and $LRAS_1$. Now, consider a big oil discovery in Manitoba in an area where no one thought oil existed. This shifts $LRAS_1$ to $LRAS_2$ at $1250 billion of real GDP. $SRAS_1$ also shifts outward horizontally to $SRAS_2$.

We summarize the possible determinants of aggregate supply in Table 8–1. These determinants will shift both the short-run or the long-run aggregate supply curve or, in the case of input prices, just the *SRAS* curve.

TABLE 8-1

Determinants of Aggregate Supply

The determinants listed here can affect short-run or long-run aggregate supply (or both), depending on whether they are temporary or permanent.

Changes That Cause an Increase in Aggregate Supply	Changes That Cause a Decrease in Aggregate Supply
Discoveries of new raw materials	Depletion of raw materials
Increased competition	Decreased competition
A reduction in international trade barriers	An increase in international trade barriers
Fewer regulatory impediments to business	More regulatory impediments to business
An increase in labour supplied	A decrease in labour supplied
Increased training and education	Decreased training and education
A decrease in marginal tax rates	An increase in marginal tax rates
A reduction in input prices	An increase in input prices

➤→ **CONCEPTS IN BRIEF**

Learning Objective 8.1: Explain the concept of the short-run aggregate supply curve.

✦ Short-run aggregate supply is the relationship between aggregate supply and the price level in the short run, all other things held constant. Most notably, we hold constant the prices of the inputs used in the production of real goods and services.

✦ Output can be expanded in the short run because firms can use existing workers and capital equipment more intensively. Also, in the short run, when input prices are fixed, a higher price level means higher profits, which induces firms to hire more workers and use existing equipment more intensively.

✦ As capacity utilization increases, the cost and difficulty of increasing output go up. Therefore, the *SRAS* curve gets steeper and steeper.

Learning Objective 8.2: Understand what factors cause shifts in the short-run and long-run aggregate supply curves.

➹ A temporary shift in input prices will shift only *SRAS*. Both long-run and short-run aggregate supply will increase with an increase in the amount of labour and natural resources used, the accumulation of capital, and improvements in the productivity of labour and capital.

8.3 *Equilibrium*

As you discovered in Chapter 3, equilibrium occurs where demand and supply curves intersect. It is a little more complicated here because we have two types of aggregate supply curves—long-run and short-run. Let us look first at short-run equilibrium.

Short-Run Equilibrium

Short-run equilibrium occurs at the intersection of aggregate demand, *AD*, and short-run aggregate supply, *SRAS*, as shown in Figure 8–6. The equilibrium price level is 120, and the equilibrium annual level of real GDP is $1200 billion. If the price level increased to 140, there would be an excess quantity of real goods and services supplied in the entire economy, and the price level would tend to fall. If the price level were 100, aggregate quantity demanded would be greater than aggregate quantity supplied, and buyers would bid up prices so that the price level would move toward 120. The key signal for firms is the changes in inventory that accompany these differences in *AD* and *SRAS*. Rising inventory indicates to firms that they should reduce production, while a shrinking inventory is a signal to increase production.

In Figure 8–6, you see that we have drawn the long-run aggregate supply curve, *LRAS*, so that there is full equilibrium in both the short run and the long run at price level 120. At price level 120, this economy can operate forever at $1200 billion without the price level changing.

Consequences of Changes in Short-Run Aggregate Supply and Demand

We now have a basic model of the entire economy. We can trace the movement of the equilibrium price level and the equilibrium real GDP when there are shocks to the

---

FIGURE 8–6
Equilibrium

Equilibrium will occur where the aggregate demand curve intersects the short-run aggregate supply curve and the long-run aggregate supply curve. In this diagram, it is at price level 120 and a real GDP of $1200 billion per year.

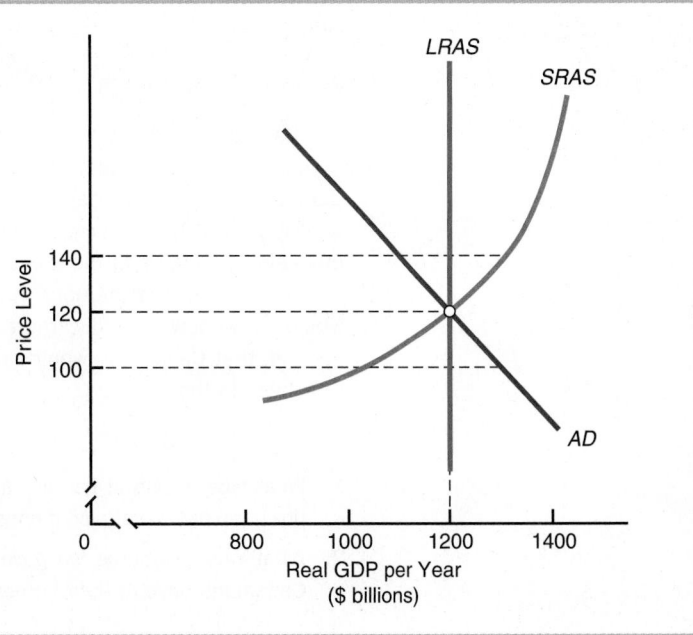

Aggregate demand shock Any economic event that causes the aggregate demand curve to shift inward or outward.

Aggregate supply shock Any economic event that causes the aggregate supply curve to shift inward or outward.

Output gap The difference between potential GDP and actual GDP.

Recessionary gap The amount by which potential GDP exceeds actual GDP.

Inflationary gap The amount by which actual GDP exceeds potential GDP.

economy. Whenever there is a shift in our economy's curves, the equilibrium price level or real GDP level (or both) may change. Any economic event that causes the aggregate demand curve to shift inward or outward is called an **aggregate demand shock**, and any economic event that causes the aggregate supply curve to shift inward or outward is called an **aggregate supply shock**.

In Chapter 3, you learned what happened to the equilibrium price and quantity when there was a shift in demand, then a shift in supply, and then shifts in both curves. In the analysis that follows, we will be using the same basic analysis, but you should remember that we are now talking about changes in the overall price level and changes in the equilibrium level of real GDP per year.

Output Gaps

In the short run, it is possible for us to be on the *SRAS* to the right or left of the intersection of the *AD* and *LRAS*, the difference between potential GDP and actual GDP being called an **output gap**. Why is it possible to have a gap? Because (as we learned in Section 8.1) a firm may temporarily choose to produce more or less than its normal capacity. These output gaps are the same ones that we encountered in Chapter 4 when we looked at business fluctuations.

When many firms are operating below their normal capacity, and we have cyclical unemployment, we have a large output gap in our economy. The size of the gap is measured as the amount by which potential GDP exceeds actual GDP and is called a **recessionary gap**. This represents lost GDP that is created when the economy experiences a shock or because potential GDP has grown more quickly than actual GDP. (It is also sometimes called a contractionary gap.)

As we also learned in Section 8.1, it is possible for firms to temporarily exceed their normal capacity. When many firms are operating above their normal capacity, we can find that the economy is experiencing strong inflationary pressures because of the shortages of inputs to production that occur. This is a condition of an "overheated" economy. The output gap created in this situation will be measured as the amount by which actual GDP exceeds potential GDP and is called an **inflationary gap**. (It is sometimes called an expansionary gap.)

The Bank of Canada controls one of the influences on aggregate demand through its control of interest rates and the money supply. Policy Example 8-1 shows how the Bank of Canada has to weigh both positive influences on aggregate demand (which might create an inflationary gap) against the influences that are negative (and therefore create a recessionary gap) in making decisions about interest rates and the money supply.

POLICY EXAMPLE 8-1 **The Bank of Canada and Output Gaps**

The Bank of Canada's job is to keep inflation under control, or in other words, to eliminate any inflationary gaps that it sees occurring in the Canadian economy. In March of 2007, the Bank of Canada announced that it was not going to raise interest rates (and did not do so until July of 2007) because it believed that the current rate of interest was appropriate for maintaining inflation at the announced 2 percent target level.

In the Bank's statement, it identified two main risks: First, that the U.S. economy would slow down rapidly, thereby hurting Canada's economy on the downside, and second, that Canadians would go on a spending spree because of the increased equity they have in their homes.

For critical analysis:

1. What type of output gap in Canada would be created if the U.S. economy were to slow down rapidly? What type if consumers would increase their spending from current levels?

2. What was the name we gave to the new spending that might arise from the equity Canadians have in their homes?

FIGURE 8–7

*The Effects of Stable Aggregate Supply
and a Decrease in Aggregate Demand:
The Recessionary Gap*

If the economy is at equilibrium at E_1, with price
level 120 and real GDP per year of $1200 billion, a
shift inward and to the left of the aggregate
demand curve to AD_2 will lead to a new short-run
equilibrium at E_2. The equilibrium price level will fall
to 115, and the short-run equilibrium level of real
GDP per year will fall to $1180 billion. There will be
a recessionary gap.

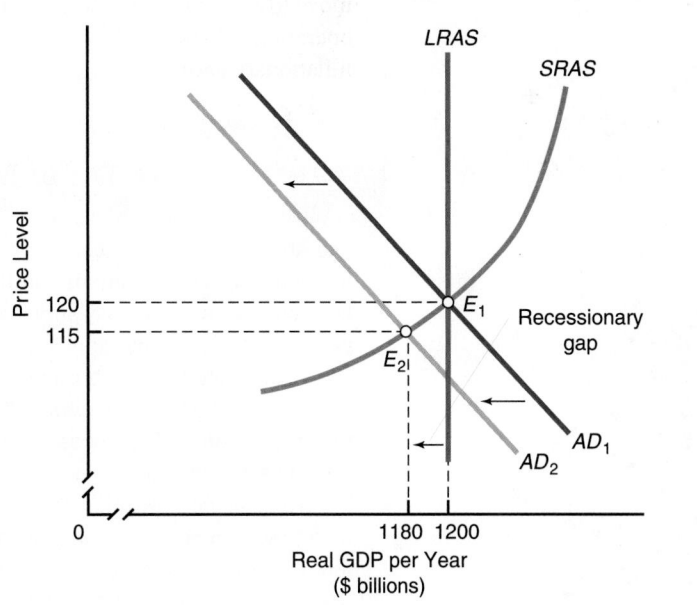

Aggregate Demand Shifts while Aggregate Supply Is Stable

Now we can show what happens when aggregate supply remains stable but aggregate
demand falls. The outcome may be the possible cause of a recession and can, under certain circumstances, explain a rise in the unemployment rate. In Figure 8–7, you see that
with AD_1, both long-run and short-run equilibriums are at $1200 billion of real GDP per
year (because $SRAS$ and $LRAS$ also intersect AD_1 at that level of real GDP). The long-
run equilibrium price level is 120. A reduction in aggregate demand shifts the aggregate
demand curve to AD_2. The new intersection with $SRAS$ is at $1180 billion per year, cre-
ating a recessionary gap. Example 8–2 illustrates how this happened in the United States.

Effect on the Economy of an Increase in Aggregate Demand

We can reverse the situation and have aggregate demand increase to AD_2, as is shown in
Figure 8–8. The initial equilibrium conditions are exactly the same as in Figure 8–7. The

FIGURE 8–8

*The Effects of Stable Aggregate Supply
and an Increase in Aggregate Demand:
The Inflationary Gap*

The economy is at equilibrium at E_1. An increase in
aggregate demand to AD_2 leads to a new short-run
equilibrium at E_2 with the price level rising from
120 to 125 and the equilibrium level of real GDP
per year rising from $1200 billion to $1220 billion.
The difference is called the inflationary gap.

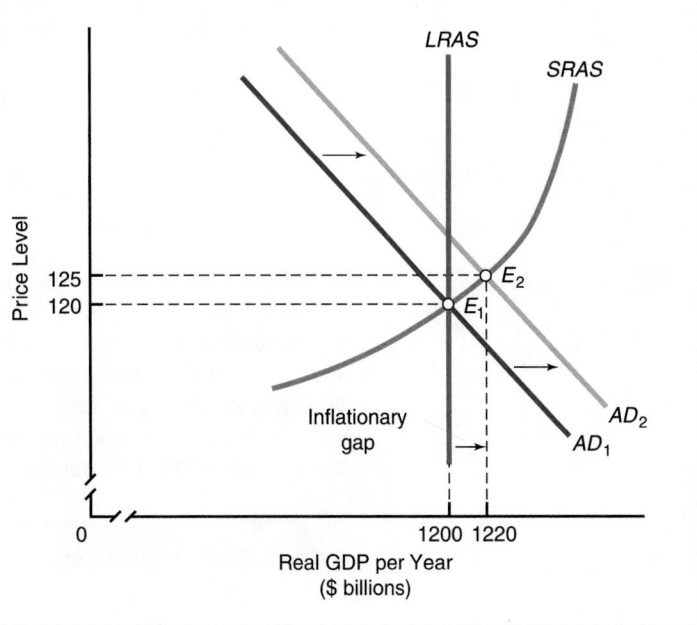

move to AD_2 increases the short-run equilibrium from E_1 to E_2 such that the economy is operating at \$1220 billion of real GDP per year, which exceeds *LRAS* (and creates an inflationary gap).

| EXAMPLE 8–2 | **A Tale of Two Economies** |

The American economy went into a short recession in 2001 and was still below its potential output in 2004. Canada, on the other hand, experienced only a short slowdown. The two economies are usually strongly linked, experiencing recessions at about the same time. Why the difference this time?

In the United States, business investment in equipment (much of it in computers and software) fell by \$100 billion between 2000 and 2001. Since then, it has rebounded. Nevertheless, this sudden drop in business equipment and software investment accounted for half of the overall decline in total American planned investment that occurred during this period.

To examine how this drop in business equipment and software investment tended to affect the American economy, consider Figure 8–9. By the late spring of 2001, annualized real GDP was close to U.S.\$9.4 trillion. The investment decline induced a leftward shift in aggregate demand from AD_1 to AD_2. Abstracting from other factors that possibly contributed to changes in aggregate demand or aggregate supply, we can conclude that this caused equilibrium to move from E_1 to E_2, implying a decrease in equilibrium real GDP and a fall in the equilibrium price level. Indeed, by early autumn 2001, American real GDP had declined to U.S.\$9.3 trillion, and the price level dropped slightly, from 109.8 to 109.7. The decline in total planned expenditures caused by the falloff in business investment spending temporarily pushed the economy to the left of its long-run aggregate supply curve.

FIGURE 8–9 *The Effects of a Short-Term Decline in Business Investment Spending*

A sharp but short-lived decline in planned investment expenditures by business shifts the aggregate demand curve leftward. Equilibrium temporarily moves from E_1 to E_2.

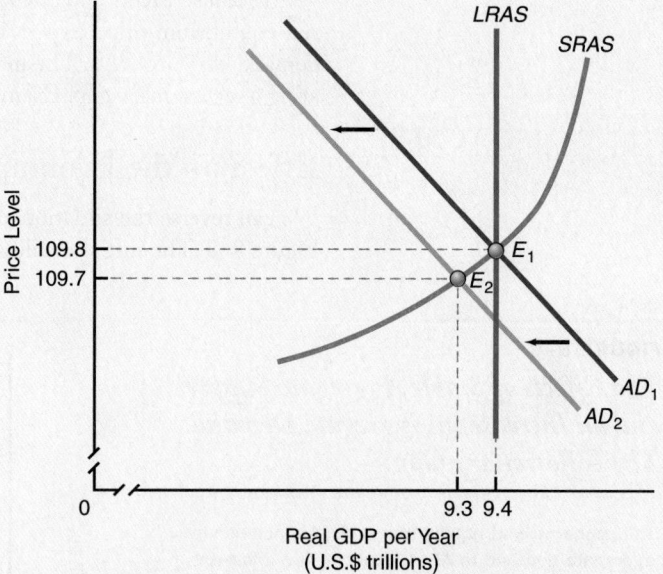

Why didn't the same thing happen in Canada? Because Canadian businesses were much slower to invest in the Internet and other computer-related industries, the change in spending was much smaller. Some well-known Canadian firms, however, did suffer greatly. Nortel Networks, a supplier of communications and Internet-related equipment, was dramatically affected. At one time, worth almost as much as the rest of the shares traded on the Toronto Stock Exchange (TSE), Nortel fell from a share value of over \$100 to less than \$1!

For critical analysis: What would have happened if the sharp drop in business investment had continued for much longer?

8.4 The Long-Run Adjustment Process

In the short run, it is possible for us to be on the *SRAS* to the right or left of the intersection of the *AD* and *LRAS*, thereby reflecting an output gap. Economists believe, however, that this situation *will not* persist in the long run.

Look at Figure 8–10. In this diagram, the economy initially has a real GDP greater than the $1200 billion year that would be consistent with long-run aggregate supply. While there is no excess demand for the final products that firms are making, firms *are* operating at a rate beyond their long-run desired capacity, and there is excess demand for inputs (shown as E_1). *Because of this excess demand for resource inputs* (such as labour), *the price of those inputs begins to rise.* When this happens, we can no longer stay with the same *SRAS* because it was drawn with input prices held constant. Higher input prices cause the *SRAS* to shift left. With no other intervention, the economy will adjust back to the long-run potential at E_2. Note that it is *not* primarily a problem of inventory that is pushing firms to adjust their output, but rather what is happening in the *input* markets that makes this adjustment happen.

If the economy finds itself on *SRAS* below and to the left of the intersection of *AD* and *LRAS*, the opposite will occur. Firms are operating well below long-run capacity, and there are too many unemployed inputs. Input prices will, in the long run, begin to fall. We can no longer stay with the same *SRAS* because it was drawn with constant input prices. *SRAS* will shift right.

The Problem of "Sticky" Wages

Many economists have come to believe that the long-run adjustment process does not work the same way for recessionary and inflationary gaps. The problem lies in trying to get labour (the major cost of inputs in the economy) to reduce its real wages in a recessionary gap. Economists believe that this is much harder than giving workers an increased real wage when an inflationary gap exists. Why? There are several reasons.

Wage contracts provide a considerable degree of certainty to wages. Many union contracts run several years in length, so companies cannot cut wage costs when prices fall. Such contracts provide for workforce adjustment through a layoff process but rarely allow for flexibility in pay rates. Even in the nonunion sector, wages are not usually adjusted more than once per year.

FIGURE 8–10

Real GDP per Year

The economy is initially at E_1. The inflationary gap in the economy will mean that input prices will rise, thereby shifting the SRAS back to E_2 in the long run.

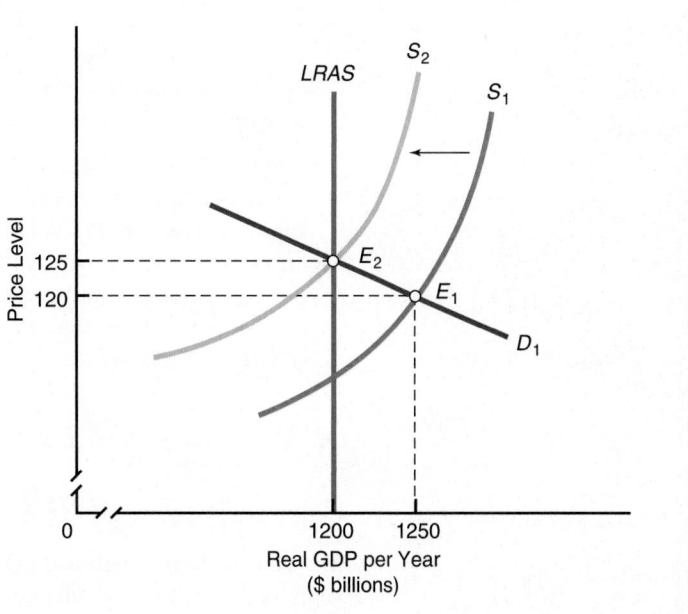

Employers may also be reluctant to reduce wages because of its effect on morale and efficiency. A high real wage may be what is called an *efficiency wage* because it encourages workers to be more productive. Lowering wages in this situation could result in a loss of productivity that offsets any gains resulting from a lower wage rate. Rising wages, of course, reduce the advantage of higher productivity, as explained in Example 8-3.

In an inflationary gap, the situation is not reversed for the workers. When wages are rising, firms may be forced to offer pay raises or lose their workers. Workers cannot be forced to stay working for a firm and are always permitted to quit their job (slavery has been outlawed!) if offered a higher wage elsewhere. Thus, the adjustment process may operate much more quickly for an inflationary gap than a recessionary one.

EXAMPLE 8-3   **Rising Labour Costs Reduce Productivity Gains**

Labour productivity growth in Canada has generally been weak throughout the 2000s, so media observers were glad to see that productivity was rising in the early part of 2007. At the same time, however, the costs of labour were rising even faster. Productivity was growing at a rate of 0.7 percent in the first quarter, but labour costs rose even faster, by 1.4 percent. As a result, the unit labour costs (as measured by the cost of wages and benefits of workers per unit of economic output) still rose 0.7 percent in the quarter, which caused some consternation amongst observers. They point out that the last time unit labour costs were rising so quickly, the Bank of Canada went on an "interest rate rampage" to squeeze out inflation and ended up pushing Canada into a recession.

For critical analysis: Why are unit labour costs considered an indicator of inflationary pressure?

SOURCES: "THE DAILY" STATISTICS CANADA, JUNE 12, 2007; http://0-www.statcan.ca.innopac.lib.bcit.ca/Daily/English/070612/d070612a.htm. "WAGE COSTS DULL OUTPUT'S EDGE", BY ERIC BEAUCHESNE, THE VANCOUVER SUN, JUNE 13, 2007 PAGE D9

➤ CONCEPTS IN BRIEF

Learning Objective 8.3: Evaluate the effects of aggregate demand and supply shocks on equilibrium real output in the short run.

- Short-run equilibrium occurs at the intersection of the aggregate demand curve, *AD*, and the short-run aggregate supply curve, *SRAS*. Any unanticipated shifts in aggregate demand or supply are called aggregate demand shocks or aggregate supply shocks.
- When aggregate demand shifts left while aggregate supply is stable, a recessionary gap can occur, defined as the difference between the equilibrium level of real GDP and how much the economy could be producing if it were operating on its *LRAS*. The reverse situation leads to an inflationary gap.

Learning Objective 8.4: Explain the long-run adjustment process.

- Long-run equilibrium occurs at the intersection of *AD* and the long-run aggregate supply curve, *LRAS*. Whenever an output gap is created in the short run, the economy will eventually close that gap through a long-run adjustment process. The process happens because of excess demand or excess supply in input markets.
- Economists believe that a recessionary gap may take much longer to close than an inflationary gap because of "sticky" wages.

8.5 *Aggregate Demand and Supply in an Open Economy*

In many of the international examples in the preceding chapters, we had to translate foreign currencies into Canadian dollars when the open economy was discussed. We used the exchange rate, or the price of the dollar relative to other currencies. In Chapter 6, you also

FIGURE 8–12

The Effects of Stable Aggregate Demand and a Decrease in Aggregate Supply: Supply-Side Inflation

If aggregate demand remains stable but $SRAS_1$ shifts to $SRAS_2$, equilibrium changes from E_1 to E_2. The price level rises from 120 to 125. If there are continual decreases in aggregate supply of this nature, the situation is called cost-push inflation.

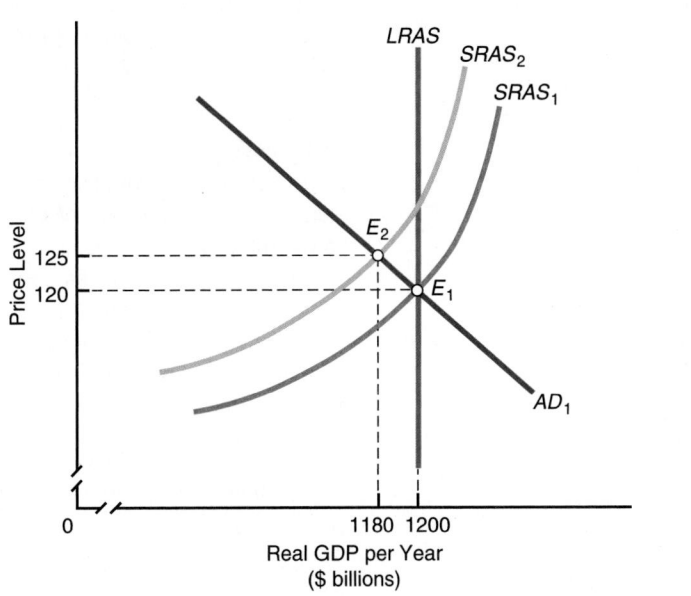

EXAMPLE 8–5   **The Effect of World War I**

One way we can show what happens to the equilibrium price level and the equilibrium real GDP level with an aggregate demand shock is to consider the effect on Canada's economy of fighting World War I (1914–18) in Europe. In Figure 8–13, you see the equilibrium price level of 133 (1900 = 100) and the equilibrium real GDP level of $1.8 billion at the long-run aggregate supply curve. The war effort shifts aggregate demand from AD_{prewar} to $AD_{World War I}$. Equilibrium moves from E_1 to E_2, and the price level moves from 133 to 176. The short-run equilibrium real GDP increases to $2.3 billion per year by 1917. The government's spending for the war caused AD to shift outward to the right. Also note that the war effort temporarily pushed the economy above its long-run aggregate supply curve.

FIGURE 8–13 *The Effects of War on Equilibrium*

World War I shifted aggregate demand to $AD_{World War I}$. Equilibrium moved from E_1 to E_2 temporarily, creating demand-pull inflation.

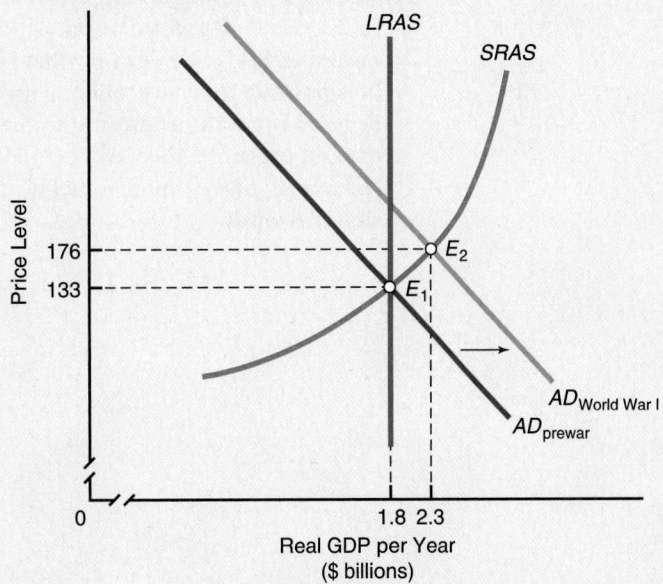

For critical analysis: What would have happened if World War I had lasted for 10 years instead of four? How would you show it on Figure 8–13?

EXAMPLE 8-6	Why Have Unemployment Rates Fallen in North America with only Low Rates of Inflation?

The American economy hovered around a 4 percent unemployment rate through the latter part of the 1990s. With such a low rate of unemployment, many economists have been wondering if the natural rate of unemployment (and the associated *LRAS*) has changed to a lower rate. Some economists are now suggesting that businesses have altered their methods of doing business so much that the shortages of labour have forced businesses to improve their productivity. In doing so, the *LRAS* curve is also shifting, and this is showing up as improved productivity in the United States and in Canada as well. Coming at the end of a long period of slow productivity growth, these improvements in productivity have been very welcome.

For critical analysis: What might happen to wages and inflation if productivity growth does not continue into the future but the unemployment rate continues to be low?

➤ CONCEPTS IN BRIEF

Learning Objective 8.5: Explain how an open economy affects aggregate demand and aggregate supply.

- A change in the international value of the dollar can affect both the *SRAS* and aggregate demand.
- A stronger dollar will reduce the cost of imported inputs, thereby causing the *SRAS* to shift outward to the right, leading to a lower price level and a higher equilibrium real GDP per year, given no change in aggregate demand.
- In contrast, a stronger dollar will lead to lower net exports, causing the aggregate demand curve to shift inward, leading to a lower price level and a lower equilibrium real GDP per year. The net effect depends on which shift is more important. The opposite analysis applies to a weakening dollar in international currency markets.

Learning Objective 8.6: Explain short-run inflation in the economy.

- With stable aggregate supply, an abrupt rightward shift in *AD* may lead to what is called demand-pull inflation. With a stable aggregate demand, an abrupt shift inward in *SRAS* may lead to what is called cost-push inflation.
- It is possible to have economic growth with or without inflation. If the aggregate demand curve shifts outward to the right at the same speed as the short-run aggregate supply curve, there will be no inflation accompanying economic growth. If the *AD* curve moves more quickly, there will be inflation and growth occurring simultaneously.

Oil Price Changes Shock the North American Economy

Concepts Applied: Aggregate Supply Shock, Short-Run Aggregate Supply Curve, Cost-Push Inflation

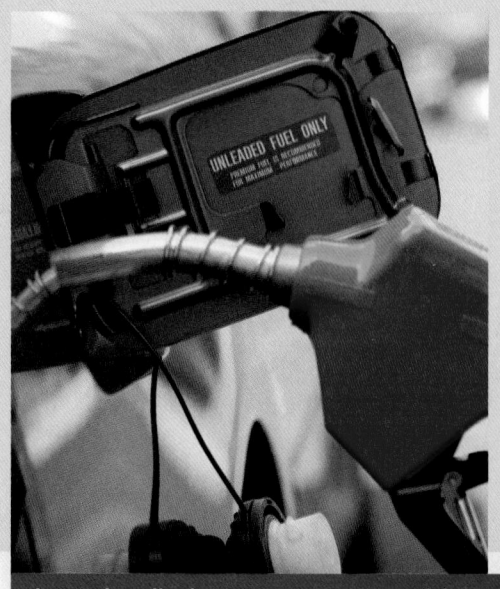

Increasing oil prices are a common complaint among consumers, but have not been as detrimental to the economy as many predicted.

As crude oil prices rose by more than U.S.$70 per barrel during the years following 1999, many commentators in the media compared the oil price run-up and its possible macroeconomic effects to North American experiences in the 1970s. Some predicted that the resulting aggregate supply shock would generate both sharply lower—and possibly negative—real GDP growth and a potentially sharp spike in inflation in oil-consuming nations.

In the end, the media commentators got it wrong. Real GDP growth rates into 2007 were respectable, and inflation rates remain close to those experienced in the 1990s.

An Aggregate Supply Shock Indeed

Crude oil is an important factor of production. It is refined to produce gasoline and heating oils that are important sources of energy. In addition, processed oil is used to lubricate machinery, and it is an input to the production of many plastics and chemical products. Consequently, substantial increases in oil prices push up production costs for many businesses, resulting in less-planned production of goods and services at any given price level. The result is a leftward shift in the short-run aggregate supply curve—an aggregate supply shock like the one we modelled in Figure 8–12.

Oil Prices Must be Adjusted for Inflation

So where did the media commentators go wrong? The first mistake they made was they did not adjust for inflation, and they confused real and nominal prices. As part (a) in Figure 8–14 indicates, this was an important oversight. Certainly, the nominal price of oil was higher in the 2000s than ever before. Once inflation is taken into account, however, it is clear that even as late as 2007, inflation-adjusted oil prices had not matched the peak reached in the early 1980s.

Reduced Sensitivity of U.S. Aggregate Supply to Oil Price Changes

Another important fact that was overlooked is that today's producers are less reliant on oil than producers were in the 1970s. To see this, take a look at part (b) of Figure 8–14. As you can see, in the 1970s about 1.3 barrels of oil were required to produce $1000 worth of real GDP, measured in 2006 dollars. Today, because items such as services and digital products are a larger share of real GDP than manufactured goods, only a little over 0.6 barrel of oil is required to produce the same amount of real GDP.

This drop in oil usage per unit of real GDP produced has had the effect of making U.S. aggregate supply less sensitive to oil price changes. A given increase in the inflation-adjusted price of oil during the 2000s reduces aggregate supply by much less than the same price increase did in the 1970s. As a consequence, oil-price induced aggregate supply shocks are smaller today than they were back then.

Effect on the Canadian Economy

Overall, the Canadian economy has not been much affected by this rise in prices either, but the effects on individual industries have been relatively large. Canada, as the largest exporter of oil to the United States, has benefited from the higher prices. Canada's oil and gas sectors, centred in Alberta, have been booming throughout this period and growth rates there have exceeded the rest of the country. From Alberta's point of view, this oil price increase represents a tremendous increase in aggregate demand, and the

FIGURE 8–14

Inflation–Adjusted Oil Prices and Oil's Role in Producing Real GDP

Part (a) shows that although inflation-adjusted oil prices increased considerably during the 2000s, they remained below the peak reached in the early 1980s. Part (b) indicates that the amount of oil used to produce $1000 worth of real GDP in the U.S. has declined over time.

SOURCE: U.S. DEPARTMENT OF ENERGY

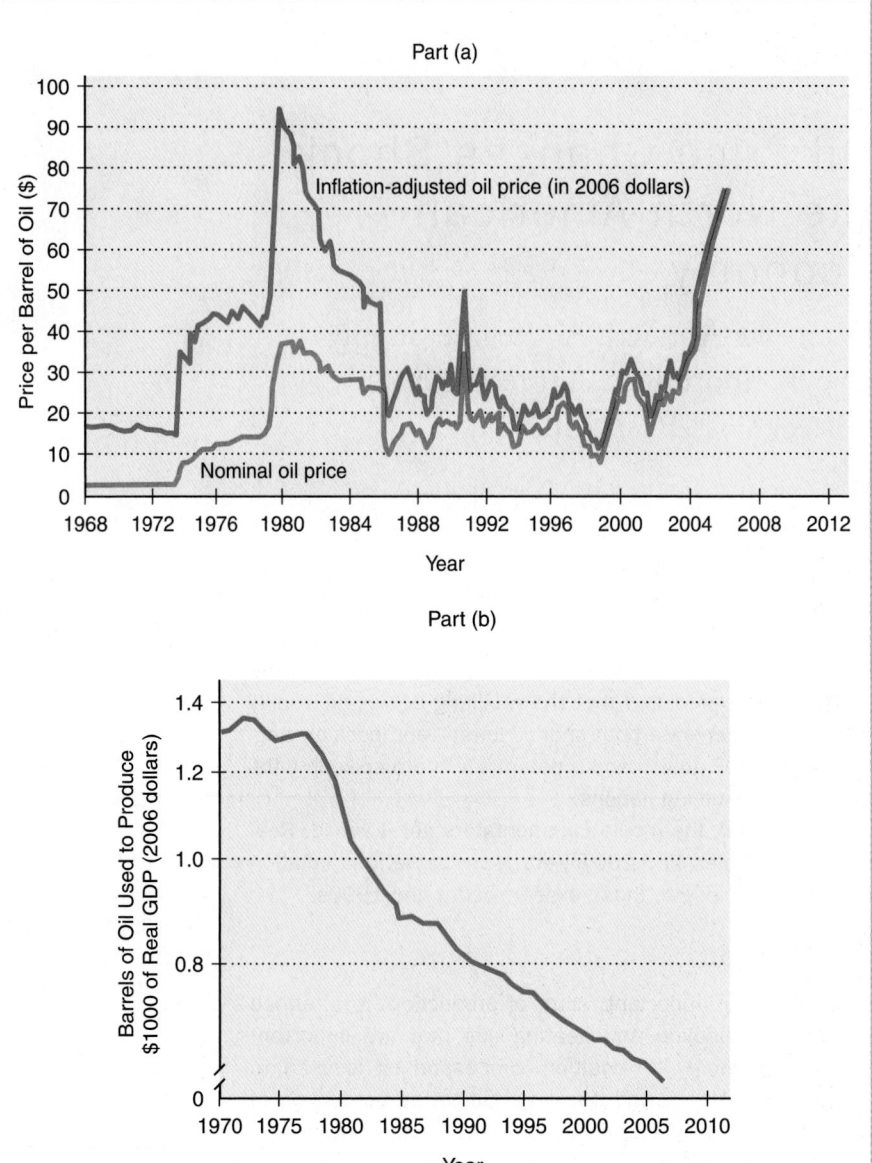

producers are hard pressed to boost their capacity to meet this demand. In Fort McMurray, where the tar sands produces much of Canadian oil, there have been tremendous problems finding enough workers, and the increased demand has driven a tremendous multi-billion-dollar investment expenditure by oil companies seeking to extract more oil.

In other parts of the country, however, the growth of oil prices has caused problems because those areas are dependent upon oil as an important resource. Furthermore, demand from the United States has been steady as well, unlike the situation in the 1970s. On the downside, for manufacturing centred in Ontario and Quebec, the cost of energy has soared. However, the sale of Canada's resources abroad has driven up the Canadian dollar, reducing the value of those exports. On top of that, the Alberta economy has attracted so many workers from across the country that unemployment has fallen to new lows in provinces not experiencing the

energy boom, making labour more expensive. All of these factors point to a supply shock.

In summary, the overall effect of higher oil prices has generally been positive for Canada. The demand effects have outweighed the supply effects, kept the unemployment rate in Canada low, kept the GDP rising, and had only small effects on the inflation rate.

For critical analysis:

1. Use the *SRAS* model to analyze the effect of rising oil prices on the Canadian economy. Separate out the effects on the demand side from those on the supply side and refer to the non-price determinants of each in your explanation. Be sure to reference the article in your explanation. Use diagrams in your answer.

⇒→ SUMMARY

Here is what you should know after reading this chapter. MyEconLab will help you identify what you know, and where to go when you need to practise. We suggest that as soon as you review one of the Learning Objective sections below, you then proceed to go through the related section in MyEconLab.

(X) **myeconlab**

⇒→ LEARNING OBJECTIVES	KEY TERMS	MYECONLAB PRACTICE
8.1 The Short-run Aggregate Supply Curve. In the short run, we assume that the prices of inputs and the available capital and equipment are fixed, while the price of output is variable. In the short run, real GDP can increase by using existing capital more intensively and hiring more labour and other variable inputs. Firms experience a temporary rise in profitability when their output prices rise but their input costs remain constant. This induces them to produce more in the short run and move along the short-run aggregate supply curve.	short-run aggregate supply, 208 short-run aggregate supply curve, 209 capacity utilization, 210	• **MyEconLab** Study Plan 8.1
8.2 Shifts in the Aggregate Supply Curves. A widespread change in the prices of factors of production—for example, an economywide change in wages can cause a shift in the short-run aggregate supply curve without affecting the long-run aggregate supply curve. Both the long-run aggregate supply curve and the short-run aggregate supply curve shift in response to changes in the availability of resources, labour, or capital, or to changes in technology and productivity.		• **MyEconLab** Study Plan 8.2
8.3 Equilibrium. An aggregate demand/ supply shock that causes the aggregate demand/supply curve to shift leftward pushes equilibrium real output below the full employment output level in the short run so that there is a recessionary gap. An aggregate demand/ supply shock that induces a rightward shift in the aggregate demand/supply curve results in an inflationary gap.	aggregate demand shock, 216 aggregate supply shock, 216 output gap, 216 recessionary gap, 216 inflationary gap, 216	• **MyEconLab** Study Plan 8.3
8.4 The Long-Run Adjustment Process. In the long run, the economy will adjust back to the intersection of the long-run aggregate supply and aggregate demand curves because of the disequilibrium in the input markets. With an inflationary gap, the costs of inputs will rise in the long run, moving the short-run aggregate supply back to potential output. With a recessionary gap, the costs of inputs will fall, moving the short-run aggregate supply up to potential output. Economists believe that the		• **MyEconLab** Study Plan 8.4

➡ LEARNING OBJECTIVES	KEY TERMS	MYECONLAB PRACTICE
long-run adjustment process acts more slowly on a recessionary gap than an inflationary gap because of "sticky" wages.		
8.5 Aggregate Demand and Supply in an Open Economy. Changes in the value of the Canadian dollar affect both aggregate supply and aggregate demand simultaneously. Aggregate supply is affected because many inputs (such as car parts from the United States) are purchased from other countries. Aggregate demand is affected because Canada sells many exports to other countries and imports many finished products from abroad. A rising Canadian dollar will tend to have a strong deflationary effect on the Canadian economy and will tend to raise unemployment because the aggregate demand effects tend to outweigh the aggregate supply effects.		• **MyEconLab** Study Plan 8.5
8.6 Inflation in the Short Run. Demand-pull inflation occurs when aggregate demand increases create an inflationary gap. Cost-push inflation occurs when supply shocks create a recessionary gap.	demand-pull inflation, 222 cost-push inflation, 222	• **MyEconLab** Study Plan 8.6

➡ PROBLEMS

LO 8.1 Explain the concept of the short-run aggregate supply curve.

1. Distinguish between short-run and long-run aggregate supply curves.

2. What determines how much real output responds to changes in the price level along the short-run aggregate supply curve?

LO 8.2 Understand what factors cause shifts in the short-run and long-run aggregate supply curves.

3. Suppose that aggregate supply decreases while aggregate demand is held constant.
   a. What happens to the price level?
   b. What happens to national output?

LO 8.3 Evaluate the effects of aggregate demand and supply shocks on equilibrium real output in the short run.

4. Given the curves in the accompanying graph, discuss why the equilibrium price level will be at P_e and not P_1 or P_2.

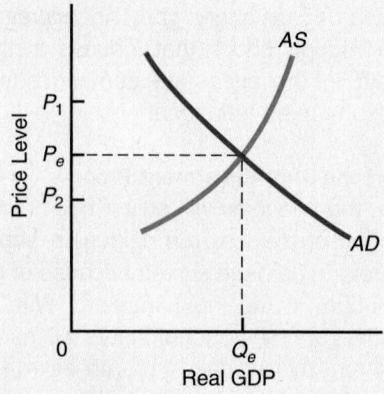

5. Natural disasters, such as an ice storm or a flood, occur frequently in Canada. They often destroy many buildings

and, occasionally, such as in earthquakes, kill many people. Model this disaster using the aggregate demand and supply curves. Be sure to distinguish the effects on the short-run and long-run aggregate supply curves.

6. Explain the effects of each of the following factors on the economy's price level and real GDP. Illustrate your explanations with appropriate diagrams.
   a. A rise in the value of the domestic currency relative to other world currencies
   b. An increase in the real interest rate
   c. A decrease in taxes
   d. A rise in incomes of Canadians
   e. An increase in the investment in technology

7. Suppose that there is a stock market crash in an economy with an upward-sloping short-run aggregate supply curve, and consumer and business confidence plummets. What are the short-run effects on the equilibrium price level?

LO 8.4 Explain the long-run adjustment process.

8. Show the effects of a decrease in aggregate demand in the long-run model, using Figure 8–6. What are the short-run consequences for the economy? Now explain, using diagrams, how the economy will adjust itself to this situation in the long run.

9. At a point along the short-run aggregate supply curve that is to the right of the point where it crosses the long-run supply curve, what must be true of the *actual* unemployment rate relative to the *natural* rate of unemployment? Why?

10. Refer back to Example 8–2, "A Tale of Two Economies." What effect does the drop in business investment have on the *LRAS*?

11. Refer back to Example 8–4, "Rising Canadian Loonie." What would the long-run equilibrium be in this economy if the economy fully adjusted?

LO 8.5 Explain how an open economy affects aggregate demand and aggregate supply.

12. What effect will an economic recession in the European Community have on the economy of Canada? Show how this would be modelled using the aggregate demand and aggregate supply curves.

13. Consider an open economy in which the aggregate supply curve slopes upward in the short run. Firms in this nation do not import raw materials or any other productive inputs from abroad, but foreign residents purchase much of the nation's output. What is the most likely short-run effect on this nation's economy if there is a significant downturn in economic activity in other nations around the world?

LO 8.6 Explain short-run inflation in the economy.

14. Suppose that an upward-sloping short-run aggregate supply curve is applicable for a nation's economy. Use

appropriate diagrams to assist in answering the following questions:
   a. What are two factors that can cause the nation's real GDP to increase in the short run?
   b. What are two factors that can cause the nation's real GDP to increase in the long run?

15. Refer back to Example 8–4, "Rising Canadian Loonie." Why would a lower-valued currency sometimes be called a "beggar thy neighbour" policy (which means that you gain at your "neighbour's" expense)?

16. How is it possible to have short-run shifts in both aggregate demand and *SRAS* curves that result in no inflation in the short run and inflation in the long run?

17. For each question below, suppose that the economy *begins* at the short-run equilibrium point A. Identify which of the other points on the diagram—point B, C, D, or E— could represent a *new* short-run equilibrium after the described events take place and move the economy away from point A. Briefly explain your answers.

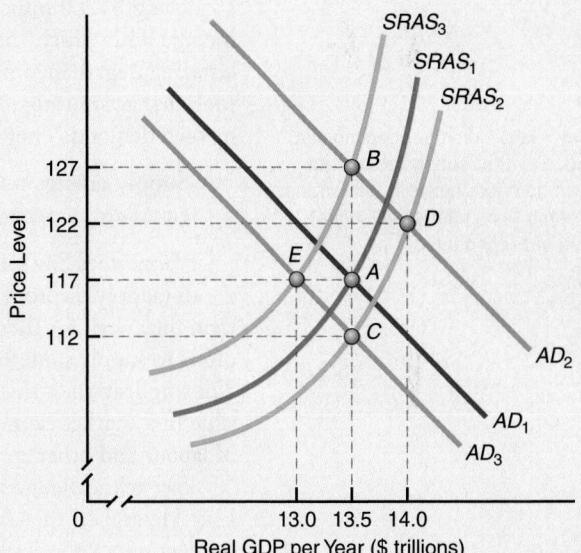

   a. Most workers in this nation's economy are union members, and unions have successfully negotiated large wage boosts. At the same time, economic conditions suddenly worsen abroad, reducing real GDP and disposable income in other nations of the world.
   b. A major hurricane has caused short-term halts in production at many firms and created major bottlenecks in the distribution of goods and services that had been produced prior to the storm. At the same time, the nation's central bank has significantly pushed up the rate of growth of the nation's money supply.
   c. A strengthening of the value of this nation's currency in terms of other countries' currencies affects both the *SRAS* curve and the *AD* curve.

The classical model, which traces its origins to the 1770s, was the first systematic attempt to explain the determinants of the price level and the national levels of output, income, employment, consumption, saving, and investment. The term *classical model* was coined by John Maynard Keynes, a Cambridge University economist, who used it to refer to the way in which earlier economists had analyzed economic aggregates. Classical economists—Adam Smith, J.B. Say, David Ricardo, John Stuart Mill, Thomas Malthus, and others—wrote from the 1770s to the 1870s. They assumed, among other things, that all wages and prices were flexible and that competitive markets existed throughout the economy. Starting in the 1870s, the so-called neoclassical economists, including Alfred Marshall, introduced a mathematical approach that allowed them to refine earlier economists' models.

Say's Law

Every time you produce something for which you receive income, you generate the income necessary to make expenditures on other goods and services. That means that an economy producing $1200 billion of GDP (final goods and services) simultaneously produces the income with which these goods and services can be supplied. As an accounting identity, *actual* aggregate income always equals *actual* aggregate expenditures. Classical economists took that accounting identity one step further by arguing that total national supply creates its own demand. They asserted what has become known as **Say's law:**

Say's law A dictum of economist J.B. Say that supply creates its own demand; hence it follows that *desired* expenditures will equal *actual* expenditures.

> Supply creates its own demand; hence it follows that *desired* expenditures will equal *actual* expenditures.

What does Say's law really mean? It states that the very process of producing specific goods (supply) is proof that other goods are desired (demand). People produce more goods than they want for their own use only if they seek to trade them for other goods. Someone offers to supply something only because that person also has a demand for something else. The implication of this, according to Say, is that no general glut, or overproduction, is possible in a market economy. From this reasoning, it seems to follow that full employment of labour and other resources would be the normal state of affairs in such an economy.

Say acknowledged that an oversupply of some goods might occur in particular markets. He argued that such surpluses would simply cause prices to fall, thereby decreasing production in the long run. The opposite would occur in markets in which shortages temporarily appeared.

All this seems reasonable enough in a simple barter economy in which households produce most of the goods they need and trade for the rest. This is shown in Figure C–1, where there is a simple circular flow. But what about a more sophisticated economy in which people work for others and there is no barter but, rather, the use of money? Can these complications create the possibility of unemployment? And does the fact that labourers receive money income, some of which can be saved, lead to unemployment? No, said the classical economists to these last two questions. They based their reasoning on a number of key assumptions.

Assumptions of the Classical Model

The classical model makes four major assumptions:

1. *Pure competition exists.* No single buyer or seller of a commodity or an input can affect its price.
2. *Wages and prices are flexible.* The assumption of pure competition leads to the notion that prices, wages, interest rates, and the like are free to move to whatever level supply and

FIGURE C–1

Say's Law and the Circular Flow

Here, we show the circular flow of income and output. The very act of supplying a certain level of goods and services necessarily equals the level of goods and services demanded, in Say's simplified world.

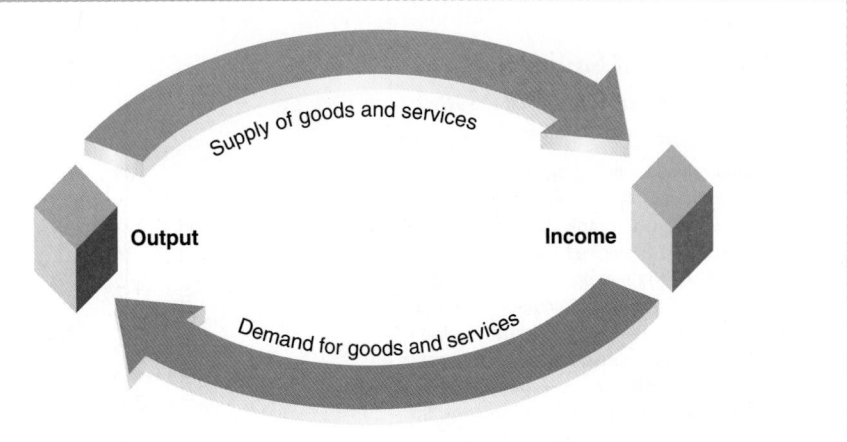

Money illusion Buyers and sellers react to changes in nominal prices and income rather than to changes in real prices and income.

demand dictate (in the long run). Although no *individual* buyer can set a price, the community of buyers or sellers can cause prices to rise or to fall to an equilibrium level.

3. *People are motivated by self-interest.* Businesses want to maximize their profits, and households want to maximize their economic well-being.

4. *People cannot be fooled by money illusion.* Buyers and sellers react to changes in nominal prices and income rather than to changes in real prices and income. That is to say, they do not suffer from **money illusion**. For example, workers will not be fooled into thinking they are better off by a doubling of wages if the price level has also doubled during the same time period.

The classical economists concluded, after taking account of the four major assumptions, that the role of government in the economy should be minimal. If all prices, wages, and markets are flexible, any problems in the macroeconomy will be temporary. The market will come to the rescue and correct itself.

Equilibrium in Financial Markets

When income is saved, it is not reflected in product demand. It is a type of *leakage* in the circular flow of income and output because saving withdraws funds from the income stream. Consumption expenditures can fall short of total output now. In such a situation, it does not appear that supply necessarily creates its own demand.

The classical economists did not believe that the complicating factor of saving in the circular flow model of income and output was a problem. They contended that each dollar saved would be invested by businesses so that the leakage of saving would be matched by the injection of business investment. *Investment* here refers only to additions to the nation's capital stock. The classical economists believed that businesses as a group would tend to invest as much as households wanted to save. Equilibrium between the saving plans of consumers and the investment plans of businesses comes about, in the classical economists' world, through the working of the credit market. In the financial markets, the *price* of credit is the interest rate. At equilibrium, the price of credit—the interest rate—is such that the quantity of credit demanded equals the quantity of credit supplied. Planned investment just equals planned saving, for saving represents the supply of credit and investment represents the demand for credit.

THE INTEREST RATE: EQUATING DESIRED SAVING AND INVESTMENT. In Figure C–2, the vertical axis measures the rate of interest in percentage terms; on the horizontal axis are the quantities of desired saving and desired investment per-unit time period. The desired saving curve is really a supply curve of saving. It shows how much individuals and businesses wish to save at various interest rates. People want to save more at higher interest rates than at lower interest rates.

Investment, primarily desired by businesses, responds in a predictable way. The higher the rate of interest, the more expensive it is to invest and the lower the level of desired

The demand curve for investment is labelled "Desired investment." The supply of resources used for investment occurs when individuals do not consume, but save instead. The desired saving curve is shown as an upward-sloping supply curve of saving. The equilibrating force here is, of course, the interest rate. At higher interest rates, people desire to save more. But at higher interest rates, businesses demand less investment because it is more expensive to invest. In this model, at an interest rate of 5 percent, the quantity of investment desired just equals the quantity of saving desired (supply), which is $70 billion per year.

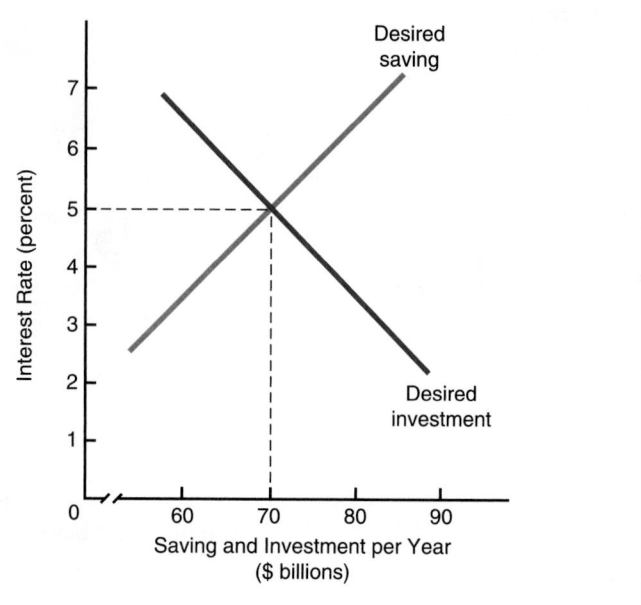

investment. The desired investment curve slopes downward. In this simplified model, the equilibrium rate of interest is 5 percent, and the equilibrium quantity of saving and investment is $70 billion per year.

Equilibrium in the Labour Market

Now, consider the labour market. If an excess quantity of labour is supplied at a particular wage level, the wage level is above equilibrium. By accepting lower wages, unemployed workers will quickly be put back to work. We show equilibrium in the labour market in Figure C–3.

Equilibrium of $12 per hour and 13.5 million workers employed represents full-employment equilibrium. If the wage rate were $14 an hour, there would be unemployment—14.5 million workers would want to work, but businesses would want to hire only

The demand for labour is downward sloping; at higher wage rates, firms will employ fewer workers. The supply of labour is upward sloping; at higher wage rates, more workers will work longer and more people will be willing to work. The equilibrium wage rate is $12, with an equilibrium employment per year of 13.5 million workers.

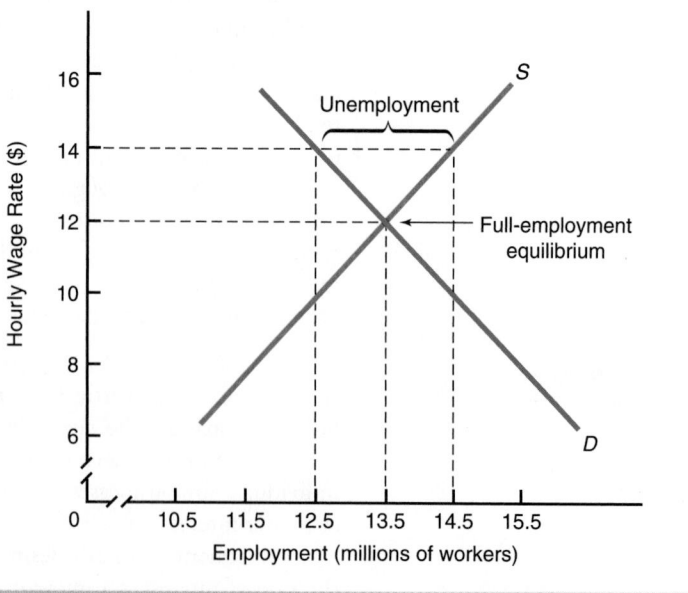

12.5 million. In the classical model, this unemployment is eliminated rather rapidly by wage rates dropping back to $12 per hour.

THE RELATIONSHIP BETWEEN EMPLOYMENT AND REAL GDP. Employment is not simply some isolated figure that government statisticians estimate. Rather, the level of employment in an economy determines its real GDP (output), other things held constant. A hypothetical relationship between input (number of employees) and output (rate of real GDP per year) is shown in Table C–1. We have highlighted the row that has 13.5 million workers per year as the labour input. That might be considered a hypothetical level of full employment, and it is related to a rate of real GDP of $1200 billion per year.

TABLE C-1

The Relationship between Employment and Real GDP Classical Theory, Vertical Aggregate Supply, and the Price Level

Labour Input per Year (millions of workers)	Real GDP per Year ($ billions)
9.8	900
10.4	1000
12.0	1100
13.5	1200
14.5	1300
16.0	1400

In the classical model, long-term unemployment is impossible. Say's law, coupled with flexible interest rates, prices, and wages, would always tend to keep workers fully employed so that the aggregate supply curve, as shown in Figure C–4, is vertical at Y_0. We have labelled the supply curve *LRAS*, consistent with the long-run aggregate supply curve introduced in Chapter 6. It was defined there as the quantity of output that would be produced in an economy with full information and full adjustment of wages and prices year in and year out. In the classical model, this happens to be the *only* aggregate supply curve that exists in equilibrium. Everything adjusts so fast that we are essentially always on or quickly moving toward *LRAS*. Furthermore, because the labour market is working well, Y_0 is always at, or soon to be at, full employment. Full employment is defined as the amount of employment that would exist year in and year out if all parties in the labour market fully anticipated any inflation or deflation that was occurring. Full employment does not mean zero unemployment because there is always some frictional unemployment (discussed in Chapter 4), even in the classical world.

FIGURE C–4

Classical Theory and Increases in Aggregate Demand

The classical theorists believed that Say's law and flexible interest rates, prices, and wages would always lead to full employment at Y_0 along the vertical aggregate supply curve, *LRAS*. With aggregate demand, AD_1, the price level is 100. An increase in aggregate demand shifts AD_1 to AD_2. At price level 110, the quantity of real GDP per year demanded is A on AD_2, or Y_1. But this is greater than at full employment. Prices rise, and the economy quickly moves from E_1 to E_2 at the higher price level of 110.

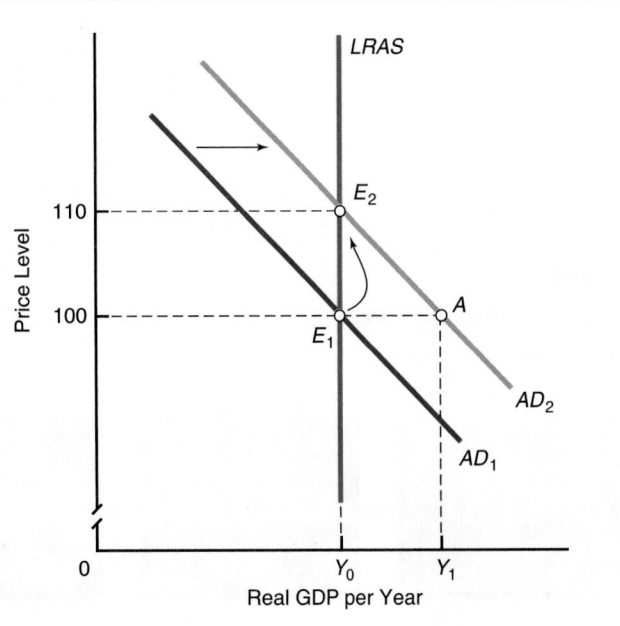

EFFECT OF AN INCREASE IN AGGREGATE DEMAND IN THE CLASSICAL MODEL. In this model, any change in aggregate demand will soon cause a change in the price level. Consider starting at E_1, at price level 100. If the aggregate demand shifts to AD_2, at price level 100, output would increase to Y_1. But that is greater than the full-employment level of output of real GDP, Y_0. The economy will attempt to get to point A, but because this is beyond full employment, prices will rise, and the economy will find itself back on the vertical *LRAS* at point E_2 at a higher price level, 110. The price level will increase at output rates in excess of the full-employment level of output because employers will end up bidding up wages for now more relatively scarce workers. In addition, factories will be bidding up the price of other inputs at this greater-than-full-employment rate of output.

The level of real GDP per year clearly does not depend on any changes in aggregate demand. Hence, we say that in the classical model, the equilibrium level of real GDP per year is completely *supply determined*. Changes in aggregate demand affect only the price level, not the output of real goods and services.

EFFECT OF A DECREASE IN AGGREGATE DEMAND IN THE CLASSICAL MODEL. The effect of a decrease in aggregate demand in the classical model is the converse of the analysis just presented for an increase in aggregate demand. You can simply reverse AD_2 and AD_1 in Figure C–4. To help you see how this analysis works, consider the flowchart in Figure C–5.

Keynesian Economics and the Keynesian Short-Run Aggregate Supply Curve

The classical economists' world was one of fully utilized resources. There would be no unused capacity and no unemployment. However, post–World War I Europe entered a period of long-term economic decline that could not be explained by the classical model. John Maynard Keynes developed an explanation that has since become known as the Keynesian model, which presented an explanation of the Great Depression in the 1930s. Keynes argued that if we are in a world in which there are large amounts of excess capacity and unemployment, a positive aggregate demand shock will not raise prices and a negative aggregate demand shock will not cause firms to lower prices. This situation is depicted in Figure C–6. The short-run equilibrium starts with aggregate demand at AD_1, the equilibrium level of real GDP per year will be Y_1 and the equilibrium price level will be P_0. If there is an aggregate demand shock such that the aggregate demand curve shifts outward to the right, to AD_2, the equilibrium price level will not change; only the equilibrium level of real GDP per year will increase, to Y_2. Conversely, if there is an aggregate demand shock that shifts the aggregate demand curve to AD_3, the equilibrium price level will again remain at P_0, but the equilibrium level of real GDP per year will fall to Y_3.

Under such circumstances, the equilibrium level of real GDP per year is completely *demand determined*. The horizontal short-run aggregate supply curve represented in

---

FIGURE C–5

Effect of a Decrease in Aggregate Demand in the Classical Model

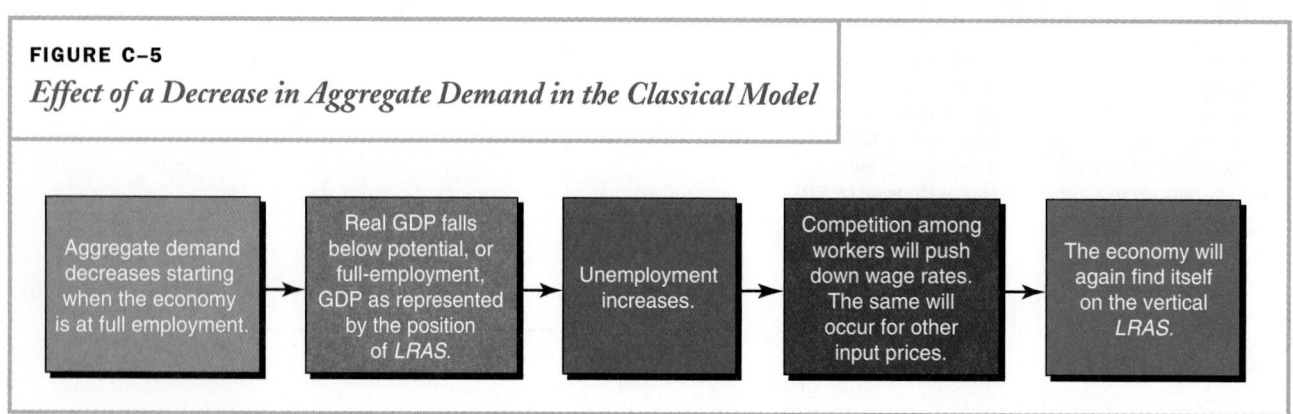

FIGURE C–6
Demand-Determined Equilibrium

If we assume that prices will not fall when aggregate demand falls and that there is excess capacity so that prices will not rise when aggregate demand increases, the short-run aggregate supply curve is simply a horizontal line at the given price level, P_0, represented by *SRAS*. An aggregate demand shock that increases aggregate demand to AD_2 will increase the equilibrium level of real GDP per year to Y_2. An aggregate demand shock that decreases aggregate demand to AD_3 will decrease equilibrium level of real GDP to Y_3. The equilibrium price level will not change.

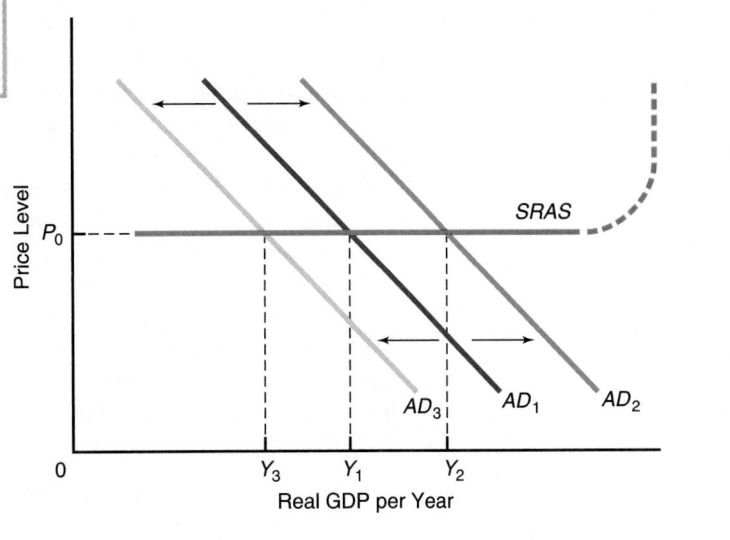

Keynesian short-run aggregate supply curve The horizontal portion of the aggregate supply curve in which there is unemployment and unused capacity in the economy.

Figure C–7 is often called the **Keynesian short-run aggregate supply curve**—the horizontal portion of the aggregate supply curve in which there is unemployment and unused capacity in the economy. It is so named because Keynes hypothesized that many prices, especially the price of labour (wages), are "sticky downward." According to Keynes, the existence of unions and of long-term contracts between workers are real-world factors that can explain the downward inflexibility of *nominal* wage rates. Such "stickiness" of wages makes *involuntary* unemployment of labour a distinct possibility. The classical assumption of everlasting full employment no longer holds.

Further, even in situations of excess capacity and large amounts of unemployment, we will not necessarily see the price level falling; rather, all we will see is continuing unemployment and a reduction in the equilibrium level of real GDP per year. Thus, general economywide equilibrium can occur and endure even if there is excess capacity. Keynes and his followers argued that capitalism was, therefore, not necessarily a self-regulating system sustaining full employment. At the time, Keynes was attacking the classical view of the world, which argued that markets would all eventually be in equilibrium—prices and wages would adjust—so that full employment would never be far away.

FIGURE C–7
Keynesian Analysis of the Great Depression

Aggregate demand dropped from AD_{1929} to AD_{1933}. The price level would have had to drop to point *A* on *LRAS* in order to avoid unemployment. In reality, it did not, so the new equilibrium shifted from E_1 to E_2. By 1933, the economy was operating at about 20 percent below its potential output.

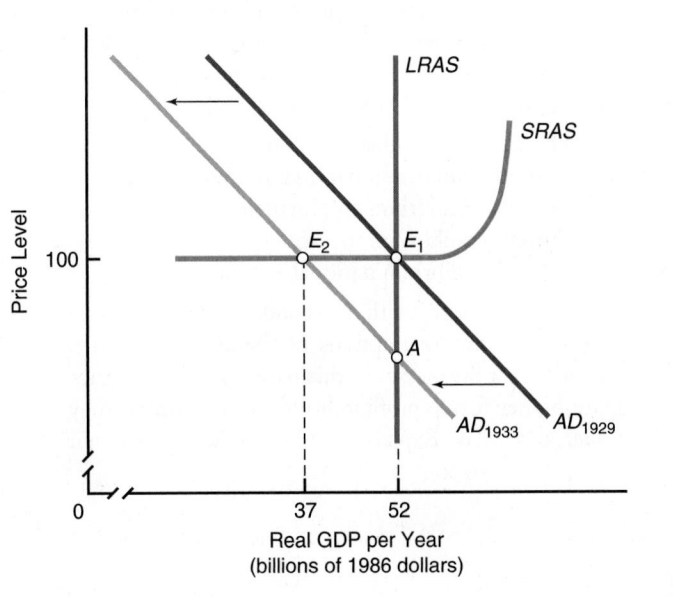

Keynesian Analysis of the Great Depression

At the beginning of 1929, the Canadian economy was doing quite well, with the unemployment rate hovering around 3 percent. A year later, it was over 9 percent, and by 1933, it had climbed to almost 20 percent. The real GDP of 1929 was not reached again until 1937, when another business downturn hit the economy. We use the Keynesian analysis shown in Figure C–7 to illustrate what happened.

Aggregate demand to start with in 1929 is AD_{1929}. According to Keynesian theory, the economy experienced a dramatic reduction in aggregate demand, represented by a shift to AD_{1933}. To prevent massive unemployment, wages and prices would have to have fallen such that a new equilibrium would have been at point A on the $LRAS$. Even though many wages and prices did fall, they did not fall sufficiently to reach such a point. Consequently, a new equilibrium was established at E_2. Real GDP fell from about $52 billion to $37 billion (expressed in 1986 dollars). By 1933, the economy was operating about 20 percent below its potential output (represented by $LRAS$).

APPENDIX PROBLEMS

(Answers to the odd-numbered problems appear at the back of the book.)

C-1. The desired investment curve intersects the desired saving curve in the economy at an interest rate of 8 percent. The current market rate of interest is 9 percent. Outline what will now take place in the economy so that the saving and investment market is in equilibrium.

C-2. Look at Figure C–3 again. At a wage rate of $12 per hour, 13.5 million workers are employed. This is called full-employment equilibrium. Does that mean there is no unemployment?

C-3. Consider a country whose economic structure matches the assumptions of the classical model. After reading a recent best-seller documenting a growing population of low-income elderly people who were ill-prepared for retirement, most residents of this country decide to increase their saving at any given interest rate. Explain whether or how this could affect the following:

a. The current equilibrium interest rate
b. Current equilibrium national output
c. Current equilibrium employment
d. Current equilibrium investment
e. Future equilibrium national output

C-4. Consider a country with an economic structure consistent with the assumptions of the classical model. Suppose that businesses in this nation suddenly anticipate higher future profitability from investment they undertake today. Explain whether or how this could affect the following:

a. The current equilibrium interest rate
b. Current equilibrium national output
c. Current equilibrium employment
d. Current equilibrium saving
e. Future equilibrium national output

C-5. "There is *absolutely no distinction* between the classical model and the model of long-run equilibrium discussed in Chapter 6." Is this statement true or false? Support your answer.

C-6. Show the effects of a decrease in aggregate demand in the classical model.

C-7. A nation in which the classical model applies experiences a decline in the quantity of money in circulation. Use an appropriate aggregate demand and aggregate supply diagram to explain what happens to equilibrium output an to the equilibrium price level.

C-8. Suppose that the classical model is appropriate for a country that has suddenly experienced an influx of immigrants who possess a wide variety of employment skills and who have reputations for saving relatively large portions of their incomes, compared with native-born residents, at any given interest rate. Evaluate the effects of this event on the following:

a. Current equilibrium employment
b. Current equilibrium national output
c. The current equilibrium interest rate
d. Current equilibrium investment

![S&P TSX Composite Index display showing 12,857.94 ▼ 190.82]

9

Consumption, Investment, and the Multiplier

➡️ **LEARNING OBJECTIVES**

After reading this chapter, you should be able to:

9.1 Distinguish between saving and savings and explain how saving and consumption are related.

9.2 Explain the key determinants of consumption and saving in the Keynesian model.

9.3 Identify the primary determinants of planned investment.

9.4 Describe how equilibrium GDP is established in the Keynesian model.

9.5 Evaluate why autonomous changes in total planned expenditures have a multiplier effect on equilibrium GDP.

9.6 Understand the relationship between total planned expenditures and the aggregate demand curve.

Whenever you buy a good or a service, you contribute to the largest component of total Canadian expenditures on goods and services. Households' annual consumption expenditure consistently accounts for about 60 percent of real GDP. At the same time, Canadian households own more shares and bonds. Does this mean that stock market volatility will bring about increased variability in aggregate spending? Will big swings in share prices also contribute to gyrations in Canadian GDP? To consider these questions, you must first learn how consumption spending and expenditures by business, governments, and foreigners together affect equilibrium GDP.

MyEconLab helps you master each objective and study more efficiently. See end of chapter for details.

DID YOU KNOW THAT... ?

Stable investment has contributed to a steady increase in GDP for Canada and the U.S. since 1991. Only a short period of decline occurred with the "dot.com" meltdown in 2001 in the United States (we had a milder slowdown in Canada) has occurred in that time frame. However, a new investment crisis is looming in the United States in 2007, the so-called "sub-prime" meltdown in the U.S. housing market. Residential housing investment declined by $140 billion dollars from the beginning of 2006 to the third quarter of 2007, a decline of about 25%. While the decline is obviously affecting the housing construction industry, other areas of the economy have largely been unaffected, and real GDP has continued to climb. How did this investment decline affect the broader economy? Did it spread to Canada?

John Maynard Keynes focused much of his research on how unanticipated changes in investment spending affect a nation's aggregate spending and income. The key to determining the broader economic effects of investment fluctuations, Keynes reasoned, was to understand the relationship between how much people earn and their willingness to engage in personal consumption expenditure. Thus, Keynes argued that a prerequisite to understanding how investment affects a nation's economy is to understand the determinants of household consumption. In this chapter, you will learn about the relationships between income and consumption expenditure and their relationship to investment, government, and foreign expenditures.

9.1 Saving and Consumption

In the Keynesian tradition, we will assume that the short-run aggregate supply curve within the relevant range is horizontal. That is to say, we assume that the equilibrium level of real GDP is entirely demand determined. That is why Keynes wished to examine the elements of desired aggregate expenditures.

Also, for the time being, we will not be concerned with the problem of inflation because, by definition, along the Keynesian short-run aggregate supply curve, inflation is impossible. Finally, given that the price level is assumed to be unchanging, all of the variables with which we will be dealing will be expressed in real terms. After all, with no change in the price level, any change in the magnitude of an economic variable, such as income, will be equivalent to a real change in terms of purchasing power. Hence we will be examining Keynes' income–expenditure model of real GDP determination in a world of inflexible prices.

To simplify the income determination model that follows, a number of assumptions are made:

1. Businesses pay no indirect taxes (for example, sales taxes).
2. Businesses distribute all of their profits to shareholders.
3. There is no depreciation (capital consumption allowance), and so gross private domestic investment equals net investment.
4. We will initially assume that the economy is closed—that is, there is no foreign trade.

Given all these simplifying assumptions, real disposable income will be equal to real national income minus taxes.[1] This relationship can be written algebraically as:

$$Y_d \equiv Y - T$$

Definitions and Relationships Revisited

You can do only two things with a dollar of income (in the absence of taxes): consume it or save it. If you consume it, it is gone forever. If you save the entire dollar, however, you will be able to consume it (and perhaps more if it earns interest) at some future time. That is the distinction between *consumption* and *saving*. **Consumption** is the act of using income for the purchase of consumption goods. **Consumption goods** are goods purchased by households for immediate satisfaction, such as food, clothing, and movies. By definition, whatever you do not consume you save and can consume at some time in the future.

Consumption The act of using income for the purchase of consumption goods.

Consumption goods Goods purchased by households for immediate satisfaction.

---

[1]Strictly speaking, we are referring here to net taxes—that is, the difference between taxes paid and transfer payments received. If taxes are $100 billion but individuals receive transfer payments—old age security benefits, employment insurance benefits, and so forth—of $30 billion, net taxes are equal to $70 billion.

Saving The act of not consuming all of one's current income.

STOCKS AND FLOWS: THE DIFFERENCE BETWEEN SAVING AND SAVINGS. It is important to distinguish between *saving* and *savings*. **Saving** is an action that occurs at a particular rate—for example, $10 a week or $520 a year—it is an act of not consuming all of one's current income. Whatever is not consumed out of spendable income is, by definition, saved. *Saving* is an action measured over time (a flow), whereas *savings* are a stock, an accumulation resulting from the act of saving in the past. You may at present have *savings* of $2000 that are the result of four years' *saving* at a rate of $500 per year. Consumption, being related to saving, is also a flow concept. You consume from after-tax income at a certain rate per week, per month, or per year.

RELATING INCOME TO SAVING AND CONSUMPTION. Obviously, a dollar of after-tax income can be either consumed or not consumed. Realizing this, we can see the relationship among saving, consumption, and disposable income:

$$\text{Consumption} + \text{Saving} = \text{Disposable income}$$

Algebraically, this is written as:

$$C + S = Y_d$$

This is called an *accounting identity*. It has to hold true regardless of the time frame in which you measure. From it we can derive the definition of saving:

$$\text{Saving} = \text{Disposable income} - \text{Consumption}$$

or algebraically:

$$S = Y_d - C$$

Recall that disposable income is what you actually have left to spend after you have paid your taxes.

Investment

Investment Expenditures by firms on new machines and buildings.

Capital goods New machines and buildings that are expected to yield a future stream of income.

Investment is also a flow concept. *Investment* as used in economics differs from the common use of the term, as we have already pointed out. In everyday speech, it is often used to describe putting money into the stock market or real estate. In economic analysis, **investment** is defined as expenditures by firms on new machines and buildings—**capital goods**—that are expected to yield a future stream of income. This we have already called *fixed investment*. We also included changes in business inventories in our definition. This we have already called *inventory investment*.

There is some debate over whether education should be included as a part of investment. This is elaborated upon in Policy Example 9-1.

POLICY EXAMPLE 9-1 | **Spending on Human Capital: Investment or Consumption?**

As a student, you are spending lots of your time and money getting an education. You are probably doing it for several reasons: for personal satisfaction, to become a better citizen, to enhance your career opportunities, and to earn greater income. Since there are a variety of reasons for getting an education, economists struggle with the classification of spending on education. The first two reasons indicate that education is a consumption service, something you are doing for fun. On the other hand, the enhanced income that results from post-secondary education makes it look more like an investment; you forgo other expenditures and money today for a return on that money in the future. So is spending on education consumption or investment?

In the official statistics for Canada, educational services are classified as consumption. Whenever people go to school it is classified as a service in the same way that going to a

continued

hockey game or a concert is a consumption item. Clearly, there is room for disagreement among economists on this issue.

For critical analysis: Based on the current classification of educational spending, if disposable income is unchanged and households spend more on education so that their total spending rises, what happens to saving?

9.2 Determinants of Planned Consumption and Planned Saving

In the classical model, the supply of saving was determined by the rate of interest: The higher the rate of interest, the more people wanted to save and the less people wanted to consume. According to Keynes, the interest rate is not the primary determinant of an individual's saving and consumption decisions. Keynes argued that saving and consumption decisions depend primarily on an individual's real current income.

Consumption function The relationship between planned consumption expenditures of households and all levels of real disposable income (all else constant).

The relationship between planned consumption expenditures of households and all levels of real disposable income (all else constant) is called the **consumption function**. It shows how much all households plan to consume per year at each level of real disposable income per year. Using for the moment only columns 1, 2, and 3 of Table 9–1, we will present a consumption function for a hypothetical household.

We see from Table 9–1 that as real disposable income rises, planned consumption also rises, but by a smaller amount, as Keynes suggested. Planned saving also increases with disposable income. Note, however, that below an income of $10 000, the planned saving of this hypothetical family is actually negative. The further that income drops below that level, the more the family engages in **dissaving**, or negative saving, a situation in which spending exceeds disposable income. Dissaving can occur when a household is able to borrow or use up existing owned assets.

Dissaving Negative saving; a situation in which spending exceeds disposable income. Dissaving can occur when a household is able to borrow or use up existing owned assets.

TABLE 9–1

Real Consumption and Saving Schedules: A Hypothetical Case

Column 1 presents real disposable income from zero up to $20 000 per year; column 2 indicates planned consumption per year; column 3 presents planned saving per year. At levels of disposable income below $10 000, planned saving is negative. Column 4 is the marginal propensity to consume, which shows the proportion of additional income that will be consumed. Finally, column 5 shows the proportion of additional income that will be saved, or the marginal propensity to save.

Combination	(1) Real Disposable Income per Year (Y_d)	(2) Planned Real Consumption per Year (C)	(3) Planned Real Saving per Year ($S = Y_d - C$) (1) – (2)	(4) Marginal Propensity to Consume ($MPC = \Delta C / \Delta Y_d$)	(5) Marginal Propensity to Save ($MPS = \Delta S / \Delta Y_d$)
A	$ 0	$ 2 000	$–2 000	–	–
B	2 000	3 600	–1 600	0.8	0.2
C	4 000	5 200	–1 200	0.8	0.2
D	6 000	6 800	– 800	0.8	0.2
E	8 000	8 400	– 400	0.8	0.2
F	10 000	10 000	0	0.8	0.2
G	12 000	11 600	400	0.8	0.2
H	14 000	13 200	800	0.8	0.2
I	16 000	14 800	1 200	0.8	0.2
J	18 000	16 400	1 600	0.8	0.2
K	20 000	18 000	2 000	0.8	0.2

Graphing the Numbers

When we constructed demand and supply curves in Chapter 3 we merely plotted the points from a table showing price-quantity pairs onto a diagram whose axes were labelled "Price" and "Quantity." We will graph the consumption and saving relationships presented in Table 9–1 in the same manner. In the upper part of Figure 9–1, the vertical axis measures the level of planned real consumption per year, and the horizontal axis measures the level of real disposable income per year. In the lower part of the figure, the horizontal axis is again real disposable income per year, but now the vertical axis is planned real saving per year. All of these are on a dollars-per-year basis, which emphasizes the point that we are measuring flows, not stocks.

As you can see, we have taken income–consumption and income–saving combinations A through K and plotted them. In the upper part of Figure 9–1, the result is called the *consumption function*. In the lower part, the result is called the *saving function*. Mathematically, the saving function is the *complement* of the consumption function because consumption plus saving always equals disposable income. What is not consumed is, by definition, saved. The difference between actual disposable income and the planned level of consumption per year *must* be the planned level of saving per year.

How can we find the rate of saving or dissaving in the upper part of Figure 9–1? We draw a line that is equidistant from both the horizontal and the vertical axes. This line is 45 degrees from either axis and is often called the **45-degree reference line**—the line along which planned real expenditures equal real disposable income per year. At every

45-degree reference line The line along which planned real expenditures equal real disposable income per year.

FIGURE 9–1

The Consumption and Saving Functions

If we plot the combinations of real disposable income and planned real consumption from columns 1 and 2 in Table 9–1, we get the consumption function. At every point on the 45-degree line, a vertical line drawn to the income axis is the same distance from the origin as a horizontal line drawn to the consumption axis. Where the consumption function crosses the 45-degree line at *F*, we know that consumption equals real disposable income and there is zero saving. The vertical distance between the 45-degree line and the consumption function measures the rate of saving or dissaving at any given income level. If we plot the relationship between column 1, real disposable income, and column 3, planned real saving, from Table 9–1, we arrive at the saving function shown in the lower part of this diagram. It is the complement of the consumption function presented above it.

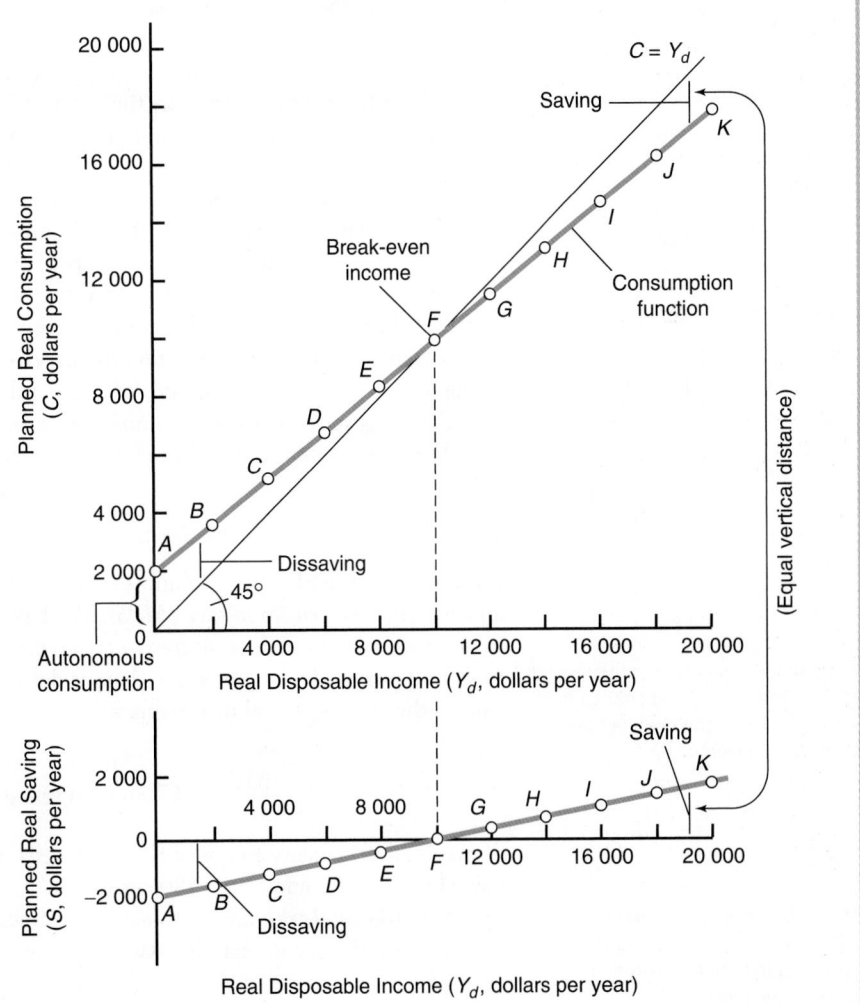

point on the 45-degree reference line, a vertical line drawn to the income axis is the same distance from the origin as a horizontal line drawn to the consumption axis. Thus, at point *F*, where the consumption function intersects the 45-degree line, real disposable income equals planned consumption. Point *F* is sometimes called the *break-even income point* because there is neither positive nor negative saving. This can be seen in the lower part of Figure 9–1 as well. The planned annual rate of saving at a real disposable income level of $10 000 is, indeed, zero.

Dissaving and Autonomous Consumption

To the left of point *F* in either part of Figure 9–1, this hypothetical family engages in dissaving, either by going into debt or by consuming existing assets, including savings. The amount of saving or dissaving in the upper part of the figure can be found by measuring the vertical distance between the 45-degree line and the consumption function. This simply tells us that if our hypothetical family starts above $10 000 of real disposable income per year and then temporarily finds its real disposable income below $10 000, it will not cut back its consumption by the full amount of the reduction. It will instead go into debt or consume existing assets in some way to compensate for part of the loss.

Now look at the point on the diagram where real disposable income is zero but planned consumption per year is $2000. This amount of planned consumption, which does not depend at all on actual disposable income, is called **autonomous consumption**. The autonomous consumption of $2000 is *independent* of the level of disposable income. That means that no matter how low the level of income of our hypothetical family falls, the family will always attempt to consume at least $2000 per year. (We are, of course, assuming here that the family's real disposable income does not equal zero year in and year out. There is certainly a limit to how long our hypothetical family could finance autonomous consumption without any income.) That $2000 of yearly consumption is determined by things other than the level of income. We do not need to specify what determines autonomous consumption; we merely state that it exists and that in our example it is $2000 per year. Just remember that the word *autonomous* means "existing independently." In our model, autonomous consumption exists independently of the hypothetical family's level of real disposable income. (Later, we will review some of the non–real-disposable-income determinants of consumption.)

There are many possible types of autonomous expenditures. Hypothetically, we can consider that investment is autonomous—independent of income. We can assume that government expenditures are autonomous. We will do just that at various times in our discussions to simplify our analysis of income determination.

On our graphs, changes in autonomous expenditure will shift the corresponding function. When autonomous expenditure increases, this shifts the function up and vice versa.

Marginal Propensity to Consume and to Save

Now, we go to the last two columns in Table 9–1: *marginal propensity to consume (MPC)* and *marginal propensity to save (MPS)*. We have used the term *marginal* before. It refers to a small incremental or decremental change (represented by Δ in Table 9–1). The **marginal propensity to consume**, then, is defined as the ratio of the change in consumption to the change in real disposable income:

$$MPC = \frac{\text{Change in consumption}}{\text{Change in real disposable income}}$$

A marginal propensity to consume of 0.8 tells us that an additional $100 in take-home pay will lead to an additional $80 consumed.

The **marginal propensity to save** is defined similarly as the ratio of the change in saving to the change in real disposable income:

$$MPS = \frac{\text{Change in saving}}{\text{Change in real disposable income}}$$

Autonomous consumption The amount of planned consumption, which does not depend at all on actual disposable income.

Marginal propensity to consume (MPC) The ratio of the change in consumption to the change in real disposable income.

Marginal propensity to save (MPS) The ratio of the change in saving to the change in real disposable income.

A marginal propensity to save of 0.2 indicates that out of an additional $100 in take-home pay, $20 will be saved. Whatever is not saved is consumed. The marginal propensity to save plus the marginal propensity to consume must always equal 1, by definition.

What do MPC and MPS tell you? They tell you what percentages of a given increase or decrease in income will go toward consumption and saving, respectively. The emphasis here is on the word *change*. The marginal propensity to consume indicates how much you will change your planned rate of consumption if there is a change in your real disposable income. If your marginal propensity to consume is 0.8, that does not mean that you consume 80 percent of *all* disposable income. An MPC of 0.8 means that you will consume 80 percent of any *increase* in your disposable income. In general, we assume that the marginal propensity to consume is between zero and 1. We assume that individuals increase their planned consumption by more than zero and less than 100 percent of any increase in real disposable income that they receive.

An Important Relationship

Consumption plus saving must equal income. Both your total real disposable income and the change in total real disposable income are either consumed or saved. The proportions of either measure must equal 1, or 100 percent. This allows us to make the following statement:

$$\text{MPC} + \text{MPS} = 1 \text{ } (= 100 \text{ percent of the } change \text{ in disposable income})$$

The marginal propensities to consume and save must total 1, or 100 percent. Check the statement by adding the figures in columns 4 and 5 for each level of real disposable income in Table 9–1.

Causes of Shifts in the Consumption Function

A change in any other relevant economic variable besides real disposable income will cause autonomous consumption to change and the consumption function to shift. There is a virtually unlimited number of such nonincome determinants of the position of the consumption function. When population increases or decreases, for example, the consumption function will shift up or down, respectively. Changes in expectations can also shift the consumption function. If the average household believes that the rate of inflation is going to fall dramatically in the years to come, the current consumption function will probably shift down: Planned consumption would be less at every level of real disposable income than before this change in expectations. Real household **wealth**—the stock of assets owned by a person, household, firm, or country—is also a determinant of the position of the consumption function. For a household, wealth can consist of a house, cars, personal belongings, bank accounts, bonds, stocks, and cash. An increase in real wealth of the average household will cause the consumption function to shift upward. A decrease in real wealth will cause it to shift downward.

In 2007, U.S. consumers faced a substantial drop in their wealth as housing prices fell. Example 9–1 analyzes the effects of this drop in wealth.

Wealth The stock of assets owned by a person, household, firm, or country.

EXAMPLE 9–1   **U.S. Consumers Are Bloodied But Unbowed**

Over the past couple of years, U.S. consumers have faced one trial after another, from soaring gas prices to the slumping housing market. Now come new worries about subprime mortgages, a jittery stock market, and growing fears that the overall economy may be at risk. Will 2007 be the year that consumers finally stop spending?

Don't count on it. Through all the hardships, strong labour markets have always ridden to the rescue, and this year is unlikely to be any different. Why?

The slowdown in 2007 was confined almost exclusively to housing and manufacturing. The services sector has been generating plenty of jobs. Services represent about 58 percent of the value of GDP in the U.S. and account for 81 percent of all private-sector payrolls. Economic growth in the sector, measured by its part of real GDP, was actually accelerating in

continued

2006, with growth of 2.4 percent in the first half, 2.8 percent in the third quarter, and 3.8 percent in the fourth quarter, the fastest quarterly pace in almost three years.

Service-sector companies showed little hesitancy in adding new workers. Recent payroll gains suggest most businesses remain committed to expanding their operations, which is providing key support for household spending. Even though joblessness in construction is over 10 percent, other areas have more than compensated. And new figures on household net worth show consumers still have a steady stream of wealth gains, through homeowner's equity and gains in the stock market, adding support to their financial condition.

For critical analysis: Why are payroll gains a "key support for household spending?"
SOURCE: BUSINESSWEEK, MARCH 26, 2007, PAGE 29, BY JAMES C. COOPER

➡ CONCEPTS IN BRIEF

Learning Objective 9.1: Distinguish between saving and savings and explain how saving and consumption are related.

- If we assume that we are operating on a horizontal short-run aggregate supply curve, the equilibrium level of real GDP per year is completely demand determined.
- Consumption is a flow that occurs repeatedly over time. It represents the purchase of consumer goods and services, such as food, clothing, and restaurant meals.
- *Saving* is also a flow, something that occurs over time. It equals disposable income minus consumption. *Savings* are a stock. They are the accumulated results of saving.
- Investment, too, is a flow. It includes expenditures on new machines, buildings, and equipment, as well as changes in business inventories.

Learning Objective 9.2: Explain the key determinants of consumption and saving in the Keynesian model.

- The consumption function shows the relationship between planned rates of consumption and real disposable income per year. The saving function is the complement of the consumption function because saving plus consumption must equal real disposable income.
- The marginal propensity to consume (MPC) is equal to the change in planned consumption divided by the change in real disposable income. The marginal propensity to save (MPS) is equal to the change in planned saving divided by the change in real disposable income.
- Any change in real disposable income will cause the planned rate of consumption to change; this is represented by a movement along the consumption function. Any change in a nonincome determinant of consumption will shift the consumption function.

9.3 Determinants of Investment

Investment, you will remember, is defined as expenditures on new buildings and equipment and changes in business inventories. Real gross private domestic investment in Canada has been extremely volatile over the years relative to real consumption. If we were to look at net private domestic investment (investment after depreciation has been deducted), we would see that in the depths of the Great Depression and at the peak of the World War II effort, the figure was negative. In other words, we were eating away at our capital stock—we were not even maintaining it by completely replacing depreciated equipment.

If we compare real investment expenditures historically with real consumption expenditures, we find that the latter are relatively less variable over time than the former (Look back to Example 5-2 on page 137.) Why is this so? The answer is that the real investment decisions of business people are based on **expectations**— subjective estimates of future economic conditions. We just discussed the role of expectations in determining the position of the consumption function. Expectations play an even greater role in determining the position of the investment function. This could account for much of the instability of investment over time.

Expectations Subjective estimates of future economic conditions.

The Planned Investment Function

Consider that at all times, businesses perceive an array of investment opportunities. These investment opportunities have rates of return ranging from zero to very high, with the number (or dollar value) of all such projects inversely related to the rate of return. Because a project is profitable only if its rate of return exceeds the opportunity cost of the investment—the rate of interest—it follows that as the interest rate falls, planned investment spending increases and vice versa. Even if firms use retained earnings (internal financing) to fund an investment, the higher the market rate of interest, the greater is the *opportunity cost* of using those retained earnings. Thus, it does not matter in our analysis whether the firm must seek financing from external sources or can obtain such financing by using retained earnings. Just consider that as the interest rate falls, more investment opportunities will be profitable, and planned investment will be higher.

It should be no surprise, therefore, that the investment function is represented as an inverse relationship between the rate of interest and the value of planned investment. A hypothetical investment schedule is given in part (a) of Figure 9–2 and plotted in part (b). We see from this schedule that if, for example, the rate of interest is 5.5 percent, the dollar value of planned investment will be $60 billion per year. Note, by the way, that planned investment is also given on a per-year basis, showing that it represents a flow, not a stock. (The stock counterpart of investment is the stock of capital in the economy measured in dollars at a point in time.)

What Causes the Investment Function to Shift?

Because planned investment is assumed to be a function of the rate of interest, any non–interest-rate variable that changes can have the potential of shifting the investment function. Expectations of business people is one of those variables. If higher future sales are expected, more machines and bigger plants will be planned for the future. More investment will be undertaken because of the expectation of higher future profits. In this case, the

---

FIGURE 9–2
Planned Investment

In the hypothetical planned investment schedule in part (a), the rate of planned investment is asserted to be inversely related to the rate of interest. If we plot the data pairs from part (a), we obtain the investment function, *I*, in part (b). It is negatively sloped.

Part (a)

Rate of Interest (percent per year)	Planned Investment per Year ($ billions)
7.5	20
7	30
6.5	40
6	50
5.5	60
5	70
4.5	80
4	90
3.5	100
3	110

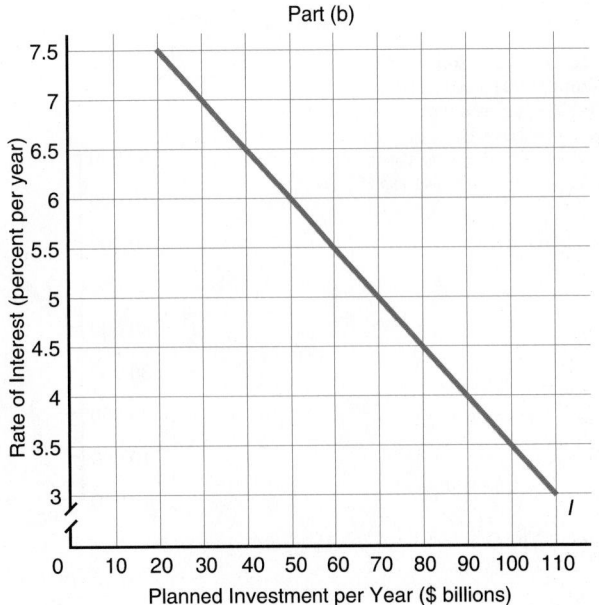

Part (b)

investment schedule, *I*, would shift outward to the right, meaning that more investment would be desired at all rates of interest. Any change in productive technology can potentially shift the investment function. A positive change in productive technology would stimulate demand for additional capital goods and shift the investment schedule, *I*, outward to the right. Changes in business taxes can also shift the investment schedule. If they increase, we predict a leftward shift in the planned investment function.

Example 9–2 shows how during the 1930s the investment undertaken by business and government declined by more than 70 percent. The consequence of these extreme changes in investment (and other components of demand) meant huge declines in employment and output in Canada.

EXAMPLE 9–2 | ## Changes in Investment and the Great Depression

A classic example of a shift in investment demand apparently occurred during the Great Depression. Indeed, some economists believe that it was an autonomous downward shift (collapse) in the investment function that provoked the Great Depression. Look at part (a) of Figure 9–3. There you see the net investment in Canada from 1929 to 1941 (expressed

FIGURE 9–3 *Net Private Domestic Investment and Real GDP During the Great Depression*

In part (a), you see how net private investment expressed in billions of 1997 dollars declined starting in 1930 and continued to decline for several years. It started to increase again in 1934. Look at part (b). There you see how changes in GDP seem to mirror changes in net private domestic investment.

SOURCE: ADAPTED FROM THE STATISTICS CANADA CANSIM DATABASE, TABLE 380-0056, AND FROM THE STATISTICS CANADA PUBLICATION *HISTORICAL STATISTICS OF CANADA*, SECOND EDITION, CATALOGUE 11-516, 1983, SERIES F41 AND F55.

Part (a)

Year	Real GDP	Net Private Domestic Investment
1926	45 897	7 650
1927	50 253	9 400
1928	54 841	11 221
1929	55 046	12 362
1930	52 700	10 051
1931	46 001	7 217
1932	41 231	3 685
1933	38 484	2 629
1934	43 157	3 362
1935	46 526	4 063
1936	48 588	4 916
1937	53 469	6 383
1938	53 909	6 177
1939	57 914	6 027
1940	66 069	7 777
1941	75 574	9 709

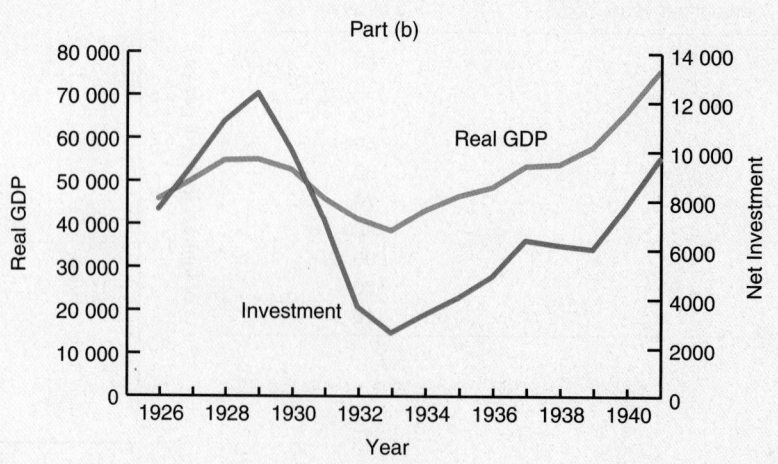

Part (b)

continued

in 1997 dollars). Clearly, during business contractions, decision makers in the business world can and do decide to postpone long-range investment plans for buildings and equipment. This causes the business recovery to be weak, unless those business plans are revised. If you examine real GDP in part (b) of Figure 9–3, you see that the contraction that started in 1929 reached its trough in 1933. The expansion was relatively strong for the following five years but then strengthened dramatically as the economy geared up to fight World War II. Some researchers argue that had World War II not occurred when it did, the Canadian economy would have remained weak, since business would have had no reason to revise investment plans upward.

For critical analysis: Relatively speaking, how healthy was the national economy in 1941? (Hint: Look at part (b) of Figure 9–3.)

➤→ **CONCEPTS IN BRIEF**

Learning Objective 9.3: Identify the primary determinants of planned investment.

- ➤ The planned investment schedule shows the relationship between investment and the rate of interest; it slopes downward.
- ➤ The non–interest-rate determinants of planned investment are expectations, innovation and technological changes, and business taxes.
- ➤ Any change in the non–interest-rate determinants of planned investment will cause the planned investment function to shift so that at each and every rate of interest, a different amount of planned investment will be obtained.

9.4 *Equilibrium in the Keynesian Model*

We are interested in determining the equilibrium level of real GDP per year. But when we examined the consumption function earlier in this chapter, it related planned consumption expenditures to the level of real disposable income per year. We have already shown where adjustments must be made to GDP in order to get real disposable income (see Table 5–2 in Chapter 5, page 142). Real disposable income turns out to be less than real GDP because net taxes (taxes minus government transfer payments) are usually about 16 to 24 percent of GDP. A representative average in the 1990s is about 20 percent, and so disposable income, on average, has in recent years been around 80 percent of GDP.

If we are willing to assume that real disposable income, Y_d, differs from real GDP by an amount T every year, we can relatively easily substitute real GDP for real disposable income in the consumption function.

We can now plot any consumption function on a diagram in which the horizontal axis is no longer real disposable income but, rather, real GDP, as in Figure 9–4. Note that there is an autonomous part of consumption that is so labelled. The difference between this graph and the graphs presented earlier in this chapter is the change in the horizontal axis from real disposable income to real GDP per year. For the rest of this chapter, assume that this calculation has been made, and the result is that the MPC out of real GDP equals 0.8, suggesting that 20 percent of changes in real GDP are either saved or paid in taxes: In other words, of an additional \$100 earned, an additional \$80 will be consumed.

The 45-Degree Reference Line

Like the earlier graphs, Figure 9–4 shows a 45-degree reference line. The 45-degree line bisects the quadrant into two equal spaces. Thus, along the 45-degree reference line, planned consumption expenditures, *C*, equal real GDP per year, *Y*. One can see, then, that at any point where the consumption function intersects the 45-degree reference line, planned consumption expenditures will be exactly equal to real GDP per year, or *C = Y*. Note that in this graph, because we are looking only at planned consumption on the vertical axis, the

FIGURE 9–4

Consumption as a Function of Real GDP

This consumption function shows the rate of planned expenditures for each level of real GDP per year. There is an autonomous component in consumption equal to $30 billion. Along the 45-degree reference line, planned consumption expenditures per year, *C*, are identical to real GDP per year, *Y*. The consumption curve intersects the 45-degree reference line at a value of $150 billion per year.

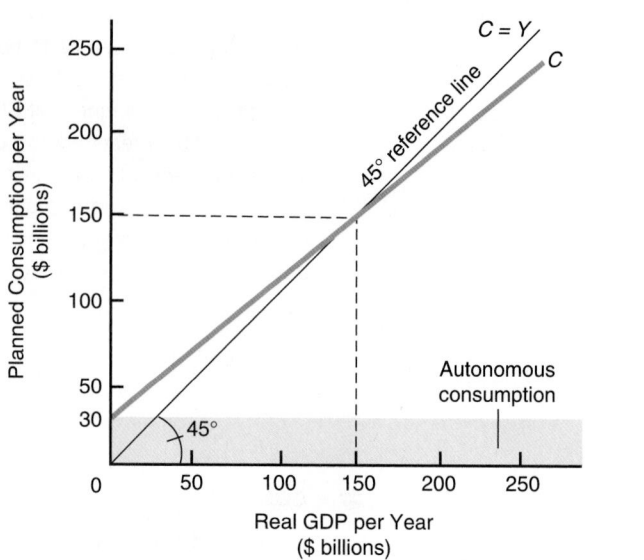

45-degree reference line is where planned consumption, *C*, is always equal to real GDP per year, *Y*. Later, when we add investment, government spending, and net exports to the graph, the 45-degree reference line with respect to *all* planned expenditures will be labelled as such on the vertical axis. In any event, consumption and real GDP are equal at $150 billion per year. That is where the consumption curve, *C*, intersects the 45-degree reference line. At that income level, all income is consumed.

Adding the Investment Function

Another component of private aggregate demand is, of course, investment spending, *I*. We have already looked at the planned investment function, which related investment to the rate of interest. You see that as the downward-sloping curve in part (a) of Figure 9–5. Recall from Figure 9–2 (page 245) that investment is determined in part by interest rates. Assume that the rate of interest is 5 percent, which results in a planned investment of $70 billion. The $70 billion of real investment per year is *autonomous* with respect to real GDP—that is, it is independent of real GDP. In other words, given that we have a determinant investment level of $70 billion at a 5 percent rate of interest, we can treat this level of investment as constant, regardless of the level of GDP. This is shown in part (a) of Figure 9–5. The vertical distance of investment spending is $70 billion. Businesses plan on investing a particular amount—$70 billion per year—and will do so no matter what the level of real GDP.

How do we add this amount of investment spending to our consumption function? We simply add a line above the *C* line that we drew in Figure 9–4 that is higher by the vertical distance equal to $70 billion of autonomous investment spending. This is shown by the arrow in part (b) of Figure 9–5. Our new line, now labelled *C + I*, is called the **total planned expenditures curve (TPE)**, which represents the relationship between spending in the economy and GDP. It tells us how expenditures will vary at all levels of income. In our simple economy without government expenditures and net exports, the *C + I* curve represents total planned expenditures as they relate to different levels of real GDP per year.

The final step in completing this highly simplified model of the economy is to plot the 45-degree reference line. This line shows where planned expenditures (*C + I* in this simplified model) equal GDP. Since GDP equals the value of national production at the point where the total planned expenditures curve crosses the 45-degree line, we will match the desires of those purchasing goods and services and the plans of producers to make

Total planned expenditures curve (TPE) Represents the relationship between spending in the economy and GDP.

FIGURE 9–5

Combining Consumption and Investment

In part (a), investment is a constant $70 billion per year. When we add this amount to the consumption line, we obtain in part (b) the $C + I$ line, which is vertically higher than the C line by exactly $70 billion. Real GDP is equal to $C + I$ at $500 billion per year where total planned expenditures, $C + I$, are equal to actual real GDP, for this is where the $C + I$ line intersects the 45-degree reference line, on which $C + I$ is equal to Y at every point.

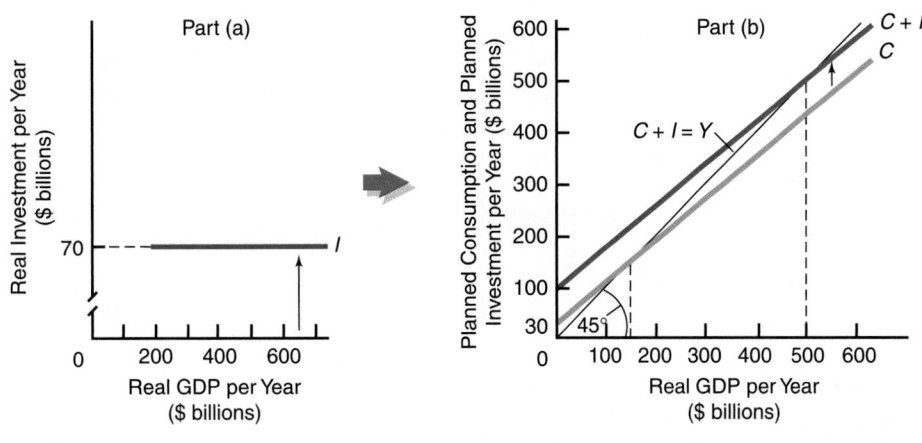

goods and services. In short, equilibrium occurs where total planned expenditures equal total planned production. In the example shown in Figure 9–5, this equilibrium occurs at $500 billion per year.

This equilibrium between production and planned expenditures does not just happen by itself. In the next sections, we will look more closely at how this equilibrium comes about.

Total Planned Expenditures with Government and the Foreign Sector Added

We have to add government spending, G, to our macroeconomic model. We assume that the level of resource-using government purchases of goods and services (federal, provincial, and municipal), *not* including transfer payments, is determined by the political process. In other words, G will be considered autonomous, just like investment (and a certain component of consumption). In Canada, resource-using government expenditures are around 20 percent of real GDP. The other side of the coin, of course, is that there are taxes, which are used to pay for much of government spending. We will simplify our model greatly by assuming that there is a constant **lump-sum tax** of $100 billion a year to finance $100 billion of government spending. A lump-sum tax does not depend on income or the circumstances of the taxpayer. An example is a $1000 tax that every family must pay, irrespective of its economic situation. This lump-sum tax will reduce disposable income and consumption by the same amount. We show this in Table 9–2 (column 2), where we give the numbers for a complete model.

> **Lump-sum tax** A tax that does not depend on income or the circumstances of the taxpayer.

The Foreign Sector

Not a week goes by without some commentary in the media about the size of our foreign trade balance. In some years, our trade balance is positive (the value of exports exceeds the value of imports), while in others it is negative (the value of imports exceeds the value of exports). The difference between exports and imports is *net exports*, which we label $X - M$ in our graphs. For simplicity, let us assume that exports exceed imports (net exports,

TABLE 9-2

The Determination of Equilibrium Real GDP with Net Exports

Figures are billions of dollars.

(1) Real GDP	(2) Taxes	(3) Real Disposable Income	(4) Planned Consumption	(5) Planned Saving	(6) Planned Investment	(7) Government Spending	(8) Net Exports (Exports − Imports)	(9) Total Planned Expenditures (4) + (6) + (7) + (8)	(10) Unplanned Inventory Changes	(11) Direction of Change in Real GDP
200	100	100	110	−10	70	100	10	290	−90	Increase
250	100	150	150	0	70	100	10	330	−80	Increase
300	100	200	190	10	70	100	10	370	−70	Increase
400	100	300	270	30	70	100	10	450	−50	Increase
500	100	400	350	50	70	100	10	530	−30	Increase
600	100	500	430	70	70	100	10	610	−10	Increase
650	100	550	470	80	70	100	10	650	0	Neither (equilibrium)
700	100	600	510	90	70	100	10	690	+10	Decrease
800	100	700	590	110	70	100	10	770	+30	Decrease

$X - M$, is positive) and furthermore that the level of net exports is autonomous—independent of GDP. Assume a level of $X - M$ of \$10 billion per year. In Table 9–2, net exports is shown in column 8 as \$10 billion per year.

In fact, the level of exports depends on international economic conditions, especially in the countries that buy our products. If there is a decline in the foreign exchange value of the Canadian dollar or if our trading partners experience economic growth, they will want to purchase more of our products. If the converse holds true, our exports will fall.

An example of this situation is the 1997 economic crisis in Asia. The economies of Japan, South Korea, and several other Asian countries faltered severely, leaving consumers and businesses in those countries less willing to purchase our goods and services. As a result, we saw our own net exports fall. This would be portrayed as a downward shift of our total planned expenditures curve.

The level of imports depends on economic conditions here in Canada. If the foreign exchange value of the Canadian dollar falls, we will purchase fewer of the now more expensive goods and services from other countries. If the federal government raises import taxes or tariffs on imported goods, those goods become more expensive for us to import, and we will purchase fewer of them. Since the value of imports is subtracted from the value of exports to find net exports, a *decrease* in the value of imports will *increase* the value of net exports and vice versa.

Determining the Equilibrium Level of Real GDP

We are now in a position to determine the equilibrium level of real GDP per year under the continuing assumptions that the short-run aggregate supply curve is horizontal; that investment, government, and the foreign sector are autonomous; and that planned consumption expenditures are determined by the level of real GDP. As can be seen in Table 9–2, total planned expenditures of \$650 billion per year equal real GDP of \$650 billion per year, and this is where we reach equilibrium.

Remember that equilibrium *always* occurs when *total planned expenditures (TPE) equal total production* (given that any amount of production in this model in the short run can occur without a change in the price level).

Now look at part (a) of Figure 9–6, which shows the equilibrium level of real GDP. There are two curves, one showing the consumption function, which is the exact duplicate

FIGURE 9–6

Equilibrium in the Keynesian Model

The consumption function shows how households' spending changes with levels of income. In the same way, the total planned expenditure function (which adds investment, government, and net export spending) shows how spending changes with GDP. The equilibrium level of real GDP is shown by the intersection of our *TPE* function and the 45-degree reference line in part (a).

Part (b) shows a situation of disequilibrium. In this diagram, planned expenditures are 530 when GDP is 500. This leads to an unplanned reduction in inventories of $30 billion. Firms will then increase their production, moving the economy back towards the equilibrium point where expenditures equal production.

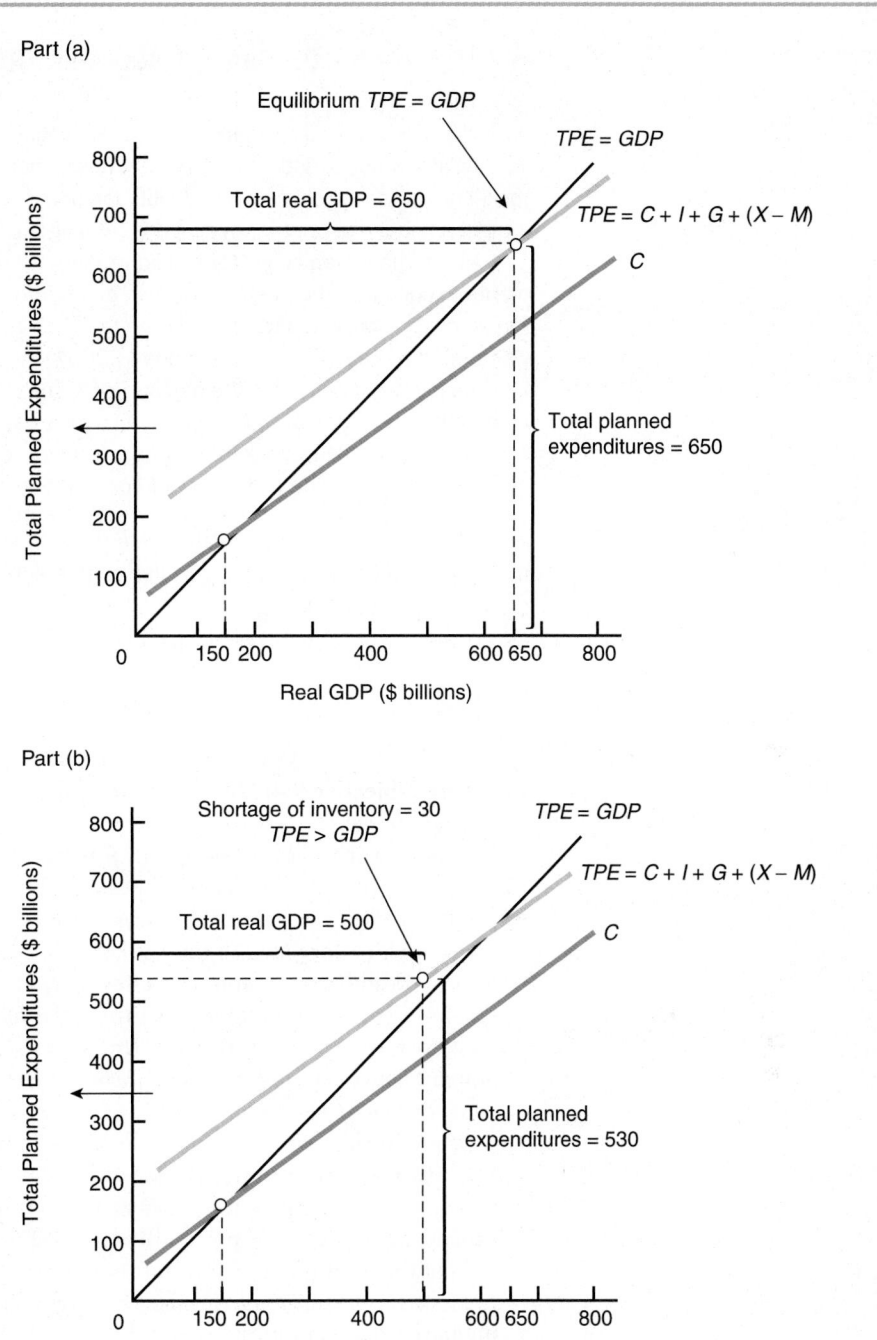

of the one shown in Figure 9–4, and the other being the *TPE* curve, which intersects the 45-degree reference line (representing equilibrium) at $650 billion per year.

Whenever total planned expenditures differ from real GDP, there are unplanned inventory changes. When total planned expenditures are greater than real GDP, inventory levels drop in an unplanned manner. To get them back up, firms seek to expand their production, which increases real GDP as shown in part (b) of Figure 9–6. Real GDP rises toward its equilibrium level. Whenever total planned expenditures are less than real GDP, the opposite occurs. There are unplanned inventory increases, causing firms to cut back on their production. The result is a drop in real GDP toward the equilibrium level.

EXAMPLE 9-3   **Oil Sands Investment Continues to Grow**

In 2007, there was a feverish pace of development in northern Alberta. An eye-popping $38 billion in deals and development plans announced in August 2007 showed that sky-rocketing construction costs had not dampened interest in the region, only that those intrigued had a blueprint for mining and refining the buried energy treasure of the oil sands.

Alberta had been crying for skilled workers for some time even before these announce-ments to cope with the staggering crush of infrastructure and energy development. Demand for oil sands labour was forecast to rise from 15 000 in 2007 to 34 000 by 2010, and that was before the announcements made in 2007.

Energy bankers believe the massive scale needed to justify an investment in the region means that the next wave of buyers of oil sands assets may be large, integrated oil and gas companies. With deep pockets and easy access to low-cost capital, the biggest firms are best able to handle the high costs of construction, operations, and labour in the region.

For critical analysis: Interest rates were rising at the time that these announcements were made. What must be happening to the investment demand function?

SOURCE: GLOBE AND MAIL, AUG 6, 2007, P B3 BY JUDY MONCHUK

➤ CONCEPTS IN BRIEF

Learning Objective 9.4: Describe how equilibrium GDP is established in the Keynesian model.

- ↲ We assume that the consumption function has an autonomous part that is inde-pendent of the level of real GDP per year. It is labelled "autonomous consumption."
- ↲ For simplicity, we assume that investment is autonomous with respect to real GDP and therefore unrelated to the level of real GDP per year.
- ↲ When we add autonomous investment, I, to the consumption function, we obtain the $C + I$ curve, which represents total planned expenditures for a closed economy with no government. With a government and a foreign sector, we add G to represent government spending and net exports, $(X - M)$. Total planned expenditures are thus equal to $C + I + G + (X - M)$.
- ↲ The equilibrium level of real GDP can be found by locating the intersection of the total planned expenditures curve with the 45-degree reference line. At that level of real GDP per year, planned consumption plus planned investment plus government expenditures plus net exports will equal real GDP.
- ↲ Whenever total planned expenditures exceed real GDP, there will be unplanned decreases in inventories; the size of the circular flow of income will increase, and a higher level of equilibrium real GDP will prevail. Whenever planned expenditures are less than real GDP, there will be unplanned increases in inventories; the size of the circular flow will shrink, and a lower equilibrium level of real GDP will prevail.

9.5 The Multiplier

Look again at part (b) of Figure 9–5. Assume for the moment that the only expenditures included in real GDP are consumption expenditures. Where would the equilibrium level of income be in this case? It would be where the consumption function *(C)* intersects the 45-degree reference line, which is at $150 billion per year. Now we add the autonomous amount of planned investment, or $70 billion and then determine what the new equili-rium level of income will be. It turns out to be $500 billion per year. Adding $70 billion per year of investment spending increased the equilibrium level of income by *five* times that amount, or by $350 billion per year.

Multiplier The number by which a permanent change in autonomous expenditure is multiplied to get the change in the equilibrium level of real GDP.

What is operating here is the multiplier effect of changes in autonomous spending. The **multiplier** is the number by which a permanent change in autonomous expenditure is multiplied to get the change in the equilibrium level of real GDP. Any permanent increases in autonomous investment or in any autonomous component of consumption or government spending or net exports will cause an even larger increase in real GDP. Similarly any permanent decreases in autonomous spending will cause even larger decreases in the equilibrium level of real GDP per year. As a formula, we use the multiplier in the following way:

Multiplier × Change in autonomous spending = Change in equilibrium level of real GDP

Knowing the multiplier for an economy does two things for us. First, it is a quick method for calculating how changes in autonomous spending will affect the equilibrium in the economy without having to go through the entire procedure of recalculating the equations or tables as we just did. Secondly, it tells us about the *stability* of the economy. A low multiplier implies that the economy will be relatively stable, and a high multiplier tells us that we will likely have a much greater degree of variability in the economy. A relatively small change in planned investment or autonomous consumption expenditure can trigger a much larger change in the equilibrium real GDP per year. Of course, an economy like Canada's that trades with other countries will reflect the stability of the economy of its major trading partners. In Canada's case, this is the United States.

The Multiplier Effect

So, where the does the multiplier effect come from? The multiplier effect happens because income received by one group is (mostly) being spent on goods and services produced by another group, reflecting the circular flow of the economy that we studied in Chapter 5. However, we also noted that not every dollar earned is re-spent. In Table 9–3, for each dollar received as income, 80¢ was passed on in a new round of spending, and 20¢ "leaked out" of the circular flow as saving (i.e., it was not spent on goods and services in the domestic economy). In turn, a portion of that 80¢ was spent, again, by the second group (and a part "leaked out"). The combined effects of these two rounds (and all the subsequent times we go around the circular flow) result in a much greater increase in economic production than the original spending.

Let us look at another simple numerical example. Suppose in Table 9–3 that planned investment increases by $10 billion. This could occur, for example, if interest rates were lowered. We see in Table 9–3 that during (what we will call) the first round in column 1, investment is increased by $10 billion; this also means an increase in real GDP of $10 billion for those who create the investment goods (in our example, the construction workers and building suppliers) which is shown in column 2. These households, in turn, spend $8 billion of their extra income (shown in column 3) and save an additional $2 billion.

That is not the end of the story, though. This additional spending will provide additional income for other individuals (pub owners on Friday afternoon, for example). Thus, during the second round, we see an increase in real income of $8 billion. Now, out of this increased real income, what will be the resultant increase in expenditures? It will equal 0.8 times $8 billion, or $6.4 billion. We continue these induced expenditure rounds until the amounts get very small and find that because of the initial increase in autonomous investment expenditure of $10 billion, the equilibrium level of real GDP has increased by $50 billion. A permanent $10 billion increase in autonomous investment spending has created an additional $40 billion in planned expenditure elsewhere in the economy, for a total increase in real GDP of $50 billion. In other words, the equilibrium level of real GDP has changed by an amount equal to five times the change in investment. The multiplier in this example would be 5.

(1) Round	(2) Annual Increase in Real GDP ($ billions per year)	(3) Annual Increase in Planned Expenditure ($ billions per year)
1 ($10 billion per year increase in I)	10.00	8.000
2	8.00	6.400
3	6.40	5.120
4	5.12	4.096
5	4.09	3.277
•	•	•
•	•	•
•	•	•
All later rounds	16.38	13.107
Totals ($C + I + G + (X - M)$)	50.00	40.000

TABLE 9–3

The Multiplier Process

We trace the effects of a permanent $10 billion increase in autonomous investment spending on the equilibrium level of real GDP. If we assume a marginal propensity to spend of 0.8, such an increase will eventually elicit a $50 billion increase in the equilibrium level of real GDP per year.

Assumption: MPC = 0.8, or $\frac{4}{5}$

The Multiplier Formula

So, where does the multiplier number come from? We will use the same figures as we did in Table 9–3 to explain. In that example, for each dollar received, 80¢ was spent. The proportion of money that is spent in the domestic economy out of every extra dollar of GDP received is called the **marginal propensity to spend**, which we will abbreviate as MPE ("E" for expenditure). (Graphically, this MPE is the slope of our Total Planned Expenditure function.) If our MPE had been smaller, say, 50¢ instead of 80¢, then the value of each round would be substantially smaller because more money would "leak" out from the circular flow and the overall multiplier would be smaller.

Marginal propensity to spend The proportion of money that is spent in the domestic economy out of every extra dollar of GDP received.

In addition to saving, there are two other such "leakages" from an economy—imports and taxes. When money is paid to purchase foreign-made goods, obviously that passes on income not to Canadian producers but, instead, to foreign producers. In the same way, taxes remove money from the economy. The higher the proportion of such leakages of each additional dollar in each round of spending, the smaller is the multiplier.

In general, the multiplier can be calculated as the *reciprocal of the proportion of leakages*, which can be calculated as (1 − MPE) or:

$$\text{Multiplier} = \frac{1}{\text{Proportion of leakages}}$$

In our first simple model, the MPE was 4/5; therefore, the proportion of leakages was equal to 1/5. The reciprocal is 5. That was our multiplier. A $10 billion increase in planned investment led to a $50 billion increase in the equilibrium level of real GDP. Our multiplier in that model is calculated as:

$$\text{Multiplier} = \frac{1}{(1 - \text{MPE})} = \frac{1}{\left(1 - \frac{4}{5}\right)} = \frac{1}{\frac{1}{5}} = 5$$

Let us examine some more cases. If the only leakage were savings and the MPS = $\frac{1}{4}$,

$$\text{Multiplier} = \frac{1}{\frac{1}{4}} = 4$$

Now, let us add imports as another leakage into our models. Look back at Table 9–3, and instead of a constant net export level of $10 billion, assume that exports are constant at $140 billion and imports are equal to 20 percent of real GDP. This means that we are spending 20 percent of our additional income on imports. This ratio of the change in imports to the change in real GDP is called the **marginal propensity to import**.

Marginal propensity to import The ratio of the change in imports to the change in real GDP.

The equilibrium value for the economy in this example will still remain at $650 billion. However, if you work through this example, you will see that since the multiplier is the reciprocal of the proportion of leakages, it will be much smaller. In this case:

$$\text{Multiplier} = \frac{1}{\text{Proportion of leakages}} = \frac{1}{\text{MPS} + \text{MPM}} = \frac{1}{0.2 + 0.2} = \frac{1}{0.4} = 2.5$$

Since we have doubled our leakages from the economy, our multiplier has been halved. In our earlier example, an increase in investment expenditure of $10 billion led to an increase in real GDP of $50 billion. With a marginal propensity to import of 0.2 added in, the multiplier will only be 2.5, and so a $10 billion increase in investment will now only lead to an increase of $25 billion in real GDP. In the same way, adding taxes that depend on GDP (such as income or sales taxes) will also reduce the multiplier.

By taking a few numerical examples, you can demonstrate to yourself an important property of the multiplier:

The smaller the marginal propensity to save, the larger is the multiplier.

The smaller the marginal propensity to import, the larger is the multiplier.

The lower the marginal income tax rate, the larger is the multiplier.

Policy Example 9–2 explains how the Chinese government has used the multiplier to boost the Chinese economy.

POLICY EXAMPLE 9–2 | **The Multiplier Effect of Forced Housing Investment in China**

For years, the government of the People's Republic of China provided housing to all workers. This "free" housing typically consisted of apartment complexes built years ago. New housing was relatively rare and consequently so expensive that only a few people could afford to purchase recently constructed houses.

Since 2000, however, the Chinese government has been promoting a market for private housing. It has required "work units"—the Chinese government's term for state-sponsored business enterprises—to make extra payments to employees, who are, in turn, required to use those funds to purchase housing. In effect, the government has embarked on a program of forced housing investment. The government's main goal was to promote private ownership of housing. Very quickly, home ownership rates more than doubled in many Chinese cities.

Naturally, the increased spending on housing has generated a boom in the Chinese construction industry and contributed to a flourishing market for home decoration services. Surging incomes of construction firms, home decorators, and other recipients of new income flows from housing construction have fuelled an expansion of retail spending, which had previously been stagnant. The mandated increase in housing investment aimed at privatizing much of China's housing market has had a significant macroeconomic spillover: a multiplier effect on planned expenditures and on equilibrium national income.

For critical analysis: If the Chinese government had spent public funds upgrading existing housing instead of requiring forced investment in new private housing, what would have been the macroeconomic effect?

The Multiplier Effect When the Price Level Can Change

Clearly, the multiplier effect on the equilibrium overall level of *real* GDP will not be as great if part of the increase in *nominal* GDP occurs because of increases in the price level. We show this in Figure 9–7. The intersection of AD_1 and $SRAS$ is at a price level of 120

FIGURE 9–7

Multiplier Effect on Equilibrium of Real GDP

A $10 billion increase in autonomous spending (investment, government, or net exports), which moves AD_1 to AD_2, will yield a full multiplier effect only if prices are constant. If the price index increases from 120 to 125, the multiplier effect is less, and the equilibrium level of real GDP goes up only to, say, $530 billion per year instead of $550 billion per year.

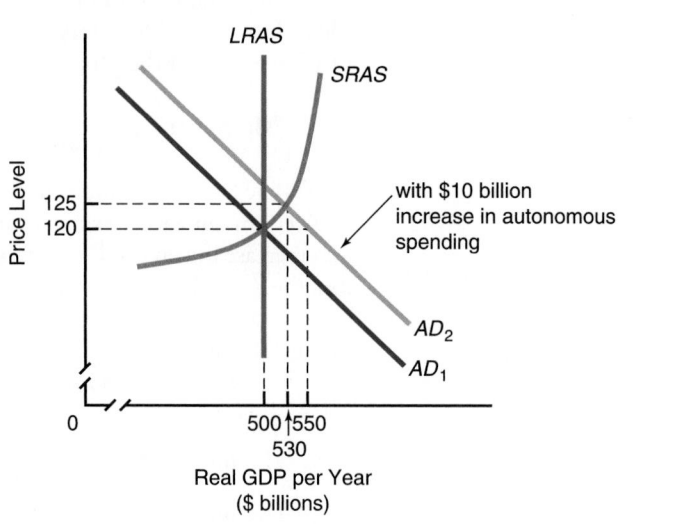

with equilibrium real GDP of $500 billion per year. An increase in autonomous spending shifts the aggregate demand curve outward to the right to AD_2. If the price level remained at 120, the short-run equilibrium level of real GDP would increase to $550 billion per year because for the $10 billion increase in autonomous spending, the multiplier would be 5, as it was in Table 9–3. But the price level does not stay fixed because ordinarily *SRAS* is positively sloped. In this diagram, the new short-run equilibrium level of real GDP is hypothetically $530 billion of real GDP per year. Instead of the multiplier being 5, the multiplier with respect to the equilibrium changes in the output of real goods and services—real GDP—is only 3. The multiplier is smaller because part of the additional income is used to pay higher prices; not all is spent on increased output, as is the case when the price level is fixed.

If the economy is at an equilibrium level of real GDP that is greater than *LRAS*, the implications for the multiplier are even more severe. Look again at Figure 9–7. The *SRAS* curve starts to slope upward more dramatically after $530 billion of real GDP per year. Therefore, any increase in aggregate demand will lead to a proportionally greater increase in the price level and a smaller increase in the equilibrium level of real GDP per year. The multiplier effect of any increase in autonomous spending will be relatively small because most of the changes will be in the price level. Moreover, any increase in the short-run equilibrium level of real GDP will tend to be temporary because the economy is temporarily above *LRAS*—the strain on its productive capacity will raise prices.

9.6 *The Relationship between Total Planned Expenditures and the Aggregate Demand Curve*

There is clearly a relationship between the aggregate demand curve that was developed in Chapter 6 and the total planned expenditures curve developed in this chapter. After all, aggregate demand consists of consumption, investment, government purchases, and net exports. There is a major difference, however, between the aggregate demand curve, *AD*, and the total planned expenditures curve: *TPE* is drawn with the price level held constant, whereas *AD* is drawn, by definition, with the price level changing. In other words, the total planned expenditures curve shown in Figure 9–6 is drawn with the price level fixed. To derive the aggregate demand curve, we must now allow the price level to change. Look at

The Relationship between AD and the Total Planned Expenditures Curve

In the upper graph, the total planned expenditures curve at a price level equal to 100 intersects the 45-degree reference line at E_1, or $800 billion of real GDP per year. That gives us point A (price level = 100; real GDP = $800 billion) in the lower graph. When the price level increases to 200, the total planned expenditures curve shifts downward, and the new equilibrium level of real GDP is at E_2 at $600 billion per year. This gives us point B in the lower graph. Connecting points A and B, we obtain the aggregate demand curve.

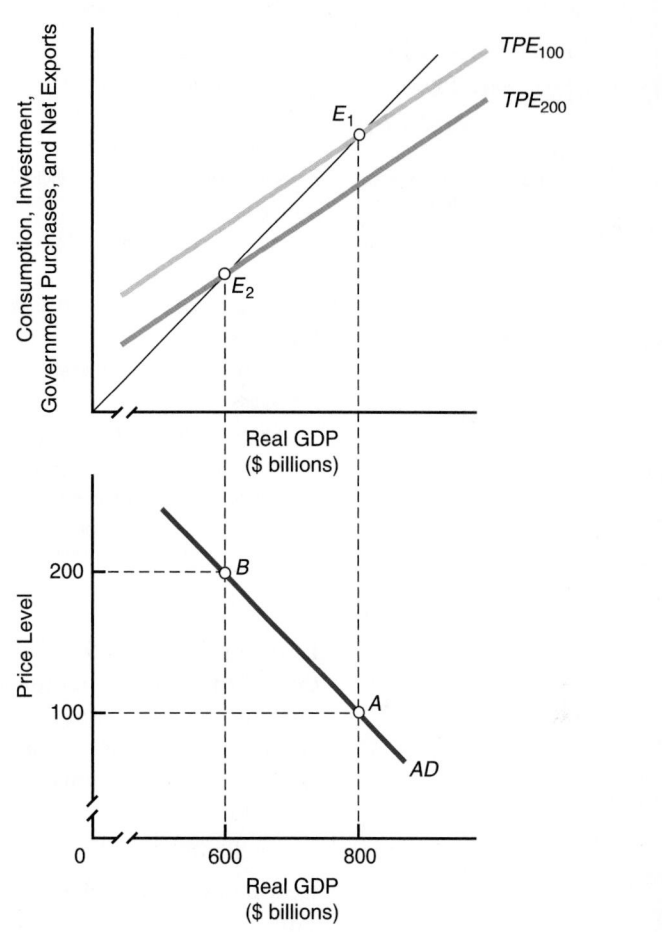

the upper part of Figure 9–8. Here, we show the total planned expenditures curve at a price level equal to 100 and equilibrium at $800 billion of GDP per year. This gives us point *A* in the lower graph, for it shows what real GDP would be at a price level of 100.

Now, let us assume that in the upper graph, the price level doubles to 200. What are the effects?

A higher price level can decrease the purchasing power of any cash that people hold (the real-balance effect). This is a decrease in real wealth, and it causes consumption expenditures, *C*, to fall, thereby putting downward pressure on the total planned expenditures curve.

Because individuals attempt to borrow more to replenish their real cash balances, interest rates will rise, which will make it more costly for people to buy houses and cars (the interest rate effect). Higher interest rates make it more costly, for example, to install new equipment and to erect new buildings. Therefore, the rise in the price level indirectly causes a reduction in the quantity of aggregate goods and services demanded.

In an open economy, our higher price level causes the foreign demand for our goods to fall (the open economy effect). Simultaneously, it increases our demand for others' goods. Since we assume the foreign exchange price of the dollar stays constant for a while, there will be an increase in imports and a decrease in exports, thereby reducing the size of *X* – *M*, again putting downward pressure on the total planned expenditures curve. The result is that a new total planned expenditures curve at a price level equal to 200 generates an equilibrium at E_2 at $600 billion of real GDP per year. This gives us point *B* in the lower part of Figure 9–8. When we connect points *A* and *B*, we obtain the aggregate demand curve, *AD*.

Table 9–4 sets out some of the nonprice factors that will change total planned expenditure and therefore affect aggregate demand.

TABLE 9-4	Increases Aggregate Demand and TPE	Decreases Aggregate Demand and TPE
Nonprice Factors That Affect Aggregate Demand and TPE	**Consumption**	
	· rise in level of personal wealth	· fall in level of personal wealth
	· fall in personal taxes	· rise in personal taxes
Changes in consumption, investment, government expenditure, and net exports can increase or decrease aggregate demand and TPE.	· fall in personal level of debt	· rise in personal level of debt
	· more optimistic expectations about the economy	· less optimistic expectations about the economy
	Investment	
	· fall in real interest rates	· rise in real interest rates
	· decrease in business taxes	· increase in business taxes
	· more optimistic expectations of profitability	· less optimistic expectations of profitability
	Government	
	· more spending in the economy	· less spending in the economy
	Net Exports	
	· decrease in value of the Canadian dollar	· increase in value of the Canadian dollar
	· increase in value of our trading partners' currency	· decrease in value of our trading partners' currency
	· increase in our trading partners' GDP	· decrease in our trading partners' GDP
	· decrease in Canadian import taxes	· increase in Canadian import taxes

➤➤ CONCEPTS IN BRIEF

Learning Objective 9.5: Evaluate why autonomous changes in total planned expenditures have a multiplier effect on equilibrium GDP.

- ❧ Any change in autonomous spending shifts the expenditure curve and causes a multiplier effect on the equilibrium level of real GDP per year.
- ❧ The multiplier is equal to the reciprocal of the proportion of leakages.
- ❧ The larger the marginal propensity to save, the marginal propensity to import, or the marginal income tax rates, the smaller is the multiplier.

Learning Objective 9.6: Understand the relationship between total planned expenditures and the aggregate demand curve.

- ❧ The total planned expenditures curve is drawn with the price level held constant, whereas the *AD* curve allows the price level to change. Each different price level generates a new total planned expenditures curve.

 ISSUES AND APPLICATIONS

Can Stock Market Crashes Affect the Economy?

Concepts Applied: Expectations, Multiplier, Investment, Wealth, Consumption

Business and consumer confidence is very important in determining national income.

Stock market crashes of the kind that occurred in October 2000 are rare and cause considerable consternation in the business world. A similar crash occurred in 1987, and the most famous crash occurred in October 1929. Yet, such crashes do not always result in recessions or depressions.

The 1987 stock market declines were not followed by a recession. As one forecaster put it, "stock market crashes have predicted seven of the last four recessions." So, what is the link between the stock market and the economy?

Linking Stock Markets and Economic Investment

The linkage between the financial investment that occurs and the real investment that economists talk about is fairly straightforward. Businesses use the financial instruments that are sold on the stock markets (such as bonds and shares) to raise money for their operations. These instruments are all different forms of borrowing. Typically, the money raised from the sale of these instruments is used to buy capital equipment or to invest in new product development and is especially important for new businesses. When financial investors are confident about the growth of the economy and the ability of the firms to repay their loans, they are much more likely to lend their money. In some cases, lending this money to these firms will reap very high returns, as the companies can often quickly grow and prosper. The value that the financial investors put on these shares and bonds is a reflection of the expectations that they have for the companies.

The Importance of Business Expectations

A stock market crash is a sign that expectations about the future have dramatically changed, sometimes because of a single event. In the October 2000 crash, the major change in expectations occurred when Nortel Networks announced that it did not meet all of the growth in sales and profitability that the market had expected. Because of this change in expectations in a company that was experiencing a very high growth rate, many investors changed their minds about the value of its shares and sold them. Because this change was experienced in only one company and, in general, limited largely to one sector, expectations for other firms were not much affected. While information technology firms experienced greater difficulty in raising new money for their operations, the expectations for the rest of the economy did not change much.

Consumers Expectations Matter As Well

Consumers experience two different "hits" to their pocketbooks when stock markets decline. They experience a tremendous loss of wealth because of the decline in the stock market and so may stop spending as much in the economy. If a recession does follow, then many will become unemployed. Unemployed people have much less money for purchasing housing, and so residential construction is usually affected. These declines in investment and in consumption expenditure (and net exports, if the phenomenon is worldwide) are all magnified because of the multiplier effect.

The Crash of 1929

Let us briefly review what happened in 1929 to illustrate how a stock market crash can be part of a bigger picture of decline in the economy. Following the famous stock market crash of October 1929 and the subsequent failure of one-third of the banks in the United States (although none went bankrupt in Canada), investment expenditure dropped nearly 80 percent of its total from the peak in 1929. (This is shown in Figure 9–3.) This was the largest percentage drop in any category of expenditure in the economy during that period and a reflection of the deep decline in confidence about the economy. Indeed, the economy did not recover to its 1929 levels until a decade later.

This loss of confidence in the future created a dramatic drop in investment in all categories of investment, residential construction, nonresidential construction, and equipment and machinery. Businesses that could not use their existing equipment saw no need to buy more. With a shattered business confidence and the subsequent decline in consumer spending, the country had to live through a very difficult period.

What Happened in 2000?

After the market crash in 2000, there was a slowdown in Canada. In the United States, where Nortel was selling most of its technology, there was a short recession that lasted from March 2001 to November 2001. So, the stock market crash did correctly predict a recession in the United States, but not in Canada.

For critical analysis:

1. How would a decline in business confidence affect the planned investment schedule in Figure 9–2? Explain your answer, and draw a graph to illustrate.
2. How would a decline in confidence affect the consumption function as drawn in Figure 9–4? Explain how it might affect both autonomous expenditure and the MPE. What effect might this have on the multiplier?

➡ SUMMARY

Here is what you should know after reading this chapter. MyEconLab will help you identify what you know, and where to go when you need to practise. We suggest that as soon as you review one of the Learning Objective sections below, you then proceed to go through the related section in MyEconLab.

⟨X⟩ myeconlab

➡ LEARNING OBJECTIVES	KEY TERMS	MYECONLAB PRACTICE
9.1 Saving and Consumption. Saving is a flow over time, whereas savings is a stock of resources at a point in time. The portion of your disposable income you do not consume during a week, a month, or a year is an addition to your stock of savings. By definition, saving during a year plus consumption during that year must equal total disposable (after tax) income earned that year.	consumption, 238 consumption goods, 238 saving, 239 investment, 239 capital goods, 239	• **MyEconLab** Study Plan 9.1
9.2 Determinants of Planned Consumption and Planned Saving. In the classical model, the interest rate is the fundamental determinant of saving, but in the Keynesian model, the primary determinant is disposable income. As real disposable income increases, so do real consumption expenditures. Because consumption and saving equal disposable income, saving must also vary with changes in disposable income. Factors other than disposable income can affect consumption and saving. The portion of consumption that is not related to disposable income is called autonomous consumption. A change in saving divided by the corresponding change in disposable income is the marginal propensity to save (MPS), and a change in consumption divided by the corresponding change in disposable income is the marginal propensity to consume (MPC).	consumption function, 240 dissaving, 240 45-degree reference line, 241 autonomous consumption, 242 marginal propensity to consume (MPC), 242 marginal propensity to save (MPS), 242 wealth, 243	• **MyEconLab** Study Plan 9.2
9.3 Determinants of Investment. An increase in the interest rate reduces the profitability of investment, and so planned investment varies inversely with the interest rate. Hence, the investment schedule slopes downward. Other factors that influence planned investment, such as business expectations, productive technology, or business taxes, can cause the investment schedule to shift. In the basic Keynesian model, changes in real GDP do not affect planned investment; investment is autonomous with respect to GDP.	expectations, 244	• **MyEconLab** Study Plan 9.3

➤➔ LEARNING OBJECTIVES	KEY TERMS	MYECONLAB PRACTICE
9.4 Equilibrium in the Keynesian Model. In equilibrium, total planned consumption, investment, government, and net export expenditures equal total GDP so that $C + I + G + X - M = Y$. This occurs at the point where the Total Planned Expenditure curve crosses the 45-degree reference line. At the equilibrium level of GDP, there is no tendency for business inventories to expand or contract.	total planned expenditures curve (TPE), 248 lump-sum tax, 249	• **MyEconLab** Study Plan 9.4
9.5 The Multiplier. Any increase in autonomous expenditures, such as an increase in investment caused by a rise in business confidence, causes a direct rise in GDP. This GDP increase, in turn, stimulates increased expenditures elsewhere in the economy. For every dollar of GDP, the proportion of money spent domestically is called the marginal propensity to spend (MPE). As this secondary expenditure occurs, however, it further creates more GDP and creates more rounds of expenditure and GDP. The ultimate expansion of GDP is equal to the multiplier, $1/(1-MPE)$, times the original increase in autonomous expenditures. The multiplier can also be calculated as 1/(proportion of leakages).	multiplier, 253 marginal propensity to spend, 254 marginal propensity to import, 254	• **MyEconLab** Study Plan 9.5
9.6 The Relationship between Total Planned Expenditures and the Aggregate Demand Curve. An increase in the price level decreases the purchasing power of money holdings, which induces households and businesses to cut back on expenditures. In addition, as individuals and firms seek to borrow to replenish their cash balances, the interest rate tends to rise, which further discourages spending. Furthermore, a higher price level reduces exports as foreign residents cut back on purchases of domestically produced goods. These effects combined shift the curve downward following a rise in the price level so that equilibrium real GDP falls. This yields the downward-sloping aggregate demand curve.		• **MyEconLab** Study Plan 9.6

PROBLEMS

(Answers to the odd-numbered problems appear at the back of the book.)

LO 9.1 Distinguish between saving and savings and explain how saving and consumption are related.

1. List each of the following under the heading "Stock" or "Flow."
   a. The Chens have $100 of savings in the bank.
   b. Smith earns $200 per week.
   c. Labatt's Breweries owns 2000 trucks.
   d. Inventories rise at 400 units per year.
   e. Brochu consumes $80 per week out of income.
   f. The equilibrium quantity is 1000 per day.
   g. The corporation spends $1 billion per year on investments.

2. Classify each of the following as either a stock or a flow:
   a. Myung Park earns $850 per week.
   b. America Online purchases $100 million in new computer equipment this month.
   c. Sally Schmidt has $1000 in a savings account at a credit union.
   d. XYZ, Inc., produces 200 units of output per week.
   e. Giorgio Giannelli owns three private jets.
   f. DaimlerChrysler's inventories decline by 750 autos per month.
   g. Russia owes $25 billion to the International Monetary Fund.

LO 9.2 Explain the key determinants of consumption and saving in the Keynesian model.

3. Make a list of determinants, other than income, that might affect your personal MPC.

4. Examine the accompanying table:

Disposable Income	Saving	Consumption
$ 200	-$ 40	_____
400	0	_____
600	40	_____
800	80	_____
1000	120	_____
1200	160	_____

   a. Complete the table.
   b. Add two columns to the right of the table. Calculate the ratio of saving to income and the ratio of consumption to income at each level of disposable income. (Round to the nearest hundredth.)
   c. Determine the marginal propensity to save and the marginal propensity to consume.

LO 9.3 Identify the primary determinants of planned investment.

5. The rate of return on an investment on new machinery is 9 percent.
   a. If the market interest rate is 9.5 percent, will the investment be carried out?
   b. If the interest rate is 8 percent, will the machinery be purchased?
   c. If the interest rate is 9 percent, will the machinery be purchased?

6. An Internet service provider (ISP) is contemplating an investment of $50 000 in new computer servers and related hardware. The ISP projects an annual rate of return on this investment of 6 percent.
   a. The current market interest rate is 5 percent per year. Will the ISP undertake the investment?
   b. Suddenly there is an economic downturn. Although the market interest rate does not change, the ISP anticipates that the projected rate of return on the investment will be only 4 percent per year. Will the ISP now undertake the investment?

7. Refer to Example 9–2, "Changes in Investment and the Great Depression." Why might a stock market crash create a situation in which firms no longer want to invest?

LO 9.4 Describe how equilibrium GDP is established in the Keynesian model.

8. Consider the table at the end of this problem when answering the following questions. For this hypothetical economy, the marginal propensity to save is constant at all levels of income, and investment spending is autonomous. There is no government or foreign trade.
   a. Complete the table. What is the marginal propensity to save? What is the marginal propensity to consume?
   b. Draw a graph of the consumption function. Then add the investment function to obtain $C + I$.
   c. Under the graph of $C + I$, draw another graph showing the saving and investment curves. Note that the curve crosses the 45-degree reference line in the upper graph at the same level of real GDP where the saving and investment curves cross in the lower graph. (If not, redraw your graphs.) What is this level of real GDP?
   d. What is the numerical value of the multiplier?
   e. What is the equilibrium level of real GDP without investment? What is the multiplier effect from the inclusion of investment?
   f. If autonomous investment declines from $400 to $200, what happens to equilibrium real GDP?

Real GDP	Consumption	Saving	Investment
$ 2 000	$2 200	$_____	$400
4 000	4 000	_____	_____
6 000	_____	_____	_____
8 000	_____	_____	_____
10 000	_____	_____	_____
12 000	_____	_____	_____

9. Consider the table below when answering the following questions. For this hypothetical economy, the marginal propensity to consume is constant at all levels of real GDP, and investment spending is autonomous. The equilibrium level of real GDP is equal to $8000. There is no government or foreign trade.

Real GDP	Consumption	Saving	Investment
$ 2 000	$ 2 000	_____	_____
4 000	3 600	_____	_____
6 000	5 200	_____	_____
8 000	6 800	_____	_____
10 000	8 400	_____	_____
12 000	10 000	_____	_____

a. Complete the table. What is the marginal propensity to consume? What is the marginal propensity to save?
b. Draw a graph of the consumption function. Then add the investment function to obtain a total planned expenditure function.
c. Now add a government sector of $400. Add this to your function. Calculate equilibrium GDP with and without the government sector. Show this on your graph by finding where your two curves cross the 45-degree reference line.
d. Why is this model unrealistic in its assumptions about production? (Hint: Why not just keep adding to autonomous consumption forever?)
e. If autonomous consumption were to rise by $100, what would happen to equilibrium real GDP?

10. Look back to Example 9-3, "Oil Sands Investment Continues to Grow." Given your answer to the critical analysis, what must be happening to the total planned expenditures for Canada, all else equal? Show this on a graph and explain in words what will happen to equilibrium GDP.

LO 9.5 Evaluate why autonomous changes in total planned expenditures have a multiplier effect on equilibrium GDP.

11. A nation's consumption function (expressed in millions of inflation-adjusted dollars) is $C = \$800 + 0.80Y$. There are no taxes in this nation and saving is the only leakage.
a. What is the value of autonomous saving?
b. What is the marginal propensity to save in this economy?
c. What is the value of the multiplier?

12. The data in the table at the bottom of this page apply to a hypothetical economy. Assume that the marginal propensity to consume is constant at all levels of income. Further assume that investment is autonomous.
a. Draw a graph of the consumption function. Then add the investment function, giving you $C + I$.
b. Right under the first graph, draw in the saving and investment curves. Does the $C + I$ curve intersect the 45-degree line in the upper graph at the same level of real GDP as where saving equals investment in the lower graph? (If not, redraw your graphs.)
c. What is the multiplier effect from the inclusion of investment?
d. What is the numerical value of the multiplier?
e. What is the equilibrium level of real GDP and output without investment? With investment?
f. What will happen to income if autonomous investment increases by $100?
g. What will the equilibrium level of real GDP be if autonomous consumption increases by $100?

13. Suppose that the European Union decides to place a ban on many Canadian products. What effect will this have on net exports? How will this shift the total planned expenditures curve? What will happen to real GDP? Draw this situation in a diagram.

14. (More advanced) Suppose that we have a consumption function given as:
$$C = 50 + 0.6 (Y - T)$$
where T = taxes, set at 100 billion, and the remaining expenditures are given by $I + G + (X - M) = 350$. Everything is measured in billions of dollars.
a. Find the equilibrium value for real GDP.
b. Suppose T is increased to 110. What happens to real GDP?
c. Now decrease T to 80. What happens to real GDP?

Real GDP	Consumption Expenditures	Saving	Investment	MPC	MPS
$1000	$1100	$_____	$100	_____	_____
2000	2000	_____	_____	_____	_____
3000		_____	_____	_____	_____
4000		_____	_____	_____	_____
5000		_____	_____	_____	_____
6000		_____	_____	_____	_____

d. How would you forecast real GDP and its relationship to taxes, knowing these outcomes?

15. Answer the following questions about the multiplier.
    a. If the MPE = 0, what is the multiplier?
    b. What happens to the multiplier as the MPC increases (all other values remaining the same)?
    c. What is the multiplier if the MPE = 0.5? If the MPE = 0.75?

16. Calculate the multiplier for the following cases. Assume that the MPC value as given shows the value as a portion of national income, not disposable income.
    a. MPC = 0.9, MPM = 0.2, Tax rate = 0.1
    b. MPS = 0.2, MPM = 0.0, Tax rate = 0.3
    c. MPS = 0.1, MPM = 0.4, Tax rate = 0.2
    d. What happens to the multiplier as a country imports a larger proportion of its income?

17. Refer to Appendix E. Recalculate the multiplier for the cases listed in Problem 16 assuming the MPC refers to disposable income, not GDP.

LO 9.6 Understand the relationship between total planned expenditures and the aggregate demand curve.

18. What component of the Canadian total planned expenditures curve will the following events affect, and will these events lead to an increase or a decrease in our aggregate demand?
    a. Japan recovers from its economic crisis and consumers start to spend again.
    b. The federal government pays out $3 million in scholarships to postsecondary students.
    c. Because of the low value of the Canadian dollar, Canadians take their summer holidays in Canada instead of in other countries.
    d. Low inflation during the last quarter causes the Bank of Canada to reduce its interest rates.

19. At an initial point on the aggregate demand curve, the price level is 125, and real income is $10 trillion. When the price level falls to a value of 120, total autonomous expenditures increase by $250 billion. The marginal propensity to spend is 0.75. What is the level of real income at the new point on the aggregate demand curve?

20. At an initial point on the aggregate demand curve, the price level is 100, and real income is $12 trillion. After the price level rises to 110, however, there is an upward movement along the aggregate demand curve, and real income declines to $11 trillion. If total autonomous spending declined by $200 billion in response to the increase in the price level, what is the marginal propensity to spend in this economy?

APPENDIX D

THE KEYNESIAN CROSS AND THE MULTIPLIER

We can see the multiplier effect more clearly if we look at Figure D-1, in which we see only a small section of the graphs that we used in Chapter 9. We start with an equilibrium level of real GDP of $650 billion per year. This equilibrium occurs with total planned expenditures represented by $C + I + G + (X - M)$. The $C + I + G + (X - M)$ curve intersects the 45-degree reference line at $650 billion per year. Now, we increase investment, I, by $10 billion. This increase in investment shifts the entire $C + I + G + (X - M)$ curve vertically to $C + I + G + (X - M)$. The vertical shift represents that $10 billion increase in autonomous investment. With the higher level of planned expenditures per year, we are no longer in equilibrium at E. Inventories are falling. Production will increase. Eventually, planned production will catch up with total planned expenditures. The new equilibrium level of real GDP is established at E' at the intersection of the new $C + I + G + (X - M)$ curve and the 45-degree reference line, along which $C + I + G + (X - M) = Y$ (total planned expenditures equal real GDP). The new equilibrium level of real GDP is $700 billion per year. Thus, the increase in equilibrium real GDP is equal to five times the permanent increase in planned investment spending.

We can translate Table 9–3 into graphic form by looking at each successive round of additional spending induced by an autonomous increase in planned investment of $10 billion. The total planned expenditures curve shifts from $C + I + G + (X - M)$, with its associated equilibrium level of real GDP of $650 billion, to a new curve labelled $C + I' + G + (X - M)$. The new equilibrium level of real GDP is $700 billion. Equilibrium is again established.

FIGURE D–1

Graphing the Multiplier

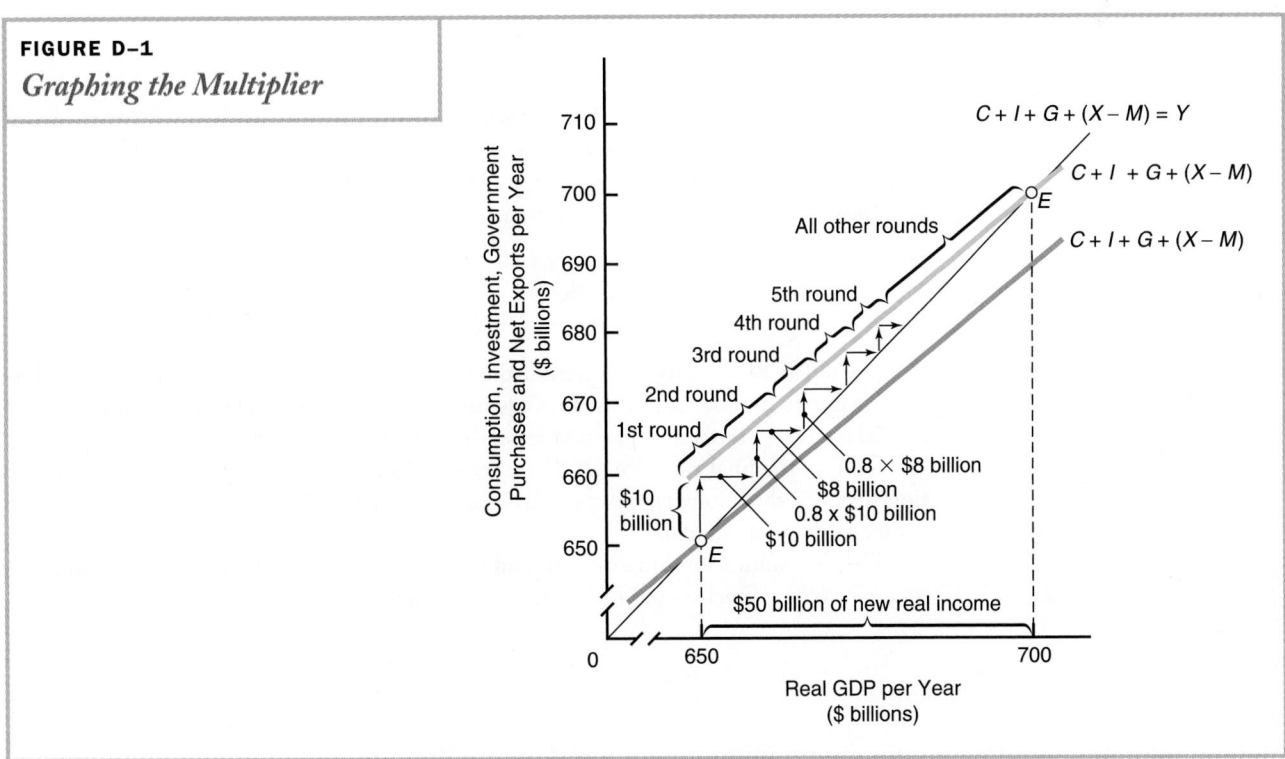

APPENDIX E

THE ALGEBRA OF THE KEYNESIAN EXPENDITURE MODEL

In this chapter, we have presented the Keynesian expenditure model with a minimum of mathematics. While this kept the model relatively simple, sometimes it is worthwhile to explore this model with a fuller presentation of the underlying mathematical model. Of course, this represents only one version of the model.

Students should not be intimidated by this model. With a little practice on actual numbers, these models are relatively easy to solve with only high-school mathematical skill and is very similar to a "break-even" model often studied in basic business mathematics courses.

In the model, the following abbreviations are used: **b** for the marginal propensity to consume (MPC), **t** for the marginal tax rate, **m** for the marginal propensity to import (MPM), and **e** for the marginal propensity to spend (MPE). The subscript "0" indicates that the term is a form of autonomous expenditure (e.g., I_0 indicates that this is autonomous investment). The following equations are basic to the Keynesian model:

(1) $$C = C_0 + b\,Y_d$$

(2) $$I = I_0$$

(3) $$G = G_0$$

(4) $$X = X_0$$

(5) $$M = M_0 + mY$$

These first five equations represent the expenditure functions that model the spending by the various groups in society. All of these equations have an autonomous component, while consumption depends upon disposable income Y_d and imports increase with GDP Y. When spending increases with income it is referred to as *induced* spending.

(6) $$T = T_0 + tY$$

(7) $$Y_d = Y - T$$

This function represents the taxation/transfer payment function of governments. Taxes are assumed to have two parts—an autonomous part composed of taxes independent of income and a constant marginal tax rate. Transfer payments can be assumed to be a "negative" tax, reducing the autonomous tax component.

(8) $$TPE = C + I + G + (X - M)$$

(9) $$TPE = Y$$

These last two equations represent the planned expenditures in the economy and its relationship to production. In the first equation, all planned expenditure is combined. The second equation shows that planned expenditures must equal national production.

To find the final value for GDP, we must reduce these equations into a single equation that will show how equilibrium GDP changes with changes in the various assumed components of the model.

First, we substitute Equations (6) and (7) into Equation (1) to alter our consumption function to be a function of GDP, rather than disposable income:

$$C = C_0 + \mathbf{b} \, (Y - T)$$

and substituting again:

$$C = C_0 + \mathbf{b} \, (Y - (T_0 + \mathbf{t}Y))$$

And reducing:

(1a) $$\qquad C = C_0 + \mathbf{b}Y - \mathbf{b}T_0 - \mathbf{b}\mathbf{t}Y$$

We then substitute (1a), (2) – (5) into (8) which gives:

$$\text{TPE} = C_0 + \mathbf{b}Y - \mathbf{b}T_0 - \mathbf{b}\mathbf{t}Y + I_0 + G_0 + X_0 - M_0 - \mathbf{m}Y$$

Now, we combine the various constant terms and Y terms separately as:

$$\text{TPE} = C_0 - \mathbf{b}T_0 + I_0 + G_0 + X_0 - M_0 - \mathbf{m}Y + \mathbf{b}Y - \mathbf{b}\mathbf{t}Y$$

Or more simply as:

(8a) $$\qquad \text{TPE} = [C_0 - \mathbf{b}T_0 + I_0 + G_0 + X_0 - M_0] + [\mathbf{b} - \mathbf{b}\mathbf{t} - \mathbf{m}] \, Y$$

The first six terms in the square brackets are all autonomous expenditures, and the second three are all induced components. Graphically, the first terms are the intercept of the line, and the next three represent the slope of the TPE function, or the marginal propensity to spend (**e**).

If we look back to our example in Section 9.4, the model can be created algebraically as:

$$C = 30 + 0.8 \, Y_d$$

$$I = 70$$

$$G = 100$$

$$X - M = 10 \; (\mathbf{m} = 0)$$

$$T = 100 \; (\mathbf{t} = 0)$$

Substituting into Equation (8a) gives us:

$$\text{TPE} = [30 - 0.8 \times 100 + 70 + 100 + 10] + [0.8 - 0.8 \times 0 - 0] \, Y \text{ or}$$

$$\text{TPE} = [130] + [0.8] \, Y$$

which can then be plotted as in Figure 9–6.

EQUILIBRIUM. Equilibrium can now be found in a straightforward manner by substituting Equation (8a) into (9). This gives:

$$[C_0 - \mathbf{b}T_0 + I_0 + G_0 + X_0 - M_0] + [\mathbf{b} - \mathbf{b}\mathbf{t} - \mathbf{m}] \, Y = Y$$

Now, factoring out all Y terms on the right-hand side gives:

$$[C_0 - \mathbf{b}T_0 + I_0 + G_0 + X_0 - M_0] = (1 - [\mathbf{b} - \mathbf{b}\mathbf{t} - \mathbf{m}]) \, Y$$

Dividing both sides by $(1 - [\mathbf{b} - \mathbf{b}\mathbf{t} - \mathbf{m}])$ and reorganizing gives:

(10) $$\qquad Y = [C_0 - \mathbf{b}T_0 + I_0 + G_0 + X_0 - M_0] / (1 - [\mathbf{b} - \mathbf{b}\mathbf{t} - \mathbf{m}])$$

Applying this to our previous example is simple.

$$130 + 0.8Y = Y$$

Combining the Y terms on the right-hand side:

$$130 = Y - 0.8Y = 0.2 \, Y$$

or $$\qquad Y^* = 130/0.2 = 650.$$

Again, this is same result as before as shown in Figure 9–6 part (a).

THE MULTIPLIER. The marginal propensity to spend (**e**) is the slope of the TPE function and is calculated here as **b** − **bt** − **m**. Note the multiplier is therefore calculated as:

(11)   Multiplier = $1/(1 − [b − bt − m])$

or more simply as $(1/(1 − e))$, which we see at the end of Equation (11). Note that all three types of leakages are included in this equation: $(1 − b)$ = marginal propensity to save, **t** = marginal taxes and **m** = marginal propensity to import.

Again, applying this to our previous example gives:

$$1/(1 − e) = 1/(1 − 0.8) = 5.$$

If we use Equation (11) and apply the approximate value for Canada we get:

$$\text{Multiplier} = 1/(1 − [0.9 − 0.9 \times 0.3 − 0.4]) = 1/1 − 0.23 = 1/0.77 = 1.30$$

This implies a very low value for the multiplier, as Canadians have average marginal tax rates and a high propensity to import.

10

The Public Sector

➤ **LEARNING OBJECTIVES**

After reading this chapter, you should be able to:

10.1 Explain the four economic functions of government.

10.2 Describe the two main political functions of government and how decision making differs depending on whether the individual is in the public or private sector.

10.3 Distinguish between average and marginal tax rates and explain the Canadian tax system.

MyEconLab helps you master each objective and study more efficiently. See end of chapter for details.

In Canada, over the course of a year, thousands of tax lawyers and accountants labour alone or with clients to help those clients reduce their tax liabilities and fill out their tax returns. Canadian taxpayers are each estimated to spend approximately 20 hours a year preparing their taxes. The opportunity cost exceeds $4 billion a year. And that is not the end of the story—many individuals spend a lot of valuable time figuring out ways to change their lifestyle so as to reduce the taxes they owe. Although there is never any way to avoid the cost of a tax system completely, there are ways to reduce compliance costs to society. One way is to switch to a more simplified tax system. To understand this issue, you need to know more about government and the public sector.

DID YOU KNOW THAT...?

The average Canadian works from January 1 through June 27 each year to pay for all municipal, provincial, and federal taxes. The average Vancouver resident works approximately two weeks longer to pay for all of the taxes owed each year when compared with the typical Ontario resident. Looked at another way, the average Canadian in a typical eight-hour day works about three hours and 54 minutes to pay for government at all levels. The average household with two or more people spends about $23 218 a year in taxes of all kinds. The total amount paid exceeds $270 billion. It would take more than 270 000 millionaires to have as much money as is spent each year by government. So, we cannot ignore the presence of government in our society. Government exists, at a minimum, to take care of what the price system does not do well.

10.1 Economic Functions of Government

Government performs many functions that affect the way in which exchange is carried out in the economy. Let us look at four economic functions of government.

PROVIDING A LEGAL SYSTEM. The courts and the police may not at first seem like economic functions of government (although judges and police personnel must be paid). Their activities, nonetheless, have important consequences on the economic activities in any country. You and I enter into contracts constantly, whether they be oral or written, express or implied. When we believe that we have been wronged, we seek redress of our grievances within our legal institutions. Moreover, consider the legal system that is necessary for the smooth functioning of our society. Our society has defined quite explicitly the legal status of businesses, the rights of private ownership, and a method for the enforcement of contracts. All relationships among consumers and businesses are governed by the legal rules of the game. We might consider government in its judicial function and then as the referee when there are disputes in the economic arena.

Much of our legal system is involved with defining and protecting *property rights*. **Property rights** are the rights of an owner to use and to exchange that property. One might say that property rights are really the rules of our economic game. When property rights are well defined, owners of property have an incentive to use the property efficiently. Any mistakes in their decision about the use of property have negative consequences that the owners suffer. Furthermore, when property rights are well defined, owners of property have an incentive to maintain that property so that if those owners ever desire to sell it, it will fetch a better price.

Property rights The rights of an owner to use and to exchange that property.

Establishing and maintaining a well-functioning legal system is not a costless activity, as you can see in Policy Example 10–1.

POLICY EXAMPLE 10–1 **Who Should Pay the High Cost of a Legal System?**

When a huge multinational corporation gets into a lengthy and expensive "shouting match" with its detractors, the public ends up footing part of the legal bill. McDonald's operates worldwide, with annual sales of about $50 billion. It has property rights in the goodwill associated with its name. When two unemployed British social activists published a pamphlet with such chapter headings as "McDollar, McGreedy, McCancer, McMurder, McRipoff, McTorture, and McGarbage," McDonald's was not pleased. The pamphlet accused the American company of torturing animals, corrupting children, and exploiting the Third World.

continued

So, McDonald's went to court in London. When the case began, there were 26 preliminary hearings spread over a four-year time period, and when it went to trial, 180 witnesses were called. McDonald's itself will end up spending many millions of dollars, but British taxpayers will foot the entire bill for the use of the court system. According to the Lord Chancellor's Department, British taxpayers paid at least £2.5 million (well over $5.5 million).

Should taxpayers continue to pay for all of the court system? No, according to policy makers in Britain. They have a plan to make litigants pay the full cost of court services, specifically judges' salaries. Such a system that forces litigants to pay for the full opportunity cost of the legal system has yet to be instituted in Canada or elsewhere.

For critical analysis: What other costs, besides judges' salaries, do citizens implicitly pay for in their legal system?

PROMOTING COMPETITION. Many people believe that the only way to attain economic efficiency is through competition. One of the roles of government is to serve as the protector of a competitive economic system. The federal and provincial governments have passed **anticombines legislation**, which makes illegal certain (but not all) economic activities that might, in legal terms, restrain trade—that is, prevent free competition among actual and potential rival firms in the marketplace. The avowed aim of anticombines legislation is to reduce the power of **monopolies**—firms that have great control over the price of the goods they sell. A number of laws have been passed that prohibit specific anticompetitive business behaviour. The Competition Bureau, which is part of Industry Canada, attempts to enforce these anticombines laws. Various provincial judicial agencies also expend efforts at maintaining competition.

Anticombines legislation Laws that make illegal certain economic activities that might restrain trade.

Monopoly A firm that has great control over the price of a good it sells.

PROVIDING PUBLIC GOODS. The goods used in our examples up to this point have been **private goods**—goods that can be consumed by only one individual at a time. When I eat a cheeseburger, you cannot eat the same one. So, you and I are rivals for that cheeseburger, just as much as rivals for the title of world champion are. When I use a CD player, you cannot use the same player. When I use the services of an auto mechanic, that person cannot work at the same time for you. That is the distinguishing feature of private goods—their use is exclusive to the people who purchase or rent them. The **principle of rival consumption** is that one person's consumption reduces the amount of private goods available for others to consume. Rival consumption is easy to understand. With private goods, either you use them or I use them.

Private goods Goods that can be consumed by only one individual at a time.

There is an entire class of goods that are not private goods. These are called **public goods**—these can be consumed jointly by many individuals simultaneously at no additional cost and with no reduction in quality or quantity. Military defence, police protection, and the legal system, for example, are public goods. If you partake of them, you do not necessarily take away from anyone else's share of those goods.

Principle of rival consumption The principle that one person's consumption reduces the amount of private goods available for others to consume.

Public goods Goods that can be consumed jointly by many individuals simultaneously at no additional cost and with no reduction in quality or quantity.

CHARACTERISTICS OF PUBLIC GOODS. Several distinguishing characteristics of public goods set them apart from all other goods.[1]

1. Public goods are indivisible. You cannot buy or sell $5 worth of a park. Public goods cannot usually be produced or sold very easily in small units.
2. Public goods can be used by more and more people at no additional cost. Once money has been spent for the park, the opportunity cost to you is zero.
3. Additional users of public goods do not deprive others of any of the services of the goods. If you use the park, it does not prevent someone else from also using it.
4. It is difficult to design a collection system for a public good on the basis of how much individuals use it. It is nearly impossible to determine how much any person uses or

---

[1]Sometimes the distinction is made between pure public goods, which have all the characteristics we have described here, and quasi- or near-public goods, which do not. The major feature of near-public goods is that they are jointly consumed, even though nonpaying customers can be, and often are, excluded—for example, movies, football games, and concerts.

FIGURE 10–1

Total Marginal Benefit of a Public Good

The total marginal benefit of a park is derived by adding the marginal benefits of all individuals.

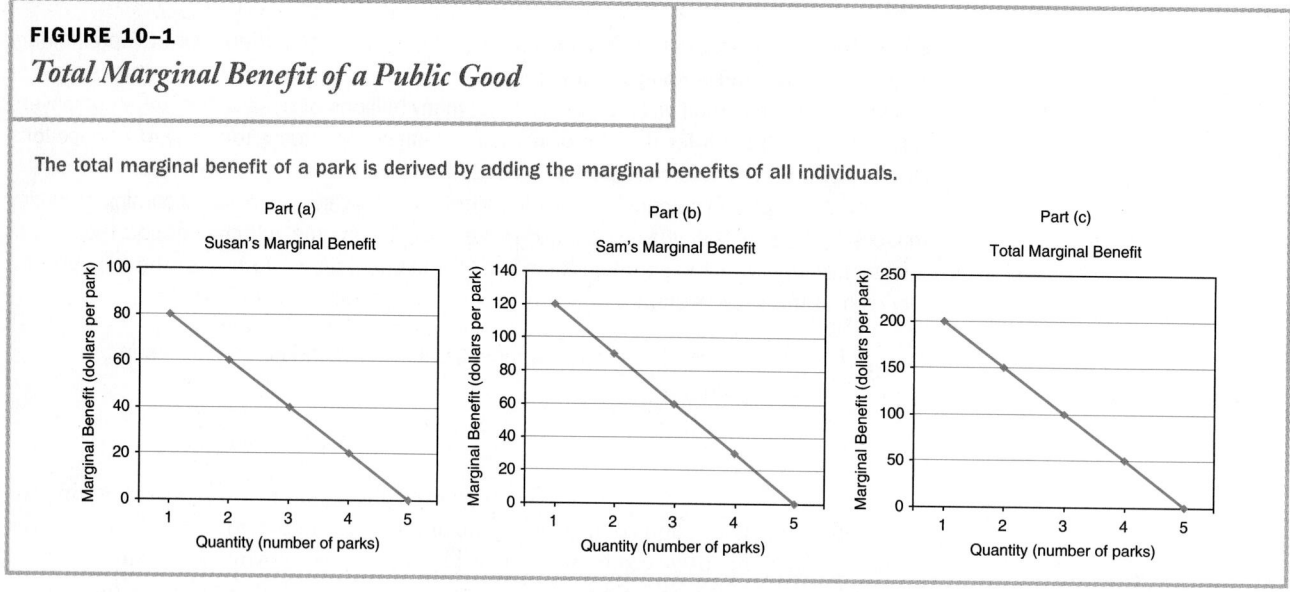

Exclusion principle The principle that no one can be denied the benefits of a public good for failing to pay for it.

values parks. No one can be denied the benefits of the park for failing to pay for that public good. This is often called the **exclusion principle**.

If we think about our park, we can determine the total marginal benefit of the park. Sam and Susan both would like some parks in their area. Each puts a different value on the park, as illustrated by Figure 10–1 above. Part (a) shows Susan's marginal benefit is $80 for the first park, part (b) shows Sam's marginal benefit is $120 for the first park, and part (c) shows the total benefit of the first park is $200. The marginal cost of a public good is determined the same way you would derive the marginal cost for a private good.

One of the problems of public goods is that the private sector has a difficult, if not impossible, time in providing them. There is little or no incentive for individuals in the private sector to offer public goods because it is so difficult to make a profit in so doing. Consequently, a true public good must necessarily be provided by government. Read Example 10–1 for further discussion.

EXAMPLE 10–1   Are Lighthouses a Public Good?

One of the most common examples of a public good is a lighthouse. Arguably, it satisfies all the criteria listed in points 1 through 4 on page 271. In one instance, however, a lighthouse was not a public good in that a collection system was devised and enforced on the basis of how much individuals used it. In the 13th century, in the city of Aigues-Mortes, a port in Southern France, a tower called the King's Tower was erected to assert the will and power of Louis IX (Saint Louis). The 32-metre-high tower served as a lighthouse for ships. More importantly, it served as a lookout so that ships sailing on the open sea, but in its view, did not escape paying for use of the lighthouse. Those payments were then used for the construction of the city walls.

For critical analysis: Explain how a lighthouse satisfies the characteristics of public goods described in points 1, 2, and 3.

Free-rider problem A situation in which some individuals take advantage of the fact that others will shoulder the burden of paying for public goods.

FREE RIDERS. The nature of public goods leads to the **free-rider problem**, a situation in which some individuals take advantage of the fact that others will shoulder the burden of paying for public goods, such as defence. Free riders will argue that they receive no value from such government services as defence and therefore really should not have to pay for them. Suppose that citizens were taxed directly in proportion to how much they told an interviewer that they valued military protection. Some people would probably say that they are unwilling to pay for it because they do not want any—it is of no value to them. Many of us may end up being free riders when we assume that others will pay for the desired public good. We may all want to be free riders if we believe that someone else will provide the commodity in question that we actually value.

The free-rider problem is a definite issue among nations with respect to the international burden of defence and how it should be shared. A country may choose to belong to a multilateral defence organization, such as the North Atlantic Treaty Organization (NATO) but then consistently attempt not to contribute funds to the organization. The nation knows it would be defended by others in NATO if it were attacked but would rather not pay for such defence. In short, it seeks a "free ride."

ENSURING ECONOMYWIDE STABILITY. Government attempts to stabilize the economy by smoothing out the ups and downs in overall business activity. Our economy sometimes faces the problems of unemployment and oscillating prices. Government, especially the federal government, has made an attempt to solve these problems by trying to stabilize the economy. The notion that the federal government should undertake actions to stabilize business activity is a relatively new idea in Canada, encouraged by high unemployment rates during the Great Depression of the 1930s and subsequent theories about possible ways by which government could reduce unemployment. In 1945, government formally assumed responsibility for economic performance. It established three goals for government accountability: full employment, price stability, and economic growth. These goals have provided the justification for many government economic programs during the post–World War II period.

➤ **CONCEPTS IN BRIEF**

Learning Objective 10.1: Explain the four economic functions of government.

- The economic activities of government include (1) providing a judicial system, (2) promoting competition, (3) producing public goods, and (4) ensuring economywide stability.
- Public goods can be consumed jointly. The principle of rival consumption does not apply as it does with private goods.
- Public goods have the following characteristics: (1) They are indivisible; (2) once they are produced, there is no opportunity cost when additional consumers use them; (3) your use of a public good does not deprive others of its simultaneous use; and (4) consumers cannot conveniently be charged on the basis of use.

10.2 *The Political Functions of Government*

At least two areas of government are in the realm of political—or normative—functions, rather than that of the economic ones discussed in the first part of this chapter. These two areas are (1) the regulation and/or provision of merit and demerit goods, and (2) income redistribution.

Merit and Demerit Goods

Merit good Any good that the political process has deemed socially desirable.

Certain goods are considered to have special merit. A **merit good** is defined as any good that the political process has deemed socially desirable. (Note that nothing inherent in any particular good makes it a merit good. It is a matter of who chooses it.) Some examples of merit goods in our society are museums, ballets, sports stadiums (see Policy Example 10–2), and concerts. In these areas, government's role is the provision of merit goods to the people in society who would not otherwise purchase them at market clearing prices or who would not purchase an amount of them judged to be sufficient. This provision may take the form of government production and distribution of merit goods. It can also take the form of reimbursement for payment on merit goods or subsidies to producers or consumers for part of the cost of merit goods. Governments do, indeed, subsidize such merit goods as concerts, ballets, and museums. In most cases, such merit goods would rarely be so numerous without subsidization.

POLICY EXAMPLE 10-2   **Do Government-Funded Sports Stadiums Have a Net Positive Effect on Local Economies?**

Probably not, even though in recent years many cities have decided that new football and baseball stadiums are merit goods worthy of public funding. Their rationale is that there is no collective mechanism besides government to ensure the construction of the stadiums that will draw big crowds. A local government, goes the argument, can regard a stadium as an investment because the crowds it draws benefit the local economy. Spending by the crowds can also generate tax revenues that help government recoup its expenses. According to economist Andrew Zimbalist, however, "there has not been an independent study by an economist over the last 30 years that suggests you can anticipate a positive economic impact" from government investments in sports facilities.

For critical analysis: In theory, explain how a sports stadium might result in positive externalities for the local economy.

Source: Noll, Roger G. & Andrew Zimbalist, editors. Sports, Jobs, and Taxes: The Economic Impact of Sports Teams and Stadiums. Brookings Institution, 1997.

Demerit good Any good that the political process has deemed socially undesirable.

Demerit goods are the opposite of merit goods—they are goods that the political process has deemed socially undesirable. Cigarettes, gambling, and illegal drugs are examples. Government exercises its role in the area of demerit goods by taxing, regulating, or prohibiting their manufacture, sale, and use. Governments justify the relatively high taxes on alcohol and tobacco by declaring them demerit goods. The best-known example of governmental exercise of power in this area is the stance against certain psychoactive drugs. Most psychoactives (except nicotine, caffeine, and alcohol) are either expressly prohibited, as is the case for heroin, cocaine, and opium, or heavily regulated, as in the case of prescription psychoactives.

Income Redistribution

Another relatively recent political function of government has been the explicit redistribution of income. This redistribution uses two systems: the progressive income tax (described later in this chapter) and transfer payments. **Transfer payments** are payments made to individuals for which no services or goods are concurrently rendered in return. The three key money transfer payments in our system are welfare, old age security payments, and employment insurance benefits. Income redistribution also includes a large amount of income **transfers in kind**—payments that are in the form of actual goods and services for which no goods or services are rendered concurrently in return. Two income transfers in kind are health care and low-cost public housing.

Transfer payments Payments made to individuals for which no services or goods are concurrently rendered in return.

Transfers in kind Payments that are in the form of actual goods and services for which no goods or services are rendered concurrently in return.

Government has also engaged in other activities as a form of redistribution of income. For example, the provision of child-care spaces is, at least in part, an attempt to redistribute income by making sure that the very poor have access to child-care (see Example 10–2).

EXAMPLE 10-2   **Child-Care Spaces**

The federal government has recently provided parents with $100 per month per child under six years old to help with child-care expenses. They are also providing provinces with money on a per- capita basis to develop child-care spaces as shown by Table 10–1.

continued

TABLE 10-1		($ millions)
Support for the Development of Child-Care Spaces, 2007–08	Newfoundland and Labrador	3.9
	Prince Edward Island	1.1
	Nova Scotia	7.1
	New Brunswick	5.7
	Quebec	58.5
	Ontario	97.5
	Manitoba	9.0
	Saskatchewan	7.5
	Alberta	25.9
	British Columbia	33.1
	Nunavut	0.2
	Northwest Territories	0.3
	Yukon	0.2
	Total Canada	**250.0**

Note: Based on equal per-capita allocation. Figures are based on Statistics Canada population projections. Totals may not add due to rounding. Provided outside of the Canadian Social Transfer in this year.

For critical analysis: Are the federal dollars given directly to the parents more beneficial to society than the money given to the provinces?

SOURCE: FEDERAL SUPPORT FOR CHILDREN. http://www.fin.gc.ca/FEDPROV/fsce.html.

Collective Decision Making: The Theory of Public Choice

The public sector has a vast influence on the Canadian economy. Yet, the economic model used until now has applied only to the behaviour of the private sector—firms and households. Such a model does not adequately explain the behaviour of the public sector. We shall attempt to do so now.

Governments consist of individuals. No government actually thinks and acts; rather, government actions are the result of decision making by individuals in their roles as elected representatives, appointed officials, and salaried bureaucrats. Therefore, to understand how government works, we must examine the incentives for the people in government as well as those who would like to be in government—avowed candidates or would-be candidates for elected or appointed positions—and special-interest lobbyists attempting to get government to do something. At issue is the analysis of *collective decision making*. **Collective decision making** involves how voters, politicians, and other interested parties act and how these actions influence nonmarket decisions. The analysis of collective decision making is usually called the **theory of public choice**. It has been given this name because it involves hypotheses about how choices are made in the public sector, as opposed to the private sector. The foundation of public-choice theory is the assumption that individuals will act within the political process to maximize their individual (not collective) well-being. In that sense, the theory is similar to our analysis of the market economy, in which we also assume that individuals are motivated by self-interest.

To understand public-choice theory, it is necessary to point out other similarities between the private market sector and the public, or government, sector; then, we will look at the differences.

Collective decision making How voters, politicians, and other interested parties act and how these actions influence nonmarket decisions.

Theory of public choice The analysis of collective decision making.

Similarities in Market and Public-Sector Decision Making

In addition to the similar assumption of self-interest being the motivating force in both sectors, there are other similarities.

SCARCITY. At any given moment, the amount of resources is fixed. This means that for the private and the public sectors combined, there is a scarcity constraint. Everything that is spent by all levels of government, plus everything that is spent by the private sector, must add up to the total income available at any point in time. Hence, every government action has an opportunity cost, just as in the market sector.

COMPETITION. Although we typically think of competition as a private market phenomenon, it is also present in collective action. Given the scarcity constraint government also faces, bureaucrats, appointed officials, and elected representatives will always be in competition for available government funds. Furthermore, the individuals within any government agency or institution will act as individuals do in the private sector: They will try to obtain higher wages, better working conditions, and higher job-level classifications. They will compete and act in their own, not society's, interests.

SIMILARITY OF INDIVIDUALS. Contrary to popular belief, there are not two types of workers, those who work in the private sector and those who work in the public sector; rather, individuals working in similar positions can be considered similar. The difference, as we shall see, is that the individuals in government face a different **incentive structure**, the system of rewards and punishments individuals face with respect to their own actions, from that in the private sector. For example, the costs and benefits of being efficient or inefficient differ when one goes from the private sector to the public sector.

One approach to predicting government bureaucratic behaviour is to ask what incentives bureaucrats face. Take Canada Post as an example. The bureaucrats running that Crown corporation are human beings with qualities similar to those possessed by workers in comparable positions at, say, Nortel or Air Canada. Yet, the post office does not function like either of these companies. The difference can be explained, at least in part, in terms of the incentives provided for the managers in the two types of institutions. When the bureaucratic managers and workers at Nortel make incorrect decisions, work slowly, produce shoddy products, and are generally "inefficient," the profitability of the company declines. The owners—millions of shareholders—express their displeasure by selling some of their shares of the company. The market value, as tracked on the stock exchange, falls. But what about Canada Post? If a manager, a worker, or a bureaucrat in the post office provides shoddy service, there is no straightforward mechanism by which the organization's owners—the taxpayers—can express their dissatisfaction. Despite the post office's status as a "government corporation," taxpayers as shareholders do not really own the organization's shares that they can sell.

The key, then, to understanding purported inefficiency in the government bureaucracy is not found in an examination of people and personalities but, rather, in an examination of incentives and institutional arrangements.

Differences between Market and Collective Decision Making

There are probably more dissimilarities between the market sector and the public sector than there are similarities.

GOVERNMENT GOODS AT ZERO PRICE. The majority of goods that governments produce are furnished to the ultimate consumers without direct money charge. **Government, or political, goods** (and services) are goods and services provided by the public sector; they can be either private or public goods. The fact that they are furnished to the ultimate consumer free of charge does not mean that the cost to society of those goods is zero, however; it only means that the price charged is zero. The full opportunity cost to society is the value of the resources used in the production of goods produced and provided by government.

For example, none of us pays directly for each unit of consumption of most highways nor for police protection. Rather, we pay for all these things indirectly through the taxes that support our governments—federal, provincial, and municipal. This special feature of government can be looked at in a different way. There is no longer a one-to-one relationship between the consumption of a government-provided good and the payment for that good. Consumers who pay taxes collectively pay for every political good, but the individual consumer may not be able to see the relationship between the taxes paid and the consumption of the good. Indeed, most taxpayers will find that their tax bill is the same whether or not they consume, or even like, government-provided goods.

Incentive structure The system of rewards and punishments individuals face with respect to their own actions.

Government, or political, goods Goods (and services) provided by the public sector; they can be either private or public goods.

USE OF FORCE. All governments are able to engage in the legal use of force in their regulation of economic affairs. For example, governments can exercise the use of expropriation, which means that if you refuse to pay your taxes, your bank account and other assets may be seized by the Canada Revenue Agency. In fact, you have no choice in the matter of paying taxes to governments. Collectively, we decide the total size of government through the political process, but individually we cannot determine how much service we pay for just for ourselves during any one year.

VOTING VERSUS SPENDING. In the private market sector, a dollar voting system is in effect. This dollar voting system is not equivalent to the voting system in the public sector. There are, at minimum, three differences:

1. In a political system, one person gets one vote, whereas in the market system, the dollars one spends count as votes.
2. The political system is run by **majority rule**, a collective decision-making system in which group decisions are made on the basis of 50.1 percent of the vote, whereas the market system is run by **proportional rule,** a decision-making system in which actions are based on the proportion of the "votes" cast and are in proportion to them.
3. The spending of dollars can indicate intensity of want, whereas because of the all-or-nothing nature of political voting, a vote cannot.

Ultimately, the main distinction between political votes and dollar votes here is that political outcomes may differ from economic outcomes. Remember that economic efficiency is a situation in which, given the prevailing distribution of income, consumers get the economic goods they want. There is no corresponding situation using political voting. Thus, we can never assume that a political voting process will lead to the same decisions that a dollar voting process will lead to in the marketplace.

Indeed, consider the dilemma every voter faces. Usually, a voter is not asked to decide on a single issue (although this happens); rather, a voter is asked to choose among candidates who present a large number of issues and state a position on each of them. Just consider the average member of parliament who has to vote on hundreds of different issues during a five-year term. When you vote for that representative, you are voting for a person who must make hundreds of decisions during the next five years.

The Role of Bureaucrats

Government programs require people to deliver them. This is manifested today in the form of well-established bureaucracies, in which **bureaucrats** (nonelected government officials) work. A **bureaucracy** is an administrative system run by a large staff following rules and procedures set down by government. Bureaucracies can exert great influence on matters concerning themselves—the amount of funding granted them and the activities in which they engage. In the political marketplace, well-organized bureaucracies can even influence the expression of public demand itself. In many cases, they organize the clientele (interest groups), coach that clientele on what is appropriate, and stick up for the "rights" of the clientele.

Gauging Bureaucratic Performance

It is tempting, but incorrect, to think of bureaucrats as mere "technocrats," executors of orders and channels of information, in this process. They have at least two incentives to make government programs larger and more resistant to attack than we might otherwise expect. First, society has decided that in general, government should not be run on a profit-making basis. Measures of performance other than bottom-line profits must be devised. In the private market, successful firms typically expand to serve more customers; although this growth is often incidental to the underlying profitability, the two frequently go hand in hand. In parallel, performance in government is often measured by the number of clients served, and rewards are distributed accordingly. As a result, bureaucrats have an incentive to expand the size of their clientele—not because it is more profitable (beneficial) to society but because that is how bureaucrats' rewards are structured.

Majority rule A collective decision-making system in which group decisions are made on the basis of 50.1 percent of the vote.

Proportional rule A decision-making system in which actions are based on the proportion of the "votes" cast and are in proportion to them.

Bureaucrats Nonelected government officials.

Bureaucracy An administrative system run by a large staff following rules and procedures set down by government.

In general, performance measures that are not based on long-run profitability are less effective at gauging true performance. This makes it potentially easier for the government bureaucrat to appear to perform well, collect rewards for measured performance, and then leave for greener pastures. To avoid this, a much larger proportion of the rewards given to bureaucrats are valuable only as long as they continue being bureaucrats—large staffs, expensive offices, generous pensions, and the like. Instead of getting large current salaries (which can be saved for a rainy day), they get rewards that disappear if their jobs disappear. Naturally, this increases the incentives of bureaucrats to make sure that their jobs do not disappear.

Rational Ignorance

At this point, you may well be wondering why this system still goes on. The answer lies in rational ignorance on the part of voters, ignorance that is carefully cultivated by the members of special interest groups.

On most issues, there is little incentive for the individual voter to expend resources to determine how to vote. Moreover, the ordinary course of living provides most of us with enough knowledge to decide whether we should invest in learning more about a given issue. For example, suppose that Canadian voters were asked to decide if the sign marking the entrance to an obscure national park should be enlarged. Most voters would decide that the potential costs and benefits of this decision are negligible: The new sign is unlikely to be the size of Prince Edward Island, and anybody who has even heard of the national park in question probably already has a pretty good idea of its location. Thus, most voters would choose to remain rationally ignorant about the exact costs and benefits of enlarging the sign, implying that (1) many will choose not to vote at all, and (2) those who do vote will simply flip a coin or cast their ballot on the basis of some other, perhaps ideological, grounds.

WHY BE RATIONALLY IGNORANT? For most political decisions, majority rule prevails. Only a coalition of voters representing slightly more than 50 percent of those who vote is needed. Whenever a vote is taken, the result is going to involve costs and benefits. Voters, then, must evaluate their share of the costs and benefits of any budgetary expenditure. Voters, however, are not perfectly informed. That is one of the crucial characteristics of the real world—information is a resource that is costly to obtain. Rational voters will, in fact, decide to remain at some level of ignorance about government programs because the benefits from obtaining more information may not be worth the cost, given each individual voter's extremely limited impact on the outcome of an election. For the same reason, voters will fail to inform themselves about taxes or other revenue sources to pay for proposed expenditures because they know that for any specific expenditure program, the cost to them individually will be small. At this point, it might be useful to contrast this situation with what exists in the nonpolitical private market sector of the economy. In the private market sector, the individual chooses a mix of purchases and bears fully the direct and indirect consequences of this selection (ignoring for the moment the problem of externalities).

➤ CONCEPTS IN BRIEF

Learning Objective 10.2: Describe the two main political functions of government and how decision making differs depending on whether the individual is in the public or private sector.
- Political, or normative, activities of government include the provision and regulation of merit and demerit goods and income redistribution.
- Merit and demerit goods do not have any inherent characteristics that qualify them as such; rather, collectively, through the political process, we make judgments about which goods and services are "good" for society and which are "bad."
- Income redistribution can be carried out by a system of progressive taxation, coupled with transfer payments, which can be made in money or in kind, such as health care and public education. Collective decision making involves the actions of voters, politicians, political parties, bureaucrats, and interest groups.

✦ The similarities between market and public-sector decision making include assumption of self-interest as the motivating force, scarcity of resources, and competition for available funds and resources.

✦ The key differences between the market and public sector include government goods at zero price, use of force, and proportional rule versus majority rule.

✦ The theory of public choice implies a situation called rational ignorance where on most issues there is little incentive for the individual voter to expend resources to determine how to vote. This allows bureaucrats and special interest groups to have a significant effect on choices in the public sector.

10.3 Tax Rates and the Canadian Tax System

Jean-Baptiste Colbert, the 17th-century French finance minister, said the art of taxation was in "plucking the goose so as to obtain the largest amount of feathers with the least possible amount of hissing." In Canada, governments have designed a variety of methods of plucking the private-sector goose. To analyze any tax system, we must first understand the distinction between marginal tax rates and average tax rates.

Marginal and Average Tax Rates

Marginal tax rate The change in taxes due divided by the change in taxable income.

If somebody says, "I pay 28 percent in taxes," you cannot really tell what that person means unless you know whether the individual is referring to average taxes paid or the tax rate on the last dollar earned. The latter concept has to do with the **marginal tax rate.**[2]

The marginal tax rate is expressed as follows:

$$\text{Marginal tax rate} = \frac{\text{Change in taxes due}}{\text{Change in taxable income}}$$

Tax bracket A specified level of taxable income to which a specific and unique marginal tax rate is applied.

It is important to understand that the marginal tax rate applies only to the income in the highest tax bracket reached, where a **tax bracket** is defined as a specified level of taxable income to which a specific and unique marginal tax rate is applied.

Average tax rate The total taxes due divided by total taxable income.

The **average tax rate** is not the same thing as the marginal tax rate; it is defined as follows:

$$\text{Average tax rate} = \frac{\text{Total taxes due}}{\text{Total taxable income}}$$

Taxation Systems

No matter how governments raise revenues—from income taxes, sales taxes, or other taxes—all of those taxes can fit into one of three types of taxation systems—proportional, progressive, and regressive, expressing a relationship between the percentage tax, or tax rate, paid and income. To determine whether a tax system is proportional, progressive, or regressive, we simply ask the question: "What is the relationship between the average tax rate and the marginal tax rate?"

Proportional taxation A tax system in which regardless of an individual's income, the tax bill comprises exactly the same proportion. Also called a *flat-rate tax.*

PROPORTIONAL TAXATION. **Proportional taxation** means that regardless of an individual's income, the taxes comprise exactly the same proportion, also called a flat-rate tax. In terms of marginal versus average tax rates, in a proportional taxation system, the marginal tax rate is always equal to the average tax rate. If every dollar is taxed at 20 percent, then the average tax rate is 20 percent, as is the marginal tax rate.

As mentioned earlier, a proportional tax system is also called a flat-rate tax. Taxpayers at all income levels end up paying the same percentage of their income in taxes. If the proportional tax rate were 20 percent, an individual with an income of $10 000 would pay $2000 in taxes, while an individual making $100 000 would pay $20 000, the identical 20 percent rate being levied on both. See the Issues and Applications for a more in-depth look at the flat tax issue.

---

[2]The word *marginal* means "incremental" (or "decremental") here.

Progressive taxation As taxable income increases, the percentage of income paid in taxes also increases.

PROGRESSIVE TAXATION. Under **progressive taxation**, as a person's taxable income increases, the percentage of income paid in taxes also increases. In terms of marginal versus average tax rates, in a progressive system, the marginal tax rate is above the average tax rate. If you are taxed 5 percent on the first $10 000 you make, 10 percent on the next $10 000 you make, and 30 percent on the last $10 000 you make, you face a progressive income tax system. Your marginal tax rate is always above your average tax rate. See Policy Example 10–3 to see how Canada compares with other countries.

Regressive taxation A smaller percentage of taxable income is taken in taxes as taxable income increases.

REGRESSIVE TAXATION. With **regressive taxation**, a smaller percentage of taxable income is taken in taxes as taxable income increases. The marginal rate is below the average rate. As income increases, the marginal tax rate falls, and so does the average tax rate. The Goods and Services Tax (GST) is regressive. Someone earning $10 000 per year pays the same sales tax on a tube of toothpaste as someone earning $100 000 per year. But the tube of toothpaste takes up a much larger proportion of the low-income earner's budget, and so the marginal tax rate for that person is higher. The federal government tries to address this inequity by giving GST rebates to low-income earners who apply for them on their income tax returns each year.

POLICY EXAMPLE 10–3   **Tax Freedom Day Around the World**

One of the measures that is getting a lot of attention from people is tax freedom day. Tax freedom day is the day people stop working to pay taxes to various governments and start working to pay themselves. It is easier for the average person to understand than a discussion on marginal and average tax rates. Canadians frequently complain that we pay too much tax, so the tax freedom day gives a quick, understandable measure of how we are doing against other nations.

TABLE 10–2

Country	Day of Year	% Burden	Date of Year
Australia	122	33.00%	April 25
Brazil	145	40.00	May 25
Canada	170	47.00	June 19
Croatia	166	45.00	June 15
Czech Republic	161	44.10	June 11
Germany	185	50.68	July 5
India	74	20.00	March 14
Israel	207	56.70	July 26
Lithuania	125	34.00	May 5
Poland	175	48.00	June 24
Slovakia	145	39.60	May 25
Slovenia	171	48.00	June 21
South Africa	112	31.00	April 22
United Kingdom	154	42.00	June 3
United States	120	32.69	April 30
Sweden	219	59.90	August 8
Estonia	114	31.10	April 24

SOURCE: http://www.answers.com/topic/tax-freedom-day, WIKIPEDIA

For critical analysis: Given that only five countries have a longer wait for their tax freedom day, what does that say about our level of taxation?

The Most Important Federal Taxes

The federal government imposes income taxes on both individuals and corporations, and collects sales taxes as well as a variety of other taxes.

The Federal Personal Income Tax

The most important tax in the Canadian economy is the federal personal income tax, which accounts for about 48 percent of all federal revenues. All Canadian citizens, resident aliens, and most others who earn income in Canada are required to pay federal income tax on all taxable income. The tax rates depend on the amount of taxable income earned, as can be seen in Table 10–3. Marginal income tax rates at the federal level have varied from as low as 4 percent after the passage of the *Income Tax Act* in 1917, to as high as 98 percent during World War II.

Advocates of a more progressive income tax system in Canada argue that such a system redistributes income from the rich to the poor, taxes people according to their ability to pay, and taxes people according to the benefits they receive from government. Although there is much controversy over the "redistributional" nature of our progressive tax system, there is no strong evidence that, in fact, the tax system has ever done much income redistribution in this country. Currently, about 80 percent of all Canadians, rich or poor, pay roughly the same proportion of their income in federal income tax.

TABLE 10-3

Federal Tax Rates

15% on first $37 178
22% over $37 178 up to $74 357
26% over $74 357 up to $120 887
29% of taxable income over $120 887

SOURCE: CANADA REVENUE AGENCY.

The Treatment of Capital Gains

Capital gain The positive difference between the buying and selling prices of an asset.

Capital loss The negative difference between the purchase price and the sale price of an asset.

The positive difference between the buying and selling prices of an asset, such as a share of stock or a plot of land, is called a **capital gain**, and the negative difference between the purchase price and the sale price of an asset is called a **capital loss**. Capital gains are taxed at ordinary income marginal tax rates. The taxable part of a capital gain is 50 percent of the net amount of your capital gains minus 50 percent of your capital losses for the year.

Capital gains are not always real. In Canada, gains on principal are not taxed, but if in one year you pay $100 000 for a house you plan to rent and sell it at a 50 percent higher price 10 years later, your nominal capital gain is $50 000. But what if, during those 10 years, there had been such inflation that average prices had also gone up by 50 percent? Your real capital gain would be zero. But you still have to pay taxes on that $50 000. To counter this problem, many economists have argued that capital gains should be indexed to the rate of inflation.

The Corporate Income Tax

Corporate income taxes account for about 14 percent of all federal taxes collected, and 3.4 percent of all provincial taxes collected. Corporations are generally taxed at a flat rate of 28 percent on the difference between their total revenues (or receipts) and their expenses.

Retained earnings Profits not given out to shareholders.

DOUBLE TAXATION. Because individual shareholders must pay taxes on the dividends they receive, paid out of after-tax profits by the corporation, corporate profits are taxed twice. If you receive $1000 in dividends, you have to declare it as income, and you must pay taxes at your marginal tax rate. Before the corporation was able to pay you those dividends, it had to pay taxes on all its profits, including any that it put back into the company or did not distribute in the form of dividends. Eventually, the new investment made possible by those **retained earnings**—profits not given out to shareholders—along with borrowed funds will be reflected in the increased value of the shares in that company. When you sell your shares in that company, you will have to pay taxes on the difference between what you paid for them and what you sold them for. In both cases, dividends and retained earnings (corporate profits) are taxed twice.

Tax incidence The distribution of tax burdens among various groups in society.

WHO REALLY PAYS THE CORPORATE INCOME TAX? Corporations can exist only as long as employees make their goods, consumers buy their products, shareholders (owners) buy their shares, and bondholders buy their bonds. Corporations *per se* do not do anything. We must ask, then, who really pays the tax on corporate income. This is a question of **tax incidence**, the distribution of tax burdens among various groups in society. (The question of tax incidence applies to all taxes, including sales and payroll taxes.) There remains considerable debate about the incidence of corporate taxation. Some economists say that corporations pass their tax burdens on to consumers by charging higher prices. Other economists believe that it is the shareholders who bear most of the tax. Still others believe that employees pay at least part of the tax by receiving lower wages than they would otherwise. Because the debate is not yet settled, we will not hazard a guess here as to what the correct conclusion should be. Suffice it to say that you should be cautious when you advocate increasing corporate income taxes. You may be the one who ends up paying the increase, at least in part, if you own shares in a corporation, buy its products, or work for it.

Unemployment and Pension Taxes

An increasing percentage of federal revenues is accounted for each year by taxes (other than income taxes) levied on payroll. These payroll taxes are for Canada Pension Plan (CPP) benefits and employment insurance (EI).

Employment insurance is a compulsory federal program that provides income assistance in the event of unemployment. EI premiums are paid by employees and matched by employers. (The employer's contribution is really paid, at least in part, in the form of a reduced wage paid to employees, as explained in Example 10–3.) Self-employed people must pay both shares. The maximum personal contribution to EI in 2007 was $720. EI premiums become part of government's general revenues; as of 1999, there was a large surplus in the EI account, which helped the federal government balance the budget for the 1999–2000 fiscal year.

EXAMPLE 10–3 **Employment Insurance**

Countless articles have been written about the problem with the employment insurance (EI) system in Canada. They all make reference to the employer and employee "contributions" to the EI fund. One gets the impression that EI premiums paid by employees go into a special government account and that employees do not pay for their employers' "contribution" to this account. Both concepts are not only flawed but grossly misleading as well. EI premiums are mixed in with the rest of government taxes collected and spent every year. The "contributions" are not contributions at all; they are merely taxes paid to the federal government. The so-called employer contribution, which matches the employee payments, is not, in fact, paid for by employers but rather, by employees because of the lower wages that they are paid. Anybody who quits a job and becomes self-employed finds this out when the time comes to pay one's self-employment taxes (employment insurance "contributions"), which effectively double the payments previously being made as an employee.

For critical analysis: Should EI premiums go into a special account?

In 2006, the Canada Pension Plan (CPP) premium payable on eligible earnings to $42 100 was 4.95 percent, with employers contributing an equal share on behalf of the employee. CPP premiums do not form part of government's general revenue but are managed separately from the government budget. The CPP is a system in which current workers subsidize already retired workers. With the coming retirement of the postwar "baby boomers," the number of retired people will grow much more rapidly than the number of current workers. In anticipation of increased outlays in pension plan benefits, the combined (employer–employee) premium has risen to 9.9 percent of eligible earnings.

The Goods and Services Tax

The Goods and Services Tax (GST) is a sales tax that makes up about 18 percent of federal government revenues. Consumers pay a 5 percent tax on virtually all goods and services they purchase in addition to any applicable provincial sales taxes. Prior to January 2008, the GST was 7 percent, and was reduced to 6 percent in 2007. The GST is a regressive tax, since it taxes consumption at the same rate for both the rich and the poor. The federal government tries to mitigate this, however, by giving a rebate of up to $76 four times a year to low-income earners. While consumers must pay GST on imports, Canadian exports are exempt.

Some economists argue that in spite of the regressive nature of sales taxes, such a tax as the GST is preferable to an income tax. Income taxes tax all income, whether it is spent or saved. Therefore, they argue, saving is discouraged. However, a sales tax taxes only income that is consumed, and so saving is encouraged. The Issues and Applications section at the end of this chapter revisits the pros and cons of this topic.

Spending, Government Size, and Tax Receipts

The size of the public sector can be measured in many different ways. One way is to count the number of public employees. Another is to look at government outlays. Government outlays include all of the government expenditures on goods and services as well as all transfer payments. Transfer payments include employment insurance benefits, welfare, and old age security. In Figure 10–2, you can see that total government outlays (as a percentage of GDP) peaked in 1995 at about 70 percent and have since declined to just under 25 percent in 2007.

Government Receipts

The main revenue raiser for all levels of government is taxes. We show in the two pie diagrams in Figure 10–3 the percentage of receipts from various taxes obtained by the federal government and by the provincial and municipal governments.

THE FEDERAL GOVERNMENT. The largest source of receipts for the federal government is the individual income tax. During the 2006–07 fiscal year, it accounted for 66 percent of all federal revenues. Next come the consumption taxes.

PROVINCIAL AND MUNICIPAL GOVERNMENTS. As can be seen in Figure 10–3, there is quite a bit of difference between the origins of receipts for the provincial and municipal governments and for the federal government. Personal and

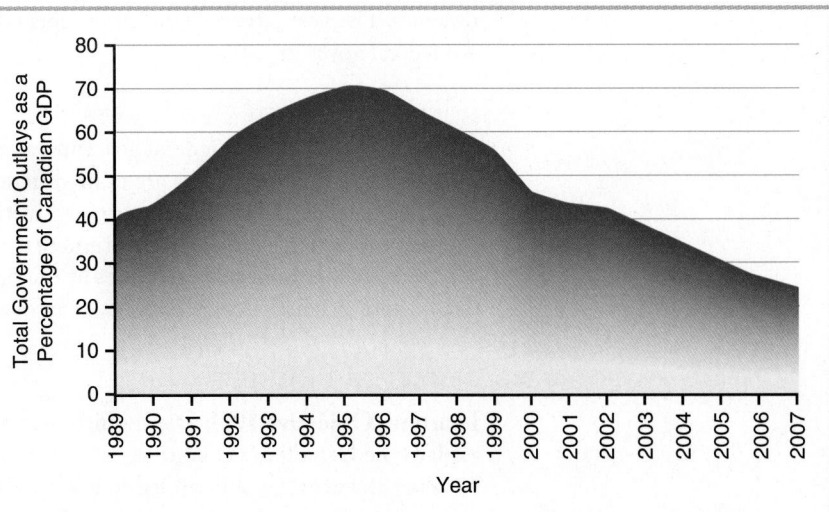

FIGURE 10–2

Government Total Outlays over Time

Total government outlays (as a percentage of GDP) peaked in 1995 and declined to just under 25 percent in 2007.

Source: http://www.oecd.org/document/61/ 0,3343,en_2649_34109_2483901_1_1_1_ 1,00.html, OECD Economic Outlook No 81 Annex Table 33 May 2007.

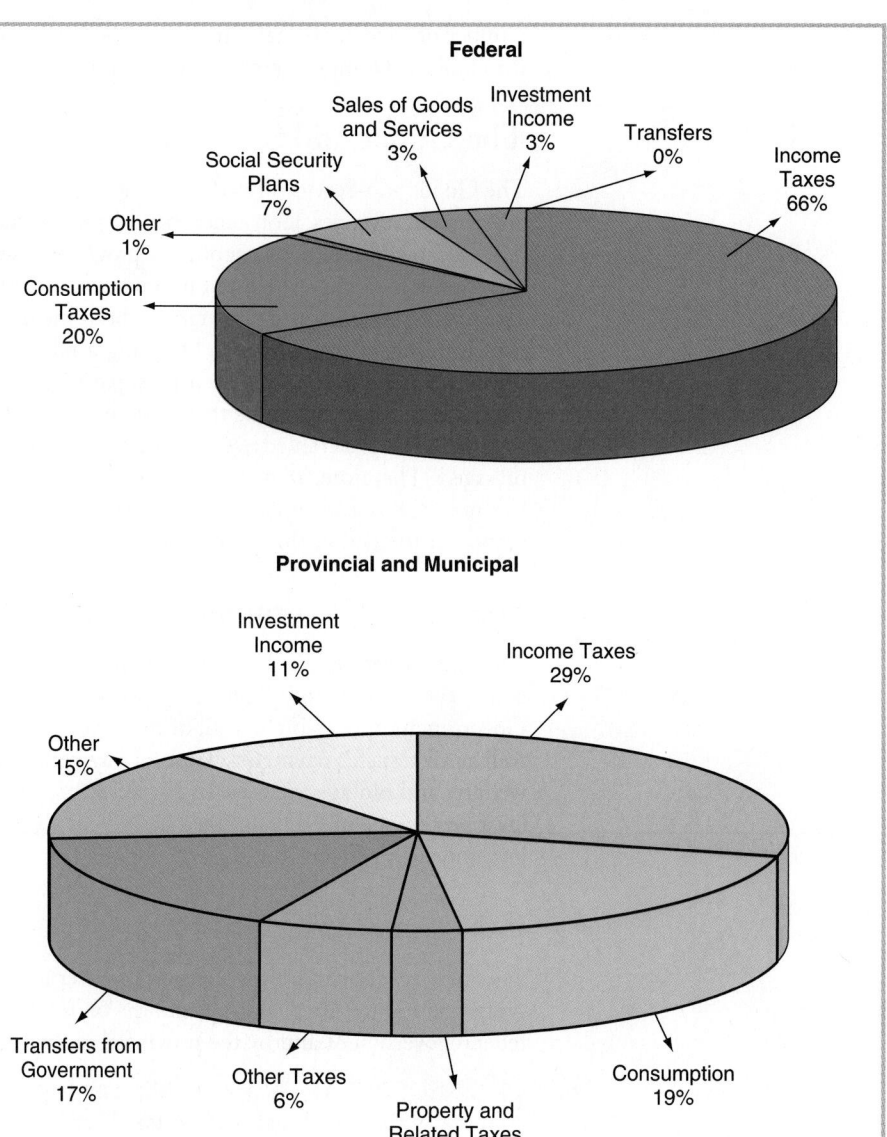

FIGURE 10–3
Sources of Government Tax Receipts, 2006–07

About 85 percent of federal revenues come from income and consumption taxes, whereas provincial and territorial government revenues are spread more evenly across sources, with less emphasis on taxes based on individual income.

SOURCES: ADAPTED FROM THE STATISTICS CANADA WEBSITE. http://www40.statcan.ca/l01/cst01/govt02a.htm, http://www40.statcan.ca/l01/cst01/govt02b.htm, http://www40.statcan.ca/ l01/cst01/govt55a.htm.

corporate income taxes account for only 29 percent of total provincial and municipal revenues. The next largest source of receipts is from consumption taxes and transfers from the federal government.

COMPARING FEDERAL SPENDING WITH PROVINCIAL AND MUNICIPAL SPENDING. A typical federal government budget is given in Figure 10–4. The federal government's spending habits are quite different from those of the provinces and territories. The categories of most importance in the federal budget are social services, debt charges, protection, and inter-governmental transfers, which make up over 67 percent. The three most important categories at the provincial and territorial level are education, health, and social services, which make up over 75 percent of the expenditures listed.

➤➤ CONCEPTS IN BRIEF

Learning Objective 10.3: Distinguish between average and marginal tax rates and explain the Canadian tax system.

✦ Marginal tax rates are applied to marginal tax brackets, defined as spreads of income over which the tax rate is constant.

FIGURE 10-4

Selected Federal Government Expenditures Compared with Selected Provincial and Municipal Expenditures

The federal government's spending habits are quite different from those of the provinces and territories. The categories of most importance in the federal budget are social services, debt charges, protection, and transfers, which make up over 67 percent of expenditures. The three most important categories at the provincial and territorial level are education, health, and social services, which make up over 75 percent of the expenditures listed.

SOURCES: ADAPTED FROM THE STATISTICS CANADA WEBSITE. http://www40.statcan.ca/l01/cst01/govt02a.htm, http://www40.statcan.ca/l01/cst01/govt02b.htm, http://www40.statcan.ca/l01/cst01/govt55a.htm,

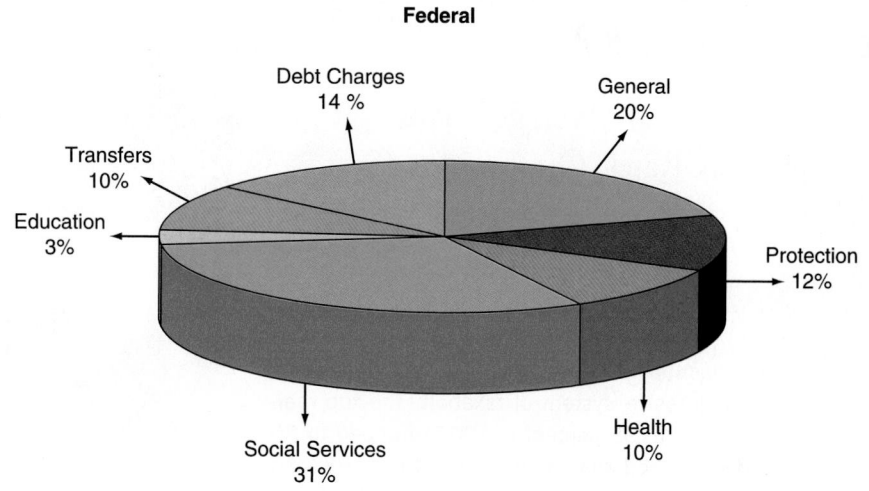

Federal

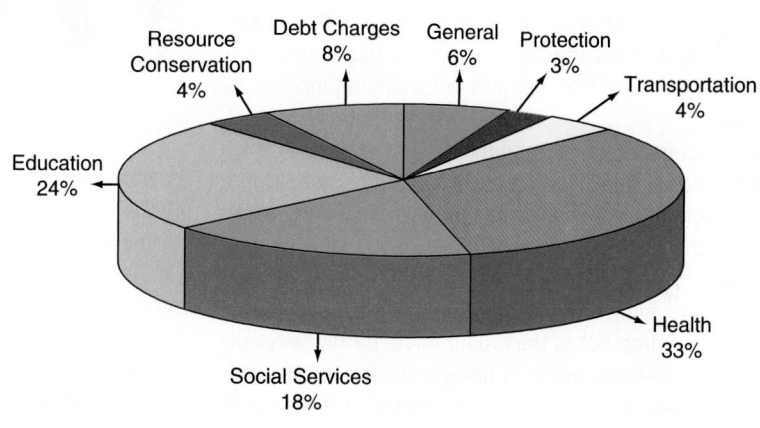

Provincial and Municipal

↟ Tax systems can be proportional, progressive, or regressive, depending on whether the marginal tax rate is the same as, greater than, or less than the average tax rate as income rises.

↟ Because corporations must first pay an income tax on most earnings, the personal income tax shareholders pay on dividends received (or realized capital gains) constitutes double taxation.

↟ The corporate income tax is paid by one or more of the following groups: shareholder-owners, consumers of corporate-produced products, and employees in corporations.

↟ In Canada, total government outlays as a percent of Canadian gross domestic product peaked in 1995 at 70 percent and declined to 25 percent in 2007.

↟ Government spending at the federal level is different from that at the provincial and municipal levels. At the federal level, interest on the debt, social services, and transfers to the provinces account for over 55 percent of the federal budget. At the provincial and municipal levels, education and health comprise over 50 percent of the expenditures graphed.

Should We Switch to a Flat Tax?

Concepts Applied: Average versus Marginal Tax Rates, Opportunity Cost, Progressive Income Tax System

Each year, Canadian taxpayers spend numerous hours preparing their taxes or hire accountants to do so for them. Switching to a national sales tax, one alternative to our current system, would lead to the downsizing of the Canada Revenue Agency and all of the expenses associated with that organization.

Since the introduction of federal income tax, Canadians have faced a progressive system of taxation. The top marginal tax rate soared to 98 percent in 1943, dropped to 80 percent in 1948, dropped again to 60 percent in 1968, and settled at 47 percent starting in 1971. Government reduced the top marginal tax rate to 34 percent in 1983; today, it stands at 29 percent. The idea behind a progressive tax system is that the "rich" should pay more. In actuality, what happens is quite a different story. In Figure 10–5, you see that regardless of what the top tax rate is, the federal government obtains around 45 percent of its annual income as tax revenues.

Why? Because people respond to incentives. At high marginal tax rates, the following occurs: (1) Rich people hire more tax lawyers and accountants to help them figure out loopholes in the tax system to avoid high marginal tax rates; (2) Some people change their investments to take advantage of loopholes that allow them to pay lower marginal tax rates; (3) Some people drop out of the labour force, particularly secondary income earners, such as lower-paid working women; and (4) More people engage in off-the-books "underground" activities for cash on which no income taxes are paid.

An Alternative: The Flat Tax

For decades, many economists have argued in favour of scrapping our progressive income tax system and replacing it with a so-called flat tax. The idea behind a flat tax is simple. To calculate what you owe, simply subtract the appropriate exemption from your income and multiply the rest by the flat tax rate, say, 20 percent. For example, a family of four might be able to earn as much as $25 000 or $35 000 a year before it paid any income tax. The major benefits of such a system, according to its advocates, would be the following: (1) fewer resources devoted to figuring out one's taxes; (2) fewer tax lawyers and accountants, who could then be engaged in more productive activities; (3) higher savings and investment; and (4) more economic growth. Opponents of a flat tax argue that (1) federal revenues will fall and a federal budget deficit will occur; and (2) the rich will pay less tax.

Another Alternative: A National Sales Tax

Alternatively, we could apply some form of a value-added tax (VAT) in place of the current income tax. VAT is common throughout Europe. VAT is assessed on the value added by a firm at each stage of production. It is a tax on the value of products that a firm sells minus the value of the materials that it bought and used to produce the products. Such a tax is collected by all businesses and remitted directly to the federal government. One of the major benefits of VAT is that it would significantly downsize the Canada Revenue Agency and the expenses associated with that government department. A VAT of, say, 15 to 20 percent in lieu of a federal income tax would be quite similar to a consumption tax.

A Consumption Tax

With a consumption tax, taxpayers pay taxes only on what they consume (spend) out of their incomes, not on all of what they earn. One way to determine such consumption in any year is simply to subtract what is saved from what is earned. The difference is consumption, and that is the base to which a consumption tax would apply. (A consumption tax is actually equivalent to the GST on all goods and services purchased.) In essence, a consumption tax provides an unlimited deduction for saving. As such, it encourages more saving. The less people choose to consume today, the faster the production possibilities curve will shift outward to the right, leading to more economic growth.

FIGURE 10–5
*Changing Maximum
Marginal Income Tax
Rates and Revenues
Collected*

At the top of the diagram, you can see listed the top marginal tax rates from 1960 to 2005. On the side is the percentage of total annual income collected by the federal government from the income tax system. No matter how high the marginal income tax rate has been, government has collected about the same percentage of national income in taxes.

Source: W. Irwin Gillespie, *Tax, Borrow & Spend: Financing Federal Spending in Canada 1867–1990.*

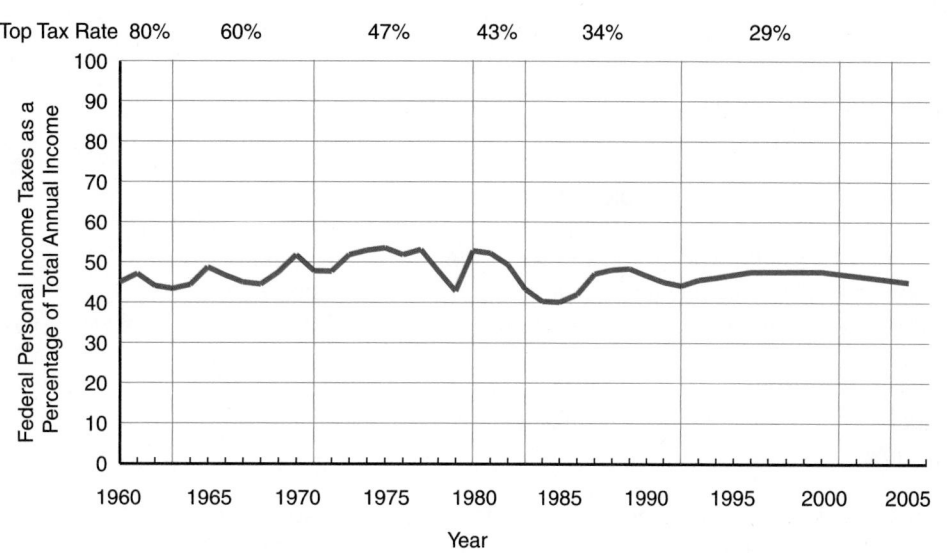

What about Fairness?

Every time a new tax system is discussed, the issue of fairness arises. Is it fair, as with a flat federal income tax, that everybody pays the same marginal tax rate, no matter how much each individual earns? Stephen Entin of the Institute for Research on the Economics of Taxation thinks it is: "It is hard to find a definition of 'fairness' more compelling than the idea that every citizen is treated equally." What about a consumption tax, which might be regressive because the poor spend a larger portion of their income than the rich? Is that a "fair" system? For most economists, these are difficult questions because they are in the realm of the normative, the value-laden. We can point out that an examination of the evidence shows what reality is. Simply stated, when marginal income

tax rates are high, the rich do not, in fact, pay a higher average tax rate than when marginal tax rates are lower. It behooves the rich to find methods to reduce tax liabilities and to expend resources to influence politicians to insert an increasing number of loopholes in the *Income Tax Act* in order to reduce effective marginal tax rates on those who earn a lot.

For critical analysis:

1. Do you think employees at the Canada Revenue Agency would be for or against the flat-tax system? Explain your choice.
2. Why is a flat-tax system more efficient than a progressive income tax system?

SUMMARY

Here is what you should know after reading this chapter. MyEconLab will help you identify what you know, and where to go when you need to practise. We suggest that as soon as you review one of the Learning Objective sections below, you then proceed to go through the related section in MyEconLab.

(X myeconlab

➔ LEARNING OBJECTIVES	KEY TERMS	MYECONLAB PRACTICE
10.1 Economic Functions of Government. Government provides a legal system in which the rights of private ownership, the enforcement of contracts, and the legal status of businesses are provided. In other words,	property rights, 270 anticombines legislation, 271 monopoly, 271 private goods, 271	• **MyEconLab** Study Plan 10.1

➤ LEARNING OBJECTIVES	KEY TERMS	MYECONLAB PRACTICE
government sets the legal rules of the game and enforces them. Public goods, once produced, can be consumed jointly by additional individuals at zero opportunity cost. If users of public goods know that they will be taxed on the basis of their expressed valuation of those public goods, their expressed valuation will be low. They expect to get a free ride.	principle of rival consumption, 271 public goods, 271 exclusion principle, 272 free-rider problem, 272	
10.2 The Political Functions of Government. Merit goods (chosen as such, collectively, through the political process) may not be purchased at all or not in sufficient quantities at market-clearing prices. Therefore, government subsidizes or provides such merit goods at a subsidized or zero price to specified classes of consumers. When it is collectively decided that something is a demerit good, government taxes, regulates, or prohibits the manufacture, sale, and use of that good. The market sector and the public sector both face scarcity, feature competition, and contain similar individuals. They differ in that many government, or political, goods are provided at zero price. Collective action may involve the use of force, and political voting can lead to different results from that of dollar voting. Bureaucrats often exert great influence on the course of policy because they are in charge of the day-to-day operation of current policy and provide much of the information needed to formulate future policy. Bureaucracies often organize their clientele, coach clients on what is appropriate, and stick up for their rights.	merit good, 273 demerit good, 274 transfer payments, 274 transfers in kind, 274 collective decision making, 275 theory of public choice, 275 incentive structure, 276 government, or political, goods, 276 majority rule, 277 proportional rule, 277 bureaucrats, 277 bureaucracy, 277	• **MyEconLab** Study Plan 10.2
10.3 Tax Rates and the Canadian Tax System. Marginal tax rates are those paid on the last dollar of income, whereas average tax rates are determined by the proportion of income paid in income taxes. With a proportional income tax system, marginal rates are constant. With a regressive system, they go down as income rises, and with a progressive system, they go up as income rises.	marginal tax rate, 279 tax bracket, 279 average tax rate, 279 proportional taxation, 279 progressive taxation, 280 regressive taxation, 280	• **MyEconLab** Study Plan 10.3

➤→ LEARNING OBJECTIVES	KEY TERMS	MYECONLAB PRACTICE
Government spending at the federal level is different from that at the provincial and municipal levels. Interest on the debt, elderly benefits, and transfers to the provinces account for almost 60 percent of the federal budget. Health care and education constitute over 40 percent of provincial government expenditures.	capital gain, 281 capital loss, 281 retained earnings, 281 tax incidence, 282	

⇨→ PROBLEMS

(Answers to the odd-numbered problems appear at the back of the book.)

LO 10.1 Explain the four economic functions of government.

1. TV signals have characteristics of public goods, yet TV stations and commercial networks are private businesses. Analyze this situation.

2. Assume that you live in a relatively small suburban neighbourhood called Parkwood. The Parkwood Homeowners' Association collects money from home-owners to pay for upkeep of the surrounding stone wall, lighting at the entrances to Parkwood, and mowing the lawn around the perimeter of the area. Each year you are asked to donate $50. No one forces you to do it. There are 100 homeowners in Parkwood.

   a. What percentage of the total yearly revenue of the homeowners' association will you account for?

   b. At what level of participation will the absence of your $50 contribution make a difference?

   c. If you do not contribute your $50, are you really receiving a totally free ride?

LO 10.2 Describe the two main political functions of government and how decision making differs depending on whether the individual is in the public or private sector.

3. A favourite political campaign theme in recent years has been to reduce the size, complexity, and bureaucratic nature of the federal government. Nonetheless, the size of the federal government, however measured, continues to increase. Use the theory of public choice to explain why.

4. Your small town would like to showcase all of the history of the town in a museum. What type of good would that be, and would government be likely to subsidize the museum or not? Why?

5. According to Policy Example 10–3, "Tax Freedom Day Around the World," Canada's tax freedom day is June 19th, while the U.S. tax freedom day is April 30th. What does that imply about Canada's level of taxation?

LO 10.3 Distinguish between average and marginal tax rates and explain the Canadian tax system.

6. Consider the following system of taxation, which has been labelled *degressive*. The first $5000 of income is not taxed. After that, all income is assessed at 20 percent (a proportional system). What is the marginal tax rate on $3000 of taxable income? $10 000? $100 000? What is the average tax rate on $3000? $10 000? $100 000? What is the maximum average tax rate?

7. You are offered two possible bonds to buy as part of your investment program. One is a corporate bond yielding 9 percent. The other is a tax-exempt municipal bond yielding only 6 percent. Assuming that you are certain you will be paid your interest and principal on these two bonds, what marginal tax bracket must you be in to decide in favour of the tax-exempt bond?

8. Consider the following tax structure:

Income Bracket	Marginal Tax Rate
$0–$1500	0%
$1501–$2000	14%
$2001–$3000	20%

Mr. Smith has an income of $2500 per annum. Calculate his tax bill for the year. What is his average tax rate? His highest marginal tax rate?

9. In 2006, Canada Pension Plan premiums were 4.95 percent on wages up to $42 100. No further CPP premiums are paid on earnings above this figure. Calculate the average CPP tax rate for annual wages of (a) $4000, (b) $51 300, (c) $56 000, (d) $100 000. Is the CPP system a progressive, proportional, or regressive tax structure?

10. According to Figure 10–4, the federal government spends only about 3 percent of the listed expenses on education, while the provinces spend about 24 percent on education. Why does it appear that the federal government spends so little on education? Do transfer payments play any part in that equation?

Fiscal Policy and the Public Debt

➡ LEARNING OBJECTIVES

After reading this chapter, you should be able to:

11.1 Use the aggregate demand/aggregate supply model to evaluate the effects of fiscal policy.

11.2 Explain the relationship between government budgets and the accumulated debt and describe the current situation for Canadian governments.

11.3 Explain the relationship between a government deficit and a current account deficit.

11.4 Discuss ways in which crowding out, direct expenditure offsets, the net export effect, supply-side economics, and the Ricardian equivalence theorem may offset the effectiveness of fiscal policy.

11.5 Explain how fiscal policy time lags complicate the use of fiscal policy to eliminate GDP gaps.

11.6 Describe how certain aspects of fiscal policy function as automatic stabilizers for the economy.

⟨X⟩ **myeconlab**

MyEconLab helps you master each objective and study more efficiently. See end of chapter for details.

The federal election of 2004 provided Canadians with another opportunity to give support and direction to their leaders on the role of government in society. The Conservative party proposed to reduce taxes below what they are elsewhere in the industrialized world, while the NDP said it would increase the role of government in many areas. The Liberals proposed a middle-of-the-road solution, arguing that the level of taxation existing at the time was necessary to keep government services at their current level.

This chapter is about the role of government in our society and, in particular, its big role in affecting the economy through its spending and taxation powers. What can we do as a society to improve the situation here and elsewhere? What role does government play in helping our economy? By studying macroeconomics, we hope to understand and improve these outcomes to make us all better off.

DID YOU KNOW THAT...

The first type of income tax was probably established in the 1200s and 1300s during times of war in the Italian city-states. Canada's first income tax, introduced in 1917 to help pay for World War I, ranged from 1 percent on incomes over $2000 a year to 6.6 percent on incomes over $20 000 per year. Two years later it was raised so that the bottom rate was 1.3 percent on incomes over $1500, and the top rate was 10.7 percent on incomes over $20 000. At first, the government promised the tax would be temporary; hence its name—"Dominion Income War Tax." Today, federal income taxes are taken for granted. More importantly for this chapter, the federal tax system is now viewed as being capable of affecting the equilibrium level of real GDP. On the spending side of the budget, changes in the federal government's expenditures are also viewed as potentially capable of changing the equilibrium level of real GDP.

11.1 Fiscal Policy

Fiscal policy The deliberate, discretionary changes in government expenditures and/or taxes in order to achieve certain national economic goals.

The realm of **fiscal policy** involves the deliberate, discretionary changes in government expenditures and/or taxes in order to achieve certain national economic goals. Some national goals are high employment (low unemployment), price stability, economic growth, and improvement in the nation's international payments balance. Fiscal policy can be thought of as a deliberate attempt to cause the economy to move to full employment and price stability more quickly than it otherwise might.

Fiscal policy has typically been associated with the economic theories of John Maynard Keynes and what is now called *traditional* Keynesian analysis. Keynes' explanation of the Great Depression was that there was insufficient aggregate demand. Because he believed that wages and prices were "sticky downward," he argued that the classical economists' view of the economy automatically moving toward full employment was inaccurate. To Keynes and his followers, government had to step in to increase aggregate demand. In other words, expansionary fiscal policy initiated by the federal government was the way to ward off recessions and depressions.

Traditional Keynesian economics dominated academic and government policy-making debates (and often actions) in the 1960s and 1970s. The federal budget of 1973, for example, was expressly focused on halting rising unemployment. In true Keynesian fashion, taxes were cut and government expenditures increased in the hope of "kickstarting" the economy.

Changes in Government Spending

Recall that in Chapter 8 (Figures 8–7 and 8–8, page 217), we looked at recessionary and inflationary gaps. The former was defined as the amount by which the current level of real GDP fell short of how much the economy could be producing if it were operating on its *LRAS*. The latter was defined as the amount by which the equilibrium level of real GDP exceeds the long-run equilibrium level as given by *LRAS*. In this section, we examine fiscal policy in the context of a recessionary gap.

WHEN THERE IS A RECESSIONARY GAP. Like firms, individuals, and foreigners, government is one of the spending agents in the economy. When government decides to spend more, all other things held constant, the dollar value of total spending must rise. Look at part (a) of Figure 11–1. We start at short-run equilibrium with AD_1 intersecting *SRAS* at $850 billion of real GDP per year. There is a recessionary gap of $50 billion of real GDP per year—the difference between *LRAS* (the economy's long-run potential) and the short-run equilibrium level of real GDP per year. When government decides to spend more, the aggregate demand curve shifts to the right to AD_2. Here we assume that government knows exactly how much more to spend so that AD_2 intersects *SRAS* at $900 billion, or at *LRAS*. Because of the upward-sloping *SRAS*, the price level has risen from 120 to 130. Real GDP has gone to $900 billion per year. (Nominal GDP has gone up by even more because it consists of the price level index times real GDP. Here, the GDP deflator has gone up by 10 ÷ 120 = 8.33 percent.)[1]

---

[1] Percent change in price index = Change in price index/Price index = (130 − 120)/120 = 8.33 percent

WHEN THE ECONOMY IS OPERATING ON ITS *LRAS*. Suppose that the economy is operating on *LRAS*, as in part (b) of Figure 11–1. An increase in government spending shifts the aggregate demand curve from AD_1 to AD_2. Both prices and real output of goods and services begin to rise toward the intersection of E_2. But this rate of real GDP per year is untenable in the long run because it exceeds *LRAS*. In the long run, expectations of input owners—workers, owners of capital and raw materials, and so on—are revised. The short-run aggregate supply curve shifts from $SRAS_1$ to $SRAS_2$ because of higher prices and higher resource costs. Real GDP returns to the *LRAS* level of $900 billion per year. The full impact of the increased government expenditures is on the price level only, which increases to 135. Therefore, an attempt to increase real GDP above its long-run equilibrium can be accomplished only in the short run.

REDUCTIONS IN GOVERNMENT SPENDING. The entire process shown in Figure 11–1 can be reversed. Government can reduce spending, thereby shifting the aggregate demand curve inward. You should be able to show how this affects the equilibrium level of the price index and the real output of goods and services (real GDP) on similar diagrams.

Changes in Taxes

The spending decisions of firms, individuals, and foreigners depend on the taxes levied on them. Individuals in their roles as consumers look to their disposable (after-tax) income when determining their desired rate of consumption. Firms look at their after-tax profits when deciding on the level of investment to undertake. Foreigners look at the tax-inclusive cost of goods when deciding whether to buy in Canada or elsewhere. Therefore, holding all other things constant, a rise in taxes may cause a reduction in aggregate demand for three reasons: (1) it reduces consumption, (2) it reduces investment, and (3) it reduces net exports. What actually happens depends, of course, on whom the taxes are levied.

WHEN THE CURRENT SHORT-RUN EQUILIBRIUM IS GREATER THAN *LRAS*. Assume that aggregate demand is AD_1 in part (a) of Figure 11–2. It intersects *SRAS* at E_1, which is at a level greater than *LRAS*. In this situation, an increase in taxes shifts the aggregate demand curve inward to the left. For argument's sake, assume that it intersects *SRAS* at E_2, or exactly where *LRAS* intersects AD_2. In this situation, the

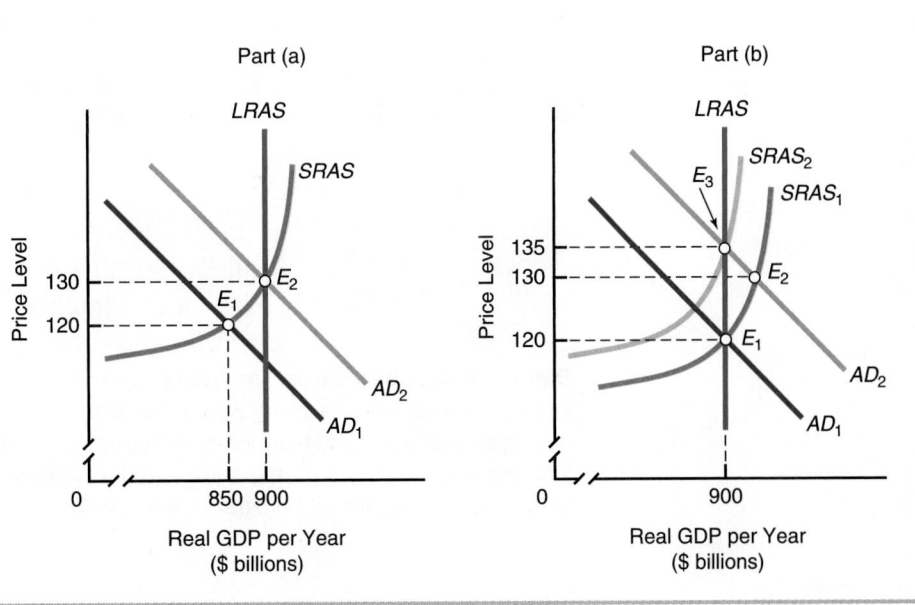

FIGURE 11–1

Expansionary Fiscal Policy: Two Scenarios

If there is a recessionary gap and equilibrium is at E_1 in part (a), fiscal policy can increase aggregate demand to AD_2. The new equilibrium is at E_2 at higher real GDP per year and a higher price level. If, though, we are already on *LRAS* as in part (b), expansionary fiscal policy will simply lead to a temporary equilibrium at E_2 and a final equilibrium at E_3, again at *LRAS* of $900 billion of real GDP per year but at a higher price level of 135.

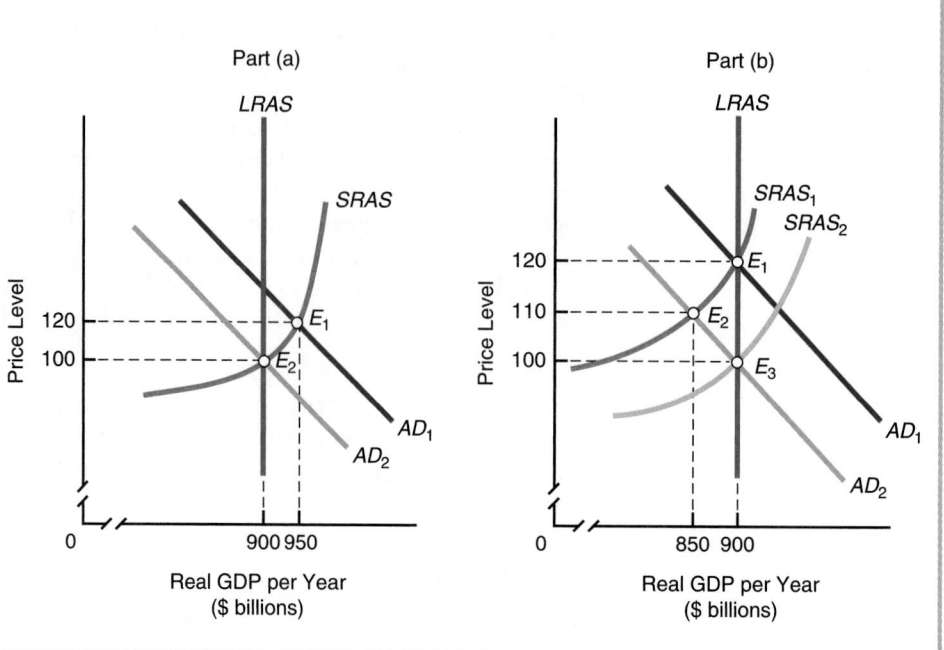

equilibrium level of real GDP falls from \$950 billion per year to \$900 billion per year. The
price level index falls from 120 to 100.

IF THE ECONOMY IS IN LONG-RUN EQUILIBRIUM. Assume that the economy
is already at short-run and long-run equilibrium as shown in part (b) of Figure 11–2. The
aggregate demand curve, AD_1, intersects both *LRAS* and *SRAS* at \$900 billion of real
GDP per year. If aggregate demand decreases to AD_2, a new temporary equilibrium
will occur at E_2 with the price level at 110 and real equilibrium GDP at \$850 billion per
year. That means that in the short run, prices and the real output of goods and services
fall. Input suppliers revise their expectations downward. The short-run aggregate supply
curve shifts to $SRAS_2$. The real level of equilibrium GDP returns to the *LRAS* level of
\$900 billion per year. The full long-run impact of fiscal policy in this situation is solely on
the price level, which falls to 100.

EFFECTS OF A REDUCTION IN TAXES. The effects of a reduction in taxes are
exactly the reverse of the effects of an increase in taxes. Figure 11–1 and the accompanying
discussion of the effects of an increase in government expenditures provide the full
analysis.

Policy Example 11–1 provides an example of how the American federal government
attempted to use fiscal policy to eliminate a large recessionary gap in the 1930s).

POLICY EXAMPLE 11–1   **Did Roosevelt's New Deal Really
Provide a Stimulus?**

During the Great Depression, American president Franklin Roosevelt implemented his "New
Deal," which was influenced by Keynes' view that government had to increase "effective"
aggregate demand to get an economy going again. To be sure, Roosevelt's New Deal
included what appeared on the surface to be large federal government expenditures and
numerous government jobs programs. We have to look at the total picture of the American

continued

economy, however. During the Great Depression, taxes were raised repeatedly. The *Revenue Act* of 1932, for example, passed during the depths of the Depression, brought the largest percentage increase in federal taxes in the history of the United States in peacetime—it almost doubled total federal tax revenues. Federal government deficits during the Depression years were small. In fact, in 1937 the total government budget—including federal, state, and local levels—was in surplus by $300 million. That means that at the same time that the federal government was increasing expenditures, local and state governments were decreasing them. If we measure the total of federal, state, and local fiscal policies, we find that they were truly expansive only in 1931 and 1936, compared with what the government was doing prior to the Great Depression. No wonder the New Deal failed to kick-start the American economy!

For critical analysis: Did the New Deal have any effect on the Canadian economy?

11.2 Government Budgets and Finances

The Rise and Fall of Government

Governments today are much more involved in the economy than they were 75 years ago. Figures 11–3A and 11–3B show how the Depression and Keynesian theory about government spending have changed the nature of government since the 1930s. The large spike in the 1940s is due to the spending that occurred during and just after World War II. However, note that since then spending on government programs (including welfare and other social benefits) has risen from about 20 percent of GDP to about 50 percent in the early 1990s and back down to less than 40 percent today. This increase is largely due to the new social programs that governments have implemented since World War II. These programs have resulted in smaller business fluctuations and have also been justified on humanitarian grounds. Note also that the peak of government spending occurred in the early 1990s and has since fallen back to levels not seen since the 1970s.

Government Budgets and Finances

Fiscal policy does not operate in a vacuum. Important questions have to be answered. If government expenditures increase, how are those expenditures financed, and by whom? If taxes are increased, what does the government do with the taxes? Governments have to answer this question every year in their budget, which is their statement of revenue and spending.

A government's **budget balance** is the amount of revenue it receives minus its spending. This is usually calculated on an annual fiscal year ending March 31. A **balanced budget** is one in which the revenue and spending are equal. A **budget surplus** occurs when the budget balance is positive or, in other words, the tax revenue is greater than what the government spends. A **budget deficit** occurs when this number is negative, that is, when government spending exceeds its revenue.

When government has a deficit, there are several ways that it can handle the problem. It can alter its budget by raising taxes or reducing spending, or, in the case of a national government, it can use **money financing**—by creating new money to pay its bills—or finally, it can borrow the money.

The first option for covering a deficit, reducing spending or increasing taxes, will have a contractionary effect on the economy. That policy would make an existing recession even larger and so was not a good option during many of the years of the 1980s and 1990s when the economy operated below its capacity.

The second option, money creation, happens when the government sells its bonds to the Bank of Canada, rather than to the public at large. The Bank of Canada pays for this purchase by creating new money. Effectively, the Bank of Canada "prints" up the money

Budget balance The amount of revenue government receives minus its spending.

Balanced budget A budget in which the revenue and spending are equal.

Budget surplus When the budget balance is positive or, in other words, the tax revenue is greater than what the government spends.

Budget deficit When government spending exceeds its revenue.

Money financing Creating new money to pay government's bills.

FIGURE 11–3A

Government Spending as a Proportion of GDP

Governments in Canada have increased their spending for most of the post-War period. This reached a peak at 50 percent of GDP in the early 1990s. Since then, governments have been cutting back on spending to about the same level (relative to the economy) as in the 1970s.

SOURCE: ADAPTED FROM THE STATISTICS CANADA PUBLICATION *HISTORICAL STATISTICS OF CANADA*, SECOND EDITION, CATALOGUE 11-516, 1983, SERIES H160, AND FROM THE STATISTICS CANADA CANSIM DATABASE, SERIES V498074, D14816, V647177.

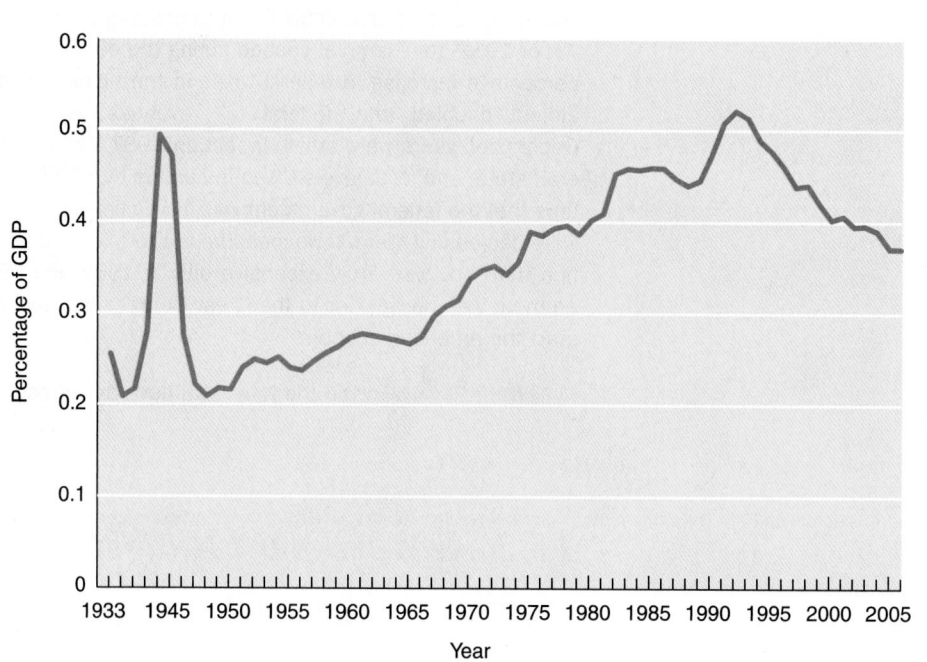

FIGURE 11–3B

Categories of Government Spending

All categories of government spending increased from the post-War period until about 1990. Debt charges have fallen to about half of what they were a decade ago, as governments have largely balanced their budgets while the economy has continued to grow and interest rates (and the resulting interest charges) have fallen.

SOURCE: ADAPTED FROM THE STATISTICS CANADA CANSIM DATABASE, SERIES V647178, V647180, V647182, V647183, V647181, AND V498074.

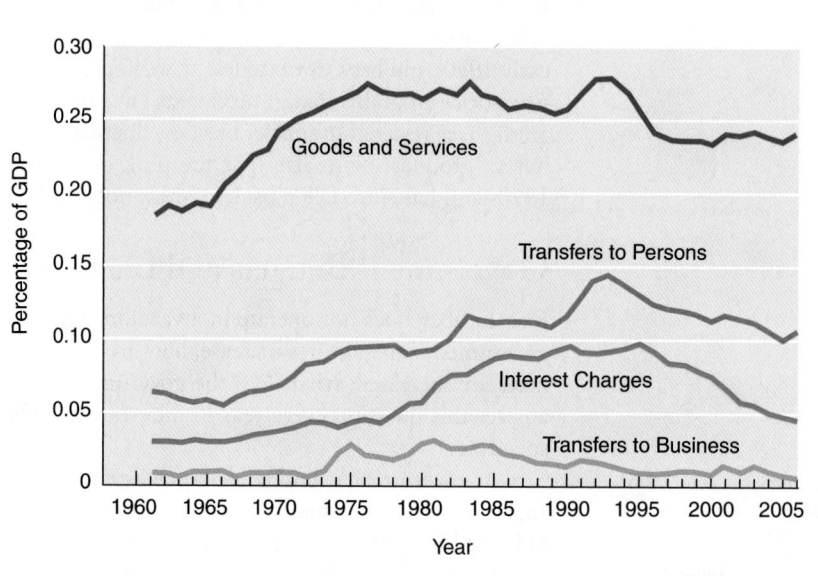

for the government to pay its bills, thus creating no new net debt. However, the amount of money that can be created to pay its bills, without other kinds of problems occurring (such as excessive inflation) is very limited—at most a few billion dollars each year. The amount that governments have needed over the years has been much larger than could be reasonably created through money creation, and so the preferred choice has been to borrow the money.

This third option, borrowing, has its own problems. First, such debt accumulates interest and so the amount we must repay is larger in the future. Second, money borrowed today must be repaid with future taxes, and thus reduces the amount available for regular program spending. We will explore some other issues around this later in the chapter after we look at some of the recent history of government spending.

The Historical Record of Deficit Financing

The federal government's record has not been good over the past 30 years, although it has been much improved recently. At the same time that governments were increasing their size, they were also increasing their deficits. Federal government tax revenues remained consistently about 20 percent of GDP while expenditures were rising to about 25 percent. The resulting deficit difference is shown as the shaded red area in part (a) of Figure 11–4. This situation was reversed in the mid-1990s and in 1998, the government recorded a budget surplus—its revenues exceeded its expenditures for the first time since 1973—and has maintained a small surplus each year since then.

The Relative Size of the Federal Budget Balance

The problem with looking at part (a) of Figure 11–4 is that the annual budget balance is expressed as a current dollar figure. In a growing economy (both through real output increases and inflation), what is perhaps more important is the relative size of the federal budget deficit or surpluses expressed as a percentage of GDP. This is shown in Figure 11–4 part (b). You can see that the federal budget deficit expressed as a percentage

FIGURE 11–4
Government Budget Balances

In part (a), federal expenditures and revenues are expressed in nominal dollars. The difference is the federal budget balance, also expressed in nominal dollars. Since the mid-1990s, a deficit has been eliminated and government has been running a small surplus. In part (b), the budget balance is shown as a percentage of GDP. Note that the "valleys" correspond to the two major recessions in the 1980s and 1990s. Provincial and local government budget balances are also shown.

SOURCES: PART (A): ADAPTED FROM THE STATISTICS CANADA CANSIM DATABASE, SERIES V156113, V156163; PART (B): ADAPTED FROM THE STATISTICS CANADA CANSIM DATABASE, SERIES V647196, V647231, V498074.

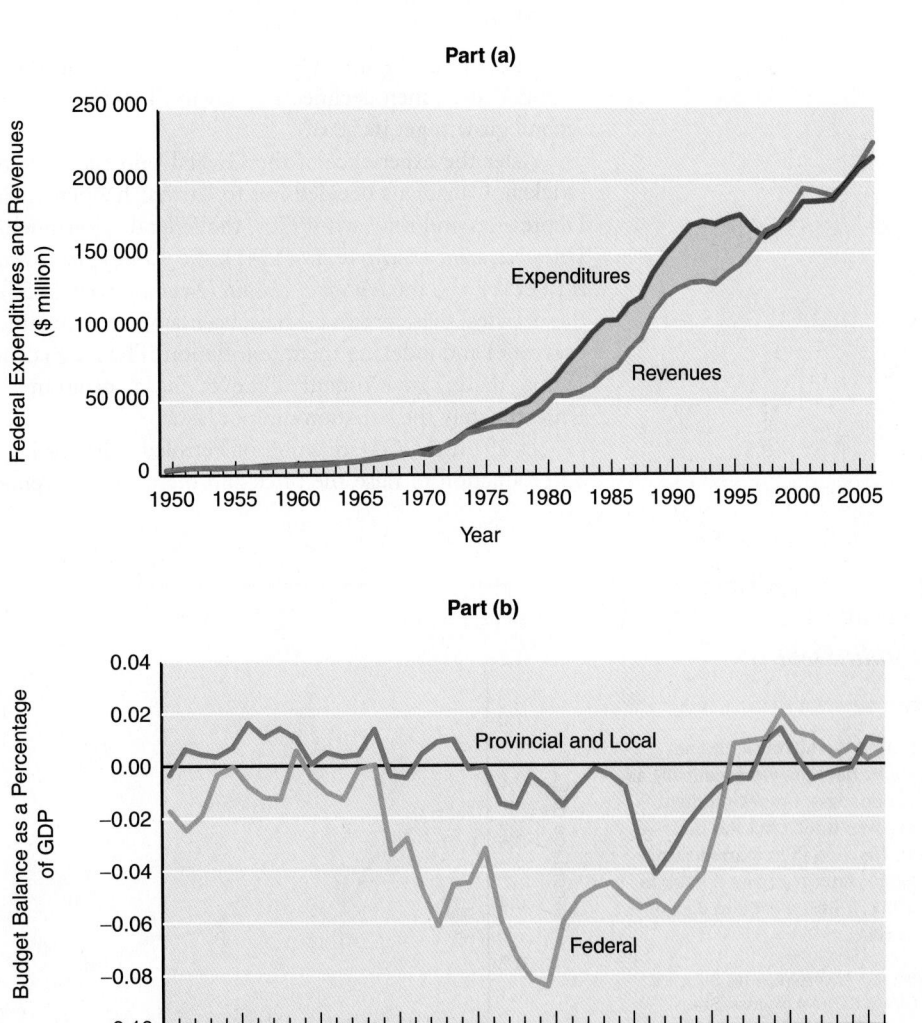

of GDP reached its peak during the late 1980s before falling back, again rose until 1993, and has been falling ever since.

From Deficits to Debt

A budget deficit or surplus is a flow, something that happens on a yearly basis or over time. Each year, these deficits or surpluses are added to the existing debt (a stock).

Gross public debt All federal public debt, taken together.

Net public debt The result of subtracting from the gross public debt the financial assets held by government agencies.

All federal public debt, taken together, is called the **gross public debt**. When we subtract from the gross public debt the financial assets held by government agencies, we arrive at the **net public debt**. The net public debt normally increases whenever the federal government runs a budget deficit—that is, whenever total government outlays are greater than total government revenues. During World War II, the 1980s, and the early 1990s, there were many years where large deficits occurred (and relatively few surpluses), and indeed, deficits came to be expected. The public debt peaked at about $590 billion in 1997 and 70 percent of GDP. In 2006, that debt is about $515 billion, or about 40 percent of GDP. Again, it is better to look at the Canadian national debt as a percentage of GDP, which we do in Figure 11–5. We see that after World War II, this ratio fell steadily until the mid-1970s. Then it rose sharply through the mid-1990s, and has recently fallen back to 35 percent of GDP. The provinces have followed a similar pattern with debt peaking at 28 percent of GDP.

How Did Our Debt Get So Big?

If you look at Figure 11–5, you will see that the net public debt soared during World War II, then declined steadily until 1974. Then the debt grew again. How did this second growth get its start?

After the experience of the Great Depression when so many families were poverty-stricken, Canadians decided not to let that happen again. Between the end of the Great Depression and the early 1970s, the federal government legislated such programs as the *Unemployment Insurance Act* (1941), the *Family Allowance Act* (1944), the *Old Age Security Act* (1951), and the *National Hospital Insurance Act* (1957), better known as medicare. Over the decades, these programs have been amended, making them universal (i.e., available to everyone) and indexing them to inflation. The long economic expansion of the 1950s and 1960s made government believe these programs would always be affordable. Unfortunately the situation did not last.

In 1973, the Organization of Petroleum Exporting Countries (OPEC) cut back on oil production to raise the price and increase its revenues. The price of oil, an input for

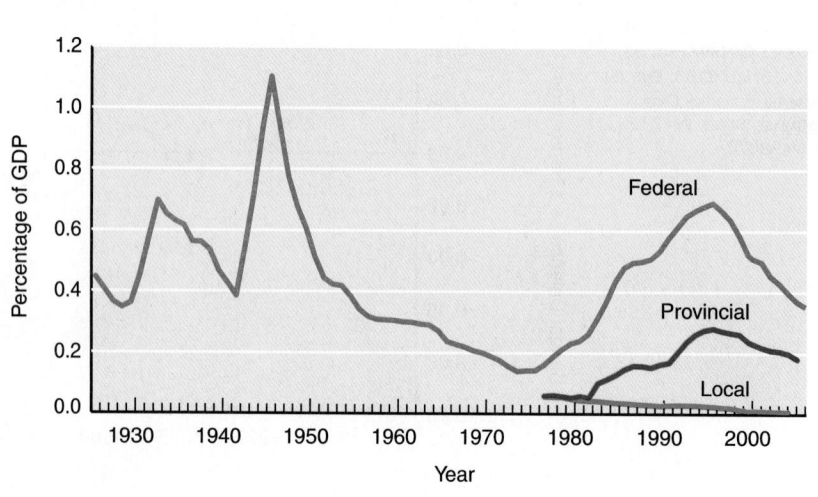

FIGURE 11–5
Public Debt

During World War II, the net public debt grew dramatically as Canada spent money to fight the war. It fell until the mid-1970s, and then started rising again. After reaching a peak in 1997, it has started to decline again.

SOURCE: ADAPTED FROM THE STATISTICS CANADA CANSIM DATABASE, SERIES V498074, V151548, V151533, V151534, V151535, AND V151536.

virtually everything produced in the West, quadrupled. Prices soared, Canadian firms went bankrupt, thousands of employees lost their jobs, and consumers cut back on spending. With universal unemployment insurance indexed to inflation, benefits paid to the unemployed mushroomed, while premiums paid in, as well as personal and corporate taxes, declined. Further, to help out struggling firms, the federal government reduced oil taxes and provided subsidies to keep them producing.

As the Canadian economy started to recover from this shock, the entire Western world slipped into the 1981–83 recession. Once again, payments out in social programs rose relative to revenues, and the debt climbed again. As well, interest payments on the (now much larger) debt were higher because interest rates rose to over 20 percent in 1980. Although economic growth in the 1980s was substantial, the Conservative government of the day did allow spending to grow and debt to continue to accumulate. By the time the 1990 recession occurred, it was even more difficult to make the adjustments needed to bring the budget balance back to appropriate levels. Interest payments on the gross public debt accounted for almost $50 billion of a budget of about $160 billion in total by the 1995 fiscal year. These interest payments were about double what the government was spending on health, post-secondary education, and social assistance.

In 1995, the federal government made a substantial change in policy direction to bring down the annual deficit.

As you can see in Figure 11–3B and part (b) of 11–4, all levels of government have reduced their spending (generally below their revenues) and have correspondingly cut their services. As well, interest rates on the debt have been dropping dramatically, giving governments greater room for spending their existing tax dollars. Since the economy has grown in size at the same time, the relative size of the debt problem continues to fall as shown in Figure 11–5, even if none of the debt is paid off.

Could it happen again? Yes, it could. The federal government is very concerned about the aging population and the demands it will make on these social safety nets and services (especially health care). It is considering raising the age for retirement under the Canada Pension Plan, and eliminating mandatory retirement rules. In Policy Example 11–2 we have a brief look at this issue.

POLICY EXAMPLE 11–2   ## The Baby Boom Generation Moves into Retirement Years

While the current problems of debt management have been brought under control, governments in Canada are already facing a new problem, that of an aging population. Figure 11–6 shows that the proportion of seniors in the population will rise dramatically by the year 2030, while the number of young people (and the number of working-age people) will decline. This change is due to the aging of the "baby-boom" population, which is the generation of people born between 1945 and 1965.

Obviously, there will be massive changes in the kinds of programs that governments will be funding in the future. Health care (now a provincial responsibility with some funding from the federal government) will experience even more pressure than currently exists. The federal government will be pressured to find more money to supplement senior citizens' incomes. As was mentioned earlier in the chapter, the Canada Pension Plan, the most basic pension that almost everyone will receive, has had to double its contribution rates to account for the fact that the population demographics are changing.

Because of the decline in the proportion of the population that is young, there will be some relief for governments. There will be less spent on child tax credits, for example.

Another proposed source of funding is to move money out of post-secondary education, as it is thought that fewer students will be enrolled. While on the surface it might appear that

continued

FIGURE 11-6

Canadian Demographic Trends

Both levels of government will face increased future spending pressures as a result of population aging.

SOURCE: THE FISCAL BALANCE IN CANADA, DEPARTMENT OF FINANCE PUBLICATION. AUGUST 2000. REPRODUCED WITH THE PERMISSION OF THE MINISTER OF PUBLIC WORKS AND GOVERNMENT SERVICES CANADA, 2004.

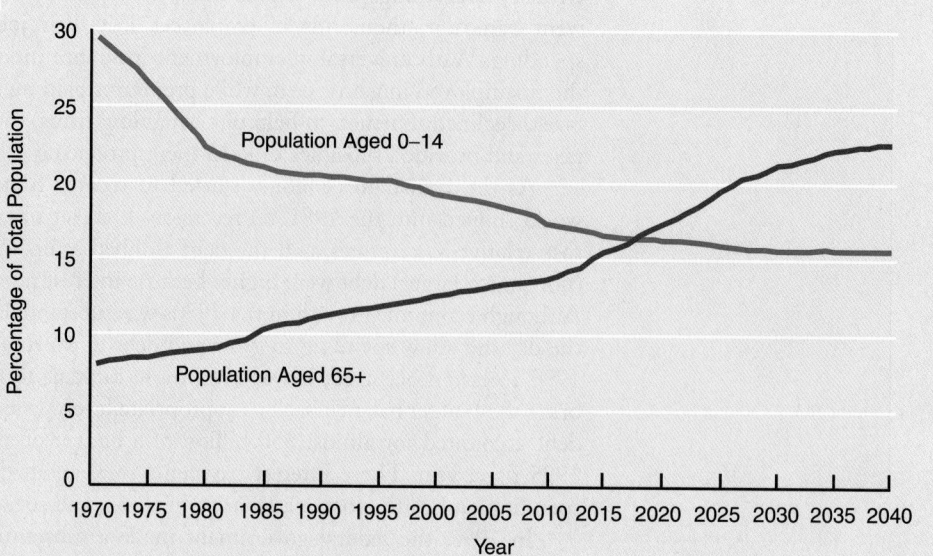

there will be fewer students coming into the system at a young age, there will be an increasing demand for post-secondary education for two reasons. First, the participation by people in the 18- to 24- year-old age group is growing. Second, the number of students enrolling and re-enrolling at older ages is also increasing. In today's world, the need for post-secondary training and lifelong learning and upgrading is more important than ever.

Finally, with the projected reduction in debt over the next 30 years, government will likely be able to re-allocate the interest payments it must now pay for other sources. Given that, in one budget, more than one-third of the budget was allocated for this purpose alone, this will represent a substantial improvement from where we are today.

For critical analysis: Why would the increase in life expectancy, if not anticipated, create problems for the Canada Pension Plan? How could this be relieved by raising the retirement age?

➡➤ CONCEPTS IN BRIEF

Learning Objective 11.1: Use the aggregate demand/aggregate supply model to evaluate the effects of fiscal policy.

- Fiscal policy is defined as the discretionary change in government expenditures and/or taxes in order to achieve such national goals as high employment or reduced inflation.
- If there is a contractionary gap and the economy is operating at less than long-run aggregate supply (*LRAS*), an increase in government spending can shift the aggregate demand curve to the right and perhaps lead to a higher equilibrium level of real GDP per year. If the economy is already operating on *LRAS*, in contrast, expansionary fiscal policy in the long run simply leads to a higher price level.
- Changes in taxes can have similar effects on the equilibrium rate of real GDP and the price level. A decrease in taxes can lead to an increase in real GDP, but if the economy is already operating on its *LRAS*, eventually such decreases in taxes will lead only to increases in the price level.

Learning Objective 11.2: Explain the relationship between government budgets and the accumulated debt and describe the current situation for Canadian governments.

- The government's budget balance is the difference between its revenues and spending. A surplus occurs when this is positive, and a deficit occurs when it is negative.

⤚ Government deficits (a flow) must be financed through money creation or by borrowing. The past accumulation of deficits has resulted in a large public debt (a stock) for the federal government.

⤚ Federal deficits peaked in the early 1990s and moved into a surplus position in the 1997–98 fiscal year. The accumulation of past deficits has meant an outstanding debt of about $500 billion.

11.3 *Federal Budget Deficits in an Open Economy*

Many economists believe that a Canadian current account deficit is just as serious a problem as a government budget deficit. The current account balance is the sum of the values of exports minus imports, plus interest payments we receive from other countries minus payments out to other countries, plus net gifts. (We will spend more time looking at the balance of payments in Chapter 17.) The current account went from a surplus of $2.6 billion in 1984 to a deficit of over $28 billion in 1993, and back to a surplus of $23 billion in 2006.

By virtue of these past current account deficits, foreigners have accumulated Canadian dollars and have purchased Canadian assets (real estate, corporate shares, bonds, and so on). If a country continues to incur these deficits, foreigners will continue to purchase assets here. This could eventually present problems. For one, what if foreign investors suddenly decide to sell such assets or take their money out of the country? Another concern is with foreigners gaining political power along with their accumulation of Canadian assets. Here, we concentrate on the linkage between federal budget deficits and current account deficits.

What the Evidence Says

Figure 11–7 shows the Canadian current account deficits and surpluses compared with federal budget deficits and surpluses. The year 1986 appears to be a watershed year, for that is when the current account took a marked turn for the worse. Concurrently, the federal budget deficit grew progressively larger.

On the basis of the evidence presented in Figure 11–7, it appears that there is a close relationship between the current account and fiscal deficits: Larger current account deficits follow shortly after larger fiscal deficits (and vice versa).

Why the Two Deficits Are Related

Intuitively, there is a reason we would expect federal budget deficits to lead to current account deficits. You might call this the unpleasant arithmetic of current account and budget deficits.

Assume that the federal government runs a budget deficit. Assume further that Canadians use their savings to buy government-issued bonds to finance the deficit. Where, then, does the money come from to finance business investment? The answer is that part of it must come from abroad. That is to say, dollar holders abroad invest in Canadian businesses by buying their shares or by investing directly in business operations. In this case, the dividends earned on their shares or the interest earned on their investments flow out of the country. The current account goes into deficit because this outflow of capital exceeds to a large measure the capital flowing into Canada from similar Canadian investment abroad. In other words, the outflow is large enough to offset the surplus on the trade account.

The reason that foreigners are induced to invest in Canadian business is that domestic Canadian interest rates will normally rise, all other things held constant, whenever there is an increase in government deficits financed by increased borrowing.

FIGURE 11–7

Canada's Twin Deficits

Canada's current account was relatively small until the mid-1970s when the federal government started running large deficits, as shown in the diagram. More recently, this situation has been reversed. Both balances are now in surplus.

SOURCE: ADAPTED FROM THE STATISTICS CANADA CANSIM DATABASE, SERIES V156245, V7792, V6599, AND V113713.

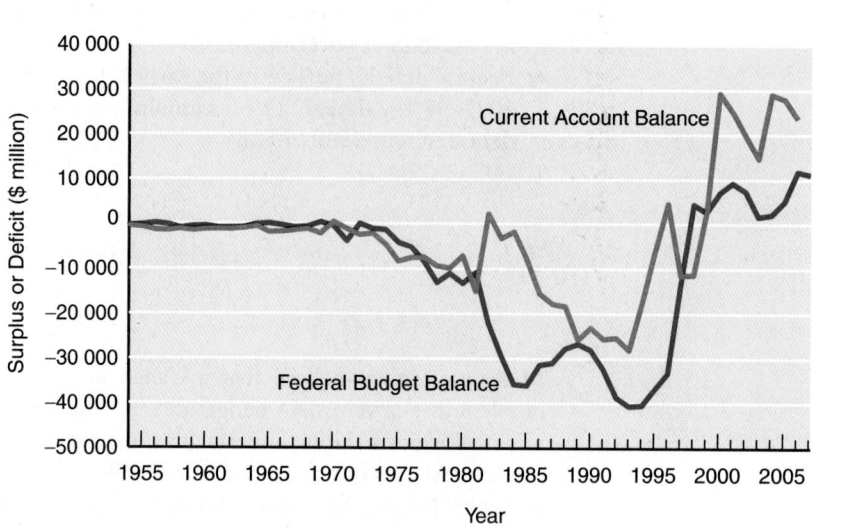

➡ **CONCEPTS IN BRIEF**

Learning Objective 11.3: Explain the relationship between a government deficit and a current account deficit.

↳ A close relationship exists between government deficits and current account deficits because government borrowing results in a large inflow of capital. The increased borrowing pushes up interest rates and the value of the Canadian dollar, resulting in a current account deficit.

11.4   Possible Offsets to Fiscal Policy

When governments choose to spend money or lower taxes, there is always a reaction by those affected. Because of these reactions, the ability of fiscal policy to work in the way that we theorized in the first section has been strongly criticized. There are plenty of ways that the effect of fiscal policy may be offset by others. Provinces and municipalities may choose to exercise their power and replace federal spending with their own or vice versa. Individuals may choose to save money today to offset future tax bills. Companies may choose to alter their investment plans because of tax increases. All of these issues involve offsets to the effects of fiscal policy and thereby reduce its effectiveness. We will look at the following reasons why fiscal policy may not work as effectively as we might hope:

1. Crowding out
2. The net export effect
3. Combined government spending effect
4. The supply-side effects of changes in taxes
5. The Ricardian equivalence theorem

Crowding Out

Consider an increase in government expenditures. If government expenditures rise and taxes are held constant, something has to give. Our government does not simply take goods and services when it wants them. It has to pay for them. When it pays for them and does not simultaneously collect the same amount in taxes, it must borrow. This means that an increase in government spending without raising taxes creates additional government borrowing from the private sector (or from foreigners as discussed the last section).

THE CROWDING-OUT EFFECT. Holding everything else constant, if the government attempts to borrow more from the private sector to pay for its increased budget deficit, it is not going to have an easy time selling its bonds. If the bond market is in equilibrium, when the government tries to sell more bonds, it is going to have to offer a better deal in order to get rid of them. A better deal means offering a higher interest rate. This is the interest rate effect of expansionary fiscal policy financed by borrowing from the public. In this sense, when the federal government finances increased spending by additional borrowing, it may push interest rates up. When interest rates go up, it is more expensive for firms to finance new construction, equipment, and inventories. It is also more expensive for individuals to finance their cars and homes. Thus, a rise in government spending, holding taxes constant (in short, deficit spending), tends to crowd out private spending, dampening the positive effect of increased government spending on aggregate demand. This is called the **crowding-out effect**. In the extreme case, the crowding out may be complete, with the increased government spending having no net effect on aggregate demand. The final result is simply more government spending and less private investment and consumption. Figures 11–8 and 11–9 show how the crowding-out effect occurs.

> **Crowding-out effect** A rise in government spending, holding taxes constant, that tends to crowd out private spending, dampening the positive effect of increased government spending on aggregate demand.

Further, as we previously discussed, as the government borrows more and more money, its overall debt climbs. As the debt grows large relative to GDP, investors may question the government's ability to use fiscal policy to manage the economy. They perceive an increased risk in buying more bonds. Thus, the government has to offer even higher interest rates to continue to finance its spending.

GRAPHICAL ANALYSIS. You see in Figure 11–8 that the initial equilibrium, E_1, is below *LRAS*. But suppose that government expansionary fiscal policy in the form of increased government spending (without increasing taxes) shifts aggregate demand from AD_1 to AD_2. In the absence of the crowding-out effect, the real output of goods and services would increase to $900 billion per year, and the price level would rise to 120 (point E_2). With the (partial) crowding-out effect, however, as investment and consumption decline, partly offsetting the rise in government spending, the aggregate demand curve shifts inward to the left to AD_3. The new equilibrium is now at E_3, with real GDP of $875 billion per year at a price level of 115.

The Net Export Effect

The crowding-out effect reduces the effectiveness of fiscal policy by reducing investment and consumption because of a rise in interest rates. However, that same rise in interest rates will also reduce our net exports because of its effect on the value of the Canadian

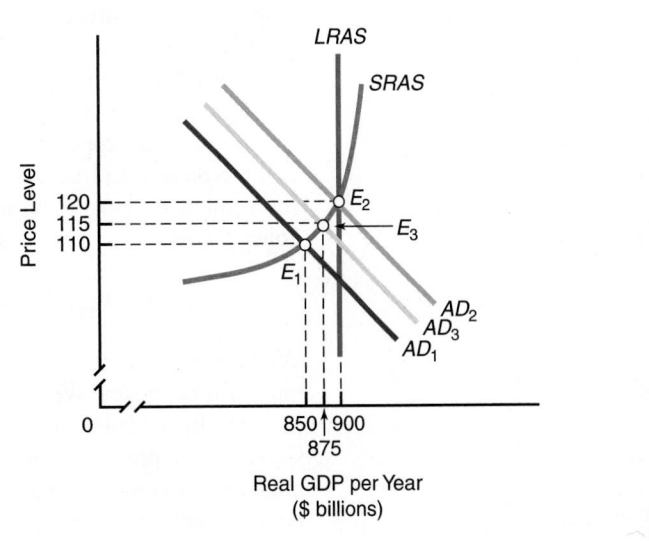

FIGURE 11–8

The Crowding-Out Effect

Expansionary fiscal policy that causes deficit financing initially shifts AD_1 to AD_2. Equilibrium initially moves toward E_2. But because of crowding out, the aggregate demand curve shifts inward to AD_3, and the new short-run equilibrium is at E_3.

FIGURE 11–9

The Crowding-Out Effect in Words

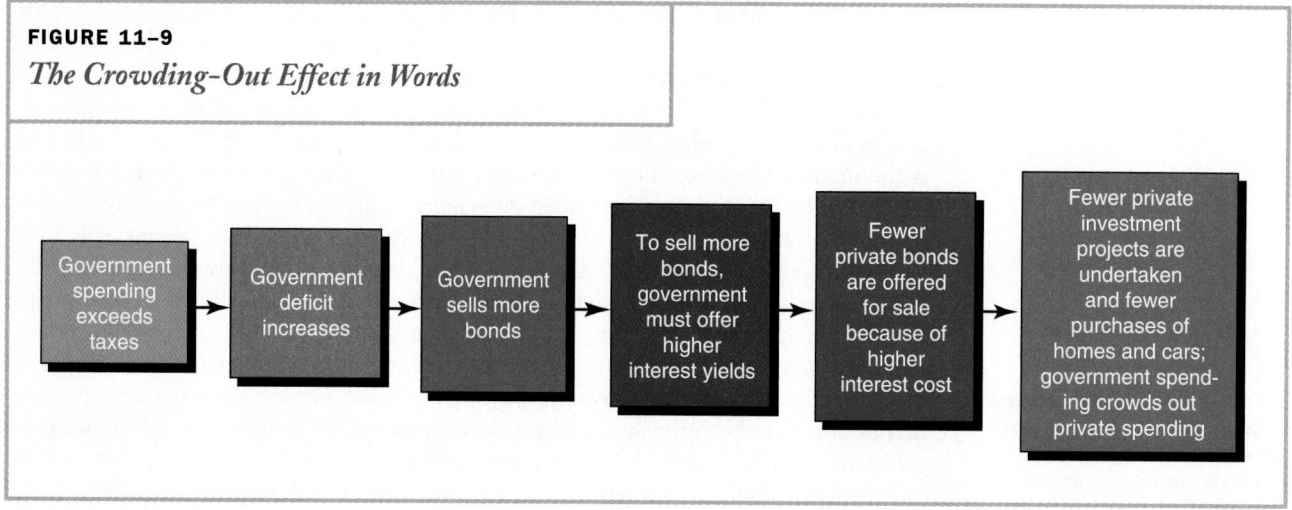

Net export effect The indirect effect that fiscal policies have on the exchange rate and net exports.

dollar. This indirect effect that fiscal policies have on the exchange rate and net exports is called the **net export effect**. How does this work? If government spending is increased without a rise in taxes, or if taxes are decreased without a reduction in government spending, the federal government must borrow more. As we pointed out, the government has to offer more attractive interest rates, and so overall interest rates go up. When interest rates go up in Canada, foreigners demand more securities, such as Canadian government bonds. When they do this, they have to pay for the bonds with dollars. After all, the typical Japanese investment firm cannot buy more Canadian government bonds without getting its hands on more Canadian dollars. This increases the demand for dollars at the same time that it increases the supply of yen. The value of the yen falls relative to the value of the dollar in international transactions. When this occurs, Japanese-made goods become cheaper in Canada, and Canadian-made goods become more expensive in Japan. Canadians want to buy more Japanese goods, and the Japanese want to buy fewer Canadian goods. This causes a reduction in net exports $(X - M)$ and cuts into any increase in aggregate demand. In sum, to the extent that federal deficit spending reduces net exports, the effect of expansionary fiscal policy will be less.

Combined Government Spending Effect

The federal government is not the only government with the power to tax and spend. We saw in Chapter 10 that provinces collect taxes to spend on highway maintenance, environmental protection, education, and welfare, for example. Cities and towns collect taxes to spend on local streets, police, and property development. Because provinces and municipalities have less access to financing through the bond market, they are typically more reluctant to finance their expenditures through debt.

This greater reluctance to deficit finance means that provinces and municipalities usually cut their expenditure during recessions as tax revenues fall, and increase spending as the economy and tax revenues improve. This procyclical behaviour can offset federal government attempts to bolster a foundering economy with deficit spending as we saw in Policy Example 11–1 (page 294).

The Supply-Side Effects of Changes in Taxes

We have talked about changing taxes and changing government spending, the traditional tools of fiscal policy. We have not really talked about the possibility of changing marginal tax rates. In our federal tax system, higher incomes are taxed at higher rates. In that sense, Canada has a progressive federal individual income tax system. Expansionary fiscal policy might involve reducing marginal tax rates. Advocates of such changes argue that (1) lower tax rates will lead to an increase in productivity because individuals will work harder and longer, save more, and invest more; and (2) increased productivity will lead to more economic growth, which will lead to higher real GDP. The government, by applying lower marginal tax rates, will not necessarily lose tax revenues, for the lower marginal tax rates will be applied to a growing tax base because of economic growth—after all, tax revenues are the product of a tax rate times a tax base. People who support this notion are called supply-side economists, whose theories we will study in Chapter 15. Due to a shift outward to the right in the aggregate supply curve, there can be greater output without upward pressure on the price level. In Policy Example 11–3, the effect of taxation on the supply side is briefly examined.

POLICY EXAMPLE 11–3 | **Boosting Tax Revenues via International Tax Competition**

Supply-side analysis indicates that people respond to lower tax rates by working more hours or making more purchases, thereby increasing the tax base. Thus, nations may be able to increase their tax revenues by reducing tax rates. A nation's government may also try to induce people and businesses abroad to move taxable activities inside the nation's borders. It can try to accomplish this by reducing its tax rate below rates prevailing in other countries, thereby boosting its overall tax revenues.

In the European Union, marginal tax rates on capital investments range from as low as under 7 percent in Greece and just over 9 percent in Ireland to as high as 25 percent in Germany and 30 percent in France. If businesspeople are otherwise equally inclined to consider capital investments in any given EU country, taking into account marginal tax rates on their investment will push them toward considering Greece and Ireland. They are less likely to consider Germany and France. Estimates indicate that each percentage-point reduction in the marginal tax rate on capital relative to the EU average tax rate tends to increase any given EU nation's inflow of capital investment by about 4 percent. For the Greek and Irish governments, the result appears to have been a net increase in total revenues from taxing returns to capital.

For critical analysis: Why do you suppose that member nations of the Organization for Economic Co-operation and Development recently threatened to impose sanctions on countries setting tax rates that the OECD deemed "too low"?

The Ricardian Equivalence Theorem

Economists have implicitly assumed that people look at changes in taxes or changes in government spending only in the present. What if people actually think about the size of *future* tax payments? Does this have an effect on how they react to an increase in government spending with no tax increases? Some economists believe that the answer is yes. What if people's horizons extend beyond this year? Don't we then have to take into account the effects of today's government policies on the future?

Consider an example. If the government wants to spend $1 today, it can raise tax revenues by $1 and the public's responsibility to the government for that particular dollar has now been met and will never return. Alternatively, the government can borrow $1 today and the public will owe $1 plus interest later. Realizing that $1 today is mathematically equivalent to $1 plus interest next year, people may save the $1 to meet the future tax liabilities. Therefore, whether the $1 spending is financed by taxation or by borrowing, the two methods of finance are equivalent.

In terms of Figure 11–8, the aggregate demand curve will shift from AD_1 to AD_3 instead of moving to AD_2 as policy makers expect. In the extreme case, if consumers fully compensate for a higher future tax liability by saving more, the aggregate demand curve

Ricardian equivalence theorem An increase in public spending is offset by a reduction in consumer spending because individuals are saving to compensate for the future tax liability.

remains at AD_1. This is the case of individuals fully discounting their increased tax liabilities. The result is that an increased budget created by new spending and no tax increase has no net effect on aggregate demand because the new government spending is fully offset by the reduction in consumption. This is known as the **Ricardian equivalence theorem**, after the 19th-century economist, David Ricardo, who first developed the argument publicly.

For economists who believe in the Ricardian equivalence theorem, it does not matter how government expenditures are financed—by taxes or by issuing debt. Is the Ricardian equivalence theorem correct? The evidence is not clear. Between 1983 and 1997, government spending exceeded taxes by over $20 billion per year. Private savings rates declined by about one-half over the same period, to the lowest they have ever been.

➤→ CONCEPTS IN BRIEF

Learning Objective 11.4: Discuss ways in which crowding out, direct expenditure offsets, the net export effect, supply-side economics, and the Ricardian equivalence theorem may offset the effectiveness of fiscal policy.

- ✦ Crowding out occurs domestically because of an interest effect in which the government's efforts to finance its deficit spending cause interest rates to rise, thereby crowding out private investment and spending, particularly on cars and houses. This is called the crowding-out effect.

- ✦ There is a net export effect that offsets fiscal policy. Like the domestic crowding-out effect, it occurs because the government's increased deficit causes interest rates to rise. This encourages foreigners to invest more in Canadian securities. When they do so, they demand more dollars, thereby increasing the international value of the dollar. As a result, Canadian-made goods become more expensive abroad and foreign goods cheaper here, and so Canada exports fewer goods and imports more.

- ✦ Changes in marginal tax rates may cause supply-side effects if a reduction in marginal tax rates induces enough additional work, saving, and investing. Government tax receipts can actually increase. This is called supply-side economics.

- ✦ Some economists believe in the Ricardian equivalence theorem, which argues that an increase in the government budget deficit has no effect on aggregate demand because individuals correctly perceive their increased future taxes and therefore save more today to pay for them.

11.5 *Discretionary Fiscal Policy in Practice*

We can discuss fiscal policy in a relatively precise way. We draw graphs with aggregate demand and supply curves to show what we are doing. We could, even in principle, estimate the offsets that were just discussed. However, even if we were able to measure all of these offsets exactly, would-be fiscal policy makers still face problems: which fiscal policy mix to choose and the various time lags involved in conducting fiscal policy.

Fiscal Policy Mix

What is the proper mix of taxes and government expenditures? Let us say that policy makers decide that a change in taxes is desirable. At least seven options are available:

1. Permanent change in personal income taxes
2. Permanent change in corporate income taxes
3. Temporary change in personal income taxes
4. Temporary change in corporate income taxes
5. Change payroll taxes, such as EI and CPP contributions
6. Change depreciation allowance on investment expenditures
7. Change specific consumption taxes, such as on oil

Note that all of these are tax changes, but their effects on individual groups will be different, and special-interest groups will be lobbying politicians to protect specific interests.

Alternatively, assume policy makers decide that a change in government expenditures is desirable. There are disadvantages to these changes. Political wrangling will arise over the amount, type, and geographic location of the expenditure change ("spend more in my city or province, less in someone else's"). Furthermore, if the expenditure is to be made on a capital goods project, such as a highway, a dam, or a public transportation system, the problem of timing arises. If started during a recession, should or could such a project be abandoned or delayed if inflation emerges before the project is finished? Are delays or reversals politically feasible, even if they are economically sensible?

Time Lags

Policy makers must be concerned with various time lags. Quite apart from the fact that it is difficult to measure economic variables, it takes time to collect and assimilate such data. Thus, policy makers must be concerned with the **recognition time lag**, the period of months that may elapse before economic problems can be identified.[2]

After an economic problem is recognized, a solution must be formulated; thus, there will be an **action time lag**, the period between the recognition of a problem and the implementation of policy to solve it. For fiscal policy, the action time lag is particularly long. It must be approved by Parliament, and much political wrangling and infighting accompany legislative fiscal policy decision making. It is not at all unusual for the action time lag to last a year or two. As well, it takes time to put the policy into effect. After Parliament enacts a fiscal policy as legislation, it takes time to decide, for example, who gets the new federal construction contract and so on.

When we add the recognition time lag to the action time lag, we get what is known as the *inside lag*. That is how long it takes to get a policy from inside the institutional structure of our federal government.

Finally, there is the **effect time lag**: After fiscal policy is enacted, it takes time for it to affect the economy. Multiplier effects take more time to work through the economy than it takes an economist to shift a curve on a chalkboard.

Because the various fiscal policy time lags are long, a policy designed to combat a recession might not produce results until the economy is experiencing inflation, in which case the fiscal policy would worsen the situation. Or a fiscal policy designed to eliminate inflation might not produce effects until the economy is in a recession; in that case, too, fiscal policy would make the economic problem worse, rather than better.

Furthermore, because fiscal policy time lags tend to be *variable* (anywhere from one to three years), policy makers have a difficult time fine-tuning the economy. Clearly, fiscal policy is more an art than a science.

11.6 Automatic Stabilizers

Not all changes in taxes (or in tax rates) or in government spending (including government transfers) constitute discretionary fiscal policy. There are several types of automatic (or nondiscretionary) fiscal policies. Such policies do not require new legislation. Specific automatic fiscal policies, called **automatic,** or **built-in, stabilizers**—special provisions of the tax and income support laws that cause changes in the economy without the direct action of the government—include the progressive federal income tax system itself and the government transfer system; the latter includes employment insurance (EI) and old age security benefits (OAS).

Recognition time lag The period of months that may elapse before economic problems can be identified.

Action time lag The period between the recognition of a problem and the implementation of policy to solve it.

Effect time lag After fiscal policy is enacted, it takes time for it to affect the economy.

Automatic, or built-in, stabilizers Special provisions of the tax and income support laws that cause changes in the economy without the direct action of the government.

---

[2]Final annual data for GDP, after various revisions, are not forthcoming for three to six months after the year's end.

The Federal Progressive Income Tax

We have in Canada a progressive income tax (in the year 2006) that ranges from no taxes for taxable incomes below $8929, 15.5 percent for taxable incomes up to $37 178, to 22 percent on additional incomes up to $74 357, 26 percent on additional incomes upto $120 887, to 29 percent on incomes above $120 887. (Provincial and municipal taxes are extra.) For an individual, as taxable income rises, the marginal tax rate rises, and as taxable income falls, so does the marginal tax rate. Think about this now in terms of the entire economy. If the nation is at full employment, personal income taxes may yield the government, say, $60 billion per year. Now, suppose that for whatever reason, business activity suddenly starts to slow down. Workers are not allowed to put in as much over-time as before. Some workers are laid off, and some must change to jobs that pay less. Some workers and executives might take voluntary pay cuts. What happens to federal income taxes when wages and salaries go down? Across the economy, taxes are still paid, but at a lower marginal rate than before, because the tax schedule is progressive. As a result of these decreased taxes, disposable income—the amount remaining after taxes—does not fall by the same percentage as before-tax income. In other words, the individual does not feel the pinch of recession as much as we might think if we ignored the progressive nature of our tax schedule. The *average* tax rate falls when less is earned.

Conversely, when the economy suddenly comes into a boom period, people's incomes tend to rise. They can work more overtime and can change to higher-paying jobs. Their *disposable* income does not, however, go up as rapidly as their total income because their average tax rates are rising at the same time. The Canada Revenue Agency ends up taking a bigger bite. In this situation, the progressive income tax system tends to stabilize any abrupt changes in economic activity. (Actually, the progressive tax structure simply magnifies any stabilization effect that might exist.)

Employment Insurance

Like the progressive income tax, employment insurance stabilizes aggregate demand. Throughout the business cycle, it reduces changes in people's disposable income. When business activity drops, most laid-off workers automatically become eligible for employ-ment insurance benefits. Their disposable income, therefore, remains positive, although certainly it is less than when they were employed. During boom periods, there is less unemployment, and consequently fewer employment insurance payments are made to the labour force. Less purchasing power is being added to the economy because fewer bene-fits are paid out. Historically, the relationship between the unemployment rate and employment insurance payouts has been strongly positive.

Stabilizing Impact

The key stabilizing impact of the progressive income tax and employment insurance is their ability to mitigate changes in disposable income, consumption, and the equilibrium level of national income. If disposable income is prevented from falling as much as it would during a recession, the downturn will be moderated. In contrast, if disposable income is prevented from rising as rapidly as it would during a boom, the boom will not get out of hand. The progressive income tax and unemployment benefits, thus, provide automatic stabilization to the economy. We present the argument graphically in Figure 11–10.

What Do We Really Know about Fiscal Policy?

There are two ways of looking at fiscal policy, one that prevails during normal times and the other during abnormal times.

Fiscal Policy during Normal Times

During normal times (without "excessive" unemployment, inflation, or problems in the national economy), we know that given the time lag between the recognition of the need

FIGURE 11–10
Automatic Stabilizers

Here, we assume that as real national income rises, tax revenues rise, and government transfers fall, other parts of the government budget remaining constant. Thus, as the economy expands from Y_f to Y_1, a budget surplus automatically arises; as the economy contracts from Y_f to Y_2, a budget deficit automatically arises. Such automatic changes tend to drive the economy back toward its full-employment output level.

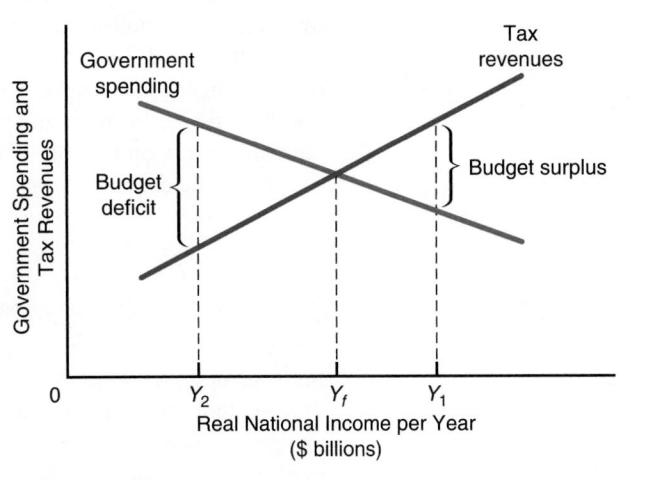

to increase aggregate demand and the impact of any expansionary fiscal policy, and given the very modest size of any fiscal policy action that the government actually will take, discretionary fiscal policy is probably not very effective. The government ends up doing too little too late to help in a minor recession. Moreover, fiscal policy that generates repeated tax changes (as it has done) creates uncertainty, which may do more harm than good. To the extent that fiscal policy has any effect during normal times, it probably achieves this by way of automatic stabilizers, rather than by way of discretionary policy.

Fiscal Policy during Abnormal Times

During abnormal times, fiscal policy can be effective. Consider some classic examples: the Great Depression and times of war.

THE GREAT DEPRESSION. When there is a substantial catastrophic drop in real GDP, as there was during the Great Depression, fiscal policy probably can do something to stimulate aggregate demand. Because so many people are cash constrained, government spending is a good way during such periods to get cash into their hands.

WARTIME. Wars are, in fact, reserved for governments. War expenditures are not good substitutes for private expenditures—they have little or no direct expenditure offsets. Consequently, war spending as part of expansionary fiscal policy usually has noteworthy effects, such as during World War II, when real GDP increased dramatically, bringing an end to the Great Depression.

The "Soothing" Effect of Keynesian Fiscal Policy

One view of traditional Keynesian fiscal policy does not relate to its being used on a regular basis. As you have learned in this chapter, there are many problems associated with attempting to use fiscal policy. But if we should encounter a severe downturn, fiscal policy is available. Knowing this may reassure consumers and investors. After all, the ability of the federal government to prevent another Great Depression—given what we know about how to use fiscal policy today—may take some of the large risk out of consumers' and particularly investors' calculations. This may induce more buoyant and stable expectations of the future, thereby smoothing investment spending.

At the same time, the supply-side effects of high levels of taxation must also be taken into account. High levels of business taxation can smother the important investment that businesses undertake. Too-high levels of welfare and personal taxation hinder the desirability of working and saving. A growing number of economists and politicians believe that governments have gone too far in trying to stabilize the economy, at the expense of long-term growth. These fundamental changes in outlook were championed in the 1980s by conservative politicians and, as we see in Policy Example 11–4, have since spread around the world. That change has shown up in the decline of governments relative to the economy in the last decade here in Canada and elsewhere as we saw in Figure 11–3A. Soothing the economy is an appropriate goal, but it should not put it to sleep! For some more discussion on the role of government, look at the Issues and Applications section at the end of the chapter.

POLICY EXAMPLE 11–4 **Keynesian Fiscal Policy Loses Its Lustre**

Some analysts argue that John Maynard Keynes was the most influential economist of the 20th century, for he supposedly armed policy makers with fiscal weapons that allowed them to fight recession. Yet, at the beginning of the 21st century, influential policy makers throughout the world are ignoring the concept of government spending as a way out of recessions.

Even though European governments have long favoured welfare spending, the 11 that joined together to use the common currency called the euro also agreed to some specific antigovernmental spending stipulations. These countries, including France and Germany, are committed to keeping public deficits at 3 percent or less of gross domestic product. Whenever a country's public deficit exceeds this figure, the offending government can be fined up to 0.5 percent of its GDP. Deficit spending—a favourite Keynesian fiscal policy action—is tightly constrained in these countries.

In 1999, Brazil's president, Fernando Enrique Cardoso, stated that in the face of the then-current recession, "we will need to put in place as rapidly as possible a fiscal austerity plan so that interest rates can fall and Brazil can begin to grow again." He publicly announced that the country's government sector should shrink by 3 percent the following year, even when his government economists predicted a probable 4 percent decrease in real GDP.

The International Monetary Fund (IMF) did a study on fiscal policy a few years ago. It examined attempts by governments to reduce public spending and public debt. It looked at 62 attempts over two and a half decades. Its conclusion was that in the 14 cases for which the governments had aggressively reduced government spending, as in Denmark and Ireland, those economies had the fastest growth rates. The IMF contended that there may have been a "virtuous circle between economic growth and debt-reduction programs."

For critical analysis: How might Keynes have responded to this increase in anti-Keynesianism?

⇒ CONCEPTS IN BRIEF

Learning Objective 11.5: Explain how fiscal policy time lags complicate the use of fiscal policy to eliminate GDP gaps.
- Time lags of various sorts reduce the effectiveness of fiscal policy. These include the recognition time lag, the action time lag, and the effect time lag.

Learning Objective 11.6: Describe how certain aspects of fiscal policy function as automatic stabilizers for the economy.
- Two automatic, or built-in, stabilizers are the progressive income tax and employment insurance.
- Built-in stabilizers tend automatically to moderate changes in disposable income resulting from changes in overall business activity.
- Though discretionary fiscal policy may not necessarily be a useful tool in normal times because of time lags and crowding out, it may work well during abnormal times, such as depressions and wartime. In addition, the existence of fiscal policy may have a soothing effect on consumers and investors.

ISSUES AND APPLICATIONS

How Much Government Is Enough?

Concepts Applied: Fiscal Policy, Stabilization, Economic Growth

Government policies can increase or decrease the role of government in society.

Consider the following two statements:

"Wherever the state undertakes to control in detail the economic activities of its citizens, wherever, that is, detailed central economic planning reigns, there ordinary citizens are in political fetters, have a low standard of living, and have little power to control their own destiny." —from *Free to Choose* by Milton Friedman, pp. 54–55

"Canada and the countries of Europe try to balance market forces with public policy, to reconcile the tendency for the rich to get richer and create an all but impenetrable elite with a social welfare state and policies to redistribute income from the haves to the have-nots. Such countries recognize individual rights but try to balance them with the rights of collectivities. These societies are more likely than Americans to realize that individuals can have too much freedom and that freedoms can be exercised irresponsibly by individuals to their own and others' detriments."—from *Fire and Ice* by Michael Adams, p. 116

The biggest economic debate that has been carried on by economists and politicians is about how much government there should be. There is no doubt that there is a need for many government functions, such as defence and a justice system, but Canada and other Western countries also have extensive social safety nets for individuals and subsidies for businesses. Political parties have advocated both for and against government intervention in the economy. Without state intervention, it is clear that many people in our society would be much worse off. On the other hand, not having a safety net would encourage some to get employment.

Governments in Canada purchase many goods and services and give them out for free, paying for them through collected taxes. (Look back to Figure 11–3B.) This includes roads, health care, education, defence, and other functions. It also regulates many industries and provides protection through the police, justice, and fire departments. This is about half of the governments' budgets. The other half primarily involves redistributing wealth through transfer payments and payments on debt, neither of which provides any services.

Governments have recently cut back on all forms of spending (relative to the size of the economy), partly because of a change in thinking in society that has favoured less government and partly because of a high debt that forced governments to rethink their priorities.

For critical analysis:

1. What changes in government spending would you favour (either more or less)? How would you finance the new services? (Assume any new services must come from new taxes.) How would you redistribute any surpluses if you favour cutting services? Who would be winners and losers from your policy? How would you or your family personally gain or lose from these policy changes?

2. What political parties would you identify with the classical approach? Which with the Keynesian approach? Why might you not vote for a party that has the economic policy you favour?

➡️ SUMMARY

Here is what you should know after reading this chapter. MyEconLab will help you identify what you know, and where to go when you need to practise. We suggest that as soon as you review one of the Learning Objective sections below, you then proceed to go through the related section in MyEconLab.

✕ myeconlab

➡️ LEARNING OBJECTIVES	KEY TERMS	MYECONLAB PRACTICE
11.1 Fiscal Policy. A deliberate increase in government spending or a reduction in taxes can raise aggregate demand. Thus, these fiscal policy actions can shift the aggregate demand curve and thereby close a recessionary gap. Likewise, an intentional reduction in government spending or a tax increase will reduce aggregate demand. These fiscal policy actions shift the aggregate demand curve inward along the short-run aggregate supply curve and close an inflationary gap.	fiscal policy, 292	• **MyEconLab** Study Plan 11.1
11.2 Government Budgets and Finances. The government's budget balance is the difference between its revenues and spending. A surplus occurs when this is positive, and a deficit occurs when it is negative. Government deficits (a flow) must be financed through money creation or by borrowing. The past accumulation of deficits has resulted in a large public debt (a stock) for the federal government. When we subtract the holdings of government agencies from government debt we get the net public debt. Federal deficits peaked in the early 1990s and moved into a surplus position in the 1997–98 fiscal year. The accumulation of past deficits has meant an outstanding debt of under $515 billion.	budget balance, 295 balanced budget, 295 budget surplus, 295 budget deficit, 295 money financing, 295 gross public debt, 298 net public debt, 298	• **MyEconLab** Study Plan 11.2
11.3 Federal Budget Deficits in an Open Economy. A close relationship exists between government deficits and current account deficits because government borrowing results in a large inflow of capital to finance those debts. The increased borrowing pushes up interest rates and the value of the Canadian dollar, resulting in a current account deficit.		• **MyEconLab** Study Plan 11.3
11.4 Possible Offsets to Fiscal Policy. Fiscal policy may not be as effective as this theory suggests for a variety of reasons. Government borrowing may raise interest rates and thus reduce domestic spending on investment and consumption goods. These higher rates may also cause the Canadian dollar to increase in value and thus reduce our net exports. Ricardian	crowding-out effect, 303 net export effect, 304 Ricardian equivalence theorem, 306	• **MyEconLab** Study Plan 11.4

➡ LEARNING OBJECTIVES	KEY TERMS	MYECONLAB PRACTICE
equivalence suggests that when the government cuts taxes and borrows to finance the deficit, people realize that eventually the government will have to repay the loan. Thus, they anticipate there will have to be tax increases in the future. This induces them to save today to meet their future tax liabilities. Current consumption is therefore unchanged even though consumers have higher disposable income. The effect of taxes on the supply side may also mean that tax rate increases and decreases may not result in large changes in total taxes collected. How strong these offsetting effects are will determine whether fiscal policy has the desired effect.		
11.5 Discretionary Fiscal Policy in Practice. Efforts to engage in fiscal policy actions intended to bring about carefully planned changes in aggregate demand are often complicated by policy time lags. One of these is the recognition lag, which is the time required to collect information about the economy's current situation. Another is the action time lag, the period between the recognition of a problem and the implementation of a policy intended to address it. Finally, there is the effect time lag, which is the interval between policy implementation and its having an effect on the economy. All of these lags can be lengthy and variable, lasting up to several years. Thus, trying to quickly adjust fiscal policy to steer the economy is very difficult.	recognition time lag, 307 action time lag, 307 effect time lag, 307	• **MyEconLab** Study Plan 11.5
11.6 Automatic Stabilizers. With discretionary fiscal policy, government spending and taxation policies are consciously applied to stabilize an economy. Automatic fiscal policy, by contrast, does not require any conscious change in policy or legislation but, rather, results from existing policies and institutional structures. Thus, a progressive tax structure and an employment insurance system (which are already in force) automatically change taxes and government outlays as national income changes. In particular, as national income falls in a recession, government outlays for unemployed workers automatically	automatic, or built-in, stabilizers, 307	• **MyEconLab** Study Plan 11.6

➤→ LEARNING OBJECTIVES   **KEY TERMS**   **MYECONLAB PRACTICE**

increase, and tax revenues fall as lower incomes mean people pay less taxes. These automatic stabilizers counteract declining national income. Similarly, automatic stabilizers reduce employment insurance benefits and increase taxes as national income rises. Therefore, changes in national income automatically affect aggregate demand because of these counteracting policies and thus give greater stability to the Canadian economy.

➤→ PROBLEMS

(Answers to the odd-numbered problems appear at the back of the book.)

LO 11.1 Use the aggregate demand/aggregate supply model to evaluate the effects of fiscal policy.

1. Assume that you are a new Member of Parliament. You believe that expansionary government fiscal policy will pull the country rapidly out of its recession. What are some of the possible tax and spending changes you could recommend? What are the possible mixes?

2. Suppose there is an inflationary gap. Discuss one discretionary fiscal policy action that might eliminate it. Illustrate your answers using the *AD-AS* model.

3. Suppose there is a recessionary gap. Discuss one discretionary fiscal policy action that might eliminate it. Illustrate your answers using the *AD-AS* model.

LO 11.2 Explain the relationship between government budgets and the accumulated debt and describe the current situation for Canadian governments.

4. In 2005, government spending is $800 billion and taxes collected are $770 billion. What is the federal budget balance in 2005?

5. Look at the accompanying table showing federal budget spending and federal budget receipts. Calculate the federal budget deficit as a percentage of GDP for each year.

Year	Federal Budget Spending ($ billions)	Federal Budget Receipts ($ billions)	GDP ($ billions)
1988	109.3	127.8	605.9
1989	117.4	137.7	650.7
1990	125.6	150.8	669.5
1991	130.9	161.1	667.5

6. What is the relationship between the annual federal government budget deficit and the net public debt?

7. Visit Canada's Finance Department at http://www.fin.gc.ca/access/fedprove.html. This site sets out the major transfers from the federal to the provincial governments. Scroll through this document until you find your province. You will find a table setting out the amount the federal government has transferred for each of the last four fiscal years. Do you think that these transfers have allowed your province to pursue expansionary or contractionary policy? Explain your answer.

8. Suppose that a government agency buys large volumes of bonds previously issued by the central treasury department of its nation's government. The treasury increases its tax collections to fund its bond purchases. What happens to the gross public debt? What happens to the net public debt?

9. Suppose that the government agency in Problem 8 purchases previously issued bonds from private individuals and companies instead of the government treasury department. What happens to the gross public debt? What happens to the net public debt?

10. Refer back to Policy Example 11–2, "The Baby Boom Generation Moves into Retirement Years." What can the government do today with RRSP programs to reduce the cost of future income support programs for the elderly?

LO 11.3 Explain the relationship between a government deficit and a current account deficit.

11. Suppose that the government agency in Problem 8 purchases previously issued bonds from foreigners who then convert that money to their native currency (assume the government uses a budget surplus to do

this). What is the effect on the value of the Canadian dollar? What effect is this likely to have on the current account balance? What effect will it have on GDP in the short run?

LO 11.4 Discuss ways in which crowding out, direct expenditure offsets, the net export effect, supply-side economics, and the Ricardian equivalence theorem may offset the effectiveness of fiscal policy.

12. Suppose that Parliament decides that economic performance is weakening and that the government should "do something" about the situation. They make no tax changes but do enact new laws increasing government spending on a variety of programs.

    a. Prior to Parliamentary action, careful studies by government economists indicated that the direct multiplier effect of a rise in government expenditures on equilibrium GDP is equal to 6. Within the 12 months after the increase in government spending, however, it has become clear that the actual ultimate multiplier effect on real GDP will be unlikely to exceed half of that amount. What factors might account for this?

    b. Another year and a half elapses following passage of the government-spending boost. The government has undertaken no additional policy actions, nor have there been any other events of significance. Nevertheless, by the end of the second year, real GDP has returned to its original level, and the price level has increased sharply. Provide a possible explanation for this outcome.

13. It may be argued that the effects of a higher public debt are the same as the effects of higher taxes. Why?

14. To reduce the size of the deficit (and reduce the growth in the net public debt), a politician suggests that "we should tax the rich." The politician makes a simple arithmetic calculation in which he applies the increased tax rate to the total income reported by "the rich" in a previous year. He says that this is how much the government could receive from the increased taxes on "the rich." What is the major fallacy in such calculations?

15. Given the existence of automatic stabilizers, a recession is expected to generate a budget deficit, and an expansion is expected to generate a budget surplus. If the generation of such budget deficits or surpluses is to be countercyclical, what assumptions must be made about how consumers react to such budget deficits or surpluses?

16. Suppose that Parliament enacts a significant tax cut with the expectation that this action will stimulate aggregate demand and push up real GDP in the short run. In fact, however, neither real GDP nor the price level changes significantly following the tax cut. What might account for this outcome?

17. Under what circumstance might a tax reduction be associated with a long-run increase in real national income and a long-run reduction in the price level?

18. If the Ricardian equivalence theorem is not relevant, then a cut in the income tax rate should affect the level of equilibrium real income per year. Explain why.

19. Suppose that Parliament enacts a lump-sum tax cut of $40 billion. The marginal propensity to consume is equal to 0.75. If Ricardian equivalence holds true, what is the effect on equilibrium real income? On saving?

20. Refer back to Policy Example 11–3, "Boosting Tax Revenues via International Tax Competition." Many governments in Canada have attempted to lower taxes, arguing that it will pay for itself in an enlarged tax base. Why is the short-run outcome of less taxes collected by the government likely to be different from what happens in the long run?

LO 11.5 Explain how fiscal policy time lags complicate the use of fiscal policy to eliminate GDP gaps.

21. Explain how time lags in discretionary fiscal policy making could thwart the efforts of government to stabilize real national income in the face of an economic downturn. Is it possible that these time lags could actually cause discretionary fiscal policy to *destabilize* real national income?

LO 11.6 Describe how certain aspects of fiscal policy function as automatic stabilizers for the economy.

22. Which of the following is an example of an automatic fiscal stabilizer? Which of the following is an example of a discretionary fiscal policy action?

    a. The Bank of Canada arranges to make loans to banks automatically whenever an economic downturn begins.

    b. As the economy heats up, the resulting increase in equilibrium income immediately results in higher income tax payments, which dampens consumption spending somewhat.

    c. As the economy starts to recover from a recession and more people go back to work, employment insurance payments begin to decline.

    d. To stem an overheated economy, the prime minister, using special powers granted by Parliament, authorizes emergency impoundment of funds previously authorized for spending on government programs.

    e. A recession occurs, and government-funded unemployment compensation payments are paid out to laid-off workers.

    f. Parliament votes to fund a new jobs program designed to put unemployed workers to work.

    g. The Bank of Canada decides to reduce the quantity of money in circulation in an effort to slow inflation.

23. What is discretionary fiscal policy? What are automatic stabilizers? Give examples of each.

24. Explain the effect that automatic stabilizers have on an economy. What is their advantage over discretionary policies?

APPENDIX F

FISCAL POLICY: A KEYNESIAN PERSPECTIVE

The traditional Keynesian approach to fiscal policy differs in three ways from that presented in Chapter 11. First, it emphasizes the underpinnings of the components of aggregate demand. Second, it assumes that government expenditures are not substitutes for private expenditures and that current taxes are the only taxes taken into account by consumers and firms. Third, the traditional Keynesian approach focuses on the short run and so assumes that, as a first approximation, the price level is constant.

Changes in Government Spending

Figure F–1 measures real GDP along the horizontal axis and total planned expenditures (aggregate demand) along the vertical axis. The components of aggregate demand are consumption *(C)*, investment *(I)*, government spending *(G)*, and net exports $(X - M)$. The height of the schedule labelled $C + I + G + (X - M)$ shows total planned expenditures (aggregate demand) as a function of income. This schedule slopes upward because consumption depends positively on income. Everywhere along the 45-degree reference line, planned spending equals income. At the point Y^*, where the $C + I + G + (X - M)$ line intersects the 45-degree line, planned spending is consistent with real national income. At any income less than Y^*, spending exceeds income, and so income and thus spending will tend to rise. At any level of income greater than Y^*, planned spending is less than income, and so income and thus spending will tend to decline. Given the determinants of *C, I, G,* and $(X - M)$, total spending (aggregate demand) will be Y^*.

The Keynesian approach assumes that changes in government spending cause no direct offsets in either consumption or investment spending because *G* is not a substitute for *C, I,* or $(X - M)$. Hence, a rise in government spending from *G* to *G′* causes the $C + I + G + (X - M)$ line to shift upward by the full amount of the rise in government spending, yielding the line $C + I + G′ + (X - M)$. The rise in government spending causes GDP to rise, which, in turn, causes consumption spending to rise, which further

FIGURE F–1

The Impact of Higher Government Spending on Aggregate Demand

Government spending increases, causing $C + I + G + (X - M)$ to move to $C + I + G′ + (X - M)$. Equilibrium increases to Y^{**}.

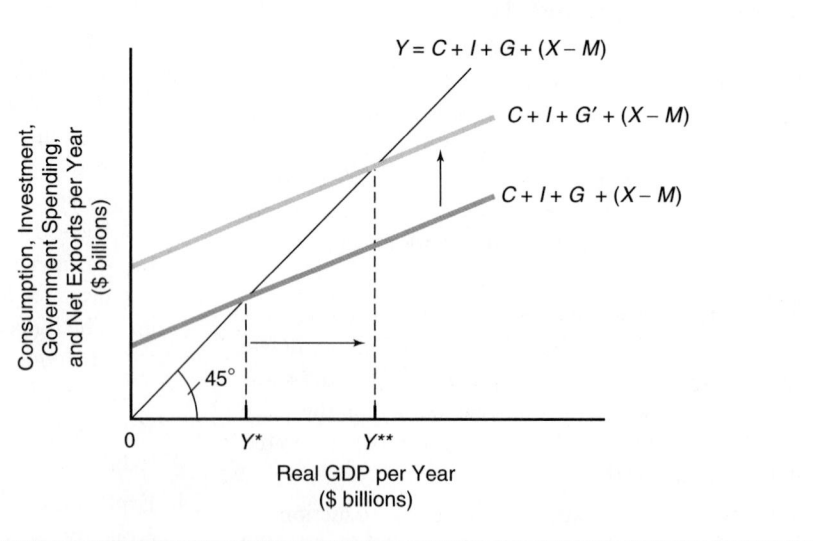

increases GDP. Ultimately, aggregate demand rises to Y^{**}, where spending again equals GDP. A key conclusion of the Keynesian analysis is that total spending rises by *more* than the original rise in government spending because consumption spending depends positively on GDP.

Changes in Taxes

According to the Keynesian approach, changes in current taxes affect aggregate demand by changing the amount of disposable (after-tax) income available to consumers. A rise in taxes reduces disposable income and thus reduces consumption; conversely, a tax cut raises disposable income and thus causes a rise in consumption spending. The effects of a tax increase are shown in Figure F–2. Higher taxes cause consumption spending to decline from C to C', causing total spending to shift downward to $C' + I + G + (X - M)$. In general, the decline in consumption will be less than the increase in taxes because people will also reduce their saving to help pay the higher taxes. Thus, although aggregate demand declines to Y^{**}, the decline is smaller than would happen if every dollar of tax increase resulted in a dollar decline of consumption.

The Balanced-Budget Multiplier

One interesting implication of the Keynesian approach concerns the impact of a balanced-budget change in government spending. Suppose that the government increases spending by $100 million and pays for it by raising current taxes by $100 million. Such a policy is called a *balanced-budget increase in spending*. The increase in spending will push aggregate demand up by a larger amount than $100 million because of the multiplier. At the same time, the tax increase will reduce consumption and therefore reduce aggregate demand by an amount larger than $100 million, again because of the multiplier effect. However, the positive effect of the spending increase is larger than the negative effect of the tax increase (as part of the tax increase is financed from reduced saving), so a most remarkable thing happens: A balanced-budget increase in G causes total spending to rise by *exactly* the amount of the rise in G—in this case, $100 million. We say that the *balanced-budget multiplier* is equal to 1. Similarly, a balanced-budget reduction in spending will cause total spending to fall by exactly the amount of the spending cut.

FIGURE F–2

The Impact of Higher Taxes on Aggregate Demand

Higher taxes cause consumption to fall to C'. Equilibrium decreases to Y^{**}.

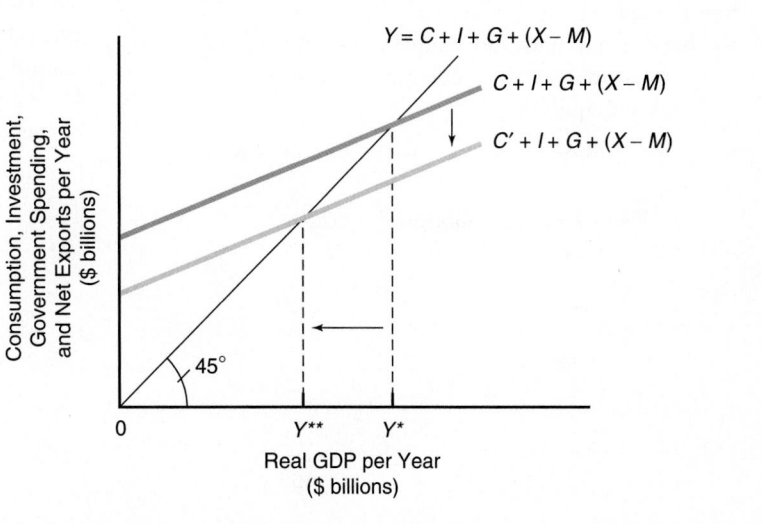

The Fixed-Price Level Assumption

The final key feature of the Keynesian approach is that it typically assumes that as a first approximation, the price level is fixed. Recall that nominal income equals the price level multiplied by real output. If the price level is fixed, an increase in government spending that causes nominal GDP to rise will show up exclusively as a rise in *real* output. This will, in turn, be accompanied by a decline in the unemployment rate because the additional output can be produced only if additional factors of production, such as labour, are utilized.

➡ PROBLEMS

F-1. In this problem, equilibrium GDP is $500 billion and full-employment equilibrium is $640 billion. The marginal propensity to save is $\frac{1}{7}$ and is the only leakage. Answer the questions using the data in the following graph:

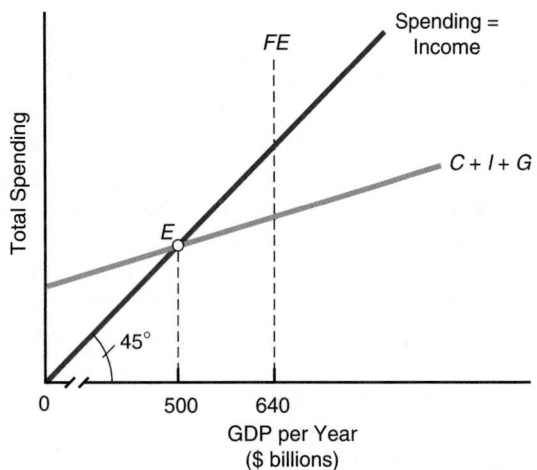

a. What is the marginal propensity to consume?
b. By how much must new investment or government spending increase to bring the economy up to full employment?
c. By how much must government cut personal taxes to stimulate the economy to the full-employment equilibrium?

F-2. Consider the following model; then answer the questions:

If $C = 30 + \frac{3}{4}Y$ and $I = 25$, equilibrium $Y = \$220$.

a. If government expenditures equal $5, what will be the new equilibrium level of GDP? (Assume Total planned expenditures = $C + I + G$.)
b. What was the government spending multiplier in this example?

F-3. Assume that MPE $= \frac{9}{10}$; then answer the following questions:

a. If government expenditures fall by $500, by how much will the total planned expenditure curve shift downward? By how much will equilibrium income change?
b. If taxes fall by $500, by how much will the total planned expenditure curve shift upward? By how much will equilibrium GDP change?

F-4. Assume that MPE $= \frac{3}{4}$; then answer the following questions:

a. If government expenditures rise by $100 million, by how much will the total planned expenditure curve shift upward?
b. If taxes rise by $100 million, by how much will the total planned expenditure curve shift downward?
c. If both taxes and government expenditures rise by $100 million, by how much will the total planned expenditure curve shift? What will happen to the equilibrium level of GDP?
d. How does our conclusion in the second part of (c) change if MPE $= \frac{9}{10}$? If MPE $= \frac{1}{2}$?

12

Money and the Banking System

LEARNING OBJECTIVES

After reading this chapter, you should be able to:

12.1 Define the functions of money.

12.2 Explain what "backs" the Canadian dollar.

12.3 Describe the various definitions of the money supply.

12.4 Describe the Canadian financial system.

MyEconLab helps you master each objective and study more efficiently. See end of chapter for details.

A couple of years ago, Argentina's government made a startling announcement. It was, it said, thinking about scrapping the nation's currency, the peso. Furthermore, it might not even replace the peso with a new national money. Instead, the government might declare American dollars to be the legal money of Argentina. Since then, a few other Latin American nations have contemplated the same plan. In Canada, some economists have floated a plan for dropping the Canadian dollar in favour of the American dollar. Why would a country think about giving up its own national currency and using American dollars instead? Before you can consider this question, you must learn about the functions of money. You must also understand how economists measure the total quantity of money in circulation. These are key topics in this chapter.

DID YOU KNOW THAT...

The typical dollar coin changes hands 50 times a year. Cash, of course, is not the only thing we use as money. As you will see in this chapter, our definition of money is much broader. Money has been important to society for thousands of years. In 300 B.C., Aristotle claimed that everything had to "be accessed in money, for this enables men always to exchange their services, and so makes society possible." Money is, indeed, a part of our everyday existence. We have to be careful, though, when we talk about money because it means two different things. Most of the time when people say "I wish I had more money," they mean that they want more income. Thus, the normal use of the term *money* implies the ability to purchase goods and services. In this chapter, in contrast, you will use the term **money** to mean anything that people generally accept in exchange for goods and services. Most people think of money as the paper bills and coins that they carry. But the concept of money is normally more inclusive. Table 12–1 provides a list of some items that various civilizations have used as money. The best way to understand how those items served this purpose is to examine the functions of money.

TABLE 12–1

Types of Money

This is a partial list of items that have been used as money. Native Canadians used wampum, beads made from shells. Fijians used whale teeth. The early colonists in North America used tobacco. And cigarettes were used in prisoner-of-war camps during World War II and in post–World War II Germany.

Iron	Boar tusk	Playing cards
Copper	Red woodpecker scalps	Leather
Brass	Feathers	Gold
Wine	Glass	Silver
Corn	Polished beads (wampum)	Knives
Salt	Rum	Pots
Horses	Molasses	Boats
Sheep	Tobacco	Pitch
Goats	Agricultural implements	Rice
Tortoise shells	Round stones with centres removed	Cows
Porpoise teeth	Crystal salt bars	Paper
Whale teeth	Snail shells	Cigarettes

Source: Roger LeRoy Miller and David D. VanHoose, *Money, Banking and Financial Markets*, 3rd ed. Cincinnati, Ohio: South Western, 2007, p. 7.

12.1 The Functions of Money

Money Anything that people generally accept in exchange for goods and services.

Money is what money does. Money traditionally serves three functions. The one that most people are familiar with is money's function as a *medium of exchange*. Money also serves as a *unit of account*, and a *store of value* or *purchasing power*. Anything that serves these three functions is money. Anything that could serve these three functions could be considered money.

Money as a Medium of Exchange

Medium of exchange Any asset that sellers will accept as payment in market transactions.

Barter A direct exchange—no intermediary good called money is used.

When we say that money serves as a **medium of exchange**, what we mean is that sellers will accept it as payment in market transactions. Without some generally accepted medium of exchange, we would have to resort to barter. In fact, before money was used, transactions took place by means of barter. **Barter** is simply a direct exchange—no intermediary good called money is used. In a barter economy, the shoemaker who wants to obtain a dozen water glasses must seek out a glassmaker who at exactly the same time is interested in obtaining a pair of shoes. For this to occur, there has to be a *double coincidence of wants*.

If it does not exist, the shoemaker must go through several trades in order to obtain the desired dozen glasses—perhaps first trading shoes for jewellery, then jewellery for some pots and pans, and then the pots and pans for the desired glasses. See Examples 12–1 and 12–2 for more discussion.

Money facilitates exchange by reducing the transaction costs associated with means-of-payment uncertainty—that is, with regard to goods that the partners in any exchange are willing to accept. The existence of money means that individuals no longer have to hold a diverse collection of goods as an exchange inventory. As a medium of exchange, money allows individuals to specialize in any area in which they have a comparative advantage and to receive money payments for their labour. Money payments can then be exchanged for the fruits of other people's labour. The use of money as a medium of exchange permits more specialization and the inherent economic efficiencies that come with it (and hence greater economic growth). Money is even more important when used for large amounts of trade.

EXAMPLE 12-1   **Will Barter Make a Comeback on the Web?**

Anyone considering barter faces a relatively high opportunity cost of locating others willing to exchange items directly. The sizable expense of finding a double coincidence of wants helps explain why societies past and present have used money.

On the Internet, however, *barter exchanges* simplify the process of searching for an exchange partner. There are more than 400 regional barter exchanges in North America, and most of these now offer their services online. At these websites, individuals and businesses can engage in bartering just as easily as they can transmit online bids through Internet auction sites, such as eBay. It is possible to trade airline tickets for advertising space, electronic security services for computer equipment, and so on.

There are two important indications that barter exchange operators do *not* believe they will eventually drive money from existence. One is that many barter exchanges have their own currencies to help facilitate exchanges. Another is that barter exchanges usually charge both sides of a barter transaction a fee of up to 4 percent of the amount traded—measured using dollars and payable only in dollars.

For critical analysis: Under what circumstances could barter transactions ever become more commonplace than exchanges settled with money?

Money as a Unit of Account

Unit of account A way of placing a specific price on economic goods and services.

A **unit of account** is a way of placing a specific price on economic goods and services. Thus, as a unit of account, the monetary unit is used to measure the value of goods and services *relative* to other goods and services. It is the common denominator, or measure, the commonly recognized unit of value measurement. The dollar is the monetary unit in Canada. It is the yardstick that allows individuals to easily compare the relative values of goods and services. Accountants at Statistics Canada use dollar prices to measure national income and domestic product, a business uses dollar prices to calculate profits and losses, and a typical household budgets regularly anticipated expenses using dollar prices as its unit of account.

Another way of describing money as a unit of account is to say that it serves as a *standard of value* that allows economic actors to compare the relative worth of various goods and services. It allows for comparison shopping, for example.

A related function of money is that it can be used as a *standard of deferred payment*. Debts that are to be settled in the future are calculated in money. Money's ability to function as a *unit of account over time* can be seriously diminished by inflation.

Money as a Store of Value

Store of value The ability to hold value over time—or purchasing power.

One of the most important functions of money is that it serves as a **store of value**—the ability to hold value over time—or purchasing power. The money you have today can be set aside to purchase things later on. In the meantime, money retains its nominal value, which you can apply to those future purchases. If you have $1000 in your chequing account, you can either spend it today on goods and services, spend it tomorrow, or spend it a month from now. In this way, money provides a way to transfer value (wealth) into the future.

EXAMPLE 12-2   Converting Dollars into African Vouchers on the Web

Many people who have immigrated to Canada and the United States from the African nations of Kenya and Uganda have been drawn to higher-wage jobs that they anticipate will provide higher incomes for themselves and for their families. In many cases, however, family members remain in Africa. If a Kenyan or Ugandan immigrant desires to convert hard-earned dollars into food products, visits to physicians, and other items for family members still living in Africa, one option is the website of Mama Mike's. This Nairobi-based service allows individuals to purchase vouchers online. The family members in Africa are then notified that vouchers can be picked up in various locations in Kenya and Uganda and used to purchase goods and services at participating merchants throughout those African nations.

For critical analysis: In what ways do vouchers, such as those issued through Mama Mike's service, function as money?

Liquidity

Liquidity Wealth in the form of money can be exchanged later for some other asset.

Money is an asset—something of value—that accounts for part of personal wealth. Wealth in the form of money can be exchanged later for some other asset—this attribute of money is called **liquidity**. Although it is not the only form of wealth that can be exchanged for goods and services, it is the one most widely and readily accepted. We say that an asset is liquid when it can easily be acquired or disposed of without high transaction costs and with relative certainty as to its value. Money is by definition the most liquid asset there is. Just compare it, for example, with a share listed on the Toronto Stock Exchange. To buy or sell that share, you usually call a stockbroker, who will place the buy or sell order for you. This generally must be done during normal business hours. You have to pay a commission to the broker. Moreover, there is a distinct probability that you will get more or less for the share than you originally paid for it. This is not the case with money. Money can easily be converted to other asset forms. Therefore, most individuals hold at least a part of their wealth in the form of the most liquid of assets, money. You can see how assets rank in liquidity relative to one another in Figure 12–1.

When we hold money, however, we pay a price for this advantage of liquidity. That price is the interest yield that could have been obtained had the asset been held in another form—for example, in the form of shares and bonds.

The cost of holding money (its opportunity cost) is measured by the alternative interest yield obtainable by holding some other asset.

FIGURE 12-1
Degrees of Liquidity

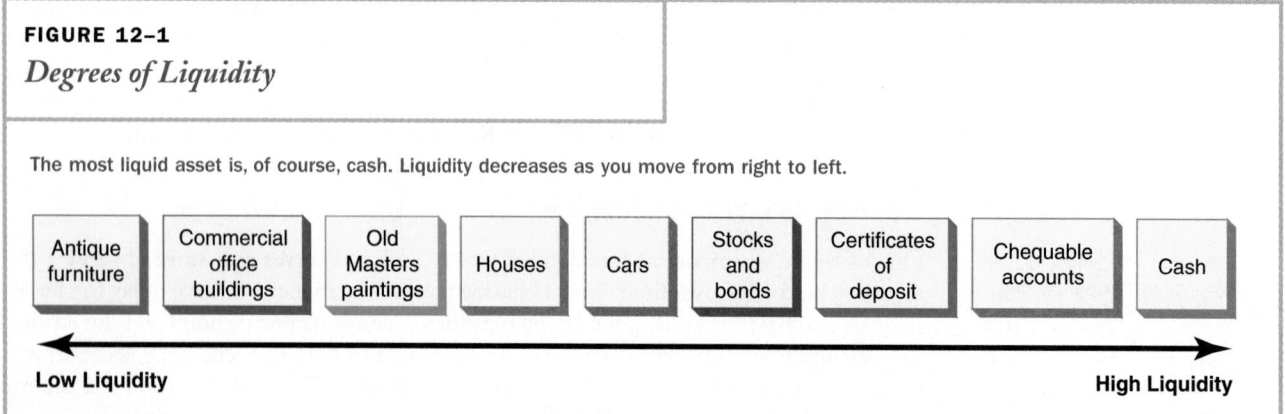

The most liquid asset is, of course, cash. Liquidity decreases as you move from right to left.

Antique furniture | Commercial office buildings | Old Masters paintings | Houses | Cars | Stocks and bonds | Certificates of deposit | Chequable accounts | Cash

Low Liquidity ←—————————————————————————————————→ **High Liquidity**

12.2 Monetary Standards, or What Backs Money

Fiduciary monetary system A system in which the value of the payments rests on the public's confidence that such payments can be exchanged for goods and services.

Fiat money Money that is widely accepted because it is declared by government to be *legal tender*.

Today, in Canada, all of us accept coins, paper currency, and cheques in exchange for items sold, including labour services. The question remains, why are we willing to accept as payment something that has no intrinsic value? After all, you could not sell cheques to anybody for use as a raw material in manufacturing. The reason is that in this country, the payments arise from a **fiduciary monetary system**, which means that the value of the payments rests on the public's confidence that such payments can be exchanged for goods and services. *Fiduciary* comes from the Latin *fiducia*, which means "trust" or "confidence." In our fiduciary monetary system, money, in the form of currency or chequing accounts, is not convertible to a fixed quantity of gold, silver, or some other precious commodity. This **fiat money** is widely accepted because it is declared by government to be *legal tender*, which means that it must be accepted in the payment of a debt. In other words, fiat money is money because the government says it is. In addition, currency and deposit accounts perform the functions of money because of their acceptability and predictability of value.

Acceptability

Currency and demand deposits are money because they are accepted in exchange for goods and services. They are accepted because people have confidence that they can later be exchanged for other goods and services. This confidence is based on the knowledge that such exchanges have occurred in the past without problems. Even during a period of relatively rapid inflation, we would still be inclined to accept money in exchange for goods and services because it is so useful. Barter is a costly and time-consuming alternative. Gold (which has served as a medium of exchange in the past) is also an inconvenient alternative. For further discussion about the present-day use of gold, see Example 12–3 and Example 12–4.

EXAMPLE 12-3 E-Gold-Backed E-Money

The Internet has served as a breeding ground for various forms of electronic money, known as e-money. One example is a throwback to the days of commodity money. This e-money, called "e-gold," is available at the website www.e-gold.com. At this site, an individual can open an account by purchasing e-gold that is fully backed by gold bars stored in repositories certified by the London Bullion Market Association. An account holder purchases an amount of e-gold based on the weight of actual gold backing the e-money. The site's online system allows an account holder to arrange to make a payment equal to, say, 20 troy ounces worth of e-gold to another authorized user located anywhere in the world. For those who prefer to keep track of their e-gold in dollars, euros, or six other national monies, the system also automatically permits denomination of e-gold payments in these currencies as well. Hence, this e-gold-backed e-money effectively provides measures of the purchasing power, in terms of gold, of several major world currencies.

For critical analysis: How is e-gold's medium-of-exchange function somewhat limited?

Realize always that money is socially defined. Acceptability is not something that you can necessarily predict. For example, you will probably have trouble spending Canadian currency in most businesses in the United States. Unless they are close to the Canadian border and deal frequently with Canadians, Americans do not have faith in Canadian money and therefore will not accept it in payment for goods and services.

EXAMPLE 12-4 **Is Gold Worth Its Weight?**

For centuries, gold has been precious because it has been scarce. Today, however, this glittering metal may be overabundant, especially for international agencies, governments, and central banks. Gold accounts for more than a third of the official international reserves of a number of developed nations. Combined gold holdings of the International Monetary Fund (IMF) and the world's central banks exceed 30 000 tonnes, or the equivalent of about a dozen years of global mining output. All this gold is very expensive to move around. For this reason, it typically just sits unused, in sturdy vaults surrounded by armed guards. This is an expensive use for a metal. Moreover, over the past 25 years, gold has turned out to be a poor store of value. Returns on relatively low-risk bonds have been much higher than the rate of return from holding gold. Switzerland, for instance, determined that the cost of interest forgone by holding gold, rather than U.S. Treasury bonds, is about $400 a year per Swiss household.

Recently, the Swiss government began selling off half its 2600 tonnes of gold reserves, third-largest in the world behind the United States and the European Monetary Union. More recently, the IMF has auctioned off some of its gold holdings to finance debt relief for poor countries. The European System of Central Banks, which began the new century with 30 percent of its reserves in the form of gold, decided to reduce this fraction to 15 percent.

Official gold sales until late 1999 contributed to a decline in the world price of gold, thereby worsening the return to holding gold. This led companies operating gold mines in the United States to lobby their representatives and senators, who successfully pushed through a law threatening a reduction of American funding of the IMF unless it agreed to scale back the gold sales it had planned for the early 2000s. It did so, and the central banks also agreed to stop selling gold.

For critical analysis: It appears that today, the central banks' portfolios are weighted too heavily in favour of gold. Under what circumstances might the central banks again determine that huge stocks of gold are worth holding?

Predictability of Value

The purchasing power of the dollar (its value) varies inversely with the price level. The more rapid the rate of increase of some price level index, such as the Consumer Price Index, the more rapid is the decrease in the value, or purchasing power, of a dollar. Money still retains its usefulness even if its value—its purchasing power—is declining year in and year out, as in periods of inflation, because it still retains the characteristic of predictability of value. If you believe that the inflation rate is going to be around 10 percent next year, you know that any dollar you receive a year from now will have a purchasing power equal to 10 percent less than that same dollar this year. Thus, you will not necessarily refuse to use money or accept it in exchange, simply because you know that its value will decline by the rate of inflation next year.

➡ CONCEPTS IN BRIEF

Learning Objective 12.1: Define the functions of money.
- Money is defined by its functions, which are as a medium of exchange, a unit of account or standard of value, and a store of value or purchasing power.

Learning Objective 12.2: Explain what "backs" the Canadian dollar.
- Because money is a highly liquid asset, it can be disposed of without high transaction costs and with relative certainty as to its value.
- Canada has a fiduciary monetary system—our money is not convertible into a fixed quantity of a commodity, such as gold or silver. It is fiat money.
- Money is accepted in exchange for goods and services because people have confidence that it can later be exchanged for other goods and services. In other words, money has acceptability and predictable value.

12.3 Defining the Canadian Money Supply

Money supply The amount of money in circulation.

Money is important. Changes in the total **money supply**—the amount of money in circulation—and changes in the rate at which the money supply increases or decreases affect important economic variables, such as the rate of inflation, interest rates, employment, and the equilibrium level of real national income. Although there is widespread agreement among economists that money is, indeed, important, they have never agreed on how to define or measure it. Therefore, we have several measures of the money supply.

The Narrowest Measure: M1

One measure of the money supply consists of the following:

1. Currency outside banks
2. Demand deposits

M1 The money supply, taken as the total value of currency plus demand deposits in chartered banks.

The narrowest official designation of the money supply, including currency outside banks and demand deposits, is **M1**—the money supply, taken as the total value of currency plus demand deposits in chartered banks. The two elements of M1 for a typical year are presented in Figure 12–2. M1 is sometimes referred to as the transactions approach to measuring money, which stresses the role of money as a medium of exchange.

CURRENCY. Currency includes Canadian coins and paper currency, usually in the form of bank notes, issued by the Bank of Canada (see Example 12–5, for a discussion of increased Canadian coin use). Although not nearly as important as chequable deposits as a percentage of the money supply, currency has increased in significance in Canada. One of the major reasons for the increased use of currency in the Canadian economy is the

FIGURE 12–2

Composition of the M1, M2, and M2+ Money Supply, 2006

This diagram shows the M1 money supply, the larger component of which is demand deposits (about 77 percent). M2 consists of M1 plus personal savings deposits and nonpersonal notice deposits at chartered banks (about 71 percent). M2+ consists of M2 plus deposits at other financial institutions.

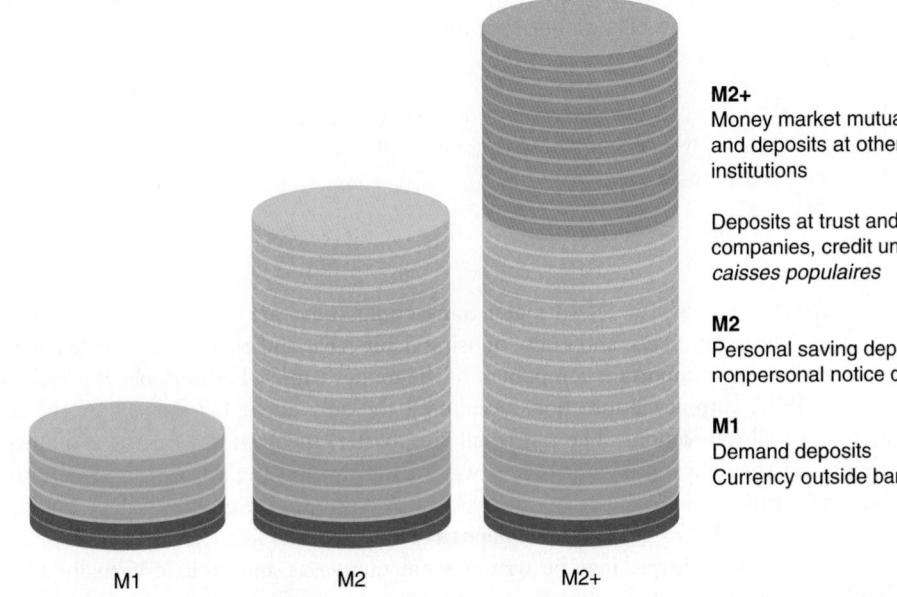

	Amount (billions of dollars)
M2+ Money market mutual funds and deposits at other institutions	**990.4**
Deposits at trust and mortgage companies, credit unions, and *caisses populaires*	258.0
M2 Personal saving deposits and nonpersonal notice deposits	**732.4** 523.3
M1 Demand deposits Currency outside banks	**209.1** 161.8 47.3

SOURCE: BANK OF CANADA, WEEKLY FINANCIAL STATISTICS, FEBRUARY 16, 2007, PP. 11–12.

growing number of illegal transactions, including under-the-table work agreements and the drug trade. McDonald's, on the other hand, is hoping its customers will stop using cash to make their purchases as discussed in Example 12–6.

EXAMPLE 12–5   Eliminating the $1 and $2 Bills

Since 1990, the federal government has replaced our $1 and $2 bills with coins—the "loonie" and the "twonie." What drove the government to weigh down our pockets and purses with heavy money? There are three reasons, all related to government revenue: coins last longer than bills, coins are quite inexpensive to produce, and the government makes a tidy profit on the replacement of bills with coins.

Coins Are Durable. You have probably been given in change a $5 bill that looks like it is about to fall apart. This is due to the wear and tear on paper currency as it is circulated in the economy. As paper currency wears out, banks and other financial institutions return to the Bank of Canada those bills that are on their last legs. The Bank then arranges for new replacement bills. A coin like the twonie, however, does not wear out quickly and has to be replaced much less frequently. A loonie or a twonie has a 20-year life span, while a paper note will last for just one year. The government saves about $12.5 million per year just on production costs of the $1 and $2 coins.

Coins Are Cheap to Produce. The government buys its coins from the Royal Canadian Mint, located in Winnipeg, at a price that includes the cost of production and a margin of profit for the Mint. While the government does not make money purchasing pennies at 1.4¢ each and nickels at 5¢ each, it makes a profit on the other coins. For example, it costs 4¢ to produce a dime, 8¢ to produce a quarter, 13¢ to produce a $1 coin, and only 16¢ to turn out a $2 coin.

Coins Earn a Profit for the Government. In 1996, the Mint turned out about 14 new coins per second, 24 hours per day, to meet the government's target of putting about 300 million $2 coins into circulation by 1997. Each time the Bank of Canada returned a $2 coin to a chartered bank in exchange for a used $2 bill, the Bank earned $1.84 in profit—after all, the chartered bank paid $2 for the coin, which cost 16¢ to make. This profit amounted to about $500 million during the first two years of twonie production.

Will we see the replacement of our $5 and $10 bills with coins in the near future? Probably not, as those bills do not circulate as quickly and therefore do not wear out as quickly.

For critical analysis: If the government decided to replace the $20 bill with a coin, what would happen to the amount of seigniorage—the profit it makes from producing our currency—that it would earn?

Chequable deposits Any deposits in a chartered bank or a near bank on which a cheque may be written.

Near bank Financial institutions, such as trust companies, credit unions, and *caisses populaires,* that offer most of the same services as chartered banks.

DEMAND DEPOSITS.   Most major transactions today are done with debit cards and cheques. The convenience and safety of using debit cards and cheques has made chequing accounts the most important component of the money supply. For example, it is estimated that in 1997, currency transactions accounted for only about 0.5 percent of the *dollar* amount of all transactions. The rest (excluding barter) involved debit cards and cheques. Debit and chequing transactions are a way of transferring the ownership of deposits in financial institutions. They are normally acceptable as a medium of exchange. The financial institutions that offer **chequable deposits**—any deposits in a chartered bank or a near bank on which a cheque may be written—are numerous and include virtually all **near banks**—financial institutions, such as trust companies, credit unions, and *caisses populaires,* that offer most of the same services as chartered banks. However, only chequing accounts held in chartered banks are included in the measure of M1.

What about Credit Cards and Debit Cards?

Even though a large percentage of transactions are accomplished by using a plastic credit card, we do not consider the credit card itself money. Remember the functions of money. A credit card is not a unit of account or a store of value. The use of your credit card is really a loan to you by the issuer of the card, be it a bank, a retail store, or a gas company. The proceeds of the loan are paid to the business that sold you something. You must pay back the loan to the issuer of the credit card, either when you get your statement or with interest throughout the year if you do not pay off your balance. (We ignore those with credit card debt that they cannot repay.) It is not a store of value. Credit cards *defer*, rather than complete, transactions that ultimately involve the use of money. Refer to Example 12–7 for insight into the use of credit cards in Canada and Example 12–8 for a discussion of digital cash and stored value cards.

A newer transaction vehicle, the *debit card* automatically withdraws money from your bank account. When you use your debit card to purchase something, you are giving an instruction to your bank to transfer money directly from your bank account to the store's bank account. If the store in which you are shopping has a direct electronic link to the bank, that transfer may be made instantaneously. Use of a debit card does not create a loan. A debit card is, therefore, not a new type of "money."

EXAMPLE 12–6 | **Why McDonald's Wants Your Card, Not Your Cash**

Fast-food giant McDonald's has equipped virtually every restaurant to accept credit- and debit-card payments. Some restaurants have also begun offering radio frequency payment tags that allow customers to wave a card across a scanning device. Equipping each restaurant has entailed a one-time system installation cost of about $2500 and a $100 monthly telecommunications expense. Processing a typical bank card transaction requires a McDonald's restaurant to pay a fee of nearly 2 percent of the transaction's dollar value. For years, McDonald's resisted accepting payment cards.

The time customers spent providing verification signatures slowed lines and made it harder for restaurants to serve their fast food fast. Banks were also unwilling to process very small denomination transactions, such as the purchase of a $1.25 soft drink. In recent years, however, banks have switched to debit-card systems that no longer require customer signatures and that process even the tiniest transactions.

McDonald's card-processing systems can complete a transaction in four to seven seconds, which is several seconds speedier than a cash exchange. This makes serving fast food even faster and, consequently, more cost-efficient for McDonald's restaurants.

For critical analysis: Why might McDonald's anticipate that promoting cashless payments could increase its overall profitability even though the company incurred large costs for the equipment to process these payments?

EXAMPLE 12–7 | **Credit Cards and Canadians**

Canadians hold more than 60 million credit cards of all types: gasoline cards, retail store cards, and all-purpose cards, such as Visa, MasterCard, and American Express.

In the early 1990s, credit card use grew by almost 60 percent in spite of slow average real income growth of about 1 percent over the same time period. Outstanding balances on Visa and MasterCard have continued to grow, boosting total consumer bank loans in the economy. These are expensive loans, however, for the average credit card interest rate is more than 10 percent above bank rates.

continued

At these high rates, what induces consumers to buy on credit? First, the convenience of purchasing now without waiting for payday is a big attraction. Second, consumers are attracted by competition between bank card companies. Some cards award credit, based on the amount of purchases each month, toward purchase of an automobile. Other cards award frequent flyer miles based on card use. Consumers have shown they find these offers hard to resist.

For critical analysis: What effect will these nonmoney transactions have on aggregate demand in the economy?

EXAMPLE 12–8 **What Will Digital Cash Replace?**

If people start to use smart cards, stored value cards, personal computers, and cellular phones to store and transmit digital cash, presumably they will have less desire to use other forms of money. To understand why, consider Table 12–2, which lists the key characteristics of cheques, government-issued currency, and digital cash.

In comparing currency with cheques, it is clear that people must trade off features that each offers. Cheques promise greater security because if a thief steals a woman's handbag containing cash and cheques, she can contact her depository institution to halt payment on all cheques in the handbag. Currency payments are final, however, and so the thief can spend all the cash he has taken from her. She can send cheques through the mail, but using currency requires face-to-face contact. In addition, currency transactions are anonymous, which may be desirable under some circumstances. Nevertheless, not everyone will accept a cheque in payment for a transaction, and a cheque payment is not final until the cheque clears. Cheque transactions are also more expensive. After evaluating these features of currency and cheques, people typically choose to hold both payment instruments.

People will likewise compare the features that digital cash offers with the features currently offered by government-provided currency and chequing accounts available from depository institutions. As Table 12–2 indicates, the acceptability of digital cash is uncertain at present. Nonetheless, we are contemplating an environment with wide acceptability, and in such an environment, digital cash would be nearly as acceptable as government-provided currency. Digital cash held on smart cards without special security features, such as personal identification numbers, will be as susceptible to theft as government currency. Some digital cash, however, may be held on devices, such as laptop computers or even wristwatches, requiring an access code before a microchip containing digital cash can be accessed. Overall, therefore, digital cash is likely to be somewhat more secure than government-provided currency, though not as secure as cheque transactions.

Digital cash transactions are likely to be less costly to undertake. People will also be able to access digital cash at home on their personal computers. In addition, they will be able to send digital cash from remote locations using the Internet, and digital cash transactions will be instantaneously final. Unlike transactions using currency, therefore, digital cash transactions need not be conducted face to face. Like currency transactions, however, most digital cash transfers will be anonymous.

In many respects, therefore, digital cash looks like a better means of payment than government-provided currency. Certainly, for some time to come, a number of items—canned beverages and candy in vending machines, for example—will be easiest to purchase using government-provided currency. Many economists, however, believe that widespread adoption of privately issued digital cash will ultimately tend to crowd out government-provided currency. The Federal Deposit Insurance Corporation (FDIC) in the United States of America has issued a proposed rule that suggests that under several conditions, stored value cards would qualify as "deposits," and that they view this rule as "evolutionary." On many college campuses, vending machines already accept stored value cards. Eventually, vending machines on street corners are likely to have smart card readers.

continued

TABLE 12-2

Features of Alternative Forms of Money

Digital cash tends to overshadow government-issued currency.

Feature	Cheques	Currency	Digital Cash
Security	High	Low	High(?)
Per-Transfer Cost	High	Medium	Low
Payment Final, Face-to-face	No	Yes	Yes
Payment Final, Non–Face-to-Face	No	No	Yes
Anonymity	No	Yes	Yes
Acceptability	Restricted	Wide	Uncertain at present

SOURCE: ALEKSANDER BERENTSEN, "MONETARY POLICY IMPLICATIONS OF DIGITAL MONEY," *KYKLOS* 51 (1998), P. 92.

For critical analysis: Explain which functions of money stored value or digital cash fulfills. What forms of money will digital cash replace?

A Broader Measure of Money: M2

A broader measure of the money supply involves taking into account not only the most liquid assets that people use as money, which are already included in the definition of M1, but also other assets that are highly liquid—that is, that can be converted into money quickly without loss of nominal dollar value and without much cost. These assets are personal savings accounts (many of which have chequing privileges) and nonpersonal notice deposits. Table 12–3 shows the components of **M2** (M1 plus (1) personal savings, and (2) nonpersonal notice deposits). We examine each of these components in turn.

SAVINGS DEPOSITS. **Savings deposits**—interest-earning funds at chartered banks that can be withdrawn at any time without payment of a penalty—are part of the M2 money supply. A savings deposit is distinguishable from a time deposit because savings funds may be withdrawn without payment of a penalty. Funds are fully protected against loss in their nominal value.

NONPERSONAL NOTICE DEPOSITS. **Nonpersonal notice deposits**—interest-earning funds at chartered banks that can, in practice, be withdrawn at any time without payment of a penalty—are similar to savings deposits but are funds deposited by firms. Although legally the firms are required to give the bank "notice" of withdrawal, this requirement is rarely observed.

OTHER MONEY SUPPLY DEFINITIONS. When all of these assets are added together, the result is M2. The composition of M2 is given in Table 12–3.

M2 M1 plus (1) personal savings and (2) non-personal notice deposits.

Savings deposits Interest-earning funds at chartered banks that can be withdrawn at any time without payment of a penalty.

Nonpersonal notice deposits Interest-earning funds at chartered banks that can, in practice, be withdrawn at any time without payment of a penalty—similar to savings deposits but are deposited by firms.

TABLE 12-3

Money in Canada, December 2006

	Millions of Dollars	Percent of M1	Percent of M2	Percent of M2+
Currency outside banks	$ 47.3	22.6	6.5	4.8
+ Demand deposits (current and personal chequing accounts)	161.8	77.4	22.1	16.3
= **M1**	209.1	100.0	28.5	21.1
+ Personal savings deposits and nonpersonal notice deposits	523.3		71.5	52.8
= **M2**	732.4		100.0	73.9
+ Deposits at trust and mortgage companies, credit unions, and *caisses populaires*	258.0			26.1
+ Money market mutual funds and deposits at other institutions				
= **M2+**	$990.4			100.0

Seasonally adjusted average monthly data

SOURCE: BANK OF CANADA, *WEEKLY FINANCIAL STATISTICS*, FEBRUARY 16, 2007, PP. 11–12.

A still broader measure, M2+, includes M2 plus the deposits held at the financial institutions that are *not* banks, the near banks such as trust and mortgage loan companies, credit unions, and *caisses populaires*. The composition of M2+ is also shown in Table 12–3.

The narrowest measure of the money supply, called M1, stresses the role of the chartered banks and money as a medium of exchange. These other measures, M2 and M2+ stress the role of money as a temporary store of value and other financial institutions. They are sometimes referred to as the liquidity approach to measuring money.

Just remember that there is no one best definition of the money supply. For different purposes, different definitions are appropriate. If we want to use a definition that seems to correlate best with economic activity on an economywide basis, M2+ is probably best.

➤➤ CONCEPTS IN BRIEF

Learning Objective 12.3: Describe the various definitions of the money supply.

- ◤ The money supply can be defined in a variety of ways. M1, which consists of currency and demand deposits in chartered banks, is the most narrowly defined.
- ◤ Demand deposits (chequing accounts) are any deposits in financial institutions on which the deposit owner can write cheques.
- ◤ Credit cards and debit cards are not part of the money supply, for they simply defer transactions that ultimately involve the use of money.
- ◤ When we add savings deposits and nonpersonal notice deposits to M1, we obtain the measure known as M2.
- ◤ When we add the deposits of near bank financial institutions to M2, we obtain the measure known as M2+.

12.4 *The Canadian Financial System*

Canada's financial system consists of a large number of commercial banks (also called chartered banks), which are privately owned, profit-seeking institutions, and near banks. Near banks, such as credit unions, *caisses populaires*, and trust and mortgage companies, may be profit-seeking institutions, or they may be mutual institutions that are owned by their depositors. In addition to the commercial banks and near banks in advanced market economies, the other type of institution is a **central bank**—for example, Canada has the Bank of Canada—which typically serves as a banker's bank and as a bank for the national treasury or finance ministry. Central banks normally regulate commercial banks. The functions and role of the Bank of Canada in Canada's financial system will be discussed in detail in Chapter 14.

Central bank A banker's bank, usually an official institution that also serves as a country's treasury's bank. Central banks normally regulate commercial banks.

Direct versus Indirect Financing

When individuals choose to hold some of their savings in new bonds issued by a corporation, their purchases of the bonds are, in effect, direct loans to the business. This is an example of *direct finance*, in which people lend funds directly to a business. Business financing is not always direct. Individuals might choose instead to hold a time deposit at a bank. The bank may then lend to the same company. In this way, the same people can provide *indirect finance* to a business. The bank makes this possible by *intermediating* the financing of the company.

Financial Intermediation

Financial intermediation The process by which financial institutions accept savings from businesses, households, and governments and lend the savings to other businesses, households, and governments.

Financial intermediaries Institutions that transfer funds between ultimate lenders (savers) and ultimate borrowers.

The process by which financial institutions accept savings from businesses, households, and governments and lend the savings to other businesses, households, and governments has become known as **financial intermediation**, and its participants—institutions that transfer funds between ultimate lenders (savers) and ultimate borrowers—are called **financial intermediaries**. Savers lend funds through financial intermediaries (banks, credit unions, and so on) to borrowers, such as businesses, governments, and home buyers. The process of financial intermediation is illustrated in Figure 12–3.

FIGURE 12–3

The Process of Financial Intermediation

The process of financial intermediation is depicted here. Note that ultimate lenders and ultimate borrowers are the same economic units—households, businesses, and governments—but not necessarily the same individuals. Whereas individual households can be net lenders or borrowers, households as an economic unit are net lenders. Specific businesses or governments similarly can be net lenders or borrowers; as economic units, both are net borrowers.

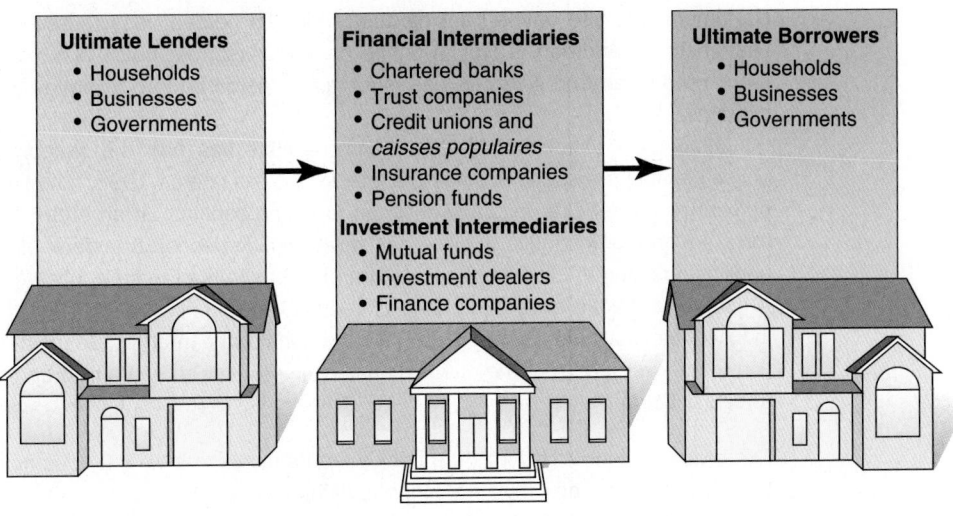

ASYMMETRIC INFORMATION, ADVERSE SELECTION, AND MORAL HAZARD. Why might people wish to direct their funds through a bank instead of lending them directly to a business? One important reason is **asymmetric information**—information possessed by one party in a financial transaction but not by the other party. The business may have better knowledge of its own current and future prospects than potential lenders do. For instance, the business may know that it intends to use borrowed funds for projects with a high risk of failure that would make repaying the loan difficult. This potential for borrowers to use the borrowed funds in high-risk projects is known as **adverse selection**. Alternatively, a business that had intended to undertake low-risk projects may change management after receiving a loan, and the new managers may use the borrowed funds in riskier ways. The possibility that a borrower might engage in behaviour that increases risk after borrowing funds is called **moral hazard**.

To minimize the possibility that a business might fail to repay a loan, people thinking about lending funds directly to the business must study the business carefully before making the loan and continue to monitor its performance afterward. Alternatively, they can choose to avoid the trouble by holding deposits with financial intermediaries, that specialize in evaluating the creditworthiness of business borrowers and keeping tabs on their progress until loans are repaid. Thus, adverse selection and moral hazard both help explain why people use financial intermediaries.

LARGER SCALE AND LOWER MANAGEMENT COSTS. An important reason why financial intermediaries exist is that they make it possible for many people to pool their funds, thereby increasing the size, or *scale*, of the total amount of savings managed by an intermediary. See Example 12–9 to read about how big banks can improve the scale of their operations with online Internet banking. This centralization of management reduces costs and risks below the levels that savers would incur if all were to manage their savings alone. *Pension fund companies*, which are institutions that specialize in managing funds that individuals save for retirement, owe their existence largely to their abilities to provide such cost savings to individual savers. Likewise, *investment companies*, which are institutions

Asymmetric information Information possessed by one party in a financial transaction but not by the other party.

Adverse selection The likelihood that individuals who seek to borrow may use the funds that they receive for high-risk projects.

Moral hazard The possibility that a borrower might engage in riskier behaviour after a loan has been obtained.

that manage portfolios of financial instruments called mutual funds on behalf of share-holders, also exist largely because of cost savings from their greater scale of operations.

EXAMPLE 12-9   Why Banks Want Their Customers to Go Online

Have you noticed that banks have been trying to persuade their customers to bank online? The reason is that the banks themselves stand to gain. Some banks have reported that customers who use online banking cost about 15 percent less to serve than traditional customers. In addition, a typical online banking customer holds about 20 percent more funds on deposit and generates as much as 50 percent more revenues than a traditional customer.

Almost every household with Internet access has had the capability to undertake online banking transactions since the late 1990s. As late as 1998, however, fewer than 10 percent of households regularly engaged in online banking. In an effort to give more customers a greater incentive to click their way to online deposit transfers, bill payments, loan applications, and the like, banks have sharply reduced the fees they charge for web access. A number of banks have eliminated or reduced most online banking fees in an effort to induce their customers to move more transactions to the Internet. So far, these efforts have convinced over a third of the nation's banking customers to use online banking services on a regular basis.

For critical analysis: How might a bank's profits increase even if it does not charge fees to those customers who utilize its online banking facilities?

Financial Intermediaries: Sources and Uses of Funds

Liabilities Amounts owed; the legal claims against a business or household by nonowners.

Each financial intermediary has its own primary source of funds, which are called **liabilities**—amounts owed; the legal claims against a business or household by nonowners. When you deposit $100 in your chequing account in the bank, the bank creates a liability—it owes you $100—in exchange for the funds deposited. A commercial bank gets its funds from chequing and savings accounts; an insurance company gets its funds from insurance policy premiums.

Assets Amounts owned; all items to which a business or household holds legal claim.

Each financial intermediary normally has a different primary use of its **assets**—amounts owned; all items to which a business or household holds legal claim. For example, a credit union usually makes small consumer loans, whereas a mortgage loan company makes mainly home mortgage loans. Table 12–4 lists the assets and liabilities of financial intermediaries. Be aware, though, that the distinction between different financial institutions is becoming more and more blurred. As the laws and regulations change, there will be less need to make any distinction. All may ultimately be treated simply as financial intermediaries.

Payment Intermediaries

Payment intermediaries Institutions that facilitate payments on behalf of holders of transaction deposits.

A commercial bank is an example of a type of financial intermediary that performs another important function. Together with the near banks, commercial banks operate as **payment intermediaries**, which are institutions that facilitate payments on behalf of holders of transaction deposits.

TRANSMITTING PAYMENTS VIA DEBIT-CARD TRANSACTIONS. Recently, the dollar volume of payments transmitted using debit cards exceeded the value of chequing transactions. To see how a debit-card transaction clears, take a look at Figure 12-4. Suppose that Bank of Montreal has provided a debit card to a college student named Jill Jones, who in turn uses the card to purchase $200 worth of clothing from Sears, which has an account at Scotiabank. The debit-card transaction generates an electronic record, which Sears transmits to Scotiabank.

TABLE 12-4

Financial Intermediaries and Their Assets and Liabilities, 2005

	Percent of Total Financial Assets	Primary Assets (Uses of Funds)	Primary Liabilities (Sources of Funds)
Financial Intermediaries			
Chartered banks and Near banks	30.6	Bank loans, mortgages, and consumer credit	Currency and bank deposits
Credit unions and *Caisses populaires*	3.5	Mortgage, consumer credit	Deposits
Trust and mortgage companies	0.3	Mortgage, consumer credit	Deposits
Contractual Intermediaries			
Life and pension funds	32.4	Bonds, short-term paper	Life insurance, pensions
Life and property insurance	8.2	Mortgages, bonds, short-term paper, and shares	Life insurance, pensions, and shares
Sales finance and consumer loan companies	1.7	Loans, consumer credit	Short-term paper, bonds
Investment Intermediaries			
Mutual funds	9.3	Short-term paper, shares, and foreign investment	Shares
Investment dealers	0.5	Short-term paper	Loans
Other financial	13.5	Consumer credit, loans	Short-term paper, bonds

SOURCE: ADAPTED FROM THE STATISTICS CANADA CANSIM DATABASE, TABLE 378-0004, DECEMBER 2005.

The debit-card system automatically uses the electronic record to determine the bank that issued the debit card used to purchase the clothing. It transmits this information to Bank of Montreal. Then Bank of Montreal verifies that Jill Jones is an account holder, deducts $200 from her chequing account, and transmits these funds electronically, via the debit-card system, to Scotiabank. Finally, Scotiabank credits $200 to Sears' transactions deposit account, and payment for the clothing purchase is complete.

FIGURE 12-4

How a Debit-Card Transaction Clears

When a college student named Jill Jones uses a debit card issued by Bank of Montreal to purchase clothing valued at $200 from Sears, which has an account with Scotiabank, the debit-card transaction creates an electronic record that is transmitted to Scotiabank. The debit-card system forwards this record to Bank of Montreal, which deducts $200 from Jill Jones's transactions deposit account. Then the debit-card system transmits the $200 payment to Scotiabank, which credits the $200 to Sears' account.

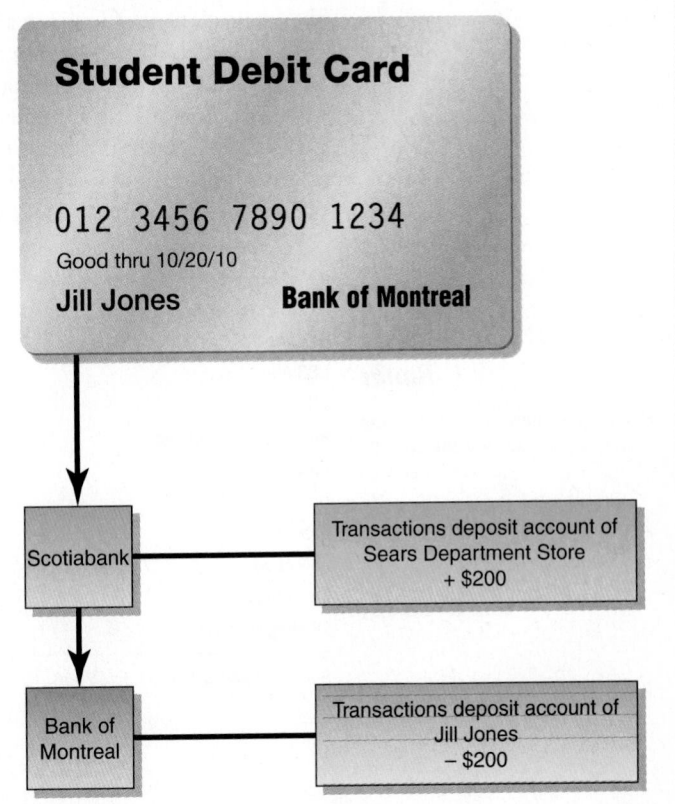

THE PAYOFF FROM PAYMENT INTERMEDIATION. Payment intermediation has traditionally been a key activity of banks. Because of the fees banks charge for payment intermediation, this has become a significant contributor to banks' earnings. Thus, payment intermediation is a fundamental aspect of the banking business.

Financial Intermediation Across National Boundaries

Some countries' governments restrict the financial intermediation process to within their national boundaries. They do so by imposing legal restraints called capital controls that bar certain flows of funds across their borders. Nevertheless, today many nations have reduced or even eliminated capital controls. This permits their residents to strive for international financial diversification by engaging in the direct or indirect financing of companies located in various nations.

Indeed, as Table 12-5 indicates, the world's largest banks are not all based in Canada or the United States. Today, most of the largest banking institutions, sometimes called megabanks, are based in Europe. These megabanks typically take in deposits and lend throughout the world. Although they report their profits and pay taxes in their home nations, these megabanks are in all other ways international banking institutions.

Multinational businesses have relationships with megabanks based in many nations. Individuals and companies increasingly retain the services of banks based outside their home countries. The business of banking varies from nation to nation, however. Each country has its own distinctive banking history, and this fact helps explain unique features of the world's banking systems.

A WORLD OF NATIONAL BANKING STRUCTURES. Countries' banking systems differ in a number of ways. In some nations, banks are the crucial component of the financial intermediation process, but in others, banking is only part of a varied financial system. In addition, some countries have only a few large banks, while others, such as the United States, have relatively large numbers of banks of various sizes. The legal environments regulating bank dealings with individual and business customers also differ considerably across nations.

The extent to which banks are the predominant means by which businesses finance their operations is a key way that national banking systems differ. For instance, in Britain, nearly 70 percent of funds raised by businesses typically stem from bank borrowings, and the proportions for Germany and Japan are 50 percent and 65 percent, respectively.

The relative sizes of banks also differ from one country to another. In Canada, the five largest banks have over three-fourths of total bank assets. The five largest banks in Belgium, Denmark, France, Italy, Luxembourg, Portugal, Spain, and the United Kingdom have over 60 percent of the deposits of their nations' residents. In Greece and the Netherlands, this figure is over 80 percent. In Germany, Japan, and Britain, about three-fourths of total bank assets are held by the largest 10 banks while in the United States, this figure is about 60 percent.

TABLE 12-5		
The World's Largest Banks		

Bank	Country	Assets ($ billions)
Barclays PLC	United Kingdom	1 587
UBS AG	Switzerland	1 563
BNP Paribas	France	1 484
Royal Bank of Scotland	United Kingdom	1 300
Crédit Agricole	France	1 252
Deutsche Bank	Germany	1 170
Bank of America	United States	1 082
ABN Amro	Netherlands	1 039
Credit Suisse	Switzerland	1 016
J.P. Morgan Chase	United States	1 014

Historically, there usually are few U.S. banks among the world's top 10.

SOURCE: *BANKER'S ALMANAC*, JULY 2006.

➤ **CONCEPTS IN BRIEF**

Learning Objective 12.4: Describe the Canadian financial system.

✦ Financial intermediaries transfer funds from ultimate lenders (savers) to ultimate borrowers. This process of financial intermediation is undertaken by chartered banks, trust companies, mortgage loan companies, credit unions and *caisses populaires*, insurance companies, mutual funds, and pension funds.

➤ **ISSUES AND APPLICATIONS**

The Dollarization Movement: Is the U.S. Fed Destined to be a Multinational Central Bank?

Concepts Applied: Federal Reserve System, Money, Currency

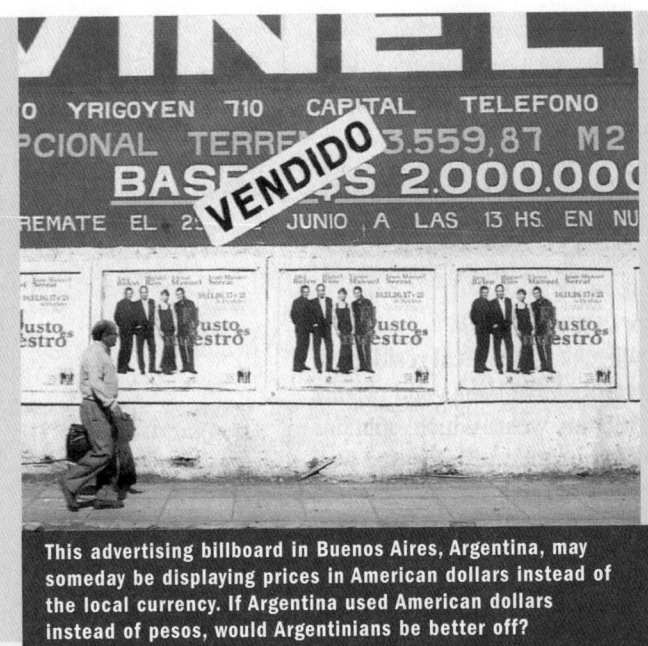

This advertising billboard in Buenos Aires, Argentina, may someday be displaying prices in American dollars instead of the local currency. If Argentina used American dollars instead of pesos, would Argentinians be better off?

In 1998, Brazil faced an economic crisis, and Brazilian interest rates shot up considerably. So did interest rates in Argentina, Brazil's main international trading partner. This spillover from Brazil's crisis induced Argentina to contemplate a radical change in its monetary arrangements.

The Prospect of Latin American Dollarization

The change that Argentina's leaders considered was *dollarization*. This would entail abandoning Argentina's peso in favour of the American dollar as a medium of exchange, unit of account, and store of value. To implement dollarization, Argentina would have to import sufficient American currency for people to use in hand-to-hand transactions. It also would have to convert all Argentine financial accounts and contracts to dollars at the prevailing fixed rate of exchange. Such a conversion would not be too difficult for Argentina, however, because it already had a *currency board* system, in which Argentina issues pesos on a one-to-one basis with the number of American dollars it has on reserve. Thus, Argentina's monetary system is already closely linked to that of the United States.

Nevertheless, Federal Reserve and U.S. Treasury officials have expressed concerns about dollarization. Fed policy actions consistent with stabilizing the American economy could have negative consequences outside the United States, fostering resentment and encouraging policy makers in dollarized countries to deflect blame onto American policy makers. This could give governments of dollarized countries political cover for dodging tough decisions regarding appropriate economic policies.

A North American Monetary Union?

Recently, a Toronto-based think tank released a study proposing "North American currency integration" by establishing the American dollar as the single circulating currency in Canada. The authors of the Canadian proposal were not quite as willing as Argentina to contemplate unilateral dollarization, however. Their proposal called for the Federal Reserve's Board of Governors to have one Canadian member.

So far, the United States has expressed little interest in sharing control of its central bank, but many Canadians seem to be coming around to the idea. After watching the value of the Canadian dollar fall from about 0.90 Canadian dollars per American dollar in 1991 to below 0.65 Canadian dollars per American dollar by 2003, more than a third of Canadians surveyed in public opinion polls indicated support for abolishing the Canadian currency altogether. Three-fourths of Canadians polled said they expected to see a common dollar for the United States and Canada by 2020. Since 2003, the Canadian dollar has risen to a high above parity with the American dollar.

For critical analysis:

1. Why would Argentina and Canada choose to dollarize their economies?

2. Do you see any merit to the arguments by critics of dollarization proposals, who argue that unilateral dollarization in Latin America and Canada would lead to "taxation without representation"?

➡➡ SUMMARY

Here is what you should know after reading this chapter. MyEconLab will help you identify what you know, and where to go when you need to practise. We suggest that as soon as you review one of the Learning Objective sections below, you then proceed to go through the related section in MyEconLab.

ⓧ myeconlab

➡➡ LEARNING OBJECTIVES	KEY TERMS	MYECONLAB PRACTICE
12.1 The Functions of Money. Money is defined by its functions. The functions of money are a medium of exchange, a unit of account (standard of value), and a store of value or purchasing power.	money, 320 medium of exchange, 320 barter, 320 unit of account, 321 store of value, 321 liquidity, 322	• **MyEconLab** Study Plan 12.1
12.2 Monetary Standards, or What Backs Money. We have a fiduciary monetary system in Canada—our money, whether in the form of currency or chequing accounts, is not convertible into a fixed quantity of a commodity, such as gold or silver. The Canadian dollar is backed only by faith—the public's confidence that it can be exchanged for goods and services. This confidence comes from the fact that other people will accept the dollar in transactions because our government has declared it legal tender and because, despite inflation, it still retains the characteristics of predictability of value.	fiduciary monetary system, 323 fiat money, 323	• **MyEconLab** Study Plan 12.2
12.3 Defining the Canadian Money System. There are numerous ways to define the money supply. The narrowest measure, called M1, stresses the role of the chartered banks and money as a medium of exchange. Other methods—M2 and M2+—stress the role of money as a temporary store of value and other financial institutions.	money supply, 325 M1, 325 chequable deposits, 326 near bank, 326 M2, 329 savings deposits, 329 nonpersonal notice deposits, 329	• **MyEconLab** Study Plan 12.3
12.4 The Canadian Financial System. Financial institutions are all in the business of financial intermediation. Financial intermediation involves the transfer of funds from savers to investors (borrowers). The ultimate lenders are the savers—households, businesses, and governments, including the federal government and provincial and municipal governments. The ultimate borrowers are also households, business and governments—the same economic units but not necessarily the same individuals. Between ultimate lenders and ultimate borrowers are financial intermediaries, including the chartered banks, trust companies, mortgage loan companies, credit unions and *caisses populaires,* insurance companies, mutual funds, and pension funds.	central bank, 330 financial intermediation, 330 financial intermediaries, 330 asymmetric information, 331 adverse selection, 331 moral hazard, 331 liabilities, 332 assets, 332 payment intermediaries, 333	• **MyEconLab** Study Plan 12.4

PROBLEMS

(Answers to the odd-numbered problems appear at the back of the book.)

LO 12.1 Define the functions of money.

1. Consider each type of asset in terms of its potential use as a medium of exchange, a unit of account, and a store of value or purchasing power. Indicate which use is most appropriately associated with each asset.
   a. A painting by Renoir
   b. A 90-day Canadian Treasury bill
   c. A notice deposit account with a trust company in St. John's, Newfoundland
   d. One IBM share
   e. A $50 Bank of Canada note
   f. A chequing account in a credit union in Manitoba

2. Elsa Lee can make several uses of her money. Indicate for each case whether her money is being used as a medium of exchange (E), a unit of account (A), or a store of value (V).
   a. Lee has accumulated $600 in her chequing account at a chartered bank.
   b. Lee decides to use this $600 to purchase a new washing machine and goes shopping to compare the prices being charged by different dealers for the machine she wishes to buy.
   c. Lee finds that the lowest price at which she can purchase the machine she wants is $498.50. She has the dealer deliver the machine and agrees to pay the dealer in 30 days.
   d. Thirty days later, Lee sends the dealer a cheque drawn on her chequing account to pay for the washer.

3. Consider a barter economy (see Example 12–1, "Will Barter Make a Comeback on the Web?") in which 10 goods and services are produced and exchanged. How many exchange rates exist in that economy, which does not use money?

LO 12.2 Explain what "backs" the Canadian dollar.

4. How have technological changes altered the form of money (see Example 12–8, "What Will Digital Cash Replace?")?

5. The value of a dollar is the reciprocal of the price index. In 1986, the CPI had a value of 1; hence the value of a dollar in 1986 equalled $1. If the price index now is 2, what is the value of the dollar in 1986 prices? If the price index is 2.5?

LO 12.3 Describe the various definitions of the money supply.

6. What are the components of M2?

7. Explain why a debit card is not a new form of money.

8. Cash and cheques account for nearly 75 percent of the total number of all payments in Canada, and wire transfers account for over 60 percent of the dollar value of all payments in Canada. How can both situations be true simultaneously?

LO 12.4 Describe the Canadian financial system.

9. Who are the three basic groups in the Canadian financial system? Give examples of individuals, parties, or enterprises in each group.

10. Match each of the rationales for financial intermediation listed below with at least one of the following financial intermediaries: commercial bank, money market mutual fund, stockbroker. Explain your choices.
    a. Adverse selection
    b. Moral hazard
    c. Lower management costs generated by larger scale

11. Match each of the rationales for financial intermediation listed below with at least one of the following financial intermediaries: insurance company, pension fund, savings bank. Explain your choices.
    a. Adverse selection
    b. Moral hazard
    c. Lower management costs generated by larger scale

12. Identify whether each of the following events poses an adverse selection problem or a moral hazard problem in financial markets.
    a. An individual, with several children, who has just learned that she has lung cancer, applies for life insurance but fails to report this recent medical diagnosis.
    b. A corporation that recently obtained a loan from several banks to finance installation of a new computer network instead directs some of the funds to executive bonuses.
    c. A state-chartered financial institution, exempt from laws requiring it to have federal deposit insurance, decides to apply for deposit insurance after experiencing severe financial problems that may bankrupt the institution.

13. Identify whether each of the following events poses an adverse selection problem or a moral hazard problem in financial markets.
    a. A manager of a savings and loan association responds to reports of a likely increase in federal deposit insurance coverage. She directs loan officers to extend mortgage loans to less credit-worthy borrowers.
    b. A loan applicant does not mention that a legal judgment in his divorce case will require him to make alimony payments to his ex-wife.
    c. An individual who was recently approved for a loan to start a new business decides to use some of the funds to take a Hawaiian vacation.

13

Money Creation and Deposit Insurance

Life used to be simple for someone who wished to finance the purchase of a house, acquire shares and bonds, take out insurance, or obtain a credit card. Each of those decisions involved going to any of a well-defined set of separate institutions. Insurance was always bought from an insurance company, for example; shares and bonds were sold only by stock brokers; and money for a house was borrowed from a bank or credit union. Today, the choices are much more complicated, and the distinctions between banks, near banks, and "nonbanks" are becoming ever more blurred. All of this comes about in an era of deregulation of depository institutions. To understand the effects of deregulation, you need to learn about the regulation of such institutions and, before that, how money is created in our economy.

➤➤ LEARNING OBJECTIVES

After reading this chapter, you should be able to:

13.1 Define the links between changes in the money supply and other economic variables.

13.2 Describe the origins of fractional reserve banking.

13.3 Define reserves.

13.4 Explain the relationship between reserves and total deposits.

13.5 Describe the money multiplier.

13.6 Describe deposit insurance and flawed bank regulation.

MyEconLab helps you master each objective and study more efficiently. See end of chapter for details.

The federal government currently insures deposits up to a limit of $100 000 per depositor per institution. Why does the federal government insure much of the nation's funds held in deposit accounts at banks? The answer has to do with the fact that many deposit funds at banks are in transactions accounts from which people can order funds to be transferred via debt cards and cheques. The widespread failure of banks would have a significant effect on the nation's money supply, thereby reducing total liquidity in the economy. A key objective of deposit insurance is to prevent such an event from occurring.

If you were to attend a luncheon of bankers and ask the question, "Do you as bankers create money?" you would get a uniformly negative response. Bankers may not believe that they create money. But through actions initiated by a central bank such as the Bank of Canada, depository institutions together do create money; they help determine the total deposits outstanding. In this chapter, we will examine the **money multiplier process**, which explains how an injection of new money into the banking system leads to an eventual multiple expansion in the total money supply. We will also take a look at deposit insurance and its role in investment decisions made by financial institutions.

Money multiplier process The process by which an injection of new money into the banking system leads to an eventual multiple expansion in the total money supply.

13.1 Links between Changes in the Money Supply and Other Economic Variables

How fast the money supply grows or does not grow is important because no matter what model of the economy is used, theories link the money supply growth rate to economic growth or to business fluctuations. There is, in fact, a longstanding relationship between changes in the money supply and changes in GDP. Some economists use this historical evidence to argue that money is an important determinant of the level of economic activity in the economy.

Another key economic variable in our economy is the price level. At least one theory attributes changes in the rate of inflation to changes in the growth rate of money in circulation. Figure 13–1 shows the relationship between the rate of growth of the money supply and the inflation rate. There seems to be a loose, albeit consistent, direct relationship between changes in the money supply and changes in the rate of inflation. Increases in the money supply growth rate seem to lead to increases in the inflation rate, after a time lag.

13.2 The Origins of Fractional Reserve Banking

As early as 1000 B.C., uncoined gold and silver were being used as money in Mesopotamia. Goldsmiths weighed and assessed the purity of those metals; later, they started issuing paper notes indicating that the bearers held gold or silver of given weights and purity on deposit with the goldsmith. These notes could be transferred in exchange for goods and became the first paper currency. The gold and silver on deposit with the goldsmiths were the first bank deposits. Eventually, goldsmiths realized that the amount of gold and silver on deposit always exceeded the amount of gold and silver withdrawn—often by a predictable ratio. These goldsmiths started issuing to borrowers paper notes that exceeded in value the amount of gold and silver they actually kept on hand. They charged interest on these loans. This constituted the earliest form of what is now called **fractional reserve banking**—a system in which depository institutions hold reserves that are less than the amount of total deposits. We know that goldsmiths operated this way in Delphi, Didyma, and Olympia in Greece as early as the seventh century B.C. In Athens, fractional reserve banking was well developed by the sixth century B.C.

Fractional reserve banking A system in which depository institutions hold reserves that are less than the amount of total deposits.

In a fractional reserve banking system, banks do not keep sufficient reserves on hand to cover 100 percent of their depositors' accounts. And the reserves that are held by depository institutions in Canada are not kept in gold and silver, as they were with the early

FIGURE 13-1

Money Supply Growth versus the Inflation Rate

These time-series curves indicate a loose correspondence between money supply growth and the inflation rate. Actually, closer inspection reveals a direct relationship between changes in the growth rate of money and changes in the inflation rate *in a later period.* Increases in the rate of growth of money seem to lead to subsequent increases in the inflation rate; decreases in

the rate of money growth seem to lead to subsequent reductions in the inflation rate.

SOURCES: ADAPTED FROM THE STATISTICS CANADA CANSIM DATABASE, SERIES V735319 AND V41552788.

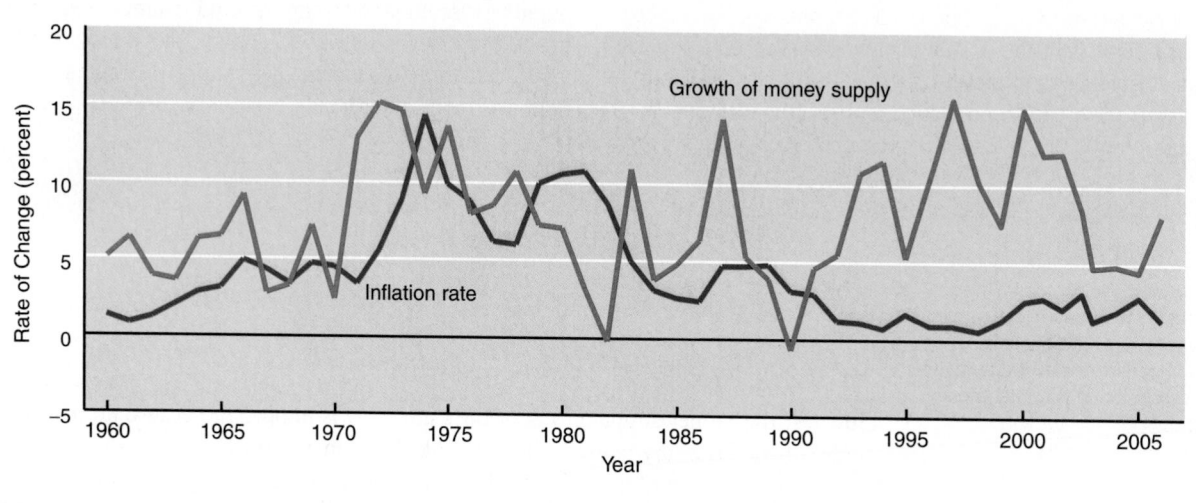

goldsmiths but, rather, in vault cash and, in the case of the chartered banks, in the form of deposits on reserve with the Bank of Canada.

13.3 Reserves

Reserves Some percentage of the customer deposits maintained by depository institutions.

Depository institutions maintain some percentage of their customer deposits as **reserves.** Different types of depository institutions hold different percentages of reserves. Normally, the larger the institution, the larger are the desired reserves. On chequing accounts, most depository institutions will keep typically 1 to 10 percent as reserves.

Take a hypothetical example. If the desired level of reserves is 10 percent and the bank[1] has $1 billion in customer chequing deposits, it will hold at least $100 million as reserves. These can be either deposits with the Bank of Canada or vault cash. Credit unions and trust companies, because they cannot hold reserves in the Bank of Canada, usually maintain accounts with the chartered banks that can act as reserves. The following discussion will focus on the chartered banks but could be broadened to include the near banks as well. There are two distinguishable types of reserves: desired and excess.

Desired reserves The *minimum* amount of reserves—vault cash plus deposits with the Bank of Canada—that a depository institution wishes to hold to back its chequable deposits.

1. *Desired reserves.* **Desired reserves** are the *minimum* amount of reserves—vault cash plus deposits with the Bank of Canada—that a depository institution wishes to hold to back its chequable deposits. They are expressed as a ratio of desired reserves to total chequable deposits (banks do not necessarily hold reserves on nonchequable deposits). In some countries minimum desired reserves are legislated and called required reserves. How this varies between Western countries is illustrated in Policy Example 13-1.

---

[1] The term *bank* is used interchangeably with the term *depository institution* in this chapter because distinctions among financial institutions are becoming less and less meaningful. However, only the chartered banks keep reserves at the Bank of Canada, and so the Bank of Canada only directly affects money creation at chartered banks.

Excess reserves The difference
between actual reserves and
desired reserves.

2. *Excess reserves.* Banks often hold reserves in excess of what they wish to hold. This difference between actual reserves and desired reserves is called **excess reserves**. Excess reserves can be negative, but they rarely are. (Negative excess reserves indicate that banks do not have sufficient reserves to meet their desired level. When this happens, they borrow from the Bank of Canada, sell such assets as securities, or call in loans.) Excess reserves are an important potential determinant of the rate of growth of the money supply, for as we shall see, it is only to the extent that banks have excess reserves that they can make new loans. Because reserves produce no income, profit-seeking financial institutions have an incentive to minimize excess reserves. They use them either to purchase income-producing securities or to make loans with which they earn income through interest payments received. In equation form, we can define excess reserves in this way:

$$\text{Excess reserves} = \text{Actual reserves} - \text{Desired reserves}$$

In the analysis that follows, we examine the relationship between the level of reserves and the size of the money supply. This analysis implies that factors influencing the level of the reserves of the banking system as a whole will ultimately affect the level of the money supply, other things held constant. We show first what happens when someone deposits currency in one depository institution. Next, we show how excess reserves can lead to an individual bank making loans that expand the money supply or create money. Then, we show how the banking system can create a multiple expansion of the money supply.

POLICY EXAMPLE 13-1   **Are Reserve Requirements on the Way Out or In?**

Several nations have reduced their required reserve ratios in recent years, as Table 13–1 illustrates.

TABLE 13-1

Required Reserve Ratios in Selected Nations

Required Reserve Ratio	1989	2007
Chequable Deposits		
Canada	10%	0%
European Monetary Union*	–	2.0
Japan	1.75	1.2
New Zealand	0	0
United Kingdom	0.45	0.35
United States	12.0	10.0
Nonchequable Deposits		
Canada	3.0	0
European Monetary Union*	–	2.0
Japan	2.5	1.3
New Zealand	0	0
United Kingdom	0.45	0.35
United States	3.0	0

*The European Monetary Union was formed in 1999.

SOURCES: GORDON SELLON JR. AND STUART WEINER. "MONETARY POLICY WITHOUT RESERVE REQUIREMENTS: ANALYTICAL ISSUES," FEDERAL RESERVE BANK OF KANSAS CITY *ECONOMIC REVIEW*, 81 (FOURTH QUARTER 1996), PP. 5–24; BANK FOR INTERNATIONAL SETTLEMENTS, 2007.

For Critical Analysis: Central banks rarely pay interest on required reserves. In what sense are banks and their customers justified in viewing reserve requirements as a type of tax?

➤→ CONCEPTS IN BRIEF

Learning Objective 13.1: Define the links between changes in the money supply and other economic variables.

✦ The money supply growth rate is linked to economic growth, business fluctuations, and the rate of inflation.

Learning Objective 13.2: Describe the origins of fractional reserve banking.

✦ Canada has a fractional banking system, in which depository institutions hold only a percentage of their deposits as reserves, either as vault cash or, in the case of the chartered banks, on deposit with the Bank of Canada.

✦ Desired reserves are usually expressed as a ratio, in percentage terms, of desired reserves to total deposits.

Learning Objective 13.3: Define reserves.

✦ Reserves are deposits held by the chartered banks at the Bank of Canada or as vault cash.

13.4 The Relationship between Reserves and Total Deposits

To show the relationship between reserves and depository institution deposits, we first analyze a single bank (existing alongside many others). A single bank is able to make new loans to its customers only to the extent that it has reserves above the desired level for covering the new deposits. When an individual bank has no excess reserves, it cannot make loans.

How a Single Bank Reacts to an Increase in Reserves

Balance sheet A statement of the assets and liabilities of any business entity, including financial institutions and the Bank of Canada.

To examine the **balance sheet**—a statement of the assets and liabilities of any business entity, including financial institutions and the Bank of Canada—of a single bank after its reserves are increased, the following assumptions are made:

1. The desired reserve ratio is 10 percent for all chequable deposits; that is, the bank holds an amount equal to 10 percent of all chequable deposits in reserve at the Bank of Canada or in vault cash.

2. Chequable deposits are the bank's only liabilities; reserves at the Bank of Canada and loans are the bank's only assets. Loans are promises made by customers to repay some amount in the future; that is, they are IOUs and, as such, are assets of the bank.

3. An individual bank can lend all it wants at current market interest rates.

4. Every time a loan is made to an individual (consumer or business), all the proceeds from the loan are put into a chequing account; no cash (currency or coins) is withdrawn.

5. Chartered banks seek to keep their excess reserves at a zero level because reserves at the Bank of Canada do not earn interest. (Chartered banks and near banks are run to make profits; we assume that all depository institutions wish to convert excess reserves that do not pay interest into interest-bearing loans.)

Look at the simplified initial position of the bank on Balance Sheet 13–1. Liabilities consist of $1 million in chequable deposits. Assets consist of $100 000 in reserves, which you can see are the desired reserves in the form of vault cash or deposits in the institution's reserve account at the Bank of Canada, and $900 000 in loans to customers. Total assets of $1 million equal total liabilities of $1 million. With a 10 percent reserve and $1 million in chequable deposits, the bank has the actual desired level of reserves of $100 000 and no excess reserves. The simplifying assumption here is that the bank has a zero net worth. A depository institution rarely has a **net worth**—the difference between assets and liabilities—of more than a small percentage of its total assets.

Net worth The difference between assets and liabilities.

BALANCE SHEET 13–1	Assets			Liabilities	
Bank 1	Total reserves		$ 100 000	Chequable deposits	$1 000 000
	Desired reserves	$100 000			
	Excess reserves	0			
	Loans		900 000		
	Total		$1 000 000	Total	$1 000 000

Assume that a *new* depositor takes $10 000 in currency out of a safety deposit box and deposits it in Bank 1. Chequing deposits in Bank 1 immediately increase by $10 000, bringing the total to $1 010 000. Total reserves of Bank 1 increase to $110 000. A $1 010 000 total in chequing deposits means that desired reserves will have to be 10 percent of $1 010 000, or $101 000. Bank 1 now has excess reserves equal to $110 000 minus $101 000, or $9000. This is shown on Balance Sheet 13–2.

BALANCE SHEET 13–2	Assets			Liabilities	
Bank 1	Total reserves		$ 110 000	Chequable deposits	$1 010 000
	Desired reserves	$101 000			
	Excess reserves	9 000			
	Loans		900 000		
	Total		$1 010 000	Total	$1 010 000

EFFECT ON THE MONEY SUPPLY.   Has the currency deposit at Bank 1 changed the economy's money supply? No. There has been a change in the composition of the money supply—chequable deposits have *increased* by $10 000 but currency in circulation has *decreased* by $10 000. Currency held by a bank is not part of the money supply.

Look at excess reserves in Balance Sheet 13–2. Excess reserves were zero before the $10 000 deposit, and now they are $9000—that is, $9000 worth of assets not earning any income. By assumption, Bank 1 will now lend out this entire $9000 in excess reserves in order to earn interest income. Loans will increase to $909 000. This is shown on Balance Sheet 13–3.

BALANCE SHEET 13–3	Assets			Liabilities	
Bank 1	Total reserves		$ 110 000	Chequable deposits	$1 019 000
(money created before cheque-clearing)	Desired reserves				
	Excess reserves				
	Loans		909 000		
	Total		$1 019 000	Total	$1 019 000

When banks lend, they create chequable deposits that are money. Bank 1 has monetized a loan or IOU. Cheques drawn against a chequable deposit are acceptable as a medium of exchange. Bank 1 has created money. It is through extension of loans by the chartered banks that the major portion of money used in our economy is created.

Borrowers borrow for a purpose. The borrower writes a $9000 cheque to buy a used car. If that cheque was deposited in another bank, actual reserves at Bank 1 will fall to $101 000 (as planned) after cheque-clearing, and deposits will fall to $1 010 000. Excess reserves will again become zero, as indicated on Balance Sheet 13–4.

BALANCE SHEET 13–4	Assets			Liabilities	
Bank 1	Total reserves		$ 101 000	Chequable deposits	$1 010 000
(after cheque-clearing)	Desired reserves	$101 000			
	Excess reserves	0			
	Loans		909 000		
	Total		$1 010 000	Total	$1 010 000

In this example, a person deposited an additional $10 000. That $10 000 became part of the reserves of Bank 1. Because that deposit immediately created excess reserves in Bank 1, further loans were possible for Bank 1. The excess reserves were lent out to earn interest. A bank will not lend more that its excess reserves because prudent banking practice dictates that it hold a certain amount of reserves at all times.

The maximum amount of new deposits that any single bank can create is equal to its excess reserves.

Money Expansion by the Banking System

Consider now the entire banking system. For practical purposes, we can look at all depository institutions taken as a whole.

NOT THE END OF THE PROCESS.   When Bank 1 made a loan for $9000 it created money or expanded the money supply. The process of money creation does not stop here.

The borrower spent the loan made by Bank 1 by writing a cheque that was deposited at Bank 2. For the sake of simplicity, ignore the previous assets and liabilities in Bank 2 and concentrate only on the balance sheet *changes* resulting from this new deposit, as shown on Balance Sheet 13–5. A plus sign indicates that the entry has increased, and a minus sign indicates that the entry has decreased. For the depository institution, Bank 2, the $9000 deposit becomes an increase in reserves (assets) as well as an increase in chequing deposits (liabilities). Because the desired reserve ratio is 10 percent, or $900, Bank 2 will have excess reserves of $8100. But, of course, excess reserves are not income producing, and so Bank 2 will reduce them to zero by making loans of $8100 (which will earn interest income) by creating deposits for borrowers equal to $8100. The money supply has increased by $8100. This is shown on Balance Sheet 13–6.

BALANCE SHEET 13-5

Bank 2

(changes only)

Assets			Liabilities	
Total reserves		$9 000	New chequable deposits	+$9 000
Desired reserves	$ 900			
Excess reserves	+8 100			
Total		+$9 000	Total	+$9 000

BALANCE SHEET 13-6

Bank 2

(money created before cheque-clearing)

Assets			Liabilities	
Total reserves		$ 9 000	Chequable deposits	+$17 100
Desired reserves				
Excess reserves				
Loans		+ 8 100		
Total		+$17 100	Total	+$17 100

Assume that a borrower who has received the $8100 loan from Bank 2 writes a cheque that is deposited in an account at Bank 3. After cheque-clearing has occurred, Bank 2's excess reserves will again be zero, as shown on Balance Sheet 13–7.

BALANCE SHEET 13-7

Bank 2

(after cheque-clearing)

Assets			Liabilities	
Total reserves		$ 900	Chequable deposits	+$9000
Desired reserves	$900			
Excess reserves	0			
Loans		+8100		
Total		+$9000	Total	+$9000

CONTINUATION OF THE DEPOSIT CREATION PROCESS. At Bank 3, chequable deposits and total reserves have increased by $8100. Look at Bank 3's simplified account on Balance Sheet 13–8, where, again, only changes in the assets and liabilities are shown.

Because the desired reserve ratio is 10 percent, or $810, Bank 3's excess reserves are therefore $7290. Bank 3 will want to lend those non–interest-earning assets (excess reserves). When it does, loans (in the form of created chequing deposits) will increase by $7290 and the money supply will have increased by $7290. Bank 3's total reserves will fall to $810, and excess reserves become zero as the $7290 loan is spent and deposited at another bank.

BALANCE SHEET 13-8

Bank 3

(changes only)

Assets			Liabilities	
Total reserves		$8100	New chequable deposits	+$8100
Desired reserves	$ 810			
Excess reserves	+7290			
Total		+$8100	Total	+$8100

PROGRESSION TO OTHER BANKS. This process continues to Banks 4, 5, 6, and so on. Each bank obtains smaller and smaller increases in deposits because 10 percent of each deposit is held in reserve; therefore, each succeeding depository institution makes correspondingly smaller loans. Table 13–2 shows the new deposits, possible loans, and desired reserves for the remaining depository institutions in the system.

EFFECT ON TOTAL MONEY SUPPLY. In this simple example, the money supply initially increases by $9000 at Bank 1. It was further increased by $8100 at Bank 2, and it was again increased by $7290 at Bank 3. Eventually, the money supply will increase by $90 000, as shown in Table 13–2. The money multiplier process is portrayed graphically in Figure 13–2.

TABLE 13-2

Maximum Money Creation with 10 Percent Desired Reserves

This table shows the maximum new loans plus investments that banks can make, given a currency deposit of $10 000 in Bank 1. The desired reserve ratio is 10 percent. We assume that all excess reserves in each bank are used for new loans or investments.

Bank	New Deposits	New Desired Reserves	Maximum New Loans Equal Maximum New Money (excess reserves)
1	$ 10 000	$ 1 000	$ 9 000
2	9 000	900	8 100
3	8 100	810	7 290
4	7 290	729	6 561
•	•	•	•
•	•	•	•
•	•	•	•
All other banks	65 610	6 561	59 049
Totals	$100 000	$10 000	$90 000

Increase in Overall Reserves

When excess reserves are created, the money supply can increase. In our example, the depository institutions use their excess reserves to make loans. It is not important how they put the money back into the system. If they bought certificates of deposit or any other security, the analysis would be the same because the party they bought those securities from would receive a cheque from the purchasing depository institution. The recipient of the cheque would then deposit it into its own depository institution. The deposit expansion process would be the same as we have already outlined.

FIGURE 13–2

The Multiple Expansion in the Money Supply Due to a Currency Deposit of $10 000 When the Desired Reserve Ratio Is 10 Percent

The banks are all aligned in decreasing order of new deposits created. Bank 1 receives the $10 000 in new currency creating new excess reserves of $9000 and lends out $9000. Bank 2 receives the $9000 and lends out $8100. The process continues through Banks 3 to 19 and then the rest of the banking system. Ultimately, assuming no leakages, the $9000 of new excess reserves results in an increase in the money supply of $90 000, or 10 times the initial excess reserves because the desired reserve ratio is 10 percent.

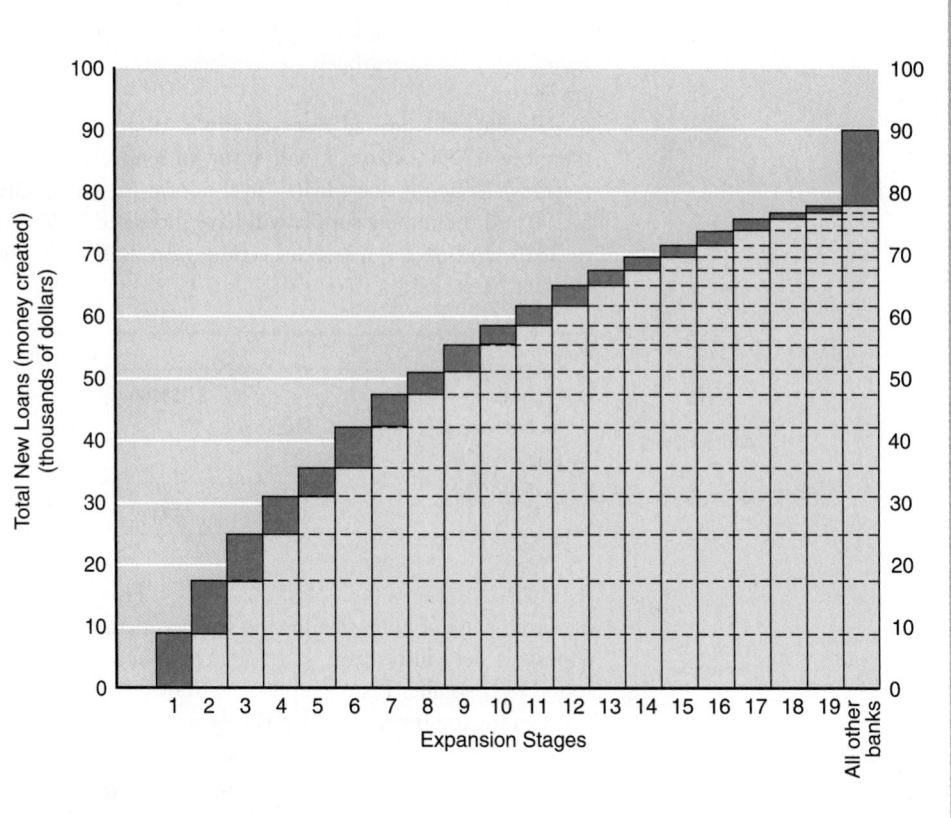

This process can work in reverse if there is a decrease in reserves, for example, when loans are repaid. The result is a multiple contraction of deposits and therefore of the total money supply in circulation.

13.5 The Money Multiplier

In the example just given, with a desired reserve ratio of 10 percent, a new $10 000 currency deposit increased excess reserves at Bank 1 by $9000 and yielded a $90 000 increase in total new loans in the banking system, an increase of $90 000 in the money supply. Loans increased by a multiple of 10 times the initial $9000 increase in overall reserves. Conversely, a $9000 decrease in excess reserves will yield a $90 000 decrease in total loans in the banking system—a decrease in the money supply; loans will decrease by a multiple of 10 times.

We can now make a generalization about the extent to which the money supply will change when the banking system's reserves are increased or decreased. The **money multiplier** gives the change in the money supply due to a change in reserves. If we assume that no excess reserves are kept and that all loan proceeds are deposited in depository institutions in the system, the following equation applies:

Money multiplier A factor that gives the change in the money supply due to a change in reserves.

$$\text{Potential money multiplier} = \frac{1}{\text{Desired reserve ratio}}$$

That is, the maximum possible value of the money multiplier is equal to 1 divided by the desired reserve ratio for chequable deposits. The *actual* change in the money supply—currency plus chequable account balances—will be equal to the following:

Actual change in money supply = Actual money multiplier × Change in excess reserves

Now we examine why there is a difference between the potential money multiplier—1 divided by the desired reserve ratio—and the actual multiplier.

Forces That Reduce the Money Multiplier

We made a number of simplifying assumptions to come up with the potential money multiplier. In the real world, the actual money multiplier is considerably smaller. Several factors account for this.

LEAKAGES. The entire loan (cheque) from one bank is not always deposited in another bank. At least two leakages can occur:

- *Currency drains.* When deposits increase, the public may want to hold more currency. Currency that is kept in a person's wallet remains outside the banking system and cannot be held by banks as reserves from which to make loans. The greater the amount of cash leakage, the smaller is the actual money multiplier.
- *Excess reserves.* Depository institutions may wish to maintain excess reserves. Depository institutions do not, in fact, always keep excess reserves at zero. To the extent that they want to keep positive excess reserves, the money multiplier will be smaller. A bank receiving $1 million in new deposits might, in our example with the 10 percent desired reserve ratio, keep more than $100 000 as reserves. The greater the excess reserves, the smaller is the actual money multiplier.

Empirically, the currency drain is more significant than the effect of excess reserves.

REAL-WORLD MONEY MULTIPLIERS. The desired reserve ratio determines the maximum potential money multiplier because the reciprocal of the desired reserve ratio tells us what that is. The maximum is never attained for the money supply as a whole because of currency drains and excess reserves. Also, each definition of the money supply, M1 or M2, will yield different results for money multipliers. For several decades, the M1 multiplier has varied between 1.5 and 2.5. The M2 multiplier, however, has shown a trend upward, ranging from 2.25 at the beginning of the 1960s, to over 12.5 in the 1990s.

➤ CONCEPTS IN BRIEF

Learning Objective 13.4: Explain the relationship between reserves and total deposits.

- Desired reserves are the vault cash a bank keeps on hand to meet the demands of its depositors when they make currency withdrawals or use their chequing accounts.
- When reserves increase at a single bank in the banking system, the result is a multiple expansion of loans and, therefore, of the money supply.
- If there is a reduction in the reserves of a bank in the banking system, the result is a multiple contraction of loans and, therefore, of the money supply.

Learning Objective 13.5: Describe the money multiplier.

- A single bank can make new loans to its customers up to its excess reserves.
- The maximum money multiplier for the banking system is equal to the reciprocal of the desired reserve ratio.
- The actual multiplier is less than the maximum money multiplier because of currency drains and excess reserves voluntarily held by banks.

13.6 Deposit Insurance and Flawed Bank Regulation

When businesses fail, they create hardships for creditors, owners, workers, and customers. But when a depository institution fails, an even greater hardship results because many individuals and businesses depend on the safety and security of banks. While Canada has a history of relatively few bank failures, we are not immune to them. Between 1967 and 1989, there were 23 failures, and there have been a further 22 failures since then. However, when compared with the American experience of 1065 failures between 1985 and 1993, the Canadian record looks quite good.

Nevertheless, in 1967 the federal government set up the **Canadian Deposit Insurance Corporation (CDIC)**—a government agency that insures the deposits held in federally incorporated financial institutions—to protect small investors who do not have the resources to accurately assess the soundness of federally incorporated financial institutions. Credit unions now have similar deposit insurance through their own institutions.

The Need for Deposit Insurance

The CDIC was established to mitigate the primary cause of bank failures, **bank runs**—the simultaneous rush of depositors to convert their demand deposits or time deposits into currency.

Consider the following scenario. A bank begins to look shaky; its assets may not seem sufficient to cover its liabilities. If the bank has no deposit insurance, depositors in this bank (and any banks associated with it) will all want to withdraw their money from the bank at the same time. Their concern is that this shaky bank will not have enough money to return their deposits to them in the form of currency. Indeed, this is what happens in a bank failure when insurance does not exist. Just as with the failure of a regular business, the creditors of the bank may not all get paid, or if they do, they will get paid less than 100 percent of what they are owed. Depositors are creditors of a bank because their funds are on loan to the bank. In a fractional reserve banking system, banks do not hold 100 percent of their depositors' money in the form of reserves. Consequently, all depositors cannot withdraw all their money at the same time. It would be desirable to assure depositors that they can have their deposits converted into cash when they wish, no matter how serious the financial situation of the bank.

The CDIC provides this assurance. By insuring deposits, the CDIC bolsters trust in the banking system and provides depositors with the incentive to leave their deposits with the bank, even in the face of rumours of bank failures. In 1967, it was sufficient for the CDIC to cover each account up to $20 000. The current maximum is $100 000.

Originally, all financial institutions insured by the CDIC paid the same premium—one-sixth of one percent of insured deposits. The Canadian Bankers' Association (CBA) opposed this method of determining premiums as it claimed that the large chartered banks are at much less risk of failing than smaller financial institutions. If, for example, economic conditions led to widespread loan defaults in British Columbia, the chartered banks could rely on their more profitable operations in the rest of the country to keep them solvent. Smaller trust and mortgage loan companies do not have that option and consequently are at greater risk of failing. The system has now changed. Chartered banks pay lower premiums than more risky financial institutions.

A Flaw in the Deposit Insurance Scheme

Because deposit insurance premiums are not based on the degree of risk of the depository institution's investments, there is no reward for investing in relatively nonrisky assets. The result is that bankers have an incentive to invest in more high-yield assets, which carry more risk, than they would if there were no deposit insurance. Thus, the premium rate is artificially low, permitting institution managers to obtain deposits at less than market price (because depositors will accept a lower interest payment on insured deposits); and even if the institution's portfolio becomes riskier, its deposit insurance premium does not rise. Consequently, depository institution managers can increase their net interest margin by using lower-cost insured deposits to purchase higher-yield, higher-risk assets. The gains to risk taking accrue to the managers and shareholders of the depository institutions; the losses go to the deposit insurer (and, as we will see, ultimately to taxpayers).

To combat the inherent flaws in the financial institution industry and in the deposit insurance system, a vast regulatory apparatus was installed. The CDIC was given regulatory powers to offset the risk-taking temptations to depository institution managers; those powers included the ability to require sound business practices by the insured institutions.

Deposit Insurance, Adverse Selection, and Moral Hazard

When financial transactions take place, one party often does not have all the knowledge needed about the other party to make correct decisions—this is known as the problem of asymmetric information. For example, borrowers generally know more than lenders about the returns and risks associated with the investment projects they intend to undertake.

ADVERSE SELECTION.   Adverse selection arises when there is asymmetric information before a transaction takes place. In financial markets, it often occurs because individuals and firms that are worse credit risks than they appear to be are the ones most willing to borrow at any given interest rate. This willingness makes them likely to be selected by lenders, yet their inferior ability to repay (relative to the interest rate being charged) means that loans to them more often yield adverse outcomes for lenders (default). The potential risks of adverse selection make lenders less likely to lend to anyone and more inclined to charge higher interest rates when they do lend.

Adverse selection is often a problem when insurance is involved because people or firms that are relatively poor risks are sometimes able to disguise that fact from insurers. It is instructive to examine the way this works with the deposit insurance provided by the CDIC. Deposit insurance shields depositors from the potential adverse effects of risky decisions and so makes depositors willing to accept riskier investment strategies by their banks. Clearly, this encourages more high-flying, risk-loving entrepreneurs to become managers of banks. The consequences for the CDIC—and often for the taxpayer—are larger losses.

MORAL HAZARD.   Moral hazard arises as the result of information asymmetry after a transaction has occurred. In financial markets, lenders face the hazard that borrowers may engage in activities that are contrary to the lender's interest and thus might be said to be immoral from the lender's perspective. For example, because lenders do not share in the profits of business ventures, they generally want borrowers to agree to invest prudently. Yet, once the loan has been made, borrower–investors have an incentive to invest in high-risk, high-return projects because they are able to keep all of the extra profits if the projects succeed. Such behaviour subjects the lender to greater hazards than are being compensated for under the terms of the loan agreement.

Moral hazard is also an important phenomenon in the presence of insurance contracts, such as the deposit insurance provided by the CDIC. Insured depositors know that they will not suffer losses if their bank fails. Hence, they have little incentive to monitor their bank's investment activities or to punish their bank by withdrawing their funds if the bank assumes too much risk. Thus, insured banks have incentives to take on more risks than they otherwise would—and with those risks come higher losses for the CDIC and for taxpayers. Policy Example 13–2 discusses the issues of bank losses for depository insurance agencies and taxpayers.

POLICY EXAMPLE 13–2   **Bailouts That Cost Taxpayers Millions**

When the Canadian Commercial Bank failed in 1985, the media alarmed us with inflated figures of how much the Canadian taxpayer was paying to bail out this bank. Although technically not inaccurate, these stories fail to point out that such bailouts always occur *after the fact*. The billion or so dollars lost by the Canadian Commercial Bank had already been lost by the time of the bailout. That is to say, the economy had already seen a $1 billion reduction in its wealth because of bad investments by the Canadian Commercial Bank.

Japan is facing a banking crisis that makes this bank failure in Canada look like child's play. The policy question is how the Japanese government is going to bail out the banking system there. The Japanese banks in the mid-1990s held problem loans equal to about $1 trillion, or a quarter of Japan's GDP. Japanese authorities continued to allow banks to lend

continued

problem debtors enough money to cover unpaid interest. If the Japanese government chooses to bail out its banking system, the estimated cost will be close to $400 billion. Alternatively, the Japanese government could simply let the weakest banks go bankrupt. Some observers believe that a third solution will eventually come about: The Japanese government will pour in enough reserves to shore up the banking system in exchange for the nation's banks' agreeing to use all of their profits for the foreseeable future to write off bad debts.

For critical analysis: Who pays for the Japanese banking bailout if the "third way" is chosen?

➤→ CONCEPTS IN BRIEF

Learning Objective 13.6: Describe deposit insurance and flawed bank regulation.
- Federal deposit insurance was created in 1967 when the Canada Deposit Insurance Corporation (CDIC) was founded to insure deposits in federally incorporated depository institutions.
- Credit unions and *caisses populaires* have their own deposit schemes.
- Deposit insurance was designed to prevent bank runs in which individual demand deposit and savings deposit holders attempt to turn their deposits into currency.
- Because of the way deposit insurance is set up in Canada, it encourages bank managers to invest in riskier assets to make higher rates of return.

➤→ ISSUES AND APPLICATIONS

Deregulating the Financial Services Industry

Concepts Applied: Regulation, Deregulation

Deregulation Step-by-Step

The first of a series of moves toward blurring the lines between financial intermediaries came in 1987 when chartered banks were given permission to acquire investment dealers. While the banks themselves could not sell shares and bonds, their wholly owned subsidiaries could.

In 1992, the insurance business was deregulated. Banks and trust and insurance companies are now allowed to carry out most of each other's business functions. For the banks, which previously could sell only mortgage insurance, this was a big step. They could now sell life insurance, property and accident insurance, and travel insurance, again through subsidiaries.

Over the early years of the 20th century, Canada created an array of regulations that constrained the behaviour of the financial services industry. Only banks could grant commercial mortgages, only licensed brokerage firms could sell shares, and only insurance companies could sell life insurance. But recently, the trend has been toward deregulation resulting in "one-stop shopping" for financial services.

Also, electronic networking allows Royal Bank customers to transfer money, pay bills, purchase airline tickets, and trade shares from their homes using computers. In a futuristic application of electronic technology to banking, Vancouver City Savings Credit Union, one of Canada's largest, purchased Citizens Trust, which it converted to a bank. However, this bank has no branches where customers talk over financial matters with their bankers. All business—from depositing and withdrawing money to applying for mortgages—is conducted electronically through the Internet or at ATMs.

More Changes to Come

The two largest banks in the world, the United Kingdom's Barlays PLC and Switzerland's UBS AG, both have loans outstanding (assets) of more than U.S. $1 trillion. The Canadian banks, which used to be relatively large, have fallen behind. The Royal Bank, Canada's largest, does not rank in the top 50 worldwide.

After a long review and lobbying by the financial services industry, early in 2001 the federal government introduced long-awaited legislation setting out a three-stage process for Canadian bank mergers. First, they would begin with a detailed application to the Competition Bureau, the Superintendent of Financial Institutions, and the Minister of Finance. Secondly, Senate and Commons committees would also hold public hearings. Finally, after all the reviews were completed, the Minister of Finance would make a final decision.

Several merger proposals from the banks have been made to government. With the exception of the Toronto-Dominion Bank merger with Canada Trust, the federal government has not proceeded with any of the bank merger proposals and continues to study the issue.

Deregulation of the financial services industry is paving the way for new kinds of banks in Canada. "VanCity had already achieved significant market penetration in British Columbia and was looking for national growth opportunities for its business and mandate of corporate social responsibility," says Dave Mowat, CEO of VanCity Credit Union. "The trendlines in our market research at the time revealed that consumers were beginning to ask for electronic banking options. Since VanCity wasn't in a position to fund the establishment of a nationwide bricks-and-mortar branch system, the opportunity became clear: a national, electronic bank serving its members by telephone, fax, ATM, and the Internet."

For critical analysis:

1. The term "nonbank bank" has been used a lot recently. What do you think it means?
2. Would there be an increased moral hazard associated with deposit insurance if banks were allowed to do everything—sell insurance, shares and bonds, and airline tickets, plus everything else a bank does?

SUMMARY

Here is what you should know after reading this chapter. MyEconLab will help you identify what you know, and where to go when you need to practise. We suggest that as soon as you review one of the Learning Objective sections below, you then proceed to go through the related section in MyEconLab.

LEARNING OBJECTIVES	KEY TERMS	WHERE TO PRACTICE
13.1 Links between Changes in the Money Supply and Other Economic Variables. The money supply growth rate is linked to economic growth, business fluctuations, and the rate of inflation.	money multiplier process, 339	• **MyEconLab** Study Plan 13.1
13.2 The Origins of Fractional Reserve Banking. Canada has a fractional banking system in which the chartered bank depository institutions hold only a percentage of their deposits as reserves, either as vault cash or on deposit with the Bank of Canada. Other financial institutions maintain reserves of deposits in the chartered banks, and vault cash.	fractional reserve banking, 339	• **MyEconLab** Study Plan 13.2

myeconlab

➡ LEARNING OBJECTIVES	KEY TERMS	MYECONLAB PRACTICE
13.3 Reserves. Reserves are deposits held by the chartered banks at the Bank of Canada or as vault cash.	reserves, 340 desired reserves, 340 excess reserves, 341	• **MyEconLab** Study Plan 13.3
13.4 The Relationship between Reserves and Total Deposits. Desired reserves are usually expressed as a ratio, in percentage terms, of desired reserves to total deposits. When depository institutions have more reserves than are desired, they are said to have excess reserves.	balance sheet, 342 net worth, 342	• **MyEconLab** Study Plan 13.4
13.5 The Money Multiplier. Single depository institutions that have no excess reserves cannot alter the money supply. A single depository institution with excess reserves can alter the money supply by making new loans up to its excess reserves. For the banking system as a whole, the money supply can be altered up to a maximum equal to the reciprocal of the desired reserve ratio. The actual multiplier is less than the maximum money multiplier because of currency drains and excess reserves voluntarily held by banks.	money multiplier, 346	• **MyEconLab** Study Plan 13.5
13.6 Deposit Insurance and Flawed Bank Regulation. The Canadian Deposit Insurance Corporation was created in 1967 to insure deposits in federally incorporated depository institutions. Credit Unions and *caisses populaires* have their own system of deposit insurance. Because of the existence of deposit insurance, the probability of a run on the banking system, even if a significant number of depository institutions were to fail, is quite small. A major flaw in the deposit insurance system has been the relatively low price for the insurance irrespective of risk. Moral hazard under the current deposit insurance system has led to overly risky and fraudulent behaviour on the part of some depository institution mangers.	Canadian Deposit Insurance Corporation (CDIC), 348 bank runs, 348 asymmetric information, 349 adverse selection, 349 moral hazard, 349	• **MyEconLab** Study Plan 13.6

→ PROBLEMS

(Answers to the odd-numbered problems appear at the back of the book.)

LO 13.1 Define the links between changes in the money supply and other economic variables.

1. What economic variables do changes in the money supply affect?

LO 13.2 Describe the origins of fractional reserve banking.

2. Describe the role of goldsmiths in the origins of fractional reserve banking. Refer back to Policy Example 13–1, "Are Reserve Requirements on the Way Out or In?", to see the current state of reserve requirements in various countries.

LO 13.3 Define reserves.

3. Arrange the following items on the proper side of a bank's balance sheet, given below.
   a. Chequing deposits
   b. Vault cash
   c. Time deposits
   d. Deposits with the Bank of Canada
   e. Loans to private businesses
   f. Loans to households
   g. Holdings of Canadian government, provincial, and municipal bonds
   h. Borrowings from other banks

Assets	Liabilities

LO 13.4 Explain the relationship between reserves and total deposits.

4. It is the year 2310. Residents of an earth colony on Titan, the largest moon of the planet Saturn, use chequable deposits at financial institutions as the only form of money. Depository institutions on Titan wish to hold 10 percent of deposits as excess reserves at all times. There are no other deposits in the banking system. If the banking system on Titan has $300 million in reserves and the total quantity of money is $1.5 billion, what is the desired reserve ratio?

5. If the desired reserve ratio is 10 percent, what will be the maximum change in the money supply in each of the following situations?
   a. Theola Smith deposits in Bank 2 a cheque drawn on Bank 3.
   b. Smith finds $1000 in coins and paper currency buried in her backyard and deposits it in her chequing account.

c. Smith writes a $1000 cheque on her own account and takes $1000 in currency and buries it in her backyard.

6. A bank has $120 million in total assets, which are composed of desired reserves, loans, and securities. Its only liabilities are $120 million in chequable deposits. The bank exactly satisfies its desired reserve ratio, and its total reserves equal $6 million. What is the desired reserve ratio?

7. The Bank of Canada purchases $1 million in government of Canada treasury bonds from a bond dealer, and the dealer's bank credits the dealer's account. The desired reserve ratio is 15 percent, and the bank typically lends any excess reserves immediately. Assuming that no currency leakage occurs, how much will the bank be able to lend to its customers following the Bank of Canada's purchase?

8. A depository institution holds $150 million in desired reserves and $10 million in excess reserves. Its remaining assets include $440 million in loans and $150 million in securities. If the institution's only liabilities are chequable deposits, what is the desired reserve ratio?

9. A bank has $260 million in total reserves, of which $10 million are excess reserves. The bank currently has $3.6 billion in loans, $1 billion in securities, and $140 million in other assets. The desired reserve ratio for chequable deposits is 10 percent.
   a. What is this bank's total amount of liabilities and net worth?
   b. What additional amount of loans could this bank make to households and firms?
   c. What is the current quantity of chequable deposits at this bank?

LO 13.5 Describe the money multiplier.

10. Assume a desired reserve ratio of 8 percent. A cheque for $60 000 is drawn on an account in Bank B and deposited in a chequable deposit in Bank A.
   a. How much have the excess reserves of Bank A increased?
   b. How much in the form of new loans is Bank A now able to extend to borrowers?
   c. By how much have reserves of Bank B decreased?
   d. By how much have excess reserves of Bank B decreased?
   e. By how much has the money supply increased ?

11. Bank 1 has received a deposit of $1 million. Assuming that the banks retain no excess reserves, answer the following questions.
   a. The desired reserve ratio is 25 percent. Fill in the blanks in the table on the next page. What is the money multiplier?

b. Now the desired reserve ratio is 5 percent. Fill in the blanks in a similar table. What is the money multiplier?

Multiple Deposit Creation			
Bank	Deposits	Reserves	Loans
Bank 1	$1 000 000	$_____	$_____
Bank 2	_____	_____	_____
Bank 3	_____	_____	_____
Bank 4	_____	_____	_____
Bank 5	_____	_____	_____
All other banks	_____	_____	_____
Totals	_____	_____	_____

12. Suppose that the total liabilities of a depository institution are chequable deposits equal to $2 billion. It has $1.65 billion in loans, and the desired reserve ratio is 15 percent. Does this institution hold any excess reserves? If so, how much?

13. Examine the following balance sheet of Bank B:

Bank B			
Assets		Liabilities	
Total reserves	$ 50	Chequable deposits	$200
Loans	100	Capital shares	200
Government securities	50		
Property	200		

Assume that the desired reserve ratio is 10 percent.
a. Calculate the excess reserves of Bank B.
b. How much money can Bank B lend out?
c. If Bank B lends the money in part (b) of this problem, what are the new values for total reserves? For chequable deposits? For loans?
d. What is the maximum expansion of the money supply if Bank B lends the amount suggested in part (b) of this problem?

LO 13.6 Describe deposit insurance and flawed bank regulation.

14. Discuss the need for deposit insurance. See Policy Example 13–2, "Bailouts That Cost Taxpayers Millions," for an example of how the Bank of Japan has had to step in because of large problems in the Japanese banking system. In Canada, with the Canada Deposit Insurance Corporation (CDIC), why would there be a need for insured depository institution oversight and regulation?

14

The Bank of Canada and Monetary Policy

If you follow any of the news stories about the policies being made in Ottawa, you cannot fail to learn about what Canada's central bank, the Bank of Canada, is doing to cool down an over-heated economy, to stop a recession, to deal with an illiquidity crisis, or something else of that nature. Whatever the Bank of Canada does, some part of the press or the academic world is apt to "bash" it for doing the wrong thing. Whenever a vacancy occurs for the Governor on the Governing Council or its Board of Directors, speculation about the political leaning of the next appointee is rampant. Some analysts argue that even though the Bank of Canada is only a quasi-government agency, it is not really independent of the government's wishes. These commentators go further and argue that the Bank of Canada

should become completely independent of the government. Is the Bank of Canada already independent? And if not, does it matter? To answer these questions, you need to know more about how monetary policy works.

?

DID YOU KNOW THAT... ●

The Governor of the Bank of Canada is often considered the second most important person politically and economically in Canada after the prime minister. Why is the head of the Bank of Canada considered so important? It is because the Governor of the Bank of Canada, the Board of Directors, and the rest of the Bank's governors determine monetary policy in Canada. A strongly worded public statement by the Governor of the Bank of Canada can cause instant reaction in Canada's financial markets and sometimes in those in the rest of the world.

This chapter will deal with the Bank of Canada and monetary policy—the Bank of Canada's altering interest rates or changing the supply of money (or the rate at which it grows) in order to achieve national economic goals. When you were introduced to aggregate demand in Chapter 6, you discovered that the position of the aggregate demand curve is determined by the willingness of firms, individuals, governments, and foreigners to purchase domestically produced goods and services. Monetary policy works in a variety of ways to change this willingness, both directly and indirectly.

Think about monetary policy in an intuitive way: An increase in the money supply adds to the amount of money that firms and individuals have on hand and so increases the amount that they wish to spend. The result is an increase in aggregate demand. A decrease in the money supply reduces the amount of money that people have on hand to spend and so decreases aggregate demand. Integral to this process is the central bank.

14.1 Central Banks and the Bank of Canada

The first central bank, which began operations in 1668, was Sweden's Sveriges Riksbank (called the Risens Standers Bank until 1867). In 1694, the British Parliament established the most historically famous of central banks, the Bank of England. It authorized the Bank of England to issue currency notes redeemable in silver, and initially, the Bank of England's notes circulated alongside currency notes issued by government and private finance companies. Until 1800, the Riksbank and the Bank of England were the only central banks. The number of central banks worldwide remained less than 10 as late as 1873. The number expanded considerably toward the end of the 19th century and again during the second half of the 20th century, as shown in Figure 14–1.

Canada's Central Banking System

The Bank of Canada is Canada's central bank. It oversees the Canadian monetary system and, as such, is considered the country's monetary authority. The Bank of Canada was established with the *Bank of Canada Act* of 1934 and opened its doors for business in 1935. At first privately owned, by 1938 the federal government had nationalized it. According to the preamble to the *Bank of Canada Act* of 1934, the Bank of Canada was expected to

> regulate credit and currency in the best interest of the economic life of the nation, to control and protect the external value of the national monetary unit and to mitigate by its influence fluctuations in the general level of production, trade, prices and employment, so far as may be possible within the scope of monetary action, and generally to promote the economic and financial welfare of the Dominion.

The preamble to the *Bank of Canada Act* has never changed; however, the Bank of Canada's primary monetary policy focus is the goal of low and stable inflation—to keep Canada's inflation at 2 percent, the midpoint of 1 to 3 percent-a-year target range.

FIGURE 14–1

The Number of Central Banking Institutions, 1670 to the Present

The 20th century witnessed considerable growth in the number of central banks.

SOURCE: DATA FROM FORREST CAPIE, CHARLES GOODHART, AND NOBERT SCHNADT, "THE DEVELOPMENT OF CENTRAL BANKING," IN FORREST CAPIE ET AL., *THE FUTURE OF CENTRAL BANKING: THE TERCENTENARY SYMPOSIUM OF THE BANK OF ENGLAND* (CAMBRIDGE: CAMBRIDGE UNIVERSITY PRESS, 1994.)

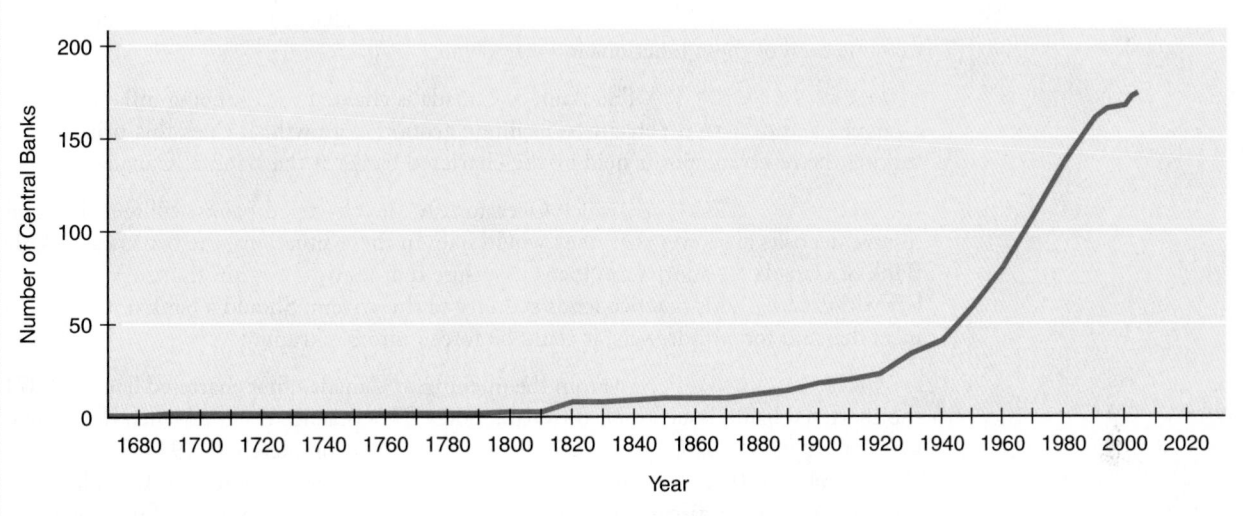

ORGANIZATION OF THE BANK OF CANADA.   The Bank of Canada is governed by a Board of Directors consisting of the Governor of the Bank of Canada, the Senior Deputy Governor, 12 directors from nonbanking occupations, and the Deputy Minister of Finance, who is a nonvoting member of the Board. The Governor is appointed by the Board, with Cabinet approval, for a seven-year term. Directors are appointed for three-year terms. Regional representation is a priority when appointing directors.

The Board of Directors must meet at least four times per year but frequently meets more often. The day-to-day operations of the Bank are directed by an executive committee of the Board, consisting of the Governor, the Senior Deputy Governor, and two to four other directors who meet weekly. While the Bank of Canada is ultimately responsible to the federal government, it is an independent body charged with maintaining price stability and economic growth in Canada. Whether this independence is beneficial is the topic of the Issues and Applications section at the end of this chapter.

THE BANK OF CANADA'S CUSTOMERS.   The Bank of Canada accepts deposits from the federal government and the chartered banks only. Almost all federal government transactions pass through the Bank of Canada, although the government also has accounts with the chartered banks.

The chartered banks hold deposits at the Bank of Canada for two reasons. First, the banks hold a large part of their reserve deposits in these accounts. Until 1992, they were required to hold reserves by law; however, the *Bank Act* of 1992 eliminated this requirement. Now, they hold reserves at the Bank of Canada as part of prudent banking practice.

The second reason the chartered banks hold reserves at the Bank of Canada is to facilitate cheque clearing. When your employer pays you with a $200 cheque drawn on the RBC Royal Bank and you deposit it in your account at Scotiabank, no money actually changes hands. All across Canada, similar transactions are taking place at financial institutions. At the end of the day, the **Canadian Payments Association (CPA)** (a regulated organization that operates a national cheque-clearing and settlements system) adds up all the money that each bank owes the other—for instance, RBC Royal Bank would owe Scotiabank $200 for your paycheque—and arrives at a net transfer of funds that should be made between banks. If TD Canada Trust owes the Bank of Montreal $1.5 million, for

Canadian Payments Association (CPA) A regulated organization that operates a national cheque-clearing and settlements system.

example, while the Bank of Montreal owes TD Canada Trust $1 million, the Canadian Payments Association would ask the Bank of Canada to transfer $500 000 out of the reserve deposits of TD Canada Trust and into the deposits of the Bank of Montreal. Near banks maintain deposits with the chartered banks so that they may participate in the cheque-clearing process as well.

Functions of the Bank of Canada

The Bank of Canada serves four basic functions. It conducts monetary policy on behalf of the federal government, it acts as a lender of last resort to the financial community, it issues bank notes, and it is fiscal agent and financial advisor to the government. Let us examine each of these functions in more detail.

MONETARY POLICY. The Bank of Canada is charged with keeping inflation within a target band of 1 to 3 percent to facilitate economic growth. It does this primarily by varying the reserve deposits held by the chartered banks at the Bank of Canada.

LENDER OF LAST RESORT. Occasionally, the chartered banks will feel that their reserve deposits are lower than they would like. In these situations, the banks can ask the Bank of Canada for short-term loans to ensure that they do not run short of cash to satisfy withdrawals. This practice lends stability to the system. Should a bank not be able to meet demand for withdrawals, it could be forced into bankruptcy.

ISSUING BANK NOTES. From the opening of Canada's first chartered bank in 1871, the chartered banks issued their own bank notes. This practice declined when the Bank of Canada began issuing Canadian currency and stopped completely in 1945. The Bank of Canada now is the only body that can issue legal bank notes in Canada. Read Example 14–1 for a discussion of another type of "currency"—Canadian Tire money.

EXAMPLE 14–1 **Is Canadian Tire Money Real Money?**

One of the functions of the Bank of Canada is to issue bank notes. Canadian Tire, however, issues its own "currency," which can be used to purchase goods and services at any Canadian Tire store. Every time you purchase merchandise with cash, you receive a small amount back in Canadian Tire money. Are these notes "real" money?

If you said, "No, Canadian Tire money is not real money," you would be right. However, in some instances, it is used in place of real money. Consider the bartender who is given Canadian Tire notes as part of a tip. If that individual's car happens to need new tires, for example, then those notes are as good as money. If the bartender does not want anything from Canadian Tire, then they are worthless.

But what if the bartender had a friend who wanted to buy tires? The two could exchange the Canadian Tire money for Canadian currency, which is real money. However, one of the tests of Canadian legal tender is that it must be accepted in payment of debts in Canada. In this instance, Canadian Tire money would not measure up.

For critical analysis: What conditions would have to exist for Canadian Tire money to act as real money in practice, if not in theory?

FISCAL AGENT AND FINANCIAL ADVISOR. The Bank of Canada acts as the federal government's fiscal agent and financial advisor. In this capacity, it manages the government's debt by arranging payment of interest to debt-holders and payment in full on maturing debt. It also holds government deposits and provides advice with respect to issuing government securities. The Bank of Canada frequently intervenes in the foreign exchange market to support the external value of the Canadian dollar and to manage the government's holdings of foreign reserves. Chapter 17 looks at the foreign exchange market in more detail.

Table 14–1 shows a consolidated balance sheet for the Bank of Canada. Its assets consist mainly of Government of Canada securities and Treasury bills. These securities form part of the public debt. The Bank's liabilities are mostly currency in circulation, with chartered bank reserve deposits a much smaller component.

TABLE 14–1

Bank of Canada Consolidated Balance Sheet as at December 31, 2006 (millions of dollars)

Assets		Liabilities	
Treasury Bills of Canada	$18 120.7	Bank notes in circulation	$48 762.2
Other Government of Canada securities	30 184.9	Government of Canada deposits	2 228.1
Foreign currency deposits	3.1	Chartered bank deposits (reserves)	9.2
Advances to members of CPA	12.0	Other deposits	446.5
Other assets	3 304.8	Other liabilities and capital	179.5
Total assets	$51 625.5	Total liabilities	$51 625.5

SOURCE: BANK OF CANADA, ANNUAL REPORT 2006.

➤ **CONCEPTS IN BRIEF**

Learning Objective 14.1: Describe the structure of the Bank of Canada and its major functions.

⤿ The Bank of Canada is Canada's central bank. It is run by a Board of Directors from nonbanking occupations, as well as the Governor and Senior Deputy Governor of the Bank.

⤿ The only customers of the Bank of Canada are the federal government and the chartered banks. The chartered banks hold reserve deposits at the Bank of Canada as a precaution in case of heavy withdrawals and to facilitate cheque clearing.

⤿ The Canadian Payments Association handles cheque clearing for the financial community.

⤿ The Bank of Canada conducts monetary policy on behalf of the federal government, acts as a lender of last resort to the financial community, issues bank notes, and provides financial advice to the federal government.

14.2 The Money Supply and Tools of Monetary Policy

Monetary policy is one means of influencing the economy through regulating the money supply. This is done by changing the reserves in the banking system.

Why do we need a monetary policy? We need monetary policy to keep our economy growing at its potential. Too little money can hamper economic growth, and too much money can cause inflation. Canada's monetary policy is conducted by the Bank of Canada. Monetary policy is the most important function of the Bank of Canada and probably is the most actively used policy in macroeconomics. In general, the Bank of Canada faces one of two economic conditions: a recessionary gap or an inflationary gap in the economy.

If the Bank is confronted with a recessionary gap in the economy, it will pursue easy money, that is, expansionary policy. Intuitively, this suggests increasing the money supply and lowering interest rates so as to increase aggregate demand, increase employment (thereby reducing unemployment), and increase real economic output to its full-employment potential.

If the Bank is confronted with an inflationary gap in the economy, it will pursue tight money, that is, restrictive or contractionary policy. Intuitively, this suggests reducing the money supply and raising interest rates to cause excessive growth of aggregate demand to fall, thereby reducing GDP to close the inflationary gap.

In general, the Bank of Canada seeks to alter consumption, investment, and aggregate demand as a whole by altering the rate of growth of the money supply. To do this, the Bank of Canada uses these tools as part of its policy-making action: open market operations, drawdowns and redeposits, and setting the target for the overnight rate.

Open Market Operations

Open market operations are the purchase and sale of *existing* government securities in the open market (the private secondary Canadian securities market) by the Bank of Canada in order to change the money supply.

A Sample Transaction: Purchase of a $100 000 Canadian Government Security by the Bank of Canada

Assume that the Bank of Canada decides to purchase $100 000 worth of Canadian government securities. The Bank pays for these securities by writing a cheque on itself for $100 000. This cheque is given to the bond dealer in exchange for the $100 000 worth of bonds. The bond dealer deposits the $100 000 cheque in its chequing account at a bank, which then sends the $100 000 cheque back to the Bank of Canada. When the Bank of Canada receives the cheque, it adds $100 000 to the reserve account of the bank that sent it the cheque. The Bank of Canada has created $100 000 of reserves. It can create reserves because it has the ability to "write up" (add to) the reserve accounts of the chartered banks whenever it buys Canadian securities. When the Bank of Canada buys a government security in the open market, it initially expands total reserves and the money supply by the amount of the purchase.

USING BALANCE SHEETS. Consider the balance sheets of the Bank of Canada and of a chartered bank receiving the cheque. Balance Sheet 14–1 shows the results for the Bank of Canada after the bond purchase and for the bank after the bond dealer deposits the $100 000 cheque. The Bank of Canada's balance sheet (which here reflects only account *changes*) shows that after the purchase, its assets have increased by $100 000 in the form of Canadian government securities. Liabilities have also increased by $100 000 in the form of an increase in the reserve account of the bank. The balance sheet for the chartered bank shows an increase in assets of $100 000 in the form of reserves with the Bank of Canada. The bank also has an increase in its liabilities in the form of $100 000 in the chequing account of the bond dealer; this is an immediate $100 000 increase in the money supply.

BALANCE SHEET 14–1

Balance sheets for the Bank of Canada and a chartered bank when a Canadian government security is purchased by the Bank of Canada, showing changes in assets and liabilities.

The Bank of Canada		Chartered Bank	
Assets	Liabilities	Assets	Liabilities
+$100 000 Canadian government securities	+$100 000 chartered bank's reserves	+$100 000 reserves	+$100 000 chequing deposit owned by bond dealer

Effect on the Money Supply

The initial increase of the money supply of $100 000, assuming a desired reserve ratio of 10 percent, requires desired reserves of $10 000, and generates new excess reserves of $90 000. For the sake of simplicity, ignore the previous assets and liabilities in the banking system and concentrate only on the balance sheet *changes* resulting from this new deposit, as shown in Balance Sheet 14–2. A plus sign indicates that the entry has increased, and a minus sign indicates that the entry has decreased.

BALANCE SHEET 14–2

Banking System

Assets			Liabilities	
Total reserves		+$100 000	New chequable deposits	+$100 000
Desired reserves	$10 000			
Excess reserves	90 000			
Total		+$100 000	Total	+$100 000

Of course, excess reserves are not income producing. Consequently, the banking system will reduce them to zero by making loans. Given a money multiplier of 10 in this example, the loans will be $900 000, which will earn interest income for the banks. The banks will have also created deposits for borrowers equal to $900 000. The money supply has therefore further increased by $900 000. This is shown in Balance Sheet 14–3. If the banks wish to increase loans to the general public, interest rates typically have to be reduced. The overall effect of this increase in the money supply and reduction in interest rates will be expansionary.

BALANCE SHEET 14-3

Banking System

Assets			Liabilities	
Total reserves		+$100 000	Chequable deposits	$ 100 000
Desired reserves	$100 000			+ 900 000
Excess reserves	0			
Loans		900 000		
Total		$1 000 000	Total	$1 000 000

Sale of a $100 000 Canadian Government Security by the Bank of Canada

The process is reversed when the Bank of Canada sells a Canadian government security from its portfolio. When the individual or institution buying the security from the Bank of Canada writes a cheque for $100 000, the Bank of Canada reduces the reserves of the chartered bank on which the cheque was written. The $100 000 sale of the Canadian government security leads to a reduction in reserves in the banking system.

Balance Sheet 14–4 shows the results for the sale of a Canadian government security by the Bank of Canada. When the $100 000 cheque goes to the Bank of Canada, it reduces by $100 000 the reserve account of the chartered bank on which the cheque is written. The Bank of Canada's assets are also reduced by $100 000 because it no longer owns the Canadian government security. The bank's liabilities are reduced by $100 000 when that amount is deducted from the account of the bond purchaser, and the money supply is thereby reduced by that amount. The chartered bank's assets are also reduced by $100 000 because the Bank of Canada has reduced its reserves by that amount.

As Balance Sheet 14–4 indicates, the reserves in the chartered banks decrease due to the sale of the securities. This implies a shortage of reserves and a reduction in lending. The scarcity of new loans will likely cause interest rates to increase. Bond purchases cause a contraction in the economy.

BALANCE SHEET 14-4

Balance sheets after the Bank of Canada has sold $100 000 of Canadian government securities, showing changes only.

The Bank of Canada		Chartered Bank	
Assets	Liabilities	Assets	Liabilities
-$100 000 Canadian government securities	-$100 000 chartered bank's reserves	-$100 000 reserves	-$100 000 chequing deposit owned by bond dealer

Drawdowns and Redeposits

Drawdown A movement of Government of Canada deposits from the accounts of the chartered banks held at the Bank of Canada into the Bank's own government accounts.

Redeposit A movement that occurs when the Bank of Canada moves government deposits into the accounts of the chartered banks, thus increasing their reserves.

The Bank of Canada changes the amount of reserves in the system through the use of *drawdowns* and *redeposits*. When the Bank of Canada conducts a **drawdown**, it moves Government of Canada deposits from the accounts of the chartered banks held at the Bank of Canada into the Bank's own government accounts. This has the effect of reducing the chartered banks' reserves, which induces the banks to call in loans to replenish their reserves. A drawdown has a contractionary effect on the money supply.

A **redeposit** occurs when the Bank of Canada moves government deposits into the accounts of the chartered banks, thus increasing their reserves. The banks then lend out their excess reserves, thereby increasing the money supply.

CONTRACTIONARY MONETARY POLICY: EFFECTS ON AGGREGATE DEMAND, THE PRICE LEVEL, AND REAL GDP. When the Bank of Canada engages in contractionary monetary policy, it conducts drawdowns. Remember that when it does so, the chartered banks will call in loans. There will be fewer reserves available for the chartered banks to lend out. The way they ration available money among potential borrowers is by raising the rate of interest they charge on loans. Some borrowers, deeming the new rate too high, will eliminate themselves from the market. Consequently, some borrowers who otherwise would have borrowed in order to spend no longer will do so at the higher rate of interest.

EXPANSIONARY MONETARY POLICY: EFFECT OF A REDEPOSIT. The Bank of Canada engages in expansionary monetary policy by conducting redeposits. Remember that a redeposit transfers Government of Canada deposits to the accounts of the chartered banks at the Bank of Canada. The chartered banks now have more reserves. Flush with excess reserves, the banks seek ways to lend them out. To induce customers to borrow more, the banks will cut interest rates even further. People who thought they were not going to be able to buy a new car, house, or whatever now find themselves able to do so. Their spending rises.

Target for the Overnight Rate

Target for the overnight rate The Bank of Canada's official interest rate (or key policy rate); it is the midpoint of the Bank's operating band for overnight financing.

Bank Rate The upper limit of the overnight operating interest rate band.

The main tool or choice of policy instrument used by the Bank of Canada (as is the choice made by most other major central banks) is to determine a target rate of short-term interest for the economy called the *target for the overnight rate*. The **target for the overnight rate** is the Bank of Canada's official interest rate (or key policy rate); it is the midpoint of the Bank's operating band for overnight financing. The band is 50-basis points (one-half of a percentage point) wide and it has the target for the overnight rate at its centre. For example, if the Bank's target rate is 4 percent, then the operating band would be from 3.75 percent to 4.25 percent. The official rate was formerly called the **Bank Rate**, which is the upper limit of the overnight operating interest rate band.

The target of the overnight rate signals to the major financial institutions the average interest rate the Bank of Canada is looking to see in the overnight marketplace. Changes in interest rates influence investors, as discussed in Example 14-2.

EXAMPLE 14-2 **Determining the Price of Bonds**

A bond is an IOU from a government or a corporation that states how much it owes you (the principal) and how much interest will be paid to you for lending it money (also called the yield). Determining the selling price of a bond depends on how much those payments are worth and on an assessment of the risk associated with the likelihood that the promised interest payments and principal repayment will occur. For example, if the company is on the verge of bankruptcy, the bond is likely not worth much. Such *risk* is important in determining the price of a bond.

The second factor in determining the price of a bond is the prevailing interest rate in the economy. There is an inverse relationship between the price of existing bonds and the rate of interest. Assume that the average yield on bonds is 5 percent. You decide to purchase a bond. A local corporation agrees to sell you a bond that will pay you $50 a year forever. What is the price you are willing to pay for it? $1000. Why? Because $50 divided by $1000 equals 5 percent. You purchase the bond. The next year something happens in the economy. For whatever reason, you can go out and obtain bonds that have effective yields of 10 percent. That is to say, the prevailing interest rate in the economy is now 10 percent. What has happened to the market price of the existing bond that you own, the one you purchased the year before? It will have fallen. If you try to sell it for $1000, you will discover that no investors will buy it from you. Why should they when they can obtain $50 a year from someone else by paying only $500? Indeed, unless you offer your bond for sale at a price

continued

of $500, no buyers will be forthcoming. Hence, an increase in the prevailing interest rate in the economy has caused the market value of your existing bond to fall.

The important point to understand is this:

The market price of existing bonds (and all fixed-income assets) is inversely related to the rate of interest prevailing in the economy.

For critical analysis: If the Bank of Canada were about to initiate an easy money policy or an expansionary monetary policy, how would this affect your assessment of an investment in a long-term bond?

Large value transfer system The electronic system through which large transactions are cleared and settled.

On a daily basis Canada's major financial institutions borrow and lend money among themselves overnight to cover their transactions during the past day. Through the **large value transfer system** (LVTS)—the electronic system through which large transactions are cleared and settled— financial institutions execute transactions with each other. At the end of the day, these transactions are reconciled, and one bank may have excess funds, while another may need money. The lending and borrowing of funds that allows all the financial institutions to cover their transactions is called the overnight market. The interest rate charged on those loans is called the overnight rate.

Since the *Bank Act* amendments of 1992, when required reserves were phased out, the banks now hold tiny reserves relative to their deposits. The reason they can do this is because the Bank of Canada stands ready to lend reserves to them to ensure that they can always meet any depositor's demands for currency. The Bank Rate, the upper limit of the overnight operating band, is the rate of interest that the Bank of Canada charges any chartered bank for any reserves that it lends. The Bank of Canada also pays interest on chartered bank deposits at the bottom limit of the overnight rate band. Because of these borrowing and lending rates, there is no reason for the banks to trade funds at rates outside the overnight operating band.

The important role of the target for the overnight rate is to communicate changes in monetary policy by announcing changes in the target for the overnight rate. A change in the target usually affects other interest rates, including mortgage rates and prime rates at the commercial banks. When the Bank of Canada wants to signal its intent to pursue tight money (contractionary monetary policy), it will increase the target for the overnight rate. Private sector interest rates will typically increase in response to the change in the official rate. If the Bank of Canada implements easy money (expansionary monetary policy), the target for the overnight rate will be lowered, prompting decreases in private sector interest rates. When the Bank chooses the target for the overnight rate, it sets the rate at a level that is consistent with keeping inflation low, stable, and predictable while maintaining a climate for sustainable growth, investment, and jobs.

The target for the overnight rate is Canada's official central bank interest rate. It is comparable with the U.S. Federal Reserve's target for the federal funds rate, the Bank of England's two-week "repo rate" and the European Central Bank's "repo rate." Refer to Policy Example 14–1 for a discussion of how the Bank of Canada's official key policy rate is announced.

| POLICY EXAMPLE 14-1 | **The Determination of the Target for the Overnight Rate** |

Bank of Canada releases dates for announcing target for the overnight rate actions

OTTAWA—The Bank of Canada on October 30, 2000, made public the dates through the year 2001 on which it will announce any changes to the official interest rate it uses to implement monetary policy. Last month, the Bank outlined its plan to adopt a new system of

continued

preset or "fixed" dates for announcing changes, which will replace the previous approach under which it could announce an adjustment on any business day in the year.

In releasing the dates, the Bank also confirmed that interest rate announcements will be made on Tuesdays at 9 a.m. (ET) eight times a year and announcement dates will be integrated with the Bank's other key monetary policy publications throughout the year to provide a more regular, frequent, and continuous process of public communication on monetary policy. The Bank would still have the option of acting between fixed dates but would exercise this option only in extraordinary circumstances.

Bank Governor Gordon Thiessen said: "I am confident that the Bank's decision to implement preset announcement dates for changes will contribute to the improved functioning of financial markets, better public understanding of the factors affecting the Bank's decisions on interest rates, and more effective Canadian monetary policy."

An announcement on each fixed date

At 9 a.m. on each announcement date, the Bank will issue a press release indicating its decision either to change the target for the overnight rate or to leave it unchanged, together with a short explanation of the factors influencing the decision and the Bank's view of the risks in the period ahead.

For critical analysis: Why has the Bank of Canada chosen preset or "fixed" dates for announcing changes to the target for the overnight rate?

The Supply of Money Curve

The Bank of Canada can direct the money supply by engaging in open market operations by buying and selling Government of Canada securities, by transferring Government of Canada deposits to and from the chartered banks, by setting the Bank Rate, and by setting the target for the overnight rate. If the monetary authorities and the financial institutions have provided the economy with a particular quantity of money, then the money supply is a vertical line relative to interest rates. In other words, at any given point in time, the money supply is fixed by the tools of monetary policy, regardless of interest rates, as in Figure 14–2.

14.3 The Demand for Money

By definition, monetary policy has to do, in the main, with money. But what is so special about money? Money is the product of a "social contract" in which we all agree to do two things:

1. Express all prices in terms of a common unit of account, which in Canada we call the dollar.
2. Use a specific medium of exchange for market transactions.

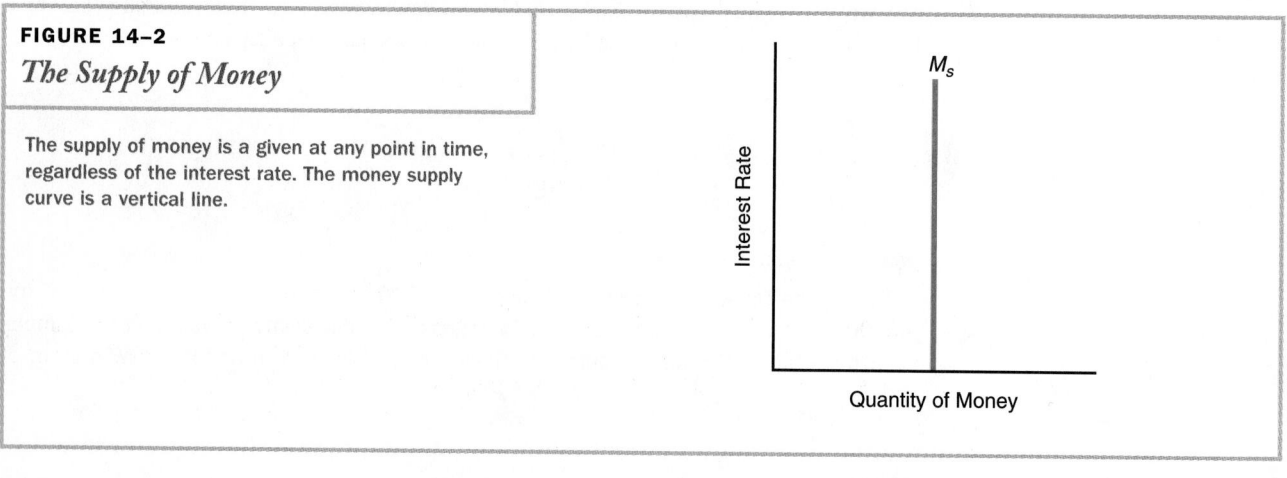

FIGURE 14–2

The Supply of Money

The supply of money is a given at any point in time, regardless of the interest rate. The money supply curve is a vertical line.

These two features of money distinguish it from all other goods in the economy. As a practical matter, money is involved on one side of every nonbarter transaction in the economy—and trillions of them occur every year. What this means is that something that changes the amount of money in circulation will have some effect on many transactions and thus on elements of GDP. If something affects the number of snowmobiles in existence, probably only the snowmobile market will be altered. But something that affects the amount of money in existence is going to affect *all* markets.

Holding Money

All of us engage in a flow of transactions. We buy and sell things all of our lives. But because we use money—dollars—as our medium of exchange, all *flows* of nonbarter transactions involve a *stock* of money. We can restate this as follows:

> To use money, one must hold money.

Given that everybody must hold money, we can now talk about the *demand* to hold it. People do not demand to hold money just to look at pictures of past prime ministers. They hold it to be able to use it to buy goods and services.

The Demand for Money: What People Wish to Hold

People have a certain motivation that makes them want to hold money balances. Individuals and firms could try to have zero non–interest-bearing money balances. But life is inconvenient without a ready supply of money balances. There is a demand for money by the public, motivated by several factors.

THE TRANSACTIONS DEMAND. The main reason people hold money is that money can be used to purchase goods and services. People are paid at specific intervals (once a week, once a month, and so on), but they wish to make purchases more or less continuously. To free themselves from making expenditures on goods and services only on payday, people find it beneficial to hold money. The benefit they receive is convenience: They willingly forgo interest earnings in order to avoid the inconvenience and expense of cashing in such nonmoney assets as bonds every time they wish to make a purchase.

Transactions demand Holding money to make regular, *expected* expenditures.

Thus, people hold money to make regular, *expected* expenditures under the **transactions demand**. As national income rises, the community will want to hold more money. Suppose that national income rises due exclusively to price level increases. If people are making the same volume of physical purchases but the goods and services cost more due to higher prices, people will want to hold more money.

Precautionary demand Holding money to make *unexpected* purchases or to meet emergencies.

THE PRECAUTIONARY DEMAND. The transactions demand involves money held to make *expected* expenditures; people hold money for the **precautionary demand** to make *unexpected* purchases or to meet emergencies. It is not unreasonable to maintain that as the price level or real national income rises, people will want to hold more money. In effect, when people hold money for the precautionary demand, they incur a cost in forgone interest earnings that is offset by the benefit that the precautionary balance provides. Nonetheless, the higher the rate of interest, the lower are the money balances people wish to hold for the precautionary demand.

Asset demand Holding money as a store of value.

THE ASSET DEMAND. Remember that one of the functions of money is as a store of value. People can hold money balances as a store of value, or they can hold bonds or shares or other interest-earning assets. The desire to hold money as a store of value leads to the **asset demand** for money. People choose to hold money, rather than other assets, for two reasons: its liquidity and the lack of risk. Moreover, if deflation is expected, holding money balances makes sense.

The disadvantage of holding money balances as an asset, of course, is the interest earnings forgone. Each individual or business decides how much money to hold as an asset by looking at the opportunity cost of holding money. The higher the interest rate—which is our proxy for the opportunity cost of holding money—the lower the money balances people will want to hold as assets. Conversely, the lower the interest rate offered on alternative assets, the higher the money balances people will want to hold as assets.

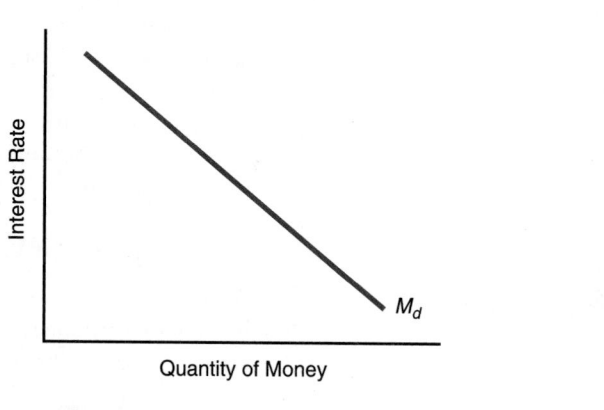

FIGURE 14–3

The Demand for Money Curve

If we use the interest rate as a proxy for the opportunity cost of holding money balances, the demand for money curve, M_d, is downward sloping, similar to other demand curves.

The Demand for Money Curve

Assume that the transactions demand for money is fixed, given a certain level of income. That leaves the precautionary and asset demands for money, both determined by the opportunity cost of holding money. If we assume that the interest rate represents the cost of holding money balances, we can graph the relationship between the interest rate and the quantity of money demanded. In Figure 14–3, the demand for money curve shows a familiar downward slope. The horizontal axis measures the quantity of money demanded, and the vertical axis is the interest rate. In this sense, the interest rate is the price of holding money. At a higher price, a lower quantity of money is demanded and vice versa.

Imagine two scenarios. In the first one, you can earn 20 percent a year if you put your cash into purchases of government securities. In the other scenario, you can earn 1 percent if you put your cash into purchases of government securities. If you have $1000 average cash balances in a non–interest-bearing chequing account, in the second scenario over a one-year period, your opportunity cost would be 1 percent of $1000, or $10. In the first scenario, your opportunity cost would be 20 percent of $1000, or $200. Under which scenario would you hold more cash?

The interest rate used here is the real interest rate. Nominal interest rates vary depending on the rate of inflation, as discussed in Example 14–3.

EXAMPLE 14-3   **The Choice between Cash and Savings Accounts in Colombia**

In countries with high inflation rates, nominal interest rates are also high. Remember that the nominal interest rate equals the real interest rate plus the expected rate of inflation. Colombia is one country that has consistently high rates of inflation. Consequently, its depository institutions usually offer high nominal interest rates to attract people's cash. In Ciudad Bolívar, about an hour from Bogotá, the *Caja Social de Ahorros* (Social Savings Bank) services a low-income area of about a million people. This depository institution was started by a Jesuit priest and continues to be overseen by a board of directors appointed by the Jesuits. On passbook savings accounts, it pays 19 percent. This sounds high, but not compared with Colombia's 22 percent annual inflation. Thus, its 10 000 depositors are willing to accept a *negative* real rate of interest of 3 percent. Why? In the first place, if they kept their cash as cash, they would suffer a 22 percent reduction in purchasing power every year. In the second place, the *Caja Social* keeps its low-income clients' money safe in a high-crime area.

For critical analysis: Why are nominal interest rates higher when a country experiences inflation?

➡→ CONCEPTS IN BRIEF

Learning Objective 14.2: Discuss how the Bank of Canada conducts monetary policy.

- Monetary policy is one means of influencing the economy through regulating the money supply.
- The tools of monetary policy are open market operations, drawdowns and redeposits, and setting the target for the overnight rate. The Bank of Canada can directly increase chartered banks' reserves by purchasing Canadian government securities in the open market; the result is a multiple expansion of deposits and, therefore, of the money supply.
- The Bank of Canada can decrease chartered banks' reserves by selling Canadian government securities in the open market; the result is a multiple contraction of deposits and therefore of the money supply.
- The Bank of Canada can affect the money supply by moving Government of Canada deposits either to (redeposits) or from (drawdowns) the accounts of the chartered banks.
- The Bank of Canada can signal either a tight or an easy money policy in the changes it makes to the target for the overnight rate.
- The money supply at a point in time is a vertical curve.

Learning Objective 14.3: Identify the factors that influence people's demand for money.

- To use money, people must hold money. Therefore, they have a demand for money balances.
- The determinants of the demand for money balances are the transactions demand, the precautionary demand, and the asset demand.
- Because holding money carries with it an opportunity cost—the interest income forgone—the demand for money curve showing the relationship between money balances and the interest rate slopes downward.

14.4 Monetary Policy in Action: The Transmission Mechanism

Monetary policy, regulating the money supply, has both indirect and direct effects. The indirect effect occurs due to a change in interest rates. In the case of expansionary monetary policy, lower interest rates induce people and businesses to spend more than they otherwise would have spent. The direct effect is simply that an increase in the money supply causes people to have excess money balances. To get rid of these excess money balances, they increase expenditures.

The Keynesian Transmission Mechanism

One school of economists believes that the indirect effect of monetary policy is the more important. This group, typically called Keynesian because of its belief in Keynes' work, asserts that the main effect of monetary policy occurs through changes in the interest rate. The Keynesian money transmission mechanism is shown in Figure 14–4. There, you see that the money supply changes the interest rate, which, in turn, changes the desired rate of investment. This transmission mechanism can be seen explicitly in Figure 14–5. In part (a), you see that an increase in the money supply reduces the interest rate. This reduction in the interest rate causes desired investment expenditures to increase from I_1 to I_2 in part (b). This increase in investment shifts aggregate demand outward from AD_1 to AD_2 in part (c).

Monetary Policy, Inflation, and Monetarists

Most theories of inflation relate to the short run. The price index in the short run can fluctuate because of such events as oil price shocks, labour union strikes, or discoveries

FIGURE 14–4

The Keynesian Money Transmission Mechanism

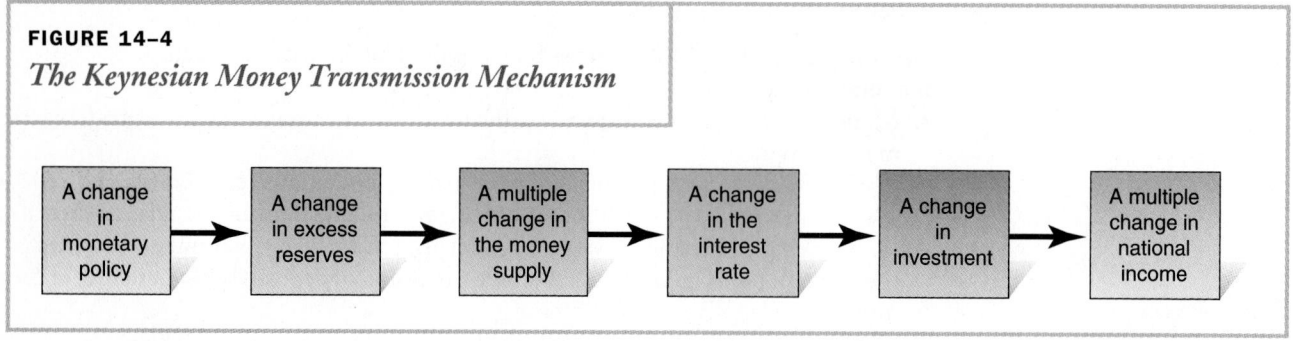

FIGURE 14–5

Adding Monetary Policy to the Keynesian Model

In part (a), we show a demand for money function, M_d. It slopes downward to show that at lower rates of interest, a larger quantity of money will be demanded. The money supply is given initially as M_s—the equilibrium rate of interest will be r_1. At this rate of interest, we see from the planned investment schedule given in part (b) that the quantity of planned investment demanded per year will be I_1. After the shift in the money supply to M'_s the resulting increase in investment from I_1 to I_2 shifts the aggregate demand curve in part (c) outward from AD_1 to AD_2. Equilibrium moves from E_1 to E_2, at $700 billion real GDP per year.

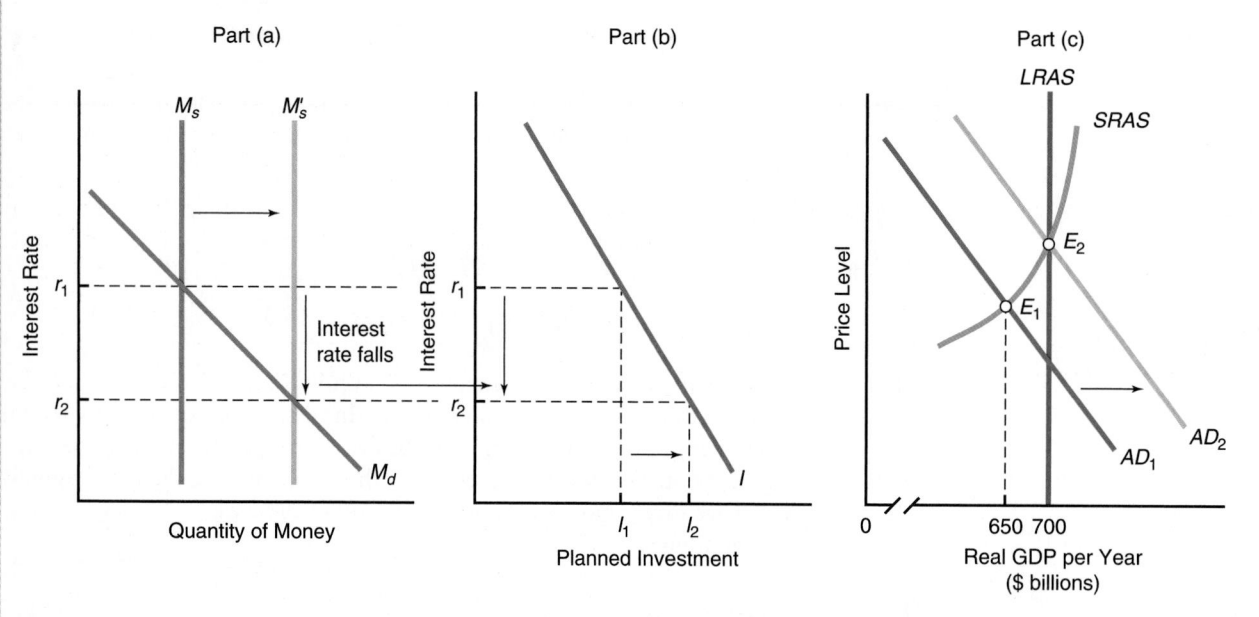

of large amounts of new natural resources. In the long run, however, empirical studies show a relatively stable relationship between excessive growth in the money supply and inflation.

Simple supply and demand can explain why the price level rises when the money supply is increased. Suppose that a major oil discovery is made, and the supply of oil increases dramatically relative to the demand for oil. The relative price of oil will fall; now it will take more units of oil to exchange for specific quantities of nonoil products. Similarly, if the supply of money rises relative to the demand for money, it will take more units of money to purchase specific quantities of goods and services. That is merely another way of stating that the price level has increased or that the purchasing power of money has fallen. In fact, the classical economists referred to inflation as a situation in which more money is chasing the same quantity of goods and services.

The Equation of Exchange and the Quantity Theory

Equation of exchange The formula indicating that the number of monetary units times the number of times each unit is spent on final goods and services is identical to the price level times output (or nominal national income).

A simple way to show the relationship between changes in the quantity of money in circulation and the price level is through the **equation of exchange**—the formula indicating that the number of monetary units times the number of times each unit is spent on final goods and services is identical to the price level times output (or nominal national income)—developed by Irving Fisher:

$$M_sV = PQ$$

where

M_s = actual money balances held by the nonbanking public
V = **income velocity of money**, or the number of times, on average, each monetary unit is spent on final goods and services
P = price level or price index
Q = real national output (real GDP)

Income velocity of money The number of times, on average, each monetary unit is spent on final goods and services.

Consider a numerical example involving a one-commodity economy. Assume that in this economy the total money supply, M_s, is $100; the quantity of output, Q, is 50 units of a good; and the average price, P, of this output is $10 per unit. Using the equation of exchange,

$$M_sV = PQ$$

$$\$100V = \$10 \times 50$$

$$\$100V = \$500$$

$$V = 5$$

Thus, each dollar is spent an average of five times a year.

THE EQUATION OF EXCHANGE AS AN IDENTITY.   The equation of exchange must always be true—it is an *accounting identity*. The equation of exchange states that the total of money spent on final output, M_sV, is equal to the total amount of money *received* for final output, PQ. Thus, a given flow of money can be seen from either the buyers' side or the producers' side. The value of goods purchased is equal to the value of goods sold. If Q represents real national output and P is the price level, PQ equals the dollar value of national output, or nominal national income. Thus,

$$M_sV = PQ = Y$$

THE CRUDE QUANTITY THEORY OF MONEY AND PRICES.   If we now make some assumptions about different variables in the equation of exchange, we come up with the simplified theory of why prices change, called the **crude quantity theory of money and prices**—the belief that changes in the money supply lead to proportional changes in the price level. If you assume that the velocity of money, V, is constant and that real national output, Q, is fixed, the simple equation of exchange tells you that a change in the money supply can lead only to a proportionate change in the price level. Continue with our numerical example. Q is 50 units of the good. V equals 5. If the money supply increases to 200, the only thing that can happen is that the price index, P, has to go up from 10 to 20. Otherwise the equation is no longer in balance.

Crude quantity theory of money and prices The belief that changes in the money supply lead to proportional changes in the price level.

EMPIRICAL VERIFICATION.   There is considerable evidence of the empirical validity of the relationship between excessive monetary growth and high rates of inflation. Look back at Figure 13–1 (page 340). There you see the loose correspondence between money supply growth and the rate of inflation in Canada from 1960 to the present. Examples 14–4 and 14–5 and Figure 14–6 show the relationship between inflation and money growth internationally.

EXAMPLE 14–4 ## Unfortunately for Germany, the Crude Quantity Theory Worked Very Well

Figure 14–6 shows that the crude quantity theory of money and prices provides a good fit for the experience of Germany during the early 1920s. As the quantity of money in circulation grew at an even-speedier rate, the price level also rose faster and faster. The dizzying pace of inflation that German residents experienced during these years is known as *hyperinflation*.

For critical analysis: Why does the crude quantity theory of money and prices prove especially useful for predicting inflation when the rate of growth of the money supply is very high?

FIGURE 14–6 *The Money Supply and Price Level in Germany in the Early 1920s*

Between early 1920 and late 1923, the German money supply and price level both grew extremely rapidly.

Source: National Bureau of Economic Research.

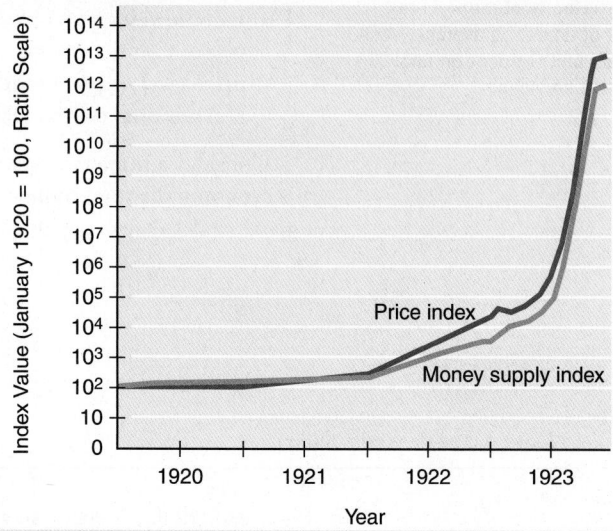

EXAMPLE 14–5 ## Inflation and Money Growth Throughout the World

Is there much evidence that the rate of inflation is closely linked to the rate of monetary growth? The answer seems to be that in the long run, there is a clear correlation between the two. Look at Figure 14–7. On the horizontal axis, in ratio form, is the rate of growth of

FIGURE 14–7 *The Relationship between Money Supply Growth Rates and Rates of Inflation*

If we plot rates of inflation and rates of monetary growth for different countries, we come up with a scatter diagram that reveals an obvious direct relationship. If you were to draw a line through the "average" of the points in this figure, it would be upward sloping, showing that an increase in the rate of growth of the money supply leads to an increase in the rate of inflation.

Sources: International Monetary Fund and national central banks. Data are for latest available periods.

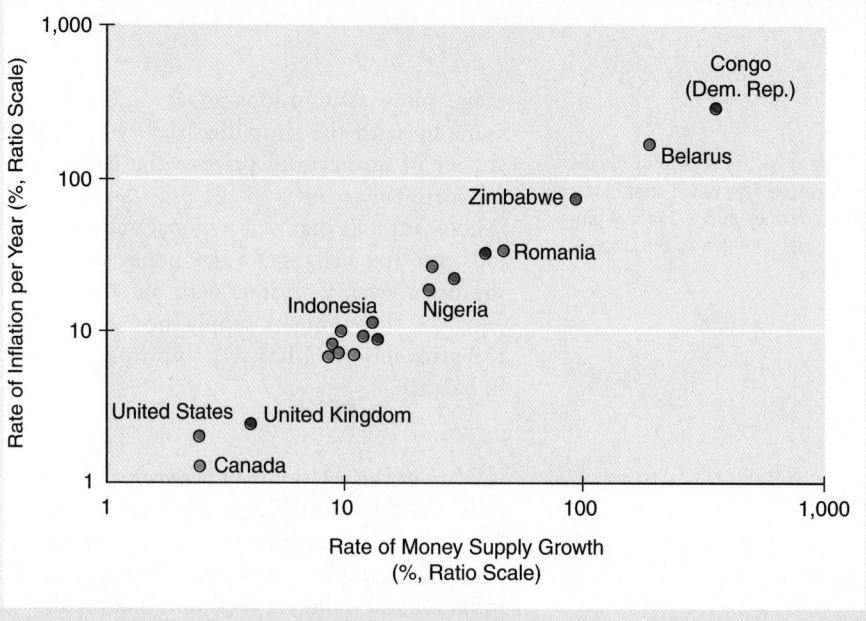

continued

the money supply. On the vertical axis is the annual rate of inflation (again, based on a ratio scale). As you can see, if you were to draw a line through the average of the points, it would slope upward: Faster monetary growth leads to a higher rate of inflation throughout different countries. This relationship appears to hold in Canada also. Decades of relatively high money supply growth are consistent with relatively higher rates of inflation and vice versa in Canada.

For critical analysis: Do the data shown in Figure 14–7 "prove" the crude quantity theory of money and prices?

Monetarists Economists who believe in a modern quantity theory of money and prices and contend that monetary policy works its way more directly into the economy.

THE MONETARISTS' VIEW OF MONEY SUPPLY CHANGES. **Monetarists,** economists who believe in a modern quantity theory of money and prices, contend that monetary policy works its way more directly into the economy. They believe that changes in the money supply lead to changes in nominal GDP in the same direction. An increase in the money supply because of expansionary open market operations (purchases of bonds) by the Bank of Canada, for example, leads the public to have larger money holdings than desired. This induces the public to buy more of everything, especially more of the durable goods, such as cars, stereos, and houses. If the economy is starting out at its long-run equilibrium rate of output, there can only be a short-run increase in real GDP. Ultimately, though, the public cannot buy more of everything; it simply bids up prices so that the price level rises. This pattern is displayed in Figure 14–8.

MONETARISTS' CRITICISM OF MONETARY POLICY. The monetarists' belief that monetary policy works through changes in desired spending does not mean that they consider such policy an appropriate government stabilization tool. According to the monetarists, although monetary policy can affect real GDP (and employment) in the short run, the length of time required before money supply changes take effect is so long and variable that such policy is difficult to conduct. For example, an expansionary monetary policy to counteract a contractionary gap may not take effect for a year and a half, by which time inflation may be a problem. At that point, the expansionary monetary policy will end up making current inflation worse. Monetarists therefore see monetary policy as a *destabilizing* force in the economy.

FIGURE 14–8

The Effects of Expansionary Monetary Policy

If we start with equilibrium at E_1, an increase in the money supply will cause the aggregate demand curve to shift to AD_2. There is an excess quantity of real goods and services demanded. The price level increases so that we move to E_2 at an output rate of $725 billion per year and a price level of 130. But input owners revise their expectations of prices upward, and $SRAS_1$ shifts to $SRAS_2$. The new long-run equilibrium is at E_3 at the long-run aggregate supply of $700 billion of real GDP per year and a price level of 135.

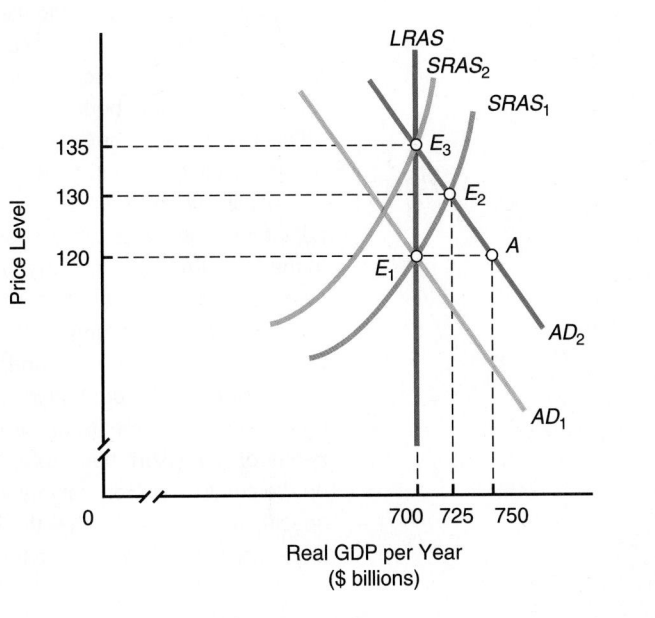

Monetary rule Increase the money supply *smoothly* at a rate consistent with the economy's long-run average growth rate.

According to the monetarists, therefore, policy makers should follow a **monetary rule**: Increase the money supply *smoothly* at a rate consistent with the economy's long-run average growth rate. *Smoothly* is an important word here. Increasing the money supply at 20 percent per year half the time and decreasing it at 17 percent per year the other half of the time would average out to about a 3 percent increase, but the results would be disastrous, say the monetarists. Instead of permitting the Bank of Canada to use its discretion in setting monetary policy, monetarists would force it to follow a rule such as "Increase the money supply smoothly at 3.5 percent per year" or "Abolish the Bank of Canada, and replace it with a computer program allowing for a steady rise in the money supply." A brief history of the evolution of the Bank of Canada's approach and its current approach appears in Policy Example 14–2. Figure 14–9 shows how the Bank of Canada has varied the overnight rate in the past decade.

POLICY EXAMPLE 14–2 **Monetary Policy: Where Are We Now?**

Gordon Thiessen, former Governor of the Bank of Canada, in a lecture at the University of Western Ontario in October 2000, reviewed monetary policy since 1935.

Monetary policy has come a long way since 1935. It is now directed toward a single long-run objective: the attainment and maintenance of price stability. Monetary authorities in Canada and elsewhere have realized that this is the best contribution that monetary policy can make to economic welfare and, indeed, the only one that they can deliver on an ongoing basis. There is no inherent conflict between price stability and most of the other objectives that are set out in the preamble to the *Bank of Canada Act*. Focusing on price stability helps us guard against the sorts of systematic errors that often occurred when we tried to aim directly at output and employment. Optimistic estimates of potential output and full employment in the early 1970s introduced a strong inflationary bias into the policy-formulation process and did not deliver any of the long-run improvements in the real economic performance that the Phillips-curve literature had promised.

Today's monetary policy differs from past approaches in yet another important way. It is conducted in a far more open and less complicated manner. Secrecy and surprise are no longer critical elements of our modus operandi. The Bank tries to work with markets, rather than against them, to avoid surprising them with unexpected actions. Greater transparency facilitates the policy-transmission process by conditioning market expectations and helps avoid unnecessary confusion about the reasons for our actions.

Various techniques for manipulating domestic credit conditions and the external value of the currency by means of direct controls, moral suasion, and active foreign exchange market intervention are no longer used. Globalization and market liberation have eliminated many of the barriers that used to separate different segments of the domestic financial system and have subjected them to increased international competition. As a result, these techniques became both less effective and more costly in terms of their impact on market efficiency. Monetary authorities now have a clearer understanding of the limitations of alternative policy measures, as well as more sympathy for indirect, market-based solutions.

Monetary policy is now implemented in a more straightforward manner. Today, policy adjustments are effected and signalled to the market mainly through announced changes in the Bank Rate and the target band for the overnight interest rate. Private agents are then free to determine how these changes will be transmitted through the rest of the financial system and the economy in general. The Bank simply issues a press release indicating what the new Bank Rate is, and this, in turn, anchors the short-term end of the yield curve.

Central bank independence and accountability have also been more clearly defined. [T]he 1967 amendments to the *Bank of Canada Act* allow the Minister of Finance, acting on behalf of the government, to issue a directive to the Governor if serious differences arise on the conduct of monetary policy that cannot be resolved. The directive must indicate the specific policy changes that the Bank is supposed to undertake. Ultimate responsibility for monetary policy, therefore, rests where it should in a democratic society—with the elected

continued

government. But, because of the consequences of issuing a directive, it is likely to be used only in unusual circumstances. Thus, a high degree of operational independence has, nevertheless, been preserved to allow the Bank to maintain its medium-term focus for monetary policy without the short-term pressures that arise in the political process.

Moreover, the explicit targets for inflation control in Canada have been set jointly by the Bank and the Minister of Finance. It is then the Bank's responsibility to achieve the agreed target. An explicit objective, a clear assignment of responsibility for achieving it, as well as the appropriate instrument and independence of action to do what is required to meet the objective, are crucial ingredients in an effective process of accountability. That is what we now have in place in Canada for monetary policy.[1]

A key part of the success over the past 15 years of the inflation-targeting system, an agreement that has been renewed through to the end of 2011, is that, according to David Dodge, Governor of the Bank of Canada, "the framework sets out a rather simple paradigm that allows people to understand and predict how the Bank will react to economic developments. If the economy is moving above the limits of its capacity, so that the trend of inflation is threatening to move above our target, we tend to raise interest rates, all other things being equal. This restrains demand in the economy and brings demand back into balance with supply, thus reducing inflationary pressures. Conversely, if the economy is moving below its capacity limits and the trend of inflation is likely to fall below the target, we tend to lower interest rates. This stimulates demand and brings it back in line with supply, thus increasing inflationary pressures. This simple paradigm is very helpful because monetary policy works better when it is understood."[2]

For critical analysis: What is the current goal of Bank of Canada monetary policy, and has it changed since 1935?

[1] Lecture by Gordon Thiessen, Governor of the Bank of Canada, to the Faculty of Social Science, University of Western Ontario, October 17, 2000. For a detailed exposition of the evolution of monetary policy at the Bank of Canada, go to "Can a Bank Change? The Evolution of Monetary Policy at the Bank of Canada, 1935–2000" at www.bankofcanada.ca/pdf/thiessen-eng-book.pdf.

[2] Remarks by David Dodge to the Canadian Netherlands Business and Professional Association and the European Union Chamber of Commerce in Toronto, January 25, 2007.

FIGURE 14–9

The Overnight Rate Target

The Bank of Canada sets a target for the overnight loans rate and then undertakes actions to keep the loans rate at the target. When the Bank wants to reduce inflation, it takes actions that raise the overnight rate target. When recession and low inflation are the concern, the Bank takes actions that lower the overnight rate target.

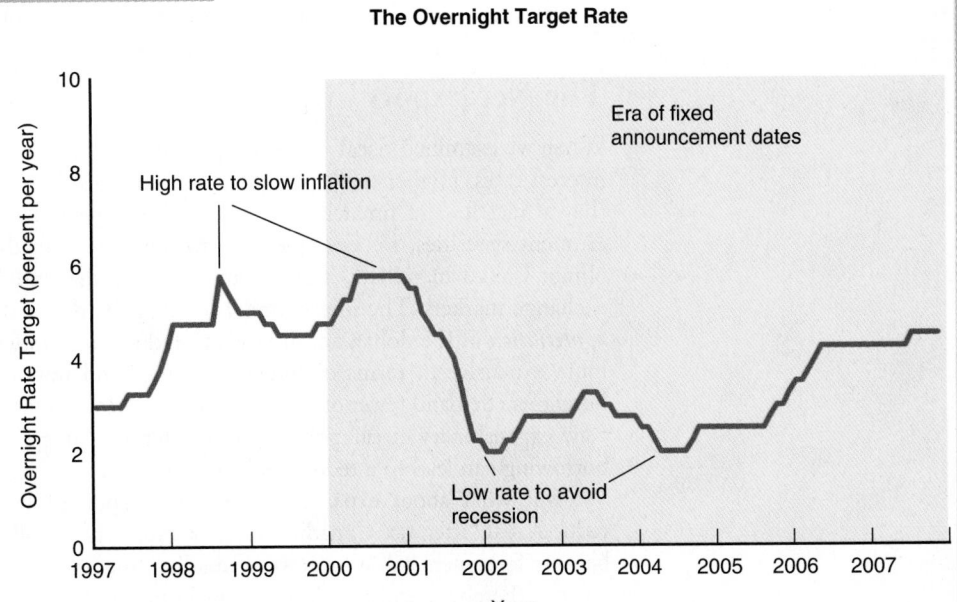

The Overnight Target Rate

➤➔ **CONCEPTS IN BRIEF**

Learning Objective 14.4: Explain two views of how monetary policy works.

- The indirect effect of an increase in the money supply works through a lowering of interest rates, which increases investment spending.
- The direct effect of an increase in the money supply arises because people desire to spend more on goods and services when they have excess money balances.
- In the Keynesian model, monetary transmission operates through a change in the interest rates, which changes investment, causing a multiple change in the equilibrium level of GDP.
- The equation of exchange states that the expenditures by some people will equal income receipts by others, or $M_sV = PQ$ (money supply times velocity equals nominal national income). Viewed as an accounting identity, the equation of exchange is always correct because the amount of money spent on final output must equal the total amount of money received for final output.
- The crude quantity theory of money and prices states that a change in the money supply will bring about an equi-proportional change in the price level.
- Monetarists believe that changes in the money supply lead to changes in nominal GDP in the same direction. The effect is both direct and indirect, however, as individuals spend their excess money balances on cars, stereos, houses, and a variety of many other things.
- Monetarists, among others, argue in favour of a monetary rule—increasing the money supply smoothly at a rate consistent with the economy's long-run average growth rate. Monetarists do not believe in discretionary monetary (or fiscal) policy.
- If we start out in long-run and short-run equilibrium, contractionary monetary policy first leads to a decrease in aggregate demand, resulting in a reduction in real GDP and in the price level. Eventually, though, the short-run aggregate supply curve shifts downward, and the new equilibrium is at *LRAS* but at an even lower price level. Expansionary monetary policy works the opposite way.

14.5 *Effectiveness of Monetary Policy*

So far, we have discussed monetary policy in a closed economy. When we move to an open economy, in which there is international trade and the international purchase and sale of all assets including dollars and other currencies, monetary policy becomes more complex. Consider first the effect on net exports of any type of monetary policy.

The Net Export Effect

When we examined fiscal policy, we pointed out that deficit financing can lead to higher interest rates. Higher (real, after-tax) interest rates do something in the foreign sector—they attract foreign financial investment. More people want to purchase Canadian government securities, for example. But to purchase Canadian assets, people first have to obtain Canadian dollars. This means that the demand for dollars goes up in foreign exchange markets. The international price of the dollar therefore rises. This is called an *appreciation* of the dollar, and it tends to reduce net exports because it makes our exports more expensive in terms of foreign currency and imports cheaper in terms of dollars. Foreigners demand fewer of our goods and services, and we demand more of theirs. In this way, expansionary fiscal policy that creates deficit spending financed by government borrowing can lead to a reduction in net exports.

But what about expansionary monetary policy? If expansionary monetary policy reduces real, after-tax Canadian interest rates, there will be a positive net export effect because foreigners will want fewer Canadian financial instruments, demanding fewer dollars and thereby causing the international price of the dollar to fall. This makes our exports cheaper for the rest of the world, which then demands a larger quantity of our exports. It also means that foreign goods and services are more expensive in Canada, and so we demand fewer imports. We come up with two conclusions:

1. Expansionary fiscal policy may cause international flows of financial capital (responding to interest rate *increases*) to offset its effectiveness to some extent. The net export effect is in the opposite direction of fiscal policy.
2. Expansionary monetary policy may cause interest rates to fall. Such a fall will induce international outflows of financial capital, thereby lowering the value of the dollar and making Canadian goods more attractive. The net export effect of expansionary monetary policy will be in the same direction as the monetary policy effect.

Now, assume that the economy is experiencing inflation and the Bank of Canada wants to use contractionary monetary policy. In so doing, it may cause interest rates to rise. Rising interest rates will cause financial capital to flow into Canada. The demand for dollars will increase, and their international price will go up. Foreign goods will now look cheaper to Canadians, and imports will rise. Because of the appreciation of the Canadian dollar, foreigners will not want our exports as much, and exports will fall. The result will be a deterioration in our international trade balance. Again, the international consequences reinforce the domestic consequences of monetary policy.

GLOBALIZATION OF INTERNATIONAL MONEY MARKETS. On a broader level, the Bank of Canada's ability to control the rate of growth of the money supply may be hampered as Canadian money markets become less isolated. With the push of a computer button, millions or even billions of dollars can change hands halfway around the world. In the world dollar market, the Bank of Canada finds an increasing number of dollars coming from *private* institutions. If the Bank of Canada reduces the growth of the money supply, individuals and firms in Canada can increasingly obtain dollars from other sources. People in Canada who want more liquidity can obtain their dollars from foreigners, or can even obtain foreign currencies and convert them into dollars in the world dollar market. Indeed, it is possible that as world markets become increasingly integrated, Canadian residents may someday conduct domestic transactions in *foreign* currencies.

Monetary Policy during Periods of Underutilized Resources

If the economy is operating at an equilibrium output level that is below that given by the long-run aggregate supply curve, monetary policy (like fiscal policy) can generate increases in the equilibrium level of real GDP per year up to a long-run equilibrium on *LRAS*. In Figure 14–10, you see initial aggregate demand as AD_1. It intersects *SRAS* at E_1, at an

FIGURE 14–10

Expansionary Monetary Policy with Underutilized Resources

If we start out with equilibrium at E_1, expansionary monetary policy will shift AD_1 to AD_2. The new equilibrium will be at E_2.

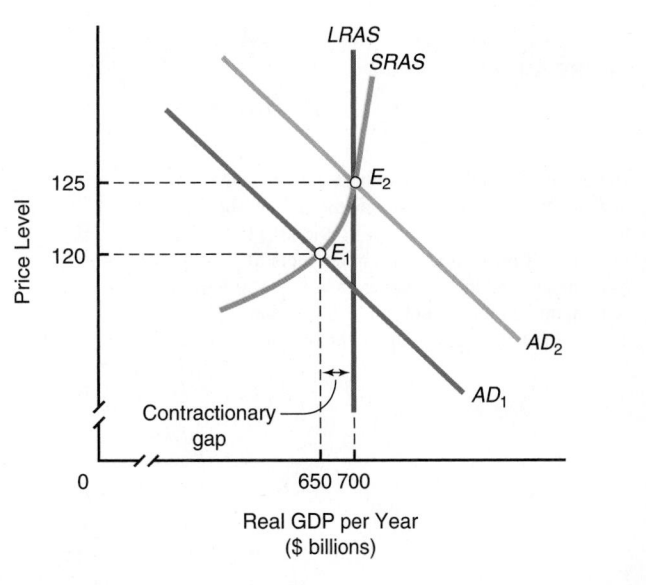

output rate of $650 billion of real GDP per year and a price level of 120. There is a contractionary gap of $50 billion. That is the difference between *LRAS* and the current equilibrium. The Bank of Canada can engage in expansionary monetary policy, the direct and indirect effects of which will cause AD_1 to shift to AD_2. The new equilibrium is at E_2, at an output rate of $700 billion of real GDP per year and a price level of 125. Note that expansionary monetary policy gets the economy to its *LRAS* sooner than otherwise.

Bank of Canada Target Choice: Interest Rates or Money Supply?

Money supply and interest rate targets cannot be pursued simultaneously. Interest rate targets force the Bank of Canada to abandon control over the money supply; money stock growth targets force it to allow interest rates to fluctuate.

Figure 14–11 shows the relationship between the total demand for money and the supply of money. Note that in the short run (in the sense that nominal national income is fixed), the demand for money is constant; short-run money supply changes leave the demand for money curve unaltered. In the short run, the Bank of Canada can choose either a particular interest rate (r_e or r_1) or a particular money supply (M_s or M'_s).

If the Bank of Canada wants interest rate r_e, it must select money supply M_s; if it desires a lower interest rate in the short run, it must increase the money supply. Thus, by targeting an interest rate, the Bank of Canada must relinquish control of the money supply. Conversely, if it wants to target the money supply at, say, M'_s, it must allow the interest rate to fall to r_1.

Consider now the case in which the Bank of Canada wants to maintain the present level of interest rates. If actual market interest rates in the future rise persistently above the present (desired) rates, it will be continuously forced to increase the money supply. The initial increase in the money supply will only temporarily lower interest rates. The increased money stock eventually will induce inflation, and inflationary premiums will be included in nominal interest rates. To pursue its low-interest-rate policy, the Bank of Canada must *again* increase the money stock because interest rates are still rising. Note that to attempt to maintain an interest rate target (stable interest rates), the Bank of Canada must abandon an independent money stock target. Symmetrical reasoning indicates that by setting growth rate targets at M_s or M'_s, the Bank of Canada must allow short-run fluctuations in interest rates when the economy experiences a contraction or an expansion.

But which should the Bank of Canada target, interest rates or monetary aggregates? (And which interest rate, or which money stock?) It is generally agreed that the answer

---

FIGURE 14–11

Choosing a Monetary Policy Target

The Bank of Canada, in the short run, can select an interest rate or a money supply target, but not both. It cannot, for example, choose r_e and M'_s; if it selects r_e, it must accept M_s; if it selects M'_s, it must allow the interest rate to fall to r_1. The Bank of Canada can obtain point *A* or *B*. It cannot get to point *C* or *D*. It must therefore choose one target or the other.

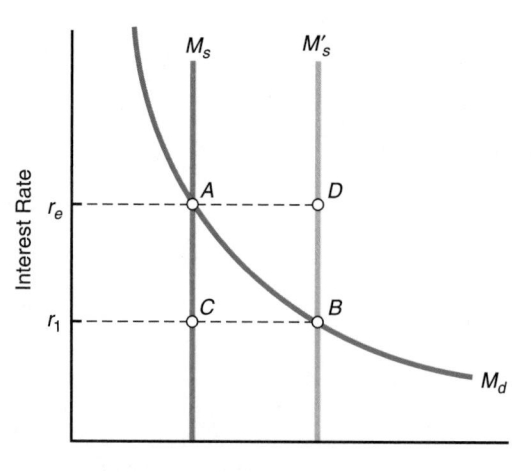

Quantity of Money Supplied and Demanded

depends on the source of instability in the economy. If the source of instability is variations in private or public spending, monetary aggregate (money supply) targets should be set and pursued. However, if the source of instability is an unstable demand for (or perhaps supply of) money, interest rate targets are preferred.

THE MONETARY CONDITIONS INDEX. From the early 1990s, the Bank of Canada has used the Monetary Conditions Index (MCI) as a rough measure of how tight monetary conditions in the economy are. The MCI is a weighted index made up of changes in short-term interest rates and changes in the foreign exchange value of the Canadian dollar.

The stated aim of the Bank of Canada is price stability. For 15 years the Bank of Canada has successfully adopted an inflation-targeting framework to keep inflation at 2 percent, the midpoint of the 1 to 3 percent inflation-control target. This inflation targeting has been renewed by agreement with the Government of Canada to 2011. We have seen that a decrease in interest rates or depreciation in the value of the Canadian dollar will stimulate aggregate demand, leading to possible price increases although these increases take some time to occur due to lags in the economy. The Bank, however, can forecast future price increases through movements in the MCI.

For example, if the foreign exchange value of the Canadian dollar fell consistently over a number of weeks, dragging the MCI down, there might be a risk of inflation recurring due to the net export effect. The Bank would estimate the seriousness of the risk and act either to raise interest rates or to support the dollar, which should ensure price stability. Conversely, if the Canadian dollar was appreciating, this could lead to a dampening of aggregate demand and falling prices. The Bank could intervene to ease monetary conditions by increasing the money supply, thus reducing interest rates.

To add to the complexity of choosing a target, other events in the Canadian (or world) economy may force the Bank of Canada to pursue a policy it does not necessarily like, as shown in Policy Example 14–3.

POLICY EXAMPLE 14-3 | **Political Uncertainty and Monetary Targeting**

In October 1995, the government of Quebec held a referendum asking Quebeckers if they wished to separate from Canada, thus creating their own nation. Leading up to the referendum there was much speculation about how the vote would turn out and what the consequences of a "Yes" vote would be.

At the same time, Canada's economy was not growing quickly, inflation was relatively low, and unemployment was relatively high. The preferred monetary policy would be one of interest rate reductions to allow spending to pick up.

However, with the uncertainty in Quebec, the Bank of Canada held interest rates high to keep foreign capital from leaving Canada. What was happening, in fact, was that the Bank of Canada was forced to add a risk premium to its bank rate due to the political uncertainty.

But Quebeckers voted "No." The "No" vote allowed the Bank of Canada to reduce interest rates over the course of 1996, which, in turn, led to some easing of the unemployment rate.

For critical analysis: What would have happened to interest rates if Quebeckers had voted "Yes"?

Other Considerations

The magnitude of expansionary and contractionary monetary policy is affected by the shapes or elasticity of the money-demand and the investment-demand curves. The steeper or more inelastic the M_d curve the larger the impact of any change in the money supply on the equilibrium interest rate. Moreover, changes in the interest rates will have a larger effect on investment spending and equilibrium GDP, if the investment-demand curve is flatter or more elastic. Monetary policy is most effective with a relatively inelastic money-demand curve and a relatively elastic investment-demand curve.

Another advantage of monetary policy is that it can be quickly altered. Compared with fiscal policy, which is forged in the political forum of Parliament, the Bank of Canada can and does buy and sell securities on a daily basis.

Finally, the Governor and Deputy Governor of the Bank of Canada are appointed for seven-year terms and can be removed only by an act of Parliament. Thus, the Bank of Canada can take a longer-term view of the national economy. Furthermore, because monetary policy works subtly and with time lags, it is usually more politically acceptable.

➤→ **CONCEPTS IN BRIEF**

Learning Objective 14.5: Assess the effectiveness of monetary policy.

- ◆ Monetary policy in an open economy has repercussions for net exports.
- ◆ If expansionary monetary policy reduces Canadian interest rates, there is a positive net export effect because foreigners will demand fewer Canadian financial instruments, thereby demanding fewer dollars and hence causing the international price of the dollar to fall. This makes our exports cheaper for the rest of the world.
- ◆ Expansionary monetary policy during periods of underutilized resources can cause the equilibrium level of real GDP to increase (sooner than it otherwise would) to the rate of real output consistent with the vertical long-run aggregate supply curve.
- ◆ The Bank of Canada can choose to stabilize interest rates or to change the money supply, but not both.
- ◆ Monetary policy is most effective with a relatively inelastic money-demand curve and a relatively elastic investment-demand curve.
- ◆ Two other advantages of monetary policy are its speed and flexibility and its relative isolation from political pressures.

➤→ **ISSUES AND APPLICATIONS**

Is the Bank of Canada Independent and, If Not, Does It Matter?

Concepts Applied: Monetary Policy, Inflation, Money Supply, Central Banking

The Bank of Canada manipulates the money supply as a way to control inflation. Evidence shows that central banks that are free of political pressure have more success in preventing inflation.

In principle, the Bank of Canada, although "owned" by the federal government, is an independent agency. Nonetheless, the prime minister appoints the directors for three-year terms, subject to cabinet approval. The prime minister also appoints the Governor of the Bank of Canada, again with cabinet approval, for a seven-year term. Given the obvious relationship between the government of the day and the Bank of Canada, is the Bank of Canada really an independent policy-making body?

What Does the Evidence Show?

The Bank of Canada was created with a view to keeping it free both of private interference and political pressure. Over the early years, it was understood that the Bank would conduct day-to-day monetary policy, but ultimately the federal government would bear responsibility for its actions.

During the late 1950s, the then-governor of the Bank of Canada was pursuing restrictive monetary policy in spite of relatively high unemployment and slow growth. The Ministers of Finance of first one government and then of a newly elected government declared that they would not take responsibility for the consequences of the Bank's policies. Academics also began to criticize the Bank, but its Governor, James Coyne, was resolute and did not change his course. Finally, the government moved to fire Coyne by introducing legislation in Parliament declaring a less restrictive monetary policy and a vacancy in the position of the Governor of the Bank of Canada. While Parliament passed the legislation, the Senate defeated it. Eventually, pressure was such that Coyne resigned. This event is now known as the *Coyne Affair*.

On taking office, the new Governor of the Bank of Canada, Louis Rasminsky, issued a statement that the Bank would be responsible for day-to-day conduct of monetary policy but that if the government issued a written directive for a change in course and if the Governor could not agree, the Governor would have to resign. To this day, no such directive has been issued.

Does Independence Matter?

Whether the Bank of Canada is more or less independent of the government is not just an academic issue. Rather, there is now evidence to show that a central bank's degree of independence over time influences a country's long-term rate of inflation. The evidence indicates that at least since the 1950s, greater central bank independence tends to lessen a nation's inflation rate during periods of high worldwide inflation.

A Case in Point: New Zealand

The government in New Zealand decided to give its central bank one job: keeping the price level stable. It passed the *Reserve Bank Act* of 1989, setting desired price stability at inflation rates of zero to 2 percent. Only if New Zealand's central bank fails to achieve these goals can its governor be fired. Consequently, New Zealand's central bank no longer has to concern itself with short-term ups and downs in GDP growth rates. So far, its new independence and explicit mission have seemed to work: In 1989, the CPI increased by 5.7 percent; today, that increase is running at less than 2.6 percent per year.

> ### For critical analysis:
> 1. Since the government is ultimately responsible for the conduct of monetary policy, is the Bank of Canada really independent?
> 2. What would you expect to see happen to New Zealand's net exports after enactment of the *Reserve Bank Act* of 1989?

➡ SUMMARY

Here is what you should know after reading this chapter. MyEconLab will help you identify what you know, and where to go when you need to practise. We suggest that as soon as you review one of the Learning Objective sections below, you then proceed to go through the related section in MyEconLab.

myeconlab

➡ LEARNING OBJECTIVES	KEY TERMS	MYECONLAB PRACTICE
14.1 Central Banks and the Bank of Canada. Our central bank is the Bank of Canada. Its governing body is the Board of Directors. The basic functions of the Bank of Canada are (a) conducting monetary policy, (b) acting as a lender of last resort, (c) issuing bank notes, and (d) advising the federal government on financial matters and acting as its fiscal agent.	Canadian Payments Association (CPA), 357	• **MyEconLab** Study Plan 14.1
14.2 The Money Supply and Tools of Monetary Policy. The Bank of Canada regulates the money supply using these tools of monetary policy: open market operations, drawdowns and redeposits, setting the target	open market operations, 360 drawdown, 361 redeposit, 361	• **MyEconLab** Study Plan 14.2

➡ LEARNING OBJECTIVES	KEY TERMS	MYECONLAB PRACTICE

for the overnight rate. In particular, the Bank of Canada can control the money supply through open market operations—by buying and selling Canadian government securities.
 	
    When the Bank of Canada buys a bond, it pays for the bond by writing a cheque on itself. This creates additional reserves for the banking system. The result will be an increase in the supply of money that is a multiple of the value of the bond purchased. If the Bank of Canada sells a bond, it reduces reserves in the banking system. The result will be a decrease in the money supply that is a multiple of the value of the bond sold. The Bank of Canada can signal changes in monetary policy by changing the target for the overnight rate. At any point in time, the money supply curve is a vertical curve.
	target for the
	    overnight rate, 362
	bank rate, 362
	large value transfer
	    system, 363	

14.3 Demand for Money. The determinants of the demand for money balance are the transactions demand, the precautionary demand, and the asset demand. Because holding money carries an opportunity cost—the interest income foregone—the demand for money curve showing the relationship between money balances and the interest rate slopes downward.	transactions demand,
	    365
	precautionary
	    demand, 365
	asset demand, 365
		• **MyEconLab** Study Plan 14.3

14.4 Monetary Policy in Action: The Transmission Mechanism. The direct effect of an increase in the money supply occurs through people desiring to spend more on real goods and services when they have excess money balances. The indirect effect of an increase in the money supply works through a lowering of the interest rate, thereby encouraging businesses to make new investments with the money loaned to them. Individuals will also engage in more consumption because of lower interest rates.
 	
    In the Keynesian model, monetary transmission operates through a change in the interest rates, which changes investment, causing a multiple change in the equilibrium level of GDP.
 	
    The equation of exchange states that the expenditures by some people will equal income receipts by others, or $M_s V = PQ$ (money supply times velocity equals nominal
	equation of
	    exchange, 369
	income velocity of
	    money, 369
	crude quantity theory
	    of money and
	    prices, 369
	monetarists, 371
	monetary rule, 372
		• **MyEconLab** Study Plan 14.4

➡ LEARNING OBJECTIVES	**KEY TERMS**	**MYECONLAB PRACTICE**

national income). Viewed as an accounting identity, the equation of exchange is always correct, because the amount of money spent on final output must equal the total amount of money received for final output. The crude quantity theory of money and prices states that a change in the money supply will bring about an equi-proportional change in the price level.

Monetarists believe that changes in the money supply lead to changes in nominal GDP in the same direction. The effect is both direct and indirect; however, as individuals spend their excess money balances on cars, stereos, houses, and a variety of many other things. Monetarists, among others, argue in favour of a monetary rule—increasing the money supply smoothly at a rate consistent with the economy's long-run average growth rate. Monetarists do not believe in discretionary monetary (or fiscal) policy.

If we start out in long-run and short-run equilibrium, contractionary monetary policy first leads to a decrease in aggregate demand, resulting in a reduction in real GDP and in the price level. Eventually, though, the short-run aggregate supply curve shifts downward, and the new equilibrium is at *LRAS* but at an even lower price level. Expansionary monetary policy works the opposite way.

14.5 Effectiveness of Monetary Policy. If expansionary monetary policy reduces Canadian interest rates, there is a positive net export effect because foreigners will demand fewer Canadian financial instruments, thereby demanding fewer dollars and hence causing the international price of the dollar to fall. This makes our exports cheaper for the rest of the world, and increases exports and decreases imports. Furthermore, expansionary monetary policy during periods of underutilized resources can cause the equilibrium level of real GDP to increase (sooner then it otherwise would) to the rate of real output consistent with the vertical long-run aggregate supply curve.

The Bank of Canada can choose to stabilize interest rates or to change the money supply, but not both.

• **MyEconLab** Study Plan 14.5

⇒→ PROBLEMS

(Answers to the odd-numbered problems appear at the back of the book.)

LO 14.1 Describe the structure of the Bank of Canada and its major functions.

1. What are the major functions of the Bank of Canada? Does Canadian Tire money, as discussed in Example 14–1, "Is Canadian Tire Money Real Money?", infringe on one of the major functions of the Bank of Canada?

LO14.2 Discuss how the Bank of Canada conducts monetary policy.

2. The Bank of Canada purchases a $1 million government security from Gulwinder Mann, who deposits the proceeds in Bank 1. Use balance sheets to show the immediate effects of this transaction on the Bank of Canada and on Bank 1.

3. Continuing the example from Problem 2:
   a. Indicate Bank 1's position more precisely if desired reserves equal 5 percent of chequable deposits.
   b. By how much can Bank 1 increase its lending?

4. Assume a 5 percent desired reserve ratio, zero excess reserves, no currency leakage, and a ready loan demand. The Bank of Canada buys a $1 million Treasury bill from a depository institution.
   a. What is the maximum money multiplier?
   b. By how much will total deposits rise?

5. Assume that the desired reserve ratio is 15 percent and that the Bank of Canada sells $3 million worth of government securities to a customer who pays with a cheque drawn on TD Canada Trust.
   a. The excess reserves of TD Canada Trust have changed by how much?
   b. By how much has the money supply changed?
   c. What is the maximum change in the money supply that can result from this sale?

6. You learned that if there is a recessionary gap in the short run, then in the long run a new equilibrium arises when input prices and expectations adjust downward, causing the aggregate supply curve to shift downward and to the right and pushing equilibrium real GDP back to its long-run potential value. In this chapter, however, you learned that the Bank of Canada can eliminate a recessionary gap in the short run by undertaking a policy action that raises aggregate demand.
   a. Propose a monetary policy action that could eliminate a recessionary gap in the short run.
   b. In what way might society gain if the Bank of Canada implements the policy you have proposed instead of simply permitting long-run adjustments to take place?

7. You have learned that if there is an inflationary gap in the short run, then in the long run a new equilibrium arises when input prices and expectations adjust upward, causing the aggregate supply curve to shift upward and to the left and pushing equilibrium real GDP back to its long-run potential value. In this chapter, however, you learned that the Bank of Canada can eliminate an inflationary gap in the short run by undertaking a policy action that reduces aggregate demand.
   a. Propose one monetary policy action that could eliminate an inflationary gap in the short run.
   b. In what way might society gain if the Bank of Canada implements the policy you have proposed instead of simply permitting long-run adjustments to take place?

LO 14.3 Identify the factors that influence people's demand for money.

8. What factors influence people's demand for money?

9. Show in the form of a chart the processes by which the Bank of Canada can reduce inflationary pressures by conducting drawdowns.

10. What motives for holding money—transactions, precautionary, or asset—explain the following holdings?
    a. Money to meet Suncor's weekly payroll deposited in the local bank.
    b. You personally carry $50 even when you have no plans to spend.
    c. An investor sells a corporate bond for cash and then deposits the cash in a lower interest rate bank savings account.
    d. Currency in the cash register of the neighbourhood convenience store.
    e. A family keeps a minimum of $2000 in its savings account.

LO 14.4 Explain two views of how monetary policy works.

11. Briefly outline the Keynesian monetary transmission mechanism.

12. The equation that indicates the value (price) right now of a nonmaturing bond (called a consol) is $V = R/i$, where V is the present value, R is the annual net income generated from the bond, and i is the going interest rate.
    a. Assume that a bond promises the holder $1000 per year forever. If the interest rate is 10 percent, what is the bond worth now (V)?
    b. Continuing part (a), what happens to the value of the bond (V) if interest rates rise to 20 percent? What if they fall to 5 percent?

Suppose that there were an indestructible machine that was expected to generate $2000 per year in revenues but costs $1000 per year to maintain—forever. How would that machine be priced relative to the bond described in part (a)?

13. Briefly outline expansionary monetary policy according to a monetarist.

14. Suppose that the quantity of money in circulation is fixed but the income velocity of money doubles. If real GDP remains at its long-run potential level, what happens to the equilibrium price level?

15. Suppose that following the events in Problem 14, the Bank of Canada cuts the money supply in half. How does the price level now compare with its value before the income velocity and the money supply changed?

16. Consider the following data: The money supply is $1 trillion, the price level equals 2, and real GDP is $5 trillion in base-year dollars. What is the income velocity of money?

17. Consider the data in Problem 16. Suppose that the money supply increases by $100 billion and real GDP and the income velocity remain unchanged.

    a. According to the quantity theory of money and prices, what is the new price level after the increase in the money supply?
    b. What is the percentage increase in the money supply?
    c. What is the percentage change in the price level?
    d. How do the percentage changes in the money supply and price level compare?

18. Assume that $M = \$30$ billion, $P = \$1.72$, and $Q = 90$ billion units per year. What is the income velocity of money?

19. Explain why the net export effect of a contractionary monetary policy reinforces the usual impact that monetary policy has on equilibrium real GDP in the short run.

20. Suppose that, initially, the Canadian economy was in an aggregate demand-aggregate supply equilibrium at point A along the aggregate demand curve AD in the diagram below. Now, however, the value of the Canadian dollar has suddenly appreciated relative to foreign currencies. This appreciation happens to have no measurable effects on either the short-run or the long-run aggregate supply curve in the Canada. It does, however, influence Canadian aggregate demand.

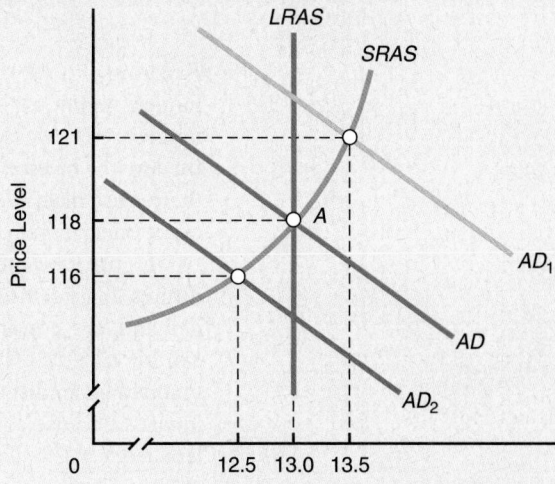

a. Explain in your own words how the dollar appreciation will affect Canadian net export expenditures.

b. Of the alternative aggregate demand curves depicted in the figure—AD_1 versus AD_2—which could represent the aggregate demand effect of the U.S. dollar's appreciation? What effects does the appreciation have on real GDP and the price level?

c. What policy action might the Bank of Canada take to prevent the dollar's appreciation from affecting equilibrium real GDP in the short run?

LO 14.5 Assess the effectiveness of monetary policy.

21. In Policy Example 14–2, "Monetary Policy: Where Are We Now?", former Governor of the Bank of Canada Gordon Thiessen outlines where monetary policy is at now in Canada. Under what conditions is monetary policy most effective? What are two advantages of monetary policy versus fiscal policy?

APPENDIX G

MONETARY POLICY: A KEYNESIAN PERSPECTIVE

According to the traditional Keynesian approach to monetary policy, changes in the money supply can affect the level of aggregate demand only through their effect on interest rates. Moreover, interest rate changes act on aggregate demand solely by changing the level of investment spending. Finally, the traditional Keynesian approach argues that there exist plausible circumstances under which monetary policy may have little or no effect on aggregate demand.

Figure G–1 measures real GDP along the horizontal axis and total planned expenditures (aggregate demand) along the vertical axis. The components of aggregate demand are consumption (C), investment (I), government spending (G), and net exports $(X - M)$. The height of the schedule labelled $C + I + G + (X - M)$ shows total planned expenditures (aggregate demand) as a function of GDP. This schedule slopes upward because consumption depends positively on GDP. Everywhere along the line labelled $Y = C + I + G + (X - M)$, planned spending equals GDP. At point Y^*, where the $C + I + G + (X - M)$ line intersects this 45-degree reference line, planned spending is consistent with GDP. At any GDP less than Y^*, spending exceeds GDP, and so GDP and thus spending will tend to rise. At any level of GDP greater than Y^*, planned spending is less than GDP, and so GDP and thus spending will tend to decline. Given the determinants of C, I, G, and $(X - M)$, total spending (aggregate demand) will be Y^*.

Increasing the Money Supply

According to the Keynesian approach, an increase in the money supply pushes interest rates down. This reduces the cost of borrowing and thus induces firms to increase the level of investment spending from I to I'. As a result, the $C + I + G + (X - M)$ line shifts upward in Figure G–1 by the full amount of the rise in investment spending, thus yielding the line $C + I' + G + (X - M)$. The rise in investment spending causes income to rise, which, in turn, causes consumption spending to rise, which further increases GDP. Ultimately, aggregate demand rises to Y^{**}, where spending again equals income. A key conclusion of

---

FIGURE G–1

An Increase in the Money Supply

An increase in the money supply increases income by lowering interest rates and thus increasing investment from I to I'.

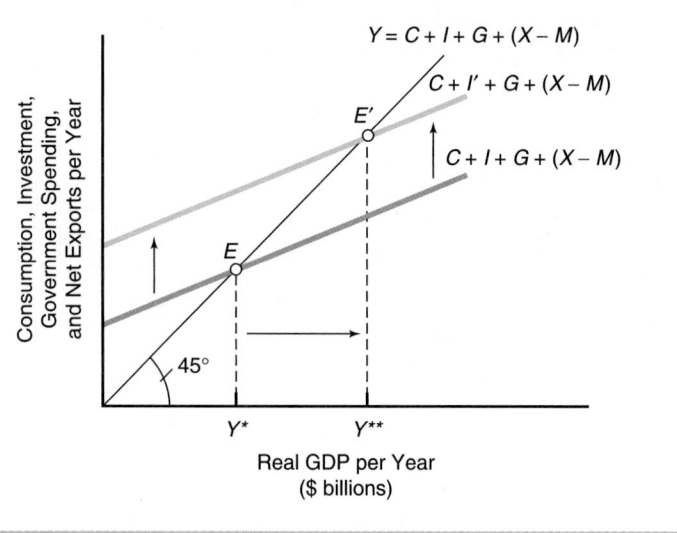

the Keynesian analysis is that total spending rises by *more* than the original rise in investment spending because consumption spending depends positively on income.

Decreasing the Money Supply

Not surprisingly, contractionary monetary policy works in exactly the reverse manner. A reduction in the money supply pushes interest rates up, which increases the cost of borrowing. Firms respond by reducing their investment spending, and this starts real GDP downward. Consumers react to the lower income by scaling back on their consumption spending, which further depresses GDP. Thus, the ultimate decline in GDP is larger than the initial drop in investment spending. Indeed, because the change in real GDP is a multiple of the change in investment, Keynesians note that changes in investment spending (similar to changes in government spending) have a *multiplier* effect on the economy.

Arguments against Monetary Policy

It might be thought that this multiplier effect would make monetary policy a potent tool in the Keynesian arsenal, particularly when it comes to getting the economy out of a recession. In fact, however, many traditional Keynesians argue that monetary policy is likely to be relatively ineffective as a recession fighter. According to their line of reasoning, although monetary policy has the potential to reduce interest rates, changes in the money supply have little actual impact on interest rates. Instead, during recessions, people try to build up as much as they can in liquid assets to protect themselves from risks of unemployment and other losses of income. When the monetary authorities increase the money supply, individuals are willing to allow most of it to accumulate in their bank accounts. This desire for increased liquidity thus prevents interest rates from falling very much, which, in turn, means that there will be virtually no change in investment spending and thus little change in aggregate demand.

⇒ PROBLEMS

LO 14.4 Explain two views of how monetary policy works.

G–1. Assume that the following conditions exist:
   a. All banks are fully loaned up—there are no excess reserves, and desired excess reserves are always zero.
   b. The money multiplier is 3.
   c. The planned investment schedule is such that at a 10 percent rate of interest, investment is $20 billion; at 9 percent, investment is $22.5 billion.
   d. The investment multiplier is 3.
   e. The initial equilibrium level of real GDP is $200 billion.
   f. The equilibrium rate of interest is 10 percent.

Now the Bank of Canada engages in expansionary monetary policy. It buys $1 million worth of bonds, which increases the money supply, which in turn lowers the market rate of interest by 1 percent. Indicate by how much the money supply increased, and then trace out the numerical consequences of the associated reduction in interest rates on all the other variables mentioned.

15

Issues in Stabilization Policy

The 1960s were an extended period of uninterrupted growth in Canada. The 1970s and 1980s were difficult times for many Canadians, as both inflation and unemployment continued to grow to double digits. We had increasing government deficits as unemployment reduced tax revenues and inflation added to the cost of maintaining programs for the unemployed. Clearly, government needed to implement a focused economic policy to turn this trend around. So, it charged the Bank of Canada with the responsibility of using contractionary monetary policy to beat inflation. Was this the best policy government could have chosen? To answer this question, you need to know more about how various economists view the economy, about its fluctuations in the short run and in the long run, and about certain issues pertaining to stabilization policies.

Active versus Passive Policy Making

Active (discretionary) policy making All actions on the part of monetary and fiscal policy makers that are undertaken in response to or in anticipation of some change in the overall economy.

Passive (nondiscretionary) policy making Policy making that is carried out in response to a rule and, therefore, is not in response to an actual or potential change in overall economic activity.

All of the actions described above constitute part of what is called **active (discretionary) policy making**—all actions on the part of monetary and fiscal policy makers that are undertaken in response to or in anticipation of some change in the overall economy. At the other extreme is **passive (nondiscretionary) policy making**—carried out in response to a rule and, therefore, not in response to an actual or potential change in overall economic activity—in which there is no deliberate stabilization policy at all. You have already been introduced to one nondiscretionary policy making idea in Chapter 14—the *monetary rule,* by which the money supply is allowed to increase at a fixed rate per year. In the fiscal arena, passive (nondiscretionary) policy might simply consist of balancing the federal budget over the business cycle. Recall that there are numerous time lags between the time that the economy enters a recession or a boom and when that event becomes known, acted on, and sensed by the economy. Proponents of passive policy argue strongly that such time lags often render short-term stabilization policy ineffective or, worse, procyclical.

To take a stand on this debate concerning active versus passive policy making, you first need to know the potential trade-offs that policy makers believe they face. Then, you need to see what the data actually show. The most important policy trade-off appears to be between price stability and unemployment. Before exploring that trade-off, we need first to look at the economy's natural, or long-run, rate of unemployment.

15.1 The Natural Rate of Unemployment

Recall from Chapter 4 that there are different types of unemployment: frictional, cyclical, seasonal, and structural. Frictional unemployment arises because individuals take the time to search for the best job opportunities. Except when the economy is in a recession or a depression, much unemployment is of this type.

Note that we did not say that frictional unemployment was the *sole* form of unemployment during normal times. *Structural unemployment* is caused by a variety of "rigidities" throughout the economy. Structural unemployment results from such factors as these:

1. Union activity that sets wages above the equilibrium level and also restricts the mobility of labour
2. Government-imposed licensing arrangements that restrict entry into specific occupations or professions
3. Government-imposed minimum wage laws and other laws that require all workers to be paid union wage rates on government contract jobs
4. Welfare and employment insurance benefits that reduce incentives to work
5. Changes in technology that make current workers' skills obsolete

In each case, these factors reduce individuals' abilities or incentives to choose employment, rather than unemployment.

Consider the effect of employment insurance benefits on the probability of an unemployed person finding a job. When employment insurance benefits run out, according to economists Lawrence Katz and Bruce Meyer, the probability of an unemployed person finding a job doubles. The conclusion is that unemployed workers are more serious about finding a job when they are no longer receiving such benefits.

FIGURE 15–1

Estimated Natural Rate of Unemployment

As you can see in this figure, the actual rate of unemployment varied widely in Canada in the second half of the 20th century. If we estimate the natural rate of unemployment by averaging unemployment rates from five years earlier to five years later at each point in time, we get the heavy solid line so labelled. It rose from the 1950s until the late 1980s and seems to be trending down since then. (Post-1999 natural rate is estimated.)

SOURCES: ADAPTED FROM THE STATISTICS CANADA PUBLICATION *HISTORICAL STATISTICS OF CANADA*, SECOND EDITION, CATALOGUE 11-516, 1983, AND FROM THE STATISTICS CANADA CANSIM DATABASE, SERIES V13682111.

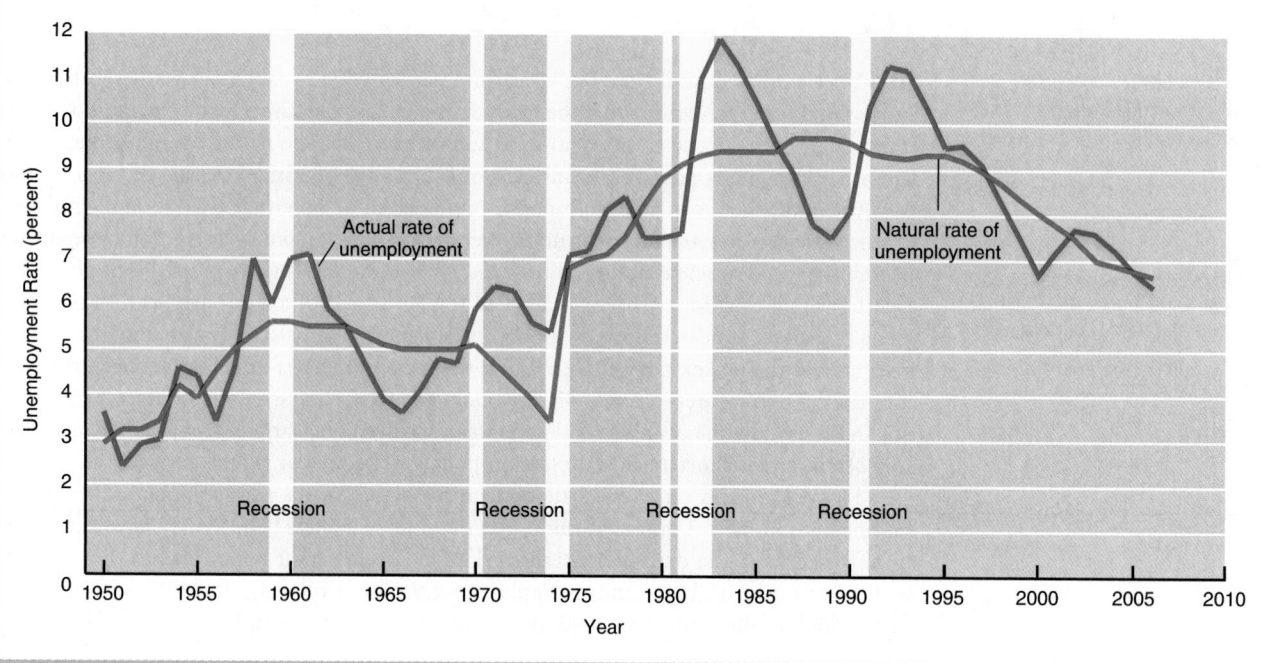

Frictional unemployment exists even when the economy is in long-run equilibrium—it is a natural consequence of costly information (the need to conduct a job search) and the existence of rigidities such as those noted. Because frictional unemployment is a natural consequence of imperfect information and rigidities, it is related to what economists call the **natural rate of unemployment**, which is defined as the rate of unemployment that would exist in the long run after everyone in the economy fully adjusted to any changes that have occurred. Recall that national output tends to return to the level implied by the long-run aggregate supply curve (*LRAS*). Thus, whatever rate of unemployment the economy tends to return to can be called the natural rate of unemployment. See Figure 15–1 for an estimate of Canada's natural rate of unemployment and Example 15–1 for a discussion of Canada's natural rate of unemployment.

Natural rate of unemployment The rate of unemployment that would exist in the long run after everyone in the economy fully adjusted to any changes that have occurred.

EXAMPLE 15–1   **Canada's Natural Rate of Unemployment**

In 1945, at the end of World War II, the unemployment rate was below 4 percent. By the early 1990s, it was above 10 percent. These two endpoints for half a century of unemployment rates prove nothing by themselves. But look at Figure 15–1. There you see not only what has happened to the unemployment rate over that same time period but also an

continued

estimate of the natural rate of unemployment. The solid line labelled "Natural rate of unemployment" is estimated by averaging unemployment rates from five years earlier to five years later at each point in time. This computation reveals that until about 1988, the natural rate of unemployment was rising. But since then, the natural rate of unemployment held steady and then began trending down.

For critical analysis: Of the factors listed on page 387 that create structural unemployment, which do you think may explain the trend upward in the natural rate of unemployment since World War II?

Departures from the Natural Rate of Unemployment

Even though the unemployment rate has a strong tendency to stay at and return to the natural rate, it is possible for fiscal and monetary policy to move the actual unemployment rate away from the natural rate, at least in the short run. Deviations of the actual unemployment rate from the natural rate are called *cyclical unemployment* because they are observed over the course of nationwide business fluctuations. During recessions, the overall unemployment rate exceeds the natural rate; cyclical unemployment is positive. During periods of economic booms, the overall unemployment rate can go below the natural rate; at such times, cyclical unemployment is in essence negative.

To see how departures from the natural rate of unemployment can occur, let us consider two examples. Referring to Figure 15–2, we begin in equilibrium at point E_1 with the associated price level P_1 and real GDP per year of level Y_1.

THE IMPACT OF EXPANSIONARY POLICY. Now, imagine that the government decides to use fiscal or monetary policy to stimulate the economy. Further suppose that this policy surprises decision makers throughout the economy in the sense that they did not anticipate that the policy would occur. The aggregate demand curve shifts from AD_1 to AD_2 in Figure 15–2, so both the price level and real GDP rise to P_2 and Y_2, respectively. In the labour market, individuals will find that conditions have improved markedly relative to what they expected. Firms seeking to expand output will want to hire more workers. To accomplish this, they will recruit more actively and possibly ask workers to work overtime so that individuals in the labour market will find more job openings and more possible hours they can work. Consequently, as you learned in Chapter 6, the average duration of unemployment will fall and the unemployment rate falls. This unexpected increase in aggregate demand simultaneously causes the price level to rise to P_2 and the

FIGURE 15–2

Impact of an Increase in Aggregate Demand on Output and Unemployment

If the economy is operating at E_1, it is in both short-run and long-run equilibrium. Here, the actual rate of unemployment is equal to the natural rate of unemployment. Subsequent to expansionary monetary or fiscal policy, the aggregate demand curve shifts outward to AD_2. The price level rises to P_2; real GDP per year increases to Y_2. The new short-run equilibrium is at E_2. The unemployment rate is now below the natural rate of unemployment. We are at a temporary equilibrium at E_2. In the long run, expectations of input owners are revised. The short-run aggregate supply curve shifts from $SRAS_1$ to $SRAS_2$ because of higher prices and higher resource costs. Real GDP returns to the $LRAS$ level of Y_1 per year. The price level has increased to P_3.

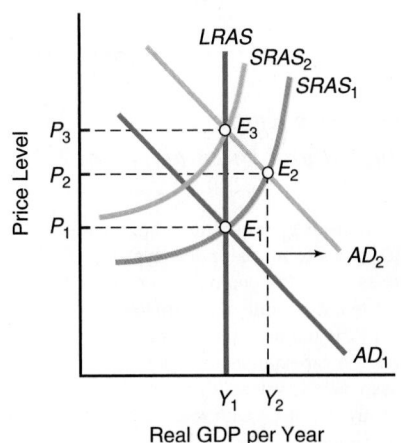

unemployment rate to fall. The *SRAS* curve will not stay at $SRAS_1$, however. A change in the expectations of input owners, such as workers and owners of capital and raw materials, will be revised. The short-run aggregate supply curve shifts to $SRAS_2$, as input prices rise. We find ourselves at a new equilibrium at E_3, which is on the *LRAS*. Long-run real GDP per year is Y_1 again, but at a higher price level, P_3. A debate on monetary policy and aggregate demand is going on in Japan, and this debate is discussed in Example 15–2.

EXAMPLE 15–2 **Monetary Policy and Aggregate Demand: The Bank of Japan Tries to Have It Both Ways**

Since the mid-1990s, the Japanese economy has experienced simultaneous declines in the price level and real output. Recently, the Diet, Japan's parliament, decided that it was time for the Bank of Japan to halt deflation and boost real GDP. To try to force the hand of central bank officials, leaders of the ruling political party in the Diet advanced a law requiring the Bank of Japan to aim for positive inflation.

Officials at the Bank of Japan first responded by pointing out that the central bank had already pushed up money growth at annual rates as high as 10 percent, yet prices of goods and services continued to fall. This experience, they argued, revealed that the Bank of Japan lacked the ability to significantly increase aggregate demand in order to raise the price level and national output.

When pressed further by the Diet, however, Bank of Japan officials changed their tune and argued that higher money growth would be "dangerous." Boosting growth of the Japanese money stock, they stated, could pose serious inflation risks.

Members of the Japanese Diet, as well as economists around the world, were left scratching their heads. How could expansionary monetary policy be ineffective and dangerous at the same time, they wondered? One Amerian economist suggested that officials at the Bank of Japan might want to retake a principles of economics course.

For critical analysis: Is it possible that an increase in the quantity of money could have hardly any short-run effects but significant long-run inflationary effects? (*Hint:* Does the aggregate demand curve necessarily shift instantaneously following a change in a factor that influences its position?)

THE CONSEQUENCES OF CONTRACTIONARY POLICY. Instead of expansionary policy, government could have decided to engage in contractionary (or deflationary) policy. As shown in Figure 15–3, the sequence of events would have been in the

FIGURE 15–3

Impact of a Decline in Aggregate Demand on Output and Unemployment

Starting from equilibrium at E_1, a decline in aggregate demand to AD_2 leads to a lower price level, P_2, and real GDP declines to Y_2. The unemployment rate will rise above the natural rate of unemployment. Equilibrium at E_2 is temporary, however. At the lower price level, the expectations of input owners will be revised. $SRAS_1$ will shift to $SRAS_2$. The new equilibrium will be at E_3, with real GDP equal to Y_1 and a price level of P_3.

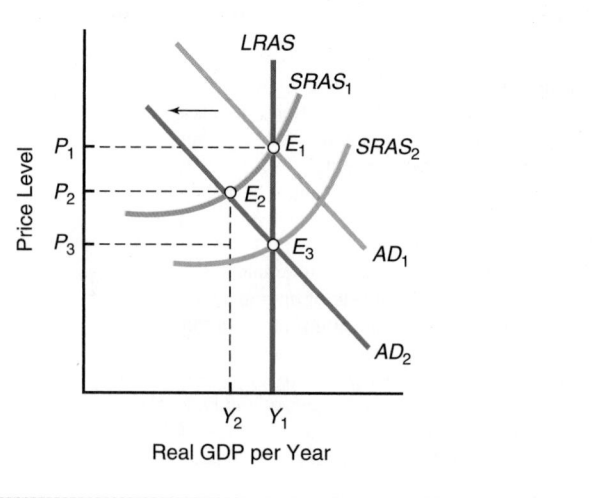

opposite direction of that in Figure 15–2. Again, beginning from an initial equilibrium E_1, an unanticipated reduction in aggregate demand puts downward pressure on both prices and real GDP; the price level falls to P_2, and real GDP declines to Y_2. Fewer firms will be hiring, and those that are hiring will offer fewer overtime possibilities. Individuals looking for jobs will find that it takes longer than predicted. As a result, unemployed individuals will remain unemployed longer. The average duration of unemployment will rise, and so, too, will the rate of unemployment. The unexpected decrease in aggregate demand simultaneously causes the price level to fall to P_2 and the unemployment rate to rise. This is a short-run situation only at E_2. $SRAS_1$ will shift to $SRAS_2$ with a change in the expectations of input owners about future prices, and input prices fall. The new equilibrium will be at E_3, which is on the long-run aggregate supply curve, $LRAS$. The price level will have fallen to P_3.

15.2 The Phillips Curve

The Phillips Curve: The Trade-Off?

Let us recap what we have just observed. An *unexpected* increase in aggregate demand causes the price level to rise and the unemployment rate to fall. Conversely, an *unexpected* decrease in aggregate demand causes the price level to fall and the unemployment rate to rise. Moreover, although not shown explicitly in either diagram, two additional points are true:

1. The greater the unexpected increase in aggregate demand, the greater is the amount of inflation that results, and the lower is the unemployment rate.
2. The greater the unexpected decrease in aggregate demand, the greater is the deflation that results, and the higher is the unemployment rate.

THE NEGATIVE SHORT-RUN RELATIONSHIP BETWEEN INFLATION AND UNEMPLOYMENT. Figure 15–4 summarizes these findings. The inflation rate (*not* the price level) is measured along the vertical axis, and the unemployment rate is measured along the horizontal axis. Point A shows an initial starting point, with the unemployment rate at the natural rate, U^*. Note that as a matter of convenience, we are starting from an equilibrium in which the price level is stable (the inflation rate is zero). Unexpected increases in aggregate demand cause the price level to rise—the inflation rate becomes positive—and cause the unemployment rate to fall. Thus, the economy moves up to the left from A to B. Conversely, unexpected decreases in aggregate demand cause the price level to fall and the unemployment rate to rise above the natural rate—the economy moves

---

FIGURE 15-4

The Phillips Curve

Unanticipated changes in aggregate demand produce a negative relationship between the inflation rate and unemployment rate. U^* is the natural rate of unemployment.

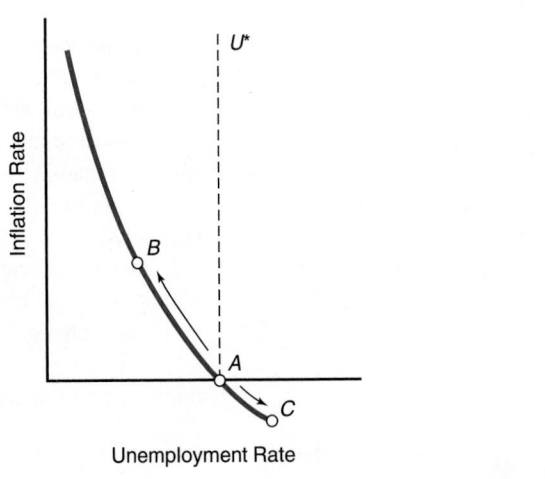

from point *A* to point *C*. If we look at both increases and decreases in aggregate demand, we see that high inflation rates tend to be associated with low unemployment rates (as at *B*) and that low (or negative) inflation rates tend to be accompanied by high unemployment rates (as at *C*).

IS THERE A TRADE-OFF? The apparent negative relationship between the inflation rate and the unemployment rate shown in Figure 15–4 has come to be called the **Phillips curve**, after A. W. Phillips, who discovered that a similar relationship existed historically in the United Kingdom. Although Phillips presented his findings only as an empirical regularity, economists quickly came to view the relationship as representing a *trade-off* between inflation and unemployment. In particular, policy makers believed they could choose alternative combinations of unemployment and inflation (or worse, that the trade-off was inevitable because you could not get more of one without giving up the other). Thus, it seemed that a government which disliked unemployment could select a point like *B* in Figure 15–4, with a positive inflation rate but a relatively low unemployment rate. Conversely, a government that feared inflation could choose a stable price level at *A*, but only at the expense of a higher associated unemployment rate. Indeed, the Phillips curve seemed to suggest that it was possible for policy makers to fine-tune the economy by selecting the policies that would produce the exact mix of unemployment and inflation that suited current government objectives. As it turned out, matters are not so simple.

THE NAIRU. If we accept that a trade-off exists between the rate of inflation and the rate of unemployment, then the notion of "noninflationary" rates of unemployment seems appropriate. In fact, some economists have proposed what they call the **nonaccelerating inflation rate of unemployment (NAIRU)**—the rate of unemployment below which the rate of inflation tends to rise and above which the rate of inflation tends to fall. If the Phillips curve trade-off exists and if the NAIRU can be estimated, that estimate will define the short-run trade-off between the rate of unemployment and the rate of inflation. Economists who have estimated the NAIRU for the world's 24 richest industrial countries claim that it has been steadily rising since the 1960s. Critics of the NAIRU concept argue that inflationary expectations must be taken into account. See Example 15–3 for a discussion of the distinction between NAIRU and the natural rate of unemployment.

Phillips curve A curve showing the apparent negative relationship between the inflation rate and the unemployment rate.

Nonaccelerating inflation rate of unemployment (NAIRU) The rate of unemployment below which the rate of inflation tends to rise and above which the rate of inflation tends to fall.

EXAMPLE 15-3 ### Distinguishing between the Natural Rate of Unemployment and the NAIRU

When the media report on the natural rate of unemployment and the NAIRU, they commonly use the terms interchangeably, as if they are identical concepts. In fact, there are important differences between the two concepts.

The natural rate of unemployment is the unemployment rate that would be observed whenever all cyclical factors have played themselves out. The natural unemployment rate thereby applies to a long-run equilibrium in which any short-run adjustments are concluded. It depends on structural factors in the labour market and typically changes gradually over relatively lengthy intervals.

In contrast, the NAIRU is simply the rate of unemployment currently consistent with a steady rate of inflation. The unemployment rate consistent with a steady inflation rate can potentially change during the course of cyclical adjustments in the economy. Thus, the NAIRU typically varies by a relatively greater amount and relatively more frequently than the natural rate of unemployment.

For critical analysis: When are the natural rate of unemployment and the NAIRU identical?

15.3   *The Importance of Expectations*

The reduction in unemployment that takes place as the economy moves from *A* to *B* in Figure 15–4 occurs because the wage offers encountered by unemployed workers are unexpectedly high. As far as the workers are concerned, these higher *nominal* wages appear, at least initially, to be increases in *real* wages; it is this fact that induces them to reduce their duration of search. This is a sensible way for the workers to view the world if aggregate demand fluctuates up and down at random, with no systematic or predictable variation one way or another. But if policy makers attempt to exploit the apparent trade-off in the Phillips curve, according to some macroeconomists, aggregate demand will no longer move up and down in an *unpredictable* way.

THE EFFECTS OF AN UNANTICIPATED POLICY.   Consider Figure 15–5, for example. If the Bank of Canada attempts to reduce the unemployment rate to U_1, it must increase the money supply enough to produce an inflation rate of π_1. If this is a one-shot affair in which the money supply is first increased and then held constant, the inflation rate will temporarily rise to π_1 and the unemployment rate will temporarily fall to U_1; but as soon as the money supply stops growing, the inflation rate will return to zero and unemployment will return to U^*, its natural rate. Thus, a one-shot increase in the money supply will move the economy from point *A* to point *B*, and the economy will move of its own accord back to *A*.

ADJUSTING EXPECTATIONS AND A SHIFTING PHILLIPS CURVE.   If the authorities wish to prevent the unemployment rate from returning to U^*, some macroeconomists argue that the Bank of Canada must keep the money supply growing fast enough to keep the inflation rate up at π_1. But if the Bank of Canada does this, all of the economic participants in the economy—workers and job seekers included—will come to *expect* that inflation rate to continue. This, in turn, will change their expectations about wages. For example, suppose that π_1 equals 5 percent per year. When the expected inflation rate was zero, a 5 percent rise in nominal wages meant a 5 percent expected rise in real wages, and this was sufficient to induce some individuals to take jobs, rather than remain unemployed. It was this perception of a rise in real wages that reduced search duration and caused the unemployment rate to drop from U^* to U_1. But if the expected inflation rate becomes 5 percent, a 5 percent rise in nominal wages means *no* rise in *real* wages. Once workers come to expect the higher inflation rate, rising

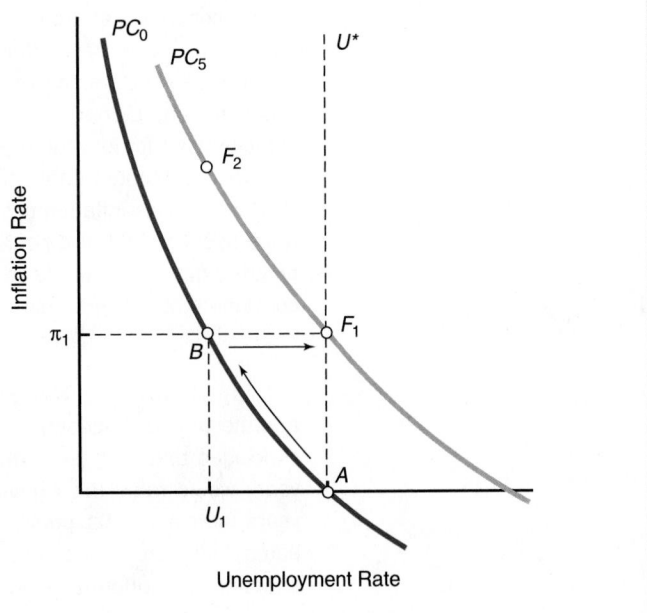

FIGURE 15–5

A Shift in the Phillips Curve

When there is a change in the expected inflation rate, the Phillips curve (PC) shifts to incorporate the new expectations. PC_0 shows expectations of zero inflation; PC_5 reflects an expected inflation rate of 5 percent.

nominal wages will no longer be sufficient to entice them out of unemployment. As a result, as the *expected* inflation rate moves up from 0 percent to 5 percent, the unemployment rate will move up also.

THE ROLE OF EXPECTED INFLATION. In terms of Figure 15–5, as authorities initially increase aggregate demand, the economy moves from point A to point B. If the authorities continue the stimulus in an effort to keep the unemployment rate down, workers' expectations will adjust, causing the unemployment rate to rise. In this second stage, the economy moves from B to point F_1: The unemployment rate returns to the natural rate, U^*, but the inflation rate is now π_1 instead of zero. Once the adjustment of expectations has taken place, any further changes in policy will have to take place along a curve such as PC_5, say, a movement from F_1 to F_2. This new schedule is also a Phillips curve, differing from the first, PC_0, in that the actual inflation rate consistent with any given unemployment rate is higher because the expected inflation rate is higher.

Not surprisingly, when economic policy makers found that economic participants engaged in such adjustment behaviour, they were both surprised and dismayed. If decision makers can adjust their expectations to conform with fiscal and monetary policies, then policy makers cannot choose a permanently lower unemployment rate of U_1, even if they are willing to tolerate an inflation rate of π_1. Instead, the policy makers would end up with an unchanged unemployment rate in the long run, at the expense of a permanently higher inflation rate, Research, such as the results reported in Example 15–4, support this conclusion.

Initially, however, there did seem to be a small consolation, for it appeared that in the short run—before expectations adjusted—the unemployment rate could be *temporarily* reduced from U^* to U_1, even though eventually it would return to the natural rate. If an important federal election were approaching, it might be possible to stimulate the economy long enough to get the unemployment rate low enough to assure re-election. However, policy makers came to learn that not even this was likely to be a sure thing.

EXAMPLE 15–4   The Effects of Higher Inflation on Inflation Expectations

Three economists at the Federal Reserve Bank of St. Louis—Andrew Levin, Fabio Natalucci, and Jeremy Piger—have attempted to measure the effects of a short-lived increase in actual inflation on expectations of future inflation. They considered what would happen to U.S., Japanese, and Euro-area inflation expectations if the actual inflation rate rose by one percentage point for just three years.

Their estimates imply that, other things being equal, even five years after this short-lived increase in inflation occurred, the public would expect the future annual inflation rate to be about a third of a percentage point higher. As much as ten years later, the expected annual inflation rate would still be one-fourth of a percentage point higher. Thus, the authors conclude that higher actual inflation has a significant holdover effect on long-term inflation expectations.

For critical analysis: The authors of this study also examined nations such as Canada and the United Kingdom, in which central banks announce formal inflation targets. They concluded that in these nations, a one percentage point rise in actual inflation for three years would raise the expected future inflation rate by only 0.09 percentage point five years later and 0.01 percentage point ten years later. Why do you suppose that higher actual inflation has a smaller effect on inflation expectations when a central bank announces inflation targets?

FIGURE 15-6

The Phillips Curve: Theory versus Data—Canada

If you plot points representing the rate of inflation and the rate of unemployment for Canada from 1950 to the present, there does not appear to be any Phillips curve trade-off between the two variables.

SOURCES: ADAPTED FROM THE STATISTICS CANADA PUBLICATION *HISTORICAL STATISTICS OF CANADA*, SECOND EDITION, CATALOGUE 11-516, 1983, SERIES D129, D132, D233, AND FROM THE STATISTICS CANADA CANSIM DATABASE, SERIES P200000, D31252, D31253, D984954, AND SERIES V41690973 AND V13682111.

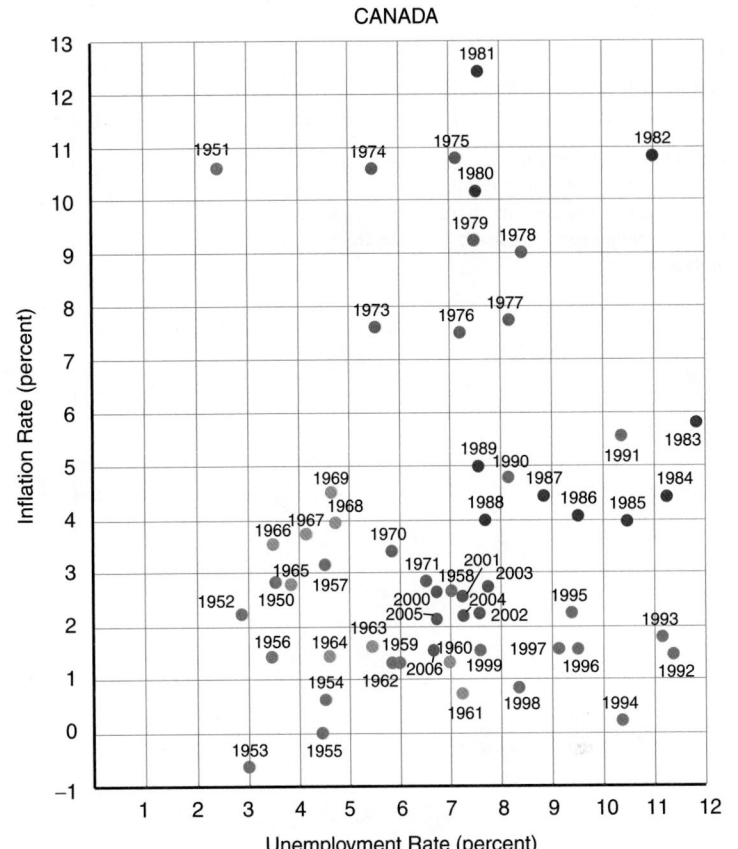

The Canadian Experience with the Phillips Curve

In separate articles in 1968, economists Milton Friedman and E. S. Phelps published pioneering studies suggesting that the apparent trade-off suggested by the Phillips curve could not be exploited by policy makers. Friedman and Phelps both argued that any attempt to reduce unemployment by inflating the economy would soon be thwarted by economic participants' incorporating the new higher inflation rate into their expectations. The Friedman–Phelps research thus implies that for any given unemployment rate, any inflation rate is possible, depending on the actions of policy makers. As reflected in Figures 15–6 and 15–7, the propositions of Friedman and Phelps were to prove remarkably accurate.

When we examine the data for unemployment and inflation in Canada (Figure 15–6) and the United States (Figure 15–7) over the past half century, we see virtually no clear relationship between them. Although there seemed to have been a Phillips curve trade-off between unemployment and inflation from the mid-1950s to the mid-1960s, apparently once people in the economy realized what was happening, they started revising their forecasts accordingly. So, once policy makers attempted to exploit the Phillips curve, the apparent trade-off between unemployment and inflation disappeared.

➤ CONCEPTS IN BRIEF

Learning Objective 15.1: Explain why the actual unemployment rate might depart from the natural rate of unemployment.

- The natural rate of unemployment is the rate that exists in long-run equilibrium, when workers' expectations are consistent with actual conditions.
- Departures from the natural rate of unemployment can occur when individuals encounter unanticipated changes in fiscal or monetary policy; an unexpected rise in aggregate demand will reduce unemployment below the natural rate, whereas an unanticipated decrease in aggregate demand will push unemployment above the natural rate.

FIGURE 15-7

The Phillips Curve: Theory versus Data—United States

If you plot points representing the rate of inflation and the rate of unemployment for the United States from 1953 to the present, there does not appear to be any Phillips curve trade-off between the two variables.

SOURCES: *ECONOMIC REPORT OF THE PRESIDENT; ECONOMIC INDICATORS,* VARIOUS ISSUES.

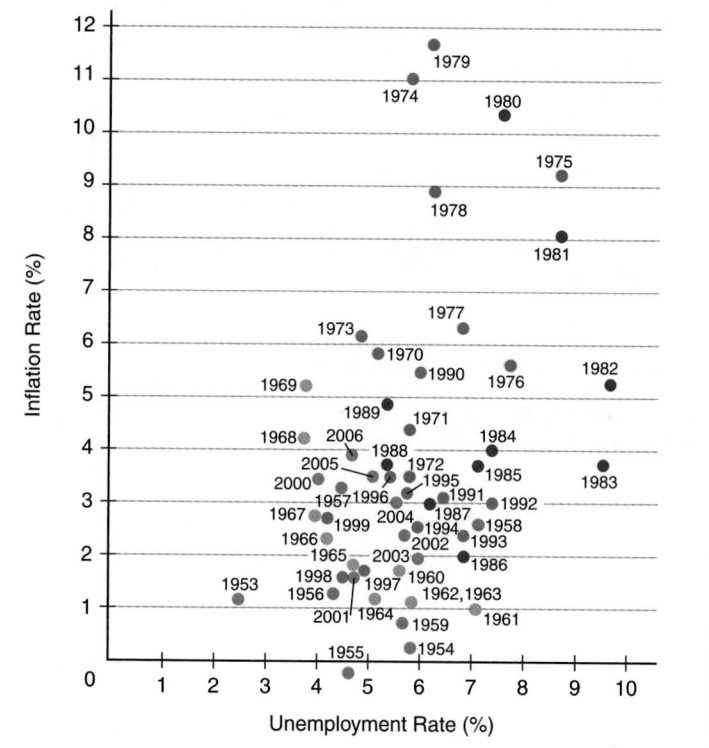

Learning Objective 15.2: Describe why there may be an inverse relationship between the inflation rate and the unemployment rate, reflected by the Phillips curve.

↪ The Phillips curve exhibits a negative relationship between the inflation rate and the unemployment rate that can be observed when there are *unanticipated* changes in aggregate demand.

Learning Objective 15.3: Evaluate how expectations affect the relationship between the actual inflation rate and the unemployment rate.

↪ It was originally believed that the Phillips curve represented a trade-off between inflation and unemployment. In fact, no trade-off exists because workers' expectations adjust to any systematic attempts to reduce unemployment below the natural rate.

15.4 Rational Expectations and the New Classical Model

You already know that economists assume that economic participants act *as though* they were rational and calculating. We think of firms that rationally maximize profits when they choose today's rate of output, and consumers who rationally maximize utility when they choose how much of what goods to consume today. One of the pivotal features of current macro policy research is the assumption that rationality also applies to the way that economic participants think about the future as well as the present. This relationship was developed by Robert Lucas, who won the Nobel Prize in 1995 for his work. In particular, there is widespread agreement among a growing group of macroeconomics researchers that the **rational expectations hypothesis**—a theory stating that people combine the effects of past policy changes on important economic variables with their own judgment about the future effects of current and future policy

Rational expectations hypothesis A theory stating that people combine the effects of past policy changes on important economic variables with their own judgment about the future effects of current and future policy changes.

changes—extends our understanding of the behaviour of the macroeconomy. There are two key elements to this hypothesis:

1. Individuals base their forecasts (or expectations) about the future values of economic variables on all available past and current information.
2. These expectations incorporate individuals' understanding about how the economy operates, including the operation of monetary and fiscal policy.

In essence, the rational expectations hypothesis assumes the old saying is correct: "It is true that you may fool all the people some of the time; you can even fool some of the people all of the time; but you can't fool *all* of the people *all* of the time."

If we further assume that there is pure competition in all markets and that all prices and wages are flexible, we obtain the **new classical model**—a modern version of the classical model in which wages and prices are flexible, there is pure competition in all markets, and the rational expectations hypothesis is assumed to be working. (This is referred to in Chapter 10 when discussing the Ricardian equivalence theorem.) To see how rational expectations operate within the context of this model, let us take a simple example of the economy's response to a change in monetary policy.

New classical model A modern version of the classical model in which wages and prices are flexible, there is pure competition in all markets, and the rational expectations hypothesis is assumed to be working.

The New Classical Model

Consider Figure 15–8, which shows the long-run aggregate supply curve (*LRAS*) for the economy, as well as the initial aggregate demand curve (AD_1) and the short-run aggregate supply curve ($SRAS_1$). The money supply is initially given by $M = M_1$, and the price level and real GDP are shown by P_1 and Q_1, respectively. Thus, point A represents the initial equilibrium.

Suppose now that the money supply is unexpectedly increased to M_2, thereby causing the aggregate demand curve to shift outward to AD_2. Given the location of the short-run aggregate supply curve, this increase in aggregate demand will cause output and the price level to rise to Q_2 and P_2, respectively. The new short-run equilibrium is at B. Because output is *above* the long-run equilibrium level of Q_1, unemployment must be below long-run levels (the natural rate), and so workers will soon respond to the higher price level by demanding higher nominal wages. This will cause the short-run aggregate supply curve to shift upward vertically (to the left), moving the economy to the new long-run equilibrium at C. The price level thus continues its rise to P_3, even as real GDP declines back down to Q_1 (and unemployment returns to the natural rate). So, as we have seen before, even

FIGURE 15–8

Response to an Unanticipated Rise in Aggregate Demand

Unanticipated changes in aggregate demand have real effects. In this case, the rise in demand causes real output to rise from Q_1 to Q_2.

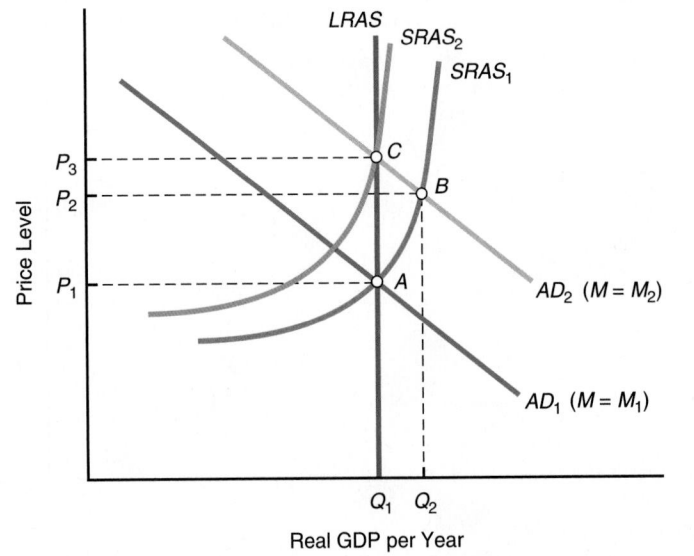

though an increase in the money supply can raise output and lower unemployment in the short run, it has no effect on either variable in the long run.

THE RESPONSE TO ANTICIPATED POLICY. Now, let us look at this disturbance with the perspective given by the rational expectations hypothesis, as it is embedded in the new classical model. Suppose that workers (and other input owners) know ahead of time that this increase in the money supply is about to take place. Assume also that they know when it is going to occur and understand that its ultimate effect will be to push the price level from P_1 to P_3. Will workers wait until after the price level has increased to insist that their nominal wages go up? The rational expectations hypothesis says that they will not. Instead, they will go to employers and insist on nominal wages that move upward in step with the higher prices. From the workers' perspective, this is the only way to protect their real wages from declining due to the anticipated increase in the money supply. You can read more about the influence of expectations on interest rates in Example 15–5.

THE POLICY IRRELEVANCE PROPOSITION. As long as economic participants behave in this manner, when we draw the *SRAS* curve, we must be explicit about the nature of their expectations. This we have done in Figure 15–9. In the initial equilibrium, the short-run aggregate supply curve is labelled to show that the expected money supply (M_e) and the actual money supply (M_1) are equal $(M_e = M_1)$. Similarly, when the money supply changes in a way that is anticipated by economic participants, the aggregate supply curve shifts to reflect this expected change in the money supply. The new short-run aggregate supply curve is labelled $(M_e = M_2)$ to reveal this. According to the rational expectations hypothesis, the short-run aggregate supply will shift upward *simultaneously* with the rise in aggregate demand. As a result, the economy will move directly from point *A* to point *C* in Figure 15–9 without passing through *B*: The *only* response to the rise in the money supply is a rise in the price level from P_1 to P_3; neither output nor unemployment changes at all. This conclusion—that fully anticipated monetary policy is irrelevant in determining the levels of real variables—is called the **policy irrelevance proposition**:

Policy irrelevance proposition The new classical and rational expectations conclusion that fully anticipated monetary policy is irrelevant in determining the levels of real variables.

> Under the assumption of rational expectations on the part of decision makers in the economy, anticipated monetary policy cannot alter either the rate of unemployment or the level of real GDP. Regardless of the nature of the anticipated policy, the unemployment rate will equal the natural rate, and real GDP will be determined solely by the economy's long-run aggregate supply curve.

FIGURE 15–9

Effects of an Anticipated Rise in Aggregate Demand

When policy is fully anticipated, a rise in the money supply causes a rise in the price level from P_1 to P_3, with no change in real output.

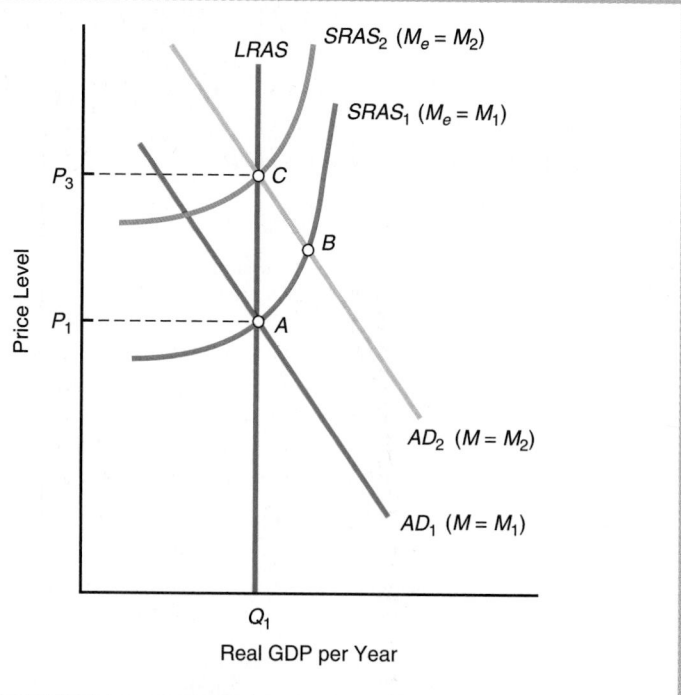

EXAMPLE 15–5 **Higher Interest Rates and "Tight" Monetary Policy**

The media often report changes in interest rates to indicate changes in monetary policy, whether they are referring to Canada or any other country. The problem with such analyses is that they fail to distinguish between real and nominal interest rates. Normally, a high interest rate is evidence that a country's central bank has been pursuing loose monetary policy in the past, rather than tight monetary policy now. Why? Because in the long run, consistent increases in the rate of growth of the money supply lead to a higher rate of inflation. A higher rate of inflation normally leads to expectations of inflation and therefore higher nominal interest rates. After all, the nominal interest rate is equal to the real rate of interest plus the expected rate of inflation. In the long run, evidence shows that monetary authorities have little effect on an economy's real rate of interest.

For critical analysis: When first home mortgages are available for 6 percent interest, is this a high, reasonable, or low rate of interest?

WHAT MUST PEOPLE KNOW? There are two important matters to keep in mind when considering this proposition. First, our discussion has assumed that economic participants know in advance exactly what the change in monetary policy is going to be and precisely when it is going to occur. In fact, the Bank of Canada does not announce exactly what the future course of monetary policy (down to the last dollar) is going to be. Instead, the Bank of Canada announces only in general terms what policy actions are intended for the future. It is tempting to conclude that because the Bank of Canada's intended policies are not freely available, they are not available at all. But such a conclusion is wrong. Economic participants have great incentives to learn how to predict the future behaviour of the monetary authorities, just as businesses try to forecast consumer behaviour and university students do their best to forecast what their next economics exam will be like. Even if the economic participants are not perfect at forecasting the course of policy, they are likely to come a lot closer than they would in total ignorance. The policy irrelevance proposition really assumes only that *people do not persistently make the same mistakes in forecasting the future.*

WHAT HAPPENS IF PEOPLE DO NOT KNOW EVERYTHING? This brings us to our second point. Once we accept the fact that people are not perfect in their ability to predict the future, the possibility emerges that some policy actions will have systematic effects that look much like the movements A to B to C in Figure 15–8. For example, just as other economic participants sometimes make mistakes, it is likely that the Bank of Canada sometimes makes mistakes—meaning that the money supply may change in ways that even the Bank of Canada does not predict. And even if the Bank of Canada always accomplished every policy action it intended, there is no guarantee that other economic participants would fully forecast those actions. What happens if the Bank of Canada makes a mistake or if firms and workers misjudge the future course of policy? Matters will look much as they do in part (a) of Figure 15–10, which shows the effects of an unanticipated increase in the money supply. Economic participants expect the money supply to be M_0, but the actual money supply turns out to be M_1. Because $M_1 > M_0$, aggregate demand shifts relative to aggregate supply. The result is a rise in real output (real GDP) in the short run from Q_1 to Q_2; corresponding to this rise in real output will be an increase in employment and hence a fall in the unemployment rate. So, even under the rational expectations hypothesis, monetary policy can have an effect on real variables in the short run, but only if the policy is unsystematic and therefore unanticipated.

In the long run, this effect on real variables will disappear because people will figure out that the Bank of Canada either accidentally increased the money supply or intentionally increased it in a way that somehow fooled individuals. Either way, people's expectations will soon be revised so that the short-run aggregate supply curve will shift upward. As shown in part (b) of Figure 15–10, real GDP will return to long-run levels, meaning that the employment and unemployment rates will as well.

FIGURE 15–10

Effects of an Unanticipated Rise in Aggregate Demand

Even with rational expectations, an unanticipated change in demand can affect output in the short run.

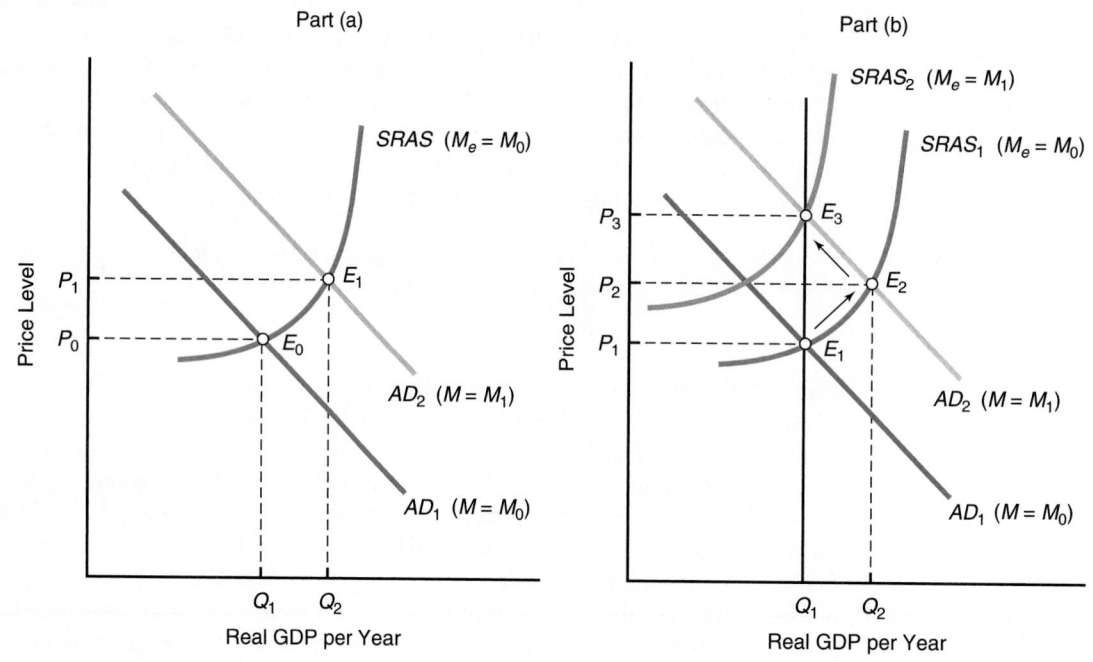

The Policy Dilemma

Perhaps the most striking and disturbing feature of the new classical model is that it seems to suggest that only mistakes can have real effects. If the Bank of Canada always does what it intends to do, and if other economic participants always correctly anticipate the Bank of Canada's actions, monetary policy will affect only the price level and nominal input prices. It appears that only if the Bank of Canada makes a mistake in executing monetary policy or people err in anticipating that policy will changes in the money supply cause fluctuations in real output and employment. If this reasoning is correct, the Bank of Canada is effectively precluded from using monetary policy in any rational way to lower the unemployment rate or to raise the level of real GDP. This is because fully anticipated changes in the money supply will lead to exactly offsetting changes in prices and hence no real effects. Many economists were disturbed at the prospect that if the economy happened to enter a recessionary period, policy makers would be powerless to push real GDP and unemployment back to long-run levels. As a result, they asked the question "In light of the rational expectations hypothesis, is it ever possible for systematic policy to have predictable real effects on the economy?" The answer has led to even more developments in the way we think about macroeconomics.

➤ CONCEPTS IN BRIEF

Learning Objective 15.4: Describe the rational expectations hypothesis and the new classical model and their implications for economic policy making.

- The rational expectations hypothesis assumes that individuals' forecasts incorporate all available information, including an understanding of government policy and its effects on the economy.
- The new classical economics assumes that the rational expectations hypothesis is valid, and also that there is pure competition and that all prices and wages are flexible.

♦ The policy irrelevance proposition says that under the assumptions of the new classical model, fully anticipated monetary policy cannot alter either the rate of unemployment or the level of real GDP.

♦ The new classical model implies that policies can alter real economic variables only if the policies are unsystematic and therefore unanticipated; otherwise people learn and defeat the desired policy goals.

15.5 Real Business Cycle Theory

The modern extension of the new classical theory involved many economists re-examining the first principles of macroeconomics that assume fully flexible wages and prices.

The Distinction between Real and Monetary Shocks

Today, many economists argue that real, as opposed to purely monetary, forces might help explain aggregate economic fluctuations.

Real business cycle theory An extension and modification of the theories of the new classical economists of the 1970s and 1980s, in which money is neutral and only real, supply-side factors matter in influencing labour employment and real output.

An important stimulus for the development of **real business cycle theory**, as it has come to be known, was the economic turmoil of the 1970s. It is an extension and modification of the theories of the new classical economists of the 1970s and 1980s, in which money is neutral and only real, supply-side factors matter in influencing labour employment and real output. During that decade, world economies were staggered by two major disruptions to the supply of oil. The first occurred in 1973, the second in 1979. In both episodes, members of the Organization of Petroleum Exporting Countries (OPEC) reduced the amount of oil they were willing to supply and raised the price at which they offered it for sale. Each time, the price level rose sharply in Canada, and real GDP declined. Thus, each episode produced a period of "stagflation"—real economic stagnation combined with high inflation. Figure 15–11 illustrates the pattern of events.

We begin at point E_1 with the economy in both short- and long-run equilibrium, with the associated supply curves, $SRAS_1$ and $LRAS_1$. Initially, the level of real GDP is Q_1, and the price level is P_1. Because the economy is in long-run equilibrium, the unemployment rate must be at the natural rate.

A reduction in the supply of oil, as occurred in 1973 and 1979, causes the $SRAS$ curve to shift to the left to $SRAS_2$ because fewer goods will be available for sale due to the reduced supplies. If the reduction in oil supplies is (or is believed to be) permanent, the $LRAS$ shifts to the left also. This assumption is reflected in Figure 15–11, where $LRAS_2$ shows the new long-run aggregate supply curve associated with the lowered output of oil.

In the short run, two adjustments begin to occur simultaneously. First, the prices of oil and petroleum-based products begin to rise so that the overall price level rises to P_2. Second, the higher costs of production occasioned by the rise in oil prices induce firms to cut back production, and so total output falls to Q_2 in the short run. The new temporary short-run equilibrium occurs at E_2, with a higher price level (P_2) and a lower level of real GDP (Q_2).

Impact on the Labour Market

If we were to focus on the labour market while this adjustment from E_1 to E_2 was taking place, we would find two developments occurring. The rise in the price level pushes the real wage rate downward, even as the scaled-back production plans of firms induce them to reduce the amount of labour inputs they are using. So, not only does the real wage rate fall, but the level of employment declines as well. On both counts, workers are made worse off due to the reduction in the supply of oil.

This is not the full story because owners of nonoil inputs (such as labour) who are willing to put up with reduced real payments in the short run simply will not tolerate them in the long run. Thus, for example, some workers who were willing to continue working at lower wages in the short run will eventually decide to retire, switch from full-time to part-time employment, or drop out of the labour force altogether. In effect, there is a

FIGURE 15–11

Effects of a Reduction in the Supply of Resources

The position of the *LRAS* depends on our endowments of all types of resources. Hence, a reduction in the supply of one of those resources, such as oil, causes a reduction—an inward shift—in the aggregate supply curve. In addition, there is a rise in the equilibrium price level and a fall in the equilibrium rate of real GDP per year (output).

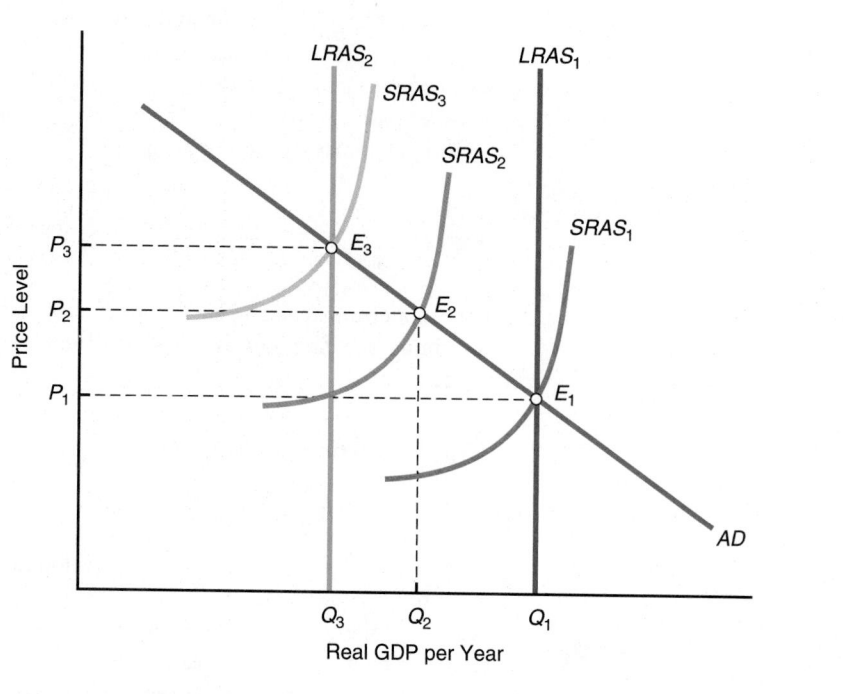

reduction in the supply of nonoil inputs, reflected in an upward shift in the *SRAS* from $SRAS_2$ to $SRAS_3$. This puts additional upward pressure on the price level and exerts a downward force on real GDP. The final long-run equilibrium thus occurs at point E_3, with the price level at P_3 and real GDP at Q_3. (In principle, because the oil supply shock has had no long-term effect on labour markets, the natural rate of unemployment does not change when equilibrium moves from E_1 to E_3.)

Generalizing the Theory

Naturally, the focus of real business cycle theory goes well beyond the simple "oil shock" that we have discussed here, for it encompasses all types of real disturbances, including technological changes and shifts in the composition of the labour force. Moreover, a complete treatment of real shocks to the economy is typically much more complex than we have allowed for in our discussion. For example, an oil shock such as is shown in Figure 15–11 would likely also have effects on the real wealth of Canadians, causing a reduction in aggregate demand as well as aggregate supply. Nevertheless, our simple example still manages to capture the flavour of the theory.

It is clear that real business cycle theory has improved our understanding of the economy's behaviour, but there is also agreement among economists that it alone is incapable of explaining all of the facets of business cycles that we observe. For example, it is difficult to imagine a real disturbance that could possibly account for the Great Depression in this country, when real income fell 30 percent and the unemployment rate rose to 20 percent. Moreover, real business cycle theory continues to assume that prices are perfectly flexible and so fails to explain a great deal of the apparent rigidity of prices throughout the economy.

15.6 Supply-Side Economics

The supply-side shocks of the 1970s, especially the reduction in the supply of oil, resulted in the worst combination of economic outcomes—high inflation, stagnation in economic output, and increasingly higher unemployment or "stagflation." But this shock caused

FIGURE 15–12

Effects of an Increase in the Supply of Resources

The position of the *LRAS* depends on our endowments of all types of natural and human-made resources. Hence, an increase in the supply of one of these resources, such as the Internet, causes an increase—an outward shift—in the aggregate supply curve. In addition, there is a decline in the equilibrium price level and a rise in the rate of real GDP per year (output).

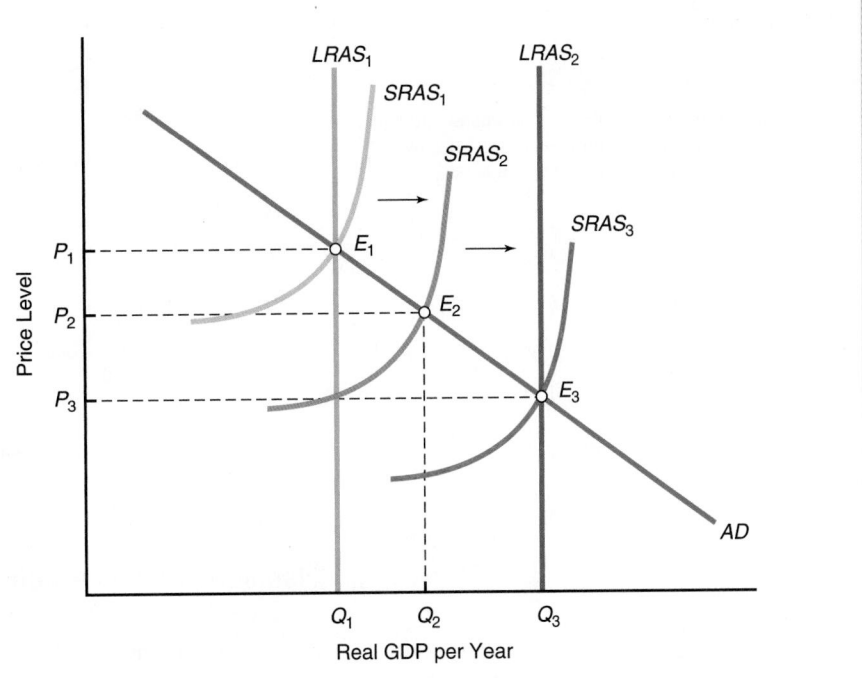

some economists to take note that virtually all attention in mainstream macroeconomic theory was focused on aggregate demand. This is focusing on only half the model.

Let us revisit the aggregate supply shock illustrated in Figure 15–11. If we could stimulate an increase in aggregate supply, could we not achieve the reverse of what had been observed? Instead of the worst combination of economic outcomes, could we not achieve the best possible combination of outcomes—low inflation, increasing real economic output, and lower unemployment? This is shown in Figure 15–12.

Supply-side economists argued that all the attention paid to demand-oriented theories distracted attention from the real problems of the economy. The real problems, according to the supply-siders, were that increasing levels of taxation and regulation were reducing incentives to work, save, and invest. What was needed were policies that would better stimulate aggregate supply, not aggregate demand. They advocated reducing marginal income tax rates, business taxes, and other business costs.

Advocates for such changes argue that lower tax rates will lead to an increase in productivity because individuals will work harder and longer, save more, and invest more; thus, increased productivity will lead to more economic growth, which will lead to higher real GDP. The government, by applying lower marginal tax rates, will not necessarily lose tax revenues, since the lower marginal taxes will be applied to a growing tax base because of economic growth. After all, tax revenues are the product of a tax rate times a tax base.

This relationship is sometimes called the Laffer Curve, named after economist Arthur Laffer, who developed it in front of some journalists and politicians in 1974. It is reproduced in Figure 15–13. On the horizontal axis are tax revenues, and on the vertical axis is the marginal tax rate. As you can see, total tax revenues rise as tax rates increase and then eventually fall after some unspecified tax-revenue-maximizing rate.

People who support the notion that reducing taxes does not necessarily lead to reduced tax revenues are called supply-side economists. **Supply-side economics** involves changing the tax structure to create incentives to increase productivity. Due to a shift in the aggregate supply curve to the right, there can be greater output without upward pressure on the price level. Refer to Example 15–6 for a historical view of supply-side economics.

Supply-side economics The notion that changing the tax structure to create incentives increases productivity.

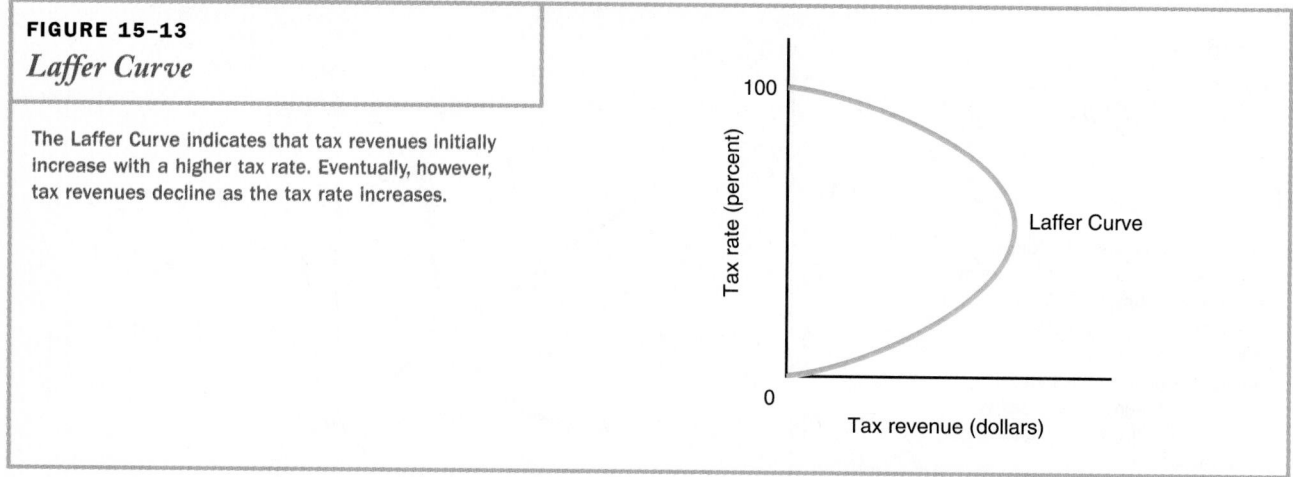

FIGURE 15–13
Laffer Curve

The Laffer Curve indicates that tax revenues initially increase with a higher tax rate. Eventually, however, tax revenues decline as the tax rate increases.

EXAMPLE 15–6   **Islam and Supply-Side Economics**

Supply-side economics has a long history, dating back to at least the 14th century. The greatest of medieval Islamic historians, Abu Zayd Abd-ar-Rahman Ibn Khaldun (1332–1406), included an Islamic view of supply-side economics in his monumental book *The Muqaddimah* (1377). He pointed out that "when tax assessments . . . upon the subjects are low, the latter have the energy and desire to do things. Cultural enterprises grow and increase . . . . [Therefore] the number of individual imposts [taxes] and assessments mounts." If taxes are increased both in size and rates, "the result is that the interest of subjects in cultural enterprises disappears, because when they compare expenditures and taxes with their income and gain and see little profit they make, they lose all hope." Ibn Khaldun concluded that "at the beginning of a dynasty, taxation yields a large revenue from small assessments. At the end of a dynasty, taxation yields a small revenue from large assessments."

For critical analysis: How do this Islamic scholar's economic theories apply to the modern world?

Criticisms of Supply-Side Economics

The supply-siders' view and the Laffer Curve have been controversial. A fundamental criticism has to do with timing and time lags. Investment does not occur overnight. Skeptics say that it is unlikely that a tax cut would have a very large impact on incentives; it would be of uncertain direction and slow to emerge. They are of small magnitude and, at best, long-term effects. In fact, most economists believe that the demand-side effects would be more immediate and overwhelm the supply-side effects.

Equally, a supply-side program is likely to have only a limited effect on inflation. Furthermore, if such policies were implemented when the economy was at the full-employment level, then the likely outcome would be inflationary. In addition, there is a different problem. Most supply-side incentives and initiatives would increase income inequality.

The supply-siders claimed that because of the Laffer Curve effect, President Reagan's substantial tax cuts in 1981 could maintain expenditures (even increasing defence spending) and balance the budget. These excessive promises proved false. In the decade after 1982, the American federal government ran huge record deficits, adding about $2 trillion to the national debt and turning the United States from the largest creditor nation in the world to the largest debtor nation in the world.

Somewhere between levels of taxation of 0 percent and 100 percent, there will be a point of maximum tax revenue. This is a logical proposition. The policy issue is where a particular economy is located on its Laffer Curve.

On balance, supply-side policies are not a substitute for short-run stabilization policy but, rather, could be approached as a way to enhance long-run economic growth.

15.7 *Alternative Models for Active Policy Making*

New Keynesian Economics

Although the new classical and real business cycle theories both incorporate pure competition and flexible prices, a body of research called the *new Keynesian economics* drops both of these assumptions. **New Keynesian economics** involves economic models based on the idea that demand creates its own supply as a result of various possible government fiscal and monetary coordination failures. The new Keynesian economists do not believe that market-clearing models of the economy can explain business cycles. Consequently, they argue that macroeconomic models must contain the "sticky" wages and prices assumption that Keynes outlined in his major work. Thus, the new Keynesian research has as its goal a refinement of the theory of aggregate supply that explains how wages and prices behave in the short run. There are several such theories. The first one relates to the cost of changing prices.

Small-Menu Cost Theory

If prices do not respond to demand changes, two conditions must be true: Someone must be consciously deciding not to change prices, and that decision must be in the decision maker's self-interest. One combination of facts that is consistent with this scenario is the **small-menu cost theory**, which supposes that much of the economy is characterized by imperfect competition and that it is costly for firms to change their prices in response to changes in demand. The costs associated with changing prices are called *menu costs*, and they include the costs of renegotiating contracts, printing price lists (such as menus), and informing customers of price changes.

Many such costs may not be very large in magnitude; that is why they are called *small-menu costs*. Some of the costs of changing prices, however, such as those incurred in bringing together business managers from points around the country or the world for meetings on price changes, or renegotiating deals with customers, may be significant.

Firms in different industries have different cost structures. Such differences explain diverse small-menu costs. Therefore, the extent to which firms hold their prices constant in the face of changes in demand for their products will vary across industries. Not all prices will be rigid. Nonetheless, new Keynesian theorists argue that many—even most—firms' prices are sticky for relatively long time intervals. As a result, the aggregate level of prices could be very nearly rigid because of small-menu costs.

Although most economists agree that such costs exist, there is considerably less agreement on whether they are sufficient to explain the extent of price rigidity that is observed.

Efficiency Wage Theory

An alternative approach within the new Keynesian framework is called the **efficiency wage theory**, which proposes that worker productivity actually *depends on* the wages that workers are paid, rather than being independent of wages, as is assumed in other theories (see Examples 15–7 and 15–8). According to this theory, higher real wages encourage workers to work harder, improve their efficiency, increase morale, and raise their loyalty to the firm. Across the board, then, higher wages tend to increase workers' productivity, which, in turn, discourages firms from cutting real wages because of the

---

New Keynesian economics Economic models based on the idea that demand creates its own supply as a result of various possible government fiscal and monetary coordination failures.

Small-menu cost theory A hypothesis that supposes that much of the economy is characterized by imperfect competition and that it is costly for firms to change their prices in response to changes in demand.

Efficiency wage theory The hypothesis that worker productivity actually *depends on* the wages that workers are paid, rather than being independent of wages.

EXAMPLE 15-7 | **Job Cuts or Pay Reductions: Which Are Less Harmful to Workers' Morale?**

Suppose that you are the manager of a firm that has experienced a decline in product demand. Should you lay off some workers while maintaining the wages of the workers you continue to employ, or should you cut wages for all your employees to avoid layoffs?

Truman Bewley of Yale University surveyed managers to find out how they would respond to this situation and why. On the basis of the managers' answers, he concluded that firms prefer layoffs. The reason is that pay cuts hurt all employees and reduce morale throughout a company. Layoffs can reduce morale among workers who retain their jobs by increasing their uncertainty about continued employment, but managers perceive that this reduced-morale effect is less dramatic and lasts for a shorter time.

Bewley argues that in bad economic times, real-world managers often behave just the way the efficiency wage concept predicts. They lay off workers instead of reducing their wages.

For critical analysis: Assuming that firms behave as the efficiency wage idea predicts, if a fall in aggregate demand causes a recession, should real wages rise or fall during the recession?

EXAMPLE 15-8 | **Henry Ford and the Efficiency Wage Model**

One of the most clear-cut examples of the efficiency wage model involved the Ford Motor Company in the United States. When nominal wage rates were about U.S.$2 to U.S.$3 a day in 1914 (about U.S.$30 in today's dollars and with no benefits, such as health insurance), Henry Ford ordered his managers to start paying workers U.S.$5 a day. Ford later argued that the increase in wages was a "cost-cutting" move. The evidence bears him out. Absenteeism dropped by over 70 percent. Moreover, labour turnover virtually disappeared. Consequently, Ford's managers had to spend less time training new workers.

For critical analysis: What alternative ways do managers have to provide incentives to their workers to become more efficient?

---

damaging effect that such an action would have on productivity and profitability. See Example 15–9 for a discussion of France's attempt to legislatively lower unemployment.

Under highly competitive conditions, there will generally be an optimal wage—called the **efficiency wage**—that the firm should continue paying, even in the face of large fluctuations in the demand for its output. If the supply of labour increases, therefore, firms may continue to hold real wages steady at the efficiency wage level. Unemployment will result. New workers will not be able to find employment at the unchanged real wage rate, at which there will be an excess quantity of labour supplied, or unemployment.

The efficiency wage theory model is a rather simple idea, but it is somewhat revolutionary. All of the models of the labour market adopted by traditional classical, traditional Keynesian, monetarist, new classical, and new Keynesian theorists alike do not consider such real-wage effects on worker productivity.

There are significant, valid elements in the efficiency wage theory, but its importance in understanding national business fluctuations remains uncertain. For example, although the theory explains rigid real wages, it does not explain rigid prices. Moreover, the theory ignores the fact that firms can (and apparently do) rely on a host of incentives other than wages to encourage their workers to be loyal, efficient, and productive.

Efficiency wage An optimal wage that the firm should continue paying, even in the face of large fluctuations in the demand for its output.

EXAMPLE 15-9 **The French Government's Direct Approach to Reducing Unemployment**

The unemployment rate in France has hovered around 10 percent for several years. In an effort to bring the unemployment rate down, the French government has required employers, except those with very small numbers of employees, to allow their employees to work no more than 35 hours per week, with some degree of flexibility in implementing weekly hour limits built in.

The theory behind this rule was that when faced with a reduction in legally permissible hours of labour from regular employees, firms would have to respond by employing previously unemployed individuals. This, the French government figured, would reduce structural unemployment, thereby boosting total employment and cutting both the actual rate of unemployment and the natural rate of unemployment.

Critics suggested the weekly work limit made already highly regulated national labour markets even more inflexible. Together with many other wage and employment restrictions, they contended, the limit hindered the ability of French companies to add workers in good times and to shed employees in bad times. This, the critics argued, actually boosted the natural unemployment rate.

There is evidence to support this position. Average unemployment rates tend to be higher in nations with less flexible labour markets. Measures of labour market flexibility indicate that French labour markets are almost 30 percent less flexible that labour markets in the United Kingdom and more than 40 percent less flexible than in the United States. This may help explain why the British and American unemployment rates have averaged about four to five percentage points lower than the unemployment rate in France during the past several years. In the end, it has become clear to even the French government that the weekly-hours limit made matters worse, not better, for the unemployment situation in France.

For critical analysis: What are some of the various types of government regulation of labour markets that might increase the overall expenses firms incur when they hire new employees?

Real GDP and the Price Level in a Sticky-Price Economy

According to the new Keynesians, sticky prices strengthen the argument favouring active policymaking as a means of preventing substantial short-run swings in real GDP and, as a consequence, employment.

NEW KEYNESIAN INFLATION DYNAMICS. To see why the idea of price stickiness strengthens the case for active policymaking, consider part (a) of Figure 15-14. If a significant portion of all prices do not adjust rapidly, then in the short run, the aggregate supply curve effectively is horizontal, as assumed in the traditional Keynesian theory. This means that a decline in aggregate demand, such as the shift from AD_1 to AD_2 shown in part (a), will induce the largest possible decline in equilibrium real GDP, from \$12 trillion to \$11.7 trillion. When prices are sticky, economic contractions induced by aggregate demand shocks are as severe as they can be.

As part (a) shows, in contrast to the traditional Keynesian theory, the new Keynesian sticky-price theory indicates that the economy will find its own way back to a long-run equilibrium. The theory presumes that small-menu costs induce firms not to change their prices in the short run. In the long run, however, the profit gains to firms from reducing their prices to induce purchases of more goods and services cause them to cut their prices. Thus, in the long run, the price level declines in response to the decrease in aggregate demand. As firms reduce their prices, the horizontal aggregate supply curve shifts downward, from $SRAS_1$ to $SRAS_2$, and equilibrium real GDP returns to its former level, other things being equal.

FIGURE 15–14

Short- and Long-Run Adjustments in the New Keynesian Sticky-Price Theory

Part (a) shows that when prices are sticky, the short-run aggregate supply curve is horizontal, here at a price level of 118. As a consequence, the short-run effect of a fall in aggregate demand from AD_1 to AD_2 generates the largest possible decline in real GDP, from $12 trillion at point E_1 to $11.7 trillion at point E_2. In the long run, producers perceive that they can increase their profits sufficiently by cutting prices and incurring the menu costs of doing so. The resulting decline in the price level implies a downward shift of the *SRAS* curve, so that the price level falls to 116 and real GDP returns to $12 trillion at point E_3. Part (b) illustrates the argument for active policymaking based on the new Keynesian theory. Instead of waiting for long-run adjustments to occur, policymakers can engage in expansionary policies that shift the aggregate demand curve back to its original position, thereby shortening or even eliminating a recession.

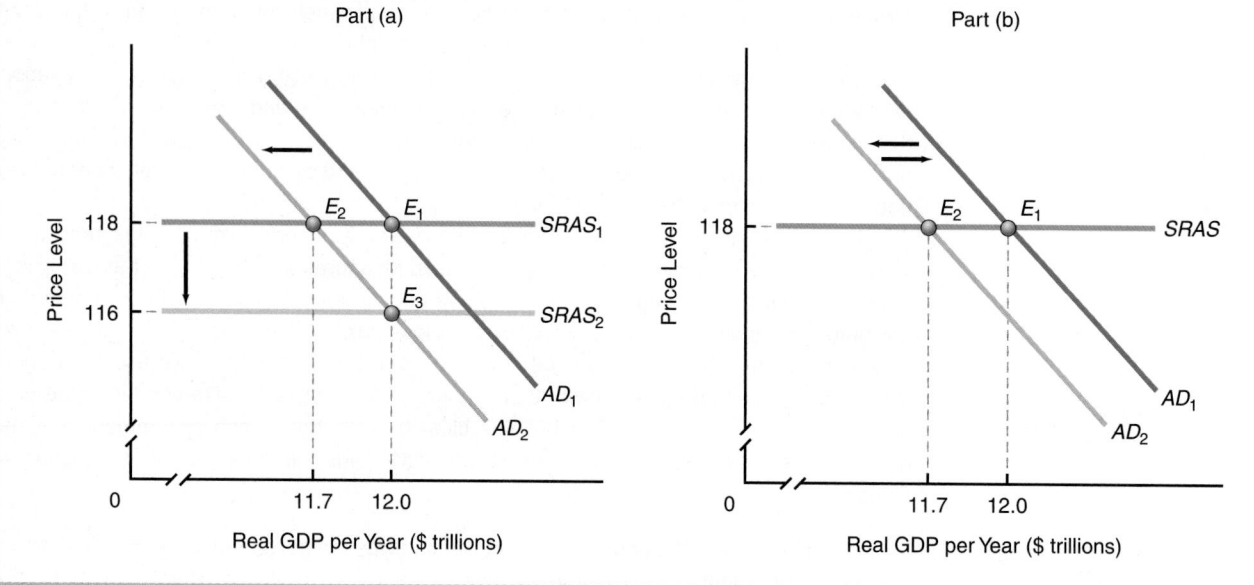

Of course, an increase in aggregate demand would have effects opposite to those depicted in part (a) of Figure 15-14. A rise in aggregate demand would cause real GDP to rise in the short run. In the long run, firms would gain sufficient profits from raising their prices to compensate for incurring menu costs, and the short-run aggregate supply curve would shift upward. Consequently, an economy with growing aggregate demand should exhibit so-called **new Keynesian inflation dynamics**: Initial sluggish adjustment of the price level in response to aggregate demand increases followed by higher inflation later on.

WHY ACTIVE POLICYMAKING CAN PAY OFF WHEN PRICES ARE STICKY. To think about why the new Keynesian sticky-price theory supports the argument for active policymaking, let's return to the case of a decline in aggregate demand illustrated in part (a) of Figure 15-14. Part (b) shows the same decline in aggregate demand as in part (a) and the resulting maximum contractionary effect on real GDP.

Monetary and fiscal policy actions that influence aggregate demand are as potent as possible when prices are sticky and short-run aggregate supply is horizontal. In principle, therefore, all that a policymaker confronted by the leftward shift in aggregate demand depicted in part (a) must do is to conduct the appropriate policy to induce a rightward shift in the *AD* curve back to its previous position. Indeed, if the policymaker acts rapidly enough, the period of contraction experienced by the economy may be very brief. Active policymaking can thereby moderate or even eliminate recessions.

New Keynesian inflation dynamics
In new Keynesian theory, the pattern of inflation exhibited by an economy with growing aggregate demand—initial sluggish adjustment of the price level in response to increased aggregate demand followed by higher inflation later.

An Alternative New Keynesian Scenario: Bounded Rationality

Not all economists are convinced that prices adjust as sluggishly as presumed in the new Keynesian sticky-price analysis presented in Figure 15-14. Indeed, not even all new Keynesian economists are convinced that prices are really so sticky.

Recently, some new Keynesian theorists have proposed an alternative theory supporting active policymaking. This theory borrows from the *bounded rationality* assumption proposed by proponents of behavioural economics. Recall that under bounded rationality, people cannot examine every possible choice available to them, so they use simple rules of thumb to guide their decision making. According to the alternative new Keynesian sticky-price rationale for active policymaking, people in the economy cannot process all the information that confronts them, so they use rules of thumb to adjust wages and prices. While wages and prices do adjust, any adjustments are potentially very incomplete. Wages and prices are not fully flexible in the short run, but they are not completely rigid either.

Thus, a key prediction of this alternative theory is that bounded rationality causes prices to *adjust* particularly sluggishly to changes in aggregate demand. Instead of price stickiness, potentially very incomplete short-run adjustments of prices prevent real GDP from rapidly reaching its full-employment level, thereby providing a channel for active policymaking to have short-run stabilizing effects. Incomplete price adjustment alone, these other new Keynesians argue, provides sufficient rationale for policymakers to engage in active efforts aimed at dampening or even preventing cycles in real GDP and, as a result, employment.

Economic Factors Favouring Active Versus Passive Policymaking

To many people who have never taken a principles of economics course, it seems apparent that the world's governments should engage in active policymaking aimed at achieving high and stable real GDP growth and a low and stable unemployment rate. As you have learned in this chapter, the advisability of policy activism is not so clear-cut.

Several factors are involved in assessing whether policy activism is really preferable to passive policymaking. Table 15-1 summarizes the issues involved in evaluating the case for active policymaking versus the case for passive policymaking.

You may have heard about U.S. President Harry Truman's remark that he wished he could find a one-armed economist, so that he would not have to hear, "On the one hand ... but on the other hand" quite so often. The current state of thinking on the relative desirability of active or passive policymaking may make you as frustrated as President Truman was in the early 1950s. On the one hand, most economists agree that active policymaking is unlikely to exert sizable long-run effects on any nation's economy. Most also agree that aggregate supply shocks contribute to business cycles. Consequently, there is general agreement that there are limits on the effectiveness of monetary and fiscal policies. On the other hand, a number of economists continue to argue that there is evidence indicating stickiness of prices and wages. They argue, therefore, that monetary and fiscal policy actions can offset, at least in the short run and perhaps even in the long run, the effects that aggregate demand shocks would otherwise have on real GDP and unemployment.

These diverging perspectives help explain why economists reach differing conclusions about the advisability of pursuing active or passive approaches to macroeconomic policymaking. Different interpretations of evidence on the issues summarized in Table 15-1 will likely continue to divide economists for years to come.

TABLE 15-1

Issues That Must Be Assessed in Determining the Desirability of Active versus Passive Policymaking

Economists who contend that active policymaking is justified argue that evidence on each issue listed in the first column supports conclusions listed in the second column. In contrast, economists who suggest that passive policymaking is appropriate argue that evidence regarding each issue in the first column leads to conclusions listed in the third column.

Issue	Support for Active Policymaking	Support for Passive Policymaking
Phillips curve inflation–unemployment trade-off	Stable in the short run; perhaps predictable in the long run	Varies with inflation expectations; at best fleeting in the short run and nonexistent in the long run
Aggregate demand shocks	Induce short-run and perhaps long-run effects on real GDP and unemployment	Have little or no short-run effects and certainly no long-run effects on real GDP and unemployment
Aggregate supply shocks	Can, along with aggregate demand shocks, influence real GDP and unemployment	Cause movements in real GDP and unemployment and hence explain most business cycles
Pure competition	Is not typical in most markets, where imperfect competition predominates	Is widespread in markets throughout the economy
Price flexibility	Is uncommon because factors such as small-menu costs induce firms to change prices infrequently	Is common because firms adjust prices immediately when demand changes
Wage flexibility	Is uncommon because labour market adjustments occur relatively slowly	Is common because nominal wages adjust speedily to price changes, making real wages flexible

➤➤ CONCEPTS IN BRIEF

Learning Objective 15.5: Identify the central features of the real business cycle challenge to policy making.

- Real business cycle theory holds that even if all prices and wages are perfectly flexible, real shocks to the economy (such as technological change and changes in the supplies of factors of production) can cause national business fluctuations.

Learning Objective 15.6: Identify the central features of supply-side economics to policy making.

- Supply-side economics is the notion that creating incentives for individuals and firms will increase productivity, cause the aggregate supply curve to shift outward, and increase tax revenues.

Learning Objective 15.7: Distinguish among alternative modern approaches to strengthening the case for active policy making.

- The new Keynesian economics explains why various features of the economy, such as small-menu costs and wage rates that affect productivity, make it possible for monetary shocks to cause real effects.
- Although there remain significant differences between the classical and Keynesian branches of macroeconomics, the rivalry between them is an important source of innovation that helps improve our understanding of the economy.
- New Keynesian approaches to understanding the sources of business fluctuations highlight wage and price stickiness. Firms that face costs of adjusting their prices may be slow to change prices in the face of variations in demand. Thus, the short-run aggregate supply curve is horizontal, and changes in aggregate demand have the largest possible effects on real GDP in the short run, which gives discretionary policies scope to offset aggregate demand shocks. Another new Keynesian approach suggests that people with bounded rationality who use rules of thumb to guide their decisions cannot fully adjust prices and wages in the short run. According to this alternative view, prices and wages are not fully sticky, but they are sufficiently inflexible in the short run that discretionary policy actions can stabilize real GDP.

The Bank of Canada's High Interest Rate Policy

Concepts Applied: Nominal and Real Interest Rates, Unemployment, Economic Growth

Gordon Thiessen, formerly the Governor of the Bank of Canada, supported the use of relatively high interest rates to dampen inflation and stabilize the economy. Critics claimed his plan kept real interest rates high and encouraged financial, rather than productive, investment in Canada.

A debate rages among economists about whether the Bank of Canada's interest rate policy is helping or harming the economy. In 1991, the Bank of Canada made a formal commitment to the federal government to keep inflation between 1 and 3 percent through to 1998 (and now beyond). The Bank has used high interest rates as its policy tool in pursuit of this goal. High interest rates discourage consumer and business spending, dampen aggregate demand, and thus keep prices from rising too quickly.

The former Governor of the Bank of Canada, Gordon Thiessen, asserted that his high interest rate policy allows businesses to make "smarter" decisions, since they can plan on a relatively stable price level into the future. This, in turn, makes Canada more conducive to expanding business activity. Further, low inflation rates contribute to lower nominal interest payments on the federal debt since nominal interest rates are the sum of real rates plus a premium for expected inflation. The combination of low debt service payments and expanding business activity will result in a lower debt-to-GDP ratio. A lower debt-to-GDP ratio makes Canada a more attractive place for investment, which will induce economic growth. Overall, Mr. Thiessen's plan was one of short-term pain—continuing high unemployment—for long-term gain—economic growth that will lead to job creation in the future.

Critics of Mr. Thiessen's plan argued that the Bank of Canada has more than one mandate: the 1934 charter of the Bank also included a directive that it should promote trade, production, and employment in Canada. By following a high interest rate policy, the Bank of Canada has kept real interest rates high. Inflation has indeed been falling, but nominal interest rates are lagging. See Figure 15–15 for a history of real interest rates. High real interest rates, argued the Bank of Canada's critics, encourage passive invest-ment—the purchase of financial instruments in order to earn a hefty return. Low real interest rates encourage active investment—investment in capital equipment and job-creating businesses because the cost of borrowing is low. With active investment the tax base increases, raising government revenues and reducing the need for costly social programs, thus making a reduction of the debt-to-GDP ratio possible.

What should students of economics make of this debate? Is it time to turn from fighting inflation to job creation? The natural rate of unemployment in Canada is thought to be about 6.7 percent (look back at Figure 15–1). The unemployment rate in 2006 was 6.7 percent, with inflation at about 1.7 percent. Has the natural rate fallen, suggesting that unemployment could be further reduced without risking renewed inflation?

For critical analysis:

1. What different effects do you think passive and active investment have on the Canadian economy?
2. According to the policy irrelevance proposition, would unemployment have been affected by former Governor Thiessen's high interest rate policy?

FIGURE 15–15

Real Interest Rates Since World War II

Real interest rates in Canada have varied from a low of minus 10 percent just after World War II to a high of about 8 percent in 1988–1990, in the wake of the OPEC oil price hikes. Real interest rates peaked again in 1994.

SOURCE: ADAPTED FROM THE STATISTICS CANADA CANSIM DATABASE, SERIES V41690973 AND V122495.

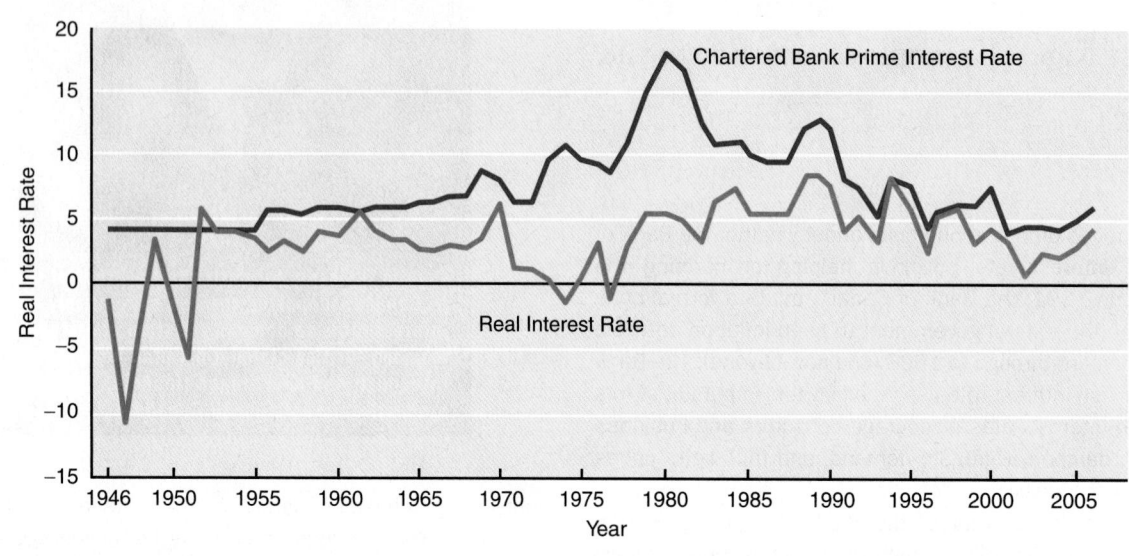

SUMMARY

Here is what you should know after reading this chapter. MyEconLab will help you identify what you know, and where to go when you need to practise. We suggest that as soon as you review one of the Learning Objective sections below, you then proceed to go through the related section in MyEconLab.

myeconlab

LEARNING OBJECTIVES	KEY TERMS	MYECONLAB PRACTICE
15.1 The Natural Rate of Unemployment. According to the basic theory of aggregate demand and short- and long-run aggregate supply, an unexpected increase in aggregate demand can cause real GDP to rise in the short run, which results in a reduction in the unemployment rate. Consequently, for a time the actual unemployment rate can fall below the natural rate of unemployment. Likewise, an unanticipated reduction in aggregate demand can push down real GDP in the short run, thereby causing the actual unemployment rate to rise above the natural unemployment rate. Therefore, the natural rate of unemployment is the rate that exists in the long-run equilibrium, when workers' expectations are consistent	active (discretionary) policy making, 387 passive (nondiscretionary) policy making, 387 natural rate of unemployment, 388	• **MyEconLab** Study Plan 15.1

⟫→ LEARNING OBJECTIVES	**KEY TERMS**	**MYECONLAB PRACTICE**

with actual conditions and departures from the natural rate of unemployment can occur when individuals are surprised by unanticipated changes in fiscal or monetary policy.

15.2 The Phillips Curve. An unexpected increase in aggregate demand that causes a drop in the unemployment rate also induces a rise in the equilibrium price level and, consequently, inflation. Thus, the basic aggregate demand–aggregate supply model indicates that, other things being equal, there should be an inverse relationship between the inflation rate and the unemployment rate. This downward-sloping relationship is called the Phillips curve. The Phillips curve shows a negative relationship between the inflation rate and the unemployment rate that can be observed when there are unanticipated changes in aggregate demand. It was originally believed that the Phillips curve represented a trade-off between inflation and unemployment. In fact, no trade-off exists because workers' expectations adjust to systematic attempts to reduce unemployment below its natural rate.	Phillips curve, 392 nonaccelerating inflation rate of unemployment (NAIRU), 392	• **MyEconLab** Study Plan 15.2
15.3 The Importance of Expectations. Theory only predicts that there will be a Phillips curve relationship when another important factor, expectations, is held unchanged. If people are able to anticipate efforts of policymakers to exploit the Phillips curve trade-off by engaging in inflationary policies to push down the unemployment rate, then basic theory also suggests that input prices such as nominal wages will adjust more rapidly to an increase in the price level. As a result, the Phillips curve will shift outward, and the economy will adjust more speedily toward the natural rate of unemployment. When plotted on a chart, therefore, the actual relationship between the inflation rate and the unemployment rate will not be a smooth, downward-sloping Phillips curve.		• **MyEconLab** Study Plan 15.3
15.4 Rational Expectations and the New Classical Model. The rational expectations hypothesis assumes that individuals' forecasts incorporate all available information,	rational expectations hypothesis, 396 new classical model, 397	• **MyEconLab** Study Plan 15.4

➤ **LEARNING OBJECTIVES**	**KEY TERMS**	**MYECONLAB PRACTICE**
including an understanding of government policy and its effects on the economy. The new classical economics assumes that the rational expectations hypothesis is valid and also that there is pure competition and that all prices and wages are flexible. A fundamental implication of the new classical theory is that only unanticipated actions can induce even short-run changes in real GDP. If people completely anticipate the actions of policy-makers, wages and the other input prices adjust immediately, so that real GDP remains unaffected. Thus a key implication of new classical theory is the policy irrelevance proposition, which states that the unemployment rate and the level of real GDP is unaffected by fully anticipated policy actions. Policies can alter real economic variables only if the policies are unsystematic and therefore unanticipated; such policies cannot affect output and employment systematically.	policy irrelevance proposition, 398	
15.5 Real Business Cycle Theory. Real business cycle theory holds that even if all prices and wages are perfectly flexible, real shocks to the economy (such as technological change, labour market shocks, and changes in the supplies of factors of production) can cause national business fluctuations. Therefore, this theory focuses on how shifts in aggregate supply curves can cause real GDP to vary over time.	real business cycle theory, 401	• **MyEconLab** Study Plan 15.5
15.6 Supply-Side Economics. Supply-side economics is the notion that creating incentives for individuals and firms will increase productivity, cause the aggregate supply curve to shift outward, and increase tax revenues.	supply-side economics, 403	• **MyEconLab** Study Plan 15.6
15.7 Alternative Models for Active Policy Making. New Keynesian approaches to understanding the sources of business fluctuations highlight wage and price stickiness. Small-menu cost theory proposes that imperfectly competitive firms that face costs of adjusting their prices may be slow to change prices in the face of variations in demand, so that real GDP may exhibit greater short-run variability than it otherwise would. Another new Keynesian approach,	New Keynesian economics, 405 small-menu cost theory, 405 efficiency wage theory, 405 efficiency wage, 406 New Keynesian inflation dynamics, 408	• **MyEconLab** Study Plan 15.7

→ LEARNING OBJECTIVES	KEY TERMS	MYECONLAB PRACTICE

efficiency wage theory, proposes that worker productivity depends on real wages that workers earn, which dissuades firms from reducing real wages and thereby leads to widespread wage stickiness. Finally, another new Keynesian approach suggests that people with bounded rationality who use rules of thumb to guide their decisions cannot fully adjust prices and wages in the short run. According to this alternative view, prices and wages are not fully sticky, but they are sufficiently inflexible in the short run that discretionary policy actions can stabilize real GDP.

⇒→ PROBLEMS

(Answers to the odd-numbered problems appear at the back of the book.)

LO 15.1 Explain why the actual unemployment rate might depart from the natural rate of unemployment.

1. Suppose that the government were to alter the composition of the unemployment rate by including people in the military as part of the labour force.
   a. How would this affect the actual unemployment rate?
   b. How would such a change affect estimates of the natural rate of unemployment?
   c. If this computational change were made, would it in any way affect the logic of the short-run and long-run Phillips curve analysis and its implications for policy making? Why might the government wish to make such a change?

2. Explain how the average duration of unemployment may be different for a given rate of unemployment.

3. What effect does the average duration of unemployment have on the rate of unemployment if we hold constant the variables you used to explain Problem 2?

4. When will the natural rate of unemployment and the NAIRU differ? When will they be the same?

5. Suppose that more unemployed people who are classified as part of frictional unemployment decide to stop looking for work and start their own businesses instead. What is likely to happen to each of the following, other things being equal?

   a. The natural unemployment rate
   b. The NAIRU

LO 15.2 Describe why there may be an inverse relationship between the inflation rate and the unemployment rate, reflected by the Phillips curve.

6. A criticism sometimes directed at the Bank of Canada is "every time growth starts to pick up the Bank of Canada pushes on the brakes, robbing working families and businesses of the benefits of faster growth." Evaluate this statement in the context of short-run and long-run perspectives on the Phillips curve.

7. Answer the following questions based on the accompanying graph:

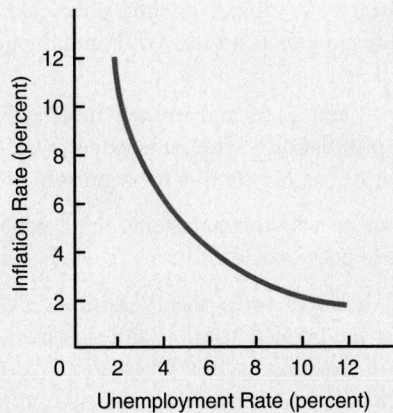

   a. If we regard this curve as showing a trade-off between inflation and unemployment, how much unemployment will it "cost" to reduce inflation to 2 percent per year?

b. What might cause this curve to shift upward?

c. Why do economists argue that there is generally no useable trade-off between unemployment and inflation?

8. The natural rate of unemployment depends on factors that affect the behaviour of both workers and firms. Make lists of possible factors affecting workers and firms that you believe are likely to influence the natural rate of unemployment.

9. Economists have not reached an agreement on how lengthy the time horizon for "the long run" is in the context of Phillips curve analysis. Would you anticipate that this period is likely to have been shortened or extended by the advent of more sophisticated computer and communications technology? Explain your reasoning.

LO 15.3 Evaluate how expectations affect the relationship between the actual inflation rate and the unemployment rate.

10. The Phillips curve exhibits a negative relationship between the inflation rate and the unemployment rate that can be observed when there are unanticipated changes in aggregate demand. If workers adjust their expectations and anticipate efforts by policy makers to exploit the Phillips curve trade-off, will the Phillips curve trade-off still occur?

LO 15.4 Describe the rational expectations hypothesis and the new classical model and their implications for economic policy making.

11. Suppose that economists were able to use Canadian economic data to demonstrate that the rational expectations hypothesis is true. Would this be sufficient to demonstrate the validity of the policy irrelevance proposition?

12. Evaluate the following statement: "In an important sense, the term 'policy irrelevance proposition' is misleading because even if the rational expectations hypothesis is valid, economic policy actions can have significant effects on real GDP and the unemployment rate."

13. If both employers and workers incorrectly perceive the rate of inflation to the same extent, would the Phillips curve still be expected to be negatively sloped?

LO 15.5 Identify the central features of the real business cycle challenge to policy making.

14. Real business cycle theory assumes that wages and prices are perfectly flexible and that markets clear. The theory explains cyclical fluctuations based on supply shocks. What might some sources of supply shocks be?

LO 15.6 Identify the central features of supply-side economics to policy making.

15. In Example 15–6, "Islam and Supply-Side Economics," an Islamic historian outlines an Islamic view of supply-side economics. What policies do supply-side economists propose today to shift the aggregate supply curve outward or to the right to increase economic growth and higher real GDP? How does this compare to the earlier Islamic view?

LO 15.7 Distinguish among alternative modern approaches to strengthening the case for active policy making.

16. Example 15–7, "Job Cuts or Pay Reductions: Which Are Less Harmful to Workers' Morale?", reported Truman Bewley's research that showed managers prefer layoffs to pay cuts consistent with the efficiency wage concept. How does the existence of contracts, small-menu costs, and efficiency wages affect the amount of discretion available to policy makers?

17. Use an aggregate demand and aggregate supply diagram to illustrate why the existence of widespread stickiness in prices established by businesses throughout the economy would be extremely important for predicting the potential effects of policy actions on real GDP.

18. Both the traditional Keynesian theory discussed in Chapter 11 and the new Keynesian theory considered in this chapter indicate that the short-run aggregate supply curve is horizontal.

a. In terms of their short-run implications for the price level and real GDP, is there any difference between the two approaches?

b. In terms of their long-run implications for the price level and real GDP, is there any difference between the two approaches?

19. Consider the diagram below, which is drawn under the assumption that the new Keynesian sticky-price theory of aggregate supply applies. Assume that at present, the economy is in equilibrium at point A. Answer the following questions

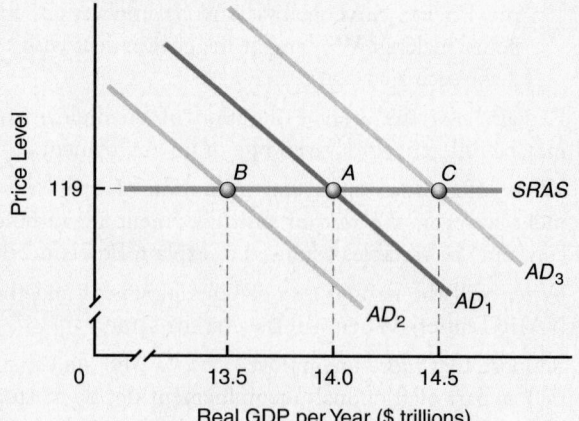

a. Suppose that there is a sudden increase in desired investment expenditures. Which of the alternative aggregate demand curves—AD_2 or AD_3—will apply after this event occurs? Other things being equal, what will happen to the equilibrium price level and to equilibrium real GDP in the short run? Explain.

b. Other things being equal, after the event and adjustments discussed in part a have taken place, what will happen to the equilibrium price level and to equilibrium real GDP in the long run? Explain.

20. Economists have established that higher productivity due to technological improvements tends to push up real wages. Now suppose that the economy experiences a host of technological improvements. If worker productivity responds positively to higher real wages, will this effect tend to add to or subtract from the economic growth initially induced by the improvements in technology?

21. Normally, firms experience an increase in profits by adjusting their prices upward when aggregate demand increases. The idea behind the small-menu-cost explanation for stickiness is that firms will leave their prices unchanged if their profit gain from adjusting prices is less than menu costs they would incur if they change prices. If firms anticipate that a rise in demand is likely to last for a long time, does this make them more or less likely to adjust their prices when they face small-menu costs? (Hint: Profits are a flow that firms earn from week to week and month to month, but small-menu costs are a one-time expense.)

16

Comparative Advantage and the Open Economy

In 1990, there were a total of 50 *bilateral trade agreements*, or special treaties governing trade between a pair of countries and *regional trade agreements*, or special treaties governing trade among a set of the world's nations. These agreements included the European Union (EU), the countries involved in the North American Free Trade Agreement (NAFTA), and the Association of Southeast Asian Nations (ASEAN). Today, there are more than 230 of these agreements. Proposals for about 70 more bilateral and regional trade agreements are under active negotiation around the globe. Why do nations enter into agreements aimed at promoting bilateral or multilateral trade of goods and services? In this chapter, you will learn about how nations can gain from engaging in international trade through the establishment of both regional and global trade agreements.

> ## ➤ LEARNING OBJECTIVES
>
> After reading this chapter, you should be able to:
>
> 16.1 Discuss the worldwide importance, trends, and patterns of trade, and the importance of trade to Canada.
>
> 16.2 Distinguish between comparative advantage and absolute advantage.
>
> 16.3 Explain why nations can gain from specializing in production and engaging in international trade.
>
> 16.4 Outline common arguments against free trade.
>
> 16.5 Describe two ways that nations restrict foreign trade.
>
> 16.6 Identify Canada's most significant international agreement and name the primary organization that adjudicates trade disputes among nations.

MyEconLab helps you master each objective and study more efficiently. See end of chapter for details.

About 25 million shipping containers, each of which offers space for up to 68 cubic metres of merchandise weighing between 16 000 and 20 000 kilograms, move along the world's sea lanes every year. The global fleet of ships that carry these containers between many pairs of ports has grown by more than 25 percent since 2000. Most of the newest ships can carry between 7000 and 8000 shipping containers each.

Without all these shipments of merchandise, many people who work to produce goods for sale to other nations would have to find other employment. Some might even have trouble finding work. Nevertheless, other people in these countries would undoubtedly stand to gain from restricting international trade. Learning about international trade will help you understand why this is so.

16.1   The Worldwide Importance, Trends, and Patterns of International Trade

Look at part (a) of Figure 16–1. Since the end of World War II, world output of goods and services (world gross domestic product, or GDP) has increased almost every year until the present, when it is almost eight times what it used to be. Look at the top line in part (a). World trade has increased to more than 26 times what it was in 1950.

Canada figured prominently in this expansion of world trade. In part (b) of Figure 16–1, you see imports and exports expressed as a percentage of total annual yearly income (GDP). While international trade was always important to Canada, with imports plus exports adding up to almost 50 percent of annual national income in 1950, today it zaccounts for almost 70 percent of GDP. A further illustration of the importance of international trade for Canada is shows in Examples 16–1 and 16–2.

Example 16-2 discusses how the Internet has contributed to increased pharmaceutical trade, because of lower Canadian prices, between Canada and the U.S. The strong Canadian dollar is contributing to more Canadians seeking competitively priced goods on the Internet from the U.S.

The pattern of Canada's merchandise trade in goods with the rest of the world is shown in the 2006 data in Figure 16–3. There, it can be seen that the United States is, by far, both Canada's largest customer at $361.0 million representing 79.2 percent of total exports and the largest source of imports at $264.9 million representing 65.5 percent of total imports. Canada's next largest trading partners are the European Union and Japan. To illustrate the magnitude of trade with the United States, Canada's trade with Home Depot is greater than its entire trade with France.

The composition of Canadian merchandise exports and imports by type is shown in Figure 16–4. Imports of manufactured goods—machinery and equipment, automotive products, and industrial goods—make up about 69 percent of imports. On the export side, manufactured goods—machinery and equipment, automotive products, and industrial goods—account for about 59.5 percent of all exports. A further 19 percent of total exports are energy.

The preceding discussion focused on Canada's merchandise trade in goods. Canada also trades in services—nonmerchandise trade—such as insurance services, banking services, consulting services, and so forth. In 2006, Canada imported $83.3 million and exported $69.0 million in services.

FIGURE 16–1

The Growth of World Trade

In part (a), you can see the growth in world trade in relative terms because we use an index of 100 to represent real world trade in 1950. By the mid-2000s, that index had increased to over 2600. At the same time, the index of world GDP (annual world income) had gone up to only around 900. World trade is clearly on the rise: In Canada, both imports and exports, expressed as a percentage of annual national income (GDP) in part (b), have been rising.

SOURCES: PART (A) STEVEN HUSTED AND MICHAEL MELVIN, *INTERNATIONAL ECONOMICS*, 3D ED. (NEW YORK: HARPERCOLLINS, 1995), P. 11, USED WITH PERMISSION; WORLD TRADE ORGANIZATION; FEDERAL RESERVE SYSTEM; U.S. DEPARTMENT OF COMMERCE; PART (B) ADAPTED FROM THE STATISTICS CANADA CANSIM DATABASE, SERIES V3860085, V3860078, AND V3680081.

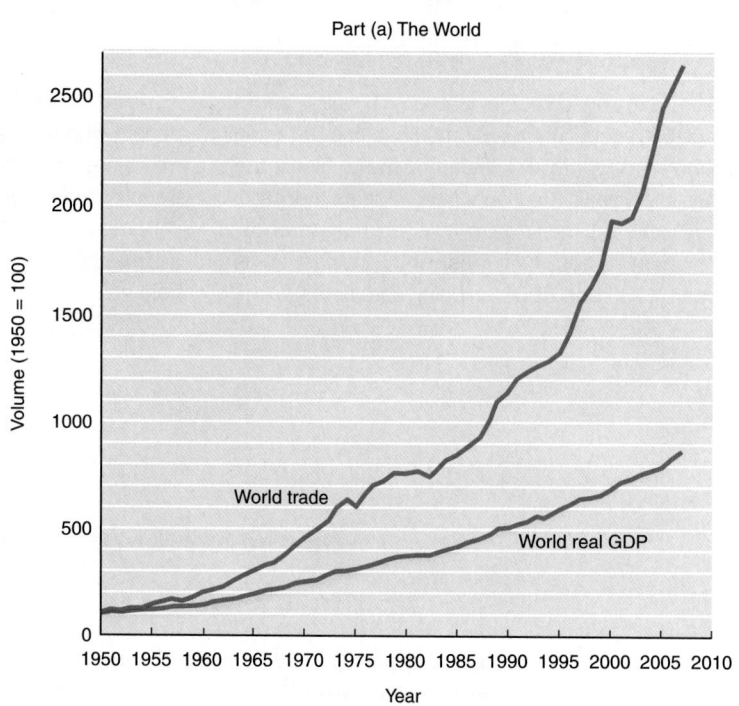

EXAMPLE 16–1

The Importance of International Trade in Various Countries

While imports and exports each account for more than 30 percent of total annual national income in Canada, in some countries, the figure is much higher. In others, it is much less, as you can see in Table 16–1. Certain nations, such as Luxembourg, must import practically everything! Another way to understand the worldwide importance of international trade is to look at trade flows on the world map in Figure 16–2.

continued

TABLE 16-1

Importance of Imports in Selected Countries

Country	Imports as a Percentage of Annual National Income	Country	Imports as a Percentage of Annual National Income
Luxembourg	95.0	United Kingdom	21.0
Netherlands	58.0	China	19.0
Canada	35.0	France	18.4
Norway	30.0	United States	12.8
Germany	23.0	Japan	6.8

SOURCE: INTERNATIONAL MONETARY FUND.

FIGURE 16-2

World Trade Flows

International merchandise trade amounts to over U.S.$6 trillion worldwide. The percentage figures show the proportion of trade flowing in the various directions.

SOURCE: WORLD TRADE ORGANIZATION (DATA ARE FOR 2003).

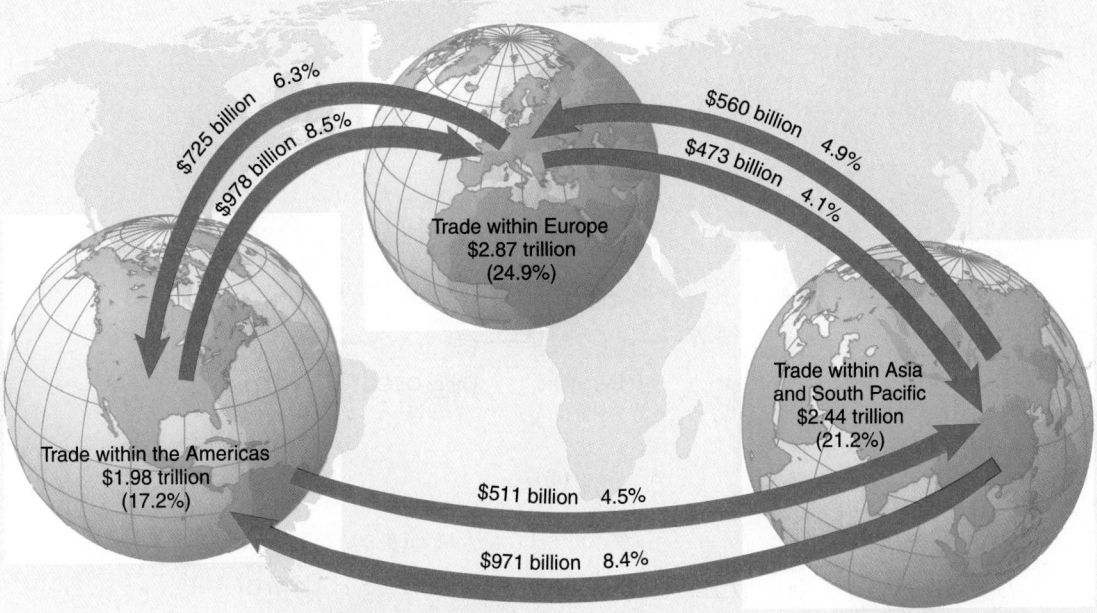

For critical analysis: How can Luxembourg have a strong economy if it imports so many goods and services?

EXAMPLE 16-2   **U.S. Consumers Go Online to Import Canadian Pharmaceuticals**

Today, about 270 pharmacies in Canada offer services to U.S. consumers. After the pharmacies receive prescriptions from U.S. physicians, Canadian physicians review the prescriptions to verify that they comply with that nation's health care laws. Then the pharmacies ship the medications across the border. All told, more than US$700 million worth of pharmaceuticals now flow southward across the U.S.–Canada border each year.

For critical analysis: Some critics claim that international trade causes nations to "lose jobs." Why do you suppose that the premier of the province of Manitoba credits international trade in pharmaceuticals with creating 2000 jobs at the province's online and mail-order pharmacies?

FIGURE 16–3

Canadian Merchandise Trade by Geographic Area, 2006

SOURCE: STATISTICS CANADA, CANSIM, TABLE 228-003.

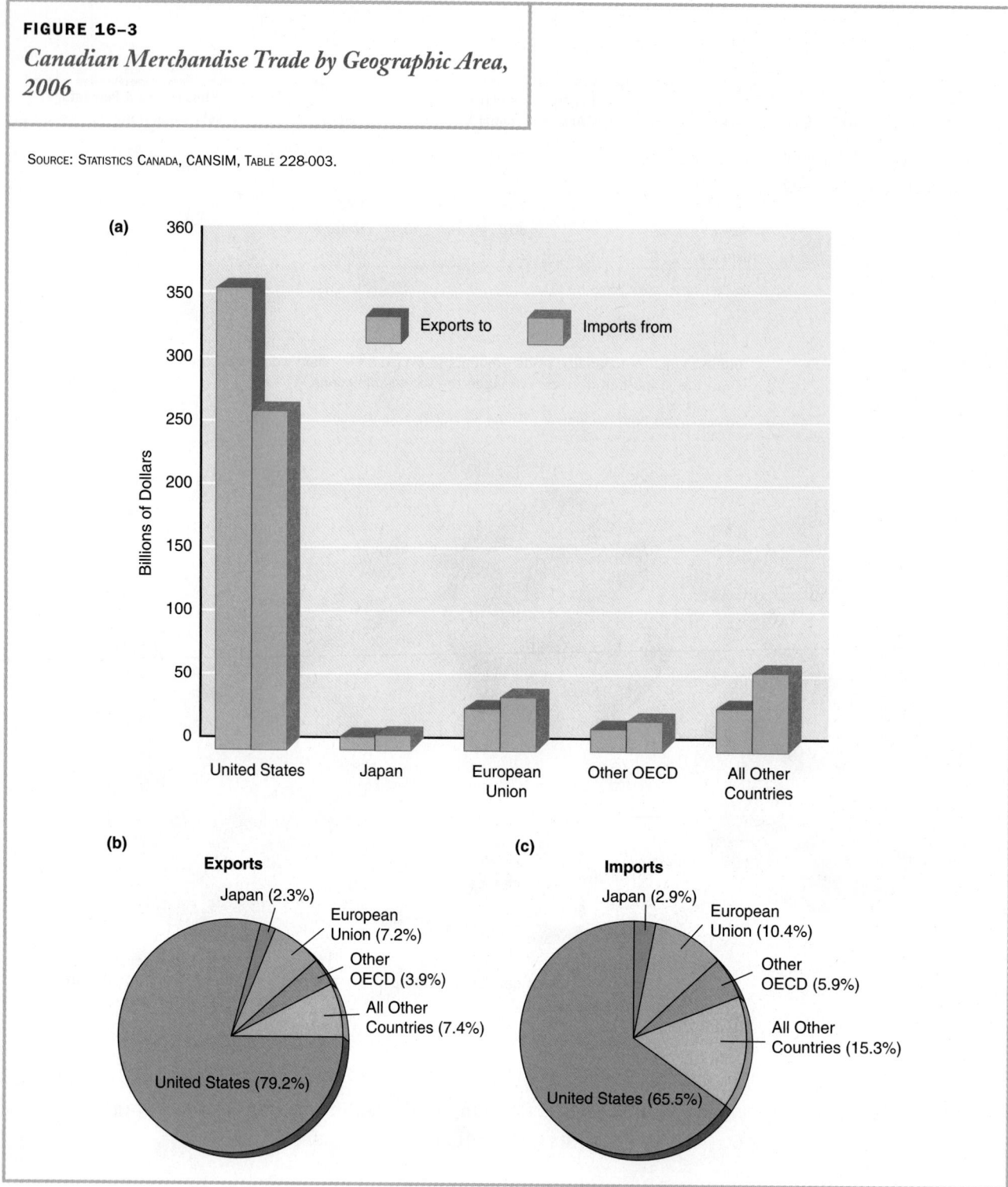

16.2 Why We Trade: Comparative Advantage and Exhausting Mutual Gains from Exchange

You have already been introduced to the concepts of specialization and mutual gains from trade in Chapter 2. These ideas are worth repeating because they are essential to understanding why the world is better off because of more international trade. The best way to understand the gains from trade among nations is first to understand the output gains from specialization between individuals.

FIGURE 16–4

Distribution of Merchandise Exports and Imports for Canada by Broad Commodity Groups, 2006

SOURCE: STATISTICS CANADA, CANSIM, TABLE 228-0003.

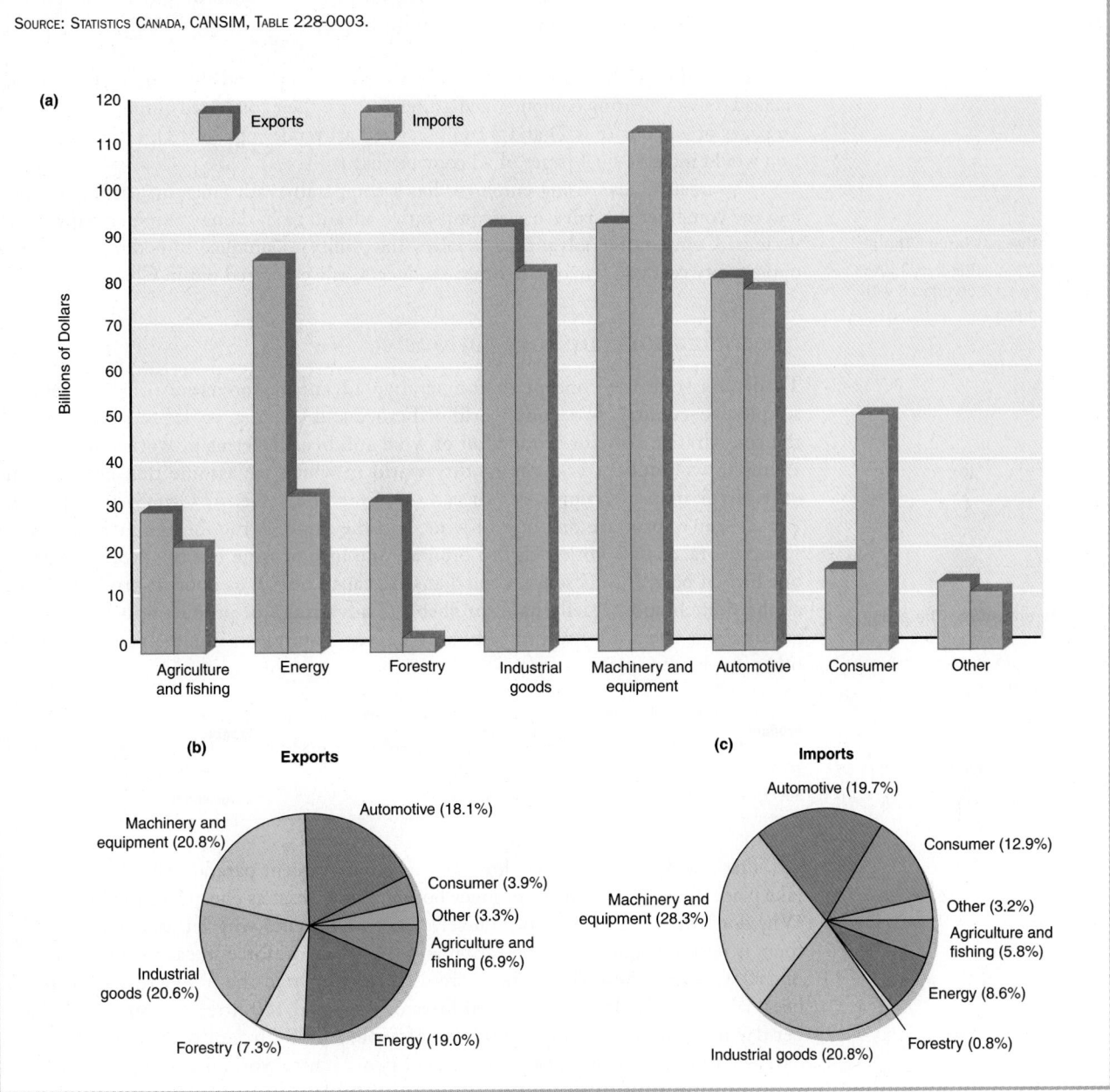

The Output Gains from Specialization

Suppose that a creative advertising specialist can generate two pages of ad copy (written words) or one computerized art rendering per hour. At the same time, a computer artist can write one page of ad copy or complete one computerized art rendering per hour. Here, the ad specialist can come up with more pages of ad copy per hour than the computer specialist and seemingly is just as good as the computer specialist at computerized art renderings. Is there any reason for the creative specialist and the computer specialist to "trade"? The answer is yes, because such trading will lead to higher output.

Consider the scenario of no trading. Assume that during each eight-hour day, the ad specialist and the computer whiz devote half of their day to writing ad copy and half to computerized art rendering. The ad specialist would create eight pages of ad copy (4 hours × 2) and four computerized art renderings (4 × 1). During that same period, the computer specialist would create four pages of ad copy (4 × 1) and four computerized art renderings (4 × 1). Each day, the combined output for the ad specialist and the computer specialist would be 12 pages of ad copy and eight computerized art renderings.

If the ad specialist specialized only in writing ad copy and the computer artist specialized only in creating computerized art renderings, their combined output would rise to 16 pages of ad copy (8 × 2) and 8 computerized art renderings (8 × 1). Overall, production would increase by 4 pages of ad copy per day.

The creative advertising employee has a comparative advantage in writing ad copy, and the computer specialist has a comparative advantage in doing computerized art renderings. **Comparative advantage** involves the ability to produce something at a lower opportunity cost compared with other producers, as we pointed out in Chapter 2.

Comparative advantage The ability to produce something at a lower opportunity cost compared with other producers.

Specialization Among Nations

To demonstrate the concept of comparative advantage for nations, let's consider a simple two-country, two-good world of France and Canada. In Table 16–2, we show the comparative costs of production of wine and beer in terms of worker-days, using a simple two-country, two-commodity world in which we assume that labour is the only factor of production. As you can see from the table, in Canada, it takes one worker-day to produce one litre of wine, and the same is true for one litre of beer. In France, it takes one worker-day to produce one litre of wine but two worker-days for one litre of beer. In this sense, Canadians appear to be just as good at producing wine as the French and actually have an **absolute advantage** in producing beer. Absolute advantage is the ability to produce more output from given inputs of resources than other producers can.

Absolute advantage The ability to produce more output from given inputs of resources than other producers can.

TABLE 16–2

Comparative Costs of Production

Product	Canada	France
Wine (1 litre)	1 worker-day	1 worker-day
Beer (1 litre)	1 worker-day	2 worker-days

Trade will still take place, however, which may seem paradoxical. How can trade take place if Canada is able to produce both goods at least as cheaply as the French can? Why don't we just produce both ourselves? To understand why, let us assume first that there is no trade and no specialization and that the workforce in each country consists of 200 workers. These 200 workers are divided equally in the production of wine and beer. We see in Table 16–3 that 100 litres of wine and 100 litres of beer are produced per day in Canada. In France, 100 litres of wine and 50 litres of beer are produced per day. The total daily world production in our two-country world is 200 litres of wine and 150 litres of beer.

TABLE 16–3

Daily World Output before Specialization

It is assumed that 200 workers are available in each country.

Product	Canada Workers	Canada Output (litres)	France Workers	France Output (litres)	World Output (litres)
Wine	100	100	100	100	200
Beer	100	100	100	50	150

Now the countries specialize. What can France produce more cheaply? Look at the comparative costs of production expressed in worker-days in Table 16–2. What is the cost of producing one litre more of wine? One worker-day. What is the cost of producing one litre more of beer? Two worker-days. We can say, then, that in France the opportunity cost of producing wine is less than that of producing beer. The residents of France realistically will choose to specialize in the activity for which they experience a lower opportunity cost. In other words, French residents will specialize in the activity in which they have comparative advantage, which is the production of wine. Likewise, residents of Canada will specialize in the area of manufacturing in which they have comparative advantage, which is the production of beer.

TABLE 16-4

Daily World Output after Specialization

It is assumed that 200 workers are available in each country.

	Canada			France		
Product	Workers	Output (litres)	Workers	Output (litres)	World Output (litres)
Wine	—	—	200	200	200
Beer	200	200	—	—	200

According to Table 16–4, after specialization, Canada produces 200 litres of beer and France produces 200 litres of wine. Note that the total world production per day has gone up from 200 litres of wine and 150 litres of beer to 200 litres of wine and 200 litres of beer per day. This was done without any increased use of resources. The gain, 50 "free" litres of beer, results from a more efficient allocation of resources worldwide. World output is greater when countries specialize in producing the goods in which they have a comparative advantage and then engage in foreign trade. Another way of looking at this is to consider the choice between two ways of producing a good. Obviously, each country would choose the less costly production process. One way of "producing" a good is to import it; so, if the imported good is, in fact, cheaper than the domestically produced good, we will "produce" it by importing it.

Gains from Trade

Trade is the means by which consumers in these two countries can consume both wine and beer.

Because 1 beer = 1 wine in Canada, if trade is to occur, Canada would expect to get more than 1 wine for every beer it sells; otherwise why specialize and engage in trade?

Similarly, because 1 wine = 0.5 beer in France, France would expect to get more than 0.5 beer for every wine.

Suppose the terms of trade falls somewhere in between these two cost conditions, say 1 wine = 0.75 beer (alternatively 1 beer = 1.33 wine) and 100 wine is exchanged for 75 beer. The gains from trade after specialization based upon comparative advantage in this situation are 25 beer for Canada and 25 beer for France. This equals the overall gain in global output of 50 beer. This result is shown in Table 16–5.

TABLE 16-5

International Specialization Based on Comparative Advantage and the Gains from Trade

Country	(1) Outputs before Specialization	(2) Outputs after Specialization	(3) Trade Exports (−) Imports (+)	(4) Outputs after Trade	(5) = (4) − (1) Gains from Specialization and Trade
Canada					
Wine	100	0	+100	100	0
Beer	100	200	−75	125	+25
France					
Wine	100	200	−100	100	0
Beer	50	0	+75	75	+25

This example shows that when nations specialize in producing goods for which they have comparative advantage and engage in international trade, considerable production and consumption gains are possible for those nations and hence for the world. Why is this so? The answer is that specializing in producing goods for which the two nations have a comparative advantage allows both nations to produce more efficiently. As a consequence, worldwide production possibilities increase. This makes greater worldwide consumption possible through international trade.

How the overall gains from international specialization and trade are divided will depend on the actual terms of trade or exchange ratio. This ratio will be determined by world supply and demand conditions.

Not everybody, of course, is better off when free trade occurs. In our example, Canadian wine makers and French beer makers are worse off because those two *domestic* industries have disappeared. Beer customers in the importing country, France, get lower-priced beer and more beer. In Canada, which has comparative advantage in beer production, customers will get more beer, but they will be paying more, the world price, for that beer.

Some people are worried that Canada (or any other country, for that matter) might someday "run out of exports" because of overaggressive foreign competition. The analysis of comparative advantage tells us the opposite. No matter how much other countries compete for our business, Canada (or any other country) will always have a comparative advantage in something that it can export. In 10 or 20 years, that something may not be what we export today, but it will be exportable, nonetheless, because we will have a comparative advantage in producing it.

As a result of specialization based on comparative advantage and trade, countries benefit. The effect of such specialization is to improve global efficiencies and to move the respective production possibilities curves outward.

Other Benefits from International Trade: The Transmission of Ideas

Beyond the fact that comparative advantage generally results in an overall increase in the output of goods produced and consumed, there is another benefit to international trade—the international transmission of ideas. According to economic historians, international trade has been the principal means by which new goods, services, and processes have spread around the world. For example, coffee was initially grown in Arabia near the Red Sea. Starting around 675 A.D., coffee beans were roasted and coffee was consumed as a beverage. Eventually, it was exported to other parts of the world, and the Dutch started cultivating it in their colonies during the 17th century and the French in the 18th century. The lowly potato is native to the Peruvian Andes. In the 16th century, it was brought to Europe by Spanish explorers. Thereafter, its cultivation and consumption spread rapidly. The alphabet was spread through international trade, as discussed in Example 16–3.

EXAMPLE 16-3 | **International Trade and the Alphabet**

Even the alphabetic system of writing that appears to be the source of most alphabets in the world today was spread through international trade. According to some scholars, the Phoenicians, who lived on the long, narrow strip of Mediterranean coast north of Israel from the ninth century B.C. to around 300 B.C., created the first true alphabet. Presumably, they developed the alphabet to keep international trading records on their ships, rather than having to take along highly trained scribes.

For critical analysis: Before alphabets were used, how might have people communicated in written form?

All of the *intellectual property* that has been introduced throughout the world is a result of international trade. This includes new music, such as rock and roll in the 1950s and hip-hop and grunge in the 1990s. It includes the software applications that are common for computer users everywhere.

New processes have been transmitted through international trade. One of those involves the Japanese manufacturing innovation that emphasized redesigning the system, rather than running the existing system in the best possible way. Inventories were reduced to just-in-time levels by re-engineering machine setup methods. Just-in-time inventory control is now common in Canadian factories.

The Relationship between Imports and Exports

The basic proposition in understanding all of international trade is this:

In the long run, imports are paid for by exports.[1]

The reason that imports are ultimately paid for by exports is that foreigners want something in exchange for the goods that are shipped to Canada. For the most part, they want goods made in Canada. From this truism comes a remarkable corollary:

Any restriction of imports ultimately reduces exports.

This is a shocking revelation to many people who want to restrict foreign competition in order to protect domestic jobs. Although it is possible to protect certain Canadian jobs by restricting foreign competition, it is impossible to make *everyone* better off by imposing import restrictions. Why? Because ultimately such restrictions lead to a reduction in employment in the export industries of the nation.

Think of exports as simply another way of producing goods. International trade is merely an economic activity like all others; it is a production process that transforms exports into imports.

| EXAMPLE 16–4 | **The Importation of Priests into Spain** |

Imports affect not only goods but also services and the movement of labour. In Spain, some 3000 priests retire each year, but barely 250 young men are ordained to replace them. Over 70 percent of the priests in Spain are now over the age of 50. The Spanish church estimated that by 2005, the number of priests would fall to half the 20 441 who were active in Spain in 1990. The Spanish church has had to seek young seminarians from Latin America under what it calls "Operation Moses." It is currently subsidizing the travel and training of an increasing number of young Latin Americans to take over where native Spaniards have been before.

For critical analysis: How might the Spanish church induce more native Spaniards to become priests?

16.3 International Competitiveness

"Canada is falling behind." "We need to stay competitive internationally." These and similar statements are often heard in government circles when the subject of international trade comes up. There are two problems with this issue. The first has to do with a simple

---

[1]We have to modify this rule by adding that in the short run, imports can also be paid for by the sale (or export) of real and financial assets, such as land, shares, and bonds, or through an extension of credit from other countries.

definition. What does "global competitiveness" really mean? When one company competes with another, it is in competition. Is Canada like one big corporation, in competition with other countries? Certainly not. The standard of living in each country is almost solely a function of how well the economy functions within *that country*, not how it functions relative to other countries.

Another problem arises with respect to the real world. According to the International Institute for Management Development in Lausanne, Switzerland, Canada has been *improving* its world competitive position. In 1994, Canada was ranked 20th in the world; in 1997, 10th; in 2003, 6th; and in 2006, 7th. Canada's improved ranking is due to better government decision-making, improving technology, and a highly productive labour force. Other factors include Canada's sophisticated financial system and better management of the private sector.

Other nations face their own challenges when competing in the international market. The unique challenges faced by some Middle Eastern nations in achieving international competitiveness are examined in Example 16–5.

EXAMPLE 16–5 **Do Legal Restrictions Reduce the International Competitiveness of Middle Eastern Nations?**

During most of the medieval period, from the 8th to 13th centuries A.D., the Middle East was an international trading centre. Mecca, located in what today is Saudi Arabia, was one of the world's key trading hubs.

Since the 14th century, the Middle East's relative contribution to world trade has declined. Today, even though the Middle Eastern population will soon surpass the American population, the international trade of these countries accounts for only 3 percent of world trade, compared with the United States' 16 percent share.

What happened? Many scholars note that both Islamic and European laws once required a partnership to dissolve if one partner died or became incapacitated. Laws set out rigid rules for splitting business inheritances among family members, such as parents, siblings, uncles, cousins, and even more distant relatives. These rules tended to limit the scale of business arrangements because the more people who were involved, the greater was the chance that the business would have to be split up unexpectedly.

Beginning in the 14th century, European laws began allowing people to give inheritances to anyone they wished. Later, people gained the right to establish corporations and spread the liability for business losses across numerous owners. These legal developments helped European businesses thrive as global trade expanded during the Renaissance. The legal foundation in much of the Middle East remained unchanged, however, which kept businesses in most of that region from adapting as readily to the new international trading environment. This handicap remains to this day.

For critical analysis: Which Middle Eastern nations would lose the most if the entire region's legal foundation were altered to match the Western framework? (*Hint*: A few Middle Eastern nations have adopted Western legal foundations.)

⇒ CONCEPTS IN BRIEF

Learning Objective 16.1: Discuss the worldwide importance, trends, and patterns of trade and the importance of trade to Canada.
- World trade is expanding more rapidly than global GDP.
- Canada has one of the highest ratios of trade to its GDP among world nations.

Learning Objective 16.2: Distinguish between comparative advantage and absolute advantage.

- Absolute advantage refers to the ability to produce a unit of output with fewer physical units of input; comparative advantage refers to producing output that has the lowest opportunity cost for a nation.
- Different nations will always have different comparative advantages because of differing opportunity costs due to different resource mixes.

Learning Objective 16.3: Explain why nations can gain from specializing in production and engaging in international trade.

- Countries can be better off materially if they specialize in producing goods for which they have a comparative advantage, and then engaging in trade.

16.4 Arguments against Free Trade

Numerous arguments are raised against free trade. They mainly point out the costs of trade; they do not consider the benefits or the possible alternatives for reducing the costs of free trade while still reaping benefits.

The Infant Industry Argument

A country may feel that if a particular industry were allowed to develop domestically, it could eventually become efficient enough to compete effectively in the world market. Therefore, if some restrictions were placed on imports, domestic producers would be given the time needed to develop their scale and efficiency to the point where they would be able to compete in the domestic market without any restrictions on imports. In graphic terminology, we would expect that if the protected industry truly does experience improvements in production techniques or technological breakthroughs toward greater efficiency in the future, the supply curve will shift outward to the right so that the domestic industry can produce larger quantities at each and every price. The **infant industry argument** is based on the contention that tariffs should be imposed to protect from import competition an industry that is trying to get started. Presumably, after the industry becomes technologically efficient, the tariff can be lifted. This infant industry argument has some merit in the short run and has been used to protect a number of industries in their infancy around the world. Such a policy can be abused, however. Often, the protective import-restricting arrangements remain even after the infant industry has matured. If other countries can still produce more cheaply, the people who benefit from this type of situation are obviously the shareholders (and specialized factors of production that will earn economic rents) in the industry that is still being protected from world competition. The people who lose out are the consumers, who must pay a price higher than the world price for the product in question. In any event, it is very difficult to know beforehand which industries will eventually survive. In other words, we cannot predict very well the specific infant industries that should be protected. Note that when we talk about which industry "should be" protected, we are in the realm of normative economics. We are making a value judgment, a subjective statement of what *ought to be*.

Infant industry argument The contention that tariffs should be imposed to protect from import competition an industry that is trying to get started. Presumably, after the industry becomes technologically efficient, the tariff can be lifted.

Countering Foreign Subsidies and Dumping

Another strong argument against unrestricted foreign trade concerns countering other nations' subsidies to their own producers. When a foreign government subsidizes its producers, our producers claim that they cannot compete fairly with these subsidized foreigners. To the extent that such subsidies fluctuate, it can be argued that unrestricted free trade will seriously disrupt domestic producers. They will not know when foreign governments are going to subsidize their producers and when they are not. Our competing industries will be expanding and contracting too frequently.

Dumping Occurs when a producer sells its products abroad at a price below its cost of production or below the price that is charged in the home market.

The phenomenon called *dumping* is also used as an argument against unrestricted trade. **Dumping** occurs when a producer sells its products abroad at a price below its cost of production or below the price that is charged in the home market (see Example 16–6 and Policy Example 16–1). Although cries of dumping are often heard against foreign producers, they typically occur only when the foreign nation is in the throes of a serious recession. The foreign producer does not want to slow down its production at home. Because it anticipates an end to the recession and does not want to hold large inventories, it dumps its products abroad at prices below its costs. This does, in fact, disrupt international trade. It also creates instability in domestic production and therefore may impair commercial well-being at home.

EXAMPLE 16–6 **Dumping Chinese Garlic**

In 1996, Canadian garlic growers complained to the Canadian International Trade Tribunal (CITT) that between 1992 and 1996, growers from mainland China had been dumping fresh garlic on the Canadian market, thus suppressing price and causing profits to decline. The domestic producers claimed that over this period Canadian demand for garlic had increased by 8 million kilograms, and at the same time the market share filled by Chinese garlic had grown from 29 percent to 68 percent.

The CITT investigated the garlic growers' complaint. It determined that the "normal" price of garlic in China—that is the price that reflects the producers' costs—would be $1.91 per kilogram. (Since China does not have a free market in garlic, the CITT determined this price by looking at prices in other garlic-growing countries, such as Mexico.) However, Chinese garlic was selling in Canada for 58 cents per kilogram, a price reduction of 70 percent.

The CITT concluded that Chinese garlic growers had dumped 6 million kilograms of garlic on the Canadian market between 1992 and 1996. As a result, importers of Chinese garlic must pay a countervailing duty sufficient to bring its selling price to $1.91 per kilogram, in line with Canadian prices.

The anti-dumping garlic duties were extended in 2001. Recently, the CITT determined anti-dumping duties be allowed to expire in 2006–07, subject to appeals or a new investigation being initiated.

For critical analysis: Since consumers benefit from the low prices of dumping, why might they be in favour of countervailing duties?

POLICY EXAMPLE 16–1 **Who Is Dumping on Whom?**

Claims of dumping are handled on a case-by-case basis under international rules. Only a few firms in an industry have to lodge a claim to justify a dumping investigation. Under international law, antidumping rules permit governments to impose *duties*—special taxes on imported goods—on the products sold by firms of offending nations. Take a look at Figure 16–5. As you can see, in the early 1990s, the developed nations filed an increasing number of claims seeking antidumping relief. The biggest filer of dumping claims during this period was the United States, which launched cases mainly against companies based in South America and Asia. The United States began to cut back on dumping claims beginning in the mid-1990s. Nevertheless, dumping claims by emerging economies—notably Argentina, Brazil, Mexico, and South Africa—rose precipitously. Whom did these emerging economies accuse of dumping? Firms in the United States.

continued

FIGURE 16-5 *Claims to the World Trade Organization for Antidumping Relief*

In recent years, the developing nations have filed at least as many claims seeking antidumping relief as the number filed by the developed nations.

SOURCE: WORLD TRADE ORGANIZATION.

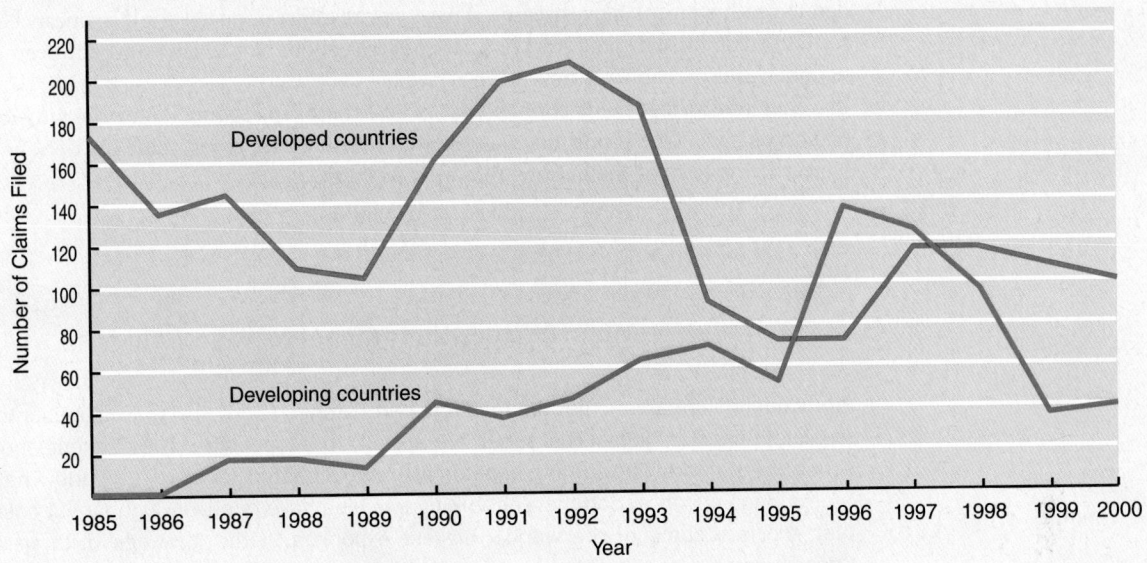

For critical analysis: Why did dumping claims by emerging nations fall as their economies expanded after the early 1990s?

Protecting Canadian Jobs

Perhaps the argument used most often against free trade is that unrestrained competition from other countries will eliminate Canadian jobs because other countries have lower-cost labour than we do. (Less restrictive environmental standards in other countries might also lower their costs relative to ours.) This is a compelling argument, particularly for politicians from areas that might be threatened by foreign competition. For example, a member of Parliament from an area with shoe factories would certainly be upset about the possibility of constituents' losing their jobs because of competition from lower-priced shoe manufacturers in Brazil and Asia. But, of course, this argument against free trade is equally applicable to trade between the provinces. See Example 16-7 for further discussion of this argument.

Economists David Gould, G. L. Woodbridge, and Roy Ruffin examined the data on the relationship between increases in imports and the rate of unemployment. Their conclusion was that there is no causal link between the two. Indeed, in half the cases they studied, when imports increased, unemployment fell.

Another issue has to do with the cost of protecting Canadian jobs by restricting international trade. Several years ago, the North–South Institute examined the cost of protection in the Canadian textile and clothing industries. It found that consumers were paying about $36 000 per year in taxes and higher prices to protect each textile and clothing industry job, which at the time paid about $10 000 per year to the average worker.

In the long run, the industries that have had the most protection—textiles, clothing, and iron and steel—have seen the most dramatic reductions in employment in Canada.

Emerging Arguments against Free Trade

In recent years, some new antitrade arguments have been advanced. One of these focuses on environmental concerns. International demonstrators have argued that some countries either have weak environmental laws and/or that enforcement of the laws is either lax or nonexistent, giving these countries a lower cost advantage. Also, many environmentalists have raised concerns that genetic engineering of plants and animals could lead to the accidental production of new diseases. These worries have induced the European Union to restrain trade in such products. Similar concerns about labour laws and enforcement and national security concerns have been raised.

Free trade proponents counter that at best these are arguments for the judicious regulation of trade. They continue to argue that by and large, broad trade restrictions mainly harm the interests of the nations that impose them.

EXAMPLE 16-7 Unfair Competition from Low-Wage Countries

Protectionists are able to get the media to carry stories about how low-wage countries are stealing Canadian jobs. The facts are exactly the opposite. The highest-labour-cost country in the world is Germany, and it is also the largest exporter in the world. The United States, Japan, France, and the United Kingdom also have relatively high labour costs, and they, too, are some of the world's biggest exporters. If the low-wage myth were true, Canada would never be able to compete with, say, Mexican labour. Yet, the reality is that Canada exports much more to Mexico than it imports. Finally, both the World Bank and the Organisation for Economic Co-operation and Development (OECD) have done exhaustive studies on the issue. Their conclusion is that there is no evidence that trade with low-wage countries results in large-scale job losses to industrial countries. The real competition for Canadian manufacturing comes from high-wage countries, such as the United States, Germany, and Japan.

For critical analysis: Who are these protectionists that are getting the media to carry stories about low-wage countries stealing Canadian jobs?

CONCEPTS IN BRIEF

Learning Objective 16.4: Outline common arguments against free trade.

- The infant industry argument against free trade contends that new industries should be protected against world competition so that they can become technologically efficient in the long run.
- Unrestricted foreign trade may allow foreign governments to subsidize exports or foreign producers to engage in dumping—selling products in other countries below their cost of production. To the extent that foreign export subsidies and dumping create more instability in domestic production, they may impair our well-being.
- Other arguments against free trade are loss of domestic jobs and the weakness of or lack of foreign enforcement of environmental, labour, and security laws.

16.5 Ways to Restrict Foreign Trade

There are many ways in which international trade can be stopped or at least stifled. These include quotas and taxes (the latter are usually called *tariffs* when applied to internationally traded items). Let us talk first about quotas.

Quotas

Quota system A government-imposed restriction on the quantity of a specific good that another country is allowed to sell in Canada.

The **quota system** is a government-imposed restriction on the quantity of a specific good that another country is allowed to sell in Canada. An import quota specifies the maximum amount of a commodity that may be imported during a specified period of time. For example, the government might not allow more than 50 million barrels of foreign crude oil to enter Canada in a particular year.

Consider the example of quotas on textiles. Figure 16–6 presents the demand and the supply curves for imported textiles. In an unrestricted import market, the equilibrium quantity imported is 90 million metres at a price of $1 per metre (expressed in constant-quality units). When an import quota is imposed, the supply curve is no longer S. Rather, the supply curve becomes vertical at some amount less than the equilibrium quantity—here, 80 million metres per year. The price to the Canadian consumer increases from $1 to $1.50. The domestic suppliers of textiles obviously benefit by an increase in revenues because they can now charge a higher price.

Voluntary export restraint agreement (VER) An official agreement with another country that "voluntarily" restricts the quantity of its exports to Canada.

VOLUNTARY QUOTAS. **Voluntary export restraint agreement (VER)** is an official agreement with another country that "voluntarily" restricts the quantity of its exports to Canada. In the early 1980s, the Canadian government asked Japan voluntarily to restrain its automobile exports to Canada for a period of three years. The Japanese government did so and even now continues to limit its automobile exports to the West.

Tariffs

We can analyze tariffs by using standard supply and demand diagrams. Let us use as our example computer software, some of which is made in the United States and some of which is made domestically. In part (a) of Figure 16–7, you see the demand and supply of American software. The equilibrium price is $100 per constant-quality unit, and the equilibrium quantity is 10 million per year. In part (b), you see the same equilibrium price of $100, and the *domestic* equilibrium quantity is 5 million units per year.

Now a tariff of $50 is imposed on all imported American software. The supply curve shifts upward by $50 to S_2. For purchasers of American software, the price increases to $125. The quantity demanded falls to 8 million per year. In part (b), you see that at the higher price of imported American software, the demand curve for Canadian-made software shifts outward to the right to D_2. The equilibrium price increases to $125, and the equilibrium quantity increases to 6.5 million units per year. So, the tariff benefits domestic

FIGURE 16–6
The Effect of Quotas on Textile Imports

Without restrictions, 90 million metres of textiles would be imported each year into Canada at the world price of $1 per metre. If the federal government imposes a quota of only 80 million metres, the effective supply curve becomes vertical at that quantity. It intersects the demand curve at the new equilibrium price of $1.50 per metre.

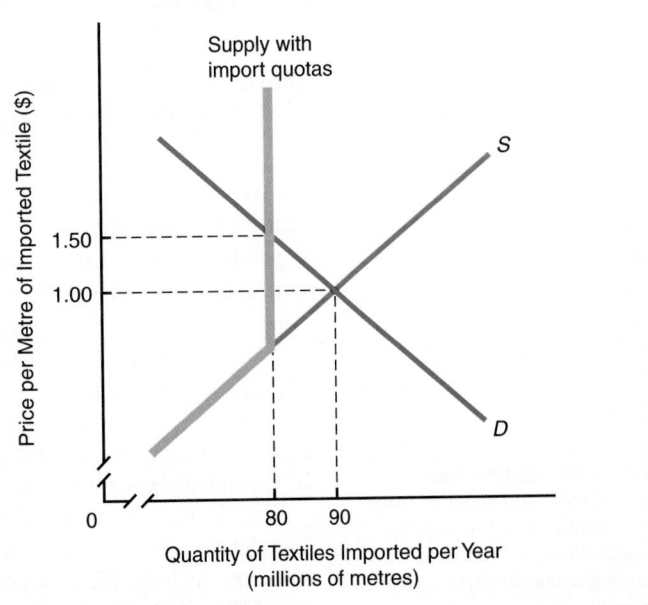

FIGURE 16–7

The Effect of a Tariff on American-Made Computer Software

Without a tariff, Canada buys 10 million units of American soft-ware per year at an average price of $100, as shown in part (a). Canadian producers sell 5 million units of domestically made software, also at $100 each, as shown in part (b). A $50-per-unit tariff will shift the American import supply curve to S_2 in part (a)

so that the new equilibrium is at E_2, with price $125 and quantity sold reduced to 8 million per year. The demand curve for Canadian-made software (for which there is no tariff) shifts to D_2 in part (b). Sales increase to 6.5 million per year.

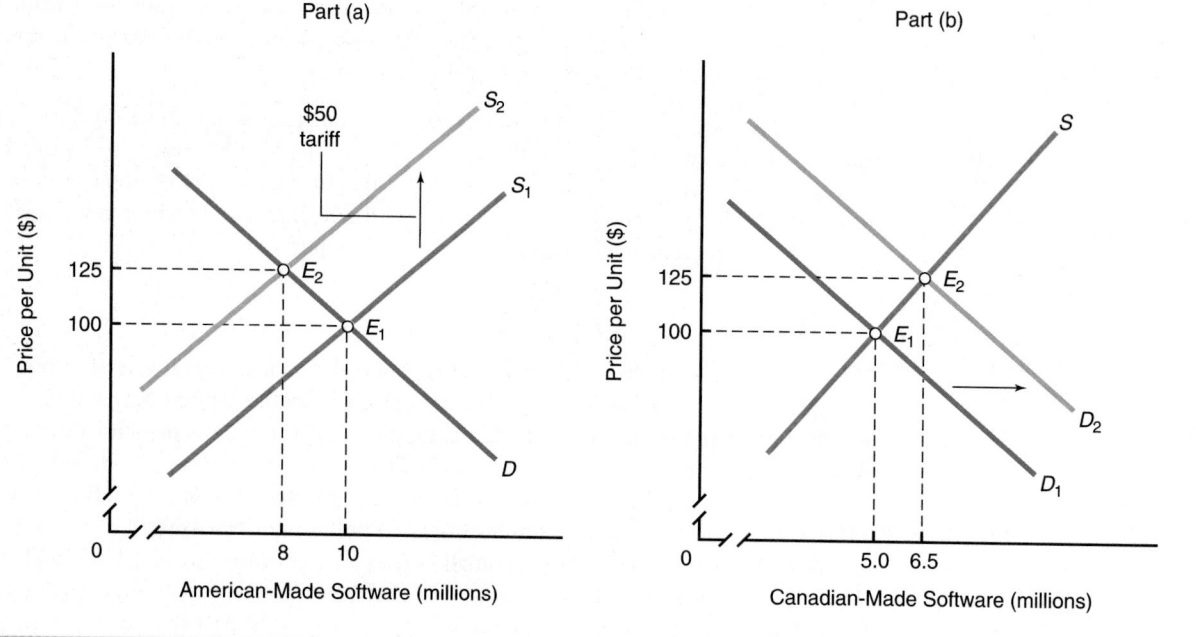

Part (a)

Part (b)

software producers because it increases the demand for their products due to the higher price of a close substitute, American software. This causes a redistribution of income from Canadian consumers of software to Canadian producers of software.

TARIFFS IN CANADA. In Figure 16–8 we see that tariffs on all imported goods have varied widely, but in general have been falling since the mid-1930s. The highest rates since Confederation occurred as part of Sir John A. Macdonald's National Policy of 1879.

CURRENT TARIFF LAWS. Canada has always depended to a large extent on trade, first with England and now with the United States. About one in three jobs in Canada depends on our exports; about 11 000 jobs are either created or sustained by each $1 billion in new exports.

16.6 *International Trade Agreements*

North American Free Trade Agreement (NAFTA) A free trade agreement among Canada, the United States, and Mexico, covering about 80 percent of our exports.

Not surprisingly, the federal government in recent years has emphasized the importance of expanded trade for Canada. In 1987, Canada signed a free trade agreement with the United States—the Canada–U.S. Free Trade Agreement (FTA), which came into effect in 1989. In 1994, Canada and the United States concluded an expanded free trade agreement to include Mexico and created the **North American Free Trade Agreement (NAFTA)**. This remains Canada's most significant trade agreement, covering more than

FIGURE 16-8

Tariff Rates in Canada since 1867

Tariff rates in Canada have varied widely; indeed, in Parliament, tariffs are a political football. Import-competing industries prefer high tariffs. In the 20th century, the highest single tariff we had was the Bennett Retaliatory Tariff (1933), which was imposed in retaliation against the United States' Smoot-Hawley Tariff of 1930. With the establishment of GATT in 1947, tariffs have been steadily reduced in a series of negotiations. The most significant of these negotiations are identified in the figure below.

SOURCE: ADAPTED FROM THE STATISTICS CANADA PUBLICATION *HISTORICAL STATISTICS OF CANADA*, SECOND EDITION, CATALOGUE 11-516, 1983, SERIES G485, AND AUTHOR'S ESTIMATES.

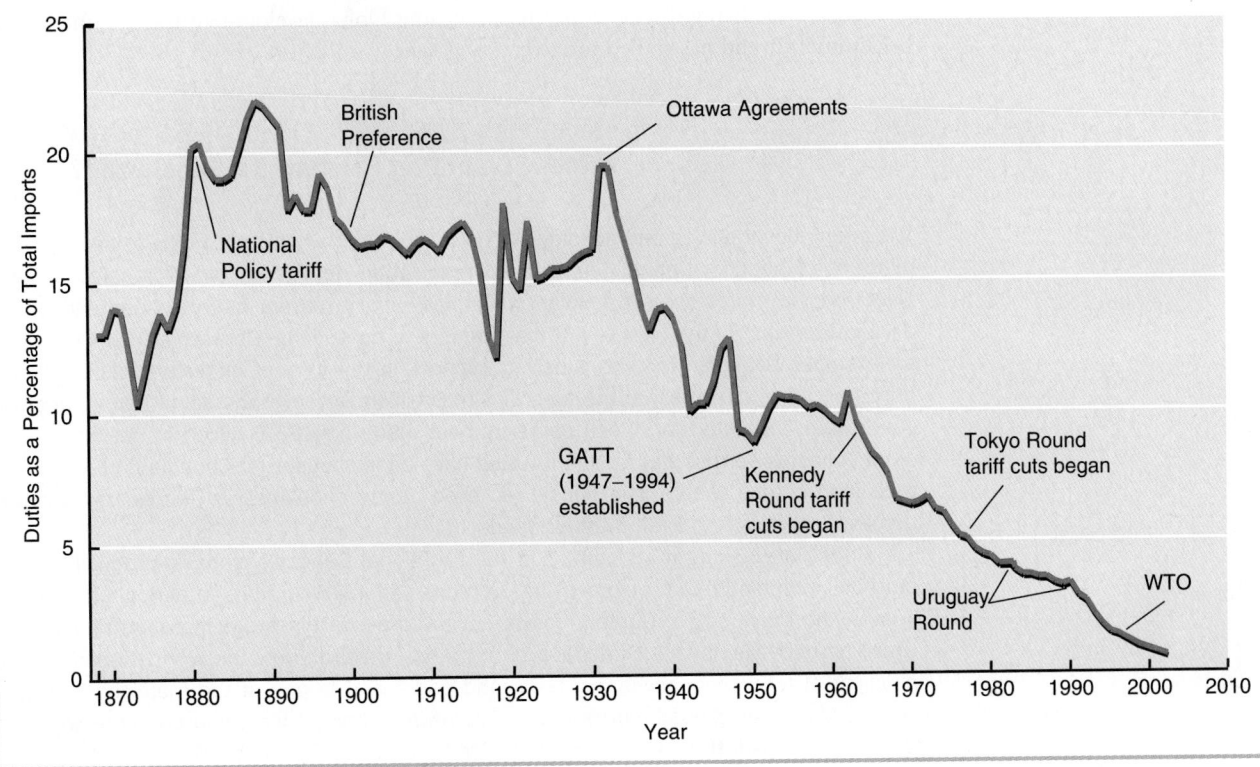

80 percent of our exports. In 1997, Canada signed a separate free trade agreement with Chile. Many other countries and groups of countries have also entered into these types of regional trading agreements. As indicated in this chapter's Issues and Applications, there are more than 130 of these agreements currently in effect.

Canada was also a signatory of the **General Agreement on Tariffs and Trade (GATT)**—an international agreement established in 1947 to further world trade by reducing barriers and tariffs. The member nations of GATT account for more than 85 percent of world trade. As you can see in Figure 16–8, there have been a number of rounds of negotiations to reduce tariffs since the early 1960s. The latest round was called the "Uruguay Round" because Uruguay is where the initial meetings were held.

General Agreement on Tariffs and Trade (GATT) An international agreement established in 1947 to further world trade by reducing barriers and tariffs.

The World Trade Organization (WTO)

The Uruguay Round of the GATT was ratified by 117 nations at the end of 1993. A year later the entire treaty was ratified. As of January 1, 1995, the new **World Trade Organization (WTO)**—the successor organization to GATT—handles all trade disputes among its 148 member nations. The ratification of GATT resulted in a cut of roughly 40 percent in tariffs worldwide.

Agricultural subsidies will be reduced and perhaps eventually eliminated. Protection for patents will be extended worldwide. The WTO will have arbitration boards to settle

World Trade Organization (WTO) The successor organization to GATT, it handles all trade disputes among its 148 member nations.

international disputes over trade issues. No country has a veto. A country that loses a WTO ruling has to comply or face trade sanctions by the country that wins arbitration.

In short, the passage of GATT and the creation of the WTO constitute the furthest-reaching global trade agreement in history. Advanced technologies, in particular, will benefit from the worldwide extension of the protection of patents. Copyrights on books and recordings will be protected from piracy better than ever before. Protectionist rules, such as "local content" requirements that force foreign firms to use locally produced inputs, will be eliminated. Also, other countries will have to treat Canadian service suppliers no less favourably than they treat their own service suppliers.

The Uruguay Round did not deal with trade distorting agricultural subsidies, which continue to increase in the developed world, including Canada (see Example 16–2). This is a major issue being discussed in the succeeding Doha development trade round which began in 2001 and has stalled for a very long time.

POLICY EXAMPLE 16-2 | **Should Canadian Farmers Be Subsidized?**

The international pricing and subsidy system is so out of whack, according to figures compiled by Statistics Canada and the Organization for Economic Co-operation and Development, that it costs Canadian consumers and taxpayers more to keep agriculture alive in this country than it would to pay farmers to do nothing. Between 1999 and 2002, for example, Canadian farmers received support, in the form of either artificially inflated prices or direct subsidies, to the tune of $24.9 billion. Yet, over the same period, after all costs were accounted for, these same farmers made only $8.8 billion in net income. In strict economic terms, that means it would have been cheaper for Canadians to buy all of their food abroad (where it is subsidized even more handsomely by foreigners) and pay domestic farmers just to sit on their hands.

Critics are asking if agriculture in the traditional Canadian sense—producing standard bulk commodities for export—has a future. Alfons Weersink, an agricultural economist at the University of Guelph, points out that new, fertile areas in countries such as Brazil produce yields that Canada cannot match. Brazil is now the world's number one exporter of feed corn, soybeans, beef, and pork—and is one of the main reasons why commodity prices globally are so low. "We always thought we could compete with the U.S. and Europe if there were a level playing field," Weersink says. "But can we compete with the Brazils of the world in producing, say number two yellow corn? I'm not sure we can. We may have to do something different." In some countries, he says, farmers are no longer being subsidized to grow crops. They are being subsidized to farm in a certain way. Switzerland, for example, pays farmers to hang bells around the necks of their cows and raze them on mountainsides. This is considered a tourist attraction. In the U.S., farmers are explicitly paid not to grow certain crops.

Weersink says the real answer for Canadian farmers is to change their way of thinking. Currently, Canadian farmers tend to produce bulk commodities, put them on the world market, and see what happens. Instead, he says, they should find out what final consumers want and produce more finished commodities to fit these demands. If consumers don't want to eat genetically modified crops, for instance, producers shouldn't waste their time complaining that city dwellers are unscientific. They should produce crops that are not genetically modified.

For critical analysis: Why are Canadian farmers heavily subsidized? Do subsidies help make Canadian farmers more competitive?

SOURCE: THE TORONTO STAR, TOM WALKOM, APRIL 16, 2005

➡ CONCEPTS IN BRIEF

Learning Objective 16.5: Describe two ways that nations restrict foreign trade.

- One means of restricting foreign trade is a quota system. Beneficiaries of quotas are the importers who get the quota rights and the domestic producers of the restricted goods.

⤳ Another means of restricting imports is a tariff, which is a tax on imports only. An import tariff benefits import-competing industries and harms consumers by raising prices.

Learning Objective 16.6: Identify Canada's most significant international agreement and name the organization that adjudicates trade disputes among nations.

⤳ Canada's most significant trade agreement is the North American Free Trade Agreement among Canada, the United States, and Mexico. The NAFTA covers over 80 percent of Canada's exports.

⤳ The other important international institution created to improve trade among nations is the World Trade Organization (WTO). The WTO is the successor organization to the General Agreement on Tariffs and Trade (GATT), which was created in 1947 and concluded with the Uruguay Round of Negotiations.

➤ ISSUES AND APPLICATIONS

Do Regional Trade Agreements Help or Hinder International Trade?

Concepts Applied: International Trade, Quota System, Voluntary Restraint Agreement, Gains from Specialization

Global trade has been a great boon to those involved in global shipping.

There are currently more than 230 bilateral or regional trade agreements in effect around the globe. These are special deals among groups of countries called *regional trade blocs.* Regional trade agreements grant trade preferences to nations in participating groups, which typically are located in the same geographic region of the world. All regional trade agreements reduce tariffs, duties, or quotas for participating nations. Many regional trade agreements completely eliminate certain trade restrictions.

Gauging the Intensity of Trade within Regional Trade Blocs

Part (a) of Figure 16–9 shows the percentages of total world trade resulting from trade within five regional trade blocs: the Andean Community and Mercosur in South America, the Association of Southeast Asian Nations (ASEAN), the European Union (EU), and the North American Free Trade Agreement (NAFTA). The EU contains 25 major developed nations and NAFTA includes the United States, Canada, and Mexico, and so trade flows within these two groups naturally account for significant portions of global trade.

The absolute trade flows within the EU and NAFTA are so large that just looking at their shares of world trade is not a good indication of the relative *intensity* of trade within the two regional trade blocs. Nations with smaller economies may account for relatively little global trade yet may trade relatively intensively with other countries with which they have regional trade agreements. Trade intensity indexes for the selected regional trade blocs appear in part (b). They indicate that the intensity of trade within the Andean Community is nearly 12 times greater than in NAFTA. Compared with NAFTA countries, Andean Community nations account for dramatically less of the world's total trade, but what trading they do is relatively more concentrated within their regional trade bloc.

Trade Creation or Diversion?

There are two ways that one might interpret relatively high trade intensity within a regional trade bloc. On the one hand, intensive trade among members of a regional trading group could indicate that their regional trade agreement has helped add to global trade.

On the other hand, intensive trade within a regional trading bloc might result from protectionist policies, such as quota systems or voluntary restraint agreements, which divert trade away from nonmember countries. If more trade is diverted from the bloc than is created within the bloc, then on net a regional trade agreement reduces trade. Then residents of participating countries fail to experience the full benefits of gains from specialization made possible by unhindered international trade. Most evidence indicates that the majority of regional trade agreements have promoted international trade, but economists agree that some regional trade blocs simply *divert* trade instead of contributing to its creation.

For critical analysis:

1. How can trade within Mercosur be more intensive than trade within the EU, even though Mercosur's share of world trade is one-thirtieth that of the EU?
2. How might companies located outside a regional trade bloc circumvent trade diversion if they can ship product components into a country within the bloc and assemble items there to export to other nations within the bloc?

FIGURE 16–9

Trade Shares and Intensities in Selected Regional Trade Blocs

Part (a) shows that trade within NAFTA accounts for more than one-fifth of world trade and that EU trade accounts for more than one-third of total international trade. Part (b) shows that the intensity of trade is greater within ASEAN, Mercosur, and the Andean Community, however.

SOURCE: INTERNATIONAL MONETARY FUND.

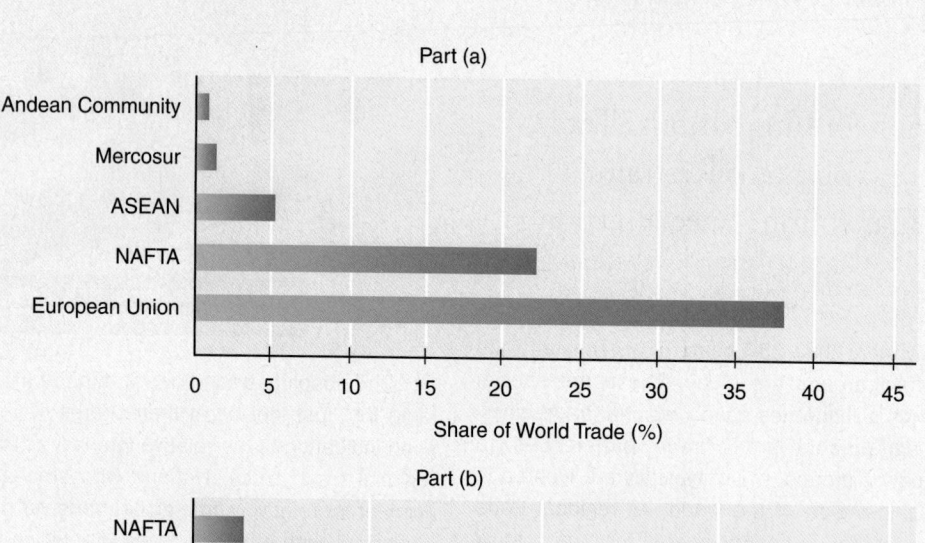

Part (a)

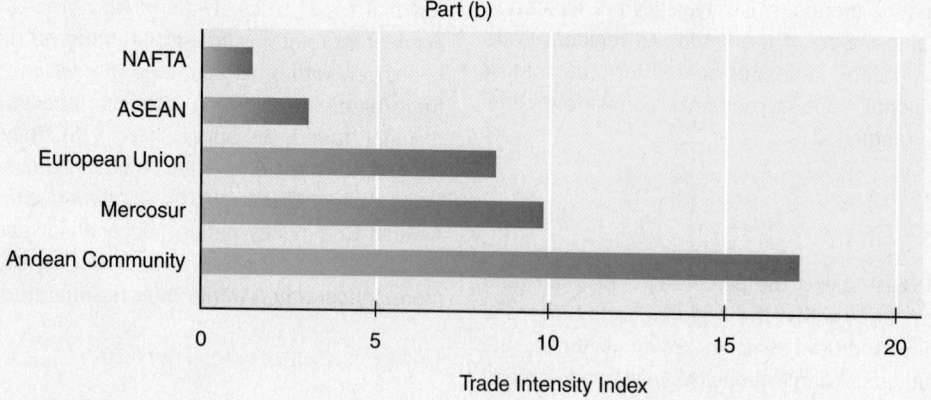

Part (b)

➡➡ SUMMARY

Here is what you should know after reading this chapter. MyEconLab will help you identify what you know, and where to go when you need to practise. We suggest that as soon as you review one of the Learning Objective sections below, you then proceed to go through the related section in MyEconLab.

ᗄ myeconlab

➡➡ LEARNING OBJECTIVES	KEY TERMS	MYECONLAB PRACTICE
16.1 Worldwide Trade and Canada. World trade is expanding more rapidly than global GDP. The direct impact of international trade on Canada, as measured by the ratio of exports to GDP, is relatively large compared with many other nations. It is hard to imagine what life would be like without international trade. Initially, many prices would rise rapidly, but eventually domestic production would begin on many goods we presently import. Consider life without imports of coffee, tea, bananas, foreign wines, motorcycles, automobiles, televisions, DVDs, and hundreds of other goods from food and clothing to electronics—not to mention vital imports such as bauxite, chromium, cobalt, platinum, and tin.	comparative advantage, 424 absolute advantage, 424	• **MyEconLab** Study Plan 16.1
16.2 Comparative and Absolute Advantage. A nation has a comparative advantage in producing a good when it can produce the good at a lower opportunity cost relative to the opportunity cost of producing the good in another nation. A nation has an absolute advantage when it can produce more output with a given set of inputs than can be produced in the other country. Nevertheless, trade can still take place if both nations have a comparative advantage in producing goods that they can agree to exchange. The reason is that it can still benefit the nation with an absolute advantage to specialize in production.		• **MyEconLab** Study Plan 16.2
16.3 Gains from Specialization and Trade. A country has a comparative advantage in producing a good if it can produce that good at a lower opportunity cost, in terms of foregone production of a second good, than another nation. If the other nation has a comparative advantage in producing the second good, both nations can gain by specializing in producing the goods in which they have a comparative advantage and engaging in international trade. Together they can then produce and consume more than they would have produced and consumed in the absence of specialization and trade. However, along with the gains, there are costs from trade. Certain	infant industry argument, 429 dumping, 430	• **MyEconLab** Study Plan 16.3

➤➤ LEARNING OBJECTIVES	KEY TERMS	MYECONLAB PRACTICE

industries and their employees may be hurt if trade is opened up. Because foreigners eventually want real goods and services as payment for the real goods and services they export to other countries, ultimately each country pays for its imports with its exports. Hence, on a worldwide basis, the value of imports must equal the value of exports.

16.4 Arguments against Free Trade. The infant industry argument maintains that new industries developing domestically need protection from foreign competitors until they are mature enough to compete with foreigners, at which time protection would be removed. One problem with this argument is that it is difficult to tell when maturity has been reached, and domestic industries will fight against weaning. Moreover, this argument is hardly relevant to most Canadian industries. It is also alleged (and is true to a large extent) that free trade leads to instability for specific domestic industries as comparative advantage changes in a dynamic world. Countries that have traditionally held a comparative advantage in the production of some goods occasionally lose that advantage (while gaining others). Regional hardships are a result, and protection of domestic jobs is demanded.

- **MyEconLab** Study Plan 16.4

16.5 Restricting Foreign Trade. One way to restrict trade is to impose a quota, or a limit, on imports of a good. This action restricts the supply of the good in the domestic market, thereby pushing up the equilibrium price of the good. Another way to reduce trade is to place a tariff on imported goods. This reduces the supply of foreign-made goods and increases the demand for domestically produced goods, which brings about a rise in the price of the good. Because each country must pay for its imports with its exports, any restriction on imports must ultimately lead to a reduction in exports. So even though restrictions on imports because of tariffs or quotas may benefit workers and business owners in the protected domestic industry, such protection will harm workers and business owners in the export sector in general.

quota system, 433
voluntary export
   restraint
   agreement (VER),
   433

- **MyEconLab** Study Plan 16.5

⇒→ LEARNING OBJECTIVES	**KEY TERMS**	**MYECONLAB PRACTICE**
16.6 Trade Treaties. Canada's most significant trade agreement is the North American Free Trade Agreement (NAFTA) among Canada, the United States, and Mexico. The NAFTA covers over 75 percent of Canada's exports. The other important international institution created to improve trade among nations is the World Trade Organization (WTO). The WTO is the successor organization to the General Agreement on Tariffs and Trade (GATT), which was created in 1947 and concluded with the Uruguay Round of Negotiations.	North American Free Trade Agreement (NAFTA), 434 General Agreement on Tariffs and Trade (GATT), 435 World Trade Organization (WTO), 435	• **MyEconLab** Study Plan 16.6

⇒→ PROBLEMS

(Answers to the odd-numbered problems appear at the back of the book.)

LO 16.1 Discuss the worldwide importance, trends, and patterns of trade and the importance of trade to Canada.

1. Example 16–1, "The Importance of International Trade in Various Countries," shows the importance of international trade in various countries, while Figure 16–1 shows the growth of trade relative to GDP in the world and for Canada. Has total trade among nations been growing faster than, at the same rate as, or slower than total world GDP? Has the growth of Canadian exports and imports relative to Canadian GDP paralleled the global trend?

LO 16.2 Distinguish between comparative advantage and absolute advantage.

2. Study the hypothetical table of worker-hours required to produce coffee and beans in Colombia and Turkey.

Product	Colombia	Turkey
Coffee (kilogram)	2 worker-hours	1 worker-hour
Beans (kilogram)	6 worker-hours	2 worker-hours

a. What is the opportunity cost to Colombia of producing one kilogram of coffee? One kilogram of beans?

b. What is the opportunity cost to Turkey of producing one kilogram of coffee? One kilogram of beans?

c. Colombia has a comparative advantage in what? Turkey has a comparative advantage in what?

3. Examine the hypothetical table of worker-hours required to produce caviar and wheat in Canada and in Russia.

Product	Canada	Russia
Caviar (kilogram)	6 worker-hours	9 worker-hours
Wheat (bushel)	3 worker-hours	6 worker-hours

a. What is the opportunity cost to Canada of producing one kilogram of caviar per time period? What is the opportunity cost to Canada of producing one bushel of wheat?

b. What is the opportunity cost to Russia of producing one kilogram of caviar per time period? What is the opportunity cost to Russia of producing one bushel of wheat?

c. Canada has a comparative advantage in what? Russia has a comparative advantage in what?

4. Examine the hypothetical table of worker-hours required to produce cheese and cloth in two countries, A and B.

Product	Country A	Country B
Cheese (kilogram)	2/3 worker-hour	2 worker-hours
Cloth (metre)	1/2 worker-hour	1 worker-hour

a. What is the opportunity cost to country A of producing one kilogram of cheese? One metre of cloth?

b. What is the opportunity cost to country B of producing one kilogram of cheese? One metre of cloth?

c. Country A has a comparative advantage in what?

d. Country B has a comparative advantage in what?

5. Assume that Canada can produce *everything* with fewer worker-hours than any other country on earth. Even under this extreme assumption, why would Canada still trade with other countries?

6. Two countries, Austral Land and Boreal Land, have the following production opportunities shown in the graphs.

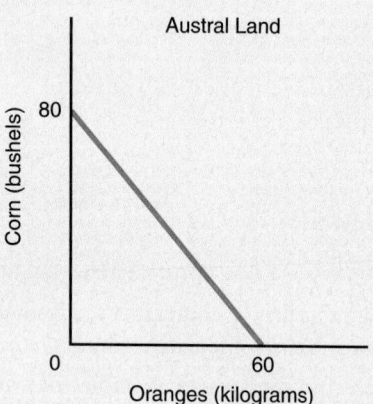

Austral Land

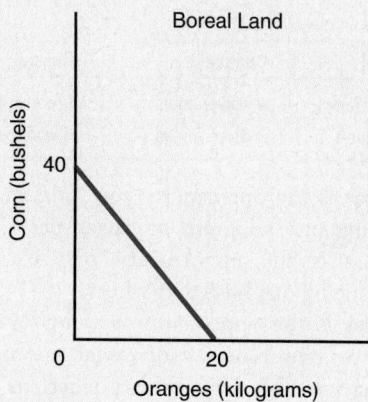

Boreal Land

a. Who has an absolute advantage in corn? In oranges?

b. Who has a comparative advantage in corn? In oranges?

c. Should Boreal Land export at all? If so, which good should it export?

d. What is Austral Land's opportunity cost of oranges in terms of corn? What is Boreal Land's opportunity cost of corn in terms of oranges?

LO 16.3 Explain why nations can gain from specializing in production and engaging in international trade.

7. Two countries, Northland and East Coast, have the hourly outputs of modems and flash drives shown in the following production opportunities table.

Northland		East Coast	
Modems	Flash Drives	Modems	Flash Drives
75	0	100	0
60	30	80	10
45	60	60	20
30	90	40	30
15	120	20	40
0	150	0	50

a. In Northland, what is the opportunity cost of producing modems? What is the opportunity cost of producing flash drives in Northland?

b. In East Coast, what is the opportunity cost of producing modems? What is the opportunity cost of producing flash drives in East Coast?

c. Which nation has a comparative advantage in producing modems? Which nation has a comparative advantage in producing flash drives?

d. Which *one* of the following rates of exchange of modems for flash drives will be acceptable to *both* nations: (i) three modems for one flash drive; (ii) one modem for one flash drive; or (iii) one flash drive for 2.5 modems?

e. Suppose that each nation decides to use all available resources to produce only the good for which it has a comparative advantage and to engage in trade at a single feasible rate of exchange you identified in part d. Prior to specialization and trade, residents of Northland chose to produce and consume 30 modems per hour and 90 flash drives per hour, and the residents of East Coast chose to produce and consume 40 modems per hour and 30 flash drives per hour. Now, residents of Northland agree to export to East Coast the same quantity of Northland's specialty good that East Coast residents were consuming prior to engaging in international trade. How many units of East Coast's specialty good does Northland import from East Coast? What are the gains for each country after they specialize in producing the good in which they have a comparative advantage and trade for the other good?

8. Two countries, Southland and West Coast, have the following production opportunities shown in the graphs.

a. Who has an absolute advantage in bottles of wine? In TVs?

b. Who has a comparative advantage in bottles of wine? In TVs?

c. Should West Coast export at all? If so, which good should it export?

d. What is Southland's opportunity cost of bottles of wine in terms of TVs? What is West Coast's opportunity cost TVs in terms of bottles of wine?

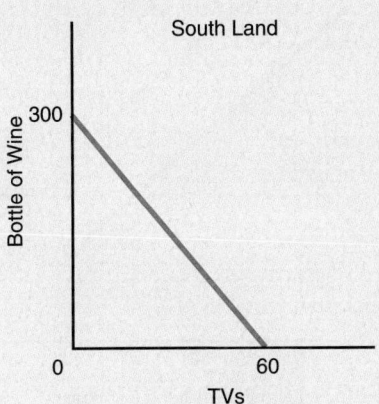

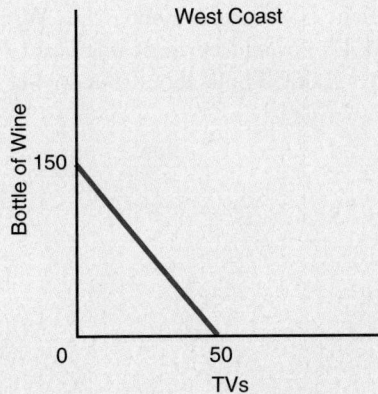

peaches is 50 cents per kilogram.

a. How many kilograms are produced domestically? How many kilograms are imported?

b. Suppose that Canada imposes a 10-cent-per-kilogram tariff. How many kilograms would now be produced domestically? How many kilograms would be imported? What are the federal government's revenues?

c. Suppose now that the government imposes a 20-cent-per-kilogram tariff. What price can domestic growers now receive for their peaches? How many

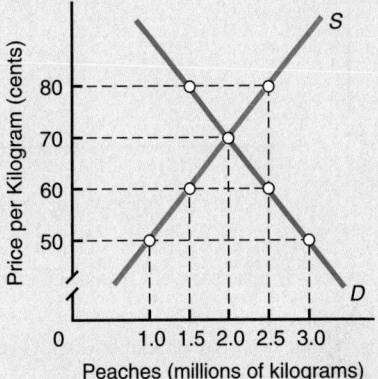

kilograms will domestic growers produce? How many kilograms will be imported? What are government revenues?

LO 16.6 Identify Canada's most significant international agreement and name the primary organization that adjudicates trade disputes among nations.

14. The diagrams on the next page illustrate the markets for imported Korean-made and Canadian manufactured PDAs before and after a tariff is imposed on imported PDAs.

a. What were the revenues of Canadian PDA manufactures before the tariff was imposed?

b. What are their total revenues after the tariff?

15. Base your answers to the following questions on the graphs accompanying Problem 14.

a. What was the amount of the tariff per PDA?

b. Before the tariff was imposed, what were the total revenues of Korean PDA exporters? After the tariff was imposed?

c. What is the tariff revenue earned by the Canadian government?

d. Based on the available information, who has gained from the tariff and who is worse off?

16. Look at the most recent edition of Canada's State of Trade from the Office of the Chief Economist on the Department of Foreign Affairs and International Trade

9. Why do nations gain from specializing in production and engaging in international trade? Does this apply universally?

LO 16.4 Outline common arguments against free trade.

10. Refer back to Example 16–7, "Unfair Competition from Low-Wage Countries," for a discussion of the protectionists' claims about how low-wage countries are stealing Canadian jobs. What are some of the arguments used against free trade?

LO 16.5 Describe two ways that nations restrict foreign trade.

11. The use of tariffs and quotas to restrict imports results in higher prices and is successful in reducing imports. In what way is using a tariff different from using a quota?

12. Explain why an increase in taxes on imports (tariffs) will reduce exports.

13. The accompanying graph gives the supply and demand for peaches. *S* and *D* are Canada's supply and demand curves, respectively. Assume that the world price of

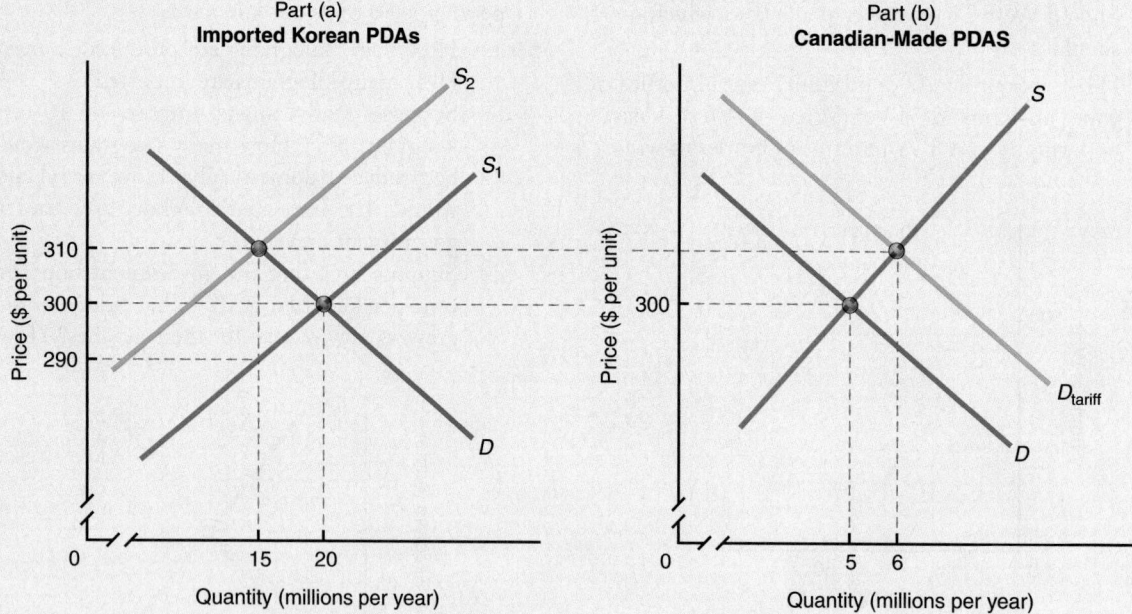

Part (a)
Imported Korean PDAs

Part (b)
Canadian-Made PDAS

website at www.international.gc.ca/eet/trade/state-of-trade-en.asp.

a. What three types of products does Canada export the most?

b. To what three countries does Canada sell the most goods and services?

c. Which trade agreement—the WHO or the NAFTA—would be most important for Canada? Why? (Hint: Think about your answer to part b.)

17

Exchange Rates and the Balance of Payments

➡→ **LEARNING OBJECTIVES**

After reading this chapter, you should be able to:

17.1 Distinguish between the balance of trade and the balance of payments.

17.2 Identify the key accounts within the balance of payments.

17.3 Outline how exchange rates are determined in the markets for foreign exchange.

17.4 Discuss factors that can induce changes in equilibrium exchange rates.

17.5 Outline how policy makers can go about attempting to fix exchange rates.

17.6 Explain alternative approaches to limiting exchange rate variability.

MyEconLab helps you master each objective and study more efficiently. See end of chapter for details.

At the time the new currency of the European Monetary Union, the euro, was established in 1999, an American resident had to pay US$1.19 to obtain one euro, and a Canadian resident had to pay Can$1.80. By the end of the summer of 2000, however, the American dollar price of a euro had dropped by nearly 30 percent, to US$0.825. Many observers began calling for the new European Central Bank (ECB) to "do something" to stop the euro's slide. For months, the ECB resisted these calls. Then, at the beginning of the autumn of 2000, the ECB "did something": It purchased billions of euros with its own reserves of dollars. In this chapter, you will learn why the ECB might have hoped to push up the dollar price of euros by purchasing American dollars. You will also consider reasons that many economists think the ECB's efforts might have been useless.

DID YOU KNOW THAT...

Every day, around the clock, over $1 trillion of foreign currencies are traded. Furthermore, the dollar prices of foreign currencies can sometimes change by 20 percent, or even more, within a few weeks. In recent years, the dollar values of the Mexican peso, the Malaysian ringgit, the Thailand baht, the Turkish lira, and the Argentine peso have experienced declines at least this large in less than a month's time. What generates monthly, weekly, or even daily variations in the relative values of these and the more than 170 other currencies in circulation? Before we consider factors that can influence the value of one currency in terms of another, we will begin by considering how we keep track of the international financial transactions that these currencies facilitate.

17.1 The Balance of Payments and International Capital Movements

Balance of trade The difference between the value of exports and imports of goods and services.

Balance of payments The total of all economic transactions between a nation and the rest of the world, usually for a period of one year.

Governments typically keep track of each year's economic activities by calculating the gross domestic product—the total of expenditures on all newly produced final domestic goods and services—and its components. In the world of international trade also, a summary information system has been developed. It relates to the balance of trade and the balance of payments. The **balance of trade** refers specifically to the difference between value of exports and imports of *goods and services*, as discussed in Chapter 16. When international trade in a nation is in balance, the value of exports equals the value of imports.

The **balance of payments** is a more general concept that expresses the total of all economic transactions between a nation and the rest of the world, usually for a period of one year. Each country's balance of payments summarizes information about that country's exports, imports, earnings by domestic residents on assets located abroad, earnings on domestic assets owned by foreign residents, international capital movements, and official transactions by central banks and governments. In essence, then, the balance of payments is a record of all the transactions between households, firms, and government of one country and the rest of the world. Any transaction that leads to a *payment* by a country's residents (or government) is a deficit item, identified by a negative sign (−) when we examine the actual numbers that might be in Table 17−1. Any transaction that leads to a *receipt* by a country's residents (or government) is a surplus item and is identified by a plus sign (+) when actual numbers are considered. Table 17−1 gives a listing of the surplus and deficit items on international accounts.

17.2 Accounting Identities

Accounting identities Definitions of equivalent values.

Accounting identities—definitions of equivalent values—exist for financial institutions and other businesses. We begin with simple accounting identities that must hold for families, and then go on to describe international accounting identities.

TABLE 17−1

Surplus (+) and Deficit (−) Items on the International Accounts

Surplus Items (+)	Deficit Items (−)
Exports of merchandise	Imports of merchandise
Private and governmental gifts from foreigners	Private and governmental gifts to foreigners
Foreign use of domestically owned transportation	Use of foreign-owned transportation
Foreign tourists' expenditures in this country	Tourism expenditures abroad
Foreign military spending in this country	Military spending abroad
Interest and dividend receipts from foreigners	Interest and dividends paid to foreigners
Sales of domestic assets to foreigners	Purchases of foreign assets
Funds deposited in this country by foreigners	Funds placed in foreign depository institutions
Sales of gold to foreigners	Purchases of gold from foreigners
Sales of domestic currency to foreigners	Purchases of foreign currency

If a family unit is spending more than its current income, such a situation necessarily implies that the family unit must be doing one of the following:

1. Drawing down its wealth. The family must reduce its money holdings, or it must sell shares, bonds, or other assets
2. Borrowing
3. Receiving gifts from friends or relatives
4. Receiving public transfers from a government, which obtained the funds by taxing others. (A transfer is a payment, in money or in goods or services, made without receiving goods or services in return.)

In effect, we can use this information to derive an identity: If a family unit is currently spending more than it is earning, it must draw on previously acquired wealth, borrow, or receive either private or public aid. Similarly, an identity exists for a family unit that is currently spending less than it is earning: It must increase its wealth by increasing its money holdings or by lending and acquiring other financial assets, or it must pay taxes or bestow gifts on others. When we consider businesses and governments, each unit in each group faces its own identities or constraints; thus, net lending by households must equal net borrowing by businesses and governments.

Even though our individual family unit's accounts must balance, in the sense that the identity discussed previously must hold, sometimes the item that brings about the balance cannot continue indefinitely. *If family expenditures exceed family income and this situation is financed by borrowing, the household may be considered to be in disequilibrium because such a situation cannot continue indefinitely.* If such a deficit is financed by drawing on previously accumulated assets, the family may also be in disequilibrium because it cannot continue indefinitely to draw on its wealth; eventually, it will become impossible for that family to continue such a lifestyle. (Of course, if the family members are retired, they may well be in equilibrium by drawing on previously acquired assets to finance current deficits; this example illustrates that it is necessary to understand circumstances fully before pronouncing an economic unit in disequilibrium.)

Individual households, businesses, and governments, as well as the entire group of households, businesses, and governments, must eventually reach equilibrium. Certain economic adjustment mechanisms have evolved to ensure equilibrium. Deficit households must eventually increase their incomes or decrease their expenditures. They will find that they have to pay higher interest rates if they wish to borrow to finance their deficits. Eventually, their credit sources will dry up, and they will be forced into equilibrium. Businesses, on occasion, must lower costs and/or prices—or go bankrupt—to reach equilibrium.

When countries trade or interact, certain identities or constraints must also hold. Countries buy goods from people in other countries; they also lend to and present gifts to people in other countries. If a country interacts with others, an accounting identity ensures a balance (but not an equilibrium, as will soon become clear). Let us look at the three categories of balance of payments transactions: current account transactions, capital account transactions, and official settlements account transactions.

Current Account Transactions

During any designated period, all payments and gifts that are related to the purchase or sale of both goods and services constitute the current account in international trade. The three major types of current account transactions are the exchange of merchandise goods, the exchange of services, and transfers.

MERCHANDISE TRADE TRANSACTIONS. The largest portion of any country's balance of payments current account is typically the importing and exporting of merchandise goods. During 2006, for example, as can be seen in Table 17–2, Canada exported $455.7 billion of merchandise and imported $404.4 billion. The balance of merchandise trade is defined as the difference between the value of merchandise exports and the value of merchandise imports. For 2006, Canada had a balance of merchandise trade surplus because the value of its merchandise exports exceeded the value of its merchandise imports. This surplus amounted to $51.3 billion.

TABLE 17-2

*Canada's Balance of
International Payments,
2006*

(in Billions of Dollars)

Current Account	Exports(+)	Imports(−)	Balance
Merchandise	455.7	404.4	51.3
Services	67.2	82.4	−15.2
Trade balance			36.1
Investment income	61.6	73.4	−11.8
Transfers	9.7	10.4	−0.7
Total current account balance			**23.6**

Capital Account			
Net capital flows [capital outflow (−)]	147.5	165.0	−17.5
Capital account balance			**−17.5**

Official Financing Account			
Statistical discrepancy*			−5.0
Official international reserves = −(23.8 − 17.5 − 5.0)			
[increases (−)]			−1.1
Official financing balance			−1.6
Balance of payments = (23.6 − 17.5 − 6.1)			**0.0**

SOURCE: ADAPTED FROM THE STATISTICS CANADA WEBSITES: http://www40.statcan.ca/101/cst01/econ01a.htm, AND
http://www40.statcan.ca/101/cst01/econ01b.htm.

*The statistical discrepancy compensates for the inability to account for some items, probably unaccounted capital
outflows, many of which relate to the underground economy.

EXAMPLE 17-1   **Perhaps the Trade Situation Isn't So Bad After All**

Virtually every month, there appears a spate of articles and TV sound bites about Canada's current account. The official numbers may be in error, however, for they ignore the multinational nature of modern firms. Canadian international trade figures exclude sales in other countries for subsidiaries of Canadian-owned companies. Because of a host of other problems, some government economists believe that they are underestimating the value of Canadian exports by as much as 10 percent. Economist Paul Krugman agrees. When he added up the value of world exports and compared it with the value of world imports, he found that the planet Earth had a trade deficit of $100 billion! Perhaps we are trading with aliens and do not know it.

For critical analysis: The balance of payments is meant to express the total of all economic transactions between a nation and the rest of the world. Which account in Canada's Balance of International Payments indicates Statistics Canada's difficulty in accounting for the total of all economic transactions with the world?

SERVICE EXPORTS AND IMPORTS. The balance of (merchandise) trade has to do with tangible items—you can feel them, touch them, and see them. Service exports and imports have to do with invisible or intangible items that are bought and sold, such as shipping, insurance, tourist expenditures, and banking services. As can be seen in Table 17–2, in 2006, service exports were $61.6 billion and service imports were $73.4 billion. Thus, the balance of services was in deficit about $11.8 billion in 2006. Exports constitute receipts or inflows into Canada and are positive; imports constitute payments abroad or outflows of money and are negative.

When we combine the balance of merchandise trade with the balance of services, we obtain a trade balance on goods and services equal to $36.1 billion in 2006.

INVESTMENT INCOME. Canadians earn investment income on assets they own in foreign countries. These earnings represent an inflow into Canada. Conversely, when Canadians pay income to foreigners who own assets in Canada, those earnings represent an outflow from Canada. You can see that net investment income for 2006 was –$11.8 billion. The fact that there is a negative sign before the number for investment income means that Canadians paid out more earnings on domestic assets owned by foreigners than they earned on assets owned in other countries.

TRANSFERS. Canadians give gifts to relatives and others abroad. The federal government grants gifts to foreign countries. Foreigners give gifts to Canadians, and some foreign governments have granted money to the Canadian government. In the current account, we see that net transfers—the total amount of gifts given by Canadians minus the total amount received by Canadians from abroad—came to –$0.7 billion in 2006.

BALANCING THE CURRENT ACCOUNT. The balance on current account tracks the value of a country's exports of goods and services, earnings on investments abroad and transfer payments (private and government) relative to the value of that country's import of goods and services, earnings on investments in Canada, and transfer payments (private and government). In 2006, it was $23.6 billion.

> If exports exceed imports, a current account surplus is said to exist; if imports exceed exports, a current account deficit is said to exist. A current account surplus means that we are exporting more than we are importing. Such a surplus must be offset by the inflow of money or money equivalent, which means (in the absence of central bank intervention) a capital account deficit.

Capital Account Transactions

In world markets, it is possible to buy and sell not only goods and services but also real and financial assets. This is what the capital accounts are concerned with in international transactions. Capital account transactions occur because of foreign investments—either foreigners investing in Canada or Canadians investing in other countries. The purchase of shares on the London Stock Exchange by a Canadian causes an outflow of funds. The building of a Japanese automobile factory in Canada causes an inflow of funds. Any time foreigners buy Canadian government securities, there is an inflow of funds. Any time Canadians buy foreign government securities, there is an outflow of funds. Loans to and from foreigners cause outflows and inflows.

Table 17–2 indicates that in 2006, the value of private and government capital going out of Canada was –$165.0 billion, and the value of private and government capital coming into Canada (including a statistical discrepancy) was +$147.5 billion. Canadian capital going abroad constitutes payments or outflows and is therefore negative. Foreign capital coming into Canada constitutes receipts or inflows and is, therefore, positive. Thus, there was a negative net capital movement of –$17.5 billion out of Canada. This is also called the balance on capital account.

There is a relationship between the current account and the capital account, assuming no interventions by the central banks of countries. *The current account and the capital account must sum to zero. In other words, the current account deficit equals the capital account surplus. Any country experiencing a current account surplus, such as Canada, should also be running a capital account deficit.*

EXAMPLE 17–2   **Does Canada's Frequent Current Account Deficit Mean It Has a Weak Economy?**

In recent years, the current account in Canada has been in deficit more than it has been in surplus. This is not something new. During the second half of the 19th century, Canada had many years of current account deficits. They were equally matched by capital account surpluses, as the rest of the world sent capital to Canada to finance the building of the

continued

railroads and the development of Canada's industrial economy. By the end of World War I, Canadians had repaid all their external debt and Canada had become a net creditor. However, this condition was short-lived, and by 1968 Canada was once again experiencing current account deficits. As can be seen in Figure 17–1, whenever Canada is in deficit in its current account, it is in surplus in its capital account.

FIGURE 17–1

The Relationship between the Current Account and the Capital Account

To some extent, the capital account is the mirror image of the current account. We can see this in the years since 1968. When the current account was in surplus, the capital account was in deficit. When the current account was in deficit, the capital account was in surplus.

SOURCE: ADAPTED FROM THE STATISTICS CANADA CANSIM DATABASE, SERIES V113713 AND V113734.

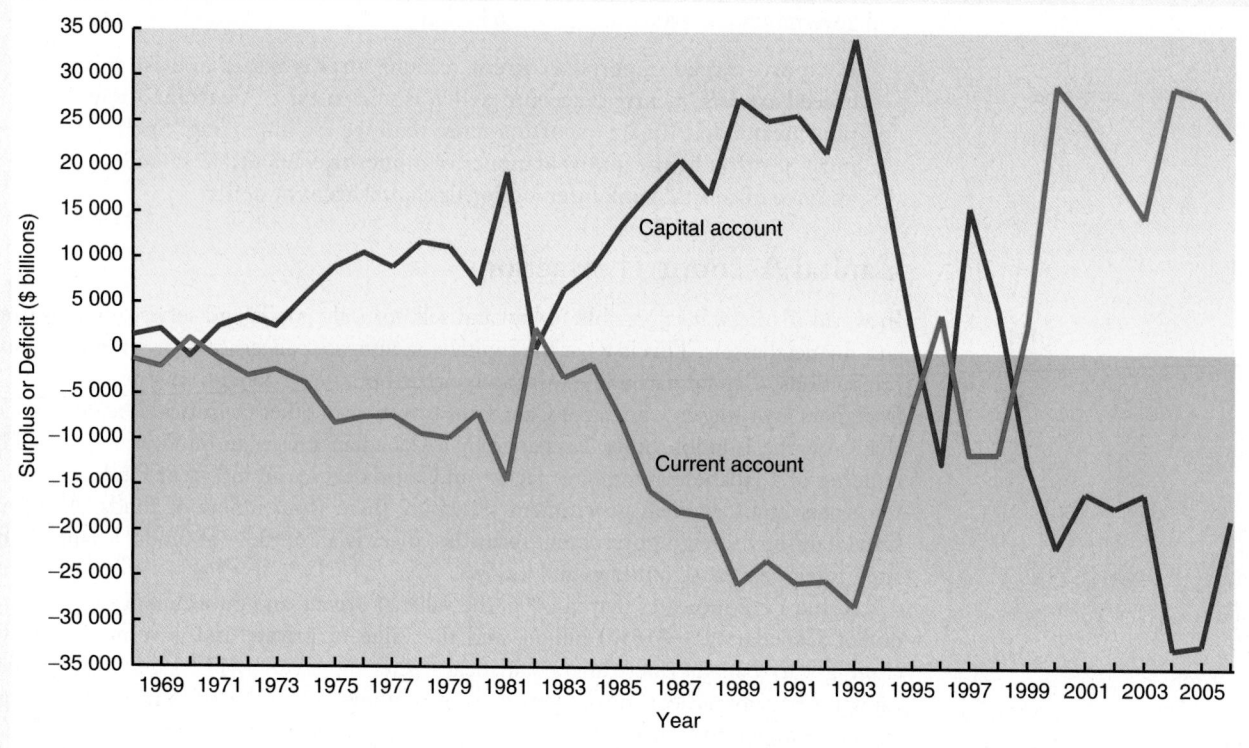

Contrary to popular belief, Canada does not necessarily have a current account deficit because it is a weak economy and cannot compete in world markets. Rather, Canada appears to be a good place to invest capital because there are strong prospects for growth and investment opportunities. So long as foreigners wish to invest more in Canada than Canadians wish to invest abroad, there will always be a deficit in our current account balance. Canadians are the beneficiaries of international capital flows.

For critical analysis: Why are politicians, nonetheless, so worried about a current account deficit?

Official Financing Account Transactions

The final section in the balance of payments concerns the statistical discrepancy and transactions in the official reserve assets of the Bank of Canada. This is referred to as the official financing account or the official settlements account.

The statistical discrepancy compensates for the inability to account for some items, probably unaccounted capital outflows, many of which relate to the underground economy.

The Bank of Canada's official reserve assets consist of the following:

Special drawing rights (SDRs)
Reserve assets that the International Monetary Fund created to be used by countries to settle international payment obligations.

1. Foreign currencies
2. Gold
3. **Special drawing rights (SDRs)**, which are reserve assets that the International Monetary Fund created to be used by countries to settle international payment obligations
4. The reserve position in the International Monetary Fund
5. Financial assets held by an official agency, such as the Bank of Canada.

To consider how official financing account transactions occur, look again at Table 17–2. The surplus in our current account was +$23.6. The deficit in our capital account was −$17.5 When you add the statistical discrepancy of −$5.0, we had a surplus on the combined accounts of −$1.1. In other words, Canada obtained more in foreign money in all its international transactions than it used.

The current account and the capital account must equal zero. The balance of payments must equal zero, as it must be with double-entry bookkeeping. It is the intervention of the Bank of Canada and changes in its official international reserves that represent the financing of the deficiency.

If the official international reserves is *negative,* as it was in 2006, the Bank of Canada has increased its reserves because of intervention in the foreign exchange market; this is a *balance of payments surplus.* When the Bank of Canada is a net purchaser of foreign exchange and a seller of Canadian dollars, this puts *downward pressure on the Canadian dollar.*

If the official international reserves is *positive,* the Bank of Canada has decreased its reserves because of intervention in the foreign exchange market; this is a *balance of payments deficit.* When the Bank of Canada is a net seller of foreign exchange and a buyer of Canadian dollars, this puts *upward pressure on the Canadian dollar.*

What Affects the Balance of Payments?

A major factor affecting our balance of payments is our rate of inflation relative to that of our trading partners. Assume that the rates of inflation in Canada and in the United States are equal. All of a sudden, our inflation rate increases. The Americans will find that Canadian products are becoming more expensive, and we will export fewer of them to the United States. Canadians will find American products relatively cheaper, and we will import more. The converse will occur if our rate of inflation suddenly falls relative to that of the United States. All other things held constant, whenever our rate of inflation exceeds that of our trading partners, we expect to see a "worsening" of our balance of trade and payments. Conversely, when our rate of inflation is less than that of our trading partners, other things being constant, we expect to see an "improvement" in our balance of trade and payments.

Another important factor that sometimes influences our balance of payments is our relative political stability. Political instability causes *capital flight:* Owners of capital in countries anticipating or experiencing political instability will often move assets to countries that are politically stable, such as Canada. However, our balance of payments is likely to worsen whenever the threat of separation looms in Quebec.

➤ **CONCEPTS IN BRIEF**

Learning Objective 17.1: Distinguish between the balance of trade and the balance of payments.

⮞ The balance of trade is defined as the difference between the value of goods and services bought and sold in the world market, usually during the period of one year. The balance of payments is a more inclusive concept that includes the value of all trade and financial transactions in the world market.

Learning Objective 17.2: Identify the key accounts within the balance of payments.

⮞ The merchandise trade balance gives us the difference between exports and imports of tangible items. Merchandise trade transactions are represented by exports and imports of tangible items.

- Service exports and imports relate to the trade of intangible items, such as shipping, insurance, and tourist expenditures.
- Investment income includes income earned by foreigners on Canadian investments and income earned by Canadians on foreign investments.
- Transfers involve international private gifts and federal government grants or gifts to foreign nations.
- When we add the balance of merchandise trade plus the balance of services and take account of net transfers, we come up with the balance on current account, which is a summary statistic taking into account the three transactions that form the current account transactions.
- There are also capital account transactions that relate to the buying and selling of financial and real assets. Foreign capital is always entering Canada, and Canadian capital is always flowing abroad. The difference is called the balance on capital account.
- Another type of balance of payments transaction concerns the official settlement assets of individual countries, or what is often simply called official transactions. By standard accounting convention, official transactions are exactly equal, but opposite in sign, to the balance of payments of Canada.
- Our balance of trade can be affected by our relative rate of inflation and by political instability elsewhere compared with the stability that exists in Canada.

17.3 Determining Foreign Exchange Rates

When you buy foreign products, such as European pharmaceuticals, you have dollars with which to pay the European manufacturer. The European manufacturer, however, cannot pay workers in dollars. The workers are European, they live in Europe, and they must have euros to buy goods and services in nations that are members of the European Monetary Union (EMU) and use the euro as their currency. There must therefore be some way of exchanging dollars for euros that the pharmaceuticals manufacturer will accept. That exchange occurs in a *foreign exchange market*, which in this case involves the exchange of euros and dollars. (When you obtain foreign currencies at a bank or an airport currency exchange, you are participating in the **foreign exchange market**—the market for buying and selling foreign currencies.)

Foreign exchange market The market for buying and selling foreign currencies.

The particular exchange rate between euros and dollars that prevails—the dollar price of the euro—depends on the current demand for and supply of euros and dollars. In a sense, then, our analysis of the exchange rate between dollars and euros will be familiar, for we have used supply and demand throughout this book. If it costs you $1.45 to buy 1 euro, that is the **foreign exchange rate**—the price of one currency in terms of another—determined by the current demand for and supply of euros in the foreign exchange market. The European person going to the foreign exchange market would need 0.69 euro to buy 1 dollar.

Foreign exchange rate The price of one currency in terms of another.

Now let's consider what determines the demand for and supply of foreign currency in the foreign exchange market. We will continue to assume that the only two regions in the world are the EMU and Canada.

Demand for and Supply of Foreign Currency

You wish to purchase European-produced pharmaceuticals directly from a manufacturer located in an EMU nation. To do so, you must have euros. You go to the foreign exchange market (or your Canadian bank). Your desire to buy the pharmaceuticals therefore causes you to offer (supply) dollars to the foreign exchange market. Your demand for EMU euros is equivalent to your supply of Canadian dollars to the foreign exchange market.

> Every Canadian transaction involving the importation of foreign goods constitutes a supply of dollars and a demand for some foreign currency, and the opposite is true for export transactions.

In this case, the import transaction constitutes a demand for EMU euros.

In our example, we will assume that only two goods are being traded, European pharmaceuticals and Canadian wireless handheld devices. The Canadian demand for European pharmaceuticals creates a supply of dollars and a demand for euros in the foreign exchange market. Similarly, the European demand for Canadian wireless handheld devices creates a supply of euros and a demand for dollars in the foreign exchange market. Under a system of **flexible exchange rates**—exchange rates that are allowed to fluctuate in the open market in response to changes in supply and demand; these rates are sometimes called *floating exchange rates*—the supply of and a demand for dollars and euros in the foreign exchange market will determine the equilibrium foreign exchange rate. The equilibrium exchange rate will tell us how many euros a dollar can be exchanged for—that is, the dollar price of euros—or how many dollars (or factions of a dollar) a euro can be exchanged for—the euro price of dollars.

> **Flexible exchange rates** Exchange rates that are allowed to fluctuate in the open market in response to changes in supply and demand. Sometimes called *floating exchange rates*.

The Equilibrium Foreign Exchange Rate

To determine the equilibrium foreign exchange rate, we have to find out what determines the demand for and supply of foreign exchange. We will ignore for the moment any speculative aspect of buying foreign exchange. That is, we assume that there are no individuals who wish to buy euros simply because they think that their price will go up in the future.

The idea of an exchange rate is no different from the idea of paying a certain price for something you want to buy. If you like coffee, you know you have to pay about $2.00 a cup. If the price went up to $3.00, you would probably buy fewer cups. If the price went down to $1.00, you would likely buy more. In other words, the demand curve for cups of coffee, expressed in terms of dollars, slopes downward following the law of demand. The demand curve for euros slopes downward also, and we will see why.

DEMAND SCHEDULE FOR EUROS. Let us think more closely about the demand schedule for euros. Let's say that it costs you $1.43 to purchase 1 euro; that is the exchange rate between dollars and euros. If tomorrow you had to pay $1.54 for the same euro, the exchange rate would have changed. Looking at such a change, we would say that there has been an **appreciation**—an increase in the value of a currency in terms of other currencies—in the value of the euro in the foreign exchange market. But another way to view this increase in the value of the euro is to say that there has been a **depreciation**—a decrease in the value of a currency in terms of other currencies—in the value of the dollar in the foreign exchange market. The dollar used to buy 0.70 euro; tomorrow, the dollar will be able to buy only 0.65 euro at a price of $1.54 per euro. If the dollar price of euros rises, you will probably demand fewer euros. Why? The answer lies in the reason you and others demand euros in the first place.

> **Appreciation** An increase in the value of a currency in terms of other currencies.
>
> **Depreciation** A decrease in the value of a currency in terms of other currencies.

How do you suppose that significant appreciations of the currencies of Central European nations relative to the euro have affected these nations' exports of goods and services to Western European countries that use the euro?

EXAMPLE 17–3   **Central European Currency Values Are Up, So Exports Are Down**

In Central European nations such as the Czech Republic, Hungary, Poland, and Slovakia, currency values have increased by 10 to 20 percent relative to the euro since the beginning of 2004. As a consequence, buyers in Western European nations that must exchange euros for the higher-valued Czech koruna, Hungarian forint, Polish zloty, and Slovakian koruna have cut back on imports from these nations by 5 to 15 percent.

For critical analysis: What would you guess has happened to imports of Western European goods into the Czech Republic, Hungary, Poland, and Slovakia since the beginning of 2004?

APPRECIATION AND DEPRECIATION OF EMU EUROS. Recall that in our example, you and others demand euros to buy European pharmaceuticals. The demand curve for European pharmaceuticals follows the law of demand and therefore slopes downward. If it costs more Canadian dollars to buy the same quantity of European pharmaceuticals, presumably you and other Canadian residents will not buy the same quantity; your quantity demanded will be less. We say that your demand for EMU euros is *derived from* your demand for European pharmaceuticals. In part (a) of Figure 17-2, we present the hypothetical demand schedule for packages of European pharmaceuticals by a representative set of Canadian consumers during a typical week. In part (b), we show graphically the Canadian demand curve for European pharmaceuticals in terms of Canadian dollars taken from part (a).

AN EXAMPLE OF DERIVED DEMAND. Let us assume that the price of a package of European pharmaceuticals in the EMU is 100 euros. Given that price, we can find the number of EMU euros required to purchase 500 packages of European pharmaceuticals. That information is given in part (c) of Figure 17-2. If purchasing one package of European pharmaceuticals requires 100 euros, 500 packages require 50 000 euros. Now we have enough information to determine the derived demand curve for EMU euros. If 1 euro costs $1.45, a package of pharmaceuticals would cost $145 (100 euros per package × $1.45 per euro = $145 per package). At $145 per package, the representative group of Canadian consumers would, we see from part (a) of Figure 17-2, demand 500 packages of pharmaceuticals.

From part (c), we see that 50 000 euros would be demanded to buy the 500 packages of pharmaceuticals. We show this quantity demanded in part (d). In part (e), we draw the derived demand curve for euros. Now consider what happens if the price of euros goes up to $1.50. A package of European pharmaceuticals priced at 100 euros in the EMU would now cost $150. From part (a), we see that at $150 per package, 300 packages of pharmaceuticals will be imported from the EMU into Canada by our representative group of Canadian consumers. From part (c), we see that 300 packages of pharmaceuticals would require 30 000 euros to be purchased; thus, in parts (d) and (e), we see that at a price of $1.50 per euro, the quantity demanded will be 30 000 euros.

We continue similar calculations all the way up to a price of $1.55 per euro. At that price, a package of European pharmaceuticals costing 100 euros in the EMU would cost $155, and our representative Canadian consumers would import only 100 packages of pharmaceuticals.

DOWNWARD-SLOPING DERIVED DEMAND. As can be expected, as the price of the euro rises, the quantity demanded will fall. The only difference here from the standard demand analysis developed in Chapter 3 and used throughout this text is that the demand for euros is derived from the demand for a final product—European pharmaceuticals in our example.

SUPPLY OF EMU EUROS. Assume that European pharmaceutical manufacturers buy Canadian wireless handheld devices. The supply of EMU euros is a derived supply in that it is derived from the European demand for Canadian wireless handheld devices. We could go through an example similar to the one for pharmaceuticals to come up with a supply schedule of euros in the EMU. It slopes upward. Obviously, Europeans want dollars to purchase Canadian goods. European residents will be willing to supply more euros when the dollar price of euros goes up, because they can then buy more Canadian goods with the same quantity of euros. That is, the euro would be worth more in exchange for Canadian goods than when the dollar price for euros was lower.

AN EXAMPLE. Let's take an example. Suppose a Canadian-produced wireless handheld device costs $200. If the exchange rate is $1.45 per euro, an EMU resident will have to come up with 137.93 euros (= $200 at $1.45 per euro) to buy one wireless handheld device. If, however, the exchange rate goes up to $1.50 per euro, an EMU resident must come up with only 133.33 euros (= $200 at $1.50 per euro) to buy a Canadian wireless handheld device. At this lower price (in euros) of Canadian wireless handheld devices, Europeans will demand a larger quantity. In other words, as the price of euros goes up in

FIGURE 17–2

Deriving the Demand for Euros

Part (a)
Demand Schedule for Packages of European Pharmaceuticals in Canada per Week

Price per Package	Quantity Demanded
$155	100
150	300
145	500
140	700

Part (b)
Canadian Demand Curve for European Pharmaceuticals

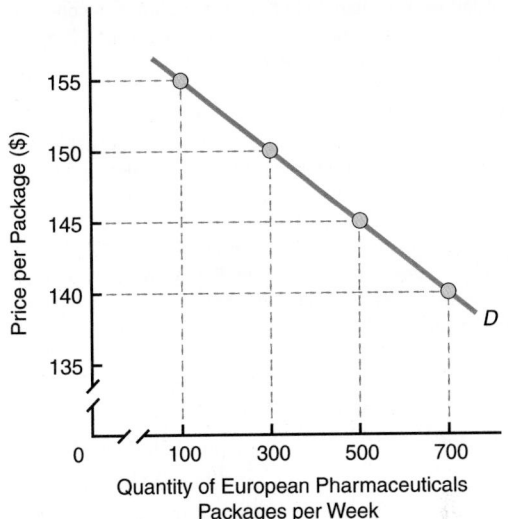

Part (c)
**Euros Required to Purchase Quantity Demanded
(at $P = 100$ euros per package of pharmaceuticals)**

Quantity Demanded	Euros Required (thousands)
100	10
300	30
500	50
700	70

Part (d)
**Derived Demand Schedule for Euros in Canada
with Which to Pay for Imports of Pharmaceuticals**

Dollar Price of One Euro	Dollar Price of Pharmaceuticals	Quantity of Pharmaceuticals Demanded	Quantity of Euros Demanded per Week (thousands)
$1.55	$155	100	10
1.50	150	300	30
1.45	145	500	50
1.40	140	700	70

Part (e)
Canadian Derived Demand for Euros

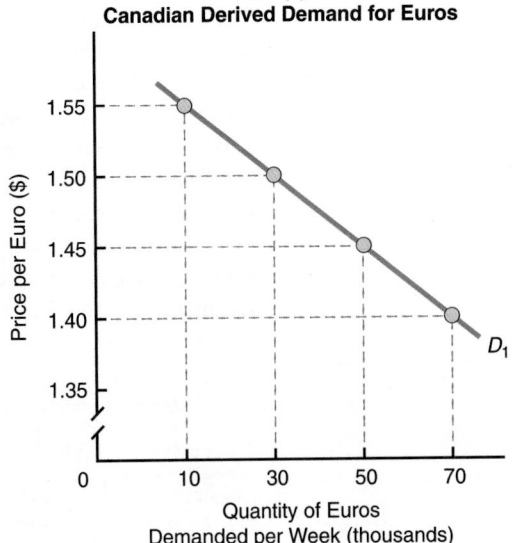

In part (a), we show the demand schedule for European pharmaceuticals in Canada, expressed in terms of dollars per package of pharmaceuticals. In part (b), we show the demand curve, *D*, which slopes downward. In part (c), we show the number of euros required to purchase up to 700 packages of pharmaceuticals. If the price per package of pharmaceuticals in the EMU is 100 euros, we can now find the quantity of euros needed to pay for the various quantities demanded. In part (d), we see the derived demand for euros in Canada in order to purchase the various quantities of pharmaceuticals given in part (a). The resultant demand curve, D_1, is shown in part (e). This is the Canadian derived demand for euros.

FIGURE 17-3
The Supply of European Monetary Union Euros

If the market price of a Canadian produced wireless handheld device is $200, then at an exchange rate of $1.45 per euro, the price of the wireless handheld device to a European consumer is 137.93 euros. If the exchange rate rises to $1.50 per euro, the European price of the wireless handheld device falls to 133.33 euros. This induces an increase in the quantity of wireless handheld devices demanded by European consumers and consequently an increase in the quantity of euros supplied in exchange for dollars in the foreign exchange market. In contrast, if the exchange rate falls to $1.40 per euro, the European price of the wireless handheld device rises to 142.86 euros. This causes a decrease in the quantity of wireless handheld devices demanded by European consumers. As a result, there is a decline in the quantity of euros supplied in exchange for dollars in the foreign exchange market.

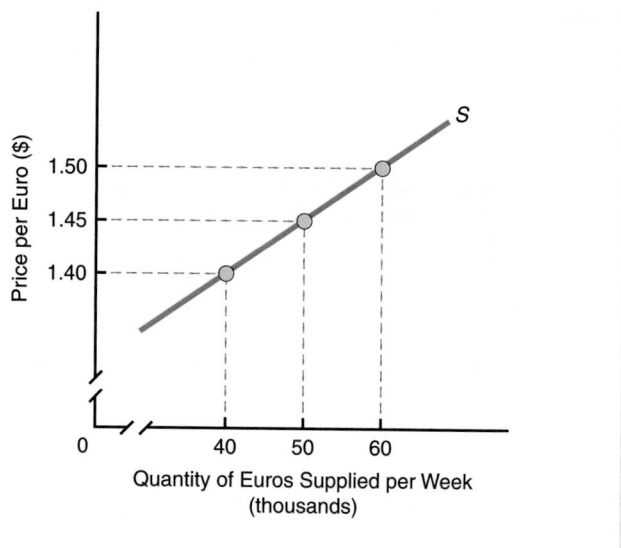

terms of dollars, the quantity of Canadian wireless handheld devices demanded will go up, and hence the quantity of euros supplied will go up. Therefore, the supply schedule of foreign currency (euros), which is derived from the European demand for Canadian goods, will slope upward.[1]

We could easily work through a detailed numerical example to show that the supply curve of EMU euros slopes upward. Rather than do that, we will simply draw it as upward sloping in Figure 17-3.

TOTAL DEMAND FOR AND SUPPLY OF EMU EUROS. Let us now look at the total demand for and supply of EMU euros. We take all Canadian consumers of European pharmaceuticals and all European consumers of Canadian wireless handheld devices and put their demands for and supplies of euros together into one diagram. Thus, we are showing the total demand for and total supply of EMU euros. The horizontal axis in Figure 17-4 represents the quantity of foreign exchange—the number of euros per year. The vertical axis represents the exchange rate—the price of foreign currency (euros) expressed in dollars (per euro). The foreign currency price of $1.50 per euro means it will cost you $1.50 to buy 1 euro. At the foreign currency price of $1.45 per euro, you know that it will cost you $1.45 to buy 1 euro. The equilibrium, *E*, is again established at $1.45 for 1 euro.

In our hypothetical example, assuming that there are only representative groups of pharmaceutical consumers in Canada and wireless handheld device consumers in the EMU, the equilibrium exchange rate will be set at $1.45 per euro.

This equilibrium is not established because Canadian residents like to buy euros or because Europeans like to buy dollars. Rather, the equilibrium exchange rate depends on how many wireless handheld devices Europeans want and how many European pharmaceuticals Canadian residents want (given their respective incomes, their tastes, and, in our example, the relative prices of pharmaceuticals and wireless handheld devices).[2]

---

[1] Actually, the supply schedule of foreign currency will be upward sloping if we assume that the demand for imported Canadian wireless handheld devices on the part of an EMU resident is price elastic. If the demand schedule for wireless handheld devices is price inelastic, the supply schedule will be negatively sloped. In the case of unit elasticity of demand, the supply schedule for euros will be a vertical line. Throughout the rest of this chapter, we will assume that demand is price elastic. Remember that the price elasticity of demand tells us whether or not total expenditures by wireless handheld device purchasers in EMU Europe will rise or fall when the euro drops in value. In the long run, it is quite realistic to think that the price elasticity of demand for imports is numerically greater than 1 anyway.

[2] Remember that we are dealing with a two-country world in which we are considering only the exchange of Canadian wireless handheld devices and European pharmaceuticals. In the real world, more than just goods and services are exchanged among countries. Some Canadians buy European financial assets; some Europeans buy Canadian financial assets. We are ignoring such transactions for the moment.

Total Demand for and Supply of European Monetary Union Euros

The market supply curve for EMU euros results from the total demand for Canadian wireless handheld devices. The demand curve, *D*, slopes downward like most demand curves, and the supply curve, *S*, slopes upward. The foreign-exchange price, or the Canadian dollar price of euros, is given on the vertical axis. The number of euros is represented on the horizontal axis. If the foreign exchange rate is $1.50—that is, if it takes $1.50 to buy 1 euro—Canadian residents will demand 20 billion euros. The equilibrium exchange rate is at the intersection of *D* and *S*, or point *E*. The equilibrium exchange rate is $1.45 per euro. At this point, 30 billion euros are both demanded and supplied each year.

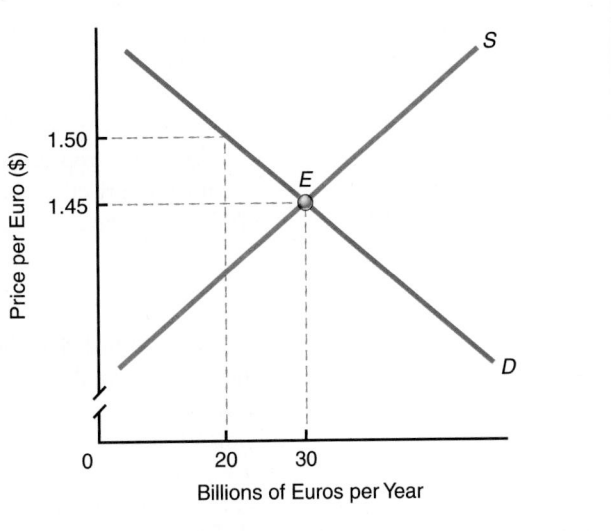

17.4 Factors That Can Induce Changes in Equilibrium Exchange Rates

A Shift in Demand

Assume that a successful advertising campaign by Canadian pharmaceutical importers has caused Canadian demand for European pharmaceuticals to rise. Canadian residents demand more pharmaceuticals at all prices. Their demand curve for European pharmaceuticals has shifted outward to the right.

The increased demand for European pharmaceuticals can be translated into an increased demand for euros. All Canadian residents clamouring for European pharmaceuticals will supply more dollars to the foreign exchange market while demanding more EMU euros to pay for the pharmaceuticals. Figure 17-5 presents a new demand schedule, D_2, for EMU euros; this demand schedule is to the right of the original demand schedule. If Europeans do not change their desire for Canadian wireless handheld devices, the supply schedule for EMU euros will remain stable.

A Shift in the Demand Schedule

The demand schedule for European pharmaceuticals shifts to the right, causing the derived demand schedule for euros to shift to the right as well. We have shown this as a shift from D_1 to D_2. We have assumed that the EMU supply schedule for euros has remained stable—that is, European demand for Canadian wireless handheld devices has remained constant. The old equilibrium foreign exchange rate was $1.45 per euro. The new equilibrium exchange rate will be E_2. It will now cost $1.50 to buy 1 euro. The higher price of euros will be translated into a higher dollar price for European pharmaceuticals and a lower EMU euro price for Canadian wireless handheld devices.

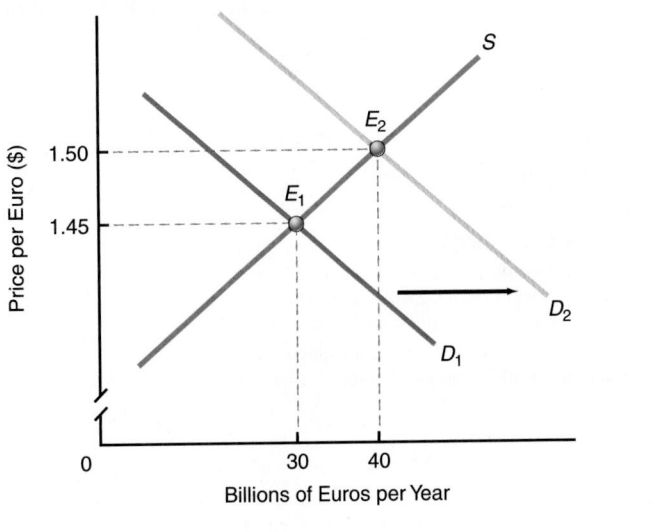

A new equilibrium will be established at a higher exchange rate. In our particular example, the new equilibrium is established at an exchange rate of $1.50 per euro. It now takes $1.50 to buy 1 EMU euro, whereas formerly it took $1.45. This will be translated into an increase in the price of European pharmaceuticals to Canadian residents and into a decrease in the price of Canadian wireless handheld devices to Europeans. For example, a package of European pharmaceuticals priced at 100 euros that sold for $145 in Canada will now be priced at $150. Conversely, a Canadian wireless handheld device priced at $200 that previously sold for 137.93 euros in the EMU will now sell for 133.33 euros.

A Shift in Supply

We just assumed that the Canadian demand for European pharmaceuticals had shifted due to a successful ad campaign. Because the demand for EMU euros is derived from the demand by Canadian residents for pharmaceuticals, this is translated into a shift in the demand curve for euros. As an alternative exercise, we might assume that the supply curve of EMU euros shifts outward to the right. Such a supply shift could occur for many reasons, one of which is a relative rise in the EMU price level. For example, if the prices of all EMU-manufactured wireless handheld devices went up 100 percent in euros, Canadian wireless handheld devices would become relatively cheaper. That would mean that European residents would want to buy more Canadian wireless handheld devices. But remember that when they want to buy more Canadian wireless handheld devices, they supply more euros to the foreign exchange market.

Thus, we see in Figure 17–6 that the supply curve of EMU euros moves from S to S_1. In the absence of restrictions—that is, in a system of flexible exchange rates—the new equilibrium exchange rate will be $1.40 equals 1 euro. The quantity of euros demanded and supplied will increase from 30 billion per year to 60 billion per year. We say, then, that in a flexible international exchange rate system, shifts in the demand for and supply of foreign currencies will cause changes in the equilibrium foreign exchange rates. Those rates will remain in effect until world supply or demand shifts.

Market Determinants of Exchange Rates

The foreign exchange market is affected by many other changes in market variables in addition to changes in relative price levels, including these:

1. *Changes in real interest rates.* If Canada's interest rate, corrected for people's expectations of inflation, abruptly increases relative to the rest of the world, international investors elsewhere will increase their demand for dollar-denominated assets, thereby increasing the demand for dollars in foreign exchange markets. An increased demand for dollars in foreign exchange markets, other things held constant, will cause the dollar to appreciate and other currencies to depreciate.

FIGURE 17–6

A Shift in the Supply of European Monetary Union Euros

There has been a shift in the supply curve for EMU euros. The new equilibrium will occur at E_1, meaning that $1.40, rather than $1.45, will now buy 1 euro. After the exchange rate adjustment, the annual amount of euros demanded and supplied will increase from 30 billion to 60 billion.

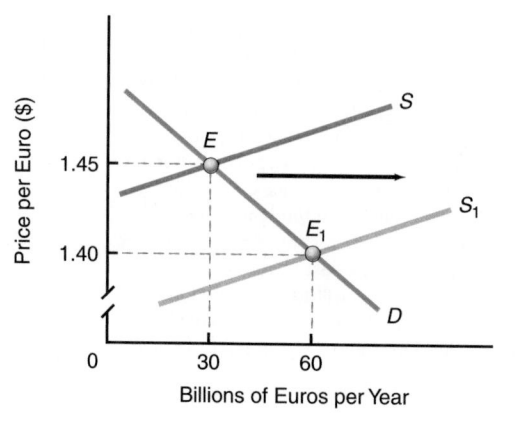

2. *Changes in productivity.* Whenever one country's productivity increases relative to another's, the former country will become more price competitive in world markets. The demand for its exports will increase, and so, too, will the demand for its currency.

3. *Changes in product preferences.* If Germany's citizens suddenly develop a taste for Canadian-made automobiles, this will increase the derived demand for Canadian dollars in foreign exchange markets.

4. *Perceptions of economic stability.* As already mentioned, if Canada looks economically and politically more stable relative to other countries, more foreigners will want to put their savings into Canadian assets than into their own domestic assets. This will increase the demand for dollars.

➤→ **CONCEPTS IN BRIEF**

Learning Objective 17.3: Outline how exchange rates are determined in the markets for foreign exchange.

↘ The foreign exchange rate is the rate at which one county's currency can be exchanged for another's.

↘ The demand for foreign exchange is a derived demand; it is derived from the demand for foreign goods and services (and financial assets). The supply of foreign exchange is derived from foreigners' demands for our goods and services.

↘ In general, the demand curve of foreign exchange slopes downward and the supply curve of foreign exchange slopes upward. The equilibrium foreign exchange rate occurs at the intersection of the demand and supply curves for a currency.

Learning Objective 17.4: Discuss factors that can induce changes in equilibrium exchange rates.

↘ A shift in the demand for foreign goods will result in a shift in the demand for foreign exchange. The equilibrium foreign exchange rate will change. A shift in the supply of foreign currency will also cause a change in the equilibrium exchange rate.

↘ The foreign exchange market is affected by nonprice factors such as changes in real interest rates, changes in productivity, changes in product preferences, and perceptions of economic stability.

17.5 *The Gold Standard and the International Monetary Fund*

The current system of more or less freely floating exchange rates is a recent development. We have had, in the past, periods of a gold standard, fixed exchange rates under the International Monetary Fund, and variants of these two.

The Gold Standard

Gold standard An international monetary system in which the values of the currencies of certain countries were tied directly to gold.

Until the 1930s, many countries were on a **gold standard**—the values of their currencies were tied directly to gold.[3] Countries operating under this gold standard agreed to redeem their currencies for a fixed amount of gold at the request of any holder of that currency. Although gold was not necessarily the means of exchange for world trade, it was the unit to which all currencies under the gold standard were pegged. And because all currencies in the system were linked to gold, exchange rates among those currencies were fixed. Indeed, the gold standard has been offered as the prototype of a fixed exchange rate system. The heyday of the gold standard was from about 1870 to 1914. England had been on such a standard as far back as the 1820s. See Policy Example 17–1, and determine whether Canada should return to the gold standard.

---

[3]This is a simplification. Most countries were on a *specie metal standard* using gold, silver, copper, and other precious metals as money. Countries operating under this standard agreed to redeem their currencies for a fixed exchange rate.

> **POLICY EXAMPLE 17-1**   **Should We Go Back to the Gold Standard?**
>
> In the past several decades, Canada has often run a current account deficit. The dollar has become weaker. We have had inflation. We have had recessions. Some economists and politicians argue that we should return to the gold standard. Canada operated under a gold standard from 1879 to 1931, except for a period during World War I. During this time, the dollar was defined as 23.22 grains of gold. Also, during that time period, general prices more than doubled during World War I, there was a major recession in 1920–21, and the Great Depression occurred.
>
> Clearly, a gold standard is not a guarantee of either stable prices or economic stability.
>
> **For critical analysis:** Why does no country today operate on a gold standard?

There was (and always is) a relationship between the balance of payments and changes in domestic money supplies throughout the world. Under a gold standard, the international financial market reached equilibrium through the effect of gold flows on each country's money supply. When a country suffered a deficit in its balance of payments, more gold would flow out than in. Because the domestic money supply was based on gold, an outflow of gold to foreigners caused an automatic reduction in the domestic money supply. This caused several things to happen. Interest rates rose, thereby attracting foreign capital and improving the balance of payments. At the same time, the reduction in the money supply was equivalent to a restrictive monetary policy, which caused national output and prices to fall. Imports were discouraged and exports were encouraged, thereby again improving the balance of payments.

Two problems plagued the gold standard. One was that by varying the value of its currency in response to changes in the quantity of gold, a nation gave up control of its domestic monetary policy. Another was that the world's commerce was at the mercy of gold discoveries. Throughout history, each time new veins of gold were found, desired domestic expenditures on goods and services increased. If production of goods and services failed to increase proportionately, inflation resulted.

Bretton Woods and the International Monetary Fund

International Monetary Fund (IMF) An institution set up under the Bretton Woods agreement to administer the agreement and to lend to member countries in balance of payments deficit.

In 1944, as World War II was ending, representatives from the world's capitalist countries met in Bretton Woods, New Hampshire, to create a new international payment system to replace the gold standard, which had collapsed during the 1930s. The Bretton Woods agreement created the **International Monetary Fund (IMF)** to administer the agreement and to lend to member countries in balance of payments deficit. The arrangements thus provided are now called the old IMF system or the Bretton Woods system.

Each member country was assigned an IMF contribution quota determined by its international trade volume and national income. Twenty-five percent of the quota was contributed in gold or American dollars and 75 percent in its own currency. At the time, therefore, the IMF consisted of a pool of gold, dollars, and other major currencies.

Par value The legally established value of the monetary unit of one country in terms of that of another; the officially determined value.

Member governments were then obligated to intervene to maintain the values of their currencies in foreign exchange markets within 1 percent of the declared **par value**— the legally established value of the monetary unit of one country in terms of that of another; the officially determined value. Except for a transitional arrangement permitting a one-time adjustment of up to 10 percent in par value, members could alter exchange rates thereafter only with the approval of the IMF. The agreement stated that such approval would be given only if the country's balance of payments was in *fundamental disequilibrium*, a term that has never been officially defined.

SPECIAL DRAWING RIGHTS. In 1967, the IMF created a new type of international money, *special drawing rights (SDRs)*. SDRs are exchanged only between monetary authorities (central banks). Their existence temporarily changed the IMF into a world central bank. The IMF creates SDRs the same way that the Bank of Canada can create dollars. The IMF allocates SDRs to member countries in accordance with their quotas. Currently, the SDR's value is determined by making one SDR equal to a bundle of currencies. In reality, the SDR rises or falls in terms of the American dollar.

END OF THE OLD IMF. In 1970, Canada moved away from the IMF peg and allowed the dollar to float. In 1971, the United States' government suspended the convertibility of the American dollar into gold. Finally, in March 1973, the finance ministers of the European Economic Community (now the European Union, or EU) announced that they would let their currencies float against the American dollar, something Japan had already begun doing with its yen. Since 1973, Canada and most other trading countries have had either freely floating exchange rates or managed ("dirty") floating exchange rates.

17.6   *Fixed versus Floating Exchange Rates*

Canada went off the Bretton Woods system of fixed exchange rates in 1970. As Figure 17–7 indicates, many other nations of the world have been less willing to permit the values of their currencies to vary in the foreign exchange markets.

Fixing the Exchange Rate

How did nations fix their exchange rates in years past? How do many countries accomplish this today in a world in which the United States dollar is the international reserve currency? Figure 17–8 shows the market for baht, the currency of Thailand. At the initial equilibrium point E_1, American residents had to give up $0.40 to obtain one baht. Suppose now that there is an increase in the supply of baht for dollars, perhaps because Thai residents wish to buy more American goods. Other things being equal, the result would be a movement to point E_2 in Figure 17–8. The dollar value of the baht would fall to $0.30.

To prevent baht depreciation from occurring, however, the Bank of Thailand, the central bank, could increase the demand for baht in the foreign exchange market by purchasing baht with dollars. The Bank of Thailand can do this using dollars that it had on hand as part of its *foreign exchange reserves*. All central banks hold reserves of foreign currencies. Because the American dollar is a key international currency, the Bank of Thailand and other central banks typically hold billions of dollars in reserve so that they can, if they wish, make transactions such as the one in this example. Note that a sufficiently large purchase of baht could, as shown in Figure 17–8, cause the demand curve to shift rightward to achieve the new equilibrium point E_3, at which the baht's value remains at $0.40. Provided that it has enough dollar reserves on hand, the Bank of Thailand could maintain— effectively fix—the exchange rate in the face of the sudden fall in the demand for baht.

This is the manner in which the Bank of Thailand fixed the dollar–baht exchange rate until 1997 (see Policy Example 17–2). This basic approach—varying the amount of the national currency demanded at any given exchange rate in foreign exchange markets

---

FIGURE 17–7
Current Exchange Rate Arrangements

Currently, 22 percent of the member nations of the International Monetary Fund have an independent float, and just over 22 percent have a managed float exchange rate arrangement. Among countries with a fixed exchange rate, about one-third use a fixed U.S. dollar exchange rate. Slightly over 21 percent of all nations use the currencies of other nations instead of issuing their own currencies.

Source: International Monetary Fund

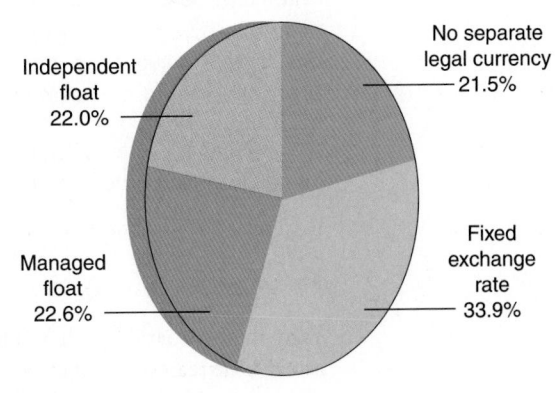

FIGURE 17–8
A Fixed Exchange Rate

This figure illustrates how the Bank of Thailand could fix the dollar–baht exchange rate in the face of an increase in the supply of baht caused by a rise in the demand for American goods by Thai residents. In the absence of any action by the Bank of Thailand, the result would be a movement from point E_1 to point E_2. The dollar value of the baht would fall from \$0.40 to \$0.30. The Bank of Thailand can prevent this exchange rate change by purchasing baht with dollars in the foreign exchange market, thereby raising the demand for baht. At the new equilibrium point E_3, the baht's value remains at \$0.40.

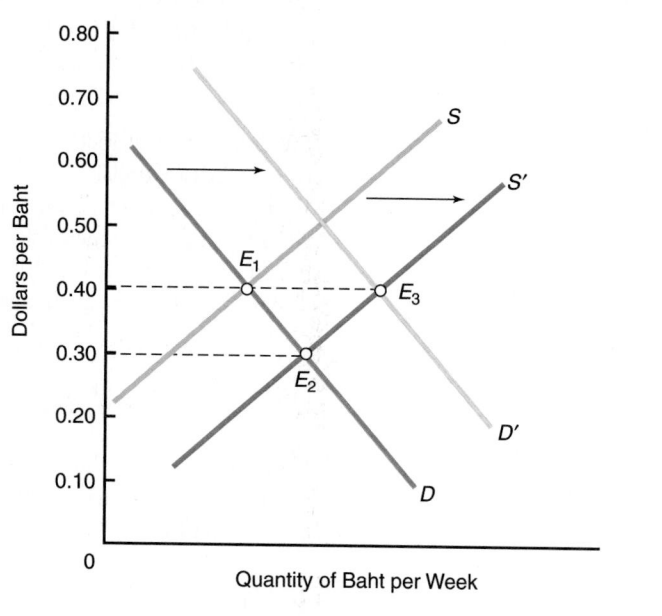

when necessary—is also the way that *any* central bank seeks to keep its nation's currency value unchanged in light of changing market forces.

Central banks can keep exchange rates fixed as long as they have enough foreign exchange reserves available to deal with potentially long-lasting changes in the demand for or supply of their nation's currency.

POLICY EXAMPLE 17–2   **Can Foreign Exchange Rates Be Fixed Forever?**

Trying to keep the exchange rate fixed in the face of foreign exchange market volatility can be a difficult policy to pursue. Consider Thailand's experience. At the beginning of 1997, the Bank of Thailand was holding \$40 billion in foreign exchange reserves. Within 10 months, those reserves had fallen to \$3 billion. Whatever the Bank of Thailand promised about not devaluing, it no longer had credibility. Not surprisingly, the baht's value relative to the dollar fell by more than 25 percent in July 1997 alone.

The Thai experience was repeated on a larger scale throughout Southeast Asia in 1997 and 1998 as efforts by the central banks of Indonesia, Malaysia, South Korea, and Vietnam to fix exchange rates ultimately collapsed, leading to sizable devaluations. Even the previously stalwart exchange rate arrangements of Singapore, Taiwan, and Hong Kong became increasingly less credible. These nations learned an old lesson: Trying to protect residents from foreign exchange risks works only as long as foreign exchange market traders believe that central banks have the financial wherewithal to keep exchange rates unchanged. Otherwise, a fixed exchange rate policy can ultimately prove unsustainable.

For critical analysis: Why do you think governments attempt to maintain the foreign exchange value of their domestic currencies?

Pros and Cons of a Fixed Exchange Rate

Why might a nation such as Thailand wish to keep the value of its currency from fluctuating? One reason is that changes in the exchange rate can affect the market value of assets that are denominated in foreign currencies. This can increase the financial risks that a nation's residents face, thereby forcing them to incur costs to avoid these risks.

Foreign exchange risk The possibility that variations in the market value of assets can take place as a result of changes in the value of a nation's currency.

FOREIGN EXCHANGE RISK.   The possibility that variations in the market value of assets can take place as a result of changes in the value of a nation's currency is called the **foreign exchange risk** that residents of a country face because their nation's currency value can vary. For instance, if companies in Thailand had many loans denominated in dollars but earned nearly all their revenues in baht from sales within Thailand, a decline in the dollar value of the baht would mean that Thai companies would have to allocate a larger portion of their earnings to make the same *dollar* loan payments as before. Thus, a fall in the baht's value would increase the operating costs of these companies, thereby reducing their profitability and raising the likelihood of eventual bankruptcy.

Limiting foreign exchange risk is a classic rationale for adopting a fixed exchange rate. Nevertheless, a country's residents are not defenceless against foreign exchange risk. They can **hedge** against such risk, meaning that they can adopt strategies intended to offset the risk arising from exchange rate variations. For example, a company in Thailand that has significant euro earnings from sales in Germany but sizable loans from American investors could arrange to convert its euro earnings into dollars via special types of foreign exchange contracts called *currency swaps*. The Thai company could thereby avoid holdings of baht and shield itself—*hedge*—against variations in the baht's value.

Hedge A financial strategy that is intended to offset the risk arising from exchange rate variations.

THE EXCHANGE RATE AS A SHOCK ABSORBER.   If fixing the exchange rate limits foreign exchange risk, why do so many nations allow the exchange rates to float? The answer must be that there are potential drawbacks associated with fixing exchange rates. One is that exchange rate variations can actually perform a valuable service for a nation's economy. Consider a situation in which residents of a nation speak only their own nation's language, which is so difficult that hardly anyone else in the world takes the trouble to learn it. As a result, the country's residents are very *immobile*: They cannot trade their labour skills outside of their own nation's borders.

Now, think about what happens if this nation chooses to fix its exchange rate. Imagine a situation in which other countries begin to sell products that are close substitutes for the products its people specialize in producing, causing a sizable drop in worldwide demand for the nation's goods. Over a short-run period in which prices and wages cannot adjust, the result will be a sharp decline in production of goods and services, a fall-off in national income, and higher unemployment. Contrast this situation with one in which the exchange rate floats. In this case, a sizable decline in outside demand for the nation's products will cause it to experience a trade deficit, which will lead to a significant drop in the demand for the nation's currency. As a result, the nation's currency will experience a sizable depreciation, making the goods that the nation offers to sell abroad much less expensive in other countries. People abroad who continue to consume the nation's products will increase their purchases, and the nation's exports will increase. Its production will begin to recover somewhat, as will its residents' incomes. Unemployment will begin to fall.

This example illustrates how exchange rate variations can be beneficial, especially if a nation's residents are relatively immobile. It can be much more difficult, for example, for a Polish resident who has never studied Portuguese to make a move to Lisbon, even if she is highly qualified for available jobs there. If many residents of Poland face similar linguistic or cultural barriers, Poland could be better off with a floating exchange rate even if its residents must incur significant costs hedging against foreign exchange risk as a result.

Splitting the Difference: Dirty Floats and Target Zones

In recent years, national policy makers have tried to soften the choice of either adopting a fixed exchange rate or allowing exchange rates full flexibility in the foreign exchange markets by "splitting the difference" between the two extremes.

Dirty float A system between flexible and fixed exchange rates in which central banks occasionally enter foreign exchange markets to influence rates.

A DIRTY FLOAT.   One way to split the difference is to let exchange rates float most of the time but "manage" exchange rate movements part of the time. Canada went off the Bretton Woods system in 1970, but it has nonetheless tried to keep certain elements of that system in play. We have occasionally engaged in what is called a **dirty float**—a system between flexible and fixed exchange rates, in which central banks occasionally enter foreign exchange markets to influence rates. The management of flexible exchange rates has usually come about through international policy cooperation. For example, the Group of Eight (G-8) nations—Canada, France, Germany, Italy, Japan, Russia the United Kingdom, and the United States—have for some time shared information on their policy objectives and procedures. They do this through regular meetings between economic policy secretaries, ministers, and staff members. One of their principal objectives has been to "smooth out" foreign exchange rates.

Is it possible for these groups to "manage" foreign exchange rates? Some economists do not think so. For example, economists Michael Bordo and Anna Schwartz studied the foreign exchange intervention actions coordinated by the Federal Reserve and the United States' Treasury for the second half of the 1980s. Besides showing that such interventions were sporadic and variable, Bordo and Schwartz came to an even more compelling conclusion: Exchange rate interventions were trivial relative to the total trading of foreign exchange on a daily basis. Thus, their conclusion is that neither the Canadian central bank nor the central banks of the other G-7 nations can influence exchange rates in the long run.

CRAWLING PEGS. Another approach to splitting the difference between fixed and floating exchange rates is called a **crawling peg**—an automatically adjusting target for the value of a nation's currency. For instance, a central bank might announce that it wants the value of its currency relative to the American dollar to decline at an annual rate of 5 percent, a rate of depreciation that it feels is consistent with long-run market forces. The central bank would then try to buy or sell foreign exchange reserves in sufficient quantities to be sure that the currency depreciation takes place gradually, thereby reducing the foreign exchange risk faced by the nation's residents.

> **Crawling peg** An automatically adjusting target for the value of a nation's currency.

In this way, a crawling peg functions like a floating exchange rate in the sense that the exchange rate can change over time. But it is like a fixed exchange rate in the sense that the central bank always tries to keep the exchange rate close to a target value. In this way, a crawling peg has elements of both kinds of exchange rate systems.

TARGET ZONES. A third way to try to split the difference between fixed and floating exchange rates is to adopt an exchange rate **target zone**—a policy under which a central bank announces that there are specific upper and lower *bands*, or limits, for permissible values for the exchange rate. Within those limits, which define the exchange rate target zone, the central bank permits the exchange rate to move flexibly. The central bank commits itself, however, to intervene in the foreign exchange markets to ensure that its nation's currency value will not rise above the upper band or fall below the lower band. For instance, if the exchange rate approaches the upper band, the central bank must sell foreign exchange reserves in sufficient amounts to halt any further currency appreciation.

> **Target zone** A policy under which a central bank announces that there are specific upper and lower *bands*, or limits, for permissible values for the exchange rate.

Starting in 1999, officials from the European Union attempted to get the United States, Japan, and several other countries' governments to agree to target zones for the exchange rate between the newly created euro and the dollar, yen, and some other currencies. Officials in the United States were not in favour. So far, no target zones have been created, and the euro has floated freely.

➡→ CONCEPTS IN BRIEF

Learning Objective 17.5: Outline how policy makers can go about attempting to fix exchange rates.

- ♣ The International Monetary Fund was developed after World War II as an institution to maintain fixed exchange rates in the world. Since 1973, however, fixed exchange rates have disappeared in most major trading countries. For these nations, exchange rates are largely determined by forces of demand and supply in foreign exchange marketplaces.

Learning Objective 17.6: Explain alternative approaches to limiting exchange rate variability.

- ♣ Many other nations, however, have tried to fix their exchange rates, with varying degrees of success. Although fixing the exchange rate helps protect a nation's residents from foreign exchange risk, this policy may make mobile residents susceptible to greater volatility in income and employment. It can also expose the central bank to sporadic currency crises arising from unpredictable changes in world capital flows.

- ♣ Countries have experimented with exchange rate systems between the extremes of fixed and floating exchange rates. Under a dirty float, a central bank permits the value of its nation's currency to float in the foreign exchange markets but intervenes from time to time to influence the exchange rate. Under a crawling peg, a central bank tries to push its nation's currency value in a desired direction. Pursuing a target zone policy, a central bank aims to keep the exchange rate between upper and lower bands, intervening only when the exchange rate approaches either limit.

➡ **ISSUES AND APPLICATIONS**

A Major Foreign Exchange Flop

Concepts Applied: Exchange Rates, Equilibrium Exchange Rates, Floating Exchange Rates, Dirty Float

Huge amounts of foreign currency are traded every day.

As the dollar value of the euro steadily declined during the months following the currency's inception in January 1999, many critics of the European Central Bank (ECB) began calling on the institution to support the currency's value. If the ECB would just buy euros with some of its billions of dollars in reserves, they argued, the euro's value would recover its lost ground against the dollar. By the summer of 2000, the financial media were abuzz with rumours that the ECB might conduct a first-ever foreign exchange market intervention to boost the euro's value. Nevertheless, when the ECB ultimately did intervene, both the central bank and its critics learned the limits of its ability to influence the euro–dollar exchange rate.

The Long-Awaited Intervention Occurs— and Fizzles

Early on the morning of September 22, 2000, the ECB launched its first effort to manage the value of the euro in foreign exchange markets. It used billions of its reserves of dollars to buy billions of euros. The Federal Reserve, the Bank of England, and the Bank of Canada supported its efforts by buying euros with their own currencies. By the middle of the morning, the euro's dollar value had increased from 81 cents to 90 cents, and it looked as though the coordinated interventions might reverse the euro's slide.

At the end of the day, however, the euro exchange rate was down to 88 cents. During the next few days, in spite of additional interventions by the ECB and the Federal Reserve, the dollar price of the euro continued to creep downward. By September 27, 2000, the euro's market value was where it had begun, at about 81 cents.

The Euro Recovers—No Thanks to the ECB

The ECB attempted several interventions during the next year, to little avail. The dollar price of the euro rose above 95 cents in early 2001, but it dropped back down near 80 cents by the summer of that year.

Then, beginning in early 2002, the euro's dollar value gradually began a sustained increase, and by July 2002, a euro once again exchanged for more than $1 in the foreign exchange market. The ECB had nothing to do with the currency's reversal of fortunes, however. Lower American interest rates and a slumping American stock market had led world investors to remove some of their funds from American financial markets, which contributed to a decline in the demand for dollars. Investors placed some of those funds in European financial markets, and this helped boost the demand for euros. Consequently, private market forces generated the higher euro value that repeated efforts by the ECB and other major central banks had been unable to accomplish.

For critical analysis:

1. What factors limited the ability of the European Central Bank, even with the assistance of other central banks, to induce a rise in the dollar price of the euro?

2. How might an observed increase in productivity in European nations that began in late 2001 have contributed to the increased dollar price of the euro?

➤ SUMMARY

Here is what you should know after reading this chapter. MyEconLab will help you identify what you know, and where to go when you need to practise. We suggest that as soon as you review one of the Learning Objective sections below, you then proceed to go through the related section in MyEconLab.

⋏ myeconlab

➤ LEARNING OBJECTIVES	KEY TERMS	MYECONLAB PRACTICE
17.1 The Balance of Payments and International Capital Movements. The balance of trade is defined as the difference between the value of exports and the value of imports. If the value of exports exceeds the value of imports, a trade surplus exists; if the value of exports is less than the value of imports, a trade deficit exists; if exports and import values are equal, we refer to this situation as a trade balance. The balance of payments is more general and takes into account the value of *all* international transactions. Thus the balance of payments identifies not only goods and services transactions among countries but also investments (financial and nonfinancial) and gifts (private and public). When the value of all these transactions is such that one country is sending more to other countries than it is receiving in return, a balance of payments deficit occurs. A payment surplus and a payments balance are the reverse.	balance of trade, 446 balance of payments, 446	• **MyEconLab** Study Plan 17.1
17.2 Accounting Identities. The balance of merchandise trade is defined as the value of goods and services bought and sold in the world market, usually during the period of one year. Investment income includes income earned by foreigners on Canadian investments and income earned by Canadians on foreign investments. Transfers involve international private gifts and federal government grants or gifts to foreign nations. When we add the balance of merchandise trade plus the balance of services and take account of net transfers, we come up with the balance on current account, which is a summary statistic taking into account the three transactions that form the current account transactions. There are also capital account transactions that relate to the buying and selling of financial and real assets. Foreign capital is always entering Canada, and Canadian capital is always flowing abroad. The difference is called the balance on capital account.	accounting identities, 446 special drawing rights (SDRs), 451	• **MyEconLab** Study Plan 17.2

➡ LEARNING OBJECTIVES	**KEY TERMS**	**MYECONLAB PRACTICE**

Finally, another type of balance of payments transaction concerns the official settlement assets of individual countries, or what is often simply called official transactions. By standard accounting convention, official transactions are exactly equal, but opposite in sign, to the balance of payments of Canada.

Our balance of trade and payments can be affected by our relative rate of inflation and by political instability elsewhere compared to the stability that exists in Canada.

17.3 Determining Foreign Exchange Rates. To transact business internationally, it is necessary to convert domestic currencies into other currencies. This is done via the foreign exchange market. If we were trading with Europe only, European producers would want to be paid in euros because they must pay their workers in euros. Canadian producers would want to be paid in dollars because Canadian workers are paid in dollars.

A Canadian's desire for European pharmaceuticals is expressed in terms of a supply of dollars, which is in turn a demand for European euros in the foreign exchange market. The opposite situation arises when Europeans wish to buy Canadian wireless handheld devices. Their demand for wireless handheld devices creates a demand for Canadian dollars and supply of European euros. We put the demand and supply schedules together to find the equilibrium foreign exchange rate. The demand schedule for foreign exchange is a derived demand—it is derived from Canadians' demand for foreign products.

With no government intervention, a market-clearing equilibrium foreign exchange rate will emerge. After a shift in demand or supply, the exchange rate will change so that it will again clear the market.

foreign exchange market, 452
foreign exchange rate, 452
flexible exchange rates, 453
appreciation, 453
depreciation, 453

• **MyEconLab** Study Plan 17.3

17.4 Factors That Can Induce Changes in Equilibrium Exchange Rates. If Canadians increase their demand for European pharmaceuticals, the demand curve for European

• **MyEconLab** Study Plan 17.4

pharmaceuticals shifts to the right. The derived demand for euros also shifts to the right. The supply schedule of euros, however, remains stable because the European demand for Canadian wireless handheld devices has remained constant. The shifted demand schedule intersects the stable supply schedule at a higher price (the foreign exchange rate increases). This is an appreciation of the value of the European euro (a depreciation of the value of the dollar against the euro).

Market determinants of exchange rates are changes in inflation, changes in real interest rates (interest rates corrected for inflation), changes in productivity, changes in product preferences and perceptions of economic and political stability.

17.5 The Gold Standard and the International Monetary Fund. If the current price of another nation's currency in terms of the home currency starts to fall below the level where the home country wants it to remain, the home country's central bank can use reserves of the other nation's currency to purchase the home currency in foreign exchange markets. This raises the demand for the home currency and thereby pushes up the currency's value in terms of the other nation's currency. In this way, the home country can keep the exchange rate fixed at a desired value, as long as it has sufficient reserves of the other currency to use for this purpose.

Under a gold standard, a type of fixed exchange rate regime, movement of gold across countries changes domestic money supplies, causing price levels to change and to correct balance of payments imbalances. The gold standard was succeeded by the Bretton Woods agreement which created the International Monetary Fund (IMF) in 1945 to maintain fixed exchange rates throughout the world.

gold standard, 459
International Monetary Fund (IMF), 460
par value, 460

• **MyEconLab** Study Plan 17.5

17.6 Fixed versus Floating Exchange Rates. The opposite alternative to a fixed exchange rate approach is flexible exchange rates. A flexible exchange rate

foreign exchange risk, 463
hedge, 463
dirty float, 463

• **MyEconLab** Study Plan 17.6

►► LEARNING OBJECTIVES	**KEY TERMS**	**MYECONLAB PRACTICE**

system is an international monetary system in which foreign exchange rates are allowed to fluctuate to reflect changes in the demand and supply for international currencies. Today, many nations permit their exchange rates to vary in foreign exchange markets. Others pursue policies that limit the variability of exchange rates. Some engage in a managed or "dirty" float, in which they manage exchange rates, often in cooperation with other nations. Some establish crawling pegs, in which the target value of the exchange rate is adjusted automatically over time. And some establish target zones, with upper and lower limits on the extent to which exchange rates are allowed to vary.

crawling peg, 464
target zone, 464

►► PROBLEMS

(Answers to the odd-numbered problems appear at the back of the book.)

LO 17.1 Distinguish between the balance of trade and the balance of payments.

1. Examine the following hypothetical data for Canadian international transactions, in billions of dollars:

   Exports: goods, 165.8; services, 130.5

   Imports: goods, −250.7; services, −99.3

   Net investment: −20.0

   Net transfers: −20.0

   a. What is the merchandise balance of trade?
   b. What is the balance on goods and services?
   c. What is the balance on current account?

2. Identify whether each of the following items creates a surplus item or a deficit item in the current account of the Canadian balance of payments.

   a. A central European company sells products to a Canadian hobby-store chain.
   b. Japanese residents pay a Canadian travel company to arrange hotel stays, ground transportation, and tours of various Canadian cities, including Vancouver, Banff, Toronto, and Montreal.

   c. A Mexican company pays a Canadian accounting firm to audit its income statements.
   d. Canadian religious groups send relief aid to Pakistan following a major earthquake in that nation.

3. Over the course of a year, a nation tracked its foreign transactions and arrived at the following amounts:

Merchandise exports	500
Service exports	75
Net unilateral transfers	10
Domestic assets abroad (capital outflows)	−200
Foreign assets at home (capital inflows)	300
Changes in official reserves	−35
Merchandise imports	600
Service imports	50

   What is the nation's balance of trade, current account balance, and capital account balance?

LO 17.2 Identify the key accounts within the balance of payments.

4. What are the three important accounts within the balance of payments? What are the major components of these three accounts?

LO 17.3 Outline how exchange rates are determined in the markets for foreign exchange.

5. In the graph, what can be said about the shift from D to D_1?

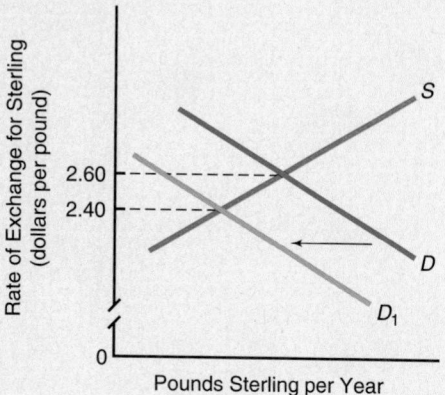

a. It could be caused by the British demanding fewer Canadian products.
b. It is a result of increased Canadian demand for British goods.
c. It causes an appreciation of the dollar relative to the pound.
d. It causes an appreciation of the pound relative to the dollar.

6. Suppose that we have the following demand schedule for German beer in Canada per week:

Price per Case	Quantity Demanded (cases)
$40	2
32	4
24	6
16	8
8	10

a. If the price is 30 euros per case, how many euros are required to purchase each quantity demanded?
b. Now derive the demand schedule for euros per week in Canada to pay for German beer.
c. At a price of 80 cents per euro, how many cases of beer would be imported from Germany per week?

7. The dollar, the pound sterling, and the euro are the currency units of Canada, the United Kingdom, and Germany, respectively. Suppose that these countries decide to go on a gold standard and define the value of their currencies in terms of gold as follows: $400 = 1 ounce of gold; 160 pounds sterling = 1 ounce of gold; and 475 euros = 1 ounce of gold. What would the exchange rate be between the dollar and the pound? Between the dollar and the euro? Between the euro and the pound?

LO 17.4 Discuss factors that can induce changes in equilibrium exchange rates.

8. Which of the following will cause the yen to appreciate? Explain.
a. Canadian real incomes increase relative to Japanese real incomes.
b. It is expected that in the future the yen will depreciate relative to the dollar.
c. The Canadian inflation rate rises relative to the Japanese inflation rate.
d. The after-tax, risk-adjusted real interest rate in Canada rises relative to that in Japan.
e. Canadian tastes change in favour of Japanese-made goods.

9. The graph below shows the supply of and demand for pounds sterling.
a. Assuming that the demand for pounds is represented by D, what is the dollar price of pounds? What is the equilibrium quantity?
b. Suppose that there is general inflation in Canada. Starting at D, which demand curve could represent this situation? If exchange rates are allowed to float freely, what would be the new dollar price of one pound? What would be the equilibrium quantity?
c. Suppose that the inflation in part (b) occurs and Canada has the dollar price of one pound fixed at $1.50. How would the Bank of Canada be able to accomplish this?
d. Now suppose that instead of inflation, there was general deflation in Canada. Which demand curve could represent this situation? How could Canada maintain a fixed price of $1.50 per pound in this situation?

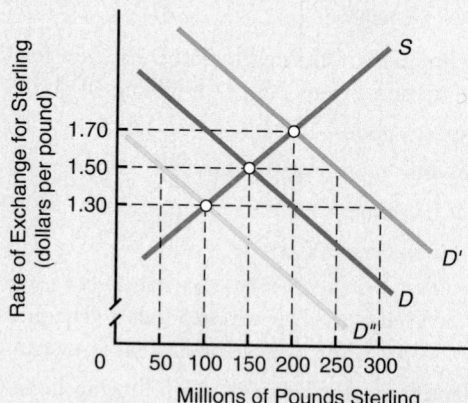

10. If the rate of exchange between the pound and the dollar is $2 for one pound, and Canada then experiences severe inflation, we would expect the exchange rate (under a flexible rate system) to change. What would be the new rate?
a. More than $2 for one pound
b. Less than $2 for one pound

c. More than one pound for $2

d. None of the above

11. On Monday, the exchange rate between the euro and the U.S. dollar was $1.37 per euro, and the exchange rate between the Canadian dollar and the U.S. dollar was $0.95 per Canadian dollar. What is the exchange rate between the Canadian dollar and the euro?

12. Suppose that signs of an improvement in the Japanese economy lead international investors to resume lending to the Japanese government and businesses. Policymakers, however, are worried about how this will influence the yen. How should the central bank, the Bank of Japan, respond to this event if it wants to keep the value of the yen unchanged?

LO 17.5 Outline how policy makers can go about attempting to fix exchange rates.

13. Maintenance of a fixed exchange rate system requires government intervention to keep exchange rates stable, as discussed in Policy Example 17–2, "Can Foreign Exchange Rates Be Fixed Forever?" What is the policy implication of this fact? (*Hint:* Think in terms of the money supply.)

LO 17.6 Explain alternative approaches to limiting exchange rate variability.

14. Policy Example 17–1, "Should We Go Back to the Gold Standard?", looks at the gold standard. Suppose that under a gold standard, the American dollar is pegged to gold at a rate of $35 per ounce and the Canadian dollar is pegged to gold at a rate of $43.75 per ounce. Explain how the gold standard constitutes an exchange rate arrangement between the American dollar and the Canadian dollar. What is the exchange rate between the American dollar and the Canadian dollar?

15. Briefly explain the difference between a flexible exchange rate system, a fixed exchange rate system, a dirty float, and the use of target zones.

Chapter 1: The Nature of Economics

1. a. Human capital
   b. Land
   c. Entrepreneurship
   d. Physical capital
   e. Labour

3. a. Macroeconomic, as the unemployment rate is national or economywide.
   b. Microeconomic, as wage increases of specific occupations, such as nurses and doctors, relate to specific parts of the economy.
   c. Microeconomic, as prices of a specific part of the economy—cigarettes—are being studied.
   d. Macroeconomic, as the inflation rate tracks the average price of all goods, which is an economy-wide measure.
   e. Macroeconomic, as the nation's total annual production is an economywide measure.
   f. Microeconomic, as an individual firm's situation, such as Eaton's bankruptcy, focuses on a specific part of the economy.

5. Jon's marginal cost of enrolling in the two month computer course equals the cost of tuition, books, and fees plus the two months of earnings he sacrifices. This amounts to: $4500 + (2 \times \$3000) = \$10\ 500$

7. No, your cash withdrawals are not free as there is an opportunity cost equal to the interest sacrificed by not putting your $5000 in an account (or another investment) giving you a higher rate of interest.

9. The decision based on availability of funds is not a rational one. In order to allocate resources in a manner that maximizes the satisfaction of the city's wants, the mayor should compare the marginal (extra) benefit of constructing the city hall with the marginal (extra) cost, including alternatives sacrificed. If the extra benefit to the city of constructing the city hall is less than the value of some other alternative that has to be sacrificed, such as paving of city roads, the mayor's decision is not rational.

11. a. We should observe younger drivers to be more frequently involved in traffic accidents than older persons.
    b. Slower monetary expansion should be associated with lower inflation.

c. Professional basketball players receiving smaller salaries should be observed to have done less well in their high-school studies.
d. Employees being promoted rapidly should have lower rates of absenteeism than those being promoted more slowly.

13. a. Positive, for it is a statement that can be tested by the facts.
    b. Normative, involving a value judgment about what should be.
    c. Normative, involving a value judgment about what should be.
    d. Positive, for it is a statement that can be tested by the facts.

Appendix A: Reading and Working with Graphs

A-1. a. Price is independent, number of notebooks is dependent.
     b. Work-study hours is independent, credit hours is dependent.
     c. Hours studied is independent, and grade is dependent.

A-3.

x	y
4	12
3	9
2	6
1	3
0	0
−1	−3
−2	−6
−3	−9
−4	−12

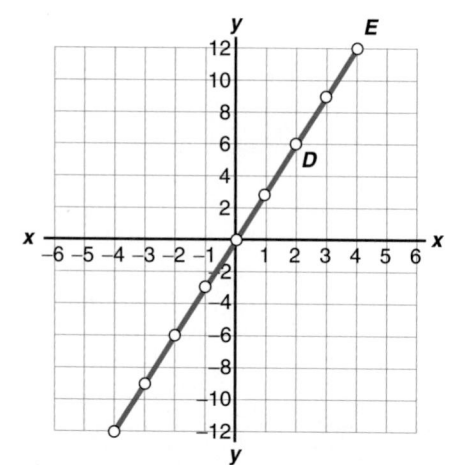

A-5.   If you move along the line in Problem A-3 from point D to point E, the slope equals the change in the y-values divided by the change in the x-values, which is:

$$(12 - 6)/(4 - 2) = 6/2 = 3.$$

A-7.   For the ordered pair (4, 16) the tangent line is upward sloping, slope is positive.

For the ordered pair (0, 0) the tangent line is horizontal, slope is zero.

For the ordered pair (−4, 16) the tangent line is downward sloping, slope is negative.

Chapter 2: Production Possibilities and Economic Systems

1. a.   The maximum amount of factories will be 2000 as shown by the production possibilities curve.

    b.   The maximum number of factories would be 5000, as shown by combination A.

    c.   A fixed amount of resources and technology prevents Epica from being able to produce combination J in 2008.

    d.   If Epica is at point I, this could conflict with the goals of productive efficiency and full employment.

    e.   i.   The opportunity cost of an additional factory when moving from point E to D would be 2 yachts.

        ii.   The opportunity cost of an additional factory when moving from point C to B would be 4 yachts.

    f.   i.   The opportunity cost of an additional yacht when moving from point A to B would be 1/5 of a factory.

        ii.   The opportunity cost of an additional yacht when moving from point E to F would be 1 factory.

    g.   The Law of Increasing Relative Cost

    h.   This situation conflicts with allocative efficiency.

    i.   Economic growth will shift the production possibilities curve outward.

3.   The plot of the product possibilities curve is displayed in the graph below.

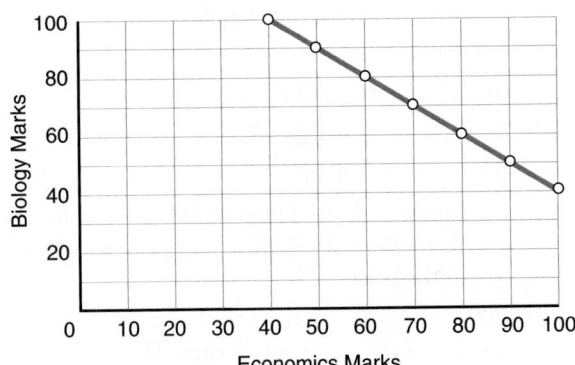

The PPC exhibits constant opportunity costs. That is, the cost of earning an additional mark in economics is always the same, in terms of additional biology marks sacrificed. In this case, the PPC is a straight line with the opportunity cost of earning an additional mark in economics always being 1 mark in biology.

5.

a.   b.

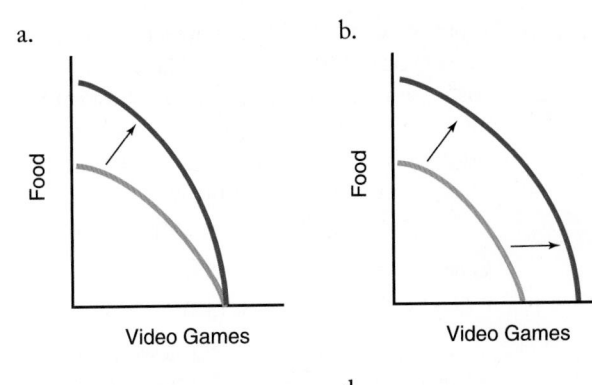

c.   d.

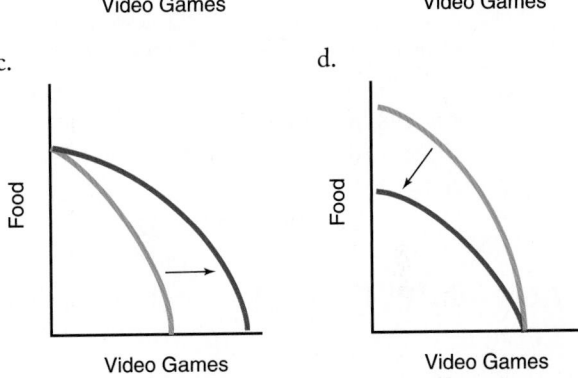

7.   If we assume that a two-year college diploma consists of four 15-week semesters, this amounts to committing 60 weeks to college studies. The opportunity cost is: 60 wks × 35 h × $7 = $14 700. The incentive for incurring this cost is that, upon graduating, you will be earning an amount significantly in excess of $7 per hour. You are sacrificing current consumption to obtain a greater amount of future consumption.

9.   Yes, you and your roommate should specialize. Since your opportunity cost of completing a basket of laundry (two meals) is lower than your roommate's (three meals), you should specialize in the laundry completion, while your roommate should specialize in the meal preparation. As an example, if you complete an extra basket of laundry, you give up only two meals. However, you free up an additional three hours of your roommate's time, which allows your roommate to produce an additional three meals. Overall, one extra meal is gained.

11.   a.   Toby has the absolute advantage in pizzas.

      b.   Tony has the lower opportunity cost in producing one lasagne supreme (gives up one pizza versus two pizzas for Toby) so Tony has a comparative advantage in lasagne.

      c.   Toby has the comparative advantage in pizza and Tony in lasagne. For each hour of specializing in the area of comparative advantage, there is a net gain of five pizzas (Toby: +10 pizzas and −5 lasagne; Tony +5 lasagne and −5 pizza)

13. The invisible hand of self-interest and competition help to ensure that firms serve the consumer, without the heavy hand of government.

15. a. In the market system, the techniques that yield the highest (positive) profits will be used.

b. Profit equals total revenue minus total cost. Because revenue from 100 units is fixed (at $100), if the firm wishes to maximize profit, this is equivalent to minimizing costs. To find total costs, simply muliply the price of each input by the amount of the input that must be used for each technique.

Costs of A = ($10)(6) + ($8)(5) = $100

Costs of B = ($10)(5) + ($8)(6) = $98

Costs of C = ($10)(4) + ($8)(7) = $96

Because technique C has the lowest costs, it also yields the highest profits ($100 − $96 = $4).

c. Following the same methods yields these costs: A = $98, B = $100, and C = $102. Technique A will be used because it is the most profitable.

d. The profits from using technique A to produce 100 units of X are $100 − $98 = $2.

Appendix B: The Production Possibilities Curve and Comparative Advantage

B-1 a. The Richard family has the absolute advantage in each product, assuming that both families use the same amount of labour input, each day.

b. For the Martin family the opportunity cost of one litre of beer is one litre of wine. For the Richard family the opportunity cost of one litre of beer is three litres of wine.

c. The Martin family has the comparative advantage (lower opportunity cost) in beer and the Richard family has the comparative advantage in wine.

d. Total combined beer production increases from three litres to four litres per day, a gain of one litre. Total combined wine production increases from 17 litres to 18 litres per day, a gain of one litre.

e. For both families to share the gains from specialization, one litre of beer should trade for somewhere between one and three litres of wine (between each family's opportunity cost for beer).

Chapter 3: Demand and Supply

1. The absolute prices of heating oil and natural gas have both increased. The relative price of heating oil decreased as it went from $1.00 / 0.80 = 1.25 to $2.00 / 3.20 = 0.63. This implies that the relative price of natural gas increased. Yes, consumers will increase their purchases of heating oil relative to natural gas, as heating oil's relative price has declined. This assumes that the prices shown in the table are per constant-quality unit.

3. a. Since the price of a substitute decreases, there will be a decrease in demand for Canadian beef and the demand curve will shift leftward.

b. An increase in demand will occur, where the demand curve shifts rightward.

c. An increase in quantity demanded will occur, which can be described as a movement along (down) the same demand curve.

d. A decrease in demand will occur, where the demand curve will shift leftward.

e. A decrease in quantity demanded will occur, which can be described as a movement along (up) the same demand curve.

5. a. P_e = $11 and Q_e = 80 million CDs.

b. At a price of $13, there would be a surplus equal to (120 − 60) = 60 million CDs. The surplus will drive down the price.

c. At a price of $10, there would be a shortage equal to (90 − 60) = 30 million CDs. The shortage will drive up the price.

7. The graph below illustrates a shift to the right in the demand curve, which indicates an *increase in demand*. The new equilibrium price and quantity are $12 and 100 million CDs. A change in any factor other than the price of CDs will cause an increase in demand, such as an increase in income or an increase in the popularity of rock music.

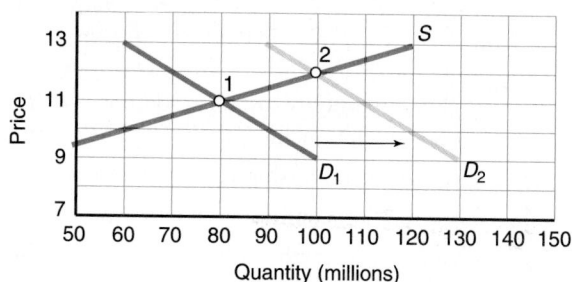

9. a. Increase in quantity demanded P_e ↓, Q_e ↑ as a result of an increase in supply.

b. Increase in demand P_e ↑, Q_e ↑

c. Increase in demand P_e ↑, Q_e ↑

d. Increase in demand P_e ↑, Q_e ↑

e. Decrease in demand P_e ↓, Q_e ↓

11. a. At a price of $1.40, there would be a surplus equal to (5 − 3) or 2000 dozen eggs. This will drive down the price.

b. At a price of $0.80, there would be a shortage equal to (6 − 2) or 4000 dozen eggs. This will drive up the price.

c. The equilibrium price and quantity is $1.20 and 4000 dozen eggs.

d. i.   Increase in demand, $P_e \uparrow, Q_e \uparrow$

ii. Decrease in supply, $P_e \uparrow, Q_e \downarrow$

iii. Decrease in demand, $P_e \downarrow, Q_e \downarrow$

iv. Increase in supply, $P_e \downarrow, Q_e \uparrow$

13. a. The equilibrium rent and quantity are $400 and 4000 units per month.

b. There will be a shortage equal to $(6 - 2)$ or 4000 units per month.

c. In the short run, by keeping the price of a substitute (one-bedroom units) lower, there will be a decrease in demand for two-bedroom units, causing a decrease in equilibrium rent and quantity of two-bedroom units. In the longer run, due to the shortage of one-bedroom units, there will be an increase in demand for two-bedroom units causing equilibrium price and quantity to increase.

15. a. Increase in demand and increase in supply. While the equilibrium quantity will increase, the combined effect on equilibrium price is indeterminate.

b. Decrease in supply and increase in demand. While the equilibrium price will increase, the combined effect on equilibrium quantity is indeterminate.

c. Increase in supply and decrease in demand. While the equilibrium price will decrease, the combined effect on equilibrium quantity is indeterminate.

Chapter 4: Introduction to Macroeconomics

1. One advantage of using models is that they are simplified versions of the real world, and are thus easier to understand and to manipulate. Another is that they can be used to predict the future, and thus allow for corrective action today. In economics, "experiments" cannot be easily repeated in the real world, especially in macroeconomics. The economic circumstances of most economies are changing rapidly, thus making a "controlled" experiment impossible.

3. Canadians in the early part of our history were much poorer than we are today. They lived in unheated, small cabins and lived very close to the land. The majority were engaged in natural resource industries such as farming, fishing, or the lumber trade. They were mostly uneducated and had much shorter life spans than we do.

5. The major symptoms of a recession are unemployment and declining real GDP. Recessions might also be accompanied by a lowering of the inflation rate, as occurred in the recessions of the 1980s and 1990s, and a drop in imports.

7. The current state of the economy can be found by looking at various sources. The business section of the newspaper may provide some reports. The Bank of Canada regularly issues reports on the state of the economy, as do most major banks.

9. a. 5 percent

b. One month

c. 5 percent

d. 10 percent

e. In this example, the unemployment rate doubled, but it is not obvious that the economy has become weaker or that workers are worse off.

11. This job bank may reduce frictional unemployment because it provides information to both employers and employees about the availability and pay scale for jobs. By providing this information, the two are able to reduce the search costs and thus reduce the duration of unemployment. Cyclical unemployment depends on the state of the economy. If demand for products does not exist, then firms will not be advertising for employees. It may provide some help when the economy is picking up and firms are rehiring in the same way that it reduces frictional unemployment.

13. a. Cyclically unemployed

b. Structurally unemployed

c. Structurally unemployed

d. Frictionally unemployed

15. a. The CPI for 2008 is calculated as below. The consumer price index for 2006 is calculated as follows:

Commodity	Quantity	2006 Price	2006 Cost	2008 Price	2008 Cost
Pop	10	$ 1	$ 10	$ 1	$ 10
Chocolate Bars	30	$ 2	$ 60	$ 4	$120
Indigestion Pills	20	$ 5	$100	$ 6	$120
Total			$170		$250

The consumer price index is therefore ($250/$170) × 100 = 147.06.

b. The rate of inflation between 2006 and 2008 is calculated as: $((147.06 - 100)/100) \times 100\% = 47.06\%$.

c. The GDP deflator is calculated as follows:

Commodity	Real GDP 2008 Quantity	Real GDP 2008 Price	Real GDP 2008 GDP	Nominal GDP 2008 Quantity	Nominal GDP 2008 Price	Nominal GDP 2008 GDP
Pop	15	$1	$ 15	15	$1	$ 15
Chocolate Bars	35	$2	$ 70	35	$4	$140
Indigestion Pills	20	$5	$100	20	$6	$120
Total			$185			$275

Therefore, the GDP deflator is calculated as: ($275/$185) × 100 = 148.65.

17. The first calculation is shown as an example. Employment = 9 million; Unemployment = Labour Force − Employed = 1 million; Unemployment rate = Unemployed/Labour force = 1 million/10 million = 10 %; Inflation Rate = $(CPI_t - CPI_{t-1})/CPI_{t-1} = (1.08-1.0)/1.0 = 8\%$

(1) Employment (millions of workers)	(2) Unemployment Rate (%)	(3) Rate of Inflation	(4) Price Level (%)
9.0	10	1.00	
9.1	9	1.08	8.0
9.2	8	1.17	8.3
9.3	7	1.28	9.4
9.4	6	1.42	10.9
9.5	5	1.59	12.0
9.6	4	1.81	13.8
9.7	3	2.10	16.0

19. Banks are less interested in long-term mortgages because of the risk involved in setting an interest rate so far into the future. If the rates were to suddenly rise, the banks could lose money because they have to pay their depositors more money and are not able to cover that expense with revenue from mortgages. This is similar to Example 4-4, "British Columbia Coal Mines" because of the long-term commitment that is being made around the price of coal.

21. The list of products owned by individuals will vary. However, most clothing, many of our cars, most of our electronics, and most manufactured goods are made elsewhere.

23. The purpose of stabilization policy is to smooth out fluctuations in the economy. It is difficult to know which is preferable without further analysis. Political parties may prefer to use government spending for ideological reasons (or avoid using taxes) during a recession. Using the Bank of Canada to stabilize the economy is quicker and less tied up with political decision making.

25. The two basic stabilization policies are fiscal policy (government spending and taxation policies) and monetary policy (interest rates and the money supply).

Chapter 5: Measuring the Economy's Performance

1. These are flow concepts. Each is measured over a period of time.

3. There would be no direct effect on GDP other than the costs of fighting the fires. Houses are capital assets which were recorded in GDP when they were built, not in the current year. Rebuilding the houses would add to GDP but would not necessarily make you better off since you are replacing assets that were lost.

5. It is likely that the underground economy will grow as welfare and unemployment benefits grow. Because working will result in a loss of benefits, there is greater incentive to not declare work when receiving benefits.

7. a. GDP falls.
   b. GDP is unchanged because illegal transactions are not measured anyway.
   c. GDP rises.

9. a. Measured GDP declines.
   b. Measured GDP increases.
   c. Measured GDP does not change (the firearms are not newly produced).

11. a. This would likely increase measured GDP as many legal operations would then start. It would be recorded as a consumption good (non-durable).
   b. Has no effect on GDP.
   c. This will increase GDP by the value of the real estate services provided as a consumption expenditure. The house itself is not included.
   d. Pizza would be recorded as a non-durable consumption expenditure.
   e. Imported wine is recorded as an import.
   f. Would be recorded as an investment expenditure. It is not a good because of its enduring nature.

13. Farms and small businesses generate "profits," but in many of those businesses there is no direct payment for the wages of the owners who are also acting as employees and the assets that the business owns. Thus "profits" in these circumstances may really represent the payment for labour, entrepreneurial ability, and perhaps other assets such as land which are owned by the business and not paid for separately as an input.

15. a. Coal; $2
   b. $3. Auto manufacturers took something worth $5 and transformed it into an auto that they sold for $8.
   c. $9 because intermediate goods are not counted.
   d. $9, resulting from adding the value added at each stage. Note that in this economy, which produces only autos, the earnings and the income approaches both yield a GDP estimate of $9.

17. a. Net domestic product = Wages (8.2) + Interest (0.8) + Rent (0.7) + Profit (2.8) + Indirect business taxes (0.8) = 13.3 billion; GDP = NDP (13.3) + Depreciation (1.3) = $14.6 trillion.
   b. Gross private domestic investment = GDP (14.6) − Consumption (11.0) − Government spending (1.8) − Net exports (−0.2) = $2.0 trillion.
   c. Personal income = GDP (14.6) − Depreciation (1.3) − Indirect business taxes (0.8) − Corporate taxes and retained earnings (0.5) = $12.0 trillion; Personal disposable income = Personal income (12) − Personal income taxes (1.7) = $10.3 trillion.

19.

Year	Nominal GDP	Real GDP	GDP Deflator (1997 = 100)
1997	125	125	100
2004	250	200	125
2007	275	225	122.22

21. a. Nominal GDP for 2006 is $2300; for 2011, nominal GDP is $2832.

    b. Real GDP for 2006 is $2300; for 2011, real GDP is $2229.

23. a. Nominal GDP for 2007 is $88 000; for 2008, nominal GDP is also $88 000.

    b. Real GDP for 2007 is $136 000; for 2008, real GDP is $88 000.

25. a. By definition, nominal GDP equals real GDP in the base year, which is at the crossing point of the two curves; thus, the base year is 2006.

    b. The GDP deflator is equal to nominal GDP divided by real GDP, or the ratio of nominal GDP to real GDP. The nominal GDP curve shows a steeper growth path of nominal GDP relative to the shallower growth path of real GDP. This means that the ratio of nominal GDP to real GDP has increased over time, implying that the GDP deflator must be rising. Hence, this country has been experiencing inflation.

27. Leisure is important for individuals to rest and recover. At the same time, having more leisure does not show up in GDP because it does not have an "accepted" value. Some economists have remeasured GDP by giving a value to leisure time and adding it to GDP. As leisure increases, this extra value is then captured in this remeasured GDP.

29. The market transactions included in GDP would be the $15 million paid to construction companies and the $5 million paid to salvage companies, for a total of $20 million included in real GDP. Any lost market value of existing homes not reclaimed would be a wealth loss not captured in GDP, because it is a loss in the value of a *stock* of resources. In addition, the $3 million in time that some devote to the reconstruction of their homes would be nonmarket transactions not included in GDP. Also not included would be the reduction in the general state of happiness—which is not valued in the marketplace—for all those affected by the hurricane.

Chapter 6: Modelling Real GDP and the Price Level in the Long Run

1. The amount of unemployment would be the sum of frictional, structural, and seasonal unemployment. Since frictional and structural unemployment are never zero, there will still be some unemployed people in this economy.

3. The real value of the new full-employment level of nominal GDP is ($1.42 trillion / 1.15) = $1.235 trillion, so the long-run aggregate supply curve has shifted rightward by $0.035 trillion.

5. There are several possible reasons for the decline in price, all of which lead to a rightward shift in the long-run aggregate supply. First, firms experience a decline in costs because of better technology used to produce computers and computer parts. Second, as demand grows for computers, they may experience economies of scale and scope in production. The shifts in aggregate supply will lead to declines in the price level in so far as computers are part of the overall GDP of the country.

7. When the price level rises, lenders who are paid by borrowers in fixed nominal dollars experience a reduction in wealth and will therefore reduce their quantity of real output demanded. However, borrowers will experience an increase in their wealth as the price level rises: they can pay off their debts with "cheaper" dollars. Borrowers will therefore increase their quantity of real output demanded. The net effect will be no change in *AD*.

9. a. When the price level falls with deflation, there is a movement downward along the *AD* curve.

    b. The decline in foreign real GDP levels reduces incomes of foreign residents, who cut back on their spending on domestic exports. Thus, the domestic *AD* curve shifts leftward.

    c. The fall in the foreign exchange value of the nation's currency makes domestic-produced goods and services less expensive to foreign residents, who increase their spending on domestic exports. Thus, the domestic *AD* curve shifts rightward.

    d. An increase in the price level causes a movement upward along the *AD* curve.

11. b, d, and e.

13. a. An increase in the capital stock causes real planned production to rise at any given price level, so the *LRAS* curve shifts rightward.

    b. An increase in the quantity of money causes the aggregate demand to shift rightward, which generates a movement upward along the *LRAS* curve.

    c. This reduction in the capital stock, which also will lead to higher energy prices, causes real planned production to decline at any given price level, so the *LRAS* curve shifts leftward.

    d. When the price level rises with inflation, there is a movement of the *AD* curve upward along the *LRAS* curve.

15. A ban on Canadian beef would initially lead to a reduction in aggregate demand. The loss of revenue and profit might lead to a reduction in the size of the beef industry in the long run. As resources are moved out of the industry through bankruptcy or by changing businesses (firms adjust to the long-run situation), this could lead to a decline in long-run aggregate supply as the resources are used less efficiently in other industries.

17. This is a somewhat unsettled issue. It can be undesirable for some of the same reasons that anticipated inflation

can be undesirable: People can incur costs as a result. For example, steady deflation could cause firms to incur menu costs, or costs of changing prices, when they adjust prices downward. Some economists (notably Milton Friedman), however, have argued that steady deflation equal to the real interest rate is desirable because then people discount present and future at the same rate and consequently hold the "socially optimal" quantity of money.

19. a. *B*: Productivity improvements cause the *LRAS* curve to shift rightward, from $LRAS_1$ to $LRAS_2$, and the increase in the quantity of money in circulation causes the *AD* curve to shift rightward, from AD_1 to AD_2.

b. *C*: The reduction in the usable portion of the capital stock reduces the economy's long-run productive capabilities, so the *LRAS* curve shifts leftward, from $LRAS_1$ to $LRAS_3$. The increase in taxes imposed on households induces them to reduce their expenditures, so the *AD* curve shifts leftward, from AD_1 to AD_3.

c. *E*: The technological improvement shifts the *LRAS* curve rightward, from $LRAS_1$ to $LRAS_2$, and the reduction in government spending shifts the *AD* curve leftward, from AD_1 to AD_3.

Chapter 7: Economic Growth and Development

1. a. J (about 10%)

b. L, M (about 2%)

3. 4 percent.

5. While increases in population will increase labour supply (shown as the shift from S_1 to S_2 in the graph below left), increased capital accumulation and technological change will shift the aggregate production function upwards from PF_1 to PF_2 (in the graph below right). The increased labour productivity will increase demand for labour from D_1 to D_2, a shift larger than the shift in supply. Thus wages can rise at the same time as an increase in population.

7. Point B is associated with the highest feasible growth rate. Capital goods implicitly represent future consumption, and point B has the highest feasible ratio of capital goods to current consumption (and thus the highest ratio of future consumption to current consumption).

9. The Canadian government uses a number of policies to encourage new technology. First, it has used the Scientific Tax Research Credit (a form of tax break) to encourage more research. Second, it funds research directly through a variety of funding agencies, such as the Medical Research Council. Finally, it funds universities and other post-secondary institutions that have as part of their mandate to engage in research.

11. a. Country Z appears to be a developing country because its GDP per person of $1500 is very low. Country X has a GDP per person of $9000, which is above the level that would normally be considered to be a developing country.

b. The life expectancy and infant mortality figures are consistent, because life expectancy is considerably lower for country Z, the developing country, and infant mortality is substantially higher. However, the literacy figures are not consistent, because we usually expect the literacy rate to be higher for developed countries, as in country X, and lower for developing countries as in country Z.

c. No, there seems to be little relationship between population and industrial development on an international level.

13. Both China and India are experiencing rapid economic growth that provides extra opportunities for people to earn high levels of income. Citizens with the knowledge and skills acquired in the North American economy would have an advantage over those people who are not as familiar with business practices in North America. These citizens would add tremendously to overall labour productivity in those countries and thereby reinforce the growth in GDP.

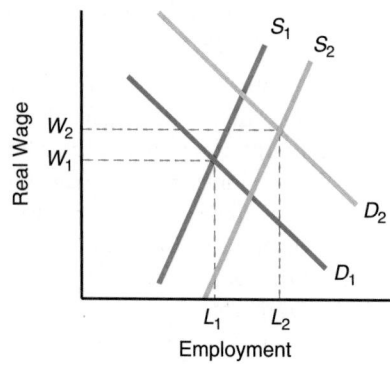

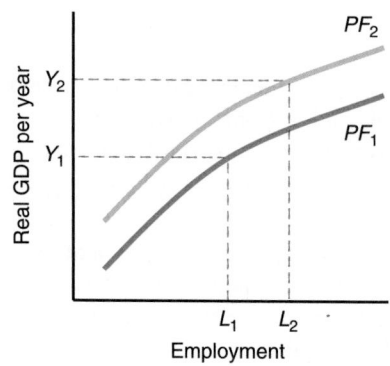

Chapter 8: Modelling Real GDP and the Price Level in the Short Run

1. The long-run aggregate supply curve is vertical at the point representing the maximum potential output possible. Prices can vary, but output cannot. In the short run, some increase in the level of output is possible with prices rising. This is possible because of the existence of some excess capacity, as well as flexibility in the nature and intensity of work. Therefore, the short-run aggregate supply curve is positively sloped.

3. a. The price level increases.

   b. National output decreases.

5. Natural disasters destroy the productive resources of the economy. They cause a decline in the level of output, and given constant demand, this increases the price level in the short run. The economy, which is assumed to be in long-run equilibrium, will undergo a period of contraction. In the long run, the output returns to the original level, as the productive resources are rebuilt.

7. With a plunge in confidence, both consumers and businesses will react by reducing their spending. Consumers will be less likely to purchase expensive items, such as cars and houses, because they expect to have greater difficulty paying for those items (as they are often purchased over time). As well, they may want to increase savings to help them through any unemployment they might experience. Businesses are also likely to reduce their investment spending, and to cut back on their capacity as confidence declines. If they expect sales to decline, then their existing capacity will probably be sufficient to meet their demand, and they would cut back on planned investment spending. This reduction in aggregate demand will result (in the short run) in a reduction in both real GDP and a lower price level, as illustrated in Figure 8–7.

9. At this point, the actual unemployment rate is below the natural rate of unemployment. The reason is that the economy is producing a level of output per year that exceeds its long-run capability, which entails employing workers that in normal times would be frictionally or structurally unemployed.

11. A rising Canadian dollar tends to shrink the economy in the short run. In the long run, this recessionary gap is removed because of the long-run adjustment effect. So in the long run, the rising dollar should lead to a lower price level with full employment.

13. Domestic producers purchase few imported inputs, and so the effect on the short-run aggregate supply curve will be minimal. Because foreign residents are key consumers of domestically produced goods, however, the fall in foreign incomes will depress aggregate demand. The equilibrium price level will decline, and equilibrium real output will decrease.

15. A lower-valued dollar encourages the exports of a country, but at the expense of a neighbouring country's industries that are exporting to you. Their higher-valued currency may force them out of the industry while you expand.

17. a. E: The union wage boost causes the $SRAS$ curve to shift leftward, from $SRAS_1$ to $SRAS_3$. The reduction in incomes abroad causes import spending in this nation to fall, which induces a leftward shift in the AD curve, from AD_1 to AD_3.

    b. B: The short-term reduction in production capabilities causes the $SRAS$ curve to shift leftward, from $SRAS_1$ to $SRAS_3$, and the increase in money supply growth generates a rightward shift in the AD curve, from AD_1 to AD_2.

    c. C: The strengthening of the value of this nation's currency reduces the prices of imported inputs that domestic firms utilize to produce goods and services, which causes the $SRAS$ curve to shift rightward, from $SRAS_1$ to $SRAS_2$. At the same time, the currency's strengthening raises the prices of exports and reduces the prices in imports, so net export spending declines, thereby inducing a leftward shift in the AD curve, from AD_1 to AD_3.

Appendix C: Classical and Keynesian Macro Analyses

C-1 If the interest rate is higher than equilibrium, desired saving exceeds desired investment. Those who desire investment funds from savers will offer to pay lower rates of interest. Savers, in competition with each other, will be willing to accept lower rates of interest. The interest rate will be bid down, which will simultaneously decrease the quantity of saving desired and increase the quantity of investment desired.

C-3 a. Because saving increases at any given interest rate, the desired saving curve shifts rightward. This causes the equilibrium interest rate to decline.

    b. There is no effect on current output because in the classical model the vertical long-run aggregate supply curve always applies.

    c. A change in the saving rate does not directly affect the demand for labour or the supply of labour in the classical model, and so equilibrium employment does not change.

    d. The decrease in the equilibrium interest rate generates a rightward and downward movement along the demand curve for investment. Consequently, desired investment increases.

    e. The rise in current investment implies greater capital accumulation. Other things being equal, this will imply increased future production.

C-5 False. In fact, there is an important distinction. The classical model of short-run output determination applies to an interval short enough that some factors of production, such as capital, are fixed. Nevertheless, the classical model implies that even in the short run, the economy's aggregate supply curve is the same as its long-run aggregate supply curve.

C-7 Because there is full information and speedy adjustment of wages and prices in the classical model, the aggregate demand curve shifts leftward along the vertical long-run aggregate supply curve. The equilibrium price level decreases, but there is no change in equilibrium national output.

Chapter 9: Consumption, Investment, and the Multiplier

1. Stock: a, c; Flow: b, d, e, f, and g

3. Time preference. If I prefer consumption now very much more than consumption in the future, my personal MPC will be higher. Wealth. The higher my level of wealth, the higher my MPC.

5. a. No. Interest costs are greater than rate of return on the investment.

   b. Yes. Rate of return exceeds interest costs.

   c. Yes. Return covers interest cost.

7. Firms may not be able to invest because the cost of borrowing might be very high. If individuals are not willing to invest new money into firms through the purchase of shares or bonds, firms may not be able to finance new investment that can be profitable.

9. a. The completed table follows (all amounts in dollars):

Real GDP	Consumption	Saving	Investment
2 000	2 000	0	1 200
4 000	3 600	400	1 200
6 000	5 200	800	1 200
8 000	6 800	1 200	1 200
10 000	8 400	1 600	1 200
12 000	10 000	2 000	1 200

   MPC = 1600/2000 = 0.8; MPS = 400/2000 = 0.2.

   b. The graph appears below.

   c. Equilibrium without the government sector occurs at 8000. With the government sector it occurs at 10 000. This is shown on the graph below.

   d. This model does not have assumptions about production other than firms can always meet any demand for output. Clearly, firms have limited capacity and cannot increase their output forever.

   e. Equilibrium GDP would rise by $500, as the slope of the *TPE* function is 0.8.

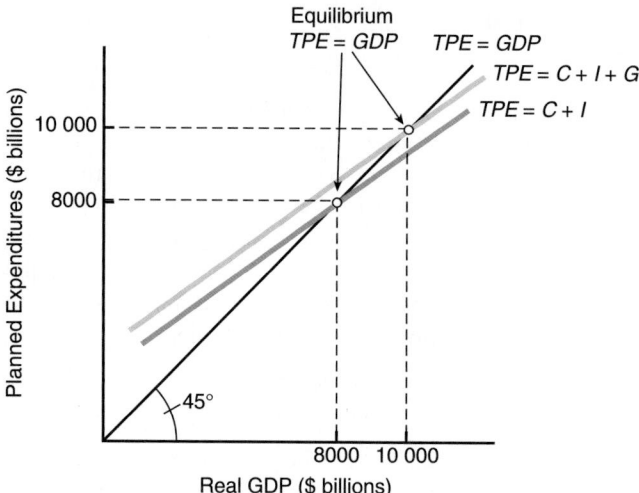

11. a. If Y = 0, autonomous consumption equals $800, which implies dissaving equal to −$800, which is the amount of autonomous saving.

    b. The marginal propensity to consume is 0.80, so the marginal propensity to save is 1 − MPC = 1 − 0.80 = 0.20.

    c. The multiplier is 1/(1−MPE) = 1/0.20 = 5.0. (Since there are no other leakages, the MPC=MPE)

13. Net exports will decline as a result of the ban. This will reduce net exports, and shift the total planned expenditures curve down. Total planned expenditures will decline, and this change will be magnified by the multiplier into a larger change (fall) in real GDP. Use a graph similar to Figure 9-6 Part (a) p. 251.

15. a. If the MPE = 0 then the multiplier = 1. Multiplier = 1 / (1 − MPE) = 1 / (1 − 0) = 1

    b. In this case, the multiplier increases as there is less saving going on.

    c. 2, 4. Multiplier = 1 / (1 − 0.5) = 1 / 0.5 = 2. Multiplier = 1 / (1 − 0.75) = 1 / 0.25 = 4.

17. a. In this case we must use the more complicated formula:

    Multiplier = 1 / (1 − [b − bt − m]). Substitute b = 0.9, t = 0.1, and m = 0.2. (See problem 16 a.)

    Substituting gives:

    Multiplier = 1 / (1 − [0.9 − 0.9 × 0.1 − 0.2])
    = 1 / (1 − [0.9 − 0.09 − 0.2])
    = 1 / (1 − [0.61]) = 1 / 0.39 = 2.56

    b. Multiplier = 2.27. Use values for b, t, and m from Problem 16 b.

    c. Multiplier = 1.47. Use values for b, t, and m from Problem 16 c.

19. The multiplier is 1/(1−MPE) = 1/(1−0.75) = 4, so the increase in equilibrium income is $250 billion × 4 = $1 trillion, and the level of real income at the new point on the aggregate demand curve is $11 trillion.

Chapter 10: The Public Sector

1. TV stations are private businesses given licences to operate by the CRTC. If they do not operate according to the rules outlined by the CRTC, they can lose their licences.

3. The theory of public choice is about collective decision making the individual will act to maximize his or her individual well-being. This often forces governments to provide more services rather than less so that the government can continue to get the votes of the people.

5. This implies that Canadians are taxed at a higher rate than Americans. Americans are free from tax much earlier than Canadians, but it might be due to the fact that Canadians get more universal programs such as health care.

7. In order for the tax-exempt bond to be more attractive, you would have to be in a marginal tax bracket where you are paying more than the 6 percent yield.

9. a. $4000 × 4.95% = $198; $198 / $4000 = 4.95%
   b. $42 100 × 4.95% = $2083.95; $2083.95 / $51 300 = 4.06%
   c. $42 100 × 4.95% = $2083.95; $2083.95 / $56 000 = 3.72%
   d. $42 100 × 4.95% = $2083.95; $2083.95 / $100 000 = 2.08%

   Thus the CPP system is an example of a regressive tax system.

Chapter 11: Fiscal Policy and the Public Debt

1. Tax Changes: Decrease the income tax, reduce the tax on capital gains, reduce the corporate income tax, reduce direct taxes.
   Spending Changes: Increase spending on public works, health care and education, or increasing transfers.

3. Using Figure 11−1, p. 293, we can illustrate a situation where discretionary fiscal policy, say, lowering the taxes or increasing the government expenditures, will bring the economy into its long-run trend level, all other components of the model held constant.

5. Two calculations are required: the magnitude of the deficit, and that magnitude relative to GDP.
   Since the deficit, which equals receipts minus spending, is a negative number, its absolute value is shown below.

Year	Deficit ($ billion)	Deficit/GDP (percent)
1988	18.5	3.1
1989	20.3	3.1
1990	25.2	3.8
1991	30.2	4.5

7. Answer to the question will vary depending on the years you are considering and the province you reside in.

9. The gross public debt remains the same, but the net public debt declines.

11. This will result in a decline in the value of the Canadian dollar as the money is flowing out of the country. It will result in a higher level of aggregate demand as our net exports rise. In effect, this is the reverse of the net export effect and should stimulate our economy.

13. Ultimately, all government debt must be repaid by means of taxation. (The government cannot forever "repay" its debt by issuing more debt because ultimately the public debt would exceed the wealth of the entire country!) Thus when the government adds to the debt, it is simultaneously adding to future taxes that must be equivalent in present value to the added debt.

15. Consumers must not regard current budget deficits as equivalent to higher future taxes and current budget surpluses as equivalent to lower future taxes. For example, if consumers regard a $1 million deficit as imposing an equivalent amount of new taxes on them in the future, they will increase current saving so as to be in a position to pay the higher future taxes. As a result, current consumption will decline, and at least some, and possibly all, of the stabilizing effect of the deficit will be wiped out.

17. This could happen if the tax cut has little net effect on aggregate demand but, as predicted by supply-side economists, causes an increase in long-run aggregate supply. The aggregate demand effect of the tax cut might be meagre if there is a significant crowding-out effect or if the Ricardian equivalence theorem is satisfied. Then, if the tax cut reduces marginal tax rates sufficiently to induce people to work more, then the long-run aggregate supply curve will shift to the right along the nearly unchanged aggregate demand curve. As a result, the equilibrium price level would decline, and real national income would increase.

19. Under Ricardian equivalence, equilibrium real income does not change. People save an extra $40 billion, the entire amount of the tax cut which they recognize they will have to repay, along with interest at a future date.

21. Because of the recognition time lag entailed in gathering information about the economy, policy makers may be slow to respond to a downturn in real national income. Parliamentary approval of policy actions to address the downturn may be delayed; hence an action time lag may also arise. Finally, there is an effect time lag because policy actions take time to exert their full effects on the economy. If these lags are sufficiently long, it is possible that by the time a policy to address a downturn has begun to have its

effects, real national income might already be rising. If so, the policy action might push real GDP up faster than intended, thereby making real national income less stable.

23. Discretionary fiscal policy is policy in which the levels of government spending and taxes change as a result of a deliberate decision by the government. Example: A change in the structure of tax rates, or a change in government expenditures not associated with a change in government revenues. Automatic stabilizers cause the level of government spending or taxes to change as a result of endogenous changes in a variable such as income, other than changes due to deliberate decisions of the government. Example: Government revenues increasing from taxes during an economic expansion.

Appendix F: Fiscal Policy: A Keynesian Perspective

F-1. a. The marginal propensity to consume is equal to 1 − MPS, or 6/7.

b. Investment or government spending must increase by $20 billion.

c. The government would have to cut taxes by $23.33 billion.

F-3. a. Aggregate demand will shift downward by $500; therefore, national income will fall by $5000.

b. Aggregate demand will shift upward by 0.9($500) = $450; therefore, national income will rise by $4500.

Chapter 12: Money and the Banking System

1. a. Store of value
   b. Store of value
   c. Medium of exchange
   d. Store of value
   e. Medium of exchange
   f. Medium of exchange

3. If there are n goods, the number of exchange rates will be $n(n − 1)/2$. In this case, $n = 10$, so the number of exchange rates will be $10(10 − 1)/2 = 90/2$.

5. If the price index now is 2, the value of the dollar in 1986 prices is 1/2 = 0.50. If the price index now is 2.5, the value of the dollar in 1986 prices is 1/2.5 = 0.40.

7. A debit card is not a new form of money because it does not satisfy the unit of account function.

9. In the Canadian financial system there are ultimate lenders, ultimate borrowers, and financial intermediaries. Lenders and borrowers include households, businesses, and government. Financial intermediaries include banks, trust companies, credit unions, *caisses*

populaires, insurance companies, pension funds, mutual funds, investment dealers, and finance companies.

11. In principle, each institution can match with each rationale; your explanations are the aspects of your answers that are most important.

a. Insurance companies limit adverse selection by screening applicants for policies.

b. Savings banks limit moral hazard by monitoring borrowers after loans have been made.

c. Pension funds reduce management costs by pooling the funds of many future pensioners.

13. a. Moral hazard problem
   b. Adverse selection problem
   c. Moral hazard problem

Chapter 13: Money Creation and Deposit Insurance

1. Changes in the money supply affect economic growth, business fluctuations, and inflation. The direct effect.

3. Assets
   b. Vault cash
   d. Deposits with the Bank of Canada
   e. Loans to private business
   f. Loans to households
   g. Holdings of Canadian government, provincial, and municipal bonds

   Liabilities
   a. Chequing deposits
   c. Time deposits
   h. Borrowings from other banks

5. a. No change.
   b. This is a little tricky. If the Bank of Canada had been "keeping track" of currency, the $1000 currency buried in Smith's backyard is accounted for; therefore, the money supply will rise by $9000 because the Bank of Canada did not have to "create" the $1000 already in existence.
   c. The money supply will decrease by $9000; see (b).

7. The dealer's bank must hold 15 percent of the $1 million, or $150 000 as desired reserves. Thus, the bank can lend out the excess reserves of $850 000.

9. a. Total liabilities and net worth = Total assets = $0.26 billion in total reserves + $3.6 billion in loans + $1 billion in securities + $0.14 billion in other assets = $5 billion.
   b. The bank could lend its $10 million in excess reserves.
   c. Chequable deposits equal desired reserves $0.25 billion / 0.1 = $2.5 billion

11. a.   Multiple Deposit Creation

Bank	Deposits	Reserves	Loans
Bank 1	$1 000 000	$ 250 000	$ 750 000
Bank 2	750 000	187 500	562 500
Bank 3	562 500	140 625	421 875
Bank 4	421 875	105 469	316 406
Bank 5	316 406	79 102	237 304
All other banks	949 219	237 304	711 915
Totals	4 000 000	1 000 000	3 000 000

The money multiplier is 4.

b.   Multiple Deposit Creation

Bank	Deposits	Reserves	Loans
Bank 1	$ 1 000 000	$ 50 000	$ 950 000
Bank 2	950 000	47 500	902 500
Bank 3	902 500	45 125	857 375
Bank 4	857 375	42 869	814 506
Bank 5	814 506	40 725	773 781
All other banks	15 475 619	773 781	14 701 838
Totals	20 000 000	1 000 000	19 000 000

The money multiplier is 20.

13. a.   The excess reserves of Bank B are $30.

b.   Bank B can lend out $30. A single bank can lend out up to, but not exceeding, its excess reserves.

c.   After the maximum loan is made, loans have increased by $30 to $130, chequable deposits have increased by $30 to $230, and there has been no change in the total reserves.

d.   The maximum expansion of the money supply that can occur if Bank B loans $30, thereby creating money, is $30. For the banking system as a whole, the money supply can increase up to a maximum of $30/.1 = $300.

Chapter 14: The Bank of Canada and Monetary Policy

1.   The basic functions of the Bank of Canada are (a) conducting monetary policy, (b) acting as a lender of last resort, (c) issuing bank notes, and (d) advising the federal government on financial matters and acting as its fiscal agent. No, Canadian Tire "money" is not real money because only the Bank of Canada can issue legal bank notes in Canada that can then be used in payment of a debt.

3.   a.

Assets		Liabilities	
Total reserves	+$1 000 000	Demand deposits	+$1 000 000
Required reserves ($50 000) + excess reserves ($950 000)			
Total	+$1 000 000	Total	+$1 000 000

b.   Bank 1 can increase its lending by $950 000.

5.   a.   The bank's excess reserves have decreased by $2 550 000.

b.   The money supply has decreased by $3 million.

c.   The money supply can decrease by as much as $20 million.

7.   a.   One possible policy action would be an open market sale of securities, which would reduce the money supply and shift the aggregate demand curve leftward.

b.   In principle, the Bank of Canada's action would reduce inflation more quickly.

9.

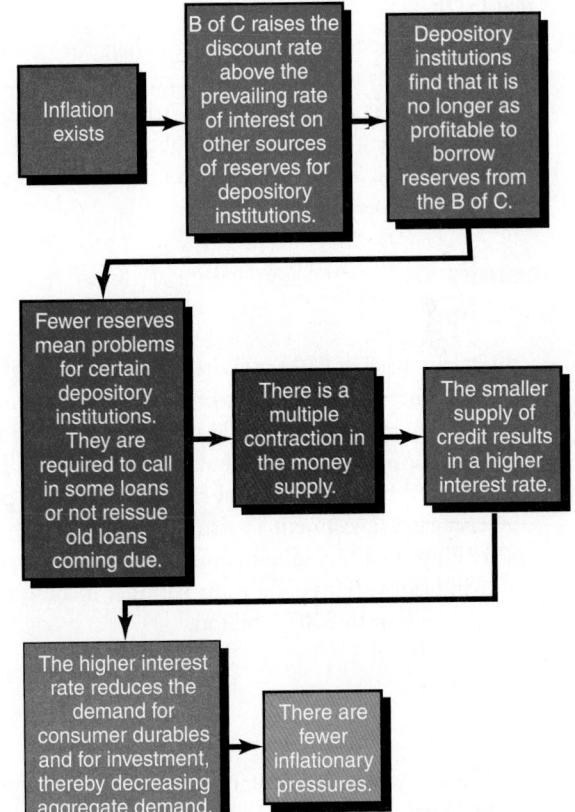

11.   A change in monetary policy leads to a change in interest rates, which leads to a change in investment. This, then, through the multiplier process, leads to a change in income.

13.   An expansionary open-market operation (purchase of bonds), for example, means that the public has larger money holdings than desired. This excess quantity of money demanded induces the public to buy more of everything, especially more durable goods. So if the economy is starting out at its long-run equilibrium rate of output, there can only be a short-run increase in real GDP. Ultimately, the public cannot buy more of everything, so it simply bids up prices, such that the price level rises.

15.   The price level remains at its original value. Because $M_sV = PQ$, V has doubled, and Q is unchanged, cutting M_s in half leaves P unchanged.

17. a. $M_sV = PQ$, so $P = M_sV / Q =$ ($1.1 trillion $\times$ 10) / $5 trillion = 2.2

b. 10 percent

c. 10 percent

d. They are equal.

19. Because a contractionary monetary policy causes interest rates to increase, financial capital begins to flow into Canada. This causes the demand for dollars to rise, which pushes up the value of the dollar and makes Canadian exports more expensive for foreigners. They cut back on their purchases of Canadian products, which tends to reduce Canadian real GDP.

21. Monetary policy is most effective when the money-demand curve is relatively inelastic and the investment-demand curve is relatively elastic. Advantages of using monetary policy versus fiscal policy are: monetary policy is faster, more flexible, and relatively isolated from political pressures.

Appendix G: Monetary Policy: A Keynesian Perspective

G-1. By its purchase of $100 million in bonds, the Bank of Canada increased excess reserves by $100 million. This ultimately caused a $300 million increase in the money supply after full multiple expansion. The 1 percent drop in the interest rate, from 10 to 9 percent, caused investment to rise by $2.5 billion, from $20 billion to $22.5 billion. An investment multiplier of 3 indicates that equilibrium national income rose by $7.5 billion to $207.5 billion.

Chapter 15: Issues in Stabilization Policy

1. a. The actual unemployment rate would decline.

b. Natural unemployment rate estimates also would be lower.

c. The logic of the short- and long-run Phillips curves would not be altered. The government might wish to make this change if it feels that those in the military "hold jobs" and thereby should be counted as employed within the economy.

3. A rise in the duration of unemployment will tend to raise the average unemployment rate because each unemployed person will be counted as unemployed more times over any given time period.

5. a. The measured unemployment rate when all adjustments have occurred will now always be lower than before, so the natural unemployment rate will be smaller.

b. The unemployment rate consistent with stable inflation will now be reduced, so the NAIRU will be smaller.

7. a. 10 percent

b. A rise in the expected rate of inflation will cause the curve to shift upward by the amount of the rise in expectations.

c. They argue thus because the systematic policies that attempt to exploit the seeming trade-off will be incorporated into workers' and firms' expectations. As a result, the expected inflation rate will move in lockstep with the actual rate (excepting random errors), so that the unemployment rate will not change when the inflation rate changes.

9. The "long run" is an interval sufficiently long that input prices fully adjust and people have full information. Adoption of more sophisticated computer and communications technology provides people with more immediate access to information, which can reduce this interval.

11. No. It could still be true that wages and other prices of factors of production adjust sluggishly to changes in the price level. Then a rise in aggregate demand that boosts the price level brings about an upward movement along the short-run aggregate supply curve, causing equilibrium real GDP to rise.

13. Yes. It is precisely the fact that both employers and workers incorrectly perceive a change in nominal demand as a change in real demand that generates the negatively sloping Phillips curve.

15. Supply-side economists propose policies that would cause the aggregate supply curve to shift outward to the right. They propose creating incentives for individuals and businesses by reducing marginal tax rates and excessive regulation. They argue this will increase productivity and GDP because of increased work, saving, and investing. Compared to the Islamic view, the proposals for reducing taxes are comparable, but the modern emphasis on reducing excessive regulation is new.

17. If there is widespread price stickiness, then the short-run aggregate supply curve would be horizontal, and the real GDP would respond strongly to a policy action that affects aggregate demand. By way of contrast, if

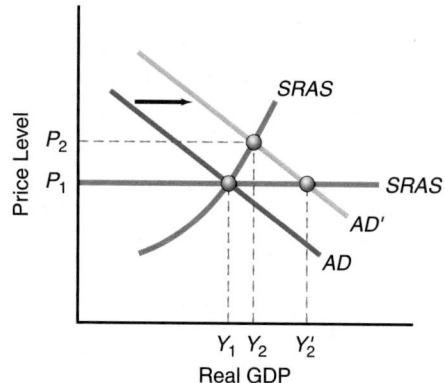

prices are highly flexible, then the short-run aggregate supply curve slopes upward, and real GDP is less responsive to the change in aggregate demand.

19. a. An increase in desired investment spending induces aggregate demand, so AD_3 applies. There is an unchanged price level in the short run, and equilibrium real GDP rises from $14 trillion at point A to $14.5 trillion at point C.

b. Over time, firms perceive that they can increase their profits by adjusting prices upward in response to the increase in aggregate demand. Thus, firms eventually will incur the menu costs required to make these price adjustments. As they do so, the aggregate supply curve will shift upward, from $SRAS_1$ to $SRAS_2$, as shown in the diagram below. Real GDP will return to its original level of $14 trillion, in base-year dollars. The price level will increase to a level above 119, such as 124. The economy moves to point D.

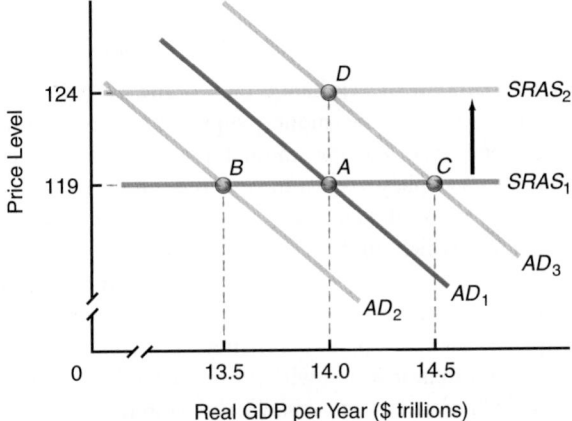

21. Increasing the price of a product in response to a long-lasting increase in demand will yield higher profits for several periods. The value of this stream of future profits is more likely to be sufficiently large to outweigh a small, one-time menu cost. In this situation, it is more likely that firms will raise their prices.

Chapter 16: Comparative Advantage and the Open Economy

1. Total trade among nations has been growing faster than total world GDP. The growth of Canadian exports and imports relative to Canadian GDP parallels this global trend. Exports and imports now equal about 40 percent and 37 percent, respectively, of Canada's GDP.

3. a. The opportunity cost to Canada of producing one kilogram of caviar is two bushels of wheat. The six hours that were needed to make the caviar could have been used to grow two bushels of wheat. The opportunity cost of producing one bushel of wheat is 0.5 kilogram of caviar.

b. The opportunity cost to Russia of producing one kilogram of caviar is 0.67 bushels of wheat. The

opportunity cost of producing a bushel of wheat in Russia is 1.5 kilograms of caviar.

c. Canada has a comparative advantage in wheat because it has a lower opportunity cost in terms of caviar. Russia has a comparative advantage in caviar. Less wheat is forgone to produce a kilogram of caviar in Russia.

5. The assumption given in the question is equivalent to Canada's having an absolute advantage in the production of all goods and services. But the basis of world trade lies in differences in comparative advantage. As long as other countries have a lower opportunity cost in producing some goods and services, Canada will benefit from international trade.

7. a. The opportunity cost of modems in Northland is two flash drives per modem. The opportunity cost of flash drives in Northland is 0.5 modem per flash drive.

b. The opportunity cost of modems in East Coast is 0.5 flash drive per modem. The opportunity cost of flash drives in East Coast is two modems per flash drive.

c. Residents of Northland have a comparative advantage in producing flash drives, and residents of East Coast have a comparative advantage in producing modems.

d. (ii) only

e. Northland will import 30 units. Gains for Northland are 30 flash drives and gains for East Coast are 30 modems

9. Nations together can produce and consume more than they would have produced and consumed in the absence of specialization and trade. While nations overall and some industries and businesses gain from specializing and engaging in trade, there are costs from trade. Certain industries and their employees may be hurt if trade is opened up.

11. Tariffs yield government revenues; quotas do not.

13. a. One million kilograms are produced and 2 million kilograms are imported.

b. With a 10 cent tariff, 1.5 million kilograms would be produced and 1 million kilograms would be imported. Government revenues would amount to ($2.5 million − $1.5 million) × $0.10 = $100 000.

c. With a 20 cent tariff, domestic growers can receive 70 cents per kilogram. They will produce 2 million kilograms, and no peaches will be imported, in which case government revenues are zero.

15. a. Because the supply curve shifts by the amount of the tariff, the tariff is $20 per PDA.

b. Total revenue was $300 per unit times 20 million units, or $6 billion, before the tariff, and it is $310 per unit times 15 million units, or $4.65 billion, after the tariff.

c.   Canadian tariff revenue is $20 per unit times 15 million units, or $300 million.

d.   Korean PDA exporters lose $1.35 billion in revenues ($6 billion minus $4.65 billion). Canadian-made PDA companies gain $360 million in revenues ($1.5 billion revenues before the tariff versus $1.860 billion after the tariff).

Chapter 17: Exchange Rates and the Balance of Payments

1.   a.   The balance of merchandise trade is a deficit of −$84.9 (165.8 − 250.7).

b.   The balance on goods and services is a deficit of −$53.7 (−84.9 + 130.5 − 99.3).

c.   The balance on current account is a deficit of −$93.7 (−53.7 − 20.0 − 20.0).

3.   The trade balance is merchandise exports minus merchandise imports, which equals 500 − 600 = −100, or a deficit of 100. Adding service exports of 75 and subtracting net unilateral transfers of 10 and service imports of 50 yields −100 + 75 − 10 − 50 = −85, or a current account balance of −85. The capital account balance equals the difference between capital inflows and capital outflows, or 300 − 200 = +100, or a capital account surplus of 100.

5.   The answer is (c). A declining dollar price of the pound implies an increasing pound price of the dollar—appreciation of the dollar. (a) is incorrect because a decrease in demand for Canadian products would affect the supply of pounds and the demand for dollars, whereas here we are dealing with the demand for pounds. (b) explains a phenomenon that would have just the opposite result as that shown in the graph: An increased Canadian demand for British goods would lead to an increase in the demand for the pound, not a decrease as shown. (d) is incorrect because the pound depreciates.

7.   One pound equals $2.50; $1 equals 0.4 pound. One euro equals 84 cents; $1 equals 1.1875 euros. One euro equals 0.33 pounds; one pound equals 2.968 euros.

9.   a.   The dollar price of pounds is $1.50. The equilibrium quantity is 150 million pounds.

b.   Curve D' describes this situation. The new dollar price of pounds would be $1.70, and the equilibrium quantity would be 200 million.

c.   At a price of $1.50 per pound, 250 million pounds sterling would be demanded and only 150 million would be supplied, so the Bank of Canada would have to supply an extra 100 million pounds to Canadian buyers of British goods or British exporters.

d.   Curve D'' describes this situation. 150 million pounds sterling would be supplied at a price of $1.50, but only 50 million pounds would be demanded. Therefore, the Bank of Canada would have to buy up 100 million pounds sterling.

11.   The Canadian dollar–euro exchange rate is found by dividing the U.S. dollar–euro exchange rate by the U.S. dollar–Canadian dollar exchange rate, or (US$1.37/euro / US$0.95/C$) = C$1.44 /euro, C$1.44 per euro.

13.   To maintain the exchange rate, domestic policy variables such as the money supply are also affected. Suppose that the government plans an expansionary monetary policy to encourage output growth. A balance of payments deficit leads the government to buy up dollars, which in turn leads to a contraction in the domestic money supply. Therefore, in order to maintain the expansionary monetary policy, the government would have to expand the money supply in larger magnitudes than it would without the balance of payments deficits with a fixed exchange rate system.

15.   A flexible exchange rate system allows the exchange value of a currency to be determined freely in the foreign exchange market with no intervention by the government. A fixed exchange rate pegs the value of the currency, and the authorities responsible for the value of the currency intervene in foreign exchange markets to maintain this value. A dirty float involves occasional intervention by the exchange authorities. A target zone allows the exchange value to fluctuate, but only within a given range of values.

Chapter 1: The Nature of Economics

Example 1–1: The Economics of Web Page Design

The web designer of a frequently visited web page, such as Yahoo!'s home page, has "unlimited wants" that include such goals as: provide maximum exposure to all of Yahoo!'s own products and services; maximize revenue from selling advertising space to other companies; present high-quality images and animations; and prevent the web page from becoming too cluttered. The "limited resources" include a limited screen space size (that one views without scrolling) and limited time to hold the web surfer's attention.

Example 1–2: The Opportunity Cost of Finding a Mate—Lower on the Internet?

There is a smaller selection of available people who match very specific characteristics. Therefore, the desire by persons to find people with very specific characteristics will involve higher search costs, in terms of the time spent dating, than would be the case with less picky requirements. In other words, the opportunity cost of dating in person is higher, which implies that people would be willing to pay more to avoid this by using the Internet alternative. This example shows how understanding opportunity cost can help the Internet firm decide on the appropriate price to charge for its different matching services.

Example 1–3: What Does a Year at College Really Cost?

Jane did not correctly determine the cost related to the decision to enroll in college full-time for eight months. She should only add the *extra* or *marginal* costs, which would be the tuition, books, college fees, and the income she sacrifices from not working full-time for eight months. This implies that the total costs of going to college would be $3600 + (8 months) × ($2000 per month) = $19 600 for the eight months spent at college. The other expenses, such as rent, food, transportation, personal care, and entertainment, can be viewed as unavoidable expenses she decided to incur before making any education decision that we would class as sunk costs. Sunk costs should not be included in computing the marginal or extra cost relating to her education decision. In order to make a rational decision, the marginal cost should be compared to the marginal benefit of enrolling in the business college program.

Policy Example 1–1: Chinese Smuggling

Any actions that reduce the benefits or increase the costs incurred from smuggling cigarettes and diesel fuel into China will reduce the incentives to smuggle. There are a number of policies that would reduce the benefits derived from smuggling. If the Chinese government lowered the domestic taxes on cigarettes manufactured in China, this would reduce the profit derived from exporting the cigarettes and then smuggling them back into China. Similarly, if the price of domestically produced diesel fuel were lowered, this would reduce the profit resulting from smuggling foreign-produced diesel fuel into the country. One way the government could increase the costs of smuggling is to significantly increase the criminal penalty attached to the act of smuggling goods into China.

Example 1–4: Giving Charity to Oneself?

The evidence that low-income households contribute a higher portion of their income to charity than those with higher incomes can be explained in terms of rational cost–benefit behaviour. When compared with a high-income household, the total extra (marginal) benefits that the low income household derives over a lifetime is much more likely to exceed the extra costs incurred from contributing to these charities.

Example 1–5: The Science Behind COLD-fX

The study examines the relationship between COLD-fX medication and the frequency of contracting colds and their duration and severity. The study attempts to apply the *ceteris paribus* assumption by holding constant other factors that might affect the frequency, duration, and severity of colds, such as having just had a flu vaccination, taking other cold medication at the same time, the placebo effect, researcher's bias in favour of finding that COLD-fX is effective, and the general health of the subjects in the study.

Example 1–6: An Economic Model of Crime

An increase in the unemployment rate reduces the opportunity cost related to the time spent planning and committing the crime and the time spent evading being caught or, if caught, time spent in jail. This reduces the marginal cost of engaging in a criminal act so we would predict that an increase in the unemployment rate would increase the crime rate.

A decrease in conviction rates reduces the expected punishment costs related to committing a crime. In turn, this reduces the marginal cost of engaging in a criminal act so we would predict that this would increase the crime rate.

Issues and Applications: Bottled Water: The Hummer of Beverages?

1. Scarcity brings home the point that resources are limited in the face of unlimited wants. Knowing this makes one concerned about whether the $100 billion bottled water industry is effectively allocating our limited

resources, as there are many other wants yet to be satisfied. Opportunity cost refers to the value of the best alternative that must be given up because a choice was made. By allocating $100 billion of resources to the bottled water industry we give up the opportunity to satisfy other wants such as promoting a pollution-free environment and increasing global access to safe water. Economics is the social science that is concerned with how our limited resources are being allocated to satisfy unlimited wants. The fact that the bottled water industry uses up a significant amount of limited resources makes it an economic issue.

2. Since this issue focuses on one industry or product area, the bottled water industry, it entails a microeconomic focus. A macroeconomic focus would relate to the level or growth of production or consumption in all Canadian industries.

3. In order to create the incentives necessary to reduce the amount of resources used to produce bottled water, the government would have to reduce the marginal benefit that firms derive from supplying bottled water. One way to do this would be to ban all exclusivity agreements, which would increase competition and reduce the prices that Coke and Pepsi could charge for bottled water.

    Another way of reducing the marginal benefit would be to mount a major educational campaign that publicized the opportunity costs related to bottled water. If the campaign could get people to reduce their demand for bottled water, it would reduce the marginal benefit derived from supplying this product.

4. Policy analysis refers to the important process of relating a proposed policy to various socio-economic goals. In this example, the Toronto City Council's proposed policy of levying a tax on the sale of bottled water was related to equity and employment. That is, the beverage companies, in arguing against the tax, noted that it would be unfair to single out just one commodity, especially a healthier product, for taxation. Also, the beverage companies projected that if the tax was implemented it would cause people to buy less bottled water (and possibly other groceries) in Toronto, which could conflict with the employment goal. On a broader level, one could look at leaving the bottled water industry alone (status quo) as another possible policy. As this issue suggests, this status quo policy can conflict with other goals such as a cleaner, healthier environment, less global warming, and providing aid to poorer nations.

Chapter 2: Production Possibilities and Economic Systems

Example 2–1: Skipping Class without Skipping Lectures

1. The example notes that if you skip class, you give up the opportunity to ask questions during the lecture, as well as to interact with other class members. Other costs that you might incur include the cost of having to take the full responsibility of pacing yourself appropriately through all the course material in all your courses. It becomes too easy to postpone viewing the online lectures so that you eventually get way behind in your course studies. By not getting to know your instructor, you might incur the cost of not being able to use your instructor as a reference for a future job opportunity.

2. Students who do attend class bear some of the opportunity cost of your absenteeism, as they have may not be able to complete the work that requires teamwork or group discussion.

Example 2–2: One Laptop per Child

One Laptop per Child promotes productive efficiency in that it seeks to deliver education to poorer nations at a much lower cost than traditional bricks-and-mortar education. As noted in the example, traditional bricks-and-mortar education is simply too expensive (thousands of dollars per student) for poorer nations to afford. With One Laptop per Child, the major education cost is the $100 laptop per student.

Policy Example 2–1: The Multibillion Dollar Park

Production Possibilities Curve: Wilderness Area Goods and Oil and Gas Goods

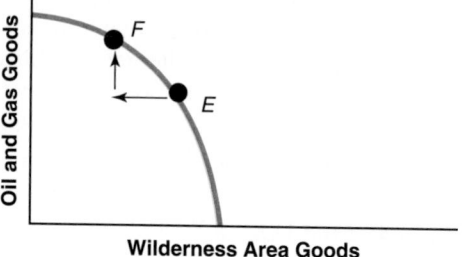

The opportunity cost of moving from E to F is the wilderness area goods sacrificed to produce more oil and gas goods, as shown by the arrows in the graph. Since E is the allocatively efficient point, the marginal cost of moving from E to F exceeds the marginal benefit of doing so, when viewing this from society's viewpoint.

Example 2–3: Canadian Post-Secondary Education Pays Off Big Time!

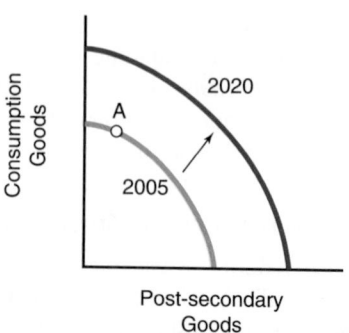

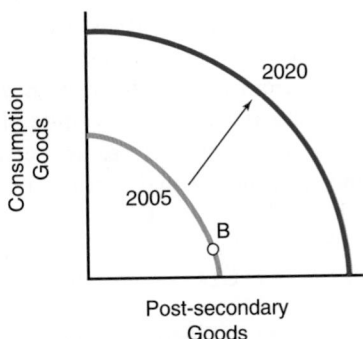

Example 2–4: Why Men Marry: Is It for Love or the Marriage Premium?

Unmarried men must divide their time between labour market goods from which they derive a paycheque and home production goods, which include food shopping, making meals, housecleaning, laundry, paying the bills, and possibly bringing up the children. Married men have greater opportunities to specialize in labour market goods (paid work) activity when their wives specialize in home production goods. The married man has the greatest opportunity to specialize in labour market activity when his wife devotes her time exclusively to home production and does not earn any income. In this example, we see that this leads to the greatest marriage premium.

Part of the gains from specialization can be explained in terms of comparative advantage to the extent that the stay-at-home wife can produce home goods at a lower opportunity cost than her husband and therefore the husband can produce labour market goods at a lower opportunity cost. As well, the gains from specialization can be due to the extra time that the husband can spend in accumulating human capital, since his wife looks after the home front.

Policy Example 2–2: Canadian Politics: Right, Left, and Centre

Policy A: Waiting time for surgeries is reduced through the expansion of government-funded surgical units located in government-run hospitals. This is more consistent with the New Democrats as this involves providing more services through the government. Policy B: Waiting time for surgeries is reduced through the provision of new surgical services through privately owned health-care clinics. This is more consistent with the Conservatives as this involves providing more services through the private sector.

Issues and Applications: Private or Public Auto Insurance: What Is Best for Canada?

1. Due to its no-fault feature, the pure command system does not have to employ the expensive legal and court-related resources to establish fault and the amount of damages experienced by injured parties. Since the government is the sole insurance provider in the province, it does not have to employ resources to market its services to the customer. Moreover, a government monopoly is able to avoid the duplication in administrative resources that typically occurs when numerous private car insurance companies compete with each other in the same province. Because the public system can offer the same insurance coverage with minimal use of resources, it is productively efficient.

2. By charging higher premiums for those individuals falling into high-risk classes, such as younger males, the private system helps to keep the riskier drivers off the road. Also, the fault system can provide an incentive to be more careful and avoid accidents. In a fault system, the injured party's right to sue for damages helps to ensure that the dollar value of the compensation resulting from an accident claim (marginal benefit) is sufficient to cover the full marginal cost related to the individual injuries and losses sustained from the accident. In this way, a fault system allocates the claim benefits (marginal benefits) in a way that matches the marginal accident costs of each individual, promoting allocative efficiency.

3. When a pure command system does not charge higher premiums based on age and gender, an equity trade-off may occur. On the one hand, equity is promoted when younger drivers with clean driving records pay lower premiums than older people who have accident histories. On the other hand, equity is compromised if the "no discrimination" practice increases collisions by encouraging riskier drivers to take to the road. In this case, older, female, safe drivers end up in more accidents caused by the riskier drivers and end up paying higher premiums.

4. With a rate freeze, the revenue from premiums stays the same but the expenses for paying out claims could increase with inflation, causing financial losses. In this situation, the private insurance companies may refuse to provide insurance in the province operating this type of mixed system. As a result, the only option would be for the government to provide the insurance.

Chapter 3: Demand and Supply

Example 3–1: Why RFID Tags are Catching On Fast

The law of demand explains the increased use of RFID tags. As this example explains, the price of RFID tags has been declining at a significant rate. As well the cost savings that companies achieve also amount to a reduced price of using the RFID technology.

Example 3–2: Chocoholics Beware

In this example, it was noted that as incomes in China increase, the demand for chocolate bars has increased. This means that chocolate bars are normal goods in China.

Because the demand for chocolate bars is increasing the market demand curve is shifting to the right, as shown in the accompanying diagram. According to the example, this shift is caused by increasing incomes in Asian countries, as well as perceived health benefits associated with eating dark chocolate.

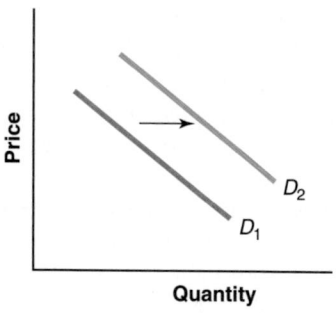

Example 3–3: Brunettes Now Have More Fun

Taste-related factors have increased the demand for brunette hair dyes. Graphically, this is reflected in a rightward shift in the demand curve for brunette hair dyes as shown below. The specific taste-related factors include: prominent female movie stars who are brunette; ethnic groups that are becoming more prominent in Canada have natural brunette hair shades; and an aging population that prefers to use brunette hair dyes to cover gray hair.

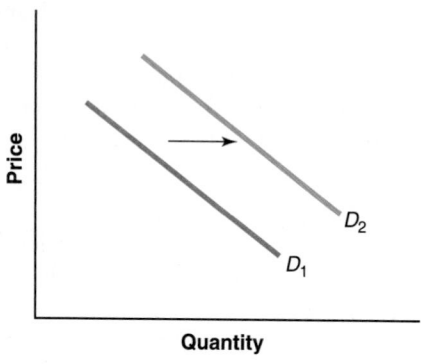

Example 3–4: Garth Brooks, Used CDs, and the Law of Demand

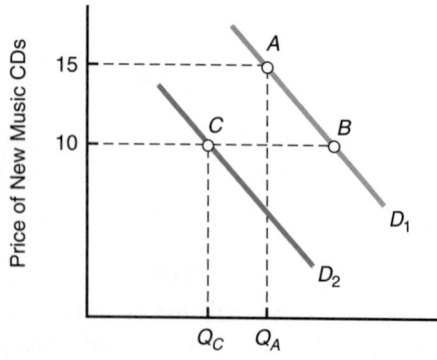

Quantity of New Music CDs

According to this example, a used-CD market lowers the net price of a CD from $15 to $10, which would result in "an increase in quantity demanded" and a movement along the demand curve from point A to point B. At the same time, used CDs serve as a cheaper substitute for new music CDs. This second effect will decrease the demand for new music CDs and shift the demand curve to the left. If this decrease in demand exceeds the increase in quantity demanded, as shown in the accompanying diagram, Garth Brooks' fear of the used-CD market is justified.

Example 3–5: Surge in Electronics Sales Follow Dramatic Drop in LCD Prices

The market supply for LCD flat screen TVs has been increasing or shifting to the right as indicated by the accompanying diagram. The determinants responsible for this shift in supply include falling prices (costs) of a key input—LCD panels, increased technology devoted to LCD flat screen TVs.

The Example predicts that in the future, the market supply for plasma TVs will start to decline or shift left, as described in the accompanying diagram.

LCD Flat Screen TVs

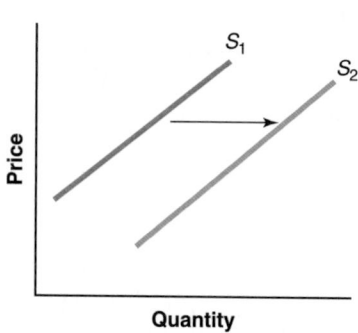

Plasma Flat Screen TVs

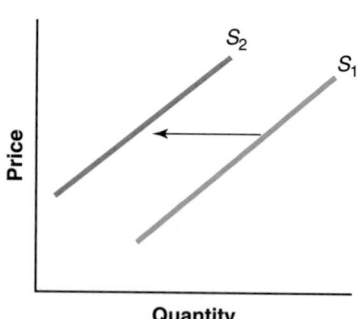

Policy Example 3–1: Having a Cow Over Milk Prices

Due to increases in the demand for milk in large nations such as India and China, the demand curve for milk is shifting rightward from D_1 to D_2 as shown in the accompanying diagram. This shift causes the equilibrium price to increase from P_1 to P_2.

The government incentives to produce more ethanol have increased the price of cattle feed (corn) and decreased the milk supply. The policy of reducing dairy farm subsidies also causes a decrease in supply of milk. Due to these decreases in the supply for milk, the supply curve for milk is

Global Milk Market

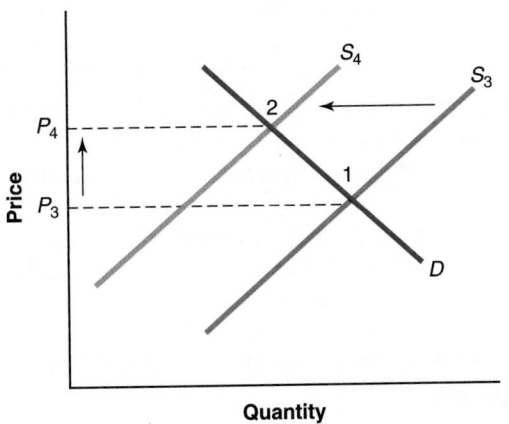

shifting leftward from S_3 to S_4, as shown in the accompanying diagram. This shift causes the equilibrium price to increase from P_3 to P_4.

Global Milk Market

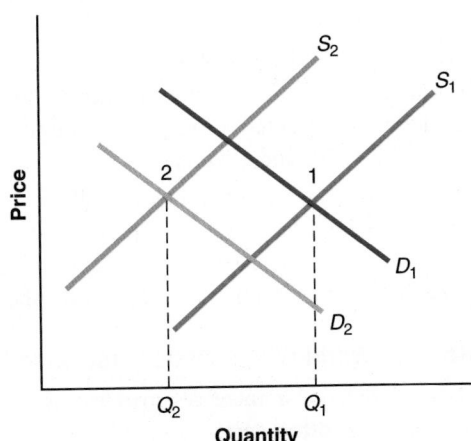

Example 3–6: Air Canada Stock Price Spins Out of Free Fall

Between 2001 and 2003, both the demand and supply for the air travel services provided by international air carriers decline. Terrorist attacks, increased use of teleconferencing technologies, and increased competition from regional airlines are factors reducing the demand for international airline services. Increased fuel, labour, and security costs were factors decreasing the supply of international airline services.

With both the demand and supply curves shifting to the left, we would predict that the equilibrium quantity of passengers using these airlines will significantly decrease. However, without additional information, the change in equilibrium air fares (price) is indeterminate. The significant decrease in quantity of passengers served has had a detrimental effect on international airlines such as Air Canada.

Since 2004, the demand for Air Canada's services has been increasing due to: passengers beging less fearful of terrorist attacks on airlines; the addition of more international flights to growth areas like China; and the demise of Canadian competitors such as Jetsgo, Canada 3000, CanJet, and Harmony.

Issues and Applications: Is Canada the Prescription for Lower Drug Prices in the United States?

1. Nonprice determinants mentioned in this Issue and Application that have the effect of increasing the demand for prescription drugs sold by Canadian Internet pharmacies include Internet promotion of Canadian drug prices in the United States; the ease of purchasing Canadian drugs using Internet and fax technology; the storefront operations located in the United States; the higher American drug prices (higher-priced substitutes); the purchase of Canadian pharmaceuticals by American government drug insurance plans (more buyers), the legalization of reimportation (if it happens).

2. Nonprice determinants mentioned in this Issue and Application that have the effect of decreasing the supply of prescription drugs sold by Canadian Internet pharmacies include the reduction in the number of Canadian doctors willing to co-sign American prescriptions, and multinational drug manufacturers' efforts to reduce the distribution of prescription drugs to Canadian Internet pharmacies.

3. The first event will tend to increase demand for prescription drugs sold by Canadian Internet pharmacies. The second event will tend to decrease the supply of prescription drugs sold by Canadian Internet pharmacies. A simultaneous increase in demand and decrease in supply will significantly increase equilibrium drug prices in Canada. The overall effect on equilibrium quantity is indeterminate.

Chapter 4 Introduction to Macroeconomics

Example 4–1: Technology and Long Cycles

The latest "boom and bust" cycle was clearly related to the computer and Internet revolution. The fastest growing (and hardest hit) firms were those that were creating and selling products related to this technological advance, which fits in with Kondratieff's idea.

Policy Example 4–1: Challenges of Measuring the Unemployment Rate in China

1. Since China has entered the global economy and has moved to a mainly capitalist system of production, it

could have economic slowdowns or recessions and thus cyclical unemployment.

2. Changes in technology, demand in the markets for goods and services, and unemployment of workers from state factories that have shut down whose skills are obsolete could lead to structural unemployment.

3. Frictional unemployment is likely because workers must search for new jobs when they become unemployed.

4. Seasonal unemployment would be the case when the planting, growing, and harvest season ends and farm workers become unemployed and seek jobs in the cities.

Example 4–2: Translating Employment into Hours on the Job

The real issue here is how productive is each hour spent by that labour. First, the education level of that worker is important. The greater the level of education, the higher the productivity. Second, labour is not the only factor that matters. The amount of machinery and the level of technology also affect the productive ability of a worker.

Policy Example 4–2: Policymakers Promote Measured Full Employment in India

Indian taxpayers provide the funds to honour the government's employment guarantee.

Example 4–3: Do Rising Nominal Wages Mean Rising Real Wages, Too?

Employers are the obvious beneficiaries of this lower wage as their labour costs decline.

Example 4–4: British Columbia Coal Mines

The risk of long-term contracts can be reduced for natural gas companies if their suppliers agree to the same structure of contracts that the consumers are agreeing to. That way there is no risk of the companies being unable to pay for higher natural gas prices.

Example 4–5: Hyperinflation

During a period of hyperinflation, prices are changing very quickly. It is in your interest to spend your money as quickly as possible, or suffer the loss of purchasing power. There would also be a strong incentive to borrow money and buy real assets unless interest rates reflected these high rates of inflation. Workers would often be paid several times a day in Germany when it experienced hyperinflation in the 1920s so that they could immediately spend their earnings.

Issues and Applications: Hyperinflation and the Collapse of the Zimbabwean Economy

1. A barter economy is less efficient because you must always find someone who has what you want to trade, rather than using money as an intermediate exchange.

Therefore, much effort is spent trying to find someone who has the correct goods to trade.

2. Printing more money does not by itself guarantee that more goods are being produced. People will not want to trade for it if they know that the value of the money is likely to be less almost as soon as they receive it.

Chapter 5: Measuring the Economy's Performance

Policy Example 5–1 The Economic Cost of Pollution

Manufacturing industries are likely to cause much more pollution than service or agricultural industries, since manufacturing usually involves the intensive transformation of physical resources into products. Manufacturing is often very energy intensive. Within that broad category there will likely be some industries that are worse than others, such as chemical-based industries, that are likely to experience more difficulty in treating by-products of their production.

Example 5–1: The Underground Economy

It can be difficult to compare data on economic performance when much of the economy is not measured. The standards of living are not easily compared if one nation has much of its economy underground and another nation does not. As well, if much of the growth of the economy is in the underground economy, it may mislead policy makers when deciding how much to stimulate or hold back an economy.

Example 5–2: Variability of GDP Expenditure Components

1. Investment falls dramatically during a recession because firms have existing equipment that is not being fully used. Firms will not be as interested in buying new equipment to add to capacity unless it is significantly better than the old equipment.

2. Investment in computers, the Internet, and related technologies represented a big part of the investment boom of the 1980s and 1990s.

3. During a recession, Canadian income falls, which leads to a decline in imports. At the same time, if other nations are not experiencing a recession, we will continue to sell our exports, leading to a positive net export balance.

Example 5–3: World GDP May Be Understated

If the value of the dollar increases in one year and then decreases relative to other currencies in the next, then the value of world GDP will be greater in the second year. The reason is that $1 will buy fewer units of foreign currencies in the second year and world GDP will be overstated compared to the first year. For example, if in 2008 world GDP was equal to 10 billion euros and $1 = €1, then world GDP (excluding the U.S.) would be $10 billion. If world GDP in 2009 did not change in terms of euros but the exchange rate became $1 = €0.5, then world GDP would become

$20 billion at the 2006 exchange rate. World GDP would appear to double.

Example 5–4: Correcting GDP for Price Level Changes, 1997–2006

Changing the price level index base year will result in a different deflator series. Since inflation has occurred since 1992, it will make the deflator numbers smaller and the resulting calculation of real GDP larger, and somewhat more comparable with today's dollars.

Example 5–5: Comparing Standards of Living

Switzerland has a much higher per-capita income than New Zealand, but according to the HDI, their human well being is nearly the same. Clearly, then, New Zealand must rank much higher on life expectancy and educational attainment.

Example 5–6: Purchasing Power Parity of World Incomes

There is a 292.7 percent increase in per-capita GDP going from the exchange rate measure to the purchasing power parity measure. The increase is calculated as:

Percent increase = $((PP - FE)/FE) \times 100$
$= ((5890 - 1500)/1500) \times 100$
$= (4390/1500) \times 100$
$= 292.7$

PP = purchasing power parity per-capita GDP
FE = foreign exchange rate per-capita GDP

Issues and Applications: Setting Goals for a Nation: What Do We Aim For?

1. The GPI would give a smaller indicator of progress because of the degradation of the environment and the loss of nonrenewable resources, which would not be accounted for in GDP.

2. Each student will have an individual answer for this question.

3. While such activities would increase measured GDP, it may not mean we are producing more output. On the other hand, having careers outside the home as a possibility may mean a better use of resources as women can capably fill these jobs, rather than be restricted to a "housewife" career.

Chapter 6: Modelling Real GDP and the Price Level in the Long Run

Policy Example 6–1: Regulation and Economic Growth

The value of the activities involved in satisfying government regulations would increase GDP, since they generate income to the resource owners who supply the information. These costs are included in the prices of goods and services produced by the firms that are required to meet the regulations.

Example 6–1: Terrorism and Economic Growth

The terrorist attack did not change the total amount of resources available but did decrease the quantity that could be used to produce goods and services. The effect of the terrorist attack will be to reduce the rate at which the economy grows because the United States will continue to devote part of its resources that would have otherwise been producing goods and services to security.

Example 6–2: Interest Rate Hikes and a Hot Loonie Are Hurting Ontario

The rising Canadian dollar and the interest rate hikes would both shift aggregate demand to the left, because of reduced net exports and reduced investment. The tax break on equipment should encourage new investment (shifting *AD* to the right) and in the long run increasing productivity and thereby shifting *LRAS* to the right as well.

Example 6–3: Information Technologies and Long-Run Aggregate Supply

Entrepreneurs are the labour resource that, among other things, brings new innovations to the market in the form of new ways of producing and new goods and services. By stimulating technological change and by bringing new products to the market, they cause the *LRAS* curve to shift outward faster than it otherwise would have.

Example 6–4: The Economic Challenge of Age

The labour supply curve will be shifting to the left as labour supply diminishes. This will increase wages and thereby reduce the quantity of labour demanded. With a lower labour input, aggregate production will be less, and thereby *LRAS* will also shift to the left.

Example 6–5: When Aggregate Demand Gets Out of Control, Watch Out!

Governments in any of these countries could have restricted the growth of the money supply so that aggregate demand would have increased at about the same rate as *LRAS*.

Issues and Applications: Why the 2004 Tsunami Did Not Swamp Asian Economies

1. If aggregate demand is increasing faster than long-run aggregate supply, then the price level will increase and real GDP will increase.

2. The country was unable to generate the saving to finance the investment needed for reconstruction of the economy, and thus negative effects on the economy were greater.

Chapter 7: Economic Growth and Development

Example 7–1: Growth Rates around the World

One would expect that growth rates could be higher in poorer countries because the same absolute increase in real

GDP would be a larger percent of a poorer country's real GDP than it would be of a rich country's real GDP.

Example 7–2: What If Canada Had Grown a Little Bit Less or More Each Year?

A difference of 0.4% over 17 years can be calculated as: $(1.004)^{17}-1 = 7.02\%$. Note that this is the difference shown in the growth rates between Canada and the U.S. in Table 7-1. Clearly, our current standards of living are much higher than our grandparents' or those living a hundred years ago.

Example 7–3: Productivity Gains

A tax on machinery and equipment will tend to reduce the purchases of those items, reducing productivity and overall production. All else equal, the demand for labour will fall, the production function will be lower, and the *LRAS* will shift left.

Example 7–4: How Does Canadian Productivity Compare with the Rest of the World?

Competitiveness as measured by the World Economic Forum is based on three variables: the macroeconomic environment, the quality of public institutions, and technology, and so Canada could easily move up the competitiveness ranking through the actions of governments in other countries. In the same way, Canada could move down. Generally, however, the differences among these countries are much smaller than would be suggested by this ranking.

Policy Example 7–1: The Mystery of Capitalism

Starting a business out of a home or garage is not as easy because the entrepreneurs in those countries cannot borrow against their home the way that we can. Because property rights are less well defined, banks are less willing to lend to these entrepreneurs because they cannot as easily count on the value of the property if the entrepreneur should fail.

Policy Example 7–2: Competing on Creativity

The Canadian government subsidizes many of the creative industries that are mentioned by Professor Florida through its various granting agencies. Further, it protects certain industries from foreign competition by requiring Canadian content and Canadian ownership, such as in the broadcasting industry.

Policy Example 7–3: Ottawa and the Kyoto Accord

Taxes can be used to reduce pollution, by having heavy polluters pay a higher tax for that pollution. This is likely to reduce demand for the products from that industry and thereby reduce the amount of pollution created. In some provinces, taxes on energy (sometimes called "carbon taxes") would severely limit the production of petroleum and would definitely limit the size of related industries.

Canadians already accept a fair amount of pollution in the air and water, although generally the amount is less for each individual polluter than it was in the industrial era. The major problem is that we have so many more firms and cars when compared with earlier times that the total amount of pollution has increased, and we still have much of the pollution around from earlier times.

As well, we also have pollution crossing borders. New developing countries are also less stringent in their standards, and thus, we are experiencing pollution coming from other countries.

Policy Example 7–4: The End of Poverty

Clearly the GDP of the country would decline as much of the commerce that goes on depends on that infrastructure to get items to market. At the same time, Canadians are still relatively wealthy, and could reinvest their other assets into these structures, creating a construction boom that would add to the investment component of GDP. Oddly enough, disasters such as flooding and hurricanes lead to economic booms for some producers.

Issues and Applications: Winners and Losers in the Brain Drain Game

1. They could subsidize the wages of highly skilled workers. They could make attractive investment opportunities available for foreign investment and domestic entrepreneurs so that the demand and wages for their own highly skilled workers would increase.

2. An increase in the supply of labour in the brain gain countries would decrease wages for highly skilled workers, other things constant.

Chapter 8: Modelling Real GDP and the Price Level in the Short Run

Example 8–1: Changing the Slope of the Short-Run Aggregate Supply Schedule?

A constant MC implies that cash increases at a fixed rate as output increases. Therefore, we do not get diminishing returns. This implies that the *SRAS* curve remains flat.

Policy Example 8–1: Controlling Inflation

1. If the U.S. economy slows rapidly, it would likely reduce aggregate demand (net exports) in Canada, creating a recessionary gap. If consumers were to increase their consumption spending (shifting aggregate demand to the right), this would create an inflationary gap.

2. This type of spending is a wealth effect, because it is not related to income but rather to the wealth that people have.

Example 8–2: A Tale of Two Economies

If the drop in investment had continued, it might have affected our *LRAS* curve more severely and limited our ability to grow in the future.

Example 8–3: Rising Labour Costs Reduce Productivity Gains

Rising labour costs will tend to move aggregate supply to the left. Without an equal sized reduction in aggregate demand, the price level will tend to rise.

Example 8–4: Rising Canadian Loonie

A lower Canadian dollar would tend to cause exports to rise, increasing aggregate demand. At the same time, it makes many (imported) inputs more expensive, shifting *SRAS* to the left. Both of these will tend to increase the price level and inflation.

Example 8–5: The Effect of World War I

If World War I had lasted 10 years instead of four, the *SRAS* curve would eventually have shifted up as input prices, like wages, rose in response to the excess demand for inputs. GDP would have approached its long-run level, but the price level would have risen beyond 176.

Example 8–6: Why Have Unemployment Rates Fallen in North America with only Low Rates of Inflation?

The problem for the economy might be that wages begin to rise in this situation faster than can be compensated for with productivity gains. If workers are used to having their real wages rise year after year, it will be difficult to say to them now that their wages cannot rise in the future. In this circumstance, costs would begin to rise and this would show up as a leftward shift in *SRAS*.

Issues and Applications: Oil Price Changes Shock the North American Economy

The rising price of oil has had a strong positive aggregate demand effect on oil-exporting provinces such as Alberta and Newfoundland, shifting *AD* to the right as shown the first graph below. The effect comes through the increased value of net exports.

Simultaneously, the rising price of oil has increased the cost of inputs for manufacturing industries, and indirectly, driven up the value of the Canadian dollar. In Ontario, this has meant a decline in the value of exports and increased costs for energy. The overall effect of these has been to shift short-run aggregate supply and aggregate demand to the left as shown in the second graph below.

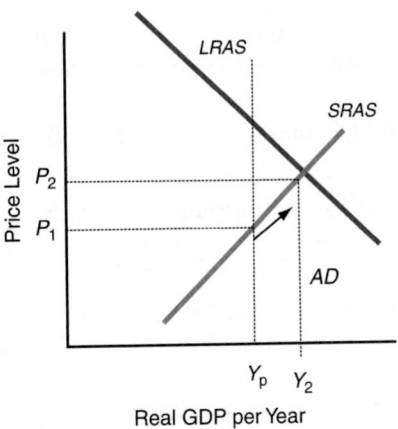

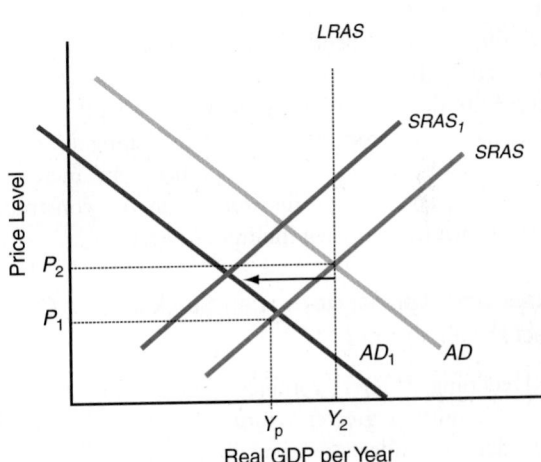

Overall, the aggregate demand effects have been roughly offsetting the aggregate supply effects for Canada as a whole. Jobs and production lost in manufacturing in Ontario and Quebec are being replaced with jobs in the oil-producing provinces, and unemployment has reached 30-year lows.

Chapter 9: Consumption, Investment, and the Multiplier

Policy Example 9–1: Spending on Human Capital: Investment or Consumption?

In this case, total savings must fall. Disposable income can only be spent or saved. With more spending on education, there must be less available for saving.

Example 9–1: U.S. Consumers Are Bloodied But Unbowed

Consumer spending depends on earning income. Payroll gains indicate that new jobs are being created, and thus income is rising.

Example 9–2: Changes in Investment and the Great Depression

The economy had recovered to its 1929 level of real GDP. Relative to the 1930s the economy was much improved.

Example 9–3: Oil Sands Investment Continues to Grow

The investment demand function for Canada must have been shifting to the right. An increase in interest rates would tend to increase the cost of the borrowing and the investment, and would indicate a reduction in investment, all else equal.

Policy Example 9–2: The Multiplier Effect of Forced Housing Investment in China

The macroeconomic effect would have been the same. By spending more to upgrade housing, the government would have still increased spending in the housing sector so that construction firms would have experienced the same increase in demand for their services except that these would have been for repair and remodelling of existing housing. Thus, there would have been an increase in employment and income for workers in the construction industry with the resulting multiplier effect.

Issues and Applications: Can Stock Market Crashes Affect the Economy?

1. Declining business confidence means that businesses will require a greater return on their investments in order to undertake that investment. This would shift the planned investment schedule to the left, as illustrated below.

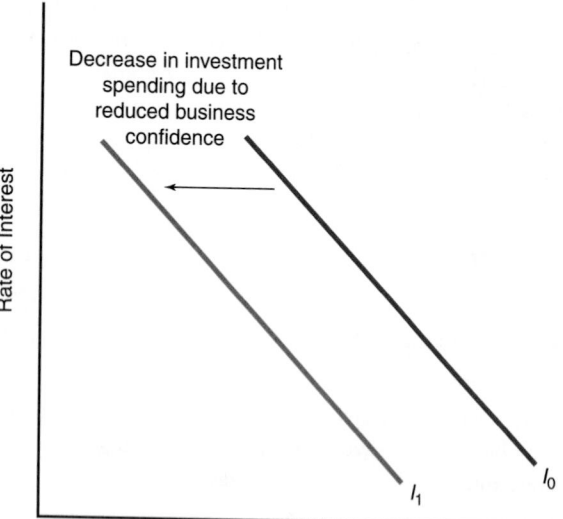

Planned Investment per Year ($ billion)

2. A decline in consumer confidence would mean a decline in consumer spending. This could result in both a reduction in autonomous spending which would shift the consumption function down in Figure 9-4, and a

reduction in the *MPC*, which would mean the consumption function was flatter. With a decline in the *MPC*, the proportion of disposable income going to savings would increase and thus reduce the value of the multiplier.

Chapter 10: The Public Sector

Policy Example 10–1: Who Should Pay the High Cost of a Legal System?

Some of the implicit costs that you could list would be time, buildings and their maintenance, court clerks, and public officers who must appear before the court.

Example 10–1: Are Lighthouses a Public Good?

In point 1, it would be difficult to sell a lighthouse to one individual. In point 2, the cost of the lighthouse does not increase if more people make use of its services, and in point 3, because one person makes use of the lighthouse, it does not mean that others cannot use it as well.

Policy Example 10–2: Do Government-Funded Sports Stadiums Have a Net Positive Effect on Local Economies?

A sports stadium will increase employment and spending within the economy. It is often seen that facilities built for the Olympics are then used by the cities for years after the event. This improves the image of the cities, as they can offer first-class facilities and attract other events, boosting their economies.

Example 10–2: Child-Care Spaces

The federal dollars given directly to all families with children benefit not only families that have children in daycare, but families that have stay-at-home Moms or Dads. This is perhaps more fair to all parents, and allows them to spend that money by choosing a method other than just daycare, such as paying relatives to look after their children. People in rural communities and parents who work shift work also benefit by having the money given to them directly, instead of money going to the provinces.

Policy Example 10–3: Tax Freedom Day Around the World

The longer you have to wait for tax freedom day, the higher your level of taxation. Swedes have to wait until August 8th for their tax freedom day, while U.S. citizens get to celebrate on April 30th. The lucky winners (on March 14th) are residents of India.

Example 10–3: Employment Insurance

Canada Pension Plan payments are not part of government's general revenue, and it might be reassuring to workers to know that EI premiums are handled the same way. If there is a surplus in the account, government should not be able to use it to balance its budget.

Issues and Applications: Should We Switch to a Flat Tax?

1. Employees at the Canada Revenue Agency (CRA) might well be against a flat-tax system. Advocates of a flat tax claim that one of the benefits would be a significantly downsized CRA, implying that many CRA employees might lose their jobs. We know from Chapter 1 that the rationality assumption tells us that people usually do not make decisions that reduce their well-being. It is likely that CRA employees would want to keep their jobs to maintain their well-being and would thus oppose a flat-tax system.

2. A flat-tax system is more efficient than a progressive tax system because the method of calculation of tax owing is much simpler: There is only one calculation to make, rather than the many calculations required in a progressive system. There would be efficiencies realized by taxpayers who could complete their tax returns easily, and by CRA employees who could check the calculation equally simply. The opportunity cost of the yearly tax return would fall, leaving resources free to pursue more productive activities.

Chapter 11: Fiscal Policy

Policy Example 11–1: Did Roosevelt's New Deal Really Provide a Stimulus?

The New Deal failed to have any effect on the Canadian economy. Any possible effect would have occurred through an increase in exports to the United States. However, during the Great Depression, the United States raised protective trade barriers that kept Canada's exports from going there in any event.

Policy Example 11–2: The Baby Boom Generation Moves into Retirement Years

A longer life expectancy means that (as a group) people will be collecting more from the Canada Pension Plan than they put in. By raising the retirement age, the government will reduce the number of years that people are collecting and raise the number of years they are contributing, thus bringing the plan back into balance.

Policy Example 11–3: Boosting Tax Revenues via International Tax Competition

These higher tax countries are clearly losing potential tax revenues as firms choose locations in Greece and Ireland. It may also be the case that some firms are moving facilities to these countries, thus causing actual reductions in tax revenues in the higher tax countries. Also, the diversion of investment to Greece and Ireland will have the effect of increasing unemployment rates in the higher tax countries.

Policy Example 11–4: Keynesian Fiscal Policy Loses Its Lustre

Keynes might have responded to this criticism in several ways. First, he would have noted that his policies were particularly designed for deep depressions, not for "fine-tuning" economies. Second, he would argue that you could not look in isolation at each instance of what is happening elsewhere in the world and in the economy. In Canada, in the 1990s, even with higher taxes and a deficit-fighting government, we still had growth, largely because of the improved world economic climate. Third, we do not know what happened with monetary policy or trade policies in those countries that also would have had big effects on economic growth.

Issues and Applications: How Much Government Is Enough?

1. No doubt many students would like to see lower tuition fees! However, you might want to think about issues that affect you beyond your immediate interests. What about policies that affect your family (such as EI or old age security)? These generally provide some stability to the system but may create a supply-side problem.

2. Generally, conservative parties favour smaller government, while socialist parties favour more government involvement. In Canada, though, we generally have a higher level of government involvement in the economy and a broader system of social safety net than in the United States or Japan. There are other reasons for voting for particular parties, such as voting for individual law makers whom you would believe to be better than the alternatives, even if they are not a member of your first-choice for political party.

Chapter 12: Money and the Banking System

Example 12–1: Will Barter Make a Comeback on the Web?

In a highly complex economy with extensive specialization, it is unlikely that the majority of everyday purchases of goods and services would ever be settled using barter, largely because most people produce very little of what they consume and would, thus, not have many goods to exchange for what they need. This suggests that for extensive barter to take place, the economy would have to be organized so that people would have to be paid in goods and then would have to have access to barter exchanges that could solve the double coincidence of wants and relative exchange ratios more cheaply in terms of opportunity cost and actual relative price paid (in terms of goods) than being paid with money for productive activity and simply going shopping in stores with money.

In any practical sense for barter to be more common than monetary exchange, the number of goods being traded would have to be smaller and production would have to be done largely by self-employed owners of businesses.

Example 12–2: Converting Dollars into African Vouchers on the Web

They act as a medium of exchange and as a store of value.

Example 12–3: E-Gold-Backed E-Money

Payments can only be made to an authorized user of the system. Thus e-gold is not generally usable as a medium of exchange.

Example 12–4: Is Gold Worth Its Weight?

Central banks would probably wish to hold large amounts of gold bullion in the event that the world monetary system had some sort of major crisis of confidence in the American dollar or there was a global depression. In such a financial climate, there would be a perception that risk could be reduced by holding gold because gold has been viewed historically as a reliable store of value.

Example 12–5: Eliminating the $1 and $2 Bills

If the government replaced the $20 bill with a $20 coin, the seigniorage it makes would increase significantly, provided the materials used to make the new coin were similar to those in the loonies and the toonies. Seigniorage derives from the difference between the face value of a coin and the cost of making it. Therefore, the higher the face value of the coin, *ceteris paribus*, the greater is the seigniorage.

Example 12–6: Why McDonald's Wants Your Card, Not Your Cash

Reducing the time it takes to conduct a transaction allows McDonald's to complete more transactions. Thus, the company can sell more of its products and make higher profits.

Example 12–7: Credit Cards and Canadians

These nonmonetary transactions increase aggregate demand in the economy. Outstanding balances on credit cards represent demand that may not have existed without the availability of instant credit.

Example 12–8: What Will Digital Cash Replace?

Digital cash or stored value cards act as a medium of exchange and as a store of value. They will begin to function as an alternative to currency and cheques.

Example 12–9: Why Banks Want Their Customers to Go Online

If more customers use online banking services and also hold higher average bank balances, then a bank could increase its lending and its interest income.

Issues and Applications: The Dollarization Movement: Is the U.S. Fed Destined to Be a Multinational Central Bank?

1. The advantage of dollarizing an economy would be increased faith in the currency (acceptability) and reduced transactions costs associated with currency conversion in international commerce. The increased transparency and predictability in prices should encourage more investment and trade. This will result in improved efficiency and increased welfare from the reduced uncertainty and better resource allocation.

2. If actual U.S. currency had to be acquired by issuing bonds to the U.S. government, then there would be payments to the United States out of Canadian and Argentine tax collections every year. If the U.S. Fed raised U.S. interest rates, then Canadian and Argentine citizens would have to pay higher taxes to the United States.

Chapter 13: Money Creation and Deposit Insurance

Policy Example 13–1: Are Reserve Requirements on the Way Out or In?

Central banks earn interest income with their customers' (financial institutions) money (the banks' reserve deposits). The customers could use the money kept in reserve accounts to earn interest on loans or securities. There is an actual reduction in earnings (interest foregone) as a result of central banks' imposition of reserve requirements.

Policy Example 13–2: Bailouts That Cost Taxpayers Millions

The interest income earned by central banks is made with their customers' (financial institutions) money. Also, these financial institutions could use the money kept in reserve accounts to earn interest on loans and securities. There is an actual reduction in earnings (interest foregone) as a result of central bank's imposition of reserve requirements.

Issues and Applications: Deregulating the Financial Services Industry

1. A bank is a business that holds funds for customers and grants loans to customers who qualify. A nonbank bank is a business that does the above but is not a bank. An example of a nonbank bank would be an insurance company, or a trust company such as Co-operative Trust Company of Canada.

2. There could be an increased moral hazard problem as banks diversify their services. With deposit insurance, banks already have an incentive to take on riskier investments than may be prudent. The additional profits the bank could earn from the sale of insurance or airline tickets would act as an increased incentive to sell to high-risk customers, or to grant credit to less-than-creditworthy

customers for air travel. Because of the existence of deposit insurance, customers would still lack the incentive to monitor the bank's decisions closely.

Chapter 14: The Bank of Canada and Monetary Policy

Example 14–1: Is Canadian Tire Money Real Money?

For Canadian Tire money to act as real money, it would have to be widely accepted by people in exchange for goods and services. The fact that Canadian Tire money would be "backed" by Canadian Tire inventory might encourage people to accept it, especially if they believed the inventory would continue to hold value into the future.

Example 14–2: Determining the Price of Bonds

If the Bank of Canada were to pursue an easy money policy, this would include lowering interest rates. Because there is an inverse relationship between the price of a bond and interest rates, lowered interest rates would result in higher bond prices in the near future. Therefore, the investor who purchased the bond immediately will realize a capital gain.

Policy Example 14–1: The Determination of the Target for the Overnight Rate

The Bank of Canada has replaced the previous approach in which it would announce an adjustment on any business day in the year with one where it would announce changes to the Overnight Rate on eight preset fixed dates throughout the year. The purpose of this change is to make Bank of Canada policy more transparent, more predictable, and less complicated. This should contribute to increased understanding and discussion of the long-term policy of the Bank of Canada, avoid surprises, and contribute to improved functioning of financial markets.

Example 14–3: The Choice between Cash and Savings Accounts in Colombia

Nominal interest rates are higher when a country experiences inflation because the demand for money increases as people attempt to buy more goods and services to "beat" inflation. In addition, higher nominal amounts must be borrowed just to buy the same quantity of goods. Borrowers become willing to pay higher nominal interest rates because their incomes are, on average, rising and the burden of their debt as a percent of their income is declining. On the other side of the equation, lenders wish to protect the purchasing power of their money and earn the real rate of interest. They will demand higher interest rates from borrowers to cover the real interest rate plus the expected rate of inflation.

Example 14–4: Unfortunately for Germany, the Crude Quantity Theory Worked Very Well

When the rate of growth of the money supply is very high, real output grows by a trifling amount compared with the growth of the money supply. Thus, very high rates of growth of the money supply will result in increases in the price level that are very close to the rate of monetary growth.

Example 14–5: Inflation and Money Growth throughout the World

The data in Figure 14–7 do not "prove" the crude quantity theory of money and prices. What they do show is that there is an association between money supply growth rates and inflation. The diagram does not show a one-to-one proportional relationship between the rate of growth of the money supply and the rate of inflation. Even those countries with very high rates of monetary growth, such as Nigeria, have rates of inflation that are less than the rate of increase in the money supply.

Policy Example 14–2: Monetary Policy: Where Are We Now?

Monetary policy is now directed toward a single long-run objective: the attainment and maintenance of price stability. It has changed since 1935. In 1935, the Bank of Canada was directed to conduct monetary policy in the best economic interest of the nation, including regulating output, trade, employment, prices, and the external value of the currency (see textbook page 356).

Policy Example 14–3: Political Uncertainty and Monetary Targeting

If Quebeckers had voted "Yes," the interest rate would have risen in the short term, reflecting uncertainty and risk in Canadian financial markets. What would happen in the long run would depend on how successful Quebeckers were at establishing a sound financial system of their own. Recently, Czechoslovakia went through a "velvet divorce" and broke up into the Czech Republic and Slovakia in January 1993. They had agreed to a common currency, but because of currency outflows, Slovakia, the economically weaker partner, was forced to opt out of this arrangement, create its own devalued currency, and raise interest rates after just over a month of independence.

Issues and Applications: Is the Bank of Canada Independent and, If Not, Does It Matter?

1. Following the *Coyne Affair*, the *Bank of Canada Act* was amended in 1967. The Act now allows the Government of Canada to issue a directive to the Bank in the event of a serious disagreement over the conduct of monetary policy. However, former Governor G. Thiessen said: "... because of the consequences of issuing a directive, it is likely to be used only in unusual circumstances. Thus, a high degree of operational independence has... been preserved." (See page 372.)

2. We would expect to see New Zealand's net exports increase. The nominal interest rate is the real interest rate plus a premium for expected inflation. If inflation decreases, interest rates decrease. When interest rates decrease, foreigners wish to hold fewer financial instruments denominated in the New Zealand currency.

Therefore there is a decrease in the demand for the currency, and its exchange rate depreciates. With a relatively less valuable currency, imports fall and exports rise, thus increasing net exports.

Chapter 15: Issues in Stabilization Policy

Example 15–1: Canada's Natural Rate of Unemployment

There are probably two primary reasons for the upward trend in the natural rate of unemployment. First, increasing welfare and employment insurance benefits reduce incentives to work. These allow workers to remain unemployed longer while they seek work. In addition, rising welfare payments have built-in disincentives for people to work because of the loss of benefits when income is earned. Second, rapid changes in technology since World War II have made many workers' skills obsolete. If these workers want to find re-employment, they often have to undergo retraining, which lengthens their duration of unemployment.

Example 15–2: Monetary Policy and Aggregate Demand: The Bank of Japan Tries to Have It Both Ways

An increase in the money supply might not have much of an impact in the short run because of time lags between the increase in the money supply and the increase in aggregate demand. In the long run, aggregate demand would increase and the time lags would not be important. If the money supply increases faster than real GDP, then in the long run, there would be inflation other things constant.

Example 15–3: Distinguishing between the Natural Rate of Unemployment and the NAIRU

The natural unemployment rate and the NAIRU would be the same when the economy was in long-run equilibrium. All short-run adjustments have been made, and there is no tendency for the inflation rate to increase or decrease.

Example 15–4: The Effects of Higher Inflation on Inflation Expectations

The public will expect a central bank that announces an inflation target will take actions that will reduce the inflation rate to the target level and that the higher inflation rate will not be likely to continue.

Example 15–5: Higher Interest Rates and "Tight" Monetary Policy

Whether an interest rate is high, reasonable, or low depends on the inflation rate. If inflation were over 10 percent, a mortgage rate of 6 percent would be very low, because the real rate of interest would be −4 percent. On the other hand, if the inflation rate were 1 percent, then a mortgage rate of 6 percent could be seen as a high real rate of interest of 5 percent. Over long periods of time, the real interest rate has averaged about 3 percent (see Figure 15–15, Real Interest Rates since World War II). If inflation were 3 percent, then a mortgage rate of 6 percent would be reasonable.

Example 15–6: Islam and Supply-Side Economics

If a tax hike pushes marginal tax rates high enough, tax revenues may actually fall when incentives to work, save, and invest are reduced. When marginal tax rates are reduced, the incentives to work, save, and invest are increased, and tax revenues may increase.

Example 15–7: Job Cuts or Pay Reductions: Which Are Less Harmful to Workers' Morale?

On the basis of the efficiency wage theory, in the case of a fall in aggregate demand causing a recession, real wages would either stay the same or rise to increase workers' productivity—workers working harder, improving their efficiency, maintaining their loyalty and morale. For this to occur, for real wages to either stay the same or rise, firms would have to lay off workers.

Example 15–8: Henry Ford and the Efficiency Wage Model

Managers can provide profit sharing plans in which workers receive a given percentage of the profits at the end of the year. Managers can pay part or all of college or university expenses that qualify workers to move up in the company and earn higher wages in the future. The same argument can be used for sending workers for additional free training.

Example 15–9: The French Government's Direct Approach to Reducing Unemployment

Governments have many legislative means to increase firms' labour costs. These can include minimum wages, employment insurance premiums, pension premiums, worker compensation premiums, employer taxes, health and safety requirements and inspections, training requirements, statutory holidays, vacation requirements, hours of work, determining who can work, and many more.

Issues and Applications: The Bank of Canada's High Interest Rate Policy

1. Passive investment in financial instruments to earn a hefty return will result in a reduction in interest rates. As we learned in Chapter 14, as bond prices rise, interest rates fall. With lower interest rates, investors will be tempted to turn to active investing in technology and businesses. Active investment in businesses and technology will stimulate aggregate demand. Depending on the output gap, the result in the

economy will be inflation if the economy is at full employment, or economic growth if the economy is not.

2. The policy irrelevance proposition states that no real variables can be affected by anticipated policy. Since former Governor Theissen announced his plan to keep interest rates relatively high to combat inflation, players in the economy are informed, and will not act to decrease unemployment.

Chapter 16: Comparative Advantage and the Open Economy

Example 16–1: The Importance of International Trade in Various Countries

Luxembourg's imports can be a large percentage of its total national income because Luxembourg imports things that it then exports. It would add value by either transforming the imports to higher valued ones or simply by acting as a middleman to reduce the transactions costs of trade.

Example 16–2: U.S. Consumers Go Online to Import Canadian Pharmaceuticals

The Canadian pharmacies have increased exports to the U.S. By expanding their businesses, they have increased the number of jobs in Canada.

Example 16–3: International Trade and the Alphabet

Before the alphabet was used, writing was in the form of abstract pictograms, such as the Chinese and Japanese use today or actual pictures, such as hieroglyphics.

Example 16–4: The Importation of Priests into Spain

One way the church might induce more Spaniards to enter the priesthood would be to offer better pay and working conditions.

Example 16–5: Do Legal Restrictions Reduce the International Competitiveness of Middle Eastern Nations?

The nations that would lose most would be those that have only limited experience with larger scale business, that is, the non–oil-exporting countries that have only small firms. They would be at a competitive disadvantage at least for a number of years.

Example 16–6: Dumping Chinese Garlic

Consumers might be in favour of countervailing duties to offset the price advantage of Chinese garlic growers. This would ensure a home-grown supply of garlic in the event of a disruption in Chinese garlic supply.

Policy Example 16–1: Who Is Dumping on Whom?

The likely explanation is that as their economies expanded, the emerging economies had fewer adverse employment effects from international competition and thus did not need the excuse of foreign dumping to protect their industries.

Example 16–7: Unfair Competition from Low-Wage Countries

As the world moves towards freer trade, there are those who gain and those who do not gain in each nation under these new circumstances. Generally speaking, those industries and companies that have comparative advantage will see their operations expand because of new export volume. On the other hand, those industries and companies that do not have comparative advantage will see their operations contract. These are the individuals who are likely to go to the media to protest their diminished circumstances.

Policy Example 16–2: Should Canadian Farmers Be Subsidized?

Subsidies are the giving of monies, tax abatements, or other concessions by governments to businesses they wish to attract or to vulnerable enterprises they want to help make more competitive. Subsidies are usually noted for their geographic concentration that often translates into political clout—the elected representative "keeps the mill running." If subsidies did increase competitiveness, then the Soviet Union, which heavily subsidized industries and businesses, would have been the most competitive economy in the world.

Issues and Applications: Do Regional Trade Agreements Help or Hinder International Trade?

1. The countries within Mercosur trade more intensively with each other than with the rest of the world. This could be because high common external barriers have diverted trade from the rest of the world to the countries in the regional trade bloc.

2. If the tariff applies to the finished product but not to the component parts, then the parts can be imported and assembled in a country in the trade bloc and sold throughout the trade bloc.

Chapter 17: Exchange Rates and the Balance of Payments

Example 17–1: Perhaps the Trade Situation Isn't So Bad After All

A major concern is that foreigners have increasing claims on Canada, which they could cash in. In the short run, the outflow of funds would have the same effect as a reduction in domestic saving and thus would reduce Canada's ability to finance investment.

Example 17–2: Does Canada's Frequent Current Account Deficit Mean It Has a Weak Economy?

The balance of payments is meant to express the total of all economic transactions between a nation and the rest of the world. Which account in Canada's Balance of International Payments indicates Statistics Canada's difficulty in accounting for the total of all economic transactions with the world?

The account in the balance of payments identified as "Statistical Discrepancy" compensates for the inability to account for some transactions, probably unaccounted capital flows such as activities related to the underground economy. Because the balance of payments has to balance, this estimate is the balancing entry.

Example 17–3: Central European Currency Values Are Up, So Exports Are Down

Central European imports of Western European goods would increase as the prices of these goods in terms of Eastern European currencies fell.

Policy Example 17–1: Should We Go Back to the Gold Standard?

To be on the gold standard is to allow a country's money supply, price level, and level of economic activity in the short run to depend, in part, on international gold movements. The governments and citizens of modern countries are unwilling to let these important macroeconomic variables depend on the international sector.

Policy Example 17–2: Can Foreign Exchange Rates Be Fixed Forever?

From an economic standpoint, governments seem to be interested in limiting foreign exchange risk. Politically, it is likely that there is some degree of prestige (from the politicians' viewpoint) in having a fixed exchange rate.

Issues and Applications: A Major Foreign Exchange Flop

1. One major factor is that the declining value of the euro was due to the market forces that were present as a result of very large capital and trade flows. To permanently increase the value of the euro against the dollar without changing the trade and capital flows originating from the private sector would have required continuous intervention on the part of the ECB and other central banks to buy up "surplus" euros.

2. An increase in productivity should decrease the average and marginal costs of production, which would reduce European prices and thus stimulate European exports to the United States while discouraging imports from the United States. The Europeans would be supplying fewer euros to the foreign exchange market so that the dollar would depreciate against the euro, *ceteris paribus*.

GLOSSARY

45-degree reference line The line along which planned real expenditures equal real disposable income per year.

Absolute advantage The ability to perform a task using the fewest number of labour hours.

Absolute advantage The ability to produce more output from given inputs of resources than other producers can.

Accounting identities Definitions of equivalent values.

Action time lag The period between the recognition of a problem and the implementation of policy to solve it.

Active (discretionary) policy making All actions on the part of monetary and fiscal policy makers that are undertaken in response to or in anticipation of some change in the overall economy.

Adverse selection A problem that arises when there is asymmetric information before a transaction takes place.

Adverse selection The likelihood that individuals who seek to borrow may use the funds that they receive for high-risk projects.

Aggregate demand The total of all planned real expenditures for the entire economy.

Aggregate demand curve A curve that gives the various quantities of all final commodities demanded at various price levels, all other things held constant.

Aggregate demand shock Any economic event that causes the aggregate demand curve to shift inward or outward.

Aggregate production function Models the relationship between the inputs to production available in the economy and the total output of an economy (usually measured as real GDP).

Aggregate supply The total of all planned production for the entire economy.

Aggregate supply shock Any economic event that causes the aggregate supply curve to shift inward or outward.

Aggregates Economy-wide measures.

Allocative efficiency Producing the mix of goods and services most valued by consumers.

Anticipated inflation The rate of inflation that individuals believe will occur in the future.

Anticombines legislation Laws that make illegal certain economic activities that might restrain trade.

Appreciation An increase in the value of a currency in terms of other currencies.

Asset demand Holding money as a store of value.

Assets Amounts owned; all items to which a business or household holds legal claim.

Asymmetric information Information possessed by one party in a financial transaction but not by the other party.

Asymmetric information When financial transactions take place, one party often does not have all the knowledge needed about the other party to make correct decisions.

Automatic, or built-in, stabilizers Special provisions of the tax and income support laws that cause changes in the economy without the direct action of the government.

Autonomous consumption The amount of planned consumption, which does not depend at all on actual disposable income.

Average tax rate The total taxes due divided by total taxable income.

Balance of payments The total of all economic transactions between a nation and the rest of the world, usually for a period of one year.

Balance of trade The difference between the value of exports and imports of goods and services.

Balance sheet A statement of the assets and liabilities of any business entity, including financial institutions and the Bank of Canada.

Balanced budget A budget in which the revenue and spending are equal.

Bank Rate The upper limit of the overnight operating interest rate band.

Bank runs The simultaneous rush of depositors to convert their demand deposits or time deposits into currency.

Barter A direct exchange—no intermediary good called money is used.

Base year The year that is chosen as the point of reference for comparison of prices in other years.

Budget balance The amount of revenue government receives minus its spending.

Budget deficit When government spending exceeds its revenue.

Budget surplus When the budget balance is positive or, in other words, the tax revenue is greater than what the government spends.

Bureaucracy An administrative system run by a large staff following rules and procedures set down by government.

Bureaucrats Nonelected government officials.

Business fluctuations The ups and downs in overall economic activity.

Canadian Deposit Insurance Corporation (CDIC) A government agency that insures the deposits held in federally incorporated financial institutions.

Canadian Payments Association (CPA) A regulated organization that operates a national cheque-clearing and settlements system.

Capacity utilization A measure of how intensively plant and equipment are being used.

Capital consumption allowance Another name for *depreciation*, the amount of the capital stock that has been consumed over a one-year period.

Capital gain The positive difference between the buying and selling prices of an asset.

Capital goods New machines and buildings that are expected to yield a future stream of income.

Capital loss The negative difference between the purchase price and the sale price of an asset.

Central bank A banker's bank, usually an official institution that also serves as a country's treasury's bank. Central banks normally regulate commercial banks.

Ceteris paribus [KAY-ter-us PEAR-uh-bus] assumption The assumption that nothing changes except the factor or factors being studied; "other things being constant," or "other things equal."

Chequable deposits Any deposits in a chartered bank or a near bank on which a cheque may be written.

Closed economy An economy that isolates itself from other countries.

Collective decision making How voters, politicians, and other interested parties act and how these actions influence non-market decisions.

Comparative advantage The ability to perform an activity at the lowest opportunity cost.

Comparative advantage The ability to produce something at a lower opportunity cost compared with other producers.

Comparative Advantage Principle states that the combined production of two producers can be enhanced if each producer specializes in the product in which it has the comparative advantage.

Complements Two goods are complements if both are used together for consumption or enjoyment.

Constant dollars The value of a sum measured in base year prices. If the values were measured at the prices that prevailed at the time measured it would be referred to as current dollars.

Consumer Price Index (CPI) A weighted average of the prices of a specified set of goods and services purchased by wage earners in urban areas.

Consumption The act of using income for the purchase of consumption goods.

Consumption The use of goods and services for direct personal satisfaction.

Consumption function The relationship between planned consumption expenditures of households and all levels of real disposable income (all else constant).

Consumption goods Goods purchased by households for immediate satisfaction.

Contraction A decline in economic output.

Cost-of-living adjustments (COLAs) Automatic increases in wage rates to take account of the increases in the price level.

Cost-push inflation Continual decreases in aggregate supply not matched by decreases in aggregate demand.

Crawling peg An automatically adjusting target for the value of a nation's currency.

Crowding-out effect A rise in government spending, holding taxes constant, that tends to crowd out private spending, dampening the positive effect of increased government spending on aggregate demand.

Crude quantity theory of money and prices The belief that changes in the money supply lead to proportional changes in the price level.

Current dollars The Statistics Canada term for nominal dollars.

Cyclical unemployment Unemployment associated with changes in business conditions—primarily recessions and depressions.

Deflation A downward movement in the average level of prices.

Demand Refers to the quantities of a specific good or service that individuals are willing to purchase at various possible prices, other things being constant.

Demand curve A graphical representation of the law of demand.

Demand-pull inflation Inflation caused by increases in aggregate demand not matched by increases in aggregate supply.

Demerit good Any good that the political process has deemed socially undesirable.

Dependent variable A variable whose value changes according to changes in the value of one or more independent variables.

Depreciation Reduction in the value of capital goods over a one-year period due to physical wear and tear and also to obsolescence; also called *capital consumption allowance*.

Depreciation A decrease in the value of a currency in terms of other currencies.

Depression An extremely deep recession.

Desired reserves The minimum amount of reserves—vault cash plus deposits with the Bank of Canada—that a depository institution wishes to hold to back its chequable deposits.

Development economics The study of why some countries grow and develop while others do not and of policies that might help the developing economies get richer.

Diminishing marginal returns means that even though we increase employment, the additional output those additional workers can make is not as great as previous workers.

Direct relationship A relationship between two variables that is positive, meaning that an increase in one variable is associated with an increase in the other, and a decrease in one variable is associated with a decrease in the other.

Dirty float A system between flexible and fixed exchange rates in which central banks occasionally enter foreign exchange markets to influence rates.

Discouraged workers People who have dropped out of the labour force and are no longer looking for a job because they believe that the job market has little to offer them.

Disposable personal income (DPI) Personal income after all personal income taxes have been subtracted.

Dissaving Negative saving; a situation in which spending exceeds disposable income. Dissaving can occur when a household is able to borrow or use up existing owned assets.

Division of labour Occurs when individuals specialize in a subset of tasks related to a specific product.

Drawdown A movement of Government of Canada deposits from the accounts of the chartered banks held at the Bank of Canada into the Bank's own government accounts.

Dumping Occurs when a producer sells its products abroad at a price below its cost of production or below the price that is charged in the home market.

Durable consumer goods Consumer items that last more than three years.

Economic growth Increases in per-capita real GDP measured by the rate of change in per-capita real GDP per year.

Economic growth The increase in economic output that nations have experienced over time.

Economic system The social arrangements or institutional means through which resources are used to satisfy human wants.

Economic way of thinking Assumes that the typical response to an economic problem of scarcity is rational behaviour.

Economics A social science that studies how people allocate their limited resources to satisfy their wants.

Effect time lag After fiscal policy is enacted, it takes time for it to affect the economy.

Efficiency wage An optimal wage that the firm should continue paying, even in the face of large fluctuations in the demand for its output.

Efficiency wage theory The hypothesis that worker productivity actually depends on the wages that workers are paid, rather than being independent of wages.

Empirical Using real-world data to test the usefulness of a model.

Employed The number of adults aged 15 years or older who have work.

Endowments The various resources in an economy, including both physical resources and human resources, such as ingenuity and management skills.

Entrepreneurship Human resources that perform the functions of risk taking, organizing, managing, and assembling other factors of production to make business ventures.

Equation of exchange The formula indicating that the number of monetary units times the number of times each unit is spent on final goods and services is identical to the price level times output (or nominal national income).

Equilibrium A point from which there tends to be no movement unless demand or supply changes.

Excess reserves The difference between actual reserves and desired reserves.

Exchange rate The amount of money that can be purchased with one unit of foreign currency.

Exclusion principle The principle that no one can be denied the benefits of a public good for failing to pay for it.

Expansion An acceleration in the pace of national economic activity.

Expectations Subjective estimates of future economic conditions.

Expenditure approach A way of computing GDP by adding up the dollar value of all final goods and services.

Fiat money Money that is widely accepted because it is declared by government to be legal tender.

Fiduciary monetary system A system in which the value of the payments rests on the public's confidence that such payments can be exchanged for goods and services.

Final goods and services Goods and services that are at their final stage of production and will not be transformed into yet other goods or services.

Financial intermediaries Institutions that transfer funds between ultimate lenders (savers) and ultimate borrowers.

Financial intermediation The process by which financial institutions accept savings from businesses, households, and governments and lend the savings to other businesses, households, and governments.

Fiscal policy The deliberate, discretionary changes in government expenditures and/or taxes in order to achieve certain national economic goals.

Fiscal policy The policies of government spending and taxation, in short, the government budget.

Fixed investment The purchase of capital goods.

Flexible exchange rates Exchange rates that are allowed to fluctuate in the open market in response to changes in supply and demand. Sometimes called *floating exchange rates*.

Floating exchange rate Occurs when countries let supply and demand determine the value of their currency.

Flow A quantity measured per unit of time that shows how fast something is changing.

Foreign exchange market The market for buying and selling foreign currencies.

Foreign exchange rate The price of one currency in terms of another.

Foreign exchange risk The possibility that variations in the market value of assets can take place as a result of changes in the value of a nation's currency.

Fractional reserve banking A system in which depository institutions hold reserves that are less than the amount of total deposits.

Free-rider problem A situation in which some individuals take advantage of the fact that others will shoulder the burden of paying for public goods.

Frictional unemployment The unemployment that arises from the continuous flow of individuals from job to job and in and out of employment, which includes those seeking a job for the first time.

Full employment Occurs if only workers who are between jobs and those whose skills are not needed in the economy are unemployed.

Full-adjustment The assumption that all markets will adjust to their long-run equilibrium values without impediment.

Full-information The assumption that all economic players are able to find and incorporate into their decision making any information that affects them.

GDP deflator A price index that measures changes in the level of prices of all new goods produced in the economy.

General Agreement on Tariffs and Trade (GATT) An international agreement established in 1947 to further world trade by reducing barriers and tariffs.

Gold standard An international monetary system in which the values of the currencies of certain countries were tied directly to gold.

Goods The physical items that consumers are willing to pay for.

Government, or political, goods Goods (and services) provided by the public sector; they can be either private or public goods.

Gross domestic product (GDP) The value of all goods and services produced in a country in a year.

Gross private domestic investment The creation of capital goods that can yield production and hence consumption in the future.

Gross public debt All federal public debt, taken together.

Hedge A financial strategy that is intended to offset the risk arising from exchange rate variations.

Human capital The education and training of workers.

Incentive Inducement to take a particular action.

Incentive structure The system of rewards and punishments individuals face with respect to their own actions.

Income approach A way of measuring GDP by adding up the income received by all factors of production, including wages, interest, rent, and profits.

Income velocity of money The number of times, on average, each monetary unit is spent on final goods and services.

Independent variable A variable whose value is determined independently of, or outside, the equation under study.

Indirect business taxes less subsidies All business taxes except the tax on corporate profits.

Infant industry argument The contention that tariffs should be imposed to protect from import competition an industry that is trying to get started. Presumably, after the industry becomes technologically efficient, the tariff can be lifted.

Inferior goods Goods for which demand falls as income rises.

Inflation A rise in average prices for goods and services across the economy.

Inflation An upward movement in the average level of prices.

Inflationary gap The amount by which actual GDP exceeds potential GDP.

Innovation The transformation of something new, such as an invention, into something that benefits the economy either by lowering production costs or providing new goods and services.

Interest Income earned by capital.

Interest rate effect A higher price level pushes up interest rates and thereby reduces borrowing and spending. (The opposite occurs if the price level declines.)

Intermediate goods Goods used up entirely in the production of final goods.

International Monetary Fund (IMF) An institution set up under the Bretton Woods agreement to administer the agreement and to lend to member countries in balance of payments deficit.

Inventory investment Investment made when a firm increases its inventories of finished products.

Inverse relationship A relationship between two variables that is negative, meaning that an increase in one variable is associated with a decrease in the other, and a decrease in one variable is associated with an increase in the other.

Investment An activity that uses resources today in such a way that they allow for greater production in the future and hence greater consumption in the future.

Investment Expenditures by firms on new machines and buildings.

Job leaver One who voluntarily ended employment.

Job loser One whose employment was involuntarily terminated or who was laid off.

Keynesian short-run aggregate supply curve The horizontal portion of the aggregate supply curve in which there is unemployment and unused capacity in the economy.

Labour Productive contributions made by individuals who work.

Labour force The total number of adults aged 15 years or older who either have a job or are looking and available for a job; the number of employed plus the number of unemployed.

Labour force participation rate The proportion of working age individuals who are employed or seeking employment.

Labour productivity Measured by dividing the total real domestic output (real GDP) by the number of workers or the number of labour hours.

Laissez-faire French term for "leave it alone"; the government should leave it (the economy) alone or "let it be."

Land Nonhuman gifts of nature.

Large value transfer system The electronic system through which large transactions are cleared and settled.

Law of demand The observation that there is an inverse relationship between the price of any good and its quantity demanded, holding other factors equal.

Law of increasing relative cost When society takes more resources and applies them to the production of any specific good, the opportunity cost increases for each additional unit produced.

Law of supply The observation that there is a direct relationship between the price of any good and its quantity supplied, holding other factors constant.

Liabilities Amounts owed; the legal claims against a business or household by nonowners.

Liquidity Wealth in the form of money can be exchanged later for some other asset.

Long-run aggregate supply The output of the economy under conditions of full employment of the available resources. It can alternatively be viewed as the potential level of real GDP after full adjustment has occurred.

Long-run aggregate supply curve A vertical line representing the long-run aggregate supply of goods and services in the economy.

Lump-sum tax A tax that does not depend on income or the circumstances of the taxpayer.

M1 The money supply, taken as the total value of currency plus demand deposits in chartered banks.

M2 M1 plus (1) personal savings and (2) non-personal notice deposits.

Macroeconomics The study of the behaviour of the economy as a whole.

Majority rule A collective decision-making system in which group decisions are made on the basis of 50.1 percent of the vote.

Marginal benefit All the extra benefits that one receives in pursuing a course of action.

Marginal cost All the extra costs or sacrifices incurred.

Marginal propensity to consume (MPC) The ratio of the change in consumption to the change in real disposable income.

Marginal propensity to import The ratio of the change in imports to the change in real GDP.

Marginal propensity to save (MPS) The ratio of the change in saving to the change in real disposable income.

Marginal propensity to spend The proportion of money that is spent in the domestic economy out of every extra dollar of GDP received.

Marginal tax rate The change in taxes due divided by the change in taxable income.

Market All of the arrangements that individuals have for exchanging with one another.

Market clearing price or **equilibrium price** The price at which market quantity demanded equals market quantity supplied.

Market demand Determined by adding the individual demand at each price for all the consumers in the market.

Medium of exchange Any asset that sellers will accept as payment in market transactions.

Merit good Any good that the political process has deemed socially desirable.

Microeconomics The study of decision making undertaken by individuals and by firms in specific parts of the economy.

Mixed economies Economies in which there is a mix of direct intervention by the government and the marketplace.

Mixed economy An economic system in which decisions about how resources are used are made partly by the private sector and partly by the public sector.

Models or theories Simplified representations of the real world used to understand and predict economic phenomena.

Monetarists Economists who believe in a modern quantity theory of money and prices and contend that monetary policy works its way more directly into the economy.

Monetary policy The policies that governments have over short-term interest rates and the rate of growth of the nation's money supply.

Monetary rule Increase the money supply smoothly at a rate consistent with the economy's long-run average growth rate.

Money Anything that people generally accept in exchange for goods and services.

Money financing Creating new money to pay government's bills.

Money illusion Buyers and sellers react to changes in nominal prices and income rather than to changes in real prices and income.

Money multiplier A factor that gives the change in the money supply due to a change in reserves.

Money multiplier process The process by which an injection of new money into the banking system leads to an eventual multiple expansion in the total money supply.

Money price The actual price that you pay in dollars and cents for any good or service at any point in time.

Money supply The amount of money in circulation.

Monopoly A firm that has great control over the price of a good it sells.

Moral hazard The possibility that a borrower might engage in riskier behaviour after a loan has been obtained.

Moral hazard A situation that arises as the result of information asymmetry after a transaction has occurred.

Multiplier The number by which a permanent change in autonomous expenditure is multiplied to get the change in the equilibrium level of real GDP.

National income accounting A measurement system used to measure national economic activity and its various components.

Natural rate of unemployment The rate of unemployment that prevails when only frictional unemployment and structural unemployment exist.

Natural rate of unemployment The rate of unemployment that would exist in the long run after everyone in the economy fully adjusted to any changes that have occurred.

Near bank Financial institutions, such as trust companies, credit unions, and *caisses populaires,* that offer most of the same services as chartered banks.

Net domestic product (NDP) The sum of all incomes arising from production, or ownership of assets used in production, within the economic territory of a country or region.

Net export effect The indirect effect that fiscal policies have on the exchange rate and net exports.

Net investment Measurement of *changes* in capital stock over time.

Net national income (NNI) The income available to Canadians for ownership of resources.

Net public debt The result of subtracting from the gross public debt the financial assets held by government agencies.

Net worth The difference between assets and liabilities.

New classical model A modern version of the classical model in which wages and prices are flexible, there is pure competition in all markets, and the rational expectations hypothesis is assumed to be working.

New entrant One who has never worked at a job.

New growth theory A theory that technology must be examined from the point of view of what drives it.

New Keynesian economics Economic models based on the idea that demand creates its own supply as a result of various possible government fiscal and monetary coordination failures.

New Keynesian inflation dynamics In new Keynesian theory, the pattern of inflation exhibited by an economy with growing aggregate demand—initial sluggish adjustment of the price level in response to increased aggregate demand followed by higher inflation later.

Nominal rate of interest The market rate of interest expressed in today's dollars.

Nominal value The value of something in today's dollars.

Nonaccelerating inflation rate of unemployment (NAIRU) The rate of unemployment below which the rate of inflation tends to rise and above which the rate of inflation tends to fall.

Nondurable consumer goods Consumer goods that are used up within three years.

Nonincome expense items Indirect business taxes less subsidies and depreciation.

Nonpersonal notice deposits Interest-earning funds at chartered banks that can, in practice, be withdrawn at any time without payment of a penalty—similar to savings deposits but are deposited by firms.

Normal goods Goods for which demand rises as income rises.

Normative economics Refers to analysis based on value judgments made about what ought to be.

North American Free Trade Agreement (NAFTA) A free trade agreement among Canada, the United States, and Mexico, covering about 80 percent of our exports.

Number line A line that can be divided into segments of equal length, each associated with a number.

Open economy An economy that engages extensively in trading and investment with other countries.

Open economy effect A price level increase tends to reduce net exports, thereby reducing the amount of real goods and services purchased in Canada. (The opposite occurs if the price level declines.)

Open market operations The purchase and sale of existing government securities in the open market (the private secondary Canadian securities market) by the Bank of Canada in order to change the money supply.

Opportunity cost The value of the best alternative that must be given up because a choice was made.

Origin The intersection of the y-axis and the x-axis in a graph.

Output gap The difference between potential GDP and actual GDP.

Par value The legally established value of the monetary unit of one country in terms of that of another; the officially determined value.

Passive (nondiscretionary) policy making Policy making that is carried out in response to a rule and, therefore, is not in response to an actual or potential change in overall economic activity.

Patent A government protection that gives an inventor the exclusive right to make, use, or sell an invention for a limited period of time, typically 20 years in Canada.

Payment intermediaries Institutions that facilitate payments on behalf of holders of transaction deposits.

Per-capita real GDP The amount of real GDP per person.

Personal income (PI) Income received by the factors of production prior to the payment of personal income taxes.

Personal savings (S) The amount that is left over from disposable personal income after consumption.

Phillips curve A curve showing the apparent negative relationship between the inflation rate and the unemployment rate.

Physical capital Factories and equipment used in production.

Policies Action plans designed to achieve goals.

Policy irrelevance proposition The new classical and rational expectations conclusion that fully anticipated monetary policy is irrelevant in determining the levels of real variables.

Positive economics Refers to analysis that can be tested by observing the facts.

Potential output The amount the economy can produce when all resources are fully employed.

Precautionary demand Holding money to make *unexpected* purchases or to meet emergencies.

Price index The cost of a market basket of goods and services in a given year expressed as a percentage of the cost of the same market basket during a base year.

Principle of rival consumption The principle that one person's consumption reduces the amount of private goods available for others to consume.

Private goods Goods that can be consumed by only one individual at a time.

Producer durable, or capital good A good that is purchased not to be consumed in its current form but to be used to make other goods and services and has an expected service life of more than three years.

Producer Price Index (PPI) A price index that measures what has happened to the price level for commodities that firms purchase from other firms.

Production Any activity that results in the conversion of resources into goods and services.

Production possibilities curve (PPC) A curve that represents all possible production combinations of two goods that can be produced.

Productive efficiency Occurs when a given output level is produced at minimal cost.

Productively inefficient point Any point below the production possibilities curve, assuming resources are fully employed.

Profit Income earned by the entrepreneur.

Progressive taxation As taxable income increases, the percentage of income paid in taxes also increases.

Property rights The rights of an owner to use and to exchange that property.

Proportional rule A decision-making system in which actions are based on the proportion of the "votes" cast and are in proportion to them.

Proportional taxation A tax system in which regardless of an individual's income, the tax bill comprises exactly the same proportion. Also called a flat-rate tax.

Public goods Goods that can be consumed jointly by many individuals simultaneously at no additional cost and with no reduction in quality or quantity.

Purchasing power The amount of goods and services a given amount of money can buy.

Purchasing power parity Calculating an exchange rate whereby money would have the same value in all countries.

Pure capitalist economy An economic system characterized by private ownership of all property resources.

Pure command economy An economic system characterized by public ownership of all property resources.

Quota system A government-imposed restriction on the quantity of a specific good that another country is allowed to sell in Canada.

Rational expectations hypothesis A theory stating that people combine the effects of past policy changes on important economic variables with their own judgment about the future effects of current and future policy changes.

Rationality assumption An individual makes decisions based on maximizing his or her own self-interest.

Re-entrant One having worked a job before but having been out of the labour force.

Real-balance effect Price level increases reduce the real value of cash balances which, in turn, reduces desired expenditures on the quantity of aggregate goods and services, all other things held constant. (The opposite occurs if the price level declines.)

Real business cycle theory An extension and modification of the theories of the new classical economists of the 1970s and 1980s, in which money is neutral and only real, supply-side factors matter in influencing labour employment and real output.

Real dollars Dollars corrected for general price level changes.

Real GDP The value of GDP adjusted for price changes.

Real income Measures how much you can purchase with a given amount of income.

Real rate of interest The nominal rate of interest minus the anticipated rate of inflation.

Real values Values that have been corrected for the changes in prices.

Recession A contractionary business fluctuation where economic output declines for two consecutive quarters or more.

Recessionary gap The amount by which potential GDP exceeds actual GDP.

Recognition time lag The period of months that may elapse before economic problems can be identified.

Redeposit A movement that occurs when the Bank of Canada moves government deposits into the accounts of the chartered banks, thus increasing their reserves.

Regressive taxation A smaller percentage of taxable income is taken in taxes as taxable income increases.

Relative price Any commodity's price in terms of another commodity.

Rent Income earned by land.

Repricing, or menu, cost of inflation A direct cost incurred by inflation in that it requires that price lists be changed.

Reserves Some percentage of the customer deposits maintained by depository institutions.

Retained earnings Profits not given out to shareholders.

Ricardian equivalence theorem An increase in public spending is offset by a reduction in consumer spending because individuals are saving to compensate for the future tax liability.

Saving The act of not consuming all of one's current income.

Savings deposits Interest-earning funds at chartered banks that can be withdrawn at any time without payment of a penalty.

Say's law A dictum of economist J.B. Say that supply creates its own demand; hence it follows that *desired* expenditures will equal *actual* expenditures.

Scarcity The condition that arises because wants always exceed what can be produced with limited resources.

Seasonal unemployment Unemployment that varies with the seasons of the year.

Secular deflation A persistently declining price level resulting from economic growth in the presence of relatively unchanged aggregate demand.

Services Intangible commodities purchased by consumers.

Services The tasks performed by others that consumers are willing to pay for.

Short-run aggregate supply The relationship between aggregate supply and the price level in the short run, all other things held constant.

Short-run aggregate supply curve An upward-sloping line representing the short-run aggregate supply of goods and services in the economy.

Shortage A situation in which the quantity demanded exceeds the quantity supplied at a price below the market clearing price.

Small-menu cost theory A hypothesis that supposes that much of the economy is characterized by imperfect competition and that it is costly for firms to change their prices in response to changes in demand.

Special drawing rights (SDRs) Reserve assets that the International Monetary Fund created to be used by countries to settle international payment obligations.

Specialization Involves working at a relatively well-defined, limited endeavour; individuals, regions, and nations produce a narrow range of products.

Stock A quantity of something at a given point in time.

Store of value The ability to hold value over time—or purchasing power.

Structural unemployment Unemployment that occurs when there is a mismatch of available jobs and available skills.

Substitutes Two goods are substitutes when either one can be used to satisfy a similar want.

Sunk costs Irreversible costs incurred prior to your decision.

Supply Refers to the quantities of a specific good or service that firms are willing to sell at various possible prices, other things being constant.

Supply curve An upward-sloping curve that shows the direct relationship between price and quantity supplied.

Supply-side economics The notion that changing the tax structure to create incentives increases productivity.

Surplus A situation in which quantity supplied is greater than quantity demanded at a price above the market clearing price.

Target for the overnight rate The Bank of Canada's official interest rate (or key policy rate); it is the midpoint of the Bank's operating band for overnight financing.

Target zone A policy under which a central bank announces that there are specific upper and lower bands, or limits, for permissible values for the exchange rate.

Tariffs Government taxes applied to imported goods.

Tax bracket A specified level of taxable income to which a specific and unique marginal tax rate is applied.

Tax incidence The distribution of tax burdens among various groups in society.

Technology Society's pool of applied knowledge concerning how goods and services can be produced.

Terms of Trade Principle Each producer will gain from specialization and trade if the terms of trade is between the producers' opportunity costs of production.

Terms of trade The amount of one product that must be traded in order to obtain an additional unit of another product.

The multiplier The multiplier is the number by which an expenditure is multiplied to get the final change in aggregate demand.

Theory of public choice The analysis of collective decision making.

Three Ps Private property, Profits, and Prices inherent in capitalism.

Total income The total of all individuals' incomes; the annual cost of producing the entire output of final goods and services.

Total planned expenditures curve (TPE) Represents the relationship between spending in the economy and GDP.

Trade surplus When exports exceed imports.

Transactions demand Holding money to make regular, *expected* expenditures.

Transfer payments Payments made to individuals for which no services or goods are concurrently rendered in return.

Transfers in kind Payments that are in the form of actual goods and services for which no services or goods are rendered concurrently in return.

Unanticipated inflation The rate of inflation that is different from what people believed it would be.

Unemployed The total number of adults aged 15 years or older who are willing and able to work, and who are actively looking for work but have not found a job.

Unit of account A way of placing a specific price on economic goods and services.

Value added The amount of dollar value contributed to a product at each stage of its production.

Voluntary export restraint agreement (VER) An official agreement with another country that "voluntarily" restricts the quantity of its exports to Canada.

Wages Income earned by labour.

Wealth The stock of assets owned by a person, household, firm, or country.

Working age population The number of people 15 years of age and older.

World Trade Organization (WTO) The successor organization to GATT, it handles all trade disputes among its 148 member nations.

x-axis The horizontal axis in a graph.

y-axis The vertical axis in a graph.

INDEX

A

absolute advantage, 41, 424
acceptability of money, 323
accounting identities
    balancing the current account, 449
    capital account transactions, 449
    current account transactions, 447–449
    defined, 446
    described, 446–447
    investment income, 448–449
    merchandise trade transactions, 447
    official financing account
      transactions, 450–451
    service exports and imports, 448
    surplus and deficit items, 446t
    transfers, 449
accounting identity, 239, 369
action time lag, 307
active (discretionary) policy making,
  387, 409, 410t
AD-AS model
    see also aggregate demand; aggregate
      supply
    economic growth, 160f
    inflation, 222
adverse selection, 331, 349
African vouchers, 322
after-tax interest, 112
age, economic challenges of, 172
aggregate demand
    see also AD-AS model
    Bank of Canada influence, 216
    classical model, 233f, 234, 234f
    and contractionary monetary
      policy, 362
    defined, 162
    determinants of, 166t
    higher taxes, impact of, 317f
    increase, effects of, 217–218, 217f
    vs. individual demand, 165
    and inflationary gap, 217f
    and monetary policy, 390
    and the multiplier, 166–167, 167f
    nonprice factors, 258f
    in open economy, 220–222
    out-of-control, 173
    output, effect on, 389f, 390f
    price level decreases, 165
    price level increases, 163–165
    and recessionary gap, 217f
    shifts, 217
    short-run aggregate demand,
      215–216
    and strong Canadian dollar,
      221–222
    unanticipated rise in, 397f, 400f
    unemployment, effect on, 389f, 390f

aggregate demand curve
    defined, 162
    described, 162, 163
    illustration of, 163f
    shifts in, 165, 166f
    and total planned expenditures,
      256–257, 257f
aggregate demand shock, 216
aggregate expenditure, 128
aggregate production function,
  156–157, 156f
aggregate supply
    see also AD-AS model
    defined, 156
    determinants of, 214t
    vs. individual supply, 208
    inflationary gap, 217f
    long-run aggregate supply,
      158, 159–161
    and oil price changes, 225
    and open economy, 220–222
    recessionary gap, 217f
    short-run aggregate supply. *See*
      short-run aggregate supply
    stable, 217
    and strong Canadian dollar, 221
aggregate supply curves
    Keynesian aggregate supply curve,
      211–212
    Keynesian short-run aggregate
      supply curve, 234–236
    long-run aggregate supply curve,
      156–159
    shifts in, 213–214, 213f, 214f
    short-run aggregate supply curve.
      See short-run aggregate supply
      curve
aggregate supply shock, 216, 225
aggregates, 5
agricultural subsidies, 435, 436
Air Canada, 86–87
Alberta oil sands, 252
allocative efficiency, 34
alphabetical system of writing, 426
Andean Community, 437
anticipated inflation, 113
anticipated policy, 398
anticombines legislation, 271
appreciation, 453, 454
Argentina, 116, 146, 319, 335, 430
Asian economies, 174–175, 250
asset demand, 365
assets, 332
Association of Southeast Asian Nations
  (ASEAN), 418, 437
assumptions, 11
asymmetric information, 331

auto insurance, 29–30, 49–52
automatic stabilizers, 307–310, 309f
autonomous consumption, 242
average tax rate, 279

B

baby boomers, 299–300
Bahamas, 146
balance of payments, 446–451
balance of payments deficit, 451
balance of payments surplus, 451
balance of trade, 446
balance sheet, 342, 360, 361t
balanced budget, 295
balanced-budget multiplier, 317
Bank Act, 357, 363
bank mergers, 351
bank notes, 358
Bank of Canada
    see also monetary policy
    aggregate demand, influence
      on, 216
    balance sheet, 360
    bank notes, issuance of, 358
    Bank Rate, 362
    as banker's bank, 330
    as central bank of Canada, 356–357
    and chartered banks, 357
    consolidated balance sheet, 359t
    customers, 357–358
    as fiscal agent, 358–359
    functions of, 358–359
    as government financial advisor,
      358–359
    Governor of, 356
    high interest rate policy, 411, 412f
    independence of, 378–379
    interest rates *vs.* money supply,
      376–377
    lender of last resort, 358
    Monetary Conditions Index
      (MCI), 377
    and monetary policy, 358
    money creation, 295–296
    money supply curve, effect on, 364
    official settlements account,
      451–452
    organization of, 357
    and output gaps, 216
    price stability, 377
    reserves, 363
    target choice, 376–377
    target for the overnight rate,
      362–363, 373f
Bank of Canada Act, 356
Bank of England, 363
Bank of Japan, 390

Bank Rate, 362
bank runs, 348
banking system
    balance sheet, 360, 361*t*
    bank failures in Canada, 347
    bank runs, 348
    deposit creation process, 345
    deposit insurance, 347–349
    deregulation and, 350–351
    flawed bank regulation, 347–349
    fractional reserve banking,
        339–340
    money expansion, 344–345
    reserves, 340–341
banks, 331–334, 334*t*, 340*n*
    see also Canadian financial system;
        depository institutions; financial
        intermediaries
Barbados, 146
Barclays PLC, 351
barter, 320, 321
base year, 110–111
behavioural models, 13–14
Belgium, 334
bilateral trade agreements, 418
bond prices, 362–363
Bordo, Michael, 464
bottled water, 16–17
bounded rationality, 409
brain drain, 180–181, 202
Brazil, 200, 310, 335, 430
Bretton Woods, 460–461
Britain, 334, 459
British Columbia coal mines, 113–114
Brooks, Garth, 72–73
Brundtland Commission, 196
budget
    balanced budget, 295
    budget balance, 295, 297–298, 297*f*
    government, 295–298
budget balance, 295, 297–298, 297*f*
budget deficit
    defined, 295
    in open economy, 301
budget surplus, 295
built-in stabilizers, 307–310
bureaucracy, 277
bureaucratic performance, 277–278
bureaucrats, 277
business cycles, 98
    see also business fluctuations
business fluctuations
    defined, 98
    idealized, 100*f*
    importance of, 99–100
    peak-to-peak, 1926–2007, 101*f*
    technology and long cycles, 99
business receipt, 127

C

Canada
    agricultural subsidies, 436
    average number of hours
        worked, 106
    bank failures, 347

Bank of Canada. *See* Bank of
    Canada
banks, sizes of, 334
brain drain to, 180–181, 202
Canada–United States exchange
    rate, 117
Canadian dollar. *See* Canadian dollar
capacity utilization, 210–211
car insurance rates, 29–30
coin use, increased, 326
credit cards, 327–328
current account deficit, 449–450
distribution of merchandise exports
    and imports, 423*f*
economic growth forecasts, 156
economic growth in, 173*f*
economic output, 97, 98*f*
first income tax, 292
free trade agreements, 434–435
Gross Progress Indicator
    accounting, 148
Human Development Index
    (HDI), 146
identity theft, 30
inflation in, 109*f*, 173*f*
inflation rates, 171*f*
international policy cooperation, 464
Internet access in, 2
Internet pharmacies, 63, 71, 88–89
interprovincial trade, 43
Kyoto Accord, 196
labour productivity growth, 220
merchandise trade by geographic
    area, 422*f*
natural rate of unemployment,
    388–389
oil prices, 207, 225–226
online pharmaceuticals, 421
patterns of international trade, 419
Phillips curve, experience with, 395
politics in, 48
post-secondary education, 39–40
production in, 126
productivity growth, 186–187, 186*f*
real gross domestic product, 98*f*
real per-capita GDP, 182, 182*f*
standard of living, 180
tariffs, 434, 435*f*
tax freedom day, 270
trade surplus, 117
twin deficits, 302*f*
Canada Pension Plan (CPP), 282–283
Canada Post, 276
Canada Trust, 351
Canada–U.S. Free Trade Agreement
    (FTA), 434
Canadian Bankers' Association
    (CBA), 348
Canadian Commercial Bank, 349
Canadian Deposit Insurance
    Corporation (CDIC), 348
Canadian dollar, 167, 221–222, 221*f*, 451
Canadian financial system
    adverse selection, 331
    asymmetric information, 331

components of, 330
deregulation and, 350–351
direct *vs.* indirect financing, 330
financial intermediation, 330–334
Internet banking, 332
moral hazard, 331
Canadian International Trade Tribunal
    (CITT), 430
Canadian Medical Association Journal, 12
Canadian Payments Association
    (CPA), 357
Canadian Tire money, 358
capacity utilization, 210–211, 211*f*
capital account, 449–450
capital consumption allowance, 141
capital flight, 451
capital gains, 281
capital goods, 37–39, 135, 239
capital loss, 281
capitalism
    features of, 45–47
    laissez-faire, 47
    The Mystery of Capitalism (de Soto),
        189–190
    pure capitalist economy, 45
    and the three economic
        questions, 47–48
capitalist model, 51
car insurance, 29–30, 49–52
Cardoso, Enrique, 310
cash, 366
central bank, 330, 356, 357*f*
    see also Bank of Canada
ceteris paribus assumption, 11
chain weighting, 115*n*
change in demand, 71–72
change in quantity demanded, 71–72
change in quantity supplied, 78
change in supply, 78
charitable giving, 10
chartered banks, 357
    see also banks; depository institutions
chequable deposits, 326
child-care spaces, 274–275
children, laptops for, 33–34
Chile, 200, 435
China
    cigarette smuggling, 13
    dumping Chinese garlic, 430
    economic cost of pollution, 132
    economic growth, 180
    forced housing investment, 255
    smuggling in, 9
    unemployment rate, 10
chocolate prices, 69
circular flow
    concept of, 126
    and economic activity, 126–128
    enhanced circular flow, 128, 129*f*
    of income and output, 127*f*
    and Say's law, 231*f*
Circular Flow Model, 45, 46*f*
classical model, 230–234
closed economy, 117, 374
Coe, David, 191

COLD-fX, 12
collective decision making, 275–277
Colman, Ron, 148
Colombia, 366
combined government spending effect, 304
command model, 51
commercial banks. *See* banks
comparative advantage
    Comparative Advantage Principle, 58–59
    defined, 41, 424
    described, 41–42
    and international specialization, 425–426, 425*t*
    and trade among nations, 43
Comparative Advantage Principle, 58–59
competition
    and capitalism, 46
    global competitiveness, 427–428
    market and public-sector decision making, 276
    promotion of, 271
    pure competition, 230
    unfair competition from low-wage countries, 432
complements, 70–71
composition of output, 131
Conservative party, 291
constant dollars, 142, 158
Consumer Price Index (CPI), 108–109, 110–111, 114, 324
consumer sovereignty, 46
consumption
    autonomous consumption, 242
    capital consumption allowance, 141
    defined, 37, 238
    forgoing current consumption, 37
    as function of real GDP, 248*f*
    and income, 239
    and investment, 249*f*
    marginal propensity to consume, 242–243
    planned consumption, determinants of, 240–244
    principle of rival consumption, 271
    real consumption and saving schedules, 240*t*
    tax, 286
    uneven consumption, worldwide, 196
consumption expenditures, 134–135
consumption function
    defined, 240
    described, 241
    graph, 241*f*
    shifts, 243
consumption goods, 37–39, 238
contraction, 98
contractionary fiscal policy, 294*f*
contractionary gap, 216
contractionary monetary policy, 362
contractionary policy
    contractionary fiscal policy, 294*f*
    contractionary monetary policy, 362

natural rate of unemployment, effect on, 390–391
corporate income tax, 281–282
corporate profits before taxes, 138
cost-of-living adjustments (COLAs), 113
cost-push inflation, 222
costs
    of economic growth, 195–196
    extra security measures, 161
    of inflation, 111–113
    inputs, 77
    labour, and exports, 432
    law of increasing relative cost, 35, 35*f*
    marginal cost, 7
    opportunity cost. *See* opportunity cost
    of pollution, 132
    repricing cost of inflation, 112
    resource cost of inflation, 111–112
    small-menu costs, 405
    sunk costs, 7
    transaction cost, 107
crawling peg, 464
creative destruction, 200
creativity, 193
credit cards, 327–328
crowding-out effect, 302–303, 303*f*, 304*t*
crude quantity theory of money and prices, 369, 370
Cuba, 200
currency
    see also exchange rate
    appreciation, 453, 454
    Central Europe, 453
    currency drains, 347
    depreciation, 453, 454
    derived demand, 454
    described, 325–326
    dollars. *See* dollars
    euro, 310, 445, 453–456, 465
    foreign currency demand and supply, 452–456, 457*f*
    supply schedule, 456*n*
    trading, 446
currency drains, 347
currency swaps, 463
current account, 447–449, 450*f*
current account deficit, 301, 449–450
current dollars, 142
cyclical unemployment, 107
Cyprus, 146
Czech Republic, 106, 453

D

Darby, Abraham, 99
Dawson, John, 160
de Soto, Hernando, 189–190
debit cards, 327, 333, 333*f*
debt. *See* public debt
decision making, 275–277
decisions at the margin, 7–8
deficit financing, 297

deficits
    balance of payments deficit, 451
    budget deficit, 295, 301
    Canada's twin deficits, 302*f*
    current account deficit, 301, 449–450
deflation
    defined, 108
    and economic growth, 169–170
    secular deflation, 169
demand
    aggregate demand. *See* aggregate demand
    change in demand, 71–72
    change in quantity demanded, 71–72
    decrease in demand, 83
    decrease in demand and decrease in supply, 85–86, 86*f*
    decrease in demand and increase in supply, 86
    defined, 64
    derived demand, 454
    determinants of demand, 69–71
    equilibrium, changes in, 82–86
    euros, 453, 455*f*, 456, 457*f*
    and expectations, 71
    foreign currency, 452–453
    and income, 69
    increase in demand, 83
    increase in demand and decrease in supply, 86
    increase in demand and increase in supply, 84–85, 85*f*
    law of demand, 64
    market demand, 66
    money demand, 364–366
    and population, 71
    and prices of related goods, 70–71
    shifts in demand, 68–72, 82–86, 82*f*, 457–458, 457*f*
    and supply, putting together, 79–81, 80*f*
    tastes and preferences, 70
demand curve
    see also demand
    aggregate demand curve. *See* aggregate demand curve
    defined, 66
    described, 65–66
    individual demand curve, 66, 66*f*
    market demand curve, 66
    movement along, 72, 72*f*
    quantity demanded, 72
    shift in, 68*f*
    straight lines, 65*n*
    and supply curve, combined, 81
demand deposits, 326
demand-determined equilibrium, 235*f*
demand-pull inflation, 222
demand schedule
    described, 65
    horizontal summation, 67*f*
    individual demand schedule, 66*f*
    market demand schedule, 67*f*
    and supply schedule, combined, 79–81

demand-side inflation, 172
demerit goods, 274
Denmark, 181, 334
dependent variable, 21
　　see also graphs
deposit creation process, 345
deposit insurance
　　and adverse selection, 349
　　bank runs, 348
　　flaw in deposit insurance
　　　scheme, 348
　　and moral hazard, 349
　　need for, 348
depository institutions
　　balance sheet, 342
　　net worth, 342
　　reaction to increase in reserves,
　　　342–344
　　reserves, 340–341
　　total deposits, 342–346
depreciation, 138, 140–141, 453, 454
depression, 98
　　see also Great Depression
deregulation, 350–351
derived demand, 454
determinants of demand, 69–71
development economies, 197
　　see also economic development
digital cash, 328–329
diminishing marginal returns, 157
direct financing, 330
direct relationships, 21, 22*f*
dirty float, 463–464
discouraged workers, 105
disequilibrium price, 81
disposable personal income (DPI), 141
dissaving, 240, 242
distribution of output, 131
division of labour, 44
dollarization movement, 335
dollars
　　see also currency
　　African vouchers, 322
　　Canadian dollar, 167, 221–222,
　　　221*f,* 451
　　constant dollars, 142, 158
　　currency trading, 446
　　current dollars, 142
　　real dollars, 142
Dominion Income War Tax, 292
double coincidence of wants, 320
double counting, 130
double taxation, 281
drawdowns, 361
dumping, 430
durable consumer goods, 134

E

e-gold, 323
Eberstadt, Nicholas, 199
economic activity
　　and business fluctuations, 97–98
　　and circular flow, 126–128
　　measurement of, 126
economic analysis, 5

economic development
　　creative destruction, 200
　　development economies, 197
　　educated population, 200
　　factors, 200
　　keys to, 199–200
　　and population growth, 197–199
　　property rights, 200
　　protectionism, limiting, 200
　　and smaller families, 199
　　stages of development, 199
　　world poverty, 197
economic functions of government
　　competition, promotion of, 271
　　economic stability, 273
　　free-rider problem, 272–273
　　legal system, provision of, 270
　　public goods, 271–272
economic growth
　　in *AD-AS* model, 160*f*
　　benefits of, 196–197
　　capital goods, 38*f*
　　costs of, 195–196
　　defined, 97, 181–182
　　definition problems, 183
　　and deflation, 169–170
　　economic development. *See*
　　　economic development
　　entrepreneurship, 188–189
　　environmental disasters, effect of,
　　　195–196
　　forecasting, 156
　　fundamental determinants,
　　　188–190
　　government, role of, 194–195
　　high growth, meaning of, 97
　　and human capital, 194
　　and ideas, 193–194
　　immigration, 190
　　income, and population
　　　growth, 197
　　and inflation in Canada, 173*f*
　　and information technologies,
　　　170
　　innovation, 192–193
　　international growth rates, 181
　　international per-capita growth
　　　rates, 182*f*
　　and knowledge, 193–194
　　limits to growth, 195–196
　　and long-run aggregate supply,
　　　159–161
　　market-driven economies, 190
　　modelling economic growth,
　　　184–187
　　new growth theory, 191–195
　　and new technology, 185–186,
　　　191, 197
　　and open economy, 192
　　political stability, 190
　　population growth, 190
　　and population increases, 185*f*
　　poverty, and environmental
　　　pressure, 196
　　price level, effects on, 168–170

production function, changes in,
　　185–187
and production possibilities curve
　(PPC), 36, 37*f*
property rights, 188–189
and regulation, 160
and research and development,
　191–192
and scarcity, 36
and secular deflation, 169, 169*f*
socioeconomic goal, 15
standard of living, 183, 197
and tariff barriers to international
　trade, 193*f*
and terrorism, 161
and uneven consumption, 196
without changing prices, 170
economic model. *See* models
economic policies. *See* policies
economic questions, 44–45, 47–48
economic stability, 273, 459
economic system
　　defined, 44
　　mixed economies, 45
　　pure capitalist economy, 45
　　pure command economy, 45
economic way of thinking, 5
economics
　　classical model, 230–234
　　defined, 3
　　Keynesian economics. *See*
　　　Keynesian approach
　　macroeconomics, 4–5
　　microeconomics, 4–5
　　negative economics, 14
　　neoclassical economists, 230
　　new Keynesian economics, 405
　　positive economics, 14
　　supply-side economics, 402–405
　　three basic economic questions,
　　　44–45, 47–48
　　of web page design, 4
The Economist, 96
economy
　　industrial economy, 212
　　information economy, 212
　　labour market model, 157*f*
　　long-run equilibrium, 168–170,
　　　168*f*
　　and stock market crashes, 258–259
　　underground economy, 132–133
Ecuador, 146
educated population, 200
effect time lag, 307
efficiency
　　see also inefficiency
　　allocative efficiency, 34
　　and production possibilities curve
　　　(PPC), 33–34
　　productive efficiency, 33
　　socioeconomic goal, 15
efficiency wage, 406
efficiency wage theory, 405–406
empirical, 12
employed, 103

employment
    see also unemployment
    full employment, 107
    India, 108
    measurement of, 103–108
    overemployment, 105
    and real GDP, 233
    translation into hours, 106
Employment Insurance, 105, 282, 308
The End of Poverty (Sachs), 201
The End of Work (Rifkin), 185
endowments, 158
enhanced circular flow, 128, 129*f*
entrepreneurship
    defined, 3
    and economic growth, 188–189
environment
    disasters, and economic growth,
        195–196
    economic cost of pollution, 132
    and free trade, 432
    and GDP, 132
    poverty and, 196
    uneven consumption, worldwide,
        196
equation of exchange, 369–372
equilibrium
    changes in, 82–86
    defined, 81
    demand-determined
        equilibrium, 235*f*
    in financial markets, 231–232
    in Keynesian model, 247–252, 251*f*
    labour market, 232–234, 232*f*
    long-run equilibrium, 168–170,
        168*f*, 294
    occurrence of, 215*f*
    real GDP, 250–251, 256*f*
    real GDP with net exports, 250*t*
    shifts in both demand and supply,
        84–86
    shifts in demand or supply,
        82–84, 82*f*
    short-run equilibrium, 215, 293–294
    World War I, 223, 223*f*
equilibrium foreign exchange rate,
    453–456, 457–459
equilibrium price, 79–80
equity, 15
An Essay on the Principle of Population
    (Malthus), 199
euro, 310, 445, 453–456, 457*f*, 465
Europe
    property rights, 189
    standard of living, 180
European Central Bank, 363, 445, 465
European Monetary Union, 445, 452
European System of Central Banks, 324
European Union, 305, 310, 418, 437, 464
excess reserves, 341, 347
exchange rate
    see also currency
    Bretton Woods, 460–461
    crawling peg, 464
    currency swaps, 463

current exchange rate
    arrangements, 461*f*
defined, 117
dirty float, 463–464
economic stability, 459
equilibrium foreign exchange rate,
    453–456, 457–459
fixed exchange rate, 461–463, 462*f*
flexible exchange rates, 453
floating exchange rate, 118, 453
foreign currency demand and
    supply, 452–453
foreign exchange rate, 146, 452–456
foreign exchange risk, 463
gold standard, 459–460
and international trade, 117
market determinants, 458–459
par value, 460
policies, 118
product preferences, 459
productivity, changes in, 459
and real rate of interest, 458
shifts in demand, 457–458, 457*f*
shifts in supply, 458, 458*f*
as shock absorber, 463
target zone, 464
exclusion principle, 272
expansion, 98
expansionary fiscal policy, 293*f*
expansionary gap, 216
expansionary monetary policy, 362,
    371*f*, 375*f*
expansionary policy
    expansionary fiscal policy, 293*f*
    expansionary monetary policy,
        362, 371*f*, 375*f*
    and natural rate of unemployment,
        389–390
expectations
    business expectations, 259
    consumer expectations, 259
    and demand, 71
    inflation, 394
    and investment, 244–245
    and stabilization policies, 393–395
    and stock market crashes, 259
    and supply, 77
expenditure approach
    consumption expenditures, 134–135
    defined, 134
    government expenditures, 135
    gross private domestic investment
        (I), 135
    mathematical representation, 138
    net exports, 135–136
exports
    described, 135–136
    distribution of merchandise exports
        and imports, 423*f*
    and imports, relationship
        between, 427
    and labour costs, 432
    net export effect, 303–304, 374–375
    net exports, 135–136
    service exports, 448

F
factor markets, 46, 128
factor payments, 137
factors of production, 3
Family Allowance Act, 298
farm income, 138
Federal Deposit Insurance Corporation
    (FDIC), 328
federal government
    see also government
    spending, 284, 285*f*
    tax receipts, 283
federal taxes
    Canada Pension Plan (CPP),
        282–283
    capital gains, 281
    corporate income tax, 281–282
    Employment Insurance, 282
    federal progressive income
        tax, 308
    Goods and Services Tax (GST), 283
    personal income tax, 281
    rates, 281*t*
fiat money, 323
fiduciary monetary system, 323
final goods and services, 127
financial intermediaries
    accounting identities, 446–451
    assets and liabilities, 332, 333*t*
    defined, 330
    large value transfer system
        (LVTS), 363
    larger scale, 331
    lower management costs, 331
    payment intermediaries, 332
    sources of funds, 332
    uses of funds, 332
    world's largest banks, 334*t*
financial intermediation
    across national boundaries, 334
    defined, 330
    process of, 331*f*
financial markets
    equilibrium, 231–232
    financial transactions, and
        GDP, 131
    possibility of saving and
        borrowing, 128
    study of, 117
financial transactions, 131
firm, 77
fiscal policy
    during abnormal times, 309
    action time lag, 307
    automatic stabilizers, 307–310, 309*f*
    built-in stabilizers, 307–310
    combined government spending
        effect, 304
    contractionary fiscal policy, 294*f*
    crowding out, 302–303,
        303*f*, 304*t*
    defined, 118, 292
    discretionary fiscal policy, in
        practice, 306–307
    effect time lag, 307

expansionary fiscal policy, 293*f*
government spending, changes in, 292–293
inside lag, 307
Keynesian perspective, 316–318
mix, 306–307
money creation, 295–296
net export effect, 303–304
during normal times, 308–309
possible offsets, 302–306
recognition time lag, 307
Ricardian equivalence theorem, 305–306
"soothing" effect of Keynesian fiscal policy, 309–310
supply-side effects of tax changes, 304–305
taxes, changes in, 293–294, 295
time lags, 307
Fisher, Irving, 369
fixed exchange rate, 461–463, 462*f*
fixed investment, 135, 239
fixed-price level assumption, 318
fixed-quantity price index, 110
flat tax, 286–287
flexible exchange rates, 453
floating exchange rate, 118, 453
Florida, Richard, 193
flow
    circular flow. *See* circular flow
    defined, 97
    of expenditures, 134
    of production, 126
    visualizing, 97*f*
    world trade flows, 421*f*
foreign currency. *See* currency
foreign exchange market, 452
foreign exchange rate, 146, 452–456
    see also exchange rate
foreign exchange reserves, 461
foreign exchange risk, 463
foreign expenditures, 135–136
foreign sector, 249–250
foreigners, 128
45-degree reference line, 241–242, 247–248
fractional reserve banking, 339–340
France, 305, 310, 334, 407, 432, 464
free-rider problem, 272–273
free trade
    see also international trade
    arguments against, 429–432
    countering foreign subsidies, 429–430
    dumping, 430
    emerging arguments against, 432
    infant industry argument, 429
    protection of Canadian jobs, 431
    unfair competition from low-wage countries, 432
frictional unemployment, 107
Friedman, Milton, 395
full-adjustment, 158
full employment, 15, 107
full-information, 158

G
gains from trade, 425–426, 425*t*
GDP. *See* gross domestic product (GDP)
GDP deflator, 114–115, 115*n*
General Agreement on Tariffs and Trade (GATT), 435
Genuine Progress Indicator, 148–149
Germany, 116, 305, 310, 334, 370, 432, 464
global competitiveness, 427–428
global economics
    see also international trade
    accounting identities, 446–451
    economic growth rates, 181
    financial intermediation across national boundaries, 334
    foreign exchange rate, 146
    global GDP, 140
    globalization of international money markets, 375
    legal structure of nations, 189
    per-capita growth rates, 182*f*
    purchasing power parity, 146, 147
    required reserve ratios, 341*t*
    standard of living, 145, 180
    world's largest banks, 334*t*
global GDP, 140
globalization of international money markets, 375
gold, 324
gold standard, 459–460
goods
    capital goods, 135, 239
    complements, 70–71
    consumption goods, 238
    defined, 2
    demerit goods, 274
    durable consumer goods, 134
    government goods, 276
    inferior goods, 69
    intermediate goods, 130
    merit goods, 273–274
    near-public goods, 271*n*
    nondurable consumer goods, 134
    normal goods, 69
    political goods, 276
    private goods, 271
    producer durable good, 135
    public goods, 271–272, 272*f*
    quasi-public goods, 271*n*
    related goods, 70–71
    second-hand goods, 131
    substitutes, 70
Goods and Services Tax (GST), 280, 283
Gould, David, 200, 431
government
    borrowing, 296
    budget balance, 295, 297–298, 297*f*
    budget deficit, 295
    budgets, 295–298
    bureaucratic performance, gauging, 277–278
    bureaucrats, role of, 277
    collective decision making, 275–277

competition, promotion of, 271
current account deficit, 301
deficit financing, 297
demerit goods, 274
differences with market decision making, 275–276
economic functions of, 270–273
economic growth, role in, 194–195
economic stability, 273
expenditures, 135
finances, 295–299
financial advisor, 358–359
fiscal agent of, 358–359
free-rider problem, 272–273
gross public debt, 298
income redistribution, 274
merit goods, 273–274
net public debt, 298
policies. *See* government policies
political functions, 273–278
public goods, provision of, 271–272
rational ignorance, 278
rise and fall, 295
role of, 311
similarities with market decision making, 275–276
spending. *See* government spending
sports stadiums, funding of, 274
tax collection, 128
tax receipts, 283–284, 284*f*
taxes as revenue raiser, 283–284
theory of public choice, 275
total outlays over time, 283*f*
transfer payments, 131, 238*n*
use of force, 277
voting *vs.* spending, 277
government expenditures. *See* government spending
government goods, 276
government intervention. *See* government policies
government policies
    see also stabilization policy issues
    exchange rate policies, 118
    fiscal policy. *See* fiscal policy
    government program spending, 117
    hyperinflation, 119–120
    monetary policy. *See* monetary policy
    trade policies, 118
    Zimbabwe, 119–120
government spending
    balanced-budget multiplier, 317
    categories of, 296*f*
    changes in, 292–293
    combined government spending effect, 304
    federal *vs.* provincial and municipal spending, 284, 285*f*
    government program spending, 117
    Keynesian perspective on fiscal policy, 316–317
    proportion of GDP, 296*f*
    reductions in, 293
GPI Atlantic Project, 148

graphs
  construction of, 21–25
  dependent variable, 21
  described, 21
  direct relationships, 21, 22f
  horizontal number line,
    22–23, 22f
  independent variable, 21
  inverse relationships, 21, 22f
  number line, 22
  numbers in a table, 23–25
  ordered set of points, 22
  origin, 23
  slope of a line, 25–27
  vertical number line, 22–23
  x-axis, 23
  y-axis, 23
Great Depression
  fiscal policy during, 309
  government intervention, 273
  investment, changes in, 246–247
  Keynesian aggregate supply
    curve, 212
  Keynesian analysis, 235f, 236, 292
  new discoveries during, 99
  stock market crash, 259
  unemployment rate, 102
  U.S. New Deal, 294–295
Greece, 305, 334
Green GDP Accounting Research
  Project, 132
gross domestic product (GDP)
  components of, 142
  defined, 97
  double counting, avoidance of, 130
  eight years of, 136f
  exclusions from, 130–132, 132
  expenditure approach, 134–136, 137
  final annual data, 307n
  as flow of production, 126
  GDP deflator, 114–115
  from GDP to disposable
    income, 142t
  vs. Genuine Progress Indicator, 148
  global GDP, 140
  and government spending, 296f
  income approach, 134, 137–138
  India, 181
  intermediate goods, exclusion
    of, 130
  international comparison, 147
  limitations of, 144–146
  measurement of, 129–138, 139f
  and money supply, 339
  net domestic product (NDP),
    140–141
  nominal GDP, 142–143, 144f
  nonincome expense items, 138
  and price level changes, 142–143
  real GDP. See real GDP
  and standard of living, 145
  and underground economy,
    132–133
  variability of nominal GDP
    expenditure components, 137

gross private domestic investment
  (I), 135
gross public debt, 298
Group of Eight (G-8) nations, 464
growth. See economic growth

H

hair colour, 70
Haiti, 202
hedge, 463
Helpman, Elhanan, 191
Hershey Co., 69
hidden unemployed, 105
historical unemployment rates,
  102–103, 102f
holding money, 365
horizontal number line, 22–23, 22f
household transactions, 131
human capital
  defined, 3
  and economic growth, 194
  spending on, 239–240
Human Development Index (HDI),
  146, 183
Hungary, 173, 453
hyperinflation, 116, 119–120

I

idealized business cycle, 100f
ideas, 193–194, 426–427
identity theft, 30, 37
illegal contraband, 9
immigration
  brain drain, 180–181, 202
  economic growth, 190
implicit rental value, 134–135
import quotas, 118
imports
  described, 135–136
  distribution of merchandise exports
    and imports, 423f
  and exports, relationship
    between, 427
  importance of, 421t
  marginal propensity to import,
    254–255
  priests, into Spain, 427
  service imports, 448
incentive structure, 276
incentives, 8
income
  and consumption, 239
  and demand, 69
  disposable personal income
    (DPI), 141
  factor payments, 137
  farm income, 138
  interest income, 138
  investment income, 138, 448–449
  net national income (NNI), 141
  nonincorporated nonfarm business
    income, 138
  per capita income, 145
  personal income (PI), 141
  and population growth, 197

real income, 111
  redistribution of, 274
  and saving, 239
  total income, 127–128
income approach
  defined, 134
  depreciation, 138
  described, 137–138
  indirect business taxes less
    subsidies, 138
income redistribution, 274
income velocity of money, 369
independence, 378–379
independent variable, 21
  see also graphs
India
  economic growth, 180
  and full employment, 108
  gross domestic product, 181
indirect business taxes less
  subsidies, 138
indirect financing, 330
individual demand curve, 66, 66f
individual similarities, 276
individual supply curve, 74f
individual supply schedule, 74f
Indonesia, 175
industrial economy, 212
Industrial Revolution, 99
inefficiency, 33
  see also efficiency
infant industry argument, 429
inferior goods, 69
inflation
  anticipated inflation, 113
  Argentina, 116
  British Columbia coal mines,
    113–114
  in Canada, 109f
  causes of, 170–174
  cost-of-living adjustments
    (COLAs), 113
  cost-push inflation, 222
  costs of, 111–113
  defined, 99, 108
  demand-pull inflation, 222
  demand-side inflation, 172
  and economic growth in
    Canada, 173f
  expectations, 394
  Germany, 116
  hyperinflation, 116
  impact of, 111
  inflation-unemployment
    trade-off, 392
  measurement of, 108–111
  menu cost of inflation, 112
  and monetary policy, 367–368
  and money growth, 370
  new Keynesian inflation dynamics,
    407–408
  nominal value, 111
  as the norm, 170
  oil prices, 225
  persistent inflation, 171f

price index, 110–111
and purchasing power of money, 111
and real income, 111
and real interest rates, 114–116
real values, 111
repricing cost of inflation, 112
resource cost of inflation, 111–112
Russia, 116
short-run, 222–224
supply-side inflation, 171–172, 223f
and taxes, 112
unanticipated inflation, 113
uncertainty, 112–113
and unemployment, 391–392
Zimbabwe, 95, 112, 116
inflation rate
and balance of payments, 451
in Canada, 171f
highest recorded inflation rates, 173t
and interest rates, 115f
measurement of, 109–111
vs. money supply growth, 340f
nonaccelerating inflation rate of unemployment (NAIRU), 392
positive inflation rate, 170
and unemployment rates, 224
inflation-unemployment trade-off, 392
inflationary gap, 216, 217f
information economy, 212
information technologies
job creation, 212
and long-run aggregate supply curve, 170
innovation, 192–193
inputs, cost of, 77
inside lag, 307
Institute for Competitiveness and Prosperity in Canada, 193
Instructional Computing Group (Harvard), 32
intellectual property, 427
interest, 3
see also interest rate
interest income, 138
interest rate
after-tax interest, 112
as Bank of Canada target choice, 376–377
Bank of Canada's high interest rate policy, 411, 412f
classical model, 231–232
and exchange rates, 458
higher interest rates, and "tight" monetary policy, 399
increases, and Ontario, 167
and inflation rates, 115f
nominal rate of interest, 114
real rate of interest, 114–116, 412f, 458
interest rate effect, 164–165
intermediate goods, 130

international accounts. *See* accounting identities
international economic development. *See* economic development
International Institute for Management Development, 428
International Monetary Fund (IMF), 147, 310, 451, 460–461
international perspective. *See* global economics
international policy cooperation, 464
international tax competition, 305
international trade
see also global economics
and the alphabet, 426
arguments against free trade, 429–432
balance of payments, 446–451, 448
balance of trade, 446
benefits of, 422–427
bilateral trade agreements, 418
and Canadian jobs, 431
and comparative advantage, 43
countering foreign subsidies, 429–430
dumping, 430
exchange rate, influence of, 117
gains from trade, 425–426, 425t
global competitiveness, 427–428
growth of, 420f
import-export relationship, 427
infant industry argument, 429
intellectual property, 427
open economies, 117
output gains from specialization, 423–424
patterns, 419–421
and production possibilities curve (PPC), 57–60
regional trade agreements, 418, 437–438
restrictions. *See* trade restrictions
shipments, 419
specialization, 43, 424–425
study of, 117
terms of trade, 59
Terms of Trade Principle, 59–60
trade agreements, 434–437
trade flows, 421f
trade policies, 118
trade surplus, 117
transmission of ideas, 426–427
trends, 419–421
worldwide importance of, 419–421
international trade agreements, 434–437
Internet
access, in Canada, 2
African vouchers, 322
banking, 332
and barter, 321
Canadian Internet pharmacies, 63, 71, 88–89
e-gold, 323
online dating, 7

online pharmaceuticals, 421
web page design, economics of, 4
interprovincial trade, 43
inventory investment, 135, 239
inventory valuation adjustment, 138
inverse relationships, 21, 22f
investment
Alberta oil sands, 252
classical model, 231, 232f
and consumption, 249f
defined, 135, 239
determinants of, 244–247
expectations, 244–245
expenditures, 135
fixed investment, 135, 239
and Great Depression, 246–247
gross private domestic investment (I), 135
income, 138, 448–449
inventory investment, 135, 239
net investment, 141
and stock markets, 259
sub-prime meltdown in U.S., 238
investment companies, 331
investment function
Keynesian model, 248–249
planned investment function, 245, 245f
shifts, 245–246
Islam, 404
Italy, 334, 464

J
Jamaica, 202
Japan
bank borrowing in, 334
Bank of Japan, 390
banking crisis, 349–350
economic crisis, 250
economic development, 200
Human Development Index (HDI), 146
international policy cooperation, 464
just-in-time inventory control, 427
Kobe earthquake, 208
labour costs, and exports, 432
real GDP, 169–170
voluntary restraint of automobile exports, 433
job creation, 212
job leaver, 104
job loser, 104
just-in-time inventory control, 427

K
Katz, Lawrence, 387
Kenya, 322
Keynes, John Maynard, 148, 212, 230, 234, 238, 292, 310
Keynesian aggregate supply curve, 211–212
Keynesian approach
algebra of Keynesian expenditure model, 266–268
balanced-budget multiplier, 317

Keynesian approach (*continued*)
  described, 234–236
  equilibrium, 247–252, 251*f*
  examination of, 238
  fiscal policy, 316–318
  fixed-price level assumption, 318
  foreign sector, 249–250
  45-degree reference line, 247–248
  government spending, 316–317
  investment function, 248–249
  Keynesian cross, 265
  monetary policy, 384–385
  and monetary policy, 368
  money supply, decrease in, 385
  money supply, increase in,
    384–385, 384*f*
  new Keynesian economics, 405
  "soothing" effect of Keynesian fiscal
    policy, 309–310
  taxes, changes in, 317
  total planned expenditures, 249
  traditional Keynesian analysis, 292
Keynesian cross, 265
Keynesian short-run aggregate supply
  curve, 234–236
Keynesian transmission mechanism,
  367, 368*f*
Khaldun, Abu Zayd Abd-ar-Rahman
  Ibn, 404
knowledge, 193–194
Kobe earthquake, 208
Kondratieff, Nikolai, 99
Korea, 146
Kuznets, Simon, 148
Kyoto Accord, 196

L

labour
  costs of, and exports, 432
  defined, 3
  rising costs, 220
labour force
  defined, 103
  increase in, effect of, 184
  measurement of, 103–108
labour force participation rate, 106, 106*f*
labour market
  age, economic challenges of, 172
  equilibrium, 232–234, 232*f*
  and long-run aggregate supply
    curve, 157–159
  shocks, impact of, 401–402
labour productivity, 184, 185, 187
  see also productivity
labour productivity growth, 220
Laffer, Arthur, 403
Laffer Curve, 403, 404*f*
laissez-faire, 47
land, 3
large value transfer system (LVTS), 363
Latin American dollarization, 335
law of demand, 64
law of increasing relative cost, 35, 35*f*
law of supply, 73–74
laws. *See* regulations

LCD prices, 78
leakages, 347
legal structure of nations, 189
legal system, 270
legal tender, 323
leisure, 131
lender of last resort, 358
Levin, Andrew, 394
liabilities, 332
lighthouses, 272
limited government, 46–47
linear curve, 25–26
liquidity, 322, 322*f*
long-run adjustment process
  described, 219
  sticky wages, 219–220
long-run aggregate supply
  decline in, 171
  defined, 158
  and economic growth, 159–161
  government spending, changes
    in, 293
  and information technologies, 170
  vs. short-run aggregate supply,
    208–210
long-run aggregate supply curve
  aggregate production function,
    156–157, 156*f*
  defined, 156, 158
  described, 156
  full-adjustment level of output, 158
  full-information level of output, 158
  labour market, 157–159
  and production possibilities, 159
  shifts in, 214, 214*f*
long-run equilibrium, 168–170, 168*f*, 294
low-wage countries, 432
Lucas, Robert, 396
lump-sum tax, 249
Luxembourg, 334

M

M1, 325–328, 325*f*
M2, 329, 329*t*
M2+, 330
macroeconomics
  aggregates, 5
  defined, 4
  importance of, 96–97
  vs. microeconomics, 4–5
majority rule, 277
Malaysia, 175
Malthus, Thomas Robert, 199, 230
Mama Mike's, 322
map, 11
marginal benefit, 7
marginal cost, 7
marginal propensity to consume, 242–243
marginal propensity to import, 254–255
marginal propensity to save, 242–243
marginal propensity to spend, 254
marginal tax rate, 279
market
  and capitalism, 46
  defined, 66

factor markets, 46, 128
financial markets. *See* financial
  markets
foreign exchange market, 452
labour market. *See* labour market
price, 66
product markets, 128
market basket of goods and services, 110
market clearing price, 79–80
market decision making, 275–277
market demand, 66
market demand curve, 66
market-driven economies, 190
market supply curve, 75, 76*f*
market supply schedule, 76*f*
marriage premium, 42–43
Mars Inc., 69
Marshall, Alfred, 230
McDonald's, 270–271, 326, 327
medicare, 298
medium of exchange, 320–321
megabanks, 334
menu cost of inflation, 112
merchandise trade transactions, 447
Mercosur, 437
merit goods, 273–274
Mexico, 430, 432, 434
Meyer, Bruce, 387
microeconomics
  defined, 4
  vs. macroeconomics, 4–5
Microsoft Corporation, 194
Middle East, 428
milk prices, 84
Mill, John Stuart, 230
mixed economies, 45, 117
mixed insurance system, 51
models
  of behaviour, 13–14
  China, 13
  classical model, 230–234
  defined, 10
  Keynesian approach. *See* Keynesian
    approach
  and realism, 11
  testing models, 12
monetarists, 371
Monetary Conditions Index (MCI), 377
monetary policy
  see also Bank of Canada
  adding to Keynesian model, 368
  and aggregate demand, 390
  arguments against, 385
  choice of monetary policy target,
    376–377, 376*f*
  closed economy, 374
  contractionary monetary
    policy, 362
  criticisms of, 371
  crude quantity theory of money and
    prices, 369, 370
  defined, 118
  drawdowns, 361
  effectiveness of, 374–378
  equation of exchange, 369–372

expansionary monetary policy, 362, 371*f*, 375*f*
globalization of international money markets, 375
Gordon Thiessen lecture, 372–373
higher interest rates, and "tight" monetary policy, 399
and inflation, 367–368
Keynesian approach, 384–385
monetarists, 371
money demand, 364–366
net export effect, 374–375
open economy, 374
open market operations, 360
other considerations, 377–378
periods of underutilized resources, 375–376
political uncertainty, 377
redeposit, 361
sale, example, 361
sample transaction, 360
target for the overnight rate, 362–363, 373*f*
tools of, 359–364
transmission mechanism, 367–372
monetary rule, 372, 387
monetary shocks, 401
monetary standards, 323–324
money
    acceptability, 323
    business receipt, 127
    creation, 295
    crude quantity theory of money and prices, 369, 370
    defined, 320
    demand. *See* money demand
    digital cash, 328–329
    e-gold, 323
    expansion, and banking system, 344–345
    fiat money, 323
    fiduciary monetary system, 323
    functions of, 320–322
    growth of, and inflation, 370
    holding money, 365
    income velocity of money, 369
    legal tender, 323
    liquidity, 322, 322*f*
    as medium of exchange, 320–321
    monetary standards, 323–324
    multiplier. *See* money multiplier
    predictability of value, 324
    purchasing power, 111
    social contract, product of, 364
    as store of value, 321
    supply. *See* money supply
    types of, 320*t*
    as unit of account, 321
    use of term, 320
money demand
    asset demand, 365
    curve, 366, 366*f*
    holding money, 365
    precautionary demand, 365
    transactions demand, 365

money financing, 295
money illusion, 231
money multiplier
    defined, 346
    equation, 346
    forces reducing the money multiplier, 347
    potential *vs.* actual, 347
    real-world money multipliers, 347
money multiplier process, 339
money price, 64–65, 65*t*
money supply
    as Bank of Canada target choice, 376–377
    changes, and monetarists' view, 371
    changes in, and other economic variables, 339
    currency, 325–326
    curve, 364
    decrease in, and Keynesian approach, 385
    defined, 325
    demand deposits, 326
    graph, 364*f*
    growth, *vs.* inflation rate, 340*f*
    increase in, and Keynesian approach, 384–385, 384*f*
    M1, 325–328
    M2, 329, 329*t*
    M2+, 330
    monetary policy, effect of, 360–361
    monetary rule, 372
    reserves, increase in, 343
monopolies, 271
moral hazard, 331, 349
Morocco, 146
the multiplier
    and aggregate demand, 166–167, 167*f*
    algebra of, 268
    balanced-budget multiplier, 317
    defined, 166, 253
    and equilibrium of real GDP, 256*f*
    forced housing investment in China, 255
    graphing, 265*f*
    and Keynesian cross, 265
    money multiplier. *See* money multiplier
    multiplier effect, 253, 255–256
    multiplier formula, 254–255
    multiplier process, 254*t*
multiplier effect, 253, 255–256, 256*f*
municipal government
    spending, 284, 285*f*
    tax receipts, 283–284
The Muqaddimah (Khaldun), 404
Muskwa-Kechika Management Area (M-KMA), 36
The Mystery of Capitalism (de Soto), 189–190

N

Natalucci, Fabio, 394
national banking structures, 334

National Hospital Insurance Act, 298
national income accounting, 126, 129
    see also gross domestic product (GDP)
national sales tax, 286
natural rate of unemployment, 107, 224, 387–391, 388*f*, 392
near banks, 326
near-public goods, 271*n*
negative economics, 14
negative slope, 26*f*
neoclassical economists, 230
net domestic product (NDP), 140–141
net export effect, 303–304, 374–375
net exports
    calculation of, 135
    described, 249–250
    equilibrium real GDP with net exports, 250*t*
    and expenditure approach, 135–136
net investment, 141
net national income (NNI), 141
net public debt, 298
net taxes, 238*n*
net worth, 342
Netherlands, 334
new classical model, 397–400
New Democratic Party, 291
new entrant, 104
new growth theory
    defined, 191
    government, role of, 194–195
    human capital, 194
    ideas, importance of, 193–194
    innovation, 192–193
    knowledge, importance of, 193–194
    open economy, 192
    research and development, 191–192
    technology, 191
new Keynesian economics, 405
new Keynesian inflation dynamics, 407–408
New Zealand, 146, 379
nominal earnings, 112*f*
nominal GDP, 144*f*
nominal rate of interest, 114
nominal value, 111
non-market-clearing price, 81
nonaccelerating inflation rate of unemployment (NAIRU), 392
nondurable consumer goods, 134
nonincome expense items, 138
nonincorporated nonfarm business income, 138
nonlinear curves, 27, 27*f*
nonmarket transactions, 131
nonpersonal notice deposits, 329
normal goods, 69
normative analysis, 14
Nortel Networks, 259
North American Free Trade Agreement (NAFTA), 118, 418, 434–435, 437
North Atlantic Treaty Organization (NATO), 273

Norway, 106
number line, 22
number of firms, 77

O

official financing account, 450–451
official settlements account, 450–451
oil prices, 207, 225–226, 298–299
oil shock, 402
Old Age Security Act, 298
One Laptop per Child (OLPC), 33–34
online banking, 332
online dating, 7
open economies
    and aggregate demand and supply,
      220–222
    budget deficit, 301
    defined, 117
    and economic growth, 192
    monetary policy, 374
open economy effect, 165
open market operations, 360
Operation Moses, 427
opportunity cost
    after specialization and before
      trade, 58
    defined, 6
    described, 6–7
    online dating, 7
    and production possibilities curve
      (PPC), 34–35
    retained earnings, 245
ordered set of points, 22
Organisation for Economic Co-operation
  and Development (OECD), 432, 436
Organization of Petroleum Exporting
  Countries (OPEC), 298–299
origin, 23
output
    aggregate demand, decline in, 390*f*
    aggregate demand, increase in, 389*f*
    composition of, 131
    distribution of, 131
    final goods and services, 127
    full-adjustment, 158
    full-information, 158
    gains from specialization, 423–424
    monetary value of, 128
    potential output, 158
    short-run expansion, 210–211
    total output, 127–128
output gaps, 216
overemployment, 105
overnight rate target. *See* target for
  the overnight rate

P

par value, 460
passive (nondiscretionary) policy
  making, 387, 410*t*
patents, 191, 435
payment intermediaries, 332
pension fund companies, 331
pension taxes, 282–283
Pentagon, 161

per capita income, 145
per-capita real GDP, 145
persistent inflation, 171*f*
personal income (PI), 141
personal income tax, 281
personal savings (S), 142
Phelps, E.S., 395
Phillips, A.W., 392
Phillips curve, 391–392, 393–394, 393*f*,
  395, 395*f*, 396*f*
physical capital, 3
Piger, Jeremy, 394
planned investment function, 245, 245*f*
Poland, 453
policies
    see also government policies;
      stabilization policy issues
    defined, 15
    principles of governing party, 48
    and socioeconomic goals, 14–15
    and theory, 15
policy irrelevance proposition, 398
political functions of government
    bureaucratic performance, gauging,
      277–278
    bureaucrats, role of, 277
    collective decision making, 275
    demerit goods, 274
    income redistribution, 274
    merit goods, 273–274
    rational ignorance, 278
    similarities with market decision
      making, 275–276
    theory of public choice, 275
political goods, 276
political stability, 190, 451
political uncertainty, 377
pollution, economic cost of, 132
population growth
    and economic development, 197–199
    and economic growth, 190
    effect of, 185*f*
    expected growth in world
      population, 198*f*
    and income, 197
Portugal, 334
positive economics, 14
positive externalities, 191–192
positive slope, 26*f*
post-secondary education, 39–40
potential output, 158
poverty
    end of poverty, 201
    and environmental pressure, 196
    world poverty, 197
precautionary demand, 365
predictability of value, 324
preferences. *See* tastes
price
    average level, 108
    bond prices, 362–363
    and capitalism, 46
    chocolate, 69
    crude quantity theory of money and
      prices, 369, 370

    disequilibrium price, 81
    equilibrium price, 79–80
    expectations, 77
    flexibility of, 230–231
    LCD prices, 78
    market, 66
    market clearing price, 79–80
    milk prices, 84
    money price, 64–65, 65*t*
    non-market-clearing price, 81
    oil prices, 207, 225–226, 298–299
    of related goods, 70–71
    relative price, 64–65, 65*t*
    stability, 377
    zero price, for government
      goods, 276
price indexes, 110–111, 114–116
price level
    changes in, and gross domestic
      product (GDP), 142–143
    and contractionary monetary
      policy, 362
    decrease in, 165
    economic growth, effects
      of, 168–170
    fixed-price level assumption, 318
    increases in, and aggregate demand,
      163–165
    interest rate effect, 164–165
    and money supply, 339
    and multiplier effect, 255–256
    open economy effect, 165
    real-balance effect, 164
    secular deflation, 169
    in sticky-price economy, 407–408
    World War I, 223
price stability, 15
priests, 427
principle of rival consumption, 271
private auto insurance, 49–52
private goods, 271
private ownership of resources, 45–46
private transfer payments, 131
producer durable good, 135
Producer Price Index (PPI), 114, 116
product markets, 46, 128
product preferences, 459
production
    aggregate production function,
      156–157, 156*f*
    in Canada, 126
    defined, 2
    factors of production, 3
    flow of production, 126
    profit and, 126–127
    value added, 130
production function
    aggregate production function,
      156–157, 156*f*
    changes in, 185–187
production possibilities curve (PPC)
    after specialization and after
      trade, 59–60
    after specialization and before
      trade, 58–59

applications, 31–36
defined, 30
described, 30–31
and economic growth, 36, 37*f*
and efficiency, 33–34
example, 31
law of increasing relative cost, 35, 35*f*
and long-run aggregate supply curve, 159
and opportunity cost, 34–35
and scarcity, 32
before specialization and trade, 57–58
and trade-offs, 32
and unemployment, 32–33
productive efficiency, 33
productively inefficient point, 33
productivity
see also economic growth
Canada, *vs.* other nations, 187
changes in, 459
gains, 187
growth in Canada, 186–187, 186*f*
labour productivity, 184, 185, 187
and retirement, 172
and rising labour costs, 220
and specialization, 41–44
and supply curves, 77
profit
corporate profits before taxes, 138
as cost of production, 126–127
defined, 3
progressive taxation, 280, 308
property rights, 188–189, 200, 270
proportional rule, 277
proportional taxation, 279
protectionism, 200
see also trade restrictions
provincial automobile insurance rates, 49–50
provincial government
see also government
spending, 284, 285*f*
tax receipts, 283–284
public auto insurance, 49–52
public debt
gross public debt, 298
net public debt, 298
size of, 298–299, 298*f*
public goods, 271–272, 272*f*
purchasing power, 111, 164
purchasing power parity, 146, 147
pure capitalist economy, 45
pure command economy, 45
pure competition, 230

Q

quality improvements, 131
quantity demanded, 71–72
quantity supplied, 78
quasi-public goods, 271*n*
Quebec, 377, 451
quota system, 433, 433*f*

R

R-word Index, 96
radio frequency identification tags (RFID), 66, 68
rational decision making
decisions at the margin, 7–8
economic way of thinking, 5–6
incentives, response to, 8
opportunity cost, 6–7
rationality assumption, 6
rational expectations hypothesis, 396–400
rational ignorance, 278
rationality assumption, 6
re-entrant, 104
Reagan, Ronald, 404
real-balance effect, 164
real business cycle theory
defined, 401
generalization of, 402
labour market, impact on, 401–402
real *vs.* monetary shocks, 401
real dollars, 142
real earnings, 112*f*
real GDP
aggregate production function, 156–157
calculation of, 115*t*
chain weighting, 115*n*
and consumption, 248*f*
and contractionary monetary policy, 362
defined, 142
described, 98*f*
and employment, 233
equilibrium real GDP, 250–251, 256*f*
equilibrium real GDP with net exports, 250*t*
fall of, in Canada, 181
Japan, 169–170
long-run growth, sample, 161*f*
per-capita real GDP, 145
per year, 219*f*
percentage change, 1926 to 2007, 100, 101*f*
plotting, 143, 144*f*
real per-capita GDP in Canada, 182, 182*f*
and regulations, 160
and savings rate, 188, 189*f*
in sticky-price economy, 407–408
World War I, 223
real income, 111
real rate of interest, 114–116, 412*f*, 458
real shocks, 401
real values, 111
real-world money multipliers, 347
realism, 11
recession
defined, 98
R-word Index, 96
in United States, 218
recessionary gap, 216, 217*f*, 292
recognition time lag, 307
Redefining Progress, 148

redeposit, 361, 362
regional trade agreements, 418, 437–438
Registered Retirement Savings Plans (RRSPs), 194
regressive taxation, 280
regulations
see also government policies
anticombines legislation, 271
deregulation, 350–351
economic growth and regulation, 160
flawed bank regulation, 347–349
and U.S. real GDP, 160
related goods, 70–71
relative price, 64–65, 65*t*
rent, 3
repricing cost of inflation, 112
required reserve ratios, 341*t*
research and development, 191–192
reserves
and Bank of Canada, 363
defined, 340
desired reserves, 340
excess reserves, 341, 347
increase in, 342–344, 345–346
required reserve ratios, 341*t*
and total deposits, 342–346
resource cost of inflation, 111–112
resources
increase in supply, 403*f*
private ownership, 45–46
reduction in supply, 402*f*
and scarcity, 2–3
underutilized resources, 375–376
used in production, 3
restrictions on international trade.
See trade restrictions
retained earnings, 281
retirement, 172, 299–300
RFID tags, 66, 68
Ricardian equivalence theorem, 305–306
Ricardo, David, 230, 306
Rifkin, Jeremy, 185
risk, foreign exchange, 463
Romer, Paul, 193
Roosevelt, Franklin, 294–295
Roubini, Nouriel, 200
Ruffin, Roy, 200, 431
Russia, 116, 464

S

Sachs, Jeffrey, 200, 201
Sala-i-Martin, Xavier, 200
Saskatchewan, 146
saving
defined, 239
dissaving, 240, 242
45-degree reference line, 241–242
and income, 239
marginal propensity to save, 242–243
planned saving, determinants of, 240–244
real consumption and saving schedules, 240*t*
vs. savings, 239

saving function
  described, 241
  graph, 241*f*
savings accounts, 366
savings deposits, 329
savings rate
  classical model, 232*f*
  and per-capita real GDP, 188, 189*f*
  and standard of living, 188
Say, J.B., 230
Say's law, 230, 231*f*
scarcity
  and choices, 6
  defined, 2
  and economic growth, 36
  as government restraint,
    275–276
  market and public-sector decision
    making, 275–276
  and production possibilities curve
    (PPC), 32
  and resources, 2–3
  and specialization, 42
  and three basic economic questions,
    44–45
  and wants, 2
Schumpeter, Joseph, 200
Schwartz, Anna, 464
scientific method
  assumptions, 11
  ceteris paribus assumption, 11
  empirical, 12
  models, 10, 11
  models of behaviour, 13–14
  realism, 11
  testing models, 12
  theories, 10
Scientific Tax Research Credits, 194
seasonal unemployment, 107
Seater, John, 160
second-hand goods, 131
secular deflation, 169, 169*f*
securities, 131
self-interest
  assumption of, 5, 9, 10
  and capitalism, 46
  classical model, 231
  and specialization, 42
semi-hidden unemployed, 105
September 11, 2001, 161
service exports and imports, 448
services, 2, 134
services sector, 199, 243–244
shocks
  aggregate demand shock, 216
  aggregate supply shock, 216, 225
  exchange rate as shock absorber, 463
  monetary shocks, 401
  oil shock, 402
  real shocks, 401
  supply-side shocks, 402–403
short-run aggregate demand, 215–216
short-run aggregate supply
  changes in, 215–216
  defined, 208

  vs. long-run aggregate supply,
    208–210
  output, short-run expansion of,
    210–211
short-run aggregate supply curve
  defined, 209
  deriving, 209*f*
  flat curve, 211
  graphing, 212
  illustration of, 211*f*
  shape of, 211–212
  shifts in, 213–214, 213*f*, 214*f*
  slope, 212
short-run equilibrium, 215, 293–294
short-run inflation, 222–224
shortages, 81
similarity of individuals, 276
slope
  derived demand for euros, 454
  of a line, 25–27
  linear curve, 25–26
  negative slope, 26*f*
  nonlinear curves, 27, 27*f*
  positive slope, 26*f*
  short-run aggregate supply
    curve, 212
Slovakia, 453
small-menu cost theory, 405
smart cards, 328
Smith, Adam, 5, 44, 230
socioeconomic goals, 14–15
South Africa, 430
South Korea, 106, 250
southeast Asia, 174–175
Spain, 334, 427
special drawing rights (SDRs), 451
specialization
  absolute advantage, 41, 424
  among nations, 424–425
  comparative advantage. *See*
    comparative advantage
  daily world output, 425*t*
  defined, 41
  division of labour, 44
  gains from trade, 425–426, 425*t*
  and international trade, 43
  output gains from, 423–424
  and production possibilities curve
    (PPC), 57–60
  and productivity, 41–44
  and scarcity, 42
  and self-interest, 42
spending
  see also government spending
  on human capital, 239–240
  vs. voting, 277
sports stadiums, 274
sports teams, 42
Sri Lanka, 175
stabilization policy issues
  see also government policies
  active (discretionary) policy making,
    387, 409, 410*t*
  alternative active policy making
    models, 405–410

  anticipated policy, 398
  bounded rationality, 409
  efficiency wage theory, 405–406
  expectations, 393–395
  expected inflation, 394
  fiscal policy. *See* fiscal policy
  monetary policy. *See* monetary
    policy
  natural rate of unemployment,
    387–391
  new classical model, 397–400
  new Keynesian economics, 405
  passive (nondiscretionary) policy
    making, 387, 410*t*
  Phillips curve, 391–392,
    393–394, 393*f*
  policy irrelevance proposition, 398
  price level in sticky-price economy,
    407–408
  rational expectations hypothesis,
    396–400
  real business cycle theory, 401–402
  real GDP in sticky-price economy,
    407–408
  small-menu cost theory, 405
  stabilization policy, described, 118
  sticky-price theory, 407–408, 408*f*
  supply-side economics, 402–405
  unanticipated policy, 393
standard of deferred payment, 321
standard of living
  and economic growth, 183, 197
  international comparisons,
    145, 180
  saving rate and, 188
standard of value, 321
Statistics Canada, 110–111, 115*n*, 125,
  142, 163, 172, 184, 187, 436
sticky-price theory, 407–408, 408*f*
sticky wages, 219–220
stock
  defined, 97
  visualizing, 97*f*
stock market crashes, 258–259
store of value, 321
structural unemployment, 107, 387
sub-Saharan Africa, 180
subsidies
  agricultural subsidies, 435, 436
  countering foreign subsidies,
    429–430
  and supply, 77
substitutes, 70
sunk costs, 7
supply
  aggregate supply. *See* aggregate
    supply
  change in quantity supplied, 78
  change in supply, 78
  and cost of inputs, 77
  decrease in demand and decrease in
    supply, 85–86, 86*f*
  decrease in demand and increase in
    supply, 86
  decrease in supply, 83

defined, 73
and demand, putting together, 79–81, 80*f*
determinants of supply, 77
equilibrium, changes in, 82–86
euros, 454–456, 456*f*, 457*f*
foreign currency, 452–453
increase in demand and decrease in supply, 86
increase in demand and increase in supply, 84–85, 85*f*
increase in supply, 83
law of supply, 73–74
money supply. *See* money supply
and number of firms, 77
price expectations, 77
shifts in supply, 76–78, 76*f*, 82–86, 82*f*, 458, 458*f*
and subsidies, 77
and taxes, 77
technology and productivity, 77
supply curve
    see also supply
    aggregate supply curve. *See* aggregate supply curves
    defined, 74
    and demand curve, combined, 81
    horizontal summation, 75*f*
    individual supply curve, 74*f*
    market supply curve, 75, 76*f*
    movement along, 78
supply schedule
    and demand schedule, combined, 79–81
    described, 74
    individual supply schedule, 74*f*
    market supply schedule, 76*f*
supply-side economics, 402–405
supply-side effects of tax changes, 304–305
supply-side inflation, 171–172, 223*f*
supply-side shocks, 402–403
surplus
    balance of payments surplus, 451
    budget surplus, 295
    described, 81
    trade surplus, 117
Switzerland, 146, 324, 351, 428

T

target for the overnight rate, 362–363, 373*f*
target zone, 464
tariffs, 118, 193*f*, 433–434, 434*f*, 435*f*
tastes
    and demand, 70
    determination of tastes, 70
    hair colour, 70
    product preferences, 459
tax freedom day, 270
tax incidence, 282
taxation systems
    progressive taxation, 280, 308
    proportional taxation, 279
    regressive taxation, 280

taxes
    after-tax interest, 112
    and aggregate demand, 317*f*
    average tax rate, 279
    capital gains, 281
    changes in, 293–294
    consumption tax, 286
    corporate income tax, 281–282
    Dominion Income War Tax, 292
    double taxation, 281
    federal personal income tax, 281
    federal tax rates, 281*t*
    first income tax in Canada, 292
    flat tax, 286–287
    Goods and Services Tax (GST), 283
    as government revenue raiser, 283–284
    and government size, 283
    and government spending, 283
    indirect business taxes less subsidies, 138
    and inflation, 112
    international tax competition, 305
    Keynesian perspective on fiscal policy, 317
    lump-sum tax, 249
    marginal tax rate, 279
    national sales tax, 286
    net taxes, 238*n*
    pension taxes, 282–283
    reduction in, 294
    and supply, 77
    supply-side effects of tax changes, 304–305
    tax freedom day, 270
    tax incidence, 282
    unemployment taxes, 282
    value-added tax, 286
technology
    and creativity, 193
    defined, 30
    and economic growth, 185–186, 191
    information technologies, 170
    innovation, 192–193
    and long cycles, 99
    and new growth theory, 191
    problem solving with, 197
    research and development, 191–192
    and supply curves, 77
terms of trade, 59
Terms of Trade Principle, 59–60
terrorism, 161
tertiary sector, 199
Thailand, 175, 461
theories, 10, 15
theory of public choice, 275
Thiessen, Gordon, 372–373, 411
time dimension, 65
time lags, 307
Toronto-Dominion Bank, 351
total income, 127–128
total output, 127–128
total planned expenditures, 250, 256–257, 257*f*, 258*f*

total planned expenditures curve (TPE), 248
trade
    international trade. *See* international trade
    interprovincial trade, 43
trade-offs
    automobiles and newsprint, 31*f*
    consumption goods and capital goods, 38–39
    inflation-unemployment trade-off, 392
    and production possibilities curve (PPC), 32
trade policies, 118
trade restrictions
    import quotas, 118
    quota system, 433, 433*f*
    tariffs, 118, 433–434, 434*f*, 435*f*
    voluntary export agreements, 118
    voluntary export restraint agreement (VER), 433
trade surplus, 117
traditional Keynesian analysis, 292
transaction cost, 107
transactions demand, 365
transfer of ownership, 135
transfer payments, 131, 238*n*, 274
transfers, 449
transfers in kind, 274
transmission mechanism, 367–372
transmission of ideas, 426–427
tsunami, 174–175

U

UBS AG, 351
Uganda, 322
unanticipated inflation, 113
unanticipated policy, 393
uncertainty, 112–113
underground economy, 132–133
underutilized resources, 375–376
unemployed, 103
    see also unemployment
unemployment
    see also employment; unemployment rate
    aggregate demand, decline in, 390*f*
    aggregate demand, increase in, 389*f*
    arithmetic determination, 103–104
    categories of individuals without work, 104
    cyclical unemployment, 107
    discouraged workers, 105
    duration of, 105
    frictional unemployment, 107
    full employment, 15
    impact of, 101–102
    and inflation, 391–392
    inflation-unemployment trade-off, 392
    job leaver, 104
    job loser, 104
    kinds of, 107

measurement of, 103–108
new entrant, 104
nonaccelerating inflation rate of
unemployment (NAIRU), 392
and production possibilities curve
(PPC), 32–33
rate. *See* unemployment rate
re-entrant, 104
seasonal unemployment, 107
structural unemployment, 107, 387
taxes, 282
and working age population,
103*f*, 104*f*
Unemployment Insurance Act, 298
unemployment rate
calculation of, 103
China, 10
France, 407
Great Depression, 102
historical unemployment rates,
102–103, 102*f*
and low inflation rates, 224
natural rate of unemployment, 107,
224, 387–391, 388*f*, 392
percentage change, 1926 to 2007,
100, 101*f*
union contracts, 219
unit of account, 321
United Kingdom, 334, 351, 432, 464
United Nations, 145, 146, 183, 196
United Nations Development
Programme (UNDP), 146
United States
average number of hours
worked, 106
Canada–United States exchange
rate, 117
and Canadian pharmaceuticals, 421

dollarization movement, 335
dumping claims, 430
free trade agreements, 434–435
Human Development Index
(HDI), 146
identity theft, 30
international policy
cooperation, 464
investment crisis, 238
labour costs and exports, 432
largest banks, 334
New Deal, 294–295
real GDP, 160
recession, 218
services sector, 243–244
standard of living, 180
Uruguay Round, 435, 436
U.S. Federal Reserve, 363, 464
use of force, 277

V

value added, 130
value-added tax, 286
vault cash, 340
vertical number line, 22–23
voluntary export agreements, 118
voluntary export restraint agreement
(VER), 433
voting, 277

W

wages
defined, 3
efficiency wage, 406
flexibility of, 230–231
and income approach, 137
low-wage countries, 432
sticky wages, 219–220

wants, 2
War of 1812, 109
wartime, 309
wealth, 243
wealth effect, 164
The Wealth of Nations (Smith),
5, 44
web page design, 4
welfare spending, 310
wireless cellular phones, 64
women, and labour force participation
rate, 106, 106*f*
Woodbridge, G.L., 431
working age population, 103,
103*f*, 104*f*
World Bank, 197, 432
World Commission on Environment
and Development, 196
World Economic Forum, 187
world population. *See* population
growth
world poverty, 197
world trade. *See* international trade
World Trade Center, 161
World Trade Organization (WTO),
118, 431*f*, 435–436
World War I, 109, 223
World War II, 108, 109, 117
world's largest banks, 334*t*

X

x-axis, 23

Y

y-axis, 23

Z

Zimbabwe, 95, 112, 116, 119–120